The Fireside Book of
TENNIS

EDITED BY
Allison Danzig
AND
Peter Schwed

SIMON AND SCHUSTER
NEW YORK

For
Dorothy
and
Antonia

Published by Simon and Schuster
Rockefeller Center, 630 Fifth Avenue
New York, New York 10020

FIRST PRINTING
SBN 671-21128-5
Library of Congress Catalog Card Number: 70-165538
Designed by Irving Perkins
Manufactured in the United States of America

Acknowledgments

Three organizations have been particularly helpful and kind in the preparation of this volume, and the Editors wish to express their sincere appreciation for the cooperation extended in granting very extensive permissions for material used.

The book would not have been possible at all without the blanket permission extended from *The New York Times* to Allison Danzig to use any articles of his own that appeared originally in that paper. In addition, the *Times* also granted permission for other tennis writers of theirs, and the articles in this book which came from this source are copyright © 1919–1971 inclusive by The New York Times Company.

Special thanks are also due Mrs. Gladys Heldman, and her magazine *World Tennis,* for equally gracious cooperation. Articles which came from this source are copyright © 1954–1969 inclusive by World Tennis, Inc.

The third organization which deserves the same sort of appreciation is the United States Lawn Tennis Association, which furnished a great many of the photographs.

In addition, the Editors wish to thank the following authors, publishers, agents and agencies for permission to quote from the books and publications listed. All possible care has been taken to ensure accuracy, to trace the ownership of each selection included and to make full acknowledgment for its use. If, however, any errors have accidentally occurred, they will be corrected in subsequent editions, provided that notification is sent to the publisher.

The Associated Press, New York: "Tilden Spells It Out" (originally "William Tilden") by Alan J. Gould, July 28, 1926; "Tilden Crowned King of the Courts" (originally "Tilden Defeats Patterson in Wimbledon Final") by Richard Larned, 1920; "Kramer Wins Wimbledon," 1947; "Savitt Crushes McGregor in Wimbledon Final," 1951; "Australian Fans Hail Olmedo" by Will Grimsley, 1958; "Peru's Just Wild About Olmedo," 1958.

A. S. Barnes & Company, Inc., Cranbury, New Jersey: "My Matches Against Helen Wills Moody" (originally "Mrs. Moody Defaults to Helen Jacobs") by Helen Jacobs, from *Gallery of Champions* by Helen Jacobs, copyright 1949.

The Boston *Globe:* "Riviera Background" by John Tunis, February 14, 1926; "Death on the Longwood Grass, Alas" by Bud Collins, August 21, 1966; "Tiny Tennis Giant" by Bud Collins, July 1965.

Bud Collins: "Robert J. Kelleher," from *Sports Illustrated*, February 5, 1968, copyright © 1968 Time Inc. Reprinted by permission of the author.

Collins Publishers, London: "Lenglen at Wimbledon," "The Four Musketeers,"

"Maureen," from *Behind the Scenes at Wimbledon* by Duncan Macaulay, St. Martin's Press, copyright © 1965.

Bob Considine: "Lenglen, Wills, Ryan, Marble," January 19, 1941; "John Bromwich," from *Colliers*, 1939.

Thomas Y. Crowell Company, New York: "The Secret of Ball Control" by Bob Harman with Keith Monroe, from *Use Your Head in Tennis* by Bob Harman and Keith Monroe, copyright 1950 by Bob Harman and Keith Monroe. Reprinted by permission of Thomas Y. Crowell Company, Inc., publisher.

The *Daily Telegraph,* London: "More Than a Tennis Tournament" (originally "Wimbledon") by Lance Tingay, June 21, 1952; "The Great Match" (originally "Lenglen-Wills Match at Cannes") by A. Wallis Myers; "Mrs. Moody's Seventh Wimbledon Triumph" by A. Wallis Myers; "Laver Wins First Wimbledon Open" by Lance Tingay.

Sarah Palfrey Cooke Danzig: "The Volley" by Sarah Palfrey, from *Winning Tennis and How to Play It* by Sarah Palfrey, Doubleday & Company, Inc., Garden City, N.Y., copyright 1946 by Sarah Palfrey.

Dodd, Mead & Company, New York, and George G. Harrap & Company Ltd., London: "Footwork and the Preservation of Balance" by Suzanne Lenglen, from *Lawn Tennis* by Suzanne Lenglen, copyright 1925.

Paul Gallico: "Helen Moody's Hope of Comeback," from the Chicago *Tribune,* January 7, 1934. Reprinted by permission of the author and Harold Ober Associates, Inc.

Harper's Magazine, New York: "Gentleman's Game" by Russell Lynes, copyright © 1967 by Minneapolis Star and Tribune Co., Inc. Reprinted from the December 1967 issue of *Harper's* Magazine by permission of the author.

Hawthorn Books, Inc., New York: "How It Feels to Be a Beginner" by Sarah Palfrey, from *Tennis for Anyone!* by Sarah Palfrey, copyright © 1966 by Sarah Palfrey Danzig. Reprinted by permission of Hawthorn Books, Inc., New York.

Herald and Weekly Times Limited, Melbourne, Australia: "Supreme Strategist" by Alan Trengove, from the Melbourne *Sun,* July 1966.

Holiday Magazine, Indianapolis: "The One and Only" (originally "The One and Only Wimbledon") by Paul E. Deutschman. Reprinted by permission from *Holiday,* copyright © 1955 The Curtis Publishing Co.

J. B. Lippincott Company, New York: "Qualities That Make a Winning Player" by Doris Hart, from *Tennis With Hart* by Doris Hart, copyright © 1955 by Doris Hart. Reprinted by permission of J. B. Lippincott Company.

Little, Brown and Company, Boston: "Major Walter C. Wingfield, Inventor of the Game" by Parke Cummings, from *American Tennis* by Parke Cummings, copyright © 1957 by Parke Cummings. Reprinted by permission of Little, Brown and Company.

London Express News and Feature Services: "Lottie Dod Won Wimbledon at 15," reproduced from the London *Sunday Express,* July 6, 1952.

Los Angeles *Times:* "The Sutton Sisters" (originally "May Bundy Recalls Her

Reign as Rose Queen") by Jeane Hoffman, copyright © 1955 Los Angeles *Times*. Reprinted by permission.

The Macmillan Company, New York: "The Ruler of the Courts" by John Kieran. Reprinted with permission of The Macmillan Company from *The American Sporting Scene* by John Kieran, with pictures by Joseph W. Golinkin. Copyright 1941 by John Kieran and Joseph W. Golinkin, renewed 1969 by John Kieran.

The New Yorker, New York: "The Story of Hazel Hotchkiss Wightman" (originally "Run, Helen") by Herbert Warren Wind, copyright 1952 The New Yorker Magazine, Inc.; "First U.S. Open Championships" (originally "September Song") by Herbert Warren Wind, copyright © 1968 The New Yorker Magazine, Inc. Reprinted by permission.

The Observer Foreign News Service, London: "Jean Borotra" (originally "Jean Borotra, Vitality Abounding") by Tony Mottram, from The *Observer*, October 26, 1958.

Jack Olsen: "Dennis Ralston," from *Sports Illustrated*, August 26, 1963, copyright © 1963 Time Inc. Reprinted by permission of the author.

Philadelphia *Inquirer:* "Margaret Smith Court" by Sande Padwe, from The Philadelphia *Inquirer*, August 14, 1969.

Paul R. Reynolds, Inc., New York: "Lili Alvarez" by Helen Hull Jacobs, copyright 1932 by San Francisco *Chronicle*. Reprinted by permission of Paul R. Reynolds, Inc., New York.

The Saturday Evening Post, New York: "A Review of Wimbledon" (originally "Wimbledon"), "Some of My Opponents" (originally "Lenglen-Wills: Some of My Opponents"), "My Match Against Mlle. Lenglen" (originally "Lenglen-Wills Match at Cannes") all by Helen Wills (Moody). Reprinted with permission from *The Saturday Evening Post,* copyright 1929–1933 The Curtis Publishing Company, copyright renewed 1957–1961.

Frederick R. Schroeder, Jr.: "U.S. Regains Davis Cup from Australia" by Ted Schroeder with Alan Trengove, from the Melbourne *Sun*.

Charles Scribner's Sons, New York: "The Doherty Brothers" (originally "Masters of the Racket") is reprinted by permission of Charles Scribner's Sons from *Kings of the Court*, pages 37–52, by Edward C. Potter, Jr. Copyright 1936 Charles Scribner's Sons; renewal copyright © 1964 Edward C. Potter, Jr.

Simon and Schuster, New York: "Brookes Versus McLoughlin—Davis Cup," "Lenglen Defaults to Mallory at Forest Hills," "Tilden-Shimizu Davis Cup Match," "Suzanne and Helen," "Tilden's Mysterious Collapse vs. Cochet at Wimbledon," "Borotra-Allison Davis Cup Match in Paris," "Crawford's Classic Defeat of Vines," "Budge-Von Cramm Davis Cup Match" all by Al Laney, from *Covering the Court* by Al Laney, copyright © 1968 by Al Laney; "A Viewpoint of the Game," "The General Technique of All Strokes," "The Drive," "Match Play Tactics and Tennis Psychology" all by William T. Tilden 2d, from *How to Play Better Tennis* by William T. Tilden 2d, copyright 1950 by William T. Tilden; "The Serve and How to

viii   ACKNOWLEDGMENTS

Vary It" by Richard (Pancho) Gonzales, from *How to Play Tennis the Professional Way* edited by Alan Trengove, copyright © 1964 by Alan Trengove.

Sports Illustrated, New York: "The Great Game of Tennis" by Robert Gordon Menzies, copyright © 1955 Time Inc.; "Newport, the Cradle of American Tennis" (originally "The Cradle of Tennis Was Meant to Be Rocky") by John Hanlon, copyright © 1968 Time Inc.; "Chuck McKinley" (originally "Little Man With a Big Wallop") by Kenneth Rudeen, copyright © 1960 Time Inc.; "Manuel Santana" (originally "The Reign in Spain of King Manolo") by Frank DeFord, copyright © 1967 Time Inc.; "Cliff and Nancy Richey" (originally "The Highest Ranking Family in Tennis") by Frank DeFord, copyright © 1965 Time Inc.; "Arthur Ashe" (originally "Service, But First a Smile") by Frank DeFord, copyright © 1966 Time Inc.; "John Newcombe" (originally "A Forgotten Aussie Refreshes the Memory") by Frank DeFord, copyright © 1966 Time Inc.; "Ustinov on Tennis" by Peter Ustinov, copyright © 1969 Time Inc.; "Italy Defeats U.S. in Davis Cup" (originally "Davis: A Cup That Got Away") by William McHale, copyright © 1961 Time Inc.; "Laver Completes His Second Grand Slam" (originally "You Can Play Laver But You Can't Beat Him") by Roy Blount, Jr., copyright © 1969 Time Inc.; "U.S. Defeats Rumania to Retain Davis Cup" (originally "Second Best Is Good Enough") by Frank DeFord, copyright © 1969 Time Inc.; "It Almost Came Up Roses for Rosewall at Wimbledon" by Walter Bingham, copyright © 1970 Time Inc.; "Sudden Death at Forest Hills" by Walter Bingham, copyright © 1970 Time Inc.; "More Joan of Arc Than Shirley Temple" by Roy Blount, Jr., copyright © 1971 Time Inc.; "A Waltz at Wimbledon" by Walter Bingham, copyright © 1971 Time Inc.

Talbert, William F.: "Tony Trabert," 1957.

The *Times,* London: "First French Open Championships" (originally "Dignity Retained by Rosewall") by Rex Bellamy, from The *Times,* June 3, 1968.

United Press International, New York: "End of the Fancy-Pants Era" (originally "Fancy Pants Era Ends") , from United Press International, October 26, 1962.

The Viking Press, Inc., New York: "The Best One I Ever Played" by Donald Budge, from *A Tennis Memoir* by Donald Budge and Frank DeFord, copyright © 1969 by Donald Budge and Frank DeFord. Reprinted by permission of The Viking Press, Inc.

The Washington *Post,* Washington, D.C.: "Good Guy or Anti-Hero?" by Bob Addie, from The Washington *Post,* June 27, 1969.

Hazel Hotchkiss Wightman: "The Wightman Cup" by Hazel Hotchkiss Wightman, from *Fifty Years of Lawn Tennis in the United States,* Lawn Tennis Association, copyright 1931.

CONTENTS

PART II *Great Moments*

PART III *Technique*

SEEING THEM IN ACTION

FOREWORD

When the idea of this book was first conceived by the publishers some time ago, one knotty problem had to be faced immediately. The "Mr. Tennis" of American writers for the past half century had been Allison Danzig of *The New York Times,* and he was the obvious and natural choice to be the volume's editor. The difficulty was that whenever on-the-spot descriptions of famous tennis matches of the past were to be selected for inclusion in the book, a great many of them would necessarily have to have been written by Danzig himself, for through the years the *Times* has been the only national newspaper to give expert, detailed coverage to the sport. Today there are many gifted tennis writers who attend every major tournament, but in the old days there were only a handful and most of them were assigned only to certain events. Any time something momentous was taking place in the tennis world, whether it was at Wimbledon or Forest Hills or Roland Garros or wherever, you could always see Allison Danzig in the press box taking notes.

Allison is the most modest of men. He was not happy about having to choose so much of his own reporting, but he recognized the fact that he'd have to do so if the entire panorama of the game's modern history was to be represented. He made the generous suggestion that I join him as co-editor of this book, and also write this Foreword explaining why the by-line of Allison Danzig appears so often in its pages.

My own role, therefore, has been somewhat that of the sedate partner in a doubles team combination. I've kept the ball in play, but Allison is the one who smashes it away. We have shared a great deal of the editorial work, and I've made a few contributions in the choice of material, but this is basically Allison's book and reflects his special tastes and enthusiasms as well as so much of his own writing. No one has been around the great players and their pitched battles against each other for so long, and no one loves the game and knows it better than he.

In recent years a number of new factors have enhanced the appeal of tennis as a popular sport, both from the spectator and the participant standpoint. These include national and regional television coverage; the opening up of the major tournaments so that the best professionals and amateurs can compete against each other; the construction throughout the country of splendid indoor courts that allow year-round play; the use of metal rackets; and the introduction into major events of new scoring experiments, such as "sudden death." Tennis has suddenly become a major sport instead of the rather exclusive country club sort of activity it once was.

The time seems ripe for this particular book, for as new interest booms, a backward look at the wonderful heritage of the game is also very rewarding. You can leaf through these pages and comprehend why there are so many old-timers who swear no tennis player was ever as good as Bill Tilden. Or no tennis match as glamorous or as fascinating as the one in which Suzanne Lenglen met Helen Wills . . . unless perhaps it was the Don Budge–Baron Von Cramm battle that decided the Davis Cup in 1937? But come to think of it, wasn't Jack Crawford's conquest of Ellsworth Vines at Wimbledon in 1933 even more dramatic? Where does Pancho Gonzales rate among All-Time greats?

Enough. Let your eye run over the Contents and you'll find your own moments in tennis history that you'll particularly want to explore, whether on a revisit or for the first time. Allison Danzig will tell you about them along with such other superb tennis chroniclers of those days as Parke Cummings, Al Laney, John Tunis, A. Wallis Myers, Edward Potter, and Fred Hawthorne. But this book by no means confines itself to ancient history. A new crop of genuinely knowledgeable and sensitive writers, including Fred Tupper, Herbert Warren Wind, Bud Collins, Lance Tingay, Neil Amdur, Rex Bellamy, David Gray, Richard Evans, Walter Bingham, Will Grimsley, Frank DeFord, and Alan Trengove, are here to recount great moments from more recent times, as the stars of today, Rod Laver, John Newcombe, Ken Rosewall, Arthur Ashe, Stan Smith, Tony Roche, and all the rest battle it out for top spot. Nor are the ladies neglected—far from it. The roster of women stars represented ranges all the way back to the Sutton sisters and Hazel Wightman, through the eras of Lenglen and Wills, Alice Marble, Althea Gibson, Maureen Connolly, up to today's outstanding players, Margaret Smith Court, Billie Jean King, Maria Bueno, Ann Jones, and those two newest sensations, Chris Evert and Evonne Goolagong.

As a final bonus, if you are more than a fan and play the game seriously yourself, you'll find much in this book to improve your own strokes and tactics. Part III is completely devoted to instruction by outstanding players who excelled in theory as well, such as Tilden, Billy Talbert, George Lott, and Pancho Gonzales. In similar vein, scattered through Part I are expert technical analyses of the games of a number of great players, written by Julius D. Heldman. I know of nothing that can compare with them in achieving what they set out to do.

Server ready?
Receiver ready?
Read!

PETER SCHWED

PART I

The Heritage of the Game

THE GREAT GAME OF TENNIS

by Robert Gordon Menzies

Lawn tennis, as games go, is a new game. It was not so many years ago that it was a polite garden-party accomplishment. I can, myself, remember the jeering remarks of the "working" youth as white-flanneled players went by. Yet today, on thousands of public and municipal courts, no other than the "working" youth is hard at it. The game of the privileged few, in less than half a century, has become the game of the many. This reflects in part a marked rise in the standards of living, but it also shows the vast attraction of the game.

A few nights ago I was astonished to hear Sir Norman Brookes, in a reminiscent mood, recall that when he first played as a boy the tennis ball had no cover as we know it today. We can say, therefore, that the development of today's game, and the implements used in it, spans the lifetime of one man.

I am a much younger man than Norman Brookes, having been born in 1894. Yet I can remember, as if it were yesterday, how some ruling woman champions served underarm, wearing skirts down to the ground, playing a steady baseline game, never venturing to the net. The first woman to go up to volley and to smash was regarded as a miracle or a monstrosity, according to the point of view.

In Australia the popularity of tennis is enormous. It is actively played by hundreds of thousands of people, and (such are our fortunate conditions) from one year's end to another. Australia's eminence in the game surprises many people. "How does it happen," they say, "that a country which has only just reached a population of 9,000,000 can so consistently have produced teams which, over a long period of years, have been outmatched in success only by the United States?"

The answer is simple enough. Australia, for tennis purposes, is one large California. The varying climates of the six states have this in common: They favor outdoor sport and outdoor living. Material standards of life are high; leisure is abundant. Good food and fresh air are the common lot. Most dwelling houses stand in their own grounds and gardens. For all these reasons, our inbred love of sport finds opportunity and expression. Even the most hardened theoretical socialist finds in games a satisfaction for his natural zest for private enterprise and individual initiative. I know that people have been heard to say reproachfully that Australians are too fond of sport. If this meant that we were a nation of mere onlookers at professional sporting spectacles, the criticism would be powerful. But the truth is that we are a nation of games-players who look at others only on occasions. There

3

are, in Australia, 250,000 registered competitive players, *plus* at least 500,000 who play nonofficial tennis in a purely private way. Behind all the traditional informality and indiscipline with which we are credited, you will find the fitness, the resourcefulness and the competitive spirit which have made the Australian soldier world famous in war and which, in peace, have wrought a national development and construction which have earned the praise of so many perceptive visitors.

Thus it is that tennis has taken its place among the great popular games in Australia and has become one of the influences which form the national characteristics.

Yet one of the fascinating things to witness is how the popularity of a game can affect the game itself, and the position of its leading players. When a game becomes so popular as a spectacle for thousands or scores of thousands, the game becomes big business. To the public or private provision of thousands of tennis courts there is *added* (I emphasize *added*, because the active playing of the game continues to expand) the large-scale and costly provision of spectator accommodations, the intensive organization of competitions, the handling of interstate and international tours.

All this has meant an inevitable change in the activities and nature of the leading amateur players. The old amateurism has been replaced by the new, and we have seen the rise of professional play.

There were great advantages in the old amateur days. I will not dwell on them too long, for there is no more weakening emotion than yearning for the "good old days." The times change and we must change with them. But I will briefly state what I believe those advantages to have been and will then examine more closely what I believe to be the reasons why the old amateurism at the top level has passed away.

As a lad, just good enough at the game to know what it was about and how strokes *ought* to be played, I first saw Norman Brookes, Rod Heath and A. W. Dunlop; some years later there was my friend Gerald Patterson. Let me assume them to be examples of what I call the "old" amateurism.

Each was a distinct individual, with unforgettable characteristics of style and play. Heath had beautifully controlled ground strokes. Dunlop was a born doubles player, with a fine sense of position. Gerald Patterson had a villainous backhand drive, but could rely on the most violent service I have ever seen. Nowadays, when so many first-rate players seem cast in the same mold, when intense coaching has created so much standardization, I frequently find it difficult to remember other than facial differences between the playing characteristics of half a dozen of the greatest players.

Put this down to my ignorance or lack of perception if you like. But is it mere perversity on my part to say that Brookes lives in my mind's eye because of his nonconformity? He was one of the first to adopt and modify the then new "American" service. In his use of it speed was secondary; placement was of the essence. It was as deep as the service line would allow. Its direction was such that the receiver always had to move quite a lot, to forehand or backhand, to play it. As soon as he served, Brookes moved in. Such was his control of service direction and length that he limited the scope of the return, and even appeared by some magic to control its actual direction. In spite of this, powerful opponents would seek to check him by driving to his feet as he advanced to the normally fatal midcourt half-volleying position. They soon discovered that to Brookes the half-volley was a weapon of attack, not of defense. Time after time I have seen him sweeping half-volleys first to one deep corner, then to the other, with his opponent sweating up and down in vain.

What a player! His long trousers perfectly pressed, on his head a peaked tweed or cloth cap, on his face the inscrutable expression of a pale-faced Red Indian, no sign of sweat or bother, no temperamental outbursts, no word to say except an occasional "well played." A slim and not very robust man, he combined an almost diabolical skill with a personal reserve, a dignity (yes, dignity) and a calm maturity of mind and judgment. I have sometimes suspected that a modern coach, given control, would have hammered out of him all the astonishing elements that made him in his day (and his day lasted for many years) the greatest player in the world.

Brookes was an "old" amateur. He had means adequate to enable him to indulge his hobby. He was not overplayed. There were few Davis Cup contests. Each match could be approached with a fresh mind and spirit.

But time has moved on. Big tennis has, as I have said, become big business. The cost of putting on good matches, with special stands and expensive organization and vast crowds of spectators, have all involved today's player in almost continuous play, in tournament or exhibition games. Under the modern circumstances of high taxation, few people can afford such "leisure." The "old" amateur has, in Australia at any rate, practically disappeared from the top ranks. And so we have entered a period when some promising boy of 14 or 15, his education hardly begun, is picked out for coaching and development and joins the staff of some sporting-goods firm. Brookes played his first Davis Cup in 1905, at the age of 28; his last in 1920, at the age of 43 when, in the Challenge Round, he took both W. T. Tilden and W. M. Johnston to four sets; one of the most remarkable feats in lawn tennis history. Today a player is described as a "veteran" by his middle 20s.

There are those who will tell you that the "old" amateurs played when the game was "slower," and "softer," and that they could never have lived with the modern champions, with their "big" services and "fierce" over-heads and "devastating" ground strokes. (You notice that I am a student of sporting journalese.) I do not decry the modern players, whose skill I admire, and who have given hundreds of thousands of us pleasure, when I say that both Tilden and Johnston, at their peak, could have beaten any 1955 amateur at his peak: and they were at their peak when Brookes played them.

But the "new" amateurism—the semiprofessionalism of the great sporting-goods firms (which, we must concede, have done much to develop the game) is here to stay, unless, indeed, it is replaced by complete professionalism or (as I think not improbably) international tennis becomes "open" to both amateur and professional, like golf or cricket. The alternative may well be that the professional promoters will come to regard the Davis Cup as a training ground for quite young amateur champions, to be recruited to the professional ranks later.

Whether we like it or not, the cost of maintaining modern international sporting teams and providing facilities for large armies of spectators to see them play inevitably tends to create a "business" atmosphere. There is another aspect of the matter. The modern proliferation of sporting journals and the expansion of the sporting pages of ordinary newspapers have led the talented, but young and mentally and emotionally immature champions into the glaring light of publicity—extravagant praise and biting criticism being more common than expert and moderate judgment. Too many are coming to regard the player as the bondslave of the public; we say that he has "obligations." If his form leaves him he is rejected and forgotten. If, at the height of his form, he abandons competitive sport in favor of a business or private career in some profession, he is not infrequently accused of "letting the public down." There are many youngish men living in some unskilled occupation today who are simply the victims of these processes. It is not to be wondered at that talented young amateurs increasingly gaze at the professional recruiter with an expectant eye.

I hope I will not be thought discourteous, if, writing for a distinguished sporting journal, I say more about the impact of a good deal of modern sporting journalism upon the lives and minds of young and talented players.

As every man engaged in public affairs knows, it takes a great deal of strength of mind and balance and experience to ignore ignorant criticism and to select and be influenced by informed and just criticism. Boys of 20, playing some game under the eyes of the entire world, under strain, would be phenomenal if they knew how to deal with the mental problems of ignoring or evaluating criticism. If some become swollen headed, as a result of extravagant praise, and others sullen or moody under extravagant blame, it is not to be wondered at. I have sometimes advised young champions at tennis or cricket to give up reading the criticisms until their current series of matches is over. This is on the very sound principle that, though real experts always write understandingly, the pungent criticism of players by those who do not and never have studied the game cannot possess much value.

There is, for those of us who love these games, nothing more pleasant than a vivid account of some match in the press or over the air. Both the ear and the imagination are stimulated. But the occasional extravagant commentator who thinks his opinions are more important than the story of the game is a constant irritant. Nor do I, for one, want to read lurid stories (usually quite fictitious) about alleged personal quarrels among players. It may be thought to be proof of advancing years if I say also that I still prefer a lively report of a Davis Cup match I cannot attend to a series of glossy paragraphs about the love life or matrimonial intentions of the players—but I do.

What is the effect of the Davis Cup or other contests on international relations? The accepted answer is "good." It appears to be widely believed that the spectacle of two or four young athletes fighting out a Davis Cup tie, or a Wimbledon or Forest Hills final, is in its very nature a contribution to international understanding and good will.

This is, I think, substantially true; but it is not inevitably true. The truth is that it depends for the most part on the players, partly on the sporting critics, and of course partly on the spectators. A skillful but ill-tempered and uncontrolled player, glaring at umpires and spectators alike, can in an hour do his own country's reputation for sportsmanship immeasurable harm. You know how fond we all are of generalizing from single instances. An American slams his racket into the ground and makes rude noises at a linesman. "Ah," says a non-American spectator, "these Americans! Always want to have their own way!" An Australian, at Forest Hills, puts on a childish act. "Look!" says an American spectator. "The trouble with these guys from down under is that they can't take a defeat without blaming somebody else." Both statements are nonsense. But they are made, all too frequently.

As the simple onlooker, I do not find the reasons for these occasional tantrums very difficult to understand. It might be useful to try to analyze the problem a little.

Sporting crowds are anything but fools, particularly when the game they are watching (which most of them have played) requires great skill and much subtlety of tactics and execution. There will, of course, be some fools among them; and some inscrutable law of Providence seems to have ordained that fools are frequently more vocal than wise men. But in Australia, about which I can speak with closer knowledge, a great crowd at a Davis Cup tie sees and understands a great deal of what is going on. It is quick to distinguish between the bad temper of a player whose conceit makes him blame somebody else for his own error, and the honest annoyance with *himself* of a player who is tensed up to do his best for his side, and falls into a blunder. No more popular player or more creditable American ever came to Australia to play Davis Cup than Ted Schroeder. Yet frequently I have seen him going back to serve after netting an easy volley, shaking his head and talking to himself with whimsical but violent disapproval. We all loved him for it. It was a natural and human part of his keenness and his will to win.

It is my own opinion that alleged "incidents" are grossly exaggerated in the reports. If we require, as we do nowadays, that mere boys should devote their lives to the game, in spite of their immaturity in general matters, we should not hypocritically expect that their demeanor will at all times and under all circumstances resemble that of a student of mental and moral philosophy. It is not uncommon to find an elderly businessman, fresh from roaring at some underling across his desk or over the telephone, glaring reprovingly at the tennis player who has displayed a sudden spark of ordinary humanity. My own complaint about the young champions of today is not that they complain too much, but that they smile too little. Perhaps it is inheritance: someone once said that the "English take their pleasures sadly."

To sum up, I think that by and large the players in Davis Cup matches have done a first-class job for international good will and understanding. The United States, since the war, has sent to Australia many fine players. With trivial exceptions, they have been outstanding athletes, intelligent and courteous. They have helped Australians to think well of Americans as a whole. I have never listened to one of them making a speech of thanks or of congratulation without marveling at their poise, their fluency, their choice of words. They have made me an admirer of American education.

I have one very happy recollection of how a player can go wrong, and then go right so splendidly that his original error is almost affectionately remembered. Tony Trabert, a superb young champion, was defeated in a crucial match at Melbourne in 1953; defeated by a stroke or two in a match he had looked like winning. In his bitter disappointment he made publicly rude remarks about the behavior of the crowd. (The crowd had, in fact, blended patriotism with judgment very fairly!) There were adverse comments on Trabert all over Australia.

Last year, at Sydney, Trabert and Seixas took the Davis Cup from us by the most concentrated exhibition of skill, fitness and determination I have seen for a long time. Speeches were made when the Cup was handed over. Trabert's turn came. There were 25,000 in the stands, and probably a couple of million listening in. Trabert had a magnificent ovation. He smiled, looked around the stands, and said: "Thank you for that. I was wondering what you would do. A year ago I said some foolish things. But I think I can tell you that I have learned from experience!" The applause was deafening. The Stars and Stripes flew high!

I wish (if you can print such a heresy) that I could be as sure of the contribution to international good will of the sporting critics and writers. The best are, of course, superb. But to paraphrase the old nursery rhyme—
But when they're bad they're horrid.

All of the great international games are deprived of some of the good they otherwise do by the type of writer who looks for mischief—ferrets out and exaggerates personal incidents; writes about tennis as if it were a civil (and not very civil) war; and ends up by producing all the news *not* fit to print.

Still, great games and great nations can survive such blemishes. When I come toward the sunset of my own life and find myself thinking of tennis, it will not be the sensation merchants I will recall. It will be the eager figures of Rosewall and Trabert and Seixas and, further back into what will be a misty past, the fierce power of Patterson's service and the calm, white-clad mastery of Norman Brookes. These are the figures that live.

MAJOR WALTER C. WINGFIELD,
INVENTOR OF THE GAME

by Parke Cummings

In the England of 1874 there were two schools of thought concerning Major Walter Clopton Wingfield, a cavalry officer who had served in China and returned to England to join the Montgomery Yeomanry. One school held that he had invented the game of lawn tennis, commonly known as tennis today. The leading, and most articulate, exponent of that school was the Major himself.

The opposite school declared he had done no such thing, and some of its members even had some rather scathing things to say about his character and motives. Looking over all the factors, it would appear that the jury is still out. Perhaps Major Wingfield did invent lawn tennis, and then again perhaps not.

England of 1874 was a bit beyond the middle of the Victorian era of gaslight and propriety. Its upper classes were becoming more and more sports conscious. The English country gentleman—the type who believed in keeping "fit"—might go in for cricket, Rugby and rowing. And it was rather likely that a croquet set was to be found on one of his lawns. The chances were that some feminine member of his family had played a part in bringing this about, since the trend was toward outdoor games that could be played by both men and women. Croquet was obviously the ladies' dish. On the other hand, it often seemed lukewarm to a male who wanted something in the way of really strenuous exercise. It seemed lukewarm, too, in comparison to several racket games with which he might be familiar. One of these was the game of court tennis. It goes back for centuries; kings have played it; Chaucer, Shakespeare and many other early writers have described it. Originally it was a form of handball, played in courtyards or monastery cloisters, but in the fifteenth and sixteenth centuries primitive forms of rackets made their appearance. The game had its ups and downs where popularity was concerned.

An English writer remarked of sixteenth-century France: "Ye would thinke they [French players] were borne with rackets in their hands. . . . There be more Tennis Players in France than ale drinkers . . . with us." But roughly a century later another English writer deplored the gambling and crookedness that accompanied it in England. "There are but few matches made, but there was either a bribed Marker, or some Gentleman that had first lost his Estate, and then his Honour, and so was forc'd to comply with the Sharpings and Tricks of the Town, to get his bread; or some Scoundrel that never had Estate or Honour either, but had acquired the game by diligent attendance upon the courts . . . and there was hardly a Set play'd but there was some sort of Falshood and Deceit practic'd."

In our year 1874, however, court tennis was not nearly as popular as ale guzzling, nor were its current abuses such as to induce any wide-scale viewing with alarm. It had become an indoor club game for relatively few well-heeled males. The same continued to hold true in 1957, both in England and in the United States, where there are less than a dozen courts in existence.

And the rules in 1874 were the same as in effect in 1957. To grasp them in their entirety is said to take months of hard cerebration, because the game is, perhaps, the most complex and bewildering ever devised by the mind of man. In the very barest essentials, court tennis is a racket-and-ball game played on a court divided by a net. The court is enclosed by walls, and the ball can be played off the walls and into various openings in them, given such esoteric names as dedans, grille, gallery. The scoring is similar to modern lawn tennis, with games scored in terms of love, 15, 30, 40 and deuce, and 6-game sets the usual custom.

A second club game played indoors by our lord—but not his lady—was rackets. . . . Its origins were not so ancient as those of court tennis, nor had it ever been styled the "game of kings." Indeed, it was believed that rackets originated in the yards of eighteenth-century English debtors' jails. Apparently these were rather swank jails. You couldn't get into a rackets-playing jail for owing a mere five shillings. You had to be in debt by a really impressive amount—probably a hundred pounds or more.

In any event, by 1874 rackets had moved out of the jails into private clubs, where, like court tennis, it has remained. It is played in a walled court without a net, the ball alternately stroked to the front wall by opponents, and scoring is in 15-point games. The modern games of squash rackets and squash tennis are smaller and less expensive outgrowths of rackets.

A third game that enjoyed popularity in 1874 was badminton. It apparently originated in India, where it was known as "poona," and was imported by British Army officers. In 1873, the story goes, they gave a demonstration of it at Badminton, the Duke of Beaufort's country estate. Badminton, of course, continues as a popular game in many countries, much more so than court tennis or rackets. It is played with a racket and a feathered shuttlecock, or "bird," over a high net on a court considerably smaller than the modern lawn tennis court.

In addition to court tennis, rackets and badminton, the wall game of "fives" was familiar to graduates of such schools as Eton and Harrow. In a few locales there had been an outdoor game, "long tennis." . . .

This was the picture that confronted Major Wingfield in February of 1874. He came from an old and distinguished family. Some ancestors had played the ancient game of court tennis. He, too, was familiar with it and with rackets. He knew these club games were denied to women—and that cricket and Rugby were too rough for them. He saw the need for an outdoor game that a woman could play and that would give her husband or brothers more of a workout than croquet. And he saw another need. His family was an illustrious one—there was a Wingfield Castle in existence when William the Conqueror invaded England—but now this gentleman at arms was a man of modest means. It would be well if he could find some way of supplementing his income, such as by inventing the game that the times called for.

This the shrewd Major proceeded to do, or to claim that he had done. In any event, he succeeded in obtaining a patent for his game. His invention consisted partly of an eight-page pamphlet giving the rules of his game, some hints on play, and a diagram of the court. On the cover was the legend "Sphairistike or Lawn Tennis." The pamphlet itself was called "The Major's Game of Lawn Tennis, Dedicated to the party assembled at Nantclwyd in December, 1873."

It appears that Wingfield had visited friends at a Christmas party in that Welsh town and discussed his proposed game with them, and perhaps carried on some experiments. In retrospect, lawn tennis seems to have had two narrow escapes. First it was burdened with the name Sphairistike, which never caught on, perhaps because detractors abbreviated this to "sticky." And since the game of badminton took its name from Badminton, the estate, it might logically have followed that lawn tennis would have been billed henceforth as Nantclwyd—a prospect to give one pause.

The Major's original pamphlet gave six rules. The most important provided for the 15-point game scoring of rackets and badminton and specified, as do these games, that a point may be scored only by the server. On the other hand, it aped court tennis by providing for a court whose two sides, as divided by the net, were not identical, and also by decreeing that the serve should be made from one side of the court only—the server to stand in the "crease" marked H in the diagram.

Because of this it was argued—and not without logic—that Wingfield actually had "invented" nothing, that his game was merely a goulash, in various proportions, of the older racket games. Wingfield denied this. He pointed to the hourglass shape of his court, narrower at the net than the baseline, and to the wing nets stretched along the sidelines near the net; both of them, he claimed, were "original" features. Moreover, he maintained that his "Sphairistike" was an adaptation of an ancient Greek game on which he had done diligent research. Detractors pooh-poohed his claims. The hourglass shape and the wing nets were of no earthly use. They were just gimmicks to make it appear that Wingfield had invented something new and therefore patentable. As for "Sphairistike," it was merely the ancient Greek command for "Play ball!"

Actually Wingfield was selling more than rules and diagrams. He was also marketing equipment for a "new and improved portable court for playing the ancient game of tennis." (Some of his advertising billed it as "wingless tennis" to distinguish it from badminton and its winged shuttlecock.) With his pamphlet came a wooden painted box 36 inches by 12 by 6. This contained poles, pegs, and netting for the net and wing nets; four tennis rackets; a bag of balls (quantity unspecified); a mallet for hammering in the net stakes; and a brush for marking out the court. The outfit was priced at five guineas, which came to a bit over twenty-six dollars, not too stiff a price for a "new and improved portable court" (plus balls and rackets) even at the purchasing value of the 1874 dollar.

This would seem to be one of sport's earliest package deals. Whether the Major was entitled to a patent I leave to other authorities, but I do maintain he laid it on more than a bit thick with at least one of his claims for his five-guinea do-it-yourself kit. This is the statement that with it a "perfect court" could be put up on any croquet ground in five minutes.

Nearly three decades ago my father and I—chiefly the former—built our own clay tennis court and spent nearly a year in doing so. This may be begging the question, since we worked in hilly, rocky New England terrain, calling for excavating, filling, and hard pick and shovel work. Wingfield was assuming a velvet-smooth English lawn with which to start—the kind for which the prescription is "Water and roll for 500 years."

But, granting that kind of lawn, no one was going to set up a court on it in any five minutes. It would have taken more time than that just to erect the net and the complicated wing nets. The lines then had to be marked out. To do so originally requires, at a minimum, two steel tapes, a working knowledge of plane geometry, and a stretch of cord to enable the marker to make straight lines between the points of intersection. I hope I may be pardoned if I claim to speak as an authority. My court has long since been laid out, with permanent pegs placed at all the intersections. For thirty years I've been marking this court with an efficient dry marker. I've spent more time marking than some people have playing. I can lay down reasonably straight lines without even bothering to stretch out a cord. In recognition of this, a group of friends who play here presented me a few years ago with a cup inscribed with the accolade "Undisputed World Champion Tennis Court Marker, Freehand Style." Of course, this tribute is overgenerous, but I'll admit to better than average skill. And on the best day I ever had I couldn't even re-mark my court—tracing for the most part over lines that are already there—in five minutes, let alone lay out one from scratch.

And let alone the matter of backstops and sidestops. Apparently these weren't contemplated on the Major's perfect court, and, indeed, they may not have been necessary. Undoubtedly the balls and rackets he supplied were less resilient than modern ones. His original net, badmintonlike, was almost five feet high—compared to the three-foot one of modern tennis— and his court was shorter. A hard-hit ball, clearing such a high net, would go beyond the baseline. We can infer that the original brand of Sphairistike was played at a much softer pace than modern lawn tennis, and hence that balls didn't go too far afield. And very likely the footman, the coachman, the butler, or the gardener could be pressed into service as ball boys. So perhaps a lack of backstops, which are indispensable on a modern court, was no detriment in the Wingfield era.

And perhaps, because of the endless hours I've spent on my own court, I'm unnecessarily indignant over the Major's claim of a perfect court in five minutes. Although it's obvious that no Wingfield customer could have come close to meeting that deadline, there is no record of complaints on that score.

Clad in gray flannel suit, Wingfield would have been able to hold his own on Madison Avenue in the mid-twentieth century. He fully understood the value of the endorsement. One of his earliest come-ons was a brochure with a list of satisfied customers. It started off with a royalty category, including the Prince of Wales, then descended through dukes and earls, and ended up with mere lords and ladies. Actually, the astute Major got an appreciable number of people to play the outdoor ball-and-racket game the times called for, but he failed to capitalize, as he had hoped, on his patent. Others took over his game and constantly altered it. Sometimes he tried to keep up with the changes, but he couldn't keep up fast enough.

Within a year after his first rules he issued a new set. He retained the rackets-badminton scoring, the wing nets, and the wasp-waisted court. But he eliminated the service crease and provided for serving from either side of the net, both now being identical. Previously his service courts had been in the *rear* of the court, as in badminton. He moved them up to the fore part, near the net, and specified that the server must move back to the baseline at the end of the court, as has been the rule ever since. It was, to say the least, a happy change. One can imagine the advantage such later-day cannonball servers as William T. Tilden or Ellsworth Vines would have had if they could have stood in the *middle* of their own court and blasted the ball all the way to their opponent's baseline!

Suggestion followed on suggestion, variation on variation. Wingfield's game became a club game as well as one for private estates. In 1875 the Marylebone Cricket Club issued rules which were, in effect, okayed by the Major. Other clubs began to take an interest in the new pastime, and there was an economic reason. The All England Croquet Club is the most famous case in point. Sphairistike, in one variation or another, was pushing croquet more and more into the background, and the club found itself with more croquet lawns than its dwindling membership could support. In 1875 it followed the sound maxim "If you can't beat 'em, join 'em." It converted one of these lawns into a lawn tennis court, and by doing so probably saved itself from bankruptcy.

Two short years later the club—which had now become the All England Croquet and Lawn Tennis Club—recodified the rules. In that year, 1877, it held the first All England Tournament for the championship of the country, the first "Wimbledon," as it is now familiarly known because of the club's location. The court was now rectangular instead of hourglass shape. The wing nets were gone, the playing net was made lower, and the badminton-rackets system of scoring had been abandoned, supplanted by the court tennis system of games and sets which survives to this day.

Wingfield's game was no longer Wingfield's. His "invention" was one over which he could not exercise control. Up to the time of his death on April 18, 1912, he stoutly maintained that he *had* made a bona fide invention. At a later day one could look at it both ways. Financially his patent brought him little because he couldn't stop the game from being altered by those who chose to do so. It seems certain that he did not die a man of wealth. (For a part of his life he had served as a justice of the peace for Montgomeryshire.) He had also tried to make additional money by writing other brochures—"The Sportsman's Guide," "Bicycle Gymkhana," "Musical Rides." On his death, the London *Times* cited him as "late His Majesty's Body Guard" in a brief paragraph in the obituary column.

Of his connection with the game of tennis there was no mention, nor was he given a detailed obituary as were some of his more noted contemporaries. However, there was at that moment a premium on space for obituaries, since many were devoted to noted passengers on the RMS *Titanic* who had perished when it struck an iceberg four days before.

The first issues of the magazines *American Lawn Tennis* and *English Lawn Tennis* to be published after the Major's death made no mention whatever of that death. From the evidence it would appear that in the popular imagination the name Walter Clopton Wingfield meant virtually nothing at the time. To the ordinary tennis follower what counted most were the leading players of the day, not the origins of the game.

But to historians of the game, the latter point seemed more important, and there were some who obviously thought that the Major's contribution had been substantial. Indeed, in the English publication *Who Was Who* he is listed, without qualification, as "inventor of the game of lawn tennis." On all the evidence, it would seem safe to say that lawn tennis was something that Major Wingfield had a hand in. Perhaps the idea was 100 per cent his, perhaps only 1 per cent. But certainly an idea was there.

SPHAIRISTIKE, HISTORY OF THE UNITED STATES LAWN TENNIS ASSOCIATION

by Allison Danzig

In December 1873, at a garden party at Nantclwyd in Wales, the game of lawn tennis was given to the world. Its inventor, who adapted it from the ancient sport of court tennis, was Major Walter Clopton Wingfield, a full-bearded sportsman whose family had established itself in Wingfield Castle in Suffolk long before the coming of William the Conqueror from Normandy. Major Wingfield gave his invention the Greek name of Sphairistike.

British games follow the Union Jack, and lawn tennis was introduced to the United States when, in the spring of 1874, Mary Ewing Outerbridge brought a tennis net, rackets, and balls back with her from Bermuda. Her brother, A. Emilius Outerbridge, got her permission to set up her net and mark out the hourglass-shaped court on the grounds of the Staten Island Cricket and Baseball Club at Camp Washington (St. George), Staten Island.

New England claimed that William Appleton's court at Nahant, Massachusetts, was the first in the United States and that Dr. James Dwight, the "father of American tennis," and F. R. Sears, brother of the first national champion, were the original players. But the late Malcolm D. Whitman, in his fascinating work *Tennis Origins and Mysteries,* settled the dispute in favor of the Outerbridges.

New York, Boston, and Philadelphia became the centers of the new game. Each city, as well as each club, had its own ideas about the rules, the size and weight of the balls, the height of the net, and the scoring system. No attempt at standardization was made until after the first important tournament, held at Staten Island in 1880, when Dr. Dwight and Richard D. Sears refused to play in the singles because they found the balls to be only two-thirds the size of those to which they were accustomed. They impressed upon the leaders the necessity of ending the chaotic conditions if the game was to grow; and Clarence M. Clark for the All-Philadelphia Lawn Tennis Committee, E. H. Outerbridge and Dr. Dwight, representative of the Beacon Park Athletic Association of Boston, called a meeting for May 21, 1881, at the Fifth Avenue Hotel in New York to organize.

Nineteen clubs sent delegates; fifteen more were represented by proxy. They formed the United States National Lawn Tennis Association and elected General R. S. Oliver of the Albany Tennis Club president. Specifications were set for the size and weight of the ball; the All-England Marylebone rules for 1881 were adopted; the 15-point system of scoring by games and sets, as used in court tennis, was made official; the height of the net, the distance of the service line from the net, and the position of the server were definitely established; and the first national championship matches were awarded to Newport.

Such were the roots of what today is the United States Lawn Tennis Association, which holds sovereignty over more than eight hundred clubs throughout the land, sanctions seven hundred tournaments, handles funds running into six figures annually, and operates through some thirty national committees, with headquarters in New York. Total receipts from the first championship were reported as $250, against expenses of $245.68.

As early as that first meeting, the question of amateurism raised its head, and the stand was taken that has held fast down through the years: none but amateurs should be allowed to enter any match played by the association. The game was entirely social; those who took part in the tournaments came from the leisure class and played solely for pleasure. The expense of competing was small. The player-writer and the "tennis bum" were a long way off. The press did not take the sport seriously enough to make lucrative offers, and the public looked with amusement, if not contempt, at the sport.

Dr. Dwight succeeded General Oliver as president of the association and served altogether for twenty-one years (there was an interval of nine years between two of his terms when T. K. Fraser, Richard D. Sears, Joseph S. Clark, and Henry W. Slocum, Jr., in turn held the office). Under Dr. Dwight's leadership the game had a gradual and steady growth. By 1885 fifty-one clubs were listed as members, sectional championships and invitation tournaments were being sponsored, the national championship had been opened to foreign players, the first ten players were being ranked, and a small balance had accumulated in the treasury. In 1889 it was moved and seconded "that the association extend its protecting wing to the Lady Lawn Tennis players of the country"—and carried. In 1893 the membership was 107 clubs and the treasury balance $1,457.48; and in that year the West Side Tennis Club, destined to become the most influential in the game on this side of the Atlantic, was founded. But in 1895 tennis entered upon a period of rapid decline; the rise of golf and the Spanish American War partly accounted for it. Membership dropped steadily, and only forty-four clubs were left in the association at the turn of the century. In 1900, however, the inauguration of the Davis Cup matches helped bring tennis new popularity. The international matches got lavish publicity, membership jumped rapidly, and so did the treasury balance. Old tournaments were revived, new ones were started.

Then Maurice McLoughlin, the California Comet, with his "revolutionary" speed, cannonball service, and spectacular net attack, made tennis something people, even those who knew nothing about the sport, would pay to see. The Davis Cup matches at Forest Hills in 1914, in which McLoughlin's play against Norman Brookes and Anthony Wilding of Australasia worked the crowd up to a high pitch of excitement, definitely served notice that tennis, formerly looked down upon by the general public as the effeminate pastime of cotillion leaders and their ladies, had become a major sport. Out of the highly profitable series at Forest Hills came an irresistible demand for serving tennis's biggest plums in New York. Frequent efforts had been made to bring the national championship to the metropolis, but the charm of Newport's velvet lawns, aristocratic setting, and hospitality was so great that the Casino remained the venue of the championship for thirty-four years. Now, finally, at the annual meeting in 1915, Julian S. Myrick and Holcombe Ward, two gentlemen whose names were to bulk large in the annals of the U.S.L.T.A., led the fight for the transfer. It was a close fight and Newport lost out by the thin margin of 129 votes to 119.

From then on, the growth of the game was lusty, and Julian Myrick figured more and more prominently in the U.S.L.T.A. Appointed to serve as president in 1917, when president George T. Adee and vice president Dwight F. Davis left for war duty, he was elected vice president in 1918 and again in 1919, and in 1920 became president. He served only three terms, but during those three years he became the most publicized leader in the history of the association, and the U.S.L.T.A. became the most influential tennis governing body in the world. The scope of the Davis Cup was doubled, with twenty-six nations in the fold. In the first year of Mr. Myrick's tenure began the joint reigns of William Tilden as the world's champion and of the United States as the supreme ruler of the courts, the winner of the Davis Cup for seven successive years. Mr. Myrick's national policy was to democratize the game and open it up to all classes. There was an aggressive campaign for the development of junior tennis, and the foundation was laid for the advance of public park tennis. Myrick liked to think of international matches as an agency for cementing friendly ties among the competing nations, and of the players as ambassadors of good will—men whose conduct on the court was impeccable and whose amateurism was authentic beyond challenge. Not only winning but the manner of winning or losing was dear to his heart, and he was responsible for hanging Kipling's quotation over the marquee steps at the West Side Tennis Club: "If you can meet with Triumph and Disaster, And treat those two impostors just the same."

The pursuit of these ideals led to a period of acrimonious controversy. For forty years the association had gone along without serious warfare within its ranks, though the question of amateurism had come up repeatedly, and it was not until Mr. Myrick's time that the players threatened to rebel against the irksome restrictions. Tennis at this time was becoming big business. At the 1923 meeting the treasurer's report showed current assets of $26,281, a Davis Cup fund of $10,000, and a surplus account of $27,632. The revenue from the Davis Cup matches in 1922 had been $22,720; from the national championship, $26,675. The West Side Tennis Club was putting up its huge concrete stadium. Money was in the air, pouring through the turnstiles at the amateur matches, and the amateurs got ideas.

The man who was responsible for bringing in most of the money was William Tatem Tilden 2d. Another drawing card was Vincent Richards. Both were individualists, and there was little they agreed on, though they won the doubles championship together. But they did agree that Mike Myrick was a dictator and that the association was tyrannical in preventing the amateurs from picking up a few pennies on their expense accounts or by writing for the papers. Considering the time they were giving to swelling the game's exchequer, they thought it was pretty small potatoes, and they said so right out loud.

As a matter of accuracy, it was not until Myrick had retired from the presidency and been succeeded by Dwight F. Davis and George W. Wightman that the issue reached a climax with the adoption of the so-called player-writer rule. George T. Adee and Holcombe Ward, as successive chairmen of the amateur rule committee, were responsible for initiating legislation delimiting the players' extracurricular activities, but Myrick was still regarded as the guiding hand behind any U.S.L.T.A. action. During the years when Tilden and Richards were inveighing against the association, he was pictured in some of the press as the symbol of star-chamber reactionaryism. Tilden, in the eyes of his friends, was the apostle of progressivism. He fought Myrick and the men he thought were Myrick's puppets on every issue in open debate on the floor of the annual meetings. It was the player-writer rule, which cut heavily into his income, that precipitated hostilities, but he fought on many other counts. In 1923 there was the memorable dressing-down of Tilden in the locker rooms of the West Side Tennis Club.

Members of the Davis Cup Committee, of which Myrick was chairman, ordered Tilden to stop playing "mixed doubles" after he and Richard Norris Williams 2d had lost two of the first three sets to Gerald Patterson and Pat O'Hara-Wood of Australia. In 1926 Tilden disagreed violently with the ranking committee's report and spoke so persuasively at the annual meeting that the delegates threw out the ranking. That same year he was breathing fire and defiance against the powers because they refused to sanction the exhibition matches he wanted to put on at Madison Square Garden with Jean Borotra, René Lacoste, and Jacques Brugnon of France and with Vincent Richards for Ann Morgan's Fund for Devastated France. Tilden said he would go through with them, sanction or no sanction. Even after the French players had declined to become embroiled with the U.S.L.T.A., he stood by this position, declaring that Richards was with him. When the youthful Richards contradicted him, he vented his wrath on his former protégé, and, having no one to play with, had to yield.

On the question of the player-writer rule and the limitations on expense payments, however, Richards was with Tilden all the way. His differences with the association on these issues had a bearing on Richards's decision to turn his back on amateur tennis at the end of the 1926 season, when he was approaching the peak of his powers, and go on a professional tour with Suzanne Lenglen and Mary K. Browne under the aegis of C. C. Pyle.

Tilden remained in the ranks for four years more. His battles with the association reached a climax in 1928, when he was removed from the Davis Cup team as captain and player while abroad for violating the player-writer rule. When the French heard of Tilden's suspension, they hollered murder. This was the first time the challenge round had ever been staged in France, and they had built a new stadium at Auteuil and cast frugality to the winds. The knowledge that the most colorful actor in the show, the one and only "Beeg Beel," was not to be allowed to go on knocked the props from under them. They burned up the cables to America.

Myron T. Herrick, the American ambassador to France, got busy. He cabled Joseph W. Wear, then chairman of the Davis Cup committee. The executives of the U.S.L.T.A. hastily convened, and word was cabled to Paris immediately that Tilden could play but that he would be brought up on charges upon his return home. The French threw their hats in the air and poured into Stade Roland Garros to see their men make a bum out of the hero of the hour. They almost had heart failure when Tilden opened the series by licking Lacoste, but, finally Tilden returned home with his beaten team, the losers in the series by four matches to one. The charges of violating the amateur rule were sustained and he was suspended from further competition that year.

Following Tilden's withdrawal from the amateur ranks in 1930, the U.S.L.T.A. has been able to relax in comparative peace. Now and then, to be sure, a rumble of discord has disturbed its serenity. In 1932 a group of players just below the top flight signed a petition to boycott one of the major grass court tournaments at Seabright, New Jersey, if the holding club did not change its practice of paying expenses only as long as the player remained in competition, and not necessarily for the whole week. That same year Ellsworth Vines, then national champion, announced that he was dropping out of the University of Southern California, apparently for the purpose of concentrating on tennis and winning a place on the Davis Cup team. His action was compared to that of John Doeg, who left Stanford in 1928 to seek a place on the cup team, with the result that Dr. Sumner Hardy, California Association president, let off a blast charging the Davis Cup committee with making bums out of the young players. Holcombe Ward, chairman of the Davis Cup committee, wired Vines to stay in school. Vines gave lack of funds as the reason for his leaving college, and was quoted as saying, "I can't even write for newspapers or work in a sporting goods store without losing my amateur status."

The restrictions that irked Vines have irked other players after him, but the trend has been to tighten rather than relax the amateur regulations. Expense accounts are more strictly inspected and the eight weeks' rule has been adopted, limiting the number of tournaments in which an amateur may accept expenses while competing on his own—that is, not as a sectional representative or as a member of an international team. Loopholes in the rules have been found and made use of, but it is the avowed intent of the U.S.L.T.A. to show little leniency to transgressors.

The purpose of the eight weeks' rule is to stop the practice of some amateurs of playing the year round; in short, to eliminate the tennis bum and to make the young player stick to school or business except in the regular summer season. Louis B. Dailey, president of the U.S.L.T.A. in 1930, was a militant advocate of such a policy, but he was regarded as an extremist by some of his contemporaries. The incumbent, Holcombe Ward, is definitely committed to it, just as he was in 1932 when he sent his telegram to Vines.

The big problem the association has faced since Tilden's exit has been how to keep its top players in the amateur ranks. Tilden made so much out of tennis that the game has attracted young men from families of modest circumstances, and it is such players who have dominated tennis in this country for the past decade. The opportunity of gaining financial independence for life in a year or two of professional touring is too tempting to be resisted, so most of the prize attractions of amateur tennis have left the fold in a steady procession.

President Ward says that this exodus is no problem and that the association is not concerned over the loss of Budge or any of the other amateurs who preceded him into professionalism. "Some people," says Ward, "have the idea that the association is interested only in making money. This is not so. Our object is to promote interest in tennis, to get more and more young people to play it all over the country, and to help the player to improve the standard of his game. Anything that assists toward this end is welcomed by us.

"We think that players like Donald Budge are an asset to tennis whether they play as amateurs or professionals. The professional reaches towns and cities that seldom, if ever, have the opportunity to see first-class tennis. Men of the type of Budge furnish the young player a wholesome example in deportment and sportsmanship. Naturally, we would like to have Budge with us this year. His absence may mean the difference between winning and losing the Davis Cup, but, while we are sorry to lose him, we don't think any the less of him. I think he made a wise decision. All of us have to think of our futures. And it is worth remembering that his going leaves the field wide open.

"Think of it from the standpoint of the players: how much more incentive they have to improve themselves, now that no one player stands out as a sure thing. During the seven years we held the cup with Tilden and Johnston, the only others who broke into the line-up were Vincent Richards, Dick Williams, Watson Washburn, and Francis Hunter. As to our position on the open tournament, I do not see any possibility of there being an open tournament in tennis in the near future. First of all, it has yet to be demonstrated that the top professionals themselves would be interested in an open championship. They take the position that they have more to lose than to gain from such a tournament. If they were beaten by amateurs, their earning power might suffer, and they realize far more from their exhibitions than they would from an open championship.

"The U.S.L.T.A. has a heavy schedule of tournaments, and we do not see where any additional tournaments could be fitted in without conflicting with our amateur events. We wish the professionals well, but our desire to cooperate with them does not go so far as to sacrifice our own amateur tournaments."

RICHARD SEARS' DEATH

by S. Wallis Merrihew

When Richard Dudley Sears died on April 8 [1943] a great and well-loved figure in the game of lawn tennis passed on to the bourne from which none return. Beginning with the first championship of the United States in 1881, he won the supreme title seven consecutive times, an achievement unequaled by anyone in our game. After 1887 he retired from tournament competition, having sustained an injury to his playing arm, and it remained for two other American players—the late William A. Larned and William T. Tilden, 2d—to equal his wins in number, but in the case of both there was an interim in making the victories.

Four years had elapsed between the advent of Major Walter Clopton Wingfield and his game of Sphairistike in England and the formation of the United States National Lawn Tennis Association. The first championship of that body was held at Newport, Rhode Island, in August 1881, and Sears came through without losing a set. He won again in 1882 and 1883, and in both years no opponent was able to win a set. It had become the opinion that something must be done, and so the challenge round was instituted. The tournament became an all-comers tournament, from which the champion was barred, and the winner had the right to challenge the champion to play a match which would decide the championship. This was no deterrent to Sears, however. He continued to "stand out" and to defend his title successfully. The end came with the 1887 championship, shortly after winning which Sears suffered an injury which compelled him to withdraw from active play. Henry W. Slocum, Jr., was runner-up to Sears in 1887, and he won the all-comers the next year and became champion through Sears' default in the challenge round.

The literature of the early and middle 1880s is replete with descriptions of Sears and his play. In combination with the records, they establish incontestably the superiority of the first champion to all other players. He began his championship play at the age of nineteen years and eleven months, for in those years the greatest honors were won by the young. It was not until 1882 that all players served overhand, "with more or less speed, mostly less, with everyone coming in to volley as soon as any good opening presented itself," as he put it. Dr. James Dwight and Sears had taken up lobbing since 1881 and did well at it. During the first seven years of the championship there was no consistent following in of the service; one reason probably being because there was no rest whatever allowed.

The 1884 English championship at Wimbledon was notable "for the first appearance of American invaders," i.e., Sears and Dr. Dwight. "Sears did not, as a fact, play, retiring in the first round," as Burrow's *Last Eight* records it. The 1884 American championship challenge round, Sears versus Howard Taylor, was a match "that calls for little comment, inasmuch as the champion, fresh from practice with the best players of England, had no difficulty in retaining his title," as Slocum says in his *Lawn Tennis in Our Own Country*. Taylor did win a set, the first that anyone had taken from Sears. Since the meeting of 1884, "Mr. Sears made another trip to England and returned" with an entirely new stroke, "the Lawford," as Slocum notes. Sears "used it with telling effect in his match with Brinley, and easily won, for the fifth time." This was in 1885. In 1886 R. L. Beeckman came through to the challenge round and won one set from Sears. In 1887 it was Slocum who challenged Sears and he won only six games in three sets.

THE DOHERTY BROTHERS

by Edward C. Potter, Jr.

For the average spectator, the most perfect technical exhibition of a game is a poor substitute for bitter rivalry and magnetic personality. The phlegmatic Englishman no less than the volatile Latin likes the smell of strife, even on the tennis court. The beautiful strokes of the unexciting Baddeleys dimmed his enthusiasm almost to the vanishing point. Receipts for the 1897 Wimbledon challenge match touched the all-time low of seventy pounds. Still, the few who saw Reggie Doherty beat Harold Mahony that day could tell their grandchildren, like the Waterloo veteran, "We were there." A new family with charm as well as skill took over the Renshaws' crown and held it almost continuously for ten years.

Lawn tennis had long since passed through the experimental stage of the eighties. Technique and tactics were already developed to a point where innovations could only be looked on as eccentricities. Yet, such is man's nature that, no matter how often the worth of classic principles has been proved, some gifted individual whose personality, environment, or training has made him the exemplar of a new style will impose that style on his generation. Sooner or later, of course, the classicist comes back into his own. Then the brilliant innovator is remembered rather for his personality than for any outstanding contribution to the fundamentals of the art.

It was the clash of the individualist, represented by Lawford, with the classicism of the Renshaws which gave the first impetus to the game. As soon as both opponents became stylists, as in the case of Pim and Baddeley, interest waned. With Reggie Doherty arrived a new family of stylists who held its place against the attacks of many different individualists, each with his own special touch of genius. It is a remarkable tribute to their influence that among the present generation of players to whom the Renshaws are only a name the "Do's" are still remembered for their personality and technical skill.

What did these brothers do for lawn tennis? They were not the first to create even one of the strokes which make up the complete game. They did not invent the perfect forehand nor the classic backhand, the high nor the low volley, the service nor the smash. They were not supreme in any single department. Others have had stronger ground strokes or more severe services or more deadly volleys. But, with perhaps one exception, there have been no players who combined all these elements to the same degree of perfection as Reggie and Laurie Doherty. There have certainly been none who added to exemplary technique a character of such personal charm and sportsmanship. It is this which has earned them fame not only as masters of the racket but as knights of the court.

There was an older brother, W. V., who went to Oxford, where he captained the varsity in 1892. Had his temperament and inclination permitted, he might have been the first Doherty to place his name on the championship roll. But he was absorbed in his theological studies and he was of indolent disposition. He was content with the reflected glory of his younger brothers. He accompanied them sometimes to a meeting at home or abroad. He often retired when within a point of victory to take a seat at the sideline of the court where the others were playing.

Reggie and Laurie were more energetic and ambitious once they developed an aptitude for their brother's favorite pastime. Reggie was the older by eight days less than two years, and throughout their lives Laurie followed closely in his footsteps. They were educated at Westminster School and Cambridge University. Both were above the average as boy players, but there was nothing to mark them as future champions. Reggie was a good footballer and cricketer. At tennis he won a boys' singles tournament at fourteen. In the same year he and W. V. won the junior doubles at Craigside. But it was not until he went to Cambridge that he gave up other sports for tennis. Interest in the game had reached such a low ebb that there were only two entries in the 1894 covered-court championship. Reggie was one of them. Though he lost to E. G. Meers, *The Field* observed that he was "a young player of great promise whose lawn tennis future will be watched with interest. He has capital ground strokes, volleys hard and clean, serves a capital length, and keeps a cool head."

No doubt all this was true enough, but if there had been more than two competitors, Reggie might have passed unnoticed. When he lost his first match at Wimbledon a few months later, his name appeared only in the summaries. There was no leap to fame at a bound like the Renshaws. But the Dohertys were none the less persistent in improving their game. If Reggie was no shining light at Wimbledon he stood out among his fellows at Cambridge. He made history in the varsity match with Oxford by winning three singles and three doubles without a defeat. Laurie showed "capital form" at Queens, and the brothers took in all the principal tournaments so as to sharpen their weapons by contact with ranking players.

At the 1895 Wimbledon, Reggie stepped into the "last eight" for the first time, but he could not take a set from Herbert Baddeley. In August he won his first open tournament at Exmouth. Now he was well enough known to be criticized. "He will never be in the first rank," it was said, "if he does not get more dash into his play." It was sound criticism. Dash was the one thing Reggie always lacked. He was already suffering from the chronic indigestion which played havoc with him later on. He made up for his lack of dash by other qualities which his critic overlooked. To prove it he won both the Scottish championship and the Welsh covered-court title.

Laurie joined Reggie at Cambridge in the fall. The varsity season was all Doherty. Wimbledon, however, was still out of reach. Both lost in the first round of the singles, Reggie going down to Mahony, the champion-to-be. . . . That winter, following the Renshaws' example, Reggie wintered on the Riviera, and Laurie joined him for some of the major tournaments. Here Reggie commenced the succession of wins which included six Monte

Carlo titles. In the spring Laurie won at Queens. Reggie beat Mahony for the Irish championship. At Wimbledon the brothers won the doubles title from the Baddeleys. Reggie went through to the singles title without losing a set. The "Do's" had arrived.

Reggie Doherty, or as he came to be known, "Big Do," was a natural player in the sense that tennis was part of him. It was not merely a talent but an instinct. He was over six feet in height. His sharply chiseled features, curly blue-black hair, and slender figure reincarnated the beauty which Ernest Renshaw brought to the court. He was cursed with a dyspepsia whose recurrent attacks led him to say resignedly that he never felt really well. But he never shirked an engagement because of his health. This devotion to the game he loved and which was so much a part of him undoubtedly shortened his days. If he had been blessed with the physique of a Lawford or a Pim he might never have been beaten. It is certain that, although Laurie succeeded him and carried the Doherty fame to new heights, the younger brother could never beat the older when Reggie was feeling fit.

Unlike the Renshaws, who never played each other when they could decently avoid it, the Dohertys were devoted brothers and got infinite pleasure out of the friendly but none the less serious matches which they played against each other in private. . . .

If there was anything one could call a weakness in Reggie's game, it was that he was slow on his feet. He made up for this defect, due largely to his health, by amazing anticipation. He was able to judge instinctively where his opponent would return the ball. More often than not, he forced his adversary to make the return where he wished it. He never allowed himself to be forced into a position where he had to make an awkward return himself. Every stroke was produced flawlessly with perfect swing and timing. His backhand in particular has always been a model for young players. Overhead he was not so severe as Laurie, though equally sure. His volleying position was somewhat farther back than that of his brother. Whether he played on Wimbledon's turf, the sand courts of Southern France, or in the high altitude of Johannesburg, all conditions were the same to him. He adapted them to his own ends as he adapted his instincts and anticipation to his bodily weakness. His strokes, his strategy, and, above all, his personality and courtliness restored vitality and prosperity to the game.

When Reggie Doherty won the championship from Mahony, a new era began for lawn tennis. Since the days when the Lawford-Renshaw duels had brought the crowds flocking to Wimbledon, even since those later and less appreciated combats between Pim and Baddeley, the evolution of the game along lines peculiar to it and no longer based on its predecessors had brought into the front rank not one or two but many players of practically equal skill. During the four years he held the title, Reggie was called on to defend it against three different players. There was no recurrent duello but a series of combats in which the champion proved his superiority over all his rivals. Among themselves these rivals were evenly matched.

The Renshaw parallel came up again when it was Laurie who was Reggie's first challenger. He was still at Cambridge and came to the front

with great strides in 1898. Eaves beat him in the covered-court championship, but he reached the final at Dublin, won the Northern, and, at
Wimbledon, beat Mahony in a terrific all-comers final. Like the first
meeting of the Renshaws, the match went to five sets, but there was no
letdown in Laurie's effort to win. Reggie simply proved he was the better
man.

Laurie was ill in 1899 and played in few tournaments. Reggie's challenger
was A. W. Gore. Gore went so far as to win the first two sets, but Reggie
found the answer to Gore's driving by placing his own strokes so close to the
left sideline that Gore could not run around them all. Reggie followed his
forcing shots to the net and volleyed the weak return. Gore's opponent in
both the 1899 and 1900 all-comers finals was also a baseliner, Sidney Smith.
In 1900 Smith won. Reggie Doherty's stomach was not bothering him this
year, and his 1899 match with Gore had shown him how to master a
baseliner.

1901 proved unlucky for Reggie. Four years of intensive competition at
home and abroad had begun to leave their mark on his frail constitution.
He was in no shape to defend his title. His doctor had specifically forbidden
him to play and it was generally understood that he would retire. But he
was still of an open mind. Whether he should stand down or defend
depended on who was his challenger. If it were Laurie, of course there could
be no question. There was some doubt about Laurie. His record of late had
not been too successful. Gore had had it all over him during 1900. He had
beaten Laurie three times—at Dublin, at Beckenham, and at Wimbledon.
Both Dohertys had an ingrained dislike for one-stroke players. There was
nothing personal about this. Their own style was so complete, so perfectly in
the tradition of the Renshaws and of Pim that neither could envisage the
possibility of handing over the title without a struggle to a player whose
equipment was as limited as Gore's or Smith's. So the lines were drawn.
Reggie hoped Laurie would come through. If it could not be Laurie, he
hoped it might be another all-court player—Barrett or Dixon or Hillyard. If
the eventual challenger should be Gore or Smith, Reggie felt he must do
battle.

No one, of course, knew Reggie's decision. Everyone expected Laurie to
be his successor. Fate intervened in the person of George Hillyard, one of
the Dohertys' closest friends. Hillyard was a retired naval officer and a
famous cricketer. He had been, with Harry Scrivener, one of the founders of
the L.T.A. He was drawn against Laurie in the third round. After "Little
Do" won the first two sets, Hillyard overwhelmed him. All he needed now
to become the champion was to beat Gore, for Reggie would not have stood
out against him any more than against his brother. Hillyard was in a fair
way to his ambition when he led Gore by two sets to one, 5–4 and 40–15. On
this crucial match point he followed Reggie's tactics by driving deep to
Gore's weak backhand and following in to the net. Gore's indecisive return
hit the net cord. It clambered up somehow, teetered on the edge, and before
Hillyard's hypnotized gaze fell over into his court. He never recovered from
the shock. Gore pulled up to even terms and went on to win the match.

Barrett and Dixon then succumbed to Gore, both in straight sets. Reggie had to decide now. His mother was pleading with him not to endanger his health by another long struggle. Was it fair to Gore, he argued, to give him the empty satisfaction of winning the championship by default when he had come to the challenge round so cleanly? No, he determined, one-stroke player or no, Gore was entitled to win, if win he must, in battle. So, chivalrous as a knight of the Round Table, he entered the lists. His lance was shaky and his shield battered. In spite of his defective weapons, he won the first set and reached 5–2 in the second. Here his strokes began to lose their length. He tried to compensate for this weakness by intensive volleying. He became exhausted. At the end he could hardly stand. Double faults streamed from his racket. Gore came through.

History was not done repeating itself. Gore's victory, like Lawford's, was well merited but ephemeral. Again it was the defeated champion's brother who avenged him. There, however, the similarity ends. Reggie played on in doubles, but he made no attempt at a singles comeback. There was no pressure on Laurie to yield his title to his elder brother. He continued to improve until he was as good if no better than Reggie in his prime. He defended his championship successfully for four years.

Although he was still unable to beat Reggie in their friendly matches, Laurie proved over these years that he was master of an even more formidable group of challengers than those Reggie had defeated. Except overhead, he had not the power nor the innate genius of Reggie. His stroke production was equally sound, but his backhand never reached the classic perfection of his brother's. He had not Reggie's sense of anticipation, but he did not need it. His footwork was exceptional. He was short and sturdily built with very long arms and considerable strength. He had no weak points anywhere, either off the ground or in his volleying. His service and his smash were unusually severe. He could kill a lob from any part of the court.

Gore, Smith, and Hillyard were among the leading aspirants for the title during Laurie's tenure of the championship. There was G. A. Caridia. There was Major J. G. Ritchie. There was the best of them, Frank L. Riseley, who was Laurie's challenger in 1903, 1904, and 1906. Riseley was an all-court player who relied particularly on a relentless service, destructive smashing, and great agility at the net. The last rounds of the 1903 and 1904 championships were almost identical. In both cases Riseley met Smith in the semi-finals and beat him by his more complete game. In both years Riseley beat Ritchie in the final. In neither year could he win a set from Laurie. Riseley and Smith met again in the 1906 semi-final, and this time Riseley needed only four sets to win. Gore was his victim in the final. In the challenge round he won the second set. It was the first set Laurie had lost in the championship since he won the title.

Though the Dohertys had invariably thwarted the ambitions of Smith and Riseley in singles, they yielded twice in doubles to this unorthodox combination. For four years after they won the title from the Baddeleys in 1897, the Dohertys were supreme in the doubles field. In 1902, however, Smith and Riseley made such effective use of their varied gifts that the

Dohertys were unable to solve the puzzle. The Dohertys won back the title in 1903 and defended it against the same pair in 1904 and 1905. In 1906 it was again the turn of Smith and Riseley.

For the "Do's" it was the end of a long trail. For ten years they had been all but invincible. Reggie had played very little singles since 1901. His stamina was constantly failing. His mother, who had pleaded in vain in 1901, was again urging him to retire for good and all. She was never absent from any match her sons played. Their distress caused her pain. But Reggie was obdurate. He would no more yield to Smith and Riseley than he had been willing to yield to Gore.

The object of the challengers' attack from first to last was Reggie. For three sets Reggie parried the thrusts successfully enough to lead two sets to one. Then, with only one more set to go for victory, the great champion had nothing left. The man whose perfection of stroke and whose charm of personality had brought the crowds flocking back to Wimbledon had lost his stout lance and his impregnable shield. While his mother looked on with tears in her eyes, he tottered about the arena he had graced with his courtly manners and his never-failing sportsmanship. His shirt was saturated with sweat. His long sleeves, unbuttoned at the cuff, flapped like white signals of distress. His curly hair was matted on his brow. He was a brave and pathetic figure.

Smith and Riseley were sure of their victory now and increased their pressure. They lost only three games in each of the last two sets. As the crowd hailed the winners and at the same time acclaimed the valiant fight of the losers, Mrs. Doherty resolved that she would never again permit either of her sons to fight beyond his strength. She made Laurie promise her, then and there, that he would not defend his singles title the next year.

When the hour arrived, a player from overseas (Norman Brookes of Australia) was the challenger. Laurie had turned him back before, in 1905. Now England was calling upon her champion to fight once more for England. Laurie was eager to respond and go down fighting as Reggie had done. But his pledge was more sacred than the call of his country Finis had been written at the end of a glorious chapter. The long Doherty reign was over. Tennis had become an international game. The Wimbledon title was to fall into the hands of overseas players for twenty-six of the next twenty-eight years.

LOTTIE DOD WON WIMBLEDON AT 15

from the Sunday Express, *London*

No one in that swirling, surging crowd round Earls Court station, London, one day last week noticed the old lady who clutched a little basket of raspberries.

With gentle eyes and the beginning of a smile, 80-year-old Charlotte Dod stood to one side and watched the crowd sweep on to Wimbledon. Then she went back to a first-floor flat—in a gray street—and her memories.

Memories of Wimbledon in the blazing summer of 1887. There stood Charlotte Dod that day. She had done a thing 17-year-old Little Mo, of America, could never do.

She had won the singles championship at the age of 15.

"Lottie, Lottie!" called the crowd that afternoon. It had quite forgotten itself. And Lottie demurely blushed.

She was wearing a long skirt which showed just a glimpse of stout black woolen stocking and just-as-stout black shoes. Her white dress had a collar which stood high around her neck. On her dark hair a white flannel cap was squarely settled.

Memories like that were in Miss Dod's mind last week as she switched on her radio for the Wimbledon commentary. "I do wish I could go," she said, "but I am far too ill. I'm quite old now."

Not too old to remember that triumphant summer. It was the first of several. For the next year Lottie won the singles championship again.

By horse and carriage they sped to Wimbledon to cheer "The Little Wonder."

Lottie Dod did it again in 1891, 1892, and 1893. In fact, every time she entered.

And then she turned to other sports—golf, hockey, archery, skating—and her triumphs there, too.

THE QUEST OF THE DAVIS CUP

by René Lacoste

Unlike Suzanne Lenglen, Tilden, according to those who knew him when he began to play tennis, did not seem at first destined to become a remarkable player. He was for a long time a middling beginner, and it took him nearly ten years of hard work to become a real champion. When Suzanne

Lenglen had beaten Mrs. Lambert Chambers at Wimbledon, she was immediately admitted to be the best player in the world. On the contrary, though Tilden won, in 1921, the championships of England and America, it was several years before he was admitted to be the best player of his time, and perhaps of all times. Tilden was not, like Suzanne Lenglen, absolutely invincible. He rarely crushed, like Suzanne Lenglen, a series of opponents, but from 1920 to 1926 Tilden was not beaten in any important match, and this, when one thinks of the number of excellent players that he met, is an extraordinary performance. It was at St. Cloud, on the same day that I saw Suzanne Lenglen beat Mrs. Mallory, that I saw for the first time Tilden, playing an exhibition match against Manuel Alonso. I admired exceedingly the speed, elegance, and ardor of the wonderful Spanish player, but was amazed by the sight of Tilden's play. It is an extraordinary thing that Tilden, who became a champion only by dint of hard work, shows on the tennis court such facility. Tilden always seems to have a thousand means of putting the ball away from his opponent's reach. He seems to exercise a strange fascination over his opponent as well as the spectators. Tilden, even when beaten, always leaves an impression on the public mind that he was superior to the victor. All the spectators seem to think he can win when he likes. Seemingly, in two steps Tilden covers the whole of the court; without any effort he executes the most various and extraordinary strokes. He seems capable of returning any shot when he likes, to put the ball out of the reach of his opponent when he thinks the moment has come to do so. Sometimes he gives the ball prodigious velocity, sometimes he caresses it and guides it to a corner of the court whither nobody but himself would have thought of directing it. One would not say that Tilden is very popular, or at all events he is not so in the same way as Borotra, who, if he does not play for the gallery, finds still the best part of his inspiration in the encouragement of the spectators. Tilden does not concern himself at all about the public. He does not seek the approval of the public, but the satisfaction of his own mind. When he refuses the benefit of a mistake of the referee, or when he complains of some injustice, he never worries about what the public thinks of his attitude. Tilden never leaves the public indifferent. One feels that he plays tennis with an inspiration which nothing will cause him to abandon. There is always much applause when Tilden plays, and if they do not applaud him they cheer his opponent on purpose. I have often seen, in the immense arena of Forest Hills, thousands of spectators having come with the idea of systematically encouraging the opponent whom Tilden would meet that day. One day when Tilden met Richards in the championships of America, ten thousand persons were applauding Richards, but only a few cheered Tilden. Tilden did not seem at all affected, did not make a gesture, nor smile in order to win the sympathy of the public, but played so wonderfully that at the end of the match all of the spectators, standing up, were applauding him.

Tilden desires something more than merely to amuse the spectators or to win their sympathy by his attitudes. He is determined to compel admiration by the quality of his play and by his personality alone.

It may be said that for quite a long time Tilden was not popular on the court. His unbroken list of victories became monotonous. But the day was to come when he had to face defeat, and he did so magnificently. Then, and only then, was he able to taste the sweetness of popularity. He had shown that he was not only a great player but a great loser. As great as Suzanne Lenglen through his victories, Tilden became greater when faced by defeat. When Tilden was beaten at Wimbledon and at St. Cloud, he did not show any of that nervous petulance which he showed and with which he was reproached when he was always winning. He did not search for any excuses, but referred to the quality of his opponent's play. His bearing in his hour of defeat set a wonderful example and compelled the admiration of all. The Tilden of 1928 is more popular and greater than ever he was in the days when he was undefeatable.

Like Suzanne Lenglen, it was not in his native land that Tilden won his first great victory. It was at Wimbledon, but a year later. In May 1920 he left New York as the second player in an American team in which he was accompanied by Johnston, Williams, and Garland. Finding inspiration which had hitherto failed him, Tilden inscribed the first American name on the records of the All-England Club by being victorious over Patterson in the challenge round. The American team for the Davis Cup triumphed easily over the English and French teams, and Tilden with his companions soon sailed for Australia. Notwithstanding the efforts of Patterson and Norman Brookes, the American team was victorious over the Australasians in the Davis Cup, and Tilden returned to the U. S. A. laden with honors.

Tilden returned to Europe in 1921 and defended with success his title at Wimbledon. He then went on to win the championship of the United States six times in succession. The American Davis Cup team beat successively, until 1927, the Australians, Japanese, and French teams who tried to take away from them the precious Davis Cup. For seven years, thanks to Tilden, Johnston, Williams, and Richards, America maintained her position as the strongest nation in the world.

William Johnston was, with Tilden, the great architect of American victories. Only beaten in America by Tilden, he won easily at Wimbledon in 1923, and until 1926 was only beaten once by a foreign player (Anderson). In the opinion of many people, Johnston was a better player than Tilden. If possible, his execution was more perfect and he was able, with limited physical advantages, to impart greater speed to the ball than his great rival. He generally beat such players as Shimizu, Kumagae, Patterson, Richards, Borotra, and myself much more decisively than Tilden could. But every time he found himself in the presence of Tilden, Johnston appeared to be dominated by the athletic superiority and the strong personality of his rival. Johnston executed perhaps more perfect strokes than Tilden. He did not give the same impression of a master as Tilden, nor did he seem capable of triumphing over any opponent in any circumstances, like the wonderful Philadelphian.

Few players on all courts had been so unanimously applauded as "Billy" Johnston. No figure was more popular in America. No player ever realized better than he the English ideal of a sportsman; no American player was more applauded at St. Cloud than he. He beat me regularly in a terrible manner several times, but always after the game I forgot the lesson that he had just given me when he said quite simply, "Bad luck. You were not in form today!"

Dick Williams was one of the most popular players in America. He had more personality than Johnston, but much less than Tilden. He does not run on a court as much as Borotra, but he executes without any effort strokes nearly as extraordinary as those of our national Basque champion. In 1914 Williams used to play well in singles but badly in doubles. After the war Williams became an admirable player in doubles, won at Wimbledon with Garland, and the championship of America with Vincent Richards. They formed a team invincible for several years.

Vincent Richards, at the time when he became a professional, was regarded as the legitimate successor to Tilden in America. His execution was not perfect; his physical advantages were not comparable to those of Tilden, but, like Cochet, he had an unusual sense of the right stroke to play. He won the Olympic Games title in Paris in 1924, but he was beaten at Wimbledon by Borotra, and in 1926 he failed twice in Paris and London, meeting Cochet, who was at his best. He was nearly always beaten pretty easily by Johnston, but defended himself very well when he met Tilden. A wonderful volleyer, he was admirable in doubles.

In 1925 France beat Australia by three matches to one, but was completely crushed in the challenge round by the holders, who won all five matches. The victory appeared to indicate a brilliant future for American tennis.

However, although in America the glory of Tilden, combined with the successes of other American players, secured for tennis an extraordinary vogue throughout the world, and especially in Europe, thousands of players were training and progressing with their eyes fixed on the American group. I think that the numerous matches in which they played enabled the best players of Europe to get greater experience than many of the young American players.

It was in 1923 that the first French tennis team sailed for America. Gobert, Cochet, and Borotra failed at Boston against Patterson and O'Hara-Wood. As in the previous year, Brugnon and Lacoste were defeated when they met Anderson and Hawkes, but little by little "The Three Musketeers," traveling from May to September and meeting the most diverse opponents, were gaining an ever greater experience.

In 1924 another defeat was suffered at the hands of the Australians. In 1925 Borotra struck his best form, beat Anderson and Patterson in singles, and France won the doubles match. But we were now up against the last barrier and the strongest, the United States. During the winter of 1925–26, having determined to play as often as possible against the Americans, The Three Musketeers were again in New York, on covered courts. Tilden and Richards won the team match for America, but two Frenchmen met in the final of the Covered Courts Championship of America.

In the spring of 1926 Richards came to Europe, but he could not win anywhere. Then came the American season. We beat with difficulty the Japanese, and on the first day of the Franco-American match Johnston and Tilden defeated Lacoste and Borotra, respectively, and the doubles match was lost. On the third day Tilden was beaten by Lacoste; this was his first defeat in an important match since 1920. Then followed the championship of America; Cochet beat Tilden, Borotra beat Richards and Johnston, and the final of the National Singles, for the first time in the history of tennis, was played between two Frenchmen, Lacoste defeating Borotra.

The Davis Cup remained in America. Tilden and Johnston no longer appeared to us invincible, but the shadow of their glory seemed still to shelter the celebrated cup and put it beyond the reach of all our efforts.

At the beginning of July 1927, when we had beaten the South African players at Eastbourne, thus winning the European zone of the Davis Cup, it was decided that we should sail as soon as possible for the United States. Our previous journeys had taught us the difficulty of becoming acclimatized to the conditions under which the American contests are carried on; the climate, the food, the balls, the courts, the atmosphere of the matches in general are so many changed factors and calculated to render difficult the task of the European player. Each year previously we commenced to play badly in the United States, but little by little, as we became more acclimatized, we met with more success. Profiting by experience, Cochet, Brugnon, and myself sailed on the 27th of July. This was two weeks earlier than in 1926, so that we had reason to hope that an extra fifteen days' training would enable us to play better when our serious tennis started.

On the boat which was carrying us, between a sky and a sea equally blue, we argonauts were wandering in search of the elusive Davis Cup, the modern Golden Fleece. Our thoughts went back to the innumerable matches played in Dublin, Rome, Copenhagen, Budapest, Eastbourne, Prague, Barcelona, and Vienna, each a stepping stone on the path to win the European eliminating contest for the Davis Cup. We recalled our emotions when Switzerland was leading by two matches to one, at Bordeaux, how little we were pleased when the referee of the Franco-Italian contest announced two matches–all. We recalled a thousand amusing incidents in our journeys and in the clubs in the places where we had played; the aspects of the various towns which had so delighted us. We thought of our past struggles in America (already a long time previously) when we had sailed as novices toward an unknown New York, and when, having beaten the Australians and the Japanese, we came to meet the American giants.

St. Cloud, played only two months previously, was fresh in our memories, and Wimbledon too, only a month before. Tilden was no longer invincible; he had been beaten, but after terrific struggles. It was impossible for us not to admit that but for some bad luck he might have won twice instead of losing. When we shall meet him in Philadelphia before his own public, on the courts where he learned to play tennis, shall we beat him in this battle for the Davis Cup, as we had beaten him in his efforts to win an individual title? Tilden was so great in his defeats that he loomed up as a formidable obstacle between us and victory.

Was there not Johnston also standing across our path? He perhaps does not give such a great impression as Tilden, but he is harder to beat; without any respite, he is able to attack from the first ball to the last, he has never been beaten by Lacoste, and Cochet has never met him. Then there is the doubles match, that unknown factor! Who is going to play for America? The great Johnston-Tilden team, or perhaps Tilden-Williams or Tilden-Hunter? And who will comprise the French team? We certainly feel that we have a chance. We feel that now it is stronger, greater than ever, but we know that it depends on imponderable trifles which cannot be foreseen or controlled. When a Tilden or a Johnston meets a Cochet or a Borotra, the result of the match may depend on the heat, on the condition of the court, on the physical condition, a shade better in one than the other. The match depends also on the greater will to win, and that spirit gives us some hope. At Wimbledon we saw Tilden lose because his nerve unaccountably failed. Tilden had played far too much in Europe. Everywhere he left a little of his will to win. While we are sailing quietly toward America, a radio message informs us that Tilden has just won his third consecutive tournament since his return home. Perhaps at Philadelphia he will be in wonderful form, but it is possible also that he will not be able to will to win.

As soon as we arrived in New York we started for Southampton to commence our training. Southampton is a wonderful place, and our reception surpassed that of any other place in the world. But we find it is not very easy to play tennis well at Southampton. Brugnon was crushed by Tilden, Lott inflicted on me a severe defeat, Cochet probably only escaped defeat because he did not play in singles. We returned to New York to meet Pierre Gillou, our captain. Pierre Gillou is the soul of the French team. He knows all of us well. He knows how to impart confidence to Cochet, to stimulate Borotra, and to cheer us up and put hope into us in our darkest hours.

After spending eight days in New York in training ourselves with scrupulous care, we played much better. We departed to play at Boston against the Japanese, who had just beaten the Canadians. At Boston, before the match, it rained for three days. It was impossible to train. We recalled our matches against the same Japanese the previous year at New York, when the rain also prevented us from training, and we very nearly lost. Fortunately the French team, which was joined by M. and Mme. Washer, was completed by the arrival of Jean Borotra. We formed a regular colony, good humor prevailed, and we were in wonderful spirits.

I played the first match of the contest against Harada with great care, because Harada plays much like Johnston and because I was anxious to try new tactics which I could use against Johnston fifteen days later. I was naturally anxious also to wipe out the memory of my defeat the previous year. Cochet won his match easily. The doubles match was also won with facility. The last two matches were canceled on account of the rain.

We then played, still at Boston, the Doubles Championship and the Mixed Doubles Championship. This was a disaster, Cochet and Brugnon were beaten by the American "hopes," Lott and Doeg, and Borotra and I were simply crushed by Hennessey and Williams. It was raining nearly every day. Borotra was quite unable to train; finally he practiced on covered courts, but the result was not brilliant. When he played again in the open air, he was no longer able to smash! The mixed doubles were a kind of revenge for us. The four French players were in the semi-finals. Unfortunately, the finals were not played until Monday afternoon, and it was not until evening of the same day that we started for Philadelphia, in order to try to perfect our game on the same courts on which the matches for the Davis Cup would be played.

Tilden seemed in wonderful condition. Hunter also played very well. On the other hand, we began to hope that Johnston, just arrived from the West, on the first day of the Doubles Championship, would not play this year as well as in previous years. We were practically certain as to who would play in the singles: Cochet and Lacoste for France, Tilden and Johnston for America. But the doubles team would only be fixed at the last moment.

Wallis Myers, who had been selected for drawing lots, asked me jokingly on the eve of the match in what order I should prefer to have them played. I replied to him that, having been beaten two years running by Johnston, I had trained especially to take my revenge, and that I was very anxious to meet him on the first day. Besides, Tilden, having to fight a hard game against Cochet on the first day, winning or losing, and playing probably the doubles on the second day, would be less able on the third day to resist the method I would employ against him, of holding out to the end; that is, if I had the good luck of prolonging the match.

Wallis Myers had a lucky hand. At half past two on Thursday, the seventh, I entered the court to play the first match against Johnston. From the beginning of the match I attacked with all my strength and was fortunate enough to find in front of me an opponent who was never able to recover his wind nor the control of his strokes [Lacoste won 6–3, 6–2, 6–2]. At half past three Cochet and Tilden, in their turn, entered the court, around which were from twelve to thirteen thousand persons in immense grandstands. Cochet played one of the greatest matches of his life. At first he played too much at the back of the court, but at the end of the match he ventured sometimes, on the contrary, to the net behind rather short attacks. Tilden that day played so wonderfully that it is doubtful if any other player in the world could have defeated him. In the middle of the fourth set Cochet, for a moment, seemed about to win, but Tilden overcame the temporary period of weakness. Perhaps the effort he had to make at that moment may have decided two days later the fate of the Davis Cup [Tilden won 6–4, 2–6, 6–4, 8–6].

That Thursday evening was not a triumphal one, but it was full of encouragement. Everything led us to suppose that Cochet would beat Johnston in the last singles match, and we still had two other cards to play when one only was sufficient. We had two fresh men to play in the doubles, and the card furnished by the opponents showed a Tilden exhausted by two strenuous and nerve-racking matches.

Borotra and Brugnon began well and won the first set six to three. Brugnon served well and executed some admirable returns. The volleys of our two players, those of Borotra especially, were fast and deep, and the few smashes that Borotra had to execute were decisive. But from the beginning of the second set Tilden and Hunter concentrated on Brugnon and, by alternating lobs and plunging drives, often put him in difficulties. He lost his service and the set, which went to the Americans by six games to three. The third set terminated in the defeat of the French pair, Brugnon losing two services and Borotra one. After the usual rest the fourth set was won magnificently by Borotra and Brugnon, but Tilden was irresistible all through the fifth set and, well supported by Hunter, scored the match for the United States.

On the evening of that day there was a banquet at the Germantown Cricket Club. So great was the impression made by Tilden in the doubles that the Americans loudly expressed their certainty of retaining the Davis Cup. In the French camp we felt that Cochet ought to beat Johnston and that Lacoste could beat Tilden, but in spite of everything, we could not persuade ourselves that we were going to win. We remembered certainly the defeats of Tilden at St. Cloud and at Wimbledon. Despite all this, however, he was a player whom one does not with impunity regard as anything less than a dangerous obstacle in the way of victory. We felt the magnetism that emanated from his personality, which compels the admiration of crowds and duly impresses his opponents. But the Tarpeian Rock is near the Capitol. At Philadelphia Tilden could not be beaten by any one player; he was beaten by a team. Cochet compelled him on Thursday to exhaust his physical powers, Borotra and Brugnon obliged him on Friday to work like a Trojan, and on Saturday Lacoste undoubtedly benefited by this attrition.

Tilden attacked with all his strength in the first set, but his aces could not compensate for his many mistakes. In the second set he adjusted his attack better, led five to two, and Lacoste was not able to come back. In the third set Tilden had to slow down his attack and accept the play of his opponent; he was beaten three sets to one [6–4, 4–6, 6–3, 6–2, for Lacoste]. When he left the court, the crowd bestowed generous applause on the winner. There would have been a wonderful scene had Tilden won. Tilden took his defeat like a great sportsman, whilst the umpiring and attitude of the public were, during the match, above all praise.

But the result created a sensational atmosphere. The match was now two–all. A silence like that of death falls over the multitude. The managers and American officials were perturbed. A wild desire surged in our hearts when Cochet and Johnston entered the court to play the fifth and last match for the Davis Cup. Generally I have the reputation of being calm, but I was so nervous during this match that I was compelled, in the warm sunlight, to put on a couple of sweaters and an overcoat! Tilden and myself sat side by side. We tried to joke, but did not succeed very well. We were looking at the match, and how can it be a joke when, according to the score, one wants to laugh and the other to cry. Cochet and Johnston, in spite of the nervousness of the public and their own tense feelings, played a magnificent game. Cochet won, without too much trouble, the first and third sets, but lost the second to Johnston, who for the moment seemed again the great Johnston of unlimited courage and resource. After an interval for rest, Cochet got quickly in action and led five games to two. He had the match several times at his mercy, on his service, but could not finish it off. Johnston, encouraged by thirteen thousand persons, won his service with four aces and led by 30–love, but Cochet succeeded in recovering his calm, stalled off the Johnston bid for recovery, and administered the final coup that brought the Davis Cup to France [6–4, 4–6, 6–2, 6–4 for Cochet].

Victory! A simple word. So short—and yet how expressive. The end of an effort begun in 1922: so many matches played in all the countries of the world, so many endless thousands of miles traveled over, so many hopes shattered as soon as formed and today finally realized. The Atlantic crossed and recrossed seven times. Months and months passed in dreaming of this day! And at last it had come.

Mme. Cochet fainted; Pierre Gillou sprang up like a child; I took off my overcoat and sweaters; Brugnon dropped his pipe; and Borotra—you can imagine him justifying his reputation of "The Bounding Basque." Everything after that seemed like a dream. The Davis Cup delivered to our team; a thousand photographs, uniting the players with the French Ambassador and American Minister for War, Dwight Davis, the giver of the Cup. The memories of it all seem like a fantasy.

Then we played for the championship of America, which I had the good fortune to win, and so brought back the National Cup with the Davis Cup. A wonderful return home, official receptions, l'Elysée and . . . calm. I cannot write it all. It is too confusing—too wonderful.

IT STARTED IN 1900

by Allison Danzig

Next to the Olympic Games, Davis Cup tennis matches are the most international of all sports competitions.

The tennis event started as a dual match between the United States and England in 1900, when Dwight F. Davis of St. Louis, a Harvard student, offered the trophy in competition. The cup now is played for annually by countries of every continent. As many as thirty-three nations have challenged for it in a single year.

Only four nations have won the cup, a massive silver bowl with tray and a huge base on which are inscribed the names of its winners. The United States, Great Britain and Australia were the only winners up to 1927. They are the three grass-court playing nations.

In 1927 France's four musketeers of the court—René Lacoste, Henri Cochet, Jean Borotra and Jacques Brugnon—ended the sway of the United States on the Germantown Cricket Club courts.

That was one of the great moments in French sports history. The celebrated Tilden and Johnston, the Big and Little Bills who had kept America supreme for seven years, were toppled. Those seven years set a record for consecutive cup victories.

In 1928 France staged the challenge round on composition courts. That was the first time it was ever played on any surface other than grass. The regulations specify that the matches may be played only on turf or on a natural or artificial fine gritty surface.

The challenge round is the climactic match of play for the cup. It brings together the nation that holds the cup and the team that survives months of qualifying play. The cup-holding nation takes part only in this one match. Its opponent may have faced as many as half a dozen other nations or more to earn the right to play in the challenge round.

The qualifying matches are held in zones. There are European, American and Eastern zones. Most of the nations compete in the European zone. This year there were sixteen in the European, five in the American and three in the Eastern.

The winners of the three zones meet in interzone matches. Italy, the winner in Europe, and the United States, the winner in America, met in the interzone semifinal in late September at Forest Hills. The United States was the winner by four matches to one.

Then the United States and India, the winner in the Eastern zone, met in the interzone final in Perth, Australia, on the Indian Ocean. Again the United States won by a score of four matches to one. It thereby qualified to face Australia here in the challenge round December 26 to 28.

A cup match between nations is known as a tie. It lasts for three days and consists of four singles and a doubles contest. Teams of not more than four players are nominated by each nation ten days in advance of a tie.

The day before play begins each captain names two men to play the singles and a draw is made. The names are put into the cup and drawn out blind to determine the pairings. On the third day the players switch opponents. The doubles match is played the second day. The doubles players may be the same as in singles or a different pair.

The team winning three of five matches advances to the next round of competition and the defeated opponent is eliminated.

The participating nations file their entries each year with the country holding the cup. That country has the responsibility of setting up the organization for conducting play. It holds the draw after the closing of entries, and the nations are drawn in the three zones. They may enter in any zone they choose.

The cup holder delegates authority to other nations to conduct play in foreign zones. The United States was in charge of play in the American zone. England usually conducts the matches in the European zone.

When Australia holds the cup, the challenge round is held in December during its summer season. When the United States, Great Britain or France holds it, the challenge round is staged at the height of their seasons, in late August in the United States.

The American season reaches its climax in the national championships at Forest Hills in early September.

Our team assembled on the West Coast in late October after defeating Italy in the interzone match at Forest Hills the previous month. It arrived in Australia the first week of November and played in several big tournaments preparatory to flying 2,500 miles across Australia to Perth to play India. It returned east to Adelaide for eight days of preparations preliminary to meeting Australia in the challenge round.

The Australian team meanwhile had been competing in big state tournaments comparable to our Eastern grass court events. Its players arrived here at the same time as ours for intensive practice to prepare them for the defense of the cup.

Such is the interest in tennis in this country that every one of the nearly 18,000 seats in the stadium here has been sold out for more than two months. The best seats cost approximately $6 each, and the two teams will share in approximately $125,000 profit from the matches. The money goes into the exchequers of national tennis associations for the development of the game.

OUR FRIENDS THE "AUSSIES"

by Allison Danzig

It was just short of three decades ago that I first had my introduction to Australian lawn tennis players. It was during an impressionable period in the life of a budding reporter on the sports scene.

Only shortly before, I had finished my schooling and entered upon a journalistic career. It was a glamorous world in which I lived—a world of excitement, thrilling sport and famous personalities from the globe over. Never before, nor since, were there so many players of the first class as held forth on the courts in those days of the 1920s.

From France there came the "Four Musketeers" who a few years later were to reap the reward for their perseverance and consecration to their mission by winning the Davis Cup for their country for the first time. They were René Lacoste, the inscrutable "Crocodile"; the dashing Jean Borotra, the "Bounding Basque"; pale-faced Henri Cochet, the supreme artist, who manipulated a racket with the touch of a Kreisler on a violin bow, and Jacques Brugnon, gentleman to the tips of polished fingers that steered a tennis ball with unerring eye for the opening in the doubles court.

Spain sent dark, handsome Manuel Alonso, the "Tiger of the Pyrenees," whose wind-up for the service was like the lashing tail of a jungle cat ready to spring for the kill and who was known to bite the throat of his racket when it betrayed him on a flubbed volley. From Japan there were diminutive Ichiya Kumagae and Zenzo Shimizu, with their unorthodox Western grips and excessive rotation of the wrist in imparting top spin to the ball. There was impish B. I. C. Norton—Brian Ivan Cobb Norton, Sir, or just plain "Babe." He arrived from South Africa with his tongue in his cheek, a twinkle in his eye for the ladies and more bounce to the ounce than a Coke, or a whiskey and soda, if you like. He had every qualification to become a world champion except the inclination to train and take time out at night to get some sleep.

There were our own Big Bill Tilden and Little Bill Johnston, twin engines of destruction who ruled the courts as absolute potentates, monarchs of all they surveyed across the net. Behind them were the other two members of our "Big Four"—Vinnie Richards, greatest of all American volleyers, and Dick Williams, with a daring brilliance that blinded when on his game or backfired into futility when his hair-trigger shots were not coming off from his risky position well inside the baseline.

Added to these, there came from Australia long, lean Jim Anderson, with the look of eagles around his eyes and a great forehand drive, and powerful Gerald Patterson, with a grace afoot unmatched by any man of his size, a corkscrew backhand, the like of which never has been unveiled on a tennis court, and the mightiest smash of all time. Well do I remember the time Borotra, in a Davis Cup doubles at Forest Hills, rushed in where angels feared to tread, instead of taking to the hills, as Patterson went up in the air for an overhead. The ball caught Jean just below the temple, knocking him flat to the ground under the net. With Patterson and Anderson came John B. Hawkes, with his kicking left-handed service that was the despair of the receiver, and Pat O'Hara-Wood, both fine doubles players.

For some reason I was more intrigued by the Australians than by any of the other great players from overseas. The giant size of Anderson and the burly sleekness of Patterson caught my eye to begin with. My imagination was stirred by the fact that they had come from so vast a distance. I was impressed, too, by the dignity and unfailing composure with which they carried themselves on the court—the carriage of thoroughbreds which has been a characteristic of the many fine players Australia has sent to America, with hardly an exception to the pattern.

Possibly I was attracted to them principally for the reason that they were of the same breed as those two giants of the court who were enshrined on as high a pedestal in tennis as were our Ty Cobb, Christy Mathewson and

Honus Wagner in baseball. I refer to Norman Brookes and Anthony Wilding. I had not had the good fortune to see them play, but neither had I seen Cobb, Mathewson and Wagner. They were all before my time. But all of them belonged to the ages as idols of the follower of sports.

I regretted then, as I regret today, that I had not been privileged to see Tony Wilding, the New Zealander, that glamorous, magnificent specimen of manhood, that shining knight of the court, who fell on the battlefield in the First World War. What would I not have given to have seen Brookes, the wizard of strategy, in that never-to-be-forgotten first set, 17–15, with Maurice (Red) McLoughlin in their 1914 Davis Cup match at Forest Hills! I was to see Sir Norman years later play doubles, at Southampton, Long Island, I believe it was. He was then close to 50, as I recall, but, though well past his playing prime, his amazing skill and cleverness were a revelation to the best of a new generation, who looked on entranced, as did this observer.

Still later, it was my privilege to gather around a radio receiving set in the Merion Cricket Club at Haverford, Pennsylvania, with Sir Norman and the members of the Australian Davis Cup team on that fateful day in 1939 when came the ominous news that Hitler had turned loose his Stukas, Messerschmitts and Panzers upon helpless Poland. It was a tragic moment for the world, the outbreak of another bloodbath for the peoples of most of the continents, and those youthful tennis players from Down Under knew they were in for it, that there would be no more cup matches for them for years, if ever. Here was one of the most fateful moments of their young lives, on the eve of the matches for which they had come thousands of miles and trained and sacrificed for many months—the same fateful moment that Brookes and Wilding had known when they got the news at the Allegheny Country Club, Pittsburgh, in the summer of 1914 that the German Kaiser had sprung his goose-steppers just a quarter of a century before.

Never shall I forget the manner in which John Bromwich, Adrian Quist, Harry Hopman and Jack Crawford heard these awful tidings—their unflinching impassiveness and the complete absence of any manifestation of dismay. Just a fleeting exchange of knowing glances and then casually, easily, they joined in the flow of conversation that filled the room, still light of heart and able to smile.

No wonder that in the galleries that saw the matches were hundreds, if not thousands, of Americans who wanted them to win and gave them wholehearted encouragement with their applause and cheers. No wonder that when they lifted the cup with their unprecedented challenge round achievement of winning the last three matches after losing the first two they captured the hearts of Americans as had no team from overseas before them.

Americans take their sports seriously and like to win. At times, possibly, they put too great an emphasis upon victory and are not sufficiently concerned with the amenities. But they are never so callous, I hope, or so consumed with thirst for success as not to recognize good sportsmanship and respond to it. No other visiting team has brought out their better side in international sporting competition quite to the degree that have Australians. All through the years in which I have watched the parade, this has been so.

And how could it be otherwise? What other nation has sent to us finer sportsmen, a higher type of young manhood, exemplifying the manly virtues both on and off the court, than the succession of clean-cut tennis players who have come to the States from Australia to play the game for all they are worth, play it always in good temper and high spirit and comport themselves alike in triumph and disaster—those two impostors—with irreproachable propriety?

It has never ceased to amaze me how these young Australian players, some of them not yet reached their majority in age, conform year after year to the same pattern. Different though they may be in their dispositions, personalities, outlook on life and abilities, each and every one of them has run true to the mould until Americans take it for granted that Australians are quietspoken, self-respecting, immaculately attired young men who bear themselves modestly but with heads aloft, conform strictly to the letter of the code and the spirit of fair play and maintain an unruffled poise regardless of the vicissitudes of fortune. They stand as models for adolescents of the sportsman par excellence. They have been ambassadors who have reflected the highest credit upon their country.

Calling the roll, in my time there have been Patterson, Anderson, Hawkes, O'Hara-Wood, Hopman, Crawford, Vivian McGrath, Adrian Quist, John Bromwich, Geoffrey Brown, Billy Sidwell, Dinny Pails, Colin Long, Frank Sedgman, Kenneth McGregor, George Worthington, Mervyn Rose and Don Candy. There were others, but these are the ones I remember well and knew the best, along with captains Hopman, Roy Cowling, Cliff Sproule, Quist and Esca Stevens.

Crawford, with his wonderfully sound ground strokes, his conservation of effort in their production, the rare ease with which he moved about the court, his serenity and total lack of temperament, was a particular favorite with us. It was a grievous disappointment to the thousands at Forest Hills when, leading by two sets to one, he lost to Fred Perry in our championship final of 1933, the year in which he won the Australian, All-England and French titles. Perry had his many well-wishers, but Jack Crawford was one of those solid men of good will whose complete naturalness, honesty and simplicity won people to him on first sight. Who ever had a better forehand than Jack?

Hopman left us with the feeling that when it came to doubles Americans were nothing more than novices. In 1939 he and Crawford reached the final of our championship when they had both passed their playing peak, and 11 years later, mirabile dictu, Harry was a sensation as he and Seymour Greenberg, an accomplished player but one who never rated in top company, qualified for the semi-finals of the championship. To arrive there they had to defeat Rose and Worthington in a match that was scored at 7–9, 15–13, 2–6, 6–3, 6–4, and in the semi-finals they gave Talbert and Mulloy a fight all the way.

No one was ever more clever on a doubles court, to our way of thinking, than Hopman. We think, too, that Davis Cup team captains do not come any shrewder or more astute than Harry, and that is one of the main reasons why the job of winning back the cup is so difficult, even though we set a high store on our new captain, Frank Shields.

Of all the Australian players who have come to the States, Bromwich has probably won the greatest celebrity in modern times. We have seen a lot of John, both before and since the war, but that alone does not account for the hold he gained on the public. The fact that he drives and volleys from the forehand with both hands gripping the racket naturally attracted attention, but neither has that explained his vogue.

Of all the players from Down Under, Bromwich is the only one I can recall who was given a sobriquet by our press. The "Melancholy Dane," they called him. I don't know how he took it, but John does not give the impression of having a hilarious time on the court, and when one shot of his in 50 goes sour it may be comedy for some people but it's nothing less than stark Shakespearean tragedy for the most self-exacting perfectionist to wield a racket. To see John at such a moment, brushing back his straight, golden mop of hair impatiently with the look of one guilty of some monstrous sin, you can understand the inspiration for the sobriquet.

The complete absorption with which Bromwich plays tennis, his intense concentration and the 100 per cent effort he gives to every shot he makes help explain his hold on tennis galleries. He never fails to give them a run for their money. He wins them, too, with the intelligence of his play, the sagaciousness with which he manipulates the ball and contrives to outwit his opponent and maneuver him into an untenable position. With him it is not a matter of speed or power but of control and generalship in exposing a vulnerable spot and trapping his rival with drop shots and lobs. It is in doubles that his artistry and cleverness best find the medium for their exposition. To see him confound the opposition as he "dinks" the ball at their feet or tosses it over their heads with identically the same motion is to behold the most masterful tactician of the four-handed game since George Lott of Chicago, with the exception of Hopman.

It was the day that Brom met Frank Parker in the final match of the 1939 challenge round series that his American vogue began. Actually, it was the opening rally of that all-important contest that did it. Parker was the personification of steadiness, the player who never missed a shot from the back of the court. No one, it was maintained, could hope to beat him from the baseline.

That first rally saw the exchange of some 50 drives, forehand to forehand. The gallery turned its heads back and forth, back and forth, as the ball crossed the net in the same line, as though drawn by a string. Then, as if by mutual consent, they switched to the backhand, and 50 times more the ball traveled from corner to corner.

It was too much for the spectators. As the rally went on and on, with both men anchored at the baseline, first there were titters of amusement, then chuckles and finally roars of mirth and an explosive cheer as Parker knocked the ball out of court (or was it into the net?). The myth of Parker the infallible machine finally had been shattered. At last the man had been found who could beat him from the back of the court. The match was won and lost with that first point. Parker knew he had met his master. He got four games in the three sets. John Bromwich then and there "sold" himself to the American public.

THE BIG BOYS OF THE DAVIS CUP

by Lance Tingay

Messrs. Ashe, Graebner, Lutz and Smith did their stuff with fine success and verve in Adelaide last Christmas and brought back the big trophy, the Davis Cup, to the U. S. It was the 57th time for which that impressive piece of plate and its accessories had been played. It looks as if the long-standing pattern of the Davis Cup is going to change a little. It is a possibility, perhaps a probability, that in 1970 the competition will admit the contracted professionals. That should enhance its prestige but it will not be quite the same. I think this a good time to have a statistical look at this competition.

The first Davis Cup tie, as most will know, was played between America and the British Isles at the Longwood Cricket Club in Boston in 1900. The Adelaide Challenge Round last Christmas was, on my reckoning, the 1282nd Davis Cup to be played.

The Davis Cup, more than any other lawn tennis event, separates the men from the boys. To win for yourself is one thing; to win for your country is another. There were two superlative performances in the cup in 1968. There was that of Arthur Ashe, who went through every tie without losing a rubber until the trophy was safely back in American keeping. Only then, in the last dead rubber of the challenge round, did he bow to Bill Bowrey. And the German, Wilhelm Bungert, helping to take Germany through to the interzone matches, was never beaten at all.

Now Ashe has played 25 Davis Cup rubbers for the U. S. (and, incidentally, lost only four of them), and Bungert has played 72 rubbers for Germany (with 46 victories). But Ashe may be regarded as a novice compared with what some, both living and dead, have accomplished in the cup, and Bungert, despite his big tally of effort, ranks only 19th in the list of stalwart cup competitors.

If the Davis Cup be measured quantitatively, one man stands out on his own. That is the Italian, Nicola Pietrangeli. He heads my list of top Davis Cup men with the stupefying total of 153 rubbers, 102 of which were singles and 51 of which were doubles. He participated in 59 ties (1954 through 1968), and no other man has done as much.

Nor, in the immediate future anyway, is anyone likely to. There are 14 on my list of Davis Cup players who have played 80 rubbers or more. Pietrangeli has announced his retirement, but it is hard to see his figures being overtaken. The only other men who have topped the century, Jackie Brichant, Gottfried von Cramm, Ulf Schmidt and Philippe Washer, have all ceased playing. Torben Ulrich, with 98 rubbers, could obviously go over the top and so could Manuel Santana, who has 96, but the gap between them and the 153 of Pietrangeli is wide. If you take your country through the European zone into the challenge round, you can take part in seven ties each season, and if you play in both singles and doubles, in every tie you can, as the top limit, build up 21 rubbers per year. That, I need hardly say, is not easily done.

Pietrangeli has played more Davis Cup than anyone. Let his name be written large in the histories of the game.

But it is not only a matter of quantity. There is quality as well, and in this context the aspect of the Davis Cup that means most is the challenge round. At that stage, the men having already been separated from the boys, the supreme overlords of the game emerge.

The statistics of the challenge round give the place of honor to an American who was, in the opinion of many, the greatest player of all time—Big Bill Tilden. You will see from the table that he played no less than 28 rubbers at challenge round level. He won 21 of them. He participated in every challenge round from 1920 through 1930. From 1920 to 1925 he never lost a singles. In all he won 13 singles on the trot before being beaten in 1926. Do they come like that any more?

The data for the challenge round, though, needs to be extended. To take part in a vital rubber in the challenge round is altogether more demanding than the test of a rubber when the tie has finished, the cup is securely in the possession of one side or the other and the outcome of a particular rubber is irrelevant to the main issue. My second challenge round list, then, is of the figures relevant only to rubbers played when the issue was still alive. Here the position changes. The man who took part in more vital challenge round rubbers than anyone else was Sir Norman Brookes of Australia. He played in 19. But the man who *won* more vital challenge round rubbers than any rival among these giants was Tilden. And he played more vital singles—12, of which he won no less than 10.

Brookes and Tilden are names from the past. Note, though, who is at number four in the list. It is Roy Emerson, victor in 13 out of 15 vital challenge round rubbers, winner of nine out of nine singles. Maybe they still do come the same way.

As an addendum I have worked out lists pertinent to the four nations who have won the cup—the U. S., Australia, Great Britain and France. Vic Seixas is the man who has played most Davis Cup for America. In all, 82 men have played Davis Cup for the U. S. Only 49 have played for Australia, 65 have played for Britain and 38 for France. The last challenge round was the 154th Davis Cup tie for America. No other nation has had so many.

Top Davis Cup Men

	TOTAL		SINGLES		DOUBLES			
	Pl'd	Won	Pl'd	Won	Pl'd	Won	Ties	
Nicola Pietrangeli	153	112	102	72	51	40	59	Italy 1954–68
Jackie Brichant	121	71	80	52	41	19	42	Belgium 1949–65
Gottfried von Cramm	102	82	69	58	33	24	37	Germany 1932–53
Ulf Schmidt	102	66	69	44	33	22	38	Sweden 1954–64
Philippe Washer	102	66	64	46	38	20	39	Belgium 1946–61
Torben Ulrich	98	46	63	31	35	15	39	Denmark 1948–68
Manuel Santana	96	72	68	54	28	18	37	Spain 1958–68
Kurt Nielsen	96	53	65	42	31	11	33	Denmark 1948–60
Ramanathan Krishnan	94	66	66	47	28	19	36	India 1953–68
Orlando Sirola	89	57	46	22	43	35	45	Italy 1953–63
Lennart Bergelin	88	62	60	43	28	19	36	Sweden 1946–65
Jan Erik Lundquist	87	64	59	47	28	17	33	Sweden 1957–67
Roderick Menzel	84	61	60	47	24	14	35	(Czech. 1928–38 Germany 1939)
Sven Davidson	84	61	53	39	31	22	35	Sweden 1950–60

Challenge Round Rubbers

	TOTAL		SINGLES		DOUBLES			
	Pl'd	Won	Pl'd	Won	Pl'd	Won	Ties	
Bill Tilden (U.S.)	28	21	22	17	6	4	11	1920–30
Norman Brookes (Aus.)	22	15	14	9	8	6	8	1907–20
Henri Cochet (Fr.)	20	14	14	11	6	3	8	1926–33
Vic Seixas (U.S.)	20	6	14	4	6	2	7	1951–57
Roy Emerson (Aus.)	18	15	12	11	6	4	9	1959–67
Jean Borotra (Fr.)	17	6	12	4	5	2	9	1925–33
Bill Johnston (U.S.)	16	13	14	11	2	2	8	1920–27
Ted Schroeder (U.S.)	15	9	11	8	4	1	6	1946–51
John Bromwich (Aus.)	14	7	8	2	6	5	6	1938–50

Vital Challenge Round Rubbers

	TOTAL		SINGLES		DOUBLES			
	Pl'd	Won	Pl'd	Won	Pl'd	Won	Ties	
Brookes	19	13	11	7	8	6	..	....
Tilden	18	14	12	10	6	4	..	....
Cochet	17	12	11	9	6	3	..	....
Emerson	15	13	9	9	6	4	..	....
Seixas	15	4	9	2	6	2	..	....
Schroeder	13	8	9	7	4	1	..	....
Borotra	13	6	8	4	5	2	..	....
Johnston	12	9	10	7	2	2	..	....
Bromwich	11	6	5	1	6	5	..	....

United States

	TOTAL		SINGLES		DOUBLES			
	Pl'd	Won	Pl'd	Won	Pl'd	Won	Ties	
Vic Seixas	55	38	36	24	19	14	19	1951–57
Wilmer Allison	45	32	29	18	16	14	20	1929–36
Bill Tilden	41	34	30	25	11	9	17	1920–30
Chuck McKinley	38	30	22	17	16	13	16	1960–65
Tony Trabert	35	27	21	16	14	11	14	1951–55
Dennis Ralston	35	25	20	14	15	11	15	1960–66

Australia

	TOTAL		SINGLES		DOUBLES			
	Pl'd	Won	Pl'd	Won	Pl'd	Won	Ties	
Jack Crawford	58	36	40	23	18	13	23	1928–37
Adrian Quist	55	42	33	23	22	19	28	1933–48
John Bromwich	52	39	31	19	21	20	23	1937–50
Gerald Patterson	46	32	31	21	15	11	16	1919–28
Roy Emerson	40	36	24	22	16	14	18	1959–67

Great Britain

	TOTAL		SINGLES		DOUBLES			
	Pl'd	Won	Pl'd	Won	Pl'd	Won	Ties	
Mike Sangster	65	43	48	29	17	14	26	1960–68
Bobby Wilson	62	41	29	16	33	25	34	1955–68
Tony Mottram	56	36	38	25	18	11	19	1947–55
Fred Perry	52	45	38	34	14	11	20	1930–36
Bunny Austin	48	36	48	36	0	0	24	1929–37

France

	TOTAL		SINGLES		DOUBLES			
	Pl'd	Won	Pl'd	Won	Pl'd	Won	Ties	
Pierre Darmon	69	47	62	44	7	3	34	1956–67
Henri Cochet	58	44	42	34	16	10	26	1922–33
Jean Borotra	54	36	31	19	23	17	32	1922–47
Paul Remy	53	33	29	16	24	17	25	1949–58
René Lacoste	51	40	40	32	11	8	26	1923–28

THE WIGHTMAN CUP

by Hazel Hotchkiss Wightman

What prompted me to offer an international tennis trophy for women's matches is a question which I have often been asked. Naturally enough, I followed with keen interest the work of the Californians in Davis Cup play—Maurice McLoughlin, Melville Long, and Billy Johnston, in particular—and soon after the World War the outstanding accomplishments of Suzanne Lenglen at Wimbledon and elsewhere increased the general appeal of women's tennis to a higher degree than ever before. The agile and gifted French girl fired the imagination of English players by her phenomenal skill, and it struck me that women's play along the lines of the Davis Cup competition would provide a new and definite objective for girls who found tennis to their liking.

Kathleen McKane (now Mrs. L. A. Godfree) had become the leading woman of the English courts, and Helen Wills (now Mrs. F. S. Moody) was just beginning to show signs of the power and genius which were to make her the outstanding player of two continents. The thought struck me that ably handled meetings which brought together the chief exponents of the game in France, England, and the United States would add new zest to women's tennis. As I recall it, the trophy was offered about 1920, but there was a lack of sympathy with the idea. Some conservatives felt that such matches would arouse only casual interest; the English tennis association was not enthusiastic. When the subject was broached, the cool attitude towards the introduction of a new international trophy was made clear, but in 1923 affairs took a different turn, and that year England decided to send an official team for women's matches.

My first inkling of the British action came in the form of a telegram, asking me if I would be able to represent the United States in matches at New York in August 1923. I was visiting my parents in Berkeley, California, at the time and rearranged my plans to come in time for the matches. The information had been forwarded that Mr. Anthony Sabelli would captain the English team, which would include Miss McKane, Mrs. Alfred E. Beamish, Mrs. R. C. Clayton, and Mrs. B. C. Covell. En route to home, I discovered from a newspaper dispatch that I had been honored with the captaincy of the first American team and that my teammates would be Mrs. F. I. Mallory (Molla Bjurstedt), Helen Wills, and Eleanor Goss.

It is a matter of history that the American team vanquished the English visitors seven matches to none, but the event served as a memorable inaugural for the new tennis stadium at the West Side Tennis Club in Forest Hills. The English girls remained here for our national championships, and they returned home with a warm feeling for the reception which they had received. Annually the competition has shuttled back and forth between Wimbledon and Forest Hills, and nothing has arisen to mar the camaraderie of the players. In each of these British-American matches there have been five singles and two doubles matches, with the No. 1 and No. 2 singles players meeting in a round robin, the No. 3 singles players competing in one match, and with each team naming two doubles teams for the competition.

The original idea of including France did not materialize, and perhaps the competition will continue indefinitely between the players of the two English-speaking nations, but regardless of what the future holds for the event, it is my conviction that the good fellowship and friendly rivalry engendered by these women's matches have made them distinctly worthwhile. When the trophy was offered, there was no thought of using a name to designate the donor. In fact the trophy, officially, is the International Ladies' Trophy, but it has become known as the Wightman Cup event, and I don't suppose anything can be done about that. I do know that it is the ambition of all of our American girls to win a blazer that goes to players selected to represent the United States against England, and this proves that the competition provides an incentive to our leading players.

Mr. Julian Myrick's tact in handling the negotiations for the inaugural match is something which should not be overlooked in a discussion of the international trophy for women. I feel strongly that similar tact is essential if the competition is to hold its high place in the calendar of amateur sport. Plans for the matches should be directed with high principle; selection of the players should be made with great care, if we would avoid a deterioration in the equality of competition. It would be possible in our broad land for sectional prejudices to exert a baneful influence on the furtherance of the thought behind the presentation of the trophy, but I am hopeful that the yearly matches will gather a tradition that will make the competition increasingly attractive to the players of the two countries and that will keep it on a high plane. This is the age of commercialization, of exploitation, yet I earnestly hope that the matches for the International Ladies' Trophy will never be stunted by too much emphasis on this phase of the competition. Certainly the results thus far attained have exceeded early expectations, and there is no doubt that the home-and-home series has been an important factor in the development of tennis interest among women, if only from the viewpoint that it provides a definite objective for the players and offers a medium of social intercourse which might have been lost without the transatlantic journeyings of the leading players of the game.

The first American team to go to England (1924) was defeated almost as decisively as the English team had been beaten in its first efforts on foreign soil. We won only a doubles match in 1924, and the final score was England 6, United States 1. The American women afterwards went to Paris to compete in the Olympic tennis competitions and brought back three Olympic championships—singles, doubles, and mixed doubles. Our men held up their end by sweeping all of the male titles. The players who competed in the Olympic play at Paris look back upon it as one of the high points of their competitive careers, and I feel that America might have been less ably represented there if it were not for the organization of the international women's competition.

Serving as a curtain raiser for the championships at Wimbledon and at Forest Hills, the women's team matches have won their place as an international fixture, and it is my sincere hope that the matches in years to come will continue to serve the useful purpose of bringing players of the two countries closer together on and off the courts.

THE STORY OF HAZEL HOTCHKISS WIGHTMAN

by Herbert Warren Wind

Of all the tight little worlds that have grown up around the popular sports of our age, the most civilized by far is the one inhabited by the people who play and follow lawn tennis. To the outsider's eye, this world appears to be an unruffled and exclusive Eden of green grass, multicolored umbrellas, crisp white duds, sunshine, good breeding, good manners, good bodies, fair enough minds, good English, and good credit at the bank. To its inhabitants, however, it can be a highly fractious and nerve-racking place, for the pressures brought on by competition, social or athletic, have made them extremely adept at the double-edged remark and the well-thrown tantrum. Cliques spring up like weeds, and it is the rare afternoon indeed when some new vendetta is not stirring uneasily on the terrace.

The comparative peace which has prevailed during the last quarter of a century in women's tennis, the Balkans of the tennis world, has been largely due to the good offices of Hazel Hotchkiss Wightman. A bouncy, warm, unpretentious accumulation of unnervous energy, Mrs. Wightman, who is now sixty-five, has reigned officially, if unregally and often invisibly, as the Queen Mother of American Tennis since the inauguration in 1923 of the Wightman Cup matches between teams of women players representing the United States and England. As the friend, tutor, and housemother of two generations of girls who wanted desperately to play championship tennis, Mrs. Wightman has probably developed more players than any other dedicated amateur, given more lessons than most professionals, and, by way of example, won more national championships than any other player in the history of the sport. When she carried off her ninth Women's Veterans' Doubles Championship in 1950 in partnership with Mrs. Marjorie Gladman Buck, a slip of a girl of forty-one, it brought the number of Mrs. Wightman's national titles to forty-three. These include four United States Women's Singles Championships (1909, '10, '11, and '19), six Women's Doubles Championships (1909, '10, '11, '15, '24, and '28), six Mixed Doubles Championships (1909, '10, '11, '15, '18, and '20), two Indoor Women's Singles Championships (1919 and 1927), ten Indoor Women's Doubles Championships (1919, '21, '24, '27, '28, '29, '30, '31, '33, and '43), five Indoor Mixed Doubles Championships (1923, '24, '26, '27, and '28), and one Clay Court Mixed Doubles Championship in 1915. This is one of the few records of our times which seems to have a fair chance of surviving our national habit of record-breaking. "Hazel had brilliant footwork and the finest sense of anticipation I've ever seen on a court," R. Norris Williams, with whom Mrs. Wightman won the mixed doubles in the 1924 Olympic Games, recently told a group discussing her astounding longevity. "To my way of thinking, though, her principal gift, the one that enabled her to win the indoor doubles with Pauline Betz in 1943—a full thirty-four years after she won her first national championship—is the way that woman can concentrate. We played our matches in the Olympics under the worst conditions imaginable. The French completed the courts at Colombes, outside of Paris, barely three days before the tournament began, so a fine spray of dust blew in our faces all week. The main stadium, where the track and field events were going on, directly adjoined the tennis courts, and there was no knowing when a pistol would suddenly go off or a national anthem blare forth or just some announcement bellowed and rebellowed in several languages. The officials running the tennis tournament allowed vendors to circulate all over the stadium and to hawk their oranges, bananas, and ice cream at the top of their lungs. On top of this, the officiating was really the poorest I have ever encountered. On several days only the umpire showed up and the line-judges had to be recruited from patrons in the stands. I was on edge the entire tournament, but nothing bothered Hazel, nothing at all. I don't think she even heard them selling those bananas."

Mrs. Wightman has lived in Boston since 1912, when she married George W. Wightman, a Bostonian who later became president of the United States Lawn Tennis Association. (They were divorced in 1940.) She has come to be regarded, along with Bunker Hill Monument and the Jordan Marsh Company, as one of the more durable features of the local landscape. A compact woman, she is just over five feet tall, and the stalwart contours of her chin, the dominant nose, the steady penetration of her gray-blue eyes, and the periphery of brisk white hair make her accommodatingly Bostonian in appearance. The qualities which have made her so able a Queen Mother, are, however, those of the nineteenth-century Californian. Mrs. Wightman, who was born of covered-wagon stock in the town of Healdsburg, sixty-five miles north of San Francisco, has the frontier woman's distaste for political and verbal maneuver, her sense of frustration in doing only one thing at a time, and her hopelessly grooved zeal for helping her neighbor. These cardinal attributes of the proper Healdsburgher, rare enough in the world at large, are almost the exact antithesis of those most often found in the microcosm of tennis. "She's been like a long, cool breath of fresh air in the hothouse," a former national women's champion said of Mrs. Wightman last spring. "She's not at all like the rest of us dames. You can't gossip about her. She's so completely old-fashioned that she thinks people can get along with each other. I don't know anybody else who'd have dared to invite Helen Wills and Helen Jacobs *and their mothers* to share the same roof at the same time, but the four of them stayed with Mrs. Wightman and they honestly enjoyed themselves."

The two sternest criticisms which are made of Mrs. Wightman are comparatively fangless when the articulateness of the tennis world is considered. Women who pride themselves on their reputations as doubles players are seldom reticent in insinuating that Mrs. Wightman's multiple triumphs in doubles depended to a large measure on the skill of her partners. This is very true. Mrs. Wightman's partners have included such players as Bill Tilden, Jean Borotra, René Lacoste, R. Norris Williams, Helen Wills, Sarah Palfrey, and Pauline Betz. The second criticism, which is also not without grounds and which is usually hurled by her exact contemporaries whose aspirations she fulfilled, is that "Hazel has done entirely too much for tennis."

The divergence between the Queen Mother and the bulk of the ladies and gentlemen of her court was never more clearly illustrated than by the appearance in 1933 of *Better Tennis,* a book which Mrs. Wightman wrote in short installments in her auto while waiting to collect her five children at their various schools. The usual autobiography of a tennis champion is couched in a high-pitched tone of self-vindication, as if the writer felt obliged to answer charges that he or she was entirely devoid of culture and had no connections on a first-name basis with celebrities on every fashionable continent. "After my fortunate victory at Wimbledon"—so runs the S.O.P. for the tennis memoir—"much as I hated to hurt Gus's feelings, I just had to tell Augustus John that the portrait he wanted me to sit for would just have to wait until I helicoptered back with the Aga Khan from St. Tropez. There, after a small festival in good taste was thrown in my honor, Aga and I played a moonlight match against our old dauntless adversaries, Noel Coward and Haile Selassie. Noel and Haile won the first set, 6–4, and then we changed courts, flying to Aga's private court in India for the second set." The autobiographical portion of *Better Tennis* is written in low-flying prose and drops only two names, John McCormack and Queen Victoria Eugenia of Spain. The section devoted to instruction is equally earthbound. Mrs. Wightman does not advise the novice to hammer nails into a wall in order to develop the basic service stroke (as Mercer Beasley has advocated) or to tie a string to the center of the racket, hold the other end of the string firmly in the left hand, and then keep the string taut when sweeping through a forehand (Bunny Austen's sure-fire gimmick for shifting the weight correctly). Good old-fashioned practice, Mrs. Wightman repeats patiently, is the only method she has ever discovered for improving strokes, balance, and rhythm. The one corner of *Better Tennis* which possesses the traditional *personalismo* of tennis literature is an alphabet of alliterative maxims presented at the end of the book. Beginning with *Always Alert, Be Better,* and *Concentrate Constantly,* Mrs. Wightman barks out her tips, hurdling the difficult Q with *Quash Qualms,* subduing the treacherous U with *Umpire Usually,* and meeting the ultimate challenge with *Xceed Xpectations, Yell Yours,* and *Zip Zip.* On the court Mrs. Wightman is a chronic talk-it-upper, and the staccato delivery of these maxims forms a running obbligato during her practice sessions with her pupils. Mrs. Wightman is not slow with a compliment, but experience has strengthened her conviction that pampering explains the failure of so many young players to fulfill their promise let alone *Xceed Xpectations.* At an early stage in the career of her protégée Sarah Palfrey, during a match in which Sarah was beginning to lose a comfortable lead, Sarah's mother turned to Mrs. Wightman and remarked worriedly that it was much too hot a day for her daughter to be playing tennis. "It's just as hot for the girl on the other side of the net," Mrs. Wightman answered. "Sarah can win this match easily if she'll only *Quash Qualms.*"

During the last two decades, although no one else has noticed a diminuendo, Mrs. Wightman has been constantly fearful that she might be losing her old *Zip Zip.* One February weekend two winters ago, when Wightman Cup business called her out of Boston, she entrusted her Saturday morning tennis class to Judy Atterbury, one of the best young players in New England, and was gigantically relieved to learn on her return that Miss Atterbury had become exhausted after the first hour and had not been able to continue with the lesson.

Mrs. Wightman has been conducting this winter-season Saturday class on the indoor linoleum courts of the Longwood Covered Courts club in Chestnut Hill every winter since 1923. In the winter of 1949 she tore a ligament in her upper right arm in a fall from an icy step. Rather than cancel her class for three weeks, she decided to see if she could play well enough with her left hand to keep the class going and was elated when she discovered that she was adequately ambidextrous. She has placed one of her children's old playpens in the balcony overlooking the covered courts so that young mothers who can't afford sitters will not have to give up the game.

Mrs. Wightman's dedication to tennis makes it difficult to get her off a tennis court once she is on it. Two summers ago Mrs. Edith Sullivan, a cohort of hers who was endeavoring to stir up interest in the game among a very untennisy set in Belmont, asked Mrs. Wightman to come out and give a stroke demonstration. Mrs. Wightman did this. She then played a set apiece with the two most advanced girls. Feeling that it would look unfair if she went away without at least rallying with the forty-odd other girls who had turned out, she gave each of them a brief individual lesson. "I don't know how she did it!" Mrs. Sullivan was exclaiming a short while ago. "It was a hot June day, a real broiler, and Mrs. Wightman stayed on the court for seven solid hours. She didn't even stop for lunch. Around two I handed her a tuna fish sandwich and she ate it out of one hand and kept right on playing with the other."

Mrs. Wightman's obstinate refusal to slow down is a source not only of wonder but of mild irritation to the younger women who partner her in doubles competitions. In 1948 she invited Mrs. Marion Zinderstein Jessup, one of her first protégées, with whom she had won four National Indoor Doubles Championships between 1919 and 1927, to play with her in the National Veterans' Doubles Championship. "It was really a thrilling experience," Mrs. Jessup had said of their reunion as a team and their subsequent victory. . . .

To the outside or unsneakered world, Mrs. Wightman, apart from her connection with the cup and the international matches that bear her name, is best known as the teacher of champions. In the last thirty years there have been few, if any, topflight American women players whose development has not been directly influenced by her. She met Helen Wills in the summer of 1920 on one of the trips she made biennially to California to visit her family and inspect the tennis crop. Helen was fourteen when Mrs. Wightman, cruising critically over the grounds of the Berkeley Tennis Club, watched her belt a series of drives and went over and introduced herself. During the remainder of her six-week stay in Berkeley, Mrs. Wightman worked with Helen on her two weakest points, her volley and her footwork, a regimen they continued the following summer when Helen and her mother came East as Mrs. Wightman's guests. Two years later, in the summer of 1923, Helen won her first national women's title, defeating Molla Bjurstedt Mallory, the sturdy Norwegian with the Gallic temperament who had held the championship almost without interruption since 1915. A substantial measure of the credit for Helen's sure and rapid rise belonged to "Pop" Fuller, the professional at the Berkeley Tennis Club, who had grounded her well; and the major share, to be certain, belonged to Helen herself, a disciplined if not an overdisciplined athlete. In Mrs. Mallory's excited opinion, however, Mrs. Wightman was wholly responsible for Helen's victory over her and had, in fact, been training Helen for that specific purpose.

"There was no truth whatsoever in Molla's accusation," Mrs. Wightman once commented on this 1923 outburst of trouble in paradise. "I just tried to bring Helen along the way I try to help any player who wants my help. Helen would have become a champion without my coaching. I may have speeded up her development so that Helen's game reached a champion's pitch a year or so before she would have otherwise got there, but that was all."

Mrs. Wightman's close friendship with Helen Wills did not deter her from giving equal tutorial and personal attention to Helen Jacobs, another product of Berkeley, who became Helen Wills' bitter and abiding rival. Mrs. Wightman met the second Helen on her visit to California in 1923 and practiced with her three hours on Monday, Wednesday, and Friday mornings as long as she was there.

"She was wonderful to work with, that girl," Mrs. Wightman has said of Helen Jacobs. "How that girl would listen to what you were trying to get across and how she'd concentrate on applying it! Helen Jacobs was the most responsive and, in a way, the most satisfying pupil I've ever taught." At one time, before it became apparent that the Wills-Jacobs feud was irreconcilable, Mrs. Wightman tried to get the two to play regular practice matches together, suggesting that these workouts would benefit both of their games. They tried it twice and then called it off, to their mutual relief. Whenever the two Helens clashed in tournament play, Mrs. Wightman, despite her efforts to enter a temporary state of Buddhistic suspension of all feelings, found her sympathies torn between the two antagonists and invariably took a deep emotional beating.

Mrs. Wightman, who can detect a natural aptitude for tennis as instantaneously as a Rodgers and Hammerstein hero can spot his true love, discovered Sarah Palfrey in the autumn of 1923, when Sarah was eleven. "Mr. Croker—he was the professional at Longwood then—told me to be sure and come down to the courts on Saturday," she recently told a friend, "and he'd show me the finest young prospect I'd ever seen. He was really crowing. On the Saturday I went to the club and watched Mr. Croker giving a lesson to a very graceful young girl, about thirteen. After the lesson Mr. Croker came over with a smile a mile wide on his face and asked me what I thought of his prize. I said that she seemed to have all the earmarks of a first-class player, and then I told him, 'There's a better player here you've missed. Take a look at that little thing on number three court. That's the one I want.' Mr. Croker's pupil was Mianne Palfrey, one of Sarah's four sisters, and I, of course, had Sarah."

Under Mrs. Wightman's tutelage Sarah became the number four player in the national rankings in 1929 when she was seventeen, but she never succeeded in winning the championship until 1941, when her husband,

Elwood Cooke, helped her, as Sarah saw it, to correct a deficient backhand. "Her backhand was always a good stroke, I thought," Mrs. Wightman told an old Longwood hand who had asked her analysis of Sarah's long-overdue arrival at the top. "I don't think Elwood gave Sarah a new backhand. He gave her a confidence she never had before in tight matches against the big guns. That's all Sarah ever needed."

An unplanned but felicitous by-product of Mrs. Wightman's coaching activities is the abundant supply she has always had of splendid women's doubles partners. She and Sarah took five National Indoor Doubles Championships. The team of Wills and Wightman won two Wightman Cup matches, two United States Championships, the Olympic tournament of 1924, and one All-England Championship at Wimbledon. They were never defeated. . . .

Alice Marble, the next great Californian to follow the two Helens, experienced little difficulty in winning our championships in the late thirties but was prone to mystifying lapses of form, particularly at Wimbledon, and was regularly defeated by players she should have outclassed. Alice was the pupil of Eleanor "Teach" Tennant, an extremely talented coach from Los Angeles. Never averse to publicity, Miss Tennant did not discourage Alice from indulging in a set of court mannerisms associated usually with Tilden and other self-consciously theatrical stars. "There was no question that the gallery ate it up when they saw an attractive girl like Alice kick the ball after a bad shot or whack it into the backstop," Mrs. Wightman has said of the touches of golden California temperament Alice injected into her matches, "but that's exactly where Alice was going wrong. She was thinking too much of the impression those displays were making on the galleries, and it was hurting her tennis." Mrs. Wightman checked herself from offering her advice until Alice approached her in a very disconsolate mood after she had been ousted by Helen Jacobs, 6–4, 6–4, in the semifinal round of the 1938 Wimbledon championship. She asked Mrs. Wightman why she thought she had lost the match. "You lost it in the eighth game of the first set," Mrs. Wightman replied. "You lost it when you began dramatizing yourself all over the court after you netted that drive, Alice—you know the one I mean. You were playing just as well as Helen. Let's see, you were behind 3–4 in games and you had 40–30 on your service, one point from tying it up. Then you netted that drive. You slipped on the shot and fell down, right? What did you do then? I'll tell you. You didn't brush off your shorts and get back into the match. No, you patted your fanny and you got a nice ripple of laughter from the gallery. So you continued to pat your fanny, and while you were amusing everyone, you netted two more simple shots and tossed Helen the set. Your mind wasn't on your tennis. It took you *two full games* before you got back to business, and after that you never caught up. Even a girl with your natural equipment can't win if she allows *anything* to break her concentration." ("She took it very well," Mrs. Wightman once remarked of her talk with Alice, "a lot better than 'Teach' did when she got word that I was tampering with her pupil. I don't think 'Teach' minded it, though, when Alice finally broke through at Wimbledon the next year.") Mrs. Wightman likes her girls to move with vigor, hit with force, and fight hard for victory, but to her way of thinking there is a definite line between feminine athletic prowess and theatrical manners. Her ideal personality, she told a tennis historian who had asked her to create a composite colossa, would have Helen Wills' concentration, Alice Marble's dash, Sarah Palfrey's grace, Louise Brough's determination, Margaret du Pont's innate sportsmanship, and Didi Vlasto's looks. "I think I'd throw in Suzanne Lenglen's shots," Mrs. Wightman added. "They might come in handy if she was having an off-day." . . .

In Mrs. Wightman's book, a champion, since she serves as a model for thousands of impressionable girls, has many responsibilities above and beyond performing with excellence. Her conduct must be exemplary in all respects, and this includes not confusing the tennis court with the stage and making too striking an appearance. This past season a contingent of fifteen-year-olds asked Mrs. Wightman what she thought of the black shorts which Gussie Moran, the game's current glamour girl, had worn in a tournament in Cairo. "I don't think there was really any need for it," Mrs. Wightman replied. "Didn't Gussie say that she had to wear those black shorts in the semifinals because she had only one pair of whites and was saving them for the final? Well, there was no reason in the world why she couldn't have worn the whites in the semifinals, washed and ironed them after the match, and had them ready for the next day."

One champion who possibly took the code a little too seriously was Helen Wills, and Mrs. Wightman is among the few people who could get along with her comfortably. In the company of Mrs. Wightman, Helen shed her poker face and the monarchical measure of her words and gestures and relaxed. On occasions she was hardly recognizable as the same girl whose life was so chained to the conservation of a pure schedule and the safeguarding of her physical resources that she had balked at visiting the battlefield at Waterloo one morning for fear that she would not be at her best for an unimportant exhibition in Brussels that afternoon. Mrs. Wightman's secret for bringing out Helen's lurking humanity was to treat her as an unqueenly and imperfect human being.

"I think Helen took it from me," Mrs. Wightman was saying a few months ago, "because I had met her when she was just a young girl, before she began to cover up from the spotlight and developed that protective layer. Helen was really an unconfident and awkward girl—you have no idea how awkward. . . . You see, where I differed from most of the tennis crowd was that I thought of Helen as an honestly shy person who was bewildered by how difficult it was to please most people. . . .

"I never found the slightest fault with Helen's behavior on the court. In tennis, after all, the idea is to win your matches as efficiently and as swiftly as you can, not to win a popularity contest. I wasn't at Forest Hills in 1933 when Helen walked off the court in the third set of her match with Helen Jacobs. How often I wish I had been! I listened to the broadcast of that match at home, and from the very beginning I had the weirdest sensation: I knew positively that something was wrong with Helen, that she was worried about her back injury and was afraid, deathly afraid, of falling and injuring herself permanently. I don't think that girl really knew what she was doing when she walked off that court or, for that matter, at any time during the match." . . .

Hazel Hotchkiss Wightman was born in Healdsburg, California, in 1886, five years after the United States Lawn Tennis Association was founded, eleven years after the All-England Lawn Tennis and Croquet Club laid out its first court at Wimbledon, and thirteen years after Major Walter C. Wingfield, a retired British Army officer, worked out a primitive form of lawn tennis to serve the same Victorian garden-party functions as croquet and bequeathed to his baby the happily short-lived name of Sphairistike. Both sets of Mrs. Wightman's grandparents made the transcontinental journey to California, though their modes of travel differed. Benoni Hotchkiss, her paternal grandfather, was living in Campbellsville, Kentucky, when he decided on the spur of the moment, in the spring of 1850, to join a covered-wagon caravan that was passing through the village and looking for one more wagon to complete the train. William Grove, her mother's father and a native of Staunton, Virginia, transported his family West after the Civil War under slightly plusher conditions. The Groves journeyed by rail most of the way and carried all their belongings with them, including the old square piano. The Hotchkisses and the Groves settled on adjoining ranches along the Russian River in the Sonoma Valley, and in the best Harold Bell Wright tradition one of the Hotchkiss boys, William Joseph, conducted a successful open-air courtship of one of the Grove girls, Emma Lucretia. They purchased a 1,500-acre ranch and proceeded to raise a family in an orderly manner. Hazel, their one daughter, was six years younger than Miller, four younger than Homer, two younger than Marius, and two years older than Linville. . . .

Mrs. Wightman's vigor and staying power stem from her mother's side of the family. When Mrs. Hotchkiss was in her sixties, she was the victim of a freak automobile accident. She had parked her electric auto on an incline and was walking away when the brake slipped and the heavy auto rolled over her left foot before she could get out of the way. Mrs. Hotchkiss stayed on her feet and managed to yank the door open and pull the brake on the runaway before she collapsed in great pain. A Christian Science reader read to her several hours that evening. The next morning she was up and bustling around the house as if nothing had happened. . . .

Hazel Hotchkiss was an extremely frail child, so subject to headaches that she could not attend school regularly. On the advice of the family doctor, her parents encouraged her to spend as many hours as possible outdoors, and her brothers were instructed to include her in their games. Hazel developed into a fair pole vaulter and halfback and a stylish baseball player. In 1900, shortly after Mr. Hotchkiss had moved his business offices to San Francisco and his family to Berkeley, a commutable distance across San Francisco Bay, the two middle boys, Homer and Marius, took up tennis and captured a local tournament the first year they played the game. In an effort to interest their sister in tennis, a suitable sport for a young lady, her brothers took her to San Rafael in the summer of 1902 to watch the Pacific Coast Championships. Hazel fell in love with tennis at her first sight of good tennis. "The feature match was the final between two of the famous Sutton sisters, Ethel and May, and they were mighty impressive," Mrs. Wightman has said of that portentous day. "Both of them had fine forcing forehands, and May particularly could soak that ball. But what caught my fancy even more than the Suttons was the doubles match put on by the Hardy brothers, Sam and Sumner. They'd been in a class by themselves on the Pacific Coast for eight or nine years, and they were a skillful team. The way girls played singles in those days, there was no net game at all. They didn't budge from the baseline. The ball passed over the net as many as fifty times in a single rally before someone made an error or finally won the point on a placement. Doubles like Sam and Sumner Hardy played it—now that appealed to me. They were awfully quick up at net, and even a greenhorn like myself could appreciate the precision with which they volleyed and smashed and their split-second maneuvers for drawing their opponents out of position and setting up their openings. I decided that afternoon that I'd go in for tennis and model my game on the Hardys'." As it turned out, the graveled back yard behind the Hotchkisses' home, where Hazel and her brothers did the bulk of their practicing since there was only one court in Berkeley, compelled them to play like the Hardys. The bounces off the gravel were so erratic that the ball had to be volleyed—that is, played before it struck the ground. It was all net play, and since the net was simply a rope strung between the house and a cluster of rosebushes, the players soon learned that if they wanted to avoid a fine patina of black-and-blue welts, they had to get their rackets in front of every ball hit at them. The brilliant anticipatory sense that later characterized Mrs. Wightman's game—and excited Wallis Myers, the English critic, to rank her alongside Suzanne Lenglen in that rare company of players whose rackets seemed to attract the ball—was born in self-defense on the graveled back yard at 2985 Claremont Avenue.

Berkeley's one tennis court at the turn of the century was an asphalt one belonging to the University of California. The court was open to the public, but girls were not allowed to play on it after eight in the morning. In order to bypass this regulation, Hazel and her brothers rose daily at five. A friend of Homer's, who made the fourth for doubles, would awaken him by jerking a string that was wound around Homer's big toe and which ran out the window and down the side of the house. Homer would then rouse Marius and Hazel. They would grab an apple from the kitchen for breakfast and eat it as they trotted the mile to the court in the ocher light of dawn. These workouts came to an end at six-thirty when Hazel returned home to practice the piano for an hour before heading for classes at Berkeley High School. Whenever Hazel could find no one to rally with on the gravel, she worked on her strokes by banging a ball against the wall of the Hotchkiss house, evolving increasingly complex patterns during these drills—forehand-backhand, two forehands-two backhands, three forehands-one backhand, and so on. She has always contended that solo practice against a bangboard, no matter how crude, can be the making of a tennis player. . . .

In December 1902, six months after she had taken up tennis, Hazel Hotchkiss entered her first tournament, the Bay Counties Women's Doubles Championship, sponsored by the San Francisco Park Department. On the ferry across the bay, she ran into a girl named Mary Radcliffe and learned that she also was going to play in the tournament. Mary, like herself, was waiting to be assigned a doubles partner by the tournament committee. The two girls decided to team up, and although neither had previously seen the other play, they went on to win the championship without the loss of a set. It was a historic day in women's tennis because of the revolutionary tactics that Hazel Hotchkiss introduced. Standing a yard and a half from the net when her partner served, she intercepted the majority of their opponents' drives and volleyed them for winners. She rushed forward during rallies whenever a short return provided that opening, and she stayed poised at the net instead of retreating to backcourt. She followed in after her better serves, just like the Hardy brothers and her brothers did, to volley the return. These measures thoroughly demoralized her opponents, who had been brought up to think that woman's place was the baseline. After Mrs. Wightman had showed the way, other women, notably Mary K. Browne, Eleonora Sears, and Elizabeth Ryan, learned to play net, and the emancipation of the woman from the backcourt was definitely under way. . . .

In doubles, Hazel was unapproachable; she could win with any partner. In singles she was a degree less formidable. Her service was well placed but not too hard to handle. Her ground strokes—when the ball is played after the bounce—were chopped and, as a result, not true attacking weapons. "If Hazel had stayed on the baseline, she would have been absolutely overpowered by a player with first-class drives," Mrs. William MacKenzie Kalt, for many years the chairman of the Women's Ranking Committee of the U.S.L.T.A., has said. "Hazel, however, was smart enough to realize that she couldn't live on the baseline. She had to get to net to win, and she knew it. She couldn't get up there behind a forcing service or drive, the way most players do it today, because she didn't have those shots. Here's how she got there. Two moves. First, after she had chopped a backhand or forehand deep into her opponent's court, she could get as far up as midcourt, about halfway between the baseline and the net. That's no man's land for a tennis player. You're easily passed down the sidelines, and most of the balls you get there land at your feet. You're lucky if you can play a strong defensive shot. Now what Hazel could do, and she *alone* among the women could do it because she could volley and half-volley like nobody's business, was to turn midcourt from a wretched defensive position into a very comfortable offensive position. Then, mind you, after she had made her volley or half-volley at midcourt, *then* she could get all the way to net and put the ball away with an angled smash."

To expose the deficiencies in Hazel Hotchkiss' singles game, a girl had to be a hard and accurate hitter, and there were no players of that caliber in the San Francisco area. When she continued to clean up all comers in tournament after tournament, the Northern Californian tennis fans began to speculate hopefully as to whether or not they had finally produced a player who could put Southern California, already its infamous rival, in its proper place by defeating all or one of the remarkable Sutton sisters.

There were five Sutton sisters in all, the daughters of an English naval captain who had transplanted his family from Plymouth to Pasadena after his retirement. Adele, the oldest, didn't care much for tennis, but Ethel, Violet, Florence, and May, who followed in that order, spent their childhood on the family court. The Suttons began to emerge around 1900 and soon dominated the tournaments they elected to enter with such unchallenged finality that even people who didn't follow tennis kept abreast of their deeds and enjoyed invoking the popular slogan, "It takes a Sutton to beat a Sutton." By 1904 Hazel Hotchkiss had widened her tournament orbit so that it took in Del Monte, Colorado Springs, and other California oases where the Suttons competed. Hazel absorbed several good lacings before she defeated her first Sutton, Ethel, in the 1906 Pacific Coast Championships at San Rafael. Shortly after this, she overhauled Violet and Florence. May, the youngest, was a different proposition. A year younger than Hazel, stocky, square-shouldered, and with the uncomplicated belligerence of a bulldog, May was *the* Sutton. She had gone East in 1904 to see what the National Championships were like and had won without exerting herself. She never chose to appear in the Nationals again during her heyday. In 1905, however, she invaded England and became the first American girl to win at Wimbledon when she outlasted the top-ranking English star, Dorothea Douglass. Miss Douglass turned the tables on May in the Wimbledon final the next summer, but in 1907 May regained that championship, again defeating Miss Douglass. That satisfied May and she never went back.

May's great stroke was her forehand drive. In the opinion of several tennis experts, the outstanding forehands of later periods—these of Molla Mallory, Helen Wills, Maureen Connolly, and May's own daughter, Dorothy Bundy—never touched May's. She used an extreme Western grip, the racket held so that the knuckles faced the ground. (In the Eastern grip, which Mrs. Wightman fell into naturally, the player more or less shakes hands with the racket.) May struck the ball low in its bounce, the racket face almost parallel with the ground, and imparted a terrific top spin to the ball. "She not only socked the ball with speed and pace but she could put it on a dime," Mrs. Wightman once commented. "I was standing near May one afternoon when a reporter asked her how she managed to put the ball in the corners time after time. She told him it was easy, that the lines on the court seemed to stand upright, like fences."

In her first match against May Sutton, the baseliner, Hazel Hotchkiss, the volleyer, gave herself, her brothers, and Northern California little to cheer about. May polished her off with the average loss of five games in two sets, blasting away with her forehand with such severity that Hazel had few opportunities to move up to midcourt. Gradually, however, Hazel began to take more and more games, and in one of their meetings, early in 1910, although she ultimately lost the third and deciding set, she did succeed in taking a set from May, something no American girl other than a Sutton had ever done before.

There were four principal reasons, as the duel progressed, why Hazel was able to keep closing the gap and to make it very warm for May. She learned to become less disturbed by May's unsettling swagger and her knack of inciting the galleries with her love of battle. She found she could cope somewhat better with May's forehand by watching the direction of May's racket head the instant before impact. . . . She perfected her smash during long practice sessions with Maurice McLoughlin, a fellow Northern Californian, who became the first men's national champion produced in the West and was renowned for the unprecedented velocity of his serve and overhead. . . . Above all, she kept hammering away at May's relatively negative backhand. There are some veteran tennis fans who think that Mrs. Wightman's years of furious concentration on breaking down May Sutton's backhand left such an indelible mark on her that ever after she automatically played everyone's backhand and thirty years later was indoctrinating her pupils to do the same even if their opponent's backhand was as impregnable and her forehand as unsteady as Helen Jacobs'.

The Sutton-Hotchkiss rivalry, which had been gathering steam as the matches became closer, erupted into a fiery full-fledged sectional feud in 1910, when Hazel was twenty-three and May twenty-two. That spring Hazel finally made it, beating May in the Ojai Valley tournament. The scores were 2–6, 6–4, 6–0, and May offered no handshake at the conclusion of the match. They faced each other six months later in the final of the Pacific Coast Championship at Del Monte. May took the first set 7–5 by running around her backhand. Hazel fought back to take the second at 6–4 with a mixture of drop shots and smashes. Feeling that she had May on the run, she was waiting on the baseline, eager to get on with the crucial third set, when May sauntered off the court without a word, announced regally to the umpire that she felt like a cup of tea, deposited herself in a wicker chair, and sat in silence until a waiter appeared from the hotel carrying her tea on a tray. Twenty minutes later, May was ready to resume play, and she pulled out the final set, 6–4. After this controversial episode—the Southern Californians considered it the resourcefulness of a true champion, the Northern Californians, shocking sportsmanship—there was seldom an empty seat in the stands when the two rivals clashed . . .

In this strong and colorful rivalry, which continued without diminution of ardor until 1912, when Hazel Hotchkiss married and moved East, the real winner was California. Hitherto the state had exhibited a patchy and rather casual concern for tennis, but the dramatic overtones of the Hotchkiss-Sutton series created in both the upper and lower sectors of the state a profound tennis-consciousness that California has never lost.

In the fall of 1908, just before this synonymity of California and tennis was established, a delegation of crack Atlantic seaboard stars, including Irving Wright, Nat Niles, and Wallace Johnson, and shepherded by the veteran Boston sportsman, George Wright, toured the West Coast with the purpose of promoting interest in tennis, a coals-to-Newcastle mission of the first scuttle. Hazel Hotchkiss was then three-quarters of the way through her conquest of the Sutton sisters, but the news of her rise had not filtered back to the East, and the unbriefed visitors were doubly impressed by her revolutionary all-court style of play. After several talks with Mr. Hotchkiss, they persuaded him to bring his daughter East the following summer to play in the National Championships. In June, when Hazel had completed her sophomore year at the University of California, she and her father crossed the country to the Philadelphia Country Club, where the women's singles, women's doubles, and mixed doubles championships were traditionally held. Hazel idled away the hours on the train by cross-stitching the design on six towels she was fashioning into Christmas presents.

It was a successful trip. Hazel won the mixed doubles with Johnson and the women's doubles with Edith Rotch of Boston. She completed her sweep of the three titles, the first player to do so, by defeating the titleholder, Mrs. Maud Barger-Wallach of Newport, in the singles. Until 1919 the defending champion did not have to play through the early rounds; she stood by as the aspirants to her title battled it out in an elimination tournament, called the All-Comers, to determine who would play the champ in the Challenge Round—roughly the same structure that obtains today in Davis Cup competition. Mrs. Barger-Wallach, a fragile artist in her thirties, had been in poor health, and she was not sure up to the last moment whether or not she would attempt to defend her title. She at length decided she would and, with her trained nurse seated in the grandstand in the event of emergency, took to the court dressed in a wide-brimmed garden hat and a flowing white gown that gave her the appearance of a displaced Renoir. It was no contest. Miss Hotchkiss ran through the first set in ten minutes with the loss of only seven points. Halfway through the second set, which was following the same pattern of an orderly rout, Hazel abruptly stopped playing Mrs. Barger-Wallach's nonexistent backhand. She also stopped coming to net. From that point on until the end of the set, which Hazel won 6–1, she fed Mrs. Barger-Wallach's forehand, and in the long and pleasant rallies which ensued, Mrs. Barger-Wallach, who had looked like no tennis player at all, played creditable forehand tennis. She walked off the court an unhumiliated ex-champion. . . .

Hazel Hotchkiss successfully defended her three titles in 1910 and again in 1911, a season in which everything went right for her and which is recognized as the high point of the "Hazel Era" of American tennis. Recurrent showers during the week of the championships threw the schedule out of kilter, and the three finals had to be squeezed into one afternoon. Hazel first took to the court at three o'clock for the singles final against Florence Sutton. With the sets at one–all, Hazel was trailing 6–5 in games and 40–30 on Florence's service, one point from defeat, when she killed a deep lob, drew up to deuce, pulled the game out of the fire, and went on to win the set and the match, 8–10, 6–1, 9–7. The final of the mixed doubles followed immediately; Hazel and Wallace Johnson took this, 6–4, 6–4. A sudden squall forced her to sit down and rest until the turf dried out, but at six o'clock she was back in action in the women's doubles final, which she and Eleonora Sears, the original Boston glamour girl, won by the scores of 6–4,

4–6, 6–2. Between three o'clock and seven-forty-two, the triple champion played eighty-nine games, a feat the more remarkable when one considers that the women players lugged around several layers of undergarments beneath their starched linen shirts and ankle-length white duck skirts. . . .

As her college graduation present, Mr. Hotchkiss allowed Hazel to stay East for four months after the 1911 championships. She made the tour of the summer circuit. . . . On the turf courts of the Queen's Royal Hotel at Niagara-on-the-Lake, Hazel and her old antagonist, May Sutton, came up against each other again in the final, their first meeting outside of California and their first on grass. . . . Hazel won, 0–6, 7–5, 6–0 . . . This was the last match between the two great rivals during their athletic primes. As they grew older, each of them mellowed to the extent that she could regard the other with objective admiration, but there remained perhaps a certain absence of warmth in their relationship. When they met in an early round in the National Championship in 1928—Mrs. Wightman won, 6–4, 11–9—both battled desperately to win, as if they were still fighting to see who was the best woman player in the country. May accepted an invitation to play on the Wightman Cup team in 1925. A decade later her daughter, Dorothy Bundy, for whom Mrs. Wightman has a tremendous affection, was on the team.

In her swing around the tournament circuit in the summer of 1911, Hazel Hotchkiss met George Wightman, a slim Bostonian who was entering his senior year at Harvard. Their engagement was announced during the visit he made to the Hotchkiss homestead in Berkeley the following winter, they were married in June, and they settled in a yellow frame house situated three flat forehands from the S. S. Pierce store at Coolidge Corner. While he was not the nationally known personality his wife was, Mr. Wightman was a sportsman of more than passing attainments. As a boy he had achieved a certain prominence in yachting circles by outsailing Charles Francis Adams in several races off the resort town of Hull, and for many years he was a contender for the national championship in court tennis, the intricate ancestor of lawn tennis. Mr. Wightman's skill as a lawn tennis player did not match his love of watching good tennis and being in the company of tennis players, but he was proficient enough to team up with Mrs. Wightman and carry off the mixed doubles in the 1913 Longwood Bowl tournament. After serving the customary apprenticeship as a committee workhorse —treasurer, secretary and vice-president—Mr. Wightman became president of the U. S. Lawn Tennis Association in 1924.

In the seven years after her marriage in 1912, Mrs. Wightman played only occasional tournament tennis, a semi-retirement occasioned for the most part by the birth of three children. In 1919 her urge to see if she could keep pace with the new stars who had come to the fore prompted her to return to tournament tennis. In the opinion of veteran tennis critics, it is questionable if Mrs. Wightman could then have stayed with the defending national champion, Mrs. Molla Bjurstedt (later Mrs. Mallory). Molla, however, did not choose to defend her indoor championship, and in the outdoor championship on grass she was eliminated in the semifinal round by Mrs.

Wightman's protégée, Marion Zinderstein. Mrs. Wightman faced Marion in both of the finals and captured them largely by giving Marion the shots she knew she was weakest on. . . .

Mrs. Wightman's successful re-entry into the lists in 1919 brought her numerous messages of congratulation from her faithful followers in the "Hazel Era" and a gracious letter, which turned out to have considerable influence, from Suzanne Lenglen, the young French whiz who had won her first Wimbledon championship that spring. At this time Mrs. Wightman was practically the only bridge between East Coast and West Coast women's tennis. For a number of years the sun-kissed prodigies sprouting in California had shied away from making the cross-country journey to the big tournaments, even if the necessary funds were available, because they had no friends on that distant shore to show them the ropes. Mrs. Wightman made it a point to meet these girls during her visits to California and to invite them, should they decide to take a crack at the eastern tournaments, to make their headquarters at her home in Brookline. An ever-increasing number accepted. In July and August, when the young Californians moved in with their several rackets and changes of bandeaux, the yellow frame house on Charles Street seethed with the coloratura hum of a girls' dormitory as their housemother gave them careful instructions on what tournaments to enter, how to line up partners, where to stay on the circuit stops, what clothes to wear, how much to tip waiters, what evening invitations were preferable, and, last but not least, how to improve their tennis.

The letter from Suzanne was the little shove Mrs. Wightman needed to expand her activities from a national to an international scale. "I'd been thinking for a long while that the women tennis players in different countries would like to get to know each other," she said recently. "The men had had the Davis Cup since 1900, and that had taken hold so well that, after the first World War, over twenty countries were entering teams. The standard of men's tennis throughout the world had been improved by the Davis Cup—no question about that. And the players had loved it. It gave them a chance to travel and see foreign countries and make many good friends. Hearing from Suzanne, whom I had never met, crystallized my feeling that the time was ripe to do something about organizing an international team match for women along the lines of the Davis Cup. I presented this idea to Mr. Myrick of the Lawn Tennis Association and told him that if they wanted a trophy for such an event, I'd be more than glad to donate one. Mr. Myrick told me to go right ahead." The next week Mrs. Wightman walked into N. G. Wood & Sons on Park Street in Boston and purchased for $300 a tall silver cup on which she had engraved Challenge Cup—Ladies Team Match. "It wasn't exactly the type I had in mind," Mrs. Wightman has said of the trophy, which is always referred to as the Wightman Cup although her name does not appear on it. "I wanted something more graceful—something more classical and flowing and urnlike. However, it was the only thing that Wood had in the shop, and by nature I'm a purchaser and not a shopper."

Upon receipt of the Wightman Cup, the U.S.L.T.A. sounded out the tennis associations of the countries which supported Davis Cup teams. Most of the replies were apathetic, pointing out that footing the bill for the Davis Cuppers made it impossible to send other players abroad. The idea of an international women's team match was quietly dropped and then forgotten. Mrs. Wightman was in California in 1923, four years after she had presented the trophy, when the first Wightman Cup match was hastily cooked up. Work on the new stadium at the West Side Tennis Club in Forest Hills had been completed that summer and the U.S.L.T.A. was pondering a distinguished opening event when someone remembered that a group of England's best women players was on its way across the Atlantic to play in our tournaments, and someone else remembered the Wightman Cup. In a ship-to-shore exchange of radiograms, an international match, England versus the United States, was arranged for Forest Hills to begin on August 10. (A day's postponement later became necessary when the tenth was set aside as a day of national mourning for President Harding, who had been fatally stricken with food poisoning in Alaska.) The first word Mrs. Wightman received of these developments was a telegram informing her that she had been selected to represent the United States in a Wightman Cup match and requesting her to return to New York immediately. When her train reached Albany, she bought the *New York Tribune* and learned that she had been appointed captain of an American team consisting of Helen Wills, Molla Mallory, Eleanor Goss, and herself. The first Wightman Cup match—they are two-day affairs—was at length unfurled at Forest Hills on August 11, 1923, in a blaze of pomp and circumlocution. Four trumpeters, serried along the top row of the west side of the stands, blew a fine series of tantaras. A military band, massed on the turf in the middle of the concrete horseshoe, solemnly rendered "God Save the King" and "The Star-Spangled Banner." Flags went up, speeches went off, and then the tennis got under way. A close contest had been predicted, but on the opening day the American side took the two singles and the one doubles, and on the second day it swept the remaining three singles and the second doubles to make the final score 7–0. . . .

In the first Wightman Cup meeting, Mrs. Wightman teamed with Eleanor Goss in the number one doubles to defeat Kathleen McKane and Mrs. Ethel Covell in a genuinely exciting duel, 10–8, 5–7, 6–4. In 1924, when the match was held on Wimbledon's number one court—in the even-numbered years England is host—Mrs. Wightman paired with Helen Wills to win the number one doubles, the only point gained by the American team in its first encounter with the English on their home grass. In 1931 Mrs. Wightman made her last appearance as the playing captain of the American team. She served as nonplaying captain, off and on, until 1949, when, believing she had been captain long enough, she asked to be relieved of that assignment and nominated Mrs. Marjorie Gladman Buck to succeed her. . . .

Mrs. Wightman's activity annually comes to its busiest bubble during the third week of August when the United States Doubles Championships are held at Longwood, eight deep lobs from the rambling brown-shingled house on Suffolk Road in Chestnut Hill, where Mrs. Wightman has lived since

1940. In order to devote her full energies to the bevy of beautiful backhands which descend on her home, Mrs. Wightman cancels for that week all outside lessons and demonstrations and gets down to the business of running a small hotel. Not counting a few itinerant competitors who knocked on the screen door late at night and were given improvised lodging for an evening, Mrs. Wightman's guests during National Doubles Week this year numbered fourteen: Doris Hart and Shirley Fry shared one upstairs bedroom; Margaret Osborne du Pont, Louise Brough, and Thelma Long (of Australia) shared another; Maureen Connolly and Anita Kanter roomed together in a third; Sachiko Kamo, the Japanese champion, and Joan and Andy Ross-Dilley, the English twins, were assigned cots on the closed-in porch; the ping-pong table was moved to one corner of the basement game room, and Kay Hubbell, Lois Felix, and Connie Bowan were moved in. Chestnut Hill, like every tennis-respecting community, is peopled with hostesses who would gladly turn over their snazziest bedroom and a private maid to any of these stars, but staying with Mrs. Wightman is tantamount to an invitation to quit the Wardman Park and move into Blair House.

During the tournament week, Mrs. Wightman rises at six o'clock, a half hour earlier than usual. While her housekeeper, Mollie Lennon, squeezes the orange juice for fourteen or more breakfasts, Mrs. Wightman, after raking the leaves from her lawn and checking her garden, jumps in her Studebaker and collects the day's provisions. On her return, she stations herself at the frying pan until the last breakfasters, invariably Brough and du Pont, have been fed and packed off to their matches. Lunch is staggered, the girls returning to Suffolk Road whenever their schedules allow. Dinner is communal and vocal. After it is over, Mrs. Wightman, who plays in the veterans' division and runs the women's part of the doubles, relaxes over a cool Bendix washing machine in a basement alcove. She regards the Bendix as a touchy instrument that needs an experienced operator, and there is an unwritten law that while guests may iron their clothes, nobody washes except Mrs. Wightman. Around eight o'clock Chestnut Hill neighbors, male competitors, old Longwood hands, boy friends, and star-struck pupils start to drop in, and for the next hour or so the decibel rate (often helped along by Mrs. Wightman's strenuous piano work on "The Maple Leaf Rag") and the floor load of the house go up enormously. When the traffic has returned to normal, Mrs. Wightman is ready for a nice long tennis talk. To make certain that she doesn't loll around unorganized at any time during the day, Mrs. Wightman scratches memos to herself on a blackboard in the pantry and so is able to remember to drive to St. Joseph's Cemetery and water the flowers on Mrs. Lennon's husband's grave, to bake two batches of brownies and Toll House cookies daily, and to write and dispatch a dozen or so post cards, a supply of which she carries in her purse. This impassioned "carpe-ing" of the "diem" is accomplished in a blaze of inconspicuousness, and it is the more astonishing in that Mrs. Wightman's vitality apparently doubles in direct proportion to its expenditure. At the conclusion of their stay at Mrs. Wightman's during the tournament week in 1940, Pauline Betz and her mother made a brave attempt to commemorate in verse the indefatigable

Zip Zip of their hostess. The Betzes tabulated her dawn-till-midnight schedule in nine frenetic stanzas, and then, still puffing a little, added as an earnest epilogue:

> No matter where our footsteps go,
> Wherever we may roam,
> For us there'll never be a place
> Like Mrs. Wightman's home.

THE GREAT AUSTRALIAN

by Arthur Daley

History has a quaint habit of repeating itself. Australia won the Davis Cup in 1914 at the outbreak of one World War and won again in 1939 just after the outbreak of another. Sir Norman Brookes had a hand in capturing the silverware in 1914 and, since he is the guiding genius behind net affairs Down Under, he was a contributing factor in lifting the trophy an even quarter of a century later.

Sir Norman was in town last week and contrived to combine a bit of pleasure with his business mission by arranging to have the United States challenge Australia next year and thus put the famed international prize back in circulation. Considering the fact that Davis Cup competition is an annual affair, it certainly has been out of circulation a lot, what with two wars interrupting its continuity.

"The circumstances surrounding the 1914 play were quite unusual," mused Sir Norman. "But I suppose most folks have forgotten about them by this time. Australia actually met Germany after our two nations were in a state of war. We played in Pittsburgh, and I still can remember Froitzheim of Germany, an officer on the Kaiser's Imperial Staff, cabling Berlin for instructions. A fine player, that Froitzheim. I'd say he was at least the equal of Von Cramm."

And how did the net war between the lads from Down Under and the disciples of the Master Race turn out?

Sir Norman looked shocked. "Tony Wilding and I beat them, of course!" he answered in pained surprise. "It was 5–0, too."

But it was not until the Brookes-Wilding pair advanced to the challenge round against the United States at brand-new Forest Hills that one of the most famous single sets of all time was held. Sir Norman squared off against a youth from the Pacific Coast. They called him the "California Comet" and he was to flame across the American tennis horizon, Maurice McLoughlin.

The hard-hitting redhead was only 24 years old then, Sir Norman a cagey veteran of 37. "I know that the old-timers refer to that match as a 'marathon,'" he said, "but it actually didn't take so long, even though the first set lasted thirty-two games. McLoughlin was positively brilliant that day and"—Sir Norman paused, cleared his throat and added modestly—"I wasn't so bad myself. He finally beat me, 17–15, and won in straight sets."

The knight from Down Under still is ranked among the all-time greats of the game. Even at the ripe old age of 44 he attempted to help defend the Davis Cup from Bill Tilden & Co., a task manifestly beyond his reach. He was the first man ever to perfect hitting a ball on the rise instead of striking it at its crest.

"I was lucky in getting started early," he admitted. "We were fortunate in having a court of our own, and, since I was the youngest of a large family, my precocious nature enabled me to learn from my elders faster than I should. Then, too, I had some excellent advice from Dr. W. V. Eaves. But I was continually experimenting.

"That's a fault I find with the present-day players. They tend to fall into the same pattern, the same stereotyped games. Too few of them have any initiative of their own. Since we in Australia have less professional coaching than you in the States, our boys have more opportunity for going off on their own. As examples I might cite the two-handed hitting of Vivian McGrath and John Bromwich."

There probably is no country in the world that has as much widespread interest in tennis as Australia. Sir Norman is indirectly—or maybe directly—responsible. "Our winning of the Davis Cup in 1907 was the greatest boon tennis ever had," he declared crisply. "It brought the sport down to another corner of the world and stimulated other countries to take part. And, of course, nothing ever could compare with the excitement aroused in Australia over our defense of the trophy the next year.

"Interest in the challenge round was enormous and they actually had to build extra stands over the streets in order to accommodate the throngs. What a match that was! It went right down to the final contest before it was decided. I'll never forget the battle I had with Beals Wright. We each had taken two sets and I had him 4–3 and 40–love with my service coming up. I still don't know how he escaped. But escape he did, as he took the set at 12–10—and in 101-degree heat, too."

Sir Norman probably has even more enthusiasm for tennis now than he did in his youth. Then he was something of a dilettante, mixing in golf with his court activities and frequently deserting the net game for astonishingly long periods of time. As one of Australia's most successful business tycoons, he's also had almost fifty years of that type of "distraction" to prevent him from making tennis a career.

From that fateful Davis Cup play of 1914 both he and Wilding went off to war. Tony was killed but the more fortunate Sir Norman wound up in Mesopotamia as a major in the British Army. "Native tribesmen made it very uncomfortable by continually sniping at us," he said and then added laconically, "but they were fearfully bad shots. The heat, however, was almost worse than the bullets since the temperature would go as high as 120 degrees."

The Australian was asked if he cared to name his choice as the outstanding tennis player of all time. "That's easy," he smiled. "Bill Tilden. He came closer than anyone else to being the 'complete player.' All he lacked was the volleying ability of Vinnie Richards, a volleyer whose skill never has been approached. Even at that, though, Tilden was nearest to perfection."

THE END OF AN ERA

by Allison Danzig

The cable from Melbourne read, "Sir Norman Brookes, president of the Lawn Tennis Association of Australia for twenty-nine years, retired today."

Fifty years after he won the All-Comers at Wimbledon, the fabulous career of Australia's most distinguished sports figure had come to an end. The man who started them jumping toward the tennis stadium in the land of the kangaroo, where they go as mad about the game as they do in England, finally was bowing out at the age of 70.

This was the Norman Everard Brookes, who in 1907 led Australasia (Australia and New Zealand) to its first victory in the Davis Cup. That same year he became the first player from overseas to win the championship at Wimbledon (in 1905 he had lost in the challenge round to H. L. Doherty).

In 1914 he revisited England and regained the title at Wimbledon. Then he came to the United States with Anthony Wilding and defeated the officers from the Kaiser's Imperial Staff on the German Davis Cup team at Pittsburgh as the first World War broke out.

Brookes played the most memorable set in Davis Cup history (17–15) against Maurice (Red) McLoughlin at Forest Hills as he and Wilding regained the cup from the United States before going off to war.

In 1915, Brookes was named Australian Red Cross representative at Cairo. He fought at Mesopotamia in 1917 while his teammate, Tony Wilding, was falling at Gallipoli. Brookes came back from the war in 1919 to play on the Australian team that successfully defended the cup as the matches were revived. He won the United States doubles championship with Gerald Patterson.

In 1926, at the age of 49, Brookes defeated Frank Hunter at Wimbledon.

Brookes was elected president of the Victoria Lawn Tennis Association and then became president of the Australian L.T.A. He received the French Legion of Honor in 1928.

Brookes led the Australian team to Europe as captain in 1935.

Then in 1939, twenty-five years after he had played on the winning team as war broke out, he came to the United States. He was present at the Merion Cricket Club, Haverford, Pennsylvania, when another Australian team, led by Captain Harry Hopman, regained the cup on the outbreak of the second World War.

Later that year, Brookes was knighted for his distinguished service to his country.

During the sixteen years after he was knighted, Sir Norman played an active part in the tennis affairs of his country. That he was still on the ball was evident only two weeks ago when he criticized Captain Hopman in connection with the marriage of Lewis Hoad, a member of the Australian Davis Cup team.

Hoad was married to Jennifer Staley, one of the top ranking players of Australia, just before the championships started at Wimbledon.

Sir Norman took Hopman to task for not letting him know about the marriage and reminded him that the team members and Hopman signed contracts that prohibited wives from being in the same country as the players during the tour.

Harry snapped in reply, "Sir Norman is a bit too far away to be in a position to criticize my actions. There is no rule which bans an Australian from getting married during the Wimbledon fortnight." He added that Hoad and his bride would observe the Australian Davis Cup team rule that says no man shall live with his wife while the players are competing in international tournaments or the Davis Cup.

Sir Norman wasn't against marriage. The Australian Association gave its blessing to the newlyweds and sent them a congratulatory cable.

From 1907 almost until the war put an end to tennis in 1914, Brookes stood with William A. Larned as the world's foremost players. Larned won our championship seven times, as William Tilden was to do later. Then McLoughlin came along with William Johnston and Dick Williams.

"The Mighty Brookes," as he was known, was possibly the greatest left-handed player in tennis history. He was a blaster at first. Then he changed his game and hit more temperately, and his astuteness and court craft became more characteristic. But he always was aggressive.

His service was drastic and all the more feared because he was left-handed. He followed it to the net in a fashion that was supposed to have started long after his day, and he was a sharp volleyer.

His match with McLoughlin, the first big tennis event to be staged at Forest Hills on the new grounds of the West Side Tennis Club, was largely fought with the serve and volley.

In the opening set of thirty-two games there was just one break through service. Brookes had his big chance in the eighteenth game. Leading by 9–8, he hit three winning returns of service for 0–40 and three set points.

Then Red McLoughlin, with his fiery style of play, his tremendous service and volcanic overhead, brought the house down. The 12,000 fans jamming the stands roared as his service pulled him out of the hole, and he went on to break through from 15–40 in the thirty-first game and take the set and ultimately the match.

That match and the fancy that the public took to McLoughlin had much to do with the popularizing of lawn tennis. The California Comet's spectacular style of play opened the eyes of the uninitiated to the fact that tennis was a vigorous sport and a stern test of physical fitness.

From this time on, and with the transfer of the national championship to Forest Hills from Newport in 1915, the game attracted an ever-widening following and audience.

Then along came Tilden to win world-wide fame, and the game spread to all parts of the globe until the Davis Cup became the most international of all annual sporting competitions.

Norman Brookes played a big part in that growth as a player and as an administrator. No other person has given so many years of distinguished service to tennis in the two capacities.

During Brookes' long administration, Australia regained the top position it had held during his playing days, thanks in part to the program of junior development which he launched in the early 1930s with the help of Gerald Patterson.

Though he retired, it is not likely that Sir Norman's interest will lessen. His counsel undoubtedly will continue to have its influence in the shaping of Australian tennis policy.

Like his old friend, Julian Myrick, former president of the United States Lawn Tennis Association, Brookes takes his place as an elder statesman behind the scene.

SUPREME STRATEGIST

by Alan Trengove

He was the father of Australian lawn tennis, representing Australasia nine times in the Davis Cup competition, and for a long period dominating world tennis with Tony Wilding of New Zealand.

Those who saw him in his prime—and there aren't many alive who did—rate him among the six greatest players of all time, ahead of players like Lew Hoad and Jack Kramer.

He was a wiry left-hander of consummate skill and cunning. And above all, he was determined. In his 44th year he went down to Bill Tilden, 8–10, 4–6, 6–1, 4–6, in a challenge round match, and Tilden said later he was thankful that Brookes had conceded him 19 years.

Today, Sir Norman Brookes is 89. Dame Mabel Brookes says of the man who hated to lose one game in a three-set match: "He was suspicious and cagey, and these characteristics came out in his tennis.

"He was the wizard who thought two shots ahead. At every change of ends he planned a little scheme.

"He was like a general without an army. His army was himself. He saw more in the strategy of the game than he did in the strategy of actual living. I think he might have been a very good general."

Thin and spare, Brookes did a little running, but otherwise scorned serious training, says the woman who held his coat for 40 years.

He never took his preparation as seriously as his business activity at the Australasian Paper and Pulp Company. Life as a businessman came harder than success at tennis.

His great gift was his co-ordination of hand and eye.

"This is why he has found old age so frustrating," says Dame Mabel. "Until a year ago he played marvelous billiards. Anything he touched requiring ball sense resulted in success. He was a champion amateur golfer and a very good cricketer."

Sir Norman Brookes' father migrated from Northampton, England, to Melbourne about the middle of last century, arriving with only £9 in his pocket. His mother was from Northern Ireland.

A bright student, the young Brookes did well at Melbourne Grammar, but was at the University only a year when his father, who had succeeded in commerce, bought the Australasian Paper Mills.

He withdrew his son from the University and, in Dame Mabel's words, "set him to licking stamps." Figuratively, she adds, he has licked stamps ever since.

William Brookes, the father, was a dour, temperate man who didn't believe in mollycoddling his children. His son Norman had to learn the business from the bottom, and if he wanted a trip overseas he had to save for it himself.

The young man did just that—and was first runner-up, then winner of the Wimbledon singles. He won the title twice.

It was at a ball given by her parents that he first met Mabel Emmerton. Her father, a lawyer, had been associated in business deals with William Brookes.

In her book *Crowded Galleries*, Dame Mabel described how Norman Brookes, then 33, proposed to her "rather suddenly" while he was nursing a jaw swollen from toothache and sitting on a log. He interrupted her as she was giving a description of early days' sheep-stealing.

"Mother and father were at once doubtful and delighted," wrote Dame Mabel. "Uncertain about age—I was 17 at the time—and pleased because they both really liked Norman, but did not even in the least understand him.

"Father sensed in him a dual personality and recognized the warring spirit that actuated his whole life's movement; and wondered if I, young and spoiled, would have strength or wisdom enough to override the temperament that had driven him so far and was still at the bottom of all his work and play."

They were married a year later in 1911. The wedding was a sensation, with crowds straining against the barricades along the streets to St. Paul's.

There were 10 bridesmaids, the bride's lace veil was made in Venice and from England came a monster wedding cake decorated with silver nets, tennis rackets and tennis balls.

Dame Mabel, who did not play tennis herself, says that she grew to love the game. She watched faithfully while her husband trounced his opponents on tennis courts all over the world.

"Tennis was a game of very pleasant coteries," she recalls. "There was a charming atmosphere especially on the Riviera, in England, and to a lesser degree in America.

"The game attracted nice people from other walks of life. It wasn't a business."

Norman Brookes, with a succession of partners, continued to win the Davis Cup for Australasia.

"He brought the Cup back in his luggage with his other cups," says Dame Mabel. "It cost him about £7-10-0. You had to do everything yourself in those days.

"Nobody much wanted the Cup. It used to sit on our sideboard, and it was so big, it dwarfed everything else. Nothing looked any good at all alongside that darned bath. We put red peonies in it."

In another chapter of *Crowded Galleries* Dame Mabel drew a very frank pen-picture of her husband.

His youth, she wrote, was marked by stubbornness, reserve and determination.

"Later he developed level evaluation," she continued, "but always possessed a fear of generosity in himself as in others. It was to him a kind of weakness and the natural desire to give which he had was something to overcome, and with which the appreciation of good living always warred.

"Intensely loyal to his friends, he kept them in a special category; others did not matter much."

She also declared that in his younger days he had a strong temper, "almost an obsession to have his own way." Over the years his temper became refined into determination.

Does Dame Mabel Brookes still believe in this appraisal?

"Norman for much of his life has been a dual personality," she says. "He had a sense of suspicion, which guided him for a while, and then a complete freedom from all of that, so that he was also a normal, athletic, very sporting person.

"In all the years he played championship tennis he suffered from a duodenal ulcer. It probably had something to do with this dual personality, which in turn made him the killer he was on the court."

As a businessman, claims Dame Mabel, Sir Norman was calm, conservative, honorable. The thrusting ambition he showed at tennis was absent in business.

When the depression came to Australia his caution, she feels, proved wise, for the Australasian Paper Mills never put off one person.

The Brookeses had three daughters, but no son to follow the tennis tradition.

In time Dame Mabel became, in her own right, as famous as her husband. She has been president of Queen Victoria Memorial Hospital since 1924, has written several books and is prominent in Melbourne social life.

It must have saddened her to see the man who pioneered tennis in Australia finally subjected to public criticism as president of the LTAA, a post he held from 1926–55.

"He tried to stem a tide that couldn't be stemmed," explains Dame Mabel. "The tide of professionalism. He was uncompromisingly straight, and when you are like that you meet criticism."

These days Sir Norman Brookes rarely looks at his trophies, which stand glistening under a Dargie portrait of him in a quiet corner of the Brookeses' graceful South Yarra house.

But he still takes an interest in Wimbledon. He is proud of Roy Emerson, for his manners and sportsmanship as much as his ability, but his special favorite is Margaret Smith.

"He doesn't say much when she wins," says Dame Mabel. "He is just so pleased. He always liked to be there when she was playing, and she knew that he was a real ally.

"They had something in common, you see. They both were the first . . ."

THE SUTTON SISTERS

by Jeane Hoffman

There used to be a saying, "It takes a Sutton to beat a Sutton."

And because it did, the historic Southern California tennis championships were nearly renamed the "Sutton California championships."

Between them, the four Sutton sisters of Santa Monica—Ethel, Florence, Violet, and May—won the tournament eighteen times. May Sutton Bundy, who accounted for nine wins, won it first in 1900. Twenty-eight years and four children later, she won it again!

All of which gives an idea of the durability of the Sutton females and explains why no one in Santa Monica is the least surprised that the four Sutton "girls" are still going strong, still playing tennis, still the greatest tennis family in America.

Ethel, at seventy-two, plays doubles four times a week, teaches three classes of private pupils, and quips, "Only a tennis ball in flight can make me run!" Florence teaches twenty-five pupils on a private court on Marguerita Avenue six days a week and grins, "Tennis? It's medicine. I feel great." Violet, twenty-five years an instructor at Marlborough, never misses her "daily doubles." "Little May," the baby who weighed fifteen pounds at birth, teaches at the Los Angeles Country Club and still sends shivers down opponents' forehands when she faces them across court.

What made them great?

"An all-consuming devotion to the game that caused my brother Henry and me to go up into Eaton's Canyon in 1899 with two shovels, horse and buggy, and haul clay down to our father's ten-acre ranch in Pasadena to build our own court," declared Ethel, oldest of the famed quartet. "The court sloped over an embankment, so we had to run uphill for forehands. But it was one of ten private courts in Pasadena, and we were proud of it. We played with tennis balls minus covers, rackets with strings missing, and taught ourselves tennis."

"We had first learned the game in England, where we were all born," explained Florence, the smallest. "Father was a captain in the navy. He had seven children: Adele, the oldest girl, two boys, then—after a lapse of four years—us four girls.

"Adele played tennis in a club near Ealing. She'd give her warped rackets to us youngsters, and my sisters and I played every game with them— rounders, croquet, cricket. When we came to America, we built the court, but we had no equipment. A nearby family, the Radcliffes, had nets and rackets but no court. We pooled our resources. We learned so well that Violet won the first tournament she entered (the first in the family, too), the Ojai championship in 1899."

"Girls were faster in our day," remembered Violet, whose children—May, Billy, Doris, and Johnny Doeg—became tennis stars. (Johnny was national champion.) "We ran more. But it's a wonder we could move at all. Do you know what we wore? A long undershirt, pair of drawers, two petticoats, white linen corset cover, duck skirt, shirtwaist, long white silk stockings, and a floppy hat. We were soaking wet when we finished a match."

"Girls today have a greater variety of strokes, but I believe we had more fight and speed, even though nobody ever dreamed of taking lessons from a professional coach," said May, whose daughter, Dorothy Bundy Cheney, became a famous player. "Girls played the net even then. It wasn't all baseline. Our weakest stroke was the serve. We just hit the ball up without much windup."

"But how May could hit that forehand!" enthused Florence. "She'd play all day without missing a forehand drive. She had power. When she won the nationals in 1904 and Wimbledon in 1905 and 1907, she weighed 160 pounds. Girls didn't worry about diets then. May even beat men. Our 'little sister' was the greatest of 'em all!"

THE GENTLER SEX

by Edward C. Potter, Jr.

The autocrats of Wimbledon waited seven years before they opened their gates to women players. The first Ladies' Championship was held in 1884 and Miss Maud Watson was the first All-England champion. She was far ahead of her contemporaries. Since 1882 she had played fifty-five matches without losing one of them. In all that time she lost only eleven sets. Even so, her game was of the pat-ball variety. Watching her, a spectator remarked, "Well! She hit the net at last after trying at least a hundred times." In the summer of 1886 she met her match in the tall, boyish, hard-hitting Charlotte Dod. She excused her defeat by saying that she "did not have the same chance of returning the ball as with other ladies."

"Lottie" Dod, as she was generally known, was one of the most remarkable players who ever came to Wimbledon. Her close-cropped hair, unusual height and strength for her fourteen years aroused curiosity. The violence of her strokes amazed the spectators. She won both the Irish and English titles in 1887 and held the English title again in 1888. The next year she was off on a cruise at the time of the Wimbledon meeting. She refused to break up the yachting party for such an unimportant event as a tennis championship. But she came back again in 1891 and won and defended for two more years. During her entire tennis career she was beaten only four times. She never lost a match at Wimbledon, and it was only on her last appearance in 1893 that she lost a set in the challenge round. After winning this match and her fifth championship, still only twenty-one, she retired and devoted herself to golf at which game she also became English champion.

When Miss Dod retired unbeaten, she was succeeded by her immediate predecessor, Blanche Bingley [Mrs. Hillyard]. Miss Bingley's career is as long and inspiring as Miss Dod's was brief and meteoric. She was a Middlesex girl and competed in the first championship, where she lost to Miss Watson. The next year Miss Watson beat her again, but in 1886 she had her revenge. Miss Dod's appearance ended Miss Bingley's reign temporarily. In 1888, after her marriage to George Hillyard, she came through to the challenge round, where Miss Dod again beat her. On Miss Dod's retirement, Mrs. Hillyard regained her crown.

Mrs. Hillyard's great asset was a powerful forehand drive executed with tremendous pace. She wore gloves to give her a better grip and had such a complete follow-through that her left shoulder was often a mass of bruises from the impact of the racket. She made up for an unreliable backhand and a lack of volleying power by superlative footwork and agility. If her form sometimes deserted her, she never worried over it. Sooner or later it always came back.

After her marriage Mrs. Hillyard never let her love for tennis interfere with her duties as wife and mother. Her championship record is marked by breaks of a year or two here and there. These indicate periods of family building. She is one of only two Englishwomen who have held the championship six times. Her span extends over a period of fourteen years and as late as 1919, thirty-five years after she first played there, she was semi-finalist at Wimbledon.

Mrs. Hillyard's chief rival after she took over the championship, and her alternate during her years of absence, was a girl with a much more varied style. "Chattie" Cooper, commencing in 1895 when Mrs. Hillyard did not defend, held the title five times. In 1902, having meanwhile become Mrs. Sterry, she lost to Miss M. E. Robb. The challenge match was halted by rain at set–all and replayed from the beginning next day. Miss Robb was comparatively unknown the year before but had strengthened her game so that she was able to beat the champion. She retired the next year, but Mrs. Sterry kept on, won for the last time in 1908, and reached the final in 1912.

Meanwhile, at Princess Helena College at Ealing, a London suburb, the daughter of the Vicar of St. Matthew's Church was just taking up the game. "Dolly" Douglass was another child prodigy but did not reach her greatest achievements until much later in life than Miss Dod. She entered her first tournament when she was only nine and won her first prize in a handicap singles at eleven. She saw Mrs. Sterry, also an Ealing girl, come from behind to win her first championship and decided to emulate her. She became marked as a player with a future when she met her fellow townswoman at Eastbourne in 1900. Though she won the first set, Mrs. Sterry came through. It was this close match against the champion which placed its stamp on Miss Douglass' game.

Mrs. Sterry relied extensively on her volleying. The fact that Mrs. Hillyard's one-shot game had prevailed against Mrs. Sterry's net attack led Miss Douglass to base her own game on accurate backcourt play. Her backhand was as reliable as her forehand, and she took the net occasionally for a finishing stroke. Her service, while soft, was well placed. Her match temperament was ideal. She was always thinking several moves ahead. She came to Wimbledon for the first time in 1902 and lost in the semi-final to Miss Robb. The next year she won the title when Miss Robb did not defend, and she held her title successfully against Mrs. Sterry in 1904.

Next year a seventeen-year-old girl from California traveled six thousand miles to Wimbledon to take an English title overseas for the first time. This was the year when the dark horse from Australia, Norman Brookes, swept everything before him up to the challenge round. Even when Brookes won the men's title in 1907, Englishmen consoled themselves with the thought that he was a British subject. In the same spirit they point out that May Sutton was the daughter of an English naval officer and was born at Plymouth.

Though she was British born, Miss Sutton was distinctly a California product. She was the first of all the great California players who derived their inspiration from the visit of Davis and the lessons the Hardys learned at his knee. She was the youngest of four sisters, all proficient players. She was only six when her father brought the family to Pasadena. Here, on his ranch, he built an asphalt court. The sisters, one after another, began winning tournaments. May was very proud when she won a set from Ethel in her first tournament. When she beat Violet in 1900 she felt she was headed for the top. The next year she won the Southern California championship. In 1904 her brother took her East. She had no trouble winning both the singles and doubles championships of the United States.

Miss Sutton's game was based on a strong and accurate forehand, a mannish service, skillful but not excessive volleying, great footwork and no nerves at all. She was rather short, but her powerful build and broad shoulders gave the impression she would take a lot of stopping. As she was so young she could wear shorter skirts than more mature women players. This not only helped her speed of foot but led to the eventual emancipation from trailing skirts, high-collared waists, and hats awkwardly held on with a hatpin.

She arrived in England in the spring of 1905. She brought a letter of introduction to the Hillyards from Marion Jones, her predecessor as American Champion. As Miss Jones had visited England without making any impression on the top-ranking players, the first sight of Miss Sutton led the Hillyards to believe that here was another disappointment. When they took her on in turn the next morning and beat her easily, they no longer feared a Wimbledon upset.

This was quite natural, for, before Miss Sutton, the American women champions were not of high class. The best of them, Juliette Atkinson, Elizabeth Moore, and Marion Jones, had held the title with one exception for nine years before Miss Sutton barged in from the West to show the Easterners a new standard of women's play.

Miss Douglass, meanwhile, had been consolidating her position as the leading Englishwoman. She had a notable series of wins at the principal county tournaments and on the Riviera. When she met the American in the Wimbledon challenge round, she was handicapped by a sprained wrist and could not win a set. Matters were reversed in 1906. She beat Miss Sutton at Liverpool and repeated the performance at Wimbledon.

For the third time in 1907 Miss Sutton commuted from California to Wimbledon. This time she allowed herself more time to become acclimated. She played in several county championships and defended her Welsh title. She beat Miss Douglass in a pre-championship match at Beckenham, and at Wimbledon inflicted an even more decisive defeat than in 1905.

Miss Sutton did not come back to England in 1908. Two years elapsed before Miss Douglass, now Mrs. Lambert Chambers, resumed her reign. When she returned to Wimbledon in 1910, it was noted that the game, which was only in its formative stages during previous years, had now reached a fruition which was to make her stand out above any other Englishwoman who has ever played tennis. The speed and accuracy of stroke which had marked her early play had been developed amazingly. She had become better as she grew older and was to go on getting better until her apogee in 1919, when she met and was beaten by a player twelve years her junior, Suzanne Lenglen.

WILLIAM LARNED

by J. Parmely Paret

There is little doubt that William A. Larned was the most consistently brilliant player this country had turned out before Tilden's skill ripened. We have had a number of brilliant performers at different times whose luster lasted for a few years, but none whose play maintained the superlative quality of Larned's for any long period. Few players of the present day realize how much he played or how long he held a pre-eminent position at the head of the American forces.

Larned began his tournament experience when quite young, but his style was too erratic to carry him early to the top of the ladder of fame. At the age of nineteen his name first appeared on the ranking lists of the first ten in 1892, when he was officially rated sixth. His first big success came when he won the intercollegiate championship for Cornell the previous autumn. From then until he retired from competition in 1912—twenty years, a long life for active tournament play—his name was missing from the elite first-ten list only once, in 1898, and then only because he was away at the Spanish-American War with the Roosevelt Rough Riders.

Think of that record! Ranked first eight years, second five years, third four years, fifth one year, and sixth one year—nineteen times ranked among the first ten of the country in twenty years. Tilden's name first appears on the list in 1918 and disappears in 1930, a run of only twelve years, although he was ranked first ten successive seasons. Larned and Tilden each won the national championship seven times.

During this long period of Larned's ascendancy, his game showed the greatest brilliance of any player we had in the country. There were many times when he was off color, when his strokes simply refused to co-ordinate, and he did not maintain at any time an unbeaten record, but always there followed soon after each defeat a fresh burst of brilliance that simply swept off their feet the best of his opponents.

Larned was a man who refused to compromise with safety. His was a most daring game; he stood or fell according to whether his play was at its best or not. He had much the same viewpoint as the celebrated English master Dr. J. Pim, who used to remark when any of his friends started to tell him of the skill of his next opponent, "I don't care what he does; it's what I do that will decide the result." It was what Larned did every time that turned the tide. He went after every shot, and when his best drives were coming off consistently—and that was with extraordinary frequency, too—the other man was always on the defensive.

The American champion was best known for his ground strokes, and his backhand stroke off the ground held the reputation of being the best that had been seen anywhere up to that time. I have seen the Doherty Brothers —played against them both, too—Pim, Mahony, and nearly all of the best of the British players, in addition to every American master of Larned's day, and I do not believe that any other had the brilliance in backhand ground strokes of Larned. H. L. Doherty, Whitman, and Mahony were perhaps steadier with this shot, and at times R. F. Doherty and Pim a bit faster, but not one of them had the variety, hid the direction so well, or cut the lines as closely as he did. Hardly any other could pass a volleyer with that dropping backhand drive so accurately as he.

On the forehand side off the ground, Larned also was very deadly at times. His direction was well hidden with this stroke, his length good, speed, drop, and accuracy all well maintained, but there was not quite as much "devil" in that shot as in his backhand, although it may have seemed that way because others played the forehand drive well and none the same shot on the backhand side. Many of the net rushers of those days were ruined by Larned's brilliant passing ability. R. D. Wrenn had many long battles with him and won some of them, but never when Larned's passing strokes were at their best.

Richard Stevens, one of the best baseline players of those days, was beaten, 6–1, 6–0, 6–0, in one of the championship matches at Newport and remarked afterward that he was playing fully up to his standard game, but that Larned was so fast and so accurate that day there was simply no chance to return the ball. "I couldn't even reach it to get my racket on the ball," he said after the match. "It was not because I couldn't handle the strokes." And Stevens was fast of foot, too.

Larned always scorned defense, as I have said, so he never practiced the lob, nor did he waste much effort in knocking the ball back without a definite attack. While the summaries of his matches showed many errors, to be sure, they were generally overbalanced by the remarkable proportion of earned points, generally clean passes, that were scored in his favor.

There has been an erroneous impression rather widely held that Larned's game was almost entirely confined to ground strokes. While there is no doubt that this was the strongest department of his play, he was nevertheless an accomplished volleyer. At horizontal volleying he was much better than in overhead work, but he was also able to put away short lobs effectively, though deep lobbing sometimes got him into trouble.

Larned's method of hitting the ball was with his racket pretty well off at his side and far from his body. His forearm and wrist were nearly horizontal, with his wrist low and inclined to be ahead of the ball. He used a good deal of top spin in his forehand, rolling the ball rapidly forward, but his backhand carried less top, although he did not undercut to any appreciable extent. His right shoulder was well extended, and he used his body weight with good rotation of the hips and shoulders to get great power into his drives.

The old master never developed the use of the American twist services. He used a powerful overhead swing with a good deal of out-twist, and he placed his services well. Attacking the far corner of the left court, he could embarrass his adversary with a deep-placed straight service, and, when anticipated by the other man to the extent of getting out of position to receive it, Larned often aced his man down the middle line with a turn of his wrist and a little added spin on the ball. At times he ran in on his service and then used the center theory to great advantage, serving down the centerline from both sides, and cutting off the other man's returns at the net with sharp crosscourt volleys. When it came to handling ground strokes, however, he rather favored placing his drives into the far corners of the other court to the conventional center theory. At short angles, both forehand and backhand, Larned was very effective, and a sharp crosscourt stroke from his adversary was more likely to be met with a reply equally sharp in angle than with a straight sideline shot. On the other hand, he did not need more than three feet of space along a sideline to slide a passing drive down the edge of the court past a volleyer running to the net or waiting there to cut off his drives.

The international record of William A. Larned was an enviable one. In 1896 he crossed over to the other side and played in a number of the largest English tournaments. In a five-set final at Liverpool he was three times within a single point of beating Mahony, the All-England champion of that year, and at Wimbledon he was beaten by H. Baddeley, one of the doubles champions of that season, only after having won the first two sets. The following year the British sent a team of three players to America made up of Mahony, Eaves, and Nisbet, and Larned was one of the Americans selected to meet them in the two international round-robin tournaments at Hoboken and Chicago. In the first, Larned beat all three of the visitors, losing only two sets out of eleven played; at Chicago, he won again from all three of the Britishers, with a loss of only two sets out of eight.

After the Davis Cup was put into competition, Larned played in eight ties, winning nine matches and losing five. In 1902, the second series for the new Cup, he beat Pim three straight sets and lost to R. F. Doherty in five sets after leading two sets to love. This match was interrupted by a thunder shower when the American was having everything his own way, and when completed the next day, Larned could never get back into winning form again and lost three straight sets. The following year he lost in five sets to H. L. Doherty and won from the older brother by default, and in 1905 in England he beat Wilding and Brookes, the two great Australasian stars, both in straight sets, only one of the six being close, but in the challenge round he lost to both the British players, S. H. Smith in four sets and H. L. Doherty in five close sets, again after leading two sets to one.

Once more he met the British in 1908, this time at Boston, and won from the great Parke in straight sets and Ritchie in four sets. The next year he beat both Parke and Dixon in straight sets, all of them easy, and in 1911 he won from Dixon in five sets and Lowe in four. That season ended his international play disastrously, for he went out to New Zealand with the American challenging team, was laid up there with rheumatism contracted during the Spanish-American War, and made a poor showing. Out of condition, he was beaten by Heath in four sets and then compelled to withdraw from the last singles match scheduled for him.

Outside of the one disastrous match in the Antipodes, Larned lost only four international matches, three of them to the great Doherty brothers, each one in five sets, and one to S. H. Smith in four sets.

The great respect in which Larned was held is eloquently testified to by the bronze tablet placed on the inner wall of the big stadium in Forest Hills in memory of one of the greatest figures of the American courts.

MAN FROM THE WEST

by Samuel J. Brookman

They called him the "Comet," and no other name could have been as appropriate, for not before or since has any player "flashed" more brilliantly on a tennis court than Maurice Evans McLoughlin. Dynamic in his attack, tireless in his court covering, dazzling in his daring, smashing game at the net and a whirlwind at serving, the Californian was the leader of the modern school of aggressive, forceful play. His rise, meteoric and startling, made him so famous wherever tennis was played that inside of a year after he made his bid for recognition in the country's leading tournaments Mac was known wherever tennis was played the world over.

It is only thirteen years ago since McLoughlin, just out of his teens, first came out of the West to meet the country's best racket wielders in the prominent tournaments in this section of the country. Only a few tennis fans in the East had heard much about him, but it was not long before the name of McLoughlin was on the tongue of every tennis fan. His dash and zest for the game, his successful advance, and his splendid personality made him a great favorite wherever he went, and devotees of the sport flocked to see him in action.

So great an impression did he make on the officials of the national association that they decided to send him to Australia to bid for the Davis Cup in the challenge round of the international tournament. William A. Larned and William J. Clothier had won the right to challenge for the trophy by beating the British Isles in the final, but both found it impossible to make the trip to the Antipodes, and the American officials, rather than default when there was some chance for victory, sent McLoughlin and his fellow Californian Melville H. Long. The youths were beaten by the famous team of Norman E. Brookes and Anthony F. Wilding, but they made a wonderful impression and a strong bid for victory, and many Australian critics predicted a brilliant future for McLoughlin.

They proved to be right. Inside two seasons McLoughlin had won the national all-comers. William A. Larned, who stood out until the challenge round, defeated him in the title match, but it took all he had to stave off defeat. The following year McLoughlin reached the goal of his ambition, forcing Larned, seven times title holder, to relinquish his championship. . . .

In 1913, the year he won the national championship for the second time, McLoughlin was a member of the American Davis Cup team that succeeded in defeating the British at Wimbledon and in bringing the international trophy back to the United States. In that famous series the issue depended on the outcome of the doubles match in which Mac played with Harold Hackett, and a remarkable recovery by McLoughlin when the British pair were within a point of victory is a vivid moment in American tennis history. The United States eventually won that match.

In 1914, just before the World War, Australia defeated the United States in the challenge round for the Davis Cup. McLoughlin, then at his best, defeated both Brookes and Wilding in singles, playing sensationally. The record set of 17–15 which opened his contest with Brookes has become famous.

Many critics contend that the terrific pace McLoughlin set in his matches caused him to burn out quickly as a player; that his was the type of game that takes too much out of a racket wielder and shortens his career. The facts appear to bear out the opinion, for following an absence of several years from the East, McLoughlin returned after the war and made an effort to regain his former position in the tennis world. Perhaps his long layoff had as much to do with it as his loss of speed, but whatever the cause, Mac was only a shadow of his former self and was beaten easily by Norris Williams in the national championship. Since then he has played no serious tournament tennis.

THE COMET

by Grantland Rice

He dropped by for a friendly call that carried you back over a long, long road. His hair was silver white, his complexion still pink, and it was easy to see that he was in good physical shape. A trifle heavy, maybe, but really healthy. He had been a star years before Babe Ruth had come along. Back when Ty Cobb was in his prime, when Matty and Three-Finger Brown were mixing up their famous duels, when Bobby Jones was still many years away from any fame at golf. The visitor was Maurice McLoughlin, better known as the "Comet" or the "California Comet." Anyway, Morrie was given credit for taking tennis from the softer game it had been before he came along with his mighty service and his smashing style. The Comet did for tennis what Tommy Hitchcock did for polo.

We were talking about his still famous 17–15 duel with Norman Brookes in the Davis Cup test of 1914, just after the first World War had broken wide open.

"That first set was the toughest I ever played," McLoughlin said. "I could get safely by on my own service, but I couldn't break through Brookes'. Norman was a great tennis player. He was smart, cool, cunning, game to the limit, with wonderful control of every shot. I happened to have my service working perfectly, and it was a good thing I did. Brookes couldn't manage a return, and I began to think we would go on forever. I was younger than he was, in fine physical shape, and it was only natural that he should tire first. The first set practically ended the match, as Norman was a pretty weary veteran when it was over."

It might be mentioned that McLoughlin beat Brookes and Wilding in that 1914 Davis Cup show, but the United States still lost the Cup, as R. Norris Williams 2d wasn't quite equal to the job of handling these two stars, who, as Morrie put it, "were just about the soundest and steadiest players I have ever met."

It was McLoughlin who proved that power also had its place.

Morrie was soon in a reminiscent mood. He was talking about Bill Larned. "A great tennis player," the Comet said. "Cool, heady, steady. Always hard to beat, since he never beat himself.

"Then there was R. Norris Williams 2d. Dick was on the brilliant but erratic side. Almost every shot was along or on the white line. He took desperate chances. If they came off, no one could beat him. If they didn't, there was another story.

"Little Bill Johnston came a bit after my time, but I think I admired him most of all. Here was a thin young fellow who weighed from 116 to 120 pounds. His arms were about the size of my two thumbs. They had broom-handle girth. But he had a forehand that could sweep you off the court. It was an even rougher forehand, a more destructive one than Bill Tilden had. And Big Bill had his share of power. Johnston was pure murder for all foreign invaders—Gerald Patterson, the Frenchmen, any others who came along in his best Davis Cup days. What a tennis player he was!" . . .

Oddly enough, the Comet lost his famous service shortly after the Davis Cup matches of 1914. He doesn't yet quite know what happened, except that he was unable to swing a racket with his old freedom. "The big punch suddenly left," he said.

After that McLoughlin took up golf. Being a natural athlete, he soon had his game from 72 to 75. "I'm happy enough to break 80 now," he said. He hasn't played a game of tennis in over thirty years. . . .

It was good to travel back some thirty-five years with the silver-haired Comet and replay a few matches that made tennis history. Also to meet in memory once more a few old-timers from Beals Wright to Bill Johnston.

GENTLEMAN'S GAME

by Russell Lynes

People who live on the Eastern Seaboard are likely to think that the National Singles Championships which are held early in September at the West Side Tennis Club in Forest Hills, New York, chop off the official tennis season the way the World Series chops off baseball. They come after a series of tournaments during the summer that has included among others the French championships in Paris, the English championships at Wimbledon, and a series of tournaments in Newport, Southampton, and the national doubles at Longwood. But for the players who lead the world in "amateur tennis" Forest Hills represents only a major, though not *the* major, stop in their rounds. Tournaments that engage the best tennis talent in the world happen all year long—in Asia, Africa, South America, Australia, and both indoors and outdoors here in this country.

Like most tennis enthusiasts I play more than I watch, but I have often wondered how a tournament like the Nationals is run, and I asked J. Clarence Davies, Jr., deputy referee of the tournament this year and the new treasurer of the United States Lawn Tennis Association, to escort me behind the scenes, which he enthusiastically and efficiently did. . . .

Mr. Davies, who is a real estate man, a two-star general in the Air Force Reserve, and a member of the Landmarks Preservation Commission in New York, used to play tennis well enough to take part in national championships. Now in his early fifties, he is one of the large, enthusiastic crowd that makes the tournament at Forest Hills work.

"It takes more than four hundred people to put this show on," he said.

These four hundred do not include the players. There are one hundred and twenty-one committee members, all of whom belong to the West Side Tennis Club, comprising twelve committees which, in a manner of speaking, grease the skids so that the players slide into the right slots at the right times with the right equipment. There are, Mr. Davies told me, "about two hundred and thirty linesmen and umpires and eighty ball boys." It takes twenty men with rollers, line markers, sod tampers, and other gadgets to take care of the finely cut turf of the courts, and there are security guards and ushers and ticket takers. These are the only professionals; the tournament is rather more amateur in the membership of its operators than of its players, though it is heresy to say so.

"We start getting ready for next year's tournament," Mr. Davies explained, "the minute this one is over. Let me show you what goes on here in the marquee."

The marquee, a long yellow and blue striped tent that closes the horseshoe of the Stadium, is the nerve center of the tournament, and the brain in charge of the nervous system is the Referee. This year it was Mr. Dan Johnson, a large man with a square face, white hair, and an air of quiet authority.

"Once the first ball is hit," Mr. Davies explained, "all decisions are the Referee's."

He decides whether a player should be disqualified, for example, if he doesn't turn up precisely on time for his scheduled match. He determines which matches will be played in the Stadium, which on the "Grandstand" court, the "Fieldstand" court, or the Field courts, of which there are thirteen, all continually busy in the early rounds of the tournament.

"You realize," Mr. Davies said, "that this isn't just one tournament; it's five tournaments—in addition to the men's singles, there's women's singles, men thirty-five to forty-five, senior men's, forty-five and older, and senior women's."

Behind the front row of boxes (in which seats for the full eleven days of the tournament cost $100) the marquee is divided into segments by wooden railings. One segment is the Referee's headquarters, where there is a battery of telephones with a couple of volunteers to man them. These phones are connected with the "Sun Deck" on the second floor of the clubhouse, which is just about as far away as one can get and still be at the West Side Tennis Club. It is to the Sun Deck that the male players report to find out when their matches are scheduled and on what courts. Another phone connects with the women's locker room, from which female contestants are dispatched.

Mr. Johnson said to me, "If there are any questions I can answer, don't hesitate to ask me."

I suggested that he must be a pretty busy man, and he replied, "It's like being the captain of a ship. It takes a lot to get it away from the pier and a lot to get it landed, but it pretty much runs on its own once it gets going."

Next to the Referee's pen is another about the same size from which umpires and linesmen, who sit in still another pen next to it, are dispatched to the courts on which they are to serve. The umpire is provided with two sets of name cards (each card a couple of feet long) with the names of the contestants of the match, one set for the master scoreboard just outside the marquee and one for the court where the match is played.

"Where do you get the umpires and linesmen?" I asked Mr. Davies.

"No problem," he said, "they come from all over, from as far as the West Coast. They come for the honor of it and for the love of the game. They get nothing. They pay their own way; they pay their own hotel bills. They're recommended by their regional associations [of the United States Lawn Tennis Association] who qualify them. I say they get nothing. They get a few free drinks and an occasional free meal, and, of course, they get abuse from the spectators from morning to night."

"What about the ball boys?" I asked.

"You know," he said, "all that's changed. It used to be considered an honor to be a ball boy at the Nationals and kids clamored to be allowed to do it. They came from tennis clubs, sons of members, from private schools, from all over. Now we have to beat the bushes for them and we pay them eighty cents an hour. It takes a good many months to train them. Perhaps you'd like to see how the operation at the Sun Deck at the club works."

The terrace of the clubhouse, a sort of 1910 Tudor mansion, was crowded. Famous tennis faces, looking rather older than one remembered them, were engaged in earnest conversation; girls in tennis dresses (the miniskirt is at home on a tennis court) gazed up at young men in tennis clothes carrying sheafs of rackets. It was any clubhouse during tournament week, only a little more so.

The Sun Deck opens out of a second-floor room with a bar where a group of men waiting to play their matches and a few old-timers were watching a baseball game on television. On the Sun Deck behind a green railing several men were looking out over the courts through field glasses.

"It's five–three in the third set on twelve," one of the men said. "They ought to be off there in a few minutes."

Mr. Davies introduced me to Mr. DeWitt Davis, who was in charge of the Sun Deck operations. Behind Mr. Davis was a large white-board on which was written "Order of Play" with black crayon and below it hastily printed pairs of names and court numbers. Matches that had been completed that day were crossed out with a large X, and in the upper right of the board was the legend: PLAYERS BE READY TO PLAY EARLY TODAY. HEAVY SCHEDULE. Next to the clubhouse wall was a counter with four or five phones on it, connecting with the marquee, with the men's and women's locker room, with the umpires' and linesmen's booth and the pen where the ball boys are corralled next to the Stadium.

"The remarkable thing about this tournament," Mr. Davis said, "is that we're all volunteers, and it's unique that we act as much like professionals as we do. . . .

"Perhaps you'd like this," Mr. Davis said and gave me several dittoed sheets from a loose-leaf notebook. They were headed "Sun Deck Operations": ". . . keeping matches going smoothly and following one another quickly on twenty or so courts at the same time," the first sheet said, "does require conscientious effort and the application of persistent ingenuity . . ."

There followed specific instructions which would seem to cover every possible exigency—missing players, missing water jugs, missing ball boys, what to do if "during play on the field courts . . . the crowds are getting out of hand" (answer: "the admissions committee should be notified") — but there are things that cannot be anticipated that require "persistent ingenuity." There were, after all, 229 players signed up for the several tournaments (the largest number, 128, was for the men's singles; 78 women played in the women's singles), which means approximately 110 matches or better than a hundred scheduled opportunities for miscalculation, misunderstanding, or mishap. Mr. Davis and his cohorts on the operations committee seemed cool in the face of these possibilities.

"The tournament at Wimbledon," Mr. Davis said, "is run by professionals."

I didn't have an opportunity to find out who or what a professional tournament operator is, but I discovered that there is a wistfulness bordering on envy at Forest Hills not only about the prestige of Wimbledon but, more importantly, about how it manages to be a sellout-and-standing-room-only proposition every single day of the tournament. At Forest Hills the only complete sale of all 12,246 seats in the Stadium happens, if it happens at all, on the day of the finals; during the early days of the tournament a good crowd is about half that number.

The weather for the tournament this year was almost perfect—bright skies free of smog, enough breeze to wave the flags on the upper rim of the Stadium but not enough to bother the players, and pleasantly cool. The rainy summer had been kind to the turf of the courts, though even when they have got a bit brown, it is possible to "green them up with top dressing in a couple of days," according to Mr. Henry Benisch, the president of the club, with whom I watched part of a match from the marquee.

I spent a good many hours at Forest Hills during tournament week, and put in much more time talking with the men who were greasing the wheels than in watching tennis. I made an attempt to talk with the woman in charge of "player hospitality," but the public-relations people, who are hired professionals, had thrown up some sort of smoke screen around her which didn't seem worth circumventing. I did get a list of the activities planned for the players; they did not lack for entertainment or hospitality when their day's work was done.

My pleasantest, and in some respects most instructive, afternoon at the tournament was on the day of the "round of sixteen"—the fourth round, that is, just before the quarter finals. There was a show between Stadium matches of tennis fashions for women in which, I am fairly sure, no self-respecting tennis players would be caught dead. ("It happens every year," one of the more prominent officials said, "and it gets worse every year. I guess they think it's good public relations; I don't get it.") When the girls in their pink (sic) sneakers got off the center courts with their pink (sic) rackets, Mr. Davies sat me down under an awning at the end of the marquee just below the loudspeaker control booth and brought several of his friends who were serving in official capacities to fill me in.

Werner C. Bruchlos, a member of the Operations Committee who that day was in charge of the marquee operations, sat with me. He is the president of the company that publishes *The American Banker* magazine. . . . I would guess that Mr. Bruchlos is in his middle sixties.

"It's up to our committee to get the players on the courts. You have to keep one eye on each player," he said; "they vanish in the wink of an eye.

We have to see that they have towels, a water cooler, salt tablets, orange juice, and Coke. . . .

"You have to be sure that the boys have a change of clothes and that they report on time. Between the third and fourth sets if the players want to rest and change they have to be back on the court exactly ten minutes from the time they leave."

Dr. Daniel H. Manfredi, in charge of the Medical Service Committee, told me that his regular job is physician to the athletes at Columbia University.

"We almost had a delivery in the Stadium the other day," he said, "a seven-month pregnancy. We're pretty well equipped for almost anything."

There is another physician besides himself and a nurse on hand during the tournament and a medical "tent," which, he explained, is a room under the Stadium.

"Players come for shots, for strapping, for supports, and, of course, for tennis elbow. We have a pretty good system for treating tennis elbow. We also treat the committeemen, and two bartenders came in yesterday with cuts on their hands."

I asked about the men who play in the senior tournament, the old boys over forty-five, and I referred to them as the "heart-attack squad."

"For a number of years," he said, "I've advocated getting cardiograms with the applications for the senior tournament, but I haven't got anywhere."

Also, I asked about the spectators.

"I've never seen tennis fans intoxicated," he said. "They're a very moderate crowd. People occasionally get sick in the stands but not from drink."

Tennis has a reputation for being a "gentleman's game," and someone, I am told, who was commenting on the finals of the tournament over television, said that it has a reputation for being snobbish; this raises several interesting questions.

Only in Australia has tennis achieved the stature of a national sport, and more there than anywhere tennis champions are national heroes. Unquestionably the climate has something to do with this: tennis there can be played all year round and potential champions can (and evidently do) think of little else. . . .

It is hard to remember how recently golf was considered a snobbish game that only the rich had time and money to play; public courses were extremely rare, and there were always more caddies in the caddy house than players who needed them. A similar declassing of tennis is, Mr. Davies assured me, taking place. There are many more schools with tennis teams than there used to be. The U.S.L.T.A. has a vigorous "junior development program" operating on a nationwide basis in which tennis professionals are teaching thousands of youngsters. There are many more tennis clubs than there used to be.

But in my estimation one of the strongest opponents of democratizing tennis is the shadowy line that separates the amateur player from the professional. In a very real sense the best players on the world circuit of amateur tournaments are on the equivalent of salaries; they make their livings, and their families' livings, with their rackets. They are supported by tennis associations and by participation in tournaments. Those who are consistent winners as amateurs are then signed to play professional exhibition tennis and compete in rather trumped-up (it seems to me) professional tournaments. Everyone knows that amateurism in topflight tennis is a sham, and nearly everyone would like to do something about it. The first step is to do what golf has long done—hold open tournaments.

"We're all for it," one of the officials at Forest Hills said when I asked him what he thought. "England and France and Australia and so on are all for it. It's the Iron Curtain countries and the small countries that vote it down every year."

The real amateurs at Forest Hills were not the players (though some, of course, were) but the men and women who put on the show, kept it going smoothly, and because they love the game give up their jobs (temporarily) or their vacations to run this complicated business operation. All around the globe this winter and during the spring there will be similar groups of men and women working doggedly at similar problems. Tennis is an addiction that once it has truly hooked a man will not let him go.

THE WEST SIDE STORY

by Allison Danzig

Half a century ago one of the most momentous moves in the history of American tennis was made. The national championships were transferred from the Newport Casino in Rhode Island to the West Side Tennis Club in Forest Hills, Long Island.

From their beginning in 1881 the championships had been held at Newport in the exclusive purlieus of society's Four Hundred. Nurtured and fostered in this cradle of blue bloods, lawn tennis won a growing following and grudging recognition in a widening circle as something more than a pale, prissy diversion for tea-drinking dandies. But it was not until the championships had been moved to the outskirts of a great metropolis and became accessible to far more people than could see them at Newport that tennis was on the way to becoming a national pastime attracting millions the country over.

Julian Myrick, Lyle Mahan and Karl Behr were the prime movers in the West Side Tennis Club who brought the United States Lawn Tennis Association to the decision to transfer the championships from Newport. It took some doing to break the grip of the Casino and its membership of great wealth and social prestige, and Myrick showed the skill and toughness of leadership in this fight that he was to exhibit in later years as president of the U.S.L.T.A. and Davis Cup chairman.

Thus it came about that the quiet, almost bucolic, little community of homeowners, some seven miles from Manhattan, started by the Sage Foundation, suddenly found itself in 1915 the foremost center of tennis in the United States. In time, after the building of a vast steel-reinforced concrete stadium seating 13,500 in 1923, it was to rival Wimbledon for world renown.

The greatest players from all the continents were to perform on the turf of the West Side Tennis Club. Tilden and Helen Wills, the two greatest names in American tennis, if not all tennis, were to win many of their most celebrated victories there in championship, Davis Cup and Wightman Cup matches.

Leading the parade into the stadium in the 1920's were Tilden, Johnston, Richards and Williams; France's Four Musketeers—Lacoste, Cochet, Borotra, and Brugnon; Spain's Manuel Alonso; Brian I. C. Norton of South Africa; Brookes, Patterson and Anderson of Australia; Japan's Shimizu and Kumagae.

In later years followed Perry and Austin of Britain; Von Cramm of Germany; Sturgess of South Africa; Drobny, the Czechoslovakian exile; Satoh and Yamagishi of Japan; Bromwich, Quist, Crawford, Sedgman, McGregor, McGrath, Rose, Hoad, Rosewall, Fraser, Cooper, Anderson, Hartwig, Emerson, Laver, Newcombe, Roche and Stolle of Australia; Nielsen and Ulrich of Denmark; Krishnan of India; Segura of Ecuador; Gimeno and Santana of Spain; Darmon, Petra and Bernard of France; Ampon of the Philippines; Olmedo of Peru; Ayala of Chile; Pietrangeli and Sirola of Italy; Jovanovic and Pilic of Yugoslavia; Sangster, Knight, Taylor and Wilson of Britain; Osuna and Palafox of Mexico; Davidson, Lundquist and Schmidt of Sweden; Bungert of Germany; and Hunter, Wood, Shields, Allison, Van Ryn, Doeg, Lott, Bell, Hennessey, Washburn, Vines, Budge, Mako, Gledhill, Kramer, Schroeder, Parker, Riggs, Hunt, McNeill, Kovacs, Van Horn, Stoefen, Patty, Larsen, Flam, Mulloy, Talbert, Savitt, Richardson, Gonzales, Trabert, MacKay, Seixas, Buchholz, Bartzen, McKinley, Ralston, Ashe, Richey, Graebner and Pasarell of the United States.

Among the women, there were Suzanne Lenglen of France and Helen Wills. Also, Kathleen McKane Godfree, Betty Nuthall, Joan Fry, Eileen Bennett Whittingstall, Katharine Stammers, Freda James, Dorothy Round, Angela Mortimer, Christine Truman and Ann Haydon of Britain; Elizabeth Ryan, Eleanor Goss, Marion Zinderstein Jessup, Helen Jacobs, Alice Marble, Sarah Palfrey, Pauline Betz, Carolin Babcock, Midge Van Ryn, Pat Todd, Louise Brough, Margaret Osborne duPont, Maureen Connolly, Doris Hart, Shirley Fry, Althea Gibson, Beverly Baker, Darlene Hard, Karen Hantze Susman, Billy Jean Moffitt, Nancy Richey and Carole Caldwell of the United States; Anita Lizana of Chile; Jadwiga Jedrzejowska of

Poland; Maria Bueno of Brazil; Sandra Reynolds of South Africa; and Margaret Smith and Lesley Turner of Australia.

Many of the most thrilling episodes tennis has known happened on the West Side turf. There was the Davis Cup challenge round match between Maurice McLoughlin and Brookes in 1914. The first set, 17–15, set a record. In 1920 Tilden beat Johnston for his first national grass court title as an airplane crashed near the stands.

In 1921 Suzanne Lenglen, rated by some the greatest of all women players, met Molla Mallory, the defending title holder, in her first match in the national championship. There was no seeded draw then. The graceful French girl came out like a ballerina in white ermine wrap and blowing kisses to the crowd while officials and photographers swarmed around her. No one paid any attention to Mrs. Mallory. Then, like a tigress, Mrs. Mallory, who was expected to be crushed, ran down every ball, took every shot possible on the forehand and gave Suzanne the shock of her life. Coughing heavily, Mlle. Lenglen said she could not continue, after losing the first set, and was assisted off the court.

In 1922 Helen Wills, sixteen years of age, got to the finals against Mrs. Mallory, and the next year she won the first of her seven championships. This same year the stadium was built at a cost of a quarter million dollars. Charles Landers, an engineer, and Kenneth Murchison, an architect, both club members, were the guiding minds with Louis Carruthers, the president. The first event staged in the stadium was the Wightman Cup matches, in which Miss Wills and Mrs. Mallory joined with Eleanor Goss, Marion Zinderstein Jessup and Mrs. Hazel Wightman, donor of the cup, in defeating the British ladies, 7 to 0. Later in the summer the Davis Cup challenge round was held in the stadium, and the United States beat Australia, 4 to 1.

In 1926 came the end of Tilden's six-year reign as national champion. On one and the same day Tilden was beaten by Cochet, and Johnston and Williams also fell in the quarter finals, Richards in the semifinals. The French stood supreme, and a year later they were to win the Davis Cup for the first time, at the Germantown Cricket Club, Philadelphia.

The 1927 final between Tilden and Lacoste was one of the greatest matches in the history of the championship. Lacoste was a faultless machine who would not miss against chop, slice or drive, and Tilden could not get a set, though he had big leads and fought like a man possessed.

In 1931, the 50th anniversary of the U.S.L.T.A., Vines won the championship. Our Secretary of the Navy, Charles Francis Adams, presided at the ceremony. Gold medallions were presented to every champion of our National Tournament. This same evening a Grand Banquet was held at the Hotel Pierre.

In 1933 came Helen Wills Moody's dramatic default to Helen Jacobs in the third set of the final. Mrs. Moody had injured her back that year and was urged not to play in the championship. That same year Jack Crawford of Australia failed by one set to make a grand slam, losing to Fred Perry of Britain in the final at Forest Hills after leading 2 sets to 1. Crawford had won the Australian, French and Wimbledon crowns. Perry won our championship a third time in 1936.

In 1937 Don Budge won the championship by defeating Baron Gottfried von Cramm of Germany in the final. Earlier in the year he had beaten the Baron in one of the greatest of all Davis Cup matches in the interzone round, before leading the United States to its first challenge round victory since 1926 to take the cup from Britain. The next year, 1938, Donald the Red completed the first grand slam in history in beating Gene Mako, his doubles partner, in the final at Forest Hills.

The West Side Tennis Club celebrated its golden anniversary in 1942 with appropriate ceremonies led by Alrick H. Man, Jr., the president, and P. Schuyler Van Bloem, who, like Dr. S. Ellsworth Davenport 2d and Dan Johnson later, rendered invaluable service for many years to the club in conducting the championships and Davis Cup matches. The net receipts from the tournament this year were turned over to the American Women's Voluntary Services, and proceeds from exhibitions during the war years went to the American Red Cross.

Fifty years before, in 1892, the West Side Tennis Club was organized by a group of thirteen players who had been using public courts that too often were not available. They began modestly with three dirt courts on Central Park West between 88th and 89th Streets. The club took its name from the location on the west side of New York. The membership increased to 43 and Harold Hackett, Raymond Little, Fred Alexander, Marion Jones and Juliette Atkinson were among those who played there.

In 1894 the club held its first tournament open to non-members. In 1897 it was awarded the Metropolitan Championship, which became an important fixture and was won by such players as Little, Hackett, Holcombe Ward and Alexander.

The club had to seek new grounds in 1902, vacating for an apartment house. It moved to 117th Street between Morningside Drive and Amsterdam Avenue, near Columbia University. It built four dirt courts. Its membership had now reached the limit of 110 and it incorporated, with Dr. James Ewing as president. Another move became necessary in 1908, and it now built a two-story clubhouse and put in a dozen grass courts and ten or more clay courts at 238th Street and Broadway, south of Van Cortlandt Park. This was a big improvement over previous quarters, and the club was now in a position to stage more important events. It put on the Davis Cup tie between the United States and the British Isles in 1911. William Larned, national champion for the seventh time this year, and McLoughlin won for the United States, 4 to 1. In 1913 it staged the tie between the United States and Australia, in which McLoughlin, Dick Williams and Hackett gained a 4 to 1 victory. Soon after, the U. S. won the challenge match with Great Britain.

Now came the third and final move. After considering a number of sites, including one in Kew Gardens, L. I., the members voted to purchase property from the Sage Foundation Homes Company in Forest Hills. With Myrick one of the prime movers, the club bought 10½ acres for approximately $77,000 in 1913, and a clubhouse costing $30,000 was erected. George Agutter was engaged as the head professional, marking the start of a distinguished career of nearly half a century with the club.

The membership of the club was now approximately 600, and plans called for the building of some 50 grass and clay courts and the installation of a piping system for watering turf. Calhoun Cragin, captain of the club, supervised the removal of the best turf from the 238th Street courts and the seeding of the new courts. He had the valuable assistance of Mike Brazil, the head groundsman.

The club was ready in 1914 to undertake its most ambitious promotion. It applied for the Davis Cup challenge round in August between Australia and the United States. It was the success of these matches, which drew capacity crowds to the stands of the West Side Tennis Club, that decided Myrick and others to go after the national championships in 1915.

The championship continued to be held at Forest Hills through 1920 (as a Patriotic Tournament in 1917). When the United States won the Davis Cup from Australia in 1920, the U.S.L.T.A. decided to stage the challenge round at the West Side Tennis Club the next three years and hold the nationals at the Germantown Cricket Club. In 1924 the nationals returned to Forest Hills, and they have been there ever since.

Editor's note: The writer acknowledges his indebtedness to Ned Potter for the use of his authoritative West Side Story *as a reference source.*

THE LONGWOOD CRICKET CLUB

by Lee Tyler

It's heading into its 73rd year now, but you really can't call Longwood an old tennis club. Several of its playing members have accumulated more years than the club has, and no one thinks of them as being particularly old.

This just goes to prove that anyone who wants to search for the past at the Longwood Cricket Club in Chestnut Hill, Massachusetts, doesn't have to look very far. There are monuments to the history of the club everywhere. The ancient steam roller that Charlie Chambers pilots over the grass courts nowadays is the same one that used to be horse-driven by his father, "Ike." The senior Chambers, who came over from England in 1884, served as groundskeeper and cricket pro at the Longwood Club. The club was in Longwood then, a very close suburb of Boston.

Scarred wooden benches around the grounds come from the original location too. And certain pictures, framed and hanging around the walls now, show that the original Longwood clubhouse was just a shack with lockers. The courts were the thing.

The stucco-covered clubhouse today has a past too—at least the middle part of it does. In 1910 it served as headquarters for the Chestnut Hill Neighborhood Club, an organization whose members held horse shows, bowled, danced, and did everything, in fact, but play tennis. Longwood bought the clubhouse rather than build a new one of its own when it moved out to Chestnut Hill after the first World War. The little building was literally raised on timbers and dragged by horses through a break in the fence, over the frozen grass, and planted where it now is, all in one day in the winter of 1921. The club, however, was not officially opened in its present location until 1924. Although the modern Longwood is generally considered to be in Chestnut Hill, actually, it can be tabbed correctly as being in Chestnut Hill, Brookline, Boston or Newton, since the club property touches all four boundaries.

The club's past is around all right. But it's largely because of its non-tennis-playing members that it is. For the Longwood Cricket Club came close to going bankrupt during the recent war years, and it was its swimming pool that brought in new members and the revenue needed to keep the club solvent. In a very real way, Longwood owes the fact that its name is still a name, and not a memory, to the happy groups of children who cavort there in bathing suits, and may not even know what the game of tennis is.

As its name indicates, Longwood came into being primarily as a cricket club. But within a few years after the club was organized in April 1877, the members' enthusiasm for lawn tennis had completely outdistanced their interest in the older English pastime. By 1895 cricket had perished in the field if not in the club name. Symbolizing the organization's growing tennis prestige was the formal debut of the Longwood Bowl for open competition in 1891. Nine years later the first Davis Cup matches were contested on the club's courts. The Bowl hasn't been offered for challenge since 1942. The Cup, of course, is still going strong.

It's a matter of pride around Longwood that six of the U.S.L.T.A.'s presidents were Longwood men, and that two of them, Dr. James Dwight and Holcombe Ward, served for a total of 32 years. Other members who have brought glory to the club name include Dick Sears, who won the first National singles championship in 1881, and kept on winning it, along with sharing in the National doubles title, for the next six years; Dwight Davis, donor of the Davis Cup; Beals Wright, who was ranked in the top ten for a decade; and, more recently, Ray Bidwell, the only Longwood member ever to win the National veterans' championship three years running.

But Longwood can claim no National singles champion since Dick Williams in 1916; no doubles champion since Williams won it with Vinnie Richards in 1926; no intercollegiate champion since G. Colket Caner in 1916 (he won the National veterans' doubles title in 1939) ; and no junior boys' champion ever.

Founded as a men's club, Longwood actually has done better by its women. Two of them, Eleonora Sears and Hazel Hotchkiss Wightman, did much to break down the invisible barrier at the turn of the century that barred members of the fair sex from seriously competing in sports.

Eleo, lean, still handsome, and almost 70 now, was "the tennis queen of Newport" in 1903 and, according to observers, was the "Gibson type of athletic girl." Famous for her 100-mile hikes and three-mile swims, she was one of the first women to fly in an airplane. As another example of her vehicular versatility, she also was one of the first of her sex to ride a horse cross-saddle.

Runner-up for the National singles title in 1912, Eleonora also was the first women's squash champion, having previously gained entry to a men's squash club in Boston by firmly announcing: "I don't care what the house rules are. I'm joining."

Long before 1927, when she donated the Sears Cup for intersectional women's play, she won the National doubles championship four times— twice with Hazel Hotchkiss (1911, 1915) and twice with Molla Bjurstedt (1916, 1917). Deeply tanned and dressed in tweeds, she turns up every year to watch the matches at Longwood. She still plays in the women's veterans' division.

Mrs. Hazel Hotchkiss Wightman, younger than Eleo, moved to Brookline, Massachusetts, from Berkeley, California, in 1912, and promptly joined Longwood, where she met her husband. She donated the famed Wightman Cup in 1923; and she's been running junior tennis clinics, junior tourna- ments, and tourneys for college girls since 1922, to say nothing of officiating over various indoor tournaments at the Longwood Covered Courts, which, incidentally, have nothing to do with the Cricket Club. Mrs. "Wightie" also donated the club's bangboard. In between coaching, running tournaments, and winning 41 national titles (to date), she's raised five children, seen all but one (son) married, and has, at last count, nine grandchildren. She lives just around the corner from the club, and opens her home during the National doubles to as many women players as she has room for. Mrs. Wightman and Eleonora Sears are two of the very few women in Long- wood's long history who have been awarded honorary memberships in the club.

Boston society has always welcomed "tennis week"—the week of the National doubles in late August—for relieving an otherwise dull "season." And when there's local interest involved, all the better. Sarah Palfrey Fabyan Cooke, who had made her debut in Boston, was the darling of the club during her youth, and in 1935, after she had won the mixed doubles title with Enrique Maier by defeating Kay Stammers and Roderich Menzel, one reporter wrote: "Mr. Maier was so delighted with Mrs. Fabyan's playing that hardly had the last shot deciding the final match hit the ground but that he was bowing over her hand and kissing it with fervent appreciation and gratitude. Mr. Marshall Fabyan, Jr., who sat in the front row watching this gruelling match with solemn mien, broke into a wide grin the minute that final shot was made and bounded out of his seat."

Other well-known feminine members of the club who made their debuts in society about the time they became known on the courts were Kay

Winthrop, now Mrs. Q. A. Shaw McKean; Virginia Rice, now Mrs. Melvin Johnson, Jr., (who won several major doubles titles with Mrs. McKean); and Marjorie Sachs, now Mrs. Carl Pickhardt, Jr.

Bostonians, when they find anything in their vicinity the center of attention, love the personal touch in publicity. They delight in seeing photos of each other in the paper, and photos published of players "with civilian clothes on." It's every young Boston girl's dream to be asked to usher during the matches.

But even when it isn't tournament time, Longwood is one place where, if you can't get away from the city for the summer, you can at least *feel* that you're away. Members behave pretty nearly as they please, with few club rules to cater to. Yet, in proper Boston tradition, Longwood is actually run more by its "old guard" than by its board of governors or its manager. Without exception, the important figures in the old guard come from the old pre-Chestnut Hill, Longwood.

One major member of this group is Irving Wright, brother of Beals, and son of the Wright of Wright and Ditson (the sporting goods firm that imported the first tennis rackets and balls). Mr. Wright won four national titles in his time, became president of Longwood, and is now on the executive committee of the U.S.L.T.A. Mrs. Wightman belongs to the unofficial order; so do Charlie Chambers and Ralph Chambers, Charlie's nephew and Ike's grandson, who never took a lesson or entered a tournament, yet has been the club's professional for the last 17 years. There is also Dave Niles, who is chairman of the pool committee and runs the Newport tournaments. A stern look from any one of these persons will bring a misbehaving youngster to heel in a hurry.

The new president of Longwood is the first top executive of the club in years to hold a current national ranking. He's Nelson Hooe of Chestnut Hill, and he holds, with his son, Nelson, Jr., the New England Father-and-Son title. The pair is nationally ranked at number ten in this division. Mr. Hooe is a Yale graduate, as were the two presidents before him. The Harvard monopoly on presidents and champions stopped long ago. Incidentally, the current club singles champions at Longwood are Baba Madden Lewis, who is ranked at 13 among the nation's women, and Chauncey D. Steele, Jr., listed at number three in the New England rankings.

Tournament life, some sigh at Longwood, hasn't been quite the colorful same since Davis Cup teams stopped sailing directly into Boston Harbor, since fans used to sit in the trees to watch the matches, and since the week in 1933 when the leading women players gave fair warning that they were going to wear shorts instead of skirts. (The board of governors had to hold a special meeting to decide if it were proper or not.) Frankie Parker turned up on court in shorts that year, too. No one thought anything of it because he was a boy and, after all, only 17 at the time. But when some of the older *boys* donned shorter pants, the club received more than a few phone calls from indignant citizens who thought the sight of so many exposed legs "disgusting."

During the war, there were five colorless years when the only tournament players were women and the over-50 age group. The grandstands around the stadium courts had been condemned as unsafe and torn down—there weren't any crowds to accommodate anyway—and all final round matches were played on the clubhouse courts. . . .

So it was a big year in 1946, when grandstands were put up again and the courts prepared for two full weeks of tournament tennis. The war was over, and faces lighted up as the club members anticipated seeing the greatest players from all over the world competing once again for prized trophies on the Longwood courts. . . .

Fresh stories are still being told of old-timers making the absent-minded mistake of getting off the train at the Longwood station and looking around for the Cricket Club, instead of traveling the 12 minutes further out to Chestnut Hill. It's obvious that Longwood is a club with a past worth remembering.

It certainly has a future worth saving.

DEATH ON THE LONGWOOD GRASS, ALAS

by Bud Collins

Pamplona is a Spanish town where the sun used to rise only if Ernest Hemingway gave the okay.

It is still an acceptable scene for orgiasts, principally American college girls pretending they are Lady Brett Ashley and boys glad they are not Jake Barnes. They gather to celebrate the Fiesta of San Fermin, which is dedicated to the killing of many bulls and much wine as eyes grow redder than the matadors' capes.

Fermin was an obscure Spanish saint, but Pamplonans and tourists are grateful that he lived. Where would they be for kicks without his fiesta?

That is the way the communicants feel about St. Dick at Longwood. (Longwood is a tennis club in Chestnut Hill, where the sun also rises unless a tournament is scheduled. Then it is 6–5 pick 'em that rain will appear.)

St. Dick, who was born as Richard Sears in 1862, came into the world humbly, covered only by a couple of trust funds. Canonization by tennis worshipers was his reward after he had won the first seven national championships played in this country. Thus elevated, he retired from the game at 27, although he did allow fellow Longwood members to touch the hem of his garments during the week when they annually observe his fiesta—the Fiesta of the Fuzzy Ball.

To outsiders, who are permitted to attend upon payment of an admission charge, the Fiesta of the Fuzzy Ball is known as the National Doubles Tennis Championships. These fiestas have been held at St. Dick's shrine, the Longwood Cricket Club, since 1917. Before that at Newport, where he performed his miracles waving a lopsided wand strung with the intestines of a lamb.

This year's fiesta begins today and carries on through next Sunday, provided there is no rain to lengthen it. Rain flows at the National Doubles like beer at a Polish wedding.

Nevertheless, the fiesta always finishes, leaving the eyes of the onlookers as bleary as those at Pamplona. Not from carousing, but from following the fuzzy balls back and forth as they make their rounds swiftly and skittishly. This can be wearing on those who line the arena as well as the performers.

The performers deal with bulls at Pamplona and with balls at Longwood. Fuzzy balls are not so dangerous to confront, perhaps, but they are more capricious, and the footwork and passes with the racket call for great skill and improvisation. It is all the more difficult at Longwood because the performers are working on grass.

Grass courts. There you have the mystique of St. Dick. Dick Sears did not walk on water—he played on grass. And there it is: St. Dick and Longwood and grass all blended into a religious fiesta of their own.

Take a Longwoodian and throw him to the lions. He will not recant. "Grass," he will cry, "is the only true surface! St. Dick played on it, and it's good enough for me." They are fundamentalists.

Grass was the surface in St. Dick's day because it was the only surface of any account. The game began on the lawns of English manors. Since his time, reformers have come along to preach the gospel of clay and cement courts—or other hard surfaces. Surfaces with a uniform bounce, resistant to wear.

Of the thousands of tennis clubs in the United States, no more than 25 of them have preserved grass courts. Yet the most important tournaments are on grass: Wimbledon in England, the National Singles at Forest Hills in New York, and the National Doubles as well as the U. S. Pro Championships at Longwood.

Why? Because they always have been. Few players learn the game on grass, but if they are to make their way in tennis they must learn to cope on turf.

Grass is the game of the no-bounce bounce. The ball skids and spins, and darts low off the lawn that is ideally as smooth as a golf green and as tough as the rough. Tennis is entirely different on grass, a faster, more intriguing game in which no bounce can be taken for granted as on clay, which is slow, or on cement, which is fast but gives a much higher bounce.

"Why the hell do we keep playing the big tournaments on this damn grass?" screeched Pancho Gonzales after he was beaten in the U. S. Pro tournament at Longwood last summer. It was a wet day, and the balls were skipping like stones on a pond.

"When is tennis going to get up to date and forget grass?" Pancho moaned. "Better surfaces have been invented. Ninety-nine per cent of the world's players are on clay or cement. Other sports keep improving playing conditions, but here we are as though it was 1881—on grass for an important tournament."

Then Pancho blasphemed, right there in the Longwood clubhouse: "They ought to blacktop the whole damn place," he sputtered. It was like proposing Billy Graham for the papacy.

Indeed the Los Angeles Tennis Club, where Pancho and a large number of America's foremost players spent their formative years, has black cement courts. "Finest courts in the world," croons Perry Jones, who runs tennis in Southern California. "Developed more champions than anywhere."

A Longwoodian would look at the place and scoff, "Why it's nothing but a parking lot with an adjoining bar."

Rod Laver, the current pro champion, is not so acidulous when he discusses grass, but he agrees with Gonzales, as do most first flighters. "Grass," says Laver, "is lovely, and fun to play on, but it's too changeable, especially in America. The courts wear out fast, not like those in England or Australia where the climate is more favorable. And the bounce is never the same. When your living depends on it, you want a consistent surface like cement or clay."

There are now National Doubles championships on cement, clay and indoors, plus the current fiesta at Longwood—four separate championships every year.

"Grass is dead," sermonize the reformers in a tone that has been used for "God is dead."

But grass and God have their backers. The only National Doubles anybody pays attention to is at Longwood; the other titles mean little.

Longwood has had grass since 1877 when St. Dick's grandfather rented a bumpy plot to a gang of cricket nuts for $40 a year. This was in Brookline's Longwood section, where Winsor School now stands. In 1922 the club moved to the wilds of Chestnut Hill, taking the fiesta and plenty of grass seed along.

Longwood Cricket Club is no longer in Longwood. Nor do its 650 members know anything more about cricket than the Boston boxing impresario Sam Silverman, who, when invited to a cricket match in England five years ago, stated: "Nah—who wants to see a couple of bugs fight?"

Cricket disappeared in 1911. Conversion of the flock had taken place in 1881, when St. Dick wore the black-and-white striped cap of Longwood into the Newport Casino to win the first U. S. championship.

The divine right of grass has been observed thereafter. "Grass," says an accomplished playing member, Z. Paul Callahan, "is sheer delight to play on. Easy on the eyes, feet and balls. Leaving grass for clay or cement is like leaving Sophia Loren to run away with Marjorie Main."

This is a trying week for Callahan and his co-religionists. They are relegated to the club's clay courts from where they can view the annual tragedy of their grass: a mob of 350 tournament players going through it like a herd of Japanese beetles.

When the fiesta ends, the courts will look as haggard as the revelers at

Pamplona. That is the price Longwoodians pay for continuing the doubles rites on their hallowed sod. But it is all in the glorious memory of St. Dick, and surely others should be allowed to run in his path.

Grass is as obsolete for tennis as cobblestones for turnpikes, but the gay blades of Longwood survive anachronistically and are still of consequence internationally. The members feel as sentimental about grass as Vito Genovese does about the Mafia, considering the courts a sporting *cosa nostra*—"our thing." They would no more abandon grass than Vito would rat on a fraternity brother.

When will St. Dick's Fiesta of the Fuzzy Ball accede to the theses of the clay or the cement protestants? On the day that the Fiesta of San Fermin bans bulls and wine.

THE MERION CRICKET CLUB

from the 1939 Davis Cup Program

"Why is it called the Merion Cricket Club?" is a question which is raised by the thousands of tennis fans who are visiting the club for the first time to see the Davis Cup matches. "Why is it called the Merion Cricket Club when it isn't in Merion and isn't a cricket club?" is the question often posed to the members of the club.

The answer lies hidden in the annals of the club. Like most of the older tennis clubs in the Eastern part of the United States the Merion Club was started for the purpose of playing cricket, and, like the others, its beginnings were most informal and unpretentious. Just the idea of a group of boys in whose veins ran the blood of settlers from the British Isles who had been bred in the tradition of cricket as the noblest of all sports.

Much of the beautiful rolling country outside Philadelphia which now forms the picturesque and aristocratic suburbs of the city was settled by English, Scotch, Irish and Welsh people. As early as 1835 cricket was introduced into Haverford College. In the early 1860s two boys, William Montgomery and Maskell Ewing, gathered together a bunch of companions to play cricket on the generous lawns of their homes, using the giant shade trees as backstops. Boys love the idea of a club. In the fall of 1865 these same two boys on a walking trip in the Blue Ridge Mountains concocted a scheme to form a real cricket club among the boys in their neighborhood in Lower Merion Township. By October they had their members all lined up and signed to an agreement to "unite together in a cricket club to meet for play next spring at least once a week." The boys, ranging in age from fourteen to twenty-two, included besides the two originators, George H. Ball, Charles

Eyre, Allen Evans, Charles W. Humphreys, Rowland Evans, Archibald R. Montgomery, Edward H. Eyre, Edward S. Sayres, Jr., Richard H. Reilly, Harry Sayres, J. Aubrey Jones, Edward H. Lycett, William Stroud and Meredith Bailey. Archibald Montgomery was not able to sign the paper because he had lost his arm by the discharge of a gun while he was serving with the Pennsylvania Light Artillery during the funeral procession of President Lincoln in Philadelphia, on April 22, 1865. Scarcely one of the founders but has from one to ten descendants in the membership of the Merion Cricket Club today.

The boys went about their enterprise in a businesslike way, called their first meeting in December 1865 at the home of the Montgomery boys on the Coopertown Road, elected "Archie" Montgomery their first president, named their club the Merion Cricket Club and appointed committees to enlist further interest among parents and friends. By April they had secured grounds. The father of one of their members, Colonel Owen Jones, came through with a plot of ground on his estate "Wynne Wood." The field was west of Wynne Wood Station of the Pennsylvania Railroad and adjoined the yard of the Wynne Wood district school. The boys were allowed to keep their equipment in the entry of the schoolhouse in a wooden box. In May 1866 the Merion eleven played and won its first match against an eleven from Haverford College. Inspired by this victory, they immediately began dreaming of a clubhouse.

It was 1873, however, before this ambition was realized. In March of that year the club was chartered and leased five acres of land at the end of the road now known as Cricket Avenue in Haverford Township about a mile south of the Ardmore Station. A small frame clubhouse was built, and in May 1875 the opening match was played.

Up to this time tennis was unthought of in the Club. But that year a cricket eleven was sent to Halifax to play a match against a team composed of officers from the English ships anchored there, and this, strangely enough, was the first link in the chain of events which brought tennis to the Merion Cricket Club. For the following year when the English officers came to Philadelphia to play the return match at the Merion Cricket Club, they brought along some contraband in their cricket gear—a tennis net, balls and bats. After the serious business of the day, the cricket match, was finished, the visitors hauled out the novel articles and proposed that they all have a try at the new game, tennis.

Tennis caught on at once with the younger fry. Girls didn't play cricket but they did play tennis and that lent an added glamour to the new sport. The older and more staid members of the Club were inclined to frown upon the innovation but the youngsters persisted and formed a tennis club within the Club, the members being allowed to put up nets and play on the grounds at their own expense.

This arrangement continued during 1880. That year the tennis membership increased so rapidly that the Club bought two and a half acres of adjoining land for tennis courts and put an addition on the clubhouse. The following year a house for Ladies and Juniors was built. That year also the

Club appointed a tennis committee composed of Rowland Evans, Edward S. Sayres and William R. Philler to govern the game. Dues of $2 a year were levied on those wishing to play tennis on the Club grounds. . . .

First real official recognition of the growing popularity of tennis in the Club was taken at a special meeting in January 1882, when it was resolved that an organization to be known as the Merion Tennis Club should be formed. This plan was carried out the ensuing spring. . . .

Tennis was finally absorbed into the regular activities of the Merion Cricket Club in 1883, with an appropriation set aside from the club funds for its promotion and no extra dues charged to members wishing to play the game.

There may be some magic in the game of tennis. In four years from the time the first net was put up on the Club grounds by the cricket visitors from Halifax, tennis had forged ahead to gain equal recognition with cricket. Who could foresee that it was to gain so amazingly in popularity that when the Club celebrated its semi-centennial tennis would be the chief activity while cricket, for which the Club had been founded, would be retained only in the name of the Club and in the fond recollection of those who played in the stirring matches against Lord Hawke's team, Prince Raniitsinhji's team, Cambridge University Eleven, Marylebone Cricket Club, Kent County Club and the Australian Elevens? . . .

Both cricket and tennis were going strong, however, in 1891, when the Club decided that even its enlarged quarters on Cricket Avenue were no longer adequate for its rapidly growing membership. Twelve and a half acres of ground were procured on Montgomery Avenue between Gray's Lane and Cheswold Lane in Haverford, the present site of the Club. There were two stone dwellings on the property. These were moved closer together and joined by a wide hall to form the main clubhouse.

The grounds of the new home were open for use in the summer of 1892, by which time a locker building known as the Cricket House had been built. The main house was opened for a housewarming in November of that year, and in August 1893 the first big cricket event, the Halifax Cup Match, was played on the new cricket crease. Bowling alleys were added to the Club in 1895.

And now the Club was to experience the first of two destructive fires. In January 1896 the main house with its furnishings, contents including the original paper signed by the founders, its original charter and many other valuable papers, pictures and relics was completely destroyed by fire.

Nothing daunted, the membership set about building a new and larger house. This was nearly completed when it too caught fire and was badly damaged in the autumn of 1896. Work of restoration was started immediately, and in April 1897 the original portion of the red brick building which is the home of the Merion Cricket Club today was opened to its members in a grand housewarming. Many important additions have been made to the building in the years which have followed, including an extensive locker house adjoining the main building, living quarters for house staff and for male members who make their home at the Club. Squash racquet courts have been built and a Ladies' Club House in early English style constructed on the Gray's Lane side of the grounds.

In fact scarcely a year has passed unmarked by some addition or improvement being made to add to the comfort of the members of this very alive and active organization. Each new activity entered into by the members has been heartily sponsored by the Club, including Ladies' Field Hockey and Soccer Football.

In 1920 adjoining land with a house on it was bought and the house altered to provide more rooms for resident members. A commodious garage was the next requirement and served also to house more squash courts, where the Women's National singles and doubles tournament was held in 1927. The big undertaking for 1928 was the modernizing of the main house, which meant the addition of three private dining rooms, six new bedrooms, new heating and lighting systems and a general redecorating and refurnishing. With its cheery sun room and many homelike lounges, card rooms and dressing rooms, the main house invites all sorts of membership activity. Badminton, bridge and dancing provide amusement for the winter months and give the club an air of warm hospitality and charm.

On the turf courts which flank the front of the clubhouse many important tennis events have taken place. The Merion Cricket Club has been the traditional scene of the Men's National Intercollegiate tournaments since 1900, this fixture taking place there with the lapse only of the years of the World War and of those from 1934–1936. Other tournaments which have been staged on the Club's courts are the Men's Pennsylvania State and the Women's Pennsylvania and Eastern States. . . .

NEWPORT, THE CRADLE OF AMERICAN TENNIS

by John Hanlon

Now that American tennis has gone frankly commercial, the diehards of the country-club, grass-court set may at last be able to face this long-forgotten fact: the Newport Casino, birthplace of U.S. tournament tennis and genteel home of the Tennis Hall of Fame, was not primarily designed for the sake of tennis at all. It was conceived in a fit of anger of the crass and flamboyant James Gordon Bennett, Jr., who was not even much of a tennis player.

Bennett, the wealthy publisher of the New York *Herald* and a front-rank Newport "cottager" when society's summer gathering place was at full flower, was not acting sportingly at all when, nettled and on his own, he put in motion the Casino project in 1879. He was prompted by what he considered an affront to a friend dealt by another Newport club: the socially formidable Newport Reading Room. The Reading Room, which was chartered in 1854 and is believed to be the country's oldest club still occupying its original building, had (and has) its quarters in a simple frame structure fronting on Bellevue Avenue, then Society's main promenade. Its title was somewhat misleading, for the Reading Room's membership—male only—was given more to socializing and wassailing than to the pursuit of literature. As Mrs. John King Van Rensselaer wrote in 1905, "The young men who throng the corridors or fill the windows are the smartest around town, and they are attractive features as they saunter about in their faultlessly cut garments, with their hats cocked in the latest fashion, with an indescribable air of self-satisfaction known only to the well-turned-out male."

That then was the atmosphere into which this friend of Bennett's rode a horse on an August afternoon in 1879. The man on horseback was one Captain Candy (inevitably nicknamed "Sugar"), a former British cavalryman and Bennett's polo-playing crony. Bennett had encountered the game in England in 1876 and with Candy's help had introduced it in this country. Whenever Candy was at Newport, which was often, he enjoyed all the privileges that close acquaintanceship with Bennett rated, including a card as Bennett's guest at the Newport Reading Room.

It has never been firmly established what caused Captain Candy to perform as he did on that August day. Perhaps it was a bet, a dare or a too-long stay at the tavern. One school holds that Bennett himself put Candy up to it. In any case, Candy and his mount set a course that brought them to the front of the yellow-colored building that houses the Reading Room. Then, to the astonishment of those thronging the corridors and filling the windows, in he rode. He went up the front steps, across the piazza, through two sets of broad doors and into the main hall. "Sir," the white-coated steward is said to have informed him at that point of the journey, "you cannot ride a horse in here." Candy ignored this. He proceeded along the hall for some 20 feet, made a left turn through an archway into what is called Reading Room No. 2, then into the South Room, which at the time housed the bar. Once there, he wheeled about, retraced his course out to the street and galloped off.

Taken purely as a feat of horsemanship, Captain Candy's ride was not much, but it had an electric effect on the membership of the Reading Room, on Newport at large and, hence, on all of Society. The act was taken as "a clear violation of the rules," as a brief reference to the happening in the Newport *Mercury* put it, and Bennett was notified that the guest card held by Captain Candy in his name was revoked.

Now James Gordon Bennett, stirred and under full throttle, was a formidable man. His drive and his news sense had made his *Herald* the most powerful publication of the day, and he ran it with a bold and totalitarian hand. Once, for example, he promoted a copy boy named Billy Bishop to the post of sports editor of the European edition simply because a pair of Bennett's Pekingese, trailing their owner through the paper's Paris office, had taken a liking to him.

Bennett was also enormously rich and, in his social as well as business life, a leader and a doer. "Mr. James Gordon Bennett reached Newport on Wednesday," the Newport *Mercury* proclaimed in its issue of August 2, 1879, "and everyone at once looked for the opening of the festivities and sports of the season, for Mr. Bennett has the energy and push needed to give the coach of gayety a good start."

Within days of the Candy incident, Bennett bought and paid $60,000 for a cottage called "Stone Villa," about one quarter of a mile up Bellevue Avenue from the Reading Room, intending to make it a rival clubhouse. He soon decided against converting, though, and took Stone Villa as his own residence, because he had a better idea. He would build an all-new structure for the new club and to that end, in early fall, he bought 126,000 square feet of land across from Stone Villa.

By October, Bennett had formed a joint stock company and offered shares in his project, at $500 each, to a select number of friends. The list of shareholders read like a reprint of the Social Register. For the architectural work, he commissioned the firm of McKim, Mead and White: Stanford White, the junior member, was to be primarily responsible for the form the Casino (as he decided to call it) would take.

What White brought from his drawing boards was a three-building complex in which space was provided for a bowling alley, a billiard parlor, reading rooms, restaurant, a court-tennis court, a theater-ballroom, bachelor lodgings and, on the ground floor facing Bellevue Avenue, space for shops to be occupied by "first-class tenants."

The main building was, and remains, three stories high, brick-faced at the street level, fish-scale shingles above. A paneled entryway on Bellevue Avenue led to the wonders within—the neatly kept tennis courts, trees, shrubs and pathways, the semicircular Horseshoe Piazza and a yellow-faced clock on a bulbous tower that struck one viewer as a copy of a London bobby's helmet. Actually the tower is shaped after a form common to the Loire Valley of France, a region much favored by White. The cost of the entire layout was said to be close to $200,000.

The grand opening was held on July 28, 1880, and the Newport *News* proclaimed: "There is nothing like it in the old world or new." The first-class tenants, most of them from New York, were installed in the shops. The 16-piece orchestra of J. M. Lander, the Meyer Davis of his time, was brought up from New York, and the cottagers all turned out to make the inaugural a dazzling success.

"It is doubtful," the Newport *News* said just three days after the opening, "if a more lively place can be found." Within a week the Casino held a gigantic housewarming attended by more than 3,000 persons, an occasion the Providence *Journal* decreed as "the greatest event of its kind ever known here." Mrs. Van Rensselaer, in her account of Newport life, was moved to note that whatever the attraction provided by the Casino—horse show, dog show, tennis tourney, *anything*—"the fashionable folk" on the grounds made "a dazzling sight" and "a picture not easily forgotten."

In short, Bennett's place was *the* place, and in record time it became the "must" place to be seen at around noon for gossiping and for lunch. Then would come tennis or whatever for the afternoon, then a play, a concert or a gala on the grounds during the evening.

Bennett himself, oddly enough, was far from the best patron the Casino had, primarily because he had expatriated himself to France and was an increasingly infrequent visitor to the U. S. But even when he was in residence at Stone Villa, Bennett did not often walk across the street to patronize his own creation; indeed there is a strong belief that he never once played tennis on the premises. Just having the Casino there and a success, apparently, was his reward.

After socializing, tennis quickly became the Casino's leading sport. The game had been growing in popularity among the American elite since it first appeared in this country from England, by way of Bermuda, around 1874. When, in 1881, the newly formed United States Lawn Tennis Association decided to hold its first national championship, the honor of serving as host for the event went to Newport and, of course, the Casino was the choice.

"The grounds were picturesque and the courts well kept," a frequent Newport participant, Henry Slocum, Jr., national champion in 1888–89, noted later, "and Newport being then as now, a very fashionable resort, the most beautiful women of the country graced the tournament with their presence." Or as another player chose to put it, "The ladies bestowed sweet smiles upon the players."

Most of the sweet smiles, undoubtedly, were initially directed at Richard Dudley Sears, Harvard '83. Sears won the singles title in the 1881 tourney, went on to defend the title for the next six years and then retired undefeated from national competition.

The national championships, singles and doubles, continued to be contested at Newport every summer until 1915, when the event was moved to the West Side Tennis Club's new quarters at Forest Hills, New York. Newporters protested this move, but the New York group was able to convince the U.S. Lawn Tennis Association that tennis at the Casino was a social event to which even championship tournaments came second. It was an argument not without fact. Newport's reply, once the switch was done, was to put on its own invitational tournament for amateurs each August. That continued, except for war years, until this summer, when the Casino elected to follow a growing tennis trend by replacing the traditional event with a tournament for professionals.

During World War II the upper floor of the Casino's main building was taken over as a club for officers at Newport's several Navy bases, but the Casino was otherwise dormant. After the war it reopened quickly and bravely. But in terms of patronage and, more so, ambiance, it somehow wasn't the same, and times became relatively hard. A corner of the Casino's property was sold off to a realtor and later became the site of a supermarket—and at the time it was thought that any good offer could have bought the rest of it for commercial uses.

Then a fourth-generation Newport cottager, James H. Van Alen, came to the fore. A wealthy, indefatigable worker for a variety of causes, whose activities included captaining the 1924 tennis team at Cambridge University, England, Van Alen was elected the Casino's president in 1952, and rescue operations began. In 1954 he obtained the U.S.L.T.A.'s sanction to establish the Tennis Hall of Fame at the Casino. He had it in business by the next year, and nearly every year since he has seen that appropriate people are named to its roster—with accompanying publicity for the Casino. He has also established a solid financial base for both the Hall and the Casino. From his office as president of the Hall of Fame's corporation, a title he assumed in 1957, Van Alen has been able to induce many of the Casino's shareholders to donate their Casino holdings to the Hall of Fame. By 1960 the Hall of Fame thus controlled more than 51 per cent of the shares and by March of 1968 it owned 75 per cent of them.

Van Alen has had all the Casino buildings and grounds spruced up, has leased out the theater-ballroom—a longtime white elephant—to a community group fostering the performing arts, and has improved the tennis setup from a spectator's viewpoint. He also has moved to give the place a more democratic mien, though not too much so. In 1965 he put on a tournament for professional players at the Casino, in addition to the regular amateur invitational.

Not all the Van Alen innovations have been totally accepted by the cottagers, but none can deny that he has made the Casino once more a going concern, and that is what the crusty Bennett, a businessman before everything else, wanted most of all.

As for Captain Candy, the man responsible, he seems to have ridden straight off to oblivion.

THE MEADOW CLUB

by Francis T. Hunter

Although the early records are a bit hazy, it can be said that the Meadow Club of Southampton is one of the oldest outdoor sports clubs in America.

The first site of the club, in 1883, was on the Charles E. Merrill property, now owned by William G. McKnight, Jr. A small clubhouse was built and two tennis courts were laid out. In 1885 the Bowers Lee property on First Neck Lane was purchased and the club moved there.

The Meadow Club became firmly established and adequately financed in the 1890s. The clubhouse was enlarged and the construction of tennis courts on the lawns was commenced and the number of courts was increased each year. In 1896, with eight lawn tennis courts in good playing condition, it was decided to hold an invitation tournament, to which all of the leading players from Newport, Seabright, Rockaway and other established tennis clubs in the East were invited.

The event was an outstanding success for the club, socially and tennis-wise, and for the Southampton community. From that year on, with the exception of a few war years and one year of omission, the Meadow Club Invitation Tennis Tournament was an outstanding event in the tennis world, attracting the world's leading players.

The ever-expanding scope and size of the Meadow Club, its facilities and activities, including the tournaments, have been under the administration, guidance and financial direction over the years of such outstanding South-ampton personalities as Dwight F. Davis, Goodhue Livingston, Lyttleton Fox, John Baker, James P. Lee, Judge Kenneth O'Brien, H. Rodgers Benjamin, Robert Stafford, Robert Magowan, Charles Merrill, Kenneth Burns, Hunter Goodrich, Grenville K. Walker, Sidney B. Wood, Jr., Frank Shields, Oliver Rodgers, Laurence R. Condon, and many others, down to the present dynamic administration of George S. Patterson, Dwight F. Davis, Jr., Joseph A. Meehan and Clifford Michel . . . assisted by the most efficiently functioning groups of committee women and committee men the Club has ever enjoyed.

A grand old club of great vintage and glorious tennis tradition is "Meadow."

A REVIEW OF WIMBLEDON

by Helen Wills

Wimbledon! The classic event of the world of tennis. First of all, it is the oldest. Secondly, it is probably the most international. And thirdly, the matches are carried out with that touch of which the English are so sure when staging an out-of-doors event in which figure green lawns, well-mannered spectators, royalty, and June showers.

Wimbledon is an event. It is marked down on the calendar almost a year ahead of time by those who intend to go. They don't mean by this that if they happen to be nearby they will run out to Wimbledon. Not at all. Their seats are bought, or are permanently there if they happen to be shareholders in the concern that is Wimbledon. The English appear to plan their summers in the most methodical way. Some may mark off in December or January a few more days for Ascot than for Wimbledon—that is, if they like horses better than tennis—but if they have planned to see some of the tennis, then they do it.

Americans arriving in London during the tournament in June, who think that it might be interesting to see Ellsworth Vines on foreign soil on the famous center court, try to get tickets and find that they were all sold in January, except for a few that are released daily at the box office at Wimbledon. Either they pay shocking prices for tickets which have found their way into the hands of some speculator, or else they take a chance at getting a ticket at the box offices at the gates of Wimbledon.

Don't ever do the latter. Although there are a certain number of tickets sold daily at the gate—never enough—the difficulty of getting one is almost insurmountable for an American. The English succeed, but it is because they love the sidewalk sport of standing in a queue. If a match is taking place that might prove exciting, it is the signal for the queue at the gate to lengthen. Sometimes queues start forming at four in the morning. That queues are a form of endurance contest is proved by the fact that those in line, anticipating long hours of waiting, bring camp stools to sit on and sandwiches to revive their failing energies. Mlle. Lenglen was responsible for more tired feet in queues than, perhaps, any other player, male or female, with William Tilden and Jean Borotra tying for second place. The American who contemplates standing in a queue at Wimbledon, or in any other queue in London, for that matter, had better discard the plan immediately. As was said before, we simply cannot compete with the British, because they regard it as a sport and are actually good-natured for hours in line.

The arrival of royalty creates a stir in the driveway at Wimbledon. The driveway always seems to be filled with people who are either going into the center court or coming out of it. A car arrives, perhaps moving softly. Gently it makes its way to the royal door. No, it isn't the King or Queen, because everyone knows their enormous cars. Black-stockinged schoolgirls press forward. They are always in the driveway in large numbers. Grownups crane their necks. An Eastern potentate descends from the car in brilliant robes. He is followed by guards who have daggers in their boots. Then the Bishop of London drives up in his very old automobile. He is past seventy, but still plays tennis on his court at Fulham Palace with an accuracy and an agility which far surpass those of some of his young curates.

If you stand by the royal doorway long enough, you will see Their Majesties, the King and Queen of England, and the Duke and Duchess of York, but not the Prince of Wales. He doesn't go to Wimbledon. Also several English princesses. Perhaps Lady Asquith. And probably the American Ambassador to the Court of St. James's. Also, Alfonso, ex-King of Spain. Last year, the ex-King of Portugal was attending Wimbledon, as was his custom. His chair in the royal box was reserved for him, as usual, and stood waiting. But one afternoon he did not come. He had died that morning of a sudden throat infection. He was Wimbledon's most faithful royal spectator and rarely missed a day of the tournament.

The most important spectators that the committee can hope to have, of course, are Their Majesties, the King and Queen. They usually appear unannounced when the matches become more exciting toward the end of the meeting. The committee does not know, or at least does not say, on what days the royal spectators are coming. They enter the royal box and quickly seat themselves. The audience rises to its feet when it sees the King and Queen. Their Majesties prefer that the players continue playing and that they do not stop their game. But it is best to stop playing—especially if you are a visiting foreign player. Also, it is very disconcerting if you continue to play while the spectators are rising to their feet and settling down again, with the buzz of conversation and flurry of excitement that the appearance of Their Majesties always brings forth.

Sometimes the Queen asks that certain players be presented to her. The American Wightman Cup team was presented to both the King and the Queen in the royal box last year. The American players mounted the stairs, rehearsing their curtsies mentally on the way.

The Queen wears dark glasses while watching the matches. She sits very straight in her chair. Her hat, worn high on her head, makes her appear taller than she is really. One might say, in regard to fashion, that the Queen of England has a style of her own and is, therefore, always in style. Her colors are mauve, powder blue, gray-blue, and silver.

My first game on the center court gave me a quite different feeling than did my last one. I was eighteen and a member of the first American Wightman Cup team that visited England. The court seemed very small, the surroundings very large. The runback from the boundary lines of the court was wider than that of any court upon which I had played. The measurements of the surroundings were greater. It was difficult for me to gauge the length of my balls. A player not only judges the length of his ball in comparison with the measurements of the court but also in regard to the measurements of the surroundings.

Because of the space about the court, and because of the height of the grandstands, the player feels that the court is smaller. Because of this illusion, he is inclined to hit his balls outside the court, until he becomes accustomed to the new surroundings. I remember that I felt somewhat bewildered by the new conditions. After a few matches, however, I discovered that I would rather play on the center court than on any other grass court. The conditions are as perfect as they can be. The turf is firm and smooth. The grass is clipped so short that the surface is as fast as a hard court. No one is permitted to play on the center court until the championship, except the Wightman Cup players. Since the Wightman Cup matches are held in England on alternate years, they do not give the court much wear and tear.

We in America look with real envy on the grass courts at Wimbledon, for there are no courts like them in our country. It is not because of lack of effort on our part. The fact is that our climate is not so favorable for grass tennis courts as is the English.

THE ONE AND ONLY

by Paul E. Deutschman

The most satisfactory occasion for an American to view the British at their most British is during the annual Lawn Tennis Meeting at Wimbledon. Coronations occur infrequently, but the tennis at Wimbledon remains the greatest year-in, year-out testament to the unmatchable British talent for combining judicious portions of drama, pageantry, and the game-for-the-game's-sake. Please note, I say, "the" tennis. For there is no doubt at all that Wimbledon is the pinnacle of world tennis—possibly the best-run, undoubtedly the best-spectatored tournament anywhere; bringing together the world's finest players and drawing out the greatest measure of excitement that the game holds. Most of our own American tournaments are definitely minor league next to the efforts of the 96 ladies and 128 gentlemen who early each summer do ceremonious battle here in the outskirts of London. By contrast, the players at Roland Garros in Paris and Foro Italico in Rome are mere untutored small boys squabbling on a sandlot.

Some 22,000 people attend each day of what has been called "this dedicated fortnight." These are the fortunate, the influential, and the brave. Plotting and juggling for tickets (at $2.25 or $2.80 each) starts in mid-January, a full six months before the actual event. The All-England Lawn Tennis and Croquet Club—which is Wimbledon's proper name, though they no longer dawdle over croquet there—has all sorts of intricate and mysterious ways of deciding your chronological eligibility to buy a ticket (with no refunds or returning if they're rained out), giving first crack to the 50 lady and 250 gentlemen permanent club members and 41 temporary members, and working down at last to the general public (who, after the first week's play, pitch overnight camp outside the gates in order to latch onto the 300 last-minute Center Court and 1,000 Number 1 Court tickets that go on sale the following noon).

Suppose this is your first Wimbledon Meeting. You should try to arrive there for opening day, even though the Main Court matches may promise mild play. Buses and cabs, in long, orderly queues, chug you the mile or so through Connecticut-looking countryside from the Wimbledon or Southfields underground stations. The polite, unjostling crowd streams through the main gates, eager to get their seats for the official opening of the Center Court at exactly two P.M. by last year's cup holder and his first-round opponent. (This court is used only during this single fortnight of play.)

Within the gates, Wimbledon strikes you, first of all, as a green vista of well-modulated excitement—with a kind of stage-set, tea-and-crumpets, garden-party quality to it. To your left are the Members' Lawn (an out-of-bounds refreshment enclave) and fifteen grass courts in triple rows—if "grass" is quite the word for this precious, pampered sea-washed Cumberland turf. To your right lie the Tea Lawn and Clubhouse, the latter making up one side of a twelve-sided stadium that encompasses the holy of holies, the Center Court. An annex nearby surrounds the Number 1 Court.

For best effect, this first day at Wimbledon should be bright and summery —with motionless white clouds puffed out overhead. The competitors, tanned and fit-looking, wander casually about the grounds, pristine in white against these greenest of lawns—lordly, confident youths, kings of the game in their home countries or local clubs, and graceful girls, made even sprightlier by artful bits of ribbon and lace peeking here and there among their carefully coutured white shorts or skirts.

In a thousand little ways during your visit here, you'll see that this *is* the big-time in tennis—in the fully seventeen officials who arrange themselves about the Center Court lines; in the efficiency of the ball boys (all orphan lads from a technical school in Herts and trained all year long for this fortnight) ; in the 900 dozen balls, kept in refrigerators to achieve best-playing temperatures (one of the few things the English *do* refrigerate) ; in the TV cameras following every second of Center Court play from the very first round; and, especially, in the reverential attitude displayed toward Wimbledon, the institution, by players and spectators alike.

But perhaps what impresses you most are the people at Wimbledon. Though there are plenty of foreigners among the spectators—in saris, turbans, and seersucker suits—it is the British hosts who predominate and give greatest flavor to the place. Among these are all the celebrated British stereotypes, seemingly straight out of Central Casting. There are buck-toothed, walrus-mustached retired colonels with marble-mouthed accents; pink-cheeked lanky young men from the City or the Guards, wearing stiff black suits and waistcoats, with umbrellas and bowlers poised in their laps. Also, sport lads of all ages, frightfully keen for tennis and wearing dark blue blazers with every imaginable kind of insignia. There are white-haired old ladies with sensible hats, large baskets of tea things, and field glasses; young matrons from the counties, with pleasingly fussed-out hair, rose-petal complexions, and not-too-becoming flowered dresses. And there are droves of uniformed little schoolgirls, like eager young penguins, in middy blouses, pigtails, and straw hats held in place by elastic bands under their chins. They are all there, as if carefully decked out for some historic pageant, and this is the wonder of Wimbledon.

But wander around a bit. Talk to people. You'll quickly discover there exists a very special type of Wimbledon fan. For England, don't forget, is an entire nation of tennis lawns. The game—with its nobility, its dash, its technique of steel and subtlety sheathed in casualness, and, above all, its emphasis on form and good manners—is a divertissement made to order for the British, even in spite of the trying days British tennis has fallen upon lately. The people gathered here make up the world's most discriminating and best-informed tennis audience, as selective as a skylark's flight to the fine nuances of the game; steeped in its past glories; alert to its future ones. Even if you're an absolute duffer at tennis or have long since given up The Game to trudge behind a golf ball, you cannot help but appreciate their wonderful esoteric knowledge; and, also, through the most random of conversations, to gain the finest possible insight into the British sporting character.

"You must understand our attitude toward games," says Colonel Duncan Macaulay, the All-England Club's secretary. "We just can't bear an ungamelike attitude. There's such a thing as being too keen at *anything*. In theory, you're supposed to be athletic but casual, to appear to be enjoying the game for its own sake but not to be too proficient at it. You should give the impression that tennis is just one of a number of games you're good at."

"We all like Miss Connolly," said the lady alongside of me in the Center Court stands, "but somehow we feel she's trained a bit like a horse!" The lady was trim, tweeded, and fiftyish, a wife of a colonial official, and we were watching "Little Mo" as she bounced grimly and self-critically through her opening-round paces against a plump, flustered girl from South Africa.

"What you don't have here is an impression of *competition*—just machinelike performance," she went on. "Of course, Miss Connolly is a gracious champion. But the terribly practiced length of those shots! Those awful devastating angles, that ferocity! for instance, she shouldn't be using those nasty little drop shots out there right now. It simply isn't ladylike—she knows that poor girl can't run very well!"

The Wimbledon fan is constantly being torn between admiring a classic performance by some virtuoso like Tilden, Lenglen, Budge, or Cochet, or going all out for some underdog from the hinterlands who is matching blow for blow with the champ. He yearns for one of his own English players to come along with the "Big Game"—the thunderbolt service, the unsubtle groundstrokes, and no-nonsense net play of a Vines, a McGregor or a Kramer—but at the same time he favors the fine slender touch of a young Rosewall, a delicate Sidney Wood, or a light-paced Bunny Austin. Also, he has the most highly sensitized loyalties. And changes of loyalties. Who ever hatched up the canard that the English are a reserved people? Repressed they are, perhaps, by form and by politeness. But reserved, never. And at Wimbledon they can often be (in their devastatingly understated way) as volatile as a piazzaful of Neapolitans.

Your Wimbledon fan likes a flash of temperament—within bounds of good taste. ("It's the Machine Age of tennis," one elderly Club member told me sadly. "I remember Borotra in his heyday—with his little beret and dashing manner. He was terribly sporting, you know, but oh so excitable!") But at the same time this is very much the gentleman's game still to the Wimbledon fan. He expects good manners on the court. Just let some Belgian, some Australian, or some American player merely frown at what the crowd *knows* is a correct call on a footfault or corner shot, and you can feel its wrath rise subtly and collectively against him. Then you see the tolerant little smirks at the spectacle of the foreigner revealing himself at his most foreign (an English player, naturally, would *never* frown over a Wimbledon official's decision) ; then you hear the annoyed underbreath little murmurs of "Come now, Washer!" or "There goes old Falkenburg again!" which are the English equivalent of hurling seat cushions or beer bottles onto the court, as might conceivably happen in Madrid or Melbourne. The malefactor, however, is finished for the fans—even though yesterday his overhead smashes from backcourt were their greatest delight.

The competitors come here from all over the world, representing some thirty countries. Each year, about 500 men and women go through the formality of sending in regular entry forms to the Committee of Management of the Championships, and paying the entrance fee (the equivalent of $4.90 for men and $3.50 for women) through which, theoretically, they can enroll in Singles, Doubles, Mixed Doubles, the All-England Plate, or Ladies' Plate Tournaments (these for players eliminated in the first two rounds) or the Boys' and Girls' Singles. But the great majority of those chosen for the actual draw are the well-known circuit riders of tennis, the journeymen expense-accounters of this, the gentleman's game.

For each player Wimbledon is the end of the road, the shining promise of having his name engraved on the Clubhouse wall with the tennis greats of other days. All through the fortnight, you see them wandering over these hallowed grounds, indulging themselves in the feel and adulation of Wimbledon, moving about like newly shining stars in an ancient honored firmament. Each is witnessed, somehow, against a backdrop of the years, and against earlier tournaments and the players involved in them.

There is, for example, the aforementioned "Big Game" that flashes across the Center Court turf so often now that an old Wimbledonian may have difficulty remembering whether this is Trabert he is watching or Budge. Or perhaps another redhead, Maurice McLoughlin, the "California Comet" of 1913, or today's Lew Hoad from Australia, with shots that explode and reel from his racket. Or any of twenty or thirty others who qualify through the sustained fury of their play, who seem to melt into the larger picture of Wimbledon.

There is also the institution of the reigning lady star, with her queenly ways, driven up along in an official car, with the crowds stopping to gape and purr as she descends at the Clubhouse door. As she passes underneath the players' portals (bearing the Wimbledon creed: "If you can meet with Triumph and Disaster, And treat those two Impostors just the same"), the all-embracing history of Wimbledon closes about her—and she may be Suzanne Lenglen, the greatest of them all, or Helen Wills Moody or "Little Mo" Connolly or the turn-of-the-century champions: Blanche Bingley Hillyard or Lottie Dod (the latter won her first Wimbledon singles at the age of fifteen) or the pre–World War I queen, Mrs. Lambert Chambers, who held the cup seven times.

Then there's the timelessness of the Royal Box, with royalty, great soldiers and statesmen elbow-to-elbow in most glittering array. You can pick them out: the chic and regal Duchess of Kent, the All-England Club's president; the Duke of Edinburgh ("Oh, there's the Duke now!" my neighbor exclaimed. "Isn't it nice of him to come! But, oh dear, he's lost all his lovely tan because of our English summer!"); Princess Margaret (the Queen, a racing fan, has never accepted an invitation here, which is a cause of much regret); the visiting King of Sweden ("Don't bother to stand up, dear boy, he's a foreigner!"); Field Marshal Montgomery; Anthony Eden (dashing in four scant hours before his plane leaves for Washington); Clement Attlee; and half a hundred others. And even an American can share in the memories: of lovely old Queen Mary, with her celebrated hats; of her shy second son, later George VI (a left-handed player good enough to enter the Gentlemen's Doubles here one meeting); of the ancient creaky tennis-mad King Gustav of Sweden (with his famous shovel forehand and his command-performance matches with the world's best); of the Asquiths, Gladstones, the triumphant generals of other wars—all of them gracing this small enclosure.

Old Wimbledon hands (and they may be any age from sixteen to ninety-six) complain that all the great colorful personalities are gone and that since the war we are living in an era of industrialized tennis, with too many deadly serious youngsters coming out of public parks and oversubsidized tennis nurseries, and with the airplane making it possible for them to play too much tournament tennis in too short a time. Thus, they say, the glamour of Wimbledon is going.

It's true the Center Court is haunted by great names, by flashes of poignant drama. But past glories—in tennis, as anywhere else—are three-quarters nostalgia. And it is entirely possible that after a suitable number of years have elapsed the events participated in by today's comparatively "colorless characters" will become invested with comparable earth-moving glamour. Last year's breakthrough to the championship by the ex-Czech Drobny may rank with the Australian Sir Norman Brookes' first coming in 1907; the 1948 Falkenburg temper tantrums may seem, in retrospect, such charming exhibits of artistic temperament as Tilden's bullying of ball boys during the twenties. Tony Trabert's blisters in 1954 may seem as dismal instruments of Fate as Reggie Doherty's poor health in the early 1900s.

There are two main periods of Wimbledon history: the "old" Wimbledon, starting in 1868, and the "new" Wimbledon, starting when the Club moved to its present grounds in 1922. At the beginning, five sportsmen got together to discuss the "laying down of croquet lawns." They petitioned several clubs devoted to other sports to give them a little space but were turned down. Whereupon they rented four acres of ground, at fifty pounds a year, on Worple Road, Wimbledon. That was the birth of the All-England Croquet Club.

The first notice on the bulletin board read: "Gentlemen are requested not to play in their shirtsleeves when ladies are present"; the first Croquet Championships were played in June 1870. In 1875 a daring innovation was suggested by one of the founders—Mr. Henry Jones—that part of the grounds should be set aside for the purpose of playing lawn tennis and badminton. At first this was considered "another little joke of Henry's," but he persuaded the members to put down twenty-five pounds for the additional equipment. Soon lawn tennis became the Club's chief interest, and in 1877 the name was changed to the All-England Croquet and Lawn Tennis Club. That same year the first championships were played, with twenty-two gentlemen competing for "The Gold Champion Prize, value twelve guineas,

with Silver Challenge Cup presented by the proprietors of 'The Field.' "
This was won by Spencer Gore after the final match had been postponed
from July 16th to July 19th on account of the Eton and Harrow cricket
match which was being played at Lord's.

At the beginning, the tournaments were rather lackadaisical, social rather
than athletic events. The first champions were merely passing players, and
they batted about a hand-stitched ball "with an honest seam to it." Also,
there was the institution of the Challenge Round (like present-day Davis
Cup matches), with entrants battling it out for the right to challenge the
previous year's winner. Not until 1922 was the All-Comers Singles inaugu-
rated, with the cupholder having to enter the draw along with everyone
else. With the 1880s, Wimbledon moved irrevocably toward becoming the
tennis classic it is today. This was when the better Ayres ball was introduced
(the present Slazenger ball was adopted in 1902), croquet was abolished,
the Club grounds were bought outright, and the first Ladies' Championships were played. Also, the Renshaws came along. They were twin brothers
who might be called the first real tennis athletes. Willie Renshaw won the
meeting six years running and was the first man to take the ball on the rise,
and he was one of the first to step into midcourt and volley the ball without
bouncing it first, thus making the first muscular inroads against "gentlemanly" court demeanor. Ernie Renshaw, who won the cup only once, was
considered by many an even better player, although, reportedly, he never
tried his best against his brother.

The Renshaws were the first of the British court kings and queens who
held open reign here until World War I. After the Renshaws there came
another set of brothers, the Dohertys. Reggie ("Big Do") was the game's
genius, the stylist par excellence, a sickly delicate man with the most delicate of games; Laurie ("Little Do"), the more robust of the two, has been
called the greatest player of all time except Tilden. Between them, the
Dohertys "made" Wimbledon, filling the new stands and holding nine
singles and eight doubles titles. Both died tragically in their thirties—
Reggie as the result of a mountaineering expedition in Switzerland and
Laurie in the R.A.F. during the war.

The first foreigner to bring a breath of internationalism to Wimbledon
was an Australian, Sir Norman Brookes (later chairman of the board of
Aussie tennis). Then came the wild Americans, with their somewhat
"unsporting" cannonball and twist services—"Big Bill" Tilden, an utterly
arrogant Shakespearean ham of a player and the greatest figure tennis has
known, and "Little Bill" Johnston, his wraithlike and determined Stateside
rival. Then the stage broadened, and the French arrived. This was the time
of Suzanne Lenglen, a heady, eruptive combination of Pavlova, Garbo, and
Babe Didrikson—Wimbledon's all-time queen, who basked in absolute
adoration almost every moment of her reign here. Also French were the
"Four Musketeers," each irresistible, each utterly different from the others:
Brugnon, the tactician and self-effacing backer-upper; Cochet, the born
player, with his every shot a flick of the rapier; Lacoste, the created player, a
student of graphs and disciplines who charted a tennis court into a complex

of engineer's squares; Borotra, the "Bounding Basque," full of courage and wit and pulling off the world's most unorthodox shots from positions no player had the right to be caught in. For six years they passed the titles back and forth. And then it was time for the Americans again—Helen Wills, who won admiration but never adulation, and Vines.

Then came the last hope of Britain flashing across the court in the person of Fred Perry, who broke all Wimbledon hearts when he turned professional. After Perry came Budge and Riggs, and then the Australians with their two-handed shots. The war changed everything. Play was suspended. Some former Continental idols emerged as *Gauleiters* and others as underground heroes; pigs and chickens were raised on the hallowed grounds and bombs fell on the Center Court stands. What comes next is the modern era—the assembly-line tennis products of Australia and America fighting it out for the war dominance, and a refugee, a former Czech ball boy named Jaroslav Drobny, battling his way to the 1954 championship with possibly the most tigerish determination ever seen on these courts.

Comparative greatness of tennis play—like memories of pain and pleasure —is interesting but futile to reconsider. There have been great players at Wimbledon during all its periods, and some of the great ones never gained the title. If you can remove emotion from your thoughts of Wimbledon tennis (and you cannot be a real tennis fan if you can do so), you will undoubtedly decide that the champions of the last twenty years were, by and large, better players (though never greater personalities) than those of former days. Kramer, Sedgman, Vines, Budge and Perry would undoubtedly beat the Renshaws, the Wildings and the Lacostes. Alice Marble, Pauline Betz and Maureen Connolly might well beat Helen Wills and Lottie Dod at their best, though perhaps not Lenglen. But these are pronouncements that could well be argued over endlessly.

What are the greatest moments of Wimbledon history? This, too, is mighty debatable. The place is so full of richness, the years so marked by poignant drama and high-spirited gaiety, your emotions are tugged in so many directions—by national pride and technical prejudice—that it is almost impossible to cull this match, that event, a single stroke of the racket or the mere landing of a ball inside or outside a chalked line, as being more important, more fateful.

There was, for example, Reggie Doherty's last singles match, in 1901. He had won the title four years running, but on doctor's advice had decided not to defend it that year, figuring his brother Laurie, "Little Do," would win the All-Comers Tournament. But Laurie was unexpectedly put out in the third round, and the final (with the right to challenge the cupholder) was won by a comparative outsider, A. W. Gore. Whereupon Reggie dragged himself out onto the Center Court for the challenge match. He managed to win the first set from Gore and led 5–2 in the second. Then he began to weaken; the crisp assurance of his shots melted; and, with the crowd looking on in well-controlled horror, the first great king of the game was humbled. He never played singles again.

There was the emergence of the great new champions: Ellsworth Vines, aged twenty-one, breezing through to the 1932 championships without the loss of a single set, with his magnificent final serve against Bunny Austin making "two clear taps . . . like a double knock on a door"; Suzanne Lenglen, in 1919, playing her first time on grass and drawing the Center Court crowds off into the outside courts, where she gave only six games to her opponents in the first four rounds while on her way to the first of her six Wimbledon singles titles. There was the deadly tension of all the Center Court matches between the "Two Helens"—Wills and Jacobs, two totally different girls from the same neighborhood in Berkeley, California, who were trained by the same coach and who carried their much-publicized feud 6000 miles across the sea.

For their last match in 1938, Jacobs appeared on court with a bandaged ankle. After the second game, she gave a cry of pain, and everyone expected her to default, as Wills had done because of a similiar injury five years before, at Forest Hills. But she didn't—and Helen Wills bore down as relentlessly as ever, while the spectators suffered in sympathetic silence.

Other high moments of most finely etched drama were Tilden's semifinal defeat by Cochet in 1927, after the American had won the first two sets and held match point, with the score 5–1, in the third set. Anxious to end the match, he began to slam, instead of hitting with his previous paced precision, and met his downfall as the younger Cochet began to counterattack. There was Fred Perry running out twelve straight games against Jack Crawford, to bring England her first men's singles title in twenty-five years. There was the terrific letdown in the 1931 finals when Frank Shields limped onto the court on his sprained ankle, exchanged a single point of play with his elegantly hitting Davis Cup teammate, Sidney Wood, and then defaulted, making Wood, at nineteen, the youngest all-time men's singles titleholder. Perhaps most poignant of all was the day in 1926 when Suzanne Lenglen refused (out of pique and misunderstanding) to play before Queen Mary and never, consequently, appeared on court at Wimbledon again.

Then there were the lighter happenings: Borotra scrambling after a ball and landing in a pretty girl's lap; Don Budge brushing his hair at the very moment the Queen entered the Royal Box—and being accused afterward of having "waved at the Queen"; Randolph Lycett, an Australian, fortifying himself first with gin, then with a whole bottle of champagne during a sixty-four-game quarter-final match against Zenzo Shimizu in 1921, on one of the hottest days of Wimbledon memory. Toward the end, between swigs and shots, he took to resting on the turf for whole minutes at a time, while his opponent looked on in inscrutable tolerance. Also: Dorothy Round's slip falling . . . Wood and Shields, still schoolboys, getting into the Royal Tent and eating the Queen's strawberries-and-cream . . . *Papa* Lenglen tossing cubes of brandy-doused sugar to his daughter during a match. All these are rich, still-savored items of Wimbledon lore.

Many Old Wimbledon Hands fear the place is changing—and for the worse. Part of this, of course, is mere intellectual snobbery—purists decrying some technical change in the play.

In 1933, for example, *The Times* carried a letter protesting against "the preposterous rule which allows two services to the server." It was signed "Sexagenarian." In 1943 the same letter appeared, probably written in the middle of an air raid, this time signed "Septuagenarian." And in 1953 it appeared again—signed "Octogenarian."

Another part is social snobbery—more and more "ordinary" people are getting into the Club grounds. Mostly, though, the Old Hands fear the ever-mounting bigness of Wimbledon. Truly, this is no longer the simple unembellished garden-party Wimbledon of Worple Road days. But Wimbledon, deep down, is basically unchanged.

You know this surely on the day of the Gentlemen's Singles Final, that moment when the drama and timelessness of Wimbledon are at their highest and the pomp and pageantry at their most untarnished. It doesn't matter much who the finalists are. They may be Tilden and Shimizu, Budge and Bunny Austin, Perry and Jack Crawford, or last year's pair, little Ken Rosewall of Australia and the ex-Czech Drobny. The moment comes, and it is a solemn one. A platoon of officials parades out and disperses itself at the proper lines and perches, with all the solemnity of the Queen's ministers at a meeting of state. The two players appear and warm up, and then a terrible, deadly silence falls over the arena—and play begins.

Last year everyone was lucky. Both men were at the top of their games— Rosewall, with the best return of service in tennis today, with the delicate, discerning touch of a Cochet or a Riggs, with the ability to thread the ball back through the narrowest of openings; Drobny, older and heavier, mixing left-handed spin with wonderful length and angles, showing a determination thick enough to cut with a knife. The match lasted 158 spectacular soul-satisfying minutes. It went to fifty-eight games, while the crowd's emotions ran like a live thing over the court, settling one moment on young Rosewall, a representative of the Commonwealth, the next on the homeless Czech. The last serve was a soft one to Rosewall's backhand, sharply angled—and he netted it. Drobny threw his racket into the air and the stadium exploded with cheers. It had happened again—the drama, the clash of personalities, the history. Some Old Hands said it was the best-played final of all time.

The day after the last final, I visited Wimbledon again. It was terribly quiet after the exertions of the previous two weeks, and a soft green serenity hung overhead. There were no guards at the gates, no waiting taxis, no beady-eyed scalpers with hot tickets in their hands. Inside the clubhouse, no reporters. It was the day after the party and Wimbledon was itself again, wearing its hallowed look of utter devotion to pure tennis, to the gentle-man's game and clean living. It was here I realized Wimbledon has nothing to fear from the future, from changes. Not even when Colonel Macaulay told me about the Russians.

"Four Russians came around to see me earlier this year," he said. "They were here for some kind of table-tennis tournament. They wanted to see everything and they asked a lot of questions about grass courts. They don't have lawn tennis in Russia, you know. I showed them all around. I gave them tea and that sort of thing, and some grass seed. They were very pleasant chaps, with a good sense of humor. So I pulled their leg a bit. 'Why not enter a Russian team next year?' I asked.

"They started gabbling among themselves and then their spokesman said, quite seriously, 'We'd like to, but we're afraid we couldn't win.'

"I think it would be really fine if those people could be pulled into Wimbledon. It would help cultural relations, and they might learn something about our attitude toward sports. They might learn what it's all about."

NINE DECADES OF SPLENDOR

by C. M. Jones

Croquet evolved from Paille-Maille, a game played in Languedoc, France, during the 13th century, and by 1850 was one of England's most popular outdoor sports.

Its connection with the highly successful Open Wimbledon Championships, staged from June 24 to July 6, 1968, dates from 1870, the year in which the All-England Croquet Club was formed at Wimbledon. This followed the first All-England Croquet Championships at Moreton-in-the-Marsh in 1867.

This is a game which demands extremely true turf, and it was while admiring the magnificent velvety square at Worple Road, Wimbledon, that three otherwise sober-minded gentlemen decided it would make an ideal surface for the lusty new game, "Sphairistike," which was then sweeping England.

So the lively three began agitating for the right to invade those sacred lawns and to stage the first Lawn Tennis Championships (Sphairistike was too clumsy a name and it soon gave way to the one by which the game is known today).

They were very persuasive, and so the honor of promoting the first "Wimbledon" was entrusted to four gentlemen, all of whom deserve the gratitude of lawn tennis players the world over. Three of them—Julian Marshall, an eminent authority on royal (or court) tennis; Henry Jones, widely known as the expert "Cavendish"; and C. G. Heathcote, a fine player himself and the stipendary magistrate at Brighton—formed the subcommittee which set up a pattern followed ever since in studying the rules then prevailing, deciding they were impossible, and so drawing up a completely new set. They brought order out of chaos, just as the present committee is convinced that its world demand for tennis honesty, backed and propagated by the Lawn Tennis Association, is the only answer to the chaos and dishonesty which prevail in world tennis today.

The fourth member of the committee was J. H. Walsh, editor of *The Field* magazine, in whose offices at 346, The Strand, London, W.C.2, the All-England Club had been founded. It was Walsh who introduced lawn tennis into the program and who, with B. C. Evelegh as seconder, carried the motion to hold a championship meeting. *The Field* presented a silver challenge cup of a value of 25 guineas, which was subsequently won outright by the late William Renshaw.

Until 1877, there were almost as many sets of rules as there were tennis courts, although the primary set in use had been drawn up by the Marylebone Cricket Club's Tennis Committee in 1875 and was the subject of much controversy.

Messrs. Heathcote, Jones and Marshall decided they would have none of this and so they framed virtually a new set of conditions and rules. History has fully justified them.

Three of the main principles laid down have stood the test of time and are still basic foundations on which the game is built, a splendid testimony to the foresight and wisdom of the revolutionary three men. These principles are: (1) a rectangular court 26 yards long by 9 yards wide, the net being suspended from posts 3 feet outside the court; (2) the adoption of tennis scoring in its entirety; and (3) the allowance of one service fault without penalty, whether the ball dropped in the net or beyond the confines of the service court itself.

The original notice to the outside world that the championship meeting was being staged was given in *The Field* of June 9, 1877. Over the signature of Henry Jones, honorary secretary of the Lawn Tennis Subcommittee, it read: "The All-England Croquet and Lawn Tennis Club, Wimbledon, propose to hold a lawn tennis meeting, open to all amateurs, on Monday July 9 and following days. Entrance fee, one pound, one shilling. Two prizes will be given—one gold champion prize to the winner, one silver to the second player."

Of the 22 players who entered, the majority were more or less familiar with tennis scoring, a circumstance which Heathcote declared fortunate for the legislators.

The winner and first champion, S. W. Gore, an old Harrovian and eminent rackets player, was naturally adept at all ball games. He possessed great mobility, a long reach and strong, flexible wrist which he used to great effect on the volley.

It must be remembered that, with the net much higher at the sides (five feet) than it is in 1968 (three feet six inches), the down-the-line pass was impossible and covering the net, therefore, much easier than today. So C. G. Heathcote, whom Gore beat in the final, later wrote: "Gore was the first to realize, as the first and great principle of lawn tennis, the necessity of forcing his opponent to the back line, when he would approach the net and, by a dextrous turn of the wrist, return the ball at considerable speed, now in the forehand, now in the backhand court, till, to borrow the expression of one of his opponents of the year, his antagonist was ready to drop." So was born the net rusher!

If volleying was decisive from the start, service was not. All entrants to the first championship used the side service used in rackets, and it was not until the following year that A. T. Myers introduced the overarm service to lawn tennis. Nevertheless, there were a fair number of aces, not because of speed but because the court, for all its smooth appearance, was terribly rough compared with the "tennis only" carefully coddled Center Court of the new (1922) Wimbledon.

Of the 601 games contested in the 70 sets played at that historic first Wimbledon, 376 went with service, 225 against. The players changed ends only at the end of the set, which had a "sudden death" after 5–all, the winner of the next game taking it. About 200 people paid one shilling each to watch the play, and the championship was adjourned during the Eton-Harrow cricket match, a great social occasion in those far-off days.

The history of tennis, like the history of war, has shown that methods of attack are, sooner or later, countered by new systems of defense. P. F. Hadow, another old Harrovian, on leave from tea planting in Ceylon, produced the answer to Gore's net attacks the following year in 1878. (These were made from so close to the net that he frequently volleyed the ball before it had reached his side. This caused a long stoppage the first time it happened. His shot was judged fair, but the rule was amended to the present one in 1880.)

Gore's closeness to the net, then four feet nine inches high at the posts, gave Hadow, a patient baseliner, the clue to success—a series of lobs hoisted over Gore as he rushed netwards. So Hadow won the Challenge Round, abolished in 1922, 7–5, 6–1, 9–7.

Earlier, L. Erskine and C. G. Hamilton played out before 700 spectators the first five-set match at Wimbledon, Erskine winning after saving two match points.

Wimbledon was now firmly launched, although interest ebbed and flowed over the next decade or so. The year 1881 produced one record which has stood ever since—the shortest men's singles final, or Challenge Round, as it was then called. Willie Renshaw took only 37 minutes to beat the Reverend J. T. Hartley. Willie Renshaw won the singles seven times in all, another record among men, although Helen Wills Moody Roark won the women's singles a total of eight times.

The great Charlotte ("Lottie") Dod made her appearance in 1887 and, although only 15 years old, she beat the holder, Blanche Bingley, in the final with the loss of only two games. This is a record which may see out the 20th century, for current ILTF rules forbid entry below the age of 16.

The first overseas winner of Wimbledon did not travel far, W. J. Hamilton crossing the Irish Channel in 1890 to beat Willie Renshaw in the last Challenge Round ever played by that illustrious stylist. One year later William Baddeley, 19, became the youngest ever winner of the men's singles.

The first "Center Court full" notices were posted in 1894, and royalty, in the person of Crown Princess Stephanie of Austria, made its first visit in 1895. The arrival of Dwight Davis and Holcombe Ward, winners of the inaugural Davis Cup championship for the U. S. in 1900, converted Wimbledon from 1901 onwards into a major international sporting event. The Slazenger ball was used for the first time and has remained the Wimbledon ball ever since. Six years later, in 1907, all titles went overseas and, in 1909, A. W. Gore became, at 41 years 7 months, the oldest man ever to win the singles.

By now, 32 years had elapsed since the inception of the championships, but already the Wimbledon legends were fast collecting. Yet it was in 1910 that the greatest to that date arose—Anthony F. Wilding of New Zealand. Nicknamed "Little Hercules" at the age of two, his clean living, persistent training and assiduous practice to eliminate weaknesses later won him hosts of friends, admirers and a wonderful reputation wherever he traveled.

Tony Wilding began with a weak backhand . . . but he knew it. So, while at Cambridge, he badgered the local authorities to let him improvise a covered court in the Corn Exchange, and there he and his friends practiced long hours after they had cleared away the remnants of the vegetable market before each session. Truly, where there is a will there is a way!

The International Lawn Tennis Federation was born in 1913, and in gratitude to England for the part she had played, the ILTF awarded to Wimbledon "in perpetuity" the championships of the world on grass, an honor which Wimbledon viewed with some misgivings and abandoned ten years later.

This year also brought to Wimbledon the "California Comet" Maurice E. McLoughlin as well as the ticket "scalpers" who asked and received 10 pounds each for Center Court tickets to view the McLoughlin-Wilding Challenge Round, won by Wilding, 8–6, 6–3, 10–8. (Scalpers got about $40 a ticket in 1968.)

Gathering war clouds did not discourage the organizers, and for the 1914 meeting the main stand was extended to accommodate a further 1,200 spectators. Norman Brookes of Australia beat Wilding in the Challenge Round, and less than one month later World War I closed the championships' gates for five terrible years. Thanks to the efforts of H. Wilson-Fox, president from 1915 to 1921, the club was kept going and it fortunately proved possible to resume the event in 1919.

DEPARTMENT OF FOREIGN AFFAIRS

by John Kieran

As originally planned, this was to have been, in part at least, home news from abroad, but the Davis Cup challenge round starting at Wimbledon today is now entirely in the realm of foreign affairs. United States citizens can go quietly about their business while Great Britain and Australia settle the matter of the lease of the Davis Cup for the coming tennis year.

Just in case it has been forgotten in the confusion, it might be mentioned again that the United States team was subdued many weeks ago on home territory by some touring Australians, the very fellows who will be bobbing up at Wimbledon this afternoon. Or this morning, rather, because afternoon in Wimbledon is morning here, within reasonable limits.

For the benefit of strangers the All-England Lawn Tennis and Croquet Club gives such explicit directions on how to get to the scene of the challenge round that it's odd how our Davis Cup squad missed the way. But this is an odd year in sports all around.

Those who tool out to Wimbledon in their motors or pop into the Underground and detrain at the Church Road station hard by the All-England Lawn Tennis and Croquet Club will receive formal notice of what's what at this party when they purchase their programs. At least part of it goes like this:

PATRON
His Majesty The King.
PRESIDENT
His Royal Highness The Duke of Kent, K. G.
VICE PRESIDENTS
The Rt. Hon. The Viscount D'Abernon, P. C., G. C. B., G. C. M. G.
The Rt. Hon. Lord Desborough, K. G., G. C. V. O.
The Rt. Hon. Sir Samuel Hoare, Bart., G. C. S. I., G. B. E., C. M. G., M. P.

Away down yonder in a corner under the heading "Tournament Executive" will be the name of D. R. Larcombe, Secretary & Manager, who is the gent who really runs the show, and if anybody within reach of him referred to him as a "gent," Major Larcombe would freeze him with an icy glance and have the bounder chucked halfway back to Charing Cross. They may have "His Majesty The King" in large letters on the front page of the program but the imperial and imperious ruler of Wimbledon is Major Larcombe. "His Majesty The King" often has talked affably with newspaper men, but Major Larcombe, by his own proud claim, never speaks to the press. One listener to this statement said that the glare that went with it was the equivalent of a further qualification, "particularly the American press." Considering that the Australians are related by the bonds of empire, he might relent a little in this Davis Cup party and talk to the Australian press through an interpreter.

This is what it would have cost some of our citizens if Allison, Budge & Co. happened to be playing and patriotic tourists from this side of the water went to the show:

All games on the famous center court. Two singles matches today, a doubles match on Monday, two singles matches on Tuesday. Three-day tickets, first eight rows of the covered stand, 2 pounds 2 shillings each, or roughly $10.50. Three-day tickets, next four rows of the covered stand, 1 pound 10, which would be about $7.50. Further back about $5.50 and the last two rows in the covered stand, $3.75.

The prices in the uncovered stand, for three-day tickets, $7.50 on the shady side and $5.50 where the spectators have to take the chance of having the sun in their eyes at the wrong time.

Further information is gladly supplied and the hopeful citizen who feels that our squad may get to Wimbledon next year may file this away for reference.

Gates open at 12:30 P.M. daily. Luncheons, table d'hôte at "four and six"—call it $1.15—or à la carte. Tea, "one and six," not quite 40 cents and well worth it. One lump or two? Car parking for the three days on the club ground, $2.50. It's cheaper to go on a bicycle.

There is generally an overflow crowd for the big Wimbledon tennis shows, the standing-room price being about 75 cents on each day of play "but not bookable in advance."

There has been frequent criticism of the turf at Forest Hills by the players, foreign and domestic, in our national singles championship. At a distance a puzzled observer can only suppose that the players have been running afoul of sunken rocks at Wimbledon this year. Either that or there are bones in the climate along Church Road.

Allison came up with a limp. Von Cramm twisted himself out of shape in his first serve against Fred Perry in the All-England final. Adrian Quist rumpled an ankle on the center court turf and Vivian McGrath (pronounced McGraw) had to take his place against Henkel in the Davis Cup Inter-Zone final. Henkel himself damaged a foot and defaulted to Jack Crawford in one of the singles matches.

There were other casualties among players of lesser note and, while nobody bothers about them, it is enough to show that playing tennis at Wimbledon this year is a dangerous pastime. But with the Davis Cup at stake, the nominees for Great Britain and Australia will grit their teeth and take a chance.

MORE THAN A TENNIS TOURNAMENT

by Lance Tingay

If legend be correct, Miss Maureen Connolly, the lawn tennis prodigy from California, is competing in the championships at Wimbledon because 75 years ago the pony roller at the All-England Club was in grievous need of repair.

Most British institutions had obscure beginnings and contained the seeds of their own growth. Lawn tennis came to the All-England Croquet Club as an afterthought, an innovation due to an empty treasury.

It is reputed—the actual figures are no longer extant—that the first Wimbledon Championship of 1877 made a profit of £10. Thus encouraged, with the roller again in good order and the croquet hoops glistening in fresh paint, the committee decided to keep on a good thing.

And a very good thing it has proved. Not only the Wimbledon Championships, with their worldwide interest and an aggregate attendance of over a quarter of a million, but the game of lawn tennis grew from that opening meeting in July three-quarters of a century ago.

In that first year, 1877, play was suspended for the duration of the Eton and Harrow cricket match at Lord's, and the winner, Spencer W. Gore, served underhand because neither he nor the 21 other competitors had thought of doing otherwise.

Lawn tennis owes much to the first championship committee. Thanks to Julian Marshall, Henry Jones, C. G. Heathcote and J. H. Walsh, the game took the right road, avoiding the pitfalls of extravagance as a new-fangled stunt. The rules they adopted have remained the bedrock of the game. They decreed the size and shape of the court, that one service fault should be permitted and that scoring should follow the venerable practice of royal tennis.

The pressure of finance has always remained. Were it not for Wimbledon the present administration of the British game could hardly continue. It is no longer a matter of a few pounds to repair a damaged roller, but of thousands to run coaching schemes, to send teams abroad, to make loans to clubs.

From Wimbledon the Lawn Tennis Association—a body younger than the All-England Club—received £22,294 in 1950, £26,022 in 1949. Its estimated share of the 1951 profits was £29,000. No doubt the Club, with heavy commitments to debenture holders who financed the building of the present ground, opened in 1922, received as much.

Championship meetings of Victorian days had the air of a garden party. Modern Wimbledon, progressive in that it looks to the future, but with an eye cast back always on its traditions, has never lost the atmosphere. More perhaps than some of the players the institution has retained an amateur spirit.

126

In the course of years Wimbledon has become something more than a lawn tennis tournament, though as such, of course, it is the most important in the world. It has become an occasion, a part of British life, a social phenomenon that will doubtless puzzle the historian of the future.

Great lawn tennis is something rather more than a sport, a mere matching of physical skill. It is a clash of personality, a test of character, a trial of temperament and an art.

In the lonely space of the Center Court—and newcomers are always quick to testify how lonely it is to be out there watched by 17,000 people—a good deal more enters into the winning or losing of matches than the mere merits of a forehand or backhand drive, a lightning service or a smash.

That indefinable quality, personality, is of vast importance. Perhaps the greatest example was Suzanne Lenglen. There was a woman, unique as a player and, as she has been described, as ugly as a totem pole, but with electric, irresistible personality. Hollywood would have described her as super colossal and meant it. She filled Wimbledon and it has gone on being full ever since.

END OF THE FANCY-PANTS ERA

from United Press International

The emphasis will be on tennis and not on panties, Wimbledon tennis officials decreed today. They said that only "all white" panties would be accepted for women's wear in the future.

Disturbed by the many-colored panties of varying lengths, color and design that have attracted spectator attention, the officials warned the women to save their creativity for the playing field.

A statement issued by club officials, who annually conduct the All-England championships here, said, "It is now a condition of entry that all players will wear white, and this will be included in the prospectus for entry into all future Wimbledon championships."

Teddy Tinling, who designs most of the costumes for the international players, first expressed horror and then annoyance when informed of the decision. But he later admitted that he had anticipated the move several months ago and had held a summit meeting with his leading clients.

Tinling said that he had convinced the South African trio of Mrs. Sandra Reynolds Price, Renée Schuurman and Valerie Forbes to go "all white" next year.

"They agreed a little reluctantly," he said, "but only after I had pointed out the shocking pink worn by Brazil's Maria Bueno this year had annoyed a small section of the crowd, and as public entertainers it was their business to please all the customers."

When asked what new designs girls would wear next summer, Tinling said, "Wait and see, but I assure you it won't be drab."

So another Wimbledon era is at an end. This one started in 1949, when Gussie Moran of the United States sported briefs with white lace showing.

Another American favorite, Karol Fageros, went one better by appearing in a pair of 18-carat gold briefs that were later auctioned for $70. Then came Mrs. Laura Lou Jahn Kunnen, who displayed her love for the Southern states by stitching a Confederate flag to her pants.

Others appeared in leopard skin and mink trimmings, wigs, tabards, transparent dresses and paper outfits. Miss Bueno's "shocking pink" panties were worn under a "twist dress." Every time Maria swung, the crowd scowled, gasped, goggled or cheered.

Colonel John Legg, the Wimbledon referee, described these creations as "being quite inconsistent with the feminine dignity desired on the Center Court. They can make the crowd restless, and this in turn upsets the player. I prefer the smart dignity of the dresses of the thirties."

PIGS AT FAIR WIMBLEDON

by Allison Danzig

The shape of things to come in England, after the wail of the sirens has heralded the clearing of the skies of the emissaries of destruction for the last time, will see far-reaching changes, it is predicted, both in the physical outlook and the social order.

Buckingham Palace, St. Paul's and Westminster have been privileged to no more immunity than the East End slums to the undiscriminating missiles of death, and the high-born lady and the little blighter with the cockney accent sharing the densely packed bomb shelter not only know how the other half lives but have a consciousness of how interdependent the two halves are upon each other for the survival of the whole. Out of that consciousness is expected to emerge an Albion fairer, more united and indivisible, with a new common denominator arising from the approach of parallel lives to infinity.

Already there has come a portentous manifestation of this changing order: Wimbledon has been given over to the breeding of pigs.

Wimbledon, the holy of tennis holies, where the Queen sat in the royal box when the strawberries were in bloom; where the fashionables familiar at Ascot, Aintree, Hurlingham, Lord's and Epsom Downs gathered for the crowning event of the social season; where the finest players from the world over experienced a feeling of exaltation just to step out on the immaculate turf of the Center Court, groomed to fastidious perfection by a corps of expert groundsmen for eleven months in preparation for two weeks of play; where 90,000 applications for tickets were received in a single year and where hundreds stood in line all night for the privilege of buying standing room—the Wimbledon of all this swank, ivy and tradition is now a nursery for pigs.

That hallowed carpet of turf, subjected daily to miscroscopic scrutiny lest a single piece of crab grass rear its monstrous head to create a national shame during the fortnight of championship play, has now been commandeered for the duration to help keep England's meat basket full while submarines infest the waters over which formerly were brought the succulent porkers from Denmark. The All-England Lawn Tennis and Croquet Club, one of the best-managed and most efficient, as well as one of the most dignified, of all sports organizations, has forgotten about the huge profits realized annually from the British championships and joined step with the country's defense program.

Little pigs, on the way to market, are now rooting where a noble German, Baron Gottfried von Cramm, charmed with his courtly style of play and his faultless sportsmanship, until he fell into disfavor with his government; where a dashing Basque in a blue beret, Jean Borotra, was wont to descend from the skies just in time to make his flashing entry and his bow to the royal box.

That box now lies in ruins. So do the competitors' stands, and the priceless Center Court turf has known the fury of the bombing planes that now fill the empyrean whence Borotra glided down with his rackets in happier days, when Vichy had a different connotation.

Will there be another Wimbledon? Will the day come when Briton, Frenchman, German, Italian, Spaniard, Japanese, Chinese, American and the nationals of a dozen other nations will all gather in the camaraderie and good sportsmanship of a world's tennis championship? The answer emphatically is yes, so long as the Union Jack flies above No. 10 Downing Street.

Whether it is a scion of the House of Marlborough or a commoner—an inflexibly tough Churchill or an equally resolute Bevin—who sits at the head of the table there, tennis, cricket, Rugby, soccer, golf and rowing are too much in the blood of the Englishman to be given up.

The playing fields of Eton may have won Waterloo, but the spirit of Eton has no monopoly in the war that is being fought in the air, on land and in most of the seven seas, to make Waterloo, by comparison, seem like a sound of revelry by night and a cap-pistol report by day. England's little man, without benefit of public school, is showing the same ability to take it in the air, on sea and in the strafed areas of devastation that is the hallmark of his Etonian buddy.

The age of chivalry is not dead and the spirit of noblesse oblige, it has been demonstrated, permeates all who breathe the free air of Britain, be they knights of the R.A.F., Lords of the Admiralty or the sturdy seafaring skippers who helped to work the miracle of Dunkerque. That spirit is the essence of Wimbledon, beneath all the swank and side, and it is too deeply ingrained to be uprooted by pigs or a changing social order.

Will there be another Wimbledon? The answer is as inevitable as to the question: Is there a Santa Claus?

SOME OF MY OPPONENTS

by Helen Wills

The greatest player that I have met upon the court is Mlle. Suzanne Lenglen. One might well call her the "Great Player," because in all the tennis world, when one thinks of all players, both men and women, Mlle. Lenglen stands out as the most interesting. Her movements upon the court, her grace in action, her stroking, footwork, tactics and strategy, and her command of difficult situations in match play were all as nearly perfect as one could hope for. There is a general impression that, while Mlle. Lenglen was a player without flaw as regards her game, she was temperamental on the court. This idea was picked up and repeated whenever tennis was discussed. I do not know what Mlle. Lenglen's disposition was off the court, but I am certain that no player had greater control over his emotions than did Mlle. Lenglen when she was engaged in a match.

She had a wonderfully strong determination. She had confidence born of her absolute faith in her ability to make the shots that she wanted to make. Her greatest ability was her power of concentration, which seldom wavered from the game at hand. Proof of this was that she could make stroke after stroke without error and finish a match against a mediumly good player with perhaps five or six errors in the whole encounter. For a player of Mlle. Lenglen's ability it is often more difficult to concentrate against a medium-good player than against a very good player, because there is the certainty of a win without the interest of competition. But to Mlle. Lenglen every ball was worthy of complete attention—not the first ball or the last ball in a rally but every ball. This is concentration.

In playing against Mlle. Lenglen, which I did at Cannes in February 1926, I was much impressed with this side of her tennis. The score of the first set, as I remember it, was 6–3, or perhaps it was 6–4; and the second set, 8–6. She won because she was the better player. We had a beautiful court, a sunny day, a slightly restless audience, which became quieter as the match went on. I believe there were two bad calls in our match, but one was for her, one for me. There are almost always a few bad calls in a tournament match. It cannot be avoided. We both received large bouquets of flowers.

It may have been that I would have met Mlle. Lenglen in a match again in Paris in May—that is, if I had been fortunate enough to reach the finals and had not fallen victim to appendicitis, which came inopportunely in the middle of the tournament. . . .

Is it safe for a tennis player to pick out some one person who is the "best-looking opponent met on the court"? In my opinion, Mlle. Didi Vlasto is quite the prettiest and most lovely-looking opponent that I have ever played against. We played against each other in the finals of the Olympic singles. She is now married and lives in Athens and does not take part in as much tennis as formerly. She is Greek but was born in Marseilles, and it was because of this that she could represent France in the Olympic Games. She arrived on the day of the finals late for the match and very much perturbed because a gendarme would not let her car come in the gate intended for the players, and it had been necessary to make a long detour, which had taken more time than had been expected. The people in the grandstand had become restless, and it was somewhat of a handicap for Mlle. Vlasto to begin her match under such circumstances. Shortly after, however, everything quieted down.

On the court I found her an opponent of the greatest grace and with unusual ease in motion. Her balls came with great speed on her forehand—a drive for which she is quite famous. Her backhand was less severe but quite steady. She was an interesting opponent, as her game was varied and intelligent, and for anyone looking on she was a picture on the court, with her skin a lovely sunburned olive, her dark hair and eyes, and her beautifully chiseled face. With her perfectly proportioned figure, she might have been a wonderfully made statue of ancient Greece come to life. Yes, I am quite certain in saying that Mlle. Didi Vlasto is the loveliest-looking tennis player that I have ever played against.

Another extremely good-looking and well-known player is Señorita de Alvarez, who is Spanish in type, with dark hair and greenish-brown eyes, and with an olive complexion. She has remarkable grace in motion. Miss Eileen Bennett of England is also charming to look at. She is taller than the Spanish player and extremely graceful. Little Cilly Aussem of Germany is yet another type. She is quite small and more of a little girl in appearance, with round brown eyes and a cherub face. Her agility on the court and the distance that she covers in spite of her shortness are really astonishing.

These three players I have met at various times in matches. Each one has, of course, strokes that are quite characteristic of herself alone. Señorita de Alvarez has a long flashing drive, both forehand and backhand, which she takes almost every time on the half volley—that is, immediately after the ball has left the ground. This means that her game is an extremely rapid one, full of brilliant strokes. This method of taking the ball is one that is full of risk, as it is the most dangerous way of playing a ground stroke. Señorita de Alvarez's game is full of daring and hairbreadth shots. One expects it of her. She is, perhaps, the most dashing and interesting of the women players to watch in action.

Miss Eileen Bennett, who has been for the past few seasons among the very best of the English players, has a game that is not quite so severe as that of Señorita de Alvarez. Like the Spanish player, she conducts her matches mainly from the back court, now and then going to the net when an opening presents itself. Miss Bennett has a long, well-topped drive, which she varies intelligently as to placing and depth. Her backhand shot is capable of quite a sharp angle to the backhand of her opponent; her service is dependable and is a hard one to return.

For several years Miss Bennett has been playing doubles with Henri Cochet in the tournaments in the South of France and has learned to play an excellent doubles game. They won the championship honors in the mixed event in Paris both this year and last. . . . Miss Bennett and Miss Betty Nuthall are two of the younger English girl players who promise to be for many seasons at the top of women's tennis in England. Miss Bennett is the older of the two by several years and has the greater number of wins to her credit over the younger player, having won five times out of the last six encounters in very interesting matches.

Little Fraulein Aussem is, perhaps, one of the steadiest players in women's tennis. Her ability in retrieving balls astonishes both onlooker and opponent. Her balls have not the speed of Miss Bennett's or Miss Nuthall's, and yet she is a worthy opponent of any of these players. Were her strokes to increase in severity and her game to become as fast as it is steady, she would be a remarkable player indeed.

LENGLEN AT WIMBLEDON

by Duncan Macaulay

The real crowd-puller at the 1922 Wimbledon (and any other Wimbledon in which she played) was the incomparable Suzanne Lenglen. Even with the extra space at the new Wimbledon, there was always a queue waiting to watch her play. It was quite impossible to put her on an outside court. The crowd grew so large that they trampled down the hedge and encroached on the neighboring courts. But the bigger the crowd the more Suzanne enjoyed it. . . .

I had never seen Suzanne Lenglen play before this Wimbledon, and it struck me at once that here was someone with such control over the ball that she hardly made a mistake; and her anticipation was so good and her footwork so perfect that she practically never did. Her game and that of "Little Mo" Connolly, the champion of 1952–1954, had much in common, except that the latter did not volley so much. Suzanne was so accurate that she could really hit the lines. Of course she was using a much looser racket and softer balls than are used today, and this enabled her to keep contact with the ball longer. But I believe she could have adapted herself to the tighter rackets and balls of the present day. She must have been heartbreaking to play against: her opponents were kept continually on the stretch, running from one side of the court to the other, only to see at the end Suzanne pushing the final volley just where her opponent was not.

Before Suzanne was due to play her first match against Miss K. McKane on the Center Court I arrived at Southfields Station to find a queue stretching all the way to the entrance of the All-England Club. People used to call it the "Leng-len trail a-winding" after the famous war song of those days. She won easily.

In 1924 Mlle. Lenglen, then holder of the title five times, seemed all set for another easy success. She won her first three rounds without losing a single game. But she had suffered a severe attack of jaundice earlier in the year, and only her devotion to Wimbledon had her play at all. Miss Elizabeth Ryan's robust attack in the next round sapped her strength and lowered her resistance. This was the thirty-sixth time these two had met, and thirty-five times running Suzanne had won. Suzanne won the first set, 6–2, then lost a gruelling second set at 6–8 and had to pull out all her reserves, both physical and mental, to win the final set, 6–4. This victory in adversity was more creditable to Suzanne than many of her easier successes. It was the first set—except the one she had lost to Mrs. Mallory in America [in 1921]—that she had lost in singles since 1919. The crowd of course was in a state of frantic excitement: if anyone got a point against Lenglen it was an achievement—a game was an event, a set unbelievable.

But immediately after the match was over, the doctors said Suzanne must retire from the tournament. Miss McKane got a walkover and then in the final defeated the brilliant young American, Helen Wills, 4–6, 6–4, 6–4. They had met only a few days earlier on the Center Court in the Wightman Cup match, when Miss McKane had won easily with the loss of only four games. But Miss Wills, inscrutable in her white eyeshade, showed her greatness by entirely disregarding this result: having won the first set, she was four times within a point of a 5–1 lead in the second. Miss McKane, however, was one of the finest match players Britain has ever had. She just never gave up. She played for every point in every game, and every game in every set, and she won—the first British victory for eleven years. . . .

In the women's singles [in 1925] Suzanne Lenglen came back to reach the zenith of her fame. And what a record she achieved! In the five matches she played she lost only five games in all. She beat Miss Ryan, 6–2, 6–0; Miss Goldsmith, 6–1, 6–0; Mrs. Beamish, 6–0, 6–0; Miss McKane, the holder of the title, 6–0, 6–0; and finally Miss Fry, 6–2, 6–0. Such ascendancy has never been achieved by any player before or since. Despite the fact that she got no games at all, Leslie Godfree has told me that he had never seen his wife [then Miss McKane] play better. In the final, Mlle. Lenglen lost only twenty-one points and scarcely ever moved from the middle of the baseline throughout the match. Poor Miss Fry—but she had done very well to get there.

Flowers and flattery were showered upon Suzanne, and all the French dressmakers fell over one another to provide her with costumes. Needless to say, Mlle. Lenglen and Miss Ryan, perhaps the finest women doubles players of all time . . . won the ladies' doubles again, for the sixth time. . . . Mlle. Lenglen achieved the triple crown for the third time when she won the mixed with Jean Borotra. . . .

Nineteen twenty-six was Jubilee Year—the fiftieth anniversary of the first championship meeting—and the Committee of the Championships had set up a special Jubilee subcommittee to prepare all the arrangements. In view of the fact that all the championships were held by French players (except for Miss Ryan), it was decided that the nominated French players should be invited to become guests of the committee during their stay for the meeting at some convenient hotel, instead of any contribution to the French Lawn Tennis Association. . . .

The opening ceremony and the presentation of commemoration medals took place on the Center Court. . . . A military band from the Royal School of Music at Kneller Hall played selections from 12:30 onwards. At 2:40 P.M. all the competitors took up their positions at both ends of the court and then the ex-champions took up their positions on the east side.

Their Majesties, King George and Queen Mary, arrived at 3 P.M. and the presentation commenced. Strips of red carpet were laid out on the court and the medals were presented in the middle. As each champion stepped forward to receive his or her medal their name was announced by Commander Hillyard. . . .

An exhibition match was played in which Mrs. Godfree and Miss K. Bouman of Holland unexpectedly beat the great doubles combination of Mlle. Lenglen and Miss Ryan. This turned out to be the last time this greatest-ever women's doubles pair were to appear together on any court. Although they were the holders, the French Lawn Tennis Association had ordered Mlle. Lenglen to break her lifelong partnership with Miss Ryan and play instead with Mlle. Didi Vlasto. And to make the parting more bitter for Mlle. Lenglen, they were drawn against Miss Ryan and Miss [Mary K.] Browne in the very first round.

At the presentation of the medals, Suzanne Lenglen had been at almost the end of the long line of champions; but she received the greatest cheer of all from the crowd. Little did anyone think—certainly not Suzanne herself—that, within a week, she would have disappeared from Wimbledon and amateur lawn tennis altogether.

The dramatic withdrawal of Lenglen, her supposed slight to the Queen, and all the emotional gossip and hearsay which surrounded the whole affair have become part of lawn tennis history, which is very critical of the greatest woman champion of all time. Suzanne Lenglen was always extremely punctilious about her matches. Either Commander Hillyard or one of the French team would bring her to the referee's office before she left the ground each day to inform her when she would have to play the next day.

In this Jubilee year, however, Suzanne was obviously not in her usual form, as in her very first round single she lost five games to Miss Browne. The previous year she had lost only five games in the whole championships. Before she left the ground on the Tuesday, she understood that on Wednesday at about 4:30 she would have to play her vital doubles match with Mlle. Vlasto against Miss Ryan and Miss Browne. But as Commander Hillyard was no longer secretary of the club, he did not take her along to the referee's office personally as was his usual custom; and she did not go herself.

Suzanne had not been feeling very well and had booked an appointment with a doctor for treatment at twelve noon next day. However, later on the Tuesday evening, the referee, Mr. Burrow, had decided that it was necessary for Suzanne to play her second-round single against Mrs. Dewhurst at 2 P.M. He quite rightly did not consider this to be a very onerous match for Suzanne. The Palace and Marlborough House were told, and the King and Queen said that they would have an early lunch and come down in time to see Suzanne play.

About 11:30 on the Wednesday morning Mlle. Vlasto told Suzanne that she had seen in a newspaper that Suzanne was down to play a single at 2 P.M. Suzanne apparently tried to get through to Wimbledon but without success. She then rang Toto Brugnon and asked him to tell the referee as soon as possible that she was unable to play at 2 P.M. but would be down on the ground in good time for her double. The announcing of matches to be played each day in the daily press at that time was a rather haphazard affair, and Suzanne had never had to rely on it for her information.

Toto Brugnon went at once to the referee's office at Wimbledon and delivered this message. But it somehow never got to the referee himself, Mr. Burrow, because he makes it clear in his book that he was expecting Suzanne to play at 2 P.M. Of course, Suzanne should have made quite certain that Mr. Burrow had got her message and that he had in fact agreed to postpone her single.

At 3:30 P.M. Suzanne arrived at Wimbledon thinking that she had a clear hour in hand before her doubles match on the Center Court. She was at once summoned before the committee and severely reprimanded for her late appearance. Suzanne, always highly strung and in any case not quite herself, retired to the ladies' dressing room in a fit of wild hysterics.

Jean Borotra was deputized by the referee to try to persuade her to go on the court. Jean claims, though not with any pride, that he was probably the only man who had ever been admitted into the ladies' dressing room at Wimbledon. As a matter of fact he is not quite correct, as, after the Second World War, a blind masseur was engaged at the request of the American Wightman Cup stars. Anyway, poor Jean Borotra was soon reduced to hysterics himself and eventually had to return to the referee's office and say that Suzanne would not play at all that day.

In these days such a contretemps would probably not occur, because the order of play for each day, in detail, is widely advertised on the television and radio, as well as in all the newspapers. Added to this, there is an intricate organization of a fleet of cars for the competitors to bring them to and from the ground, and the secretary's transport official is in close touch with the referee all the time and can tell him exactly when each competitor arrives on the grounds.

The committee went into a huddle to decide whether Suzanne should be scratched. But after a long discussion it was decided that both her matches should be postponed until the next day and that, in accordance with her own wishes, her double should be played first. The doubles match was duly played on a rainy and not too pleasant afternoon and was won by Miss Ryan and Miss Browne, 3–6, 9–7, 6–2, after Mlle. Lenglen and Mlle. Didi Vlasto had twice been within a point of winning it. Suzanne's single against Mrs. Dewhurst had to be postponed until the Friday owing to rain. Mlle. Lenglen won it easily, 6–2, 6–2, but complained of feeling unwell.

On the Saturday she had only one match to play—a mixed double with Jean Borotra. The Center Court crowd gave Lenglen a cold and hostile reception—how fickle crowds can be! However, Jean Borotra saved the situation with a bit of inimitable clowning which soon had everyone laughing. They won, 6–3, 6–0. But Lenglen had been very severely criticized in the press and that, together with the fact that she was not physically or mentally at the top of her form, decided her, over the weekend, to scratch first from the singles and then from the tournament altogether. She had always lived a good deal on her nerves, and the strain of being at the top for so many years had begun to tell. Inevitably she became surrounded by a host of sycophants and self-appointed advisers, some of whom gave her very bad advice.

But it was a very great pity that this magnificent player, who had given so much pleasure to so many thousands of people—and indeed had done so much to popularize lawn tennis as a world game and to swell the finances of the All-England Club—should have taken leave of Wimbledon in such unfortunate circumstances. She never played amateur lawn tennis again. Shortly afterwards she signed a lucrative contract and turned professional. Twelve years later she was dead. The doctors put down her premature death to years of overstrain. . . .

I thought it would be interesting to ask one of our great British women champions, Mrs. L. A. (Biddy) Godfree, what she thought of some of the great players of this era. Biddy had played against Suzanne Lenglen and Helen Wills and many other well-known players of those days. She had also been an acute observer of the lawn tennis scene at Wimbledon right up to the present day and still plays regularly on the club courts herself. I therefore recorded her views and give them verbatim.

I first asked Biddy what it was like to play against Lenglen, and she replied:

"Well, I played her about ten times in all, and of all the people I have ever had to play she was undoubtedly the most difficult to win a point from, because she was so tremendously accurate and never gave anything away. She was a tremendously sporting player. I can never remember her trying to take a point she was not entitled to or glaring at a linesman or an umpire. She played completely fairly. I was a great fan and admirer of hers, and she was always very nice to me. But she spoke very little English and my French was bad, and so we never got very close to one another.

"Suzanne never slogged the ball hard, but she hit it with adequate pace and absolute control. Her service was well placed and had a nasty swerve which took you right out of court. Her footwork was wonderful, and she had almost uncanny anticipation so that she was always in the right position to take the ball as she wanted to take it, from anyplace on the court. Her game was perfectly rounded so that all the shots came alike to her. I think that as I played her more and watched her more over the years, I came a bit nearer to her standard, and therefore we had better games and longer rallies. Her extreme accuracy nearly always gave her the initiative, but she could run all night if she was made to.

"But I felt that, towards the end of her career, she might crack—because, after all, she had kept at the top for so many years and no one can go on indefinitely. It must have been a tremendous strain for her."

My next question was how she thought Suzanne compared with Helen Wills and other leading players of that time and of the present day.

"Oh, I am sure Suzanne Lenglen was the greatest of them all, and she also made a far greater impact on the game of lawn tennis than anyone else. She altered the whole aspect of women's tennis. Few women before her played the all-court game; but Suzanne volleyed like a man and continually played with the best men of her country in practice in doubles. She also entirely altered the style of women's dress, not with the idea of being sensational, but to gain greater mobility. And her lovely one-piece dresses, much shorter than any woman had ever worn before, looked very attractive.

"Alvarez, of course, was a lovely player with the most perfect shots, taken sometimes on the half volley. But she never had any stamina; that was her weakness—she got tired. And she could not really be as serious and concentrate on the game as some of her rivals. But I think she was one of the most fascinating people to watch I have ever seen.

"Suzanne was a very different type of player from Helen Wills, who preferred to play entirely from the back of the court. But I feel sure that Suzanne at her best was the greatest of them all. There is only one other player I am not sure about and that is Alice Marble, who won the triple crown at Wimbledon in 1939 but never had an opportunity of appearing again owing to the war. Otherwise she might have gone on winning Wimbledon for years. And I thought Bobbie Heine of South Africa had the makings of a very fine player, but she was, I think, upset by an airplane accident on one occasion and was never quite so good afterwards."

What about the modern champions? I asked her.

"I think Maria Bueno, the two years she won the championship, was terrific and most fascinating to watch. But she did not last like Suzanne and Helen Wills, although I realize that may be due to her illness. And, of course, Maureen Connolly was marvelous and hit the ball as hard or harder than anyone else. But her game was much more limited and she hardly volleyed at all. She was no good as a doubles player, whereas Suzanne was brilliant. One must remember, of course, that rackets and balls are both tighter now than in my day, and that makes for harder hitting and more speed—but I feel sure Suzanne could have adapted her game to modern conditions."

It is interesting to compare here some of the opinions expressed by Helen Wills Moody, whom most people would rank as No. 2 to Suzanne Lenglen in a list of the all-time great. Helen gave her views in her book, which was published in 1937: she considers that concentration is the keynote to success at lawn tennis and that this is a matter of "disciplining one's mind to shut out conflicting thoughts and impressions." She does not agree that some players are by nature better able to concentrate than others: she considers that the best concentrators she met in women's tennis were Mlle. Lenglen and Mrs. Mallory. Among the men, she considers that René Lacoste stood out as "being the possessor of almost unbelievable powers of concentration."

Helen Wills was of the opinion that severity of ground stroke is the key to success in the world's ladies' class, rather than the all-court game, although she agrees that every player must work out her own type of game. Her views would certainly seem to be borne out by the success of Maureen Connolly, whose game so much resembled that of Helen Wills Moody and whose actual achievements might have been just as great had she been able to continue with her lawn tennis career.

Helen Wills Moody considered that the farther anyone went up the lawn tennis ladder the simpler the game became in its fundamentals: there is no game like the direct attack, and fancy strokes and excess of spin do not bring the results which a fast driving game does. In this opinion, too, she agrees with so many of the great champions.

THE BATTLE OF THE CENTURY

by Allison Danzig

Everything was the same, except that a few eucalyptus and mimosa trees were missing, as on the day of one of the fabulous matches of tennis history. Except, too, that now you were there, thirty-four years after Suzanne Lenglen and Helen Wills, greatest of all women players, met for the only time.

The fans paid fifty francs ($12.50) then and perched in trees and jammed the surrounding hotel and housetops to see La Belle Suzanne defeat Little Miss Poker Face, 6–3, 8–6, in 1926. It was the tennis battle of the century in sports' golden age.

It was at the Carlton Tennis Club that Suzanne and Helen played, and a pilgrimage to the shrine was a "must" for the sojourner on the Riviera Côte d'Azur. Imagine his joy on arriving at the club, a few hundred meters from the turquoise blue Mediterranean, to find that Tom Burke still was the head professional and manager.

And imagine how the thin-faced Tom's faded blue eyes lighted and danced at the opportunity to relive the most exciting day of his career. Tom has countless friends of all ages who greet him at the courts, but this day he had hardly a word for them as he discoursed for more than an hour on the match that made Cannes the tennis capital of the world for a week.

Over and over the effort was made to get Burke to say who was the better player—Suzanne or Helen. Always he was off on a tangent.

"My brothers, Albert and Edmund, and I were good friends of Suzanne and her father and mother," he began. "My father came to France from Dublin in the nineties and was probably the first lawn tennis professional in this country. I was born in Cannes. I knew Suzanne as a girl. She would practice for hours daily. Her father would bring a box of balls and she would hit them at a handkerchief which he moved from one spot to another. In this way she developed her wonderful accuracy.

"Suzanne's game was built on control of the ball and placing it to open the court. She was a great one for catching you on the wrong foot. She was a back-court player. She was apprehensive about going to the net and rarely went up voluntarily to volley. She was not the powerful hitter that Helen was. Her forehand was made with a minimum of top spin. Her backhand was underhit.

"She had a gift for anticipating her opponent's shot and being in the right place. Her footwork was wonderful. She was quick and there was an elegance about the way she moved on her toes. She looked more like a dancer.

"Suzanne was like wine, bubbling. The day she played Helen she was nervous and she missed shots she never did ordinarily. The crowd was bigger than anything we've ever seen here and you never saw so much betting. Suzanne was a 3-to-1 favorite, but there were a lot of Americans to back Helen. Suzanne was distracted by the crowd and she insisted the camera men stop taking pictures. There was a dispute about the ball and Suzanne refused to play unless the one she liked was used.

"I sat next to Mme. Lenglen. She was accustomed to seeing Suzanne beat her opponents, 6–0. She got so excited over Helen winning so many games, she called to Suzanne, 'You shouldn't lose a game. You should win easily,' and she gave her brandy. I told her to calm down.

"Suzanne got more and more nervous in the second set. She had match ball in the tenth game. She hit a drive and the umpire was about to call 'game, set, match,' when a linesman said the ball was out. Suzanne never would speak to that linesman again. He was an English Lord.

"Helen won the game to make it 5–all and Suzanne became more and more worked up as the score went to 6–all. When she finally won at 8–6, she was on the verge of collapse. If she had lost the set she would have been finished."

Tom was finally inveigled into committing himself.

"If the match had been played in private," he said, "Lenglen would have proved definitely the superior player. She was too nervous to play her best tennis."

But Tom conceded that Helen in 1926 had not reached the full maturity of her powerful game, the most powerful two-sided driving attack women's tennis had known. He readily agreed, too, that on grass Helen's speed and pace of stroke would have been more effective than on the slow clay surface.

Suzanne and Helen never met again. Helen was stricken with appendicitis in Paris and was unable to play at Wimbledon. Suzanne fell into disfavor at Wimbledon for keeping Queen Mary waiting half an hour for her appearance on the court and later that year she turned professional. Helen won at Wimbledon eight times and the American crown seven times and ruled incontestably as the queen of the courts, as Suzanne had reigned from 1919 to 1926.

RIVIERA BACKGROUND

by John Tunis

Now to get a full understanding of the visit which Miss Helen Wills is paying to the French Riviera, you have to be behind the scenes a little and realize just how things work along this sunny stretch of sea coast between Toulon and San Remo. For the Riviera in general, and Nice in particular, is the bailiwick of the great and only Suzanne Lenglen. If she plays in a tennis tournament, that tournament is made.

I remember being in the office of W. G. Henley, the genial secretary of the La Festa Tennis Club at Monte Carlo, several years ago before their big international meeting. An elderly Englishwoman entered and asked Mr. Henley whether she could reserve three seats for the tournament.

"Certainly," said the secretary. "What day?" The old lady thought a minute.

"Aaah, errh, what day is Mademoiselle Lenglen playing?"

Henley looked over at me and smiled. He had been waiting for just that question. "I'm sorry," he said. "You know she's not been well this season and she isn't playing."

"Aaah." The old lady thought a minute. "Well, in that case I dare say I shan't want any." And out she went, only to return a minute later. "Errh, do you think Mademoiselle Lenglen will be ovah to watch the tennis at all this week?"

Ever willing to oblige, the genial secretary replied, "Surely, she has reserved seats for Sunday, the date of the finals."

"Oh, yes. Well, will you please give me three seats for that day."

Now in case you think this is an exaggeration, let me hasten to assure you that such scenes are not extraordinary on the Riviera, where Suzanne Lenglen is really a national figure. In a nation not passionately or notoriously addicted to sports, she rules supreme. Never beaten in her own country or in Europe, she has never been close to being beaten except for her meeting with Mrs. Mallory in America in 1921. The French football teams may go down to defeat, Carpentier takes a sock from Dempsey and remains inert, the French champions of tennis like Lacoste and Borotra are powerless before Tilden and Johnston; but Suzanne—Suzanne is still what she has been ever since the war, the queen of queens, the champion of champions.

Now naturally when a great player like Suzanne Lenglen appears on the court, everyone wants to see her. In fact a visit to the Riviera without seeing Suzanne play is like a visit to Rome without seeing St. Peter's. And obviously if she does not play, there will be a vast void of empty seats and a slim gate receipt. If she does play—well if she does play, that's something else again. I know for a fact that when she omitted the Monte Carlo meeting several years ago it cost the Société des Baines de Mer, who run the Casino and the tennis and the golf and the theater and the opera and everything else at Monte, exactly 40,000 francs. And even in its present depreciated state, 40,000 francs is a lot of money to lose in one week.

So that every club along the coast—and there is a different meeting each week from December until May—importunes Suzanne for her favors. And of course Suzanne reserves her favors for her home club at Nice. Not that she does not play occasionally in a mixed doubles at Cannes or Monte, but the singles she plays only at Nice, on her own courts, under surroundings she knows and likes best of all. This is her yearly program and this was her program for this winter, when suddenly without warning a thunderstorm broke with the advent of Miss Helen Wills. The whole Riviera at once stood on its toes at the thought of a meeting between the two.

Never has the Riviera been like this before, at least in the six winters that I have known it. Tennis and Suzanne, tennis and Helen Wills, that is the chief topic of conversation. People who until last week did not know whether tennis was a game or something to eat now discuss footwork and a difference in balls or climate with the greatest authority.

When Miss Wills landed in Paris, she was met by a delegation from the French Tennis Federation and an army corps of newspapermen, French and American. At Cannes she was met at the station by another army corps of newspapermen, supported by a number of press cameramen, all effectively marshaled by Charlie Aeschliman, the Swiss champion who married Miss Leslie Bancroft of Boston and who is a great friend of the American girl. At a short visit of half an hour at the Wills hotel the other day, no less than three reporters sent up their cards with requests for interviews. Every big press association has its man here, there are men from papers as far away as Norway and South America. All come to see a match which may have taken place before these lines see print, and which, on the other hand, may never take place at all.

Indeed, my good friend Sparrow Robertson of the Paris edition of the New York *Herald* asserts both in word and in writing that the match never will take place. He intimates and I imagine, though I have never talked to him about it, he believes that Suzanne is afraid. I think this is unfair. That Suzanne will play I am convinced; but she will play under the conditions that suit her best and with the balls she believes best suited to her game. However, she is the champion, she is the holder, she is the one who has everything to lose and nothing to gain by the match. Despite the fact that she should win, and win fairly comfortably, I really think she is nervous. I think she realizes that her reign, though not over yet, is ending.

For insofar as Miss Wills' chances of winning go, the Riviera has changed from their views before her arrival. At first the American girl was not considered worthy of real notice. Then she came and they observed her physique with interest. She played once, and people began to see that here was a real champion. She won her first tournament, and although her performance against indifferent players was far from startling, she showed a surprising ability to acclimatize herself to the strange conditions.

Then the crowd began to wonder. They watched that powerful drive of the Girl of the Golden West, and they became reflective. I sat next to Suzanne's mother at the finals of Helen's first tournament the other day, and that lady was strangely uncommunicative. I believe she saw a real rival for her daughter.

Meanwhile, the whole Riviera is on its toes, wondering whether Helen will beat Suzanne or Suzanne will beat Helen, and in the interim those in the know stand back, watch the whole proceeding, and, if they are at all cynically inclined, get a great big laugh. For it is a fact that if Tex Rickard had charge of this match, he could clean up at least $500,000. Of course, that would be professionalizing amateur tennis. But one wonders sometimes whether amateur tennis can be any more professionalized than it is at present. . . .

Picture the scene at Nice when the two finally clash—the sunswept court, the green hills beyond in the distance, the blue Mediterranean stretching out to the horizon. And around the court the socially elite of Europe, the King and the Crown Prince of Sweden, the ex-King Manuel of Portugal, the Duke of Connaught, the uncle of the King of England, the Duke of Westminster, who owns half of the city of London and is the richest peer in Great Britain, besides hundreds of other lesser nobility from all over the Continent.

LENGLEN AND WILLS

by Grantland Rice

The argument as to who is the greatest woman tennis player of all time stops definitely in the immediate vicinity of two people—Suzanne Lenglen, of France, and Helen Wills Moody, of California.

One might go back to the starring days of May Sutton and Mary K. Browne and from there move on up to Helen Jacobs, another California tennis queen, now ruling the United States. But the all-time answer would still be Suzanne Lenglen vs. Helen Wills.

And between these two, the larger section of the crown will have to go to the lady from France. She wins by her margin in one vital count—speed.

I first saw Mlle. Lenglen play in the French championship of 1921. Outside of Bill Tilden, she was about as good as most of the men playing in that field. And even as fine a woman player and as great a competitor as Molla Mallory was outclassed in the final test.

Mlle. Lenglen had flawless form, amazing skill and almost perfect control of every shot. She had no crushing power—but she had an abundance of speed.

Her one vital weakness was lack of any keen competitive spirit. She had to outclass an opponent to win, as even the thought of defeat sent her into the jitters more than once. In her case, the jitters meant prompt retirement, for that day, anyway.

Mlle. Lenglen was not to be set up as any female beauty, but she was beautiful as an athlete when the flaming color she wore began to move around—a red or orange lightness blown by the wind.

It was impossible to detect any form of effort in anything she did. Her grace was of the nonpareil type. As she had been trained since early childhood in the correct execution of every stroke, the combination was more than any woman could meet.

The tennis paths of Mlle. Lenglen and Mrs. Moody, at that time Helen Wills, crossed but once, at Cannes, where the French star won in two hard straight sets. Shortly after that meeting, in 1926, the French star heard the lyrical call of Charley Pyle and abandoned amateur ranks, leaving Helen Wills in full control of the amateur side.

Mrs. Moody at her best has had a combination of tennis qualities only slightly below that of her French rival for all-time honors.

In the first place, she has always had a far better competitive spirit—much better competitive courage under fire.

In the second place, she has carried greater power. But she was never quite able to reach the all-round skill or finesse of Lenglen, and she was never born with the foot speed that Sizzling Suzanne used around the court, where, like Tilden, she was always at perfect balance for the next stroke.

I have followed Helen Wills' tennis career since I first saw her as a kid of 15, wearing the famous pig-tails of her early days. It was apparent then that her only slip below tennis greatness for women would be in the matter of speed. Not that she was slow or lumbering. She wasn't. But she was distinctly away from the twinkling feet of the shifty Suzanne, who, at times, was an acrobat upon attack or defense.

Another reason for naming Suzanne Lenglen in front of the parade is this—every woman tennis player who happened to meet both always picked the French entry. And there was almost no sign of hesitation when this choice was made.

The fact that Mrs. Moody, after a two-year layoff demanded by a back injury, could still return to Wimbledon and win is proof enough that she is top today.

Strangely enough, both Suzanne Lenglen and Mrs. Moody figured in defaults that brought on a volley of adverse criticism at the time, but Mrs. Moody's long absence under a physician's care proved that she had a pretty good reason, despite the manner of its presentation.

A dramatic highlight in Suzanne Lenglen's career and in tennis history came in the women's national championships of 1921, when Miss Lenglen, facing certain defeat and asserting she was not able physically to continue the match, walked off the main court at Forest Hills, defaulting to Molla Mallory, who went on to win the crown.

Miss Jacobs has played fine tennis the last three years and Molla Mallory had one of the greatest of all tennis careers, but the two leaders remain where this article starts—and Lenglen is still the pick.

LENGLEN, WILLS, RYAN, MARBLE

by Bob Considine

Remember Elizabeth Ryan? She would have been the greatest woman's tennis player of all time—if there hadn't been a Suzanne Lenglen and a Helen Wills and an Alice Marble. She could never quite make the top, but she could beat everybody else. In all she won or was runner-up in 1,500 tournaments and won 19 Wimbledon titles alone during her 20 tough years of campaigning.

Well, she's a pro now and is out here coaching at the Royal Hawaiian Hotel courts. Holcombe Ward, the president of the U.S. Lawn Tennis Association, has put her in charge of what is called Junior Davis Cup and Junior Wightman Cup tennis—which is the partly underwritten training of promising players.

Elizabeth Ryan developed the chop stroke into a sharp, attacking weapon. With this savagely undercut shot, and a keen generalship and great stamina, she twice beat Helen Wills in the latter's prime and became the best women's doubles player who ever played. Her chop skidded like a goose on ice and, when socked right, was virtually unreturnable by man or woman. But Miss Ryan doesn't teach it to her pupils. She schools them in the standard topspin forehand and the flat-as-possible backhand. She calls these shots the meat and vegetables of tennis. And if they master them, she'll teach them that saber-tooth slice which developed more cricks in the back, among lady opponents, than the combined March winds since 1914.

She played them all, in her day. So we asked her who was the best among Suzanne, Wills and Marble.

"Suzanne, of course," she snapped, without hesitation. "She owned every kind of shot, plus a genius for knowing how and when to use them. I worked with her quite a bit around the start of the World War, when she was fourteen or fifteen. In fact I beat her in one of those early tournaments. But just after that she won the championship of France. And she never was beaten thereafter. You realize what that means? She just never lost. She walked off the court, after Molla Mallory won a set from her at Forest Hills, but she could have beaten Molla any other day by almost any score she chose.

"She never gave an opponent the same kind of shot to hit, twice in a row. She'd make you run miles. She wouldn't sock more than two shots a set . . . her game was all placement and deception, and steadiness. I had the best dropshot anybody ever had, but she could not only get up to it but was so fast that often she could score a placement off of it. She had a stride a foot and a half longer than any known woman who ever ran, but all those crazy leaps she used to take were done after she hit the ball. Sure, she was a poser . . . a ham, in the theatrical sense. She had been spoiled by tremendous adulation from the time she was a kid . . . all nose and bones. But she was the greatest woman player of them all. Never doubt that.

"Moody was all muscle . . . brute strength. She'd blow you off the court with her power, though Suzanne knew what to do about it when she beat Helen 6–3, 8–6 at Cannes in 1926. I don't think any tennis player ever got as many hard first serves in as Helen did. When we played doubles together I usually could count on her serving two aces or set-up returns per game. A lot of people think she couldn't run, but she could—back and forth across the baseline. Where she was slow was up and back. Her only weakness was that her game tended to break down if you could go out there and carry the fight to her.

"Marble? She's a nice courageous girl, with the kind of boys' type game I like to teach. But Moody's power would have cracked Alice's game. And Suzanne would have made her look very bad. Alice has the shots, but no craft. She hasn't got much to beat nowadays, either. But you've got to admire the way she tossed off that illness of hers. That takes guts. Yeah, guts, you heard me."

HELEN WILLS

by Allison Danzig

Six years ago this month a fifteen-year-old girl came out of the Far West heralded as one who would emerge as the outstanding woman tennis player of the United States. Her hair was worn in pigtails down her back, and she never appeared on the courts without a white visor to shield her from the sun. These were sufficient in themselves to set her apart at once from the crowd, and, of course, her youth also drew the spotlight upon her.

But it was not merely these outward attributes that set the stamp of distinction upon Helen Wills, nor was it the fact that she could hit the ball with surprising force. Her personality, the quiet dignity of her manner, and her unfailing poise and reserve were unusual in a girl of her years.

Today, at the age of twenty-one years and nine months, Helen Wills stands as the greatest amateur woman player of the world, and as the first American woman to triumph at Wimbledon in the twenty years since May Sutton Bundy, also a Californian, scored her second victory there in 1907. There are some who, in their unbounded enthusiasm over her annihilating performances in England, would bestow the mantle of Suzanne Lenglen upon Miss Wills as the greatest player of all time. But this is a moot question that cannot be answered unless Miss Wills turns professional and thus makes a meeting between the two possible. This she has declared she will not do. It is glory enough for the California girl that she has fought her way through one of the most formidable fields ever assembled at Wimbledon and had the whole tennis world at her feet, marveling at what one English tennis critic termed the "revolutionary power" of her hitting.

It is a long span from those days in July of 1921, when the fifteen-year-old girl ventured forth to storm the tennis citadels of the East, to that afternoon a fortnight ago when, before almost 20,000 spectators, that same girl defeated Señorita Elia de Alvarez of Spain in the final round at Wimbledon to establish her world supremacy.

In time it is merely six short years, hardly longer than it took William Tilden to develop from a third-rater into one of the country's best, but in the annals of achievement it is a period that encompasses some of the most thrilling moments the world of sport has known. Who of those who saw the match will ever forget that day in August of 1923 when the Berkeley girl hammered her way to victory over Mrs. Molla Mallory at Forest Hills to end the reign of the woman who had dominated American tennis almost continuously since 1915?

Who of those who hung eagerly on the cables for word from Europe can ever forget her match with Mlle. Lenglen at Cannes in February of 1926, one of the most celebrated and advertised sporting events of all time? And who of those who were touched a few months later by the news that Helen Wills was lying in a French hospital, stricken with appendicitis on the eve of a second meeting with her French rival of the courts, can recall a more poignant situation than the thought of this young girl, who had come to meet her rival on her own stamping ground, frustrated in her ambition by a stroke of fate?

The history of sports records few parallels to the comeback of Helen Wills from a sickbed to scale the greatest heights in tennis. Just a year ago she was a spectator at Wimbledon, still convalescing after her operation. Forced out of the international matches for the Wightman Cup and denied the chance to play again for the title which she had failed to win only by the narrowest margin to Mrs. Kathleen McKane Godfree in the final at Wimbledon in 1924, the American girl returned to this country, hopeful that she might at least be sufficiently mended in health by August to defend her national crown.

But after taking part in three tournaments and being defeated by Miss Elizabeth Ryan at Seabright and Mrs. Mallory at Rye, Miss Wills realized that she was still below her normal strength. Yet she insisted on playing in the championship, and it was only after she had been warned by her physician that she might injure her health permanently if she did not give up tournament play for the season that she finally capitulated.

And so the three-year reign of Helen Wills as American champion came to an end, and a broken-hearted girl, bereft of her title, turned her face toward the West, but vowing her determination to come back. There were some who shook their heads sadly after her, who thought that Helen Wills, in spite of her youth, had seen her greatest playing days and that in Kathleen McKane Godfree, Miss Ryan, and Señorita de Alvarez she would henceforth find opponents whom she could not subdue. But these skeptics reckoned without her spirit and her powers of concentration. The girl who had won the American title in 1923 despite the sting of her defeat by Miss Eleanor Goss only two weeks before, who in 1924 went on to win the Olympic championship in France immediately after twice losing to Mrs. Godfree in England, who had refused to be discouraged by her defeat by Miss Ryan on the eve of the 1925 championship, and who was plucky enough to cross the Atlantic to seek a meeting with the invincible Mlle. Lenglen—this girl was not one to surrender to circumstances.

For months Helen Wills prepared quietly for her comeback. Few words came from California of the work she was doing and of the schedule she was following in her training, and it was not until she arrived in New York early last May that it was learned that she had been practicing five times a week during the winter and early spring with the best men players in California. Even when she went out on the court at Forest Hills for a last practice preparatory to sailing, it was impossible to determine with any certainty whether she was as good a player as the Helen Wills of 1925.

Once Miss Wills reached England, however, and got back into tournament play, the world learned the truth quickly enough. She was better than ever, harder in her hitting, more active on her feet, and more resourceful in her ability to cope with an attack of changing pattern and also to shift the strategy of her own offense. When Miss Ryan was defeated at 6–2, 6–2 in the

North London championship, it was proof enough that the Berkeley girl had moved ahead. When, a week later, Mrs. Molla Mallory, who regained the American crown last year, was beaten at 6–0, 6–1 under a terrific cannonading of drives, it was evident that Helen Wills carried greater dynamite in her racket than ever before. That score was almost unbelievable. Not since 1922 in her match at Wimbledon with Mlle. Lenglen had Mrs. Mallory been so overwhelmingly beaten. And then Mrs. Godfree fell before her at 6–2, 6–4. The last skeptic was convinced, and Miss Wills became the favorite to win at Wimbledon.

English critics were agreed that no woman in the tournament could stand up against such murderous drives as Miss Wills commanded. Except for an unaccountably stiff match she had with Gwendolin Sterry in the first round, the Californian never was extended until she met Señorita de Alvarez, the dashing, daring shotmaker, in the final. The match was described as unexcelled in Wimbledon history for brilliancy of strokes and the high tactical skill of the players. It is not to be wondered that some of the English critics, after watching Miss Wills dispose of the brilliant Spanish girl in two sets, were ready to rate her as the equal of Mlle. Lenglen. . . .

There have been many episodes that reveal Helen Wills' poise. Two years ago when she walked out on the court at Forest Hills, unavoidably late for her doubles match, to be greeted by an outburst of "boos," her features furnished not the slightest indication of the dismay and shock that she must have experienced, though it was apparent in the raggedness of her play for a brief period at the outset. The ability to mask her feelings, to maintain an inscrutable countenance in the face of the vicissitudes of match play, was the characteristic that made the deepest impression upon tennis galleries on her first appearance in the East. "Little Miss Poker Face" she was nicknamed and, as incongruous as it was in association with a girl of her character, it struck home. This imperturbability is one of her biggest assets. It is disconcerting to an opponent to find that no matter how well she is playing she can never disturb the calm of Helen Wills.

In no game played with a ball is concentration a greater virtue than in tennis, and Miss Wills has the faculty of letting nothing distract her as she goes about the business of dispatching her adversary. So complete is her absorption in her play that everything else about her, including the gallery, is forgotten. A tennis court, to the Berkeley girl, is a place to do just one thing, and that is play tennis and play it to the end.

In her match with Mlle. Lenglen at Cannes, played under conditions that were almost intolerable—when first the notoriety growing out of the commercial aspects of the match and then the behavior of the crowds that stormed the gate must have taxed the nerves of the players to the utmost—Miss Wills showed in her play how impervious she can be to all distractions. Mlle. Lenglen, on the other hand, was plainly in distress. The unceasing chatter in the stands so aroused her wrath that she repeatedly ordered the spectators to remain silent, and finally, seeing that they paid no attention to her, she pleaded with them to "please keep quiet."

Perhaps there is no better way of conveying a picture of Helen Wills as she is on the court than to contrast her with the girl who, until she abandoned the amateur ranks, stood as her rival and who held sway at Wimbledon for six years. Temperamentally, they are completely the antithesis of each other. To Suzanne Lenglen, all the court's a stage, and she has played the leading role. The presence of the gallery is as strongly impressed upon her consciousness as is her opponent. Helen Wills could no more fit this role than she could fly. Quiet-spoken, totally undemonstrative, and unaffected by plaudits of the multitudes, she yields the stage to Mlle. Lenglen when it comes to pyrotechnics.

Power under control and ability to hit a ball harder than any other woman on the courts have been largely responsible for Miss Wills' rise. Mere power in itself would have been of little avail. It is the almost flawless control that she combines with this pace that has carried her to the heights. It took years of practice to acquire this control, years that began when, as a child, she was given a racket by her father, Dr. Clarence A. Wills, and launched on her career. Few women players have had the benefit of better coaching than she has had. Dr. Wills, finding the time had come when there was nothing further that he could teach his daughter on the courts, turned her over to "Pop" Fuller, the veteran coach who had trained many of the best players that have come out of California. Then, like Mlle. Lenglen, Miss Wills took to playing against men. Opposed to players of the caliber of William Johnston, she learned to time her shots against blistering pace and to increase the tempo of her attack. When she came East she was taken in hand by Mrs. Hazel Hotchkiss Wightman of Boston, who formerly lived on the Pacific Coast and who is generally classed as the greatest strategist women's tennis has produced in this country. After a season of association with Mrs. Wightman, Miss Wills knew considerably more about court generalship, but still there was much for her to learn; rather, she needed more experience in high-class competition before she could put into practice the things she had been taught to do.

Even when she dethroned Mrs. Mallory in 1923 her game was lacking in certain elements. Her sense of anticipation needed sharpening; her footwork suffered by comparison with that of Mlle. Lenglen and Kathleen McKane; the knack of changing pace was still beyond her; and, above all, she was yet powerless to deal with an attack of the subtlety and variety of Miss Ryan's, as she was to show in 1925 and 1926.

During the three years that Helen Wills held the American title she ruled almost entirely by virtue of her withering drives and her stout-heartedness, just as Mrs. Mallory had ruled before her. The California girl was a sound volleyer, one of the extremely few that this country has developed, but in the main her game was founded on that old theory that a strong offense is the best defense, and her forehand drive almost entirely constituted that offense. Her meeting with Mlle. Lenglen must have opened Miss Wills' eyes to the loopholes in her game, and when she fell a victim again to the drop shots of Miss Ryan, she knew that she had her work cut out for her when she went back home.

All through the winter and early spring Helen Wills labored to develop a stronger, more diversified, and better-rounded game, just as Dempsey, shorn of his title, has been seeking to build up the defense that he neglected in the days when he scoffed at the idea that he needed anything more than his sledgehammer fists. In Clarence Griffin, as crafty a tactician as California has produced, with his elusive chop strokes and spinning drop shots, she found an opponent qualified to show up the weaknesses in her game, and she asked him not to spare her feelings.

Five months of unceasing, conscientious practice with Griffin and other men on the Coast made a different player of Helen Wills, if the accounts of her play in England have not been exaggerated. Not only is she hitting now with "revolutionary power," but her footwork is immeasurably better, her backhand is a stronger attacking weapon, and drop shots have lost their subtlety against her. Her 6–2, 6–2 victory over Miss Ryan would seem to indicate that.

Helen Wills, as she takes her place on the tennis Olympus today, is a living example of what hard work, self-sacrifice, and zeal for self-improvement can do. Another player, on winning the national championship, might have complacently told herself that her work was done and that she could rest on her laurels. Helen Wills had the good sense to know better.

Last May, on the night that she sailed for England, she spent her last few moments at the Hotel Roosevelt putting the finishing touches on some sketches of Mrs. Mallory, Miss Ryan, and Mrs. Godfree. As she held up her board to ask judgment on the naturalness of the drawings, she had words of praise for each of the subjects. But when asked what she thought were her chances of defeating them, she evaded the issue with "Oh, they're all awfully good."

If Helen Wills felt in her heart at the time that she could defeat them, that answer was as near as she ever came to showing anything approaching vanity.

HELEN MOODY'S HOPE OF COMEBACK

by Paul Gallico

We stood on top of Telegraph Hill, the girl and the reporter, and looked out over one of the loveliest sights in all the world—the blue hills and blue waters of San Francisco Bay and the golden gate, Alcatraz the grim, lying like a steel stud on the ultra-marine surfaces, the black hulls and gay funnels of the Orient steamers tucked in their berths below.

Behind us the gray towers of San Francisco, to the left the Presidio and white flat buildings shining in the afternoon sun, buildings that somehow remind you of Havana of the Antilles. Across the bay, Berkeley gleamed dim and distant. A gray tramp steamer stole out from under a bluff, and moaned a wistful homecoming with its siren, a white plume of steam at the throat of the rusty stack. From behind us came the roar of the city. In the air was the smell of peat smoke and salt air and fish and spices and waterfront things.

The girl had gleaming light blue eyes, a straight nose and the pure Greek profile. She wore a simple black frock, with white lace at the neck and shoulders, a small close fitting black hat and a silver fox. She motioned toward the town and said: "See how all those buildings merge into a sort of a gray wash—no detail, but just the feeling of a great city."

May I present to you, Mrs. Helen Wills Moody at home. Now, if you are looking for a sensational story or inside information on what happened at Forest Hills last fall when the most famous woman tennis player in the world walked off the courts and left victory and the championship to her deadliest rival, Miss Helen Jacobs, we part company here, because this is just the story of two people who went sightseeing, who fell under the spell of San Francisco and who talked of things that interested them.

This much I can tell you: In all probability, and if it's humanly possible, you will see Helen Wills Moody on the No. 1 court at Forest Hills next August fighting for the championship which for so many years had been hers. Something is driving her on to it.

She spoke wistfully and with a faraway look in her eyes when she said: "I want to play in the nationals—very much—if I possibly can." Her expression changed. She left the rest unspoken. But I thought that her nostrils dilated a little and that she was scenting battle. Rest, until March, or until the pain leaves her spine; practice—and then a date at Forest Hills. For many reasons, or perhaps for no particular reason, it is hard to tell, she is a strange, introspective girl.

We lunched in the mural room of the St. Francis. She sipped sherry from a tiny thin-stemmed glass, one glass. She told how desperately she missed the exercise of tennis and the fun of playing it. She found that she had to have a substitute and so she swam—and loved it. There was a constant ache at the base of her spine. Only rest would help. Until that disappeared she was not to touch a racket. It was hard. She loved to play with her friends around Frisco and Berkeley. Did I know whether athletes who were injured ever went to osteopaths?

She hadn't given up her painting—had two canvases finished and was working on a third. With a spoon, she drew on the tablecloth a makeshift skeleton and showed me where the doctors said the trouble lies—but the doctors weren't sure. They said rest was the best doctor. I asked her to sign the tablecloth sketch and she laughed, showing even white teeth.

It had been a strange physical experience for her, she said, that adventure back East. "I'm not used to feeling tired, you know," she said. "I've never been tired. Playing with a drag took all the fun out of it. I love tennis. I miss it dreadfully now, I know if I start to play before this injury clears up, I'll just start it all over. But it is a terrible temptation."

After lunch we walked for a while and poked into curio shops and looked at ancient jades and silks and crystals. There were still two hours before my ship returned to Los Angeles. We stopped at the garage for her car and, with pride and excitement, Helen Wills Moody showed me the city she loves. We drove to the waterfront that smells of hemp and tar and tea and spices, where the great liners head west to the Orient, and passed the fish wharf where hundreds of little fishing boats are tied in orderly rows, where Eyetalians with gallant black mustaches fish gigantic gleaming pink crabs out of steaming caldrons on the sidewalks and sell them, hot and glistening; where the gray gulls perch bright-eyed on the roofs of the fish stalls and the parked cars. We laughed at the indignant look on a gull that was sitting on a car that was backing out and that refused to get off.

We climbed hills so steep that it seemed the car must drop over backward. We went to see Mrs. Moody's own little joke—the indoor tennis courts in the palace of fine arts, an enormous semicircular building, pillared and colonnaded in front, bare in back. The roof is of glass, the floor of asphalt. Mrs. Moody persuaded the city fathers it would be a perfect place for indoor tennis courts when the building was not in use for exhibitions. They put them in. They are the finest indoor courts in the world now.

We drove through the Presidio and saw ancient abandoned gun emplacements where the mortars once roared and we came out at a high point and saw far below at our feet the Pacific Ocean battering white froth at the black crags of the cliffs. On the way back to town we fell to talking again about people and newspapers, and I asked her whether the reams of publicity meant anything to her, whether she had been disturbed by the many columns of criticism of the past year. She said gravely and quietly, "I bear no grudges. Everyone is entitled to his opinion. I read only a few of the sports writers, those whose writing I like. I read Tunis and Danzig and Hawthorne and Rice, and some of the things that you write. Whatever is written, is written. I love peace more than anything."

We finished the drive, threading down through the once bold, bad Pacific Street, the Barbary Coast, past Spider Kelly's and the beautiful bas reliefs outside the wicked Thalia, then up to the top of Nob Hill, the old residential section, and back to the St. Francis. The most famous girl tennis player in the world waved good-bye. Something tells me the next time I see her will be in Forest Hills in August, and I wouldn't miss that one for millions.

MOLLA

by Allison Danzig

Mrs. Molla Bjurstedt Mallory came from Norway to establish herself among the most famous of the world's tennis players.

Seven times she won the championship of the United States on grass courts, the record, equaled by Mrs. Helen Wills Moody. In addition she carried off the national patriotic tournament of 1917, substituted for the

championship in this war year. As Molla Bjurstedt she won the championship
the first time she competed for it, in 1915. She repeated in 1916, 1918, 1920,
1921, and 1922 and came back in 1926, after yielding the crown to Helen
Wills in 1923, to score her seventh triumph.

Mrs. Mallory, who married Franklin I. Mallory, a New York stockbroker,
in 1919, was ranked in the first ten thirteen times from 1915 through 1928—
seven times at No. 1, twice at No. 2, three times at No. 3, and once at No. 4.
There was no ranking for 1917.

She won the national doubles with Miss Eleonora Sears in 1916 and 1917
and the national mixed doubles with Irving Wright in 1917 and with
William Tilden in 1922 and 1923. She was national indoor champion in
1915, 1916, 1918, 1921, and 1922.

Five times Mrs. Mallory played for the United States in the Wightman Cup
matches with Great Britain. She was a member of the inaugural team in 1923
and played in 1924, 1925, 1927, and 1928.

Mrs. Mallory never had the satisfaction of winning the All-England
championship at Wimbledon. Mlle. Suzanne Lenglen was ruling the courts
as the recognized greatest woman tennis player of all time after the First
World War, and the tournament was not held from 1915 to 1918. In 1922
she got to the title round at Wimbledon and lost to the celebrated Frenchwoman.

The year before that, 1921, Mrs. Mallory scored what was undoubtedly
the most cherished victory of her career. It was at the expense of Mlle.
Lenglen at the West Side Tennis Club in Forest Hills, New York.

The great French player came to this country to play for the championship for the first time. There was no seeded draw at that time, and she and
Mrs. Mallory met in the second round, after Mlle. Lenglen had won by
default in the first round from Miss Eleanor Goss.

The match was one of the red-letter events of world tennis of all time.
Mlle. Lenglen, invincible and a prohibitive favorite to beat any player in
the world by a crushing margin, came out on the court in an ermine wrap,
smiling and throwing kisses to an enraptured gallery that packed the stands
for her première in America. It was the entrance of a prima donna of the
opera, or rather of the ballet, for Mlle. Lenglen had all the grace of movement of a dancer.

Mrs. Mallory, almost neglected in the rush of officials to convoy the great
celebrity out on the turf courts, was a grim figure. This was the day she had
looked forward to, to make amends for crushing defeats she had suffered at
the hands of the world champion abroad. No one conceded her the ghost of
a chance.

Mrs. Mallory played with implacable determination. One of the strongest-
hearted players tennis has known, she was a fighting fury that day, whaling
the ball with her powerful forehand, the only really strong stroke she possessed, and retrieving unflaggingly.

The crowd could scarcely credit its eyes, for Mrs. Mallory was running
away with the match. Mlle. Lenglen developed a cough, which became
progressively worse. Mrs. Mallory won the first set, 6–2, and early in the

second Mlle. Lenglen, coughing heavily, said she was too ill to continue any longer. The score was 1–0 and 30–0 against her in the second game when she retired. She was led off the court in tears, and Mrs. Mallory was given an ovation for her victory.

For days a controversy raged as to whether Mlle. Lenglen was really too ill to continue or whether she became panicky at finding herself losing in her first match in America before she had had the opportunity to adapt herself to the new conditions of turf, ball, climate, food, water, etc.

Probably the next most treasured triumph for Mrs. Mallory was her victory over Miss Elizabeth Ryan in the final of the 1926 championship at Forest Hills. Helen Wills had ended her reign in 1923. No one believed that Mrs. Mallory ever would have a chance of winning the crown again.

Miss Wills in 1926 underwent an operation for appendicitis, after losing to Mlle. Lenglen in their celebrated match at Cannes on the French Riviera, and was unable to defend her title at Forest Hills. Mrs. Mallory and Miss Ryan, a Californian who had lived abroad for years and won many championships in doubles as Mlle. Lenglen's partner as well as ranked among the top singles players, advanced to the final round of the tournament. The play went to a third set, and Miss Ryan established a lead of 4–0 in games. She looked to be a certain winner.

At this point Mrs. Mallory staged one of the most remarkable rallies in the history of the championship and pulled out the set at 9–7 for the match and title. Later, Mrs. Mallory explained that her rally was made possible by the fact that she had the gallery overwhelmingly behind her, and their cheers inspired her on.

YOU'VE GOT TO HIT THE BALL HARD

by Emma Harrison

Women's tennis today lacks the vigor of the days when Molla Bjurstedt Mallory and Suzanne Lenglen were burning the grass with their deadly baseline drives and cooling the air with their real or imagined three-continent feud.

The authority for that? Mrs. Mallory herself, who, though retired, is not retiring in sizing up the current ladies of the court. Mrs. Mallory, who invaded our courts in 1915 as Molla Bjurstedt, a hard-hitting aggressor from Norway, won the United States championship seven times.

Commenting on last year's final at Forest Hills between Doris Hart and Louise Brough, she hesitated, then said softly, but with typical frankness: "I didn't think it was very good.

"I don't know what it is. I don't think they have the stamina."

She paused, then continued:

"They won't like me for saying this, but I think maybe they pamper themselves too much.

"They don't seem to have any fun. You know, I think they go to bed at 9 o'clock. In my day we had fun. I went out dancing, even the night before a match."

Mrs. Mallory advises the girl players to brush up on their passing shots and to stop relying on net play.

"In my day, we played more for the baselines and hit harder," she says. "Today all they do is struggle to get up to the net.

"You've got to hit the ball hard and have passing shots—Maureen Connolly had them."

Without sounding immodest, she added: "They couldn't beat my passing shots at the net."

Another thing missing today she finds is the placement.

"You must have placements, but don't let it interfere with hard hitting. You can beat anybody at the net with placements, hard hitting and passing shots.

"Put the ball where the other fellow ain't. Don't hit it back and wait for him to make an error."

Mrs. Mallory is unequivocally in favor of the earned point over the error. The preponderance of errors in last year's title match annoyed her.

"There's something on a tennis ball called top spin and they haven't got it," she said. "Louise Brough has it.

"I didn't know I had it until Bill Tilden told me. I said to Bill, 'Really I don't know very much about tennis.' "

In spite of her lack of technical training, Tilden was effusive in praise of her.

In 1921, after she had beaten Mlle. Lenglen in one smashing set followed by the mercurial French star's default, he called Molla "the greatest tennis player among women of all time."

Although she has put away all physical reminders of her tennis days—scrapbooks, rackets and trophies—she is not beyond a reminiscence.

"In those days we never thought of taking a rest between sets," she recalls. "That started later. You know, in the twenties they even started going into the dressing room and having a massage in between sets. Ridiculous."

She remembers she once played four matches in one day. The only ill effect was the loss of one match, the women's doubles.

Mrs. Mallory's tennis reign was ended by another hard hitter, Helen Wills. Mrs. Mallory lost to her the last time in 1929 at Forest Hills in a withering 6–0, 6–0 match that Molla played despite a bad knee.

Wimbledon and Mlle. Lenglen revive the most frustrating experience for Mrs. Mallory.

Of Wimbledon she remembers: "I just never could play there. Sometimes I wonder if it wasn't psychological."

It was in her return match with Mlle. Lenglen there in 1922 that the

French star beat her. Mrs. Mallory says the reports of their post-game exchange were exaggerated.

What did she say to Mlle. Lenglen?

"Nothing! But I'll tell you what I did say when she beat me at St. Cloud. I said to Bill Tilden, 'Wait till I get her on a grass court, I'll beat her.' And do you know what? She was standing right in back of me!"

Mrs. Mallory retired in 1939. After her broker husband died, she served as a censor in the New York Office of Censorship. She became a saleswoman at Lord & Taylor after World War II.

The former champion, who plays nothing more strenuous than a game of cards now, will spend her Sundays at Forest Hills as usual during the championships. She figures Miss Brough will win the title. But she has reservations:

"When Helen Wills played, they knew she was going to win. When I played, they knew I was going to win. They just aren't as good."

"LITTLE BILL"

by George Lott

When sports historians write about the Fabulous Twenties, their superlatives are usually reserved for William T. Tilden II. Tilden and tennis became synonymous, and his contributions to the advancement of the game were enormous. But there was another player whose presence on the scene contributed almost as much. This gentleman, and I use this word in its highest sense, was the most popular tennist ever to step on a court. He was called "Little Bill" Johnston. In the tennis rivalry between Tilden and Johnston, "Little Bill" was the "good guy" but, unlike the movie scripts, he didn't get the girl. But if he lost most of the cups, he won most of the fans—and with good reason. After Tilden perfected his backhand, our hero suffered a string of heart-rending defeats. Even in defeat he never once lost his hold on the love and affection of the fans. He reached everyone—people in country clubs, public parks, pool halls and hospitals. I remember a truck driver going by the courts on South Park Avenue in Chicago, who stopped to ask if we thought "Little Bill" could do it this time.

Compared to Tilden, who was an independent and controversial figure, "Little Bill" was a model of deportment and as close to being a pure amateur and gentleman tennis player as I ever saw. Whereas Tilden provided Webster with a new definition of "expense account," "Little Bill" stayed strictly within the rules. He not only was a delight to the millions of sports fans but also to the amateur gentlemen of the USLTA. It was one of the few times within my memory when tennis players, tennis fans and the USLTA agreed 100 per cent.

Johnston's game was something to behold. He was slight of stature, weighed about 120 pounds, and he had the most devastating forehand I ever saw. It was a Western, but unlike so many Westerns, there was not excessive topspin. From the waist up he hit almost a flat shot, and on low balls there was just enough topspin to clear the net. There was no suggestion of the loop. His backhand was also a Western hit with a slight undercut. It was by no means weak. His whole plan was to advance to the net behind his forehand and to volley severely off both sides if there was a return, which there wasn't. On overhead and service he was steady and forceful but not severe. These two parts of his game contained the only elements of subtlety in his repertoire, "Little Bill" here preferring placement over the power which characterized the rest of his game.

When you faced this little bantam you felt that he was all over you. You never dared to take a deep breath because if you did, you would find yourself saying "good shot." He swarmed over his opponents with that forehand, as a great number of top players will testify. Until the twilight of his career he overwhelmed everyone. His Davis Cup Challenge Round record reveals eleven wins and one loss. During these years he won 35 sets and lost only seven. In one tie against Australia's Gerald Patterson and J. O. Anderson, he lost only 11 games in six sets. In another tie against Frenchmen René Lacoste and Jean Borotra, he lost a total of 18 games in two matches, crushing Borotra with the loss of only five games. In this tie he lost one set 6–8 to Lacoste; in the other six sets he dropped only ten games!

Then the inevitable happened. The United States lost the Cup and "Little Bill" lost both his matches to the French. It was the saddest weekend of my life. It was not that we had lost the Cup, but it was so obvious that this great player and magnificent sportsman was not the "Little Bill" we had known. I, for one, do not believe it should have happened at that particular time. Our armchair strategists at USLTA headquarters decided "Little Bill" was too frail to prepare for the Challenge Round by playing the Eastern Circuit on grass, so they induced him to come East just a little over two weeks before the tie. Due to lack of competition he was no more in condition for this type of play than I was to fight Jack Dempsey. He was a hollow shell of himself and won only one set in two matches, whereas the year before he had lost only one set. It may be that tuberculosis, which later took his life, had gotten its initial hold at this time, but you would have never known it from watching "Little Bill." He lost as he had won for so long, in the same gracious business-like manner, although his thunder was gone. There was no suggestion of an alibi. Win or lose, "Little Bill" played the game as the poem suggests. He was small physically, but he was a BIG man. I thank the Lord that I was privileged to know him. It was the best thing that happened to me during my tennis career.

TRY, TRY AGAIN

by Allison Danzig

"Once you've tasted of success, try and try again" is the motto of William Johnston of San Francisco. "Little Bill" has been trying so long to regain the national tennis title from William Tilden that the struggles between the two have become an established fixture. It makes no difference what other attractions there are on the tennis calendar, the climax is always the Battle of the Bills in the final of the national championship.

Back in 1915 a slender freckle-faced youngster barely out of his teens came East to furnish the tennis world with another sensation of the Pacific Coast variety. Maurice McLoughlin, the California Comet, and R. Norris Williams 2d, the defending champion, two of the immortals of American tennis, were humbled in defeat by this youngster, and Johnston won his first national championship.

Four years passed. Johnston laid aside his navy uniform and came East to Forest Hills to begin a struggle that has been going on ever since. There, on the greensward of the country's leading tennis club, the Battle of the Bills began. Norman Brookes and Gerald Patterson of Australia, McLoughlin, Williams, Ichiya Kumagae of Japan, R. Lindley Murray, Charles S. Garland and Wallace Johnson were included in the field arrayed for the title. When the final round was reached, there stood Tilden and Johnston, Big Bill and Little Bill, the two men who were to dominate world tennis from then on.

For the second time Johnston won the title. Tilden, the man who stands today as the mightiest player who ever trod a court, did not get a set. The score was 6–3, 6–3, 6–4.

In 1920 Johnston came back, and lost his title to Tilden. In 1921 he sought to regain it and was defeated again; in 1922 also; in 1923 ditto; the same in 1924, and once again in the same place last year. Each time the story was the same: Tilden, Tilden, Tilden, Tilden, Tilden, Tilden, an echo that to Johnston said, "Nevermore."

In 1922, 12,000 tennis lovers sat enthralled in their seats at the Germantown Cricket Club, Philadelphia, as Johnston made his supreme effort to overcome that one great obstacle that persistently bobbed up between him and the championship. He won the first set; he swept through the second set. All that was needed for victory was one more set.

The thousands in the stands were stirred deeply as the struggle went on. They were Tilden's fellow townsmen for the most part. They were happy— for Johnston's sake. Little Bill was realizing the goal of his dreams. He was not through, as the papers were saying. He was not a has-been. Who else in the world could sweep through two sets against Tilden as he had done?

On a table off to one side of the court, in full view of all, glistened the national championship cup, a magnificent piece of silver bearing the names of a half dozen giants of tennis who had won it. Twice had Johnston tasted of the ambrosia of Victory from it. Once more let him lift it to his lips and the cup would be his for all time.

Already his hands were upon it. He was lifting it to his lips, his parched throat thirsting for its cooling fruit of victory, and in his mind's eye he saw reflected in the handsome piece of silver his face smiling in the prospect.

And then Tilden let loose the lightning of his strokes.

An hour later a grim, stricken little player, worn to the point of exhaustion, wan and pale, made his way through a lane of worshiping and sympathetic admirers. His ears were deaf to their cheers, his eyes saw no one—not even his wife, who hurried to comfort him on his downfall and to pour out her admiration for his grand, game fight. Heartbroken and disappointed in his great ambition, he pushed brusquely on down the lane, a lane that he knew would have no turning and that would always lead to the couch of the defeated man.

The cup was gone forever, for Tilden had won it for the third time—Tilden, the super player, master of all time, who could rise to unassailable heights in moments of stress and confound his opponent with the wizardry of his racket—Tilden, the giant who toyed with his opponent until he had him primed with confidence and then brought the world down about his ears with the devastating hail of his matchless shots.

Anyone who had seen the champion, serene in the face of apparent defeat, suddenly become rampant and make child's play of Johnston's most desperate efforts would have said that it was hopeless for Little Bill to try to beat him. Perhaps Johnston believed so himself, but when the play came down to the title round in the championship the following year, there again was Johnston across the net from Tilden, trying again.

Johnston tried his hardest and so did Tilden from the beginning, with the result that Johnston took the worst licking he has suffered in a national championship. "Try again!" said Little Bill, and in 1924 he came back once more. In the path of the Californian in the semi-final round stood Gerald Patterson, the giant from the Antipodes, he of the crashing service and the reverberating overhead kill.

In thirty minutes Patterson's remains were removed from the scene, annihilated by the pitiless fury of the 125 pounds of deadly machinery across the net. "The greatest tennis Johnston has played in his life," said the critics. "Let Tilden beware." But Johnston wasn't impressed. They hadn't seen anything yet. Primed with confidence in himself, he took to the court the next day against Tilden.

Twelve thousand fans filled the stadium at the West Side Tennis Club, Forest Hills, for the sixth annual Battle of the Bills, twelve thousand who had been thrilled by the great playing of their idol the day before and whose hearts were high with the hope that at last he was going to break through on the turf on which he had first sprung into prominence in 1915.

Forty-five minutes later those twelve thousand fans made their way silently out of the stadium, sadly disillusioned. Once more had Johnston withered before the devastating attack of his opponent. The flawless machine that had mowed down Patterson the day before never got started. The spark was killed.

Who can hope to portray the sensations of the Californian as he walked off the court? Such tennis as he had played against Patterson had seemed unsurpassable, as magnificent and perfect a performance as any that had been seen on a court in this country. Yet, he might have been a babe in arms so helpless was he when arrayed against Tilden. Johnston's heart must have cried out against this desecration of a perfect work of art. It was almost inhuman. It was Tilden, the superman of the courts, the colossus of the racket, the master.

And still Johnston had not had enough. Last year he came back again, exactly ten years since he had won the title for the first time. The air was filled with all sorts of rumors about Tilden. His narrow escapes from defeat at the hands of George Lott in the national clay court championship and Harvey Snodgrass and Howard Kinsey in the Illinois State championship gave those rumors birth, and they grew to huge proportions when Borotra and Lacoste of France had the champion tottering on the brink of defeat in the Davis Cup challenge round.

Here was Johnston's big chance, it was agreed. Play began between them in the final round again of the championship. Johnston went to the net for beautiful punching volleys, he ripped the grass with his vicious forehand drives. He took the first set, he gained a big lead in the second. Now he stood on the very brink of winning this set; 1922 was starting all over again.

But nervousness or overanxiousness ruined Johnston's big chance. A single stroke was all that stood between him and a 2–0 lead in sets, and he could not make that stroke. Who can blame Johnston for being nervous at a moment like this, arrayed against his nemesis, even though he did have ten years of championship experience behind him.

Tilden, cool and smiling, was not worried for a minute. One would never have dreamed that there was a national championship at stake in this match, so apparently unconcerned was he at all times. He won the second set, and the third set. After the rest period they came back and Johnston kept the thousands on the edge of their seats as he tied the score at 2–all. And that was all. Tilden settled himself to the task, and Johnston's hopes went aglimmering in short fashion for the sixth year in succession.

Will 1926 be a different story? If Tilden's performances on the court this year can be taken as an indication, there is reason for Johnston to take heart. Five times the champion has been beaten—by Borotra in the national indoor championship, by Lacoste in the international indoor match, twice by Richards in the South and by Al Chapin at New Haven. There are many who believe that the great Philadelphian is beginning to slip.

Johnston doesn't believe it. He says that tennis and the stage do not mix and that Tilden's defeats are to be charged up to his giving so much of his time to theatrical work. Nevertheless, he is coming back to try again. Someday someone has got to defeat Tilden in the national turf court championship, and Johnston believes that he is the man to do it. Little Bill is going to have another try for the blooming mug.

THE RULER OF THE COURTS

by John Kieran

There have been three outstanding figures on the tennis courts of this country: William A. Larned, Maurice McLoughlin, and William Tatem Tilden 2d. Larned was not the first but the last and probably the greatest of the old masters. He ruled in the days when Newport, Rhode Island, was the center of the Smart Set of gay summer days, and it was there that the tennis championships were settled, with high society looking on and the vulgar barred by mutual consent as well as by the scarcity of seats in the sacred enclosure and the high price of tickets.

There was an aura of aristocracy, a touch of hauteur, to the game in those days. The courts of the class-conscious Casino were not to be profaned by the common herd. And in the last decade of this austere era, William A. Larned was the Nestor at the net, the stand-out champion who waited with due dignity while some knightly challenger fought his way through the lists— the tourney of the royal racket week—for the honor of being baffled by Champion Larned in the ultimate challenge round.

Then came a larruping Lochinvar out of the West: Maurice E. McLoughlin, the California Comet, with a slashing, smashing game and a flaming thatch of red hair to make his rise more colorful. In three years Red McLoughlin dispersed the lavender and old lace trappings of the upstage game of tennis. He brought tennis down to the common ground. It was no longer a game for the Four Hundred—not the way Red McLoughlin played it. He made it a game for the millions, for the young fellows at the small clubs about the country and the youngsters just starting out on the courts in the public parks.

Thus was tennis happily knocked off its lofty perch and put on a footing where the kids of the country could go at it with vim and vigor. No longer was it a select diversion of the society set. No longer did the man in the street or the boy in public school regard it disdainfully as a sissy sport. The way Red McLoughlin laid about him with the racket it was a slam-bang game, all-out give-and-take tussle that was just as much fun for the masses as it had been for the classes before the kid from California came from a public park court to raise hob on the conservative turf of the Newport Casino enclosure.

The shock was more than Newport could stand. Probably with a feeling of some relief but with an assumed air of "noblesse oblige," society bade farewell, not au revoir, to the holding of the national tennis championship each season as part of the glittering program of summer gaiety for the swanky set at Newport, Rhode Island. The national championship was shifted to Forest Hills, Long Island, in 1915, shifted to the Germantown Cricket Club of Philadelphia in 1921, then back again to Forest Hills in 1924, when the concrete tennis bowl was finished and ready for occupancy by championship crowds and players. Where it may be shifted in the future, deponent sayeth not; but the sun will never rise on championship tennis at Newport again, unless it is in some nostalgic memorial celebration of the quaint days of old.

When the flaming Red McLoughlin wrenched the game away from the patricians and brought it down to the crowd, the kids of the country went for it avidly and made the most of it. With millions slamming away at it where only thousands had toyed with it before, something drastic was bound to come out of the program. And the something drastic was William Tatem Tilden 2d: Big Bill from Philadelphia, for six full years the king of the courts of all the world. England, Australia, the Continent, the United States—with racket in hand, Big Bill was monarch of all he surveyed. No one could stand before him.

Big Bill was more than a monarch. He was a great artist and a great actor. He combed his dark hair with an air. He strode the courts like a confident conqueror. He rebuked the crowds at tournaments and sent critical officials scurrying to cover. He carved up his opponents as a royal chef would carve meat to the king's taste. He had a fine flair for the dramatic; and, with his vast height and reach and boundless zest and energy over a span of years, he was the most striking and commanding figure the game of tennis had ever put on court.

There wasn't anything in the game that he couldn't do superlatively. His service was a cannonball. His ground strokes were lightning thrusts. His volleying was superb. With his long legs he could cover the court in three strides. He was as light on his feet as a ballet dancer. His backhand was baffling. His chops and drop shots were feats of legerdemain. And for tactics and strategy he had all his opponents backed off the board. When Tilden was Tilden, nobody could touch him. In fact, nobody could compare with him. And King William knew it and reveled in it. He wrote for the newspapers and magazines. He trod the boards as an actor. He lectured. He laid down the law. He bestrode the tennis world like a Colossus between whose legs the lesser figures of the game ran about and found themselves dishonorable graves.

On the expense accounts afforded by the modern game, he traveled in style and lived in comparative luxury. Paris, London, Southampton, Hot Springs, Sydney, Cannes knew his footprints and his regal ways. With Master Justice Shallow, he had heard the chimes at midnight. He played bridge until all hours. He smoked cigarettes as one to the manner born. It was a terrific shock, then, to learn that one day, shortly after his retirement from the championship heights, he had lectured a group of open-mouthed and innocent younglings on the virtues of copybook conduct, the benefits of deep breathing, early rising, modest manners, simple ways, pure food, noble aims, and all that jolly sort of thing. From the flamboyant and imperial King William, who had partaken of and enjoyed all the luxuries and fripperies that three or four continents and a decade of traveling on a generous expense account could provide in the modern world! Copybook conduct held out as the road to success by the superman of the racket game who himself, by right of eminent domain, had trampled on tournament committees, defiantly broken laws that were designed to hem in his ambitious and adventurous spirit, and kicked the stuffing out of some of the finest stuffed shirts bulging along the official front of the game.

It must have been a wonderful speech. But the context is lost to history. In its place is offered a substitute as William Tatem Tilden 2d might have delivered his message in the meter and manner of Quintus Horatius Flaccus, with the famous "Integer Vitae" (*Carmina,* Liber I. XXIII) as a model, with or without the permission of the estate of Q. H. Flaccus, deceased:

Advice from an Expert

Eat but simple food; go for early rising;
Follow out my plan, daily exercising;
Then your tennis game you will find surprising;
    So, too, will others!

Drink but water pure, not the wine that glitters;
Whiskey let alone, for it brings the jitters;
Sip not even one little taste of bitters;
    Sun it, my brothers!

Thus I reached the top, and thus you should follow,
If, across the net, you would beat all hollow
Playboys of the court. Though they call you Rollo,
    Stick to it cheerly.

Then upon the court, with some crafty blending,
Power, skill and speed you will have for spending.
When the wastrels sag, for a happy ending,
    Ace them severely!

Once we were beset, with the French besetting;
Threats from Anzacs, too, we were always getting;
On my upright life did they base the betting
    I would outlast 'em.

Primed with ozone pure (and with a speed a trifle),
Strong with simple food (and a service rifle),
Fresh from calm, sweet sleep (what a tennis eyeful!)
      Say, did I blast 'em!

Place me in a land where it may be snowing
Or 'neath tropic skies, with the warm winds blowing,
Bring your young net star. When the game gets going,
      I'll dust his jacket.

Thank the simple life (and a service stringing)
That at forty-odd, with the loud cheers ringing,
· I—King William still—on the courts am swinging,
      Boy, what a racket!

Aside from Tilden, most of the net stars have been fine players but, beyond that, nothing in particular to write home about. They had their idiosyncrasies in tactics on and off the court; but, in either direction, they were mild compared to the great King William. One exception might be cited, however, and he was not by any means of the Tilden heights on the court. But Alain Gerbault, not a score of years ago, was good enough to earn a reserve place on the French Davis Cup team, and his subsequent career, in contrast with the hemmed-in hitting he did at Auteuil and Forest Hills, set him far apart from the ordinary tennis player of the top-flight set.

Alain Gerbault, at the heights of his tennis game, suddenly walked off the court, turned up his nose at the caviar and champagne provided by the tournament committee, and went the way of loaves and fishes. Discarding his playing flannels, he donned dungarees. He became a sailor, a lone sailor. He was "the crew and the captain bold and the mate" of the *Firecrest,* a twenty-nine-foot sloop in which he attempted and completed a one-man westward voyage of forty-five hundred miles across the Atlantic. Others had attempted it. Alain Gerbault, a rather small, thin, wiry and melancholy-looking French refugee from the high life of the tennis tournament circuit, was the first to complete the trip. He had read of a predecessor who set out on such a long voyage. Away out at sea, in such difficulties as lone sailors may meet, this predecessor had written in his log: "I am going out to the end of the bowsprit. Shall I return?" The answer was evident when his empty boat was picked up later by a transatlantic steamer and the question in the log was scanned by the salvaging officer.

In a book that he wrote of his own voyages in the *Firecrest,* M. Gerbault confesses that he remembered that incident when he had to go out to the end of his own bowsprit in mid-ocean with a storm raging. But he came back even though there were moments during which, clinging with legs and arms, he was hanging head foremost under three feet of water out there. He was 101 days from Gibraltar to Fort Totten, Long Island, and for months he never saw another human being. His drinking water spoiled. He suffered severely from thirst. His salt meat rotted. His sails were ripped and torn time and again by wild winds at sea.

Racked with fever, soaked with spray and rain, with his throat swollen from thirst, short of food, possibly Alain Gerbault on the wild waste of the tossing Atlantic thought of his tennis days on the Riviera when during the luncheon period—and at the expense of the willing tournament committee—the club waiter or restaurant captain would offer the tennis stars at a select table a menu starting:

Hors D'Oeuvres Varieés   Pamplemousse Rafraichi au Kirsch

Celeri en Branches   Olives Noires

Potages

Crème Fontanges

Consommé Andalouse

Consommé Froid en Tasse

Soupe à L'Oignon, Gratinée (10 minutes)

Possibly the lone sailor thought of that the day he had to heave his salt beef overboard because it was just too bad. But the strange thing was that Gerbault, after sampling the sybaritic existence of the top-flight tennis player and the hard life of the lone voyager at sea, preferred the life on the ocean wave and his home on the rolling deep. He went on around the world in his *Firecrest,* and his own written record of his voyaging is something to make any tennis story seem "weary, stale, flat and unprofitable."

THE RECORDS PROVE IT

by George Lott

Not many people will be startled when they hear me say that Bill Tilden was the greatest tennis player of all time. The record books prove it conclusively. No other player's record is close to that of Tilden's. There have been players with better individual strokes, viz., Budge's backhand, but no player had the all-round equipment to equal Tilden's. And, when the occasion demanded, he would produce a backhand shot better than Budge ever dreamed of making.

But what kind of a man was this giant colossus of the court? What made him tick? How did he get to be so great?

Tilden was often called a genius. Genius he was, but of his own making. Until he reached the age of 27 he was just a so-so player. Practically all our past and present champions reached that level in their teens or early twenties. When Tilden was 25, he was a struggling chop-stroke artist, and not a very good one. He spent the better part of his youth as a fringe player.

When he was 26 he reached the National Singles final and was beaten by "Little Bill" Johnston, who was the idol of the public. "Big Bill's" backhand betrayed him. Johnston's forehand, the best in the world at that time, pulverized Tilden's backhand, which was a chop stroke.

Determined to become champion and realizing he did not have the equipment, Tilden moved to Providence, where he played daily the entire winter on Jed Jones' indoor clay court. If Arnold Jones had a dollar for every ball he hit to Tilden's backhand that winter, he would have been as rich as his father, who was a millionaire. Hour after hour, day after day and week after week Tilden worked on his backhand until it became his strength. The following summer he won the U.S. Singles, handling Johnston's ferocious forehand so well that he broke "Little Bill's" heart. To the public's dismay, Johnston could never beat him again in an important match.

Thus began a six-year reign in the world of tennis by a man who was to become an enigma to those around him.

I was associated with Bill for the better part of fourteen years, on and off the court. I played tennis against him. I played with him. We argued and seldom agreed. We traveled the world over together. At the bridge table, the only time we were both happy was when we were opponents. When we met on the tennis court, there was one less happy person. I saw him under all types of conditions and I came to know him as well as it was possible for one human being to know another.

My first impressions of Tilden were mixed. Immediately there was a feeling of awe, as though you were in the presence of royalty. The atmosphere became charged and there was almost a sensation of lightness when he left. You felt completely dominated and you breathed a sigh of relief for not having ventured an opinion of any sort. At the same time, you knew you were in contact with greatness, even if only remotely. You either liked this man or you didn't. No halfway measures. My first reaction was the latter.

All through his life one of Tilden's idiosyncrasies was expressing his opinion (in no uncertain terms) of the future of young players. His first pronouncement concerning me was that I would get nowhere in the tennis world and that Julius Sagalowsky, who had beaten me in the Boys' Nationals, was the comer. I was too young then to know that he had put the kiss of death on Sagalowsky. The only youngster ever touted by Tilden to accomplish anything was Vincent Richards, and after that his batting average was a big zero. His choices were dictated by likes and dislikes and not by what he saw on the court.

And yet Bill had a tremendous sense of fair play; if he saw something he thought was wrong, he would move heaven and earth to change it. He and I were never very close friends, especially in my younger days as National Junior Champion. That year I had a good singles record and deserved a place in the First Ten. The ranking came out with me at No. 11. Who do you suppose raised such a holler and yell that the rankings were changed at the Annual Meeting? You guessed it.

He carried this desire for fair play to the tennis court. It is true that he could and did intimidate linesmen, but it was never his intention to frighten them into favorable calls. All he wanted was linesmen who were alert and accurate. Heaven help the poor linesman who let his attention wander. I never once saw Tilden take a point that he believed did not belong to him.

Tilden had an inordinate amount of pride and confidence in himself. He felt during his reign that he was Mr. Tennis. So much was this apparent that he made many enemies, especially among USLTA officials. But in actuality he was Mr. Tennis—on the court and to the public.

During 1928, these unfriendly officials finally got him. They had incorporated a rule forbidding any player from writing current reports on a tournament in which he was playing. This hit Bill in a sensitive spot—the pocketbook. However, he negotiated a contract with a news service in which his stories were to be printed 24 hours after the action, the legal USLTA limit. During Wimbledon, three weeks before the Challenge Round in Paris against the French, one of these articles was printed ahead of time and the anti-Tilden forces insisted that the USLTA bar him from Davis Cup competition. However, public opinion in France became so incensed that the French Government asked the American Ambassador, Myron Herrick, to contact the U.S. State Department in Washington to have Tilden reinstated for the Challenge Round in the interest of international goodwill, which was done. After all this furor, Tilden played what I consider his greatest match of all time.

He beat René Lacoste with a display of versatility that has never been equaled. Bear in mind that Lacoste at this time had beaten Tilden on several occasions and was a 2–1 favorite. Tilden defeated this great baseliner with chops, slices, drop shots, lobs and power shots, conceived and executed by the greatest tennis brain of all time. And he was on his way down at the time! I know, from practicing with him before this match, that he was upset mentally and physically by the hubbub, and for him to pull himself together to win this match was a victory of determination and intense pride.

I doubt if there has ever been anyone who loved the game as much as Bill. Many times I have seen him out on the public courts helping youngsters. His sole purpose in having the youngsters go to tournaments with him was his desire to develop them into champions. He worked with them hour after hour and got them in tournament after tournament, much to the dismay of many tournament chairmen. If a tournament got Tilden, it also got the entourage. In the end, everyone was happy. Tilden was such a great draw that he overcame the expenses of his pupils.

Bill's relaxation from tennis took two forms. One was the stage, which was so disastrous financially that even he became convinced. One winter he came into an inheritance of about $30,000, so he backed a play called *Dracula* in which he played Dracula—with the inevitable result. Bill was an actor all right, but on the tennis court, where he had the tools.

The other form was bridge. He played this game as he did everything else—he had to be in complete charge. If his partner bid hearts, he would insist on being the declarer, even with a weaker suit. On one boat trip to Europe Gene Dixon, our Davis Cup Captain, and I almost cured him of this habit—but his money held out. Tilden and Frank Hunter lost to us every afternoon and evening across the ocean, but even at the end Tilden's stubbornness was in evidence.

Bill's disregard for money made me feel that he was the man Walter Hagen had in mind when he said: "I don't want to be a millionaire. I just want to live like one." And he did, practically his entire life.

If they play tennis Upstairs, you may rest assured Big Bill has taken over. Just a word of warning to the angels who are linesmen: Pay attention or you'll be back at your harp in no time flat!

TILDEN SPELLS IT OUT

by Alan J. Gould

"Little Bill" Johnston, if he never knew it before, can here and now learn of the stroke "Big Bill" Tilden had to acquire and master seven years ago in order to defeat Johnston at tennis. And Tilden not only gives credit to Johnston for having been instrumental in pointing out to Tilden the latter's weakness in the game but, in an interview with the Associated Press, he also expressed his gratefulness to Johnston, who, Tilden says, had greater experience and "match temperament" in 1919 when for the first time the two met in contest.

"It was Johnston's ability to pound my backhand stroke to a pulp," said Tilden, "that taught me I had to have an offensive backhand stroke. So during the following winter I worked indoors four days a week on my backhand at Providence, Rhode Island. Before we went to England in 1920 for the Davis Cup matches, I had acquired, through intensive practice, an offensive as well as a defensive backhand shot.

"It was the difference between my backhand of 1919 and that of 1920, plus additional experience, that enabled me to win the Wimbledon tournament, carrying with it the world's title at that time, and later the American championship. In the American final that year Johnston set out to pound my backhand as he had done the year before. But it wouldn't be pounded that time.

"It is just this difference in backhand strokes which I believe has provided the margin of my victories over Johnston through the past six years."

For the mass of young tennis players who aspire to lift themselves out of the ranks of the ordinary, Tilden has a formula for success, compounded out of the elements of his own career of unprecedented triumph on the courts. It is the formula that has given Tilden the magic touch and made him the champion of champions in an era of stirring competition, but there is no secret key to it, no short cut to the final product, for its chief ingredients are sacrifices, concentration and an all-around game.

They are the factors that stand for success in the game of life as well as sports; their product is championship stuff and if you could hear Tilden himself—as he expounded for the Associated Press their application to his career as well as to others—you would know the intensity with which he has lived them, made them the cornerstone of his own existence and sought to spread their gospel to others.

There is sacrifice of the most Spartan sort in the story of Tilden's early career, of how, after being a "bust" for some seven or eight years, he was willing to spend a half dozen more overcoming obstacles and developing the game that has lifted him to the top. There was concentration of a single-track variety in this, too, and concentration now in his lean figure, his almost gaunt features, as he drives home for another generation the lesson of his rise.

Perhaps nothing else carries home this lesson so forcefully or characteristically as Tilden's own story of his rise, told with his own sense of the dramatic, with the clearness of a keen student and the soundness of a thorough teacher.

"I started to play as soon as I was old enough to hold a racket, at the age of five," he began. "I was pretty good for a youngster for my age, and got a great deal of incentive from helping as a ball boy at the Germantown Cricket Club, watching Parke and Dixon, the British stars, play such Americans as Larned, Clothier, Beals Wright, and Ward.

"My brother, Herbert, seven years my senior, was one of the best young players in the Philadelphia district at the time. The most valuable thing he did was to give me a general bawling out after every tournament I played in. That made me 'sore' and I tried to do better."

As he recalled those days of his gangling youth, Tilden glanced reflectively at one of his protégés—"Junior" Coen, who has come East after making his mark in Middle Western ranks. The champion, a few minutes before, had been making imaginary slices with a collection of new rackets under Coen's admiring gaze.

"From the age of twelve to about nineteen or twenty," he went on, "I played pretty badly. I was wild as a hawk. My shots were not particularly sound. I was just a 'swatter-type.' At about eighteen I made up my mind to remodel my game, which at the time was very erratic off the ground and had as its only redeeming feature a fast service. I realized it wouldn't get me anywhere and that I needed a sound ground game. On that theory, I analyzed my play along common-sense scientific lines, and for the next half dozen years, or until I was twenty-five, I worked on an all-court game.

"Everyone, including my friends, told me I was foolish; that I couldn't be both a baseline and net player, but fortunately I was pig-headed enough not to believe them and kept at it. As a result, in 1918 I got to the finals of the national singles, losing to Lindley Murray, and found a place in the 'first ten' for the first time.

"In 1919 Bill Johnston and I began our long span of rivalry, meeting four times altogether [that year]. I defeated him the first time we met at Newport, and also won in the East-West matches, but he turned the tables in the clay court tournament and again in the title round of the national singles. Two factors accounted for Johnston's decisive victories—first, his greater experience in match temperament; second, his ability to pound my backhand to a pulp." Tilden then told how he developed an offensive backhand in Providence during the winter of 1919–1920. Applying the object lessons of his career, Tilden went on:

"I am convinced that any player who wants to can master any stroke in the game. And no player will hold the American championship in the future who has any pronounced weakness. Therefore, any young player who aspires to be a national champion must be willing to go through the long, tedious and, at times, seemingly hopeless grind of learning the fundamentals of an all-court game.

"Style too must be acquired. By that I mean correct form, which is a combination of racket technique and footwork. The ability to keep the eye on the ball at all times and correct court position are absolutely essential to success. Every player to reach the top must acquire these fundamentals, yet these alone won't make a champion. It's the willingness and the knowledge of when to sacrifice to gain this form that make a great champion.

"Bill Johnston, a model of style, will sacrifice comfort, looks and dignity to win a crucial point if that point happens to mean victory or defeat. It is this ability, which I term the ability to 'scramble,' the determination to go after everything, which carries most players out of the mass of the good into the select circle of the great. Lacoste has it. So have Richards and Borotra, but they are a few among many. . . .

"I can not too strongly urge young players to attempt the impossible in recoveries. At least 75 per cent of the shots considered impossible are actually recoverable if the effort is made for them. Let no player cramp his style by worrying about the gallery thinking he is playing to the grandstand when he is trying for sensational recoveries."

Tilden himself, it should be noted, lives up to his own advice to "scramble." In his long stride and with his tremendous reach, the champion has physical advantages that enable him to make difficult "gets" with seeming ease, but at the same time he is always ready to dash far out of court or to plunge to the net, risking possible injury to recover the ball.

"I am a great believer in imitation; not that a player can accurately copy another's stroke, but in attempting to do so he is apt to discover a valuable stroke of his own. My forehand drive, which actually bears no resemblance to J. O. Anderson's, is the nearest to it which I am able to produce. My backhand slice, which has no family connection with that of J. J. Armstrong, former Harvard star . . . started as an imitation of his famous slice.

"My advice to young players is to see as much good tennis as possible and attempt to copy the outstanding strokes of the famous stars.

"In attempting to develop the game of various juniors, I have found the road to greatest success lies in taking their natural game and modifying it for orthodoxy without destroying its individuality. The greatest danger of professional coaching lies in the fact that every professional strives to make a duplicate of his own game, whereas a sound teacher should treat each pupil as an individual case to be developed along different lines, rather than as a standardized product. I could not have developed Carl Fischer, the former intercollegiate champion, along the lines of Vincent Richards, nor Sandy Wiener and Junior Coen on parallel planes. Each is great in his own way. Had I tried to make them play my game I would have ruined them all."

The guide lines which Tilden stakes out for boys would not, however, apply to feminine players, he believes.

"One hears discussion of the relative merits of the tennis of leading men and women, but their games are entirely different," the champion pointed out. "To me the ideal type of game for a woman is the baseline game. I consider it impossible for a woman to play an all-court game for three sets. They are not physically able to do so. Even as great a star and unusually strong a woman as our own national champion, Helen Wills, or our former champion, Mrs. Molla Mallory, or Elizabeth Ryan cannot consistently go to the net through three sets and stand it. It is common knowledge that Suzanne Lenglen, notwithstanding the sensational photographs of her playing, only goes to the net when drawn in by her opponent."

Tilden deftly parried a request to explain some of the playing psychology that has been so conspicuous in his many close matches, his frequent uphill victories in international play. He did so because he feels this is a peculiar attribute of his own game and that no explanation or analysis of it would be beneficial to any other player.

"Tell us, then, what match was your hardest?" he was asked.

"Unquestionably my five-set struggle with René Lacoste in the challenge round of the Davis Cup play last year," replied the champion. "I never was in a worse hole and I never took any greater physical punishment getting out of it than I did in that match. I was physically 'dead on my feet' in the first set, losing it as well as the second set and the first four games of the third set before striking my stride. I was four times within a point of losing the match before I took the third set and turned the tide, but even then it was a terrific battle right down to the finish."

"What are your views as to professional tennis?" he was asked, and he replied:

"I do not believe in professional tennis. My faith and interest is in the amateur game, but at the same time I think professional tennis might succeed. Personally, I have never considered turning professional and have no thought of it now. Necessity would be the only thing that would interest me in it."

THE GREATEST OF ALL TIME

by Allison Danzig

As months of play for the Davis Cup come to a climax this week in Australia, it is difficult to believe that this is the first time in four years that the United States has qualified for the challenge round. It is even more difficult to believe that only twice since 1949 has the U. S. won the cup, which was first offered in 1900 by Dwight F. Davis of St. Louis, and is played for annually by more than 40 nations. In all the other years since 1949, Australia, with a population of under 11 million, has been the winner.

For those who remember the 1920's—"Sport's Golden Age"—it is especially hard to understand why our teams have fared so poorly so long. For in those years the United States was supreme in tennis—indeed, it established a record of seven consecutive victories that has been unmatched by any other nation (though France won the cup from 1927 through 1932). It was supreme because the mainstay of the team for those seven years was the greatest tennis player the world has seen.

William Tatem Tilden 2d was his name. He was the autocrat of the courts as no other player has been since, an absolute monarch in a period when American tennis was at its most resplendent and great players were developed in many lands. He was not only the supreme, the most complete, player of all time; he was also one of the most colorful and controversial figures the world of sports has known.

His flair for the theatrical stemmed from a fascination with the stage that had held him since boyhood. He would have given his right arm, and his racket with it, to have been a successful, idolized actor. Instead, he was almost the worst that ever played on Broadway; and he squandered the fortune he made from tennis backing stock companies and Broadway productions.

To Tilden, a tall, gaunt figure with hulking shoulders and the leanest of shanks, the tennis court became a stage. He was in love with it and with the crowds before whom he performed. Most of the time they were against him—or at least for his opponent, the underdog. To win them to his side, he went to lengths that seemed to border on lunacy. He would allow his opponent to gain so big a lead as to make his own defeat appear inevitable. Then, from this precarious position, he would launch a spectacular comeback that had the crowd cheering him and that invariably ended with an ovation from the stands when he won.

Only Tilden would have dared set the stage as he did to make himself the hero instead of the villain. Such was the might of his racket, so unquestioned was his authority on the court, that he could predict the scores of his matches with almost any player the world over when he was in his prime. That was from 1920 through 1925, when he reigned as national champion, won every one of his twelve Davis Cup challenge-round singles matches and carried off the Wimbledon crown both times he competed for it.

In 1925, Tilden played Howard Kinsey in the Illinois State championship at the Skokie Country Club in Glencoe. Kinsey was the fourth-ranking player in the country and national doubles champion with his brother, Robert, that year. After winning the first two sets, Tilden lost the next two. Leading 2–0 in the fifth set, he then lost the next five games. The crowd of 5,000 buzzed with excitement. Could it be that the great Tilden was going down in defeat?

The court was close to Lake Michigan and a cold wind was blowing. The spectators were bundled in coats and blankets. As the players changed sides with the score 2–5, Tilden took off his sweater for the first time, picked up a pitcher of ice water at the umpire's chair and poured it over his head.

A shiver went through the crowd. Tilden kept them waiting as he carefully dried his head and hands. Finally, he walked to the base line and prepared to serve. Then, adding to the suspense, he beckoned to a ball boy to bring him a towel with the imperious gesture he used so often when holding court before his tennis audiences.

Meticulously, he wiped the last bit of moisture from his hands. By now the gallery was limp from tension. With the stage set as he wanted it, Tilden picked up racket and balls and cut loose. Kinsey could win only one more game—after Tilden had won four. Final score: 8–6. The cheers for Big Bill at the end were wild.

This ability of Tilden's to extricate himself from seemingly hopeless positions (deliberately arrived at) even against players superior to Kinsey was a manifestation of his unrivaled supremacy. To establish that he ranks above all others, not only of his time but of all time, it is necessary to examine his attributes—his physical and mental capacities and stroke equipment—and the abilities of his contemporaries.

In some sports, particularly track and swimming, it is easy enough to compare athletes of one generation with those of another by citing time and distance figures. In tennis, as in prizefighting, there are no such yardsticks. The only pertinent arguments must be concerned with how much of a punch the athlete had with his right or left (forehand or backhand) and how good were the men he beat.

Tilden held absolute sway in a period when there were probably more truly first-class players than either before or since. In the twenties, France, Spain and Japan produced their most renowned players. Australia was represented by the giant Gerald Patterson, with the devastating service and overhead smash, and Jim Anderson with the rifled forehand. There was Brian Ivan Cobb (Babe) Norton from South Africa. Manuel Alonso was the greatest player ever developed in Spain, and for Japan there were Zenzo Shimizu and Ichiya Kumagae. The French had Henri Cochet, René Lacoste and Jean Borotra, who, with Jacques Brugnon, were to end Tilden's reign and break the United States' seven-year hold on the Davis Cup.

The French were formidable. Cochet was a born artist of the racket, with more natural ability and "touch" than probably any other player in history.

It was he who ended Tilden's six-year reign as national champion in the 1926 quarter-finals at Forest Hills. Lacoste came as close to being an infallible machine—in the inevitability of his return against any amount of pace, power or spin—as any player who ever lived. He won at Wimbledon in 1925 and 1928. Borotra—"The Bounding Basque from Biarritz"—played tennis like a man possessed, with a mania for getting to the net, but was wily, too. He was Wimbledon champion in 1924 and 1926.

In our own country there were two immortals: "Little Bill" Johnston of San Francisco and Vincent Richards, the boy wonder of Yonkers, New York. It was Johnston's great misfortune that he was a contemporary of Tilden. Had their careers not coincided, "Little Bill" might have won the championship eight times instead of twice (in 1915 and 1919). Johnston's Davis Cup record was virtually the equal of Tilden's except that he did not play singles in 1924. He ranks among the half dozen top players of all time.

Richards was another player of the first class. The game has not seen his superior as a volleyer. He had extraordinary control of the ball, even in returning Tilden's cannonball service, and a temperament and instinct for the game that have hardly been surpassed.

These, then, were the players over whom Tilden held sway. He was their master for the following reasons:

(1) He had the greatest combination forehand and backhand drive the game has known. No other player could hit with such pace and control from both sides. Donald Budge's backhand is usually rated today ahead of all others, but not by those who saw Tilden in his prime.

With his great strength in the fundamental strokes and his zest for moving his opponent about, he preferred to stay in the back court rather than rush to the net. There are those, therefore, who mistakenly assert that he could not volley. Tilden was not the equal of Johnston or Richards at the net, nor was he as strong overhead as would have been expected of so tremendous a server, but when he chose to, or had to, go in, he was a master of the drop volley, as he was of the drop shot.

(2) His service ranks with the greatest. His cannonball first serve was as consistently fast as any with the possible exception of Ellsworth Vines's and the frequency with which he could make the chalk fly on the center line when he was behind was discouraging to his opponents. There have been few American twist services to compare in "kick" with his second ball.

(3) He was unrivaled as a student and master of spin. He could blow his opponent off the court with pace or he could break down his control with a chop or slice used alternately with a flat or a top-spin drive.

(4) No player had a better physique for the game. Tilden stood 6 foot 1 and weighed 165 pounds; he had broad shoulders, a lean waistline and long, tapering legs that carried him swiftly with giant strides. Invariably he was in perfect condition and could battle interminably, despite the fact that he smoked incessantly off the court and ate prodigious amounts of food an hour or two before playing.

(5) No player moved more gracefully or with footwork that was more

secure. His speed has hardly been excelled except by Fred Perry's, and no matter how fast he ran or how far he reached, he rarely made a shot off balance.

(6) There never has been a more thorough student of the game or greater master of tactics. This is evidenced not only by his craft on the court but also in his writings, particularly in his classic work, *Match Play and Spin of the Ball*.

(7) No player ever loved the game more, got more pleasure from the play or gave his life to tennis so wholeheartedly as did Tilden, from the age of 7 until he died at 60 in 1953.

It is also true that there never was a more temperamental player than Tilden, nor one more opinionated. He was a supreme egoist, although off the court he could be gracious and charming. He had a deep love of music, acquired from his mother. He was always ready for a game of bridge; he liked to talk rather than listen. He had friends who were devoted to him— among them Mary Garden, the singer, and Mrs. Molla Bjurstedt Mallory, seven times the winner of the national championship, a woman of great courage and pride.

On the court, too, Tilden could be winning and generous. But he could also be carping, demanding and fault-finding to a point where the gallery turned against him. Linesmen and ball boys were often the objects of his ire. With arms akimbo, he could wither a linesman with a glare or contemptuous grin if the decision did not please him. More than one official thus humiliated refused to serve on a line at Tilden's matches.

There were occasions when Tilden threatened to walk off the court because of the condition of the turf or the partisanship of the gallery for his opponent. At the Orange Lawn Tennis Club in South Orange, New Jersey, where the turf is now as good as any in the country, he informed the chairman that he was not accustomed to playing in a cow pasture.

At the Westchester Country Club in Rye, New York, he was losing badly to Clifford Sutter in their quarter-final match in the 1930 Eastern grass court championships. The gallery was on him for his poor tennis and temperamental displays and finally a woman in the stands shouted, "Play tennis!" In a rage, he walked off the court, and defaulted.

In 1923, Brian Norton was quoted in the New York *Times* as saying that he was confident he could win the national championship if he defeated Richard Norris Williams 2d the next day in the quarter-finals at Germantown, Pennsylvania (Tilden's home town). Tilden was so infuriated that he threatened to withdraw from the tournament if Norton did not apologize to him for the implied slight. Norton did not apologize and Tilden did not withdraw. Norton did beat Williams—and in the semi-finals Tilden gave him a fearful licking.

There was scarcely a question in anyone's mind in Tilden's heyday that he was the greatest player the world had seen. Old-timers who saw him at his peak still hold to the belief, with few exceptions, that he is the greatest to this day. Those among them who may give preference to Budge, Kramer,

Gonzales, Vines, Perry or some other will respect the choice of Tilden and argue rationally for their man. Not so the younger generation, who saw Tilden, if at all, only in the late stages of his career.

To the young players currently active it is like waving a red flag before a bull so much as to suggest that Tilden or any other player of his time would have the ghost of a chance against Gonzales or Kramer or Lewis Hoad or some other of the famous modern-day champions who play the Big Game. Nothing can convince them that the game Tilden played would not now he hopelessly outdated and outclassed.

They maintain flatly that the game of Big Serve and Volley came in with Kramer and Ted Schroeder and point out that it was Australia's changing to this type of play after taking a series of bad lickings from the United States in the Davis Cup matches in the late 1940's that put the boys from Down Under up yonder. They are convinced that Tilden would be out-matched.

The fact is that tennis was played identically in Tilden's time as it is today, except that there were not as many net rushers and the rallies were longer. There was never a more daring game than that played by Dick Williams, who went in on his big serve and made most of his shots on the half volley or the full volley, winning in 1914 and 1916. Who ever rushed the net more than Borotra or Wilmer Allison?

Tilden was supreme over the great volleyers and servers until 1926 and at times defeated them years later, primarily because of the strength of his ground strokes. He could return the Big Serve wrathfully and he repulsed the volleyer with passing shots from either side. It would be the same today as it was 40 years ago.

Sir Norman Brookes, for many years president of the Lawn Tennis Association of Australia, and himself one of the top-ranking players of all time, ranked Tilden as the greatest in 1956. Vines, in 1958, said that he always had felt that Tilden was the greatest. In 1934—10 years after his prime—Tilden played Vines in a professional match in Los Angeles. Tilden was 41; Vines was 22. Big Bill lost, but he battled for three hours before yielding. The final score was 6–0, 21–23, 7–5, 3–6, 6–2. Bobby Riggs wrote that Tilden, at the age of 52, had pushed him (when he was 28) to the limit in a tournament match, a fact that convinced him that Tilden must have been the greatest of all time. Allison wrote:

"I have gotten tired of people who should know better saying that Tilden wasn't the greatest that ever lived. I never played Tilden at his best but I have never felt so helpless in all the time I played as I did against him in the finals at Wimbledon in 1930. Of course, I haven't played Hoad or Gonzales, but I did play Vines, Budge, Perry, Kramer . . . while they were great players, they certainly weren't the equal of Tilden."

Frank Hunter, who was Tilden's partner in the U.S. and Wimbledon doubles championships and on Davis Cup teams, and who was twice runner-up for the national singles title, has summed it up this way:

"Tilden could have changed his game if necessary and played the Big

Game. He could play any kind of game. He had a wonderfully analytical mind in sizing up the other fellow's game—its strengths and weaknesses— and deciding what methods and tactics to use. He had the equipment to beat them all—past and present. There's never been anyone like him."

THE TOP SHOTMAKERS

by Allison Danzig

By coincidence, Theodore Roosevelt Pell was encountered on the North Shore of Long Island the day *Esquire* magazine came out with its poll on the greatest shot makers in tennis.

For the benefit of the younger fry in the class, be it said that once upon a time there was a princely youth by the name of Theodore Roosevelt Pell who went forth bent on conquest and unsheathed a backhand that was as much of a sensation as Donald Budge's was to become a generation later. Our hero never made a grand slam nor did he win the national championship, but in his day he could turn loose a port broadside that blew them off the court.

That was thirty-odd years ago. Tennis was in its ice-cream pants, and any man caught off base with a racket on the city streets was fair game for the Dead End Kids. Maurice McLoughlin had yet to convince them with his comet speed that the sport was he-man stuff. But Pell's backhand, which won him a ranking five times in the top ten, has become so legendary that some of the Old Blues today will tolerantly let you sound off about Budge and Bill Tilden and then enlighten you pell-mell about a backhand that was a backhand.

Mr. Pell declines the honor with a chuckle. The backhand of backhands, for his money, belongs to Budge. The top player of them all, however, is neither Budge nor Tilden. Rated on peak form, he likes Ellsworth Vines, who had a very fine backhand but a more murderous forehand. Mr. Pell can get an argument on both counts, but that's no way to treat a guest.

"Fifty per cent of winning tennis," says Mr. Pell, "is good footwork. That is why Suzanne Lenglen was so great. She was a ballet dancer on the court."

He might have added that that was one reason why Tilden was greatest of them all, if he agreed with this corner. Today, at 51, Tilden's footwork is something to marvel at. In his prime he was the most graceful, sure-footed and best-balanced athlete ever to step on a court.

Fred Perry of England was a good second, and Gerald Patterson of Australia had amazing grace for a man of his bulk. Jean Borotra of France, Gregory Mangin, Wilmer Allison and Brian Norton of South Africa were exceptionally fast and quick, to make them feared volleyers, but they were a bit too impetuous to be perfect in their footwork.

Thanking Mr. Pell and *Esquire* for starting the argument, we now proceed to get contrary. The best forehand of the moderns belonged to Bill Johnston—a tremendous Western top-spin drive that lifted his 120 pounds off the ground in the execution.

The best flat forehand was Tilden's, and Big Bill had the best two-sided attack. Vines' was the most lethal flat forehand but not as consistent. Perry had the best running forehand and Henri Cochet's was next.

J. Gilbert Hall has a solid forehand that would satisfy any player. Other good ones have belonged to Jack Crawford and Jim Anderson of Australia, Baron von Cramm and Hans Nusslein of Germany, Manuel Alonso of Spain, René Lacoste of France, Frank Hunter and Dick Williams.

Tilden, Budge and Pell are the backhand names. Probably none has struck such terror to his opponents' hearts as has Budge's, but Tilden could crucify a net player with his backhand down the line or across court, and he could hit over or under the ball or straight through it.

The most skilled volleyer was Vincent Richards. Johnston, McLoughlin, Borotra, Allison, Mangin, Cochet, Joe Hunt, Williams, Perry and Robert Riggs also sparkled at the net, and Tilden could volley superbly, though he preferred to stay back most of the time.

The great smashers included McLoughlin, Patterson, Borotra, Budge and Vines. John Doeg, Frank Shields, Cochet, Lacoste, Allison and Frank Kovacs also excelled overhead. This was the one shot of which Tilden was not the master.

The kings of the lob were George Lott, Lacoste, Riggs, Bryan Grant and the Kinsey brothers, Howard and Robert. Tilden, exploding fifteen cannonball aces in two sets against Kovacs at the age of 51, is the pick for the best service. There were others almost as good—Vines, Budge, Doeg (the most natural), Shields and McLoughlin.

That leaves only the chop. The master here was Wallace Johnson. His was the unkindest cut of all, or is there a rebuttal?

MAN OF THE HALF CENTURY

by Allison Danzig

Anyone who has seen the parade for the entire fifty years may go for Little Do Doherty, Norman Brookes, William Larned, Maurice McLoughlin, or one of the other relatively ancient heroes of the early 1900s, but the nomination here for tennis's man of the half century is William Tatem Tilden 2d.

Further than that, when, in all the years since Major Walter Clopton Wingfield brought forth the game in 1873 under the patented name of Sphairistike, has the world seen a greater master of the racket than the Germantown iconoclast who told Dempsey, Ruth, Jones, Grange, and Hitchcock to move over in the Golden Twenties?

Big Bill Tilden held absolute sway on the courts in a period unapproached before or since in the number of players of the first class developed the world over. In France there were the Four Musketeers—Lacoste, Cochet, Borotra, and Brugnon. From Spain came Manuel Alonso, the Tiger of the Pyrenees; from South Africa, Brian Ivan Cobb Norton (that is all one man).

Big Jim Anderson and burly Gerald Patterson stood for Australia; Zenzo Shimizu and Ichiya Kumagae for Japan. In the United States Little Bill Johnston, Vincent Richards, and Richard Norris Williams 2d, one of the breathtaking shotmakers of all time, formed the Big Four with Tilden. Behind them were Francis Hunter, Wallace Johnson, and Howard Kinsey.

From 1920 through 1925 Big Bill was so supreme that no one among all of these could carry his racket. Still, he had some close scrapes.

Impish Babe Norton, with more bounce to the ounce than a cooler of cola, had him match point in the 1921 challenge round at Wimbledon. Tiny grinning Shimizu, lost under his flapping sou'wester hat and reeling under the impact of Tilden's cannonball, was within two strokes of slaying him in three sets in the Davis Cup challenge round that same year at Forest Hills. Alonso, a raging señor who sometimes bit the throat of his racket, almost turned the trick at Newport, and Johnston took the first two sets from Big Bill in the championship final at Germantown in 1922.

But Tilden, the showman who would have given his racket hand to be an actor, usually got into hot water because of his flair for the dramatic. His idea of a good time was to get the gallery seething with excitement by giving his opponent a dangerous lead and then, with the stage properly set and the crowd won over to his side by the seeming desperateness of his plight, come on in a cyclonic rally to victory.

Johnston, with his unparalleled Western top-spin forehand, his almost unequaled volleying ability, and his great fighting spirit, could practically call the score against any other player in the world, but Tilden broke his heart. Little Bill would go out and slaughter one of the foreign greats, and the next day he would find himself at the mercy of Big Bill. "I can't lick that big bum," he said once as he came off the court dripping wet with perspiration and worn to exhaustion after having the cup of victory dashed from his lips.

Tilden had the greatest two-sided attack from the baseline the world has seen. They can talk about Donald Budge's backhand and Ellsworth Vines's paralyzing forehand. Tilden was just as strong from either side.

Big Bill could hit his backhand straight down or across court with the velocity of a bullet. He had one of the best cannonballs that ever belched aces, and his twist had a terrific kick. He was a master of spin without an equal. He could beat you with flat speed from the back of the court or he could win by destroying your control with forehand chops and sliced backhands.

Tilden was a tactician compared to whom most rivals were novices. He had a magnificent physique for the game and a grace and nimbleness of foot that Fred Perry alone equaled in the last thirty years. He wasn't the volleyer that was Vincent Richards or Johnston, and he wasn't secure overhead, but he did not need to go to the net until he began to slip and the French caught up with him after 1925.

Cochet brought him down in the championship quarter-finals in 1926. Lacoste did it in the Davis Cup challenge round that year and again in 1927 and beat him once more in one of the greatest championship finals on record with an exhibition of defensive play that bordered on the miraculous.

Tilden insisted that the tennis the French played went beyond his game. He wouldn't admit that his own game was slipping, even at the age of 34 in 1927, when he was having trouble with his knee.

Cochet was the greatest natural player the world has seen, with a touch out of this world. He did through sheer genius what Tilden did through years of slavery to the racket in practicing hours daily, week after week, month after month.

No one had such control of the ball as the inscrutable Lacoste, the Crocodile, or a better match temperament. But for all their greatness on the court, and the mad volleying of the dashing, debonair Borotra, there was only one Tilden. He was the master of his time and for all time.

OUR GREATEST ATHLETE

by Al Laney

For more than a month now the mailbox has called insistently for some comment from this quarter on the passing of William T. Tilden, which occurred in Los Angeles on June 5. The obituaries were inadequate, it was said, since Tilden was a unique personality aside from his unmatched achievements as a tennis player. He had continued in his game so long after passing his peak, it was suggested, that people had forgotten how great a man he was.

All this is true. Tilden was active in his game for more than a quarter of a century after his decline had set in and his many troubles in late years had taken the sheen from his earlier exploits. But these achievements must stand forever and no shadow should be cast over them.

Let us, as the saying is, take a look at the record for a moment. Tilden was twenty-seven years old when he first became champion in 1920. From that day to 1926 he never lost a championship match anywhere in the world in an era of the greatest concentration of tennis talent the game has known. He was nearly thirty-four when first beaten and thirty-seven when he became champion at Wimbledon for the third time in 1930.

Consider the names of the players who had come and mostly gone during that ten year span: Norris Williams, Billy Johnston, Gerald Patterson, Vincent Richards, René Lacoste, Henri Cochet, Jean Borotra. Tilden had beaten them all when at their best.

Tilden was sixty when he died and it is only about a year since he played in the professional championship, where he defeated Wayne Sabin and played a close match with Frank Kovacs. This represents a period of thirty-five years of continuous championship play in a game as strenuous as any. And at fifty-nine Tilden still was the world's finest tennis player over the short span of one set.

To win his last big title at Wimbledon in 1930 Tilden defeated Wilmer Allison, one of our finest players, in straight sets in the final. Nine years later, in 1939, he defeated Ellsworth Vines in a professional tournament at Wembley, in London, in a match on which considerable money rode.

The usual thing is to say that Tilden belonged to the so-called Golden Age of sport, the age of Bob Jones, Jack Dempsey, Red Grange, the Four Horsemen and Babe Ruth, that he was one of the great ones. Well, there above is the evidence to support the contention that Tilden was our greatest athlete in any sport.

From the standpoint of technique Tilden certainly was without a peer in tennis, quite possibly in any game. He had incomparably the finest forehand ever seen and, during that wonderful stretch of years which extended almost through the 1920s, the finest backhand ever seen also. He lost this latter shot somewhere toward the end of that period but his second best, the sliced one which he used for twenty more years, was better than all other backhands save that of Donald Budge.

Those who did not see Tilden in the 1920s do not know about this wonderful backhand and some of those who did see him then have forgotten about it. But there is plenty of ground for believing it the greatest single shot ever developed in the game of lawn tennis.

Tilden also was the finest server the game has known and a lot of people have forgotten that too in the age of slam-bang tennis. He was the best for the simple reason that the so-called cannonball, as hard a serve as any ever hit and which he could put into court eight times out of ten, was held in reserve. You saw it when Tilden wanted you to see it, which was an average of about once a service game. It was only when advancing age forced Tilden to use the big service constantly in an effort to shorten his service games that he began to be beaten.

With these three fundamental strokes alone Tilden no doubt would have been all-conquering, but he had developed to the highest point of efficiency every other stroke known. Moreover, he introduced strokes that others had not used. One of these was the drop shot, which, though he did not invent it, he introduced as an effective attacking weapon. For this he was booed at

Wimbledon, but a few years after that memorable occasion the drop shot had become a fundamental part of the equipment of every player. But none ever made it so well as Tilden.

Many have said that Tilden could not volley and smash, but they do not know what they say. He was the safest smasher imaginable and when he chose to volley he could do it with deadly effect. He did not seem to be a volleyer and smasher because he nearly always controlled the game from back court, but there was no single stroke of the game he had not perfected. He was a master of spin and slice and he could use what in baseball is called change of pace in a more bewildering way than the greatest pitcher who ever lived.

We remember Tilden as a fierce attacker, always after his man like a tiger, but the fact is he was basically and fundamentally a defender and the greatest of all there, too, for the man never lived who could break down that defense. That is a fact which young players of our day might ponder carefully. Tilden was the greatest attacker because he was first the greatest defender.

The mere thought of Tilden brings on a flood of tennis memories. Tilden at Forest Hills, Merion and Germantown, at Wimbledon and St. Cloud and Roland Garros and the Racing Club in Paris. These were the great days of the game. With most players legitimately rated as great ones, you may remember one, maybe two outstanding matches. With Tilden the list is endless. Tilden and Williams, Tilden and Johnston, Tilden and Patterson, Tilden and Lacoste three or four times, Tilden and Cochet as many, Tilden and Richards, Borotra and many others. Great and memorable matches and a hundred dramatic incidents in which Tilden was the chief figure.

Great as he was as a player, it is impossible to consider Tilden outside the rich soil of his nature. He was arrogant, quarrelsome, unreasonable; very hard to get along with and all his life an unhappy man. It is not generally known that Tilden was a wealthy man and that he ran through at least two substantial family fortunes to die with ten dollars in his pocket. And he probably made more money out of tennis than even the modern plutocrats of the professional exhibition racket.

Throughout his life he lived on a scale befitting an Indian Prince. Through the wonderful era of the 1920s he spent with a lavish hand.

Tilden longed beyond all else to be a great actor, and he dropped a small fortune producing plays with himself as the star, plays that failed miserably. For Tilden, who was indisputably a great actor on the tennis court—who ever can forget those majestic entrances and exits at Forest Hills and Wimbledon?—was a tragic failure behind the footlights.

There all his peculiarities of personality were accentuated and made ridiculous . . . His unquenchable thirst for victory never was slaked by his many triumphs on the courts of the world, and off them he was, most of his life, a desperately unhappy man, unloved and perhaps unloving, searching always for something he could not find, something which possibly did not exist.

It always is annoying to hear from someone else how fine were things you have not seen but, taking that risk, one cannot say other than that those who did not see Tilden at his peak against the finest players of his time have not seen the game of lawn tennis on the highest level it has yet reached.

Tilden, unquestionably, was one of the great personalities of our time. He died alone, in poverty. But even those who defeated him on the courts could never hope to be his equal. Probably we shall never see his like again.

AN IDEAL GAME

by Richard Norris Williams 2d

When discussing the ability of our greatest tennis player, W. T. Tilden, it is only natural that we turn for a few moments to the game itself and find out to what level it has progressed, say when Bill was just beginning his game and playing in the second class of some club handicap event, with a handicap of, say, plus 15—and he no doubt did it just like the rest of us mortals.

The great players of those days were of the steady kind, what we now speak of as the stonewall variety. Nothing spectacular, playing a rather slow all-round game, very well grounded but more or less of a defensive game, with but little power, especially on the attack. This was the natural development from the pat ball beginning of the game. It had acquired and digested the principles of "safety first." It now needed something new to carry it on one step higher. This "something new" was personified and came in the person of M. E. McLoughlin; and what he brought with him and gave to the game was the spectacular part, the tremendous power of the attack.

The game grows by what each generation of players gives to it; this is then digested, assimilated, into what we call the game of that particular period. Thus it was that when Bill started to get his head just above the great mass of the "also rans" he was confronted with a game that was, no doubt, too greatly devoted to the attack. He, however, had started in the days of "safety first," and, being a great student of the game and the time being ripe, he was able to amalgamate the two at first antagonistic games into his great game of today.

Mind you, when I mention McLoughlin as bringing in the fireworks and Tilden the modern game, I in no way mean to give the impression that they were the only ones that gave anything to the game. Each player makes his little contribution, which is just as valuable to the whole as that which is given by the man that represents the combination of those parts. Ward and Davis gave the powerful service; Wright, Brookes and many others gave different units of the attack, thus making it possible for McLoughlin to combine them and bring to a climax that great attacking game.

Just as McLoughlin profited by what went before him, so Tilden profited by what he found. Tilden, however, deserves the greater credit. McLoughlin disregarded part of the past—he was young, full of fire, he would not listen to the wisdom of the ages, he did not stop, look and listen; safety-first was nothing to him. Tilden, a naturally great player and a great student, realized the value of soundness as well as of fire, and he was able to combine those two into a game that is far and away superior to that played by McLoughlin.

To a great many readers this will probably sound as very meager praise. My only answer to them is, try it! For a good many years it was thought impossible, and yet Tilden did it.

In a few words, it is just a change of pace, and yet it's a tremendous stride. He has brought the fireworks down and the safety-first up, making it into a far more scientific game. Curiously enough, he leans towards the conservative, and this is said in spite of newspaper articles filled with adjectives which give the impression that every time he touches the ball it becomes invisible from speed. Not that he cannot produce speed; he can and often does. But he waits for the proper time and then he produces it when needed.

It is a really wonderful game, an ideal game: a great variety of strokes, easily executed, with very little effort; a great deal of pace and "weight" and the shot admirably placed—just easily waiting for the break or the opening. If the break does not come, the opening must—then the execution.

JOSEPH W. WEAR

by Allison Danzig

Joseph W. Wear of Philadelphia, chairman of the Davis Cup Committee of the United States Lawn Tennis Association since 1928, informed the New York *Times* yesterday of his retirement from active participation in lawn tennis affairs.

Pressure of his private business affairs and the exacting duties required of him as chairman of the alumni board of Yale University were given by Mr. Wear as the reasons for his decision to give up the work in which he has served with distinction for three years and added to the luster of his international reputation as one of the country's most distinguished sportsmen.

Coming on the heels of the announcement of Louis B. Dailey's retirement as president at the expiration of his term in February and William Tilden's renunciation of his amateur status, Mr. Wear's withdrawal marks the third big loss the U.S.L.T.A. has suffered in its jubilee year.

No formal letter of resignation has been forwarded to the association as yet by Mr. Wear. His announcement to the *Times* is his first official statement, though one or two officials of the association have understood that he was disinclined to accept the post again. It has been expected that Mr. Dailey's successor as president, who in all probability will be Louis J. Carruthers, now first vice president, woud name Mr. Wear as chairman again to serve for 1931. Not only will Mr. Wear not consider the Davis Cup portfolio again, but he also will decline to accept the office of vice president of the U.S.L.T.A.

Asked as to whom he considered the man best qualified to succeed to the chairmanship, Mr. Wear named Fitz-Eugene Dixon of Philadelphia, who has been his right-hand man for the last two years as captain of the Davis Cup team.

"Mr. Dixon's services," said Mr. Wear, "have been invaluable. I know of no man who could do a better job and I hope that the association will see that he is kept interested in tennis. If the choice were left to me, I would appoint him to serve both as chairman of the committee and captain of the team."

Coincident with the announcement of his retirement from the post he has occupied during the three years in which the United States has been a challenger for the cup lost to France in 1927, Mr. Wear took occasion to make known his disagreement with certain changes in Davis Cup regulations and policy that have been advocated recently. It is his inflexible position that so long as the Davis Cup is held by another country, it reflects upon the good sportsmanship of the U.S.L.T.A. to advocate any changes which might detract in any degree from the victory of the holding nation or minimize its satisfaction thereover.

"I agree," said Mr. Wear, "that certain changes should be made in the play for the Davis Cup. Ever since I became chairman of the Davis Cup Committee I have thought that the Davis Cup competition had grown to such dimensions and so much time was required of the players representing us that the U.S.L.T.A. should do something to minimize the time a boy should be away from his business or collegiate work. The only question in my mind was when to make the necessary reforms.

"I am firmly of the opinion that, in fairness to France and the other nations, we should do nothing until we have brought the cup back to the United States. We must be careful not to create the impression that we might at times be unable to use our best players and, therefore, were entering the competition under a handicap. France, England, Germany, Japan or any other nation who wins from our representatives should have the satisfaction of feeling that they have won from our best. We must not dim the luster of any victory over us.

"Over a year ago I wrote to Mr. Dwight F. Davis, the donor of the cup, that I thought reforms were necessary, and in his answer to me he agreed that the proper time to make any changes in our eligibility rules should be when we became the defending nation again." Mr. Wear's reference to changes in the eligibility rules concerned the proposal made to limit the eligibility of Davis Cup players to three years of competition, and to bar married players from the team.

"The whole idea back of the Davis Cup," said the retiring chairman, "is to establish the champion team. The idea is not to give a player a few years of experience in international play and then drop him. It is for each nation to put its strongest representatives upon the field and determine the champion nation. If we disqualify a player because he is married or has represented us three years, obviously we are not going to put our greatest strength on the court and the matches do not represent a championship.

"If it is decided that it is to the best interests of tennis and sport that the purpose of the matches be changed, that is well and good. But while another country holds the cup, it ill becomes us to advocate this change or to attempt to make it binding on other nations.

"France met us under the regulations that now exist and proved her superiority and right to the cup, and as the nation that sponsored the matches in 1900 we should abide by them as a challenger and not create the impression that we are seeking to gain an advantage through legislation. That seems to me to be good sportsmanship, while the other course may serve to create resentment in the French association."

Instead of barring the players who have represented us for three years or who are married, Mr. Wear recommends that George M. Lott, Jr., of Chicago, Wilmer Allison, Jr., of Austin, Texas, and John Van Ryn of East Orange, New Jersey, all of whom fall in both categories, be selected for the squad again this year, as well as John Hope Doeg, the national champion, if he is available. Along with these, he would name also Gregory Mangin of the 1930 squad, Sidney B. Wood, Jr., and Frank Shields, whose play stood out prominently, and possibly Clifford Sutter and Ellsworth Vines. . . .

The retirement of the Davis Cup chairman will be a serious loss not only to tennis in the United States but to the game in general. No one in tennis is held in higher regard than the Philadelphian, who won prominence at Yale as a baseball player and in court tennis and racquets after his graduation. Mr. Wear won the national racquets doubles with Dwight Davis in 1914 and the national doubles in court tennis with Jay Gould six times. His appointment as Davis Cup chairman in 1928 was hailed as the entry of one of the country's most representative sportsmen into its lawn tennis councils and was foreseen as a guarantee of the maintenance of the association's international relations upon their high plane of noblesse oblige.

A man of wealth and the highest social position, Mr. Wear took up his work with an enthusiasm and energy that have been characteristic of him in everything that he has done. He immediately laid his plans for the 1928 team, arranged with the Augusta Country Club at Augusta, Georgia, to hold trials for the squad on its courts, and went down personally with Mrs. Wear to supervise the play. From the beginning he won the confidence of the candidates for the team and became their warm friend, and no one was ever a more welcome or respected figure in an American Davis Cup camp.

In 1929, Mr. Dixon, his friend of many years standing, became associated with Mr. Wear in the handling of Davis Cup affairs, and between the two of them they have not only established a spirit of splendid morale in the Davis Cup squad but have added to the prestige abroad of American standards of sportsmanship. Mr. Wear found it impossible to accompany the team abroad in 1929 and 1930, owing to the demands of his business affairs, but he was in constant touch with them by cablegram and transatlantic telephone and directed the campaign from Philadelphia.

In 1928, it was to Mr. Wear that the late ambassador to France, Myron T. Herrick, appealed for the restoration of Tilden to the team for the challenge round match with France after he had been disbarred for violation of the player-writer rule at Wimbledon. This controversy was one of several centering around Tilden to which Wear necessarily was drawn in, and his decisions in every instance reflected his executive capacity for clear thinking and quick action.

Not all of his decisions met with unanimous approval, naturally, since each year the team failed to bring back the cup, but no one ever questioned them on the grounds of good sportsmanship or fairness, and Mr. Wear retires with the satisfaction of knowing that any mistakes he may have made, if he did make any, were mistakes in picking a man who lost instead of a man who might not have lost. Mr. Wear was never troubled by criticism. He is by nature too buoyant and serene to be disturbed by it, and his decision to retire was in no way influenced by opposition of any kind. Outside of the above mentioned criticism there has been no opposition to him, and his retirement will occasion only regret that the game has lost so outstanding a sportsman and so zealous a worker for its welfare.

VINCENT RICHARDS, THE FIRST BOY WONDER

by Arthur Daley

When Vincent Richards was only 15 years old, he paired with Bill Tilden to win the national doubles championship in tennis and he never quite lost the label of boy wonder even when his blond hair turned gray. Vinnie was a popular figure along the sports scene over the decades and it just doesn't seem right that his passing be unmarked by the farewell he deserved.

Yet his death at 56 came at a time when the sports pages were boiling with so much news that an appreciaton of his talents had to be delayed. Certainly he ranks with the great stars of the court, although his proper rung on the ladder will always be clouded. The fuzziness is caused by the fact that Richards had not even reached his peak when he turned professional at the age of 23 in 1926.

That was the year when Vinnie had beaten Tilden with such frequency that he was slated to gain the distinction of No. 1 in the national rankings. But the tennis fathers, frowning on commercialism, dropped Richards from their list, much to the indignation of press and public.

If it had not been for his decision to go on the C. C. (Cash and Carry) Pyle tour with Suzanne Lenglen, Mary K. Browne, Howard Kinsey, et al., Vinnie unquestionably would have taken his place with such greats as Tilden, Don Budge, Jack Kramer and the like. But professional tennis was a bumbling thing then and the pros didn't get the recognition accorded today to such as Pancho Gonzales, Lew Hoad and the like.

For one thing, Vinnie was victimized by a canard foisted by the mischievous Francis Albertanti, the somewhat zany sports editor of the old *Evening Mail*. According to Francis, a man whose tongue was always firmly in his cheek, his newspaper saved time by keeping a stock headline always standing. It proclaimed: "Tilden Beats Richards Again."

Maybe it seemed that way when Vinnie was a 15-year-old kid from Fordham Prep and Big Bill was a magnificently coordinated wizard of 25. But as Richards developed in strength and skill, the gap between them narrowed. One of the greatest volleyers the sport ever had, the boy from Yonkers more than held his own.

Statisticians once toiled through results over a thirty-seven-year span. According to these calculations, Tilden and Richards met in 1,002 matches, counting singles and doubles. Richards was on the winning side of the net 502 times, Tilden 500. As a doubles team, they won three national championships and were unbeatable in Davis Cup play.

"Funny thing," Vinnie once remarked with a wry grin, "but Tilden was too much of an individualist to be a good doubles player. He always thought he was entitled to cover three-quarters of the court. I always held that half of it was mine. So I kidded him constantly about it, a ribbing he never appreciated. Once Bill got on a court he had no sense of humor."

Nor was the shrewd Vinnie beyond exploiting that lack of a funny bone or of stirring the temperamental Tilden into petulant rages. One year, Richards had beaten Big Bill in successive tournaments and Tilden was seething because defeat rankled within him. They were in Jacksonville when Vinnie approached his rival on the veranda.

"Bill," said Vinnie, manfully keeping a straight face, "I don't like the looks of that big tree at the end of the court. You and I are a cinch to play a five-set match and by late afternoon that tree will cast distracting shadows over the court. You ought to do something about it."

Tilden stalked over to the tournament chairman.

"Cut down that tree," he demanded in his usual imperious manner. He was told it was impossible.

"Then cut off the branches," snapped Tilden, building up a head of steam. That also was impossible.

Tilden threatened to withdraw and was so mad when he did play, Richards beat him in five sets—in the distracting shadows, too.

Of all the honors to accrue to Vinnie, the one he treasured most was the winning of the only Olympic men's singles tournament ever staged. It not only was the first in history but also undoubtedly will be the last. This was in Paris in 1924 under the merciless sun that flooded Roland Garros Stadium. Vinnie started the tournament weighing 170 pounds. He finished it at 152.

The notable part of this was that he polished off in successive days the colorful Three Musketeers of the tennis world, the flamboyant Frenchmen who were to dominate international play for many years—René Lacoste, Jean Borotra and Henri Cochet. Each match went five sets.

Vincent Richards was not only a top-flight tennis player but he also was a top-flight person, a welcome decoration to any sports event in our town. He will be grievously missed.

JULIAN MYRICK

by George McGann

In thinking back over a career in tennis which is as old as the century, Julian (Uncle Mike) Myrick can take pride in the big role he played in moving the National Championships from Newport to Forest Hills in 1915 and the subsequent building of the Stadium at the West Side Tennis Club. The first event opened up the game to the public and the second made tennis a big-time sport in this country. For these early achievements, and for his many later ones, he is being honored this month with the Marlboro Award.

Now in his eighty-fifth year and retired from active duties with the USLTA, Uncle Mike still retains a keen interest in all phases of the game. He is particularly concerned about the recurrent movement to award the Nationals to Los Angeles or some other city and is firmly against it.

"Lawn tennis is a grass court game and our Championships should always be played on that surface," Uncle Mike said in a conversation the other day at his club in midtown Manhattan. "The Stadium at Forest Hills is still the finest in the country. There is no reason to go elsewhere. All that is needed is better promotion of the event. Instead of waiting until August to publicize the Championships, it should be made a year-round effort. With the foreign players now coming each year, it is a truly international tournament. New York is the best place for it."

When he reached the pinnacle of 80, the newspapers devoted a lot of space to Uncle Mike's achievements in tennis and selling life insurance and the way he dominated both fields during his heyday in the 1920s. They also dwelt on his daily setting-up exercises, his thrice-weekly tennis doubles matches and his multiple martinis before dinner.

"I still do calisthenics with dumbbells every morning," said the trim white-haired gentleman the other day, his eyes alertly snapping behind rimless spectacles. "Unfortunately since an eye operation I am no longer able to play tennis. Instead I go round to the River Club regularly to hit with the pro. I tell you I miss my regular games, as much for their companionship as for the exercise. As for the martinis, I enjoy a drink or two in the evening."

Uncle Mike, a legendary success story in the competitive life insurance field, still goes to his office at the Mutual of New York Company. He tried to retire several years ago but idleness bored him and he went back to work as a consultant. As a young man, his dynamism and drive sent him to the top of his profession when he and partner Charles Ives formed their own insurance agency. Myrick often won selection on the exclusive "million dollar a year" group of insurance salesmen. Ives was as well known in the field of music as Myrick was in tennis; he won a Pulitzer Prize for composing symphonies and sonatas on American themes.

As president of the USLTA and chairman of the Davis Cup Committee in the decade following World War I, when tennis and most other pastimes basked in the glow of the Golden Era of Sports, Uncle Mike was a strong—often headstrong, according to his critics—and vital leader. His accession to power coincided with the rise of another dynamic figure, the incomparable Bill Tilden, who was every bit as headstrong, and they clashed frequently and publicly, particularly over Tilden's violations of the amateur code and its prohibition against players writing for pay. Tilden fancied himself as a writer and often signed up to report tournaments for newspapers or news syndicates. Each time he did so, Uncle Mike would step in and forbid Tilden to go through with the job. This led to many a squabble and, on one occasion in 1928, caused Tilden's removal for a time from the U.S. Davis Cup team (of which he was the leading player). Tilden called Uncle Mike a "czar" and Uncle Mike, in turn, was quoted as calling Tilden "an evil influence in the game."

Tilden, whom Uncle Mike regards as "the greatest player I ever saw" despite their many differences, helped dramatize the Davis Cup competition during the years when the Four Musketeers—Lacoste, Cochet, Brugnon and Borotra—dominated the international scene. With Tilden packing the crowds into tennis arenas with his flamboyant style and Uncle Mike working diligently behind the scenes to build up the structure of the game, tennis in this country reached its all-time peak in public interest and participation. The overnight rise of tennis as a major sport in the immediate postwar years led to the erection of the 13,500-seat stadium at Forest Hills in 1923, and Uncle Mike was the leading spirit behind this major move in the game.

Ten years earlier, Uncle Mike had headed the committee of members who moved the West Side Tennis Club from Van Cortlandt Park in upper Manhattan to its present site alongside the Long Island Railroad in Forest Hills. In 1914 he succeeded in bringing the Challenge Round with Australasia to the new club grounds for the historic meeting between Norman Brookes and Maurice McLoughlin of California.

"The tremendous crowds we got for those Cup matches inspired us to try to get the National Championships away from Newport," Uncle Mike recalled. "The Newport faction was well entrenched in the USLTA. We had what you might call a heated meeting of the Executive Committee at the old Waldorf Astoria in 1915 and won by a narrow vote after I had promised we would make more money at Forest Hills than any tournament ever held at Newport. We got the Championships and made good on the promise. Tennis was restricted during the war years, but when the armistice came we started thinking about a stadium. With the help of a ten-year contract from the USLTA for the Championships, enabling us to sell ten-year seats and boxes, we built the stadium and opened it in 1923 with the Wightman Cup matches. They were a great success. In those days we never had any trouble selling seats. I used to stand by the window near my locker in the Club, looking out at the railroad station—everybody came by train—and watch the people streaming along Burns Street towards the stadium. It was a pleasant sight."

Tennis has brought many other pleasant moments to Uncle Mike, and he cherishes two particular memories. In 1954 he accompanied Billy Talbert (whom he considers one of the finest American captains in the history of the game) and the Davis Cup team to Australia in the capacity of official representative of the USLTA.

"I was particularly happy to be in Australia, not only to meet so many old associates such as Norman Brookes and Gerald Patterson, but to get to play doubles with friends at the Kooyong courts in Melbourne," Uncle Mike remarked. "That completed my personal 'grand slam' of playing at all the world's major tennis centers. I had already played at Forest Hills, of course, and at Wimbledon and Paris."

His other pet recollection is of the European tour he made with the U.S. Olympic Tennis Team of Vincent Richards and Helen Wills in 1924. "When we got to Spain, I arranged a mixed doubles match for Queen Victoria, who was very keen on tennis," Uncle Mike reminisced. "The Queen and Vinnie Richards beat Hazel Wightman and me, 8–6. In 1938 at Wimbledon I was again presented to the Queen and she recalled the incident very pleasantly. One of her sons, now the Duke of Barcelona, had admired our rackets during the match in Spain, and I gave him one. His father, King Alfonso, told me that no present could have given the boy greater pleasure."

Uncle Mike was never a tournament player as a youth but has always been an excellent "club" player. He has played most of his tennis at the Seventh Regiment Indoor Courts in Manhattan (he joined the Regiment in 1899!) and at the West Side and Maidstone Club near his summer home in Easthampton, Long Island. In recent years he has played at the River Club in Manhattan during the winters.

Uncle Mike is a member of an extensive tennis family. One of his nephews is Sidney Wood, the former Wimbledon winner who is founder and president of the Town Tennis Club in Manhattan's fashionable Sutton Place area. Watson Washburn, who played Davis Cup tennis during the early twenties, is a brother-in-law.

Born in Murfreesboro, North Carolina—"my father raised mules and horses and grew cotton and peanuts"—young Mike grew up in suburban Dobbs Ferry near New York City and attended Trinity School. He still retains the soft Southern-accented speech of childhood. He never attended college—"the Seventh Regiment was my college"—but got into the insurance business at an early age and quickly was a financial success. As a member of the Seventh he not only played tennis but competed on the regimental track team, running the 220 yard dash. He has continued the training habits he learned as a runner into his later years. "As you get older you should take exercise to keep up your muscle tone," he points out. "Otherwise the muscles get flabby and you let yourself down physically and mentally."

Julian Myrick is 84 years young. Age has mellowed him, and from being an arch-tennis-conservative in the twenties he has become a flaming liberal in the sixties. He walks briskly, thinks keenly and is even more charming than in his early years. He looks 60, acts 50, has the vigor of a man of 40, the love of sports of a man of 30, and the forward-looking attitude of a man of 20.

"Here's how," from one martini drinker to another.

WILLIAMS AND WASHBURN

by George Carens

Ten years ago at Philadelphia, Watson Washburn and Richard N. Williams 2d faced each other in the final round of the intercollegiate doubles tournament, Washburn teamed with Joe Armstrong of St. Paul and Williams with Ted Whitney of Boston. In the battle between the two Harvard teams Washburn's side won.

Tomorrow at the Chestnut Hill courts of the Longwood Cricket Club these old Crimson racket wielders will be on the same side of the net, expending every ounce of energy and resorting to every legitimate device to keep the national doubles championship in America. They made it certain yesterday that the honors would not go wholly out of the country by eliminating the Australian Davis Cup team of James O. Anderson and John B. Hawkes after four sets of excellent combination play on the part of the

Bryn Mawr and New York residents. Whether the W-W team will face William T. Tilden 2d of Germantown, Pennsylvania, and B. C. Norton of South Africa or the Spanish-American team of Manuel Alonso of Bethlehem, Pennsylvania, and Wallace F. Johnson of Cynwyd, Pennsylvania, will be determined when the second semi-final is played this afternoon.

Two years ago, one week before Williams and Washburn successfully carried the Davis Cup doubles burden against the Japanese, they were runners-up to Tilden and Vincent Richards in the national doubles. Thus it is the second chance that the W-W team will have had to capture the title.

The names of Williams and Washburn have been linked so often in tennis that one might suppose that they have been inseparable since their college days, but that has not been the case. They played together first in the spring of 1914 and during the summer of 1915 won the Eastern doubles championship. The elimination series for the sectional title winners was held on the turf courts of the Onwentsia Club in Chicago that year and Williams and Washburn were beaten by Wallace Johnson and Clarence J. Griffin.

Williams concentrated on singles in 1916 and won the national title for the second time, and Washburn competed in doubles that year with Richard Harte. In 1917 and 1918 the famous W-W team was in khaki, but with the close of the World War they resumed partnership and won a good doubles tournament and the A.E.F. title at Cannes, France. Upon their return from France, they again won the Eastern doubles but were beaten in the nationals at Longwood by Norman E. Brookes and Gerald L. Patterson, the Australian team which subsequently defeated Johnston and Griffin in the final round and then downed Tilden and Richards in the last challenge round on record.

The 1920 campaign found Washburn teaming with Dean Mathey, and Williams with Harte. Williams and Washburn hooked up again in 1921, the year they were finalists in the national doubles, and formed the doubles team in the Davis Cup challenge round, and since then they have stuck together. . . .

Whether the all-American team can prevent a foreigner from figuring in winning the national doubles for the fourth time in forty-three years is the main topic of conversation at Chestnut Hill today. All observers are agreed that Williams is playing better tennis than he has shown since the war. But the feeling will not down that Washburn will be unequal to the task of holding up his end of the partnership. The New Yorker with the classical attitude on the courts . . . who is a sensible, manly chap and extremely popular with all of the players, has a weakness that may prove fatal if Tilden gets into the final. This is his overhead, which does not compare favorably with the flat drives that he angles with exasperating frequency (for his opponent) for placement aces. If Washburn's overhead withstands the test and if Williams selects the proper moments for his fancy shots that no other player would attempt, then the Yankees may be able to reach the pinnacle in American doubles. Their methods of attack were well devised against the Australians and they may profit by an afternoon of restful observation while their prospective opponents are toiling through today's semi-final contest.

RICHARD NORRIS WILLIAMS 2D

by Allison Danzig

Richard Norris (Dick) Williams 2d was one of the most brilliant lawn tennis players the world has known.

Born of American parents, January 29, 1891, in Geneva, Switzerland, where he was coached from boyhood by his father, Williams came to the United States in 1912. His trip was made on the ill-fated *Titanic,* which went down after striking an iceberg in the North Atlantic. He was picked out of the icy water after swimming for over an hour. His father was lost.

Williams established himself immediately after his arrival in the United States as one of the foremost tennis players. For fifteen years he was in the headlines (with time out for war service) as the winner of national championships, Wimbledon and Olympic titles and as a member and captain of United States Davis Cup teams.

They called Williams the "beau sabreur" of the tennis courts. He was a player of breathtaking daring in his tactics and stroke production, who either beat his opponent with his sheer brilliance of stroke in taking the ball on the rise or defeated himself with his errors if his touch was lacking. Never content to play safe or to win with prosaic measures, he might scale the heights or plumb the depths, according to whether he was on or off his game.

At his best Williams was more dazzling than William Tilden, leaving galleries spellbound with the volleys and half-volleys that rippled off his racket with the minimum margin of safety. Lithe, trim and straight as an arrow to the tip of his bristling shock of hair, and hitting to the hilt on every shot with complete disregard for the consequences, he was an immediate sensation. To the end of his tournament playing days in his middle forties, he remained the same bold, uncompromising antagonist who would rather lose with a stroke of daring than win with the commonplace.

Twice Williams won the national championship. The first time it was the great Maurice McLoughlin, the California Comet, whom he beat in the final, ending his two-year reign, in 1914. Such was the belief in McLoughlin's invincibility, particularly after his great victory over the celebrated Norman Brookes of Australia in the Davis Cup challenge round, that his defeat by the comparative newcomer from Switzerland caused a sensation. The match was played in Newport, the last national championship held there.

Williams, who had been runner-up to McLoughlin in 1913, won the championship a second time in 1916. In the final he beat William (Little Bill) Johnston, champion in 1915 and 1919 and ruler of the courts from 1919 up to 1926 with Tilden.

In his first season of play in this country, 1912, Williams won a national ranking second only to McLoughlin. From then until 1925 he was ranked in the first ten eleven times, remaining at 2 through 1915 and going to the top in 1916. McLoughlin was ranked ahead of him in 1914, despite the fact that Williams won the crown.

Within a year after coming to the United States Williams was put on the Davis Cup team, in 1913. Going abroad, he won his two singles matches against Australasia, Germany and Canada. Against Great Britain in the challenge round he won one match and lost the other. He was in the challenge round against Australasia in 1914 and lost to Brookes and Anthony Wilding. There was no Davis Cup play again until the war ended, and the United States remained out in 1919.

Williams went to the officers' training camp at Plattsburg in 1917 and left for France as a lieutenant of artillery. He won his captaincy and was an aide to Major General James Harbord, with whom he was decorated with the French War Cross for distinguished service in the second battle of the Marne. . . .

With his return home, Williams took up his racket again in 1919 and was ranked sixth in the country. In 1920, when the United States resumed Davis Cup competition, he was a member of the team but, with Tilden and Johnston on deck, he did not play a part in the challenge round victory over Australasia in New Zealand. He was captain of the team from 1921 through 1925 as a playing member and was non-playing captain in 1934. In 1921, 1923, 1925 and 1926 he played in the challenge round doubles, winning with Watson Washburn in 1921 against Japan, with Tilden in 1923 against Australasia and with Vincent Richards in 1925 and 1926 against France.

Eleven national titles fell to Williams. Besides the two in singles on grass, he won the doubles with Richards in 1925 and 1926, the mixed doubles with Mary K. Browne in 1912 and the clay court singles in 1912 and 1915.

Also, he won the intercollegiate singles in 1913 and 1915 as the representative of Harvard and the intercollegiate doubles with Richard Harte in 1914 and 1915.

In 1920 Williams won the British doubles championship at Wimbledon with Charles S. Garland. In 1924 he was runner-up there with Washburn, and he won the Olympic mixed doubles in Paris with Mrs. Hazel Wightman.

THE FOUR MUSKETEERS

by Duncan Macaulay

Nineteen twenty-four was the beginning of six years of French domination at Wimbledon. The "Four Musketeers" of France were great players individually and also a great team—probably the greatest national team there has ever been since the game of lawn tennis began. Lacoste, Borotra, Cochet and Brugnon were all very different in style and temperament, and they sometimes clashed bitterly with one another on the courts. But whenever they felt they were playing for France, whether it was in defense of the Davis Cup—or at Wimbledon—they always put France first. Thus it was the combined pressure of Lacoste and Cochet which began to rock the great Bill Tilden on his pedestal, and which finally toppled him off it.

Although Jean Borotra was the most volatile of the four, it was he who really supplied the inspiration and the cement which bound the team together—just as it was Toto Brugnon who was the rock upon which most of their doubles successes rested. Toto was not only a very delightful character but one of the greatest doubles partners in the game. He was everyone's "invitation to the waltz"; and whether he played with Borotra or Cochet, with each of whom he won two Wimbledon titles, he always subordinated himself to the brilliance and opportunism of his partner. Toto always played in the right court, as he said he had no backhand—although he managed to beat a lot of high-class singles opponents in his time. But all his strokes were safe, steady, well placed and directed by an acute lawn tennis brain—to give his partner a winning opening either on volley or smash.

Jean Borotra was a great athlete and showman, bounding about the court in his black beret; but underneath the gaiety, the charm, and often the deliberate fooling, lay a body of steel and a will of iron. His victories over René Lacoste in singles were a great triumph of will and endurance, directed by a very keen lawn tennis brain, because René was really the better singles player, and Tilden always feared him more than he did Borotra. But if Jean could get one of the first two sets against René, he could generally win the match in the fifth, by the careful parcelling out of his reserves. Jean Borotra loved the red wine and the pretty ladies, but by a combination of rationing and strict self-discipline he maintained a very high degree of physical fitness—so much so that he has outlasted them all and, in his sixties, must be one of the greatest athletes of his age in the world. Jean was also a very fine doubles player and won the Wimbledon doubles three times, once with Lacoste—who was never in the same class in doubles as in singles—and twice with Brugnon.

Lacoste was the youngest of the four and the most austere. He studied his strokes and tactics far more than any of the other three did, or could. The crocodile, which he adopted as his mascot and which he had embroidered on

196

all his tennis vests, symbolized his determination to keep on keeping on and devour his opponents in the end. It was a tragedy that ill health should have put an end to his tennis when he was in his very early twenties and had the whole world at his feet.

Henri Cochet was a magician, and I don't think he knew himself how he made his strokes. He was the quickest thing ever seen on a lawn tennis court; and also the coolest and the most nonchalant. He could demoralize the hardest hitter by standing right inside the court and taking all the speediest shots on the rise. He had no service to speak of and no backhand; yet for about five years running he was ranked as the foremost player in the world. But he had the defects of his virtues and he was sometimes beaten in an important match by someone not in his class at all.

JEAN BOROTRA

by Tony Mottram

Yesterday and Friday at Queen's Club, Jean Borotra, now turned 60, paid his annual playing visit to London on the occasion of the match between the International Lawn Tennis Clubs of Great Britain and France.

For those who care to watch only the finest lawn tennis in the world, this event will have aroused no great interest.

For those whose lawn tennis extends to the early years of the All-England Club at its present Church Road site in Wimbledon, Borotra's presence must have conjured up memories of what was probably the game's most exciting era when international lawn tennis came of age and great personalities of the courts like Tilden, Suzanne Lenglen, and Borotra himself, aroused tremendous interest throughout the world.

Tilden and Suzanne Lenglen are with us no more, and to most of today's younger players the name of Borotra means little more than an oft-repeated entry in the record book.

Yet Borotra, with 40 years of playing experience behind him, continues to bring all his immense vitality, personality, and activity to bear on the game.

Jean Borotra was born in Biarritz on August 13, 1898. By the age of 24 he had established himself as one of France's greatest players. His winning exploits, along with those of his compatriots, Henri Cochet, Jacques Brugnon (who, now 63, was also in action at Queen's Club this weekend) and René Lacoste, took France to the top in lawn tennis. These "four musketeers" together dominated the Davis Cup and world tennis generally and the great personality among them was undoubtedly Jean Borotra.

Borotra—"the bounding Basque" they called him—won twice at Wimbledon, in 1924 and 1926. He was a net-rusher purely and simply. There was none of the touch and finesse in his game that characterized the play of Cochet, Brugnon in doubles, or of Lacoste. Borotra's speed of eye and foot was fantastic; his volleying acrobatic and punishing. Everything about his play was spectacular, and keyed to his colorful performance was an inborn love of showmanship. He was at his best when his play was appreciated. Borotra loved a crowd and the crowd loved Borotra.

This was "the bounding Basque" at his best. Yet today Borotra can still enthrall the gallery at Queen's as he dashes forward to make a winning coup. The beret has now been discarded and a pair of necessary but incongruous-looking spectacles take away much of the pantherlike appearance he had in earlier days. There remains the same urgent manner, if the step is less springy; the acrobatics still come naturally, if in a slightly more restrained form.

It is a point for argument as to whether Borotra at his best would have proved capable of winning in the company of today's greatest players. Technically his game could not measure up to the efficiency of modern champions. It was, and still is, individualistic in the extreme. He thrusts and parries, lunges and strikes like a duellist, his racket flashing backward and forward like a rapier. And behind his tennis, which at 60 puts to shame the efforts of men half his age, lies the driving spirit of a true champion.

How does he do it? The answer must lie in fitness. Borotra is a slave to it. Every morning without fail he goes through a rigorous routine of physical jerks on the balcony of his flat in Paris's Avenue Foch. His regular games of tennis are treated with the same seriousness as a business appointment.

To play against Borotra was and still is a great experience. Under his spell Borotra's partners come alive with fresh purpose. Lazy players bestir themselves, and some, playing more for the experience than for the honor of winning, suddenly find themselves fighting with all the fervor they would summon to a Davis Cup tie.

In mixed doubles the Borotra magic continues to weave its spell with undeniable charm and effect. Mixed doubles was made for a player of Borotra's speed and anticipation. But in triumph or in defeat the lady of his choice invariably receives a token of his appreciation with the gift of perfume—a thought which endears him to all his mixed doubles partners, which is considerably more than most of us are able to claim.

TOTO BRUGNON

by Gerald Perreau-Saussine

The closest thing to boasting ever heard from Jacques Brugnon is a quiet explanation to a persistent questioner that the four little insignias on his tennis sweater each stand for a victory in the finals of the world's doubles championship. The little man with the slight French accent has won four Wimbledon titles!

No little praise has been heaped on the diffident Frenchman. The incomparable Tilden called Toto "the equal in doubles of anyone who ever lived"; Lacoste considered that his unorthodox strokes made him one of the most difficult players in the world to beat. His backswing was almost nonexistent, which made it practically impossible to anticipate the direction of his shots. His volley, a quick slap of unerring depth and accuracy, was perhaps his best shot, but the true brilliance of his game was based on superb reflexes and a canny sense of tactics. Rarely did he play the wrong shot.

At nineteen, when he went into the army, Monsieur Brugnon was an unspectacular tennis player, but three years later he emerged from his military service several classes better than he had gone in, without ever having picked up a racket! He promptly won his first National Championship, achieving a measure of note by winning the Indoor Singles Championship of France in 1921.

Toto established himself as the greatest doubles player in the world in 1925. In the next few years, he won the national titles of France, England, Australia and Germany a total of twelve different times with several different partners including Dupont, Cochet, Borotra, Boussous, Lacoste and Von Cramm. It seemed to matter very little who his partner was—he nearly always won. His victims included Tilden-Hunter, Allison-Van Ryn, Vines-Gledhill, Tilden-Richards and Perry-Hughes among others. Every doubles team he met felt the rapier thrust, and between 1925 and 1933 losses were relatively few.

Toto's peak was reached during the Golden Age of Tilden and Lenglen, an era of tremendous popularity for the great champions. Many of the celebrities of this period were avid tennis enthusiasts, and they took the Frenchman with the shy charm and easy, elegant game to their hearts. The effervescent Borotra and the quiet Brugnon were the doubles attraction of their day and great favorites with the Wimbledon gallery.

Perhaps the greatest glory of a champion lies not with the individual successes but with the Davis Cup. Toto's presence was felt at thirty International meetings, and for six years he was Captain of the French Davis Cup Team. The Four Musketeers held the Cup from 1927 to 1932.

While he will always be remembered for his exploits in doubles, his ability in singles is too often underemphasized. On the Center Court at Wimbledon in 1929, he displayed absolutely top class tennis in eliminating Johnny Van Ryn in straight sets, and he holds major victories over Frank Hunter, Henri Cochet, Jean Borotra, Jack Crawford, Gerald Patterson, Bunny Austin, René Lacoste, Manuel Alonso and Gottfried von Cramm. . . .

In 1928 he won the French and Australian titles with Borotra and the Wimbledon title with Cochet. His great hope was to become the first man to win the four major doubles titles of the world in one year. The Grand Slam eluded him.

The sole major title that eluded the magic racket of the great Frenchman in doubles was the USLTA Championship. He won our National Indoor Doubles title with Borotra in 1927 and lost to his partner in the singles final. With Meade Woodson he won the USLTA Senior title in 1941, but the big one slipped by. . . .

Now, in 1954, Jacques Brugnon lives quietly in Hollywood, California. He works in the Foreign Department of MGM Studios as a technical assistant, and he numbers many of the movieland personalities among his friends. He rarely makes a tournament appearance, preferring to play doubles once or twice a week at the Los Angeles Tennis Club, where he is an honorary member. . . .

Every year an old friend and tennis rival comes to Los Angeles for the Pacific Southwest with a squad of fine young players under his guidance. Harry Hopman and Toto Brugnon have been a fixture in the Senior Doubles event for the past few years. . . . In 1953 they swept the senior field without losing a set. A spectator watched the two in the finals with unconcealed admiration as they put the ball away for game, set, match and tournament. He turned to his companion and said, "Y'know something? He won four Wimbledon titles!"

And that's where we came in.

RENÉ LACOSTE

by Allison Danzig

This is the scientific age in lawn tennis, and the man who would be king of the game must be able not only to outstroke his opponent but to outthink him as well. In William Tilden, who has at last given up his throne after six years of absolute monarchy, the tennis world has recognized one of the most thoroughgoing students of stroke production and court tactics that the game has known—a player thoroughly grounded in the mechanics of tennis, with a mastery over spin and pace that amounts to science and an analytical mind as eternally vigilant in the deployment of his strokes as a chess player in moving his pawns.

The great match player, says Tilden, is always a shot ahead of the one he is making. He must be a psychologist and understand what he is trying to do with every stroke in a set plan of attack.

In Jean René Lacoste, the 22-year-old youth of France, on Army leave, who has succeeded to Tilden's scepter, the tennis world recognizes another mastermind of the Tilden pattern. Lacking in the American's variety of stroke production and complete mastery of spin and the delicate nuances of racket manipulation, Lacoste is nevertheless equipped with the most classic fundamental strokes in tennis and is a psychologist par excellence.

Tilden was among the first to recognize in this phlegmatic, nerveless young Frenchman with the brooding eyes the man of destiny in tennis. Tilden, the consummate strategist of the game, saw in this young rival from across the sea a mind of his own pattern and heralded him as the coming champion of the world when others leaned toward Vincent Richards.

The psychology of Lacoste is applied not only to his own scheme of attack but also to the weaknesses of that of his opponent. More than any other player now in the game, more so even than Tilden, Lacoste makes an analysis of his opponent's vulnerable points, and once they are face to face on the court proceeds to concentrate upon them.

It was in 1923 that America first saw this young Frenchman. His performances during that season in Davis Cup play and in our national championship were not sufficiently impressive to arouse general enthusiasm, but among those who appreciate perfection of form and the finer points of match play, the rise of the Gallic youth to a place among the topnotchers was looked upon as only a matter of time.

To the field of battle Lacoste brought with him ostensibly only his rackets; but he also brought a mind keenly sensitive to the peculiarities of his opponent's methods and style; and after each match, in the seclusion of his room, the French player methodically entered in his record book the results of his observations. That book of Lacoste's now contains the names of all the leading players of the world. By the side of each of them is set down an analysis of his game, his strong points and his weak points, and also the methods to be employed against him.

Against the name of Vincent Richards, for instance, the dictum is entered: "Play deep to his backhand and go to the net." Richards' backhand is a defensive stroke, one of the weakest of any topnotch player in tennis. A forcing shot to his backhand, therefore, is sound strategy, paving the way for a safe advance and provoking a weak return. Against Tilden such tactics would not do, for Tilden's backhand is the most dangerous in the game. "Play the ball down the center of the court in going to the net against Tilden" was Lacoste's prescription, though in general he uses a straight line drive down the side of the court to reduce the enemy's redoubt.

How well this 22-year-old youth fathoms the weaknesses of his opponents and builds to capitalize them was shown in his final match with Jean Borotra in the national championship. Borotra is fundamentally a net player, ruthless in his volleying and deadly overhead, though his ground strokes, which get away like a flash, are anything but weak. To break up this short-range attack of his countryman, Lacoste perfected himself in the use of the lob until his accuracy with it has become uncanny. A short lob against Borotra is fatal, and to get the proper length on the parabola without putting it over the baseline requires perfect control and judgment of distance.

It was Lacoste's lobbing that killed off Borotra in their match at Forest Hills. By the time that he had laid two or three of those high returns within an inch of the baseline to bring Borotra's headlong rushes to the net to an abrupt halt, the Basque knew that he was a beaten man; the heart was taken out of him. The same procedure is always followed by Lacoste against Borotra in their every meeting, and invariably with the same result. There is no player in the world that Borotra dreads meeting more than he does this cool young strategist. Even Tilden does not strike such terror to his heart. After Borotra had beaten the Philadelphian in the indoor championship last February he told of the trepidation with which he faced his match in the final against Lacoste, who had advanced by putting out Richards. "René kills me," said Jean.

The rise of Lacoste to his position at the top of tennis marks the attainment of a goal set for him by his father five years ago. It was only six years ago that he entered upon his tournament career, from which his father sought to lure him away, importuning him upon the necessity for his entering the family business. Finding that his arguments were of no avail, the elder Lacoste finally capitulated, but in sending his son back to the courts he made this final reservation, "Play tennis if you must, but remember that you must become the world's champion." At least this is the story that has grown up about Lacoste, and if it is a myth it has taken on too great a sentimental value, like folk lore, to be dismissed.

One year after he started to play the game seriously Lacoste took a firm step up the ladder of fame when he received his first ranking as a French player. By 1922 he had gained international recognition, defeating Borotra, who played on the Davis Cup team that year, in the Coupe de Noël, and also Barrett of England in a tournament in Brussels. In 1923 Lacoste made his debut as a member of the French team and also before American galleries. His play here then, as has been said, was not particularly impressive, except for the potentialities it revealed. In the national championship he was beaten by Francis T. Hunter of New Rochelle. The following year found Lacoste reaping the reward of the intensive study and practice that he had given to the game. He reached the final round of the English championship at Wimbledon, in which he lost to Borotra, and was also runner-up to the same player in the French championship. Dick Williams, Manuel Alonso and Jean Washer fell before him at Wimbledon.

Coming to the United States again, he defeated both Gerald Patterson, Australia's leading player, and Pat O'Hara-Wood in the Davis Cup matches; and had Borotra given him the support expected, France would have reached the challenge round for the first time. The opportunity of meeting these giants of tennis was bringing a constant improvement in Lacoste's game, and his notebook was continually growing thicker. In 1925 the then 21-year-old youth reached the goal which was formerly looked upon as the ultimate in tennis. Reaching the final round of the classic Wimbledon championship, he again met Borotra, and this time he was the winner. The English tournament, however, no longer carries with it the title of "world's championship," and so, turning his face toward the west, Lacoste set out for bigger game in America.

Against the Australians in the Davis Cup interzone match last year the young Frenchman was sadly disappointing. He was totally unable to adapt himself to the climate and conditions of play in the short time between his arrival and the start of the matches, and this time it was his weakness that threatened to ruin France's chances again of reaching the challenge round. But Borotra filled the breach, redeeming himself for 1924, and in spite of Lacoste's poor showing, France earned the right to meet the United States.

Now came Lacoste's opportunity to prove his worth. Meeting Tilden in the challenge round, the young Frenchman held a gallery of 10,000 spectators spellbound as he rushed through the first two sets and gained match point in the third. Four times in this set he was within a single stroke of victory over the player who had not lost a Davis Cup singles match in the six years that he had played for the United States. Tilden, staging one of his characteristic rallies, managed finally to save himself, but only after the bitterest struggle he had gone through since his historic match with Zenzo Shimizu in 1921.

That struggle seemed to have robbed Lacoste of his keenness, for in the national championship his play was of an inferior standard and he fell an easy victim to Vincent Richards. Borotra's game showed the same decline, and the Basque was disposed of in summary fashion by Dick Williams. Last February Lacoste returned to the United States as a member of the French international indoor team to defeat both Richards and Tilden. These victories did not cause any undue alarm among Americans, scored as they were on indoor courts, on which the French play more extensively than is the practice in this country.

Returning home with a cold, which developed into bronchial trouble, Lacoste curtailed his play and for a while it was feared that he might not be seen on the courts again this year. But he recovered from his illness and represented France in the European Davis Cup ties, though his army duties did not permit him to play at Wimbledon. He obtained leave to come to the United States, and when he lost to Takeichi Harada of Japan in the Davis Cup interzone match, it seemed that he had not fully regained his health. He showed improvement, though, in his second match, and then came the challenge round in Philadelphia. It was there, at the Germantown Cricket Club, that Lacoste gained the greatest single victory of his career.

HENRI COCHET

by Allison Danzig

Of all the players of renown who have passed in review during half a century of tennis history there is one who, it seems generally agreed, stands out transcendently in the natural gift that he has had for the game.

Arguments will never cease as to which of the "immortals" developed his game to the highest point of efficiency. There probably never will be complete unanimity of opinion as to who was the greatest of them all, for the generation of the past had as deep a veneration for "Little Do," Brookes, Wilding, Wright, Larned and McLoughlin as Tilden, Johnston and their French contemporaries are held in today. But the old generation of tennis followers and the new, and the old world and the new, are fairly definitely in accord in holding to the belief that never before has a player come to the courts with so pronounced an instinct for the game, with so gifted a hand for the racket as has Henri Cochet.

There is an English song famous some thirty years ago, in which are to be found the words "Of course you can never be like us, but be as like us as you are able to be." That sentence might be taken as a text by the preceptor of tennis, teaching the young idea to shoot after the fashion of Cochet. The second part of it, indeed, already has been taken by Tilden, who has held up the model of Cochet as the one to be followed by American youth if we are to re-establish ourselves in France's place at the top.

But while one may become schooled in the methods of Cochet, his execution defies imitation. His is the hand that was born to the tennis racket as divinely as the right by which the monarch of yore of princely blood and ancient lineage held the scepter of power. One might have his strength of wrist and forearm but still lack the touch that rises superior to the tenets of orthodox stroke production. One might have his quickness and accuracy of eye and still lack the perfection of timing, which, with his wrist flick, is the mainspring of his unsuspected pace off the ground.

What player is there in the world that makes his volleys, not in front of him, but at his side, with the head of the racket in line with the extended arm? Who is there that plays a rising ball while moving forward, with such stability and accuracy? Where is there a player with such hair-trigger reflexes, with such unerring instinct for being on the ball with the center of his racket? What player is there who affords so perfect an example of the conservation of energy, both in his lithe footwork and in the restricted length of his backswing, and who gets the maximum return for the minimum expenditure of effort?

Who but Cochet? Who but the pale-faced, curly-haired Lyonnais, the youth who brought Tilden's six-year reign to an end at Forest Hills in 1926, winner of the deciding victory in the challenge round of 1927, the "great artisan" of France's victory in 1928, mainstay of her defense in 1929 and the man of the hour in Paris today. . . .

Of all the players who have worn the mythical mantle of world's champion none has remained more inscrutable to the general public than has this same Cochet. Just as Maude Adams, in the heyday of her sweeping success as interpreter of Barrie, revealed only her stage personality to a captivated world that was completely in the dark as to her private life, so has this quiet-spoken young man with his winning smile remained cloaked in mystery outside of the tennis enclosure.

Of Tilden, Lacoste and Borotra there is a wealth of stories and tradition. Of Cochet we know almost nothing except that he owns a highly successful sporting goods shop and that he is the "ball boy of Lyons." In all the reams of "copy" that have been written about him this is the single lone tag that has been affixed to him.

We know Tilden as the "stormy petrel," the "thespian of the courts," the "iconoclast," the player-writer, etc. Borotra is the "bounding Basque," the volatile Basque with the blue beret, the automotive pump salesman, the aviator, the pullman car's best patron, the raconteur, the prince charming of the courts. Lacoste is the "crocodile," the phlegmatic young Parisian, the schoolboy wonder, the machine, the scion of a wealthy manufacturer of motor cars, the inventor of a practice machine for pumping forth tennis balls. Cochet, who has been coming to this country since 1922, we know only as the ball boy of Lyons.

This dearth of information about the greatest player on the courts may be ascribed in part to the fact that he understands very little English and speaks even less, or at least he did on his visit here in 1928. So interviewers have not been able to "pump" him as they have his compatriots. For another thing, he is taciturn except to his intimates, and it is not easy to penetrate his reserve. By contrast with the effervescent, happy-go-lucky Borotra, who has a sunny smile and a warm handshake for every acquaintance, he is almost frigid in his quiet indifference to all save his closest associates, and even Lacoste, the sphinx of the courts, is almost voluble by comparison.

On the court, Cochet is practically never heard to speak. A shake of the head, affirmative or negative; a quizzical lifting of the eyebrows, or a Gallic shrug of the shoulders is the only outlet he allows his feelings. On rare occasions, at the end of an important match or in answer to the badinage of Borotra, a radiant smile lights up his pale features.

On the occasion of his first visit to the United States in 1922, Cochet was hardly more than another name in tennis. He had done little up to the time to attract notice outside of Europe and had been sent here, with Borotra and the veteran André Gobert, as a young player who showed considerable promise. This was the beginning of France's far-sighted program of development of her younger players in which she sowed the seeds of the harvest that was to be reaped five years later.

In 1923 Lacoste and Jacques Brugnon were sent over and each succeeding year saw these same players representing the Tricolor, though Cochet did not come over each time. Lacoste, from his first visit, was judged to have a brighter future than Cochet, and, indeed, few American critics were able to visualize the latter at all as a potentially great player. Even the schoolboy wonder did not look any too good by comparison with Tilden, Johnston and Richards, and it was not until 1925 that American students of tennis form began to have a wholesome respect for any of the young French players.

Even then no fears were entertained for the immediate safety of the cup, for it seemed that the representatives of the Tricolor were unable to produce on American courts the form that they showed at home and at Wimbledon. So when the holocaust came in 1926 with the defeat of Tilden, Johnston, Richards and Williams in the national championship it was like a bolt out of the blue. Cochet, in spite of the fact that he was the one to defeat Tilden, was still playing second fiddle to Lacoste, who defeated him in the semi-finals after being hopelessly outplayed in the first two sets.

It was not until 1928 that the Lyonnais came to be recognized as the world's greatest player when he won three victories in the Davis Cup challenge round, while Lacoste was losing to Tilden, and captured both the American and French titles. Since then, with Lacoste invalided out of service, his right to the top position in any world's ranking has been unchallengeable, and he stands today as the same towering obstacle in the path of invading Davis Cup teams that Tilden was from 1920 to 1927.

It was at the tender age of seven that Cochet, who was born December 14, 1901, was introduced to tennis. His father at the time was manager of the Lyons Lawn Tennis Club, and so fond was Henri of watching the matches that he acted as ball boy in order to see the play better. When everyone had left the courts he would take an old racket and ball and practice against a wall, running home from school as quickly as he could in order to lose no time in practicing.

"I consider wall practice the best way to learn strokes," Cochet is quoted as saying. . . .

"I believe that a beginner should play at least six months against a wall before entering a tennis court. After this practice, holding a racket will seem natural to him and he will improve rapidly. . . . Having learned to hit back the ball, one will try to acquire good footwork and to play every stroke with the shoulder sideway to the net. In my opinion, the position of the upper part of the body is more important than that of the feet."

Two years after he first began to hit balls against a wall, Cochet was permitted to play once a week on the courts with his school friends. So keen was he for the game and so rapidly did he improve, that he soon became the best youngster in Lyons. It was not until after the war that he began to acquire fame that was more than local. In 1919 he played in his first tournament of consequence and two years later his star definitely began to rise when he won the Regional championship played in Lyons and went to Paris to win the military championship of France, his first national title.

The following year saw Cochet playing extensively during the winter and spring and his fame spreading beyond the borders of his country. He won the world's covered court championship in singles and doubles at St. Moritz, where he defeated Borotra in the final. He also captured the world's hard court title at Brussels, where his victims included Manuel Alonso and Count de Gomar of Spain and Nicholas Mishu of Roumania. That year, also, he won the French hard court championship at Paris, defeating Borotra, and as a reward for his fine record he was named on the Davis Cup team. After winning a singles match and a doubles, with Borotra, against Denmark, he came to the United States and accounted for France's only victory in the tie with Australia, defeating Pat O'Hara-Wood. He did not compete in our national championship, and before coming to the United States he had fallen an easy victim at Wimbledon to James O. Anderson of Australia.

In 1923 Cochet retained his world covered court crown at Barcelona but lost to Jean Washer in the hard court tournament at Paris, the last of these tournaments to be designated as a world's championship. The esteem in which the young Lyonnais was held at this time was indicated by the fact that Suzanne Lenglen, then at the height of her career, chose him as her mixed doubles partner and together they won the hard court title. Cochet did not come to the United States in 1923 nor did he compete at Wimbledon. He played against Denmark, Ireland and Switzerland in the Davis Cup matches and won all of his engagements except one.

In 1924 he lost to Lacoste in five sets in the French championships and was runner-up to Vincent Richards in the Olympics. He played only in the European Davis Cup matches and was beaten by J. Brian Gilbert of England after winning the first two sets. The following year saw him out of the Davis Cup and playing in only a few tournaments, losing to Washer in the French championships and to Borotra at Wimbledon.

Cochet was not in the best of health at this time and an injury to his wrist further handicapped his tennis. Lacoste, writing of him during this year, summed up his game as follows:

"He has a marvelous drive and a terrific overhead, great agility and anticipation, but only the shadow of a backhand and no service. For three years he did not work to improve his service or to attack with his backhand. Now he is a marvelous natural player, playing in the most fluent style the most difficult shots of the game and then missing the easiest balls. He is the French Patterson. Careless in practice, a little lazy in matches, he can beat everybody when his shots are working, he can be beaten by everybody when they are not going in."

It was in 1926 that Cochet definitely started up the ladder on his way to world recognition as the greatest player in the game. He was beaten at Wimbledon in five sets by Borotra, who was the one player who seemed to have the "Indian sign" on him, but prior to meeting the Basque he had beaten Vincent Richards.

In the French championship he beat both Richards and Lacoste to win the title. Coming to the United States, he was beaten by Takeichi Harada of Japan, as also was Lacoste, in the interzone round, and he was not chosen for the singles in the challenge round. Two weeks later, however, came his stunning, history-making victory over Tilden in the national championship and there no longer was any doubt that he rated among the two or three greatest players of the world.

In the English championships of 1927 Cochet turned in one of the most remarkable feats in the history of this classic. In three successive rounds, starting with the quarter-finals, he lost the first two sets and then went on, in each case, to win the match. His opponents were Frank Hunter, Tilden and Borotra, in that order, and against Borotra he was six times within a stroke of defeat, while against Tilden he trailed at 5–1 in the third set.

These three successive rallies stamped Cochet as the greatest fifth set player in the world. . . .

Before winning the English title, Cochet had lost to Tilden in the final of the French championships, and in the Davis Cup challenge round at Philadelphia the American again defeated him on the opening day; but it was Cochet's victory in the fifth match of the series against Johnston that gave the cup to France for the first time in history.

Cochet, writing his impressions of that great victory, said, "Our Captain, Pierre Gillou, was very nervous, especially before our last match; but he kept his sangfroid to the end. The proof: after I had won he refrained from kissing me. He remembered that he was not at the races. . . . The French ambassador warmly congratulated us; in his excitement, he asked me if Johnston was a good player. It was hard for me to answer, 'No!' " . . .

In 1928 Cochet beat Lacoste and Borotra to win the French championship but he lost to the former in the final at Wimbledon. Then came his glorious three days in the challenge round against the United States, when almost single-handed he saved the cup and became the hero of France.

Following the challenge round, Cochet came to the United States to win the American title, which Lacoste failed to defend and for which Tilden was ineligible to compete. In 1929 the English crown fell to him and in the Davis Cup challenge round he was again the savior of the cup with his victories over Tilden and Lott after Lacoste had been lost to the team through illness.

THE MEN FROM THE EAST

by Edward C. Potter, Jr.

The Davis Cup tie between Australia and Japan, held at the Nassau Country Club in Glen Cove, Long Island, over the August 7 weekend, was the occasion for a long-awaited reunion with Takeichi Harada, Captain of the Japanese team and one of the four immortal Japanese players who have been included in A. Wallis Myers' World's First Tens. The others were Ichiya Kumagae, who captained his country's team last year, Zenzo Shimizu and Jiro Satoh.

Kumagae was the first of the four to appear on the American scene. A student at Keio University, he took part in our championship in 1916 and played a sensational match against George Church, a Princeton lad who had modeled his game on that of the hard-serving, net-rushing Californian, Maurice McLoughlin. "Itchy," as Kumagae was nicknamed, was a left-hander with a completely self-taught style. His forehand was a looping drive. His backhand and service were negligible. His volleying was almost nonexistent. He was so persistent and so eager to improve that he soon learned to adapt himself to the methods of his opponents. His later successes gave the first impetus to the game in Japan.

When the United States entered the first World War, Kumagae returned to Japan but came back to America in 1919 and again took part in our championship. Tilden beat him in an early round.

In 1920 the second great Japanese player, Shimizu, appeared at Wimbledon. He was a few months older than Kumagae and had perfected his game in India, where he held the Bengal championship for five years. He had profited not only by Kumagae's experience in America but also by his own matches with English players in India. Shimizu's style was far from classic. His ground strokes were awkward but effective and his volleying was distinctly better than Kumagae's. Nevertheless, "Shimmy" was the surprise of the tournament. He had beaten the great French player, André Gobert, and had come through to the All-Comers' final where his opponent was the redoubtable Bill Tilden, who, up to then, had been considered only second fiddle to Billy Johnston. But Johnston had lost to Parke, and Dick Williams to Mavrogordato, while Tilden had beaten both Parke and Kingscote, mainstays of the British Davis Cup team. Shimizu was no match for Tilden and won only four games in each of the first two sets. Then Tilden twisted his knee. Shimizu carried the third set to twenty-four games before the limping American won it.

The Japanese now had two players worthy to represent them in Davis Cup competition and in 1921 challenged for the first time. After winning from the Philippines and Belgium by default, Japan met India in the third round at the Onwentsia Club in Chicago and won by 5 rubbers to none. Australasia was Japan's opponent in the final round, played at the Newport Casino at the end of August. Jim Anderson, Jack Hawkes and Clarence Todd composed the Australasian team. Anderson was a big hitter and in the opening match against Shimizu the wily Japanese never gave his opponent a ball that carried any pace. He hit the ball hard when he was trying to beat Anderson to the shot but at other times he hit it gently. He kept his service low and well placed and made few errors. Anderson seemed to be semi-paralyzed by Shimizu's crafty play and lost in straight sets.

In his match against Hawkes, Kumagae started erratically and dropped the first two sets. Hawkes reached 5–4 in the third but then the Japanese recovered, won the set at 8–6 and the next two easily. The doubles went to

Anderson and Todd, but Kumagae clinched the tie with a five-set win over Anderson who again seemed confused with the Japanese tactics. Shimizu ended matters with a four-set win from Hawkes, and the Japanese, in their first try, had reached the challenge round. Never since then have they come so far.

There was no challenge in 1922 but Shimizu returned in 1923 with new partners. Kumagae had retired and Fukuda and Kashio accompanied Shimmy. This was the first year in which the draw had been divided into zones and four teams—Japan, Canada, Australia and Hawaii—entered in the American Zone. The Japanese beat Canada at Montreal 5 to 0 and met Australia, the other finalist, at Chicago. Shimizu's win over Hawkes in five sets was the only Japanese victory. Anderson revenged himself with a straight-set win from the little Japanese.

Harada's first appearance as a member of Japan's team came in the following year. Playing only doubles, with Shimizu and Okamoto taking care of the singles, Harada and Okamoto lost the only point against Canada in a 4–1 win but were smothered by the Australians at Providence, winning only two sets in the five matches.

Harada had now come into his own, and in 1925 he and Shimizu took care of both singles and doubles when they met Spain in Baltimore. Harada beat both Flaquer and Alonso while Shimizu lost to the two Spaniards but the vital doubles was won in five sets. Again in the final against Australia Harada accounted for Japan's only point when he beat Gerald Patterson in four sets.

Beaten by France in the 1925 Interzone final, Australia did not challenge in 1926, and the Japanese team of Harada and Tawara had an easy road in the American Zone. After beating Mexico 4–1, no rubbers were lost against the Philippines and Cuba, and the Interzone tie against the French was a personal triumph for Harada, who won both his singles from Lacoste and Cochet, each in four sets. But the doubles loss and Tawara's two defeats put France in the Challenge Round for the second time.

Shimizu returned to America for the last time in 1927 and played only one match, a doubles with Harada, in which they were beaten by the Mexican team of Bob Kinsey and Claude Butlin, both Americans by birth. The Japanese team again went to the Interzone final and this time could not win a match against the French, who, a few weeks later, were to win the Cup from Tilden, Johnston and Hunter.

Harada took no part in the 1928 or 1929 matches and, with the Cup now in Europe and America dominating the American Zone, Japan in 1930 challenged in the European Zone. Harada returned to the team, won his matches against Von Kehrling of Hungary, Charanjiva of India and Menzel and Jan Kozeluh of Czechoslovakia and won the doubles with Abe in all three ties, thus reaching the final round. Here a strong Italian team was met and though Harada beat both De Morpurgo and De Stefani, Ohta lost both his singles and the doubles also went to the Italians in a close five-set match.

Now a new Japanese, perhaps the greatest of them all, succeeded his three predecessors as the mainstay of his country's team. Jiro Satoh, with his brother and Kawachi, went to the semi-final of the European Zone in 1931, where they were beaten by Great Britain, the eventual challengers, by 5 to 0.

The Japanese had come far from the days of Kumagae and Shimizu's awkward style, for both Harada and now Satoh were completely orthodox. Satoh was quick on his feet. He was perfect master of himself. He could wait for an opening with true Oriental patience. He liked to tire his opponents with soft, accurate drives. Then, when the moment came, he took the ball on the rise with Cochet-like speed and fury. His swift and unexpected return left his victim at his mercy.

Satoh's greatest year was in 1933. In the French championship he beat Perry to reach the semi-final, where he lost to Crawford. At Wimbledon he beat Austin and again lost to Crawford in the semi-final. In the Davis Cup he beat Von Kehrling and Gabrowitz of Hungary, McGuire and Rogers of Ireland, Von Cramm and Jaenecke of Germany and, with Nunoi, won the doubles in all three ties. In the European Zone semi-final against Australia at Paris, he revenged his French championship loss by defeating Crawford in five sets but lost to McGrath to give the Australians a 3–2 victory.

Another year might have brought Satoh to the top of the heap but it was not to be. He had played the year around for the glory of Japan. He was ill and despondent when the call came to get ready for another European tour. Stoically he accepted against his better judgment. He bade his fiancée goodbye and left with the team. As the ship steamed out of Singapore he could no longer carry on. He made his last obeisance to his gods and plunged into the sea.

FRANK HUNTER

by Fred Hawthorne

It was in 1922 that Francis T. Hunter, then a burly, stalwart young fellow with a bulldog jaw, first broke into the first ten of the American rankings. Within the next few years, he was to become a tennis headliner.

Today, Frank Hunter transacts his business behind a desk instead of on a court. He can be found daily in a plush office on New York City's West 52nd Street. His title: President of "21" Brands, Inc. . . .

Many tennis players have been noted for their business acumen. Hunter is one striking example. He has been active (and successful) in several different vocations. He once owned and edited a newspaper in Beckley, West Virginia. He later tried his hand in the bituminous coal industry, and also invested in a steamship line. Then he reverted to the newspaper field again, publishing a chain of newspapers in New York State. In 1933 he founded, with others, "21" Brands, and more recently, the "21" Brands Distillers Corporation. He is currently president of both concerns.

Hunter, now, probably is better known as a businessman than as a tennis player. But in his day he ranked with the best in the racket game. In 1924, he paired with Vincent Richards to win the Olympic doubles championship, and in 1927, the year he played on the Davis Cup team, he and Bill Tilden won the Wimbledon doubles title. His singles record also was impressive. He was the runner-up two years in a row for the National men's championship at Forest Hills. He lost in the 1928 finals to France's brilliant Henri Cochet, and bowed to the mighty Tilden in the 1929 final round.

What made this record really astonishing was the fact that the Francis T. Hunter of 1922 and for several years thereafter was virtually a one-stroke player. He relied mainly on the crushing power of his forehand drive to bring him victory, and this stroke rarely let him down. No one has ever pounded a ball off the right side with more concentrated fury than Hunter did in those days. His backhand always was vastly inferior to his forehand during his competitive career, although he did manage to strengthen it defensively. It never, however, became an attacking weapon.

To offset the lack of variety in his game, Hunter always came on court with a fixed determination to win. This determination—his great fighting spirit—more than made up for any technical shortcomings. During a match, Hunter often ran around the ball so that he could take it on his forehand. He never relaxed his furious assault. Many players of the period displayed a better-rounded game than this dark-haired battler, but comparatively few walked off a court the winner after a match with him. His forehand undoubtedly was an invaluable asset. When great forehand strokes of past and present are discussed, such as were wielded by S. H. Smith, Frank L. Riseley and Fred Perry of England, and by Tilden, Bill Johnston, Ellsworth Vines, J. Gilbert Hall and Jack Kramer of the United States, Hunter's does not have to take a back seat to any.

He was built along the lines of a fullback in the days when power and aggressiveness were not considered necessary assets on a tennis court, and he looked little like a tennis player of merit when he first competed on the circuit in the early '20s. He had been captain of the hockey team at Cornell, and when I first glimpsed him I thought he should have stuck to the rough ice sport. In the beginning, he frequently would shift his racket from the right to left hand in an attempt to bypass his feeble backhand stroke. But his game improved, and rapidly. He advanced step by step up the tennis ladder until he was recognized among the mighty. I doubt if any other high ranking player ever advanced to such a position with so limited equipment. Frank had a tremendous forehand and a burning will to win. They proved enough to give him a number two ranking in the country—right behind Tilden—in 1928 and 1929.

Hunter made many lasting friendships in tennis. One of the earliest and firmest had its beginnings during the first World War. Frank was a Lieutenant Commander in the Navy, and was stationed on British Admiral

David Beatty's flagship when the German fleet struck its colors to the British-American flotilla at the war's end. Beatty was an avid tennis fan, and a warm friendship developed between him and the young American officer. After the war terminated, Hunter and the admiral played several times as doubles partners. Later, Frank wrote a book about his experiences as an officer serving with Beatty.

Hunter entered the professional tennis ranks with Tilden in 1931, and he later was the promoter of a professional tour in which Ellsworth Vines and Fred Perry were the headliners. Now he is outside tennis almost completely. His favorite sports activities are golf, hunting and fishing. . . .

Hunter's office walls would be a taxidermist's delight. Animal heads—elk, moose, tiger, mountain lion, and even rhinoceros—surround the former tennis star's desk. There are also stuffed fish, from the sailfish to the tuna, and various mounted birds. . . .

Hunter feels that tennis as played today is better than the game was years ago. "The game has improved in every particular since those days," he said. "This is due mainly to the fact that the action has speeded up because of the use of the forcing volley in modern tennis. It is a matter of consistent attack nowadays, and the attacker is the man who is going to win. Jack Kramer and Richard Gonzales are outstanding examples of the importance of the all-out attacking type of game."

Hunter, incidentally, does not yet rank Gonzales with the all-time greats. He rates his top ten in this fashion: 1. Bill Tilden; 2. Norman E. Brookes (Australia) ; 3. Don Budge; 4. Ellsworth Vines; 5. René Lacoste (France) ; 6. William Johnston; 7. Jack Kramer; 8. Anthony F. Wilding (New Zealand) ; 9. Reginald Doherty (England) ; 10. Fred Perry (England).

Hunter believes that a 1927 match between Tilden and Lacoste in Paris was the finest singles contest he ever saw. "It was a five-set contest," he recalled. "Bill held match point six times and six times Lacoste turned him back. The little Frenchman just wouldn't make an error when the big points came up, even though Bill tried everything he had. No one can ever convince me that this wasn't the finest singles match ever played."

Frank saw this contest, but he, himself, was a participant in the doubles match he remembers best. It was in 1927, also, and turned out to be one of the highlights of the Davis Cup competition that year between France and the United States. The two nations had split their opening singles matches, Lacoste defeating Bill Johnston, and Tilden evening the score with a victory over Henri Cochet. The doubles loomed then as the decisive battle of the Challenge Round.

"On that day," Hunter told me, "Tilden and I faced Jean Borotra and Jacques Brugnon. The French were great that day, but Bill was unbeatable. The match went five sets. The first four were nip-and-tuck affairs. But by the final set Borotra and Brugnon had played themselves out. The match was ours, 3–6, 6–3, 6–3, 4–6, 6–0."

This doubles triumph gave the United States a 2–1 lead in matches, but the inspired French players won the final two singles tilts to gain the coveted bowl for the first time in history.

JOHN DOEG

by Allison Danzig

He has the build of a young Goliath and the bronzed complexion and tawny locks of a true son of the Pacific. He has a grin that reaches from here to the Golden Gate and a southpaw service that brings out the roar of the crowd as unmistakably as does the crack of the Babe's fungo against a fast one on the inside.

He was born to the purple of tennis, and now, five years after his arresting physique first caught the eyes of Eastern galleries, sits, at the age of 21, on the throne which no other American save William Tilden has occupied for the last ten years.

The first time John Doeg stepped on a court in the East, a spectator in the stands was heard to remark: "What a champion he'd make!"

Standing straight as an arrow, more than 6 feet tall, proportioned like a young Hercules and with the self-possession of a past master at the game, the then 16-year-old giant from the Coast captured the public fancy with his home-run service and boyish grin, in the same manner as did that other flaming native son, Maurice McLoughlin, the California Comet.

Mrs. Helen Wills Moody, on her first appearance in the East in 1921, created no more of a stir than did the arrival of this strapping scion of a family long famed in lawn tennis, nor was her future painted in more glowing colors.

Reared in an atmosphere of tennis from the cradle, imbibing its precepts from such illustrious forebears as his mother, Mrs. Violet Sutton Doeg, and his aunt, Mrs. May Sutton Bundy, and blessed with a magnificent physique and natural gift for the game, John Hope Doeg was born to rule the courts.

The road of this heir-apparent to the throne, however, was a tortuous path, strewn with the thorns of disillusionment such as few princes of the blood have to travel. Indeed, so labored had become his progress along that road, so many checkmates had he encountered, that his stanchest adherents had begun to abandon hope for him and to turn to other idols of the clay and grass courts.

There were only two people who continued to maintain their faith in the manifest destiny of this strapping young Californian. One was Doeg himself. The other was his mother, and of the two, Mrs. Doeg was decidedly the more unalterable in her conviction.

John was beginning to lose some of his keenness for the game as he weighed its glory against the demands it imposed, and he decided it was time for him to think of his business career. It was not so much faith in himself that carried him to the crown as it was his loyalty to his mother's unswerving confidence in him and his dogged determination to confute those who began to say he never would be champion.

A year ago last July his critics were sounding a requiem over his career. That was after Doeg had been beaten twice in succession by Eddie Jacobs. The season before he had failed to gain a place on the Davis Cup team, making a disappointing showing in the trials at Augusta, Georgia; and these setbacks at the hands of an unranked player on his return to the East in 1929 apparently pointed to his definite eclipse as a member of the tennis elect.

A few days after his second defeat by Jacobs in the intercollegiate championship at Haverford, Pennsylvania, the writer was talking with Mrs. Doeg at the Women's National Golf and Tennis Club at Glenhead, Long Island. With her eyes kindled in resentment, Mrs. Doeg demanded to know why many seemed to have lost faith in the 20-year-old boy.

"John's ground strokes are not weak," she insisted emphatically. "No one in California thinks so. There's a big difference in playing on asphalt and grass. Why don't they give him time to adjust himself to the difference? After all, he is only a boy."

While Mrs. Doeg was speaking, John was playing only a few miles away at Glen Cove. Before three days had passed his traducers were beginning to recant, as he won the Nassau Country Club tournament, and for the next three weeks he was the outstanding player of the American season, as he captured the Rhode Island championship and the Longwood and Seabright bowls.

Almost overnight, Doeg had become a different player, and the chief reason was that he had discarded the forehand drive he had been trying to master and had gone back to the chop that he had used on his first visit to the East.

With this chop he developed an accuracy in picking off openings that was almost uncanny, and this correction of a weakness that had hopelessly handicapped him had a tonic effect upon his whole game, energizing his service and volley again and dissipating the blight of doubt that had robbed him of his aggressiveness.

When the 1929 national championship was held Doeg was so vastly improved over the player who had lost to George Lott in three sets in the 1928 tournament that he smothered H. W. Austin of England and extended Tilden as did no other player in the championship, leading him 2 sets to 1.

Last Winter the Californian compiled a splendid record in the Southern tournaments and won his first berth on the Davis Cup team.

His trip to Europe with the team, his initial visit abroad, was in the nature of a return of the native, for his antecedents are British. His grandfather on his mother's side was an English sailing captain and the fame of his mother and aunts, the celebrated Sutton sisters of a generation ago, was as cherished abroad as it was in this country.

Needless to say, Doeg received a warm reception when he made his debut at Wimbledon on the turf, where his aunt, Mrs. May Sutton Bundy, twice had carried off the English championship. His play there helped to swell the paean of praise for America's representatives and it was only by a narrow margin that he failed to defeat Wilmer Allison, the conqueror of Henri Cochet.

In spite of the excellence of his tennis, he was not used in the cup matches and upon his return home he and the other members of the team were eclipsed in the public eye by the deeds of a younger crop of players— Wood, Shields, Sutter and Vines.

When the draw for the championship was made, both Wood and Sutter were seeded ahead of him and the name of Doeg was scarcely mentioned among those who were conceded a chance of defeating Tilden. In spite of his showing against the champion in 1929 and his fine record for the past two seasons, the Californian's lack of a forcing forehand drive continued to foster skepticism. No one who depended upon a chop, it was felt, could be considered seriously as a championship contender, regardless of the fact that he had the most dreaded service in tennis and an affinity for net play.

But with that chop Doeg fully held his own against Tilden's immaculate drives, though it was his service and volleys that won the match, and against the hard-hitting Shields that chop again stood up beautifully to break up the young New Yorker's advances to the net and to keep him rushing headlong across the court in vain pursuit of a spinning ball that skimmed the tape and barely rose from the turf.

Extremely few players in the history of the game have risen to the top with a chop stroke. That Doeg should have done so makes his victory all the more notable and praiseworthy, and in the face of the adverse criticism and discouraging setbacks he experienced it testifies to the stout heart and perseverance of this unaffected, self-reliant young giant of 21 years.

Winner of both the national singles and doubles and assured of first place in the next ranking, Doeg sits in the seat of the mighty at an age when his best years are before him, and has put the scoffers to rout.

It is his intention to confine his tennis in the future to two or three tournaments at the most and to forsake Davis Cup play in order to make a start in his life's career.

Those who know him for the level-headed youth that he is, with an admirable sense of proportion and values, do not doubt his sincerity in planning to restrict the time he gives to tennis, nor will they take issue with the wisdom of his course.

If he should yield, however, to the pressure that undoubtedly will be brought to bear upon him as a national champion to make him postpone his withdrawal from the tennis courts, there are thousands who will be so selfish as to rejoice.

It is not every year that the game produces a champion of the arresting physique, spontaneity and boyish grin of this young Hercules with the service of the century and the greatest grin since the days of Huckleberry Finn.

KAREL KOZELUH, HANS NUSSLEIN, AND FRITZ MERCUR

by George Lott

The name of Karel Kozeluh means little or nothing to the current young tennis star, possibly because it is nowhere listed in the record books, but it connotes memories of many a great match to tennis stars of the past.

Kozzie was never an amateur. In his native Czechoslovakia he was an international soccer player as well as a tennis pro. He moved like an athlete and could run all day. His confidence in himself any time he stepped on a court was well founded; he had as good a pair of groundstrokes as ever swung at a ball and he was aware of what to do in a given situation. Additionally he had the best drop shot I have ever seen, plus magnificent lobbing ability.

When you played Kozzie, you had to be prepared to run forever and never to lose patience, because no match against him ended in a hurry. He was a Bitsy Grant type player but (with apologies to Bitsy) much better than the original. Bitsy let you beat yourself; Karel also permitted you to do so, but additionally he could beat you into the ground. He was the ultimate retriever but he could also force.

My first experience with Kozzie came during my novitiate year on the Davis Cup team. We were in Paris preparing for the Challenge Round, and Kozzie had been hired as our coach and practice player. He was much more valuable in the latter capacity, as his English consisted mostly of "Uppy uppy" and "dollar." He used the former to encourage Hennessey and me as we chased wildly after his drop shots, and the latter represented a subject very close to his heart.

When Kozeluh was first hired I was not impressed. I knew that his matches with Vinnie Richards in the pro finals at Forest Hills had been considered tennis classics, but it seemed to me that as Vinnie had beaten him, it only substantiated the often-proved theory that a good net player would usually beat a good baseliner. I also believed that Vinnie was not as good as he had been as an amateur and that therefore Kozeluh must be just another European baseliner who could scurry around and get a lot of balls back but who couldn't be much to worry about. I was wrong on both counts. As I found out in practice, "this European" was something more than a baseliner and, if Richards beat him, he had to be playing his top game. The year before I had beaten Lacoste, who was considered the world's No. 1 baseliner. How could I have any trouble with Kozeluh? I was wrong again. The one who had no trouble was Kozeluh. He separated the men from the boys.

There existed an undercurrent of rivalry between Kozzie and Tilden. Bill was still very near the best in the world. As an amateur he had received incredible publicity, whereas comparatively few people had heard of Kozeluh. It was this lack of recognition that got under Kozzie's skin, because he was absolutely certain he was a better player than Tilden and he wanted nothing more than a chance to prove it. One morning, as Karel and I were having breakfast, I was listening for the umpteenth time to Kozzie's pronouncements on how he could beat Tilden. In waltzed Big Bill, announcing to one and all that he wanted to get "match play tough." He asked Karel to be at the Stade Roland Garros at 11 A.M., prepared to play a five-set match. Kozzie looked as though he had just been crowned king of Czechoslovakia.

We adjourned to the courts and the match commenced before the members of our group. I was intrigued because I knew that with Tilden involved, anything could happen. It did. They played seven games, every point a masterpiece. Everything connected with great tennis was on exhibition. There were few errors and then only by inches. The points were won either by beautiful tactics or magnificent strokes. The score was 5–2 in favor of Kozzie. They changed sides and I noticed Tilden talking to Kozeluh. This had to be good, so I edged up. The conversation went along these lines:

Tilden: "I'm not hitting my backhand just right. I want you to serve some balls so I can get my timing."

Kozeluh: "Beel, five-set match . . ."

Tilden: "It's more important that I get my timing."

Kozeluh: ". . . . . ." (This was in Czech, which I didn't understand, but I have an idea.)

Tilden stopped the match and Karel had to serve balls to his backhand. I really don't know who would have won if they had finished. Poor Kozzie! His dream of playing a match against Bill was rudely ended. If Karel had known that he was destined to play Bill over a hundred times in professional tennis, it would not have seemed so important.

Kozzie was a real pro. His game was the same, day in and day out. His strokes never faltered. He didn't know the meaning of the word "off day." As the saying goes, the dice never ran cold. It was with real sadness that I heard of his death in Czechoslovakia where he had been made Sports Commissioner.

Hans Nusslein, a handsome German youth, was comparatively unknown in the United States. He had always been a pro in Europe and had received very little publicity. If he had been an amateur, Germany would have been a real factor in world tennis, for Hans, to my mind, was a little bit better than Gottfried von Cramm. He had a game similar to that of Kozeluh, but he hit his ground shots just a bit more securely and, upon occasion, would advance to the net in singles, whereas the area between the net and the service line was no-man's land for the Czech.

During the fall of my first year as a professional I met Hans in singles at Wembley. I played well against him the first set. I served with depth, came in and volleyed to the corners, hit overheads with authority and lost the first set, 6–0! I was able to scramble four games the second set. . . . There was never a gentler, less argumentative person than Nusslein. There was no sportsmanship award in those days, but if there had been, Hans would have been a leading candidate and a very likely winner.

A smile automatically comes to my face when I think of Fritz Mercur. As a tennis player he ranked seventh and sixth during part of the reign of Tilden. As a man, he ranked higher than that. If ever a person enjoyed life, it was Fritz, whether he was playing tennis or selling insurance. He was one of the few players who never questioned a decision of a linesman, taking the good with the bad and both with a smile. That charming smile hardly ever left his face, and, until you knew Fritz, you might think he was laughing at you, especially if he was beating you. But if you were beating him it was still there. He was one of the charter members of a very hardy battalion that used to make the southern circuit. It consisted of "Pop" Baggs, Freddy Hawthorne, Allison Danzig, Beals Wright, Doc Rosenbaum, Berkeley Bell, Gil Hall and Jack Stockton. That was a very tough group of competitors at anything you care to name. . . . Fritz was a very fine doubles player. He and Gil Hall used to be very hard to beat and they gave Doeg and me many uncomfortable moments. Always an amateur as defined by the U.S.L.T.A., Fritz Mercur came closest to being an amateur as defined by Mr. Webster— quote: one who plays a sport for the joy of competition without recompense.

ELLSWORTH VINES

by Allison Danzig

Somewhere west of Chicago, on a transcontinental Pullman clicking the rails toward California, is a sandy-haired, hazel-eyed young man, dangling his lengthy legs over the seat and watching the world go by through rose-colored glasses. Telegrams are scattered all about him and likenesses of his thin, solemn face look up from the newspapers beside him.

H. Ellsworth Vines, Jr., of Pasadena, California, just another youngster with a tennis racket fifteen months ago, is homeward bound, the greatest amateur player in all the United States.

Sitting alongside of him is Keith Gledhill, the other half of the famous "Gled-Vines System," a combination seldom known to get set at contract or to yield more than two sets on the doubles courts. Between the two of them they have won all the honors in every major grass court tournament of the entire season with the exception of the Seabright and national doubles and the Eastern and Southampton singles. In addition they hold the national clay court singles and doubles.

For all of the adulation which has been heaped upon them the world over, there will not be found two more casual, matter-of-fact youngsters than these 19-year-old six-footers returning with such rich booty from their second invasion of the "foreign" precincts of tennis turfdom. Only one thing can stampede them—that is anyone who takes liberties with the fair name and overflowing blessings of the Golden Gate State. Two more loyal native sons never came out of California.

When the dour-visaged young Vines steps down from the train at Pasadena, it will mark the first time a Californian has returned home with the men's national championship since 1919, the year of William Johnston's second victory. John Doeg, last year's winner, who hails from Santa Monica, did not go back to the Coast, taking up his residence in Newark.

The praises of this Pasadena stripling have been sung continuously all season. The whole tennis world, or at least the major part of it, is familiar by now with the fact that he has the most devastating drive in amateur competition; that, along with his meteoric speed off the ground, his annihilating service and overhead smash, he combines a repertory of strokes second to none in the game today.

No one player has arisen on the American scene during the past decade whose play has so fired the imagination of the tennis public or who has come so close to attaining the stature of a national idol. They have compared him to McLoughlin in the ferocity of his kill; to Johnston in the paralyzing speed of his forehand (though his is a flat, Eastern forehand while "Little Bill's" was a Western, top-spin drive) ; to Tilden in the full-rounded efficacy of his game in general and in the potency of his backhand and service in particular. Most striking of all in his resemblance to Tilden is his faculty for lifting his game to Olympian heights in a crisis, regardless of the opposition, as he did against George Lott on Saturday.

All of this is old in story, a story of success that is cause to marvel, remembering that until a year ago last July the name of Vines was almost unknown outside of his native bailiwick and that he started playing tournament tennis only five years ago.

Vines is probably the youngest-looking player ever to win the national crown, though there have been others to come to the throne at a slightly more tender age. It is the extreme youthfulness of his appearance that makes the solemnity of his expression so pronounced, an expression so serious that one might think he carried the burdens of the world on his slim shoulders. That expression is apt to be misleading, though not on the courts, for there it is indicative of the thought and concentration Vines is bringing to bear on his play, a concentration manifested in the comprehension and shrewdness of his stroking. Off the court, however, it is deceiving.

It is often the case that the humorist is the man with the saddest face. Vines has a keenly accentuated sense of humor and this is one of his most winning qualities. He has a grin, too, that breaks out all over his face and leaves it in scores of wrinkles. There is no player in the game more "regular," more companionable and more thoroughly likable than this gangling youngster with his quiet drawl and ambling gait. Success and adulation have left him totally unaffected and modest to the core.

Here is a genuine character, a personality who makes an unmistakable appeal to the gallery, not through temperamental pyrotechnics but through the compelling force of his personality and simplicity, aside from the magnetism of his strokes. When Vines goes on the courts he goes to play ball, and anything else is irrelevant, including arguments with the linesmen and plays to the grandstand. That was the attitude taken by tournament players in the prewar days but unfortunately it has not obtained generally during the past decade.

It is a stroke of fortune for the game that the youth who sits on the champion's throne sets so impeccable an example of sportsmanlike deportment. Not only is it to the good of the game but it is to the good of Vines, too.

When you are summing up the assets of his success put down "temperament" at the top. No man on the courts has a better one for tennis than this 19-year-old youngster. Nothing perturbs him, nothing interrupts his concentration or distracts his attention to make him lose sight of his goal. Neither adversity nor the perversity of the breaks of the game can stampede him out of his self-possession. This is why he can make so many bad errors and still come through to victory. All season long he has shown this self-possession, winning two of his most important triumphs after being two sets down to John Doeg and Frederick Perry at Seabright and Forest Hills. Any man who can do that against the formidable opposition which Vines faced on those two occasions, not to speak of his victory over the superb play of Lott, is perforce among the great players of his day.

A yet greater Vines will be seen in the years ahead, with his acquisition of more control. Master of himself, he needs only to get more thorough mastery over his magnificent armory of weapons to take his place definitely among the immortals of American tennis.

THE STYLE OF VINES

by Julius D. Heldman

In 1931, a brilliant and personable 19-year-old slashed and whipped his way to the U.S. National Singles title. He was a lanky 6′ 1″ and weighed only 145 pounds. He shambled when he walked like the great basketball player he was, but he was beautiful in motion. Ellsworth Vines was the "players' player" of his era. He had the flattest set of ground strokes ever seen and they were hit so hard, particularly on the forehand, that they could not clear the net by more than a few inches without going out.

Vines came up the public parks route in Pasadena. He was the hardest hitter among the juniors but also one of the most erratic. His flat strokes were gorgeous but never safe or secure. The antithesis of the Vines game was that of his doubles partner, Keith Gledhill of Santa Barbara, who was a spin artist. In their junior years it was usually Gledhill who came out on top. Then, for some reason, Ellsworth suddenly consolidated his game and became the top amateur in the world for two successive years. He hit the No. 1 spot with meteoric speed, climbing from a junior with potentiality to the top American man in the space of one year. All of a sudden the ball started to go in, and the gawky junior who was then only a mild threat became the sensation of Forest Hills.

Vines attended the University of Southern California while still a junior in tennis and was the star of the freshman basketball team. Tennis and basketball are the two most compatible games for men; the same physical skills other than racket handling are involved. In winter, basketball is good for every tennis player to increase or aid stamina and speed of foot. Ellsworth, otherwise known as "Hank," "Slim" or "Elly," showed the results of the double training in his excellent footwork and use of his body on the volley and overhead. He was sinuous and agile, leaping in the air for an overhead like a center on the opening jump. He knew how to make maximum use of his body, moving and stretching for volleys but still keeping his flat, hard approach.

I have always likened Elly's wind-up action on the serve to that of a writhing snake. His body seemed to amass energy as he stretched up to maximum height for the first ball. Think of an Indian fakir piping a snake into standing erect and you can then visualize Vines climbing up to the top of his swing. It was a beautiful motion which was followed by a stinging, heavy whip at the ball.

The first serve was almost flat. It had the same heaviness of the great Budge delivery, but the motion was freer and deceptively easy. His second ball often had a heavy kick, with placement being his primary objective. The serve was the most reliable part of his game, for although his ground strokes could desert him badly, he seldom had a day of double-faults. Unlike the player who resembles him most today, Barry MacKay, Vines chose to put enough heavy spin on the second ball to maintain the attack without frequent double-faulting.

I ballboyed for Vines when I was 12 years old. He was playing Fred Perry in the finals of the Pacific Southwest. A very vivid recollection is that of catching one of Vines' aces as it whizzed by Perry. It was leaden—heavy and hard, with enough spin to hurt. My hand stung for an hour. I have played against many other serves since, but none had the same leaden feeling with the exception, perhaps, of those of Budge, Gonzales and occasionally Savitt.

Elly had a four-fingered grip not only on the serve but on the forehand as well. He simply extended his leverage by sliding his little finger—and sometimes his last two fingers—off the racket. It gave him the famous whip stroke but it was also the cause of his highly erratic play. When his timing went off he had no stiff wrist shot on which to fall back. Only four fingers controlled the wiggle of the racket. They were strong as iron, but even the very slightest misjudgment produced a monstrous error.

When Vines was warming up with new balls, he would hit them so flat with his forehand that you could read the marking as they went over the net. Then, as he started to hit them harder, you could clearly see them spinning sideways, not rolling over or under. Only Kramer, following Vines, ever had this approach to the forehand, and of course he modeled his after Ellsworth. Jack, at age 15, used to practice with Vines regularly and it was inevitable that he would pick up many of Elly's characteristics. Vines could hit an overspin crosscourt but it was not a stroke he used often or from choice. If he were pulled wide, he preferred to blast the ball for a down-the-line placement, and the trajectory would keep the ball actually wide of the court until it hit on the sideline.

Vines never temporized by hitting a foot inside the line. He made more chalk fly on grass than any other player who ever lived. Roscwall's backhand passing shot, while not in the style of Vines, is also a chalk-raiser. The fact that Vines hit so flat or with sidespin meant that the ball slithered off the ground. It never set up "fat" for his opponent.

Although Elly hit hard off the backhand, it was not the equal of his starboard side. He preferred low or waist-high balls and perhaps this was the reason he was so good on grass. He got down well. He had a little natural underspin on his backhand, particularly when he would temporize, but he was at his best in hard-driving baseline rallies where he would work his opponent into an impossible position off either side. He never knew what it was to move back; he moved beautifully sideways and attacked as a natural consequence of his forcing game.

Vines' game is the direct opposite of the current "chippers." His return of serve alone would annihilate the poorly founded youngsters of today. He did not chip or block: he stroked returns of serve because his muscle-eye coordination was so good.

Vines was a very unsafe volleyer. He had little spin clearance and he went for winners most of the time. He did not play too close in to the net and he did not mind taking balls off his shoe tops on either side, hitting almost flat, low put-aways. His volley was great but fundamentally risky. It is surprising with his almost perfect overhead that he did not play in a little closer in singles.

He was not a true net-rusher such as Kramer. He came in occasionally behind his serve, more so on grass than on any other surface. He attacked the barrier more than Tilden but he has to be considered a baseliner in comparison with today's net-campers.

Despite the fact that Vines at his best was unbeatable, his style of game made him inevitably the victim of serious slumps. After two years at the top in which he mopped up the opposition, he suffered a disastrous third season. Vines went to Europe with the Davis Cup team and literally collapsed in his match against Fred Perry at Roland Garros. Then he was beaten by Jack

Crawford at Wimbledon. On his return to the States, Bitsy Grant threw every ball back at him in the Nationals and Vines promptly hit every ball out. He was beaten in three straight sets. Then, in the Pacific Southwest, Elly went to pieces against Jack Tidball after amassing an almost unbeatable lead. This was his last amateur singles match. He turned pro shortly thereafter and dominated the play-for-pay group until the advent of Don Budge five years later.

BETTY NUTHALL

by Allison Danzig

At the top of the short flight of steps leading from the marquee to the stadium courts of the West Side Tennis Club there hangs suspended an English plaque bearing these lines from the Kipling poem which stands as the credo of British sportsmanship: "If you can meet with Triumph and Disaster,/And treat those two impostors just the same."

A week ago yesterday as fair and representative a daughter of John Bull and his healthy attitude toward sport as has passed down those steps walked off the Forest Hills courts acclaimed as the first woman to carry the American tennis championship out of the country.

No player was ever more deserving of such a tribute, for Betty Nuthall, in the short span of her nineteen years, has been treating those two impostors with the same sunny smile and unaffected good sportsmanship from a time when she was scarcely old enough to have been introduced to the stanzas of "If."

Ever since she was seven years old this winsome, sturdily built girl from fair Albion's shore has wielded a racket, placed there originally by her father, and from the time she was nine she has competed in open tournaments.

Titles were hers when she had scarcely reached her teens, the English junior championship falling to her in 1924, 1925 and 1926, and in 1927, with her victory in the women's hard-court championship, came a wider fame and then laudation as she defeated Mrs. Molla Mallory, then the American titleholder, at Wimbledon.

A trip to America as a member of the English Wightman Cup team, a victory over Miss Helen Jacobs in the international matches and a stirring battle with Mrs. Helen Wills Moody in the final of the national championship all added additional lustre to the fame of the sixteen-year-old girl. Then came a testimonial from René Lacoste of France to "perhaps the future champion lady player of the world."

Up to this time, 1927, Miss Nuthall had really known only one of those

two impostors, but the girl with the golden ringlets was soon to make the
acquaintance of the other, and it was her perseverance, her smiling acceptance of defeat without the loss of faith in herself or any of her intense
ambition to improve her game during her adversity of 1928, 1929 and most
of 1930, that bespoke the championship quality of her mettle more than did
her sweeping success in the years before.

Beaten at every turn in 1928, when Miss Marjorie Morrill, among others,
scored over her on the Riviera, and turned back repeatedly in 1929, when
her 8–6, 8–6 match with Mrs. Moody in the Wightman Cup play was the
only redeeming feature of a season that saw her lose to Mrs. Peggy Saunders
Mitchell in the second round at Wimbledon and to Mrs. Mallory at Forest
Hills, Miss Nuthall's career seemed to be definitely on the wane.

So much ground had she lost that when the English Wightman Cup team
was picked this year she gave way to Miss Joan Fry and Miss Phyllis
Mudford, a newcomer, to the surprise of the tennis world, and in the English
championships she was put out by Miss Elizabeth Ryan, who was winning
doubles titles at Wimbledon before Miss Nuthall was heard of.

The outlook was dark in the extreme for the former "child wonder" of
the courts, but if everyone else had lost faith in her, Miss Nuthall remained
undiscouraged.

Instead of resigning herself to accepting the prevailing opinion that the
future held nothing further in store for her, this blue-eyed young Diana of
the courts, who had the initiative in 1928 to forsake a lifelong underhand
service for an overhead delivery, packed her trunks and, accompanied by
her young brother, Jimmy, who is the junior champion of England, set out
across the Atlantic to prove differently.

Winning the American championship without Mrs. Moody or Miss Helen
Jacobs in the lists is considerably short of the feat of winning it in opposition to those two players, but this triumph of the popular young British girl
stands in some ways as the most creditable performance of her brilliant, if
erratic, career.

Miss Nuthall had no idea when she left England that Mrs. Moody would
not defend her crown. She set out with the intent and hope of meeting the
foremost woman player of the world and, considering the adversity she had
undergone, that is testimonial enough to her courage and enterprise.

In defeating Miss Morrill in the semi-finals Miss Nuthall again showed
her fortitude by overcoming an opponent who for a set and a half put on
the closest thing to a Helen Wills exhibition of blinding speed under control
that any player has given at Forest Hills in years.

To have won in the face of such a withering attack after losing the first
set and trailing at 2–4 in the second speaks both for her unwavering courage
and the effectiveness of her own weapons, as well as for the astuteness with
which she uses them.

Speed, the distinctive attribute of the championship player of this generation, is the essence of Miss Nuthall's game. Like Mrs. Moody, she uses her
racket as a flail with which she flogs the ball with utter disdain for
temporizations.

Speed alone, however, would not have beaten Miss Morrill. With her speed Miss Nuthall combines a sagacity and discernment in divining the winning avenues in the opposing court and in surveying them with strokes of corrected angles and length that make keenness of anticipation and mobility of foot a prerequisite of success for her opponent.

Immaculate in her length, resourceful and enterprising in the range of her strokes, strong of endurance and agile in her movements, Miss Nuthall is as well endowed and equipped to throw down the gauntlet to Mrs. Moody as any player on the courts and it may be that the prophecy of Lacoste may yet be borne out.

LILI ALVAREZ

by Helen Hull Jacobs

The majority of tennis enthusiasts who follow Lili Alvarez, the picturesque Spanish player, do not know that she is an accomplished ice skater and skier. In fact, the winter season at St. Moritz is usually completed by the appearance of Alvarez, who excels in all the winter sports and amuses the guests by her daring activities.

Two winters ago she decided that she wanted to go mountain climbing in the Alps in order to make motion pictures. She spent several months in the snow, and when she finally emerged to play in the Beausite tournament at Cannes on the French Riviera she was so snowburned that for a time she was almost unrecognizable. The snowburn proved to be so discomforting, in fact, that she had to withdraw from the singles and was far from her usual standard even in the doubles, which Elizabeth Ryan and I won.

The general impression of Americans regarding women tennis players abroad is that they keep to the one sport and are not apt to branch out to other things, as so many of our American players do. Personally I have found this to be an erroneous impression. If there is any difference in the versatility of American and foreign players, the edge is with the foreigners.

Alvarez, while perhaps unusually versatile, is nevertheless a good example of the sort of thing I mean. With her, the end of the tennis season does not mean the end of sport, although sometimes she will go through the winter without touching a tennis racket. We played a practice match together two weeks before the French championship last year and she told me it was the first time she had been on a court since the French championships of the year before.

Alvarez is said to be the only tennis player of the present time who really resembles the former world champion, Suzanne Lenglen. Lenglen was before my time, so I have had the pleasure of seeing her play only once, as a professional in Oakland. However, a friend of mine and an intimate friend of Lenglen's and Alvarez' has told me that if Alvarez had 15 per cent more stability she would have been capable of passing as a prototype of Lenglen. My personal opinion, after having played and watched Alvarez for five years, is that she would require 50 per cent more stability to duplicate the performances and the game of the Lenglen I saw in Oakland—and those who knew Lenglen's game say she was quite below par in her California matches.

I think the greatest point of similarity between the two is undoubtedly their temperaments. Both are vivacious, temperamental, and colorful. On the court Alvarez is perhaps the most attractive player in the world. Both her face and figure are striking, the latter especially so in its graceful and rhythmic movements. The impression of agility and expertness that she invariably gives to the gallery is as much a result of her strokes as anything else. They are long, sweeping Continental strokes that make full use of the arm, giving it a free look, rather than just the bent and rather compact appearance of the forearm.

All of her shots are played on the half-volley and for this reason have great pace and speed. However, this very fact accounts for her frequent unsteadiness. If the slightest wind happens to be blowing, Alvarez has great difficulty because, as she has admitted herself, she never watches the ball. Her net game is at times inspiring. This too can drop to mediocrity with her mood, but when it is at its height it is almost impossible to pass her or give her a lob she can't reach and hit for a placement.

Lili has always been a favorite of the former King of Spain. Whenever he came to Wimbledon she was put on the center court and usually performed her best. That is Alvarez. With inspiration she can become a really remarkable player, but with discouragement or a lack of confidence in her shots she is likely to be defeated by anyone, as indeed she was at Wimbledon in 1929.

THERE NEVER WAS A FEUD

by Helen Hull Jacobs

If I had ever saved all the newspaper clippings, I could have filled a scrapbook with stories of the "feud" between Helen Wills and myself. It was a wonderful story from the newspaper point of view but it could not have been farther from the truth. During all the years in which we both were playing, we never once exchanged an unpleasant word!

Helen and I had similar backgrounds. We both played at the Berkeley Tennis Club, both attended Anna Head's School, and both went on to the University of California. We even lived in the same house. When we moved to Berkeley from San Francisco, our family took the old Wills home. My mother was friendly with Mrs. Wills as was my father with Dr. Wills. And there was so much that was parallel in both our careers. We were in a different age bracket, she being two years older than I, but we followed the same general pattern. She won the National Junior Championships two years in a row as did I, and we both practiced with and competed against the same players.

We were probably most friendly when I was in the juniors. In 1924, my mother and I were guests of Mrs. Wightman along with Helen and Mrs. Wills. Helen had just returned from the Olympic Games, and we frequently went shopping together or sat around and chatted. Starting in 1927, we began to meet in the finals of tournaments although, in an eleven-year period, we played only seven or eight times. I suppose it was only natural that when we played, our friends would be divided into two camps. However, they had nothing to do with this myth of a feud. Helen and I were rivals, certainly, but never enemies.

Helen was a magnificent player from the back court. She had power, control and a great sense of strategy. Her only "weakness" was her net game, which was merely adequate. For five or six years she was the superior player in each of our meetings, but by 1933 I felt I had learned to play her. It happened during the French Championships. Suzanne Lenglen then told me that the only way to defeat Helen was to force her to move for the short crosscourts. She offered to rally with me each day so that I could develop a sharp crosscourt from any section of the court. We rallied endlessly. Lenglen was incredibly accurate. She would drive down the line, deep or short, to teach me to hit the crosscourt from any spot between the baseline and the service line. This, combined with going to net at every opportunity, gave me the edge in our famous singles final of 1933.

The story of this match has been told and retold. It was the finals of the National Singles Championship. We had divided the first two sets and I was leading 3–0. I turned around to the ballboy to receive the balls, but he was looking in the other direction.

"May I have the balls, please?" I asked.

He pointed toward the other end of the court. Helen was walking toward the umpire's stand and had begun to put on her sweater. I walked toward her and asked if anything was wrong.

"My leg is hurting," she replied. "I can't go on."

"Would you like to rest for a minute?" I asked.

"No," she replied. "I can't go on."

That sums up our entire conversation, although one reporter quoted me as begging her to continue. I was later asked as to whether I thought Helen should have defaulted. In my opinion, only the player himself knows if he can go on, and who can presume to say that an opponent is or is not in great physical pain?

In 1935, we met again in the finals of Wimbledon. This time I was leading 5–3, 40–30, match point in the third set. After an exchange of shots, Helen threw up a lob. The wind carried the ball down, and by the time I was ready to hit the overhead, I was practically on my knees! My shot taped the net, and Helen went on to win. She certainly deserves all credit for pulling out a victory. As for me, I have replayed that overhead a thousand times!

We met once again in 1938 in the finals of Wimbledon. In the quarter-finals, I had torn the sheath of my Achilles tendon while playing Jadviga Jedrzejowska. My leg was strapped for my next match against Alice Marble, but I managed to beat her 6–4, 6–4 in a battle that was closer than the score indicates.

We had a day of rest before playing the final. Once again my ankle was strapped and we both started out to play what looked to be a fine match. Then at 4–all, 40–30, on my serve in the first set, I leaped for a sharp crosscourt and landed heavily on my foot. My ankle started to swell above the bandage and, although I could stand on it, I could not run. Mrs. Wightman came down on the court to ask me to default, but I told her that I was able to continue. I played on, although unable to do more than just move from side to side of the court, losing the next eight games and the match at 6–4, 6–0. Helen did the right thing in playing each point as hard as she could, for it was obvious that she was going to win and there was no reason to prolong the agony.

Our famous "feud" may perhaps have inspired a professional offer that I received in 1935. I don't know what happened when Helen was approached, but I was offered $50,000 to tour against her. I sat up all night before making up my mind. I had never won Wimbledon, which was my biggest ambition, and I turned down the offer to make another try at the Wimbledon title the next year. By great good luck, I won it.

Helen and I were never together off the court for we each had our different personalities and our own friends. Her personality toward tennis opponents was definitely on the cold side, but I, too, had made most of my friends outside the tennis circle. We always spoke when we passed, but to read the papers you would have believed that we turned our heads as we went by! This "feud" was perhaps merely a matter of two players who were neutral toward each other, for I know that I certainly never felt any dislike toward my namesake. . . .

Helen is living in Southern California and I have made my home in the East. Our paths have never crossed since our tournament days. The last time I saw her was the last match we played in 1938!

BOOK REVIEW OF *BEYOND THE GAME*

from the London Post

The public is quite humanly interested in the private life of its sporting champions. Much has been written about Miss Jacobs, both fact and fiction, with the result that, as the person "in possession of the facts," she has written her own life. We find that her interests are far from being circumscribed by tennis. Miss Jacobs is remarkably shrewd and I trust it is not exceeding my scope to suggest that I believe the unconscious motive in writing this book was the reasonable desire to establish a truer perspective between Mrs. Moody and herself.

It becomes apparent that the background of these two women was not as unsimilar as has been occasionally indicated. Miss Jacobs' restrained self-editing is admirably done. She once chose between journalism and tennis as a career; her talent for both cannot be questioned.

But those who look to this book for Miss Jacobs' views concerning her great rival will be disappointed. Though readers may derive some amusement from the fact that they both lived successively in the same house and knew one another, however casually, far better than their behavior on the tennis court could even remotely suggest, there springs to mind that dramatic study in high tension during their final match at Wimbledon last year. It is a pity that the nature of tennis demands an inevitable duel which has more to do with prestige than the game itself.

Miss Jacobs aptly appraises most of her opponents, but her references to Mrs. Moody's game are discreetly few. Psychologically speaking, and the author has studied psychology with excellent results, it is noticeable that in losing to others it is always with genuine generosity "to the better player." When losing to Mrs. Moody, though unfailingly just, there are explanations. "Some expected me to win the final against Helen Wills (1927), which I didn't do. Probably among other reasons because I was so anxious to win." Again we find, "I knew that Helen's better play had beaten me, but I feel that most of my bad play was pure stupidity." Of her defeat last year she remarks "that it has been an exhausting, in some respects a bewildering match." Incidentally Miss Jacobs is in error when stating that the late King and Queen Mary were present at this match (1935).

However, it is pleasant reading in these days of self-praise in autobiographies to discover in one who has every reason to think well of herself a charming modesty. Her victories are explained sympathetically. "Hilda Krahwinkel was tired and decided to take a rest." Much of her success she gratefully attributes to her mother, her doctor and the understanding of such distinguished friends as Lord d'Abernon, the American Ambassador and Mrs. Bingham, Lady Cairns and the Beaumonts—and as far as tennis alone is concerned to the helpful coaching of Mrs. Mallory, Mlle. Lenglen and Tilden.

Obviously one learns much about Miss Jacobs' character in her book. She is determined, she is conscientious, she is independent; all qualities which help to build her excellent game. Once the possessor of a temper, "to say the least deplorable," she now verges upon the philosophical. Her adaptability is evident from the fact that she always learns from defeat. Sensitive, and encouraged by sympathetic approval, she is fortunate in many friends.

Miss Jacobs describes the exhilarating realization of victory, though one cannot afford to be hopeful, or relinquish hope, until the last point is played. There are those who suffer from the "stadium complex," never doing as well before a gallery as those to whom it is an "infectious excitement." Mrs. Mallory is paid a graceful tribute. "She had never to stop and consider the sporting thing to do on any occasion. She knew instinctively because she never forgot that tennis was a game. . . . I liked Mrs. Mallory for her spontaneous smile in defeat and her considerately repressed pleasure in victory." The author is a consistent admirer of the old school of players who, she contends, are not subject to the limitations which the younger players suffer when modern "perfect conditions" are lacking.

There are reflections upon conditions past and present at Wimbledon; thoughtful consideration is bestowed upon the fate of former champions. Miss Jacobs is determined to avoid overspecialization to the exclusion of other interests. About her own game she maintains a cool detachment, preferring only the subtlety of a grass court to the hard. It seems, also, that tennis tournaments in England are arranged with more efficiency than on the Continent.

Miss Jacobs is hard-hitting over the amateurs and the money problem. Her case is justly expressed and should be read in her own outspoken words. Briefly, her contention is that "no amateur has been able to make money at amateur tennis except by writing upon it." This statement will be questioned by some. She points out that the conditions of practice, including the occasional permanent sacrifice of good health, to produce the necessary results are strenuous. "The pleasures, the advantages, the personal tests of character in first-class tennis are greater, but the risks are also great. If a player gives twenty years to the game, if he gives far less, I do not see what possible justification there can be for the demand that he shall not profit in any way from the sacrifice."

In France, England, and Australia amateur players may represent tennis firms. In America the U.S. Lawn Tennis Association eight-weeks rule (i.e., no amateur player may compete in tournaments where his expenses are paid for more than eight weeks throughout the year unless he is asked to play for his country) gives, in Miss Jacobs' opinion, an unfair advantage to the well to-do over the less fortunate. She concludes: "Championship tennis requires patience, competition and intelligence, it requires calm nerves, strong bodies, and clear minds. It is an all-time job. Why not therefore define the professional rather than the amateur?"

Miss Jacobs is a good sportswoman. Sheer vitality makes her book almost as stimulating to read as she is to watch. Tennis has made travel possible for Miss Jacobs, and she emerges, rather wistfully, from her chronicle as one who would enjoy embarking upon other adventures as well if time and tennis would only permit. My guess is that she can accomplish anything she makes up her mind to do. She is refreshingly honest, capable, and intelligent. So read for yourself this book by a grand player about a great game.

SIDNEY WOOD

by Allison Danzig

The note read: "Give me a ring some day and come up to the house for lunch." The signature was Sidney Wood's.

The date was made, and at the appointed hour I was at his apartment. My host was not there. Probably a big day at the office. I was a few pages along in *Guinea Pigs No More* when he arrived, breathing heavily and apologetic. He had left his brief case in the taxi and remembered it in time to set out in pursuit, overtaking his quarry and rescuing the prize.

"Look here a minute," he called from the next room, after excusing himself to wash up. From a chiffonier he took a small bottle and held it up smilingly.

"There's the fellow that caused all the rumpus," he explained. It was his appendix (pickled in alcohol), removed in an emergency operation in the small town of Boone, Iowa, after he had been stricken on the train en route to California.

I looked and my thoughts turned back to the awful match Sidney Wood had played against Wilmer Allison in the final of the National Tennis Championship last September. Through my mind flashed the memory of his repeated disappointing performances and of his long quest for robust health on trips to the Far West. Did that small bottle, with its intriguing contents, furnish the answer after all these years?

"The doctor told me that I would feel like a new man and put on more weight than I ever had in my life," he revealed.

"How much did you weigh last summer?" I asked.

He grinned guiltily. "Less than 140." His guilt was in stating in May 1935 that he was up to 150. He was afraid at the time that if his real weight were known it would kill his Davis Cup chances. And having made his bed, he slept in it. He had no alibi to offer for the season for the terrible licking he received from Allison after the latter, more magnificent than ever I saw him before, had beaten Fred Perry. He took his unmerciful panning in the press without a word of protest and laughed when shown a clipping that gave the world to know that Sidney Wood couldn't produce when the chips were down.

I was glad that I hadn't said that as I looked at the bottle on the chiffonier. That fuzzy, curling piece of vermiform tissue in alcohol, whose intertwining with the colon had raised havoc with the digestive process, took on the aspect of a big question mark: If a man with a strangulated appendix in his innards could play well enough to reach the finals of the National Championship, what might he not accomplish with the evil genie corked up in a bottle?

I put the question to him as we fenced with the artichoke salad. Before he could answer, the telephone rang again—for the seventh time in half an hour. The serving girl conveyed the message with an apologetic shrug of the shoulders. It was another "must" call.

So I understood when, later on, he gave me to know that he was indifferent to whether or not he played any more Davis Cup tennis. A man with so many business obligations wasn't likely to give serious consideration to a game.

In truth, I couldn't recall ever seeing Sidney Wood when winning meant life or death to him. Of all the tennis players I have watched pass in review, he, more than any other, symbolized the spirit that plays the game for the sheer love of playing. None could attach smaller consequence to victory or accept defeat more light-heartedly.

That is not to say that he shirked the task or gave up the fight or did not want to win. No one could say that who saw his pitifully futile efforts to get his game going against the merciless onslaught of Allison in the final at Forest Hills. No one could possibly question his gameness after seeing the amazing performance he put on in 1930 at Southampton, where, in successive rounds, Frank Shields, Allison and George Lott fell before him after Lott and Shields had collectively stood at match point seven times. Three gorgeous backhand passing shots straight down the line that Wood made against Lott, as the latter came up behind powerful forehand drives at match point, stand out as vividly in memory as though they were made only yesterday.

The transcendent artistry of those backhand shots gave you to know for the first time that Sidney Wood belonged among the great virtuosos of the racket. A week before, he had made the headlines with a masterpiece of politic play at Seabright, where his tactical discernment in the exploitation of the soft ball turned away the wrath and broke the heart of Ellsworth Vines, then the sensation of the country with double victories over Shields and Frank Hunter. But it was not until those almost unbelievable circumventions against Shields, Allison and Lott at Southampton that the majestic radiance of his attack stood forth to stamp him as one born to wear the purple. From that day on, this observer was on the bandwagon of this jovial, flaxen-haired stripling, and his triumph at Wimbledon in 1931 at the age of nineteen was regarded as the beginning of a great reign.

But, instead, it actually marked the climax. Sidney Wood has never since reached the same stature, and his great gifts, including a tactical shrewdness comparable to Tilden's, have availed him little against the more prosaic but more substantial and dependable tennis of Vines, Perry and Allison. From time to time we saw flashes of the real Wood. His match with Jack Crawford in the championship at Forest Hills in 1933 was regarded as the best of the tournament, though I thought the finest tennis of the week was furnished in his engagement with Gene Mako on an outside court, the first and last really first-class tennis the blond Californian has played in the East.

His match with Crawford in the Davis Cup in 1934, won in the fifth set, was another reminder of the profundity of his generalship and the masterful quality of his stroke production, and in the challenge round a week later his undeniable genius asserted itself again as he led Perry two sets to one in spite of the handicap of repeated foot-faults called against him. But then came his crushing defeat by Allison in the championship that year and again in the final in 1935.

Coming in the wake of his displacement by Budge in the Davis Cup singles abroad, as well as his overwhelming defeat by Shields at Rye in his first tournament after returning home, the debacle at Forest Hills last year seemed definitely to write *finis* to a career that had gained international attention so long ago as 1927, when, as a mere spindling boy of fifteen, Wood appeared on the center court at Wimbledon in linen knickerbockers against René Lacoste, of France. Even his stanchest and most loyal adherents wavered in their allegiance. Apparently the limitations of the flesh were an insurmountable handicap for one of the brainiest strategists and most entrancing shot-makers tennis has known.

It may be, indeed, that 1935 marked the swan song of Wood as an internationalist. The Davis Cup squad for 1936 as designated for the match with Mexico failed to reveal his name, and Allison and Budge, on the record, are the logical choices for the singles berths. But to one who for years found more inspiration for his scribbling in the glamorous, shimmering strokes and rare powers of divination of Sidney Wood than in the attributes of any other player on the courts, that bottle on the chiffonier was fascinating in its implications. Tilden, a great player in 1922, became even more formidable after the amputation of half of his middle finger on his racket hand. May it not be possible that Sidney Wood, through the amputation of his appendix, will finally reap the reward, after all these years, of one of the most gifted hands and minds tennis has produced?

FRANK SHIELDS

by Alice Marble

My first recollection of Francis X. Shields, our new Davis Cup captain, takes me back to William Randolph Hearst's fabulous ranch, San Simeon, California. The guest list was, as always, studded with the names of newspaper celebrities and glamorous movie folk, but it was the twenty-three-year-old Frank, handsome as any male star and considerably more virile than the majority, who was on the receiving end of more than casual glances from the movie queens.

He was there primarily to study dramatics with Marion Davies' coach. A New Yorker by birth, he had gone out to California to play in the Pacific Southwest tournament, where his good looks and gallery appeal were spotted by a sharp-eyed agent. Leaving his insurance business in the capable hands of his partner, Julius Seligson, Frank remained in Hollywood through three and a half depression years. Under contract to one of the major studios, he earned a handsome salary of three hundred and fifty dollars a week while cooling his heels, making screen tests, and—sensible man—opening a branch office on the West Coast for the firm of Seligson and Shields.

Frank is anything but a glamour boy. He is a sincere, honest, hard-working insurance broker, and he is able to look back on those gay days in Hollywood with much amusement at his own expense. In his opinion he wasn't any great shakes as an actor. Though he appeared in several movies, he admits, most of his emoting ended up on the proverbial cutting-room floor. This might well be true, but he seems to have every bit as much gallery appeal at the ripe old age of forty as he had in his prime in the early 1930s. The tennis gallery, that is. Last February, when he defeated one of the first-ten ranking players, Vic Seixas, in an early round of the national indoor championships, the name of Frank Shields was on the lips of the spectators for days afterward.

Frank was never a national or Wimbledon champion, but he came very close to winning England's great tournament. Unfortunately, in defeating Jean Borotra in the semi-finals in 1931, Frank tore the ligaments around his knee and was forced to default to Sidney Wood. (The year before he was runner-up to John Doeg for the United States championship.)

Shields' record as a member of the Davis Cup team is an excellent one. He defeated the great Fred Perry and later won the deciding match against the Australians.

Over a period of years Frank has beaten practically everybody worthy of the name of tennis champion. He was, and is, a fine player and one of the best competitors I have ever known. Possibly this is true because he is such a sound, natural athlete. I have read his boyhood clippings and know he was in the sports headlines practically every day of the year for his prowess on the baseball diamond, the basketball court and the gridiron. As a prep school star he could toss a football seventy yards, and the Yale coach at that time said Frank was the finest natural football player he had ever seen.

Frank also began his tennis career very early, with the encouragement of his father, a certified public accountant. He won the national boys' fifteen-and-under championship at the age of thirteen and won the national junior championship twice. Of this he says, "I never practiced a day in my life."

Players were not taught then as they are today, and Frank, with all his fine natural ability, never learned a backhand drive. Against sound, well-taught players he was consequently under a terrific handicap, and his record against them speaks for itself. Now, of course, he realizes the need to learn the fundamentals of any game. In three short years he has developed into a ranking star at court tennis, one of the most difficult games in the world to learn, and plays every weekend against the world champion, a fifty-six-year-old phenomenon named Pierre Etchebaster. Shields is also a ten-handicap golfer. In discussing his present attitude toward learning, he sighed and said, "Allie, if I had studied and practiced tennis as much as I have the game of court tennis, I might have been a real champion." I think he's right.

THE REDHEAD

by Allison Danzig

The return of Donald Budge to the lists under the management of Jack Kramer brings back into the touring fold a player of established position high among the greatest masters of the racket of all time. No less established and every bit as high is the place he holds in the regard of tennis lovers everywhere as a thoroughbred sportsman whose devotion to the best interests of the game and its code of fair play is unexcelled.

There are those who rank Budge as the supreme player of them all, ahead of Tilden, Cochet, Lacoste, Johnston, Brookes, the Dohertys, Williams, Perry, Vines, Beals Wright, McLoughlin, Wilding, Parker, and Kramer. Not every one will go along with that, and in any such argument Tilden gets the vote here.

But any such speculation can be only that, falling short of convincing anyone who has his mind made up and his heart set on his particular idol. It is as idle as any attempt to establish the pre-eminence of Dempsey, Louis, Sullivan, Corbett, Fitzsimmons, Johnson, Jeffries, or Tunney among the heavyweight champions of the ring.

The feats of Budge on the court are sufficient to leave no doubt that he stands with the greatest, regardless of who rates the No. 1 spot. His record does not match Tilden's in longevity, in part because he left the amateur ranks when he was only twenty-three years old—an age at which Tilden was four years short of winning the first of his seven national championships—and also because his career was interrupted by the war, and a sore shoulder impaired his game when he returned from the service. But before he entered professional tennis, Budge had established himself beyond dispute as the world's foremost player, his backhand had won recognition as probably the most potent the world had seen, and he had accomplished something that neither Tilden nor any other man in history has achieved.

In his last year as an amateur, 1938, Donald the Red scored the only grand slam recorded in men's tennis. In one and the same year he won all four of the world's major crowns—the Australian, French, British and American. Quite likely Tilden would have been equal to making the slam had he attempted it, but the fact remains that the freckled, flaming-haired six-footer from Oakland, California, stands as the only one who has adapted his game and himself to the varying conditions of climate, water, food, court surface, grass texture, ball differences and gallery behavior to sweep the boards at Melbourne, Auteuil, Wimbledon and Forest Hills.

That same year Budge was voted by the sports writers of the country the top athlete—amateur or pro—of 1938. He had also been voted the top athlete of 1937 and won the Sullivan Trophy, the first tennis player to be so honored as the outstanding amateur athlete of the nation.

It was in 1937 that Budge gave Americans one of their greatest thrills in many years. It was his victory over Baron Gottfried von Cramm of Germany that enabled the United States to bring back the Davis Cup, ten years after it had been lost to France at the Germantown Cricket Club in Philadelphia.

The match between the handsome baron and the red-thatched youth from California was the big one in the interzone round. The winning nation still had to play England in the challenge round, but Fred Perry had entered the professional ranks and it was a foregone conclusion that without him the British would be unable to make another successful defense of the cup, which they had won from France in 1933.

In all the history of the cup it is doubtful if there has been a greater match than this meeting between Budge and von Cramm. Certainly none had a more thrilling finish or produced more glorious tennis under nerve-wracking tension and pressure. No wonder, after that almost miraculous victory over so magnificent an opponent as was von Cramm, that Pate to this day maintains that no player who ever lived was Budge's superior.

After that, Donald the Red led his team to victory over Great Britain in the challenge round and won the championship at Wimbledon also. Returning home a conquering hero, he added to his stature by winning the national crown at Forest Hills. The world was at his feet. He was the undisputed master of the courts, seven years after his brother, Lloyd, had persuaded him to forget about the many other games he played and take up tennis.

It was inevitable that professional promoters should besiege the 22-year-old youth with tempting offers. It was taken for granted that he would yield to them and sign for a fabulous sum that would give him and his family security and a share in the comforts and luxuries that had been beyond their means.

Now it was that Budge showed more than ever the character that has marked him throughout his career. He turned down a contract that would have guaranteed him $50,000 or more for a year of play as a professional. His reason? He thought he owed it to amateur tennis, in return for all it had done for him and the opportunity it had given him to see the world, become famous and make something of himself, to remain an amateur for another year and help defend the cup the United States had been so long in regaining.

So he turned down the offers and stayed an amateur, though he knew the risk he was running of losing a fortune that he might not have another chance to make. It was the risk that he might suffer an injury that would put an end to his career, that another player might arise to put him in eclipse as a professional attraction, that he might not enjoy another season of such transcendent success as in 1937.

The risk did not materialize. Donald the Red went on to score an even more sweeping triumph in 1938, with his grand slam and his leadership of the United States team in its successful defense of the cup in the challenge round.

Now, clear of conscience in having fulfilled his obligation and helped to keep the cup in this country, he took the $50,000. And, for the first time, the United States Lawn Tennis Association was officially represented at the signing of a professional contract by one of its top drawing cards.

To the law offices of Captain Pate, Holcombe Ward, then president of the U.S.L.T.A. and an inflexible advocate of uncompromising enforcement of the amateur code, came to offer Budge his congratulations and best wishes for a successful career as a score of reporters looked on. Never before nor since has a player left the amateur ranks with the blessing bestowed upon Budge by the ruling powers of 120 Broadway. It was a fitting testimonial to the place that Donald the Red, with his sportsmanship, loyalty and integrity, as well as with his mighty racket, holds in the hearts of all who are devoted to lawn tennis.

WINNING THE BIG FOUR

by Donald Budge

The other evening, my brother Lloyd and I were talking about Lew Hoad and the reason for his inability to win the Big Four. He had won the Australian, French and Wimbledon crowns and was only two sets away from taking the Forest Hills title over Rosewall. Only Jack Crawford had come closer; he took three of the Big Four and led Fred Perry two sets to one in the final round of the Nationals. I said that Lew had failed for two reasons: first, Rosewall had the advantage of having had a tough match against Dick Savitt, who serves and hits as hard as Hoad, while Lew had had an easy path to the finals; secondly, Hoad got here late and played only

Longwood before entering the Nationals, which didn't allow him enough time to become acclimatized.

My brother said that perhaps the reason I won the four titles was because I hadn't set out to win them. He was wrong. Everything I did that year was aimed at winning them. I was due to go to Australia in the latter part of 1937 to play in the Victorian Championships in Melbourne and the Australian Championships in Adelaide. I had been forewarned by Wilmer Allison, Johnny Van Ryn and Elly Vines about the Aussie Test Matches. They unanimously agreed that if I went to Australia, I would play myself out in the Test Matches and would be practically no good the rest of the year. However, I had already said I would go, but I took advantage of the advice given me and did not take the Test Matches as seriously as the Australian boys did. As a consequence, I was fresh and eager when I played the two tournaments.

I liken my tactics down there to Hoad's this year, with the one exception. I think Hoad overplayed his hand by not arriving in this country one or two weeks earlier than he did. . . .

Because I played these matches without any stress or strain, I was fresh and eager for any event in which I wanted to do my best. If I had tried my hardest and played every exhibition as though it were the finals of Wimbledon, I would have been putting myself in a position where I might have been mentally tired for the big one. Naturally, after losing 8 out of 10 Test Matches, the Aussie press felt that, although I might be a reasonable player, I wasn't head and shoulders above the rest of the boys. How else could they explain my losses? Little did they know that I was doing my road work and exercises regularly and that I could hardly wait for the opening day of the Australian Championships. Then I'd show them a Budge who had come to their country to do a job!

I had one plan in mind, and that was to hit every ball as hard as I could, beat everyone 6–0 if I could, and get each match over with as quickly as possible. This is understandable since the coolest day in the tournament was 105° and the hottest was 115°. I was very lucky, didn't drop a set in any of my matches, and beat Bromwich in the final, 6–3, 6–1, 6–2. . . .

Playing the French Championships was my biggest test. Several of the European players felt that when I got onto en-tout-cas, I'd find the going much tougher. I wanted to prove to them that my game was equally the same on all surfaces. Conditions are different in tournaments all over the world, which is an important factor in keeping one's game at its highest peak. I suffered throughout the whole French Championships from a stomach disorder, and as a consequence, in practically every singles match I played, I had to have a sandwich sent down to the court in the middle of the match.

I did lose two sets in this tournament, both to Franjo Kukuljevic. . . . I finally got through this match, winning the fifth set comfortably and I went ahead to defeat Roderick Menzel in straight sets in the final.

One of the biggest thrills of my life occurred during the French Championships. Each day Russell Kingman came out to the tennis matches with Pablo Casals, who is considered the world's greatest living instrumentalist. We always had tea together after my singles, and after the final with Menzel, Pablo said: "Don, I got so much enjoyment from watching you play that I would like to invite you back to my house tonight to play for you." I accepted with great enthusiasm, and after dinner ten of us climbed up to Pablo's studio overlooking the city of Paris and sat on the floor as Pablo, with the spotlight on him, played to the rapture of all of us for some two hours.

For some reason or other, Wimbledon that year offered no problems. I had played so well the week before at Queens, defeating Bunny Austin in the finals, 6–0, 6–1, that I felt I was at the top of my game for this stage of my life. I went through the tournament without the loss of a set, beating Austin in the finals, 6–1, 6–0, 6–3. I played a good match that day.

I returned to the States in time for the Eastern Grass Court Championships, in which I played only the doubles. Then I won my third leg on the Newport trophy. I was now beginning to get a little nervous about winning the Big Four. Fortunately, I did not encounter any problems in getting to the finals at Forest Hills. I had been pulling for Mako to do well in the singles, for he had been playing very well ever since the French Championships. He had a most impressive tournament, beating Kovacs in the first round, then Gil Hunt and Puncec, and finally Bromwich in the semis to gain the title round.

I knew this was going to be a difficult final, even though I knew Gene's game inside out. Nobody seemed to take the match seriously except me. After we each won our semi-finals, we had one week of solid rain and the final round wasn't played until seven days later! I won in four sets and was very astonished to hear that some people thought Mako got the second because we were friends! Let me assure you that when one is out to establish a record, the idea is to win the match as quickly and as painlessly as possible.

I had finally done it. I hadn't lost a singles since the Test Matches and I had won the Big Four. I went out to California to play in the Pacific Southwest and the Pacific Coast. I was so tired mentally that I affected everyone in the tournament! I lost to Quist in the Southwest and Harry Hopman in the Coast. It was awful, but I couldn't have cared less and I couldn't help it.

Every player who has gone after the Big Four has geared himself for it. A few who might have tried for it automatically eliminated themselves by playing too many tournaments. I never played Italy, the Riviera, Egypt, South America or India because I didn't want to poop myself out for the more important events. I spent the winter working with Tom Stow on correcting my faults so that I would have less to worry about the following year. A lot of players make the mistake of playing too many tournaments instead of working on their bad points.

Seeing Them
in Action
THE EARLY YEARS

Richard D. Sears,
first U.S. champion,
1881–1887 inclusive   (USLTA)

Dr. James Dwight,
President of the USLTA,
1882–1884, 1894–1911   (USLTA)

Wimbledon All Comers, H. F. Lawford vs. E. Renshaw, 1887   (THE GRAPHIC)

"Lawn Tennis at Newport," drawn by C. D. Weldon   (BETTMANN ARCHIVE, INC.)

The first U.S. Davis Cup team, 1900:
Malcolm Whitman, Dwight Davis, Holcombe Ward
(BETTMANN ARCHIVE, INC.)

May Sutton (Bundy),
Wimbledon champion,
1905, 1907; U.S., 1904
(PHOTOWORLD–FPG)

William A. Larned,
seven-time U.S. champion,
1901–1902, 1907–1911 inclusive
(PHOTOWORLD–FPG)

Maurice E. McLoughlin,
U.S. champion, 1912, 1913
(USLTA)

Mary K. Browne, U.S. champion,
1912, 1913, and runner-up, 1921,
at which time she was also
one of the nation's
finest golfers
(PHOTOWORLD–FPG)

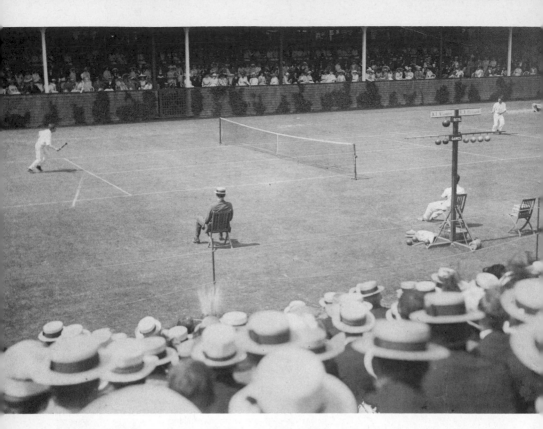

The Newport final, 1913,
Maurice E. McLoughlin vs.
R. Norris Williams
(CULVER)

R. Norris Williams,
U.S. champion,
1914, 1916   (PHOTOWORLD–FPG)

Molla Bjurstedt (Mallory), eight-time U.S. champion between 1915 and 1926

Molla Mallory's historic victory over Suzanne Lenglen, Forest Hills, 1921 . . .

. . . and its aftermath   (PHOTOWORLD–FPG)

"Little Bill" Johnston and "Big Bill" Tilden, for seven consecutive years the pair that held the Davis Cup for the U.S., 1920–1926 inclusive   (PHOTOWORLD–FPG)

Zenzo Shimizu of Japan
and Bill Tilden
just before their classic
Davis Cup match
which Tilden won after
being two sets down
and two points
from defeat—
in the third set
(PHOTOWORLD–FPG)

Bill Johnston's
famous Western
forehand drive
(PHOTOWORLD–FPG)

A legendary ladies' foursome in the early twenties: Eleanor Goss, Elizabeth Ryan, Mary K. Browne, and the then new young star, Helen Wills   (USLTA)

Vincent Richards, Tilden's greatest protégé, one of America's finest doubles players of all time and winner of the Olympic singles title in 1924   (USLTA)

1926—and the U.S. has just defeated France 4–1 in the Davis Cup Challenge Round at Germantown for their last victory before the next six-year domination by the French. Julian S. Myrick, Bill Johnston, Bill Tilden, Dwight F. Davis, R. Norris Williams, George Wightman, Vincent Richards and Charles S. Garland   (USLTA)

The all-conquering
Helen Wills (Moody)
in 1927, winning the first
of her eight
Wimbledon championships.
She also won the U.S. title
at Forest Hills
seven times between
1923 and 1931.

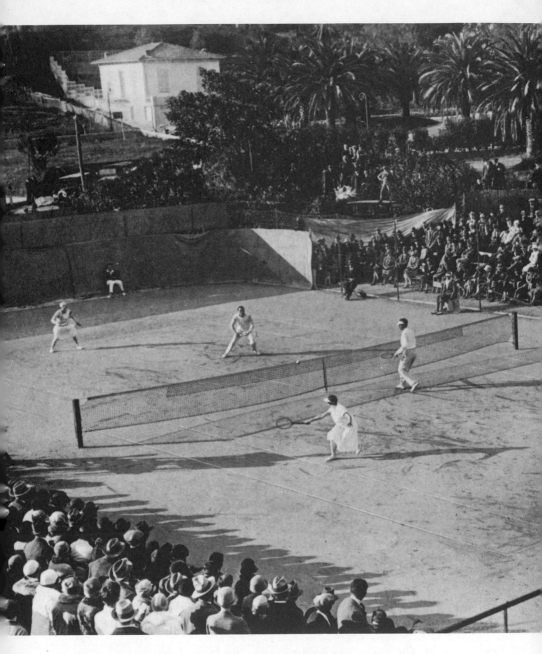

The first meeting of Suzanne Lenglen and Helen Wills was here at Nice in a mixed-doubles match. This was followed soon after by their "Match of the Century" singles encounter at Cannes in 1926.   (WIDE WORLD)

Two of France's "Four Musketeers" in 1927
as they took over the tennis world:
René Lacoste and Jean Borotra
(PHOTOWORLD–FPG)

Henri Cochet who,
along with Lacoste,
was the best of
the "Musketeers"
(USLTA)

The most flamboyant
of the French quartet,
"The Bounding Basque,"
Jean Borotra   (USLTA)

In 1927 René Lacoste
played an early round match
at Wimbledon against the
15-year-old American
youngster Sidney B. Wood.
He won handily.
Four years later,
Wood won the Wimbledon
championship.   (USLTA)

George M. Lott, Jr.,
and John Doeg,
winners of the U.S.
men's doubles in 1929
and 1930. Doeg also won
the singles title in 1930.
(USLTA)

John Van Ryn and Wilmer Allison, U.S. doubles titleholders in 1931 and 1935, and Wimbledon champions in 1929 and 1930   (USLTA)

George Lott with Lester Stoefen. They paired to win at Wimbledon in 1934 and to take the American title in 1933 and 1934. Lott was so outstanding a doubles partner that he'd be likely to win with any good partner, but Stoefen was his favorite one.   (PHOTOWORLD–FPG)

Ellsworth Vines, Jr., who dominated American tennis after Tilden, and who won at Forest Hills in 1931 and 1932 and at Wimbledon as well in the latter year (PHOTOWORLD–FPG)

England's Fred Perry,
U.S. champion in 1933, 1934,
and 1936, Wimbledon champion
from 1934–1936 inclusive,
and the mainstay of the
British Davis Cup team which took
the cup from 1933–1936 inclusive
(USLTA)

Jack Crawford, of Australia, beat Vines in the Wimbledon final of 1933 in one of the finest matches ever played, but Perry beat him in five sets that year in the finals at Forest Hills.   (USLTA)

Another memorable encounter of the thirties was Donald Budge's epic victory over Baron Gottfried von Cramm of Germany in their celebrated Davis Cup match of 1937. Here is a von Cramm smash.   (WIDE WORLD)

Two months later,
in September 1937, Budge
once again defeated von Cramm
(foreground) in another
five-set match to win
the American title.
(WIDE WORLD)

The Budge backhand was
one of the most elegant
and powerful shots in the game,
and he was still making it
many years after the two epic
duels against von Cramm.
(PHOTOWORLD—FPG)

With Helen Wills (Moody) in semi-retirement, Helen Jacobs dominated American women's tennis from 1932–1935 inclusive, beating Mrs. Moody in 1933 in their most controversial match. Miss Jacobs also took the Wimbledon title in 1936. (USLTA)

But Mrs. Moody had the last word, returning to Wimbledon in 1935 and in 1938 to beat Miss Jacobs both times and to win her seventh and eighth All-England championships. (PHOTOWORLD–FPG)

THE BUDGE STYLE

by Julius D. Heldman

I was one of those players who grew up in the era of Don Budge. He was the King of the Tennis World from 1937 until World War II, and to those of us who were on the circuit with him he was not only untouchable but the greatest player of all time. The same arguments as to who was the better, Tilden or Budge, started in 1937 and are still going on.

"Untouchable" was the right word to describe Don. He never allowed his opponent to get his teeth in the match, and his overwhelming power was not subject to bad streaks. His unfortunate victim had the feeling of complete helplessness, for there was no way in which he could touch Don. The situation would be the same today if Pancho Gonzales were playing against the current crop of amateurs.

Budge grew up in Oakland, California, and was soon the best junior in Northern California. His backhand was always sound and aggressive, but until he was 19 he had a rolling Western forehand. He was one of those players who was anxious to improve and willing to listen. He heard enough from his tennis friends to determine him to switch to the more appropriate Eastern grip. He made the change in the winter of 1935. From then on, it was only a matter of time as to when he would win the world title.

Budge, like his arch-rival Fred Perry, made a magnificent court appearance. Dressed in immaculate long flannels, carefully whited shoes, imported woolen shirts, traditional cable-stitch tennis sweaters, and a white Davis Cup blazer, he looked every inch the champion. In contrast to Perry, Budge was always serious and straightforward. There were no casual quips, no light-hearted behavior, and absolutely no comments during the match. He never questioned a call during his entire amateur career and he was always a perfect gentleman, even during those rare occasions when the going got rough. The game was everything to him and he always gave it 100 per cent effort.

Don was well liked by all the players, but his special friend during his playing days was his doubles partner, Gene Mako. Gene was already a famous young player in 1933, and when Don beat him in the final of the National Juniors it was considered a tremendous upset. After that the two became inseparable. They were inveterate jazz listeners to the extent that they never traveled without their portable record player and a large collection of their discs. I remember rooming next door to them at Westchester during the Eastern Grass Courts and hearing them shave to the accompaniment of Benny Goodman.

Because Don's forehand was a completely trained stroke, it is unique among the strokes of all the champions. Technically it was flawless. It was mechanical in that it was not original with him, but although it did not

241

have the personal flair of his backhand, it was a magnificent, forceful weapon. Of all the strokes of the great champions, this was the one that was always hit properly. He was drilled so thoroughly by Tom Stow and he was so willing and apt a pupil that he never hit it in any manner but letter-perfect. He always approached the ball in the same way, hitting with a closed stance but moving forward. He did not chop, chip or hit on the dead run; he wheeled into position, aimed and fired. The result was a heavy ball to a corner followed, if there was a return, by an equally heavy ball to the other corner.

Budge's forehand was a relentless bludgeon. He took the ball on the top of the bounce, although his eye was good enough so that he could hit on the rise if he had so chosen. He hit on the rise only when it was necessary on a deep ball. This was in strong contrast to the styles of Fred Perry and Henri Cochet, both masters of the half-volley. Budge preferred to take a careful, calculated swing that was sure to put his opponent in the soup. However, although he was no net rusher in the sense of a Schroeder, he never let a ball drop and followed all short ones into net. He hit so well on a short ball that he seldom had to hit anything but a set-up volley or an overhead.

Don's timing was fantastic. He saw the ball better than anyone else. Contrary to most professional advice, he did not "feel" the ball on his racket for any length of time. Most players will flatten or lay back their wrists as they hit in order to hold the racket on the ball as long as possible. If they then mis-time the ball, they still have a very good margin for error. There was no margin on Don's shot. The wrist was locked and not laid back, and if his eye had been poor he would have been a most erratic player. Instead he had perfect coordination and he hit the ball clean and true.

Every Budge forehand was the same. He gracefully two-stepped into position, pivoting as the wind-up started. His backswing was a compact semicircular motion, the hit was wristless, and the follow-through was over the left shoulder. On return of serve, the only forehand shot which he hit with an open stance, he was always on balance and his weight was moving forward.

Don had a slight amount of overspin on the forehand. The overspin was heavier on the crosscourts and for this reason he was one of the few men capable of hitting a sharp crosscourt with a lot of pace. While there was a slight knee bend on waist-high balls, rather than bending his knees he spread his legs for the low ones. The racket head never dropped, but Don never really crouched over either. He got far enough away from the ball so that he was not cramped, but he always stretched rather than bent when digging up a grounder.

Budge's backhand is the most famous ground stroke in tennis. Technically it was very much like his forehand, but it had that extra flair, that great freedom of motion, which made it the envy of every player who ever lived. Only once in his life did it ever go "off," and that was in the early days of a Wimbledon tournament; he regained the feel for the stroke after a few worried hours and took the title handily.

The backhand was hit with a slight amount of topspin, although he often used sidespin when hitting down the line. He was capable of underspinning but he did so rarely, and then mostly in doubles play. His forte was sustained power, not touch tennis. He could hit a placement from any spot in the court to any other spot in the court. His opponent just could not possibly get Don in trouble off the backhand. No matter what you did, he would reply offensively off this wing. The player who attempted to serve and come in on Budge generally lost the point outright, but he was in even more hot water if he tried to serve to the forehand and come in! This left the contestant with no choice but to serve to the backhand and stay back. Years later, when Don was past his prime, the big net rushers such as Kramer, Gonzales and Sedgman found that they could not stay on even terms with him if they tried to follow their serve in.

The backhand was a free motion which basically consisted of taking the racket back rather straight and then literally throwing arm and racket toward the opponent's back fence. The arm straightened out during the hit. It is a simple stroke for anyone to hit and does not require split-second timing—unless one hits it as hard as Budge. It has been a stroke that has been used successfully by a variety of Northern Californians such as Frank Kovacs, Tom Brown and Dorothy Knode. Practically the only other top players who hit the backhand with overspin in the game today are Dick Savitt and Tony Trabert. It is a pity that more players have not learned this easily timed and potent overspin weapon since the underspin fails repeatedly against the big net attack.

Don served his share of aces, but not to the extent of an Ellsworth Vines or a Barry MacKay. It was a great serve nevertheless because the ball was so heavy, deep and well placed. He had a lot of confidence in it during his amateur days, and he took a full roundhouse swing. The toss was always perfect and he used his full height. After the war he developed a slight hitch in the backswing due to a previous arm injury, and he was never quite able to regain his former freedom of motion.

Budge's second serve was hit almost as hard as his first. There was possibly a bit more spin but it was never pronounced. He was not a spin artist and he never used the American twist. He put just enough slice or overspin on the ball to give him control. It takes a lot of confidence to hit that way since the ball skims so close to the net. Don had supreme confidence not only in service but in all other strokes. When he was in his prime he never clutched because he never doubted that he would win. Therefore there were no double-faults or easing up of the power game.

Don did not take the net behind his service. He was a good athlete and could have come in, but it was not his style of play. He was not the type to scurry or scramble; he chose instead to put the pressure on from the ground, coming in only for the assured kill.

Budge hit the overhead just as he did the serve. He had a big round swing in contrast to most players, who choose a smaller backswing on the smash. It was a bludgeon based on heavy rather than wrist-snap power. Behind it was the full weight of his 170 pounds, backed by perfect timing.

In later years it was the first stroke to go off since he refused to temporize or shorten the swing.

Because Don's overhead was like his serve, it was hit with a small amount of slice. The average big overhead is hit quite flat since the player is always standing inside the baseline and often inside the service line. A serve must be sliced because of the distance to the net, but the smash can safely be hit without spin. This weakness in Don's overhead never appeared when he was playing top tennis. In his tournament days it was a great if somewhat unusual shot.

Don was a stroke volleyer by preference. Anything above net level was stroked rather than punched. The only difference between Budge's stroke volley and ground strokes was a shorter backswing and shorter follow-through. It was lethal off both sides. This was the finishing touch of the killer who had prepared his way up to net very carefully. He could stroke-volley the way other players could punch-volley. In general his volleys had no spin and were hit almost completely flat, and the fact that he was so consistent was a tribute to his magnificent timing.

Don could also slice-volley. It was still a big stroke compared with most punches, but he did turn his racket head under for all low balls and for those where he was necessarily cramped. He did not get down too well but he was surprisingly good as a low volleyer. Here he proved that he could have touch, and he could drop-angle volley with the best of them. He was a great doubles player; the only time he ever really camped at the net was in a doubles match. He was also a good poacher and could leap well when required.

Budge's physical condition was always perfect. He never got tired in his life, the one exception being when he had a bad cold. He had a big chest and a wonderful breathing apparatus, but mostly it was because he hit so hard that it was his opponent rather than he who was on the run. His carriage was kingly and he was one of the few big men who were graceful. In his junior days he was as thin as a Buchholz, but as he reached his prime as an amateur he developed a physique in accordance with his powerful frame.

Don Budge was the only man ever to win the Big Four. In one year he took the titles in Australia, France, England and the United States. After dominating the amateur game for two years, he turned professional with the blessings of the USLTA officials. He had stayed amateur another year at their request to defend the Davis Cup, and because he had made a personal financial sacrifice, there were no hard feelings when he eventually made the decision to tour. He dominated the pro world until he went into the Army.

Budge is still a name to conjure with in the world of tennis. When the young players come East for the first time after having fraternized with the "name" players on the tournament circuit, the one personality who can still awe them simply by his presence is J. Donald Budge. The big redhead with the friendly personality is still "Mr. Tennis."

THE BEST ONE I EVER PLAYED

by Donald Budge

I am usually hesitant to answer when an interviewer asks me to put a superlative on one or another moment in my career, but I find no difficulty whatever in naming the greatest tennis match I ever played in. It was an Interzone finals match for the Davis Cup, played on the center court at Wimbledon before a packed stand that included England's Queen Mary, and I was pitted against Germany's Baron Gottfried von Cramm.

As one of the participants, it has always been impossible for me to evaluate objectively all that happened on that July afternoon in 1937. I do know, though, that I never played better tennis nor did I ever play anyone as good as Cramm. Walter Pate, the U.S. team captain, said later, "No other player—living or dead—could have beaten either man that day."

Henner Henkel had just beaten Bitsy Grant in four sets to tie the score in the pairing between the U.S. and Germany at 2–2. The winner of this pairing would still have to meet the defender, England, in the Challenge Round, but in just about everyone's view the 1937 Davis Cup would certainly go to the survivor of the U.S.–Germany meeting. Fred Perry, who had led the English to victory in the competition for the previous four years, had turned pro, weakening the British team to a point where they would be definite underdogs against either of the challengers.

If I won this one match the U.S. would almost certainly get the cup back across the Atlantic after a full decade in Europe. On the other hand, if Cramm beat me, the Germans seemed certain to win their first Davis Cup ever. This possibility was not lost on a man called Hitler whose Nazi pride was still chafing over the Olympic triumphs in Berlin a year earlier of a non-Aryan named Jesse Owens. Before the match had even begun, Hitler's interest in it was to become apparent.

I think I realized early in the match that the crowd was slightly in favor of Cramm, but I had a few British fans rooting for me, as well as a spirited U.S. cheering section that included Paul Lukas, the tennis-loving movie star who had declared himself an unofficial member of our team; his friend, Jack Benny; and Ed Sullivan, then a newspaper columnist.

Still, as the match wore on, I got the feeling that there was no one present who was really *against* either one of us, Gottfried or me. It seemed as if the longer we played and the more exciting and better the tennis became, the less the crowd really cared who won.

The ironic thing about the match was that right up to the time it started I had hopes that it really wouldn't have to count for a thing. When I came into the locker room Tuesday before the first match was over, I was just hoping that Bitsy would beat Henkel, put us ahead 3–1, and make my match against Cramm relaxed and pro forma.

Unfortunately, however, Henkel defeated Bitsy easily, and before I really had time to console him, Teddy Tinling, the tennis clothes designer who was acting as sort of a sergeant at arms, had me by one arm and Cramm by the other and was marching us off to play. Gottfried and I were bustled along so that we hardly had time to acknowledge each other, and Tinling had just about swept us out into the stadium when a phone rang. None of us paid any attention, but a locker room man picked it up and called to Gottfried. "Mr. von Cramm," he said. "Long distance for you, sir."

"Come on, you can't keep Queen Mary waiting," Tinling said.

"But it might be an emergency," Cramm replied. Tinling frowned but let Cramm pull free and go over and pick up the receiver. "Yes, hello," he said. "This is Gottfried Cramm." He spoke English impeccably, just as he did half a dozen other languages. Teddy and I relaxed and did not pay much more attention until Gottfried finished speaking to the operator and suddenly switched to German. *"Ja, mein Führer,"* was the first thing he said.

He said, in fact, little else but *"Ja, mein Führer,"* for the rest of the conversation. He spoke with respect but showed no emotion. Teddy and I (and Hitler, for that matter) knew that Gottfried was less than enchanted with the Nazis. Finally, after a couple of minutes or so, Cramm hung up, turned sharply and walked over to Tinling. Teddy handed him his rackets back. "Excuse me, gentlemen," Gottfried said matter-of-factly. "It was Hitler. I don't know why he called me." That was all he offered and there was time for no more. In a few steps we were marching into center court, with the crowd rising and roaring all about us.

I think one reason why Gottfried irritated the Nazis so particularly in refusing to go along with them was that he looked and acted exactly as the Nazi propaganda said all Germans should. He was six feet tall, with blond hair, of course, and cold blue eyes, and a face that was handsome to a fault. And more, Gottfried emitted a personal magnetism that made him dominate any scene he was a part of.

But on to the center court: Cramm won the toss and elected to serve first—which, as it worked out, was to be the case in each set. He held that first serve at love, I came back to win mine at 30, and we moved on that way, sharing service through the first eight games. In the ninth I broke through. I didn't know it then, of course, but this was to be the longest game in the match—until the very last one. But then, at that time, ahead 5–4, I just felt pretty good. Hold the serve, I told myself, take the set 6–4 and I'm winging.

There was no reason, either, why I shouldn't hold serve. It was moving well, I was getting it in deep and Cramm had not been able to take more than two points off it in any game so far. First serve, I smashed a beauty at Cramm. It clicked right in. I never touched his return. I moved over and hit another beautiful first serve. I never touched his return. I hit another beautiful first serve. I never touched his return. I hit my fourth straight beautiful first serve. As a matter of fact, the only thing I hit in that game was beautiful first serves. And that was all he hit back. I never touched the fourth return either. Cramm had broken me back at love with four fantastic placements. I did not win the set at 6–4. He broke me again four games later, and *he* won the set 8–6.

The second set was much like the first, only now, increasingly, it was his serve that was more dominant. I was holding my own and matching him, but with more difficulty. Tactically we were both playing well, but he was having more success at getting to the net and staying there. He attacked incessantly and kept me on the run and tried to exploit a bad patch of my forehand that showed up here.

For my part, as the set wore on, I found it more difficult to get to the net at all behind my serve. Therefore I decided to put the extra effort all into the serve—hit it really hard—but lay back and try to take his return on the rise. Then I would attempt to come into the net. This worked well, but I still had no defense for the placements he kept drilling past me no matter where I was. It was becoming a little discouraging. I was sure that I was playing tennis as well as I ever had before, but here I was one set down and struggling to stay even in the second. The fewer mistakes I made, he made fewer still, and he held serve to 6–5.

Then in the twelfth game I roared right out to 40–love, but I let him off the hook and he took the next three points to catch me. We battled through two more advantages, and then for the first time, Gottfried got the advantage—and set point. He played to win it. He followed my serve into the net and then took my return with a go-for-broke volley that swept past me and chipped the chalk off the back line. I was down two sets to none.

At this point I remember becoming more angry than analytical and that may have been a good thing, for I promptly went out and broke his serve in the first game of the third set. For the second time in the match I was ahead, and I held on to 2–1. At this point I was serving, I had new balls and I immediately fired off a beautiful batch of first serves. If all of this sounds slightly reminiscent of something else, it was. Exactly as in the first set, the last time I had been ahead, he blasted back four straight passing shots, broke me at love and tied up the set. I was the unwitting pioneer of the instant replay, and to say it shook me up would be every bit of the truth. Happily, it was all so astounding I think it also shook up Cramm. I came right back in the next game, broke *him* at love and finished out the set at 6–4 before hurrying off to the locker room for a welcome rest.

Cramm seemed oddly off his game after the rest period. I not only broke him at love in the first game, but held and then broke him again to go ahead 3–0. We went through the motions of playing it out to 6–2 and the set was done. Then Gottfried picked up the balls and began to serve for the fifth set.

This was to be the first time I ever played Cramm in a fifth set. I had a pretty good record in five-set matches but his was unbelievable. Only a few days before, he had won the key match against Czechoslovakia in the finals of the European Zone by the score of 3–6, 4–6, 6–4, 6–3, 6–2. Perhaps even more impressive than that, Cramm had won the French championships the previous year by lasting to five sets in almost all of his matches and then finishing it off by beating Fred Perry 6–0 in the fifth set of the finals.

So now, as we entered our fifth set, I knew quite well that Cramm would give no indication if he was tired. It didn't take me long to find out that that wasn't even worth speculating about. He took charge from the first, picked up momentum, broke my serve in the fourth game and held his to move ahead 4–1. He had only to hold serve to run out the set easily.

In the stands there was a new, excited buzz, one of obvious anticipation. I did not notice it myself at the time, but over where the other players were seated in one section of the stadium there was an even livelier response. I was to hear about it in the greatest detail later.

It revolved about Bill Tilden who—oddly enough—was serving as coach of the German team. It was, of course, not at all unusual for a pro in one country to coach another nation's Davis Cup team. But it was highly uncommon for a coach to maintain the post when it meant working against his own nation. A lot of people considered it, if not downright unpatriotic, at the least a little tactless of Bill.

But if his loyalties were divided, Tilden made it plain enough that his tennis allegiance was strictly with his employer. He was seated a few rows in front of our team's show business friends. They in turn were a few rows in front of Henner Henkel, who had come back to watch our match after beating Grant. Now, with Cramm ahead 4–1 in this last set, Tilden could not contain himself any longer.

He stood up in his seat and turned fully around, looking up past Benny and Sullivan and Lukas to where Henkel was sitting. Then, without a word, only a large smug grin on his face, Tilden held up his hand, forming a circle with his thumb and forefinger—the traditional "it's in the bag" sign. Sullivan and the others saw it right away and were furious. Immediately, Sullivan leaped to his feet and began to try to tear his coat off, at the same time hissing—tennis manners, you now—imprecations at Tilden. Lukas and Benny jumped up themselves and managed to pull Sullivan down and hold him. Tilden just smiled back and then sat down again.

At this moment, out on the court, I was changing sides with Gottfried. I kept thinking, Is he really this invincible in the fifth set, am I going to go down just like all the others? Pate threw me a towel and I rubbed myself with it. "Don't count us out yet, Cap," I told him, perhaps with more optimism than logic. "Look, I'm not tired and I feel great." And that was the truth. I won my serve at love and came back to 4–2.

I was at the net when I took the last point in the game, and in the walk back to receive serve I decided that it was time for me to try something new. After all, I no longer could take any solace in the hope that playing better than Cramm would reward me with the win. We were both playing too well and I was only one or two games from extinction. I had to get lucky and I had to make my own luck. Okay, without thinking too much about the odds I planned to play it half-safe and gamble on his second serve. I decided that if he missed the first one I would creep up several steps and attack his second serve and then come to the net quickly behind it.

Looking back, it was not really that bright a strategy because Cramm had such a controlled first serve that it was seldom he did not get it in. Even when he missed, it was invariably off only by a hair. But if he missed—ah, *if*—well then I was in good shape because his second serve was typed pretty well for me. His second serve tended to be a high kicker. Against most players it was terribly effective, but in my case it just so happened that I had the type of backhand that made it possible for me to pick up the serve on the rise before the ball could take off on that big bounce.

I have often wondered what happened to Gottfried at this point. Maybe I just got lucky with the law of averages. But I remember how anxious he was to get the balls to serve, and I think he became just a little too impatient. The victory was so close now that for once in his life he lost the composure he always guarded so well. His first service, which had been consistent throughout the match, failed him all but once in this game. And that was to be the only point he won. The other four times he served, he missed getting the ball in by just about the same slim margin each time. Each hit in almost the identical spot, at no more than two inches back.

And each time, of course, that gave me the chance to employ my new strategy. I moved up for that second serve. And located there, just as I had calculated, I was able to catch his second serve before it could bounce up and away. I hit each one back, hard and deep, putting Cramm on the defensive and myself at the net. Each of the four points I won were made exactly the same way with a well-placed net volley on my second shot. I had the break I had to have and I was back to 3–4.

He almost came right back and broke me in the next game, but twice in a row, as the score stood at his advantage, he punched backhands that went out, in the same spot, by inches. How many times in this match did these crazy things repeat themselves? After this sort of double jeopardy I managed to hold and tie the score at 4–4 and, as the tension grew to almost unbearable proportions, we matched each other's serve to 6–all. Then, remarkably and suddenly, and without really any shots of distinction, I broke Cramm in the lucky thirteenth game and stood ahead for the first time in hours, 7–6.

Now at last I had only to hold my serve to win the match and the opportunity for the United States to play England in the Challenge Round. Clearly, after hours of play, I was now immune to pressure. This is why my first serve in the game went right smack into the *bottom* of the net. That either steadied me or embarrassed me, for I did manage to get the second serve in and even to win the point. He tied at 15–all, and then we repeated the sequence: 30–15, 30–all, and 40–30, the first match point of the long afternoon.

So, I guess, I played it too safe again. I was too tentative with both my serve and second shot. Cramm took the net easily, volleyed past me and we were deuce. I came right back with a placement of my own for a second match point, but he took the net away from me again and once more tied the game. Moreover, when he was able to repeat the ploy on the next point, he moved ahead. Later he also had one more game point so that by the time I gained my fifth match point it was the eighteenth point of the game, and all of five minutes had passed since we had first played a match point way back there at 40–30. Five minutes under circumstances like these are like a month of 3–2 counts in baseball.

So once more I served. It was the 175th time that day I had made a first serve. What there had been of my cannonball had gone, but I managed to get enough on this one to clear the net and send it sufficiently deep so that Gottfried could not begin to move up and gain the net from me. But he made a beautiful long return that kept me far back in the court too. All I could do was trade long ground strokes with him. I hit a good backhand.

Cramm moved over to his right-hand corner, so that we were now both on the same side of the court—facing each other down my left-hand side. He caught my shot with a forehand and hit it crosscourt. It was a beautiful shot, firmly hit, and it gave him the opening to move toward the net. He came up, crossing the court catty-cornered, following, essentially, the direction of his shot.

The ball was landing just inside my right sideline, a bit deep of mid-court. I had hit my last shot far back on the other side of the court and I had begun to move toward the center as soon as I hit it. Now, however, when I saw Cramm place the ball so far over, I had to break into a dead run if I wanted to catch up to it. I could not worry about position at all any longer. In fact, nearing the ball just as it bounced in, I realized that my speed had brought my body too far forward. There was no way I could brace to hit the ball. As a matter of fact, there was suddenly no way I could keep from falling.

Instead, resigned to this indignity, I did the only thing I could. I kept going at full speed and just took a swipe at the ball. What did I have to lose? I was going to fall anyway. Then, immediately after I swung, I dived for the ground, preparing to break my fall. I could tell, though, as soon as I hit the ball, that I had smacked it solidly, but only as I crashed onto the grass did I turn to look. The ball whipped down the line, just past Cramm's outstretched racket. He had come up fast and could cover all but about the last two feet on the right side of the net (his left). At my angle, I could not have returned the shot crosscourt. I had been forced to try for a shot right down the line. Now I saw the ball slip past his reach.

By this point I was flat out on the ground but so far outside the alley line that I could see around the net into much of the other side of the court. I could see the ball hit. I watched it kick up. But I had no perspective and no idea where the ball had landed. I waited for the call and then, suddenly, even before the linesman could begin to flatten out his hands in the "safe" sign, I could hear the cheers begin to swell. They were different cheers. The ball had landed, miraculously but perfectly in the corner. I had hit the one possible winning shot. I was told later that the ball landed at a point that was less than six inches from being out *two* ways, to the side or long.

But now the roars were greater and more excited and here I was, still lying flat out on the ground. Gottfried, the noble loser, had to stand at the net, waiting patiently for me, the winner, to get up off the ground. I rose, finally, bewildered, and rushed toward him. I tried to hug him, but before I could he stopped me and took my hand. "Don," he said, evenly and with a remarkable composure, "this was absolutely the finest match I have ever played in my life. I'm very happy that I could have played it against you, whom I like so much." And then he pumped my hand. "Congratulations." Only then was it, at once, that we threw our arms about each other. I think we both wanted to cry.

HOLCOMBE WARD

by Allison Danzig

Thirty-two years ago four young Harvard tennis players banded together under the leadership of George Wright of Boston, one of the grand old men of American sport, to undertake a missionary trip to California. Their mission was to help promote interest in the game of lawn tennis on the Pacific Coast, where they engaged to play with Samuel Hardy, Sumner Hardy, George F. Whitney and Robert N. Whitney.

These four young men were Dwight F. Davis, Malcolm D. Whitman, Beals C. Wright and Holcombe Ward, all of whom were to earn a place among the most distinguished figures in American tennis.

It was during this expedition that Mr. Davis, impressed with the nation-wide interest manifested in the America's Cup yacht races, was struck with the idea of offering his now historic trophy in competition for an international team match with England.

A year later the international Davis Cup championship was an accomplished fact, and the first team to defend the trophy against the English at the Longwood Cricket Club in Boston was composed of Mr. Davis and Mr. Whitman as singles players and Mr. Davis and Mr. Ward as the doubles team.

The coupling of the names of Davis and Ward in tennis, which started in their sophomore year at Harvard in 1898, when they originated the American twist service, and which brought them three national doubles championships and the intercollegiate crown, has its renewal in 1931.

Last week Louis J. Carruthers, president of the United States Lawn Tennis Association, appointed Mr. Ward as chairman of the Davis Cup committee to succeed Joseph W. Wear of Philadelphia.

The new holder of the international tennis portfolio stands among a group of men who have rendered invaluable service to the game for years and yet have managed to keep their identity largely an unknown entity to the public.

Although he has been a devoted worker for tennis for more than a quarter of a century, from the time that he was named on the executive committee by Dr. James Dwight, Mr. Ward has never held elective office in the association, though the office has repeatedly sought the man.

Mr. Ward's work has all been done in committee, and the less public recognition his part in this work received the more satisfaction it gave him, simply because of his instinctive dislike for publicity.

A member of the advisory and finance committee from its formation in 1925 and at various times of the ranking Davis Cup honorary membership and executive committees, it has been as chairman of the amateur rule committee that Mr. Ward has made his most important contributions to tennis.

Since 1924 he has held this post, during the most trying and vexatious period of grappling with the amateur problem in the fifty years' history of the U.S.L.T.A. Any one knowing his sensitiveness and extreme antipathy to becoming involved in anything remotely approaching the airing of controversy in public can appreciate how strong was the sense of duty that kept him in this work during the years of bitter controversy over the player-writer interpretation of the amateur rule.

The continual repercussions centering about this interpretation, which put a check upon the journalistic efforts of the players, constituted only one phase of the disagreeable task that fell to Mr. Ward and his associates.

There was also the problem of putting a curb upon the indiscriminate payment of expenses to players who gave most of their time the year round to the game.

Needless to say, it was a thankless task, one that was bound to create hostility toward the committee among some of the players, who found the amateur rule irksome. But the rule was there, upon the books as revised by representatives of the players themselves, and Mr. Ward was not to be swayed an iota by criticism or any other consideration in its enforcement.

Inflexible in his stand against violators of the rule once he was convinced of wrongdoing, Mr. Ward leaned over backward in the effort to give the player the benefit of the doubt.

At times he stretched the regulations to the limit to give him the chance to show that he had not intentionally done wrong. It was nothing unusual for him to stay up all hours of the night, analyzing and sifting the evidence against the player and seeking a loophole for him. But once he made up his mind that there had been a violation he gave no quarter.

This work, as chairman of the amateur rule committee, was not only of the most exacting character, but called for a tremendous amount of time. It has been estimated by some of the past presidents of the U.S.L.T.A. that it cost them in the neighborhood of $25,000 annually to hold the office, so much time did they have to sacrifice from their private affairs.

In carrying out his duties Mr. Ward has easily made an equal sacrifice. As he lays down this task to take charge of all international play sponsored by the U.S.L.T.A. he has the satisfaction of knowing that he has upheld the amateur code without fear or favor, and those who have been associated with him during the past seven years will appreciate his work for its full worth as a service to tennis that is unsurpassed in its devotion to the good of the game.

As chairman of the Davis Cup committee, a post for which he is a happy choice both because of his executive capacity and his ability, as a former national champion and Davis Cup player, to analyze form, Mr. Ward has no intention of making any radical departures from the policies of his predecessors.

At the same time, he has gone on record as being opposed to putting too great a demand upon the time of young players who have their college and business careers before them, and it may be expected that he will seek to reduce this time to the minimum without jeopardizing the success of the team. . . .

In view of the reputation for scrupulous fairness which he gained as chairman of the amateur rule committee, it may be vouchsafed that Mr. Ward's selection as the Davis Cup chairman will be accepted by the players with great satisfaction. The United States renews its campaign for the reclamation of the cup under the happiest of auspices.

THE STYLE OF FRED PERRY

by Julius D. Heldman

England's greatest player since the days of the Dohertys was the flamboyant Fred Perry. Dressed in beautifully tailored white flannels and a matching white blazer, Fred looked and was the amateur champion of the world. He had the personal magnetism that is "star" quality. He dominated the scene from the moment he walked on the court, casually carrying a half dozen rackets under his arm and waving pleasantly at select acquaintances in the gallery. He was the idol of thousands of young players, though more for his poise and court demeanor than for his style, which was beautiful but highly personalized. He made the game fun for the spectators, joshing with the ballboys when he was ahead, dazzling the crowd with his tricky shots and chatting with the boxholders in between games. When the going got tough Perry got down to work and concentrated as any great champion must. He was a showman but nevertheless a magnificent competitor.

When Bill Tilden was incensed by a call, he would argue with the linesman or demand his removal. Perry never got as upset, but when he was the victim of a questionable decision he would smile at the linesman, humorously shake his finger at him and remark: "Naughty boy!" He wasn't a temperamental player. He had spark, fire and verve and an enormous amount of self-confidence. He did not "blow" because of emotional problems, and his game was so grooved that he seldom had a really bad day.

Fred Perry had the greatest running forehand the game has ever known. His serve was quite good, albeit not great; his backhand was very accurate, his net game vastly underrated and his overhead absolutely deadly. He had a cocked-wrist Continental game with more wrist power than any other player before or since. His eye was superb; it had to be, for he took every ball on the rise. He was fast as lightning and was always in top physical condition.

Perry won every big title in the amateur game. He appeared on the international scene during Ellsworth Vines' last amateur year. Jack Crawford of Australia was the heir apparent and won the Australian, French and British titles before losing out in the finals at Forest Hills to Perry. Fred teamed with Bunny Austin to take the Davis Cup for his country, and the two of them held the Cup against all challenges for three more years. During this period Perry was the world's best amateur, winning Wimbledon three times, the French title once, Forest Hills three times and Australia once. He turned professional to play Vines in a very successful tour. He continued to compete professionally, despite interludes at other enterprises, until his late thirties. He became a well-established teaching professional, retiring last year when he reached the age of 50. His is still the magic name in England, and three years ago when he made a rare public appearance at the Art Larsen Benefit, thousands turned out to watch the unique Perry game in action.

Just as Don Budge had a backhand that never went "off," so Fred Perry had a forehand that was aggressive and always consistent. It was a table tennis forehand, hit with an extreme Continental grip and a pronounced cocked-wrist action. Fred was the World Table Tennis Champ before he ever took up lawn tennis. As a result of his background and great athletic ability, he had magnificent wrist control. He could fool his opponent on any shot on the forehand, whether he hit from an open stance or on the dead run. It was a graceful stroke, without the extra frills that many Continental artists use. Both the backswing and follow-through were extremely short, the whole stroke being simply a wrist snap.

Footwork meant nothing to Perry on the forehand side. He could just as well hit by snapping the ball from behind him while facing the net. However, he was never off balance; his body was always right for every shot and he was never caught in an awkward stance. He was most famous for his forehands hit on the run coming into net. These were lethal. His opponents used to say it was more dangerous to run him wide on his forehand than to play the center of the court! He had complete angle control, and when he was pulled out of court he could just as easily hit a sharp, short crosscourt as a deadly down-the-line. Vines, for example, could not hit a sharp crosscourt well when forced. Budge could hit the crosscourt with as much power but not as sharp. Only a looper or a Continental artist can execute this riposte with any pace, the rare exceptions being Maureen Connolly and Dick Savitt among the classical Eastern players.

Perry generally hit a flat forehand with a wrist snap at the moment of impact. He used topspin occasionally, particularly when picking up a low ball. The topspin was manufactured by pulling up sharply, somewhat in the manner of Hoad, although Perry's stroke was much shorter. He never chipped, chopped or sliced on the starboard side. His return against a powerful service was small enough to be called a block, yet it was actually a drive. A block is merely a backboard response to a hard stroke, with the racket held stiff and essentially motionless. Perry did more than this: a short wrist flick often sent the ball back harder than it came to him. There was no arm motion to his return. All the power came from wrist action and body balance.

Perry was a fine player in all departments but a great player only on the forehand. In the ranking lists of most tennis aficionados, Perry's name appears among the All-Time Top Ten. To achieve this distinction a player cannot have a weakness. When I say his backhand was not in the same league as his forehand, it is not meant as a derogatory remark. His backhand would be the envy of every top junior today. It was not a defensive shot and he passed extremely well with it. However, when he was engaged in a baseline backhand rally, he was content to keep the ball deep and in the corners. He did not let fly like Budge or even Savitt, nor did he come in behind it like Rosewall. The key for him on the backhand was control. He and Vines would often have long backhand exchanges, the ball going back and forth 8 to 10 times in one rally, neither player daring a down-the-line to the opponent's murderous forehand.

The backhand was just as short a stroke as the forehand. All of Perry's actions were quick. There were no long, flowing motions except the sweep of his running advance to net. The rapid backhand motion was also a wrist flick, with the same cocked wrist as on the forehand. This small, neat action was capable of executing both the flat and underspin drives. He would pull his wrist under at the last minute to hit the down-the-line but would hit with relatively little spin when exchanging backhand crosscourts. It was a full-length drive rather than a chip since the wrist always snapped or came through, but it was a very short action. He never shoved the ball or hacked at it.

Perry was essentially a baseliner who came to net when the opportunity arose. He never followed his serve in. His coming-in shots were so forceful that he seldom had to volley more than competently. Spectators rarely saw him leaping since his way to net had been so thoroughly prepared. He was no Wilmer Allison at the barrier, the latter being far more at home at the net than at the baseline.

Perry got down well for his low forehand volleys, which he took to the side of him or even hooked from behind him. His forte was his high volley on both forehand and backhand. He was a short stroke-volleyer, the wrist being the dominant part of the action. All volleys above the net were stroked, the motion being quick and sharp. His net play was in keeping with the rest of his game—crisp, neat and lightning-quick. There were no false moves, no awkward pushes. Everything was done with grace and dispatch and every shot was executed with the same flair.

Perry's overhead was absolutely lethal. He never bludgeoned the ball, but he never missed and he always outguessed his opponent. He was uncanny in his ability to pick the right spot. He was agile, quick, and he leapt well. Those who saw Fred in action will always remember him springing in the air to bring down a tough lob. His legs were as springy as a basketball player's, and he always seemed to be on the balls of his feet.

The overhead action was just as small as his other shots. There was no massive wind-up. He simply brought his racket head behind him with a cocked wrist and snapped the ball where he wanted it. The shot was distinguished by his ability to leap, most other players appearing dead on their feet in comparison.

Fred Perry was the quick-server of all time. His whole game was characterized by rapidity of movement during and in between points. He was always ready before his opponent and he always wanted to get on with the next point. He was frequently accused of serving too fast, and although this may not have been deliberate, it was nevertheless a fact. He had a short wind-up and a fast action, and this undoubtedly contributed to his opponents' dismay. Don Budge often held up his hand and asked to have a let played. I can remember myself, when playing him in the Pacific Southwest, feeling hurried whenever Perry served.

Perry had a rather flat first serve with just a little overspin to bring it in. There wasn't enough spin to call it "slice" or "twist." He hit it reasonably hard, but he depended more on accuracy than blinding pace. A very high percentage of his first balls went in; when they didn't, the second was on its way! This second ball usually had American twist, although he could slice in the right court. His American twist was not one of these big high-bouncing balls that pulls you out of court and is hit with a back bent almost double. Again, it was a neat, short wrist-snap designed to keep him out of trouble and open a baseline rally. It was good enough to prevent his opponent from taking net off it.

Any man who made his move too soon while Perry was serving was a dead duck. Fred had a very quick eye, and his reactions were so fast that he could change direction in the middle of a stroke with accuracy. Even though his second serve was far from murderous, he would ace an opponent who tried to outguess him almost every time.

All champions are in excellent physical condition when they reach the top. They have to be. However, few have all the physical attributes that compose the perfect athlete. Ken Rosewall has the disadvantage of small stature; Lew Hoad is almost over-muscular; Dick Savitt is so big that it is sometimes hard for him to maneuver; Bunny Austin was too frail to stand up to a five-setter; Welby Van Horn, Billy Talbert, Ham Richardson and Doris Hart had to overcome actual physical handicaps. Only occasionally does a Frank Parker, a Gardnar Mulloy, a Pancho Gonzales or a Fred Perry come along. These are perfect athletes with ideal tennis builds. They have an edge which is given only to a few. I never saw Perry tired in the course of a match. His great eye, natural talent, and physical ability enabled him to compensate for any weaknesses inherent in the overly wristy Continental game.

THE FINEST ATHLETE I EVER SAW

by George Lott

During the second week of July in the year 1934, I was sitting in the players' section of the Wimbledon Center Court pulling for my friend, Jack Crawford, to beat the daylights out of a cocky Englishman named Fred Perry. An hour and one half later I was still sitting in the players' section, contemplating the drama that had taken place. On that particular day, in that particular match, I had seen the perfectly conditioned athlete play the perfect match.

Perry had the swashbuckling good looks and the air of supreme confidence of a Walter Hagen; the grace and ease of a Joe DiMaggio gathering in a fly ball; the cleverness and agility of a Billy Conn; the brute strength of a Man Mountain Dean; and the skill and know-how of a Tilden. Here was a man who not only possessed but also exhibited the qualities so necessary in a champion, namely, confidence, concentration, condition, co-ordination, courage and fortitude, determination, stamina, quickness and speed.

It was an awe-inspiring exhibition. Perry played many important matches before this one and many after, but I know (and I am sure that Fred also knows) that on this day he reached the peak of his effectiveness. I see Perry from time to time and we always wind up talking about Fred's 1934 Wimbledon. Ordinarily this would bore me considerably, but it gives me almost as much pleasure to go over the details as it does Fred. I appreciate a champion and on that day I saw one. Then again, during the reminiscences with Fred, while he recounts his victorious march through the field, I occasionally get a word in to the effect that Stoefen and I won the doubles that year, and I receive a "Righto" from Fred which increases the enjoyment of the memory.

I first came across Perry in 1928 or 1929 when the English Association sent a team to play at Newport, Longwood and Forest Hills. He had a match with John Van Ryn on a side court at Newport. It was a close one and I was quite impressed with this Englishman who didn't seem quite like an Englishman. I thought he was an American with an English accent and a pipe. The accent came naturally but not the pipe. He carried it around unlit because he thought it would make him seem more British—and British was what he wanted to be. In those days English society peered down its nose at anyone who didn't wear the old school tie. Fred's parents were in "trade" and, consequently, Fred's education did not include Eton or Harrow, which left him outside the inner circle. This class consciousness always annoyed Fred but it acted in his favor; it made him more determined than ever to reach the top. His compatriot and teammate, Bunny Austin, did wear the old school tie and, consequently, was the darling of the English officials and tennis fans. Fred was a new breed of Englishman and, in the end, he won them all with his ability.

In 1931 the United States had a Davis Cup team that looked, on paper, a certain bet to bring back the Cup from France. Our singles players were Ellsworth Vines and Wilmer Allison; John Van Ryn and I were the doubles team. We spent considerable time figuring out how we would defeat the French in the Challenge Round and very little thought was given to the Inter-Zone Final against Great Britain. Our chickens were never hatched and, in a tie that featured Vines' famous lunch of cream of tomato soup, cucumbers, pork chops, vanilla ice cream with chocolate sauce and grapefruit juice, Mr. Perry and company took care of us to the tune of 4–1. We were able to salvage only the doubles. Perry won over Vines when Elly collapsed in the heat, but at this point in his career Fred was beginning to "arrive." I believe he could have eaten Elly's lunch that day and still won.

After the tie, Fred commented to me that "your boys seemed very overconfident and they are really not that good, you know." This observation, while not grammatically perfect, was factually correct. Perry was on the way up and we did not realize it at the time. He had been World Champion at Table Tennis and he knew what it was to be a winner.

Perry finally arrived at or very near the top in the year 1933. He always had a really great forehand, but it was his backhand that had been keeping him back. I used to tell him that he looked like he was swatting a fly when he hit a backhand. He undercut it and even then he did not have much control. Under severe pressure it would give way, but by 1933 he had firmed it up and, while it never reached the efficiency and dispatch of his forehand, it was equal to most occasions. This year he led the British team to a Challenge Round victory over the French, who had held the Cup for six years. To win this tie it was absolutely necessary for Perry to beat Henri Cochet, and in those days it was no easy matter. Cochet was the idol of 15,000 fans and had an equally high standing with all French linesmen (see Wilmer Allison for confirmation). Six games to one in the fifth set was the margin by which Perry won, and a great accomplishment it was. At Forest Hills that year I asked Fred how he did it. Censorship forbids an exact quote, but the gist was that he ran Cochet into the ground until the Frenchman ran out of gas.

For the next three years Fred won two singles in each Challenge Round and firmly established himself as an English hero as well as World Champion. His final Challenge Round record was nine won against one lost. The only loss occurred in 1931 when, after having beaten Vines and Allison in the Inter-Zone Final, he was beaten by Cochet.

Tennis fans occasionally ask me about an all-time world ranking, and when I place Perry in the First Three they are amazed. What is not generally realized is that during a four year span (1933–36) Perry won eight Challenge Round singles matches, three successive Wimbledons (1934–35–36), one French Singles, three U.S. singles (1933, '34 and '36) and, for good measure, one Australian Singles (1934). I know of no player who so dominated the tennis scene over an equal period of time.

When Perry lost in the semi-finals to Allison at Forest Hills, it only confirmed my opinion that I had been watching a champion. Allison beat him handily, and there were rumors galore about Fred's condition. He certainly wasn't the Perry I had seen on so many other occasions. I, being of a curious nature, went to the locker room after the match and waited until the reporters had left. I asked him what happened. No alibis were forthcoming. He simply commented that "I got the bloody hell beat out of me." However, I knew for a fact he was lucky to be able to lift his arm high enough to serve.

Fred Perry was a real champion, in spite of the pipe.

WILMER ALLISON

by Allison Danzig

Six years ago, at an intercollegiate tennis dinner at the Merion Cricket Club in Haverford, Pennsylvania, an unassuming, soft-spoken little man, whose kindly eyes radiated friendliness from behind their gold-rimmed glasses, made the prediction that the time was not far distant when Texas would take as much pride in the products of her tennis courts as in the yield of her cotton fields.

At the time that Dr. D. A. Penick, professor of Romance languages at the University of Texas, made this prophecy, the Lone Star State was practically a nonentity in tennis. The summer before, Lewis N. White and Louis Thalheimer had carried off the national intercollegiate doubles to Texas, and the name of J. B. Adoue had been well known in the game for years, but otherwise the Southwest was looked upon as a hinterland whose natives were much more at home with the lasso than with a racket.

It wasn't more than two years after Dr. Penick's dip into the future that Texas qualified a man for the "first ten" of the national ranking, when White was rated sixth, and since then the Lone Star has risen higher and higher in the tennis firmament as her young emissaries—White, Bell,

Thalheimer, Quick, Barr, Barnes and Mather, to name a few—have taken the trail eastward to challenge the best of the country over.

Today one of these young emissaries holds the spotlight on European soil as no other male American player, with the exception of William Tilden, has held it in years. When Wilmer Allison of Austin, 25-year-old son of a Fort Worth physician, defeated Henri Cochet at Wimbledon, he fired a shot that was heard around the tennis world. When he followed up that stunning triumph by playing a major role in last week's victories of the United States Davis Cup team over Italy, the detonation in Texas was as loud as anything heard in the Alamo.

The victory of Allison over Cochet so far transcends anything else that he has done as to stand out as the most startling upset in the game since Tilden, Johnston, Richards and Williams all went down in the French uprising of 1926 at Forest Hills. When it is remembered that no other American has lowered the colors of the recognized world's champion since September 1927 and that Allison was not even seeded in the English championship, the monumental size of his feat may be appreciated.

Cochet has been beaten before this year, but beating him at Wimbledon had become the exclusive privilege of his illustrious compatriots, and even they had come to regard it not as a privilege but as a thankless job. In a way, English and Continental galleries were better prepared for Allison's conquests this year than were Americans. Last year the Texan had given them an inkling of the magnificent tennis of which he is capable when he and his inseparable doubles partner, John Van Ryn, spread-eagled a field of the world's best teams to win the Wimbledon doubles and then went on to defeat Prenn and Moldenhauer of Germany in the interzone Davis Cup doubles and Cochet and Borotra in the challenge round. Allison had never attained such form on his native heath as he displayed on the velvety English turf and the hard courts of Berlin and Auteuil.

But, revelation that the Texan was in four-handed play, no one, either at home or abroad, conceived of his being a threat in singles. True, he had beaten George Lott in the national championship last year, and Lott and John Doeg fell before him at White Sulphur Springs, West Virginia, last April, but outside of those victories, which were followed by his decisive defeat by Van Ryn in the final at White Sulphur Springs, his singles record had been lacking in distinction from the time he won the intercollegiate title in 1927.

Because of the instability of his form, the conclusion had been reached generally that his future lay in doubles rather than in singles, in spite of the fact that "on his day" he was capable of rising to great heights.

The instruments by which he reached such heights were the best overhead smash in America, a flat smash service that kicks from the turf with the sting of a Texas mustang, a volley second only to Lott's in this country and a backhand drive that yields only to Van Ryn's and Tilden's.

The one thing that appeared to be holding Allison back was lack of confidence. One day arresting, volatile and hot for the kill, the next day would find his game afflicted by the blight of doubt and a lamentable stream of errors. Thus it was that the Davis Cup Committee, while appreciating the potentialities of his game, was preparing to turn to others less spectacular but more consistent in its quest for singles candidates.

The difference in the European climate may account in part for the marked improvement in Allison's play abroad. The broiling heat and particularly the humidity of the Eastern summer have affected him noticeably, and his fellow Texans have maintained all along that on his home courts he is so much better a player that the East has no idea of what his real game is like. There the sun beats down just as fiercely, but it is a dry heat, without the humidity that he finds so enervating.

No one has been more deserving of the honors that have accrued to him in tennis than has this unassuming, warm-hearted Texan. Few know of the handicap under which he has labored as a result of an operation in his side, which might have discouraged another from subjecting himself to the wear and tear of tournament play. When Allison serves, it will be noticed that he stands with his body squarely parallel to the net and both feet on a line pointing straight forward. This position was forced upon him because of the strain on his side when he served from the orthodox stance. One would little suspect this alteration in his service from the searing pace he puts on the first ball, but the fact remains that he has had to adapt it to circumstances, and so all the more credit is due him for developing one of the swiftest deliveries in the game. . . .

Last night word came from the Davis Cup Committee that Tilden will be back in the line-up when the United States meets France in the challenge round and that Allison appears to be in need of a rest from the rigorous strain he has been under. This announcement probably means that Allison will not be used in the singles against France, giving way to Tilden and Lott, the latter being better on clay than he is on grass.

But, regardless of the role Allison is assigned, his fame is secure and it may be predicted that if he should be left out of the singles he will accept the decision with the same good sportsmanship for which he has been held in esteem throughout his career and which has reflected so highly on Texas tennis.

CRAWFORD

by George McGann

Gentlemanly Jack Crawford, with his sweeping backhand and effortless strokes, was a dominant figure in the tennis world twenty years ago, a giant among the greats of the Tilden, Cochet, Perry and Vines eras. Of them all, Jack is the only one still playing in the major amateur tournaments.

At 43, genial Jack has slowed up. The inevitable years, plus the beers which Jack imbibes in moderation, have put a few pounds on that once lean and graceful frame. But as late as 1948 Crawford won a major Australian singles title, the New South Wales hard court championship, a title he first attained twenty years earlier.

Jack rarely gets past the first round of a singles tournament these days, but he still packs the galleries whenever he steps onto the serving line in his immaculate old-fashioned full-length white flannels. There is still the same old magic in his strokes, executed without hurry or effort but which still impart pace and authority to the ball.

In the recent Australian championships at Sydney, Jack drew the largest gallery at the White City Club for his first-round match with G. Hartwig, a promising younger player. . . . Among those who watched Jack bow gracefully to his younger opponent was Don Budge, who had engaged Jack in many a memorable joust back in the mid-thirties. Budge rates Crawford as the greatest Australian player he ever met and places him far above Bromwich, Quist, Pails and Sedgman. He discounts the notion that Crawford was so artistic and effortless in his stroking that he did not hit the ball hard. Budge asserts that Crawford hit a "heavier" ball than most power players.

Norman Brookes, from an earlier generation, is Crawford's only possible rival for the title of all-time Australian great. But Brookes, and for that matter any other Australian player, cannot approach Crawford in mass appeal. The winning Crawford personality and his impeccable behavior on the court and his good sportsmanship always earned him the affection of the galleries. Stanley Doust, dean of English tennis reporters, names Crawford as the most popular Wimbledon winner in history.

John Herbert Crawford was born in 1908 on a farm at Albury, on the border of the Australian states of New South Wales and Victoria, where the chaotic railway system forces passengers on standard-gauge New South Wales trains to switch to wide-gauge Victorian trains.

Jack was one of six children and was fortunate in having a father with sufficient foresight to build a tennis court. Jack as second youngest child in the family did not get a game with his brothers too often and was forced to spend most of his time hitting a ball against a wall. Somehow he picked up the rudiments of the game and at 12, as a tall, skinny kid with a leisurely way of moving, he was playing in local events. He moved up to "big time" tennis in 1923, when he entered the New South Wales state championships in Sydney and bowed out in an early round. Crawford was put out of the same tournament in an early round this year, twenty-eight years later.

Jack won the Wimbledon singles title in 1933, his best year, beating Ellsworth Vines in the final, 4–6, 11–9, 6–2, 2–6, 6–4. He won the Wimbledon doubles with Quist in 1935, defeating the American pair of Allison and Van Ryn in the final.

Crawford won all of the world's major singles titles except the American, which always eluded him, but it is his Davis Cup record which endears him most to Australians. He was a member of nine Australian Davis Cup teams from 1928 to 1939, which is probably some kind of record. He was so dedicated to the pursuit of the cup that he turned down an attractive professional offer in 1933, at the peak of his game and fame, to continue in Davis Cup competition. He was a member of the Australian team that finally wrested the cup from the United States in 1939, although he did not play in the challenge round.

Crawford's dominance of Australian tennis in the early thirties is proven by the fact that he won the national title in 1931, 1932, 1933 and 1935. Fred Perry broke that sequence by beating Jack in the 1934 finals. Crawford won the Australian doubles title four times—with Harry Hopman in 1929 and 1930, with E. F. Moon in 1932, and with Viv McGrath in 1935. In all Crawford has won 27 Australian state and national titles in singles and doubles in 20 years. His greatest year, 1933, was also the year in which he won undeserved notoriety for mixing alcohol and iced tea during his memorable Forest Hills final with Fred Perry.

In that year Crawford went after a grand slam of the Australian, French, English and American titles and came within a whisker—or a whiskey glass, as the stories went—of getting it. He started off in January by beating the American Keith Gledhill in the finals of the Australian championship (Vines having been surprisingly eliminated by Viv McGrath); he went on to defeat Henri Cochet in straight sets in May for the French title, and then won at Wimbledon in June, beating Vines.

By the time the American nationals came up in early September, Crawford was badly overtennised. He was suffering horribly from insomnia, complicated by the sweltering heat of his hotel room, where he was only two stories above the unaccustomed din of traffic. Such was Crawford's state of tension that he hardly slept a wink for an entire month, beginning two weeks before the finals at Forest Hills.

"I used to play tennis all afternoon at Forest Hills," Jack recalls, "go back to that hot little room in the hotel and play tennis all night, going over and over in my mind matches I had played years before."

On the day of the finals, in which Crawford was pitted against Fred Perry, Jack told his friend Vincent Richards of his chronic insomnia and inability to relax.

"You'll never beat Perry all wound up like that," Richards told Crawford. "But leave it to me. I'll fix you up with a nerve tonic I've used myself."

Later, as Jack walked onto the court for his match with the English star, Richards approached him. "I've slipped the tonic into your iced tea," Vincent told Crawford. "Just sip it each time you change courts and you'll forget all your tension."

Jack started the match with his nerves taut as piano strings but with the help of Richards' tonic he gradually unwound. The match was a brilliant battle, but Crawford succumbed to the inspired Englishman, 6–3, 11–13, 4–6, 6–0, 6–1.

Afterwards Richards approached Crawford in the clubhouse and asked him how the tonic had worked. It was fine, Crawford responded. "By the way, what was it?" he asked. Richards chortled, "Just good old Kentucky bourbon."

The story got around, and the New York papers enlarged on it and gave Crawford a completely undeserved reputation as a tippler. The irony of the situation was that Crawford never before had tasted bourbon or any other kind of whiskey. He never tried Richards' nerve remedy in subsequent matches in California that year either.

THE STYLE OF JACK CRAWFORD

by Julius D. Heldman

The only man ever to win the Big Four titles in the same year was Don Budge. However, his predecessor by a few years, Jack Crawford, came within one set of sweeping all the major tournaments in 1933. The wavy-haired Australian won his own national championships, took the French and Wimbledon titles and reached the finals of Forest Hills, only to lose to Fred Perry.

Crawford was an old-fashioned classicist. He had flowing strokes and moved gracefully on the baseline. His accuracy has been matched only by Bobby Riggs. Bobby's strokes were better founded but Crawford had more of a flair for the unusual or surprising shot. Whereas Riggs was often predictable in his choice of passing shot or lob, Crawford could pull off any number of unexpected angles. Jack always drove the ball, but you could never predict the direction or pace.

Jack's appearance on the court matched his style of play. He walked slowly, almost ambling between points. His manner was mild, soft-spoken and always gentlemanly. He wore long-sleeved shirts, sometimes open at the cuffs, and the long white flannels typical of that era. His whole demeanor was distinctive and impressive. The spectator was aware that this was Jack Crawford, a strong personality force and a great champion. He gave the impression of maturity and sensibility, and in many ways his outward appearance resembled that of Ham Richardson.

Crawford was almost the last of his generation of Australians to play championship tennis from the backcourt. He was an attacker from the baseline, so secure in his ground strokes that he came to net only when drawn in on a short ball. He used the whole court like a chess board, maneuvering and parrying with intelligence and subtlety. He was not a bone crusher by any means, although he could hit hard on the forehand side. Instead he aimed for accuracy, control and disguise. He was as graceful as any man who ever stepped on a court: his strokes flowed effortlessly and he moved so well that one was hardly aware of it. He was a big man but he trod lightly.

Jack's big handicap was his asthma. He might have continued to dominate amateur tennis if he had had no breathing problems. Asthma attacks are unpredictable, and Jack's would often come at crucial times. When he had a bad spell during a match, he would dip a lump of sugar into brandy and suck it to gain some relief. He lost many an important match because he simply could not last through five sets when he had breathing problems. Even so, his stamina was remarkable and oftentimes after a very poor start he would get stronger as the match continued. Asthma may have been responsible for his loss at Forest Hills when he was only one set away from the Grand Slam.

Although Jack did not have a bludgeon forehand, his stroke had pace and bite. The ball would jump at you after it bounced. The pace was created by just the right amount of topspin, which was imparted to the ball by a wrist snap. His swing had less topspin than Lew Hoad's but just about the same amount of wrist. It was free and easy and particularly effective on low balls. It is quite remarkable that with this amount of wrist he was still able to have so much control, but it also explains his magnificent disguise and change of pace. Crawford could whistle the ball by an opponent, seemingly with the same action which he used on a defensive shot. It was very disconcerting since one could never get grooved against his style of play. This is a type of tennis that is never seen today, to the great regret of the older lovers of the game.

"Chess tennis" was the order of the day in the twenties and early thirties. Bill Tilden was a master of the chess board, as were Henri Cochet, René Lacoste, Norman Brookes and even Fred Perry. Crawford, too, played the all-court game in the sense of using all of his opponent's court. He stayed on the baseline by preference, and from there he teased his unfortunate victim with shots that seemed to be just beyond reach.

He had a rolling backswing and a rather short follow-through. It was a loose and, in some respects, rather floppy stroke; it certainly did not go "by the count" like the highly trained Budge forehand. It was not as short and not as precise as the Talbert swing, but Jack in common with Billy had wrist control. It was a relaxed motion, rhythmic and easily produced. It was a magnificent stroke, and the only reason it was not known as one of the great weapons of all time is that Crawford did not always apply merciless pressure with it.

I think that Jack's backhand had the same weakness as did that of Sidney Wood. It was too long and had too much underspin. It was flowing, long and graceful, but it lacked power and it sat up too much against a net-rusher. The more the underspin, the less the pace. While Crawford could handle everything well off his backhand side, he could not hurt his opponent with it. Many a great player such as Ken Rosewall will use a certain amount of underspin, but never to the extreme of a Crawford or Wood. If Jack had used his flat or topspin drive more frequently, he might have turned into a more forceful player on the port side.

The Crawford serve was also a beautiful action. It was produced with no apparent effort, and it looked as though he could serve for five hours without tiring. The toss was no higher than required, the wind-up was short and there was plenty of wrist action. The hit was usually sliced, although he could hit a flat ball. Again he got the maximum pace with minimum effort. The service was characteristic of his whole game—it was strong but not terrifying. He usually put you in trouble with it but it was no cannonball. There were aces and there were wide ones that forced poor returns, but this was not the Budge or Gonzales brand of delivery. It was more like Kramer's second serve if the latter had chosen to remain on the baseline.

Crawford was a superb low volleyer. He handled himself beautifully at net but he stayed too far back as though to cover the lobs. He was just not the killer in the forecourt. However, had he attacked regularly and closed in for the winner, his artistry as a volleyer would have been better recognized. He could take a ball an inch above the ground or half-volley from his shoe laces. With his great racket control nothing was beyond him, and in this sense he was very much like Hoad.

Jack had an excellent and precise overhead. He was not a big jumper, and perhaps the fact that he was more comfortable on the ground led him to play back too far. The overhead was hit very much like his service, but surprisingly often with some slice.

Jack's best year was in 1933, but he continued to play amateur tennis until the war. The last time he played in the States was in 1939. He was then past his prime and not the great Crawford of five years before. He was still with the Australian Davis Cup team, but Bromwich and Quist were the stars and Jack was third man behind them. I played him at Forest Hills that year and have a vivid memory of his characteristic mannerisms—the ambling, relaxed walk, the soft and lazy speech, the almost careless play and the beautiful strokes that had by then lost some of their effectiveness. He started very slowly and was down two sets to none in 45 minutes. He eventually won in five sets, thanks to some sugar and brandy, but he went out in the next round to Joe Hunt.

Two years ago Jack Kramer and his pros contributed the proceeds from a day's play to Jack Crawford Day. The old magic of the Crawford name and the popularity of the man himself attracted sell-out crowds. It was a wonderful gesture on the part of Kramer and a fine tribute to a very great star.

BRYAN (BITSY) GRANT

by Allison Danzig

Pound for pound, Bryan M. Grant, Jr. (or Bitsy, to be less formal), has been as great a tennis competitor as the world has seen. On second thought you can strike out the "tennis." For sheer fight and bulldog tenacity in hanging on against overpowering force, I never saw his superior in any game.

I have seen the "Mighty Atom" in action throughout his career and he is a dead game scrapper—all heart, or almost all of his 120 pounds. You could run him across the baseline until he was panting and holding his hand over his ticker and shaking that bristly-haired head in desperation, but no one—not Budge, nor Perry, nor Von Cramm, nor Vines, nor any of the greats—could ever make him quit on the match.

Read the roll call of the players he beat and you have a world ranking. He beat Ellsworth Vines, possessor of one of the fastest forehands the world ever saw. And he beat him in 1933 when Vines ranked first in the world after winning our title and Wimbledon. Bitsy beat him at Forest Hills in the championship, and that was the last match Ellsworth ever played on grass as an amateur. He cut the gut out of his racket after that 6–3, 6–3, 6–3 beating and said wearily, "I'm through."

I saw Bitsy beat Don Budge at White Sulphur Springs on clay, and you should have heard the Rebel yells that went up as he brought down the red terror who was to become the first and only player in history to make a grand slam of the world's four top championships—Australian, American, British, and French.

The little "Giant Killer," 5 feet, 4 inches in height, was commonly looked upon as a defensive player. His defense was the strongest part of his game. He could retrieve as could no one else I ever saw, and his control of the ball was as near to infallible as I ever saw. To beat him you had to attack might and main and go to the net.

On clay as powerful a hitter as Budge could not stay at the baseline against him. It was an endless endurance test against an opponent who forever kept the ball going back until you made the error. On grass, where pace pays more dividends, Bitsy was not quite as formidable, though some of his greatest victories were gained on the faster surface. But on grass he demonstrated that there was more attack to his game than was generally realized.

Stung by the dismissal of his game as purely defensive, he often would go to the net as much as his opponent, and he was a good volleyer. His lack of height and reach told against him at the net, for he could not bring down the lobs that a six-footer could, and also he did not have the powerful service to open the court for his volley that Budge, Vines, and others possessed. It was largely for these reasons that Bitsy elected to play mostly in the back court.

Considering his limitations of height, reach, power, and service, it is all the more remarkable that he has victories to his credit over so many of the great players of the past quarter of a century. It is a testimonial to his wonderful fighting heart and to the headiness of his court tactics in using the correct methods and coming up with the right shot in every circumstance.

Grant started proving that he was all man as early as 1927. As a 16-year-old shaver he won the Southern Championship. In all, he won this title eleven times, and the last time was in 1952, twenty-five years after he first carried it off. There are few spans of success to equal this.

Other titles to fall to Bitsy were the National Clay Court, the Eastern Grass Court, the Texas and Western Championships. He won the National Clay Court singles crown in 1930, 1934, and 1935, and in 1932 he won the doubles with George Lott.

Although he was competing in a period when Budge, Lott, Frank Shields, Sidney Wood, Lester Stoefen, Wilmer Allison, Frank Parker, and Robert Riggs were riding high, Grant was chosen a number of times for the Davis Cup team. His most impressive victories in the cup matches were scored over Australia's John Bromwich and Jack Crawford in the American Zone in 1937. He beat both of them without the loss of a single set.

Among Grant's most memorable matches at Forest Hills in the championships were his five-set struggle with Budge in 1934, his four-setter with Budge in 1935, his four-setter with Fred Perry in 1936, and his five-setter with Baron Gottfried von Cramm in 1937.

Bitsy was ranked in the first ten in 1930, 1933, 1934, 1935, 1936, 1937, 1938, 1939, and 1941. He was third in the country in 1935 and 1936. He might have been ranked among the elect again, but he was in the service during the war and that interrupted his career as a national figure.

In 1955, Bitsy returned to the National scene, competing for the first time in the Senior Division. Playing in the stadium built and named in his honor by the City of Atlanta, Georgia, he took the National Senior Clay Court Singles title, defeating Jack Staton 6–0, 6–4 in the finals. He then teamed with Malon C. Courts to win the National Senior Doubles crown. In 1956, he successfully defended his National Clay Court Senior Singles title in St. Louis, Missouri, defeating Dave Freed 6–3, 6–2 in the finals.

After a long absence, Bitsy went back to Forest Hills in September 1956 to compete, on grass, in the National Senior Championship. Playing for this title the first time, he won it, with the loss of only one set, against a field that included Jean Borotra of France, Berkeley Bell and Phillip Hanna, the 1955 champion, whom he beat in the final round—7–5, 6–4.

The Atlanta delegation in the stands held nothing back in letting Bitsy know how they felt about his victory. Atlantans have been doing that for years. And here's a Texan who also wants to stand up and sound the Rebel yell for a big warrior who never asked any quarter, no matter how big or famous they came and who beat most of the foremost players of his time. The Sovereign State of Georgia has given sports possibly its greatest triumvirate of all the forty-eight—Ty Cobb, Bobby Jones, and Bitsy Grant.

J. GILBERT HALL

by Fred Hawthorne

There are some athletes who seem to defy the laws of advancing age by becoming more proficient at their chosen sport as they grow older.

Tennis has its J. Gilbert Hall, who, at 51, is still a semi-regular on the tournament circuit and currently is limbering up his racket arm in preparation for another defense of his national veterans' singles crown. . . . Hall has won the title for six consecutive years. There is not much doubt that he is the greatest player over 50 years of age in the world today. Until the recent national indoor championship, I had been inclined to regard the great French Basque, Jean Borotra, as the man entitled to that distinction. . . .

Hall's game is better today than at any time since he first won the title in 1944. One thing is certain: Hall has made a greater niche for himself in the world as a veteran than he ever did as an "undergraduate." He has been ranked in the first ten of the men's division only twice. He was 37 when the ranking committee listed him at No. 8 in 1935, and he was 46 and the veterans' champion when the committee placed him at No. 10 in the 1944 rankings.

Hall waited until he was 22 years old before he lifted a racket for the first time. As a youngster in Springdale, New Jersey, he played football and baseball and built up quite a reputation as an ice skater, showing proficiency both at hockey and figure skating. To this day, Gil maintains a full sports schedule throughout the year, but the key sport for this bachelor, who in business is associated with a printing and lithographic firm in the Wall Street district of New York, has been tennis for the past several decades.

Gil entered his first tournament in 1923 at South Orange, New Jersey. He has accumulated some 350 trophies and has given away at least a score of these prizes to friends. Several times he has won outright possession of challenge trophies, only to return them to competition. Nothing of the mughunter in Gil's court career.

Hall's great weapon today is his forehand, and from the beginning of his career his forehand drive has been an awesome attacking shot. Hit solidly and with considerable top spin, the drive was—and still is—so powerful, and accurate in its placement, that it really opened up the opposing court and placed the opponent on the defensive. And Hall was never a man to hang back after this forcing shot, racing up to forecourt for the following volley. His heavily topped first service, an American twist delivery that hammered the ball so hard it took on the shape of an egg, was as potent as his forehand drive.

The fame of his forehand became legend wherever tennis players gathered, and his name became prominent in the winning lists. He hung up occasional victories over players such as Jean Borotra, George Lott and Greg Mangin, and he carried Sidney Wood to three five-setters over a period of four years. . . . Ask Gil who was the greatest player of all time and he answers with a booming question himself: "Who do you think? Why Tilden, of course."

Through the years Hall has built up a reputation as one of the game's finest sportsmen. Although over the draft age, Gil volunteered for Army duty in the Second World War. He served as a top sergeant in the Eighth Armored Division.

MARY HARDWICK

by Allison Danzig

Mary Hardwick is a name that is becoming more and more familiar in the training camps of this country. It is the name of a blond, blue-eyed British girl who is well known wherever lawn tennis is played and whose conquests with her racket, including a victory over Mrs. Helen Wills Roark, never gave her the satisfaction she feels in putting on tennis shows for the enjoyment of the armed forces.

In September 1939 Mary Hardwick was in this country when the war broke out in Europe. A cable from her family, concerned over the peril lurking beneath the Atlantic waters with the U-boats on the loose, directed her not to undertake the hazardous trip home.

She has remained here ever since, and America and Britain have both benefited by her stay. She has been one of the most devoted workers in the cause of the Allies, with a zeal that has amounted to consecration.

Reared in the careful protection surrounding the family ancestral estate and a Paris finishing school, Miss Hardwick is an example of what the war has done to unite a people and give them all a common working purpose. This slender, vividly attractive daughter of John Bull has a vitality that probably would have burst the confinements of the social calendar, war or no war, but quite likely she would have caught her breath at the mere thought, prior to 1939, of the tangent her life was to take from the circumscribed orbit.

First of all she joined the ranks of the professional players to go on tour with Miss Alice Marble. The necessity of supporting herself, when Government restrictions on the export of money cut off funds from home, dictated this step, which probably dumbfounded friends in England. They could hardly be said to have been as pleased as Punch. It was a step taken in stride by Miss Hardwick and without any qualms, even though the professional enters by the back door at Wimbledon, within a stone's throw of the family town house.

A career as a professional player enabled her not only to be self-supporting but to remit money home to the Red Cross along with the extra funds she raised in the course of her tour by devoting every possible spare moment to the war cause.

When the tour ended she went into war work all the way. Tennis became a means to an end, though she probably has derived as much fun from the game as any player who ever lived. Such was her infatuation with it that she was on the courts when she should have been learning French at finishing school.

From June 1941 until the end of 1942 Miss Hardwick raised $43,000 with her racket for the American and Canadian Red Cross, the British War Relief and the USO. During the time of the terrible bombing of London the Mary Hardwick Wimbledon Fund was launched and she sent three mobile canteens home.

In these fund-raising exhibitions she was assisted principally by Charles Hare, former member of the British Davis Cup team and a resident of this country since 1937, to whom she was married this year. Hare, who has taken out his citizenship papers, is in the Army Special Service School at Washington and Lee University.

Last February Miss Hardwick went to Arizona and for ten weeks she played exhibitions in every air force camp in the State, both RAF and American. When she finished her daily stint any of the young eagles who wanted to take off against her with a racket was accommodated and dispatched.

Most of them, though, were satisfied just to sit and look. It could have been that it was her radiant loveliness rather than her tennis that held them in their seats. Some persons have no appreciation at all for classical stroke production.

Upon her return to the East this amazingly vital British girl launched another series of exhibitions for the fighting forces in camps, bases and stations all along the Atlantic seaboard. She enlisted such prominent players as Miss Marble, Dorothy Round Little, Vincent Richards, Ladislav Hecht, Karel Kozeluh and Hare for the matches, which drew 4,000 service men at Atlantic City.

Now Miss Hardwick is off again on another tour, this time for the entertainment of the Wacs. With Miss Marble, starting Tuesday, she will play exhibitions and give instruction in Wac camps of the Middle West, South and East under the sponsorship of the USO Camp Shows.

It's a grand name, Mary Hardwick. She has been a grand ally for the United States, or, perhaps it should be said, for Great Britain. For as the wife of Corporal Charles Hare of the United States Army, Mary Hardwick is here to stay.

MERCER BEASLEY

by George McGann

A trim white-haired gentleman wearing tennis shoes, slacks, a checked button-down sport shirt, striped silk bow tie, hound's-tooth belted jacket and jockey cap walked onto the courts at the Flamingo Hotel in Miami Beach. Around his neck hung a whistle and clutched in his right hand was the inevitable pad of yellow paper covered with pencil-written notes. Under his left arm were boxing gloves, a baseball bat, some placards, a tennis racket and a golf club. Mercer Beasley was about to hold a clinic.

He was greeted with warmth by his good friend Doris Hart, the Flamingo's famous pro. Among the spectators were a number of other dear friends, including several children under eight, a group of "name" players, a dozen admiring parents, cohort Mike Blanchard, and Mr. Beasley's cat, Ace, who accompanies his master wherever he goes.

"Beas" immediately caught his audience's attention by blowing the whistle. Sudden silence. He then put his paraphernalia on the ground and proceeded to talk. His opening remark caused the gallery to smile. Within one minute he had them in the palm of his hand. He spoke clearly, deliberately and with great humor. The clinic was off to an immediate success.

The "Old Pro" used every gimmick in the book, plus two hitherto unknown, to capture the audience's attention. He put on a catcher's mask and tossed a ball to Doris, he swung at a tennis ball with a golf club, and he sparred for a moment with an awed youngster. Doris demonstrated the strokes while Beas lectured and blew his whistle. At his command, the children in the gallery walked onto the court and got a practical lesson in stroke production. He rallied with a 7-year-old and dropped his racket in amazement when his tiny opponent whipped a hard forehand over the net. Mike Blanchard and Doris were smiling, for the "Old Pro" was in rare form.

But Mercer Beasley is always in rare form. He walks with the spring of a junior, follows the tournaments like a circuit player, and has an unending interest in the tennis careers of all players. His gruff voice and fierce eyebrows belie his friendly disposition. His colorful wardrobe, which includes plaid vests, tennis sweaters and a dozen jockey caps, is heightened by his sky-blue eyes and shock of white hair. Most men retire at the age of 65; "Beas" is 77, and still charging full speed all over the East Coast. . . .

Mercer Beasley's two most famous pupils were Frankie Parker and Ellsworth Vines. Frankie was Beas' adopted son as well as his most distinguished protégé. He was two times National Champion and seventeen times listed in the country's First Ten. The most important traits instilled into Parker by his mentor were the ability to devote himself completely to tennis, to play the game without ever being disturbed by outside factors, and the wonderful quality of perfect sportsmanship. Parker was the ideal opponent. There was never any "incident" in a match in which he played. He just went about the business of winning.

Frank's serious attitude was in part the result of Beas' insistence that nothing should interfere with a businesslike attention to the game. He arrived at the courts on time for each match, played, showered, dressed and left. He was even-tempered and friendly with all the players and universally liked. On the court he was a deadpan, again the result of Mercer's training.

Parker's backhand was one of the famous strokes in tennis. It was very precise, clean and neat. There were no elaborate frills. He hit with a locked wrist, and he could hit flat or with slight overspin or underspin. If there was any criticism at all of the backhand, it was that he tended to underspin when under attack, and the ball therefore rose to the net man rather than dipped.

His forehand changed every year. Each spring, as the buds blossomed and the birds flew north, sports writers all over the country would speculate on the new Forehand Model. There was always a hitch in the wind-up, and nothing that Beas or Parker ever tried would eliminate it. One year, the New Model had absolutely no wind-up; another year the forehand resembled a side-arm delivery in baseball; and his present forehand still bears Beasley's last imprint. The service was a neat, short action, well-disguised and the volley on the backhand side was excellent. He was as consistent as Bitsy Grant, and he tried for every point in the manner of a Vic Seixas. His game was thoroughly respected.

Ellsworth Vines came to The Coach when he was a mature player. Beas' job here was to talk strategy and tactics, keep Vines from overhitting and to teach him to temper his game. Vines was one of the hardest hitters the game has ever known. On his good days he was unbeatable; on his poor days he was still tough but wild enough to be beaten. The Old Pro used to paste pieces of paper around Vines' racket handle with pithy instructions inscribed thereon. They admonished him to "Get the first serve in," "Hop into position," and "Clear that net!"

Beasley accompanied Vines to Wimbledon. When his pupil took the court, Mercer seated himself in the stands and scribbled undecipherable notes on yellow sheets of paper. After each match, Beas was able to tell Vines how many errors were made on backhands down the line or how many outright points were won on low forehand volleys. The English newspapers paid almost as much attention to Beas as to young Ellsworth. One sports writer claimed that The Coach was using mental telepathy; another insisted that Vines raised his eyes after every point to catch the signal as to how he should play the next point.

KRAMER

by Allison Danzig

When Jack Kramer was a schoolboy with shining morning face in Las Vegas, Nevada, the one thing in all the world he wanted to be was a big-league baseball player; the last thing, a sissy tennis player—"And for gosh sakes, maw, don't let the fellers know you bought me that racket."

By the time he came up to high school in Montebello, California, Jack had changed his mind. Today, the six-foot one-inch national champion with deep-set blue eyes and sandy stand-uppish hair, cut to crew, is the player on whom the United States is laying its blue chips to bring back the Davis Cup from Australia.

The Anzacs, it will be remembered, took the cup away from us in 1939 at Philadelphia as the Second World War broke out. Maybe the answer to putting an end to these global conflicts is to keep the Aussies at home. The Kaiser turned loose his goose-steppers as another Australian team (actually Australian and New Zealand combined) was winning the Davis Cup at Forest Hills in 1914. It's getting to be a habit, and if we get that hunk of silver back this year, with the renewal of the challenge round for the first time since 1939, in Melbourne, December 26, 27 and 28, we'd better make the peace stick, or, sure as shooting, the lads from Down Under will be back gunning again with their rackets.

Now Jack and his mates on the team, led by Captain Walter L. Pate, are in Kangaroo Land on a 14,000-mile round-trip expedition out of California to bring the mug back. Frank Parker, Ted Schroeder, Tom Brown and Gardnar Mulloy and William Talbert, the national doubles champions, are the other playing members. The issue will be joined with Messrs. John Bromwich, Adrian Quist, Dinny Pails and Geoffrey Brown in Kooyong Stadium in Melbourne.

The Davis Cup is the most international of all sporting competitions with the exception of the Olympic Games. The play for the trophy offered in 1900 by Dwight F. Davis, who was later to become Secretary of War and Governor General of the Philippines, is distinctly a team proposition. No one man alone can win the cup, for the challenge round, as well as all preliminary rounds (or ties), is decided by winning three of the five matches. The most any one member can contribute is to win two of the four singles and share half the burden of winning the one doubles match.

But while the Davis Cup is a team affair, the history of the matches reveals that one outstanding individual has most often been the key to success. First it was Malcolm Whitman for the United States, with Dwight Davis and William Larned to support him. Then H. L. Doherty made Britain top bulldog from 1903 through 1906, aided and abetted by brother Reginald Doherty and Sidney Smith. Norman Brookes, the Australian wizard, put the Anzacs on top in 1909, 1910 and 1911 and again in 1914, with help from Anthony Wilding and Rodney Heath.

Then along came William Tilden, and the United States was supreme for seven years. Little Bill Johnston stood shoulder to shoulder with Big Bill, and he used to deal out some murderous lickings, too, and Vinnie Richards had a crack at the singles as well as teamed in the doubles with Tilden or Dick Williams as his partner. But it was Tilden the great who was every man's poison in those days.

Next along came Henri Cochet to end the Tilden dynasty and the American cycle in 1927 and keep the Tricolor on top. René Lacoste was just as great as Henri, but Lacoste had to retire on account of his health, and it was the Ball Boy of Lyons who carried the burden, with help from Jean Borotra and Jacques Brugnon, until along came another world champion in the person of Fred Perry, in 1933.

The greatest player England has had since the First World War, if not since "Little Do" Doherty, Perry stood off Wilmer Allison, Frank Shields, Sidney Wood and Donald Budge, as well as the Australians, until he turned professional. Bunny Austin and Pat Hughes assisted in keeping the Union Jack on high.

Then Budge—Donald the Red—came of tennis age and no one could stand before him. He won back the cup in 1937, ten years after it had been lost to France; turned down a pro offer of $50,000 and defended the cup in 1938; and then said farewell to amateur tennis and Frank Parker, Bobby Riggs and Gene Mako, his teammates.

Upon the stage now stepped John Bromwich, with Adrian Quist. An unorthodox player, who has no backhand but two forehands, Brom hits what would be backhand shots with his left hand. On his forehand he uses both hands, a two-fisted grip, and what he does to the ball on that side is murder in the first degree. He serves with one hand, his right. He is a natural right-hander who taught himself to hit with his left.

In the 1939 challenge round, the last to be played, Bromwich met Parker in the deciding match at the Merion Cricket Club near Philadelphia, with each nation holding two victories. Frank was the backcourt player par excellence, the mechanical man who never missed, the thinking robot of the racket, the human backboard, whom Mercer Beasley had brought along from a Milwaukee ballboy to the precisionist second to Lacoste in the infallibility of his return.

In the opening rally of that deciding match, the two players stood on their baselines and exchanged fifty drives from the forehand. Then, as if by mutual agreement, they swung and swayed over to the backhand (Brom's southpaw forehand) , and it was give and take, nip and tuck, see and saw for fifty more shots, until the gallery's neck muscles gave out and astigmatism set in from turning their heads and clicking their eyeballs north and south so many times. The rally finally ended with Parker, the infallible machine, knocking the ball into the net, and that was it. Frank couldn't help knowing that he had met his master at baseline play. He got four games in the three sets.

That was the Bromwich who took the cup away from us seven years ago, with material help from Quist, who beat Bobby Riggs in the singles and won the doubles with Bromwich after the Australians had dropped the two opening singles. According to reports, it's a Bromwich every bit as good, despite his layoff while in the military service during the war, who bars the way to our designs on the cup in December. If you take it from Bobby Barnes and Jim Russell, two good fellows and knowing ones from Down Under, Brom is the top amateur of the world, a superman of the courts lying in wait to ambush the invader of Kangaroo Land. If they show any slightest reservation about the outcome of the challenge round, it is only in their respect for Jack Kramer.

Jack is the one player Australia fears. That's our man who has got to make the Aussies say Uncle Sam if the huge silver cup (actually a bowl) and its accompanying tray, which have been holed up in a vault for seven long years, are to be brought back.

If the bad luck that has dogged Kramer throughout his career, in the way of hand blisters, operations and digestive afflictions from sea food, lets up on him—as it seemed to have done when he won the national championship in September—there is a good chance that he will do it.

Jack Kramer was twenty-five years old August first last, but he looks more like a kid of eighteen, and as nice and respectful and unpretentious a kid as you ever knew. Friendly and trustful as a puppy dog, almost naïve in his faith in people and as regular with the fellows as if he were just another member of the gang and not the best amateur tennis player in the United States, he has nothing but well-wishers and not an enemy or critic anywhere on the entire tennis circuit. From the time he first came East I have never seen him that he wasn't in the best of spirits and enjoying himself.

Even after he came back from England, where he had to default in his first big tournament since returning from two years' service in the Pacific as an officer in the United States Coast Guard, owing to blisters on his hand, and where he was beaten at Wimbledon, largely because of that affliction, he had no complaint or alibi to offer. He said that Drobny, the Czech who beat him, to the amazement of the tennis world, was simply too good for him. His blisters kept him out of singles competition on grass all season except for Seabright; still he took it with that big boyish smile and had no fears about being ready for the national championship. When he was unexpectedly beaten in the national doubles at Longwood with Ted Schroeder, and the treasured challenge bowls, on which they held two legs and had designs of winning outright, passed permanently into the possession of Talbert and Mulloy, his instinct was to rush to his partner and throw his arms about him and console him, forgetting his own keen disappointment.

Generous, thoughtful and honest to the core in his every word and action, Jack Kramer, or Jake, as they call him, has the character of a champion. The tougher side of him comes out on the court, when that smile gives way to frowning concentration and intensity of purpose as he pulls himself up on his toes, lets go with that big serve and whales the daylights out of every ball without a letup. If you have seen Donald Budge or Ellsworth Vines in action, making the chalk fly on the lines with deep, skimming drives and twisting services, and closing in for the kill with drilling volleys and thundering overheads, you have an idea of how Kramer plays tennis and why the crowds go for him. It's the killer with the big punch that they pay to see on the courts as well as in the ring, and the friendly kid from Montebello changes into a killer from way back and up at the net when he gets a racket in his hand.

Jack started out on the long hard row to the championship at the age of thirteen. Up to that time he had been interested in every sport except tennis, with football, baseball and basketball as his favorites. Baseball came before all others, and his father, who had been denied the chance to enjoy sports as a youth, indulged his son by buying him every kind of equipment he wished for.

When he was seven years old, Jack had seven baseball mitts, a catcher's mask and half a dozen bats and balls, all regulation equipment. Arriving on the playing field one day in Las Vegas, his birthplace, he objected because he wasn't picked first in choosing up sides and announced he wouldn't play and would take all of his gloves and bats if he couldn't be No. 1. His father, standing nearby, informed him he wouldn't play that day under any circumstances, nor any day if he acted that way. That was one of many lessons that Jack received from his father in sportsmanship.

Jack's introduction to tennis came about as a result of injuries he suffered in football. Playing with older boys, he sustained a broken nose and later a separation of several ribs in scrimmages. His mother wanted no more of this and decided to try and interest him in another sport for the fall, after baseball was over. She bought a secondhand racket. When she gave it to him he begged her not to let his friends know about it. Tennis is a game for sissies, he protested. But she persuaded him to try playing tennis, and he did a few times on the school courts.

That was in the fall of 1934, when Jack was 13 years old. A few months later the family moved from Las Vegas to San Bernardino, California. Tennis was a big sport there, played by all the boys, and Jack changed his ideas. His father bought a racket, too, to get exercise, and they played together on the high school courts. Three months after arriving at San Bernardino, Jack played in his first tournament and won it, despite the fact that he had received no coaching whatever. That was the end of Jack's plans to become a big-league baseball player.

His family then took Jack to play in the Dudley Cup tournament for boys at Santa Monica. There he was beaten by the late Ted Olewine, who was to win national prominence. His father decided he needed coaching and put him in a class conducted by Dick Skeen. Aside from some help that Vines gave him, that was the only coaching he has ever received, though Budge gave him some tips in practice matches on the coast.

Kramer won the national boys' championship at Culver, Indiana, and also the interscholastic title. He failed to win the junior crown. Schroeder, who was to become his partner in winning the national doubles twice, defeated him one year after Jack had suffered the first of the many bad breaks that were to mark his career. He pulled ligaments in his side at Culver and couldn't serve and was beaten by Schroeder in the semi-finals. By a coincidence, it was the year that Schroeder won the national men's title, 1942, that Jack, who was thought about due to get to the top, underwent an operation for appendicitis the day before he was to have left for the East.

The year Schroeder beat him in the junior championship, Jack was bothered for the first time by blisters, and he has been troubled with them off and on ever since, though never to the degree that he was this year. Some thought that they came from his service on an LST in the Pacific, during which he was in five invasions, but his mother says that it is simply a matter of his hands being sensitive.

In 1943, while in training at the Coast Guard Academy at New London, Connecticut, Jack was given permission to go down to New York to play in the national championship at Forest Hills. He reached the final, and there lost to the late Lieutenant Joe Hunt of the U.S. Navy, with whom he had played the Davis Cup doubles match against Australia in 1939. Hunt played beautiful tennis and might well have won regardless, but Jack was taken ill the day before the match, after eating clams, and weakened in the final. Characteristically, he refused to offer any alibi and gave Hunt full credit for his victory. (It wasn't many months later that Hunt, training as a fighter pilot, lost his life in the crash of his plane, after serving as a deck officer in both the Atlantic and Pacific theaters of the war.)

The next two years found Jack serving aboard his LST in the Pacific. Then came word that he had received his discharge, and the East eagerly waited for his return. Early in 1946 he defeated Parker, national champion in 1944 and 1945, in a California tournament, and the report was that he was in fine shape and playing better than ever. That immediately established him as the player of the year to watch. He was selected to go to Wimbledon and everyone expected he would win hands down. Came the dismaying information of his default because of blisters, and then his stunning defeat by Drobny. It was the same old story, and it got worse as he returned and had to lay off for weeks to give his hand a chance to heal. It took a long time before he discovered the right treatment. Then came the national championship.

Could Kramer beat Parker? That was the big question. Frank had played no grass tournaments all season except the national doubles, and Jack had played only at Seabright and in the doubles. The question was never answered. Tom Brown, Jr., who had come out of the Army, which meant nowheres in a tennis way, and had been the surprise of Wimbledon, knocked Parker out of the championship with the most devastating speed unleashed at Forest Hills since Vines' day.

That was the sensation of the year, and when Brown, in the semi-finals, next knocked out Mulloy, who had been in the finals of the four big grass tournaments of the year and won two, the question became "Can Kramer beat Brown?" They met in the final and for one thrilling long set it was a battle of heavyweight hitters, with Brown coming from behind and breaking service for a 7–6 lead. After that, Jack took charge, and against the grinding, unrelaxing pressure of his all-court attack, Tom's control buckled, and nothing could stop Kramer. At long last, Jack was the champion everyone had predicted he would be when he was a junior.

The prediction was that Kramer would become not only a national champion but another Budge or Vines, meaning a world champion. The Davis Cup matches in Kooyong Stadium in Melbourne will furnish the answer. The only man that can conceivably stop him there is Bromwich, and, playing on his own turf courts, harder and faster than ours, and under familiar conditions, Brom may do it. But if Jack is able to adapt himself to his surroundings and plays the tennis he showed at Forest Hills, it should take an even better Bromwich than the one of 1939 to beat him. . . . It should be the greatest match of the year anywhere. Good luck to the hard luck kid, and don't eat any clams, Jake.

THE STYLE OF JACK KRAMER

by Julius D. Heldman

The Kramer theory of modern tennis completely changed the complexion of the game. Jack popularized the terms "attack," "the Big Game" and "percentage tennis." There were many attacking players before Kramer but none who consistently came in behind every serve. The big serve combined with the big volley became known as the Big Game. The words "percentage tennis" described a theory of play which included such Kramerisms as hitting every forehand approach shot down the line, serving at three-quarter speed to the backhand on important points, and coasting on the opponent's delivery until the opportunity came for the break.

Jack Kramer did not start to play tournament tennis until the age of 13. When he was 14 he became a member of a select group of young players who were being developed by Dick Skeen. The latter, a classical baseliner, had organized a method of training for some 15 youngsters which was designed to make them into champions. The group met almost daily at various courts, including Poinsettia Playground in Hollywood, the Palomar in Culver City (now the California Racquet Club) and private courts in Altadena, Beverly Hills and San Diego. Whenever Skeen gave a lesson on a private court he took some of the group with him. Most of these youngsters were from relatively poor families; Skeen's fee of $10 to $20 a month included rackets, balls and lessons. Kramer, who lived way out in Montebello, would be driven in several times a week by his mother or his aunt to work out with the Skeen group. The brush action on Kramer's forehand was a typical Skeen stroke, and the undercut backhand also bore the Skeen stamp.

Jack developed remarkably fast. He came from a family of moderate means but he was able to play the National Boys' Championships at Culver Military Academy due to the fact that his father was a railroad engineer, which entitled young Kramer to a free ticket. He played at Culver at the age of 15, winning the title although he had not been the pre-tournament favorite. Larry Dee and Jimmy Wade were the top seeds, but Dee was upset by Harper Ink, and Wade, who was sick, was eliminated by Kramer.

Almost from the beginning Jack showed great court presence and good match temperament. He never got flustered or fell apart under pressure. In the 15-and-Under division Jack's game was noted for its consistency in the backcourt. He was a steady player but not a soft-ball artist, and he was definitely not a net rusher. He was not a great natural athlete since he was always a little heavy on his feet. He could not change direction fast or run down a ball that got behind him as could a young Vic Seixas or a Pancho Gonzales. However, he had a great eye, an infinite capacity to work on his game and a champion's determination to win.

Jack was the top future prospect when he returned from Culver as National Boys' Champion. Southern California officialdom lured him away from the Skeen group by offering him playing privileges at the famous Los Angeles Tennis Club. Here he got the opportunity of a lifetime. He worked out with Ellsworth Vines, the world's best player, almost daily. Other youngsters before and since Jack have had similar opportunities, but never developed into championship caliber. Kramer stayed hungry and eager. He consolidated his strokes and learned to handle speed. Within a year he had all the earmarks of a world-beater. He was often beaten but he never played foolish tennis and never stayed disheartened.

Just about this time an automotive engineer named Cliff Roche convinced Kramer that the winning game should be played in set patterns. Roche, who played reasonably well himself, had worked in Detroit as a mass production designer and had formalized a theory of the game based on repetitive action. Every ball, he said, should be hit in a certain pattern. The forehand down-the-line approach shot, for example, became 100 per cent automatic since it was not a function of the opponent's position or strength. Every time the "automatic player" came into net behind a forehand, he hit for an area two feet from the sideline and three feet from the baseline. Crosscourt forehand approach shots were never to be used since, on a percentage basis, they would lead to more passing shots on the return. The crosscourt forehand could be played only as an outright placement, never as a forcing approach.

Roche had been expounding his theories of the game for many years but no player had ever thought to follow his strategy religiously. Jack Kramer and his young doubles partner, Ted Schroeder, were the first Roche disciples. The court tactics in which they were drilled became the ABCs of modern tennis. Today every top player adheres to the basic Roche tenet of coming to net behind every serve and, whenever possible, behind every return. Kramer and Schroeder, from being steady baseliners, became net rushers.

The Roche strategy, as exemplified by Kramer, contains much more than the principle of attack. Coach Roche wanted Jack to limit himself to a few grooved shots. Every backhand exchange from the baseline was a deep crosscourt. The backhand down the line was to be used only for the sure winner. The term "percentage" was the key to championship tennis: if backhand crosscourts earned more points than backhands down the line, then never use the backhand down the line. Considered in the calculations were the errors and placements of the player as well as the errors and placements of the opponent. Roche did not attempt to modify Kramer's stroke technique. He was interested only in overall strategy.

Kramer became the automatic player. He served every ball to the backhand except when he saw the big opening. He never tried for an ace on an important point. His first serve went in a remarkable percentage of the time. His forehand became so grooved that he could hit the 2-foot-by-3-foot rectangle consistently. He never learned a defensive game other than the necessary lob. He went all out to win every service game but elected to go all out on his opponent's service only when he felt he had a real opportunity for the break. He was tireless in a five-setter because he always conserved his strength on his opponent's delivery except when he felt the opportunity for the "kill." He played pattern tennis.

Jack's career in the game puts him in the category of one of the all-time great players. At 18 he was selected to play Davis Cup doubles with Joe Hunt. The war interrupted his meteoric rise and he scarcely played any competitive tennis for five years. He returned to the circuit as the top amateur. Jaroslav Drobny upset him at Wimbledon in 1946, but thereafter Kramer was untouchable. He won the U.S. National Singles title twice, the Wimbledon Singles once, the U.S. National Doubles with Schroeder, and the Wimbledon Doubles with both Tom Brown and Bob Falkenburg. When he turned pro he completely dominated the pay-for-play circuit. On his first tour he defeated Bobby Riggs and thereafter he downed Pancho Gonzales, Frank Sedgman and Pancho Segura. He retired undefeated when Gonzales came into his own.

Jack's strongest weapons were his forehand and serve. The volley was great only because the approach was great. Every stroke in his repertoire was thoroughly grooved, and he even had a preferential spot for his overheads. His one weakness was the undercut backhand, which did not have enough pace to be an effective passing shot. He was a good drop-volleyer and knew the value of the dump shot as a winner. He played close to net, knowing that the percentage was against his opponent in placement lobs and that the percentage was with him in scoring with close-in volleys.

His forehand was hit with a laid-back wrist. When he hit down the line he pulled the racket slightly across his body. The sidespin on the down-the-line side was a heavy ball to return. When he hit crosscourt he used overspin by pulling up on the follow-through. The stroke was a relatively short one, always hit with an open stance. It was a great grooved approach shot which forced the opponent into errors or pop-ups.

The backhand was steady but not powerful. Jack led with his elbow always, which meant that there was sidespin as well as underspin on the ball. The sidespin was on the down-the-line and the underspin on the crosscourt. He hit with good depth, but unless he followed the ball to net his backhand never worried his opponent. It was a small stroke, and the action and style were only slightly longer than the "chip" shot.

Although Jack did not serve as many aces as Bob Falkenburg or Pancho Gonzales, he was considered by all those he played to have one of the truly great serves. His second serve was almost as hard to handle as his first. It was a slight slice service with great depth and placement. The ball was heavy and invariably pulled his opponent wide, and of course Kramer was into net waiting for the return. The action was highly stylized, and for five years every junior attempted the Kramer wind-up. Jack leaned way back, almost on his haunches, at the beginning of the wind-up, pulling up to full height at the hit. The overhead, which was hit with the same action as the serve, had that high left hand pointing at the ball just as he pointed at the end of the service toss.

The forehand volley was hit with a laid-back wrist and resembled his down-the-line forehand without a follow-through. He did not make leap-volley kills nor did he powder the ball. He hit with great placement and consistency, not with bludgeon power. His first volley behind service was just like his forehand: it was always placed deep to the backhand unless he had a set-up kill. He did not attempt to put away the first volley but merely to set himself up for the killer second where he was in close.

The backhand volley was hit with a fair amount of underspin and had the same action on high and low balls. It carried slightly less pace than the forehand volley but he had excellent control. He never rallied from the net: when the first volley was not a put-away, he was either passed or made a winner on the second. He tried to force his opponent into hitting set-ups or errors by his great depth and blanketing of the net.

The Kramer Pros are carbon copies of Jack tactically, although individual styles and stroke techniques vary. Each one has learned that percentage tennis as exemplified by Jack is vital to survival in the top leagues.

FRANK KOVACS

by Jason December

Francis Louis Kovacs II was born on December 4, 1919, in Oakland, California. He began to play tennis when he was 12 years old and he won his first tournament, the Men's Singles Championship of Oakland (4th Class), on April Fool's Day in 1934, a date that was indicative of things to come.

There has never been anyone in tennis quite like Frank. He never won the National Championship yet he was often better known than the National Champ. He played havoc with the USLTA with his antics, he delighted the bobbysoxers with his good looks, he was the terror of the tournament circuit, yet he was universally liked by the players. Frank never had a mean word to say about another player, but he thoroughly earned his nickname of The Clown Prince.

Don Budge calls Frank "The greatest player in the world who never won a big tournament." As an amateur he was ranked No. 3 in 1940 and No. 2 in 1941, when he was runner-up to Bobby Riggs at Forest Hills. He annexed the National Indoor crown that same year over Wayne Sabin. As a professional he defeated Pancho Segura for the World Pro singles title, making a left-handed shot to pull out the match! No matter what the tournament or who the opponent, he could never resist the gesture, remark or stroke that would amuse the gallery. To all external appearances Frank could never be serious.

For the first few years of his tennis career Frank, amazingly enough, had a poor backhand, but by dint of hard work he acquired a stroke which is recognized as one of the greatest in the world (his standard greeting to Don Budge: "How's the second best backhand in the world?"). In 1937 he scored his first great win, toppling the Atlanta Atom, Bitsy Grant, who was then ranked No. 3 nationally. In 1938 Frank took the California State title and, after playing the Eastern Circuit, was ranked No. 10 in the country.

In 1939 Frank successfully defended his California State championship, then got a "tennis elbow" and was informed by his doctors that he could never play again. This was a terrible blow to the Happy Hungarian, but he refused to give up and commenced to learn tennis all over again with his left hand. When the Pacific Coast Championships came along in the fall, the committee asked Kovacs to enter to stimulate publicity. Frank agreed and decided to play right-handed. Much to his surprise the ache departed when he hit hard. He defeated Adrian Quist, the Australian champion, 6–2, 6–0 and reached the finals despite a five-month lay-off, bowing only to Bobby Riggs, then No. 2 in the nation.

Frank made his first Eastern trip in 1937 when he was still a junior. He astounded the East with his Wild West tactics. No point was lost until Kovacs hashed and rehashed it with the linesmen, umpire and the audience.

It was hard to believe that tournaments could be so completely disrupted by one individual. The crowds loved his antics, as did the press. In spite of official reprimands, Kovacs kept on heckling his opponents just as they were about to kill easy overheads, threatening the linesmen and chewing on tennis balls. During the summer of 1940, at the Newport invitation tournament, he brought down the house when he acknowledged an umpire's order to "play tennis" by clicking his heels, coming to attention stiffly and giving a perfect Nazi salute. . . .

In the quarter-finals of the 1940 national championships Frank was a chief participant in one of the most unusual events in the history of sports—a sit-down strike in the stadium. Kovacs had played in 20 consecutive tournaments and was both weary and stale. He had been seeded No. 3 and was supposed to eliminate seventh-seeded Joe Hunt, but Kovacs had no heart for the match. He had already reserved space that night on a California-bound plane and he decided to enjoy his exit from the championships. Frankie fooled away the first two sets and was trailing, 3–1, in the third. He hit balls behind his back and between his legs. He tossed up three balls on the service and blasted the middle one over for an ace. Even though Hunt was winning, he was the only one in the crowd of 15,000 who was not enjoying the show.

Hunt halted play and asked the umpire to request Kovacs not to clown any more. He wanted a straightforward victory, and it was obvious that Frank was throwing the match. Kovacs refused to give in to the umpire on the grounds that he always enjoyed winning and he now wanted to enjoy losing. Hunt refused to continue the match. The Clown Prince then plopped down on the turf, strumming his racket as if it were a guitar and he were some carefree cowboy out on the range. At the opposite end of the court Hunt, too, sat down on the baseline, wishing, no doubt, to conserve his energy.

Officials sprang up from all quarters, converging on happy-go-lucky Frankie. They begged, cajoled, stormed, threatened, but Frank was adamant. The officials then switched their attack to Joe. Hunt, after fifteen minutes of deliberation, was finally persuaded to resume play. Joe quickly ran out the last three games as Kovacs had lost all desire to be comical, much to the dismay of the gallery. When the rankings appeared at the end of the year, Kovacs was ranked No. 3, two notches ahead of Joe Hunt at No. 5.

In 1938 Kovacs was playing at Forest Hills in the traditional "longs" of the day. The weather was so hot that in the middle of the fifth set of an encounter with Vic Seixas, Frank chopped his pants off three inches above the knee. The gallery laughed hysterically and Frankie ran out the next three games. . . .

Frank is 36 years old, and although he is still delightfully amusing, he is becoming relatively serious. For the past two years he has been instructing Northern California juniors and he has earned a reputation as a fine tennis pro. Every day he teaches at beautiful Davie Stadium in Piedmont on the edge of Oakland. . . . Frank is not out of competitive tennis. He just recently had two match points against Pancho Gonzales, but, although his playing days are far from over, the large percentage of his time is spent in teaching.

WALTER L. PATE

by Axel Kaufmann

It is sometimes difficult to realize, considering the worldwide interest in and scope of tennis, that the entire history of the sport encompasses a period of time which still falls within the lifespan of people still on the scene who have contributed to making it great. One such person, and undoubtedly the dean of the group, is Walter L. ("Cap") Pate, who can today look back upon nearly three quarters of a century of observation, participation and service.

Born in 1878 (a year which comes close to coinciding with the introduction of the game in America), this still-active lawyer saw the first Davis Cup encounter between the United States and the British Isles in 1900, was a player of note from the turn of the century through the twenties, won two national senior doubles championships, and served the United States Lawn Tennis Association in numerous capacities, including that of captain of the Davis Cup team. His name is associated with the regaining of the cup in 1937 and again in 1946 and its successful defense in 1938; with the founding of the Brooklyn Tennis Club; with the initiation of the Nassau Country Club invitation tournament; and with the start of the film library of great players. But most of all he is proud of having been responsible for the international standardization of the tennis ball.

"Cap" is a true Easterner by origin and residence, having spent nearly all of his life in and around New York City. He was born in Brooklyn and there attended Adelphi Academy, going on to Cornell University to combine liberal arts studies with those of the law. He was graduated with honors in 1899 and was admitted to the bar the following year.

His first tennis was played as a youngster on the courts in Prospect Park, but only in a minor way. Only after graduation did he take up tennis again. The lack of courts near home presented no obstacle to the enterprising young lawyer. A vacant lot on Atlantic near Franklin Avenue, large enough for three courts and a dressing shack, caught his eye, and a short while later the Brooklyn Tennis Club came into existence. Cap was both its president and perennial club champion.

In 1904 he was married to Marian Davol and in 1906 he ventured far north to the West Side Tennis Club, then near Columbia University, to compete in his first sanctioned tournament, the Metropolitan championship. During the ensuing years Cap became a "regular" on the circuit and was ranked nationally many times. He played in every national championship from 1906 to 1920, when he suffered a dislocated hip, the result of a bad fall. While he recovered, the injury caused a permanent lameness.

In 1912 he was instrumental in adding the Nassau Country Club invitation to the list of annual grass court events, placing in competition a magnificent challenge bowl which today bears the names of many national champions and has never been retired. Tilden, Dick Williams and Bobby Riggs each have two legs on the bowl. Pate had moved to Locust Valley, Long Island, with his wife and children, joined Nassau and felt that it was an ideal setting for a tournament. It was the only big tournament which did not charge either the participants or spectators.

The year 1912 marked two other occurrences. Cap's name first appeared on the letterhead of his law firm as a partner, and he began his long association with the USLTA in official capacity by serving on the ranking committee. During his third term on this committee, he made historic headlines when *American Lawn Tennis* magazine published his report setting forth the reasons for ranking Maurie McLoughlin at No. 1, although he had been beaten in the finals of the Nationals. It was the first time that the champion did not head the list. "Maurie had not lost a match all year," Cap recalls, "except to R. Norris Williams 2d in the final of the national championships." The USLTA annual meeting upheld the ranking.

World War I temporarily interrupted Cap's tennis activities. While his efforts to join the armed forces were unsuccessful because of over-age, he did see overseas service with a YMCA group in France. . . . In 1924 he won his first national title, the senior doubles. Sam Hardy was his partner, and they repeated the following year. In 1926, however, the misfortune of a broken ankle (acquired during the final match in the same event) called a wholly involuntary halt to Cap's competitive career.

In the meantime, his USLTA activities had expanded considerably and he had graduated from the ranking committee to the ball committee (later tennis supplies committee). It was in this innocuous-sounding post, which he held for 39 years, that he feels he has made his greatest contribution to tennis. . . . In order to further international competition by eliminating the handicap of an unfamiliar ball (and he feels that before standardization the type of ball used had much to do with the outcome of Davis Cup matches), Cap suggested to the International Lawn Tennis Federation that an international ball committee be appointed to study the matter and reach an agreement on standards acceptable to all. He met with a favorable response and in 1924 was made chairman of a committee of five, one each from Britain, France, Germany, Australia and the United States. This committee met in London in the spring of the following year, consulted various ball manufacturers, and after numerous sessions reached compromise agreements on all four specifications (weight, size, bounce and hardness or compression). These were embodied in Rule 3 of the Rules of Lawn Tennis, which was adopted unanimously by the Federation. . . .

Several years after the adoption of Rule 3, Cap embarked on another project which, if it was not as far-reaching in effect, was at least of major significance. By taking and directing the first slow-motion films of great players, he insured that their styles would be perpetuated and available for study and record. Cap personally filmed over 20,000 feet of champions in action, later edited his material and added explanatory titles (sound was not yet available) until he had six reels of 1,000 feet each of Tilden, Johnston, Helen Wills and several other leading players. These films became the nucleus of the USLTA's film library and were shown all over the country at clubs, schools and colleges. Cap himself lectured with them at Princeton, Columbia, Cornell and many high schools and clubs.

As his involuntary retirement from competition left more time available for service in official capacity, Cap became one of the backbones of the USLTA. In addition to the chairmanships already described, he was placed on the executive committee, the court construction committee and others, was president of the Eastern Lawn Tennis Association in 1926, a member of the committee that built the Forest Hills Stadium, vice president of the West Side Tennis Club, president of the Cornell Club of New York and the Nassau Country Club, a member of the International Lawn Tennis Club of England, France, Australia and the United States. In 1935 he was named by Walter Merrill Hall captain of the Davis Cup team. . . .

In 1937 the encounter with the German Davis Cup team (in the interzone round) turned into one of the high points of Davis Cup history. On the final day, with the score tied 2 all, Budge and Baron Gottfried von Cramm took the court for what was to be perhaps the greatest match ever played.

"Since Don had beaten Gottfried in straight sets in both the Queen's and Wimbledon finals, I was not particularly worried," Cap reminisces. "How wrong I was! Von Cramm won the first two sets, lost the next two to Don's superlative play and pulled ahead 4–1 in the fifth. As they crossed sides I handed Don a towel and patted him on the back. He then made the famous remark that has so often been quoted: 'Don't worry, Cap, I won't let you down.' He didn't. Nine games and eight match points later he won. Both men scored over fifty per cent earned points, which indicates the quality of the play."

The challenge round was almost anticlimactic. Fred Perry had turned professional, and Budge, Gene Mako and Frank Parker joined forces to win from the English by 4–1. On the return trip Cap was presented with a surprise package, a watch bearing the inscription "To Cap, from the United States Davis Cup Team, 1937."

In 1938 Cap's team successfully staved off Australia's challenge, but the following year Bromwich and Quist ruled over a new Budge-less team, and the cup once more went overseas, where it remained for the duration of the Second World War.

In 1946 Cap was again the logical choice to mastermind and supervise the American effort, and he acceded to the USLTA's request that he lead the journey Down Under. Kramer, Schroeder, Parker, Talbert, Mulloy and Tom Brown received the nod of the selection committee for the trip, with a free rein going to Cap for the actual choice of the team. He picked Kramer, then the world's outstanding player, and Schroeder, whose aggressive tactics, he felt, stood the best chance against Bromwich's baseline consistency. The team in a 5–1 vote for Ted supported his thinking. The collective judgment was borne out by the result, a sweeping 5–0 victory despite 8–5 betting odds against the U. S.

DON MCNEILL

by F. G. McMurray

Well, readers of the *Lone Star Tennis* magazine, I hardly expected to be able to write about an Oklahoman as national amateur champion, in this, my second message to you. Of course, I am delighted to be able to do so.

Our new national champion, Don McNeill, first came into public notice generally by his good showing in 1937, when he zoomed to a ninth rank among the nation's best players. This was his second season playing in the Eastern grass court tournaments. He was then a sophomore in Kenyon College, Gambier, Ohio.

During the 1938 season Don dropped to number 13 in the rankings. But in the fall he was invited to become a member of an American team which was to tour Europe and Asia. He left his studies at Kenyon College and, with three other American tennis players, toured and played in Hawaii, Japan, India, Egypt, Greece, France, Sweden and England. He met and defeated the best players in these countries, including Gottfried von Cramm, then regarded as the world's best amateur.

The tour gave Don a polish and certainty about his game which, no doubt, contributed greatly to his climax win of the French hard court championship in 1939. He returned to Kenyon some weeks late but worked with the same concentration that has helped him pull out many a tough match and was graduated cum laude in June 1940. During the year he was a member of the school fencing team and of the debating team.

Don played brilliantly in the Oklahoma indoor tournament during the Christmas holidays last winter and went to New Orleans, where he won the Sugar Bowl tourney. Bruce Barnes, now a professional and a former University of Texas player, went to Kenyon to take up the tennis coaching duties. He was quoted as saying Don had the makings of a champion.

Don started his summer of play in June and since then he has been defeated only three times. In each case the winner was Robert Riggs. They have battled repeatedly since the days when they were both juniors, with Riggs holding a slight edge in matches. But now that Don has defeated him for the French hard court, the U.S. clay court and the national grass titles, I guess we cannot begrudge the wins Bobby has had.

You might enjoy some of the personal sidelights on the making of a champion. It has been my good fortune to know Don since he was twelve years old. He was born at Chickasha, Oklahoma, on April 30, 1918, and is therefore 22 years of age. Don attended Taft Junior High School in Oklahoma City, and under Coach Mace Spangler learned the principles of volleying. He approached the net with great flat-footed strides. In his gangly teen-age his movements seemed made up of elbow and knee action. Nevertheless, he became state junior high singles champion, then went to Classen High School, where Coach Earl Coffey put him through the sprouts of court strategy and continuous attack and hard, controlled driving.

Don accounted for the state high school title in both his junior and senior years and in February, after graduation, entered Kenyon College. During these preliminary years I have seen him with George Counts and Ed Lindsey sweeping rain puddles or snowspots off the Oklahoma Tennis Club courts in order to practice.

I heard Bob say to Don Kamrath during the state indoor tournament here last winter, "Don, do you remember that I asked you to show me how to hit a backhand after you defeated me in a junior match? We went on the court and you demonstrated your method. I have never changed the fundamentals." Now the stroke is Don's forte. It comes off the court faster than his forehand, and his backhand crosscourt shot from a short ball is the envy of all who have watched it. It was this shot Ted Husing could only gasp about in the last game of the championship match at Forest Hills. Ted said, "This is match point. Riggs serves with deliberation and great concentration. He rushes the net. McNeill returns with a crosscourt backhand and the ball is— Oh! McNeill is the new national champion!" . . .

Don's sportsmanship was evidenced in his giving Riggs the second point of the last game in the championship because the net judge ruled Bobby had touched the net with his foot on a close volley while Bobby thought he did not so lose the point. . . . Don's square-shooting is based on the background of a very wonderful family, of mother, father and sister Mary Helen. I have heard Mrs. McNeill say, "I'd rather the sports writers would say Don was a true gentleman than to have him win the greatest title on earth."

That the writers have said just that, that Don has won the title which, since the war, is the greatest on earth, and that he is ours—here in the Southwest—I guess we can all fill up our lungs and strut a bit. Anyhow, it is lots of fun.

JOE HUNT

by Allison Danzig

The blow fell several weeks ago, but the impact is no less hard to take today. A Grumman Hellcat making a run on a target 10,000 feet over Daytona Beach in a routine gunnery practice flight went into a spin and crashed into the sea. Before rescue and crash boats could reach the scene the plane sank.

The pilot of that Hellcat was Lieutenant Joseph Raphael Hunt, USN, national tennis champion in 1943 and a member of the varsity football squad at Annapolis for two years.

Every fine young life snuffed out in the daily grist of war brings tragedy to some home and grief to many. It makes no difference who the boy was or what he had accomplished in his brief span of years. The loss is as overwhelming to someone in the casualty of a lad off the farm or a truck as when a young athlete or celebrity of any calling is taken. In the latter case the blow simply is more far-reaching in bringing home the terrible price that youth pays for the mistakes of the older generation and the fact that there are no distinctions in the toll that war takes.

The loss of Joe Hunt happens to bring this home to the writer of these lines more than has any other. Here was a youth who represented the finest in young manhood. Physically he was an Apollo, magnificently proportioned and strikingly handsome in a masculine way, with the jaw of a fighter.

No finer specimen of an athlete has been seen in the Forest Hills Stadium, nor a straighter living one. For a youngster he had a remarkably sound sense of values from the time he first came East from Los Angeles as a junior. Fame did not go to his head. He was serious in his outlook but did not take himself or his position in tennis that way.

Tennis was never more than a game to him, to be played to win for all he was worth but not to be regarded as the be-all and object of his life. He had a code and he lived up to it without any thought of being a beau sabreur. He did the right and fair thing instinctively.

At Annapolis he was the most famous tennis player ever to matriculate in the academy, but the upper classmen never found it necessary to make him forget it. He took his lumps on the B squad when he went out for football and spent most of the time on the bench when he was promoted to the varsity without a sign of temperament.

Coach Swede Larsen spoke highly of his ability, but there were too many good, experienced backs at Annapolis at the time for him to see much action. He was grateful that he had a chance to play briefly against Army. Annapolis and West Point know how to handle boys who are too big for their britches. There is no instance of where Joe had to be given any part of the treatment.

After getting his ensign's stripe, Hunt went to sea. He served aboard a destroyer in the Pacific when there wasn't much left of our fleet in that ocean and in 1943 he saw action in the Atlantic. Between those tours of duty, while awaiting orders, he won the national championship at Forest Hills.

Back at sea in the Atlantic, Joe got the bug to be a flier. Some tried to discourage him, but he made up his mind. Returning to port late in 1943, he applied for transfer to the Naval Air Force. It wasn't alone the glamour and thrill of being a fighter pilot that appealed to him. Aviation, he decided, was to be the big thing in the future and he wanted to get in on it.

So, shortly before Christmas in 1943, Joe set out for the Naval Air Training Station at Dallas, Texas, with his lovely wife, who had made a name for herself in tennis as Jacque Virgil.

Young Hunt had looked forward to resuming his tennis when the war should end. He wanted to defend his championship at least once. He hoped that he might be a member of the team that would go to Australia to challenge for the Davis Cup when the international matches are resumed. His father, Reuben Hunt, who was a player of rank himself on the Pacific Coast, shared those hopes, as did his mother.

There are other fathers whose hopes have been similarly ended. There can hardly be any among them who has more cherished memories to comfort him in his loss than has Reuben Hunt. Joe was every inch the ideal of what every parent would like his son to be. He was fine all the way through. Tennis isn't going to be the same without him.

FROM FLANNELS TO KHAKI AND BLUE

by Allison Danzig

Possibly Nostradamus, who could dip centuries into the future and come up with the sixty-four-dollar answers, foresaw it back in the distant ages, but who else could have suspected it? A weary old warrior calls in an erstwhile Austrian corporal and paperhanger to take over the reins of Government in Berlin in 1933, and ten years later, four thousand miles away, Newport, Seabright, Longwood, Nassau, Spring Lake, East Hampton and Manchester are wiped off the tennis map.

Admittedly, direr consequences have attended the fateful decision of Hindenburg than the temporary eclipse of a game in some of its most

292 THE FIRESIDE BOOK OF TENNIS

pleasurable capitals, to which might be added Wimbledon, St. Cloud and Melbourne. To Rotterdam, Lidice and Coventry, being wiped off the map is something more than a figure of speech.

But to one who would ordinarily be lazying in the Southampton surf (when he ought to be on duty watching the tennis at the Meadow Club) on this day in August and finds himself, instead, between stints such as this, wrestling with the sweet mystery of life in onion, tomato, corn and cabbage seed, the fate of Newport, Seabright, etc., brings the war closer to home.

It isn't the denial of the pleasant life that goes with tournament week in these watering colonies that hits home, though the current crop on Bailey's Beach would be a welcome change from spinach and squash. It is the thought of the young men who would be cavorting on the courts there had not the aged field marshal given in to a rabble-rouser whom his Prussian caste held in the contempt Badoglio had for the deserter who led the march on Rome in 1922.

The tennis amateur has not been the most popular of the nation's athletic idols. It was a long fight before the public accepted him as an athlete. The social background of the game, the politeness of the players to each other and of the gallery in keeping a decorous silence, and the nomenclature of the sport, particularly the "love" element in the scoring, gave rise to an unjust conception of the character of the game.

Tennis players just didn't rate with the virile breed of he-men represented by Babe Ruth, Jack Dempsey, Red Grange, Johnny Weissmuller, Tommy Hitchcock, Walter Hagen and Bobby Jones. Today, however, with most of the famous tournaments on the grass court circuit closed down, the tennis player is showing that he does rate.

There's Wilmer Allison, national champion in 1935. It's Lieutenant Colonel Allison now. A radio expert with his own amateur sending station before the war, Allison has practically been living in Army bombers, flying the oceans to set up radio installations. There's his doubles partner, Johnny Van Ryn, a lieutenant in the Navy.

Ramsay Potts didn't make the headlines with his racket but Captain Potts was decorated with the Air Medal by Major General Lewis H. Brereton for valor in the Middle East. Robert Vaupell of Seattle was another amateur who won even less distinction on the courts, but Captain Vaupell, the dive-bombing ace, won the Purple Heart, the Navy Cross and the Air Medal in action at Guadalcanal.

Lieutenant Ernest Sutter, former intercollegiate champion from Tulane, was in the landing force that invaded French North Africa and has a shattered right arm that may never wield a racket again in tournament competition. Little Frank Guernsey, another winner of the intercollegiate crown, from Rice, is one of the Army's crack pilots and proved it in the Aleutians. Ensign Kendall Cramm, still another college player, died a hero's death in the Pacific after getting all his men safely off his torpedoed ship.

There's Gil Hall. It's Sergeant Hall now. Gil was in the tanks in World War One. He couldn't get in fast enough after Pearl Harbor. Though well past 40, he's taking his lumps again in those fire-spitting steel monsters, which is a lot different from taking lumps in his spot of tea on Bailey's Beach.

Off went Bitsy Grant, too. He didn't get in quite so soon, but it wasn't his fault. Bitsy is so small he was shooed off by dozens of recruiting sergeants before he finally talked his way into the Army. It's Sergeant Grant who tells the company to fall in, and no nonsense and wipe that smile off.

They called Frank Kovacs "screwball" when he was staging his sitdown strike at Forest Hills, but, aside from reporting to his training camp with golf sticks and ukulele, he's been strictly business in the job of soldiering. From buck private he has worked his way up to lieutenant in the Southwest Pacific, as Hal Surface has done in India.

Ted Schroeder, national champion, is a lieutenant in the Navy, and so is Gardnar Mulloy, third in the ranking. Frank Parker, No. 2, is in the Army.

Donald McNeill, Joe Hunt, Frank Shields, Elwood Cooke, Frank Bowden, Russell Bobbitt, Sandy Davenport, Norman Anderson, Chauncey Steele, Charles Mattmann, Harris Everett and Bruce Barnes, all recent headliners, hold commissions.

These are only some of the better-known players in service. It's enough to show that tennis has gone off to war as have all other sports and that, despite their love–forty and lip service to the social amenities, the boys in the ice cream pants aren't any comfort to Tojo or Adolf.

THE UNSEEDED SEMI-FINALIST

by Welby Van Horn

In 1939, Australia defeated the United States in the Challenge Round at Merion in Pennsylvania. One week after Merion, I won my most exciting amateur match by beating Jack Bromwich in the semi-finals of the National Singles at Forest Hills. Bromwich was No. 2 in the world and, with Adrian Quist, shared in the Aussie Davis Cup win.

I was unseeded at Forest Hills and had only a Class "A" men's ranking (Class "A" often represented a ranking of No. 30 to 50 among the U.S. men) and a U.S. junior ranking of No. 2 from the previous year. I managed to squeeze by two early round matches and this set the stage for an unexpected four-set win over Elwood Cooke in the round before the quarter-finals (Cooke was Wimbledon finalist to Riggs during the summer of 1939). In the quarter-finals, I scored another upset in five sets against Wayne Sabin (Sabin had eliminated Adrian Quist in the previous round).

My semi-final with Bromwich was expected to result in an easy win for my opponent. I had no business being in the semi-finals, much less against such formidable opposition. Although I was determined to do my best, the match turned into an immediate rout as Brom won the first set 6–2 and ran the first five games in the second set. At this point it was "farewell to Welby," and the words "bewildered" and "desperate" would best describe my confused efforts to stem the tide. However, from here on, the changeable fortunes of the match would more aptly fit a ring battle ("he's down, he's up, he's down again, he's up again") than a tennis encounter. The rapid reverses in the match had the crowd and Bromwich bewildered, and I was the only calm one in the enclosure.

At 0–5, I ran four games in a row with drop shots and lobs (almost unthinkable in today's "big game" tactics), but Brom won the tenth game for the set, 6–4. I pursued the same strategy in the third set and won, 6–2. After the rest period, we traded serves and then Brom went to 4–1, forty-love. That clinched it—almost! Just as quickly as I had lost my touch, I regained it again and ran five successive games for the set, 6–4. I leave it to your imagination to visualize the physical and mental pressure on one who is within a set of being the youngest player ever to reach the final of the U.S. men's singles championship.

We fought to 6–6 in games in the fifth set. Having served first, I was never worse than even and had the opportunity of going ahead if I could break Brom's delivery. At 6–7, Brom's serve, I did just that. I was in the finals! Few spectators could spell my name correctly and fewer had ever heard of me. It was the most exciting experience of my brief amateur career and, though Riggs made short work of me in the finals (6–4, 6–2, 6–4), it was a long time before I returned to orbit.

PANCHO

by Allison Danzig

The world champion in sport, so the book says, reaches the top only after years of striving to improve himself through sacrifice and abnegation. To remain there entails a continuation of the hard work and the abjuring of the things of the flesh.

Not so with Richard (Pancho) Gonzales.

The supreme ruler of the tennis courts came up the easy way in an almost unbelievably sudden ascension. And staying on top has meant no more for him than doing what comes naturally. It has been fun all the way, and no sacrifice at all. That's his story, and what this handsome six-foot three-inch athlete from Los Angeles tells you, in his positive, uninhibited way, you believe.

Twenty-nine years old this month, Pancho Gonzales is sitting on top of the world, with money in the bank, a pretty, tiny wife, Henrietta, who bubbles with fun (except when anyone calls her Richard "Pancho"), three healthy sons, and no one on the immediate horizon to challenge his suzerainty of the courts. He expects to receive around $60,000 from promoter Jack Kramer when the American phase of his tour with Kenneth Rosewall of Australia—which began in Melbourne last January—ends May 27 in California. And he could add another $25,000 during the year from tournaments in this country and abroad, although he may have contract trouble with Kramer if his demand for a greater share of the take than the 25 per cent he has been getting is not granted.

"The only worry I have," says Gonzales, "is the income tax." Possibly the fact that Uncle Sam will take so large a percentage of anything additional he makes in 1957 may help to explain his decision not to go on a South American tour with the Kramer ensemble in June. He says the reason is that he wants to rest and be with his family.

On the subject of what being the world's top player has meant in the way of hard work and denying himself the pleasures of life, Pancho says:

"I never felt I had to sacrifice or work, because I enjoy tennis so much. To me this is fun—as a professional the same as it was when I was an amateur. The hardest part of it is when you lay off and have to work to keep in condition. While on tour I don't regard it as work. I can't go to the movies or watch television as often as I would like because of the eye strain. There are eight hours during the day when you have nothing to do, lying around for the match in the evening. It can get boring. But once I'm on the court I'm doing the thing I want to do, and I am very happy with my life."

It may have been fun for Gonzales as an amateur, but until he got to the top he had lean pickings and very little change in his pocket to satisfy his big appetite. In 1947, his first year on the Eastern grass court circuit, the leggy, swarthy kid from the Coast was grubbing it in a small, isolated rooming house, some miles away from the club where he was competing in the national doubles championship matches. When a tennis reporter asked him to dinner, the home-cooked meal was a royal treat. And his host's children took a greater liking to him than they have to almost any other tennis player.

It was only a year later that Gonzales won the championship of the United States at Forest Hills. He had had no professional coaching—in fact, he was entirely self-taught. It was not only his second season of play on grass courts but his second in men's competition on any surface, incredible as it seems. In all the history of tennis no one has even approached this amazingly quick rise to the pinnacle. William Tilden, recognized generally as the greatest player of all time, had slaved for years on the practice court and in tournaments before he won the national championship for the first time at the age of 27.

Pancho began to play in boys' tournaments in 1942 at the age of 14, two years after his mother had given him a 50-cent racket for Christmas (he had quickly come to the decision that tennis, rather than baseball, was his game because of its speed). In 1943 he was ranked as the No. 1 boy in Southern California.

Then his tournament career came to an abrupt halt. He was disqualified for not going to school ("I was playing hooky," he admits with a grin). Not until 1947, after a hitch in the Navy, did he play against ranking players. He won the Southern California championship in May of that year to gain the first ranking ever accorded him—No. 17 nationally. Sixteen months later, in September 1948, he won the national crown at Forest Hills as an outsider who was seeded last.

Once he became national champion, Gonzales' fortunes began to improve. He was a drawing card with his "big" game, his speed and grace of movement, superb physique and swarthy handsomeness. He no longer had to room out in the sticks. He ate regularly and to his fill.

But he wasn't getting rich, as tennis champions are commonly supposed to. He won the championship again in 1949, played on the Davis Cup team, helping the United States retain the trophy, and then in October 1949 began his professional career, going on tour with Kramer.

"As an amateur," says Gonzales, "I saved enough from the expense money I received to be able to practice and play occasionally in the off season. You can't hold a steady job and hope to be a top amateur player. You have to keep in competition most of the year to keep your game up with the others' and maintain the physical condition tennis requires. I just managed to get by when I was out of competition, but I had to scrape. When I got married, I really had to pinch pennies. Lucky that Henrietta is so small and doesn't eat much."

Now, as a professional, Pancho lives it up the year round with no financial worries. He travels in style, with his brother Ralph at the wheel, in one of his hot-rod cars that he loves to tinker with—a Ford with a 350-horsepower Cadillac engine. A drag racing enthusiast who has driven 114.8 miles per hour (his service, recorded electronically, travels 112.88 miles per hour), Pancho is taking no chances while in the prime of his tennis career and earning power. He will have no part of road racing but drives only in carefully supervised tests on airstrips.

Comparing professional and amateur tennis, Gonzales says that there is a certain amount of strain to playing now that was missing when he was competing just for the fun.

"There is more involved now," he explains. "As an amateur you don't work at it as a business, but purely for the enjoyment. As a pro, every time I lose or come close to losing it is a strain. It takes away from your livelihood. You never let up on your opponent. Every victory helps to ensure your ending up on top in the tour and staying in the big money the next year. Also, the amateur plays under ideal conditions and in the daytime. The pro plays mostly at night, indoors. He jumps from town to town.

"But, in one respect, there is more strain in amateur tennis. When you play on the Davis Cup team, the pressure is greater than I have known as a pro. You are representing your country and you can't let your team down. Also, you are younger and not as able to overcome the nervousness.

"The top amateur meets a lot of rich people and gets invitations to their homes. But if he isn't careful all the partying can hurt his training. The pro doesn't find himself in the limelight as much. The only thing comparable in professional tennis is when you play in Australia, where they go mad about any kind of tennis.

"The competition is tougher in pro tennis. It stands to reason that it should be. You are playing against the best men in the world."

Asked to compare his game now with what it was when he was amateur champion and to rate himself with the other professionals, Pancho does so with his characteristic realism. He has no false modesty. He believes he is the world's best player and says so. He said so publicly a short while ago when he announced that he was dissatisfied with his contract and threatened to break with Kramer.

"I'm the best player in the world," he declared. "I am in a position to call the shots."

At the same time, Gonzales readily admits to weaknesses in his game, says that his forehand and backhand are not so good as were Kramer's and Donald Budge's ground strokes, and agrees that he would not be on top were it not for his service and quickness of movement and the advantage these give him on indoor courts.

"I am more consistent now than I was before I turned pro," he says. "As an amateur I was good one day and bad the next. Now I keep my game on a high level fairly regularly, though I have my losses. My service has always been strong. It came to me naturally and has been my biggest asset. My service is no better now than it was in my amateur days, but I volley and hit my ground strokes better. My return of service has always been the weak part of my game. I have a tendency to step backward instead of forward.

"I think I am entitled to the top position in pro tennis and that my record against Tony Trabert and Ken Rosewall and against other players in tournaments proves it. [Pancho defeated Trabert, 74 matches to 27, on tour last season and has won 40 of his first 60 matches with Rosewall on their current tour.] It is my service and the fact that the matches are played mostly indoors that give me my advantage. My serve is strongest indoors and I have the reach for the net attack which is so important in the indoor game.

"My toughest opponents have been Frank Sedgman and Kramer. Sedgman is capable of lifting his game to great heights. Kramer was too good for me when I first turned professional [he defeated Gonzales, 96 matches to 27, in their 1949–50 tour], but I think that my game has improved since then. Segura is a tough little opponent, too."

Francisco (Pancho) Segura, a little South American from Guayaquil, Ecuador, who has the best two-handed forehand the game probably has known, won the Australian professional championship recently. He rates Gonzales the world's No. 1 player, but only because of his service.

Little Pancho goes so far as to declare that big Pancho would not be an outstanding player were it not for his serve. He says that on any surface Rosewall is a better player than Gonzales, except in the service department. "Rosewall," says Segura, "is sounder off the ground. He returns service more consistently and his passing shots are better. Gonzales has more great shots but he is not as reliable. He uses a little too much wrist. He flicks the ball and has no long follow-through."

But no one, Segura concedes, is more consistent than Gonzales in getting his first service into play. When he does, he adds, "You can't attack him. You can't make him work indoors. Outdoors, you can return his service with more length and make him work more to win the points.

"Pancho is a natural athlete. If he worked more on his strokes and trained more, he could be even tougher than he is. He misses a lot of returns of service and he could improve his lobbing and passing shots."

As Segura points out, Gonzales does not work or train as seriously as do others. On tour, Rosewall is in bed half an hour after his match. Pancho will go out for a steak, and it may be 2 or 3 in the morning before he is in bed. "Pancho is a very individual person," says Segura. "He likes to be alone and doesn't pal around much. But he's a good guy."

Gonzales admits to taking training less seriously than Rosewall. "That little guy is in bed at 11," he objects. "His determination and incentive keep you on your toes to beat him."

Big Pancho likes to stay up late and to sleep late. He likes to bowl and play snooker, to go hunting in the mountains. On Sundays when he is at home in Los Angeles, he and Henrietta spend the entire day at the drag races. "Tennis has been good to me," he says. "You wonder why some players get so much and others who work so hard get so little."

Gonzales is one of the few top professionals who have declared themselves ready to take part in an open tournament should one be held. He thinks that an open championship would give a tremendous boost to tennis, just as it has to golf, awakening wider interest in the game and helping to build up the standard of play.

"I would like to be a part of an open tournament," says Pancho, "and would help even though it would hurt me financially. It would hurt me, the top amateur who turns professional and the promoter who books our tour. But the top pros should play even if they take a loss."

Gonzales finds the standard of amateur play in the United States very poor and sees no chance of Australia's losing the Davis Cup this year. He considers Ashley Cooper, the new Australian champion, probably the best amateur in the world.

"We keep using the older players," he objects. "We don't give the younger players enough of a chance. Sam Giammalva was given a chance last year and made the best showing in Australia. We should work with the kids coming up and see that they get in shape. Those who show the desire and work hard should be sent to Wimbledon and put on the Davis Cup team."

It can be pointed out that the state of American amateur tennis is not quite so bad as it seems, considering the many losses of top players to the professional ranks. It can be pointed out further that had not a certain Pancho Gonzales turned pro after licking the Australians in 1949, the United States probably would still have the Davis Cup.

"You got a point," Pancho admits with a grin.

GOOD GUY OR ANTI-HERO?

by Bob Addie

Richard (Pancho) Gonzales-Gonzales is up to his old tricks of confusing the public. Some of the confusion is over the spelling of his name and some is whether to regard the volcanic Californian as a hero or a villain.

The 41-year-old veteran was asked yesterday how he spells his name, because it has been carried with a "z" interchangeably with an "s" on the end.

"The correct spelling of my last name is with a final 'z,' " he said, "but it has been spelled with a final 's' so long that now I must sign my checks that way. From now on just make it Gonzales."

So that clears that up. If a man's castle is his home, his checkbook signature is his personal coat of arms. But what about the other confusion? Is Pancho Gonzales one of the good guys or is he an anti-hero?

Gonzales irritated proper Britishers at Wimbledon Tuesday afternoon while playing Charles Pasarell. Gonzales kept complaining it was so dark he couldn't see the ball. The 25-year-old Pasarell won the first two sets, 24–22 and 6–1. Everybody figured that when the match resumed, the old boy would be worn out.

Gonzales, never known for his couth, kept beefing all the way off the center court Tuesday and the normally polite Wimbledon crowd jeered. The boorish conduct displayed by the American chap just isn't tolerated, doncha know.

On Wednesday, Pasarell and Gonzales were at it again. But the gasping old pro took the next three sets, 16–14, 6–3 and 11–9, to win the match. The 112 games set a Wimbledon record.

Yesterday, apparently refreshed, Gonzales knocked off a Swedish player named Ove Bengtson in straight sets. But the sports world still was buzzing over the Gonzales-Pasarell match and the dogged courage of the fading veteran. That always gets a crowd, and at the end of the marathon Wednesday, Wimbledon spectators forgot their dislike for the conduct of the American and cheered him wildly. It had to be a great moment in sports and perhaps a wry satisfaction for loner Gonzales.

Pasarell was only 5 years old when Gonzales won his second straight U.S. amateur title at Forest Hills in 1949 by beating Ted Schroeder in a match remarkably similar to the Wimbledon marathon. Schroeder won the first two sets, 18–16 and 6–2. But Gonzales was on 21-year-old legs then and he came back to win the next three sets and the championship.

Gonzales, one of seven children, was a high school dropout. His mother, Mexican-born Mrs. Manuel Gonzalez (with a "z" on the end), hired out as a seamstress in Los Angeles. Young Gonzales became interested in tennis when his mother bought him a 50-cent drugstore racket for Christmas.

The boy played on public courts and was not invited to tournaments at exclusive country clubs. Yet he beat another California boy, Herbie Flam, five out of six times when Flam was national junior champion.

Gonzales enlisted in the Navy at 17. And when he returned to civilian life, his military service opened doors his public courts background could not.

Gonzales finally was sponsored by the Southern California Tennis Association, which financed his trip East. . . .

Gonzales signed as a pro with Jack Kramer and the two had a series of contract squabbles. In 1958 Gonzales was playing Lew Hoad in Melbourne and objected to a linesman's call which eventually lost him the match. Gonzales then slammed a ball into the crowd and stomped off. Not even Ted Williams got oneupsmanship on his critics so dramatically.

In 1963 Gonzales was suspended by his fellow pros for signing for a television series without the group's permission. Only in January, again in Australia, Gonzales was playing doubles with Spain's Andres Gimeno when he suddenly walked off the courts. "I'm tired," he shouted. "I'm leaving."

Apparently, Gonzales was not about to leave in his match against Pasarell. Gonzales is a hair shirt. He's been an angry young man and now he's an angry middle-aged man.

And yet he proved that an athlete who gives his last full measure of determination still is admired and applauded. Gonzales may have the mind of a scold but he has the heart of a champion.

HIS TOUGHEST RIVAL

by Dave Anderson

In reflecting on more than two decades of quality tennis, Richard (Pancho) Gonzales chose Lew Hoad, one of his many Australian rivals, as "probably the best and toughest player when he wanted to be" of all his famous opponents.

Gonzales put Hoad, Rod Laver, Don Budge, Jack Kramer and Frank Sedgman on the same competitive plateau. He selected Francisco (Pancho) Segura as the "most underrated" player.

At the age of 41, Gonzales has remained a headline performer. He will oppose Laver tonight at Madison Square Garden in a $10,000 winner-take-all match, the start of the Tennis Champions, Inc., $200,000 classic challenge series. But his career as a touring pro began two decades ago after he had twice won as an amateur at Forest Hills.

"Budge was still playing then," Gonzales said, "and he was past his peak. He gave up quickly when he got tired, but I would've dreaded playing him at his best. He had a great backhand, he always hit it firmly whether driving it or placing it. Budge would've been tough for Laver because Rod's natural left-handed serve would have spun to Don's backhand.

"Jack Kramer wasn't a natural player. He wasn't too fast or too quick, but he had a knack of winning.

"Hoad was probably the best and toughest player when he wanted to be. After his first two years on the tour, his back injury plagued him so much he lost his desire to practice. He was the only man to beat me in a head-to-head tour, 15 to 13. I had blisters under my blisters from the punishment. But after that tour, he never had the desire again.

"Sedgman was one of the physically strongest players—he, Hoad and Laver. He never labored in a long match. He might get tired from nervous energy, but never physically. Only two players beat him consistently—Jack and myself.

"What makes Laver great is his desire and his ability to lift his game when the going is tough. And being a left-hander gives him a 5 per cent advantage, because you don't play a left-hander that often. He is so great offensively that you forget he's great defensively. He intimidates most players by flicking the ball, but Hoad would've flicked it back."

Of his other opponents, including Ken Rosewall, Gonzales said, "None of them could come close to beating Segura at his best," meaning around 1954.

"As strong as Budge's backhand was, Segura's forehand was even stronger," Gonzales said. "Segura was very accurate with his forehand . . . and he had a great lob off his backhand, which meant you needed a good overhead. Segura demoralized Rosewall a decade ago when we were on the tour. What I did to Rosewall, Segura did even worse."

Of the younger players, he selected Tom Okker of the Netherlands as "having the most potential," but criticized the others.

"Arthur Ashe doesn't train or practice hard enough; there are ten players better than he is. John Newcombe isn't that fast afoot. Tony Roche lacks something some place. I don't think he knows how to train. He's too chunky and it affects him."

Asked to name the players who best exemplified each stroke, Gonzales had a surprise for his backhand volley.

"Rex Hartwig," he said, referring to an Australian of another decade. "He was a strange player. He was in a fog out there on the court. He once told me, 'I don't know what I'm doing,' but he could hit a backhand volley perfectly every time. He was amazing. Segura had the best forehand volley and Hoad had the best overhead.

"Segura and Jack had the best forehands, Budge and Rosewall the best backhands, Rosewall had the best half-volley off the backhand, Segura the best off the forehand. The best baseline players were Kramer, Rosewall and Segura. And for the serve, Jack had a great serve. I'd say that the best servers were Jack and myself."

THE STYLE OF PANCHO GONZALES

by Julius D. Heldman

It is my belief that Pancho Gonzales is the most natural player who ever lived. He never had a tennis lesson and he had almost no tournament competition during his formative years. When he dropped out of school in the tenth grade, the Southern California Tennis Association did not permit him to play in junior tournaments. He was 19 when he played his first big event, which was the Southern California Championships. He defeated 19-year-old Herb Flam, the National Junior Champion.

Two months later, Pancho went back East to play the clay and grass court circuit. His play was spotty, but he managed to earn a No. 17 ranking. The following year (1948) he was No. 1 in the country, beating Eric Sturgess to win at Forest Hills. The next year he again won the Nationals, defeating his old nemesis, Ted Schroeder. He turned professional a few months later and was decisively beaten by Jack Kramer. He had actually had only three summers of top amateur competition and was far from a finished tennis player.

His loss to Kramer put him out of the "big time" in professional tennis. He waited on the sidelines while Kramer annually played against the neophyte pro of the year. Gonzales was eager to get back on the pro tour. His annual competition was limited almost solely to Jack March's World Pro Championships in Cleveland, which he won with monotonous regularity, and yet he did not receive a bid to tour with Kramer's boys. Eventually Pancho got his opportunity. Jake offered him $15,000—an all-time low for a feature player—to play against Tony Trabert, who was to receive $95,000. Gonzales reluctantly accepted, although the amount he received left him with bitter feelings towards his boss which have lasted to this day.

From here on Gonzales was the World Champion. He beat Trabert, Sedgman, Segura, Rosewall, Hoad and Olmedo. He barely edged past Hoad last year, losing in Ampol (tournament) points but winning out on day-by-day play. This year, in a limited tour, he lost fewer matches than ever before in two-night tournament stands against Rosewall, Segura and Olmedo. Last month he announced his retirement from professional competition.

The Gonzales game has always been admired by every top player. He has no critics. He is universally recognized as a great stylist, a hungry competitor and a winner. It is a tennis aphorism that it is far easier to become a world champion than to stay at the top. Once a player has reached the pinnacle he can suffer from fear of losing or he can lose his hunger for winning. Pancho was always courageous and success never softened him. He is as hard today as he was when he was struggling for recognition 13 years ago. He is as tough a competitor as the world has ever known. He gives no quarter, and the old venom that made him become a winner is still the most significant characteristic of his court personality. He is a tennis killer in the best sense of the word.

Gonzales has a great temperament for the game, albeit not in the grand manner of a Gottfried von Cramm or J. Donald Budge. Despite the fact that his attack seems to be motivated by sullen, cold fury or murderous determination, his inner turmoil has never caused him to lose a match. He can play badly and be beaten, or on a given day he can be trounced by a colossus such as Hoad, but his temperamental displays have never affected his own game. If he is licked by Hoad on a Monday, he is more than liable to reverse the score on Tuesday. Losing has the effect of stirring him up, and when he starts winning he is never headed.

At the beginning of a tour, after a four- to six-month layoff, Gonzales has frequently been ten to fifteen pounds too heavy. Within a few weeks he is back to his regular playing weight, leaner and meaner than ever before. Although he has a friendly personality which will immediately make a stranger warm to him, he is basically a "loner"—a little withdrawn and aloof and living very much to himself. He can kid with Segura, josh with Olmedo and horse with Hoad, but mostly he would prefer to travel by himself. Among his close pals he still numbers many old friends from his Exposition Park days. His lack of desire to meet new faces or move in a different group is balanced by long-term friendships with loyal buddies such as Segura.

The Gonzales game has nothing but virtues. Every stroke is beautifully executed, he plays with consummate grace, and he never makes the wrong shot. He makes tennis look too easy. Gonzales has always been known as a great attacker, but he is equally as great in the role of defensive player. Everyone acknowledges the magnificence of his service, volleying and overheads, but he is equally as strong in lobbing, running down balls and nailing placements on passing shots. Segura once said that Gonzales was the only big man who attacked who could also defend well. There is no hint of clumsiness in his game. He covers a prodigious amount of court with so little effort that few spectators realize how well he retrieves.

The Gonzales service is a natural action that epitomizes grace, power, control and placement. The top players sigh when they see the smooth, easy action. There is no trace of a hitch and no extra furbelows. I have never seen a serve so beautifully executed. The toss is no higher than it has to be and it is timed so that he is fully stretched when he hits it. The backswing is continuous, not as big as Trabert's nor as concise as Talbert's. The motion of the backswing blends into the hit and continues into the follow-through without a pause.

Pancho is not a heavy spin artist. His first serve is almost flat and the second has a modicum of slice or roll. Slice, as most players know, is produced by moving the racket face across the ball from right to left; American twist is given to the ball by moving the racket face from left to right with a pronounced wrist snap; the roll is halfway between the slice and twist and gives the ball forward spin rather than spin to the left or right. The slice or roll that Gonzales gives to the ball is just enough for control on second serve.

The strongest part of Gonzales' serve is his ability to put the first ball into play when the chips are down. At 0–40, 15–40 and 30–40, his batting average on first serves must be .950. It is incredible to have so high a percentage while still hitting hard and almost flat. The number of aces served on these important points is also astounding. No other player has so regularly been able to perform this feat, although Budge for two years was probably as tough on the serve. Vines could do it on a given day, but not day in and day out.

Pancho is not a leaper on the overhead and he does not have that wristy, flat snap that bounces them very high. He hits the ball with a little spin in a motion that is almost identical with his serve. He literally pole-axes the overhead just as he punishes the serve. Gonzales seems to have an infallible sense of where to hit the ball; more than any other player he catches his opponent going the wrong way. Bobby Riggs was deceptive, too, and so is Pancho Segura, but Gonzales has the edge of size.

Pancho is a natural net player because of his anticipation and great coordination. He is not a particularly hard volleyer, except for high forehands which he tends to stroke as do so many of the top players. He has excellent control over sharp angle shots, which he hits rather than "dumps." Most players will use a very small action in "dumping" an angle shot, but Gonzales actually punches the ball to make his angle volley. He plays extremely close to the net except, of course, when he is coming in behind service for the first volley. Standing this far in is dangerous but gives Gonzales an almost sure winner if he can touch the ball. He chooses mostly angle shots and only volleys deep on the first ball when he is caught behind the service line. Only a player with great height, reach and anticipation can use this type of tactics; the pros would lob a lesser man unmercifully.

Both the forehand and backhand volley are characterized by underspin. He holds the racket with fingers close in a "hammer grip" on the forehand side. Consistency in the volley is the mark of a top pro in today's game since the leading players literally camp on the net. Gonzales is consistent in his first volleys, which he plays deep, and in his angle volleys, which he hits sharp.

In the old days, the half-volley was a trick shot used by a player caught in "no man's land." Today it is standard equipment and is used regularly by the server in his approach to net. Gonzales on the forehand side will take a rather full swing on the half-volley. On the backhand he prefers to take a backward step so that the ball will rise off the ground. Then he uses heavy underspin, preferably crosscourt, and closes in on the net. He uses this technique so frequently that it is an integral part of his style.

Pancho is one of the few great players who has been able to use the "hammer grip" successfully. The four fingers of the hand are held together rather than spread. Most players feel that the spread fingers give more feel and control, and yet Pancho has excellent touch and precision with the tight grip. His forehand is not grooved in a distinctive pattern: he will hit with closed or open stance, with a big backswing or none at all, and with a high or low follow-through. He would be the despair of a current teaching pro, but Bill Tilden would have loved him. Pancho uses many spins, although none is as pronounced as Tilden's. The latter used them consciously to affect his opponent's play, but Gonzales is simply doing what comes naturally.

Only when Pancho stays back does his forehand take on a grooved look. The backswing is lengthened and the follow-through definitely shows overspin. If you give him any short ball he is completely unpredictable. He may shove it from the hip down the line or leisurely come over it for the crosscourt or snap his wrist to hit the desired spot on the court. He will block, chip or stroke on return of serve, hitting with all his might when he so desires. Mostly he will chip against the big serves since he is a "percentage" player and feels the odds are with the chip in keeping the ball in play. On passing shots he is not afraid to strike out very hard. He is flat and sharp and accurate. It is surprising since it comes in such contrast to his chip return of serve.

The forehand is a good one although not the greatest part of his game. It is certainly not as great a stroke as Segura's, and yet it is one of the better forehands in the pro game. It is not a vulnerable stroke and it stands up well in the heat of battle.

Gonzales can hit the backhand in any of the three classical modes—with underspin, flat or with overspin. He prefers the underspin but will use one of the other two on passing shots. His flat backhand is extremely powerful, particularly when he is run out of court. The underspin is used on return of serve, which is usually a low crosscourt in the left court. This is his chosen gambit to slow down the game momentarily.

His control on the backhand is excellent. It is smooth as silk and well grooved. He generally slices when he comes in, but he will vary his backhands when he stays in the backcourt. Most people never appreciated the soundness of his ground game, but the recent pro tour featuring the three-bounce rule permitted Pancho to demonstrate his all-round competence. He can handle Segura or Rosewall from the baseline!

For a decade players argued the relative merits of Tilden and Budge when discussing the never-ending question of the greatest player of all time.

Budge himself now feels that "Gorgo" has earned the No. 1 spot. The players will never agree on an answer, but the general consensus among top players is a three-way split among Tilden, Budge and Gonzales. The present pros vote for Pancho because he has whipped them all with the net attack. He could not have beaten Don in a baseline duel, and whether he could have dominated Budge via the serve and volley is a question that unfortunately will never be answered.

TOM BROWN

by Jason December

Thomas Pollok Brown, Jr., has a thoroughly unusual tournament history. In 1946, his first big tournament year, he was ranked No. 4 in the nation but was only No. 9 in his own section, Northern California! He was superb at both Wimbledon and Forest Hills, but his early season record in San Francisco was a succession of losses to lesser players. Fortunate for Brown, and the one factor that made him a true champion, was his ability to play at his peak in the important events.

Brown played the complete circuit for three years only, from 1946 through 1948, while he was attending Boalt Law School at the University of California. Ever since, his play has been restricted to interclub matches in San Francisco and local California events. But toward the end of the summer he always comes out of the West like young Lochinvar to make a spectacular appearance at Forest Hills. Strange as it may seem, Brown is playing far less erratic tennis now than in the days when he was a finalist at Wimbledon and Forest Hills. In the late 40's he was known as an in-and-out player, capable of knocking off the best or going out to an unknown; now he seldom falls before a lesser player.

Brown has a game that matches in uniqueness his tennis personality. He is known to his opponents as "The Flailer." Every stroke is a jerky wallop, and he remains one of the last of the attacking baseliners. He has no nerves on the tennis court, for he will whack the ball just as hard on match point as he will at 15–0. He is the most relentless player in the game as well as the most dogged, for he stays in the match until the last point. This was shown in his only Davis Cup match, played in 1950 against Australia, when he defeated Ken McGregor after being two sets down and behind a service break in the fifth set.

Both forehand and backhand are unconventional slam-bang shots. The forehand is hit close to the body with sidespin, the same difficult forehand to handle as that of Maureen Connolly. The backhand is almost as severe, with the power gained from a pulling up of the body at the moment of impact. In the days when he was losing all his lesser matches, his forehand was more of a thunderbolt but less steady. Today his backhand is better than ever and his game has steadied down so that he rarely has those "off days." . . . His serve is one of the best, particularly on the fast grass courts of the Eastern Circuit. He uses a heavy slice that feels like lead on his opponent's racket and he has never been known to serve an American Twist. His second serve is almost an exact replica of his first, although placed not quite so close to the corners. His volley is good but not dazzling, and his overhead is almost always reliable.

Tom works at his tennis with the same tirelessness that he applies to everything he attempts. He is a hard practicer who works on schedule, and his thorough workmanship has made him as dangerous, surprisingly enough, on slow clay as on fast cement. . . .

He was born on September 26, 1922, in Washington, D.C. His family moved West in 1924 and his father, a newspaperman, became publicity manager for the Western Pacific Railroad. His mother is an instructor at San Francisco State College. He started to play on the public courts of Golden Gate Park at the age of 11, the same year that he entered Lowell High School. He first played the circuit in 1942, at the age of 20. He lost to Gardnar Mulloy at Forest Hills in a good five-setter in the round of 16, and was ranked No. 16 in the nation. The same year he won the Pacific Coast by defeating Bill Canning, and the following May he won the California State over Norman Brookes.

In July of 1943, Brown represented the University of California at the National Intercollegiates where he went out to Pancho Segura in the final. . . . Immediately after the Intercollegiates, he entered the Army, serving as a private first class in the infantry. He played very little during the next three years. . . .

Tom considers that he played his best tennis in 1946. He defeated Parker, Mulloy, Segura and Puncec, reaching the semi-finals of Wimbledon on his first try and the finals of Forest Hills. In the former tournament, he led the eventual champion, Yvon Petra, by two sets to love. Then Brown's game deteriorated and Petra's rose until the Frenchman was leading 5–2 in the fifth set. Brown evened the score but was eked out at 8–6. He climaxed the season by beating Parker and Mulloy in the National Championships, losing out to Kramer in the finals after a good opportunity in the first set.

1947 and 1948 were considered "bad years" by Brown! "I was in law school at the University of California and was playing practically not at all during the school year, which lasted nine months. I returned to Wimbledon in 1947 and had a bit of belated revenge by ousting Petra in the quarter-finals. I was lucky against Budge Patty, who was exhausted after long matches against Drobny and Bromwich. I reached the finals but did not play well against Kramer." 1948 was Tom's last attempt in England. He fell in the quarter-finals to Josef Asboth, the human backboard from Hungary. . . .

In 1946, Brown was ranked No. 4 in the country. Last year he was ranked No. 6. This year his ranking will undoubtedly be lower since he played few of the major tournaments . . . He flew back for the National Champion-ships and played two thoroughly remarkable matches. In the second round he won over Gardnar Mulloy in four sets . . . Then he met up with Herb Flam in a match that was perhaps the most exciting of the tournament. He had four match points against Herb in the fourth set, then fought off a half dozen match points for Flam. Each time Brown saved a match point, Herb would throw up his hands and shriek "Gad"; Brown said nothing. He never so much as raised an eyebrow or allowed a smile to escape during the entire five sets. He played as he does every match—he exhibited perfect concentra-tion, whaled the ball for placements on match point against him, and took every call, good or bad, with the same impassiveness. He lost with the same expression he would have worn had he won.

Off the court Tom is affable and always pleasant. He has a sly sense of humor and a quiet charm. . . .

When Tom was asked to give a few words of advice to younger players, he replied: "Occasional coaching on the fundamentals is helpful, but the most important method for improvement is practice. I would recommend that they hit a very large number of tennis balls, say about 3,371,583. . . ."

ERIC STURGESS

by Owen Williams

Born in Johannesburg on May 10th, 1920, Eric William Sturgess began to batter a ball about at the age of nine. Encouraged then as now by his mother, the young Sturgess graduated into the men's ranks by winning the Border title in East London while still 17. At this stage, tennis was very much a weekend occupation, for Chartered Accountancy examinations de-manded most of his concentration. Such was his ability, however, that in 1939, at the age of 18, he defeated Eustace Fannin to gain his first South African title.

The following year Eric retained his title with a victory over Max Bertram, a previous titleholder, but a matter of months later he had en-listed in the South African Air Force. The early part of Eric's Air Force career was spent as a flying instructor in the Union. Later, as a captain, Eric went north to the battle zones of North Africa and Italy and, as a flight commander piloting Spitfires, he did a tour of operational flights, dive-bombing and strafing.

On the 20th of October, 1944, Eric was flying on an extended tour of operations near Boulogne. The anti-aircraft fire was particularly heavy and he was hit at a height of only 50 feet. He managed to climb to a height of

600 feet before parachuting to the comparative safety of a Prisoner of War camp. He spent the rest of the war in the now famous Stalag Luft 3 Camp, from which he was released by the Russians in May, 1945. He returned to South Africa and to serious tennis after a complete break of five years.

The South African Championships were reinaugurated in 1946, and veteran Norman Farquharson played his way into the final, only to meet with sudden defeat at the hands of an eager Sturgess. In 1947 Eric, now 27, visited Europe and Wimbledon for the first time, but not before he had relinquished his grip on the South African title to Davis Cup teammate, Eustace Fannin, in a fluctuating five-set battle. In the five years that followed, Eric was ranked in the First Ten of the world. He now traveled the world prodigiously, and together with South Africa's golfing maestro, Bobby Locke, he probably held the South African record for hours in the air. He played in Europe, the United States, Mexico, South America and Australia, winning titles, making friends, beating the big names in tennis—always a consistently good performer, but always those big titles proved elusive.

A glance at the record books of Wimbledon, Forest Hills and Roland Garros reveals the consistency with which Eric reached the quarter-finals, semi-finals and finals of these tournaments. At Forest Hills, in his one attempt at winning the title, he battled his way to the final, only to encounter an inspired Pancho Gonzales, and once again he met defeat while on the brink of winning a major crown.

Eric is primarily a baseliner who earns his points through exceptional footwork, speed and solid ground strokes. The fact that he has never gained one of the three major titles has always been attributed to his weak service. . . .

Eric considers he played his greatest match against Frank Parker, whom he defeated 6–3 in the fifth set in a Wimbledon quarter-final. . . . His best match in South Africa was his straight set victory over Budge Patty in the semi-final of the 1954 nationals at Ellis Park, Johannesburg.

Eric would not rank a World's First Ten, as he does not feel competent to rate players he has never seen at their best. However, he lines up those players he encountered in Europe and the States from 1947 to 1952 as follows: 1. Jack Kramer, 2. Pancho Gonzales, 3. Ted Schroeder, 4. Frank Parker (whom he considers best on clay) , 5. Frank Sedgman, 6. Jaroslav Drobny, 7. Dick Savitt, 8. Budge Patty, 9. Vic Seixas. He does not include Lew Hoad, Tony Trabert and Ken Rosewall, as he did not see them at their peak.

Eric is quiet and unassuming off the court and yet singlemindedly determined in his approach to tennis. He is phlegmatic under pressure but ruthless in sight of victory. He is lean, wiry, impeccable in court attire, and is regarded as the most agile player of our age. He is known the world over for his exceptional court behavior. At Easter this year, he won his 11th victory in the South African Men's Singles. This month he gained his 11th Southern Transvaal title. His record in national play is unexcelled by any player in any major tennis country. The players of South Africa salute a great champion!

PANCHO SEGURA

by Mike Davies

While nothing can bring back the hour of splendor on the grass or glory in the original achievement, for a moment in such things as this month's Marlboro Award to Pancho Segura we can know them briefly again, with his recognition.

When reporting on such awards, the temptation is strong to rummage through our Little Tribute Kit for the perforated platitudes (Untiring in his efforts to . . . Selfless in his desire . . .) and pregummed laurels (Proud, but not vain; kind, but without condescension) which suit most recipients and require least effort. It is not possible with Segura. He defies the cliché and confounds the facile. He is a person, as Raintree County was a place, not of perishable fact but of enduring fiction, as much a legend as Red Grange and Babe Ruth.

Biographically, Pancho was born in poverty on June 20, 1921, in Guayaquil, Ecuador, one of nine children (six sisters and two brothers), and his life has been at times the Grimmest of fairy tales. At eleven he had rickets and malaria, was weak and spindly, derided by other children with the nickname "parrot foot." Yet even the poor can do extravagant things for their children, and Segura says today that his family gave him love and understanding and a great sense of security which belied their surroundings. He gained a chance entrée into the rarefied world of tennis when his father landed a job as caretaker of the local tennis club and he learned to play, in secret, when the courts were not otherwise occupied. Because he was too small to swing the racket with one hand, he developed his now-famous two-handed forehand. He made such rapid, natural progress that the class-conscious club had to swallow its pride and select Pancho to represent them in an interclub challenge match with Quito. He won and became a hero overnight. Soon after, he was sent to the Bolivian Olympics and gained fame by his victory there. (In 1940 the Guayaquil Club changed its name to the Pancho Segura Tennis Club and it was there, in June, that the United States was defeated in the Davis Cup competition.)

In 1941, at 20, Pancho came to the United States to play in the Nationals at Forest Hills. He lost to Bitsy Grant in five sets, but Gar Mulloy, who saw the match, was so impressed that he arranged a scholarship for Segura to the University of Miami in Coral Gables, Florida. There Segura majored in (he says, cryptically) "Business Administration, Canoeing and Forestry." He made history for the University of Miami when he became the only man ever to win the U.S. Intercollegiate Championships three years in a row (1942–43–44).

It is said that, though he was twice ranked No. 3 nationally, he never hit his stride as an amateur. However, since turning professional in late 1947 he has had a phenomenal career. In 1949 he played Frank Parker on the tour and overwhelmed him completely. In 1951 he was runner-up for the pro title. In 1952 he beat Gonzales at Forest Hills 6–2, 6–2, 6–2 and he won a tour against former Aussie Davis Cupper Ken McGregor by 74 matches to 25. In 1954 he finished behind Gonzales in a round robin tour featuring Gonzales, Sedgman, Budge and himself. In 1956 he swept Rex Hartwig off the court 56 matches to 22. In 1957 he won the big AMPOL tournament in Sydney, and in the London Indoor Professionals at Wembley he defeated Gonzales in the semi-finals, only to lose a tough five-setter to Rosewall. Then, in 1958, in a round robin (the Masters) in Los Angeles, on successive days he beat Hoad, Gonzales, Sedgman, Trabert, Hartwig and Rosewall to win the tournament hands-down.

Pancho is no stranger to awards. He has been presented with every imaginable kind of trophy, and every conceivable kind of honor has been bestowed upon him. Jack Kramer dedicated the first court at his Palos Verdes Tennis Club to "Seg," as did the new Brook Club in Milwaukee. In 1966, on "Pancho Segura Night" at the Los Angeles Sports Arena, he was given a Corvette and a gaggle of lesser gifts, as well as a standing ovation from a crowd of over 5000.

Jack Kramer has said that Segura has done more to make professional tennis the honest and honorable profession it is today than any other individual. Segura started when pros got $300 per week, win or lose, and were playing four and five matches a day and traveling 300 to 3,000 miles to get to the next town. But in spite of the absence of financial incentives for winning, Seg always played his best. He could not conceive of playing any other way. He imparted this spirit to others as they turned professional and it has had a salutary effect on the pro game. (Just incidentally, Kramer considers that forehand of Seg's to be the best single shot in tennis.)

Segura has a fantastic ability to spot a player's weakness and he is eager to tell people how to use it to their advantage. Ken Rosewall recalls a match he was to play against Lew Hoad in Europe. In the locker room before the match, he overheard Segura coaching Hoad on how to beat him. Then, noticing that Ken had overheard, Segura came over sheepishly and began telling Ken how to beat Lew. He is a noted court tactician and Andres Gimeno confesses that Seg has done wonders for his own crosscourt forehand volley and that he would never have had his successes against Gonzales had it not been for Seg's advice.

From his 37th to his 39th year he played the best tennis of his life. Although he is 46 now, only two weeks ago he beat Dennis Ralston 6–1 in the third at Berkeley. He has the best concentration of any player in the game, and his only concern when he is playing is the competition itself. The money involved does not occur to him and he loses, when he loses, without rancor or bitterness, either at himself or at others. Fans know him to be a genial, fierce and inspiring sight during a match, and that's a large combination of qualities.

Today at 46 he is still touring. When he is not on the road he works as the resident pro at the Beverly Hills Tennis Club, but he devotes five hours each Saturday to working at a tennis clinic for youngsters in Pasadena. With his wife, Beverly, and his two children (Spencer, 14, and Maria, 4½), he lives in a $100,000 home in Woodland Hills with a garage full of cars. He says wryly: "That's not bad for a guy who started life on a burro."

He continues, as he always has, to help players whenever they request it. No active player comes to town without calling Seg at the club. He is the most hospitable man alive, the most willing to arrange matches, honorary club memberships, housing, transportation, social engagements and all the practice sessions one could wish. Maria Bueno, Thomas Koch and countless others depend on his endless kindness.

To the Don Quixote that professional tennis sometimes seems, Segura is a faithful Pancho Sanza. But to all of tennis he is a friend and an institution. He is not only the most colorful but the most valuable asset the game could have.

ALICE MARBLE TURNS PRO

by Allison Danzig

From force of habit, a number of people will make the usual trek to the Seventh Regiment Armory today to take in the national junior indoor tennis championships. Once arrived there, they will learn, to their chagrin, that the tournament has been transferred to Camden, New Jersey, and that the armory is no longer interested in volleys other than anti-aircraft fire.

The same experience, in all probability, is in store for some of those who have been accustomed to going to the Park Avenue bastion for the men's and women's national indoor championships. The government's restriction against the use of the armories for non-military purposes points to the dispossession of the McNeills and Riggses, too, in the name of national defense.

There are at least a few New Yorkers by whom the removal of the indoor championships will be taken in stride without any deep sense of personal loss. But though the quality of the competition was not to be compared with that at Forest Hills, except in the late rounds of the senior event, there are those who will find it difficult to reconcile themselves to a complete void of tennis through the winter. To these, then, the return of professional tennis to Madison Square Garden will be doubly welcome, tiding them over in their craving for cannonball aces and straight backhand passing shots until the outdoor parade gets under way in the spring.

In turning out for the professional debut of Miss Alice Marble on the night of January 6, the tennis public will be saying farewell to the one player in the amateur ranks who has measured up to the full stature of an international drawing card since Donald Budge won his last championship at Forest Hills.

There have been extremely few women players who were big box-office attractions. Miss Marble rates with Mrs. Helen Wills Roark and the late Mlle. Suzanne Lenglen. She may not have been as great a player as these two on unswerving consistency of form over a period of years but she excelled them in the virtuosity of her command of all the strokes in the game.

Miss Marble plays more like a man than any other woman to win championship honors. She does not hit as hard as did Mrs. Roark, but in her speed around the court, her skill as a volleyer, her severity overhead and her cleverness in the change of pace—exemplified in her use of the drop shot— her game went beyond Mrs. Roark's. This observer would pick Mrs. Roark to win in a series of matches, but Miss Marble, on a day when she had complete confidence and security of touch, would likely have beaten any woman player in history.

Winner of four national championships and of the last Wimbledon tournament, Miss Marble enters upon her professional tour with a record of invincibility in 1940 that compares with Budge's in 1938. She went through the season without losing a match, as she did also in 1939, and no one was able to win a set from her at Forest Hills.

Miss Marble is not only a great player. She is also a particularly attractive one who has never let her public down in her scrupulous regard for her appearance, and she has been equally faultless in her sportsmanship. In this respect, as well as in her pre-eminence, she stands where Budge stood when he left the amateur ranks two years ago.

THE STYLE OF ALICE MARBLE

by Julius D. Heldman

"Meteoric" is the word to describe Alice Marble's magnificent tennis career. In 1931 she was a promising young player at Golden Gate Park in San Francisco. The next year she was No. 7 in the country and the following year No. 3. She was just approaching the apex of her career when she was stricken by pleurisy. From the medical reports it seemed that her tournament tennis days were ended, but two years later she made one of the most remarkable comebacks of all time to win her first National title. She was the No. 1 American player for five years, turning professional in late 1940 to tour with Mary Hardwick, Don Budge and Bill Tilden. Some years later she suffered a recurrence of her illness. A lung was removed, ending her serious playing days, but she still keeps active in the game with occasional social doubles, and she has a prize protégée in Southern California's young Billie Jean Moffitt.

I first saw Alice when she was making her comeback in 1936. She was very trim and tan from a winter of training in Palm Springs, and it was already clear that she would be the world champion if her health held out. Everything about her game had the mark of greatness. Just as, two years ago, every tournament player immediately spotted the future world champion in Maria Bueno, so did all those who saw Alice recognize her fantastic talent. It was more than just athletic ability, although there are hardly four or five women in the history of tennis who have had as much. It was a knack for playing the game more aggressively than any of her competitors; it was a man's approach to the game, from the American twist serve to the leaping volleys and jump overheads. Added to this was her fierce competitive spirit and coolness under pressure. She was head and shoulders above her closest rivals, and she dominated the women's field to the same degree as did Don Budge in the men's.

Only occasionally do the leading male players come out to watch their female counterpart. The men on the circuit turned out en masse for Alice. Her appearance was trim, her manner brisk and businesslike, and her style of play exciting. She managed to play like a man and still maintain her feminine appeal. She went for the kills at net and she angle-volleyed like Gene Mako, one of her famous mixed doubles partners. She played without restraint, running wide-legged, stretching full out for the wide balls, and walloping serves and overheads. Her game was the product of her tomboy days of baseball in Golden Gate Park. The throwing action and batting stance learned there carried through directly to their tennis counterparts, the serve and forehand.

Alice had a flat Eastern grip on the forehand, which she hit with a loose wrist action. Her fingers were held close together and she did not get that feeling of control which comes when the fingers are spread out. The combination of floppy wrist and bunched fingers resulted in more errors than necessary. Her forehand was a powerful baseball-type swing, with an almost flat-back wind-up. There were no curlicues, rolls or figure eights in the backswing, which was very short. There was a snap of the wrist at the moment of impact and then, like all wristy Eastern grip players, sidespin for the down-the-line or a pull-up, short loop action for the crosscourt.

Marble's forehand was powerful albeit not as hard as Maureen Connolly's. She used it to attack and was one of the first women players to follow her forehand to net at every opportunity. I have seen her rally from the baseline on the starboard side, but to me she always appeared uncomfortable here since she was not steady enough to maintain her dominance. Her forehand was a weapon to get her to net, but it was neither chip nor push; it was forceful in that it produced a weak return, but it was not an outright point winner.

Alice had two distinct follow-throughs. Neither was big, even when she hit her hardest. When she hit with sidespin down the line, her racket face came across the ball and the follow-through was more likely to end at waist rather than shoulder level. Among the men, Ellsworth Vines was the most famous exponent of the sidespin forehand, although his whole action was longer than Alice's. Louise Brough's sidespin drive resembled Marble's, but Maureen Connolly's famous sidespin was more like Vines'. Alice's topspin drive was a little wristy and was not the Rock of Gibraltar by any means. Sometimes she literally came over the ball, turning the racket face over after the hit, while other times she simply pulled up and ended high on the follow-through. Her wrist enabled her to become a master of the sharp angles, which characterized her style of play.

If Alice had not had so much athletic talent, her loose wrist tendency on forehand and backhand would have been a serious handicap. Instead this same wristy action enabled her to disguise her shots, to change directions at the last minute and to give added pace to the ball. She had good body control and she stepped into the ball solidly. Everything else about her game was classically executed.

The Marble backhand was also a short stroke. It was rather flat, but she often added overspin by rolling her wrist slightly. When she hit down the line, she preferred to use sidespin rather than underspin. In other words, she held the head of the racket behind her wrist and let the elbow guide it down the line.

Alice could hit on the dead run on both sides, and there was nothing she liked so much as to wallop a ball and charge the net. This style was a revelation in women's tennis. She was playing in a league of solid baseliners, all of whom were sharp with passing shots, and so her approach shots had to be forceful. This philosophy led her to more ground stroke errors than her contemporaries, but she made up for it by the advantage she gained from her constant attack. Marble was the all-court player *par excellence*. Her movements were rangy, her ground strokes aggressive, and she leaped and jumped like a top man athlete.

There have been only a few great serves in women's tennis, and among them most players would number those of Alice, Althea Gibson, Maria Bueno, Doris Hart, Margaret Osborne duPont and Louise Brough Clapp in her prime. To me Marble's delivery was by far the best from three standpoints: her first serve was as hard as any and more consistent; her second serve had more bite and was better placed than the other women's; and her attack, particularly in doubles play, behind the service, was incomparable. She was the most sought-after mixed doubles partner in the history of the game. Budge and Mako alternated cleaning up the major titles with her. It was a foregone conclusion that if she had a reasonable partner they would win. It was like having two men serve on the same side!

Marble was completely unrestrained on her service action. She could stretch more from the chest, bend more from the back and kick more from the knee than any other woman. This was a free, relaxed motion. She could clout an ace on the first serve or kick a high spinner on the second. She did not follow her serve to net in singles as much as Althea does, but if she were playing in the current era there would be no problem in adapting her game to the philosophy of 100 per cent attack.

The backswing on the serve was not as long as Bueno's or Gibson's. It was a fairly short action in the style of the top Aussie players of the last decade. The racket came up from the waist to the shoulder rather quickly, then was followed by the sharp elbow bend and back-scratching action. The hit was made with a wrist snap of real power or spin. She was not quite the feminine counterpart of Vines, who snaked up to the ball, but she had a definite body slither in the style of some top batters.

If a single outstanding feature had to be picked out of Alice's game, it would have to be the serve. I have a vivid mental picture of her standing up to the line, batting an ace and moving briskly into the next court to serve again. She had supreme confidence in her serve and it was thoroughly justified. The rest of her game could go off key, but the delivery was her faithful standby. There was never any rash of double-faults, and when the first serve did not go in, she had that kicking American twist serve to fall back on.

The overhead was as good as her serve—free and unrestrained. She leapt beautifully, and this enabled her to play closer in when she attacked. Occasionally she might have a spell of missing, but she never babied an overhead. It most resembled Darlene Hard's among the current players, although Alice had more wrist in the hit. She hit for the angles, and a lob from her opponent invariably meant the end of the point either way.

Alice was a killer volleyer. She played in close and she went for the short, sharp angles. She was death on the high ones, but her wrist sometimes played her false, causing her to miss a sitter. She was a great net player because she anticipated and moved so well. She was also fearless. Technically her volleys were a little too flat, perhaps too much like a short stroke rather than an underspin punch. For this reason low volleys sometimes gave her trouble. She did have a great eye and fast reflexes, and she never lost that tomboy attitude at net.

In doubles she was a delight. She had the knack of poaching for the kill and she ate up the other man's speed. When she played with Budge or, alternatively, Mako, she started the fashion of standing in on her partner's return. She was the first woman to do so, just as Budge and Mako were the first men's team to stand in on each other's returns. Alice was as good a doubles partner as any but the very top men except for the fact that her return of serve was not consistent enough. She was also as pleasant a partner as one could hope to have.

Alice had a most attractive court personality. She was able to be warm without losing concentration, and nothing won over a gallery quite so fast as the smile and wave of the racket which she gave in recognition of her opponent's good play. She was a fierce competitor and did not like to lose, but she was never a gamesman. There were no sulks or moans or unhappy expressions during the play, but after the match was over she could cry if she lost. Everyone liked her, from her closest competitors to the linesmen and ballboys who worked her matches. She was as friendly a World Champion as the game has ever known.

Alice's record places her among the all-time greats. She won the Nationals in 1936, 1938, 1939 and 1940, Wimbledon in 1939, the National Women's Doubles four times with Sarah Palfrey, and the National Mixed Doubles with Gene Mako, Don Budge, Harry Hopman and Bobby Riggs. Following her tennis career she became a successful nightclub singer. Currently she is living in Southern California, where she works in a medical clinic.

MY PICK OF THE BEST

by Alice Marble

Exercising my newly found talent for raising controversial issues, I'm going to attempt to answer a question fans ask me very often. What makes a tennis champion? What distinguishes the champion from the "almost" player? In my opinion, it can be summed up in the predominance of the following: natural ability, will to win, hard work, soundness of body and mind, superior reflexes, and a natural ball sense.

This is not to suggest that all champions have all of the above qualifications, of course. There has never been a perfect champion, but if I could draw from the strength of the all-time greats to create Miss Champion of the past quarter century, these are the strokes I would borrow from each.

FOREHAND: JADWIGA JEDRZEJOWSKA

Jaja, as everyone called her, hit a tremendously hard forehand, which carried so much topspin that it hit one's racket like a rock. With little else but that booming forehand, she was twice runner-up at Wimbledon and once at Forest Hills.

BACKHAND: PAULINE BETZ ADDIE

Until I played against Pauline, Helen Wills Roark had the strongest backhand I encountered, but the current pro champion brought an entirely different kind of stroke into women's tennis. Not satisfied to be able to rally all day from the baseline, making safe crosscourts and down-the-line shots, she can—and does—make spectacular winners. The rapidity of her swing is also more deceptive than that of Mrs. Roark.

SERVICE: HART, ROARK, BROUGH

Since no one combines the three distinctly different services perfectly, I would choose these three women to exemplify each:

Flat service. For outright aces, Doris Hart is queen of this category in my book. She has a lovely natural swing and excellent placement, and her direction is particularly well disguised. Like some of us, Doris depends on her service a great deal. If the first ball is catching the line, she is at the top of her game. If not, her worry causes her other strokes to suffer.

Slice service. Helen Wills Roark had such a wide-breaking slice that one was forced well out of court to receive it. With her sound ground strokes, she had the ability to make an opponent feel rushed in order to get back in court for her return. On a fast court, such as cement or grass, this type of service is so effective that I wonder why more players don't develop it.

Topspin. The topspin service is not new to women's tennis; Mary K. Browne employed it some thirty years ago. The finest American twist I know, though, belongs to our present Wimbledon champion, Louise Brough, who has streamlined it to match that of many of our men. She gets an enormously high bounce on this serve, and women are notoriously feeble in their efforts to return it, especially on the backhand. If Louise's service costs her in energy spent, it pays off dividends in games won.

VOLLEY: ELIZABETH RYAN

Bunny Ryan should go down in history as the greatest woman volleyer of all times. Players like Margaret du Pont and Sarah Cooke execute this shot beautifully, but they lack the "killer" force that identifies Elizabeth Ryan. I never saw her make a really defensive volley. Hugging the net, hitting high volleys like rifle shots, she had every angle known to the game at her command.

OVERHEAD SMASH: ALTHEA GIBSON

I thought I had seen everything in women's tennis until Miss Gibson came along to demonstrate the power and ease with which a smash ought to be hit. To be sure, she flubs plenty of them because she takes liberties with the ball, asking, as Tilden says, "too much of the little white pill," but there has never been anything like that overhead in the distaff department of tennis.

DROP SHOT: ANITA LIZANA

Perhaps only a handful of people will remember our 1937 champion, diminutive Anita Lizana of Chile, though she has been compared to the great Suzanne Lenglen in her approach to the game. She was a comparatively soft hitter, but her drop shot, beautifully disguised, was the most frustrating single shot I ever played against. I don't believe this shot can be taught; it is, rather, a natural talent, like angled volleys, that a player either has or has not. Anita's game showed a fine imagination, and I'm sorry that she faded out of the tennis picture so quickly.

FOOTWORK: SUZANNE LENGLEN

I regret to say that I only saw Mlle. Lenglen play on two occasions. I've lost my mental picture of what must have been classic strokes, but I can still see the "Pavlova of the courts" taking her tiny dancing steps into position. Pauline Betz Addie is as fast as a streak, but it was Suzanne who gave the word "footwork" to tennis.

ANTICIPATION: HELEN WILLS ROARK

A great player, Helen Wills was never fast on her feet, and yet she never seemed rushed. She seemed to run no more than the rest of us, but she always appeared in the right spot at the right time. The answer is, of course, anticipation. Helen was such an ardent student of the game that she knew where the ball would be hit and was able to get there first.

STRATEGY: HELEN WILLS ROARK

Here, too, the nod falls to Mrs. Roark. I can't recall having seen her in the stands, watching tennis, but she must have studied her opponents very carefully. I once heard her say that she always planned four or five shots ahead of the point in play, and certainly she knew when to play a weakness and when, contrarily, she could make a winner off her opponent's strength.

NATURAL ABILITY: ALTHEA GIBSON

Tennis players are not necessarily natural athletes, as Margaret du Pont, and Doris Hart are, as was Lili de Alvarez, the lovely Spanish player of twenty years ago. I think Althea has more natural facilities than any of the above mentioned. She has complete freedom of muscle and motion, even enough to be a handicap (as well I know) if she relies on it too much instead of learning fundamentals.

FIGHTING SPIRIT: HELEN JACOBS

It would be difficult to point out any outstanding shot Helen Jacobs had—her service was sound, her backhand good, her forehand bad; she had a well-made defensive slice, a fair volley and overhead. But she had something else: more will to win, more drive and guts than anyone else. Plagued by sprains and other injuries throughout her tennis career, Helen never gave up. That she was four times National Champion and once Wimbledon titleholder is proof enough that you can win if your desire is big enough.

POISE: HELEN WILLS ROARK

Queen Helen retires the selection trophy for the third time. It has been said of her that she was nerveless; obviously she had to have the impetus of a certain nervous energy to rise as high as she did. It is also true, though, that she earned her nickname of "Poker Face" by remaining cool and unruffled under fire. The ability to retain her poise, whatever the circumstances, is one of the assets that made her eight times a Wimbledon champion.

COLOR: SUZANNE LENGLEN

Mlle. Lenglen won her last Wimbledon championship more than a score of years ago. Today, wherever tennis is discussed, some player, some official or fan still recalls a fascinating story about the great temperamental French star. She might not have been liked by everyone, but she had the intangible, irresistible quality of personal magnetism; her game was no more exciting than her personality.

PLEASING PERSONALITIES:
KAY STAMMERS MENZIES—BETTY NUTHALL

These two girls gave me, as a player, more pleasure from the stands than any other players. If they were not great champions, they both gave a lovely vitality and warmth to tennis—Kay with her wonderful sense of humor, beauty and charm, and the never-to-be-forgotten "Bouncing Betty" who won our national championship in 1930 and captured all our hearts while she was at it.

This, then, is my perfect champion, chosen from my own experience and observation. Since I wasn't privileged to see the other all-time greats, I could not include them here. Dissenters will kindly form a line to the right of the doorway of the ALT offices. No pushing, please.

GEORGE AGUTTER

by Al Laney

They are throwing a party for George Agutter at the West Side Tennis Club in Forest Hills tonight and the tennis world ought to pay a great deal more attention to the event than it probably will. George has been the professional at the club ever since it opened in Queens in 1913. That is 46 years gone now and George is retiring to his place at Falmouth, on Cape Cod, to the leisure that he has earned.

The West Side club is the No. 1 tennis institution in this country, one might almost say the headquarters of the game in the United States, as Wimbledon is in England. Most people just say Forest Hills when they mean the club, and the very name brings a thousand tennis memories crowding in from the past. And just as this is the No. 1 club, so, too, is George Agutter the country's No. 1 tennis professional.

Ah, no! Not one of those dashing fellows who go trouping about the world putting on their shows is the top man in this profession. Not they. Fine players every one, all they could do is beat George on the court. They could never hope to be his equal as a tennis pro.

It used to be in this game that when you employed the word professional you meant men like George, men attached to a club for instruction purposes and to run a shop. Each club had one, still does, and he was the most important person at the club, most likely, besides being in most cases the club's finest player.

These men have had an influence for good on the game that is not properly understood by the tennis people themselves. And George Agutter has been all these years the outstanding example of what the tennis professional is and should be. In his own person he exemplified the ideal and sets the standard by which they should be judged.

It tells much of the personality of this man that to call him Mr. Agutter would be a sort of an affront. He is George to everyone and he loses no part of his dignity when small boy and girl pupils so address him. He has an altogether winsome quality about him and his expression often indicates that he is enjoying a private joke which he is too polite to make public. George is 73 now, and 63 of these years have been devoted exclusively to tennis.

He was born in the West Kensington section of London, the son of a small tradesman, and he gravitated quite naturally toward the nearby Queen's Club. By the time he was ten he was earning a few bob a week retrieving balls for such as the Dohertys, Hugh and Reggie, two of the game's immortals. But small boy George was doing more than shagging balls. Already he was drinking at the fount of tennis knowledge, and those who go back so far as he say that still to this day there is, however faint, a reflection of the marvelous strokes of H. L. Doherty in his own game. For George already was a tennis professional in his own young mind, never gave a thought to being anything else, and when he was 16 he had his first job at a club in Wales.

At 18 George was in Paris as professional at the Tennis Club de Paris and after a couple of years on the Continent, which included the occasional instruction of royalty at such places as Baden Baden, destiny stepped in to take him by the hand in 1904 and make an American of him. Representing destiny in this case was George Rublee, a wealthy international lawyer, who brought George to this country as his personal professional. It was fairly common in those days for a man who had the means and was a good player to have a personal pro. At any rate, young Agutter, now turned 20, was established at the Rublee summer home in Windsor, Vermont, where he played with and taught such famous neighbors as Ethel Barrymore; Homer St. Gaudens, the sculptor; the American novelist Winston Churchill; Norman Hapgood; and some other prominent persons of the day.

George went that winter to the Royal Poinciana of happy Palm Beach memory (for the rich), where the likes of Goulds and Whitneys played the game. When the time came to go back to Europe George didn't want to, so Rublee got him a job at the Homestead in Hot Springs, Virginia. For eight years then he was there summers and at Palm Beach winters until finally the West Side club moved from Manhattan to Queens and George made his last move until today.

They will be talking about these things at George's party tonight but mostly, no doubt, about the things that have happened since 1913. For you might say that the club has little or no history of which George has not been a part, although it was not so young when it took up residence on Long Island. Its real life began, though, when George showed up.

Some of the younger ones there tonight will not know and some of the older ones may have forgotten that George was a very fine player of the game besides being an outstanding instructor. There scarcely has been a ranking player of the last 40 years with whom he has not engaged in friendly matches, and it ought to be kept in mind tonight that there are precious few of them against whom George could not just hold his own between his 25th and 50th birthdays.

And especially let it be recalled that he helped many of them to be better players, some to become champions. They should remember also that it was George who started the Long Island and New York State junior and boys' tournaments and kept them going until they were firmly established. So they will be saying a lot of nice things about George tonight but surely not too many and probably not enough. As many will be there as the joint will hold, but if all the people who esteem George were to come they'd have to hold it in Yankee Stadium.

Not many have served the game so well as he. They honor him tonight for that and because they love him, but they cannot honor him so much as he has honored them by his mere presence during 46 years.

THE STYLE OF BOBBY RIGGS

by Julius D. Heldman

The best founded strokes in the tennis game belonged to Bobby Riggs, a Southern Californian who came up the hard way. He did not have a power game, particularly as an amateur, but he did everything right and was capable of hitting hard when he had to. He was undoubtedly the cagiest player of all time and was a superb "gamesman" as well. He was small as tennis players go, standing only 5′ 8″; he had a duck-footed walk, which is untypical of athletes; but he was speedy, enormously talented and, more than any other player, exemplified the champion's "will to win."

Bobby had the spark from his earliest days. He used to play at Highland Park, wearing street clothes and a pair of sneakers, but the tiny 12-year-old was already steady enough to win sideline bets for his brother John. At the age of 12, one of the top local players, Dr. Esther Bartosh, spotted him and immediately realized his amazing potential. Esther and Jerry Bartosh rallied with him, drove him to tournaments, saw that he had rackets and gave him those fundamentally sound strokes. He had no other coaching, and while other young Los Angeles players were growing up with flippy Continental strokes, Bobby acquired a clean, solid, wristless Eastern game.

At the age of 13 it was already clear that he was going to be a top player. None of the men players wanted to admit it since Riggs at that time could only bloop the ball. Nevertheless he was amazingly accurate on passing shots, he lobbed perfectly and he eked out ranking Southern California men. The mark of the comer is the ability to win matches that he is supposed to lose, and Riggs always outplayed the rankings and seedings. At 15 he was winning men's tournaments. His only loss that year was in the finals of the National Boys' when Bobby Harman beat him. At 16 he defeated Frank Shields, then the No. 2 man in the country. This defeat, plus his loss to Don McNeill in the finals of the Nationals in 1940, were his only reversals in major competition. His entire tournament record is astonishing for its consistency, yet he always came back from a beating stronger than ever.

Riggs was a monkeyer in his early round matches. He frequently dropped sets to "unknowns," yet when he got to the quarters and semis he often won with the loss of only a game or two. As a result, players paradoxically boasted that Bobby beat them 6–0, 6–1, to prove that he respected their game enough to work on the match!

Bobby Riggs' forehand was absolutely correct in every particular. It had the least wrist of all the big forehands and therefore was not as hard as some of the others. Because of that lack of wrist his accuracy was fantastic both in depth and direction. His fingers were separated well on the racket, his wrist was slightly laid back, and he had only the faintest trace of a semicircle on the wind-up. He had rather a short backswing, which helped his disguise, and he got his accuracy out of perfect timing. He did not flick his wrist for change of direction but instead hit the ball slightly earlier or later. Never in his life did he drop his racket head, which is further proof of his iron wrist.

On all his ground strokes he was not ashamed to clear the net by five feet or more. This was to get depth when his opponent was in the backcourt. When his opponent attacked he could skim the net on a passing shot, and that locked wrist and very slight overspin would put the ball just where he wanted it. With the same action he could lift lobs, which were just deep forehands to him. Occasionally he would underspin a very high defensive lob in order to get back into the game, but the lob was primarily an offensive passing shot for Bobby.

Riggs was not a bone-crusher on his forehand. He was primarily a parrier off of his opponent's thrusts. He could do something with every forehand he could touch and he seldom made errors except when he was "monkeying" in those early rounds. His footwork was marvelous. In the early days he was not an "open stance" man. He had the old-fashioned classical approach that the Bartoshes gave him, with the left foot placed well forward toward the net. In later years he began to chip with an open stance to get the net position.

Bobby was just as letter-perfect on the backhand. The stroke was essentially flat, but he could apply a little overspin for passing shots or a little underspin for baseline rallies. He had a small, neat backswing, he guided the ball by holding it on his racket as long as possible, and although he lacked real power, he was able to utilize his opponent's pace effectively. His ground strokes were not colorful because he never really teed off on the ball.

Riggs was a great touch artist. He could drop shot off either side and he was always working the angles of the court. He hit short crosscourts successfully because he did not hit too hard. His backhand motion on the lob was as good as his forehand, and it was death to take the net against him. Joey Hunt at that time epitomized the attacking game, but in the hundred or so meetings between the two, Riggs only lost three times. Hunt had a big serve, a powerful overhead and a murderous volley. Bobby would lob a lot, losing points frequently in the earlier sets in order to pull Joe back from the barrier. Then the passing shots would begin to sneak by, and brother John would win another bet.

Bobby never had a hard serve until he was a top amateur. He always had a competent delivery and the first ball came in 90 per cent of the time. Riggs did not see the percentage in missing and could go months without ever double-faulting. His was the most underrated serve in the game. He had just enough American twist to put his opponent on the defensive. He served deep into the corners, never following his service into net as an amateur. Gradually his delivery hardened up, and by the time he was National Champion he was able to throw in an occasional ace.

The serve was also a classical action, distinguished by the fact that he used his height so well. It was competent and clean but seldom a cannonball. He was giving his opponents at least four or five inches in height so that he could not hope to keep up with them on blistering aces. The motion was beautiful without extra frills. It came from the book and, like all his other strokes, was manufactured without a hitch.

Bobby became a true net player only when he came up against Jack Kramer as a pro. His answer to Kramer's relentless drive to the net was to follow his own serve in every time. The game had changed and Bobby changed with it. After 15 years of playing tournament tennis mainly from the baseline, Riggs became a volleyer. It is a great tribute to his basic ability that he was able to make this change. His height, reach and lack of power were against him, and yet he managed to beat all but Kramer with his new tactics.

Whatever Bobby did he did well. The forehand volley was practically wristless, pulled from the shoulder with an extremely short swing. He sometimes stroke-volleyed high forehands, which is practically the rule in top-flight tennis. His backhand volley was simply a foreshortened version of his backhand ground stroke, with a little bit of underspin added for control. On both sides he got down well for low balls, but he never bent his knees unnecessarily.

Riggs had always been a competent volleyer. However, as a pro he made the volley his forte. If there was ever a time when he hit the ball hard it was on a high stroke forehand volley. Generally he was a percentage volleyer who never hit harder than he had to. Bobby was interested in winning the maximum number of points, which from his point of view meant consistency.

Bobby knew the angles on the overhead. Again he was equipped with a good fundamental stroke and he chose to use it as a placement weapon rather than a bludgeon. Whereas other players would leap backwards in an attempt to kill a difficult lob, Bobby would be content just to tap the ball back deeply to get into position. He was lethal on short to medium lobs and careful on the deep ones.

To beat Bobby you simply had to outhit him. Nobody could outsteady or outthink him. No one could "outpsych" him—usually the shoe was on the other foot! He had to be outpowered, and it took a consistent hitter like Budge, and later Kramer with his grooved shots, to beat the little "guts" player. Those who played him in tournaments had the utmost respect for his game. He was a clutch artist, a money player and a competitor who was never out of the match until the last point was over.

In his amateur career he won the National Juniors, the National Clay Courts, the U.S. National Singles twice and Wimbledon. At the age of 18, he was ranked No. 4 in the men's division. He took the Nationals for the first time when he was 20. He was unsuccessful in defending it the next year, losing to Don McNeill, but the following year he came back stronger than ever to win back the crown and to turn pro. He was out of competition during the war years. To Bobby, his biggest success was beating Don Budge in their pro tour. The margin was only one match, but Riggs had at last beaten the man who has often been called the greatest player of all time.

SARAH PALFREY DANZIG

by Allison Danzig

"If you can meet with Triumph and Disaster, And treat those two impostors just the same," read the lines from Kipling that meet the eye of the player descending the marquee steps to the stadium turf at Forest Hills, Queens.

No one has more genuinely typified the Kipling spirit on the tennis court than did Sarah Palfrey in her unfailing graciousness and the radiance of her smile in adversity or victory. Sportsmanship has had no truer exemplar than the slip of a Boston blueblood who fought unrelentingly to win, but never at all costs, and ever mindful that it was a game.

If American tennis has had a sweetheart comparable to the movies' Mary Pickford, Sarah is her name. In her exquisite daintiness, her starry-eyed infatuation with the wonder of life and the excitement and fellowship of the match, and her complete naturalness and overflowing friendliness, this New England girl with the culture and careful rearing of upper-register Boston won adoring homage from galleries at home and abroad at Wimbledon and Stade Roland Garros in Paris. She may not have ruled the courts as supremely the queen as was Mary's sway over the movies, but she won no less than 37 United States championships as girl and adult, and her celebrity has been international.

It has been a good many years since Sarah Palfrey (now Mrs. Jerry Danzig) played her last big match. But her identity with the game in which she was twice national champion, nine times doubles champion (with Betty Nuthall, Helen Jacobs, Alice Marble and Margaret Osborne duPont) and won many a Wightman Cup match for the United States, has been maintained with undiminishing enthusiasm while rearing a family.

Tennis has had no more loyal worker or devoted patron. She has contributed some of the most readable and valued books and magazine articles on the game. Three years ago, in recognition of her distinguished service to the game, as well as her pre-eminence as a player, she was elected to the National Lawn Tennis Hall of Fame at Newport, Rhode Island.

Now, with her daughter, Diane, married and her son, Jerry, at Hotchkiss, Sarah Palfrey Danzig has committed herself to a new career as an executive of *World Tennis* in association with Mrs. Gladys Heldman, the editor and publisher of the most widely read and entertaining tennis magazine the world over.

Her undertaking so demanding a position is indicative of her boundless energy and enthusiasm for the game she has played since childhood with her four sisters, all of whom became national junior champions, and brother John (in later years a dean of Columbia College).

As the wife of Jerry Danzig, a radio and television executive who is special assistant to Governor Rockefeller, she presides over an eight-room Park Avenue apartment and a summer residence in Pawling, New York.

Sitdown dinners, cocktail parties and buffet suppers bring to her table Governor Dewey, Lowell Thomas, Ed Sullivan, Budd Schulberg, Mrs. Kermit Roosevelt, Marlene Dietrich, Bert Lahr, Jack Paar, Julian Myrick, Mrs. Hazel Wightman, Helen Jacobs, Althea Gibson, Leontyne Price, Mrs. August Belmont, divers numbers of her nineteen nieces and nephews, and itinerant tennis players, both domestic and foreign, caught off expense account between tournaments.

Charity work occupies much of Sarah Danzig's time with the Community Service Society of New York, of which she is women's division chairman; the Visiting Nurse Service of New York; the Child Study Association of America; and the Junior League.

Over and over she has responded to calls for help in tennis, assisting in clinics for underprivileged youth, finding quarters, often in her own home, for overseas players competing at Forest Hills, and helping with the international tennis ball. With all her activities and duties, she still finds time for an occasional social game of tennis or golf, to play the piano, do some of the household cooking and gardening and work at her typewriter.

Her books have included *Winning Tennis and How to Play It* and *Tennis For Anyone,* recently off the press. She has contributed articles to the *Saturday Evening Post, Sports Illustrated* and *Seventeen,* and she has given radio reports on the tennis championships at Forest Hills and made appearances on the *Today* and *Home* television programs. And through it all she has never lost for a minute that radiant smile and loveliness that made her the sweetheart of tennis.

PAULINE BETZ ADDIE

from World Tennis

There is something special one can say to describe every great champion. Tilden had the greatest variety in his shots. Helen Wills had both hard and steady ground strokes, Don Budge had the biggest backhand, Jack Kramer epitomized the aggressive style of play. Pauline Betz was the most popular.

Pauline, or "Bobby," as her friends call her, didn't begin tennis until the age of 14. Her mother, who was a physical education teacher, taught her the game and it wasn't until she reached the age of 16 that she was able to defeat her parent. . . .

One of Pauline's most vivid memories goes back to the age of 15, when she was competing in the Pacific Southwest championships. Gracyn Wheeler, then ranked No. 5 in the United States, was serving a big basket of balls on a back court. The awed Pauline went up to the champ and asked, "May I gather the balls up for you?" Gracyn won her heart forever by replying, "Why don't we hit some together?"

From the very beginning Pauline lived only for tennis. At the age of 17, she and the 12-year-old Budge Patty would get up at five to be at the courts at six so that they would be sure to get a court. During all her long amateur tennis career, she never took off a Saturday afternoon to see a football game, never stayed out late before a big match and never laid off when the courts were dry enough for play. She was always eager on the way up and never felt "stale" until she began to defend her title. . . .

Bobby never played in the national juniors because "I never had the money to go and no one offered to send me." She made her first trip on the Eastern circuit at the age of 19, succeeded in beating Dodo Bundy and Virginia Wolfenden, had a three-set match with Alice Marble and won the national indoors. She was ranked No. 8 and the next year rose to No. 3 behind Marble and Helen Jacobs. That year she had wins over Bundy, Jacobs and Mary Hardwick. The win over Jacobs was both thrilling and disillusioning. She defeated her in the quarter-finals of Essex but felt sorry at the same time that "Helen should lose to a player like me." . . .

Pauline won four national singles titles, 1942, 1943, 1944 and 1946, and one Wimbledon singles title, in 1946. Her game was based on a tremendously strong backhand which she could hit crosscourt or down the line, a steady and well-controlled forehand which lacked the power of her left side, and a better than average net game. Her biggest defect, she says, was her overhead. Her strongest point was her fight and stamina. She never tired during a match at any time in her life! Although she had the nervousness common to so many players before a match, she was never bothered by nerves on the court.

During the winter of 1947 Pauline went to the Riviera to play the international tournaments at San Remo, Cannes, Beaulieu, Monte Carlo and Nice. When overseas she received a cablegram from the U.S.L.T.A. asking her if she had authorized Elwood Cooke to send out letters of inquiry to various country clubs sounding them out on possible exhibitions for herself and Sarah Cooke. The following day she received another telegram, informing her that she could accept no further expense money until her status had been clarified. That afternoon she went out to Magda Rurac in the Monte Carlo tournament, from which time Magda was known as "the girl who beat Pauline Betz on the Riviera."

A few days later, Pauline learned that the association had definitely suspended her from amateur competition and that she would be allowed a hearing only after Wimbledon and the nationals. The newspapers described Pauline as "bursting into tears when she received the news," although it actually affected her very little. She was feeling overtennised and was anxious to consider a professional career. The only disappointment was the fact that she could not defend her Wimbledon and national titles. At this time, her good friend Barbara Hutton invited Pauline to visit her and her new husband, Prince Igor Troubetzkoy, in Zurich, Switzerland. After a week of lazy Swiss life, she received a phone call from Sarah announcing that Elwood had had a wonderful response on their pro inquiry, and would Pauline please fly home immediately to arrange the tour? With that, Pauline turned professional. . . .

In 1949 Pauline married Washington, D.C. sports columnist Bob Addie. She had always said she would marry either a really good tennis player or someone who didn't play at all. Bob fell into the second category. He doesn't play tennis because, Pauline says, she won't allow it. In their five years of marriage Pauline has acquired three children, one by adoption. Rusty will be three in December, Jon (who was adopted when he was three weeks old) is 15 months and Kim is four weeks.

Pauline still keeps in close touch with tennis. She designs her own rackets for Cortland and is on their tennis staff. She frequently plays with the men professionals at various clubs in and around Bethesda, Maryland, their current home, and has even entered the men's events of professional tournaments. . . . She won against Sarah Cooke in 1948 and she toured against Gussie Moran in 1951, winning the big majority of the matches. For four years she topped the amateur rankings and for seven more she has headed the professionals.

JOHN BROMWICH

by Bob Considine

One summery morning in January 1925, in the back yard of No. 52 Illawarra Street, Kogarah, New South Wales, where the seasons of the year are reversed, a six-year-old boy named John Edward Bromwich resolved to beat the stuffings out of a ragged tennis ball.

He was aided by two advantages: His father, a man of moderate means, had scraped together enough money to build a tennis court in the rear of his modest property. His father, in addition, owned a good stout tennis racket. And this the boy lugged out on the court and took the first curious swing of an even more curious sports career.

It was a heavy racket, suited to the slow backcourt game his father and mother played. To swing it with any degree of accuracy or pleasure the boy had to hold it with two hands. But that was natural as well as handy. Because from the time he could toddle he had seen and played rudimentary forms of cricket. Thus, though he knew his father and mother didn't hit a tennis ball that way, and certainly wouldn't approve, he decided to use a cricketer's grip and a cricket swing. He could hit that tennis ball harder that way.

When they saw this strange hybrid of a stroke, half tennis and half cricket, his father and mother laughed at the sober kid and made a mental note to teach him the right style when he was older. But John couldn't wait. Left to his own devices, he began adding strokes to his two-fisted forehand.

He decided, after trial and error, that it was all right to use two hands on his service, too, like a boy beating a carpet strung high above his head. He decided further that backhands were too difficult to make, either with one or two hands, so he simply decided to eliminate the troublesome backhand from his game. He was ambidextrous, so what he did when a ball came to his left, or backhand, side was suddenly shift the racket to his left hand.

Jack got around the problem of how to throw the ball up in the air on his service, what with both hands busy holding the racket, by gripping the handle with four fingers of each hand and sticking his index fingers straight out to form a little platform on which to hold the ball—and from which to catapult it into the air by suddenly bringing his arms up.

Before his parents could get around to curing him of all these absurdities, John had become the neighborhood champion. He couldn't swing the heavy racket fast enough to hit the ball for placements, but he could run like a frisky young deer, and for a longer time, and any ball that he could reach he could push back over the net. Even in those tender years, when the world's most eccentric tennis game was jelling about him, he seemed to sense that tennis matches are lost by errors, and never won by brilliant shots.

This month Jack Bromwich, now a diffident yellow-haired boy of twenty who looks like a slenderized Tommy Farr and talks in a quick and almost Cockney voice, when he talks, is destined to become the world's No. 1 amateur tennis player. On September 2d, 3d and 4th, on the grass courts of the Merion Cricket Club (prophetically enough) the cricketerlike Australian boy is expected singlehanded to capture the Davis Cup for his country by winning both his singles matches against the defending Americans and by dominating the important doubles match. . . .

The singular part of Bromwich's rise from hopeless obscurity . . . is that he has achieved his rank with almost the identical game his child's mind fashioned in the Kogarah back yard. His game is childishly absurd, but it works. It is almost as unorthodox as if a ballplayer stood with his legs straddling home plate and tried to hit a wicked curve with the swing of a man driving a nail. A golfing counterpart of Bromwich would be an eccentric who used only one hand on all approach shots. The difference is that Bromwich wins tough, grueling matches with this child's game.

The pile of victims in his short and turbulent wake include Budge, whom he beat in an exhibition in Australia when he was eighteen, and the great Baron Gottfried von Cramm, from whom he nonchalantly won the German singles championship at the age of seventeen.

Bromwich has made one concession to tennis' rigid form book. When he was thirteen he gave up serving with two hands, but he still has misgivings

about the decision because his service, the one orthodox shot he owns, is the
weakest link in his game. When he decided to go normal on his serve, he
chose a soft and conventional slice serve which any crisp-driving opponent
could lean into with great glee. But lately, as if moved by the same happy
perversity that made him distort all the rules on how to hit a tennis ball, he
has been hitting himself on the lower right leg in the midst of his windup
for his serve. The shock of the collision often causes the ball to take a
slightly different flight across the net than the progress of the swing would
indicate, simply because the face of the racket tends to wobble from the
impact with his leg. Now, due to this apparently brainless leg-whacking, his
serve is harder to receive. His opponent is never quite sure where the thing
is going and, judging from his worry-creased pan, neither is Bromwich.

Today, when he is about to attain the top peak of world tennis,
Bromwich doesn't hit the ball as hard as the average public playground
player. He will be the softest hitter in the National Singles, and in the Davis
Cup matches his American opponent will sock the ball at a speed of from 20
to 40 miles per hour faster than he. But Bromwich will keep the ball in play
all day. That's his strength.

"He's the closest thing to a practice wall I've ever seen," Vincent Richards,
who alternates with George Lott as Bromwich's American coach, told us
recently.

Did you ever play a practice wall? If you ever did you took the worst
beating you'll ever take in tennis, for you didn't win one point. You
couldn't, for the wall returned the ball as often as you hit it against it. A
practice wall always has the last word, or shot. Playing against Bromwich
gives players a similar feeling of futility. He looks easy at the start, for his
shots carry no particularly visible power, and while they are extremely well
placed, it isn't too difficult to reach the first five or six of them he hits during
a single rally. However, the disheartening thing is that Bromwich keeps
sending your returns back over the net, and back and back and back. And
sooner or later, with mounting vexation or the recklessness born of weariness, his opponent slams the ball so hard, in the hope of winning the point
outright, that he drives it into the net or out of bounds.

The one hard-to-cure weakness in the game of Jack Bromwich is Jack
Bromwich. The fellow is a strange nest of moods. Last year in the finals of
the National Doubles he played in a way which should have caused the
customers at the Longwood Cricket Club to yell for their money back. He
and Adrian Quist lost to Don Budge and Gene Mako, 6–3, 6–2, 6–1. Bromwich was as unsteady as the franc, and when those queer shots of his go
haywire he looks like a comic valentine of a tennis player, even to the mop
of yellow hair hanging in his eyes.

But ten days later at Germantown, Pennsylvania, in the Challenge
Round of the Davis Cup matches, he pressed Don Budge to Big Red's
hardest match of the year and stood within one shot of sending it into the
fifth set, where anything could have happened. For Budge was winded and
tired. Bromwich lost gallantly, fighting like a demon for every point, 6–2,
6–3, 4–6, 7–5. In the doubles the next day, against the same team of Budge

and Mako, which had annihilated him and Quist at Longwood, Bromwich played some of the greatest tennis ever seen in this country to dominate the Australians' 0–6, 6–3, 6–4, 6–2 victory. Standing well inside the baseline, and hitting the Americans' whistling serves with a kind of hay-pitching swing, Bromwich made dozens of returns that had Budge and Mako pawing at the air like stricken fighters.

On the third and final day of the 1938 Challenge Round, Bromwich dusted off Bobby Riggs, 6–4, 4–6, 6–0, 6–2, ending the match with an absolutely flawless streak of tennis. As a result of that 3-day performance he was named the No. 1 seeded foreign player in the National Singles and a certain bet to oppose Budge in the finals. But some kind of adolescent listlessness overcame him at Forest Hills. He barely squeezed through Frank Shields in five sets and finally was knocked out of the tournament in the semifinal round by Gene Mako, who normally couldn't take a set from him with a court order. Nobody could understand it, and Bromwich, who is reporter-proof, wouldn't explain.

Though his current ambition is to be a sports writer, Bromwich has a fear and mistrust of reporters. Like a considerable proportion of our big-league baseball players—whom he greatly admires, by the way—he freezes up at the sight of a newspaper man or woman bearing down on him for an interview. But this is not wholly a personal trait. It is contrary to the rules of the Australian Lawn Tennis Association, and other Anzac sports bodies, for a member of an Australian team to speak to a member of the press. All interviews must be obtained from the captain of the team or by his leave.

This quaint rule is a throwback to the nasty little scandal kicked up a few years ago when an Australian bowler was accused of deliberately trying to bean one of England's finest cricketers in the celebrated contest for "The Ashes."

Bromwich is a brilliant volleyer. Indeed, it is at the net that his unearthly, catlike speed is best exhibited. For there, in the very teeth of his opponent's driving, he still is able to make a two-handed forehand volley, follow it up if necessary with a quick shift of the racket to his left hand, for a left-handed forehand volley and finish off the point, if given the chance, with a one-handed (right-handed) overhead smash. And he can do all this racket-shifting and artful swinging in the briefest flick of time, while he dives this way and that, propelled by two brisk legs and a sense of anticipation that is definitely not of this world. . . .

Jack has worked out his own method of relaxing from what must be—for all its country-clubbish luxury—downright hard work. In America he gets up quite early, eats a carefully selected breakfast, and starts the phonograph he takes everywhere with him. Unlike the jitterbug American players, he abhors swing. His records go as deep into music as Tchaikovsky. In mid-morning he begins playing bridge and at noon he eats again, lightly, and goes to the courts. If he doesn't have to play that day he'll play his phonograph nice and loud after lunch, then go to a ball game or to a race track, if one is handy. At night he goes to a movie. He doesn't have a very good time with girls, nor a great deal of money to spend on them.

Bromwich is a subsidized amateur. He works for Slazenger, the British sports-goods house. He's a salesman without portfolio. He uses their equipment and for this he gets a retainer of five pounds a week. Adrian Quist, his teammate, has a similar arrangement with Dunlop. It takes some of the strain off the Australian amateur net body, which looks upon such subsidies with favor, but the greatest bulk of Bromwich's annual expenses are borne by the Australian association.

In a much less hypocritical manner than our U.S.L.T.A. supports our more prominent players, the Australian association has been more or less supporting Bromwich since he was fifteen. He attended Hurstville Technical School, at home, but by the time he got through what amounts to a junior-high education he was too valuable a piece of amateur tennis property to permit to go to college—as was the case with Budge. In 1934, when he was fifteen, he won the junior championships of Queensland, New South Wales, South Australia and Australia, and repeated in all these tournaments the following year. That same year, 1935, he was so good that the association gave him a spot on the Australian men's team which met an all-European team in Adelaide, and he won his match. That same year, at sixteen, he beat Crawford, Quist and McGrath, and in 1937 he began the globe-trotting that will continue until his springs run down.

George Agutter, the veteran professional at Forest Hills, believes that in Bromwich is ingrained one of the finest cases of "tennis sense" he has seen in forty years of watching tennis. "When he beat Riggs in the Davis Cup matches last year he did it by deliberately softening every shot he hit to Riggs' backhand," Agutter says. "That kept Riggs busy trying to put some speed into his backhands, but whenever he seemed to be mastering Bromwich's slow shots Jack would wallop one to Riggs' forehand. In other words Bromwich reversed the usual procedure and simply outwitted his man. I think he's the steadiest, brainiest player we've seen since Lacoste, and with a better all-round game than the Frenchman had."

HARRY HOPMAN

by Harry Gordon

Seven earnest and single-minded young men, whose average age is 19, will make Australia's annual pilgrimage to the All-England lawn tennis championships at Wimbledon this July. From London they will continue on what for most teen-age tourists would be a dream trip. They will play in a number of Continental tournaments, fly the Atlantic to tackle the American tennis circuit, then head for home in time for the Australian summer.

But for Australia's tennis tourists this journey won't be any tourists' jaunt. They won't see Montmartre, because it could be tiring. They won't eat ravioli in Rome, because it could be fattening. They won't, when they arrive back in Australia, be able to assess the current plays on Broadway, but they will be able to debate, with considerable authority, the respective merits of the clay surface at the Stade Roland Garros and the grass courts at Forest Hills.

The man who will see that they are not up late nights or fattened by ravioli—and who will receive a large share of the honors they bring back—is Harry Hopman, the non-playing captain of Australia's team and an outstanding—if not great—player in his own day. He will watch their plane reservations and their weight, their hotel bookings and their manners. If they get homesick he will talk to them like a parent; if their strokes get sloppy he will lecture them like a coach.

Hopman, the foundation about whom present-day Australian tennis has been built, is an exceptionally hard taskmaster. "We are not off on a pleasure trip," he says. "We are going away to win what we can, and to give our youngsters experience. It will entail a good deal of hard work."

A perky nut-brown man of 47, Hopman is generally acknowledged to be the shrewdest tennis brain in the world. He is invariably admired, often feared, and sometimes hated by tennis followers in every country, including his own. He has been called a variety of names—a good many of them unflattering. Probably the most appropriate description came from America's Tony Trabert, after Australia had been presented with the Davis Cup for the fourth year in a row. "We were beaten," he said, "by two babies and a fox."

The babies were Lew Hoad and Ken Rosewall, both only 19—the two brightest pupils in the current Hopman crop. The fox, of course, was Hopman. Less complimentary critics than Trabert have called him a whip-cracker in a tennis chain gang, a producer of magnificent robots.

The Hopman era began after World War II, when Hopman, appalled at the comparative inferiority of Australian players, decided to build for the future. He developed Frank Sedgman and Ken McGregor, both outstanding juniors, into two of the finest players in the world. In 1950, appointed non-playing captain for the first time, he substituted McGregor for the veteran John Bromwich against Ted Schroeder in the first singles. McGregor won, and so did Australia.

Hopman has continued to concentrate on youngsters—so much so, that when Sedgman and McGregor became professionals, he was able to hold the cup with newcomers like Lew Hoad and Ken Rosewall. That is the basis of the Hopman legend, a legend which is becoming a big psychological weapon in Australia's tennis favor.

How has he done it? In the United States and England there is a widening belief that Hopman has evolved some secret, almost magic, formula. The men close to Hopman regard this as nonsense; they attribute his undoubted success to a combination of firm, practical measures.

Hopman prefers, for the most part, to maintain a discreet and knowing silence on the subject. Some of the most knowledgeable men in Australian tennis have declared emphatically that the key to Hopman's undoubted greatness lies mainly in the tough, almost merciless, conditioning process to which he submits his protégés. Other contributing factors, they say, are his great tactical ability and the vast amount of time he is able to devote to his duties as mentor. They believe also that he has not imparted a great deal of purely tennis knowledge to them, pointing out that he has not, to any large degree, altered the styles of the youngsters whose training he has taken over. Most critics point out that he does not work on raw material, that he hand-picks his pupils from Australia's finest junior talent.

Former Davis Cup captain Colin Long has definite views about Hopman's methods. "The man is a physical-fitness fanatic," he says. "His object is to have his boys faster, sharper, peppier than their opposition. He drives them hard with five-mile runs before breakfast and long sessions of squash and gym work. Then, when they think they are as fit as they can be, he drives them harder. When he gets them on a tennis court, it is usually to shoot balls at them from all sorts of angles, with the object of sharpening the reflexes. He spends a relatively small amount of time perfecting their stroke play."

What is the Hopman conditioning plan that has helped to achieve such magnificent results? According to Frank Findlay, the chunky, powerfully built physical culturist at whose gymnasium the Hopman charges work out with pulleys, oars and weights, there isn't any set plan. The youngsters train to individual schedules, he says.

"Look at Sedgman, for instance," says Findlay. "When he came to the gymnasium he was long and skinny, so Harry and I gave him plenty of weight-lifting. He developed so fast that we soon had to put the brakes on. We didn't want him to get top-heavy. What we were aiming at was speed, flexibility, the agility to reach up high for overhead smashes and the strength to bang down winners.

"Always, we work that way, tailoring our program to the needs of each tennis player. If they are flat-footed, big-hipped or heavy-shouldered, we try to compensate for these features. In general, the training programs resemble those of sprinters, but we've incorporated a lot of exercises peculiarly for tennis players. Some of our exercises have been taken from adagio and ballet movements. They're to give the boys extra spring and bounce.

"When we got Hoad, he had no use for body-building; he was built like a lumberjack at 17. So we gave him large doses of squash and track work—made him whippy and able to keep attacking. Rosewall needed off-season body-building. We let him work with the pulleys and do light weight-lifting to get some power into his shoulder muscles."

Findlay, on Hopman's instructions, takes all members of Australia's Davis Cup squads on runs of up to five miles. Sometimes he takes just one along and sometimes they run in packs. They walk a while, run a while, throw stones at trees and stumps, vault fences, and often peel off and swim. These runs, he says, are aimed at building up speed without losing stamina.

The conditioning plant may be the most important section of the

Hopman factory for champions, but there is certainly no secret blueprint for it. Recently, Findlay received a letter from an American coach asking if he would send a copy of the Australians' training schedules. Findlay referred the letter to Hopman "because I didn't want to be disloyal," and was promptly told to give the American all the information he could.

As a tennis coach, the dice are heavily loaded in Hopman's favor. His stable consists of single, easy-to-handle boys who are happy to let him make the big decisions for them; he is backed by a powerful newspaper; and he is able to devote more time to tennis than most other non-professional coaches.

Hopman, a sports columnist on the 450,000-circulation Melbourne *Herald,* starts his working day around 7 A.M. and is through by noon. He does the indexing of his very complete files at night, so that he has his afternoons free. He is almost a teetotaler and has a surprisingly small circle of intimate friends. Few home interests keep him from the tennis courts. Childless and a non-gardener, he is quite happy to spend his weekends away from home. His tennis friends say that he is extremely fond of children and would have made a wonderful father. He has certainly taken a fatherly interest in his boys and has taught them a good deal more than tennis. Under him, they learn to wear good clothes and to mind their manners.

His system of fining the boys for misdemeanors on and off the court has come in for a good deal of criticism. . . . While many tennis officials regard these fines as dictatorial nonsense on Hopman's part, the view of his co-trainer, Findlay, is interesting. "In the main, they are high-spirited and irresponsible boys," he says, "and Harry feels that they must be turned into good ambassadors for Australia. He has to teach them how to pass the butter and how to use their forks, and fining them is a good way of doing it. . . ."

Hopman's system of supervision on and off the court has produced fine-looking athletes of good character, but most of his products appear to have been singularly lacking in personality. This fact was never more clearly demonstrated than on the center court at Kooyong on that clear December day last year when Australia retained the Davis Cup. Each member of the American team called to the microphone gave a short and witty speech. Their Australian rivals, who had been glacier cool in play, were nervous and gauche.

Although it should be conceded that the Australian Davis Cup players are of a lower educational standard than their American counterparts, this absence of personality must be regarded largely as a Hopman by-product, since he has never encouraged his boys to talk to press or radio interviewers.

As an official, Hopman often seems to newspapermen to be suspicious and unwilling to cooperate. These qualities may seem strange, coming from a working reporter, but Hopman stops being one the moment he and his boys go on tour. He has, in fact, good reason to be cagey with the press. On almost every tour, he has had to take a beating from some newspaper critics—not because of poor behavior on the part of his teams, but mainly as a result of their tennis perfection. Hopman is usually terse and scathing, but not very enlightening, when asked to reply to these criticisms.

When a leading English columnist, Peter Wilson, attacked "High Priest Harry's conveyor-belt methods" last year, Hopman answered: "We don't take dear old Peter seriously. . . . The boys sit around the TV set after dinner, listen to Peter Wilson and have a good laugh. He knows nothing about it. . . ."

He can be selfish at times. Many claim that he did nothing to encourage young players when he himself was playing and began to take an interest in them only after he had retired. But he can be exceedingly kind and helpful to the mediocre tennis players, weak-armed jockeys, and overweight swimmers who come in contact with him on his daily sporting rounds. . . .

Throughout his career, Hopman has admitted no diversion to sidetrack him—and he expects his "babies" to be equally single-minded. He has had to push a great many people aside, but he has fought his battles with tremendous fairness. He has never chiseled a point, and would never allow his protégés to do so. Back in 1926 he was one of the world's leading tennis players—but he was never great. In his own country, he was overshadowed by the lank, austere-looking Jack Crawford. Hopman's name crops up in the record books mainly in the doubles—with Crawford and with Mrs. Hopman.

Hopman is hard to pin down on just how he has achieved his successes. "I think that the experience that I have been able to impart quickly to our top players has helped as much as the fitness I've insisted upon," he says. "A big factor is that Australia has excellent tennis conditions—a suitable round-the-year climate and many competitions and schemes for juniors." Of his coaching methods, Hopman will say that they consist of "watching closely and studying closely and then worrying about how to counter the opposition's good points and overcoming one's own weaknesses. . . .

"I arrange training to fit in with the tennis program. The average retiring hour of the boys while on tour is 11 P.M., and before-breakfast runs are ordered only when players aren't as fit as they should be.

"The boys don't drink or smoke. Players at their top don't need alcohol and are usually too young to know drinking discretion when they start. My main worry is to see that they don't eat too much."

It is quite conceivable that Harry Hopman will be a big power in Australian tennis for another five, ten or even twenty years. But one thing is certain: the man who succeeds him will have an unenviable job.

Colin Long, the top-ranking candidate for the position, puts it this way: "For the man who follows Hoppy, there will be little credit if his teams win; to the vast tennis public, Harry Hopman will still be the man responsible.

"But if his teams lose, people will say, 'Look at that—they just can't do without Hopman.' "

Whatever happens, it seems, the dice will still be loaded in favor of "Harry the Hop."

GUSSIE MORAN

from World Tennis

I shall never forget the first time I saw Gussie Moran. It was one of those typically unusual Northern California days—damp, foggy and cold. The door of the Berkeley Tennis Club flew open, and as the cold blast of air hit us, we looked up. I was sitting in an overcoat with my feet hanging over the lone small floor heater in the clubhouse. Three other players, swabbed in mufflers and overcoats, were beating their arms against their legs and jumping in rhythm to keep warm.

As Gussie slowly walked into the club, the soft thud of arms flapping against bodies died away. Two or three vets who had been standing by the soft drink bar discussing their forehands stopped their conversation. One of them had even pursed his lips in readiness to give a low wolf call before he caught himself.

I have only a vague memory of her apparel—a multicolored skirt, a snug sweater, a large coat thrown over it, hair pulled tightly back behind the ears and one or two hair ribbons twined through the straight black hair. As she walked, she threw one leg in front of her as far as she could without tearing a muscle, landing on the ball of her foot. Then the other leg followed in long stride, landing smack on the same imaginary line. The whole was accompanied with a jaunty bounce which was unusual enough to cause the oldest vet and the youngest junior to turn around for a second look.

She stopped in the middle of the room, turned around and gave everyone a friendly smile which you may be sure was returned by every man present. The Maestro, Tom Stow, emerged from his office and strolled toward Gussie swinging his hips in imitation Moran-stride. He smiled, Gussie smiled, and he introduced us.

Gussie, to my surprise, was as well liked by women as she was by men. She was always sweet and friendly, slightly on the shy side, good-natured and kind, and she never had a mean word for anyone, even when they weren't there. She had several other distinguishing characteristics besides The Walk, the sleek hair-do and the colorful clothes. One was her laugh, which sounded like a series of rapid hiccups. The other was her voice, which gave the impression, if your eyes were closed, of a raised eyebrow. Everything combined gave her that touch of glamour which tennis had never had before.

Gertrude Augusta Moran's fabulous career started 30 years ago in Santa Monica when she was born. . . . When Gussie entered high school she took up tennis. Being one of the best natural athletes that ever hit the ball, she became very good almost immediately. She and Louise Brough were the two best in the Southern California area, although Louise gradually passed her by the time they were seventeen. Gussie had a good record in the juniors,

losing to Doris Hart in the quarters of the Nationals twice but making an
outstanding impression wherever she played.

Gussie was never the great player she could have been. She was universally recognized as having the best coordination, the soundest strokes and
the most potential ability of anyone in her group as an amateur. Her highest
national ranking was No. 4 in 1948. As Gussie herself puts it, she never
fought, she never trained, and she never knew what it was to want to win
until she took a terrible shellacking from Pauline Betz on the pro tour.

When Gussie graduated into the women's ranks, she played only locally
for several years. In the summer, instead of going East, she worked around
the movie studios. For a while she was a stand-in for her good friend Jinx
Falkenburg. . . .

Gussie finally went East in 1945 and created a sensation but was not
ranked. The next year she made No. 13, and then No. 7, No. 4 and No. 7,
after which she turned professional. During this period, she played Wimbledon twice. The first year, she played on the center court and went out to
little Gem Hoahing in the first round. The next year she bowed to Margaret
duPont in the round of 16. But in spite of her failure to win the world
championship, Gussie was the hit of the show. She became world famous at
Wimbledon, thanks to a bit of tennis apparel designed by Teddy Tinling.

When Teddy designed the lace panties, neither he nor Gussie had any
inkling of the international repercussions that would ensue. Practically
every tennis dress that had been sold for the last ten years had come with a
matching pair of panties, just in case the wind blew or the player crouched
low to receive service. Gussie's panties were distinguished only by a small
ribbing of lace around the edges.

When Gussie made her appearance accoutered in the lace panties,
swarms of tennis enthusiasts lined the path to the courts in the hopes of a
glimpse of her famous underapparel. Several fans even stretched out on the
ground. Newspaper photographers begged for a shot that revealed the lace
ribbing. The results were sensational. Within weeks, every radio comic had
at least one joke about the lace panties, and Gussie became to tennis what
Marilyn Monroe was to the movies.

But Gussie stayed the same old Gussie—a little giggly, a little shy, and
very much overwhelmed by all the publicity.

In 1949, Gussie was staying with Mickey Falkenburg Wagstaff, mother of
Jinx, Bob and Tom, while she was playing the national indoors in New
York City. Gussie was so nervous before each match that Lee, Mickey's
husband, suggested that she pay a visit to the zoo in Central Park and pick
up a little courage from the lions. Gussie went to the zoo and watched the
lions every day, then went to the courts and played like a tiger. She won the
tournament, and from then on she was a zoo addict. Gussie claims she has
been to zoos in every country she has played in. . . .

Gussie's travels took her all over the world—Australia, Egypt, France,
England and every section of the United States. Wherever she went, she left
a trail of swooning men. . . . She made headlines in Egypt—she appeared
in black shorts for the finals. She was front page news in India—she went on

a safari with the Maharajah of Cooch Behar and shot a leopard. She never wore the lace panties again, but wherever she went she was known as Gussie of the lace pants. . . . Wherever she played she was greeted with whistles and wolf calls.

Gloria Butler claims that any inferiority complex that she possesses is due to a series of exhibitions that she played with Gussie. Gloria, who is a beauty in her own right, played a year of exhibitions as arranged by Bill Tilden. It was during the war, and Gussie and Gloria gladly donated all their free time to playing before vets in a 135-mile radius of the Los Angeles area. Tilden would pick up the two girls as early as 6 A.M. every Saturday and Sunday. Gussie would pile in the car, sans make-up, carrying a small kit with which to put on her face. Then away they would go, into the desert or out to a small town, to play before returning G.I.'s and hospitalized vets.

Each time Big Bill introduced Gussie, the house would come down. Gussie would walk out in form-fitting shorts and a form-fitting pink angora sweater, while G.I.'s shouted, "Take off your sweater!" When the hullabaloo quieted down, Gloria was introduced.

Says Gloria, "That wasn't the worst. She beat me with monotonous regularity. I should have ended up hating her."

Then came the day that Bobby Riggs signed up Gussie for the pro tour. Gussie was to get $75,000 and to be matched against the best player, amateur or professional, in the game—Pauline Betz.

Gussie says she still hates to think about opening night in the Garden in New York. The last thing she remembers was the band playing "The Star-Spangled Banner" and the lights going out. When the match was over, Mrs. Fred Small came over and offered her a drink of brandy.

"Thanks," said Gussie, "but why couldn't you have given it to me before the match?"

The tour was slightly one-sided, with Pauline dominating the play. Toward the middle of the tour, Gussie showed some improvement but there were still, she admits, many dog matches. By the end, Gussie was a different person.

"I took enough beatings," says Gussie, "to learn my lesson. I'm not sorry I turned pro, because it made me grow up. I stopped fooling around, I trained and I practiced more as a pro than I did in all my years as an amateur."

With the tour over, Gussie settled down to the quiet life of a hostess at Charlie Farrell's Racquet Club in Palm Springs, California. She was on the court from nine to six every day. . . .

During the nationals this year, Maureen Connolly created quite a sensation every time she walked from the clubhouse to the stadium. The tennis fans turned and stared when old-timers like Nancy Chaffee Kiner and big Dick Savitt put in an appearance to watch the matches. Jack Kramer and Bobby Riggs drew their quotas of "oooohs" and "aaahs." But when Gussie showed up, you could hear the buzz-buzz run through the crowds like wildfire. Gussie gave the game a touch of glamour and beauty that won't soon be forgotten. Gussie has been tennisdom's most spectacular press agent!

THE GREATEST IN WOMEN'S TENNIS

by George Lott

Helen Wills Moody receives my nomination as the greatest woman tennis player of all time. Her record of winning seven United States titles, an unprecedented eight Wimbledon championships and four French crowns gives her a total of major championships unequaled by any other player. In Wightman Cup competition, which is not considered in the scoring system of this tabulation, Mrs. Moody won sixteen out of eighteen matches, the last fourteen in succession.

Little Miss Poker Face, as she was dubbed by Grantland Rice, the great sportswriter of the Golden Twenties, was the female apotheosis of the great athletes of that era. Her male counterparts were Red Grange, Babe Ruth, Jack Dempsey, Bobby Jones and Bill Tilden. Helen thoroughly dominated women's tennis, she had color and mystery, and, in race-track parlance, she had class. I never understood how "Granny" arrived at the nickname of Little Miss Poker Face. It is true that Helen's facial expression rarely varied and that she always tended strictly to business, but her opponents were never in doubt as to what she held: 1, an excellent service; 2, a powerful forehand; 3, a strong backhand; 4, a killer instinct, and 5, no weaknesses. Five of a kind! Who would want to draw against this kind of hand?

One of the most famous matches in the history of women's tennis was played between Helen and the great French champion, Suzanne Lenglen, on the French Riviera, and the French girl won, 6–3, 8–6. Although at the time of this contest Helen was already a three-time American champion, I do not believe she had reached her peak. On the other hand, Suzanne was nearing the end of her career. I like to imagine the results of a match between the Suzanne of 1921 and the Helen of 1928. It would be so close that picking a winner would be strictly a guess. This is all anyone can do in comparing champions of different eras. The only way they can be ranked is on their recorded accomplishments, and on this basis Helen Wills Moody is clearly the No. 1 woman player of all time.

Strangely enough, at least to me, Maureen Connolly is entitled to second place. Her record of nine major championships within three years was a great achievement, but it was her grand slam of 1953 which allows her to edge out Lenglen for second place. "Little Mo" is one of four women players in the entire history of tennis who won a championship in each of the four major tennis countries. The others are Margaret Smith, Doris Hart and Shirley Fry. It was unfortunate that Mo's career was ended with an accident before she reached her majority. It seems quite possible that, given time, she might have earned the top position.

The fabulous Suzanne is ranked third, and I expect to hear from General De Gaulle about this heresy. She ruled the tennis world from 1919 to 1925 and was undoubtedly the most colorful female ever to swing a racket. She didn't have the power of Mrs. Moody or "Little Mo," but she had a rare artistry that was unsurpassed. She was lightning-fast and her footwork was perfect. I doubt if any tennis player, man or woman, was as accurate as Suzanne. . . .

There are two players in this ranking who are still active and who have the opportunity to move up higher as the years pass. One is Margaret Smith, who is now in the No. 4 position, with nine major championships distributed around the world—a very definite sign of greatness. The other is Maria Bueno, who is currently No. 9, with six titles. There cannot be any doubt that either, or both, will go up the ladder.

Mrs. Mallory, the fifth-ranking all-time player, won the U.S. singles seven times, and the wartime patriotic tournament in 1917 also. She was a one-shot woman who had great determination. Her forehand was severe, she could hit it anywhere, and the only time she ever quit in a match was after the final point.

In the sixth position we find Doris Hart, with six championships that were won in four countries. Her rise to such a high ranking is a great tribute to her capacity to overcome physical disabilities. Her life is one of the great stories of the sports world. Louise Brough and Margaret duPont are ranked at Nos. 7 and 8. They have identical records: each won six titles in three countries. Maria Bueno follows at No. 9 with the same number of championships, but she won them in only two countries.

The rest of the rankings are very close in relative records. The woman who has my sympathy is Helen Jacobs, who won a total of five major titles

All-Time Women's Singles Ranking

		U.S.	Wimbledon	Australia	France	Total
1.	Helen Wills Moody	7	8	0	4	19
2.	Maureen Connolly	3	3	1	2*	13
3.	Suzanne Lenglen	0	6	0	6	12
4.	Margaret Smith	1	1	5	2	9
5.	Molla Mallory	8	0	0	0	8
6.	Doris Hart	2	1	1	2	6
7-8.	Margaret duPont	3	1	0	2	6
7-8.	Louise Brough	1	4	1	0	6
9.	Maria Bueno	3	3	0	0	6
10.	Althea Gibson	2	2	0	1	5
11-13.	Helen Jacobs	4	1	0	0	5
11-13.	Alice Marble	4	1	0	0	5
11-13.	Pauline Betz	4	1	0	0	5
14.	Shirley Fry	1	1	1	1	4
15.	Hazel Wightman	4	0	0	0	4
16.	Mrs. L. Chambers	0	4	0	0	4
17.	Dorothy Round	0	2	1	0	3
18.	Darlene Hard	2	0	0	1	3
19.	Mary K. Browne	3	0	0	0	3
20.	Angela Mortimer	0	1	1	1	3

SCORING: *1 point for each major title*
    * *4 points for Grand Slam in 1953*

All-Time Women's Doubles Ranking

	U.S.	Wimbledon	Australia	France	Total
1. Brough-duPont	12	5	0	3	20
2. Hart-Fry	4	3	0	4	11
3. Palfrey-Marble	4	2	0	0	6
4. Lenglen-Ryan	0	6	0	0	6
5. Hard-Bueno	2	2	0	1	5
6. Mathieu-Ryan	0	2	0	2	4
7. Mathieu-Yorke	0	1	0	3	4
8. Wills-Ryan	0	1	0	2	3
9. Smith-Ebbern	1	0	2	0	3
10. Jacobs-Palfrey	3	0	0	0	3

SCORING: *1 point for each major title*

but who was runner-up at Forest Hills four times and at Wimbledon five times. What a difference a few wins would have made! Helen Jacobs was one of my favorites. I always thought she got the furthest with the leastest. To be exact, she had a forehand chop, a sound backhand, and lots and lots of stomach muscles. She was buffeted from pillar to post by Helen Wills and still came back for more. I have seen Helen Wills beat her 6–0, 6–0 in matches that would discourage anyone. I can well imagine the satisfaction she must have felt when she finally beat the other Helen in the finals of Forest Hills in 1933, despite the unfortunate ending.

The team of Louise Brough and Margaret duPont was the greatest of all time. Their record is one of the best in any sport. Their domination began in 1942 and their last title was won in 1957. After taking the U.S. title in 1942, they won for nine consecutive years through 1950. Their reign was interrupted for four years (1951–1954) by the runners-up in this ranking, Doris Hart and Shirley Fry. Then they resumed as titleholders for three more years. They are truly the greatest of the great!

THE REBUTTAL TO LOTT'S RANKING OF WOMEN

by Peter Wilson

I should never presume to criticize George Lott's ability to choose the "All-Time Greats"; it is the method he has adopted which I dispute. I do not, for instance, think it's equitable to go only on the number of "Top Four" tournaments won in making a ranking list. Before the Second World War scarcely any top-ranking overseas women players ever competed in the Australian Championships. Indeed, before the *Queen Mary* had her maiden voyage in 1936, it took nearly five days to get from Britain to the U. S. A.

—and the almost total lack of long distance flying meant that top American women players usually came to Continental Europe only every other year when the Wightman Cup was played at Wimbledon. In fact, from 1925 to 1946, only one American woman won the French Singles—although that one player, Helen Wills Moody, triumphed four times.

But let's go on to specific comparisons between George Lott's ranking lists and the rearrangements I should make. I have to omit Mrs. Lambert Chambers because I never saw her in action, although those old enough to have watched her Wimbledon final against Suzanne Lenglen in 1919 in which she held two match points before losing 8–10, 6–4, 7–9, say it was one of the greatest ever. Suzanne, also, I never saw play competitively. But one of the greatest disappointments of my (sporting) life was when, at the old Dulwich covered courts near London, I was asked to make up a friendly mixed doubles with "the Queen"—who had then been retired from competitive play for over five years—only for the missing members of the foursome to turn up just in time. Or, in my case, just too soon!

I saw Suzanne play then and I have seen her on film, and it really is correct to describe her as "incomparable." She wedded ballet to sport in a way no other player has duplicated, even though Maria Bueno has approached it. Furthermore she DID beat Mrs. Moody (or Miss Wills, as she was then) 6–3, 8–6 on the one occasion they met. That was in February 1926, at Cannes. I know that Mrs. Moody had not reached her best then—she was not yet 21—but equally Mlle. Lenglen was slightly past her best at 27; in fact she turned professional at the end of that year. I would have said that Suzanne's greater mobility and her superior volleying put her above Mrs. Moody, although physical strength and certainly indomitable temperament would have been on the American's side.

Is the Frenchwoman my No. 2, then? No. That position, I maintain, is reserved for a girl whom neither I, nor anyone else, ever saw at her best. I refer, of course, to Maureen "Little Mo" Connolly. I was extraordinarily lucky enough to see her in the first international match which gained her mentions on the front pages of the world. I actually wrote one of them! This was her first appearance as "third string" (!) singles player in the 1951 Wightman Cup at Boston. I also saw her win her last of three Wimbledon titles in 1954. Her victory over Doris Hart in two straight but tense sets in 1953 remains as the best women's singles final I have ever watched at Wimbledon.

In between that first Wightman Cup match "Little Mo," who was then still 16, went on to win the U.S. title every time she competed for it, AND Wimbledon, AND the French Championship AND the Australian the only year she played in it—1953, the year of her Grand Slam. The fantastic thing is that had it not been for that career-crippling disastrous accident, she would almost certainly have been the favorite for Wimbledon—for since her day we have seen none better there—and the other major titles this year for she would still be only 30 by the time they were played. Mrs. Moody, for instance, won Wimbledon for the eighth time when she was 33. This year, by the way, could have made "Mo's" FOURTEENTH consecutive victory.

I say no one ever saw her at her best, and of that I am sure, for she still had a certain weakness on her service and with her volleying, on which she was still working. But after the time she got to the top—finishing *before* her 20th birthday—as far as I know she lost only two important matches. I firmly believe that her greater speed about the court, her equal consistency and hitting power *plus* the reasonable supposition that she would have improved had her career continued—Mrs. Moody was, of course, beaten in her first Wimbledon final when she was 18½—would have put Miss Connolly ahead of Mrs. Moody and would have gradually destroyed the gossamer touch of Mlle. Lenglen.

So much for the first three. Of the remaining "Top Ten" in George Lott's rankings I agree that Margaret Smith, who will not quite be 23 by the time she plays in this year's Wimbledon, may well garner more championships, which would move her up "Lott's list." *But* unless she experiences a complete temperament change she will never be the good bet which Mrs. Moody and Miss Connolly were when the chips were down. As for Maria Bueno, delight though she is to watch and capable of beating any contemporary on her day, I can't see her consistently combating the power game of Australia's greatest woman player. At the last count the Australian and the Brazilian were reported to have met fifteen times, with the score 11 4 in Miss Smith's favor. And Miss Bueno is nearly three years the older.

I would not quarrel overmuch with the placing of the other Top Ten except to say that I thought, at their best, that Louise Brough was a slightly superior singles player to Mrs. duPont and that I should not put Althea Gibson quite so high. I think Helen Jacobs and Alice Marble, for differing reasons, were more complete players. I never saw Mrs. Mallory.

But one player I am certain has been very harshly treated by the "statistical" rating system. She is Pauline Betz. When the Second World War came to Europe Miss Betz was only twenty. She won the U.S. title from 1942–44 and again in 1946; in 1945 she was beaten in the final by my old friend Sarah Palfrey Cooke in what Bill Tilden said was one of the greatest women's matches he had ever seen. In 1946, when she was not quite 27, she came to Wimbledon for the first and, as it turned out, the last time and joined the elite who won what I still regard with perhaps pardonable patriotic pride as the world's finest tournament at her first attempt; a feat which eluded every other overseas player except Mlle. Lenglen and Miss Connolly.

There was no doubt among those lawn tennis-starved enthusiasts who saw the first postwar Wimbledon of 1946, which "Bobbie" Betz won, that she stood out even in the immensely powerful U.S. Wightman Cup team of that year—herself, Margaret Osborne, Louise Brough and Doris Hart—who between them won no fewer than 23 of the "Big Four" championships. As Miss Betz turned professional in 1947 and as her peak period had been so restricted by the war, I think she has always been very much underrated; proof of this came when, as Mrs. Addie, with four children and at over forty, she took the eight years younger Althea Gibson to 7–5 in the third set of a professional match before, as she told me, "my old pins let me down."

With her wonderful court-covering ability, her truly glorious backhand and particularly, her ability to "scramble" so much back, she would have been a test for anyone—particularly "Little Mo," who never really cared for this sort of opponent. I should unhesitatingly put Pauline Betz in the Top Six—perhaps even in the Top Four rankings.

THE GREATEST IN MEN'S TENNIS

by Sir John Smyth

I was very interested in "Passing Shots" by Ned Potter in the April number, wherein he discusses the "all-time great" amongst the male lawn tennis players.

I agree with him when he ranks Bill Tilden as "the greatest player who ever lived." I also agree with him when he says, "It is impossible, actually, to compare great players of entirely different eras and to say categorically that one was better than another." . . .

In this fascinating game of ranking the world's best, we are all apt to be particularly fascinated by our own national heroes. . . .

Most British critics consider that lawn tennis began and ended with the Dohertys and Fred Perry. The French will look no further than René Lacoste, Henri Cochet and Jean Borotra. And the Americans put Bill Tilden, Don Budge and Jack Kramer as the greatest of all. In fact Ned Potter does just this—and he may well be right.

In my book *Lawn Tennis* in the series of British Sports: Past and Present (1953), which was dedicated to His Royal Highness the Duke of Edinburgh, I had the temerity to produce an "all-time great" ranking. . . .

The really bitter criticism I got from the United States was not that I had only included five American players amongst my first twelve—and that very great player Don Budge was not amongst them—but that I had only put little Bill Johnston Number Ten instead of Number Two.

Now I had seen all my first twelve in action but I tried to be logical and quite "non-British" in my approach. I agreed with Ned Potter that Bill Tilden was the greatest of them all. And I argued therefore that, if I were correct in that assumption, those players who, in that great Tilden era, pressed him hard, and indeed beat him on occasions, must find some place in my world ranking. So I ranked René Lacoste Number Three, Henri Cochet Number Nine and W. M. Johnston Number Ten. I rather bow to the Americans' criticism over the latter and think that, on pure logic, I should have ranked Johnston higher.

Now there is a great body of expert opinion which does not agree with

Ned Potter and me that Tilden was a better player than H. L. Doherty. The latter won the Wimbledon singles title five years running from 1902–1906 and the doubles eight times with his brother R. F. Doherty. Tilden won the American Championships six times from 1920–25 and again in 1929 and the American doubles six times. But they were supreme in different eras, so I have been un-British enough to place H. L. Doherty at Number Two.

Now between the Tilden and Doherty eras there was another very great player who provided a link—the Australian wizard, Norman Brookes. He was not at his peak when he was beaten by Doherty at Wimbledon in 1905, and he was 43 and Tilden only 27 when they met in the Challenge Round of the Davis Cup in 1920. Yet Tilden only beat him 10–8, 6–4, 1–6, 6–4 and Tilden said of him then, "Norman E. Brookes is the greatest match player the world has ever known." He had, of course, just beaten him in four sets!

But still, one must acknowledge that Norman Brookes was a very great player in an era of greatness—and I placed him Number Four.

I was then faced with a dilemma as to whether I should include any more of the ancients such as R. F. Doherty, winner of the Wimbledon singles title four times and the doubles eight times; Anthony Wilding, who won at Wimbledon four years running; or such other stalwarts as S. H. Smith, J. C. Parke and M. E. McLoughlin. Should I next consider the great era of the French predominance from 1924–1929, or the Vines-Crawford era of 1932–33, or the Perry-Budge era of 1934–38—or should I come right down to the postwar era? I decided on the latter and gave fifth, sixth and seventh places to Jack Kramer, Frank Sedgman and Pancho Gonzales, ranking the latter, of course, on his achievements in the amateur game.

I gave the eighth and ninth places to Ellsworth Vines and Henri Cochet. We have never seen such tennis at Wimbledon as Vines played when he won the title in 1932 at his first attempt. His career at the top of the amateur game was of course a short one, but I am ranking these great players on the degree of their excellence.

And Cochet at his best was a magician. Tilden said about him in 1928, "In these inspired moments of his Cochet is the greatest of all Frenchmen, and in my opinion possibly the greatest player who has ever lived." . . .

Well, I was now left with two more places in my first twelve and the outstanding candidates—even if I left out those great figures such as the Renshaws and W. Baddeley—were R. F. Doherty, Anthony Wilding, S. H. Smith, J. C. Parke, M. E. McLoughlin, J. H. Crawford, Jean Borotra, F. J. Perry and Donald Budge.

I chose F. J. Perry and Jean Borotra. It was a very difficult choice between Perry and Budge. Perry staved off the challenge of the latter during his three years' supremacy from 1934–36 and Budge then reigned supreme for two years. Maybe they were better than the Doherty era, the Tilden era, the reign of the three musketeers of France, or the postwar era of Kramer, Sedgman and Gonzales. As Ned Potter says, it is impossible to make an exact comparison except amongst exact contemporaries.

I saw that in the April issue Sir Norman Brookes agrees with me about Bill Tilden being Number One, and he ranks next both the Dohertys, Tony Wilding and Billy Johnston—all players who had beaten him in his peak years and one or two of whom he had beaten. But that is only human nature.

Kramer was a disciple of Budge and Budge of Perry. To them and their public their era was a very great one. It may possibly have been the greatest of all. That must always be a matter of opinion.

But I think most people would agree to this. There have been several great lawn tennis eras in this century. The first was the Doherty, Norman Brookes, Anthony Wilding era. The second was that of Bill Tilden, Billy Johnston and their contemporaries. The third was that of the famous musketeers of France—Lacoste, Cochet, Borotra. The fourth was that of Vines, Crawford, Perry and Budge. And the fifth was the postwar era headed by Jack Kramer, who actually only won Wimbledon once but was quite obviously one of the all-time greats.

I am not one of those who always consider the old champions were best. The modern generations have broken records in every other sport and it is reasonable to suppose that their brand of lawn tennis was at least as good as any other. It is really a matter of opinion—but it is certainly not a matter anyone can be dogmatic about.

"You pays your money—and you takes your choice!"

THE DIFFERENCE

by G. P. Hughes

Whatever you say about modern lawn tennis, there can be no doubt that the men's doubles game, at any rate from the spectators' angle, has deteriorated. It is no longer the great attraction it used to be—that was proved at this year's Wimbledon, when the final, won by Hoad and Hartwig of Australia, was watched by only mildly enthusiastic people in half-full stands.

Exactly when the deterioration began it is difficult to say, but I do know that in the prewar era a good men's doubles match was regarded as the best spectacle of all. In those days the ball was longer in play. There were frequent rallies which roused the galleries to the highest pitch of excitement. Defense was combined with attack. Players fought themselves out of precarious situations by retreating, and if the lobs thrown up were often given a terrible bashing, every point was disputed to the end.

Today the tactics are different. Defense has been discarded, and even when the players are at a great disadvantage they "have a go." Brilliant shots are followed by errors, and with everybody practicing the same aggressive theory the rallies are rarely long enough to provide the thrills which the public enjoy. The feelings of spectators, however, are a secondary consideration, and the important issue is whether or not the modern game is of as high a standard as the old.

Watching one of the best men's doubles matches at Wimbledon this year, I was asked my opinion of the standard as compared with that of the mid-thirties, when Raymond Tuckey and I won the title. I gave what I thought the most effective answer: "Ask Adrian Quist."

Quist, of Australia, won the Wimbledon doubles with Jack Crawford in 1935, returned to win again in 1950 with John Bromwich, and then came back this year as manager of the Australian women's team. . . .

Quist's view is that the doubles game has deteriorated, not because the present-day men are incapable of top-class play, but because they are 100 per cent concentrated on singles. In other words, they look on doubles as the "poor relation."

The late Bill Tilden put things bluntly 30 years ago when he wrote that singles is a game of speed and doubles a game of finesse. In his opinion the two games are poles apart and I feel that most successful doubles players would agree with him. Tilden freely admitted that he was far from being an expert exponent of doubles, but he had many fine doubles successes—due to his extraordinary versatility. In the same way, Fred Perry was not an ideal doubles player, but he could not help having good results in that department.

There are exceptions to every rule, but history shows that the greatest doubles pairs have owed their success to mutual understanding and team-work. Only on rare occasions have two individualists made a good team, and in general, the best results have been obtained where the right-court player has made the openings to enable his partner to jump in with the "kill."

Brugnon and Cochet were a great pair and so were Brugnon and Borotra, but Borotra and Cochet together were a comparative misfit. Both wanted too much of the net and neither could do the preparatory work to help the other.

In the same way, the great American combinations of Allison-Van Ryn (Wimbledon winners in 1929 and 1930) and Lott-Van Ryn (1931) depended on perfect blending of styles. In each case, Van Ryn dipped the ball over from the right court and his partner stepped in at the psychological moment with the final volley.

Perhaps the best examples of all were that tremendous team of Quist and Bromwich, Wimbledon and American champions, who won the Australian title for the three years before the war and for the five years that followed it. Neither was so outstanding in singles. Both were good, but they were at their best in partnership.

One must be frank. Any comparison between the technique of the Bromwich-Quist pairing and that of the leading pairs of today is ridiculous. Bromwich, in the right court, rarely missed a return of service. If the service was wide to his forehand he had three replies—a short chip to the incoming server's feet, a fierce double-handed drive, or a lob over the man at the net. If the serve came down the middle line he merely took the racket in his left hand and made a dipping return, or, with no change of action, played a "dome" shot over the server's partner.

Only those who have had the task of serving to him can have any appreciation of his extraordinary ability. He was not a great quick volleyer, so he hung far enough back to give himself the extra time. But he missed nothing, and all his play was concentrated on putting his opponents into difficulties. Once that was achieved, Quist did the rest. Anything the slightest bit "uppish" was immediately thumped for a winner.

What happens today? Hoad serves with tremendous power to, say, Hartwig, who, despite the difficulties, has a crack. The return may be a good one—or it may go anywhere. Nobody worries. Within a few minutes the position is reversed and Hartwig is serving. He too has a great serve, but Hoad attacks it. The rallies are short. The games are quick. It is one-all, two-all and level-pegging all the way until one side breaks through for the set. Succeeding sets are played in the same way—the entire match being dominated by the service.

General opinion is that modern tactics are dictated by the increased power of present-day serving, but I agree with Quist that the service today is no faster than it was 20 years ago. Who, in 1955, has a better serve than that of Frank Shields, Ellsworth Vines or Donald Budge, to mention only a few? George Lott, Lester Stoefen, Wilmer Allison, Harry Hopman, Don Turnbull and many others packed in serves of the highest quality. To hear some people talk, anyone would think that Fred Perry, Raymond Tuckey and Gottfried von Cramm merely pushed the ball!

No, people forget. The physical power of athletes does not alter from one generation to another. There have always been powerful services, but in past generations players went to greater trouble in their attempts to return them. Prewar doubles players, when under pressure, realized that the odds were against them, and were prepared to defend. They saw the chance of extricating themselves by a lob and they appreciated the possibility of their opponents missing the smash or not putting the ball away. They worked on the principle that while the ball was in play there was always a hope, however small. Points were not ceded lightly.

My most vivid recollection is of having to deal with high lobs while Lott and Van Ryn were 10 yards outside the baseline ready to retrieve my smashes. Sometimes they succeeded. Their defense was magnificent and it was most tantalizing and nerve-racking to be faced with such a perfect barrier. Their system was the generally accepted one; it was to defend when in trouble and to attack when they saw the chance. I felt this combination of attack and defense made for the highest brand of doubles, and it certainly provided a much more interesting show for the spectators.

That, then, is the difference as I see it. As an onlooker now, I find doubles to be somewhat mechanical and to lack variety. It is all attack. The player in difficulties takes a chance even if his hope of success is remote. He is not prepared to defend and to retrieve and to give his opponents an opportunity to make errors.

And the explanation for the change? I can only attribute it to the revolution which has taken place in lawn tennis since the war. Whether or not we like to admit it, the game today is on a semi-professional basis. "Expenses" are paid according to a player's drawing power, and this depends on his world ranking in singles.

His doubles achievements are of comparatively trivial value, so naturally he concentrates on singles. He becomes a singles specialist and plays doubles only because he has got to do so. It is not surprising, therefore, that doubles quality has slumped.

THE GREAT DOUBLES TEAMS

by George Lott

If all the great doubles teams in history could meet each other while each was at its respective peak, it would provide a sport spectacle that would make the gladiator show in Rome look as tame as a tiddlywinks tournament. After all, every lion looks pretty much like every other lion, but the doubles teams in my dream tournament embody all the varieties of great athletic endeavor. There are the big servers, the touch artists, the great half-volleyers, the shot-makers, the big smashers, the superb dinkers. . . .

In limiting this fanciful tournament to sixteen pairs, I am forced to leave out some very fine teams. There were great players who teamed together only occasionally, viz. Tilden and Johnston and Sedgman and Bromwich. They regularly paired with other players and were just put together in Davis Cup matches. Either one of these two teams was capable of beating anyone.

But, before it gets too late, on with the tournament. . . . The teams in this blue-ribbon affair are:

VINCENT RICHARDS AND R. NORRIS WILLIAMS

These two were never beaten in major competition. They won the U.S. Doubles and the Challenge Round Doubles in 1925 and 1926. They formed the best doubles combination I ever saw or played against. Williams, on his day, was the finest doubles player of all time. Richards was not far behind and they blended perfectly. Vinnie was from the Bronx and liked the bright lights. Williams was a steady, reliable type. Yet, on the court, their person-alities were reversed. Richards was the steady player, brilliant at net but conservative in service and return of service. Williams, on the other hand, was the daring, brilliant shot-maker, setting up the points for Richards and going all out on his shots. His sharply angled returns of service were the work of an artist, the ball being taken on the rise at all times. Watching Williams at his best gave the equivalent pleasure a music-lover would receive from listening to Heifetz play his violin. He was truly a genius.

GARDNAR MULLOY AND WILLIAM TALBERT

My judgment of this team is from observation only. If one takes Al Smith's advice about looking at the record, one would have to go back to the turn of the century to find a combination that could equal their achievement of four National Doubles titles. Consider also that they were runners-up twice and that, with different partners, Mulloy was a runner-up three times and so was Billy. From the years 1940–1948 either one or both played in the finals of the National Doubles each year. Never were two players more consistent for such a long period.

JOHN BROMWICH AND ADRIAN QUIST

Here again is a team so good that it is difficult to say that anyone would beat them. They won their own country's doubles championship on nine occasions and the U.S. Doubles once, in 1939. Bromwich was a master technician and an excellent student of the game, and Quist was a perfect foil. In 1938 I had been hired by Harry Hopman to help with the doubles team for the Challenge Round. Budge and Mako had beaten Bromwich and Quist at Longwood, but in losing we all learned something. Bromwich was the first to notice that in certain exchanges at the net, Mako had a tendency to angle his volley crosscourt. In the Challenge Round, the Aussies laid for this shot, and while this one factor may not have been responsible for the victory, the fact remains that Bromwich and Quist reversed the Longwood result.

KEN McGREGOR AND FRANK SEDGMAN

My first look at this pair of giants was in the Boston Garden when they were playing a top pro combination. As I watched their two big serves, Sedgman's incredible speed at the net and their amazing overheads, I thought how lucky I was to have played tennis before these lads arrived. I believe that I and any of my partners would have been shaking hands with McGregor and Sedgman about twenty minutes after the match started.

WILLIAM TILDEN AND VINCENT RICHARDS

This team might have gone on to establish a record that would have been very hard to equal, but a difference in personalities caused a break. After winning three U.S. titles, the team split up and never played together again. In winning their third U.S. title in 1922, they defeated Gerald Patterson and Pat O'Hara-Wood in the final. Later that year they lost to this same team in the Challenge Round by scores of 6–3, 6–0, 6–4, so the friction was evident. The breaking up of this team really led to a mess the following year as a genius on the Selection Committee decided to put Tilden and Dick Williams together. Both were left-court players! This led to a razzle-dazzle in the clubhouse during the rest period between the aforementioned genius and Tilden. The Americans were down two sets to one and tempers were flaring. It ended shortly; Dick and Bill got together and won the last two sets 6–3, 6–2. They never teamed again; they should never have been teamed in the first place. All the Selection Committee had on hand was the two best doubles teams of all time, namely Richards-Williams and Tilden-Johnston.

KEITH GLEDHILL AND ELLSWORTH VINES

The first time I saw Keith Gledhill was at a luncheon party during the Newport Invitation given by Mrs. Astor. As we were leaving the Astor home, a line of players formed to thank their hostess. One player made a rather articulate thank-you speech. Keith leaned over his shoulder, stuck out his hand and said, "Same goes for me, Mrs. Astor."

Keith was an excellent doubles player mixing a loop forehand with judicious lobs. He also had an excellent knowledge of the game. However, the team won or lost according to the form of Vines on that particular day. I vividly remember a match at Longwood where this team led Doeg and me two sets to one and 4–1 in the fourth. Ellsworth chose this moment to start missing overhead smashes, so we got out of the barrel. When Elly was on, he simply overpowered the opposition.

WILMER ALLISON AND JOHN VAN RYN

There were never two happier lads than Wilmer and John when they won their first Wimbledon in 1929. The man who put them together as a team and who was responsible for their success, Fitz Eugene Dixon, was happy too. I have always thought that this year was their greatest, due mainly to their enthusiasm and the newness of their glory. They went on to Paris to defeat Cochet and Borotra in straight sets. During these two months they reached the realm of greatness, and while they won many championships afterwards, it was then that they impressed me the most—and I looked at them across the net many times.

JACQUES BRUGNON AND HENRI COCHET, JACQUES BRUGNON AND JEAN BOROTRA, JEAN BOROTRA AND HENRI COCHET

I would never separate these three teams. Of course they were all very good, but it did seem to me that Cochet might have been the weakest doubles player of the three. Borotra, with that bounding Basque business at the net, was the toughest. His backhand volley was as good as I have seen and his overhead was deadly. The only counterattack against Jean was the dink shot, followed by a quick crowding of the net. Toto Brugnon won four Wimbledons and was runner-up twice, but no French team was ever able to win the American Doubles.

FRANCIS T. HUNTER AND WILLIAM TILDEN

These two great players were an excellent team in 1927 when they won Wimbledon, the U.S. Doubles, and the Challenge Round Doubles. Their success was due mainly to Tilden's all-round play and the bulldog determination of Frank and his forehand. Actually, they played a doubles game all their own. Court position meant nothing, but win they did. And, believe me, it was fun to play them. The practice matches we had in Paris in 1928 were most enjoyable because, with Tilden around, even a practice match got you keyed up. I have always had a great deal of admiration for Hunter. He got "the furthest with the leastest." Bluntly put, he had guts galore.

CHARLES GARLAND AND NORRIS WILLIAMS

Placing the 1920 Wimbledon winner in this dream tournament may surprise some, and I admit I never saw them together as a team. However, I know about Williams and have played against Chuck many times in friendly doubles matches. During the years Stoefen and I were touring with Tilden and Vines, and during my visits to my home in Chicago, I always seized the opportunity to have games with Chuck—not only because I liked him but because he was a challenge. I was not able to move him out of position and, more often than not, his superb drop volley caught me in an awkward spot. He and Williams must have been a fine team. They also must be the only Harvard-Yale combination to win a Wimbledon.

HOWARD AND BOB KINSEY

From these two men I learned the value of the lob. At the Longwood Cricket Club in Boston I won the National Junior Singles the day the Kinsey brothers beat Gerald Patterson and Pat O'Hara-Wood in the National Doubles final. You had to see this one to believe it. Before the match, Tilden and the rest of the experts gave the Californians about as much of a chance to win as the boxing experts gave Clay against Liston. At the start of the final the Australians were putting away the lobs and going about their business with brisk efficiency. As the match progressed, errors crept in and soon the lobs got deeper, the looped drives and chops got loopier and choppier, and the Australians got dizzier. Eventually the Aussies collapsed completely. . . . Bob and Howard . . . were a team you had to beat; they would not beat themselves.

DON BUDGE AND GENE MAKO

Here was a great team along the lines of Vines and Gledhill. Mako was the play maker and a very capable one, but the success of the team depended on Don. He was the power—not an artist like Williams, but he got the job done. That backhand of his was tremendous, as we all knew, but so were his volley and serve. For three years (1936–38) they were the best American team, winning two U.S. titles, one Wimbledon and one Challenge Round match. They were beaten in the Challenge Round in 1938 by Quist and Bromwich.

GERALD PATTERSON AND PAT O'HARA-WOOD

These two Australians reached their peak in the 1922 Challenge Round when they defeated Tilden and Richards rather easily. They failed to win a major tournament other than their own Australian Doubles in 1925, but during these years they were the team to beat and it took some doing.

GEORGE LOTT AND LESTER STOEFEN

It might be presumptuous of the writer to put this team in the tournament, but I am doing the dreaming. This was a pretty fair team, and against the other combinations we would win a little and lose a little. But one thing is certain: no matter how hard I might try, there seems to be no way in the world I can dream a win over Richards and Williams. It always comes out the same and, I imagine, for a very good reason. They were the best.

Doubles Championship of Utopia

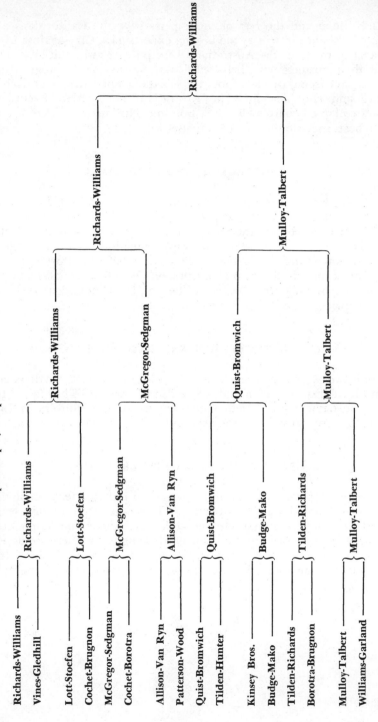

ART LARSEN

by Jeane Hoffman

Every war produces a champion in some sport. World War I saw Gene Tunney emerge from the Marines to become world's heavyweight boxing champion, and Marcel Cerdan put the French Navy on the map in the last war; but Art "Tappy" Larsen is probably the first to become a national champion as the direct cause of conflict. Art's tennis career was spawned on the battlefields of France and sparked to a triumphant zenith on the center court of Forest Hills.

"I'd played tennis before I went in the Army, in fact, since I was 11," said the new national singles champion of the U. S., still a little dazed by his rapid ascendency. "But I didn't take up tennis seriously until after the war, on orders of my doctors. I was so nervous and shell-shocked that the exercise in the open air, through tennis, was the only thing that cured me."

What happened at Brest was enough to shake anyone. Art, three years in the Army, saw one and one half years' action of the roughest fighting in Europe. He landed on Omaha Beach on D-Day plus 30 with the 17th Cavalry Squadron of the 9th Army. Most of his buddies were killed at landing. Art fought his way to Brest as a tommy-gunner. "Suddenly, out of nowhere, a fleet of bombers began strafing and bombing us. Our own air force had mistaken us for Nazis. Before the holocaust was over, half the troop was killed, ambulances were lined up for miles. I came through unscratched. Then and there I developed the complex which I'm still trying to shake.

"I figured I'd done something lucky that day, that some good omen was watching out for me. I remembered I'd changed my socks, putting on the left one first, and ate breakfast at a certain hour. The next day I followed the same routine, and the next, all through France, Belgium and Luxembourg.

"By the time I got out of the Army and home to California, I had cultivated a whole string of superstitions and jinxes. Gosh, I had so many I couldn't count them. I was too nervous to hold a job. I worked a calculating machine for a while, then gave it up. My hands were too shaky. My mother says that when I used to go out in the morning to look for a job, I'd go up and down the front steps four or five times, retracing my steps, figuring that one such trip would insure luck."

The wise counsel of a Veterans Administration doctor got Art back on the right track, via the tennis court, but Art promptly transferred the fear of getting killed to fear of getting licked. He brought along his growing corps of complexes, and added new ones. "You name 'em, I had 'em," laughs Art. "I wouldn't step on any kind of a chalkline. I always had to have the winning ball to put back in play. I'd cross on the opposite side of the net from my opponent, tiptoe over baselines, even in competition, tap the base-line three times before serving, stand for a second with my back to the court. Then I had a number ritual that is too complicated to explain. The doctor told me my 'jinxes' were 'compulsory suggestiveness' and he convinced me of one thing: I was wasting a heck of a lot of energy on them." . . .

Rivals are constantly amazed at wiry Art's boundless energy. He's one of the smallest players afloat, at five foot, nine inches, weighs only 150; but in the Nationals he was in such superb shape against Savitt and Flam that he didn't even sit down to rest changing courts. "I just wanted to get it over with fast," says Art. "I wasn't even perspiring at the end of those matches." His amazing endurance and indefatigable retrieving ability wear out bigger and stronger players. Nothing tires Larsen, including smoking. He didn't sleep a wink the night before he played Flam, yet he was raring to go after the fifth set while Flam was near collapse—triumphant testimony that Art has recovered from his war experiences and a sickly childhood.

MR. JONES

by Gussie Moran

Perry T. Jones is a familiar name to tennis devotees. Perry T. Jones is a new name to those who don't assiduously follow tennis but who recognize the words "Davis Cup" when they see them. On February 9, 1958, Perry T. Jones was named non-playing captain of the Davis Cup team, to succeed William Talbert.

The logical question at this juncture is—"Why?"

There may be many reasons. It could be that the West Coast is now most prominent in USLTA representation. It might be that we haven't won the Cup since 1954 and only once since 1950. When informed of his dismissal, Billy Talbert had occasion to speak to Jack Kramer moments later.

"Who do you suppose will replace me?" Billy asked of Jack.

"Darned if I know," Jack replied. They considered Vic Seixas and elimi-nated him. Then Jack and Billy thought of Gardnar Mulloy. He, too, didn't seem a likely threat, due to past relations in Australia. They were puzzled. And then came the news. Even Jack couldn't believe it!

What kind of a man is Perry T. Jones?

I was brought up under Jones' regime in Southern California, although not quite under his wing, and I have been exposed to Mr. Jones since I was 13 years old. I still call him MR. JONES.

My first emotion on meeting him was fear. Here was Mr. Tennis, himself. Through tennis and Perry Jones, a wide, wide world opened for me. I include Mr. Jones, as he was the one who made it possible for me to attend my first "away from home" tournament. It was an annual event at the Hotel del Coronado near San Diego, and it was there, in their sumptuous dining room, that I learned that finger bowls were for fingers and not for watermelon seeds.

My knees would quiver when he watched me play. I so much wanted to make great shots for him. Others experienced similar reactions. Barbara Winslow, well on her way to defeating national champion Anita Lizana of Chile on the No. 4 court of the Los Angeles Tennis Club during the 1937 Southwest, fell apart and lost the match when Mr. Jones appeared momentarily on the court.

He hasn't changed much through the years. He still wears white flannels, black and white shoes, long-sleeved white shirts and a Panama hat.

Mr. Jones was always a stickler for proper dress on and off the court, and for many years he frowned on tennis shorts. Only after his favorite doubles combination, Kramer and Schroeder, won the national doubles wearing shorts did he give in. Jones had given them white trousers that year, and it was said that Schroeder cut his off. . . .

Mr. Jones was equally as fussy about the girls wearing skirts. However, he always made a particular point of complimenting a youngster for a neat and tidy appearance. He exuded great plaudits for my mother when she made me a Jones-pleasing dress which hung to my knees.

In 1941 Perry Jones, with his sister, Mrs. Llewellyn Brown, as chaperone, took a group of us to Mexico City. The travelers were Jack Kramer, Ted Schroeder, Bob Peacock, Doug Woodbury, Louise Brough, Pearl Harland, Joanne Brooke and myself. Our suitcases were brimming with starched white tennis dresses and clean white sneakers. Perry Jones was wonderful to us on this trip. He was tolerant, considerate, a good organizer, a fine promoter and a grand gentleman. It was a long flight to Mexico City in those days, and for Mr. Jones and Mrs. Brown the trip must have seemed interminable, with eight teen-agers on their hands. . . .

My only run-in with Mr. Jones came in 1943. Bill Tilden had asked me to play some exhibitions with his group for the armed services. I asked Mr. Jones for his permission, which he refused to give. Nevertheless, I went along with Bill, Walter Wesbrook and Gloria Butler, all of whom were donating their services, to entertain at various Army, Navy and Marine bases and hospitals for many months.

Apparently I wasn't the only one to have a run-in with Mr. Jones. When Pancho Gonzales was still in the juniors, he found school distasteful and decided not to attend classes. He dropped out in the tenth grade and was immediately barred from all tournaments. Pancho resented the suspension, but all is well now between them. Recently Pancho said, "He's a fine man. There were always rumors we didn't get along, and Perry took a lot of criticism. But he had his rules to enforce . . . and he enforced them. He's wonderful with kids. He knows them and helps them." Gonzales is now one of Jones' stand-bys in teaching tennis to youngsters in the Los Angeles area.

Perry Jones has had fantastically susccessful results in producing tennis players. No other section in the world can approach his record. Not all Southern Californians have been his protégés, viz. Bobby Riggs and Pauline Betz. Down through the years he has been unconcerned about public acclaim and averse to personal publicity. A few years ago Allan Grant, a *Life* photographer seeking anecdotal material on Pancho Gonzales, arrived at the Jones office. Mr. Jones cooperated but made it quite clear that no pictures were to be taken of him. . . .

The great Babe Didrickson, desirous of becoming the champ, once sought his advice. "Get some white tennis dresses," he told her. "Then," he added, "find a good coach."

He has his likes and dislikes, and I believe he never forgets a favor or an injury. His demeanor is serious, sometimes with humor. I am still amazed when I hear him laugh or say something mundane. He is quite a politician, shuffling movie stars, admirals, senators and dowagers during tournament time.

His advice to tennis players, which I have heard for years is: "You're only in trouble when you think."

GARDNAR MULLOY

by Jeane Hoffman

Baseball has its Luke Appling, football its Sammy Baugh, boxing its Joe Walcott and tennis its Gardnar Mulloy. We're talking about the Grand Old Men in sports, and although it will probably make Irishman Mulloy's crew haircut stand on end to be classified as the "old man of tennis," the fact remains that at 38 he's the miracle man of the game—the best-conditioned athlete in tennis today, and certainly one of its greatest players.

When handsome Gar faced Herbie Flam in the semi-finals of the national championship last September, few in the gallery at Forest Hills were aware that the lithe, sunburned Floridian was exactly 16 years older than his California rival; that he had, in fact, been playing competitive tennis before Flam was born! Mulloy came within a whisker (not his own) of defeating Flam to realize his dream of making the finals of the U.S. singles for the first time. . . .

Mulloy has been in the first ten for nine years, played on the circuit for fourteen years, with time out for three years of war duty; has been four times national men's doubles champ, has been a member of five Davis Cup teams, and dashed the hopes of so many youngsters coming up to the big time that he's known as the Gibraltar of the trade. There are few kids today who can match him in endurance and ability.

"What do I attribute my ability to stay at the top to?" ponders Mulloy, who looks like a collegian on the courts. "Well, I'd say strict self-discipline and training. Training is a year-round proposition with me; I don't get in shape just for tennis season. You'll find me in bed by 11 P.M. almost every night of the year, and during the season I hit lights-out at 10:30." . . .

Mulloy doesn't drink or smoke, he remains 170 pounds in weight, slim for his six feet one inch in height. He gives the appearance of being lackadaisical on the courts occasionally, but it's just his system of conserving energy for more crucial points.

Compared to California kids, Gardnar was a Johnny-come-lately to tennis. He didn't get interested in the sport till he was 15. "Football was my game," affirmed Gar. "My dad was a rabid tennis fan, but he couldn't sell the bill of goods to me. Finally he took me to the Miami High School tennis finals. I watched sort of bored and finally observed, 'Heck, I could beat those guys!'

" 'I know you could,' said my dad. 'That's what I've been trying to tell you.' " Gar went out for the team and made No. 1 position. It is not generally known that Gar and his father, R. B. Mulloy, were three-time national father-and-son champs ('39, '41 and '42) .

Mulloy entered the University of Miami on a football scholarship and became one of its greatest all-round athletes. He was on the boxing team, made the football varsity as end and halfback, and excelled as both passer and kicker. A broken right wrist and collarbone helped to convince him that tennis would pay longer dividends, and after competing in the Eastern intercollegiates he set out for the tennis trails in 1936. So far, his most serious injury has been athlete's foot.

Gar is a graduate lawyer and is now a member of the firm of Pallot, Silver, Tatham, Abdo and Mulloy. He was graduate manager of athletics at the University of Miami for several years and advisory coach of the tennis team. . . . Plus which he's vice president of the Florida Tennis Association. . . . Married, he's the father of two daughters, aged five and seven.

For a guy who got into tennis via football, Mulloy is a long way from his original ambition, which was to be an architect. The nearest he got to that port of call was as part of the blueprint for the Allied victory in World War II. As commander of an LST 32, known in the ranks as "Mulloy's Joy Ship," the Irishman bagged his share of prisoners and took part in five invasions—Sicily, Salerno, Anzio, Isle of Melba and Southern France.

Sometime during the war, stay-at-home fans were startled to read that one Lieutenant Commander Mulloy, temporarily stationed on a large man-of-war, had set up a portable tennis court on the top deck and, using the superstructure as a practice wall, was industriously banging away in mid-ocean. It was typical of the guy. Not even a war and oceans of water could keep him away from training.

WILLIAM TALBERT

by Richard Evans

Whenever the *World Tennis* editor telephones Billy Talbert, he immediately recognizes her voice and says, "How much?" Last week it was the money for the boat trip during Forest Hills, the week before it was the invitations for the tennis ball, and the time before it was to pay the round-trip fare of a personality—but only from England to New York. Next month she will hit him for something big. . . .

William F. Talbert is the game's second greatest benefactor. He gives incredible amounts of time and money and he participates in the sport to a greater extent than most people realize. He has been housing tournament competitors for twenty years. He arranges a half dozen tournaments with "name" players and always manages to squeeze in a couple of "hungry" unknowns. He lives for the sport as it was yesterday, as it will be tomorrow and as it is today.

Billy has been a diabetic since he was 9. At the age of 13 he made medical history when he became the first diabetic to participate in an active sport. Before that he seldom ventured from his parents' small apartment in Cincinnati. He had a protective mother, a carefully watched diet and a comfortable chair. He felt great but he was not allowed to do a thing. Total inactivity was the only treatment for diabetics. But Billy, who had been a keen baseball and basketball player before his illness, couldn't adjust to a sedentary life. He persuaded his father and his doctor to let him take exercise, which was a revolutionary medical hypothesis. Tennis was selected. All the energy bottled inside for four years shot out like a whoosh of compressed steam. Billy threw himself into the sport like a starved Dickensian foundling sitting down to his first full-course meal. In six months this so-called invalid was the tenth ranking junior of the country. . . .

In 1938—he was 19 then and studying at the University of Cincinnati— "Talb" was selected for the first United States junior Davis Cup squad. When the war years came, diabetes prevented him from enlisting, so he worked as a civilian for the Navy and continued to play tennis with increasing success. Twice, in 1944 and 1945, he reached the finals of the national singles at Forest Hills, losing on both occasions to Frankie Parker. . . .

But already doubles was the game that fascinated him most and when he went to Australia in 1946 in a squad headed by Jack Kramer and Ted Schroeder, the man with whom he formed one of the great partnerships of all time was also on the team—Gardnar Mulloy. Gar and Billy fitted well together. They had the two ingredients that are essential to all good doubles teams—Billy had the touch and Gar the power. Says Talbert: "With

Mulloy and later with Tony Trabert I was lucky in having two of the all-time great left-court players." . . .

The extent to which Talbert understands doubles is best represented by his record. Of the 33 national titles he won, 30 were in doubles. During a 10-year period he and Gar Mulloy played 90 tournaments and won 84. Between 1950 and 1953 Trabert and he played 28 tournaments and won 27. Patty and Schroeder nailed them in the final of the Pacific Southwest; that was the only one they lost.

Of all Billy's unceasing efforts to help young players, none was more successful than his long association with Tony Trabert. Apart from an odd similarity in name, they both grew up in Cincinnati and Tony was only 12 when his future doubles partner saw him practicing, recognized the boy's potential and offered to help. Because he got him so early, Billy was able to mold him into what he thought a player should be.

When Tony was 19, Talbert took him to Europe and, typically, paid all the expenses out of his own pocket. By this time he was in a position to do so, for not all his time had been spent on the tennis court. In 1948 Billy had joined what is now called the United States Bank Note Corporation and in a very few years was made a vice-president. He is now the senior V-P. Tony never forgot what Billy did for him. When I reached Tony by phone at the Tahoe Racquet Club, he told me: "It is no coincidence that I am up here doing a bit of coaching with the kids. The fact that a player of Talb's stature was so interested in helping a youngster like myself made an impression on me that will last forever." Trabert later played Davis Cup under Billy (from 1953 to 1957) and again the conversation turned to superlatives.

"Psychologically and tactically, he was great," said Trabert. "In those challenge rounds against Australia, he could tell us whether Hoad would go down the line with his backhand or crosscourt—and why. I don't intend to knock anyone who has had the job since when I say that, in my opinion, Billy Talbert is easily the most qualified Davis Cup captain we have in this country at the moment." . . .

Butch Buchholz and Chuck McKinley are two other players who have benefited enormously from Talbert's wisdom, friendship and generous support. Nothing is ever too much trouble. It was Billy and his charming wife who laid on Frank and Fran Froehling's wedding when the couple decided to get married at short notice. . . .

Talbert quit the big-time circuit in 1954 ("By then I was back to No. 10 in the ranking, the position I had started in, so I decided it was time to get out") but in some ways his real contribution to the game was only beginning. For more than a decade now he has traveled endlessly around the country, giving as many as fifty exhibitions or clinics a year, rarely accepting expenses (only when the trip involves an extended air fare), and content, if asked, to play and teach from nine-thirty in the morning to five at night—free!

"I'm not that young any more," says Billy, who turns 49 on September 4, "but it's still fun. I get a kick out of all sports, whether it's watching Ryun run or playing golf with Arnie Palmer, Jack Nicklaus and Gary Player [three pros Billy has under contract for his company to play with business colleagues]. And then there's court tennis, which I play at the club quite a bit. Now there's a fascinating game."

LOUISE BROUGH

by Allison Danzig

Louise Brough is a champion who came back. Five years after her third victory at Wimbledon she has won the crown a fourth time.

The tall blond Californian, with the shy smile and the quietest manner of anyone playing tournament tennis, had this victory coming to her. Last year she was runner-up at Wimbledon to Maureen Connolly and also to Doris Hart at Forest Hills. Three times she was within a stroke of victory over Miss Hart before the Florida girl was finally rewarded for her years of perseverance with her first United States singles championship.

That was the fifth time Miss Brough had been in the final at Forest Hills. Despite the fact that she excels most women players at the net, her only triumph there was in 1947. Three times she was runner-up at Wimbledon.

One might say that Mrs. Beverly Baker Fleitz had victory coming to her also. A year ago, on the comeback trail after dropping out of tennis to rear a family, she defeated Miss Connolly at La Jolla Beach and Tennis Club in California and won five successive tournaments, only to suffer an ankle injury and have to default in the national championship. In one of the tournaments, the Pennsylvania State championship, she defeated Miss Brough.

This year Beverly started out by defeating Miss Brough again at La Jolla. In the semi-finals at Wimbledon she gave Miss Hart one of the severest trouncings Doris has ever experienced.

But Mrs. Fleitz is still looking for her first major championship despite the terrific beating she gives the ball with both hands.

Miss Brough was born in Oklahoma City and began to play tennis at the age of 13. She was the national girls' champion in 1940 and 1941 and has ranked in the top four since 1942, except for the year 1951. She won the Australian championship in 1950 and she has an amazing record in doubles with Mrs. Margaret Osborne duPont.

They won the United States championship nine years in succession from 1942 through 1950, the Wimbledon doubles in 1946, 1948, 1949, 1950 and 1954, and the French doubles in 1946, 1947 and 1949.

Miss Brough has been a member of the Wightman Cup team every year since 1947, except 1949 and 1951.

MARGARET OSBORNE DUPONT

by Bryan Field

In Spokane, Washington, a little girl 9 years old was walking to a music lesson with her brother, about the same age, and their path lay past some tennis courts. As they continued to go back and forth for their lessons they stopped frequently to watch a game that looked very nice, and seemed to be a good game to play. The next season mother gave both children swim suits and tennis rackets. The boy, now grown to manhood, is just a routine tennis player; but for the girl there thus began one of the greatest tennis careers the competitive tennis world has known.

Margaret Osborne was the girl and she now is Mrs. William duPont, Jr., mistress of Bellevue Hall just north of Wilmington, a plantation that, in addition to indoor and outdoor tennis courts, is possessed of rolling fields, a racetrack one mile and an eighth in circumference, a dairy, foxhunting installations, horses, cattle, an arboretum and the other things one might expect to find on the estate of a famous sportsman devoted to the out-of-doors.

Margaret's son, young Billy, is now about 11 and he is at school and being taught team games for the same reason that Prince Charlie in England is getting similar instruction. The children of famous parents have a way of getting spoiled by adulation. William duPont, Jr., in addition to his sports abilities, is one of the best known bankers and business executives in the nation. And Margaret's career, which had its germination in Spokane, is still going on.

Rightly Margaret is called a product of California tennis, for it was there in San Francisco that she became a sensational junior and went on to dozens of championships. And it is there today that a sign reads: "Margaret Osborne duPont Tennis Courts." The dedication was made January 29, 1959, by one of California's great tennis leaders, Jim Moffet, and Mayor Christopher of San Francisco.

In 1963, month of December, Margaret laughed over the telephone and said: "I guess I'm still a national champion, as in 1962 we won the women's senior national squash rackets championship, and it wasn't played for in 1963." In that same year, 1962, she won the Wimbledon mixed doubles with Neale Fraser. Previously at Wimbledon she captured the women's singles, and five times was victorious in the women's doubles, but it would take a page of type merely to list her string of championships, including three United States singles and thirteen doubles.

Wilmington and Philadelphia are in the Middle States section of the U.S.L.T.A., and in the latter city is Mrs. Harrison Smith, a mature judge of all that is great in women's tennis. She is the one who said that Margaret duPont has won more national grass court titles than any other woman.

Grass is Margaret's favorite surface, although she learned on the hard courts of the Far West. But Margaret can step off the courts and into the classroom, as in the summer of 1963 when she taught with her colleague, Margaret Varner, at Texas Women's University.

Mrs. duPont also is a writer of considerable ability and is presently engaged in preparing the article on tennis in general and the Wightman Cup in particular for the Book of Knowledge encyclopedia. Between times she has given and is giving clinics at Penn State, Delaware University, and locally for the Delaware Lawn Tennis Association, of which her husband is such a stalwart supporter.

MAUREEN

by Duncan Macaulay

The 1952 Wimbledon was a splendid one; with wonderful weather, record crowds, players from thirty-five different nations competing, thrills galore, and the eventual emergence of two new singles champions in Frank Sedgman of Australia, who had been competing for the crown since 1945, and little Maureen Connolly of the U. S. A., who was making her debut at Wimbledon. . . .

The seeded players in the ladies' singles were: 1, Miss Doris Hart; 2, Miss Connolly; 3, Miss Shirley Fry; 4, Miss Louise Brough; 5, Mrs. Patricia Todd; 6, Mrs. Jean Walker-Smith; 7, Mrs. Thelma Long; 8, Mrs. Jean Rinkel-Quertier.

Miss Hart, the holder, was eager to retain her championship and prove that her defeat by seventeen-year-old "Little Mo" Connolly at Forest Hills (in 1951) was all wrong. Miss Connolly was eager to show her best form on her first visit to Britain. Miss Fry wanted to improve her record of being the eternal second; and Miss Brough wanted to make a much more championshiplike bow to Wimbledon than her injured arm had permitted her to do the previous year. Mrs. Todd, the greatest fighter of them all, was out for anybody's blood and, as far as she was concerned, the higher they were the harder they would fall.

A few days before the championships started, Miss Connolly suffered a minor injury to her shoulder during practice. This little upset, combined with all the emotional atmosphere which surrounds such a person on these occasions, almost persuaded her to scratch. But her own good sense and sportsmanship eventually prevailed. However, she was far below her Forest Hills form to start with, and would have lost to Britain's Sue Partridge in the fourth round had the latter grasped her opportunity when leading a sorely worried opponent in the critical stage of the final set. "Little Mo" then lost a set to Thelma Long of Australia before reaching the semi-final.

Britain's leading player, Jean Walker-Smith, reached the last eight and was then beaten all ends up by Miss Fry. Jean Rinkel also reached the last eight and then went down in two sets to Louise Brough. The gallant Pat Todd brought off her greatest singles triumph when she beat the holder, Doris Hart, 6–8, 7–5, 6–4. The intense heat and Mrs. Todd's tremendous fighting spirit wore down Miss Hart's nervous and physical resources. Louise Brough lost the middle set to Pat Todd in one semi-final, and Maureen beat Shirley Fry in the other by 6–4, 6–3. It was good to see Louise Brough contesting the final again, but the old fire and fury of her game had gone and, try as she would, she could not counter the stream of hard-hit drives that flowed from Maureen's racket.

The feat of Miss Connolly in winning the ladies' championship at such a tender age was without precedent at Wimbledon since 1887, when the fabulous Miss Lottie Dod won at the age of fifteen. In addition to her stroke equipment, Maureen showed remarkable qualities of concentration, self-confidence, and determination. . . .

Nineteen fifty-three was Coronation year. There had been only three Coronation years in the history of the championships—and indeed of lawn tennis—for Queen Victoria had been thirty-nine years on the throne before the first Wimbledon was held in 1877, and that was only a few years after the game of lawn tennis had been invented. The first Coronation year was that of King Edward VII in 1902. That was the golden era of British lawn tennis, when the Doherty brothers reigned supreme. King George V's Coronation year was 1911, when the Wimbledon entry had risen to over a hundred. The year signalized the second successive championship of the great New Zealander, Anthony Wilding. The famous Mrs. Lambert Chambers won the fifth of her seven Wimbledon singles titles, beating her challenger, Miss D. Boothby, by the overwhelming score of 6–0, 6–0. The year was remarkable for the first French victory at Wimbledon; in the challenge round, M. Decugis and A. H. Gobert beat the holders, A. F. Wilding and M. J. G. Ritchie, who had never been defeated in a championship before.

The last Coronation year in lawn tennis history was that of King George VI in 1937. The famous British champion, F. J. Perry, who had won the men's title three years running, had departed the year before to the professional ranks, and his place was taken by that fine American player, J. D. Budge, who was then only twenty-one. In the absence of Mrs. Helen Wills Moody, Britain's Dorothy Round gained her second Wimbledon singles title. And now, in 1953, we had come to Wimbledon's fourth Coronation year—that of our beloved young Queen Elizabeth. . . .

The semi-finalists (in the ladies' singles) were Miss Hart, Mrs. Dorothy Knode, Miss Fry, and Miss Connolly. . . . Miss Hart, playing at the top of her form, tore Mrs. Knode's industrious driving game to shreds, and Miss Connolly likewise overwhelmed Shirley Fry in thirty-five minutes with the loss of only two games.

The stage was thus set for the meeting of the two top women in the world, and they certainly did not disappoint their audience. The match was a great display of classic tennis. Doris Hart, the more accomplished and versatile stroke player of the two, did everything she could to break up the rhythm of the Californian's stream of accurate hard-hit drives on either wing. She attacked in the forecourt behind her more penetrating service, she slow-balled, and she tried the slice, but "Little Mo" Connolly never wilted or relaxed, and she eventually ran out a very worthy winner by 8–6, 7–5. It was one of the best ladies' singles finals since the war.

When, later in the year, Maureen Connolly won the American singles title for the third successive year, she became the first woman to win the "Grand Slam" championships of England, France, Australia and the U. S. A., all in one year. It must be remembered, however, that Suzanne Lenglen and Helen Wills Moody never competed in Australia. . . .

In the ladies singles (in 1954) all eight of the seeded players came through to the quarter-finals. They were Miss Connolly, Miss Hart, Miss Fry, Miss Brough, Mrs. Margaret duPont, and Mrs. Betty Pratt—all of the United States—and two British players, Miss Angela Mortimer and Miss Helen Fletcher. Miss Hart beat Miss Fletcher, 6–1, 6–3, and Miss Brough beat Miss Mortimer by the same score. Mrs. Pratt (formerly Miss Rosenquest) covered herself with glory by beating Shirley Fry, 6–4, 9–11, 6–3, and Miss Connolly overwhelmed Mrs. duPont, who was appearing for the first time since 1951.

The Duke of Edinburgh was in the Royal Box for the semi-finals. Miss Connolly beat Mrs. duPont with the loss of only two games, but it must be remembered that Miss Connolly was only seven years old when Margaret duPont had won her first national championship. In the other semi-final Louise Brough, returning after a year's interval to reach her sixth Wimbledon final since 1946, brought off the big upset of the event by defeating Doris Hart. It was twelve years since Louise had won her first national title in the United States.

In the final Miss Brough made a gallant fight of it, employing a mixture of spin, slice, and flat-hit shots to try to break up Miss Connolly's rhythm. Miss Connolly, however, won again, for the third year running, 6–2, 7–5, and she always looked like a winner.

Only a few weeks later Miss Connolly sustained a severe injury to her leg whilst horse-riding. And this ended her championship career. Her short time in the top-most ranks was quite remarkable. From September 1951, when she won the United States championship at the age of sixteen, to July 1954, when she gained her third successive title at Wimbledon, she was beaten only once anywhere in the world, in California in March 1954. Without a powerful service or volley, she built up her supremacy on the solidarity and accuracy of her ground strokes, which she hit with amazing power for one so small.

In only three years she won a unique sequence of nine major world championships—before she was twenty. Had she been able to compete for another five or six years, her total number of championships could well have been quite unparalleled. As it was, she deserves to be ranked among the very greatest women singles players that have ever lived. And her character and temperament remained durable and unruffled in all circumstances.

QUEEN AT SEVENTEEN

by Allison Danzig

The ladies in lawn tennis have taken a back seat to the men for many years but a 17-year-old girl from California has wrested the play away from the stronger sex. When the national championships are held at Forest Hills in August, the Sedgmans, Savitts, McGregors, Seixases, Pattys, Larsens and Flams are likely to find themselves playing second string to Maureen Connolly.

When Miss Connolly defeated Doris Hart and Shirley Fry last September to win the crown at Forest Hills, a new personality had arrived to give women's tennis its biggest shot in the arm in a long, long time. When she triumphed a few weeks ago at Wimbledon, where our men were shut out of the finals, this little blond scrapper with the bobbing head, twinkling toes and the killer instinct on the court of a Jack Dempsey in the ring commanded comparison with no one less than Helen Wills.

One has to go back all the way to the days of the rivalry between Helen Wills and Suzanne Lenglen of France for a parallel to the interest created in women's tennis by Miss Connolly. There have been many other fine players of the fair sex over the years. Alice Marble was the most complete tennis player of modern times, with more versatility in her armory of weapons than Helen Wills boasted, and she more nearly approached the type of game played by men than any other woman since Mary K. Browne.

Helen Jacobs, Sarah Palfrey Cooke, Pauline Betz, Margaret Osborne duPont, Louise Brough and Miss Hart have also been excellent players in winning the championship. But none of them caught the public fancy to the degree that has Miss Connolly.

Women's tennis had little attraction and was totally eclipsed by the men's tournaments. This was so even for some of the years when Helen Wills Moody was at the top. The women's championship drew so few people to Forest Hills that it was decided to combine it with the men's, and the Wightman Cup matches with the British were transferred to smaller clubs because of the pitifully small galleries.

Miss Connolly has changed all of that and the prediction is made that she will prove to be the biggest magnet in years during the coming combined championships at Forest Hills in August. The center and No. 1 courts at Wimbledon were packed to the fill of their standing room for the little Californian's appearances.

The British are so tennis-minded that they will queue up and stand to see almost anyone play at Wimbledon. But there was no mistaking the eager intensity of the interest when Little Mo walked on the court. Her extreme youth was part of the explanation. But the bigger part was the personality of this remarkable youngster and the fierce competitive spirit she brings to the court.

When she is not playing tennis, Maureen Connolly is the normal healthy teen-age bobby-soxer. She loves music of any kind and the movies and dates and dancing. But when she walks out before a gallery with her racket she becomes another personality. Her every thought and energy are bent on destroying her opponent with the most lethal two-sided driving attack mounted by a woman player since Helen Wills.

The concentration this 17-year-old youngster brings to the court is almost unequaled. Her fighting spirit is even more pronounced. The tougher the going, the greater the danger, the harder she fights and the more of a threat she becomes.

She was in serious difficulties twice in early rounds at Wimbledon and against opponents whom she was supposed to defeat easily but who were playing tennis far superior to their suspected capacities. Miss Connolly had been going through difficult days as a result of publicity of which she was the innocent victim. She was in an unhappy frame of mind because of the exaggerated reports about her shoulder "injury" and the critical letters they drew upon her.

The combination of her mental state and the punishing ordeal she was subjected to on the court might have broken the morale of an older and more experienced player. It did nothing of the kind in Miss Connolly's case. She settled herself more grimly to the task, attacked with boldness, rather than played safe to hang on, and hammered her opponents into submission.

Here in this girl from San Diego is one of the most courageous competitors this observer has ever seen in any sport. Anyone who hopes to beat her at Forest Hills or Wimbledon from now on will have to play the game of her life and fight as she never fought before.

HORSE DE COMBAT

by Allison Danzig

Like Helen Wills, as in so many other respects, Maureen Connolly has been the victim of a sudden crippling blow, ending her hopes of winning the national tennis championship a fourth successive time.

In 1926, Little Miss Poker Face, as Queen Helen was known, was stricken with appendicitis during the French hard court tournament. She was rushed to the American Hospital at Neuilly for an operation. That was the end of her tennis for the year. The title she had won at Forest Hills in 1923, 1924 and 1925 went undefended.

Now Little Mo, every inch the queen of the courts that was Helen Wills, must apparently forgo the defense of the crown she has won the past three years. Unless she has a miraculously speedy recovery from her leg fracture of last week, when her horse took fright and whirled into a cement-mixer truck in San Diego, there is no possibility of her playing in the championships. They start August 28.

Last year Miss Connolly defended her title without the loss of a set in the tournament. She previously had won the championships of England, France and Australia. So, at the age of 18, she became the first woman to achieve the grand slam that Donald Budge had gained in men's tennis in 1938. And for the third successive time she was voted the woman athlete of the year in The Associated Press poll.

This year the blond little California girl defended her French and British crowns, then flew to Dublin to win the Irish championship before hopping the Atlantic to retain the national clay court crown. Until her sad mishap, her triumph in the forthcoming championships at Forest Hills was accepted as foregone, just as was Helen Wills' in 1926.

Helen never had the satisfaction of winning the title four times running, though she was champion seven times in all. She was supreme again in 1927, 1928 and 1929. But in 1930, after winning at Wimbledon for the fourth successive year and at Paris for the third, she elected to go home to California and let her national title go. Betty Nuthall of England won it, the first player to take it out of the country.

In 1926 it had been Mrs. Molla Bjurstedt Mallory who triumphed in Miss Wills' absence, the same Molla whose reign was ended by Helen in 1923. That was Mrs. Mallory's seventh championship and probably the most satisfying of them all. For the first time, she said afterward, she had the gallery with her as the non-favorite, and it was the support from the stands that helped her to overcome Elizabeth Ryan's 4–0 lead in the third set of the final.

They came no gamer than the Norwegian-born Mrs. Mallory, who had nothing more than a forehand in the way of stroke equipment but had the heart of a lion. Mrs. Mallory won the national tournament from 1915 through 1918, but in 1917 it was designated as a "patriotic" tournament. No title was involved. Helen Jacobs is the only player to win the championship four times consecutively, from 1932 through 1935.

With Miss Connolly out of action, the biggest scramble in years for the women's title is in prospect. Any one of a half dozen players might win it without causing any surprise.

There is Doris Hart, five times a finalist but never a winner, though she was 1951 Wimbledon champion. Last year she was runner-up to Little Mo at Paris, London and Forest Hills. Hardly seems fair. There will be many pulling for Doris, who lets go with everything she's got without ever changing expression.

There is Louise Brough, a big girl with power and blond hair overhead. She won three times at Wimbledon and once at Forest Hills. She beat Miss Hart in London and gave Miss Connolly a rough second set.

Mrs. Margaret Osborne duPont, American champion three times, is one of the most knowing and versatile players. She is the cleverest of them all up forward and in the use of spin, but has she the lasting powers? Shirley Fry, a runner-up at Forest Hills and Wimbledon, and Mrs. Betty Rosenquest Pratt, who beat her at Wimbledon, are other possible winners among the more experienced players.

Of the more youthful ones, Mrs. Beverly Baker Fleitz seems the most dangerous. She's 24, red-haired and ambidextrous. She changes the racket from one hand to the other and hits nothing but forehands; hits with jolting speed, too.

Beverly beat Little Mo in the La Jolla Beach and Tennis Club invitation semi-finals in March, 6–0, 6–4.

"Everything I hit at her she sent back," said Maureen. "She was just too, too good."

Maybe Maureen was a little off, in her first tournament in months, but there's no denying that Beverly can belt the ball. She dropped out of tennis for two years after four seasons in the top ten. Now the mother of 1-year-old Kimberlee Fleitz is back in the lists, and she thinks she can win. What player doesn't, with mighty Little Mo horse de combat?

LITTLE MO

by Ann Jones

I first met Maureen many years ago, but it was not until we were in Melbourne for the Federation Cup matches in January 1965 that we got to know each other. A quite exceptional friendship developed which I like to think was of mutual benefit. Certainly I can say without any hesitation that I found new inspiration both in my tennis and in my private life through my association with her. Maureen had a tremendous zest for life which was unbelievably infectious to those who were close to her, as I was privileged to be. She had an insatiable curiosity and many times we sat late into the night and early morning, discussing a wide variety of subjects. I would stagger onto the tennis court next day in anything but first-rate physical condition, but mentally I was more than 100 per cent.

The Brinker establishment, whether in Dallas, Palm Desert or Santa Barbara, became a second home for me and I had personal insight into the very close family ties which existed. The first time I visited Dallas, which was just before Forest Hills, I was asked to share Maureen's love of horses; the fact that I had never sat on a horse before daunted neither of us. So I duly climbed on top of "Kansas Boy," a 14-year-old polo pony who, I was promised, was very lazy and "wouldn't do a thing." He lived up to his reputation and refused to move at all. After several minutes of frustration, Maureen presented me with Norm's polo whip. Now we were off. I found it impossible to hold reins, saddle and whip correctly, and with each stride the whip firmly and repeatedly landed on Kansas Boy's rump. Obediently he went faster and faster around the field while I hung on grimly. Ten minutes later Maureen's agonized cry of "drop the whip" got through to me and we finally came to a halt. Maureen galloped anxiously over, expecting to find me frightened out of my wits, but I was beaming from ear to ear. I had loved every minute of it. But my back was stiff during the opening rounds of Forest Hills on that and subsequent years.

Last August we were faced with the problem of moving the Brinker family plus Pip and myself, 9 horses and other contents of a house from Santa Barbara to Dallas. Only Maureen could have planned such an epic. Off we set with Maureen leading the way in the station wagon, towing a two-horse trailer. Norm followed behind in the truck, pulling eight horses. It took us four days and nights to reach our destination, and if you have never experienced looking for lock-up stabling with food and water for the horses after midnight in small townships in the California desert or on the plains of New Mexico, then seeking food and lodgings for six people, try it sometime. It has its moments.

We were stopped only four times by the police for one thing or another, mainly because the lights in the trailer refused to function, and when we eventually arrived home at 2 A.M. there was no water in the stables. It had been turned off. The horses were eventually watered from a bucket on the front doorstep. We had no key to the front door, and a German shepherd dog was desperately anxious to tear us to pieces. But in Maureen's inimitable never-give-up manner, we finally managed to overcome all problems and got to bed just in time to get up next morning—to find the car battery flat since we had left the headlights on.

So many similar happy memories of a courageous, generous and inspiring personality will be treasured by me over the coming years and will go a little way to fill the void created by her tragic and premature death.

BUDGE PATTY

by Allison Danzig

In women's tennis it's Gorgeous Gussie Moran with the lacy creation that brought every monocle into position at Wimbledon to a delighted chorus of "Bah Joves!" and who is knocking some of the stuffiness out of the old guard at Forest Hills, too. Now men's tennis has its glamour boy to give Gussie some real competition as a magnet of the first magnitude for those who don't know very much about lobs and volleys but suddenly have acquired a craving for learning.

Budge Patty has had them swooning on the French Riviera the past few years. It wasn't fair to American womanhood that any one so tall and handsome, with that je ne sais quoi which defies translation but compels capitulation, should spend all of his time on the Continent when he had a good home in California.

Only on rare occasions did Patty favor his own country by putting in a tournament appearance. France had an irresistible attraction for him and so, outside of Jinx Falkenburg and her mother, "Mickey," who have known all about him since they gave Budgey cookies and milk as a little boy, the fair sex of America had no idea of what they were missing.

The spell of the Riviera and Paris was on Patty almost from the time he won our national junior title in 1941 and 1942. He played for the men's championship in 1941 but hardly anyone knew it, for Ted Schroeder knocked him out early, and that was the last Forest Hills saw of him until 1946.

Back from service in the Army in the European theater, Patty competed in the championship four years ago and scored a sensational victory over Yvon Petra, the 6-foot 6-inch Frenchman, who had just won the British title at Wimbledon. When a reporter congratulated him and told him enthusiastically he had a great future in tennis, Budge gave him an amused smile that somehow made the reporter feel a bit silly. Why get excited over a game of tennis?

The next day the California youngster took a bad beating from Bob Falkenburg, the first he had suffered in some twenty meetings between them, and then he was off to France again. It was two years before he was back, and again it was Falkenburg, then the champion of Wimbledon, who beat him.

Last year, Patty defeated Pancho Gonzales, our national titleholder, in the French championship and lost to Frank Parker in the final. He played at Wimbledon and was beaten by Jaroslav Drobny of Czechoslovakia in five sets, but Forest Hills saw him not.

Now Budge has come home again and Forest Hills is going to see him—a lot of him. For he returns as the champion of Great Britain and the champion of France, and he comes home fired up about a silly game of tennis. With him it's no longer a case of meeting with Triumph and Disaster and treating both those Kipling impostors just the same. Winning has taken on a new importance, and there's no fun in losing.

How are they going to keep him off the Davis Cup team after his twin victories over Bill Talbert in the French and British championships and his conquest of Jaroslav Drobny and Frank Sedgman in the finals of those two tournaments? Sedgman is the champion of Australia and the No. 1 hope of the team that likely will challenge us for the cup at Forest Hills, August 25, 26 and 27. After that will come the national championships, and if there is any one player who stands out as the man to beat for the title, it is J. Edward (Budge) Patty.

It was a body blow to amateur tennis when Pancho Gonzales followed Jack Kramer, Bobby Riggs, Donald Budge, and Pancho Segura into the professional ranks after winning the crown for the second time last September, taking Frank Parker with him. There was no one on the horizon who could fill the void he left as a crowd pleaser to make the turnstiles hum, and badge wearers of the West Side Tennis Club and the United States Lawn Tennis Association have been wearing long faces.

Now they're all wearing smiles again. They have a successor to Gonzales who has not only won the two big foreign titles that escaped Pancho but who should have an even greater appeal for the distaff side of the gallery as the Prince Charming of the courts.

No relation to Donald (The Red) Budge, who had them swooning over one of the greatest backhands the game has seen when he was scoring the only grand slam in history, Budge Patty may become the first player to win the American, British and French crowns in the same season since his namesake did it in 1938. Whether he makes it or not, there will be plenty of swooning in the Forest Hills Stadium. Gorgeous Gussie can look to her laurels.

TUT BARTZEN

by George McGann

Tut Bartzen is anything but the stereotyped Texan. No long-limbed, swaggering extrovert he. Tut is short, soft-spoken, serious-minded, dedicated. Not the charged-up cowpoke pounding into town for a night's spree. Rather, the solitary figure outlined against the sky, gazing somberly into the canyon as the sun sinks behind him into the Golden West. Well, enough of movieland metaphors.

Bernard Bartzen, 29, formerly of San Angelo and now of Dallas, Texas. That is a listing you find year after year, with only the age altered, among the top tennis players in the United States. Number five in the country this year, number four (his highest) last year— always well up with the more spectacular and more celebrated players, the crowd pleasers.

Tut—the nickname might well have derived from that other thin-lipped and silent fellow, King Tut-ankh-amen, memorable mummy of the Nile—is a player whose strong points are determination, doggedness and devotion to the game. He is a left-hander who plays with all the solemnity of his celebrated southpaw predecessor, Sir Norman Brookes of Australian Davis Cup renown.

Tut's principal problem is that he is seemingly allergic to grass. His type of game is better suited to clay than to the traditional turf in use at the Eastern tennis centers—Merion, Orange, Newport, Southampton and Forest Hills or at Wimbledon and in Australia. On grass Tut has never been fully effective against the big-serve, big-volley boys so beloved by Davis Cup selection committees. That is the reason that players below Tut in the national ranking whom he has handled with ease on non-turf surfaces have made the trip to Australia on the Cup team while he has never been selected for an assignment more important than American zone competition.

Davis Cup captain Billy Talbert likens Tut to that amazing court coverer of a generation ago, Bitsy Grant. But as far as considering the little Texan for the next Cup quest Down Under, Talbert shakes his head: "I'm afraid Tut is not really big enough for top-flight Cup play and his game is not severe enough." . . .

Tut has tended to avoid the grass court circuit since he got out of the Army in 1953, depending upon his stand-out performances elsewhere to earn him his high rankings. His record on clay and cement has always been superb: he almost never loses to anyone ranked below him; he invariably beats one or two players ranked above him, and his scores are decisive, to say the least. . . . He plays mainly from the baseline and depends upon his smooth ground strokes from either side, hit with moderate pace, to elicit errors. . . .

"The first big thrill I had on the circuit," he says, "was the time my pardner, Gardy Larned, and I beat Kramer and Schroeder at Southampton. My second 'big moment' came in 1954 when I won the national clay court by defeating both Vic Seixas and Tony Trabert. But the biggest thrill of all was playing Davis Cup for the United States against Cuba. The moment I stepped onto the court and heard 'The Star-Spangled Banner,' I felt rewarded for all the years of hard work I put into the game." . . .

FRANK SEDGMAN

by Jeane Hoffman

If Frank Sedgman is the world's greatest amateur tennis player, as has often been said, he is also the world's most inarticulate person on the subject of Frank Sedgman. But we managed to find out a segment or two on Sedgman, aside from the fact that his hobby seems to be beating Americans and walking off with the silverware.

Born in Melbourne in 1928, Frank played his first tennis at eight years of age but entered his first major tournament only five years ago. He was just another tennis-talented youth batting the little white ball around when Harry Hopman discovered him at the age of 12. It's Hopman who must be given the lion's share in the development of the Aussie ace. Hopman invited Frank to join his tennis classes, took over the boy's coaching, especially on tactics, and urged him to join a local suburban club.

"B.H.," which is to say before Hopman, Frank had been well on his way to becoming an all-round athlete, starring in schoolboy cricket, football and track, where he was a top hurdler (that experience comes in handy for jumping the tennis net now). But after World War II, which Frank was too young to see much of, it was all tennis.

His first appearance overseas was in 1948, when he tagged along after the Australian Davis Cup team as a sort of tennis tourist or spare tire. That same year, at 19, he won the Wimbledon doubles championship with Jack Bromwich, which should have warned the Yanks of things to come. He also won the Kent title, but he didn't do so well in the United States, losing to Tom Brown at Southampton and Earl Cochell at Newport, and bowing out to Frank Parker in the nationals—all early-round defeats. In 1949 he leaped into the limelight by defeating Bromwich for the Australian championship, but lost to Eric Sturgess at Queen's and Ted Schroeder at Wimbledon, both quarter-final losses. Pancho Gonzales and Schroeder beat him in the Davis Cup matches (he was on the team by this time), so it still wasn't his year.

But in 1950 the "Aussie lamb" turned into a mighty mutton. He won the Australian championship again, took the South African title, lost to Art Larsen at Queen's, but beat Larsen, Philippe Washer, Fred Kovaleski and Jar Drobny to get to the finals at Wimbledon, where Budge Patty eliminated him. In the Davis Cup matches, as the world knows, he defeated Tom Brown and Schroeder, then teamed up with Bromwich to score a smashing victory in doubles.

As for 1951, his followers hadn't seen anything yet. By the end of the summer he was invincible. Larsen was his final-round opponent and runner-up in Aussie tourneys at Victoria, Queensland and South Australia, while Sedgman came out second best at New South Wales and lost to Dick Savitt in the semis of the Australian championship. Paris was his next stop. There he lost in the semis of the French championship to Drobny. Frank's talent was recognized at Wimbledon and he was seeded first, only to lose to Herb Flam in a quarter-final five-set upset. He then made a brief but memorable invasion of the U. S. He lost to Bill Talbert in the quarters at Orange, won Newport, took the national doubles with Ken McGregor, breezed through the nationals singles, exhibiting the finest tennis of his career and defeating Vic Seixas in the final, and added another trophy to his already crowded shelf when he walked off with the Pacific Southwest. He has now returned Down Under, leaving a dejected American populace and many defeated U.S. tennis stars in his wake.

In Australia Sedgman and Bromwich are like sugar and spice, tea and crumpets, ham and eggs—an inseparable combination, a daily double of destiny in the public esteem. Frank has had a half-dozen offers to turn pro, but it's doubtful if even the U.S. mint at Fort Knox could move him until he's had a chance to defend the Davis Cup in his home country. "Then I might be interested," he says, "although I've really never thought of turning pro. I just like to play tennis."

Frank plays basketball all winter, starring at center. His hobby is collecting records—phonograph ones, not just tennis. He leans towards swing music, likes to dance, has a steady girl in Australia, likes to swim.

Sedgman likes America, once considered staying over here to go to school. About 5 feet 10 inches, he has blond hair, blue eyes, calls West Preston, Victoria, his home. He hopes to realize his ambition to win the U.S., Wimbledon and Aussie championships all in the same year; figures Australia will win the Davis Cup again and also figures to be around when they're doing it.

ALEX OLMEDO

by Allison Danzig

"Style," said Buffon, "is the man himself." (*Le style c'est l'homme même.*)

The style of Alejandro Olmedo has made him the man of the moment in tennis. Chief artisan of the United States Davis Cup team's stunning victory Down Under, he captivated Australians with the magic of his racket in defeating their Ashley Cooper and Malcolm Anderson. Now he has taken the hearts and fancy of New Yorkers with his delicate handicraft in winning the national indoor championship.

Not in years had so many people thronged to the 7th Regiment Armory as gathered there daily to see the young Peruvian work the wonders of his feathery touch and steely wrist.

For close to three hours, in the final, they looked on spellbound at the wizardry of this slight, poised youth of inflexible purpose in turning away the wrath of the powerful Dick Savitt's lightning-bolt serves and thundering drives.

In a match ranking with the most memorable of all time for the high level of the play, sustained to the end of a thrilling 22-game fifth set of fantastic exploits, Alex Olmedo stood forth as a true virtuoso of the racket. He stood, too, as a resolute fighter of unshakable spirit, as well as a master craftsman, a weaver of the most delicately wrought subtleties of shading and timing.

A year ago the Chief was just another good tennis player. His only accomplishment of note was his winning of the national intercollegiate championship twice for the University of Southern California, where he is in his senior year.

Today he stands as the player to beat in amateur tennis the world over. He stands, too, as the game's top attraction, with probably even greater appeal than has any of the world champions of the past and present Jack Kramer is bringing into Madison Square Garden Sunday afternoon. He may not be their equal in ability but the style of his game, his artistry in manipulating a piece of ash and gut as a magic wand, has even greater charm than the cannonball serve and the dreadnaught drive.

This has come about since Olmedo was named on the United States Davis Cup team, the second player so honored who was not a native of this country. Possibly in time he would have attained his stature of the moment even had he not been put on the team.

But heretofore the Chief has been a player lacking in desire. He showed at Merion last July, in a tremendous match with Barry MacKay, that he had the game to challenge the best. But in other appearances he appeared indifferent and disappointed.

The opportunity to represent the United States, and at the same time to stand for his native country, Peru, has brought a change. It is the ambition of every player worthy of his salt to participate in the Davis Cup matches, greatest of all tennis competitions.

Given the chance he never hoped for, since Peru does not have a Davis Cup team, Olmedo found the incentive he apparently needed to realize his potential.

In defeating the world's two ranking amateurs in the challenge round, in winning the Australian championship and, now, our indoor title, the Chief has shown the desire and intensity of purpose required to bring his game to full flower.

There has been sharp criticism of the United States Lawn Tennis Association for using Olmedo to help bring back the Davis Cup, though Australia and many other nations sent their congratulations and approval of his participation. The fact that the Chief is not an American citizen and has expressed no desire to become one, or to subject himself to the military draft, has irked some.

What should be kept in mind is that in naming Olmedo, the USLTA little suspected he would win the cup for us. There was doubt that he would even get into the singles. Hamilton Richardson and MacKay were rated every bit his equal, if not superior, at the time.

The association simply was rewarding Olmedo for his tennis and good sportsmanship and character. His game had been developed in this country during his five-year residence, he was ranked in our national list and he had earned the place on merit. Also, it was entirely proper to put him on the team under long-standing Davis Cup regulations establishing eligibility with three years of residence.

Olmedo was not the first to so qualify. Among others, John Doeg was not a citizen when he played on the United States team against Canada and Mexico in 1930, the year he won the national championship.

The USLTA was demonstrating that it gives equal opportunity to every player, to the foreign-born as well as the homebred. It was also carrying out the good-neighbor policy and putting the United States in a favorable light in Latin American countries.

In Peru there has been great rejoicing and pride in Olmedo's triumph, and gratitude to the United States for giving him his chance.

A hero's welcome awaits him in Lima when he returns with the cup on a tour sponsored by our State Department.

On the matter of citizenship, Alex says, "I have never been able to plan ahead. I am here on a student visa. If I decide to remain in the United States permanently, I will become a citizen. I don't mind going into the Army. You can learn a lot of things in the Army."

To anyone close to this modest, likable youth, it is unthinkable and cruelly unfair to suspect him of being a draft dodger.

DORIS HART

by Emma Harrison

Doris Hart played the final of her thirteenth national tennis championship yesterday and—with concentration, determination and a maximum of hard work—found that number lucky.

Ever since the slender, serious girl from Coral Gables, Florida, entered her first United States championship match at the age of 16 in 1941 and nearly upset high-ranking Pauline Betz, older tennis hands had been solacing her.

"You're young, yet. You have time to win," they'd tell her after she'd lost a close one. But she was 29 years old and had won the British, French, Egyptian, South African and other far-flung titles before she became champion in her own country.

Besides Miss Hart's "always a bridesmaid" role at Forest Hills, there was another reason for the polite partisanship shown to her by the spectators who watched her win the hard three-set match from Louise Brough, the 1947 champion. The new champion obviously is impeded in her coverage of the court by a childhood knee injury.

When she was about a year old, she injured her right knee in a fall. There was the threat of amputation, because of infection, and a doctor performed an emergency operation on the knee on the family's kitchen table.

Doris plays a hard, aggressive game to compensate for her lack of speed.

"I can't run too well, so I try to hit the ball a little harder and make up in other ways. I dropshot a lot and make them run." Also her hard ground shots are among the best in women's tennis.

Miss Hart, a tall, brown-eyed woman, who tends to look more serious and calm than she admits to being on the court, is a strict disciplinarian of her own game and court behavior. Her slower gait, looking more like a deliberate saunter than an impediment, adds to her general cool court presence. She rarely indulges in court emotions, occasionally permitting herself a gasp at a missed return or giving a little kick at a short shot she missed with her racket.

Since she began playing at the age of 10 after an abdominal operation in a hospital which overlooked some tennis courts, Doris Hart has found the game an absorbing and "full-time job." She was within one semester of graduation from the University of Miami when an attractive match loomed and she gave up her degree. Lately she's been thinking of tapering off a bit, at least on her foreign treks.

"Travel was fine in the beginning, but, like anything else, it gets tiresome," she said, thinking of her last five years of almost constant travel on the tennis circuit.

"I'm looking for a good reason to settle down. It's hard to stop something without a good reason," she said, adding that she thought "the best" reason would be marriage.

After the match the winner, her arms full of silver trophies, told the crowd she hoped "to keep playing a few more years."

Among her friends, with whom she has toured and played for many years, she is known as a dedicated tennis player, a generous and loyal friend and a witty, likable companion. She attends church regularly, even while on tour. Players report at least one instance when she has helped a teammate out with needed fare to some tennis contest.

Doris' close tie with her family is also well known among her friends. When not on tour, she lives with her parents, Mr. and Mrs. Robert J. Hart, in Coral Gables. Now, because her father is a mutuels manager at race tracks and works in Chicago in the summer, the family is there. Mrs. Hart, who used to travel with Miss Hart, gave it up long ago "because it made me too nervous to watch."

The most interested spectator yesterday appeared to be Richard Hart, the brother who taught her to play. Having flown in from Chicago for the sixth time to see his sister in the final at Forest Hills, he told friends he would break a habit and root out loud. He did. Then Miss Hart broke her old habit of losing the final.

SHIRLEY FRY

from the New York Times

Shirley Fry has been trying to quit tennis for five years.

She took a second large step backward yesterday when she won her first United States championship at Forest Hills. Her first big mis-step was at Wimbledon last July when she won the English title. She has been as unsuccessful as can be in her pursuit of retirement.

Until she "gave up" tennis, the major titles had eluded the tenacious, hard-hitting young woman from Akron during her twenty-one-year career on the courts of the world. A great believer in the importance of mental attitude in tennis players, she credits it for her Wimbledon victory.

"I play better when it doesn't matter if I win or lose," she explained. "After eight attempts at Wimbledon, I didn't feel I was going to win." This theory must have made her twice as good at Forest Hills yesterday. It was her sixteenth try.

Then, too, she had other incentives. When Doris Hart, her doubles partner and the country's top-ranking woman amateur player, turned professional this year, Miss Fry, who ranked second, moved up. She was in the embarrassing position of being the ranking United States woman player without having won the title.

"Some people thought I hadn't earned it, so I decided to go out and win this year. That's what I'm doing," she announced in a matter-of-fact way even before she marched out to the center court and defeated the formidable Althea Gibson.

Her second incentive, which probably ranks first, was to justify the work her father, Lester R. Fry, had put into developing her as a tennis player. He introduced her to the game when she was 8 and by the time she was 9 had given her a paternal order: "Wimbledon by 1945."

She's also been needled a bit by Doris Hart. The pair dominated women's doubles for several years, winning the United States title from 1951 to 1954, the Wimbledon title from 1951 through 1953 and the French championship from 1950 through 1953. Those titles, with the national girls' in 1944 and 1945 and the French championship she won in 1951, were Shirley's major triumphs until this year.

Since Miss Hart turned professional, she's been urging Shirley on with telegraphed messages. Before a match with Louise Brough, the message would be: "Get rough; beat Brough." Doris came from Coral Gables, Florida, to see yesterday's match.

Some of the players around Forest Hills remember Shirley when she first toddled on the scene out there, "a little girl, out without her mother."

Some remember one of her achievements there in the early days that had little to do with tennis. Too shy to ask anyone where the World's Fair was, she put on her hiking shoes—father Fry believed in hiking, too—and hiked around Queens till she found it.

There's very little repose for anyone on the other side of the net from Miss Fry. She is known as one of the most persistent retrievers among all the women in tennis today. Yesterday she took ample advantage of Miss Gibson's relatively soft return of service to draw her into position for some telling passing shots.

After the match she said she hadn't enjoyed the strain at all.

In pursuit of retirement a couple of years ago, Miss Fry moved to St. Petersburg, Florida, and took a job on a newspaper. But she drifted back into tennis. She holds a Bachelor of Arts degree from Rollins College in what she describes as a "very general course." About quitting tennis, now she can't say.

She was definite about one thing after the match, however.

"No more tennis this year," she said firmly as she headed for the clubhouse.

BIG AUSTRALIAN

from the New York Times

Late in 1954, a husky blond youngster with the build of a football guard threw down his racket in disgust after losing to Vic Seixas in the Victorian tennis championship. Irritated by the jeers of his Australian countrymen and the succession of setbacks he had suffered, with the resulting criticism of his poor play in the press, he gave vent to his feelings in a rare outburst. "I'm just fed up," he snapped. "Sure, I didn't care whether or not I won. I'm just tired of tennis, and I've gotten so I don't give a rap."

That teen-age Sydney youth, whose mother went to his defense and blamed his crack-up on too much team discipline and year-round regulation of his every move, won the championship at Wimbledon yesterday. He sits on the throne where Tilden, Budge, Vines, Cochet, Lacoste, Perry, Crawford and Kramer sat before him as recognized world champions, kings of the amateurs.

Lewis Hoad is his name. In Australia, where tennis is second to no other sport and where the inhabitants get as excited over a Davis Cup challenge round as we do when the Dodgers and Yankees meet in baseball's world series, his name is in front page headlines. And they may put it in bolder headlines than have been seen since the end of World War II if he wins the United States championship in September.

With that additional victory, 21-year-old Hoad would stand as the first Australian player ever and the first player from any country since 1938 to score a grand slam in tennis. J. Donald Budge of the United States did it eighteen years ago, and Donald the Red was both the first and the last to do it. A grand slam takes in the world's four major tennis crowns—the British, American, Australian and French.

Until this year, Hoad had not won one of the four crowns and it didn't look as if he would ever reach Olympus. For all of his great facility and power, his lightning reflexes, the great strength of a wrist that did wonders with a volley and also a backhand drive and the most thundering service in tennis, he apparently wasn't going to fulfill the promise of his great talent. He could win isolated victories of note in Davis Cup tournament play, but he wasn't temperamentally conditioned to be a world champion.

As a 17-year-old kid Lew and his junior buddy, Ken Rosewall, stampeded 16,000 customers at Wimbledon out of their British reserve. The center court clientele was jumping with joy at the sheer wizardry of stroke and, most of all, tactics of these teen-agers as they beat the American giants, Dick Savitt and Gardnar Mulloy. They beat them with a poise and composure that never wavered at any time during the two hours of electrifying doubles play.

A year later Hoad was electrifying his own people in Australia. Frank Sedgman and Kenneth McGregor had turned professional after winning the Davis Cup for their country in 1950, 1951 and 1952, and there was little hope that it could be held for another year against the challenge of Trabert and Seixas.

It was too much to expect of the inexperienced Hoad and Rosewall. So, when Hoad beat first Seixas and then Trabert, to score two of the three necessary victories in Kooyong Stadium, Melbourne, he became the national hero.

The tennis world was at the feet of Hoad now. So it seemed. But he was called into military service in January.

When he took off his khaki and returned to the courts in May 1954, his game was far below what it had been. He lost to Mulloy in the French championship, to Jaroslav Drobny at Wimbledon and to Ham Richardson at Forest Hills. Then, following his outburst in the Victorian championship, he and Rosewall were beaten for the Davis Cup by Trabert and Seixas.

Then came 1955, and defeat after defeat followed for Hoad. More than that, he was showing more and more temperament, something the British frown upon more than upon defeat. He lost to little Rosewall in his national championship. At Wimbledon he was beaten by Budge Patty.

Before Wimbledon started, it was a front-page sensation when Hoad and Jennifer Staley, a member of the Australian women's team, were married in England. The president of the Australian Lawn Tennis Association issued a statement in Melbourne that members of Australian teams abroad weren't supposed to have their wives with them. Nettled by the criticism, Harry Hopman, the Australian team captain, issued a strong statement in London in defense of matrimony.

Then it was off to the United States for Lew after his wife had taken a plane from England to Australia. Hoad hardly rated as a world beater when he arrived here. But when the Davis Cup challenge round came around, he was ready to play the tennis of his life.

Perhaps it was his way of showing his gratitude to his captain for standing up in his behalf; perhaps it was the inspiration of his bride. At any rate, he beat Trabert, the man who won three 1955 championships, in the key match of the challenge round at Forest Hills. The next day, with Australia leading by 2–0 after Rosewall had defeated Seixas, Hoad went out with Rex Hartwig to win the doubles and regain the cup for Australia.

The United States championship was an anti-climax after the winning of the Davis Cup, and Hoad made no great effort in the tournament. But, starting with 1956, he was out to win everything in sight.

He started by beating Rosewall for the Australian championship in January. Since then it has become apparent that Hoad is not only superior to the highly gifted but smaller and less powerful Rosewall but also to all other amateurs the world over.

THE STYLE OF LEW HOAD

by Julius D. Heldman

When Lew Hoad was 17, he made his first overseas tour with his smaller, slighter counterpart, Ken Rosewall. Within two years, this sleepy blond god, the idol of galleries all over the world, was one of the world's best players. He was playing Davis Cup singles and doubles for his country, he was one of the favorites for the Wimbledon title and he had already received and turned down a pro offer. Before he left the amateur ranks he had won three of the four major titles—Australia, France and Wimbledon. He reached the finals of Forest Hills the same year, only to lose to his rival, Rosewall. He took his defeat, which kept him from becoming the second player of all time to make the Grand Slam, with the same stolid and phlegmatic countenance as he took his victories.

I saw Hoad immediately after he had defeated Pancho Gonzales at Forest Hills in 1959 in one of the all-time great matches. Everything was working for him that day. He was hitting winner first volleys from midcourt, hard-angled ground strokes on the rise, and he consistently outguessed his opponent. Hoad wore Gonzales down: Pancho was drawn and puffing, but Lew was still the young bull at the close of the match. Lew and Jenny spent the evening with us. The match was completely gone from his mind. It might have been a practice set from his point of view, even though to many it was the final proof that he had arrived as the world's premier player.

Hoad never won a tour from Gonzales, although he was up on him in "Ampol points" (tournament competition). Lew on any day was by far the best player in the world, although in consistency Gonzales could still edge him. He has always had a spotty record. The year he won the Big Three, he was beaten in almost every minor event. His brilliance showed when the chips were down. The year he turned pro, he was to receive a bonus if he won the Wimbledon title. He came through brilliantly, winning the final over Ashley Cooper by a more decisive score than had ever been registered in the past. One week later he was playing for Jack Kramer.

From the very beginning Hoad had an electric court personality. His demeanor was almost cold, his bearing athletic but very poised, and his stroke production a miracle. He was always immaculately but casually attired. When the going got tough, he looked as relaxed as in the warm-up; he seemed immune to nerves. He was utterly indifferent to the pressures that practically all players feel when playing a vital match. He was like a big sleepy cat—capable of stretching out on a couch for a 10-minute nap an hour before a final, then of rousing himself to his full and magnificent powers on the court.

Hoad was one of the least temperamental of all players. He was capable of knocking a ball into the air, dropping his racket or even glaring at a linesman. One second later the point or the decision had been forgotten. His professional confreres consider him unrivaled as a sportsman. He was never a gamesman and was incapable of such questionable practices as needling, stalling, extended groaning or complaining. All he wanted to do was play, and as soon as the match was over it was immediately forgotten. No other champion was ever able to take his losses so phlegmatically or his wins so nonchalantly.

Off the court he was as well liked as he was on. His distant look belied his friendly disposition. He and Jenny had the same casual attitude toward life as they did toward tennis. They would rather go to a movie than a party, or to a diner than a restaurant, because it was less effort. Hoad's tie, which was always askew, was a symbol of his relaxed personality. One player, contrasting Lew with another famous professional, said of the latter that he would dive in front of a truck for a nickel, whereas Lew would not cross the street for $100,000 if he weren't in the mood.

Lew, like every great postwar player, based his game primarily on a big serve and a net attack. He was extremely quick and he moved in very close so that almost all his volleys were put-aways. He gambled on outguessing his opponent, and often when he was out of position he would end up right in front of the ball like a magnet. He was the all-time exponent of a controlled wrist whip, and consequently he could hit sharper hard ground strokes than any man in the game. It was impossible to cope with him when he was on his game: a series of winners flew off his racket to confound his opponent.

Most of the Australians use what is almost a Continental grip. The forehand is only an eighth of a turn from the backhand. Perhaps this is because they stress net play so much, and in their formative years they become accustomed to situations where there is no time to change grips. More likely it is because the young athlete is imitative and most great Australians in the recent past have had Continental or semi-Continental grips. Even before the war Quist, Hopman and Bromwich set the pattern. In the postwar era the style was perpetuated by Sedgman and McGregor. Only Ashley Cooper among the recent Australian Davis Cuppers has had a classical Eastern grip.

Hoad holds the racket with his fingers almost locked. His stroke is based on wrist, but not the usual slap action that the word connotes. His wrist is used to come up and over the ball. It is responsible for the pronounced overspin on all his shots. He is as strong as a bull moose, his arm is as muscled as a weight-lifter's, and his wrist is a steel pivot. Lew has a round-house wind-up that is rather compact when compared with Rod Laver's. It is a very quick semicircular motion, and the follow-through is short and rather high.

Although Hoad can hit as hard as any man, the stroke was never noted for its depth. He can hit sharp angles or dippers when his opponent is at net. Both are the result of overspin and the wrist action. In this crazy game where there is hardly ever a baseline rally, depth becomes less important. If Lew were to play a lot of clay tennis, he would undoubtedly develop better length. This he could do by either allowing himself more margin over the net or by taking off some of the topspin.

I have always liked Hoad's forehand because of its versatility, but he pays for it with frequent errors. There have not been too many shots like this in the game, although lefties Jaroslav Drobny and Rod Laver have similar strokes. It is always aggressive and I can't imagine his "playing steady" with it.

On return of serve, Hoad will sometimes use his full forehand swing because his muscle-eye coordination is so good. When he does, it is like a bullet. However, he chips a fair amount. Then the wind-up disappears while the shoulder, arm and wrist lock and move as a unit. It is not a Seixas chip where the stroke begins a foot in front of the body and the wrist turns under; Hoad's chip starts slightly behind the waist and is more like a flat block or a sideways shove. Lew also uses this for approach shots occasionally, particularly when he is more anxious to get to net than to hit a decisive ground stroke.

Hoad is one of the few players whose backhand looks like a mirror image of his forehand. There is the same roundhouse semicircle wind-up and the same pulling up on the follow-through, although sometimes he will finish with his racket turned over. The stroke is remarkable. It requires a powerful arm and wrist, which is one of Lew's principal tennis endowments. Only Trabert, with this action, can hit the ball as hard, although Lew has the sharper angles.

On return of serve Hoad will underspin or chip when necessary. The overspin on his regular backhand drive is very pronounced. As a matter of fact, Lew hardly has a flat shot in his repertoire.

The prettiest part of the backhand, and of the forehand as well, is the way Hoad gets down to the ball. His knees almost touch the ground on low balls, while his back is like a ramrod. He never makes an ungraceful move. The footwork is classical on the port side as he moves into the ball.

On low balls Lew gets down in the same beautiful way. The action is like his forehand chip: it starts slightly behind him and there is almost no wrist motion. These low volleys are extremely consistent. On the backhand side he practically never makes an error, and the approach to the ball is meticulous. There is a little more sidespin or underspin on the backhand, which has a slightly shorter motion.

If Lew has a weakness, it is his tendency to put too much overspin on waist-level or higher volleys. He handles these as full strokes by choice, and they are always winners when they go in. He nets them more than he should, for many of them are setups. However, it is a frightening sight to see Lew haul off and crack a high volley on either side. There is no more murderous shot in tennis and the point is over one way or the other.

The Hoad service is one of the most powerful weapons in the game. With the same wind-up action he can bludgeon a flat ace or whip a high-bouncing twist to the backhand. It is a fast and full wind-up, with the ball hit at the top of the toss. A typical Hoad mannerism is the small step which he takes with his hind foot as the action begins. It is perfectly legal service since the left foot does not move across the line.

When the foot-fault rule was changed, Lew utilized the jump. As he hits the ball now, it is almost as though his feet were doing a scissors in the air. To some players, it is the only way they can get their full height without tensing up. While the subject of jumping is controversial, it is now legal and being used by players such as Hoad and Segura.

Lew's toss is rather far over to the left, and for this reason he can use the same action on flat and spin serves.

The Hoad overhead is hit like his flat service. Its only weakness is the fact that he overhits. There is no restraint or temporizing. He tends to hit them a little short but he does have great angle choice. Every player who stands as close in as Lew has to leap well, and at this Hoad is a master.

Lew is a superb athlete who is already considered one of the all-time greats although his career is not over. Only two factors stand in the way of a 1961 world title. He has a recurrent back injury, of which he never complains, and on the nightly grind of the pro tour he is inclined occasionally to lose his edge. A few loose matches can make the difference in the final outcome against his rivals.

ROSEWALL

from the New York Times

When slight, freckle-faced Kenneth R. Rosewall gained his amazing victory at Forest Hills yesterday, it represented a triumph of artistry over greatly superior strength.

Rosewall stands 5 feet 7 inches and weighs 145 pounds. His opponent in the contest for the men's national tennis championship was four inches taller and twenty pounds heavier. But Rosewall's classic technique turned the trick, as it had two days before when he overpowered Richard Savitt.

A long-standing friendly rivalry underlay yesterday's contest. Rosewall and Lewis Hoad have been playing each other since they were boys of 12 in their native Australia. They were born only three weeks and nine miles apart.

At 17, their wizardry sent 16,000 spectators at Wimbledon into a frenzy. Together they played on victorious Australian teams in the Davis Cup matches. Rosewall won the Australian championship in 1953 and again in 1955. Hoad took it away from him this year.

Yesterday Rosewall destroyed his rival's hope to become the first man since Don Budge to make tennis' grand slam in one year—the Australian, French, Wimbledon and United States championships.

A diffident young man of 21, with hazel-blue eyes and a shock of black hair, Rosewall has been playing tennis since he was 7. It came naturally; his parents operated tennis courts in Sydney. At 17, he was the junior champion of Australia.

For the last four years, he and Hoad, together and separately, have held virtually every major tennis title. But until yesterday Hoad had been considered the superior player.

How long Rosewall will resist offers to turn professional is a subject of debate. In 1955, after the Davis Cup victory, Jack Kramer offered him and Hoad $50,000 and the players reportedly gave tentative acceptance.

But they returned to Australia—where the popularity of tennis compares with that of baseball in this country—and were persuaded to remain amateurs. Australian sporting goods firms gave them "jobs."

Recently a United States concern that prepares canned milk contracted with Rosewall to represent it in Australia. He intends to spend some time at the organization's Los Angeles office before going home.

In manner, Rosewall is unassuming and approachable. He has a wide, quick smile.

Patiently, on Saturday, after his hard-won triumph over Victor Seixas, he gave autographs to the youngsters who swarmed after him as he left the stadium. He posed for a picture with an Indonesian visitor who said he just wanted one "to take home."

He waited upon a capricious sun with cameramen for a magazine. He borrowed a pocket mirror first to comb his hair—"just in case my fiancée sees the pictures."

On October 6, Rosewall will marry Wilma McIver of Brisbane. They met when both were playing in an Australian junior tennis match.

As a hobby, Rosewall collects recordings, mostly popular. He likes Mario Lanza, but his general preference is for piano selections. "I always wanted to play the piano," he says.

He received his education in the public schools of Sydney. His parents now operate a delicatessen business in a Sydney suburb.

MY LIFE AND TIMES

by Ken Rosewall

When I was a small boy in Rockdale, I wanted more than anything else to be champion of Australia. Today my intensity of feeling about the game has changed only in scope. Many of my ambitions have been achieved, but there are many more challenges ahead of me. As a youngster, I learned to play on the three courts owned by my father. My idol was Frank Sedgman and my boyhood rival was Lew Hoad. . . .

My "life and times" follows the pattern of so many other tennis players in its ups and downs—up when I won the French championship at the age of 17, and down when I failed to defend it successfully the following year; on top of the world when Lew and I kept the Davis Cup for Australia in 1953, and ready for the gas chamber when Seixas and Trabert took it away from us in 1954. . . .

My dad taught me how to play tennis. He was an A-grade player with excellent athletic ability and quick reflexes. He was very keen on the game and he read every book he could get his hands on. He taught me my strokes and they are not so different today from what they were under his tutelage. . . . Although dad had three courts at Rockdale, we had to sell them when he went into the Air Force, because we could not look after them. These courts were literally in our back yard, and when we gave them up they had become the basis for a small club which was used regularly by all the Rosewalls. I played there exclusively until I was 11.

I first heard of Lew Hoad when we were twelve years of age. I had never seen him, but I was aware of the stir he created when he played in the Manly open junior tournament. He was very small and slight, but he managed to knock off a six-foot junior player. This was just after the Davis Cup challenge round. Jack Kramer and Ted Schroeder had won the cup for the United States, and Kramer and Tom Brown were to play a few exhibitions against John Bromwich and Adrian Quist. One of the matches was scheduled for Rockdale, and Lew and I were selected to play a preliminary exhibition. This was the first match between Rosewall and Hoad, and I went about it as though I were playing for my life. I won, 6–0, 6–0.

Even at the age of 12 Lew was an aggressive player. He hit the ball! I was the consistent one, and although I did not have much pace, I played the ball fairly well. As for my net game, I pooped my serve in and then retreated.

Lew and I were living in different parts of Sydney, and the only time we ever saw each other was at tournaments. We respected each other's games, but we scarcely knew each other. Our first tournament match (and our third meeting) was in the New South Wales school and age championships in May of that year. We played in both the 13 and 15-and-under finals, and I won both times.

When I was growing up in tennis John Bromwich was my first hero. He belonged to the same association and he had grown up in the same district. I worshiped silently for four years, and then I finally got to meet him through Arthur Huxley. Huxley and George Worthington, who was then a leading junior, used to watch . . . youngsters who showed promise. I was picked by them as a possibility, and from then on I was given rackets and helped in many other ways by Slazengers. One day, when I was 14, Huxley asked me if I would like to play doubles with Bromwich at an Easter tournament in Orange. I was so eager that I would have walked the 200 miles from Sydney to Orange. . . .

Bromwich and I won the doubles. I played with him a few times thereafter. I always felt I had only to cover one-quarter of the court and that he would take care of the rest. He was one of the best doubles players I have ever seen. First he confused his opponents with spin and touch, and then he would whip one past them. He had a fantastic return of serve. I believe he and Adrian Quist were the greatest doubles combination of all time. They were in their prime in 1938 and 1939, but in 1950 they won Wimbledon! They were an unconventional team, as opposed to the very correct Mulloy-Talbert tandem. Bromwich was not only a great player; he was also an unusual person who was very popular with all those who knew him. He was a great sportsman in the true sense of the word.

My second hero was Frank Sedgman. I met him in 1949, when I was 15. I was entered in the men's doubles with Ken McGregor, and we played Sedgman and George Worthington. My serve was pretty weak and my volley was not sound or safe. We lost in straight sets, 6–3, 6–4, 6–3. . . . That same year Lew and I teamed in doubles for the first time. Adrian Quist phoned my dad and suggested that we enter the New South Wales juniors, and so Lew and I paired together. We lost in the final of the 19-and-under event, but we won it for the next three years running.

Many people have asked me how Lew and I got along. We were both tremendously competitive, particularly against each other, but we were always thrown together as juniors during the tournament season. Then, when we were 17, we were both selected for the overseas team. We traveled together and we played doubles together, but when we were on the court in singles, we tried to beat each other as badly as possible. We were both grown men now and we got more enjoyment out of being together than ever before. Lew is happy-go-lucky, friendly and easy to get along with. . . .

I traveled with Harry Hopman from 1952 to 1955, and Cliff Sproule was the team manager in 1956. Cliff was easy to get along with, as was "Hop," although the latter was more strict. But Lew and I were young and we had no objections. It meant that our choice of tournaments was very limited. . . .

Frank Sedgman was the first Australian to travel privately, for the Lawn Tennis Association of Australia permitted him a "honeymoon tour" in

1952. Mervyn Rose was married shortly after, and he too toured privately. Lew Hoad was the next, after his marriage to Jenny. I never asked to travel privately because I never really thought about it too much.

The part that Hopman played in the development of Hoad and myself has been a matter for much discussion. Harry has been credited with being both a great coach and a great trainer. He does not feel he deserves this credit, although he does not deny it. I was traveling with Hop when I was beaten in the finals of Wimbledon by Drobny and again when Nielsen defeated me. I do not believe I would have lost to either of these players if I had known as much about tennis then as I do now. I was strictly a baseliner, and I won or lost from the backcourt. When I turned professional I discovered more about the game, but I had to play Gonzales, Trabert and Segura to do so. Hop did try to help me, particularly with my serve, but I was never encouraged to be a net-rusher.

Harry has been kind in many ways, but I find him hard to understand. None of the Aussies, as amateurs or pros, ever openly criticized Hopman or discussed his coaching ability. But after we turned professional, we dropped out of his life. Occasionally he would say in the papers that we were better players when we were amateurs. When we played a pro tournament, he never came over to say hello or shake hands. It was as though Mal Anderson, Ashley Cooper, Frank Sedgman, Mervyn Rose, Rex Hartwig, Lew Hoad and myself no longer existed for him. . . .

Lew and I were so good when we were 16 that we attracted a fair-sized gallery whenever we played. I remember my first big match in men's singles. I was 16 and I played Dick Savitt in Sydney. It was my first time against an overseas player. I was beaten, 8–6, 6–8, 7–5, 6–3, but it was a pretty good match. I started to play well the following year, when I was 17. Frank Sedgman, then the best player in the country, beat me in five sets in Queensland. He went through me in the semi-finals of Sydney fairly easily. Then, in the Australian nationals, Rose beat me in the quarter-finals at 6–2 in the fifth set. Lew was also coming up very fast. On the basis of our showing, he and I were both picked for the overseas team.

This 1952 team was a congenial one. The other members were Ken McGregor and Mervyn Rose (Sedgman was traveling privately). Rosie and Harry Hopman had several arguments, but Mac was very easy to travel with. No one had any problems with Lew and me because we were so new to it all. We flew directly to London (it took three days and two nights on a Super Constellation). Upon our arrival, we practiced four or five days on the clay at Wimbledon, then played some exhibitions before entering the French championships. I was defeated in the first round by Fausto Gardini at 6–3 in the fifth. Fausto, a weird-looking player, was not much to look at but he kept the ball coming back. Unlike his fellow Italians, he was a real fighter. I could not help but admire Gardini because he always tried. Lew was beaten by Eric Sturgess, one of the top seeds, in three good sets.

At Wimbledon that year, I lost to Gar Mulloy in the second round in three straight. It was my first time on the center court. We flew to the United States. At Orange I was beaten on a wet court by Dick Savitt, 7–5,

6–3. Lew and I played together in the national doubles at Longwood. We got to the semi-finals, where we took a set off Sedgman and McGregor. At Forest Hills I had a win over Vic Seixas, then lost to Mulloy in five sets.

In January of 1953 Sedgman and McGregor turned professional. This left Mervyn Rose as the number one player in the country. But in the Australian championships at Melbourne, I beat Straight Clark, Vic Seixas and Mervyn Rose to win the title. I was the youngest ever to win it, and it was my most thrilling experience to date. It was what my dad had always hoped for. Lew was beaten by Clive Wilderspin, and on the basis of his win Clive got his 1953 overseas trip. Ian Ayre, who had almost beaten Rose in the semi-finals, also made the team. We were also joined by Rex Hartwig.

This 1953 trip was a long one. We went to Rome for the Italian championships. Jaroslav Drobny won the title, beating me in the semi-finals and Lew in the last round. The next big tournament was the French championship, which I won, beating Enrique Morea in the semi-finals and Seixas in the final. Vic had surprised Drobny in the semi-finals.

I was seeded No. 1 at Wimbledon. Kurt Nielsen beat me in the quarters. I was disappointed, but not nearly as much as when he beat me the second time at Wimbledon in 1955. This [1953] was the year of the Drobny-Patty marathon. Drobny was so exhausted after this match that he could do nothing against Nielsen in the semis. The Wimbledon title went to Vic Seixas. He beat Lew in a long, close match in the quarters, he won over Rosie in the semis, and he raced right through Nielsen in the final.

I lost a lot of matches in those days, mainly through inexperience. . . . My failing was that I was a counter-puncher rather than an attacker. I put the ball in play, but I made my play off the opponent's next shot. I put no pressure on. The year I lost to Drobny in the Wimbledon final, I seldom followed my serve to the net. More than 50 per cent of the match he had time to play his backhand, which meant I was not putting enough pressure on his weakness. My strokes were solid, but I was not yet playing the game correctly.

In the U. S. that year I lost to Lew at Orange, and I was beaten by Tony Trabert in the semi-finals of Forest Hills. Tony then won the title over Seixas.

The 1953 year ended with the challenge round. It was the first time that Lew and I had played Davis Cup. Lew won both his singles. I lost my first match to Tony and beat Vic in my last match. This tie was famous for the great Trabert-Hoad match.

I failed to keep my Australian title in January of 1954. Mervyn Rose beat me in the semis and then won over Hartwig in the final. Lew was doing his National Service and did not compete.

Lew and I, at 19, were the "veterans" of the 1954 overseas team, along with Rose. The youngsters were Neale Fraser, Roy Emerson and Ashley Cooper. Roy and Ashley were just 17. Our first tournament was the French championship, where I was beaten by Sven Davidson in the round of 16. . . . At Wimbledon I was beaten in the final by Jaroslav Drobny, who was not among the top eight seeds. Drob, twice before a bridesmaid at Wimbledon, was the sentimental favorite. The crowd was for him, but I was not unduly conscious of any partisanship.

At Forest Hills Hartwig beat me in the semi-finals while Seixas defeated Lew in the other half. Vic then won the title over Rex. Rex was awfully good. He had knocked out Trabert in the previous round. He was a great player, but his stumbling block in singles was his temperament.

In 1953 I had won two of the Big Four titles; in 1954 I won none. In 1953, Lew and I kept the cup for Australia; in 1954 we were beaten. Australia was favored in the challenge round. . . . Both Trabert and Seixas played very well. It is said that Vic beat me by coming in on my forehand. We played a lot of matches thereafter and I won them all.

Our 1955 overseas trip was a "Davis Cup tour," for we now had to fight our way up the ranks to the challenge round. The team consisted of Hartwig, Fraser, Cooper, Hoad and myself. We did not play in the French championship. At Wimbledon Lew lost to Budge Patty, I was beaten by Nielsen in the semis, and Tony Trabert beat Kurt in the final. Our American tour consisted almost solely of the Davis Cup tie. We met the United States in the challenge round at Forest Hills, and we won, 5–0. First I defeated Vic, then Lew defeated Tony. Rex played with Lew in the doubles and they won over Seixas-Trabert in an excellent five-setter. Rex was the star of the match. After the tie had been clinched, Lew defeated Seixas and I beat Ham Richardson.

In January of 1956, Lew beat me in the final of the Australian nationals. Again we prepared to go overseas, this time with Cliff Sproule as manager. Harry Hopman was unavailable to take the team. Lew was on a "honeymoon" tour, and the team consisted of Fraser, Cooper, Emerson, Mal Anderson and myself. We skipped the French championships (won by Hoad) and we played two tournaments before Wimbledon. I was very lucky to beat Seixas in the Wimbledon semi-finals, for I was down 2–5 in the fifth. Lew defeated me for the title.

Lew came to the States with three of the Big Four titles to his credit. The two "veterans" met in the Forest Hills final, and this time I beat Hoad. Lew and I now played our last Davis Cup match for Australia. The American team consisted of Vic Seixas, Herbie Flam and Sammy Giammalva. I now played my last Australian amateur season. At Queensland Ashley Cooper came into prominence. He beat me in the semis and Lew in the final. I won New South Wales, South Australia and Victoria. I had married Wilma McIver in October of 1956, and I decided to turn pro early in 1957 for a total of $65,000 for 14 months of play.

My opponent on the pro tour was Pancho Gonzales. We played 11 matches in Australia and New Zealand and then we had a series of one-night stands in the U. S. Pancho beat me, 50 to 26. There was an enormous difference between Gonzales and the amateurs of that year. . . . His ground strokes were solid and his only weakness seemed to be return of serve.

In July of 1957 Hoad turned professional and toured with Pancho in late 1957 and 1958. I had three months at home with Wilma, but I joined the tour toward the end when Lew developed back problems. At Forest Hills Pancho beat me in a terrific match in the round-robin final. When the tour ended I was the No. 2 player. In 1959 I was again No. 2 behind Gonzales. He stayed at No. 1 until his retirement, although I had the edge on him the last year in tournament play. On the pro circuit there are only two or, at most, three major tournaments. They are Wembley in England, Roland Garros in France, and, on those occasions when it is held, Forest Hills in the U. S. My record was best at Wembley and Roland Garros.

In 1960 I won Paris by beating Hoad (Lew had eliminated Gonzales in the semis) and Wembley by beating Segura. In 1961 I beat Gonzales in Paris and Lew at Wembley (Lew defeated Gonzales). In 1962 I beat Andres Gimeno at Paris and Hoad at Wembley.

I am an admirer of the Gonzales game. He is a great competitor. But so are Segura and Trabert. "Segoo" has a great fighting spirit and no one tries any harder than Tony. But Pancho is the toughest opponent I have ever faced. On my first tour against him, I felt like I was being thrown to the lions. Night after night we played, and I doubt if he let up in two matches during the entire tour. He is difficult to play because of his big serve and his all-round ability indoors. He is still a great player outdoors, but he is best on canvas. Pancho is not only a great athlete but a great retriever as well. I have to class him as a notch above Hoad, although the latter is the greatest of all time when he is "on."

TONY TRABERT

by William F. Talbert

With the 1955 season completed, Tony Trabert had compiled one of the most outstanding records in tennis history. No tennis critic in the world would dispute his position as the top ranking amateur. His series of victories includes the French and Wimbledon titles, the latter without the loss of a set. He also showed his superiority in the American scene by winning the National Indoor Singles, the National Clay Court Singles, and the National Singles at Forest Hills. He won his second American title, again without the loss of a set. Other important tournament wins were in the Pacific Southwest and the Pacific Coast.

Tony began his tennis career at the age of six. He lived next door to some public courts where he played until the age of twelve when he joined the Cincinnati Tennis Club. He had professional instruction from two fine Cincinnati professionals, Earl Bossong and Howard Zaeh, between the ages of nine and eleven. They were both sound teachers and gave him good fundamental teaching in the ground game, the volley and the all court game.

My interest in Trabert was a natural one. I, too, was from Cincinnati, but a few years older. We started to work out together when he was twelve, for he was interested, hard-working and eager to improve. He was obviously a fine athlete with a natural ball sense, hampered only by being a bit slow on his feet. I could see in him a duplicate of myself at the same age—an intense desire to be a good player and a willingness to spend the long hours required to make the grade. Our friendship, which began then, continued through a doubles partnership of one year and a captain-player relationship of three years.

Tony was limited in his playing to local events until the age of fourteen. He entered his first tournament at the age of ten and lost in the first round by scores of 6–0, 6–1. . . . Tony was an outstanding athlete in high school and college. He was adept at all sports, but gradually limited himself to basketball and tennis. . . . He was outstanding at basketball, yet played on the Cincinnati team mainly to sharpen up his footwork for tennis.

As a younger player, he was promising but far from the best. He never won either the National Boys' or the National Junior title.

His first big year came in 1950 at the age of nineteen. He defeated Ted Schroeder in the Western Championships, although he lost to him the next week in the semi-final round of the National Clay Court Championships. He went out in the first round of the National singles to John Bromwich in straight sets, yet nevertheless was ranked No. 12 in the Nation. This was the year Tony made his first trip to Europe, where he and I in partnership won every tournament in which we played— . . . the Italian Championships, the French Championships and various lesser ones.

Tony was the epitome of the Big Game. He uses the Kramer-style strategy of serve and advance to the net. However, Trabert has the additional capacity to return serves clean and hard and to make spectacular passing shots. In the National Championships this year he outstroked and outvolleyed both Rosewall and Hoad.

Tony's climb to the top was aided by the faith of those who believed in him. He was given the opportunity to play the European circuit at nineteen, and this experience enabled him to progress twice as fast as he would have ordinarily. The following year he was No. 3 in the Nation. Tony was out of competition most of the next years when he served in the United States Navy. He was granted a leave to play for the Davis Cup in Australia. One year later Tony won his first American singles crown and was ranked No. 1 in the country for 1953.

Trabert's biggest victory was his Davis Cup win over Lew Hoad in the opening match of the December 1954 Challenge Round. For three months both he and Vic Seixas had been pointing only toward one match. Every earlier Australian tournament and each practice session was designed to work the player up to a peak. Tony made his third appearance in the Challenge Round in perfect physical shape, at the top of his game and with a nervous eagerness that insured concentration and fight. This could perhaps be called the greatest singles match of his career. He served at three-quarter speed in the windy arena, never softened up or allowed his nervousness to get out of hand, and won in four exciting sets.

One of the major disappointments in Tony's amateur career was the loss of United States to Australia in the Davis Cup in 1955. He was on top with a series of spectacular victories when he lost to Lew Hoad and this could have been a serious blow to his confidence for the remainder of the season. It, however, takes a great champion to come back stronger than ever just one week after the biggest loss of his career. Tony did it by winning the singles at Forest Hills, defeating Flam, Hoad and Rosewall with power and authority. He was now universally recognized as the world's outstanding amateur and was being approached by Jack Kramer relative to a professional tour. Tony received advice from all sides and thought carefully before he made his decision, which was to accept the offer.

Wherever Tony goes he is universally liked. He has the easy speech and manner of a diplomat, the poise of one far older than his years and a generally pleasant disposition.

I sincerely hope that his new career will bring him the success and good fortune that he so well deserves.

VIC SEIXAS

by Axel Kaufmann

When all tournaments have become open and all good players have become pros, new generations of tennis followers will look back with amazement at an era of tennis when champions thought of winning simply as a means of proving themselves best rather than as a way of securing financial gain. During the Forties and Fifties, the era's last golden glow, American tennis produced a few strong proponents of this love-of-the-game attitude. They were headed by E. Victor Seixas, Jr., a Philadelphian whose name has been indelibly written across the pages of tennis history and whose outstanding devotion and contribution to the game, both in achievement and sportsmanship, make him the September choice for the Marlboro Award. Three times the top-ranking player of the country, twice a national singles champion, holder of 13 other national titles, Wimbledon winner, member of several battling Davis Cup teams and recipient of the William Johnston Trophy, Vic has consistently exemplified throughout his long career all of the highest amateur ideals. Today, at 38, he is a weekend player, albeit still a dangerous competitor.

Vic is that relatively rare member of the family of prominent modern-day tennis players—the true Easterner. Born in Overbrook, Pennsylvania, in

1923, he has resided within the Philadelphia city limits ever since. His latest move last fall was only into a new house in Villanova.

Vic was an only child. As the son of a tennis enthusiast, his opportunity to contemplate a court and the activities connected with it came early in life. His father belonged to a Community Neighborhood Club, and since baby-sitters were unknown in those days, he was taken along quite regularly. He started playing when he was five and owned his first racket soon afterward. His schooling was public through the eighth grade. Thereafter he attended Penn Charter for four years. Once at prep school, he branched out into all kinds of sports, earning letters in baseball, track, squash and basketball, in addition to tennis.

"I have always considered myself a frustrated baseball player," he says. "I stuck to tennis only because I was better at it." . . . Vic's great-grandfather played for the old Phillies and invented the figure-eight stitch for baseballs. Summers during these years were given to playing in local boys' and junior tennis tournaments, in which his only real competition was provided by his Penn Charter teammate, Bill Vogt. . . .

Although Vic was seeded No. 1 in the 1938 national boys' championship, he was not the winner of the tournament (nor ever in the national junior). In 1940, however, he won both the national interscholastic singles and doubles (with Bill, of course), the first of his many national titles. Later that year, on his 17th birthday, he played a first-round match against Frank Kovacs at Forest Hills, which he counts as one of his most memorable. . . .

In the 1941 juniors, Vic's quarter-final round encounter with Budge Patty became one of the all-time great junior matches. It was lost by Vic after he held match point. That fall he entered the University of North Carolina, and the following year, his first in the men's division, he broke into the coveted first-ten rankings in the No. 9 spot.

As was the case with so many others, Vic's tennis and college career became a temporary victim of the war. He was called into the Air Force early in 1943 and sent to Maxwell Field for pilot training. During the next three years he was to play but two weeks of tennis, one of them in the 1944 nationals. His service stint included a period as flight instructor and a year and a half in the Pacific, divided equally between New Guinea (where he tested planes which had been assembled overseas) and, following V-J Day, Tokyo. He returned home just in time to enter Merion in July of 1946 and won it. It was one of his seven wins of this major tournament. He has now competed 21 times and retired two challenge bowls.

Following his discharge, he resumed both college and tennis. . . . He left Chapel Hill in 1949 with a B.S. in Commerce, but not without taking with him one of the university's prettiest and most charming co-eds—his wife Dolly. Their honeymoon trip was a tennis tour of South Africa and Europe, culminating at Wimbledon, where he reached the 1950 semi-finals. . . . In 1951 Vic won Merion once again, reached the final of the nationals, where he lost to an unbeatable Frank Sedgman and was picked to go to Australia as a member of the controversial Davis Cup team captained by Frank Shields.

"We started out as a 3-man team," he says of the trip. "There were Savitt, Trabert and myself. Not until we reached California did we learn that Schroeder was also going along. Actually, I considered myself the bottom man as far as chances to play went, although before Ted joined us I had been hopeful of a doubles berth. Once in Australia, though, I played myself into position by splitting with Sedgman in two tournaments and beating Schroeder and Tony in a third." . . .

Although his 1952 season, which brought him a No. 2 ranking, cannot exactly be regarded lightly, Vic's best years came in 1953 and 1954. First one and then the other of these years saw him realize two dreams—to win Wimbledon and the U.S. nationals. In 1954, with Trabert, he was instrumental in wresting the Davis Cup from the Australians, defeating Rosewall in a magnificent four-set singles match and, with Trabert, scoring over Hoad and Rosewall in the doubles. He was ranked No. 2 in 1955, No. 3 in 1956, and he stood again at the top of the list in 1957, the year which saw him play—and win—his final Davis Cup match at Kooyong Stadium (Australia), 13–11, in the fifth set against Mal Anderson, an opponent 11 years his junior.

Since 1957, when he went into the securities business by joining the Philadelphia office of Goldman, Sachs, Vic has gradually tapered off the amount of his competitive play. . . . He has played all over the world, with the exception of India and Japan, and his six Australian trips are topped by seven visits to Europe. . . . Of the players he has met in competition—and he is careful to point out that he has never played Kramer, Riggs, Budge or Falkenburg—he rates Sedgman best. "When Frank was on his game, he was unbeatable," he says.

ASHLEY COOPER

from the New York Times

When Ashley Cooper won the tennis championship of the United States at Forest Hills yesterday he was asked whether he was going to telephone Helen Wood in Melbourne.

"I don't think so," was the answer. But immediately Esca Stephens, the manager of the touring Australian team, said: "I am putting in the call for Ashley as a present for his winning today."

Helen Wood is Miss Australia and the expectations are that before another year has gone by it will be in order for them to be receiving gifts jointly.

Ashley is the quietest, least talkative and most meditative of the Australians. He comes from an academic family.

It was his father and mother who first taught the game to the youth who stands as the world's amateur champion. He played with them for some years on the family court in the country outside of Melbourne.

Football was another sport of which he was fond and he played on his high school team. But in time he forgot about football and also photography, his hobby, as he made rapid progress on the court.

He was never more serious about anything than he became about tennis. To develop his game, he became a fanatic on physical condition.

He spends hours doing road work and exercising in the gymnasium. That accounts for his strong physique and his great lasting powers, which were a factor in his victory yesterday.

The first thing he did on his arrival from Wimbledon in July was to go to the New York A. C. There he worked out for five days before playing in his first tournament at the Orange Lawn Tennis Club early last month.

While competing at Orange, Cooper was stricken with pains in his back and he was the victim of the most stunning upset of the year, a loss to John Cranston.

At Newport the following week the pain continued. A physician found that he was suffering from a shortage of sugar in his blood and prescribed glucose. He lost in the final to Anderson in three sets.

Cooper also has been troubled at times by a bad ankle, which occasionally affects his play and which has kept him out of the compulsory national armed service.

Cooper's father, a Melbourne schoolmaster, had hoped his son would become a physician. But Ashley, an honor student at school, was determined to play tennis.

Father and son reached a compromise after Ashley's graduation from secondary school. The boy was to play tournament tennis for two years. If he didn't become one of Australia's top players at the end of that time, he would return to his studies.

That was the start of a career in which yesterday's triumph was only one of several big moments.

MAL ANDERSON

by Murray Illson

Malcolm Anderson, the winner of the United States men's singles championship at Forest Hills yesterday, used to be a cow puncher on his father's cattle ranch in Australia. He expects to be one again when he quits tennis competition.

The 22-year-old Anderson, unseeded in the national tournament, stunned the experts with his victory over Ashley Cooper. But one who wasn't completely surprised was Clifford Sproule of Sydney, the captain of Australia's touring tennis team.

Sproule described the dark-haired, jut-jawed 6-footer as having "the greatest potential of all our boys." Anderson, he said, plays "a very well-balanced game" and outside of a tendency to try and make his shots look too good, shows no weaknesses.

The Aussie captain wasn't second-guessing. He made these statements before Anderson took the court against Cooper, the Australian champion. Cooper, who will be 21 years old next Sunday, was expected to have little trouble in taking the American championship home to Melbourne as a birthday present. He had been touted as on his way to becoming the best amateur in the world, and had beaten Anderson five times in six tournament matches.

Now it is Anderson who will take the American title home, as a wedding present. He is engaged to Daphne Emerson of Brisbane, a sister of Roy Emerson, the fourth-ranking member of the Australian team. They plan to be married on October 5.

Anderson was born on his father's ranch in Queensland. His father, mother and three older brothers (he has a younger brother, too) are all good tennis players and all have taken a hand in coaching him from the time he was 13. . . .

The new titleholder said he owed a lot to tennis because of the people he had met, the sights he had seen and the things he had learned in four years of travel about the world. But he went on to say:

"I get home only one week out of the year and have been doing that for four years. It gets a little monotonous living in a suitcase, packing and unpacking and having no real home."

Compared with the husky Cooper, who is 6 feet 1 inch and weighs 170 pounds, Anderson at 150 pounds looks almost frail. He is considerably narrower through the chest and, according to Sproule, needs to be beefed up somewhat.

The Australian captain described Anderson as a tense youth who, though affable, "likes to be on his own."

Anderson also plays golf, cricket and football, and Sproule says he has become an enthusiastic bowler. "The other night he bowled 198, and remember that we don't have the game at home."

Sproule added that both Anderson and Cooper "love baseball, too, and have become terrific Dodger fans—I'm a Yankee fan, and of course we have terrible arguments."

NEALE FRASER

by George McGann

Saturday, August 23, 1958, was a black day in the life of Australian south-paw Neale Fraser. In the afternoon he was roundly booed, hooted and Bronx-cheered by impolite people in the gallery at the national doubles championships who urged him to depart the premises of the Longwood Cricket Club with "Aussie go home" and similar unfriendly taunts. That night at a rooftop party in the ordinarily quiet Back Bay area of Boston, a trio of cops arrived at the height of festivities and the height of the noise and peremptorily ordered all the guests, including Fraser, to depart at once, under implied threat of arrest for disturbing the peace.

Fraser later was philosophical about the uncharitable acts of the Bostonian public and gendarmerie, just as he is philosophical about other and more important things in his life—his failures to get into the Davis Cup competition in the annual challenge round, his 13 consecutive losses to Ashley Cooper, and his monopoly of the No. 3 position in Australian tennis. His disappointments have never soured him, and his disposition on the court and his charm at social functions have won him more friends than any other player. The title "Most Popular Man in Tennis Competition" is thoroughly deserved. It is perhaps the most desirable of all the Mary Chess awards.

Fraser has been a member of three of his country's Davis Cup teams but has yet to see action with any of them in either singles or doubles. And yet he is recognized as one of the world's best doubles players and is the 1957 U.S. doubles champion with Ashley Cooper. The trouble is there is always someone just ahead of Neale. In doubles last year it was the other southpaw, Mervyn Rose, who got the nod in the challenge round tandem competition. Before that, it was Hoad and Rosewall in doubles as well as singles.

This year an American sportswriter asked Neale how he was ranked in Australia. The handsome Victorian replied: "Number three—as usual. Only now, I'm just behind Ashley Cooper and Mal Anderson. I used to be just behind Hoad and Rosewall."

It's an old story for the 24-year-old Fraser, dating back to his days of interstate junior competition in the famous Australian Linton Cup series. Fraser headed the team from Victoria, which was strong enough to defeat every other state except New South Wales and boasted the "Whiz Kids," Lew Hoad and Ken Rosewall. Neale could beat any junior in Australia with the exception of these two. When first Rosewall, then Hoad, entered Jack Kramer's professional troupe, Neale's chances for Davis Cup stardom brightened. Unfortunately for him, his fellow Victorian, Cooper, was just coming into his own at the time, and Mal Anderson astonished the world by sweeping past the world's top amateurs to take the U.S. title in 1957. Fraser missed out to both these players when it came time to choose the Australian singles players in the last challenge round. . . .

Neale comes from a family of professional people in Melbourne. His father, a lawyer, is a judge of the Licensing Board and his two brothers are also lawyers. His father wanted Neale to enter the University of Melbourne, as his brothers did, upon graduation from St. Kevin's College, a private Catholic preparatory school, at the age of 17. But by that time Neale was one of Australia's outstanding juniors, having been publicly praised by Jack Kramer as a "comer" after taking a set from Wimbledon champ Dick Savitt, and he was much keener about continuing with tennis than continuing with his education. . . .

Neale learned to play tennis at age 11 on a neighbor's court with his brother John. They were permitted to play as much as they wanted in return for rolling and lining the court. . . . Neither of Neale's parents ever played tennis. His father had played football at the University of Perth. Neale started to play in tournaments just after the end of the war, when Australia was reviving its interest in all sports, and he was caught up in the national fever of competition. At 12 he won his first tournament, an under-13 competition. By the time he was fifteen he was beating most players in Victorian junior ranks, and at 17 he won the junior championship.

In his first year out of junior ranks Neale was not too successful. "But the next year, 1953," he says, "was a big one for me. In the Victorian championships I took the first two sets from Hoad and led 4–2 in the third. He beat me, but that performance won me a spot on an overseas team for Malaya. I also toured New Zealand the same year with Rex Hartwig, Ian Ayre and Clive Wilderspin. When time came to choose the overseas team for 1954, I was considered good enough to tour along with Hoad, Rosewall, Rose, Cooper and Emerson, under the direction of Harry Hopman. I have been on every overseas team since. I was not chosen for the Cup team in 1954, when we lost to the U. S. I have been on every winning team since, although I am still waiting to play."

Fraser owns a unique but unenviable Wimbledon record, having played five finals at the All-England Club without winning a single one. They were three men's doubles, one singles (this year against Cooper) and one mixed.

"My toughest opponent has been Ashley Cooper," says Neale. "We have met thirteen times since our junior days and I have never beaten him, although I have been awfully close. One of the matches that stands out in my mind is my win over Lew Hoad in the South Australian championships after being two sets down. That victory came after 14 straight losses to Lew. Another win that I remember is beating Budge Patty at Wimbledon in 1957 on a terrifically hot day after he had led me two sets to love with match points in the third set. . . . The biggest thrill I ever got out of winning was taking the U.S. doubles title in 1957 with Coop."

Editor's note: Since this article was written, Fraser won the championship of the United States in 1959 and 1960 and took the crown at Wimbledon in 1960. He made his debut as a Davis Cup player in 1958, losing the doubles with Emerson to Alex Olmedo and Ham Richardson as the United States won the cup. He was a member of the victorious teams of 1959, 1960, 1961 and 1962, winning both of his singles and the doubles with Emerson in 1959, winning one singles and the doubles with Emerson in 1960, winning the doubles with Emerson again in 1961, when Laver and Emerson played the singles, and won both of his singles in 1962 against Mexico. In his final appearance, in 1963, he lost the doubles with Emerson as the U. S. regained the cup.

ROY EMERSON

by Harry Gordon

In Brussels for the space of just one day, during the first trip overseas he had ever made, Roy Emerson enjoyed a reputation as a large-scale tipper. For a tennis player, his handouts were surprisingly generous; for an Australian tennis player—a notoriously careful breed, this—they were massive. As a result, the staff at his hotel lavished special care upon him; headwaiters bowed deeply, bellhops fawned and the man who looked after room service arrived breathlessly, within seconds, every time he was summoned.

Roy Emerson was 17 at the time, and until that journey had spent the bulk of his life on a farm in the Queensland outback, milking 160 cows every morning. Because he could hit a tennis ball hard and accurately, he had been yanked from the bosom of his family and exposed suddenly to the wonders of the international circuit. Emerson was traveling as a member of an earnest young team, under the managership of Harry Hopman, and Hopman, who believed in asking his youngsters to shoulder some responsibilities, had asked him to handle the petty cash for several of the team who were flying from Paris to Brussels ahead of the main party.

In France that summer, 11 years ago, an Australian pound was worth about 1,000 francs; in Belgium it brought a little over 100 francs. Mervyn Rose, the oldest member of that Hopman team, recalls today, "To Emmo then a franc was a franc was a franc. That was all there was to it. He had noticed that the usual tip in France was 100 francs, or a tenth of an Australian pound, and he just kept on tipping 100 francs when we arrived in Brussels. That meant he was giving away a pound every time a waiter approached him, and that was often; this at a time when 20 pounds a week was an excellent wage in Australia.

"We were having a lot of food in our room, and those waiters loved Emmo. They wouldn't leave him alone. Sure . . . the rest of us knew he was paying out ten times too much, but we figured it was Australian Lawn Tennis Association money anyway. Hopman arrived next day and he looked as if he was going to explode when he saw what had happened. From then until the tour ended, he didn't let Emerson handle another penny."

Roy Emerson has come a long way since that first trip in 1954—as a tennis player (he is a prime choice to win the men's singles in the French matches starting tomorrow), a sophisticate and a handler of finance. A regular visitor to such places as the Caribbean, Panama, Naples, Rome, Barcelona, Paris, Berlin, Deauville, London, Istanbul, Athens, Beirut, New York and Los Angeles, he can nowadays convert pesetas to dollars and marks to drachmas almost without a blink. He mixes easily with movie stars, wears the finest clothes, drinks the best wines, stays at the plushest hotels. He is the best amateur tennis player in the world, and it follows, in the phony twilight zone of amateurism which belongs exclusively to lawn tennis, that he is the "highest paid."

Emerson, who is a very honest young man, has often observed that "there is no such thing as amateur tennis." At the international level of tennis, amateurs are not amateurs in the accepted dictionary sense. They earn money out of tennis, just as emphatically as the professionals do. The big difference is simply the method of payment. Whereas the professionals earn their money openly, and sign receipts for it, the amateurs have to resort to various subterfuges. They get their money from "expenses," which are not expenses so much as appearance fees, and from retainers paid by manufacturers who want to cash in on their reputations. Sometimes patriotic individuals pay them large lump sums so they can afford to reject professional offers and stay "amateur" and available for Davis Cup matches.

If the set-up smacks of hypocrisy and deceit, it is not the amateurs-who-really-aren't who should be blamed; it is the administrators who condone the massive masquerade. . . . Australian professionals joke openly about the manner in which they used to earn their extra "expenses." Sometimes they would perform some simple feat like jumping over a suitcase on a "bet"; sometimes they would be asked to play poker, knowing that their hand was loaded with aces; sometimes they might just find an envelope packed with bills wedged inside one of their shoes in the locker room.

None of this is very new. A well-known story of the tennis circuits concerns the way Continental officials used to bet Suzanne Lenglen's father 1,000 pounds (sterling) that she wouldn't arrive for a certain tournament. She would turn up and he would pocket the 1,000 pounds. . . .

It would be wrong to infer from all this that players like Emerson are guilty of any misbehavior. They simply conform to the accepted pattern. It is a fair bet that every top amateur player since the last war has been, by the strict Olympic standards of Mr. Avery Brundage (in charge of the Games since 1952), a professional. . . . A player like Emerson, who has the largest reputation in the business—and therefore the largest income—looks upon amateur tennis as an industry which allows him to move around the world in reasonable luxury, sometimes accompanied by his family, and so far he has refused to swap it, even for an offer of $85,000, for the life of a professional.

Emerson is in the top income bracket of amateurism for one reason: he is remarkably good at winning. He has won virtually every title of any significance, singles and doubles, in the world. This year it is generally conceded that he has an excellent chance of winning the quartet of major singles championships which constitutes the "grand slam"—the Australian, French, Wimbledon and American titles. Only two players in history, Donald Budge and Rodney Laver, have won the four in any one year.

Even more imposing, though, than his string of tournament wins is Emerson's record in Davis Cup play. He is unbeaten in Cup singles, and is undoubtedly the reason why Australia holds the Cup today. He has been a member of the Australian Davis Cup squad since he was 17 and has played in six challenge rounds. Only one Australian, the late Sir Norman Brookes, ever played in more, and Emerson seems certain to top his record of eight if he remains an amateur.

Several times before Emerson has been tagged as a likely winner of the "grand slam." In 1963, after Laver turned professional and left the amateur field comparatively clear, the slim and lanky (6 feet, 165 pounds) Queenslander got halfway there by winning the Australian and French singles titles. Then he went down in a quarter-final at Wimbledon, and was bundled out of the American championship by the unseeded Frank Froehling. After that defeat, Emerson announced, "I reckon I'm ready for the pasture"—but he was back the following year and won three of the four big ones. He took the Wimbledon title (his ninth try) but missed out in the French championship. . . .

Emerson's biggest asset as a tennis player is his superb physical fitness. He was a schoolboy track and field champion. Harry Hopman, who is something of a fanatic on the subject of conditioning, says that he has never handled a fitter, more athletic player than Emerson. . . .

The Emerson game is neither colorful nor dramatic. He hits the ball very hard and spreads himself around the court more efficiently than any other man in the game. He is not a great tactician; he moves more by instinct than by generalship, and the weakest single factor of his game is his service. He wins matches mainly by just hitting the ball back and wearing his opponents down. His fitness and his great courage make him very hard to beat in a long match. He demonstrated his fighting qualities in this year's Australian singles final, when he came back to win after losing the first two sets and trailing 1–3 in the third against Fred Stolle. . . .

Neale Fraser, who was Emerson's Davis Cup buddy in three winning doubles matches, is frank in his assessment of Emerson's ability.

"Roy is the fastest man I've ever seen around a tennis court, amateur or pro," he says. "You can never be sure of winning a point against him until the ball is out of play. His forehand is not as strong as his backhand, which can be a match winner. I've often been amazed at the way he punches back his return of service, and some of his interceptions at the net are unbelievable. One big fault is his inability to alter his game when things are going against him. He's very stereotyped, and has trouble changing a losing game into a winning one."

Alf Chave, a veteran Queensland official who has known Emerson since he was a boy and has managed him on several overseas trips, claims that his one real failing is his lack of variety. "On grass courts, his speed gives him the ability to win any tournament," says Chave. "But there's a sameness about his stroke-making that makes him vulnerable when anything goes wrong. His shots come off the court at the expected height and pace. There just isn't much element of surprise in his equipment."

Rod Laver, who was unbeaten in six singles and two doubles during Davis Cup challenge rounds, claims that the only possible way to beat Emerson is to hustle him. "You've got to keep the pressure up from the first ball, and just not relax concentration," he says. "The German Wilhelm Bungert, who isn't a great player, proved at Wimbledon a couple of years ago that Emerson can falter under pressure." . . .

Hopman claims that Emerson has improved his forehand and his service greatly in the last 18 months, and that he has finally achieved excellent ball control: "He used to hit that forehand far too flatly, but he's worked on it desperately hard in the last year or so. I'd say that the only aspect of his play that bears improvement now is his second service. It's too flat. It lacks spin and just isn't penetrating."

Emerson's service is a weird thing to behold. He is the only player in the world who winds up three times, in the manner of a baseball pitcher, before he belts down on the ball. His corkscrew action has earned him the nickname "Old Crankshaft." . . .

Emerson admits that he doesn't bother a great deal about strategy. "If I know an opponent has a weak point, I attack it," he says. "That's elementary. But I don't think you need to keep changing your game. All you can do is play your bloody best. You either have the ability to win or you don't. That's all there is to it." This attitude is characteristic of Emerson's whole approach to the game.

Even as a very young teen-ager, Roy Emerson never wanted to be anything other than an international tennis player. Born in the peanut-growing township of Kingaroy, he grew up on his father's 800-acre dairy farm near Blackbutt, about 100 miles from Brisbane, with his parents, two older sisters (Daphne and Hazel), 160 cows and a tennis court for company. (The tennis court was not a remarkable feature for an Australian farm. The sport is not limited to any income group Down Under, and many homes, both in the country and in suburban areas, are equipped with either lawn, en-tout-cas, or asphalt courts.) Emerson claims quite seriously that the steady milking helped his tennis by making his wrists grow big and strong.

In 1951 his father sold half his share in the farm and moved to Brisbane. Mr. Emerson admits today that the major motive for the move was to promote the tennis ambitions of young Roy. By the time he was 17 and a member of the Australian Davis Cup squad, the lad had won every junior Queensland title from under-11 up. He took his first overseas tour in 1954. He beat Lew Hoad in a tournament at Newport, Rhode Island.

During the next few years, though, Emerson seemed unable to fulfill his early high promise. He found himself low man among a batch of remarkably gifted Australian youngsters which included Hoad, Ken Rosewall, Ashley Cooper, Neale Fraser and Mal Anderson. Anderson, a close friend whose lithe, clean-cut, toothy good looks bore an astonishing resemblance to Emerson's own, began to overshadow him. . . . Anderson, who later married

Emerson's sister Daphne, went on to play in two challenge rounds before he turned professional in 1959.

At 21, Emerson, disappointed by his own lack of improvement but still nagged by his tennis ambitions, made a difficult decision. He withdrew from the official 1958 Australian touring team and spent the winter at home, brushing up his forehand and his service under guidance of Frank Sedgman. The sacrifice of the trip paid dividends the following year: after taking his bride, Joy, on a honeymoon tour around the world circuits, he joined the Australian Davis Cup team for the challenge round in America. He shone first as a Cup doubles player, with Neale Fraser; later, after Fraser was forced out of the game by a knee injury and Rod Laver decided to join the Jack Kramer troupe, he inherited the world singles championship. . . .

At Wimbledon last year, and in the last couple of challenge rounds, the quality of his tennis was generally rated superior to that of many recent amateur "greats."

Emerson is a devoted family man. He lives across the street from his parents in a fashionable suburb of Brisbane with his wife and two very young children. Last year he took his wife and son, Anthony, around the world with him. This year he is traveling alone, having delayed his departure until after the birth of his daughter, Heidi, at the end of March. When he rejected the offer of $85,000 to turn professional last November, he explained, "It would mean spending too much time away from my family . . . a lot more than I do now."

He is a gracious young man who does not conform to the old Australian tradition of dumb tennis players. Bob Mitchell, a Melbourne businessman who acted as Emerson's patron in the late nineteen fifties, is emphatic that he is the most intelligent Australian player since the war. . . . "He's an excellent conversationalist, interested in everything that's happening. He's a music lover, a student of Spanish dancing, and he has a very discriminating palate for wine. He's a real cosmopolitan."

Strangely, in view of his urbanity, Emerson is something of a rebel. He has skirmished often with the Establishment of Australian tennis, mainly on the subject of expense payments, and has at times refused point-blank to play in championships rather than accept expenses which he considered inadequate. He founded the Australian Tennis Players' Association, which is a kind of militant trade union in white shorts, and last year he led a mutiny against the L.T.A.A. With five other players, he refused to accept an order to play in Australian bush towns rather than visit the Caribbean, where the pickings are excellent.

They were all suspended, and thus banned from last year's challenge round in Cleveland, Ohio. But after some vigorous off-stage maneuvering by Harry Hopman and a face-saving demand by officials for an apology, the L.T.A.A. climbed down and allowed Emerson and Stolle to play. This surrender undoubtedly won back the Cup for Australia, but it also cost the L.T.A.A. much respect.

For three years now, Emerson has been employed as a public relations officer for the Philip Morris cigarette company. At home he does office work and travels for the company, but mostly the job consists of looking good on the tennis court and carrying packs of cigarettes around (even though he's not an enthusiastic smoker). . . . He is very serious about his work with Philip Morris, whose president, Joe Cullman 3d, has been generous with him. He receives a retainer of around $8,000 a year. . . . It is possible that he will receive another big offer to turn professional this year. Despite his unwillingness to leave his family for long periods, he has let it be known that he is "always willing to listen."

THE ROCKET

by Dave Anderson

In the locker room at the West Side Tennis Club in Forest Hills, Rod Laver was changing into his working clothes when he picked up one of his rackets and examined the grip.

"Got to fix this," he mumbled to himself. As he began to repair the grip, a friend of his strolled by and began to make casual conversation.

"Sorry," Laver said, looking up, "I'd rather not talk now. I've got to fix this, and I've got a match to play in a few minutes."

"Sure, Rod," his friend said, "but I just wanted to ask you if—"

"Not now," Laver said firmly, but pleasantly. "I'd rather not talk about anything right now, thank you. I've got a match."

Laver, a little left-hander who is gunning for the Grand Slam of amateur tennis, wasn't trying to be nasty. He was trying to do his job: win tennis matches. As he tours the world, winning tournament after tournament, the red-headed Australian plays an occasional round of golf or drinks an occasional beer or goes out on an occasional date. But as he sat on the locker-room bench the other day, it was obvious that tennis is his business. So much so that, if he wins the current national singles tournament, he could be in line for a $100,000 professional contract as the second amateur player—Don Budge was the other one—to sweep the Grand Slam: the four major titles of Australia, France, Wimbledon and United States in the same year. Laver is thinking about the Grand Slam but he's not talking about it.

"All I know," he says, "is that I have to win seven matches in the tournament."

Such sentences are typical of Laver's pleasant but close-mouthed manner. He lives, as he plays tennis, with an almost mechanical precision. There is no showboat in him. He will be remembered as one of the great amateur tennis players. And he will also be remembered as a sort of automaton who, when wound up, whips in bullet serves and flicks off winning volleys and collects silverware everywhere he goes.

"Laver," says Don Budge, "can do everything on a tennis court. He's got all the shots and he's a fine competitor."

On the court it may not be obvious but, on closer inspection, there is no doubt where Laver gets the strength to do everything on a tennis court. He's not big—only 5-8 and 145. But compare his left arm to his right. His left arm, after years of hitting thousands upon thousands of tennis shots, is much larger than his right arm; so much so that his right arm appears almost deformed. From the wrist to the elbow, his left arm is huge.

"This strength in his left arm," Bill Talbert, the former U.S. Davis Cup captain, says, "is the reason why Laver is able to adjust the angle of his wrist in hitting certain shots."

Laver is known as a "wristy" player, similar to such recent Australian champions as Lew Hoad and Neale Fraser and unlike the big names of U.S. amateur tennis, Jack Kramer and Pancho Gonzales, in the days shortly after World War II. Ordinarily, wristy players don't possess the control necessary to become a great champion. But Laver disproves that theory, just as he has disproved the theory that his shyness would prevent him from gaining the confidence necessary to become a great champion.

"Rod got that confidence," says Fred Perry, the one-time British champ who won Wimbledon in 1934, 1935 and 1936, "at Paris this year." In the final of the French championship against his Australian Davis Cup team-mate, Roy Emerson, Laver was trailing 2 sets to love, and 4–5 on Emerson's serve. Then, suddenly, he rallied to win the set and the match and keep alive his hopes for the Grand Slam. "You could see his confidence bloom after that," Perry says. "It was just like the petals of a flower opening up." . . .

Off his record, Laver is so much the best of the amateurs that there are those who predict that he could crash the pros and win as a rookie. Even Pancho Gonzales, the now retired pro king, didn't win as a rookie. Jack Kramer mopped him up. . . .

Laver, now 24, has come a long way from the ant-bed tennis court on his family's small ranch a few miles from Rockhampton, Queensland, in the cattle country of Australia.

"My father built a tennis court for me when I was 13," Rod once said. "An ant-bed court out of the dirt from the red-ant hills. You crush it up fine and spread it on clay and roll it in. They're common in Australia—Roy Emerson learned to play on one too—and it's the best dirt surface in the world for a tennis court."

Compared to such teen-age Australian pheenoms as Lew Hoad and Ken Rosewall, who were touring the world at 17, Laver was an unknown until his father drove him into Brisbane one day for a tennis clinic. Harry Hopman, the famous Australian Davis Cup captain, took one look at Laver hitting a few shots and, the next year, took the skinny 18-year-old redhead with him on a world tour. In his first trip to the United States he won the U.S. junior championship. That was in 1956. The next year he disappeared from tennis in order to put in his time in the Australian Army. But in 1958 he was back and nearly upset Dick Savitt, the semi-retired 1951 Wimbledon champion, in the round of 16 at Forest Hills. Three months later he was named to the Australian Davis Cup team but didn't play as Alex Olmedo won the cup for the U. S.

When Ashley Cooper and Mal Anderson turned pro, Laver suddenly was a Davis Cup singles player, along with Neale Fraser, in 1959 at Forest Hills. But Laver was forgotten as Fraser, winning two singles and teaming with Roy Emerson in the doubles, recaptured the cup. In 1960 Fraser won at Wimbledon and it was the second straight year that Laver lost in the final. In 1959 he had lost to Alex Olmedo. But, despite Fraser's headlines, Laver was considered to be the superior player. One day in the summer of 1960, Adrian Quist, the manager of the world-touring Australian team, said, "Fraser has a better serve, that's all. Laver has a better backhand, a better forehand, a better volley. Give him a little more time. He'll be the best in the world."

That summer Laver swept the four grass court tournaments on the Eastern circuit—Merion, Southampton, South Orange and Newport—but lost again to Fraser in the final at Forest Hills. In 1961 Laver finally won at Wimbledon, crushing Chuck McKinley in the final, but lost in the Forest Hills final to Emerson.

This year, however, Laver defeated Emerson in three man-to-man duels in the finals of the Australian, Italian and French championships. At Wimbledon Emerson had to default early in the tournament with a badly bruised toe, and Laver coasted to the title, routing unseeded Aussie Martin Mulligan in a near-record 52-minute final.

"I feel," Laver said after the match, "that I played very well."

This, of course, was the understatement of the year in tennis. Chuckling about it, Alf Chave, the manager of the Aussie team this year, said, "Mulligan's only chance would have been to use a rifle."

That's the way things shape up at Forest Hills, too. No snipers, please.

TINY TENNIS GIANT

by Bud Collins

Rodney the L is what's happening, baby, in tennis these days. He goes onto the Longwood veldt this afternoon to resume his rain-delayed pursuit of another professional singles championship, and if he wore a top hat you'd think he was Mandrake the Magician.

Instead he'll be wearing a crinkled white cloche that looks as though a flapper had slept in it. It was probably willed to him by Clara Bow, but it does the job. It keeps the sun out of his eyes and off a face of painfully fair complexion. Laver gets a second-degree burn every time somebody lights a match within 20 feet of his face. His eyes seem like a pair of blueberries in a tureen of borscht.

Rodney's hat may be investigated by the Pure Food and Drugs Administration because he uses it for a salad bowl. His friends call him Mr. Wiggs of the Cabbage Patch and Cole Slaw Head. On very hot days Laver lines his hat with wet cabbage leaves. "Keeps a bloke cool," he says. He used to plaster his hair with Vitalis, but regardless of what the commercial says, it's kid stuff as salad dressing.

Now Rodney pomades himself with roquefort. Swell. It enhances his orange hair and goes great with the cabbage.

Twenty years ago Rodney Laver's parents made him take up tennis to get him off the streets. This was a little hysterical because there aren't any streets in a place like Rockhampton, Queensland. Just kangaroo trails. The thing was, the folks didn't like his companions on the corner. Wombats, kangaroos, koala bears, and wallabies. Rodney was getting bad habits. He was developing a hop, and slept in a tree.

Mama was a tennis player, and she knew best. Her little Rodney had a rare gift and flair for the game, and became a wonderplayer: the unique athlete whose moves blend sport with art. Laver is as unimposing a figure as Rubinstein on a concert stage in a cabana set. A little guy with a jog in his nose, a bow in his legs, splotched with 15,000 freckles. Looks cannot disguise genius for long. He flies at the ball, his racket flashing and working miracles.

At 26, Rodney the L is a left-handed whirlpool whose spin sucks everybody under. He is running the crookedest game since Doc Kearns was a faro dealer in the Klondike. Rodney never hit a ball straight in his life. When he quits playing tennis, he'll be able to scare up dinner like an Aborigine, with a boomerang. His left wrist is so strong that he'd knock his own teeth out if he didn't brush them right-handed.

Pancho Gonzales said it for the opposition: "Laver is one guy I consider dangerous because he can hit a winning shot when you think you've got him way out of position."

His wondrous backhand looks so casual, like a guy flinging rice at newlyweds. The stern wrist, though, is snapping and loading the ball with that googly topspin that kangaroos away when it strikes the ground. He can kill you on shots with his back to the net, and his quickness is appalling.

Rodney's crashing backhand returns of service against Gonzales in last year's final were the most incredible shots I've seen.

More incredible, perhaps, was the way he moved in the rainstorm and the bog that the court had become. It was then I decided that there was a duckbilled platypus somewhere in the Laver family tree. His feet must be webbed.

THE STYLE OF ROD LAVER

by Julius D. Heldman

Rod Laver was 18 years old when he first came to the United States to play our circuit. He looked very much then as he does now, although his red hair was usually hidden under a floppy hat and he often had a handkerchief tied around his neck à la Rosewall. He was only of medium build, he looked fragile and he hit the ball a ton. That year he won the U.S. junior title. Six years later he was to become the second man in history to win the grand slam—Australia, France, Wimbledon and the United States championships. Within another two years he became the No. 1 professional and today he is still acknowledged the No. 1 player of the world. He is the only man today who can go through the last rounds of a major international tournament without dropping a set, because he is the only player who can literally crush the opposition with his power. He is capable of being upset (he lost to Cliff Drysdale in the 1968 U.S. open and to Cliff Richey in the 1969 Madison Square Garden open) but only he could win the 1968 Wimbledon open and the 1969 South African and French opens so decisively.

Rod swings at everything hard and fast. His timing, eye and wrist action are nothing short of miraculous. On either side, forehand or backhand, he takes a full roundhouse-loop crack at the ball, which comes back so hard it can knock the racket out of your hand. I saw Rod play Rafe Osuna in the semi-finals at Forest Hills in 1962. It was murder. In the last game, Rafe bravely served and ran for the net. Rod cracked a backhand back full speed, free swing—so hard that Rafe's racket wavered in his hand. Not so amazing, perhaps, but the same scene was repeated four points in a row. Rod literally knocked Osuna down with four successive returns of serve, and Osuna was one of the quickest and best racket handlers who ever played.

On the backhand side, Laver often uses a heavy underspin. Most players who come under the ball slow it up. Not so Rod; he is also moving in and hitting so hard that the shot is deep and attacking and has unusual pace. He often takes high backhands this way, but he is just as liable to come over the ball with a tremendous wallop, ending with wrist turning the racket head over, and the ball going with incredible speed and accuracy.

From the ground, about the only shot that Rod does not clobber is a forehand underspin or chip. I don't recall his using the shot much or at all when he was younger, but as he matured he began occasionally to hold the ball on his racket with some underspin and place it carefully while he ran for the net. But the next time he would literally jump and throw his racket at the ball with all the force he could muster, wrist and arms snapping over at the hit. The shot is unreturnable. It always ends the point, one way or the other, and you can never predict when the lightning will strike, although you know it will be often.

Volleying in top international tennis is more than technical proficiency. Rod is not a great low volleyer, but he is merciless when he gets half a chance. He is competent on low balls, handling them with underspin for control (more on the backhand than forehand, which he can net occasionally), but he will cream any ball at waist level or higher. As time goes on, Laver takes fewer unnecessary big swings at set-up high put-aways; he taps or punches them away. But if he needs to, he can and does hit high volleys with all his might as swinging drives or, on his backhand, sharp underspin angles as well. It is hard to believe a ball can be hit that hard and with that much angle, but Rod does it. No wonder he is the terror of all opponents.

There is not an Aussie netrusher who does not have a great overhead to back his attack. Otherwise he would be lobbed to death. Rod has one of the best, quite flat, angled to his left sharply by preference but capable of being placed anywhere. While Rod is not tall, he is agile and leaps well and is hard to lob over. What is worse, if you do get a lob over him, he will run it down and, with his powerful stiff wrist, rifle a full loop past his helpless opponent. This happens so often that players have begun to say that they prefer to lob short to Rod, at least on his backhand. Actually, if Laver has a weakness, it is on his backhand overhead, on which he does err, but in a way that is silly: how are you going to get in position to play that shot to Rod often?

Some lefties make it primarily by virtue of their serve, John Doeg and Neale Fraser being good examples. Not so Rod. His first serve has always been hard and flat, and he makes his share of aces, but he never had a heavy, deep spin second ball. It was just adequate, at least in the context of world class. In the last year, Rod has made a conscious effort to harden up his second delivery. For a while, all his timing seemed to be affected—he had some eye trouble at the same time—but now he is serving better than ever.

Someone once told Chuck McKinley that he should just try to be steady because he was too small to hit the ball hard. He paid no attention and he won Wimbledon. A few well-meaning coaches advised Rod to temporize more on his shots if he wanted to win a big tournament. It went in one ear and out the other, and Rod rose to the greatest heights in the game. His shots are breathtaking, his talent is enormous and his drive to be the No. 1 has made him the most successful player in the world today.

DARLENE HARD

from World Tennis

Darlene Hard, who turned professional this spring to teach at John Gardiner's Tennis Ranch, is the No. 1 player in Southern California and the No. 1 in the United States. She is 28 years old, and in the eleven years in which she has competed in national events she has ten times been ranked in the First Ten and four times been No. 1. Only three women in the history of American tennis have been ranked No. 1 more often than she (Molla Bjurstedt Mallory, Helen Wills Moody and Alice Marble) and only two others have equaled her record (Helen Jacobs and Pauline Betz).

In doubles, Darlene's record is even more superb. She won the U.S. title five times with three different partners, a feat equalled or exceeded by only five other women in tennis annals—Margaret Osborne duPont (13 wins), Louise Brough (12), Sarah Palfrey Fabyan (9), Juliette Atkinson (7) and Hazel Wightman (6). She won the Wimbledon Women's Doubles four times with three different partners, and here she was only topped by the great Elizabeth Ryan (12 wins), Suzanne Lenglen (6), and Louise Brough-Margaret duPont (5), and equaled by Doris Hart (4). She has won national doubles titles with a Junior (Paulette Verzin) and a Senior (Dodo Cheney), with Aussies (Lesley Turner, Mervyn Rose, Rod Laver), Americans (Althea Gibson, Jeanne Arth, Billie Jean Moffitt, Sue Behlmar, Beverly Fleitz), a Brazilian (Maria Bueno), an English girl (Shirley Bloomer) and a South African (Gordon Forbes).

In singles, Darlene has won the Nationals (twice), the Hard Courts and the French Championships. In doubles she has taken the U.S. title five times, the Hard Courts twice, the Clay Courts four times, the Italian women's doubles, the French women's doubles three times, the French mixed twice, the Wimbledon women's doubles four times and the Wimbledon mixed three times.

Darlene will not be eligible for an amateur ranking this year since she turned professional early in the season. However, her success in South Africa this winter was little short of sensational. She dominated the tournaments over such stars as Maria Bueno, Ann Jones and Annette van Zyl.

Darlene was born in Los Angeles on January 6, 1936. Her mother, Ruth, was an excellent local tournament player (Darlene could not beat her until she was 18), and young Darlene started to play seriously at the age of 13. At the end of the year she was ranked No. 2 sectionally behind Leigh Hay in the 13 and Under division. She won her first title when she beat Mary Lou Maxwell to win the Southern California Girls' 13 Championships.

Darlene at 16 was one of the most promising young players in the country. Her rival was Barbara Breit, who matched Darlene's attack with a beautiful baseline game. Barbara twice won the National Junior Girls' title, teaming with Darlene to win the Doubles in 1954. Two years later Miss Breit married and retired from the tournament game.

Darlene credits a number of coaches with helping her. She was taught by Tani Tanasescu at the age of 14, by Bobby Harman at 16, by Alice Marble at 19, by Pauline Betz at 20 and by Sarah Danzig at 24. Originally she had a Continental forehand which she changed to an Eastern, with the help of Miss Marble, when she was 19.

MARIA BUENO

by Julie M. Heldman

Maria Bueno is 5′ 6″ and weighs 115 lbs. She has a magnificent figure, a sultry look and an air of fragility. She walks with great beauty, she runs with the grace of an antelope and her overall appearance is one of queenliness. Her coterie is small and her worshipers are legion.

If one looks back into the old volumes of *World Tennis*, Maria's name first appears when she was 14 years old. Shirley Fry, one of the leading players in the world, dropped a set to young Maria in a tournament in South America. Two years later Maria appeared in Puerto Rico—a shy, talented, inexperienced young athlete with an English vocabulary of three words ("Yes," "No" and "Thank-you"). Even at this early stage it was evident that she was going to be a great champion: she had far more talent than the other women on the circuit and she was completely dedicated to tennis.

During her career, Maria won almost every major title in tennis in both singles and doubles. She was the Wimbledon Singles Champion three times, the Forest Hills Champion four times and the Italian Champion three times. In doubles she took the U.S. title three times with Darlene Hard and in 1966 she won it again with Nancy Richey. She was five times Wimbledon Doubles Champion and she took the French, Italian and Australian Doubles once each. When Althea Gibson turned professional, Maria Bueno became the undisputed queen of the game.

Rumors of Maria's great talent preceded her before her first trip to Europe. When she arrived in Rome to play her first Italian Championships, respect for her game turned into idolatry. The fans chanted "Bueno, Bueno" as she played. Her matches were put on the center court of Il Foro Italico, which is more like a gladiator's arena than a tennis court. Señorita Bueno became the Italian Champion on her first try.

The British press and Teddy Tinling first discovered Maria on their yearly pilgrimage to the Championships at Rome. The press was unrestrained in its superlatives about the South American beauty and Teddy found another spectacular queen to worship. T.T. had designed tennis clothes for the great Suzanne Lenglen, and although he had dressed many champions in the '40's and '50's, he had not discovered a star with similar appeal since the days of Gussie Moran. Teddy spared no expense to add to Maria's extraordinary appearance on the tennis court, and his costumes for her were beautiful to the point of being scandalous. One year Maria lost in the semi-finals of Wimbledon and many attributed her downfall to her spectacular clothing. Her magnificent dress was capped (or bottomed) with purple panties. Whenever she served or whenever the wind came up in the Stadium, the crowd "oohed" and "ahed" or went "tsk tsk" as they had when they first saw Gussie Moran's lace panties in 1951. Later that year the staid Wimbledon promoters banned color on tennis apparel, a crushing blow to the star couturier's originality.

The card tables in the men's locker room are deserted when Maria Bueno goes out to play a big tennis match, a tribute no other female racket handler has received since Maureen Connolly and Beverly Baker Fleitz. Her movements are exquisite and she plays with a beauty reminiscent of Suzanne Lenglen. Maria is not built like the average woman tennis player. The run-of-the-mill champion has to develop a complex muscular structure which often includes big shoulders and a gluteus maximus of similar proportions. The chest and back muscles expand from the constant hitting of big serves and overheads and the lower part of the body becomes muscular from running with knees bent and with the center of gravity close to the ground. I believe that Maria runs differently from the other champions: she looks more graceful and her legs slither delicately from what seems to be the middle of her spine rather than a protruding muscular rear end.

Señorita Bueno's strokes are the personification of her temperament. Her forehand and backhand are long, flowing, flat and uncompromising. Her serve has always been good but she is now reputed to have the best second serve in the game because it is consistently hard and deep. She has a hitch in the middle of her serve when she rocks back and forth for timing and power, but the extra motion does not seem to take away from the end effect. Maria's excellent timing has given her the best stroke volley in the game (Billie Jean King has the quickest volley and Margaret Smith Court the volley with the most crunch). However, the weak point in Maria's game can be revealed by chipping the return of serve at her feet and coming in to volley. But nothing works against Maria when she is inspired and imagination comes to her at vital moments. She is a different player during the two weeks of Wimbledon. Sometimes a flash of genius from her racket will renew her confidence, no matter where she is playing, just as a few bad shots will bring her game down to plebeian level.

The stroke that tells the tale is one that Maria learned from Armando Vieira, a fellow Brazilian. When the opponent lobs over Maria's head and she cannot take the ball in the air, she runs back and hits it with all her might with her back to the opponent. She does so by flicking her wrist for power and she often ends up with her right hand over her left shoulder, having turned somewhat around toward the opponent by the momentum of the stroke. If this shot is a winner, Maria is likely to play well for a few games; if it fails, she might not. This is a stroke she uses no matter what the score and it is symptomatic of her uncompromising attitude.

If you look at the stamp on the letter from your Brazilian pen pal, you might see a picture of Pele, the soccer hero, or the likeness of Maria Bueno, Brazil's national heroine. A statue has been erected in Sao Paulo to this modern Aztec goddess. But although Maria has countless admirers in her own country and in every major tennis center in the world, she is regal without being haughty. She never walks by an acquaintance without stopping to talk and she is friendly in five languages—Portuguese, Spanish, English, French and Italian. She was never alone at the top since she was ever surrounded with a court of admirers and a close circle of friends.

Eighteen months ago Maria encountered a relatively unknown Rosie Casals in the semi-finals of Forest Hills. Rosie, with a talent just as great and a pixie personality, played the match of her life. Here is where Maria's stature as a player became so apparent. As the crowd pulled for Rosie and as the score became closer, Maria pulled herself out of a bad patch with the coolness and dignity of a queen. Pride makes the true champion, and on the tennis court no other player can approach Maria's magnificent demeanor. She has been on the top or near it for almost 10 years, despite having been plagued by illness. She was sick for a year with hepatitis but came back again into the winner's circle. She had several leg injuries resulting from the cramps which attacked her in the finals of the Australian Championships when she was forced to default to Margaret Smith in brutal heat. Currently she is suffering from calcium deposits in her right elbow and shoulder and she has not played a tournament since Wimbledon. No one is sure when she will be able to go back on the tournament trail. Perhaps the thought of her moments of glory will inspire her to overcome these most recent injuries.

The queen of the courts deserves the many honors she has received. Germaine Monteil this month adds to her quantity of trophies with another tribute to her greatness.

ANN HAYDON JONES

by Julie M. Heldman

Ann Jones had a reasonably satisfactory record last year. She won the French, German and Scandinavian Indoors, the British Hard Courts, the Italian and French Championships and reached the semi-finals of Wimbledon. She beat King in Federation Cup, Bueno in the French and Richey in the finals of the French. This year she did a little better. Her sideline companion and husband, Pip Jones, could not have been overly disappointed.

Ann has been married to Pip for 4 years. The first year she suffered from the typical tennis let-down that immediately follows marriage. Many women tennis players mysteriously lose the desire to win and acquire a strange yen to stay at home, viz., Carol Aucamp (née Hanks), Betty Pratt (née Rosenquest), Donna Fales (née Floyd) and Barbara Davidson (née Scofield) —but not Billie Jean King (née Moffitt). All of the husbands of the above-mentioned ladies have been interested in tennis, and the wives have generally come back stronger than ever. . . .

Pip is as much a fixture on the international tennis scene as Ann. When his wife is playing a big match, Pip is always around to give encouragement and Ann looks to his corner for support at crucial moments. They have a beautiful relationship. This kind, very sweet, happy, red-faced, bald English businessman writes beautiful letters to his wife, and the pink-cheeked Ann turns two shades pinker on receiving one of his missives. He plays Robert Browning to her Elizabeth Barrett, although perhaps not Richard Burton to her Liz Taylor.

The 18-year-old Ann Haydon was a table-tennis champion originally and was ranked No. 2 in the world. She took up lawn tennis after giving up the paddle, and this extremely competitive, strong-willed woman, still in her teens, began to win big matches. At this period in her life, Britain's tennis women were showered with glory. Christine Truman was the darling of the British public and Angela Mortimer (one of Ann's heroines and closest friends) was to win the Wimbledon Championship.

And then there was Ann, a solid player with excellent groundstrokes and sharp wits. She was the stage actress competing against the movie stars, the Geraldine Page who vied against a 6 ft., 160 lb. Shirley Temple. It was frustrating because no matter how well she played, the sweet-faced, magnificent Christine Truman always "owned" the British public. Ann had to accept the fact that her closest rival was the idol not only of all British schoolgirls but of everyone who read the English newspapers. It is something you can't fight and, when you know Chris, something you don't mind. My closest British supporters—the elevator man at the Westbury, the waiter at Lyon's Corner House and the newspaperwoman at the Green Park tube station—said, "Sorry, old dear," when they heard I was to play Chris in the 16s of Wimbledon. They had pulled for me through four rounds but after all, they explained, "Christine is a British institution." And so when Ann goes on the court to play her teammate and rival, it is like fighting the Established Church—or the Throne.

Mrs. Jones has a big, loopy lefty forehand which she occasionally takes behind her. She pulls up sharply on the follow-through but she is also capable of hitting the forehand with sidespin. Her backhand is underspin and accurate. She developed these strokes from her table tennis. It was from her earlier experience with a ping pong paddle that she learned the "feel" of when to hit certain shots and when to be steady or aggressive. The unfamiliar facets of lawn tennis were the serve, overhead and volley, which are not exactly useful on a table. As Ann Haydon she was hesitant about her net play, but as Ann Jones she learned to come in on the right shots and developed a fine volley and overhead, although her groundstrokes and strategy are still her strengths. Ann's game is deceptive. She appears to be a pleasant, steady clay court Briton but she is, in actuality, an attacking, ferocious fighter who rarely misses and never gives up.

One day in Rome last year (I vividly remember the occasion and the hour) Ann came up to me and asked: "Would you like to play doubles in the French Championships?" I accepted in two seconds flat. We got to the semis where we met two lobbing Australians. They discovered I was weak on overheads and I found myself hitting five or ten every point and missing about four a game. Ann encouraged me for three straight sets. Finally she casually suggested that I let a few bounce. I did but we still lost because my game was shattered from looking at the sun so long. This was the year that Ann won both the singles and the mixed. When we got off the court, Pip consoled me with a hearty "You tried hard and that's what counts."

Ann Jones is deeper than her peaches-and-cream complexion indicates. I call her top-heavy because she is a shrewd thinker. She enjoys sitting around and talking in a friendly, comfortable manner and she has a good time at parties. But if you look closely, you can see the ambition bubbling up under the surface. The champion in her makes her practice hard, mostly with the top women. The shrewd strategist in her allowed her to absorb Maureen Connolly's knowledge when the former champ coached the British Wightman Cup team in 1965 at Cleveland. Only after their meeting was Ann able to assemble her incredible string of major titles. Maureen was not only her inspiration and her mentor but also her closest friend.

If you travel with Ann on a tournament circuit, the routine is simple. She only expects you to practice with her three or four hours a day; after all, why tire yourself if you have singles, doubles and mixed to follow? She encourages you to go to cocktail parties and receptions, but just when you are loosening up (1 A.M.?) she pulls you away since she has a practice court for you at 9 A.M. If there is a free week and you are in the vicinity of North, South or Central America, she drags you with her to Dallas to get a dash of inspiration from Maureen. At the end of the circuit you are exhausted and frustrated but you are playing the best tennis of your life. If you don't believe me, ask Virginia Wade.

When Ann Jones is on her game, she is one hell of a fine tennis player whom even Dick Savitt enjoys watching. She is also a mature woman who balances the various sides of her life, knows how much to play before getting stale and when to quit the circuit and go home to Pip. Perhaps the newspapermen will someday discover just how good she is and give her star billing.

Ann becomes the third international recipient of the Germaine Monteil Cup, which honors distinguished women in the game. Her name adds additional lustre to the famous trophy.

MARGARET SMITH COURT

by Sande Padwe

She is tall and lean, with soft blue eyes and blondish-brown hair, a pretty face, and a soft voice and smile. She also is one of the world's outstanding tennis players, winner of more national singles championships than anyone in women's tennis history.

Margaret Smith Court is at Merion this week en route to Forest Hills and a chance for her fourth United States singles crown.

She is now 27 and married and, she says, enjoying tennis more than ever. Three years ago, Mrs. Court, then just Margaret Smith, decided to retire from tennis. "I couldn't take the traveling," she said. "For almost six years I was playing tennis 11 months a year, eight months away from home."

Home is Australia, where tennis is the game. But until Margaret Smith's debut in the early 1960s, women's tennis in Australia was about as popular as a loss in the Davis Cup Challenge Round.

"There were four of us who came along at the same time," Mrs. Court said, "and then the women became popular like the men. Lesley Turner, now Lesley Bowrey, was one of the girls. Jan Lehane was another and Robyn Ebbern the other."

But it was Margaret Smith who consistently wound up in the first paragraph of the news stories and, consequently, with the most hardware and notoriety.

"My goal at the time," she said, "was to become the first Australian girl to win at Wimbledon." She later did win Wimbledon, and suddenly her name was as big in Australia as those of Rod Laver, Ken Rosewall, Lew Hoad, Fred Stolle and Roy Emerson.

A solid, well-muscled 5-10, Margaret combined speed and power with such precision that she seemed, at times, to be ready to challenge some of the male stars.

She had such good speed that there was, at one point in her career, a time when there was a possibility of an Olympic berth. One Australian track coach tried to persuade her to forget tennis and concentrate on the 440 and 880 instead.

But she didn't and continued to improve her tennis. To build strength, she lifted weights. "It's not too feminine I suppose," she once said, "but I can lift 150 pounds."

During her early years on the world circuit she perfected her game in practice sessions with some of the better Australian males. "Harry Hopman [Australian Davis Cup captain] would always encourage the girls if he thought they had talent," she said. "So sometimes I would work out with Fred [Stolle] and Emmo [Roy Emerson], but we never played any real matches. I doubt if I could have taken many games from them."

Mrs. Court's retirement shocked a number of tennis people, who figured she could complete a grand slam or at least add a few more Wimbledon or U.S. titles before leaving the game.

"The traveling wears you out," she said. "You stop enjoying the things you did. When you begin to feel unhappy like that your tennis starts to go bad. I had lost all my keenness. I was making myself play and it seemed stupid. So I decided to try something else."

That something else was running a sports boutique in Perth. Having a "name" didn't hurt business. "I didn't touch a racket for 16 months," she said. "I had no urge to play at all. I just did all the things I have always wanted to do and waited until I felt like starting again.

"Now that I'm playing again, I can see the difference in how much I have matured as a player. When you are younger you are not able to cope with little things that bother you. Now I am."

Having her husband, Barry, along on some of the trips—like this one to Merion—helps a bit. "What other people don't realize," she said, "is how lonely it gets out there. It makes a world of difference knowing there is someone to share the good and bad with you."

This could be her last full swing around the American and European circuits. "Next year," she said, "I'll probably just play the British tournaments leading up to Wimbledon, and then Wimbledon. I wanted the grand slam this year, but it didn't happen." She won the Australian and French titles before losing in the semifinals to the eventual Wimbledon champion, Ann Jones of Great Britain. [She also won the U.S. crown.] . . .

You think of the names from the tennis past like Suzanne Lenglen, Helen Wills, Alice Marble, Helen Jacobs, Maureen Connolly, Maria Bueno.

In terms of major championships, Margaret Smith Court has surpassed them all. In fact, if you are one for those endless sporting debates, Margaret Smith Court may be the best of all.

ANDRES GIMENO

by Neil Amdur

In Salt Lake City, he was introduced as "Mr. Hamandeggs." At a posh Miami Beach hotel, the tennis poster read "Jimeno." Last Wednesday night at Madison Square Garden, the umpire called him "Gimenyo."

Yesterday, he was not registered at the Roosevelt Hotel.

"I'm sorry," said a switchboard operator at the hotel. "There is no Mr. Geemino registered here."

It figured. Andres Gimeno (pronounced Heemeno) had been staying at the hotel for the last week.

Seldom has a professional athlete won so often and been accorded so little. Gimeno is the No. 3 player in professional tennis today, behind only the Australian mini-giants, Rod Laver and Ken Rosewall. But no one talks of Gimeno with the superlatives found for Billy Casper or Buckpasser, two other number threes.

Even in his native country, Spain, Gimeno is only No. 2. And to an amateur, no less, Manuel Santana.

Gimeno beat Pancho Gonzales, 15–13, 6–4, Wednesday night in the opening match of the Garden's $30,000 pro tournament. It was his 12th victory in 18 matches on the current National Tennis League tour and his third triumph in five matches with Gonzales.

"I knew the crowd would root for Gonzales," said Gimeno, whose victory gave him a berth in tonight's semi-final round against Rosewall. "But it made me play that much harder."

Gimeno is 30 years old with a lean, lithe body that is spread over a 6-foot-1½-inch frame. He is polite and pleasant and his carefree conduct on the court is a sincere reflection of his personality, not a pretentious exhibition.

Gimeno's problem is convincing the public that his $40,000 a year earnings are as meaningful as Gene Littler's or Tom Weiskopf's.

A typical example of Gimeno's situation occurred in England recently when he beat Roy Emerson in straight sets. "The next day, the papers say, 'Emerson was very erratic,' " Gimeno said. Gimeno's performances are consistently underplayed because he is so consistent. . . .

"For a while it bothered me that no one cared about my play," Gimeno said. "Newspapers at home [Barcelona] hardly talked to me. Everything is Santana. But now I don't worry. I play for money and my own self-respect."

With a $7,000 first prize going to the Garden's men's singles winner, Gimeno has the incentive, although Rosewall was picked to win the title by a computer last week. . . .

"I would like to win this tournament," Gimeno said. "I still think I can become the best in the world."

Will he ever live down his difficult-to-pronounce last name?

"Not as long as people call me Hamandeggs," Gimeno said.

CHUCK MCKINLEY

by Kenneth Rudeen

The most exciting tennis player in the United States today is a broad-backed, brown-eyed, irrepressible Missourian named Charles Robert McKinley. A year ago he was just another talented youngster. Now, at the still tender age of 19, he is whipping some of the finest amateurs in the game. To the delight of the galleries, he plays with a headlong exuberance seldom seen in amateur tennis since the days of Pancho Segura. Not in years has an American fledgling combined so much box-office appeal with so much pure ability—or crashed the tight little world of big-time tennis with so much confidence. "If I didn't think I could be the best tennis player in the world," Chuck McKinley says, "I don't think I'd want to play."

McKinley looks more like a stocky fullback than a tennis player. Only 5 feet 8 inches tall, he is as short as Bobby Riggs but, at 160, he weighs some 20 pounds more than Riggs did when he was winning at Wimbledon and Forest Hills. McKinley has broad shoulders, thick biceps and the wrists and hands of a blacksmith. He is what most top-flight American tennis players are not—an honest-to-goodness athlete who would stand out in almost any sport.

On the court McKinley's nerves are stretched as tautly as the strings of his racket ("It all builds up inside me; if I'm not nervous, I lose"), and it is transparently clear that he does not intend to finish where nice guys traditionally do. "You don't want to give 'em anything," he says. "You're out there to win the same as they are, and you can't for one minute be nice. If you get ahead, you can't afford to let up and let 'em win a few games."

As McKinley leaps, lunges, runs full tilt and whacks the ball violently, he burns energy at a furious rate. When he really leans into an overhead smash he looks as though he is going to bounce the ball into the next township. A fine shot brings a quick broad grin to his face, and when an opponent misses, he often chirps a falsetto "Out!" to supplement the linesman's call. But when he commits an error he is likely to bring his racket savagely downward as if clubbing a snake, or to tell himself, so courtsiders can hear him, "Oh, Charley, you missed that one."

Since all this is spontaneous and unmarred by the sulkiness so commonly seen on tennis courts today, spectators who have watched McKinley in action are fascinated by him. He has color, a rare and precious quality for which they are grateful, but beyond that they sense his impending arrival as a major star. . . .

"There is nothing he can't do on the court," Bill Talbert says. "He has all the strokes. He's fast. He's strong. He has marvelous reflexes. He has the eyes of a hawk—sees the ball as well as anyone in the game." . . .

McKinley began beating the country's best players as long ago as last August, when he gave the veteran Dick Savitt a 6–4, 6–8, 6–4 licking in the Eastern grass court championship. In September he removed the Mexican champion, Antonio Palafox, from the national championships at Forest Hills before losing in the fourth round to Alex Olmedo, who later lost in the final to Neale Fraser. From Forest Hills McKinley went to San Antonio to enroll as a freshman at little Trinity University, a Presbyterian school with 1,600 students, year-round tennis weather and an aggressive recruiting policy that has put Trinity tennis in a class with the country's best. . . .

In the national indoor championships in New York this February he disposed of Sweden's Ulf Schmidt with such vigor that Allison Danzig, the New York *Times* tennis writer, was moved to salute flamboyantly "the fury of his service, the vengefulness of his volley and the murderous effectiveness of his overspin drives." Next to fall was Holmberg, who is ranked fourth in the U. S. Finally, McKinley extended Savitt (ranked fifth) to four sets before losing in the semi-finals. Then came Pittsburgh and the first important men's tournament victory of McKinley's career. His victims were Vic Seixas, ranked tenth, whose best years, of course, are behind him, and Barry MacKay, ranked third. . . .

"I used to be so scared when I'd play a top man," he said. "Now maybe they're a little bit scared of me."

The remarkable thing about McKinley is not that he has arrived in the big-time but that he ever got started in the first place. The son of a St. Louis pipe fitter, he spent his earliest years in a "rough neighborhood" on the north side of town. Baseball was his first love, Marty Marion and Stan Musial of the Cards his sports heroes. During winters, when it was too cold for baseball, McKinley went to the Y, where he swam and played table tennis. He came under the influence of a volunteer instructor named Bill Price, who dropped in now and then to give pointers on the game the kids called ping-pong. Price was one of the best table-tennis players in the country and a tennis pro as well.

The Price-McKinley relationship might have ended when, at 10, Chuck moved with his family to the suburban community of St. Ann. But McKinley made frequent trips back into town to play at the Y. One time, in 1953, just to be with the crowd, young McKinley trooped out to a public tennis court with his buddies and Price. He discovered that he got a kick out of slamming the ball around. Before long he cared enough about tennis to cry after losing a match and to defend the game with his fists against sneering schoolmates with whom he had, as he puts it, "a few differences of opinion." . . .

When it became apparent that Chuck could be a superior player, Price advised him to forget about other sports and to concentrate on tennis. He plunged into a long series of boys' and then junior tournaments, forsaking other sports except table tennis and, when in high school, basketball. . . . Last spring a capped and gowned Chuck McKinley accepted his high school diploma one evening at 8:30 and half an hour later was flying out of St. Louis on the first leg of an all-summer tennis tour. With time out for classes at Trinity, he has been traveling steadily to tournaments ever since.

Editor's note: McKinley won the Wimbledon Championship in 1963 and was runner-up to Rod Laver in 1961. He was a member of the Champion U.S. Davis Cup team in 1963.

DENNIS RALSTON

by Jack Olsen

If the ancient statesmen of amateur tennis agree on anything as the national championships get under way at Forest Hills, it is that only two men are capable of preventing 21-year-old Dennis Ralston from becoming the national champion. One is Chuck McKinley, the Wimbledon champion, who in 1963 has been playing the best tennis of his career; the other is R. (for Richard) Dennis Ralston.

Chances are that when the tournament is over, Ralston will have continued to confound and confuse the experts—much as he did last week in the U.S.-Mexico Davis Cup matches, in which he beat both Rafael Osuna and Antonio Palafox with ease. He may have roared through the nationals untouched, leaving the top seeds strewn behind him, or he may have blown his stack and been knocked out in the first round by a player known only to his own next of kin and a few close family friends. That is the very nature of Dennis Ralston, a fretful young man who, for several years, has been the heir apparent to the throne of American amateur tennis.

It has been twelve years since Ralston came down U.S. 99 from Bakersfield to amaze the nabos of Southern California tennis with a sample case of strokes and techniques worthy of a person three times his age. And it has been fifteen years since he played his first official tournament. . . .

By the time he was old enough to fool around with his father's shaver, Ralston had filled half a dozen shelves with trophies, including the national junior singles championship. At 17 he went to Wimbledon, paired with Rafael Osuna of Mexico. Together they brought off the first victory for an unseeded team in the history of that old dowager of tournaments. The same year Ralston became the youngest player ever to reach the semi-finals at Forest Hills. At 19 he was national doubles champion with Chuck McKinley. And in his twentieth year, which ended last month, he knocked off the national indoor singles and doubles championships, the national intercollegiate singles and doubles championships and more than a few other major tournaments. Perry T. Jones, the paterfamilias of Southern California tennis and a former Davis Cup captain, says, "No player of Ralston's age has ever made a record to match this. Not Gonzales, not Budge, not Tilden, not Vines. He has looked like a champion since he was nine years old."

The indisputable fact, however, is that Dennis Ralston is not the U.S. champion. Tennis has set up the throne, waxed it and polished it for him, and still something keeps Dennis from sitting on it. The something is his own quixotic disposition. He seems, at times, to be a man firmly arrayed against himself. It is not only that he has a bad temper, and that he is his own favorite target. He also has trouble concentrating on his game. . . .

He repeatedly has been in trouble for disturbing domestic and international tranquility by throwing his racket and making "menacing gestures" at the crowd. What manner of ruffian is this?

Well, Dennis Ralston is, in simple fact, a 6-foot 2-inch 165 pounder who looks like Hiram Hayshaker, parts his short, straight reddish-blond hair neatly on the side, uses greasy kid stuff and has close-set, vivid blue eyes. Off the court he is courteous and gracious and has as much poise as Prince Philip. He is kind to old ladies and little children (not in the literary sense but in the actual) : at buffet dinners he is to be seen helping elderly women carry away their delicacies, and he devotes two days a week, when he is in California, to instructing children under the direction of the Youth Tennis Foundation. . . . But Ralston's busiest hours, in a sense, are from midnight to dawn, when he talks to himself and fights furious battles in his sleep. When he drives he keeps up a running commentary of annoyance at rotten drivers. . . .

Ralston stalks out on the tennis court with a scowl, as if something nearby smells bad. He looks mean. It is his normal countenance when he plays. Even his walk is aggressive. The effect is accentuated by the fact that he is a big strong kid with solid legs, heavily muscled thighs and a powerful shoulder development.

When he starts playing, everything is silence until he misses a shot—any shot. Then he begins talking loudly to himself: "Oh, you idiot!" "Gosh, that's just the worst!" "You're so bad, it's unbelievable!" When the wind blows one of his lobs out, he will shout, "Thanks, wind, thanks a lot!" And pretty soon Ralston finds the crowd against him.

"My attitude on the court," says Ralston ruefully, "is not a crowd-pleasing type, I guess." He has a rationalization for this: he says he needs to goad himself to raise his game to the necessary pitch. So he cusses himself out when he misses.

Ralston is not, by a long shot, the first tennis player with this attitude. "I've known plenty of great players who looked around for ways to get mad, people to get mad at: their opponents, umpires, anybody or anything," says his University of Southern California coach, George Toley. "Bill Tilden would select a line judge and convince himself that the fellow was doing him dirt. Pancho Gonzales developed his 'hatred' by refusing to travel in the same car with his pro tour opponents. . . ."

The prime difference between Ralston and the others is that his anger is directed only at himself. But tennis fans, like U.S.L.T.A. officials, are not mind-readers, and when they see Ralston kick his racket, thump the net or slam a ball over the officials' stand, they are entitled to believe that he is acting like a poor sport and, in effect, insulting his opponent. For this misapprehension, Ralston has had to pay dearly.

Three years ago, playing in a tournament in Australia, Ralston behaved badly. He stomped off the court after losing, he drove a ball over the stands because he was fed up with his own play and he asked to have a roving photographer removed from the sidelines. For these offenses against the Commonwealth and for other offenses at home, he was placed on a year's probation. In August 1961 at the American Zone Davis Cup finals in Cleveland, there was more trouble. . . .

The U.S.L.T.A. suspended Ralston for four months. A fuss went up from all quarters, and for weeks nearly every ranking player in the world was busy signing petitions beseeching the U.S.L.T.A. to change its bureaucratic mind. Included in the signers: the Mexican Davis Cup captain whom Ralston supposedly had insulted. Ralston went home to Bakersfield and brooded. At one point he decided, childishly, never to represent the United States again in a Davis Cup match. At another, he made up his mind to quit tennis altogether.

Then old Perry Jones, who had known him since he was 9 years old, called Ralston to Los Angeles and sat him down in his office at the Los Angeles Tennis Club. "I told him something," says Jones, "that Helen Wills once said right in this office: 'Nobody is interested in how you lose. They're only interested in how you win.' I said, 'Now you've been suspended, and you think it was unfair. And you're right. But you *are* suspended, and I recommend that you say nothing. Take your punishment.' After that, and to this very day, he has never complained about that suspension. I say he should get a good sportsmanship award for keeping his mouth shut!"

The suspension lasted until the beginning of 1962, and then the next affaire Ralston happened. Representing the United States in the Davis Cup doubles in Mexico City, with Chuck McKinley as his partner, Ralston double-faulted fifteen times in the first three sets, including five times in a row. The U.S. team lost the doubles to Palafox and Osuna, with Ralston chalking up a grand total of 18 double faults in the five sets.

"Ever since then," Ralston says dryly, "all you hear is how I lost the Davis Cup with my double faults. Well, we won two of the first three sets where I double-faulted fifteen times. We lost the last two sets where I double-faulted only two or three times." Ralston had a legitimate excuse: a cartilage in his left knee was damaged. (He was operated on shortly thereafter.) But instead of alibiing he went home. His mother recalled: "Those articles that came out in the papers saying how he lost the Davis Cup, they just about tore him to bits. He was in awful shape. He goes to pieces over something like that. He was talking in his sleep all night. I would lie awake and listen to him. He'd say, 'We've got to win this. I've got to get this one back.' He relived the whole thing in his dreams. In the mornings I would be practically in tears." . . .

"He is the most competitive athlete I have ever seen," says the brilliant Osuna, who is in a unique position to evaluate Ralston, having been his roommate at USC, his partner in winning Wimbledon and his arch-opponent in Davis Cup competition. "When I miss a shot, I say, 'Well, it is only a shot. I will get the next one.' But to Dennis it is like losing his life to miss a single shot." . . .

Dennis's father, a transmission man for the telephone company and a fine tennis player himself, says, "He wants to win everything. He demands four strokes a side when we play golf, even though he plays too good for that. He always wants to beat me, whether it's gin rummy or cribbage or whatever.

Five minutes after he gets in the house from a long trip he wants to play me cards."

"Yes," says Gail, "he just seems to want to beat his father at everything. And yet they've got a very close relationship, a wonderful relationship."

Dennis Ralston's introduction to tennis, its play and its attitudes, came when he was an infant. When he was barely out of diapers, his father gave him a cut-down racket. "From then on," says his sister Roberta, two years older, "he would go out to a brick wall we had in the back of the house and hit balls against it for hours, while all the other kids were out making mud pies."

Ralston's early tutelage on the courts was handled by his parents. . . . "I made him mad when I played him," said Mr. Ralston. "It was gamesmanship. I tried to get him mad for a definite purpose. I would do it hoping he would finally get to the point where he could see that it wouldn't do him any good to get that mad." . . .

Whatever else he may have picked up from his parental mentors, Dennis Ralston vaulted into junior tennis tournaments with as fine a set of basic strokes as could be seen short of a training film. Perry Jones had had his first look at the young Ralston, who was then being taught independence and resourcefulness by his parents, in 1951. They had loaded him on the bus from Bakersfield to Los Angeles, and at age 9, all alone, he appeared for a junior tournament at the Los Angeles Tennis Club.

"His eyes barely came up to the counter," Jones said, "and right next to him was the biggest valise you ever saw. He looked up at me and said, 'I'm Dennis.'

"I said, 'Dennis who?'

"He said, 'Why, I'm Dennis Ralston. Where do I stay?'

"Well, I must say I almost fell over at the sight of this little kid telling me he was Dennis as if I ought to know." . . .

It was not uncommon, in those days, for the youthful prodigy to work out with the likes of the Panchos, Gonzales and Segura, and other fine players who hung around the Los Angeles Tennis Club. When Dennis was 16, Ken Rosewall came through Los Angeles on the way to Wimbledon and paid a visit to Jones, who savors the story:

"Rosewall said, 'Mr. Jones, I've just a few hours here but I'd like to have a rally.' I said, 'There's nobody that could give you any kind of game.' He said, 'That doesn't make any difference. Just somebody that can bat a ball.' 'Well,' I said, 'I got a boy 16 years old here, and he'd get a tremendous thrill batting balls with you. But of course he can't give you too much of a game.'

"I took Dennis out there to Court No. 2, and he beat the heck out of Rosewall. Beat him, beat him, beat his ears back. Rosewall wasn't concentrating. And he was just working out, loosening up. But he never expected to see a 16-year-old with that collection of strokes and so much finesse. Right then Denny certified that he was going to be a great player."

Ralston's repertoire of shots, most of them learned from his mother, blends with an innate tennis sense that cannot be taught. As Jones explains it, "When you look at slow-motion pictures of Vines, of Budge, of Kramer, you find they're in the exact place they should be in order to return the ball *most comfortably*. This is an uncanny quality, and Dennis has it." . . .

Other facets of Ralston's game mark him as a special case. For one thing, he is an all-court player without a stroke weakness (with the occasional exception of the first serve, which has gotten better since the Mexico City debacle, but which can still use further improvement). He can play steady baseline tennis with anybody. There is no solace to be gained from hitting to his backhand; it is as strong as his forehand. He is an expert volleyer and has perhaps the best offensive lob in amateur tennis.

With a superb pair of eyes, Ralston picks up the ball sooner than most other players and thus is able to play it faster, an important advantage in top tennis. Explained Coach Toley: "Dennis plays the ball on the rise; he plays it early, when the ball has barely left the ground after bouncing, like a shortstop charging a ball instead of backing up on it. . . . Eighty per cent of the top players can't play the ball early. It takes a great eye and great timing. Ellie Vines played the ball on the rise, and so did Don Budge. Dennis is as close to Budge in all-court ability as any player we've had for a long time. He's got that short backswing and those eyes, and he has the ability to hold off doing what he's going to do until the last second. He doesn't commit himself, and that's murder on the opponent. That's why he gets a lot of lobs over people's heads. They don't know it's going to be a lob."

Now with his bad knee corrected (his left leg had become shorter than his right), all that stands between Ralston and the top spot is his disposition, a fact of which he is well aware. He wishfully thinks he has his temper well under control. He thinks his main problem now is an inability to concentrate. . . .

"I know that's what is on his mind these days," says his roommate, Osuna. "The other night I was reading and he was sleeping, and all of a sudden he started shouting in his sleep: 'Concentrate! Concentrate!' "

OSUNA

by Gerald Eskenazi

Rafael Herrera Osuna first returned a ball across a net when he was 10 years old. The sport was table tennis, and he is remembered as a tiny fellow who could hardly see over the top of the table.

An older brother, Jesus, then put a tennis racket in Rafael's hand and told him to play. But Rafael found it frustrating and turned his attention instead to team sports such as basketball and softball.

Finally, eight years ago, when he was 17 years old, Rafael Osuna took up the game with a vengeance. His earlier, frustrating experience was forgotten yesterday at Forest Hills, as he defeated Frank Froehling 3d in straight sets to win the United States tennis championship.

The title came one week before his 25th birthday. It culminated four years of hard work—four years in which Osuna also learned to speak English. The language barrier had made Osuna a shy athlete when he came to the United States in the spring of 1959.

He was born in Mexico City. He left there to enroll at the University of Southern California. George Toley, the school's tennis coach, remembered yesterday that Rafael could hardly speak English. Toley said:

"Rafe was bashful. Maybe it was because he barely understood the language. As for tennis, all he had was a talent that had to be developed—he could move well, but he had no finesse in his strokes."

Osuna was advised to pass up tournament play during his first summer at U.S.C. He attended summer school classes each day until noon, then headed for the Los Angeles Tennis Club. At the club he practiced until it was too dark to see. Then he went back to his dormitory and studied.

Osuna's family lives in Mexico City. His father, an engineer, played basketball and his mother was a swimmer. He has three brothers and two sisters.

His mother recalled that Rafael was afraid of becoming too good at tennis. Too many of his countrymen left home when they became famous.

Osuna's English is now flawless. He delights in amusing dressing-room habitués with such time-worn saws as "I used the old bean today" and "I put my noodle to good use."

His sister Elena, speaking from Mexico City yesterday, said that Rafael always had a joke ready. His informality with people and with family led him to walk around the house barefooted, Elena recalled.

Osuna, at 5 feet 10 inches and 155 pounds, has protean eating habits. He likes Chinese and Japanese foods. But when in training, he says, "I gotta stay away from those old beans."

Frijoles, a bean dish, is a great favorite of the champion when he's home. Yesterday, his mother promised to make him mole—chicken and chili—and tacos when he returns. Tacos is a dry corn pancake.

Osuna is entering his senior year at U.S.C., where he is majoring in business economics. He probably will do graduate work in France.

Toley said that Osuna often talked of life on a cosmic level. Osuna is a tireless reader and an interested traveler. Much of what he sees or reads becomes a topic of conversation.

If Osuna has a failing, it is perhaps part of the quality that made him a champion. He has a tendency, said Toley, to be too calm.

On the court, nothing appears to bother Osuna. Indeed, that is a strong point of his game—his constancy. But, said his coach, "I spend a lot of time convincing Rafe that he should be up for the small match as well as the big one. He has a tendency to sag when the match isn't important."

Osuna is not bothered by his slender frame when he plays chunkier opponents.

"I have great confidence in myself," he says. "When I get up in the morning I know I am good. And I keep in shape. After all, being good is my business, isn't it?"

HAPPY MEMORIES OF RAFE

by Gladys Heldman

On Wednesday, June 4, 1969, an airplane crashed into a mountain while attempting to land in Monterrey, Mexico. All 79 passengers were killed instantaneously. Among the passengers was Rafael Osuna, one of the best-loved men that tennis has ever known.

When you think of Rafe, don't think sadly. Remember instead his color-ful nature, his great talent, and, above all, his zest for living. He led a happy life and he was full of humor and laughter. He loved everybody and he was equally well loved. He had 5,000 friends and no enemies.

The player who was closest to him was, of course, Antonio Palafox. Rafe and Antonio were teammates and traveling companions from 1958 on. Antonio shared a suite with him in New York the year Rafe won his biggest international title, Forest Hills (Antonio went to bed promptly each night at 10 P.M. while Rafe stayed up talking to his pals until 3 A.M.). Antonio is a quiet, gentle, talented tennist. Rafe was effervescent and bubbly. He dubbed Antonio "the world's most inscrutable man" and did everything he could to make Antonio sparkle—at night. . . .

Rafe got his first opportunity in tennis in 1958 when he became a last-minute substitute for Gustavo Palafox (Antonio's cousin) on the Mexican Davis Cup team. . . . He was asked if he would like to go to Finland as a member of the team. Rafe thought someone was trying to play a joke on him; two days later he was in Finland. After Mexico took an unbeatable lead against Finland, Osuna was chosen to play the fifth and last match. He won. . . .

The next year Rafe got a scholarship to the University of Southern California. Two of the men who immediately befriended him became two of his closest friends. One was Corny Jackson, a retired advertising executive who was for many years the president of the Los Angeles Tennis Club, and the other was George Toley, the club pro and the coach at U.S.C. Rafe had not yet achieved any tennis renown. He was fast as lightning, but he had not developed a style of play or a tennis brain. . . . Corny and George became advisers and confidants. George got him into top physical condition and both men stood *in loco parentis*. . . .

Rafe liked to phone his friends. When Antonio moved to Texas, Rafe telephoned him every week. One evening Dick Savitt got a call from Rafe, who was passing through New York on the way to Europe: "Hey, Dick, do you want to hit some?"

"Sure, kid, sure." At midnight the two of them were hitting balls at Lenny Hartman's indoor court in Long Island.

One day I was the recipient of a call: "Mrs. Heldman," said the soft, familiar voice, "this is the Associated Press. We are going to do a story on you. May I ask you some questions?"

"Certainly, Rafe." . . .

Pancho Contreras knew Rafe both as a close friend and as his captain. Pancho was the Davis Cup captain when Rafe and Antonio did the impossible: they reached the challenge round against Australia. On the way to the final, Mexico played India in Madras. Rafe played the Indian national hero, Ramanathan Krishnan, and although the fans wished Krish to win, they also loved Krish's opponent. Who wouldn't? He was an artist and a genius with a racket and he had a flair, like Santana (another very close friend) for capturing the hearts of the crowd. Rafe beat Krish and received a deafening ovation. . . .

Nicki Pietrangeli was another intimate friend of Osuna. Whenever Rafe came to Rome, Nicki and he would have lunch together—a simple 7-course affair at the club with a bottle of wine. . . .

Two years ago Osuna had to decide between tennis and his career with Philip Morris. His close friend George MacCall offered him a professional contract at $80,000. Rafe turned it down. He thought his international tennis career was over. It was, from the viewpoint of regular tournament competition, but the best was yet to come. A few weeks before his death Rafe once again played Davis Cup for Mexico and he led his team to an astonishing American Zone victory over Australia.

Rafe had a wonderful, full life. His gentle nature, his soft manner and his humor endeared him to many people. He had two dozen intimate friends— Pancho Gonzales, Roy Emerson, Pancho Segura, Joe Cullman, Corny, Antonio, Nicki and Manolo, to name a few—several hundred good friends and several thousand others who adored him. Most of all, he had Leslie, the wife he loved, and Rafe, Jr., his 4-month-old son. Little Rafe has the same beautiful eyes that his father had, but where Rafe's were deep brown with thick black lashes (a young girl once said, "Rafe, don't rub your eyes, or you will ruin your eye makeup"), little Rafe's are pure blue with thick black lashes.

Rafe died young but he will live forever in our memories.

MANUEL SANTANA

by Frank DeFord

It was almost as if all Spain, not just Manuel Santana, had been the defending champion of Wimbledon, so that when Monday, on center court, Santana was upset by Charlie Pasarell of the U. S., Spain, too, had lost. No athlete in the world is so revered by his countrymen, and no defeat will alter that feeling. He is, in fact, the nation's leading hero by any measure, and by the personal decree of Generalissimo Franco, he is known as Illustrisimo.

Santana did not reach this position of esteem until two summers ago when, at the age of 27, he anchored the Spanish Davis Cup team that whipped the U. S. in Barcelona. The outcome was hardly a surprise to anyone but the Spanish people, who, with little appreciation or knowledge of the game, had naturally assumed that Spain had as much chance of beating the U. S. in tennis as in nuclear warfare. When Manuel, or Manolo, as he is known, and his teammates charged out and wrapped up the competition, 3–0, the whole country went berserk. Franco, watching on television from his yacht in the Mediterranean, had the silver medal of sport struck for the whole team, except Santana. Manolo was awarded the *gold* medal of sport, an honor so rarely accorded that only one other Spaniard— a soccer player named Alfredo di Estesano—has earned it.

After he beat the U. S., Santana kept on winning. He took the U. S. nationals the next month, midway in a streak from May to December in which he did not lose a single match. Spain's newfound interest in tennis grew to a passion, and even though Santana and his Davis Cup teammates were beaten in Australia in the challenge round, Manolo revived the joy last July by winning at Wimbledon. This time when he returned to Madrid, he was larger than life. Summoned to Franco's palace, Santana played an exhibition on the Generalissimo's private court against his doubles partner, Lis Arilla. Afterward, with the elite of Spanish society and government in attendance and with the light, gay music of the band playing in the background, General Franco called up his honored guest and pinned upon his chest one of the highest medals that Spain can bestow upon a citizen—the Isabel la Catolica. Then, beaming, Franco embraced Manuel Santana, the first champion of his Spain.

It had been many years since Santana's father, Braulio, came to live in Madrid. He moved there from Valladolid, a city in northwest Spain. . . . Santana's father died when he was 16. Manolo was the second of four boys, born in Madrid on May 10, 1938. The city was seething in the grip of the civil war, and a year after Manolito was born food rationing was forced upon the torn, besieged population.

Chamartin, where the Santanas lived, was then almost on the outskirts of the city. None of the Santanas live there now. Today, when he is not traveling the tennis circuit, Manolo winters in Madrid but moves each summer to La Coruña, a resort where his wife, Maria—the daughter of one of the most prominent lawyers in Spain—comes from. They have two children, Manolito, who is 4, and Beatrice, 2. It is a proper, comfortable existence they enjoy, complete with a nannie who lives with them and takes care of the children. Manolo, after all, commands the highest expense fees (with Roy Emerson) in the game. When Maria travels with him in the pursuit of more titles, Manolo's widowed mother, Mercedes, moves in to help the nannie with the kids. But there is less and less need for that, for Santana is employed by Philip Morris and is now home for months at a time, working in the Madrid office.

In Madrid, Santana's mere presence in public leads to immediate mobbing and hugging. He walks down the street, and the children, some of them dragging rackets that they use to hit balls against walls (for there are no tennis courts), scramble to get nearest to him. A policeman at an intersection abandons his job of sorting out the darting Spanish traffic and, while motor chaos ensues, hustles over for an autograph. Manolo smiles brightly, his teeth gleaming, and writes his name.

It is this way everywhere. Because his Davis Cup matches were brought into Spain by Eurovision from all over the Continent, Santana is nearly as much TV personality as athlete. Certainly no other athlete in Spain gets anywhere near the reception that he does. . . .

Santana carved his first racket out of wood when he was 12, a skinny truant drifting toward an illiterate life. He had quietly abandoned school when he was 10 after he discovered one day that he could pick up tips as a ball boy at the Club Tenis de Velasquez. Soon he was going to the club every day and not at all to school, and he would bring some of the money home.

For little Manolito it was an existence not unlike Peter Pan's. The Club Tenis was right in the heart of Madrid, and Manolito, like any businessman, would casually take a streetcar in from Chamartin every morning. When he was 13, a club member gave young Santana an old racket, and later that year he won a ball boys' tournament at the club. Young Santana had experienced his first touch of recognition. . . . Then, when Manolo was 16, Braulio Santana, an electrician for the streetcar company in Madrid, died. "And that was when my whole life changed completely," Santana says. When he talks about this his voice deepens with emotion.

To comprehend what happened to Santana next, it is necessary, really, to understand his manner. He is always positively joyous, so full of good will, so perpetually smiling, that there is no one in tennis who is not genuinely fond of him. Smiling, hugging, laughing, he invests a whole gathering with good spirits. His jutting teeth deny him good looks, but his face—somewhat reminiscent of Fernandel's—is so expressive, his mood so infectiously charming, that the teeth are quickly forgotten.

It is not hard to imagine, then, how appealing the little waif scrambling after balls at the Club Tenis must have been to the members. Shortly after his father died, one family at the club approached him and asked him to come live with them. "It was unbelievable, just like a book," Santana says. "I look back now and I really cannot believe that this happened to me. It was the family of Romero Giron. Señor Giron was dead and they were not very wealthy people. They lived comfortably—one house, one car. And when they asked me to come into their house, the last thing they wanted was to take me away from my own family. They made me go home every day for lunch with my mother and brothers and they also sent money home to my mother. And listen, the important thing: they did not take me because they thought I would be a great tennis player. Who could tell then anyway? They took me because there are just some people in the world who want to do good. That is the family of Romero Giron."

The Girons undertook to remake young Santana. Most involved in the project were Señora Gloria Giron, the family matriarch and widow of Romero (Santana always first refers to his benefactors as an entity, however, "La familia de Romero Giron"), and two of her children—Alvaro, who was to be Manolo's best man, and Aurora, who was to be named godmother of his first child. He fell into a disciplined new routine. He would arise and go to the gymnasium to lift weights, return to the Girons' for breakfast and then go to the club for tennis lessons for the balance of the morning. He would next board the streetcar for Chamartin and the other life, eat lunch with his mother and brothers and then return to the Giron house for a full afternoon of studies with a tutor. It was not easy, having been five years away from school, but eventually he earned what would amount to a high school diploma in the U. S. The Girons also began to expose him to religion again (he is today very devout) and they were just as solicitous in his social development; they would not let him travel alone until they considered him both mature and socially adroit.

Santana first visited America in 1959. He was wide-eyed and spoke little English. Frank Froehling, the American amateur, remembers meeting Santana. That night Froehling and two others ended up having dinner with the young Spaniard. The check came and Santana pounced on it. "You've got to remember," Froehling says, "that he was a nobody then, making minimum expenses. The check ran to $25, and he wouldn't let us pay a cent! I remember still. All he said was 'These are my friends. I will pay for them.'"

Indeed, the two qualities that those close to Santana invariably ascribe to him are pride and loyalty. . . . Once he refused to accept any expense money when, well into a tournament, Maria lost a baby and he was called home. And when a California promoter reneged on him and then upped his price drastically to get Santana back, Manolo would not even go to the phone to talk to the man. Neither, as some suggest to him, will he deny his true upbringing. "They tell me," he says sadly, shaking his head, "that I should say I was always with the family of Romero Giron, but no. I am proud of my whole life and my own family. I am luckier than most. I have two families, so why should I try to lose one?" . . .

Considering that his tennis development was on clay, Santana's individual accomplishment of winning the two major grass tournaments—Wimbledon and Forest Hills—which no other Continental European had managed since the 1920s, is perhaps an even more impressive feat than carrying little Spain to Australia. His grass game suddenly matured about three years ago, when he gained confidence in it. In fact, his game on the turf does not differ all that much from his clay maneuvers. He does serve harder on grass and tries to gain the net more quickly, but his serve is so relatively weak, even in the matter of placement, that it would be impossible for him to win in the traditional slam-bang manner. Instead, he must depend upon much the same strategy and nuances that work for him on slower surfaces. Anticipation, quickness, guile are as much a part of his repertoire as are his marvelous strokes. He is always switching his style to catch an opponent off guard and take control of the match from the harder hitter. He varies spin, cuts and slices, and, above all, he gets the ball back. . . .

Santana's chances of successfully defending his Wimbledon title were always questionable, for a ligament operation on his right ankle this past winter left him a bit tentative in his movements. . . . Santana is not himself interested in the Grand Slam or other cumulative honors that demand a full year's rigorous campaigning. It seems, in fact, that his passion for the game diminishes each year. . . .

"I cannot ask for much more, can I?" says Santana. "I'm No. 1, some people say; No. 2, others. It really doesn't matter. I am not a champion in the way they have been—like Perry and Budge and Sedgman and Laver. I'll never be a real bloody champion, so I can't expect much more."

Instead, his greater concern for the future is with Philip Morris, where he is determined to prove he is not just a used tennis celebrity.

"This is a wonderful thing," Santana says of his businessman's role, "and I will never lose this opportunity by playing tennis week after week, all year. . . . After all my life in tennis, I want to prove to myself that I can do something else besides tennis. The life I would prefer is to finish in my office, and on the way home to Maria and my children, I would stop and play tennis with my friends, and then say thank you to God for the opportunity to play tennis and see the world for all these years."

CLIFF AND NANCY RICHEY

by Frank DeFord

The Richeys of Dallas are a family consumed by a single passion that binds them together and gives meaning to their lives. The passion is tennis, although it seems not to matter what it is—it could be music or politics or cocker spaniels—because the significant aspect is the extent of the family's commitment. It is natural enough that the dedication is to tennis, for George and Betty Richey are both teaching professionals, and their children Nancy and Cliff are among the top amateur players in the world. But for the Richeys tennis has long been more than simply vocational, more than a game.

The Richeys' love for tennis and for each other—they are a joyously happy family—is so overwhelming that it has both isolated and insulated them. "Often we don't realize that things we say or do strike other people as different," George Richey says. "We are so close and we live with such a common purpose that sometimes, why, we just forget how other people may look at us."

The family lives in an atmosphere of despotic togetherness, believing in each other and especially in George, whose firm control is directed by an overriding concern for his children's success. Toward that end he will subjugate himself completely, even if it means abandoning parental dignity and authority. When practicing with his father, Cliff—who is still in his teens—will snarl appallingly rude abuse: "Shut up and just hit me the ball!" Or, "Well, I don't want to quit, so stay there and hit me some more!" But George Richey takes it because he believes that Cliff must release his tensions in this way. "I do nothing but try to please him and give him what he wants," he told an old Houston friend a short time ago.

George and Betty travel almost everywhere in this country to see their children play but, though George Richey is a tough little man, he is afraid of airplanes and never has been in one. So the Richeys tour the country in their 1959 Cadillac, carting the kids from tournament to tournament. In the summer they take their vacation from the swank Brook Hollow Golf Club, where Richey is the tennis pro, and make a long circuit. "I guess we've never had a real vacation," Betty Richey says.

Anyway, there is always practice. Nancy and Cliff practice incessantly, hours every day, and they go at each other without compassion. "We never play what Daddy calls 'giggle tennis,'" says Nancy. (Giggle tennis encompasses just about all tennis not played in the determined Richey manner.) The family has stopped the car on a whim to practice on a strange court. Nancy and Cliff have gotten off a plane and practiced at midnight. They have rallied long hours in the tropical midday sun when every other tour player was asleep or sunning. The two kids invariably practice before a match, and often they start hitting at dusk after both have played singles and doubles that day.

"I need some grooving," Cliff will whine, and there go all the Richeys, changing clothes, picking up tennis paraphernalia, charging into action just like down at the firehouse. "Just that extra 15 to 20 minutes can make the difference," George Richey says, explaining it all.

Many people consider the Richeys' attitude odd, but the Richeys are singularly proud of themselves and their accomplishments. They are straightforward, pragmatic people, firmly believing that discipline, competition and victory offer greater rewards than a more prosaic life. The results seem to bear them out.

Nancy Richey, 22, has grown up to be an attractive woman, the best player of her sex in the United States, and the fourth best in the world. Cliff Richey is 18 and still maturing, but already he is ranked eleventh among U.S. men. . . . Before Nancy and Cliff grew up, Richey's best pupil was Tut Bartzen, who was a high-ranked U.S. player. Eight years ago, when he was at his peak, Bartzen said, "George Richey is a thoroughly fine person who adores the game. It's his whole life. He is not in teaching for the money but because tennis means so much to him. His only interest is in helping my game. He will stay out as long as I want to and do anything I want." That could be Cliff Richey talking now. . . .

As a boy in San Angelo, George Richey was a boxer and an outstanding baseball prospect, good enough at 13 to pitch against 18-year-olds in American Legion ball. At 14, however, he injured his right elbow when he fell out of an automobile, and in a lengthy, complicated convalescence he took up tennis, the only one-armed sport he knew of. Even today the only thing George Richey does left-handed is play tennis.

Richey quickly became proficient enough in the sport to earn scholarships to two Texas colleges. After marriage, the war and a half-hearted attempt at chicken farming back in San Angelo, he became a tennis pro. . . . As a teacher Richey can be a martinet, but he tempers his demands, with the understanding that he is only interested in meeting you all the way—or not at all. "I never cared if Nancy and Cliff played tennis," he says, "but, if they wanted to, all I asked was that they really devote themselves to it."

The charges that Richey has driven his children unmercifully are, taken as a lot, patently foolish. Richey drives them, yes, he saturates them with this game and the importance of victory, but the children approve of his demanding methods. Mrs. Richey explains. . . .

"They used to kid Cliff at school, always asking him why he didn't want to have any fun. He would just grit his teeth and try to explain. I remember how wonderful I felt a couple years ago when we were all driving back to Dallas after the Sugar Bowl tournament. Cliff had won a great big trophy— oh my, you should see it—and we were just driving along together when all of a sudden Cliff grabbed that trophy and hugged it and said, 'They talk about me not having any fun. Why, this is the greatest fun in the world. This is the kind of fun that lasts all year.' " . . .

Cliff was batting a tennis ball around from the time he was old enough to walk. He actually gave up tennis when he was eight; he took it up again when he was about 12 upon discovering that his school tennis team took auto trips to matches. . . .

On the circuit Nancy and Cliff spend most of their time together. They keep strict training, up at 9, in bed by 11. In between there is practice and matches. Seldom indeed do they bother with social functions. Nancy is thus something of an unknown quantity to her touring companions. She is petite, only 5 feet 3, with auburn hair, delicate skin and the intense look of her father. But there are three things that everybody says (in order) about Nancy Richey: she is sweet, she is domesticated and she will make somebody a good wife. And these are things that also describe her mother.

Betty Richey can be as frank as her husband, but she has tact and grace. She is a kind, sensitive woman. . . . When she moved from Electra, Texas, to San Angelo Junior College, where she met her husband, she knew nothing of tennis. Today she is her husband's assistant, teaching beginners and helping to run the tennis shop at Brook Hollow. Despite their devotion to a sport, however, both Mrs. Richey and her daughter remain refreshingly feminine, content in the old Southern style to be overshadowed by the men in the family.

Not surprisingly, Nancy rarely creates any sort of public commotion. The one exception is her fondness for wearing shorts instead of a skirt when she is playing. Writing in *World Tennis* magazine last year about the Italian championships, correspondent Gloria Butler suggested that mass Italian male apoplexy had been occasioned by Miss Richey's unfeminine apparel. "Nancy was a curiosity to the Italians," the article said. "They are very woman-conscious and they just could not understand how such a pretty girl could ruin herself by wearing unbecoming clothes. The face is adorable, but she wears a floppy hat which hides it, a T-shirt and long Bermuda shorts which emphasize the wrong part of her anatomy."

Mr. Richey himself designed and sells the hats ("mesh panels on the side of the crown for coolness and air circulation"), and Nancy gave up on the fetching little swishy skirts for reasons even more utilitarian: she likes to keep the extra ball in her pocket and sometimes she has caught her racket in her skirt.

The rest of Nancy's court manner draws little attention, because her excellence is so mechanical. She appears to be a player constructed, a wind-up doll. While playing she is mute, a bundle of combative pugnacity. She speaks not at all to her opponent, no matter how well she may know the girl, and emits only unladylike grunts—"oomm"—nearly every time she hits a ball. She looks over at her parents less than Cliff does when he is playing, but her gaze is more painful and beseeching, as if she were trying to communicate on some new level. The other girls on the circuit believe that Nancy must have her father in attendance to play her best, and Nancy herself admits that she is happier now that Cliff is traveling with her.

On the court Nancy seldom ventures from the baseline, stroking the ball perfectly, boom, "oomm," again and again. Because her ground strokes are nearly flawless, she plays her best tennis on slow surfaces such as clay, where the stress is off the serve and volley. Having improved her volley and overhead, Nancy now comes to the net with more confidence and regularity. After four years of being ranked near the top, she attained the No. 1 U.S. ranking in 1964, and she is well on her way to retaining it for 1965.

To become the world's top woman player, however, Nancy must improve her performance on grass. She has never progressed beyond the quarter-finals at Wimbledon nor the semi-finals at Forest Hills, and you don't become No. 1 like that. But her all-round play has never been better than this year, and on clay and composition surfaces she has consistently beaten the three women ranked ahead of her: Maria Bueno (1–1), Margaret Smith (3–1) and Lesley Turner (3–1). . . .

Nancy loves the tennis life more than ever and is quite content to do Cliff's laundry while waiting for that somebody to be a good wife to.

"Nancy took every home economics course there was at Southern Methodist University and then left," Mrs. Richey says. "She is very domesticated and can cook, and she sews quite well. I wish Cliff would have some other interest. . . . He's so intense that it's—well, it's scary. You ought to see his notebooks. Why, every page is just lists of players that he beat and their records." . . .

At 18 Cliff remains something of a child. He has an unbecoming butch haircut, and when he plays his shirt flaps right out and stays out. He is 5 feet 9, a bit taller than his father, and he has taken off about 15 pounds, down to 165, but he still gives the impression of chubbiness. It may be just his round, full face and his big oval gray eyes that give this impression. . . .

Cliff's explosions on the court are a side product of his competitive intensity. Like all members of his family, he has an extremely good sense of humor, but on the court there is no lightness. He is obsessed, determined not to be diverted from the single goal of victory. . . . He has been rude to referees and opponents at the price of becoming unpopular with his fellow players and losing all favor with crowds, even in Dallas. . . . In his headlong rush toward victory Cliff has somehow equated courtesy with being sissy. Fortunately, George Richey has cautioned Cliff about the folly of further frenetic disorders. Last year, when Cliff called home after a series of frightful episodes in Italy and England, his father instructed him that no matter how right he might be he was "to go about things more diplomatically."

Cliff is so enveloped in tennis that many tour players believe he does nothing at night but go to his room and read his scrapbooks and tennis magazines. Cliff is not only a tennis player but a tennisophile. He knows virtually every score of every match he has ever played and—with the important and semi-important matches—he also has a total recall of point scores, key shots, bad calls, crowd noises, temperature, wind conditions, his father's reaction and other attendant information. . . .

Stubborn and cocky, Cliff has always been a more difficult tennis student than the amenable Nancy. It took months for George Richey to convince his son that he must eliminate the loop in his backhand but, characteristically, when Cliff finally agreed he went right out and hit 4,562,182 balls to improve it. Like his sister, his ground strokes are the strength of his game, but he has far more court imagination and variety.

His deficiency is his serve—particularly the second one—which is neither tricky nor deep. One who does not agree with this widespread analysis, however, is Pancho Gonzales. "A weak serve in comparison to what?" Gonzales says. "Weak compared to Kramer? Weak compared to Gonzales? Weak compared to who? It's the results that count."

Cliff and Nancy are at Wimbledon now—center stage, the shrine of tennis. They are hiding under their floppy hats, gritting their teeth, not smiling and not talking to prospective opponents—generally behaving like the gladiators they consider themselves. They are practicing all the time, consoling and helping each other, watching out for each other, cheering for each other and walking off the court with each other, because George Richey, for once, is not there. . . .

"There is a wonderful satisfaction in seeing something succeed that you developed yourself," says George Richey, talking of that moment when he stands there waiting for his child who has won. . . . His child comes off the court and to him. This time it is Nancy. George Richey ushers her through the crowd, but sometimes he gets lost in it, so that he must drop behind, and many do not know that he is the father of the player, tagging along. Betty Richey, still in her seat, and Cliff, somewhere nearby, glance fondly at each other and then watch them as the other two go off. It is the same every time, they know. At the very first chance, past the press of the crowd, George Richey will reach out and put his arm about his child, and they will walk off that way, talking tennis. They have great love for each other, they have pride in their life, and they have won.

VIRGINIA WADE

by Julie M. Heldman

While Sergei Prokofiev, Rudyard Kipling, Aesop, Walt Disney, La Fontaine and one or two TV programs have given human characteristics to members of the four-legged world, we of the international tennis circuit have chosen animal designations for our two-legged friends. Is there a player of 20 years' standing who does not know that Fausto Gardini is "The Spider" (*Araneida*) or that Bob Perry is "The Snake" (*Ophidia*), that Mike Franks' wife is "The Mouse" (*Mus Musulus*) or Gussie Moran "The Goose" (*Anserinae*)? Tennis has had a famous "Birdie" (one of the immortal Sutton Sisters), a "Dodo" (niece of Birdie), several "Kittys," a couple of "Chicks" and a fabulous "Mousie" (Mrs. William Powell). It is therefore not beyond the realm of imagination for me to designate Virginia Wade, the subject of this encomium, as a Lioness, albeit only a cub.

The species Felidae, as every biologist knows, includes the lion, the tiger, the leopard, the puma, the jaguar, the lynx, the cheetah and the housecat. The Felidae characteristically have lithe bodies, handsome fur, powerful muscles, retractable claws and formidable teeth. The lion is distinguished by his pride, his roar, his courage and his killer instinct; our heroine is just as famous for these very same qualities. The lion is King of the Jungle; our protagonist is Queen of the British Courts. She becomes frustrated when her right paw does not connect correctly with fleeting victory and then we are treated to the roar of pain of the wounded cub who goes off to the corner to lick her wounds.

Virginia was made for combat in the great arenas. She rises to the occasion on the Center Court of Wimbledon. She is a proud creature, capable of affection and frequent loud purrs when contented, equally capable of violence and mayhem in actual combat, visibly hungry for conquest and physically able to tear the opposition limb from limb. Her talent for the game has made her the greatest female British prospect in years. But she is still a cub and not yet a full-fledged lioness; she must learn to conquer the smaller beasts, one by one, before she can successfully eat up her bigger rivals. She has stalked her victims relentlessly in the jungles of Johannesburg and the hills of Rome, killing off the antelopes and knocking down the trees, but she has yet to prove herself against the mighty elephant or the vicious crocodile.

The lion cannot be domesticated but it will breed in captivity. It can be taught to jump through hoops and play "follow the leader" and it will do a trick at the crack of a whip. Virginia is the most educated lioness in captivity, having earned a high degree in mathematics at Sussex University. Her assets are a bright and a disciplined mind, great athletic ability and an indomitable desire to succeed. Her only problem is her temperament. To her the tennis court is a field of mortal combat. When she is ahead, she stalks about the court with deadly efficiency, slashing balls at all conceivable angles, but when the foe begins to look unconquerable, her discouragement becomes evident to the onlookers. If unhappiness could be measured in decibels, Virginia's vociferousness would probably be counted second only to my own hearty screams.

Virginia has the best first serve in women's tennis. She hits it with a very natural action and a good deal of confidence. With this same action she can serve hard down the middle or slice wide to the righty's forehand. Although she has tempered her game in the last few years, Virginia still tends to hit very hard on all her strokes. She has a wristy Continental forehand which she likes to roll crosscourt. It is a shot which, when successful, is a winner; occasionally it becomes erratic. Her backhand is mostly hit with underspin. It is steady and the ball bounces low. It is a fine coming-in shot, especially on grass, where the ball does not bounce up much anyway. Her sliding shot makes the opponent hit up at the ball so that Virginia can finish the point on a volley or an overhead. She is basically an attacking player with a good, though at times erratic, volley and a strong overhead because she has the same feel and action as on her serve.

Virginia Wade was born in England but her parents moved to South Africa one year later, in 1946. Her father had the post of Archdeacon of the Episcopal Church in Durban, and the family lived there for 15 years. It was inevitable that Virginia would learn to play tennis since the whole family enjoyed the game and they lived next door to a club. Tennis is an all-year game in Durban, and Virginia had plenty of time to establish a style of her own without much professional assistance on her strokes. She was a fair junior but not in the same league as Maryna Godwin who, she says, was "miles better."

Only recently has Virginia come into her own as a tennis player, and now that Ann Jones has turned pro, Virginia has become the No. 1 amateur in Britain. Maureen Connolly Brinker has been very helpful to both Virginia and Ann, molding their minds and attitudes as well as aiding them technically. This relationship of former champion to future greats began in 1965 when Little Mo coached the British Wightman Cup team in Cleveland. It has continued and both the British girls have gone out of their way to visit Dallas for rest and friendly advice. Both Virginia and Ann have played their best tennis since coming under Maureen's tutelage. In 1965, Virginia was a set up and 5–4 with her serve to follow against Nancy Richey but could not quite close out the match against the American groundie slammer. The next year, in the middle of her final exams, Virginia had 5–3 in the third against Richey to win the Wightman Cup for Britain, but she was still not mature enough to deliver the mortal blow. This year she beat Nancy! Her other two great performances came against her steady rival, Ann Jones. . . .

The young British lass reckons she played the best match of her career when she won the title at Bournemouth over Ann 6–2, 8–6 in 1967. This year the dark-haired, slim, athletic Virginia has looked impressive while winning tournaments in Nairobi and Kampala, gathering a win over Margaret Court in the latter, and taking a second title at Bournemouth over Winnie Shaw in the final. She also got to the finals of the South African Championships and Hurlingham where she lost to the very powerful Margaret Court. . . .

BILLIE JEAN KING

by Hal Higdon

When she first started playing in tennis tournaments, little Billie Jean Moffitt found her aggressive net-rushing style ineffective against the "back-courters"—"the kids that are very steady, and play from the back of the court, and hit lobs all day," waiting for the opponent to make the first mistake. "They used to say, 'Ha, ha, all we need to do is to get two or three back on you and you'll miss the fourth shot.' And I said, 'We'll see who's winning when we're 16.' "

It didn't take that long. When she was 15 she won her first big tournament with her own hard-hitting style, and since then she hasn't slackened a bit: she still plays a man's game, darting toward the net and glowering over it like an angry bear, covering the net as a fly covers a sugar bowl, slamming serves and mixing ground shots the way Juan Marichal mixes pitches. Her hard, grueling game has led her to the top of women's amateur tennis, and following this summer's capture of the "Triple Crown" at Wimbledon—her second consecutive women's singles title, her fourth women's doubles championship and the mixed doubles title—Mrs. Billie Jean Moffitt King is now comfortably lodged as the world's No. 1 women's tennis player. One of the few honors to elude the dynamic Mrs. King is, oddly enough, the championship of her own country.

The world's top-ranked women's player is 23 years old, stands 5 feet 6 inches tall and weighs 140 pounds ("That is, when things are going right—I love to eat") . . . . With short, wavy brown hair, blue harlequin glasses, 5 million freckles and a Doris Day face, Mrs. King seems an ordinary attractive young lady. But she is probably amateur tennis's most colorful and controversial player today. "I have a tendency to say things that should be off the record," she admits. "I don't know if our men really want to be the best in the world," she once told a reporter asking about American tennis players. "There's no glory in this country!" And when a Chicago newspaperman recently approached Billie Jean with a request to interview her for a feature on the women's page, she blurted angrily, "That's the trouble with this sport. We've got to get it off the society pages and onto the sports pages!"

Recently, in the clubhouse of the elite Town Club in the Milwaukee suburb of Fox Point, where she was playing in the national clay court championships, Billie Jean held forth in her usual outspoken way on one of her favorite subjects: What's wrong with American tennis. "Tennis is a very good sport," she began, "but you've got to get it away from the club atmosphere and into the public places, the parks, arenas like Madison Square Garden. You've got to get tennis into places where everyone feels welcome. I don't think the average person feels welcome in a club atmosphere like this unless he's a member"—and she looked pointedly around her at the ornately fashioned bar and the ornately fashioned men and women sitting around it. . . .

"Tennis takes stamina, so much stamina, but you never think of it as a sport. You picture people sipping mint juleps under an umbrella, and it's not that way. People think of tennis as a sissy sport and this is what we have to get away from." . . .

Mrs. King is as outspoken and controversial on the court as off. "Billie Jean's a ham," says her husband Larry. "She likes to play before fans. And she lets them know when she's angry." If the call of an official displeases her, she does not hesitate to raise her voice to tell him.

In addition to haranguing officials, Billie Jean maintains a constant conversation with herself, particularly after a bad shot and always in a voice clearly audible in the grandstand. "Oh, Billie, think!" she'll shout, or, "Boy, I'm telling you!" or, "You've got the touch of an ox!" or her favorite expression: "Nuts!" She also has been known to mutter a few other less homey expressions under her breath, and in fact several years ago the U.S.L.T.A. apparently considered censuring her for her language on court.

. . . Billie Jean also dislikes the sepulchral atmosphere at most tennis tournaments and would like to see the fans shout and cheer and even boo for a change.

Controversy seems to snap around Billie Jean's heels. After the 1965 season, during which she reached the finals at Forest Hills (losing to Australia's Margaret Smith) and won for the third time the doubles crown at Wimbledon (with Brazil's Maria Bueno as partner), Billie Jean seemed assured of ranking No. 1 in America. The U.S.L.T.A.'s national ranking committee did list her in that position, an action approved by its executive committee. But Al Bumann, president of the Texas Lawn Tennis Association, wanted the top ranking for Nancy Richey of Dallas, who had won the national clay court championship, a tournament Billie Jean had skipped. Bumann's proposal that Billie Jean be dumped to No. 2 lost before the U.S.L.T.A. membership. Finally Bumann suggested that Billie Jean and Nancy be allowed to share the No. 1 ranking. This compromise proposal passed. . . .

Billie Jean won Wimbledon the following season, but when she appeared at Forest Hills for a second-round match with Australia's Kerry Melville, she found Texas official Bumann sitting in the raised umpire's chair. She promptly kicked up a storm and asked that another umpire be substituted, but the officials denied her request and Bumann himself declined to move. Billie Jean proceeded to blow higher than a lob to the baseline, losing her match in straight sets even though she had beaten Kerry Melville just two weeks before, 6–1, 6–2. . . .

Billie Jean has risen to the top of women's tennis by following a daily training regimen that would impress even Jim Ryun. When not traveling the tournament circuit, the Kings live in a one-bedroom apartment in Berkeley, California, where Larry attends the University of California. They selected their apartment because of the view across the street, which happens to be of the Berkeley Tennis Club.

Billie Jean rises between 8 and 8:30 and by 10 she is on the court for two hours of drills aimed at perfecting her shots and improving her conditioning. She may also mix in some exercise or run short sprints, preferring speed work to long-distance running. She practices at Berkeley seven days a week unless Rosemary Casals—who herself reached the semi-finals at Wimbledon this year—is in town and then the two girls will split their practice time between Berkeley and Golden Gate Park near Rosie's home. Following lunch, Billie Jean will play a match with one of the men players ("because men players are tougher") and three or four sets of doubles with Rosie. Larry, a handsome blond law student . . . rarely plays tennis with his wife, figuring she can benefit more by playing different players. He is a shrewd analyst of tennis style, but prefers to leave the actual coaching of his wife to Frank Brennan, who runs a tennis clinic in Upper Saddle River, New Jersey, and with whom the Kings stay between summer tournaments. . . .

Billie Jean finishes practice around 6 or 7 and then cooks dinner, usually steak. She likes to read, particularly books on psychology, and eventually hopes to complete her college degree in that subject. Partly to aid her concentration, Larry taught his wife to play bridge.

"Billie Jean also likes to dance," says her father, Bill Moffitt, a fireman in Long Beach, California. . . .

Billie Jean seems to have been endowed with a certain athletic talent at birth on November 22, 1943. Her father played basketball, baseball and ran track; her mother is an excellent swimmer. This summer Randy Moffitt, her 18-year-old brother, pitched three no-hitters and one one-hitter in four games in the local Connie Mack baseball tournament. "Whenever the Fire Department had a picnic," says her father, "the men would always want Billie Jean to play shortstop or third base. She had natural ability in hitting the ball and fielding and throwing."

When Billie Jean was 10 she played shortstop with a group of girls mostly 14 or 15 years old. Billie Jean realized her potential in that sport (softball) was limited. "I told my mother, 'You know I love softball, but I'd still like to be in a sport where you could be considered a lady.' My parents, especially Dad, suggested I play tennis, and I said, 'What's tennis?' "

When she learned tennis was a game in which you could both run and hit a ball, Billie Jean decided to try it. . . . Tennis professional Clyde Walker gave free lessons once a week at each of five public parks in Long Beach, and Billie Jean would trail him from park to park. She played few games those first years, spending most of her time standing with a bucket of balls, hitting them one at a time over the net. For a while she walked three and a half miles to school each day, to strengthen her legs. When she started entering tournaments, invariably she would lose in the first round to the backcourters, who would play steadily while Billie Jean charged all over the court. "I've always played a net game," she says. "It's part of my personality. It's *me!* One day Clyde asked me, 'What are you doing at the net?' I said, 'I don't know. This is fun, whatever I'm doing.' He said, 'You get back in the backcourt and learn those ground strokes first!' "

Billie Jean's ground strokes, relatively speaking, remain the weak point of her game, but she feels that she now profits from the flexibility she learned at that very early age. "I was very erratic when I started playing tournaments," she says. "But I learned an all-round game, and it paid off, even though I suffered." . . .

In 1958 tennis fans from Long Beach raised money to send her and her mother (as chaperon) to the national girls' 15-and-under championships in Middletown, Ohio. Billie Jean lost in the quarter-finals. . . . The following year Billie Jean played in the Eastern grass court championships against 1959 Wimbledon champion Maria Bueno. She lost, but her showing impressed tennis coach Frank Brennan. "You're going to be good someday," he said, and he has continued as her coach and adviser to this day.

In 1960 Billie Jean reached the finals of the national girls' 18-and-under championships, losing to Karen Hantze. The following year she traveled to Wimbledon, where she and Karen won the women's doubles title. Billie Jean was 17 and Karen 18, the youngest pair to achieve such a victory.

Billie Jean returned to Wimbledon in 1962 and startled the tennis world by defeating top-seeded Margaret Smith in the opening round, the first time a first-ranked player had lost that early. She made the quarter-finals and with Karen repeated her doubles victory. In 1963 she went to Wimbledon and, still unseeded, upset three seeded players—Maria Bueno, Ann Jones and Lesley Turner—to make the finals, where she lost to Margaret Smith. Margaret told her, "You know, Billie Jean, you've got all the shots, but I always wear you out. I know you don't practice. You just don't play enough. I know you could win Wimbledon. Why don't you give it a go?"

But Billie Jean wasn't yet ready to give it a go. "I was in love," she says of 1964. "I was in another world." She had met Larry King one night in the library and soon they began to talk of marriage. Nevertheless, she made the semi-finals at Wimbledon that year—on what amounted to a week's practice—then decided she either had to take tennis seriously or give it up. Billie Jean and Larry became engaged that fall and two weeks later she left for Australia to train three months under Mervyn Rose. . . . The Australians had her running, doing exercises and participating in two-on-one drills where two players guard one side of the net with the single purpose of returning all shots to the remotest possible corners of the court. When she first began two-on-one drills she found herself unable to last more than five minutes; after three months she could retrieve shots for an entire hour.

Learning a whole new game did not come easy for Billie Jean. In an attempt to improve her consistency, Rose shortened all her strokes, which immediately affected her timing. . . . Merv said, "Don't get discouraged. I promise you that in six months you're going to notice the difference." And September 1965, says Billie Jean, "is when I played Margaret Smith and realized that the work I had done had made all the difference in the world."

Billie Jean lost in the finals at Forest Hills to Margaret, but said, "I realized that I could beat her and that I could beat anyone in the world." The following spring she did beat Margaret in the South African championships, then won the singles title at Wimbledon (1966) and again this year. Even the U.S.L.T.A. has had to acknowledge her as the best woman tennis player in the world.

It is Billie Jean's early-developed ability to play an all-round game that has brought her to this peak, plus the sheer speed of a well-tuned body. "She's a hell of an athlete," says Arthur Ashe, the top-ranked American amateur. "That's the most important thing for a woman. Forget the strokes—if you can move on your feet, you can win." And her husband Larry adds, "She can run down balls that other girls won't even try for."

Billie Jean originally used a "Continental" grip, but now she has modified this so it is closer to the more standard "Eastern" grip. She also has changed rackets. She now uses a new steel-frame racket which she claims is faster and whippier than the old wooden ones.

Her strongest shot is her volley at the net. Her backhand (which she can hit with topspin, underspin or even sidespin) is stronger than her forehand. Her main serve is the standard slicer, although occasionally she will change pace by offering a flat serve, harder for the server to control. For the second serve she can utilize either the spin or the American twist, the latter a serve most other girls can't master because of the strain imposed on back and stomach muscles. . . .

Does Billie Jean deserve to be ranked with the great women tennis players of the past? Perry T. Jones, president of the Southern California Tennis Association, says: "Mrs. King so far is the best of her day. That is, 1967. . . . I can't put Mrs. King in the same class with somebody like Suzanne Lenglen or Helen Wills Moody, who won Wimbledon eight times. She's going to have to stand the test of time before she can be ranked as one of the all-time greats." . . . According to Jack Kramer: "I don't think she's reached the caliber of the real best of the Americans I've seen—such as Helen Wills Moody or Alice Marble or Maureen Connolly or Pauline Betz—and I think that Margaret Smith and Maria Bueno at their top would have an edge. But I think she's about ready to jump into that group."

ARTHUR ASHE

by Frank DeFord

Among the tennis trophies arrayed in the living room of the Ashe home in Richmond, Virginia, is a decree attesting—quite officially, with one pompous "whereas" after another—to the honors and attributes of Arthur Ashe Jr. and to the fame that he has brought to his native city. The house, marked for demolition now, is at the edge of Brookfield Park, a Negro playground where Arthur Ashe Sr. is guardian and caretaker. The park includes two major recreational facilities, though one of them, a pool, no longer holds any water. Richmond, in another, but less inspired, moment declared that it was better to empty all its pools than to permit the races to cool off together.

About midway between the wasted pool and the warm words on the living-room wall is the tennis court where the young man who may someday be the best player in the world started to learn the game. Somehow he also learned to endure the capriciousness of a time that so arbitrarily gives and takes from his race. He is the only Negro player in a white tennis world. He is very easy to spot. But he sometimes has difficulty finding himself, for he must also serve as an image, that of the American Dream, minority division. Further, because of his unique status, he is invariably pestered by fawning Negroes whom he does not know and by patronizing whites keen to display their latent brotherhood now that they have a colored boy right here at the club.

It is a difficult role for a 23-year-old, but Ashe bears it all with ease. "His head is not big enough," says Dr. Walter Johnson, an old coach and friend. "He tries to be too accommodating and popular with everyone." Nevertheless, were Ashe not possessed of mature balance and a discerning appreciation of the ironies about him, it is not likely that he would ever have become the 100th player in the nation, much less the best or second best. It is often that whites—whether out of condescension or sincerity—say of him: "There would be no race trouble if all Negroes were like Arthur Ashe." But the complete response is: there would be no race trouble if all *people* were like Arthur Ashe.

Ashe's qualities, such as his stability, have derived from a large reservoir of family strength. His development has been further enhanced by able advisers at every level. Still, the prime influence remains his father, a proud man with a deep sense of honor. Arthur Ashe Sr., 47, is stocky and slightly Oriental-looking, with a philosophy to match: "No one will care a hundred years from now." It helped to sustain him through a deprived childhood and the loss of a wife. That the philosophy is not lost on Arthur Jr. helps explain why he can so easily accept victory or defeat in a mere tennis game with apparent equanimity.

Ashe evidences so little concern when he plays that he is often accused of being lazy, of simply not caring. "I've heard it so often that I'm beginning to believe it myself," he says. His coaches disagree. George MacCall and Pancho Gonzales, the U.S. Davis Cup team captain and coach, and J. D. Morgan, the UCLA athletic director and former tennis coach, all marvel at Ashe's ability to pace himself. Morgan also notes that Ashe shows at least some emotion on the court now. When he first arrived at college he was much too shy and introverted.

But Ashe is always trying to check himself. "No matter how tense I am inside," he says, "I will never blow up on the court. If you want to know, I'm just too conscious of the effect it might have on my image. Wait, next question: And do you worry about your image, Arthur? You're damn right I do."

It is ridiculous that there should be any debate at all on the question of whether Arthur's court conduct is too restrained. After all, Americans have suffered far too long with petulant young tennis tigers. But people just like to worry about Arthur. They are particularly determined to know if he has that great American athlete virtue, the fire that is supposed to separate the men from the boys. That is, the killer instinct. Everybody who boosts Arthur says you bet he has the killer instinct. Kid from a minority, had to fight his way up, may look loose out there, but such determination.

"Killer instinct? O.K., let's be hypothetical," Ashe says, tilting up the glasses he wears most of the time off the court. "O.K., it's the Davis Cup. Challenge round, Australia. Uh-huh. Two matches apiece. O.K., and I'm playing Emerson. Do I have a killer instinct? No. Sorry. I just don't have a killer instinct. I play the game. That's me. I give it all I've got—people are wrong about that—but if it's not enough I figure they'll just get someone else."

His demeanor on the court was shaped by Dr. Johnson, a Negro general practitioner in Lynchburg, Virginia, who was Ashe's first coach away from Brookfield. To limit controversy as his player broke color lines, Dr. Johnson invoked rules of tennis nonviolence long before such strategy became a widely employed device. He instructed Arthur and other young charges to play balls hit an inch or so out by opponents as if they were good shots, and he told them to smile at their mistakes. Ashe still does. It drives teeth-gritting, racket-throwing opponents to distraction. "They think I must be goofy," Arthur says.

Ashe was discovered at Brookfield by Ronald Charity, a part-time playground instructor who is now a partner in CJL Associates, a successful public relations firm in Richmond. Charity remembers: "It was difficult to tell whether Arthur was dragging the racket or the racket was dragging Arthur, but he was soon so obviously good that I arranged to have him go to Dr. Johnson's for a summer. It was one place a Negro could get teaching and good competition."

In spite of his limited means, Dr. Johnson is a true philanthropist. He has helped young Negro players for two decades now. National women's champion Althea Gibson was previously his most famous graduate. . . . Dr. J., as they call him, puts them up, feeds them (Arthur, Dr. J. recalls, had a weird craving for rice), teaches them and carries them around to tournaments. They practice and play on his court—all day and even into the evening under the lights. . . .

It was the same sort of sticky Southern summer when Arthur first came up to Lynchburg at the age of 10. "He was the youngest in the group and so skinny he looked like he had rickets," Dr. Johnson says. Ashe was not as good or as natural as many of the others, but he was quick, he had fast eyes and he always worked harder. The only time he caused any trouble was upon his arrival, when he refused to do anything that clashed with what Ronald Charity had taught him. Dr. Johnson called Arthur's father, who patiently explained to his son that it was Charity who had sent him here. He might as well come home if he was not going to do what Dr. Johnson said. Arthur listened to his father. He thought it over and stayed.

"I have never once in all my life talked back to my father," Arthur says. "My younger brother, Johnny—he's in the Marines ready to go to Vietnam now—he'd question him sometimes, and I'd shudder. I'd feel awful if I ever did anything at all bad that my father found out about. He trusts me completely."

Ashe's mother, Mattie Cunningham Ashe, died when he was 6, following an operation. Ronald Charity remembers . . . when Mr. Ashe came out of the house and called Arthur. Charity watched the skinny little boy go to his father and then into the house with him, where he learned the news. "Well, Daddy, as long as we are together," Arthur said, "everything will be all right."

Ashe Sr. maintains that nothing Arthur has done since has made him so proud. "Look at these trophies," he says, his arm sweeping over the living room. "I'd just as soon take them, the ones in the attic and that placard from the city, and throw them all into the junk heap if he ever did anything to disgrace me." . . .

Mr. Ashe refused to farm his sons out to relatives but instead brought in a housekeeper until he remarried a few years later. He was determined to have a family life, as he had not had as a boy, and he was keeping a promise to his wife. . . .

It is his mother that Arthur takes after, in manner and appearance. On the mantel there is a picture of Mattie Ashe, an elegant, lovely lady in a long pink dress. The delicate features and the light skin are almost perfectly repeated in her oldest son. "Arthur Jr. has always been just like her," Mr. Ashe says. "Timid, quiet. She wouldn't swap three words with anyone. She wouldn't argue with a soul."

Despite this resemblance, Ashe's determination and ease, as well as his athletic ability, most surely come from his paternal forebears, especially Edward Ashe, the amazing man who was Arthur Ashe Sr.'s father. And Arthur Jr. shares something else with his grandfather—an ambiguous racial situation. For in a race-conscious society Edward Ashe had to manage as neither white nor black. He was half American Indian, half Mexican and known as Pink Ashe. "He wore a big turned-up mustache out to here," Arthur Sr. says. . . .

Arthur Sr. has been as diligent as his father was flamboyant. He came to Richmond from Lincolnton, North Carolina, to work for $2.50 a week. Now, besides his city park job, he has his own landscaping business. He has two trucks for that, a car and a 21-foot motorboat, and he has just built a new house out in Louisa County with virtually nothing but his own two hands.

Arthur Jr. is the distillation of such conflicting strains. "The most impressive thing is that he is so able to take things as they are," says Charlie Pasarell, his best friend, teammate and roommate at UCLA. "He can be absolutely objective. I think of Arthur as a multiracial person."

"My favorite quote is Voltaire's," Ashe says. "I disapprove of what you say but I will defend to the death your right to say it." This is hardly a revelation, for Mr. Ashe reared Arthur with his own favorite homemade homily: "Respect everyone, whether they respect you or not."

"I worry sometimes that I'm too open-minded," Arthur Jr. says. "But then, being open-minded and strongly convicted just can't go hand in hand, can they? And, besides, I have opinions on everything. I'm always thinking. I don't care how tired I am. Once I get into bed I can't go to sleep for an hour. There's just so much to think about. Really, I mean it. Ask me about anything and I'll have an opinion right on the tip of my tongue."

Unfortunately, too much of this intellectual meandering takes place on court. Most players agree that the best way to beat Ashe is just to hang with him until his concentration starts to wander or until his booming service begins to falter. His serve is much the best among the amateurs. It is almost entirely the result of flowing coordination, since he scatters only 147 pounds over six feet and looks, when serving, like a bow and arrow. But more often than not the serve disappears in tandem with the concentration. "He wins or loses every match," says George Toley, the University of Southern California coach. "Nobody really beats him in that sense."

Ashe does not have a stroke that can be rated poor, although his forehand and second serve are the more vulnerable aspects of his game. At his peak, he cannot be touched. He slaughtered Pancho Gonzales 6–0 in Jamaica one day last spring. "And listen," Gonzales emphasizes, "I was really trying. I was playing, I tell you, it was the greatest set of tennis I ever saw played; yes, including any of the ones I played." But Ashe's inability to concentrate and his predilection for experiment hold him back.

"I guess," says UCLA's J. D. Morgan, "that the biggest thing he has going for him is also his biggest fault—his imagination." Arthur himself is quite in agreement.

"I'll start thinking about anything but the match—girls, a horse race. I don't know. At Sydney this past year, I was playing John Newcombe in the finals. I won the first set. Then all of a sudden I started thinking about this stewardess, Bella, I had met. Oh-h-h-h. She was Miss Trinidad of 1962. I just kept seeing her—this gorgeous face, this beautiful creature—and the next thing I know the match is over and Newcombe's won." . . .

Ashe searches for such inadequacies in himself. In the same way, he likes to uncover reasons to fret about the spate of good things that have happened to him. He feels guilty that he won a free college education. He is depressed that he travels all over the world and is no longer impressed by it. He graduated from UCLA in June with a B-minus average and a feeling that he should have done better, since it "came so easy." He seems constantly in pursuit of a trauma, as if concerned over his inability to be disturbed like normal people.

Instead, he adapts so well that he even got to liking the Army this summer when he had to serve six weeks at a R.O.T.C. camp. Typically, he volunteered for KP and other odious tasks so that he could not be accused of slacking. "He's worried about the Cassius Clay thing," Pancho Gonzales says. Ashe finished second in his platoon in over-all achievement and will be inducted into active service for two years in February as a second lieutenant in the Adjutant General's Corps. . . .

"I don't know how the Army, the two years, will affect Arthur's tennis career," Gonzales says, "but I know this. He is at peace in his mind. He won't duck a thing, and he won't let anybody down."

Ashe himself is fully aware of the special responsibilities that weigh upon him. "You never forget that you are a Negro, and you certainly can't in my case," he says. . . . "It's not unusual for me to go a month without a date. Of course, wherever I go there are usually Negroes who look me up. But that can be difficult. I try to be nice, but I'm fickle, I'm choosy no matter what your race happens to be. And however well-meaning these people are, I just can't embrace them because we happen to be the only two lumps of coal in the snowbank.

"For me it's a phony world." He stopped to consider that. "No, that's not fair. That's wrong. It isn't a phony world. It's an *abnormal* world I live in. I don't belong anywhere. It's like I'm floating down the middle. I'm never quite sure where I am. I guess Charlie is my best friend, but I never felt that we were really as close as we should be. It's simply that he's white and I'm Negro. I joined a Negro fraternity at UCLA. You know, I felt I had to at least make the effort. But I was never really part of it—our interests were so different. It's just this: no matter how you happen to look at it, the two things—tennis and a Negro social life—are mutually exclusive."

In many ways being a Negro serves to accentuate the nomadic, lonely life of the tennis circuit. "I'd like to get married now. I really would," he sheepishly admits. A year ago the idea repelled Ashe, but most of his tennis contemporaries are married, and it seems to be getting to him. "It'd be nice to have someone. I mean, the last thing I am is a loner. I'm a real extrovert around people I know. I have to have noise. I carry a radio around all the time."

This spring, "strictly on one of his crazy impulses," according to Pasarell, Ashe got himself engaged. The memory makes him more sheepish. It made all the columns before Ashe and his girl decided against it.

"But I do get lonely," he says, "and it does bother me that I'm in this predicament. But I don't dwell on it, because I know it will resolve itself. If I valued peace of mind or security more than tennis I could get off the tightrope now, and I will someday. Then, things being the way they are, I'll fall back onto the Negro side."

Before that (and after the Army) it is probable—though not yet settled in is mind—that he will turn pro. To be a prime asset, however, he must first win one of the big ones—Wimbledon or Forest Hills—or be the decisive factor in a Davis Cup challenge. Ashe's game is now at a level where all of this is quite possible. . . .

After Forest Hills, Ashe may well pass Dennis Ralston and become the No. 1 U.S. player. He should be ranked no lower than fifth in the world. The pros are already drooling. Not only does he have the big exciting game, but as the first Negro pro—apparently Ashe is forever doomed to being identified as the first Negro something-or-other—he has special drawing quality. . . .

Ashe is already on a retainer to promote Coca-Cola and he has been hired by Philip Morris Incorporated to work in its Clark Gum and American Safety Razor divisions. . . .

"A lot of people say I should do more boasting and bragging about Arthur Jr.," Mr. Ashe says. "But that can get aggravating. I plan to live to 100—and I'll never make it that way." . . .

Last year in Dallas, two days before the Davis Cup round with Mexico, the most important match of Ashe's career at that point, he had to attend a fancy luncheon in a tall building. He was able finally to escape to a far corner and hide there with some friends. Suddenly, however, he spied two determined matrons steering toward him. He knew their look.

"Uh-uh," he said, "here come the ones who have been assigned to put me at ease." He smiled. "Why does everyone want to put me at ease?" he asked. "I *am* at ease. I'm *always* at ease." The two ladies came and took him away. They did their duty. Arthur put them at ease.

JOHN NEWCOMBE

by Frank DeFord

At 23, John Newcombe is handsome, attractive, popular, quick, confident and—as winner at Wimbledon in July—champion of the amateur tennis world. He fears no one except his fellow Australian, Roy Emerson—and that fear is more one of respect for an elder than an actual competitive concern. Newcombe's powerful services and strokes can eventually wear down and crush the most diligent of opponents and he should, without great difficulty, win the U.S. singles championship that is under way at Forest Hills this week.

Newcombe is a strong young man in top shape, fit and taut—yet he has achieved this stature comfortably and amiably, without denying himself the more pleasant blandishments of good fellowship. The "keg he put on" after his victory at New South Wales two years ago remains a party of some substantial legend. Nor were his ample baby blues altogether denied to the beautiful ladies who distribute themselves about tennis tournaments—prior to his marriage in February 1966 to the charming blond German player, Angelique Pfannenberg. . . .

Newcombe has such a warm, engaging personality and such bright championship prospects that in any other sport but tennis his future would be unlimited. But tennis is not a game for these times, and Newcombe already anticipates retirement in about four years. Contradictions like this abound in tennis. Newcombe's style is power and attack—the same charged-up essentials that dominate and give bone to practically every other sport. But in tennis the power game is repetitive, lifeless—the serve-and-volley offense has all the eloquence and plot a recital of the alphabet would provide.

Newcombe's game bores most spectators, but the high level of competence he has brought it to amazes most of his countrymen, who are rather surprised that he is champion. They invariably describe him, sparingly, if politely, as "craftsman" or "tradesman." Says Sydney tennis columnist Alan Clarkson, "What we need is a colorful player. Newcombe just isn't the answer." . . .

In the rest of the world Newcombe is dismissed as "another Aussie"—just as Emerson, another Australian craftsman, was before him. Newcombe thinks his style is similar to Emerson's, although he believes he depends on the serve more than Emerson does. But Newcombe does not agree that his game is mere serve and volley. "The game we play—I play, the Australians play—is to pressure an opponent," he says. "Serve and volley works best—so we use it. But it's just a means to an end. We could change.

"I think one of the reasons for our success is that we always have had such good leaders to look up to, to follow. I'm certainly influenced by Emerson, but the basic game we all play can be traced back to Sedgman and Mc-Gregor. Rosewall was the only major exception. Maybe if Hoad hadn't come at the same time as Rosewall we would all have been ground-strokers after that."

Fred Stolle, a pro now but the man who beat Newcombe in the dreary serve-and-volley final at Forest Hills last year, was visiting his old cohorts and "checking out to see how they pay the amateurs this year—under the table or over it." Newcombe called over to him, "Hey, Fred, if I wanted to play the pros, what would I have to improve? My backhand and my second serve, would you say?"

"I guess so," Stolle answered, "but that comes with play. It's more the thinking you have to improve—which shots to try for winners off of."

"That's the truth," Newcombe said. "That's true with me. It comes from confidence—knowing your shots. Instead of going for silly shots and missing, you know to hit the right ones. You do that twice a set at 30–40, say, and in two shots you can turn the whole set around."

"That comes with time," Stolle said. "People are always amazed when we come up with another champion. Where did he come from? Well, look at John. Only 23, sure, but this was his seventh year at Wimbledon. You look back. All our winners—even the ones who win it young, like John—seven years. I got in the final after four."

"But you didn't win," Newcombe said.

"That's my point," Stolle said.

If anyone were to have broken that pattern, it should have been New-combe. At 19—when he had *seen* Davis Cup competition only once—he was picked over Stolle and Neale Fraser to play singles in the challenge round. He had excellent chances in both his matches—against Chuck McKinley and Dennis Ralston—but lost both. His mother, Lillian, remembers that John came home without depression. "Well, I lost, but I did my best," he told her evenly. "And I needed the experience."

Today, however, Newcombe feels that the unusually early Davis Cup adventure somehow inhibited his career. "I can't really say how," he says, "but I've got the feeling that it set me back, if only psychologically." And, in fact, it was not until Newcombe made the final at Forest Hills last year that the logjam in his career was finally broken again. Shortly thereafter he finally beat Emerson for the first time, an experience more therapeutic, perhaps, than Forest Hills. And then, in a series of events, Newcombe's world competition faded before him. Stolle and Ralston turned pro. Manuel Santana had a serious ankle operation. Arthur Ashe went into the Army. Tony Roche came up overtennised and stale. Emerson, 30 now, came up old. Can he come back? Emmo turns his thumb to the ground. "The only way left to go," he says. And then, cryptically, shaking his head toward Newcombe, just: "John."

There are a few who could upset Newcombe at Forest Hills—Charlie Pasarell on one of his unpredictable good days; Emerson on a young day; lefties Pilic or Roger Taylor of England on a day they outslug Newcombe. But Newcombe really should be a more overwhelming favorite than his record suggests. On grass, anyway, he could dominate the game for the next few years.

The potential for such excellence has been evident practically since he was 9 and first learning to play tennis in the street in front of the home his parents still live in, in Longueville, a Sydney suburb. Exceptional athletic ability was in the family—a cousin, Warren Bardsley, was one of Australia's great cricketeers—but John's father, George Newcombe, a retired dentist, did not play tennis, and his mother and two sisters have been no more than casual social players.

When John was only 11, Newcombe's parents were already concerned that he was devoting too much time to tennis, and by the time he was 16 all hope for a respectable accountant's career—which he had envisioned—went careening into obscurity when Newcombe became the third youngest player ever named to an Australian overseas team. No wonder his countrymen find him such an old letdown at 23. . . .

But he is champion now, and the suspicion here is that he is not going to be the nondescript everyday type that he has already been written off as. The confidence that is now turning tentative shots into winners seems capable of transmuting the accountant's entire game into one with a champion's flash and style. The big game, so repetitive and jejune, could become thunderous and ebullient. Even now, Newcombe plays the net with his own special daring—on top of it, challenging like a third baseman moving in close, defying a potential bunter to hit away. And his on-court peculiarities—shirttail out, tousled towhead, a large inurbane grunt that he dispenses with each serve—can become crowd-pleasing characteristics. The considerable charm of the private Newcombe is unlikely to remain hidden within the public one. He may well prove to be a special Aussie, and not just another one.

FRED STOLLE

from the New York Times

Hunched over, waiting for a serve, Fred Sidney Stolle looks like a dehydrated octopus. With only 162 pounds stretched tightly around a 6-foot-3-inch frame, he has elbows and knees that jut out like stunted tentacles.

But when he uncoils, the former cricketeer moves with a fluid grace that has propelled him to the finals of the world's major tennis championships during his career. Yet, until he won the United States singles championship yesterday at Forest Hills, Queens, Stolle had been blanketed in the shadow of his countryman and teammate, Roy Emerson.

Stolle had firmly established himself as sports' most consistent runner-up. For three straight years, from 1963 through 1965, he had finished second, twice to Emerson, in the Wimbledon championship. He had been beaten three times in the final of the Australian championship and once, by Emerson, at Forest Hills.

However, the blond, blue-eyed Australian rarely allowed his frustration to show. The top Australian tennis players are trained and disciplined in behavior. It is said they are drilled in table manners, how to make speeches and how to behave with spectators and officials.

So Stolle developed a dry sense of humor and plugged away. He rose to the No. 3 ranking in the world, won the French championship in 1965 and developed a sharp business acumen.

On the court, Stolle talks to himself, sometimes exclaiming, "I don't believe it!" when an opponent makes an exceptionally good shot.

He has turned down a $60,000 offer to be a professional. Like most top amateurs, he can be choosy. Employment in a public relations capacity for cigarette and sporting goods companies plus expenses paid to him as a member of the Australian national team, make him financially solvent.

"I'm not interested in being just another pro," he said yesterday. "If they want to talk real money, I'll listen."

While a youngster Stolle earned spending money as a ball boy on the Sydney courts. He showed promise in cricket, but as the wicket keeper he kept getting his hands banged up, so his mother ordered him to stick to tennis.

He progressed slowly. As a junior (age 18 and under), he ranked only seventh in Australia. But at 22 he was good enough to be named to the official Australian touring team.

Stolle (pronounced Stahlee) first gained international prominence in 1962, when he teamed with Bob Hewitt to win the Wimbledon doubles title. Last year he beat Manuel Santana and Juan Gisbert in singles as Australia turned back Spain in the Davis Cup challenge round. He has teamed with Emerson and Hewitt to win many other doubles titles.

Stolle was born in Sydney on October 8, 1938. He lives there in an attractive house built a year ago. His wife Pat, an Australian country girl, decorated the house while he was touring and surprised him when he returned. They have a 21-month-old daughter, Monique.

Stolle, who capitalizes on a powerful serve and an attacking game, keeps in shape all the time but hates to run, which is part of the Australians' training regimen.

A few years ago he turned down the pro job at the prestigious All-England Club. Indications are he will be back on the amateur circuit in 1967.

"You hate to give it away when you are going so good," he said.

And, anyway, Big Bill Tilden, possibly the greatest tennis player ever, won quite a few major championships after he had turned 27.

ROBERT J. KELLEHER

by Bud Collins

On his first day as president of the U.S. Lawn Tennis Association, Bob Kelleher was bitten by a dog and threatened by a man with a machine gun. It may have been the least trying day of his first year in office and good preparation for leading an organization that, in terms of efficiency and coordination, rivals the New York Mets.

Kelleher's involvement with the belligerent dog and its armed master occurred in Puerto Rico where, searching for the home of a friend in a rural area, he was challenged as a trespasser. Though the hound was unconvinced of Kelleher's merit, the man with the machine gun was fairly reasonable and did not pull the trigger.

As Robert J. Kelleher, a Los Angeles lawyer out of Williams College and Harvard Law, winds up his first year in the unpaid job of presiding over amateur tennis in this country, several of his fellow officers have concluded that the dog in Puerto Rico had the right idea. These are the men who have kept tennis in the Victorian era, who consider themselves watchdogs guarding the old homestead—guarding it from progressing into the 20th century, that is.

Kelleher may be outdistancing the watchdogs, though (he prefers to classify them, zoologically, as "the old goats"). During the year he has moved ambitiously and impressively to pull the organization together—or at least to connect with a financial pipeline that will enable the musty USLTA to update itself in several ways. Most recently he has been vigorously campaigning to get the USLTA to allow U.S. amateurs to participate in an open Wimbledon. Whether or not he has convinced the old goats will be revealed this week in Coronado, California, when the organization holds its annual meeting and makes its decision.

Although southern California has produced more championship players than the other 16 sections of the USLTA combined—and Los Angeles is the country's tennis mecca—Kelleher is the first southern Californian to become chief executive of the 87-year-old organization. Maybe this isn't so strange. Sectionalism is strong in the USLTA. The East—the New England and Eastern sections—has nearly enough votes to run the show. Allied with the Western (Midwest) sections it can carry anything.

Apparently Kelleher was acceptable because he is a blend of East and West. Raised within a mile of the game's American showplace—The West Side Tennis Club—in Forest Hills, New York, he migrated to Los Angeles in 1940 with his wife, Gracyn, a Santa Monica native.

Foremost reason for Kelleher's near-universal appeal was his success as Davis Cup captain. His victory in 1963 over Australia brought the cup back to the U. S. for a brief visit, the only look Americans have had at it in five years, and it convinced tennis officials that Kelleher had supernatural powers. Kelleher accepted the nomination, he says, "primarily to keep the job from going to one of the backward old goats—some New Englander dedicated to tennis but completely out of touch with the sporting picture in America.

"Tennis is a marvelous sport to play and watch," says Kelleher, "but we've swallowed some of our own myths about its popularity. Look at the sports pages, look at TV. Where is tennis? It is a minor sport that has a chance to realize its potential as a healthful recreational and consequential spectator sport if it will get up-to-date."

Such frankness does not please the old goats, few of whom can see beyond their own sectional strongholds and club gates. To them, a crowd of 2,000 at a big match is a major happening.

Soon after his inauguration, moving so quickly that the goats had no time to butt in, Kelleher made three significant moves in the USLTA's behalf: 1) he became a client of Licensing Corporation of America, which could mean added income of $50,000 to $100,000 annually for the USLTA; 2) he signed a deal with Madison Square Garden for a yearly international indoor tournament in the new building, which will give amateur tennis its first exposure in a prime Manhattan arena and put a minimum of $30,000 in the kitty; and 3) he hired the organization's first full-time salaried executive assistant, Bob Malaga of Cleveland, whose role corresponds to that of Joe Dey in golf.

A tall, easy-moving, dark-haired man of 54, Kelleher periodically asks himself, understandably, "What am I doing this for?" He can sit on the bricked terrace in front of his handsome home—an aerie in the Coldwater Canyon section of Beverly Hills—and peer across Los Angeles to the Pacific and Catalina Island. His lighted tennis court is at his feet, and next door is the only clay court in Los Angeles, belonging to Ginger Rogers. Kelleher has often played there.

As USLTA president there is little time for sitting on the terrace with his wife, two children and their collie. The ceremonial appearances demanded of the president keep him on the road most of the time. His own tennis game suffers, and the summer home on the beach near San Diego is hardly used. The Kellehers have been married 27 years. Gracyn Wheeler was Bob's best win when he was playing the Eastern Circuit during the late '30s. He was a good college player, winning the Eastern Intercollegiate Doubles for Williams. He still plays well, having stood as national Senior Hard Court Doubles champ in 1958, 1959, 1960 and 1962. But it was by marrying Gracyn that he forever etched the name Kelleher in the national rankings. She was No. 5 among the women in 1940.

Kelleher's progressive thinking naturally has made him a number of enemies in the conservative, old USLTA. "Money, money, money—that's all Kelleher and Malaga think about," says one oldtimer. "There's too much emphasis on tournaments and talk about opens. Open tennis will kill the amateur game as we know it."

"Possibly," says Kelleher, "open tennis would diminish the current amateur fixtures. I don't know." But he does know that people who talk about "the great amateur game" are dreaming and that none of the top amateurs have been actually amateur for about 40 years. Kelleher thinks that opens might bring the game into perspective. If pros become the stars he won't mind very much. "I would hope the USLTA would take steps to control open play—as the USGA does the U.S. Golf Open—to profit by it. And perhaps then the USLTA would slowly go back to what it was intended to be—an organization to spread the gospel of tennis on an elementary level."

HAMTRAMCK

by Fred Kovaleski

Fifteen years ago, Hamtramck had one court, no players and a budding coach, Jean Hoxie. The town is a typical industrial center. Probably 85% of the residents work for Ford, Dodge or Chrysler, and 99% of the population are second-generation Slavic. The town depends completely on the automotive industry. If there is a strike or autos take a turn for the worse, the people are affected immediately.

Tennis in Hamtramck was always connected with money and fancy country clubs. To the second-generation Slavs, tennis was for the aristocracy. They favored strong backs, big muscles and football. When I was twelve, I remember walking from my house to the courts at the junior high school carrying my racket. At least two or three times a month I would get in a fight with a couple of kids before they would let me by. The enthusiasm for tennis in Hamtramck was on the same level as their desire to learn the finer points of hopscotch.

Mrs. Hoxie used to drum up trade for the tennis courts by invading the schools and picking out the best handball players. When I was eleven, I won the grade school handball championship and was immediately collared by Mrs. Hoxie and whisked off to Hamtramck's asphalt court.

She actually started us out on a wall in the school gym. She drew a line and had us play games of five points similar to handball except that we used only one wall. She had wastebaskets filled with balls. We would serve a couple of hundred, then hit a few hundred forehands and backhands. She had the temperament of a volcano and transmitted to us her enthusiasm for the "patsy game."

Hamtramck was no Newport. No one dreamt of going down to the local sports store and ordering a new racket or of paying the local professional for weekly lessons. Mrs. Hoxie never charged for lessons and provided the rackets and balls. She bought the first three rackets I ever owned. She dug in her own pocket for tennis clothes, trips and equipment and when the expenses were too big, she talked the city into helping.

In the summers, Mrs. H. piled us into her Dodge and we took off for the tournaments. I traveled with her on the circuit for four years, often driving until late at night to get to the next tournament. During these hours in the car, I got my education. She taught me clothes, manners, neatness, deportment, etc. I remember when I was in junior high school she gave me some tennis shirts that buttoned up to the neck. I was indoctrinated by her to button the top button, and in spite of pointed remarks from the Falkenburg brothers and the 100-degree heat during 5-set matches, I never unbuttoned it!

All of us were from Polish families with 9-syllable last names, all consonants. Almost all of us went to college through her efforts. She would arrange some sort of scholarship and she would see that we got there. As a matter of fact, she could arrange anything. In the evenings when I had a date, she would see that I had a corsage for the girl and a convertible to call for her. She was a coach, a teacher, a friend and a second mother to me.

Mrs. Hoxie was heavy on the guts department, her slogan being "I like 'em when they fight!" She was through with me once when I lost a bad match as a junior. I was sixteen and was playing in the Michigan State Championships. My opponent was a mediocre player from California, but when I heard where he was from, I dropped dead. I was a steady player at the time but I actually threw the match that day by clobbering every ball as hard as I could in an "I can't win it anyway so I might as well slam 'em" attitude.

She was through with me several other times. Once I was late for a team match because I had a flat tire. I didn't phone, and when I finally arrived at the courts, I was sternly reprimanded and bounced off the team.

When we were beginners she arranged for good players to come to Hamtramck as often as possible to give us tough competition. When I went away to college, she would corner me on my vacations and get me to play with the younger kids at the State Fairgrounds Indoors Courts. As we grew older, a new bunch of Hamtramck kids took our places. After Gene Russell and me came Ted Jax, Alex Hetzeck, Elaine Lewicki, Jerry Parchute, June Stack, Phyllis Saganski and Gwen McEvans. In all, her pupils won 19 National Championships and Mrs. Hoxie herself received the National Sports Award, the Coach of the Year Award and the honor of being Woman of the Year in 1952.

I am sorry, because of her, I never got in the first five of our rankings. She had so much trust in my ability that my biggest regret is that I didn't give tennis a more serious try. Like all her pupils, I followed her most important precept. "Play tennis a couple of years after college, then settle down to a respectable job." I would probably still be playing if it hadn't been for her.

The players in Hamtramck don't have to hide their rackets or knock off a few heads on their way to the courts any more. Over 300 kids in the

Pulaski School have their own rackets. There are eight courts instead of one. There are indoor courts instead of a wall in the gym with a line drawn across it. The Polish town of Hamtramck has finally been Australianized by a fiery, enthusiastic Irish woman!

STEEL RACKETS

by Charles Friedman

"It's faster, whippier."

"It takes a lot of adjusting."

"My serve is 30 per cent more effective."

"I wouldn't trust it; too dangerous to control."

Fans at Forest Hills are excited about the controversial steel tennis racket being used in the national championships for the first time. In fact, the round-headed racket, developed by René Lacoste, the old-time French Musketeer, is almost as popular a topic of conversation as who will win what has become, through casualties, a wide-open tournament.

On opening day, Jean Borotra, the 70-year-old Bounding Basque, another of the unforgettable Musketeers, walked onto the court and unveiled the racket. It had already been used in United States tournaments, but never at Forest Hills.

The old warrior flailed away with it and gallantly went down to defeat in the senior division. He missed a lot of shots, but never, as many players do, did he look at the racket as if to say, "You're to blame, you rat, not me."

And, at the end, he lovingly tucked it under his arm, convinced that it was not his comrade, Lacoste, who had let him down, but plain old hardening of the arteries.

The racket is made of chrome-plated tubing and stainless wire, a frame supposedly more durable and resilient than wood, much like the steel-shafted golf clubs, which first gave Lacoste the idea. It takes conventional nylon or gut stringing. A major innovation is the open throat, which reduces wind resistance in the act of stroking. The theory is that this results in a faster, more powerful shot.

While many top players have besieged the Wilson Sporting Goods Company, which manufactures it, for information about the racket, only nine have made the switch from wood for the nationals. They are Mrs. Billie Jean King, Rosemary Casals, Kathy Harter, Chuck McKinley, Clark Graebner and his wife, Carole, and Stephanie DeFina, Gene Scott, Joaquin Loyo-Mayo of Mexico.

Others are eager to try it, including Charlie Pasarell, but they are committed to the wooden rackets put out by rival manufacturers, which they get free, or are unwilling to change at this point of the season. Of course, they could buy the steel racket, but they'd better not get caught playing with it, or the free service ends. Also, they would have to spend $40 to $52 for it, the current retail price. That is about $10 to $22 more than what a first-class wooden racket costs.

For players who don't get rackets free, the difference in price apparently is not a great obstacle to sales of the Wilson T2000, as the "steelie" is labeled. It has hit the market hard in recent weeks through a combination of published advertising and comments by those using it.

For instance, when Mrs. King and Miss Casals showed up with it at the Eastern grass tournaments, they told everyone they were getting better results. Mrs. King, the Wimbledon champion and the top favorite in the nationals, said it gave her a faster, whippier stroke.

Immediately a host of players began looking for Joe Boggia, Wilson's liaison man, who travels the tournament circuit.

McKinley, the former Davis Cup hero and now a part-time player, surprisingly began showing the form of his glory years, earning the respect he used to command.

"I'm a little guy, which puts me at a disadvantage in serving," he said. "But the racket, I found, has put more power into my serve and I'm getting the ball in more often."

Scott said the only complaint he had was that the racket was so easy to maneuver that sometimes "I don't feel I'm part of the game." He conceded that it took time to adjust to it, "just as when the steel shaft was introduced in golf."

Mrs. Graebner, who has come back strongly after a year's retirement, during which she had a baby, wanted to play with the racket at Wimbledon, but Boggia couldn't get her more than two. Her husband confiscated one and she didn't want to be left with just the other for the big tournaments.

"I did pretty well with the wooden one at Wimbledon, so I'm continuing to use it for the rest of the season," said the attractive star. "But I'm going to switch to steel next year.

"That racket does all the work. The ball comes off so fast that your opponent finds it hard to tell where it's going. It gives you more touch and you can make more flick shots."

Her husband chimed in: "I like the feel of the ball on the strings. For me, it's easier to serve and volley."

For the average swinger, however, a few doubts persist, mainly on the matter of control.

"It seems that you just tip the ball and it goes over the baseline," said one. "I've found it good for certain shots and not so good for others. And I'm not sure whether to have it strung loosely or tightly, or with nylon or gut."

Another had this to say:

"It's strictly a fad thing. Let's face it. It's the player wielding the racket who tells the ball what to do, not the racket."

A woman club player said she was through with the racket after having given it a week's trial.

"See this," she said, pointing to a blood-scabbed shin. "That damn steel hurts like hell." Unfortunately she had a serving flaw.

ALUMINUM RACKETS

by Parton Keese

Tennis, which has undergone a revolution in the last few years with new scoring systems, synthetic playing surfaces, steel rackets and open tournaments, introduced an aluminum racket yesterday.

With this latest development, A. G. Spalding & Bros. brings a third alternative to tennis players who already can choose between wood and steel.

Wilson Sporting Goods Company, which pioneered the development of the steel racket, says the demand in the United States for its product is still greater than the supply. The Sterling Automotive Manufacturing Company of Elk Grove Village, Illinois, which last week came out with its own steel racket, with conventional stringing and a five-year guarantee, foresees a tremendous response from the public.

Jim Long, the vice president of product design for Spalding, explained at a news conference at the Vanderbilt Athletic Club here why Spalding had turned to aluminum.

"Not many people realize that Spalding, as far back as 1932, produced a racket with an aluminum bow and wooden shaft. But it wasn't until recently that the necessary technology—mainly from the aerospace industry—was able to come up with the alloys and extrusion processes to make a superior tennis racket."

Dennis Ralston and Cliff Drysdale, the barnstorming tennis pros, have been testing the new concept for the last few weeks and, with Doris Hart and Gardnar Mulloy, demonstrated the racket on the Vanderbilt's rubber courts.

"I like it a lot," Ralston said. "It's easier to get used to than the steel racket because it's less resilient and the ball doesn't fly off the surface as it does with steel. It's really more like a wood racket, except that there's much less wind resistance with the open throat, and it feels more controllable in your hand."

Ralston also thought it would take him only a month to become completely adjusted to aluminum, while Mulloy said with a smile that it should take him "only 10 minutes the way I'm playing."

"The best thing about this aluminum racket," Mulloy said, "is when you partly miss a shot or strike the ball on the edge of the frame, you don't get the terrific vibration as you do with wood."

"This," Long explained, "is because aluminum dampens vibration, while wood and steel don't." Long, who designed the revolutionary racket in the Chicopee, Massachusetts, plant, doesn't consider himself a tennis player, although he "fools around" at the game with his sons.

When his sons went back to school, they took the new racket with them to help test it, and they enjoyed telling fascinated observers that it was "just something our father designed for us."

The aluminum racket is a half-inch shorter than a wood model and round instead of oval. It is strung the same as wood, and Spalding has put a suggested price of $31 on an unstrung frame, which is comparable to the price of a steel racket. If the company's claims for durability come true, they may sell one racket to every player in the world and then take up another business.

JAMES H. VAN ALEN

by Allison Danzig

They don't laugh when Jimmy Van Alen sits down to the piano. They know that he can tickle those ivories—or the gut of a guitar or a ukulele.

They stopped laughing a long time ago at James H. (VASSS) Van Alen. He has a habit of seeing it through on anything he starts, and he has started some beauts. For openers, he started an intercollegiate tournament in the ancient game of kings, court tennis, and there isn't a college in the country that has a court. (The last private court that was built, in 1914, set Payne Whitney back a quarter of a million.)

Jimmy picked out some squash racquets players at Yale, Princeton and Harvard and arranged with the Racquet Clubs in New York, Boston and Philadelphia to permit them to use their court tennis facilities for free. In no time at all they picked up the intricate game so fast that he not only put on a successful tournament but within a year started an international match with Oxford-Cambridge.

For years the idea of a tennis hall of fame was kicked around and got nowhere. Then Jimmy stepped in and, presto! they opened the hall of fame in the Newport Casino, of which he is the overlord. Where could you have a more appropriate one than on the site of the national grass court championships from the first in 1881 through 1914? Moreover, Jimmy got enough Casino stockholders to donate their shares to give the hall of fame controlling interest, thereby assuring the permanence of its home.

The only thing I know of that ever licked Jimmy was his project of importing English robins. He thought our own red breasts were disgustingly bosomy and he formed a syndicate to replace them with their more svelte British cousins. Something went wrong somewhere. The imports wouldn't mate together over here, after the males popped an eye at the Mae Westian vital statistics of our aborigines, and Jimmy packed them off back to Piccadilly and dissolved the syndicate.

Another thing that disgusted Jimmy was going to a tennis tournament to see a particular match and never getting a peep at it because it was held up for hours by some dreary, interminable marathon ahead of it. He decided that deuce-advantage games and sets were an abomination—and the result was VASSS—the Van Alen Simplified Scoring System that uses the scoring method of table tennis, badminton and squash and makes it possible to control the length of a match to within a few minutes.

They called Jimmy a revolutionary and a lot of other things when he first tried to interest the U.S. Lawn Tennis Association in it. The fact is, he was being a reactionary. He was reverting all the way back to the beginnings of tennis in the 1870s. For the game was introduced with the badminton scoring. It was later that the 15, 30, 40, deuce-advantage scoring of court tennis was substituted.

It looked like a hopeless undertaking for Jimmy and VASSS. For several years it was good for a lot of laughs—especially half VASSS for juniors—and nothing more. But our hero is a bulldog for sinking his teeth into a fight and refusing to let go. He wrote letters and made trips all over the country, spreading the gospel and putting up money to help with the promotion and pay for the prizes for any tournament that would try VASSS, with its great advantages for handicapping. And he kept working on his system, changing it and eliminating the bugs.

He still wasn't getting anywhere much, outside of Newport, when last year the pros signed to play at the Casino and use his system. Bonanza! Eureka! At last, Jimmy had hit the jackpot.

Life, Sports Illustrated and the New York and Boston papers were there to record history as Gonzales, Laver, Rosewell and the rest played VASSS before big galleries. This year at the Vanderbilt A.C. in the Grand Central Building in New York, Santana, Ashe, McKinley, Pasarell, Osuna, Froehling and Scott played in a VASSS tournament that went over big. Now VASSS is coming to Forest Hills, with the top pros playing for $30,000 in prize money. A tournament was recently held in England with Jimmy's system, and things are popping around the country.

Last Laugh Van Alen has done it again.

A VASSSLY ENTERTAINING WEEKEND

by George McGann

Only Wimbledon and Jimmy had them—electric scoreboards, that is. But Jimmy conjured up far more for the wide-eyed galleries at his first VASSS tournament than was ever dreamed of in Wimbledon's philosophy. In addition to the scoreboards, which registered not only points played but money won by the competing professionals, Jimmy introduced a "loveless" tennis scoring system similar to ping pong and a service line drawn three feet behind the baseline to inhibit net-rushers; he rang a ship's bell to signal the end of matches and rigged up banks of lights for night play which created an other-worldly scene as fog swirled in from Narragansett Bay to the accompaniment of bellowing foghorns and whistling buoys. Unplanned, but adding a pop-art touch to the Van Alen concept of New Wave Tennis were town fireworks which crackled, sizzled and rocketed across the astonished heavens.

Somewhere in the fog out there, Luis Ayala was playing his fellow South American, Pancho Segura. It was Saturday night and the crowd was enjoying itself hugely. Not the least of the fun was trying to tell which player was which, particularly when the rolling fogbank obscured Segura's famed parenthetical underpinnings. At the stroke of 10 Ayala (I say it was Ayala; there are those who disagree) lifted his racket to serve, innocent of the knowledge that at that very moment the weekly Newport fireworks display was to start at the nearby town beach. As he threw up the ball, the first sky-rocket of the night canaveraled high overhead. Ayala (I think) watched it, fascinated. As it exploded with a wild crackle, he dropped racket and balls to the Casino turf and gracefully followed them in a ballerina's swoon, as if drilled through the heart by one of Jimmy's partridge guns. Not a few among the dazzled onlookers must have thought that Jimmy had planned the fireworks as he had the rest of the pyrotechnics that transformed the once-staid Newport Casino into a mad avant-garde arena for the most revolutionary weekend in the history of tennis. The thought that it was all happening on sacred soil in the Holy of Holies, the Casino where this whole tennis bit got started in America eighty-four years before, was nothing short of overwhelming. Pros at Newport? Electric cash registers? Who *is* this man Van Alen, anyway?

The joke is, of course, that Jimmy—a show in himself with his big-brimmed planter's hat, Casino-striped tie, beige slacks and suede shoes, all tethered to his dog VASSS (that's right)—is Mr. Newport Casino, born, reared and matured in its traditions and the only man on earth who could commercialize the charming old institution with such a radical format as this professional tournament and get away with it. Get away with it? The crowds were nuts about it. For days afterward Jimmy was stopped on

Bellevue Avenue by people who shook his hand, thanked him for putting VASSS into action after years of fruitless missionary work among the heathen of the USLTA, and begged him to repeat the show next year.

What seemed to get them all worked up about VASSS (Van Alen Simplified Scoring System) was that it intensified their enjoyment of the tennis produced by the talented troupe of Rod Laver, Ken Rosewall, Andres Gimeno, Mal Anderson, Pancho Gonzales, Pancho Segura, Butch Buchholz, Barry MacKay, Luis Ayala and Mike Davies.

The moved-back service line prevented the big hitters, particularly Gonzales (who never stopped screaming in protest) and Laver (who calmed down as he found he could win anyway), from rushing in after serving for the putaway volley and the quick winner. But it produced delightful rallies as players gradually worked their way to the net from the baseline. It put a premium on good ground strokes and, as Laver admitted, proved to be an "equalizer" for the less powerful servers. Jimmy Van Alen drew his service line for two reasons actually—not only to prolong rallies for the crowd's sake but to preserve the baseline turf of the main exhibition court, where all VASSS matches were played, for the sake of the amateur Newport Invitation Tournament scheduled to get under way six weeks later. Inasmuch as rain and nightly fog dampened the turf to the extent that the pros had to use spikes to remain upright, this precaution proved wise. (It might be noted that the special service line is not an integral part of the VASSS innovation; it is most effective on fast grass courts but might not be needed on slower surfaces.)

The heart of VASSS is its scoring system, which resembles that of ping pong. The 31-point set (or match) at Newport lasted one-half hour unless tied at 30–30, in which case it required about three minutes to play five more points to decide the issue. Jimmy Van Alen, who knows from long, bitter experience as a tournament director what a marathon five-set tennis match can do to the schedule, pointed delightedly to the statistics of the four days of play in the VASSS tournament. Ten matches were played daily (in afternoon and evening sessions) under a round-robin system which gave the spectators a chance to see *every player in action each day*. "That meant a total of two hours and thirty minutes of playing time," Jimmy gloated, "and we never exceeded it on any day by more than fifteen minutes!"

The pros were playing for a total of $10,000 put up by Jimmy, possibly with help from some wealthy friends, and each point won was worth a five-dollar bill to each pro—with the five dollars registering on the scoreboard along with the point. The scoreboards were specially constructed for the VASSS tournament by a shooting pal of Jimmy's and put Newport one up on every other tennis ground in America, most of which, including Forest Hills, still use primitive methods involving small boys and colored balls or cardboard numbers.

At the beginning the pros reacted in a decidedly unprofessional manner towards the radical Van Alen innovations. Losers griped loudly; winners found VASSS vasssinating. One of the Latin Americans complained about "Senor Vassseline's goofy system." Pancho Gonzales demonstrated a remarkable lack of maturity in taking a 31–16 trouncing from Andres Gimeno on Saturday night in the fog. The big ex-champion of the world yelped throughout the match, firing a linesman, moaning about the lighting and generally misbehaving like a tennis brat half his age. Pancho packed his bags after that walloping and stalked out of the dressing room, ready to desert his doubles partner à la Dennis Ralston, but he was physically restrained by his wife from leaving the Casino grounds. At 37 Gonzales is obviously facing the moment of truth about his career and finding it highly unpalatable. . . .

Laver, the eventful winner, was unhappy about the whole thing after Ayala murdered him in his first VASSS match. "Bloody ridiculous!" exploded the redhaired southpaw. But by the time Rod had won his way through to the finals he was far more receptive to the new system. Said he: "It was tough coming onto grass after playing on hard courts, then trying to cope with the new service line and a 31-point match. It took a while to learn. The system needs a longer trial before you can make up your mind about it." . . .

All three of Laver's matches on the final night were see-saw battles in which he had to come from behind to win. In the last contest of the tournament, Laver took an early edge of 9–0 over Rosewall, who bounced back to lead 15–10. Rosewall ground out a 23–16 lead, mainly on Laver's errors. But Rod fought back, taking the last four points in a row for a 31–28 victory, top money of $1,770.25 (including victory in doubles with Buchholz) and the gleaming silver Cartier Cup—donated by *the* Cartier's of Fifth Avenue and Paris. The fact that Laver, who has won more matches and more money than the rest of the pros on the current American tour, also emerged on top in the VASSS contest, seemed to dissipate early arguments that it was not a "true test" of tennis ability.

Butch Buchholz, who failed to reach the final round, was open-minded nevertheless. "I think we should give VASSS a chance," he said. "That's the trouble with tennis. Nobody wants to change anything. If golf had been like that it would not have become the hottest thing on TV. Golf tried an open and medal play. This is medal play in tennis." At the Saturday night dance on the Casino porch, Butch told Jimmy: "This is the most exciting week we've ever had on the tour."

Jimmy called in his old friend, Frank Pace, to "talk sense" to the pros when they were in the acute griping stage. Pace, former Secretary of the Army and a leading industrialist, is an ardent golfer and former college tennis player. As president of the International Golf Association he had much to do with the enormous growth of that sport in recent years, particularly on television, where the pros dominate the screen on weekends in specially staged matches.

"Pro tennis needs a gimmick to sell itself to the public on TV," Pace pointed out. "VASSS could be it. The point-scoring system can be understood by anyone switching to a tennis match for the first time. The length of matches can be precisely fitted to TV time segments. And the extended rallies give the public a better show." Jimmy Van Alen, who puts his money where his mouth is, promptly offered the pros a $2,000 donation to produce a TV pilot film using VASSS which could be shown to networks and sponsors. . . .

Jimmy, who never doubted for a moment that the VASSS experiment would work, spent the weekend on a cloud of euphoria as matches proceeded with clocklike regularity, as the long rallies brought cries of delight from the galleries and as the crowds streamed through the portals of the rococo Casino, groping their way through night fog to their seats in the quaint old relic of a grandstand. Criticism from disgruntled players left him untouched. He carried an article by Bud Collins of the Boston *Globe* about with him and insisted on reading it in its entirety to acquaintances—even this passage:

"One of the players suggested that Jimmy borrow the Liberty Bell because it and Jimmy would make a great couple—they're both cracked." "Isn't that marvelous?" Jimmy chortled each time he read the line. . . .

Jimmy will never stop trying to sell VASSS to somebody. The pros could do worse than buy it. In any event, three cheers for Jimmy and his enthusiasm and his spirit. As they say in Australia, his blood should be bottled.

USTINOV ON TENNIS

by Peter Ustinov

I became conscious of tennis at a very early age, stimulated by the fact that I detested cricket, a hate that has never left me. I got out of cricket, but then I had to row instead and that didn't interest me either, as I don't like going backward. Of all the games, I always had the most flair for tennis—an instinct for it.

As early as when I was 8 or 9, I can remember absolutely insisting on accompanying my father, who was a journalist, to Wimbledon. I'll give you an idea of how long ago that was: I can remember a lady player with an eyeshade beginning to wind up to serve and suddenly shouting at the top of her voice, "Underarmmm!" And then she belted across a withering underarm service, which aced the opponent, who looked as if she had been cheated.

Nowadays the cry would be taken as a deodorant advertisement, but in that distant past, serving underarm—while providing shrill warning at the same time—was a form of bad sportsmanship cleverly disguised to look like good sportsmanship. In other words, it was vintage gamesmanship.

Wimbledon supplied me, then, with a certain amount of rudimentary instruction, which was helpful, because at an English school there were very few opportunities to play tennis. I was never taught. In those days one was never taught; one was allowed to play. Also, I was, for some obscure reason, kept off the team for some time, and when at last I was allowed on the tennis squad, I had already formed certain bad habits from playing squash and fives, which is a three-wall game rather like handball.

I still hold the racket the wrong way whenever I play, and so I have a great deal of excitement. My best shot is my forehand. It's not good enough to generate speed, but if somebody hits a ball hard at me I can sometimes get it back even faster. I'm absolutely inconsistent, but I sometimes do spectacular bits of nonsense, which gives me immense satisfaction. What I find magical about the game is that if you play sufficiently well, then your play against a fine player will improve instead of going downhill.

I can speak with some authority on that subject, since some of the best players in the world have been sympathetic enough with my passion for the game to go on the court with me. I've played with Frank Sedgman, Neale Fraser, Roy Emerson, Fred Stolle and, most recently, John Newcombe, which seems like the whole Australian Davis Cup roster since the war. I hit with Newcombe in San Antonio, where I was making the movie *Viva Max.*

The best birthday present I ever had was one time when I was in New York appearing in a play and some friends said they would take me to the Town Tennis Club for the occasion. When I reached the courts, there were all my friends in the galleries, and on the court stood my surprise partner and opponents—Gardnar Mulloy, Bill Talbert and Donald Budge. Mulloy and I lost 5–7, 5–7, and I was delighted to escape without casualty.

I'm really not built for tennis. I'm built in a very Slavonic way, and the player I have always had the most empathy—and sympathy—for is Jaroslav Drobny, because we are the same age, built in the same way and by now he's got rather stouter than I, which is a fine advertisement for Czech beer. I have had affection for Drobny ever since he fell in at Wimbledon—a stocky Slav amid all those lissome Australians and lithe Americans—and won. He was also supposed to have a suspect temperament, although I never understood that, because he was forever playing those 37–35 sets with Budge Patty and standing up under them. I think, really, it is the British who have a suspect temperament, because they have this complex about losing and then winning by their grace on the way back to the changing room.

The British really are extraordinary. The only trouble with them—well, I once said that a British education is the best in the world if you can survive it. If you can't, there's nothing for you but the diplomatic corps. I have two Oscars and two Emmys—two emasculated men and two emasculated women who play tame mixed doubles on my desk—and when I won my first Oscar and had to make a speech I was really lost for words. At last I said something from the heart, apologizing for being unable to make a speech but explaining that I was educated in a British school, where an enormous amount of time was spent in teaching us how to lose gracefully but absolutely no time was spent on how to win gracefully because it wasn't expected that we would win.

I'm British by passport and I was born there, but I'm really not very

British. There was anomaly from the first because I was born in the section of London known as Swiss Cottage, and I had been conceived in Leningrad (then St. Petersburg)—I have that on the best authority. I admire the British enormously, though, because I was in the British Army during the war, surrounded by British characters, and there is nothing like a war to make you feel foreign.

I think that through history the British have been extremely ingenious in inventing sports, but when other people would catch up with them in one—which was not long—they would drop it and invent another. They stuck with cricket because there was no competition. Tennis is really very un-British, very specialized in that it is linked so to Wimbledon, which is unquestionably the championship of the world. Why, in the British calendar, I would say that Wimbledon is at least comparable to the ceremony that used to be held for the new victory of India.

Wimbledon is just so much more agreeable than Forest Hills, or Roland Garros or the Foro Italico. So very little seems to mar it, though I do recall Jean Borotra once saying that his ideal death would be serving an ace at center court. I reminded him that you must be very careful in this endeavor because the linesmen are so slow that after you fall to the turf there is liable to be a voice calling "Outtt!"

More seriously, I find it truly sad that there are certain aspects of the snobbishness of tennis that still remain at Wimbledon. A great friend of mine, and I think one of the most admirable of men, is Bunny Austin, who was the last Englishman to make the singles finals of Wimbledon and who teamed with Fred Perry to bring the British their greatest triumphs in the Davis Cup in the 1930s. Bunny is a successful businessman but at the same time is one of the pillars of the Moral Re-Armament movement—with which I'm not very much in sympathy, although I am enormously in sympathy with Bunny and his wife. And yet, because he is in the Moral Re-Armament program, he is not a member of the All-England Club. This I find absolutely insupportable, that people can be so ungrateful as to deny him entrance to the place where he so rightfully deserves to be. It is as impossible as imagining Olympus without Jupiter.

But then, the people who administer tennis the world over are absolutely surpassed by the events. They treat their players as though they were gladiators, in the most cavalier and stupid fashion. What a shame for the game that the usual lawn tennis association people are of such an extraordinary low level. I think they are even worse than film distributors.

I remember one marvelous exchange which I overheard at the Pacific Southwest tournament in Hollywood, when Mr. Perry Jones approached Ramanathan Krishnan and said he was fed up with his behavior and would have to report him to his federation. "In that case," Krishnan replied, "you had better give the letter to me, because I am the Indian federation."

There is this element in my love for tennis, that it is such an international sport—like soccer, which I enjoy watching, but don't care for playing, since it is sometimes a little difficult to find 21 others to play with you. Tennis does take on national characteristics so very easily. Krishnan, for instance, is capable of beating anyone with his soft, accurate shots, psyching opponents with a game that is obviously related to the Indian character. Manolo Santana and Maria Bueno, and even your Gonzales and Segura—so marvelously Latin, their strength and their weakness.

My own is a touch game, although too often the touch finds the net or the netting at the back. I roam quite a bit because I have quick reflexes and am better at the net than at the baseline. I see both the theater and tennis as sports of quick reflexes. Because, in fact, the theater is such a sport, I disapprove of the so-called Method—it is so analytical that it slows down everybody's reactions. I believe, obviously, that you must go into depth in your own mind when you're going to attack a character, but I believe also that the whole Method approach to acting is as though you asked everybody to consider every ball in a tennis game and work it out on a plan. You're so hidebound at the end that you miss all the excitement—the quick reactions in the theater or in sport.

There are also psychological things which are, to my mind, especially interesting. For instance, when there is a quick exchange of balls and suddenly at an instant somebody lobs, you somehow know the other lad is going to miss it because all at once he has too much time to think after a passage in which his instinct alone guided him. It is that disruption which is terribly similar to the moment in the theater when you blow your lines. It is invariably the moment on stage when you take time out and say to yourself, "Ah, thank God, I'm over the awkward bit and this bit I know." Aaaaiii! You're stuck. That is it, the sudden variation of pace which is so liable to throw the mind, or the stroke, off its rhythm.

I was doing a film in Rome a few years ago and three players arrived unexpectedly and wanted me to make a fourth. They were Neale Fraser, who was then at the top of the tree; a Californian named Jack Frost; and my old friend Abe Segal from South Africa. They were wonderful to ask me. I felt very cosseted by them, lullabyed, because they know I'm a fanatic but don't really play very well. They put up with me because they know that sometimes I will take them out to dinner, though that should not be sufficient reason.

For some reason it was decided—I suppose again to flatter me—that a fair team, a fair one, would be Fraser and Segal vs. Frost and me. Absolutely ludicrous. The first thing I had to face was Fraser's service, which I had never seen from that angle before except in the newsreels. I saw him winding up and aiming, and suddenly I noticed an aspirin flying at me.

I put my racket in the way and felt an enormous wrench, and the ball went flying back, to Fraser's surprise—and mine. He was coming into the net, but he hadn't gotten in quite far enough and so he hit the ball back at me again, and I remember thinking—a kind of emergency semaphore—if it's possible once, it's possible again. Once more I felt an enormous wrench and the ball flew back again.

This time it really surprised him—he was up at the net—and he sent a rather soft ball—that is, soft by his standards—to my backhand. I was embarrassed by it, because my backhand is notoriously weak, and all I could do was pat it back. In the air the aspirin became a beach ball, and though he was right at the net, he was so surprised he put it into the net.

I looked around in triumph. A friend who was standing there but not watching asked if I were winning. Ah, 15–love on Fraser's service. But I didn't reply, which was wise, for thereafter I was like a war correspondent, just watching the bullets pass.

Tennis at its best is a game of endless surprises. If Goliath wins, you think, yes of course that is logical, but if David wins, you think only how marvelous. It is also, of course, a thing of stamina. Any big tournament, like Wimbledon, is a marathon. You must win seven matches just to get into the final and it is a tremendous physical and mental drain. That's why I think the Davis Cup—which I love—is not quite fair. I don't see why the champion nation can sit it out. It should be in the thing from the beginning. It would also be more interesting for defenders to have to take risks, to try out their good people.

Tennis seems to me a game of tremendous subtlety—which is perhaps why it has never become enormously popular. Certainly, it must be subtle when you think that the United States can be defeated by Ecuador, when you think that at just some moment a country can produce two great players who can take the Davis Cup. And yet it seems to be very difficult to produce a player of world rank. There are many efficient players but it is so rare that you find one subtle enough to be the champion.

I remember at the Pacific Southwests the first time I saw a young Spanish player—very young and unknown at the time—Santana. He was not supposed to beat anybody, but he was playing marvelously well and we happened to meet. He suddenly asked me for my autograph. I said, I'll give you my autograph if you'll give me yours, and so we exchanged. He was playing Alex Olmedo next, and Olmedo was near the height of his career, but I said to Santana that he was going to win.

He protested that that was impossible, but he won the first set against Olmedo. Santana lost the second, but as he changed sides to begin the deciding set I did a thumbs-up sign, because he said he had liked Nero in *Quo Vadis*. And Manolo won the last set 6–0.

I lost sight of him completely then, but a little bit later he was in the French championships in 1961 and I read that he had reached the quarter-finals. I was crossing France by car when I learned of this, so I stopped and sent Manolo a telegram just saying *"Olé!"* The next day I opened the paper and saw he had won his way to the semifinals, so I sent him a cable saying, *"Olé, Olé!"* And he won that and went into the finals for a chance at his first major title against Pietrangeli. So now I sent him a cable saying, *"Olé, Olé, Olé!"*

I could not find the results of the finals till late the next evening in the south of France, when I got an evening paper that described Santana's victory and said he had jumped the net shouting, *"Olé, Olé, Olé!"* Long afterward I saw him and he thanked me for my encouragement, so whenever he is in a big match, Australia or anywhere, I always send him a cable. Of course, it doesn't always work.

Though I most enjoy watching a player like Santana, I never look for one thing when I go to any match because I don't think that any tennis player ever lives by himself. The most marvelous thing is when you find two players of contrasting techniques. In that sense I think it must be like chess—although I don't play chess myself—for when I see a great tennis match I think this must be like that scene in Moscow, where you have the great crowds watching the chess scoreboards and gasping whenever somebody makes an odd move. It's this to me, but of course at a very, very high speed.

I don't think, really, that most people realize it is not good enough to be a champion in tennis: it takes two to make greatness. A great match needs a loser as well as a winner. This is something on a much deeper and more profound basis that we don't usually realize. I'm writing a play now about Pontius Pilate, simply because there was a much maligned man; without him there would have been no match, and Jesus could not have won and entered history. It is always this way. You needed Pétain to make de Gaulle. There's always someone you have to step over to get to where you are, someone who contributes to your success. That's my point. I don't believe in either villains or heroes but in everybody's contribution to a story—or a match.

HOW TO RUN A TOURNAMENT

by Edward Gordy

This article has been prepared despite an awareness that many experts know far more about tournaments than the author. That is partly why it was written. The experienced people find it hard to believe that a new tournament chairman is so ignorant. They therefore neglect to tell him the simple facts of tournament life. This memorandum will provide information acquired the hard way during the 1960 Illinois State Juniors. For simplicity, opinions and conclusions will be given in an unduly dogmatic way. Please read into all statements, ". . . at least in our experience," or ". . . in our opinion."

GENERAL POLICY

If yours is a state tournament or covers some other large area, keep it open. Touring stars will win many trophies, but they give zing to the tournament and your local players enjoy playing against them. Include all the junior age groups, but omit doubles for Boys' 11 and Girls' 11. If it is a big tournament, announce in your notice that events with fewer than 8 entries will be canceled. Restrict players to 3 events. Plan for five days of play. Four will do it, but some players will be overtaxed. Also, you may have a day of rain.

Apply early for your USLTA sanction. The chairman of schedules and sanctions for your district must coordinate your event with others.

FACILITIES

Thirty courts are not too many for a state tournament. For the early rounds, borrow school and other courts. Players will complain about concrete beforehand, but many will tell you afterwards they liked it. Remind the others that California has nothing else. If you do use outlying courts, plan to have each location supervised.

COMMITTEE

You will need, at least for the first few days:

1. General chairman.
2. Vice chairman (who can schedule matches and also double as Referee).
3. Umpires chairman.
4. Transportation chairman.
5. Financial chairman, presumably your club treasurer.
6. Registration chairman (the local district will help).
7. Check-in chairman, who should also be prepared to receive doubles fees.
8. Food chairman, if there are no eating facilities.
9. Housing chairman, if you are providing housing.

NOTICES AND ENTRY BLANKS

Your notices can be printed, but multilithed notices are quite satisfactory. They should state clearly the information about: the events included, eligibility rules, fees, name to go on checks, closing time for entries, starting time for each age class, location of courts and the type, any special restrictions as to type of shoes or playing apparel, living and eating accommodations, how additional entry blanks can be obtained, and the name and address of the general chairman.

The entry blank should include space for: name, telephone number, street address, *town or city,* date of birth, USLTA registration number, previous year's ranking or other guide to ability, doubles partner, the age groups entered and whether boy or girl. The underlined item is important. In the 1960 Illinois State Juniors, 37 players gave the street address but not the town.

Distribute your notices widely. Send multiple copies to all the member clubs of your district and to the junior development chairmen of other districts. Use the USLTA list of clubs and associations freely, as well as the list from the previous year's tournament.

TROPHIES

Trophies should be taken care of early; otherwise you will have a mailing chore after the tournament. Some organization in your community has awarded trophies and can recommend a supplier. Spend all you can reasonably afford. Cheap trophies cause adverse comments.

Trophies should be engraved with the name of the event but not the winner. Get an idea of the shape of the nameplate, and fit economical lettering into it: "2nd, Girls' 13, Illinois, 1961." "Runner-up" is too long; "State" can be assumed. Lettering will cost 4¢ to 7¢ a letter, depending on the number of trophies you buy and the deal you make.

On the subject of cups versus figurines, this observer is confused. Cups were well received in our tournament. Some of the winners of figurines said they would have preferred cups, yet the trophy houses say the demand is for figurines. Better do some checking.

FINANCES

With 179 players entered, many in several events, finances broke down as follows:

Income		$582.00
Expenditures		
Mailing	$ 35.12	
Balls	335.25	
Trophies	90.49	
Engraving	39.62	500.48
Net income from tournament		$ 81.52

The costs were unrealistically low because multilithing of the notices and entry blanks was obtained gratis. Fees were $2.50 for singles players and $3.00 for each doubles team. They were based on an actual cost of $1.50 for the two balls issued to each player, plus $1 for trophies and general tournament expenses. Fees 50¢ higher could hardly be considered exorbitant.

Insist absolutely that fees accompany entry blanks. Otherwise, players will sign up on a tentative basis and then fail to show, with resulting great damage to the draw, the seedings, and the scheduling of matches.

THE DRAW

Make sure plenty of entry blanks are available, then refuse to accept phoned entries or list of names given you by coaches. Here again, the presumed entries tend to end up as "no-shows." Announce a firm deadline for singles entries. Set a time and place for the singles draw, immediately after the entry deadline. Then *refuse absolutely to make an exception.* If you make one exception, you have set a precedent for twenty. You will end up remaking the draw, and you will spend your next two days on special cases instead of on improving the tournament for the legitimate entries.

In the case of doubles, it is good practice to accept entries (and fees) up to the end of the first day's play. Many doubles teams get together at the tournament.

Before making any draw, read carefully the rules in the USLTA Year-book and Guide.

There is a big pay-off on extra copies of the draw sheets—one set to be posted, one for the scheduler of matches, one for the person who takes down the scores for phoning to the papers, and one to send *World Tennis* immediately upon completion of all events. At least 24 hours before the start of the tournament, file a complete set of draw sheets with each local paper or with the city news bureau, if there is one. The multi-copy pads of draw sheets provided by the USLTA are a great help. Unfortunately, they provide too little space for players' names and affiliations. You will probably need to type the sets for the papers. Your ball supplier will furnish draw sheets for posting at the courts.

CONDUCT OF THE TOURNAMENT

Your tournament notice should include staggered starting times: 9:00 A.M. for one age group, 10:00 A.M. for another, and so on. Perhaps one group should not report until 1:00 P.M. Your check-in person should have a typed list, preferably in a notebook, with the names of all the players and spaces to note fees paid, balls issued, USLTA registration number, and so on.

You should not need umpires in the early rounds. However, any player has a right to ask for an umpire if he feels one is necessary. This should be pointed out. Players in the older age groups are generally glad to umpire while waiting for their matches. For the finals, the local district should provide at least one experienced umpire, but even in the finals the players can carry most of the load. You may have three final round matches going on simultaneously. In one tournament there were 13 finals. (Tip: don't put a Girls' 13 doubles final on the court next to your Junior Singles final.)

In the opinion of this observer, there is too much tendency to feel that the supplier of the balls has an obligation to come up with an umpire. The manufacturer's profit on $300 worth of balls will not pay for many days of a salesman's time.

Tell the players you are going to call footfaults and you will be surprised to see how completely footfaulting is eliminated. Disqualify any player guilty of unsportsmanlike conduct. Pay no attention to the rule requiring that Junior finals be 3 out of 5. This generally cannot be done.

Despite the work involved, you will find that holding a tournament is a worthwhile, rewarding and enjoyable experience.

CLARK GRAEBNER

by Neil Amdur

A woman watching the first Wimbledon open tournament on television became distraught with the court behavior of Clark Graebner and Lieutenant Arthur Ashe and wrote a letter to the American tennis players.

"I dislike terribly the way you just drop the ball out of your pocket when you're serving after you've won the point," she wrote.

"You just drop the ball and make the ball boy pick it up, and Graebner's the worst. He picks the ball out of his pocket and throws it back to the fence."

Criticism for Clark Graebner is not new, but it has reached a new low. Impressive Davis Cup victories and overpowering performances at Queen's Club and Wimbledon this year have wiped away the frustrations and failures that followed most of his amateur career.

Now when the critics come calling, their excuses are that Graebner "doesn't bend his knees enough," or "doesn't smile enough on the court," or mistreats ball boys.

After Graebner won an early round match in the United States clay-court championships at the Town Club this week, a youngster was intrigued by his straight-back stride as he left the court.

"Watch the way he struts," the youngster said to a friend. "He looks stuck-up."

Obviously, the youngster had never seen Braulio Baeza, the great jockey, sitting imperiously atop a horse. Nor would he have known that Graebner, as a rapidly growing teen-ager, had worn a back brace for two years to correct vertebrae calcifying in his back.

The effects of the brace account for Graebner's marine-like posture and his inability to bend for low balls as well as he should.

Few people have understood Graebner in the past and few understand him now that he is one of the top 10 players in the world, amateur or professional. Behind those dark-rimmed spectacles is a glib, candid personality that comes full cycle once Graebner steps onto a tennis court.

"I guess I'm a lot like Dennis Ralston in that respect," Graebner said. "I've always had this intense desire to win and it bothered me if I didn't win, because I felt I had let myself down."

Graebner has let no one down this year. He is unbeaten in five Davis Cup singles matches, was co-champion of the rain-terminated London grass-court championships at Queen's Club and reached the semi-final round at Wimbledon before bowing to Tony Roche, a professional, in four sets. . . .

Victories have done more than restore Graebner's confidence in himself. They have brought him the same belated recognition that Ralston now is accorded as a top-ranking professional. Little kids who rooted against

Graebner because he was a Northwestern University stereotype instead of a Manuel Santana or Rafael Osuna now stand in line for his autograph and envy his serve, one of the strongest in tennis. Acquaintances are eagerly as hospitable, quick with can't-miss tips on the stock market and "Is there anything else you need, Clark?" Professional promoters, the men with the money that really talks, confer with Graebner and sound like they finally mean business.

Graebner, 24 years old, "has not really changed as a person," his mother, Mrs. Paul Graebner of Cleveland, said the other day. If Clark has changed at all, she said, it is "mentally and emotionally as a player."

"Maybe in the past I hadn't been able to take the mental anguish on all surfaces and be willing to fight for as long as I do now," Graebner said. . . .

"But no one bothered to ask me the way I felt about things. They just took it for granted that Graebner was what they wanted me to be—whatever that was."

Friends have said that Graebner's marriage to the former Carole Cald-well—herself a one-time ranking American amateur player—his responsibilities as a father, and his promising position with the Hobson-Miller Paper Company in New York are other reasons for his solidarity and improvement.

"He's maturing," his mother said, "but Clark has always been opinionated and individualistic like his father. Instead of looking just to tennis now, he's enjoying it and playing with more personal enthusiasm."

Graebner is happy and this confidence carries over to the court. He rarely stalks around the baseline, looks trim at 6 feet 2 inches and 180 pounds (he once weighed 200 at Northwestern), and is frank and honest with himself and reporters.

Graebner attributes part of his success to Donald Dell, the United States Davis Cup captain. Dell, he said, "can make you do something even if you don't want to do it, and make you realize that you're doing it for your own good."

Graebner's business commitments are the reason why he has remained an amateur. Few young executives can afford a month away from the office without incurring the wrath of their superiors, but Graebner travels with his boss's blessings.

Only a professional offer that will please him, his employer, his family and his prospective pro sponsors will change his playing status. Lamar Hunt, however, has been known to make matters financially attractive enough for his stable of athletes.

"I'm willing to listen," Graebner said, "but I'm not going to make tennis my life. Right now the Davis Cup is the biggest thing. I'm going to take one thing at a time."

CHARLEY PASARELL

by Neil Amdur

He is the No. 1 tennis player in the United States, but critics still call him lazy. He can match shots with the great Ken Rosewall for five thrilling sets at Wimbledon, then lose in straight sets to an obscure amateur the following week.

On the court, he can be the picture of confidence with his roosterlike strut and that trademark of determination, a protruding tongue that grabs for the top of his mouth as he is about to unwind his picturesque serve. But there are those uncontrollable moments when, in frustration or anger, he will berate himself in a combination of English and Spanish that emerges as gibberish. Then he will lose not only his serve, but sets and matches.

For the last six years, Charles Pasarell has been the handsome, enigmatic, bright hope in United States tennis, precariously playing between very brilliant and bad. Great victories over Manuel Santana and Roy Emerson have been offset by embarrassing losses to David Reed and Lenny Schloss. Gifted physical talent and strong, almost classic strokes have succumbed to intense mental pressure.

Pasarell's position as America's top amateur rests uneasy if one is to believe a phrase in the United States Lawn Tennis Association Guide. In describing his style, the guide says: "Hard hitter, brilliant but erratic." The phrase has been repeated for four years.

Shaking a label of inconsistency has been Pasarell's biggest problem since he won the national junior championship in 1961 and became one of Puerto Rico's most prominent sports products. The situation is pronounced now because he is Private Charles Pasarell, United States Army, 24 years old, and at the top of the rankings.

Pasarell has responded to the challenge. Last week, after losing the first two sets to Clark Graebner in the Eastern grass-court men's singles final, he won the next three sets and the match.

This week, he is on the spot again. He has been selected as one of the four playing members of the United States Davis Cup team that will meet Spain in the interzone competition at Cleveland. The 5-point series will be held Friday through Sunday on a fast asphalt court.

Pasarell's selection has put Donald Dell, the United States captain, in a delicate position. To name Pasarell, Dell had to split up America's No. 1 doubles team of Bob Lutz and Stan Smith, a combination that had won its two Davis Cup doubles assignments this year.

"I could hardly afford to leave Charlie off the squad the way he's playing," said Dell, who also named Lieutenant Arthur Ashe, Clark Graebner and Lutz to the team. "I think he'll give our squad more flexibility and I have confidence that he can do the job." . . .

Pasarell has played and won two Davis Cup singles matches. Both were against the British Caribbean.

"I'm confident I can do the job," he said the other day, "and I'm glad Donald is giving me the opportunity to play."

Pasarell's size (6 feet 1½ inches, 171 pounds), strokes and rugged Latin features have always endeared him to the purists, who compared his arrival to that of Pancho Gonzales two decades ago.

Pasarell and Pancho are similar in their intensity on the court and strokemanship. But Pasarell, at this stage of his career, is considerably closer to rival players and much more open as an individual. He is just as apt to play with Clark Graebner's little daughter as tease Donald Dell over expense money for the Davis Cup team.

Pasarell's warm personality is a reflection of his parents, both former singles champions in Puerto Rico and active in the island's expanding junior tennis program. Dora Pasarell is a charming, energetic woman; Charles Pasarell Sr., dubbed "Big Charlie" by friends, is easy to spot at his son's matches.

"Just look for a man smoking two cigarettes at the same time," Charles Jr., or Charlito as he is known, said. "Big Charlie" is 6-4.

"Charlie is one of these players who will blossom late," said Dell, who renewed Pasarell's confidence, lost after 10 weeks of basic training. "Like Clark Graebner, Pasarell's best tennis is still to come."

Military commitments could cause Pasarell to lose his No. 1 ranking this year. But if he can help the United States regain the Davis Cup, he will have succeeded where others, in recent years, have failed miserably.

TOM OKKER

by Charles Friedman

Tom Okker, the slight, speedy Dutchman who moved into the quarter-finals at Forest Hills yesterday, enjoys the best of two worlds in tennis.

As a "registered player," the new category sanctioned by the international rules makers, he may play for prize money or expenses in open tournaments. He may also play in European amateur events. But in the United States he is limited to the two opens and the national amateur championship.

So far this year he has won $5,000 in prize money. "It's a kind of gamble, though, because if you lose early, you don't take home a penny," he said.

In Haarlem, were he lives, his fiancée is waiting impatiently for him to take time off from the circuit and get married. But Okker has had the sweet smell of success and wants to become the world's No. 1 amateur. Many experts now rate him Europe's best player. He is weighing offers to turn professional, and has no fears about doing well in that league. In recent tournaments he has defeated Nikki Pilic, Dennis Ralston, Rod Laver and Roy Emerson.

"I've been doing all right as a registered player," he said. "I really haven't done too much serious thinking about going professional. I might, some time."

Playing Peter Curtis, the conqueror of Fred Stolle, on the beat-up grandstand court yesterday, Okker was muttering that the grass resembled some of the ball fields in his homeland. He yielded a set, then got his murderous topspin forehand working, began sawing off the volleys with more authority and discouraged the Briton with his remarkable recoveries. He is so fast that rarely does a ball escape his racket.

But right now he is a tired young man. "I've been playing steadily since October, and while the competition has sharpened my game, it's taken a bit out of me," he said.

"I don't think I can win this tournament. There are others who are stronger physically."

Three years ago at the age of 21, he played at Forest Hills for the first time and was knocked out in the opening round by Arthur Ashe. Now, however, the quiet curly-haired swinger is a man to be reckoned with. He meets Pancho Gonzales today.

"If I play well, I'll make a lot of money," he said. "Nothing wrong with that." At Forest Hills he's already picked up $3,500 and if he beats Gonzales it means $1,500 more in the bank.

Off the court, Okker likes to fish and dabble in photography. His father is a dress manufacturer and encouraged him to smack tennis balls at an early age. Tom doesn't think he wants to go into the dress business. "I'm associated with sporting goods," he said. So are a lot of other tennis players. It must be convenient work.

ALASTAIR B. MARTIN

by Neil Amdur

From his 36th-floor Park Avenue office, Alastair B. Martin has a picturesque view of the city and its skyline. He also has some eye-opening thoughts about streamlining the structure of tennis in this country.

On February 8 Martin will move into a position to accelerate his ideas. As president of the United States Lawn Tennis Association, he will have the responsibility of charting the course of a sport that has reached its most profitable and provocative period.

"Tennis has two courses of action," Martin said recently during a break in his duties as a beneficiary with the Bessemer Securities Corporation, a family holding company. "We can pull in the horns and remain amateur, or widen our view and let all of tennis work together under one umbrella."

Martin has selected the second alternative. When the U.S.L.T.A. holds its annual meeting in Clearwater, Florida, he will outline a program that he hopes will preserve the game's growth of last year and expand into previously overlooked areas.

Among Martin's proposals are to update antiquated U.S.L.T.A. committees, delegate more duties to officers and work more closely with teaching professionals. He also hopes to incorporate the association ("to protect its officers and personnel and take advantage of corporate benefits") and establish a nonpartisan committee that can work with the two professional groups to tap the potentially lucrative open tennis market.

"We're moving into tennis as big business," Martin said. "It's too much for part-time officials to administrate. We have to professionalize and streamline, or we'll lose certain aspects of the game. There will probably be some individuals who will be against change. They think it will decrease their personal activities. Some amateur officials are loath to turn over their duties to professionals, but there's a place for both in the organization. The U.S.L.T.A. is not an end in itself. It's a tool to even greater things."

One of the association's most delicate matters is the open tennis question and whether the professional promoters and the U.S.L.T.A. can co-exist. Martin believes they can and he sees a settlement to current problems that have threatened to eliminate the excitement generated by the amateur-pro confrontations of last year.

"The professional managers did a service to tennis by playing in the opens last year," Martin said. "I don't think the International Lawn Tennis Federation people feel this way, but I think the professionals should be recompensed for this."

If Martin sounds somewhat liberal, he is—at least by staid U.S.L.T.A. standards. This viewpoint may surprise some skeptics who viewed his election as a product of the Park Avenue–Princeton–Eastern establishment. Martin is aware of the undercurrent surrounding his nomination. He also realizes that his tenure in office could be the make-or-break year for tennis.

"I have a knack of getting along with people," he said. "But I think this attitude can be misinterpreted. If some think that getting along with people means taking a passive line, then they don't know me very well."

What people do not know about Martin is his maverick sense of independence—an undefined quest that beckons even those born to beautiful backgrounds. In Martin's case the challenge is art, tennis and six radio stations he owns in Syracuse, New York; Grand Rapids, Michigan; Kingston, New York; Meadville, Pennsylvania; Muskegon, Michigan; and Sharon, Pennsylvania.

A former court tennis champion who twice challenged for world honors, Martin, 53 years old, delights in the fact that his assorted collection of medieval, folk and pre-Columbian paintings will go on display in the Metropolitan Museum of Art later this year.

"Friends told me you had to specialize in one form of art to have it accepted," he said, his blue eyes radiating a moment of pride. "But I wanted a wide range of paintings, and decided to go into different areas."

A proxy fight in the Eastern Lawn Tennis Association brought Martin and several liberal-leaning colleagues into tennis. He emerged on the national level as a compromise vice president during another petty, and all too familiar, personality power struggle in the U.S.L.T.A.

Martin is not, in the strictest sense, a true fan. Not like Townsend B., his brother and business associate, who is chairman of the board of the New York Jets pro football team and advertises his allegiance with a green-and-white "Go, Jets, Go" decal on one of the office windows.

Alastair B. is resolute and unassuming. If anything, his detached qualities—the folded hands and interested ear—make him an adroit listener. He frequently will probe a questioner for answers by ending a sentence with the phrases "Don't you think so?" or "Don't you agree?" It is a skillful way of soliciting an opinion and producing a free forum for thought.

Martin favors an open Davis Cup (pros and amateurs), provided the machinery can be established to maintain the current competitive principles. He also hopes to improve the association's ragged public relations policies.

"I don't see the amateur tennis player dying," said Martin, who was born in New York and lives with his wife, Edith, a tennis devotee and player. "We should have a niche for the amateur. But let him stand for what he is, not what we want to make him."

And what is the challenge for Martin?

"One does get an appetite for competition," he said. "I don't feel I'm an officials' official. People ask me why collect art? I can't say. Maybe it's just the satisfaction of putting something together. That's what I would like to do—put something together in tennis. It does deserve it, don't you agree?"

PART II
Great Moments

1877

THE FIRST WIMBLEDON

by A. Wallis Myers

The salient fact about lawn tennis, and therefore about Wimbledon, which is its capital, is not its age but its youth. Compared with the veteran of cricket and the patriarch of golf, lawn tennis is a mere stripling. No legends of its precocious infancy are chronicled; no daily newspapers championed its future. Many people, indeed, derided the game; none of its early disciples trained to excel at it; its introduction was an accident in the social life of placid Victorianism, and, but for the faith and fortitude of a few zealots, who nursed the weakling, lawn tennis might have enjoyed no greater fame or fashion than rinking.

Fifty years ago, on a croquet lawn at Wimbledon, a company of sober-minded gentlemen, divided in their allegiance to racquets and tennis, both indoor games, launched a ship to which they attached the name of "The Lawn Tennis Championship." The mariners were sailing on uncharted seas; their Eldorado was nothing more dazzling than a desire to bestow permanence on a pastime the potentialities of which had only been vaguely visualized. Buffetings, and satire from larger craft, befell them. If their land of promise was revealed in the 'eighties, it was to recede in the 'nineties; not until the new century was its rich outline really exposed. Of the fertility of this realm, its rapid growth in population and power, the interest which its life would excite in all parts of the world, and, above all, in the proof it would furnish of women's athletic emancipation—that dream, realized today, had but few portents in 1877.

Round numbers, Dr. Johnson declared, are false. Lawn tennis had been invented before 1877, but the first Wimbledon founded in that year gave the new pastime a style and status of its own. It clarified conflicting codes, lent form and substance to conditions of play that had been primitive and crude, invested lawn tennis with the dignity of corporate life.

The game is young enough for its early struggles and vicissitudes to be remembered by many living men. It is old enough to have reached a prosperity and a permanence that entitle it to be called the pastime of all peoples. It has a larger army of disciples than any ball game in the world. Whether lawn tennis was an adaptation of the ancient game of [court] tennis to the needs of society—a claim urged by Major Wingfield when he deposited a specification in 1874 with a view of patenting his "new and improved portable court"; whether lawn tennis assumed a vogue in England because it demanded more violent exercise than croquet, the province of which it usurped in the private garden; whether its early appeal was due to the fact that women could pursue it as diligently as, and in company with, men—these speculations do not affect its commanding position today. They only serve to demonstrate that, in spite of obscure origin, initial privation and public ridicule, lawn tennis occupies today a unique place in the physical and social life of the world's inhabitants.

Popular as it is in England, the land of its birth, lawn tennis has even greater vogue in other lands. It is the summer game of America's youth; the Continent of Europe pays it universal homage; every French boy and French girl of athletic tendency has been inspired by the prowess of French champions; it holds the Oversea Dominions in a firm and strengthening grip; its recent development in the prosperous countries of South America has been extraordinary; it is pursued throughout India and the Orient; the Japanese have embraced it fervently; from China to Peru the net has been spread.

In this great development the share of Wimbledon needs no advertisement. Wimbledon was the nursery of the game; it bred the giants of the past, men who, by the exercise of their art, the vigor of their physique and the force of their personality, inspired countries beyond to accept and pursue the cult of lawn tennis. As and when this oversea talent ripened, Wimbledon became the clearing-house of the world's skill, the final assessor of form, the standard by which championship mettle was measured. It has long ceased to be a national tournament; time, competition and sentiment have made it international. As such, its prestige is unique and its educational value incalculable. It unites on common ground players of all nationality. It provides for the champions of other lands a neutral court on which, with conditions equitable to each side, the question of supremacy may be decided.

"On the Lawns of the All-England Club," the words of Mr. Rudyard Kipling, engraved over the portals of the Center Court—"If you can meet with Triumph and Disaster, And treat those two Impostors just the same"— have their meaning understood.

There have been many matches of historic interest on those "Lawns of the All-England Club." . . . The championship meeting is greater than any champion. Wimbledon has given more to the world than a register of skillful men and women. It has founded and permeated beyond its boundaries a spirit of camaraderie and fair play that has oiled the wheels of sport in every land. It may justly claim to have "set the cause above renown."

Croquet, racquets and [court] tennis (the ancient and royal game) were all associated, in greater and less degree, with the first Lawn Tennis Championship Meeting. Disciples of these games were its founders; they swaddled the then infant game of lawn tennis, took it out for its public airing, so to speak, and offered it food and shelter in a cold and critical world. Croquet's sympathy, it is true, may have been a species of cupboard love. The All-England Croquet Club, which had been founded in 1868, discovered after a rather precarious life of seven years that croquet had its limitations; the club exchequer was almost empty. The sacred lawns at Worple Road, Wimbledon, had been invaded by a few members who preferred to hit a moving ball with a racket rather than tap a stationary ball with a mallet. These heretics doubtless found that a neatly groomed surface, free from bush or other obstruction, and permitting the ball to bound with some uniformity, offered new and alluring scope to a pastime which, in its common or garden form, had been pursued under crude and cramping conditions. They began, like youthful porridge eaters in a famous novel, to ask for more, and they got it, first by the addition of "Lawn Tennis" to the title of the Club, and then, a few months later, by the institution of a Lawn Tennis Championship.

The honor of promoting and organizing the first Wimbledon must be given to four gentlemen, all of whom deserve the gratitude of lawn tennis players the world over. Three of them—Mr. Julian Marshall, the eminent authority on [court] tennis; Mr. Henry Jones (widely known and respected as "Cavendish"); and Mr. C. G. Heathcote, a tennis player of repute and stipendiary magistrate at Brighton—formed the subcommittee which, bringing order out of chaos and practical wisdom out of conflicting prejudice, framed not only the rules of the Championship, but virtually the rules of the game itself. The fourth was Mr. J. H. Walsh, the editor of the *Field*, in whose office at 346 Strand (now the site of the *Morning Post* office) the All-England Club had been founded. It was Mr. Walsh who introduced lawn tennis into the program at Wimbledon and who, with Mr. B. C. Evelegh as seconder, carried the motion to hold a championship meeting. Mr. Walsh induced the proprietors of the *Field* to offer for competition a silver challenge trophy of the value of twenty-five guineas—a cup won outright by the late William Renshaw and now in possession of his family.

"If of late years," says Mr. Heathcote, "many a local committee has been able to offer more costly prizes, a special and almost sacred value will, in the opinion of lawn tennis enthusiasts, forever attach to the trophy which, in the infancy of the game and amid all the uncertainties which necessarily surround a new and difficult experiment, the generosity of the *Field* newspaper and the energy of Mr. Walsh enabled the committee of the All-England Croquet and Lawn Tennis Club to offer to the lawn tennis players of England."

Chief among these uncertainties and difficulties was the question of rules. No important match had hitherto been played and no tournament had been conducted under the code drawn up in 1875 by the Tennis Committee of the Marylebone Cricket Club. That code, valuable as it may have been at the time, had obvious imperfections. Its compilers adopted the hourglass-shaped court, claimed as part of his invention by Major Walter Wingfield, the author of Sphairistike. It provided that the court should be divided into two equal parts by posts 7 feet in height and 24 feet apart, with a net 5 feet high at the posts and four feet high at the center. Baselines 30 feet in length were to be drawn at a distance of 39 feet, and service lines at a distance of 26 feet from the net. The players were to be distinguished as "Hand-in" and "Hand-out." Hand-in alone could serve or score; and on losing a stroke he became Hand-out. The service was to be delivered with one foot outside the baseline, and was required to drop between the net and the service line of the court diagonally opposite to that in which the server stood. If he failed to serve the ball over the net, the player lost the stroke and became Hand-out, but it was a fault only if the ball bounded in the wrong court or over the service line. The balls were to be 2¼ inches in diameter and 1½ ounces in weight. The game was 15–up, as in racquets. . . . In doubles matches the partner of the striker-out might take a service dropping in the wrong court.

The M.C.C. code had excited controversy both by speech and written word among the adherents of the new game. Most of these had graduated in racquets and tennis; the rival methods of scoring these games had their advocates in lawn tennis. Nor was there more unanimity over the size of the court, the height of the net, the position of the service line and the question of faults. The subcommittee already mentioned might have been more discreet than valorous and based the championship rules on the existing code. They took the bolder line and framed what was virtually a new set of conditions and rules. Their enterprise was criticized, even vehemently; history has proved that their instinct was sound; for, in the main, with amendments and adjustments rendered necessary by progress and the passage of time, their charter holds good today, not only at Wimbledon, where it was first interpreted, but on every court throughout the world. The unqualified success of the first championship meeting proved that revolution was demanded.

Three of the principles laid down in 1877 have stood the test of time and are still law—an adequate tribute to the original legislators. These three may be tabulated:

1. A rectangular court 26 yards long by 9 yards wide, the net being suspended from posts placed three feet outside the court.

2. The adoption of tennis [court tennis] scoring in its entirety.

3. The allowance of one fault without penalty, whether the service dropped in the net, in the wrong court, or beyond the service line.

In regard to the service line, that was still left at 26 feet from the net; the server had his feet *à cheval* the baseline, and a service which touched the net was declared to be good. In these three instances experience had dictated a change. The height of the net was 5 feet at the posts and 3 feet 3 inches at the center; the balls were prescribed to be of not less than 2¼ inches and not more than 2⅝ inches in diameter, and 1¼ ounces to 1½ ounces in weight. Here, too, there has been evolution.

The first intimation to the outside world of the championship meeting was given in a notice appearing in the *Field* of June 9, 1877. It was signed by Henry Jones, Hon. Secretary of the Lawn Tennis Subcommittee:

"The All England Croquet and Lawn Tennis Club, Wimbledon, propose to hold a lawn tennis meeting, open to all amateurs, on Monday, July 9th, and following days. Entrance fee 1 pound, 1 shilling. Two prizes will be given—one gold champion prize to the winner, one silver to the second player."

It was added that "Players must provide their own racquets and must wear shoes without heels," while intending competitors were informed that balls could be obtained for practice by personal application to the gardener.

Twenty-two gentlemen sent in their names, which were duly drawn at the *Field* office two days before the meeting opened. The majority were more or less familiar with [court] tennis scoring, a circumstance which, says Mr. Heathcote, "was perhaps fortunate for the legislators, as it prevented any marked dissatisfaction with the rules." One of the competitors—Mr. Spencer W. Gore, who proved to be the winner—has, however, placed on record that the innovations (i.e., the new regulations imposed by the subcommittee) caused some dissatisfaction. "We detested the tennis scoring, which was then for the first time introduced and which puzzled us 'pretty considerable.' The service line, under the new laws, was actually 5 feet farther from the net than it is at present, and the balls were smaller and lighter than those now in use." But the first champion is careful to add that without the bold policy of the original championship committee "we might still be groveling in an hourglass court, with balls of all sorts and sizes, and governed by laws varying according to the size of the lawn and surrounding accidents of nature." Such has ever been the tendency of the British citizen. He may croak a little in private; in public he upholds the laws which he himself, by elected representatives, has shaped. Well has it been for lawn tennis that a game so cosmopolitan in its future development should have had as its original legislators men of courage, foresight and character.

It must not be supposed, however, that the first championship meeting was held without hitch or hindrance. Laws had been laid down; the question was to provide implements which should subscribe to them. The balls, for example, had to be made for the occasion. They were required to be of certain weight and to be sewn in a particular way. The influence of the wind could not be overlooked. Their white cloth covers (in the earliest days the balls were uncovered) had to be sewn on like the cloth of a tennis ball, and not with cross stitches; the thread had to be unbleached carpet thread; the dyed thread, used by certain makers "for the sake of prettiness," was barred. Of the fifteen dozen used, according to the *Field,* there was "not a bad one among them." Wells, by the way, were used to hold the balls when not in flight; these were supplied specially by a firm in the Strand. As for the nets they were all of the "right size and texture," and the posts of the "right height and stoutness." The lines were marked very distinctly, the machine having been taken over them twice. The umpires, who sat in raised seats between the guy ropes supporting the net posts, had both score cards and measuring rods—for the net, even at Wimbledon in 1877, was pegged down in the middle. That the first umpires, like the last, sometimes sinned against the light was only too true. Even "Cavendish," the referee, wrote after the meeting: "It is hopeless to expect exceptional umpires at Wimbledon; players must take the chance of a mistake, which, after all, is as fair to one side as to the other." But he did not suggest that the umpires' seats should be raised two feet or three feet; they are nearly twice as high today.

The first Wimbledon proved that whatever the winning style at lawn tennis might ultimately become, the style of the real [court] tennis player was doomed. The graduate in real tennis had every advantage on this occasion. The net was high at the sides and low in the middle; he was encouraged to play his shots diagonally from corner to corner; the service line was so far from the net as to give his heavily cut service every scope. Yet the competition was won, and won comfortably, by a racquets player, Spencer W. Gore, an old Harrovian. He met and defeated several players who were proficient at real tennis, notably C. G. Heathcote and W. C. Marshall. Endowed with a natural aptitude for all games, possessing great activity, a long reach and a strong and flexible wrist, he went up to the net and volleyed the drives of his adversaries. His volleys, novel in their conception and in their effort, were no mere pat over the net. As Mr. Heathcote says, he was "the first to realize, as the first and great principle of lawn tennis, the necessity of forcing his opponent to the back line, when he would approach the net, and by a dexterous turn of the wrist would return the ball at considerable speed, now in the forehand and now in the backhand court, till, to borrow the expression of one of his best opponents of that year, his antagonist was ready to drop." But if volleying was successful at the first championship meeting it was due to the fact that, with the net high at the sides, players did not attempt the drive down the line.

Nearly all the competitors used a service that was delivered from a point level with the shoulder. Some of these services were unplayable, doubtless because the lawns at Wimbledon at that time, employed exclusively for croquet, were smoother and softer than they afterwards became, but we know that many of them were faults. Indeed, Spencer Gore declared that at least one third of the services in the matches in which he participated were invalid. Of the 601 games contested in the 70 sets, 376 were won by the server and 225 by the striker-out, showing a preponderance of about 5 to 3. Spencer Gore's service was more varied than any other; he "kept up his sleeve" an underhand service with a double dose of cut. Of course, if a modern overhead service had then been adopted the service superiority, having regard to the distance of the service line from the net, would have been overwhelming.

Two or three other points may be noted about the original Wimbledon. Sudden death was decreed after "five–all." Players changed courts after every set—a condition that placed a premium on the service, especially when the server had both the sun and the wind in his favor, as he often had. The layout of the old ground, doubtless because of its croquet origin, took no account of the sun's incidence, and even some of the greatest matches on the Center Court, as we shall see presently, suffered from this unconscionable penalty—the sun hitting the eyes of players on the pavilion side of the court. The tournament was adjourned over the Eton and Harrow match; indeed, for some years play was not continuous from day to day. About 200 spectators watched the final, paying one shilling each for the privilege. The weather was unfavorable and the court dead and slippery; the match was played, indeed, in order not to disappoint the "crowd," between heavy showers. Gore won the first set at 6–1 after fifteen minutes' play, the second set at 6–2 after thirteen minutes, and the third set at 6–4 after twenty minutes. It was a contest between Gore's racquet style and Marshall's tennis style, and the result was conclusive.

The championship was founded, but the game did not shake itself free from the shackles of tennis and racquets—that is, from the strokes of men who had grafted lawn tennis onto another game and were not young enough to create a style really applicable to the new pastime—for three years. The daring volley of Spencer Gore actually became obsolete—to be revived in another and more brilliant form by the youth and activity of the Renshaw twins. . . . Meanwhile from 1878 to 1880, the patient baseliner, the player who made certainty of return his rule and the long rest his ambition, governed, and, by the monotony of his stroke, threatened the game. For the second meeting in 1878, by a new code framed jointly by the M.C.C. and the All-England Club, the height of the net had been reduced to 4 feet 9 inches at the posts, and 3 feet at the center. The service line was brought 4 feet nearer to the net. The balls were increased in weight to 2 ounces. These changes, though they exerted their influence later and were a sign of progress, only served to emphasize the need for an independent style. The game was there: the men to exploit its possibilities of speed and counter-speed had not yet appeared.

Nevertheless P. Frank Hadow and J. T. (now Canon) Hartley, who held the title in 1878 and in 1879 and 1890 respectively, were both players of skill and fortitude. The first, like Spencer Gore, had been a Harrow boy and proficient at racquets. He had been in Ceylon, coffee planting for three years and, returning to England for a short holiday, left cricket and devoted his time to lawn tennis, first on a covered court at Maida Vale (the nursery of many fine players of the 'eighties, by the way) and then on turf. All June he went down to Wimbledon and practiced with H. F. Lawford, whose power was then developing in a massive frame, and with L. Erskine. Mr. Hadow, who is now 71, has told of a sequel in a letter to the writer:

"I felt very fit and well up to the break-off for the Eton and Harrow match, when I somehow got a touch of the sun and was otherwise ill, with the result that the Saturday, Sunday and Monday I had to keep quiet with ice on my head. On the Tuesday I had to go down to play in the final against Erskine, but was fairly fit though feeling pretty cheap, and was glad when it was over and able to get to bed again with a horrible headache, where I remained all the next day. On the following day I had to play Spencer Gore, the previous year's champion. I confess I was not feeling even as well as when playing Erskine, taking a frantic headache with me in the train to Wimbledon, which got worse and worse.

"It was not easy to drive down the sidelines, like a racquet stroke down the sidewall, with the net sagging to the center from the posts and fastened below the top of each post, instead of being level. I was told the 'lob' had not been introduced before—certainly I had never tried it before. It was only natural enough though, with a tall, long-legged and long-armed man sprawling over the net, ready to reach over at the ball before it had even reached the net. My attempts to pass Gore, I can remember, with a low, hard stroke, when he was at the net, usually failed."

Mr. Hadow left both England and lawn tennis after his victory. Nor has he ever been to Wimbledon nor seen first-class tennis since.

The entry rose to 34 in 1878. It was larger because the game was better known and understood. The agreement between the M.C.C. and the A.E.C. had cleared the air, and in a few weeks over 7,000 copies of the revised rules were sold. Whereas the previous year it had been the exception to find tennis scoring used (out of Wimbledon), this year it was considered rather an affront to ask an opponent whether he scored by that method. The lawns at Wimbledon had all been levelled in the winter; the courts were adjudged in excellent condition. Improved implements were used, and the famous Tate racket, with an oval face, made its appearance. There were complaints that the net cord was not stout enough and not the right color; also that the post came above the staple which fixed the rope. These were the shadows of coming improvements.

The match between Erskine and C. G. Hamilton in the fourth round deserves passing mention because it was the first in Wimbledon's history that yielded five sets and depended on its issue on one stroke. Hamilton had represented Cambridge University at tennis and employed a severe cut on both wings. Seven hundred spectators applauded a very evenly balanced contest. Hamilton led 5–3 in the last set and was twice within a point of winning; after 5–5 there were four deuces and a desperate finish. The winner put out H. F. Lawford quite easily in the next round—Lawford was then only distinguished for his accuracy; his speed was to come—but fell to Hadow in three sets in the final. The latter never let a ball pass him that was within reach. In the challenge round Spencer Gore's volleying propensities caused his racket on one occasion to be over the net before the ball crossed it. There was a halt and a discussion before it was decided that the rules did not bar him from holding his racket anywhere within reach. So Gore continued to commit an act that today is illegal. But more often than not when the holder ran in, the challenger tossed the ball over his head. Hadow won by lobbing; it was a revelation to the crowd. On the cruelly hot day the regulation enjoining 'vantage sets in the last stage—the first time they had been necessary—added to the strain of the competitors. After five–all in the third set there was talk of adjourning, but the volleyer and the lobber got together again and finished the sixteenth game. "A terrific set" was the *Field*'s comment.

The volleying incident mentioned provoked a heated debate. The volleyer became a target for abuse. Not only, declared his enemies, were the best strokes of his adversary killed; he even invaded the latter's territory. "It was proposed, on the one hand," says Mr. Heathcote, "that a penalty should be imposed on touching the net in striking, while others wished to limit the possibility of volleying at the net by the addition of a volleying line within which the player was not to stand, while others even desired to prohibit the practice altogether." It was argued that the umpire had enough burdens already, but the objection was overruled and players were forbidden to volley a ball before it had passed the net. The volleyer, as we have seen, retired for the time being.

1 8 8 1

THE FIRST AMERICAN CHAMPIONSHIPS

by Richard D. Sears

By the year 1880 quite a number of clubs had taken up lawn tennis, and, in addition to an open tournament at Staten Island, New York, there was an inter-club, four-handed match arranged between the Young America Club of Philadelphia and the Staten Islanders, which was played in Philadelphia. The Philadelphians had been playing over a net of different height, and with balls of a different size and weight than those used at Staten Island. At this time dealers here had been selling any sort of ball, stamping them, without any recognized authority, "Regulation." Hardly any two dealers used the same weight or size, and the various club committees were all at sea with their own particular balls.

This condition of affairs finally decided three clubs, one each in New York, Philadelphia and Boston, to send out an invitation to such other clubs as they knew were playing the game for a meeting in order to form a national association to bring order out of chaos. Thirty-three clubs met in New York on May 21, 1881, and the United States Lawn Tennis Association was formed. A date was set for the first championship, August 31, the place chosen for this being Newport, Rhode Island, and, after some discussion, the English rules were adopted as well as the English ball made by Ayres.

When the time arrived, twenty-five players turned up to try their luck in the singles, and thirteen pairs entered for the doubles. Dr. Dwight, who had been more instrumental than anyone else in the formation of the Association, did not enter for the singles, but with me as partner he entered in the doubles. The entrants knew about the various styles of play of their club-mates, but nothing whatever of the others.

As already mentioned, the Ayres ball was used and the nets were 4 feet at the posts and 3 feet at the center. This had led to a scheme of attack by playing, whenever possible, across court to avoid lifting the drives over the highest part of the net along the sidelines. This method just suited me, as I had taken up a mild form of volleying, in practice, and all I had to do was to tap the balls as they came over, first to one side and then to the other, running my opponent all over the court. My racket this year weighed sixteen ounces!

All of the players entered came from the East and most of the doubles teams were made up on the spur of the moment, with the result that there was little teamwork and the partners were constantly interfering with each other. The ultimate winners of the pairs showed much better team play than anyone else, with the result that they won without much difficulty. These winners, Clarence Clark and Fred Taylor of Philadelphia, played one man close to the net with the other in the back court. Lobbing had not come in at this time and when this pair met Dwight (who also volleyed) and myself they won handily. Our volleying, as I have stated in my account of the singles play, did not have enough speed to worry their net man.

A large number of the players wore knickerbockers, with blazers, belts, cravats, and woolen stockings in their club colors. Their shoes were rubber-soled and generally of white canvas or buckskin. None of their sleeves were cut off, and while a large majority rolled them up, a few left them at full length. They all wore caps or round hats with a rolling brim that could be turned down in front to ward off the glare of the sun. The rackets were generally lopsided slightly as in the old court tennis bats.

There were no grandstands, the courts being roped off, and the gallery sat on camp stools or light chairs set out in two or three rows, and those who arrived late were obliged to stand. The nets were made of much lighter materials than today and were not reinforced at the center, and the center strap was made of iron. The flimsiness of the net did not make much difference at first because none of the services was particularly severe; in fact a few of the players served underhand, but I must confess without much success. There were no heavy rollers to keep the court surface in good condition, only hand rollers being in use.

The winners in both singles and doubles in this first championship were given medals instead of the usual cups, and the conditions were the best two of three sets until the finals, which were the best of five. No 'vantage sets were played and the players changed courts only at the end of each set.

The second year of the championship found all of the players serving overhand with more or less speed, mostly less, with everyone coming in to volley as soon as any good opening presented itself; but as Dwight and I had both taken up lobbing, a stroke which, to be effective, requires a great deal of practice, a certain amount of discouragement appeared, and when these players also tried this stroke they generally lobbed much too short, giving us an easy kill. In addition, we no longer tapped our volleys as in 1881, but hit them with a good deal of speed. I had discarded my 16-ounce racket and was using one of only 14 ounces. When it came to the doubles, Dwight and I had developed as good teamwork as any other pair, a condition of affairs quite different from the year before. This extra speed, together with our lobbing, when it seemed wise to use this stroke, put the formation used by Clark and Taylor in 1881, and this year copied by most of the other pairs, in a very difficult position, and we managed to carry off this championship.

This year also, in addition to a championship cup, another cup was put up to be won three times, but under rather severe terms, inasmuch as it not only required three years to win it, but these three years must be successive before it became the property of the champion. A change was also made in the playing rules instructing the referee to allow a change of court at the end of the first, third, fifth and each following odd game, providing the request for this was made before the toss; otherwise no change was allowed until the deciding set.

It was in this year, also, that Mr. Horsman, a New York dealer in sporting goods, offered the so-called Diamond Racket. This was a full-sized racket made of various inlaid woods with a gold cap at the end of the handle, a gold ban with places for ten names around the head, and another gold band around the throat, three diamonds being set here surrounded by small pearls. The strings were harp strings. The strings attached to this prize, however, were so absurd that I could not see my way to take it, and, upon my refusal, the Association also turned it down and returned it to the donor. . . .

The only step in the development of the game in 1883 was a change in the rules introducing 'vantage sets in the final round, and in the following year the height of the net at the posts was lowered from four feet to three feet six inches, the champion was barred from the All-Comers and was to defend his title against the winner, and the Bagnall-Wilde system of the draw, which brought all the byes, if there were any, into the first round (which, for some unknown reason, we called the preliminary round), was adopted.

This was the year when steel points appeared for the first time. I do not speak of these points as spikes as I do not want to confuse them with the long spikes of the present time. I had been in England with Dwight in the early summer of this year and we found practically all the English players using these points. On our arrival at Newport we persuaded the governors of the Casino to mark out a court and let us play a set with some other pair; we to wear these points and they to play in rubber soles, and at the finish an inspection to be made of the condition of the turf on both sides of the net.

It was damp and the court was rather "greasy." The side that we had used showed hardly a scar, while the other court was in a terrible condition. The result was that the Casino management preferred to have these points worn rather than the rubber soles. Unfortunately, these points clogged up more or less with grass after a short time, and every once in a while a few seconds had to be taken out to clear them. These points were only one-eighth of an inch long and were too short to go down into the turf to any extent and naturally failed to hold one up as well as those in present use, but they held immeasurably better than the rubber soles in use at that time.

The championship this year brought out, for the first time here, the so-called Lawford stroke. I use the term "so-called" in this connection because that was the name given to it by the press, but never by me. When asked where I had learned it, I replied that the idea came to me from watching Lawford and from playing with him. I do not think that anyone could have exactly copied Lawford. He was a heavily built man who had not taken up the game until he was twenty-six years old. He was not very light on his feet, and certainly not easy or graceful. In spite of these handi-caps, however, he was one of the greatest players of his time. He seldom came up to the net, but when he did he generally killed the ball. His usual manner of playing his forehand stroke was to wait until the ball was drop-ping; his racket was almost perpendicular to the ground, with his wrist and hand slightly more forward than the head of his racket; then, hitting the ball with a great deal of force and at the same time pulling up on it, he gave it a tremendous over-spin, causing it to drop sharply after crossing the net and making it a very difficult stroke to volley successfully. By allowing the ball to drop a little before hitting it, the over-spin was considerably in-creased. When he was further forward in the court and hit the ball nearer the top of the bound, he hit with his racket more nearly horizontal with the ground, very much as the stroke is played today. This latter stroke was both much easier to play and much easier to volley well. The perpendicular method also had this advantage: the direction in which you meant to send the ball was more easily concealed, as the slightest little turn of the wrist at the last moment would change it from one corner to the other. I remember that I called this a lifting stroke, not a Lawford, as it felt to me as though I were lifting the ball. When I next saw Lawford he was very curious to know what we meant in America by the term "Lawford" stroke, as he claimed that, except for his awkwardness, he hit the ball just the same as Renshaw or any other first-class player, and that any drop that took place was simply due to gravity. It was not until some time later that one could persuade even the English cricketers that a ball could be made to curve in the air.

As the first championship cup under the three successive winnings became my property this year, another cup, under the same conditions, was put up at the annual meeting of the Association in 1885, and 'vantage sets in the earlier best-two-in-three matches were decided upon. Another change was the adoption of the Peck and Snyder ball in place of the Ayres English ball. The reason for this change was due to the fact that the English balls varied quite perceptibly in both size and weight. At that time, in America, the committee did not test each individual ball as was done in England. There, outside the club house on the old Wimbledon grounds, could be seen a large mesh bag into which all the balls which varied from the regulation weight or size in the slightest degree were thrown.

No other changes were made this year, but in 1886 the number of sets in the early rounds was made the best of five instead of the best of three but no 'vantage sets were played in these rounds unless the score reached two sets–all, in which event the deciding set was 'vantage. In addition, the Peck and Snyder ball, not having proved as satisfactory as the Ayres ball which it had replaced the year before, was given up and a return was made to the English ball. At the next annual meeting the Ayres ball was again thrown out and this time the Wright and Ditson ball was adopted.

Until this time it had been the custom at Newport, the venue of the championships, to play a round of singles in the morning and a round of doubles in the afternoon, and as it had now been decided that all sets, both in singles and doubles, should be the best of five 'vantage sets, it was decided to play the singles, only, at Newport, and the doubles were awarded to the Orange Club in Orange, New Jersey. The date for the doubles was set for three weeks after the finish of the singles. This did not prove as satisfactory as had been hoped, for, as all the players thought so much more of the singles than the doubles, the latter event became much of an anticlimax and the play fell off considerably.

During these first seven years of the championships there was no consistent following in of the service. If a player had attempted to do this in a five-set match with any player about his equal, and his opponent had only done this occasionally, when a good opening offered, the man who continually rushed in would certainly have been obliged to win before five sets had been played as there was no rest whatever allowed in those years. It is quite true that I did follow in at times, but certainly not as a habit, as became so often the custom in later years after the rests were allowed; and owing to this, it seems to me that our leading players had a more evenly developed all-round game than a great majority of the later ones. Of course, in the doubles, most of us followed in on every point as you only have your service once in every four games. After the first year the most successful method of doubles play was the same as today, the partners keeping as much as possible alongside of each other.

Until the Bagnall-Wilde system of the draw came in, a new drawing was made after each round, whether there had been any byes in the completed round or not, so that you never knew when you would come up against any particular entrant in case you were both successful.

During the first two or three years the general trend in the shape of the rackets was to work away from the old court tennis shape and to straighten out more like the rackets of today, though nearly all of the center pieces were convex for some reason or other, while today they are mostly concave. There appeared, however, during this period, three abnormally shaped frames. One was about twelve inches long in the head by about seven inches wide, and another was almost triangular in shape, with a flat head and with the sides slightly bowed, just enough to withstand the strain of stringing. The theory for the first one I do not recall, but the idea governing the triangular shaped one was that it would facilitate making a half volley. I tried them both but I did not find either of them as satisfactory as my oval-shaped one.

The third one was the invention of Fred Taylor of Philadelphia, the doubles champion in 1881. In this racket, when you came to the center piece, it first curved backwards and then came forward again, like a table fork or coal shovel, bringing the plane of the playing surface at a slight angle forward from the handle. I do not remember that Taylor used this for any length of time but certainly no one else that I know of ever used it. I can only suppose that Mr. Taylor found himself a little late in striking the ball and, instead of altering his stroke, tried to correct it in this way. I tried it once in a knock-up as a handicap and I must confess that I was surprised to do as well as I did with it.

The history of one other racket, anything but a freak, was remarkable. It was given me in 1884 by William Renshaw as I was leaving England to defend my championship at home. Much to my surprise and delight he gave this to me with best wishes for my success, saying that it was the best racket that he had ever had in his hand. It was made by Thomas J. Tate, by far the best racket maker in England at that time. Renshaw had won the Irish and English singles and doubles championships with it that year and it was still as good as when new, except for the need of restringing. The balance was perfect. When I got home I had it carefully restrung, won the singles with it, and, for precaution, used it only in the final of the doubles, winning again. I then cut out the stringing, gave the frame a slight oiling, placed it very carefully in a press and put it away. When the 1885 championship came around it was restrung, holding its shape wonderfully, and I won both the singles and doubles with it again. All told, it won eight championships!

1 9 0 0

THE FIRST DAVIS CUP MATCHES

by A. Wallis Myers

The story of the Davis Cup challenge round competition is a rich record of international rivalry, patriotic fervor, and strenuous endeavor. The massive solid silver punchbowl, lined with gold, valued at about 200 pounds, and presented by Mr. Dwight F. Davis of St. Louis, bears a relationship to lawn tennis somewhat akin to that of the America's Cup in yachting. And so far as public interest in America is concerned, the fight for this trophy, symbol of international supremacy, has aroused as much excitement and attracted as many onlookers as the struggles of British and American racing craft off Sandy Hook. We may even draw a more specific analogy between these two contests. Both have sprung from American enterprise and from the inherent desire of Americans to assert their supremacy in every branch of sport. Both are governed by hard and fast regulations, which, though they have never impaired the cordial relations of the rival authorities, have yielded a demand for modification or adjustment. Both, on the days of actual conflict, have been influenced in result by the vagaries of the weather and by conditions peculiar to the scene of action; and both have brought out the distinctively constructive methods, as well as the sporting tempera-ments, of the two countries. At first sight the maritime passage of a wind-propelled yacht may appear to have little or nothing in common with the human-projected flight of a tennis ball on a lawn. Yet the successful issue of the first depends largely on human effort—on the skillful handling of the wheel, the care of the canvas, the training and control of the crew, and a complete knowledge of the course. If we substitute a racket for the wheel, regard the crew as human muscles and the course as confined within the limits of a court, the comparison becomes more intelligible.

But there is this great difference between the contests for the Davis Cup and the America's Cup: Many valiant efforts have been made by this country to gain the blue riband of yachting. These have not yet been crowned with success; the theater of war still remains American waters. For three years the lawn tennis players in the States victoriously defended the Davis Cup against the attack of the invader—not always a well-balanced attack, let me add. But in 1903 the superior skill, greater consistency, and wonderful tenacity of the British team prevailed—the trophy was exported for the first time to British soil. Three more years, and though the field widened and challengers came from the Continent and even from distant Colonies, the custody of that cup was safeguarded. The Dohertys had captured it; they were its trusty defenders. But in 1907, a bad year for England's sporting prestige and one in which neither the Dohertys nor S. H. Smith and Frank Riseley were available for home service, the Davis Cup exhibited further globe-trotting tendencies, and as the result of a brilliant campaign by Norman Brookes, the Australian, and Anthony Wilding, the New Zealander, set off on a long journey to the uttermost ends of the earth. Happily its destination was a Commonwealth alined to us by Imperial ties. The Davis Cup is still a family possession, despatched across the seas as tangible proof of our sons' prowess. That it will come back sooner or later to the Motherland, untarnished by its sojourn abroad, we may confidently predict.

There can be little question that the first British team that went over in 1900 to challenge for the Davis Cup suffered from several disadvantages. For one thing, it lacked the administrative assistance and paternal influence of a non-playing manager. It was new to the climatic conditions of America; the tour was strictly limited and its members had no time to feel their feet on American soil. The conditions of play were likewise novel and in some measure primitive. Perhaps our team had underestimated the strength and skill of their opponents. Certainly they were repulsed in a manner which suggested, even if it did not proclaim, their inferiority, while the confidence of the British authorities seemed scarcely justified. But let me interpolate here the interesting and untoned impression of this, the pioneer tour of an official British team, kindly supplied for this volume by Mr. H. Roper Barrett, one of its three members:

"After many disappointments (the Dohertys and several other leading players were unable to accept the invitation of the Lawn Tennis Association) the team that actually set sail was Arthur Wentworth Gore, Ernest D. Black, and Herbert Roper Barrett—poetically referred to in the official organ as the 'Dauntless Three.' The *Campania* landed us at New York on a Saturday morning. Here we were met and welcomed by Mr. Stevens' (he was an American player of those days) man. We appreciated Mr. Stevens' kindness in sending down his man; it seemed so friendly and kind and much better than coming himself. Having had no particular facilities offered us for practice, it was unanimously decided, Gore being in the chair, that we should forthwith visit Niagara. Accordingly, on the same night we took the train and went right through to Buffalo, where we saw the wonderful Falls, crossed over to Canada and subsequently went beneath them. The Falls beggar description; it is impossible to describe their grandeur and power and, as you know, I am no poet. Let that go. We saw many hundred thousand tons of water rushing over the Falls each minute and throwing up spray three or four hundred feet above the level of the land, the sun meantime forming beautiful rainbows. Well, having inspected this bewildering sight and the awful whirlpool where Captain Webb tempted Providence once too often, we journeyed back to Boston. Here we were heartily welcomed by Palmer Presbrey, M. D. Whitman, Leo Ware, James Dwight, Leyman, A. Codman and many others famous in the lawn tennis world of America. Palmer Presbrey looked after us right royally, made us members of all the leading clubs and had us put up at the University Club. I should like to express our special appreciation of the unremitting attention we received from Palmer Presbrey and James Dwight, and particularly to mention the farewell dinner they gave us at the Somerset Club, with Mr. Leyman in the chair.

"Now as to conditions of play at Longwood, the venue of the international matches. The ground was abominable. The grass was long. Picture to yourself a court in England where the grass has been the longest you ever encountered; double the length of that grass and you have the courts as they were at Longwood at that time. The net was a disgrace to civilized lawn tennis, held up by guy ropes which were continually sagging, giving way as much as two or three inches every few games and frequently requiring adjustment. As for the balls, I hardly like to mention them. They were awful—soft and mothery—and when served with the American twist came at you like an animated egg-plum. I do not exaggerate. Neither Beals Wright nor Holcombe Ward nor Karl Behr can make the balls used at Wimbledon break as much as these did. They not only swerved in the air, but, in hitting the ground, broke surely four to five feet. Our team was altogether taken at a disadvantage. We had never experienced this service before and it quite nonplussed us. The spectators were most impartial and the female portion thereof not at all unpleasant to gaze upon. [This last sentence may explain something.]

"M. D. Whitman, Dwight Davis and Holcombe Ward were a fine team, certainly the best group America ever had. Taking into consideration the adverse conditions under which we played (the thermometer was 136 degrees Fahrenheit in the sun—a dry heat) I do not think we did so badly. [America won by 3 matches to nil, ten sets to one, and 76 games to 50. Rain interrupted the last day's play, which was never completed.] The umpires, who sat on chairs perched on tables, and the linesmen discharged their duties most satisfactorily. Indeed, we had nothing to complain about in regard to American sportsmanship and hospitality.

"Personally I had to catch the *Campania* back to Liverpool on the next Saturday. I was only in America a week, and I often laugh to myself over the fact that I journeyed some 6800 miles to play thirty games. Still I do not grumble. There was no one else to represent England and I felt I had to go despite the inconvenience and personal expense to which we were put.

"Whitman, let me conclude, was one of the finest singles players I ever saw, but I think Gore was a match for Davis. (A thunderstorm stopped the match between Gore and Davis. Davis won the first set 9–7; the second was drawn at 9–9.)"

Mr. Barrett's outspoken criticism of the playing conditions at Longwood are doubtless justified; these must have seriously militated against the chances of the British team, which had been familiar with up-to-date English accessories. But I do not think that even on perfect courts with perfect nets and in a more normal temperature the Englishmen would have triumphed. Nor do I gather that Mr. Barrett holds any other opinion. The American writer who said that "it will always remain a mystery why the English players should not have had some inkling of what they had to expect" was not referring to the conditions, though he might have been, but to the American service. "The Englishmen," this chronicler goes on, "were taken on the flank and utterly routed. To those across the water it was some consolation to know the three players who represented Great Britain, good as they were, were not the three best men to send over." Possibly they may not have been, but that reflection does not absolve the Lawn Tennis Association from a charge of overconfidence or relieve them from a share in the defeat. The truth is, probably, that estimations of American form were based on the results of an unofficial tour made by Dr. Eaves, H. A. Nisbet and H. S. Mahony through the States in 1897. At Newport, Nisbet beat both Whitman and Larned, while Dr. Eaves, defeating Nisbet in the final, came within a few points of winning the American championship. But in the intervening three years American players had made great strides. Apart from their service, which they developed with such enterprise and conspicuous success, the players in the States were adding new strokes to their repertoire each season. Commenting on their progress, the late H. S. Mahony observed about this time: "The Americans dart in and kill many a volley which an English player would either let drop, half-volley, or volley very weakly. Of their ground-play, especially on the forehand, there is nothing to be said but praise, and those who saw Larned's beautiful ground strokes in this country will thoroughly endorse this opinion."

In 1901, anxious to re-establish the supremacy which it was felt the result of the first conflict had impaired, the English Association challenged again, and visions of an early revenge began to float before the eyes of the English players. But this dream had to be postponed. No team whose chances of success might have been considered superior to those of the 1900 combination could be raised, and it was wisely decided to wait another year. Obviously, the desire of the Association was to pit the invincible skill of the Doherty brothers against the American holders; it was therefore necessary to await the convenience of the champions. The wisdom of this course was proved by the remarkable success which attended the visit to Wimbledon of the American doubles champions, Holcombe Ward and Dwight Davis, in the summer of 1901. Not until this redoubtable pair served, smashed and lobbed their way through to the challenge round did the average Englishman appreciate the real potency of their game, nor give Black, Gore and Barrett their righteous due. Even in the challenge round itself, when only the potential resistance of the Dohertys divided the invaders from the championship, the extraordinary powers of Ward and Davis and the efficacy of American methods were so far demonstrated that, had not rain cut the match short on the first day, the visitors might have triumphed. As it was, the Dohertys were tested to the utmost to save their title on the following day. A team more aggressive and synergetic had never been seen on the center court of Wimbledon.

It is no exaggeration to say that when R. F. and H. L. Doherty, Dr. Joshua Pim, and "Captain" W. H. Collins were selected to take up the second challenge for the Davis Cup, every player in this country proudly pictured the trophy coming back with the team. This confidence was justified; why it was not fulfilled we shall presently discover.

When one considers that the British travelers were going to exhibit their prowess before the assembled gaze of 10,000 spectators in New York, it is remarkable—indeed an indication of newspaper apathy in regard to lawn tennis at that time—that the party should have slipped out of England unattended by even the faintest trumpeting in the daily press. It is true one paper sent its representative to Euston to interview the champions, but the result when published was so obviously lacking in illumination as to be practically worthless—it seems to have provoked great hilarity on the other side. Perhaps there was some desire on the part of the tourists themselves to "lie low," for the medical member of the team (who sailed a week later) was mysteriously referred to as "Mr. X" and "A Famous Player" and seems indeed to have left these shores rather in the character of a stowaway than as a champion whose name was a household word on every tennis lawn. Doubtless there were sound professional reasons for this secrecy, but it must be recorded that the voracious journalists on the other side scarcely tasted "Mr. X" while greedily swallowing Dr. Pim.

With a view to winning the Eastern Doubles and thus gaining a passport to Newport, the team went through at once to Boston, and after enjoying a trip to Nahant on Mr. Charles Hayden's yacht, immediately began operations on the Longwood courts. The British players seemed to have impressed themselves most favorably on the spectators. The Dohertys' appearance on court was described as "very pleasing." "Wearing the light blue colors of Cambridge University and attired in white clothes, they contrasted favorably with the grotesque and disheveled appearance of some of the American players" (said the Boston *Globe*). As the brothers' only object in competing at Longwood (apart from their desire to win the Eastern Doubles, which they fulfilled) was to gain practice in singles, H. L. retired after winning three rounds comfortably, R. F. a little earlier. Had they not done so, as Mr. Collins points out, "they might, one or the other of them, have had to play two hard matches on both Friday and Saturday, or have been compelled to retire in the final round of the singles."

"What the press will have to say tomorrow," wrote the English captain in his diary, "is none of our business." As a matter of fact the press only wrote nice things. "The decision to withdraw," said one of the leading dailies, "can in no wise be criticized. The Dohertys availed themselves of an opportunity to become accustomed to the American style of playing and to acquire a familiarity with American turf and balls. Nobody should question the propriety of their withdrawing if it seems policy to do so."

It is interesting to note, in view of the criticisms leveled against the Longwood courts by the first British team, that Mr. Collins stated at a complimentary dinner before leaving Boston that he considered the differences in conditions of play in America and England so slight "that any player could get accustomed to them with two days' practice." The Dohertys themselves admitted that the "American conditions, except for the great heat, are quite up to ours; and we could not wish to have better courts than those at Brookline near Boston." Doubtless there had been great improvement in the two years.

There can be little question that when the Dohertys, now joined by Dr. Pim, arrived at Bay Ridge, New York, to contest the international matches, they were fairly confident of winning the Davis Cup. Their achievements at Longwood, slight as they were, included victories over both Larned and Ware and the brothers Wrenn in the doubles, each with the loss of only one set. It is true neither had yet met Whitman in a single, but both had met and defeated players who employed Whitman's service and most of his methods. As to Ward and Davis, the Dohertys had vanquished them at Wimbledon a year ago. Among Americans, however, there was a feeling of quiet confidence. "The visitors," we are told (in the New York *Sun*), "decline to express any opinion on the outcome, but seem to be very confident under the surface. Their experience at Longwood helped this feeling immensely. Captain Collins declared yesterday that every condition was satisfactory to himself and his men. He had tested the American balls and found them very similar to the English and apparently quite as good. The turf suited him and he said all three of his men were in excellent condition."

Now we come to a question of policy on the part of the British captain that later evoked much comment on both sides of the Atlantic. Mr. Collins nominated R. F. Doherty and Dr. Pim for the four singles and the brothers Doherty for the one doubles. "People are constantly asking me," said Mr. Collins subsequently, "why the Doctor was chosen instead of H. L. Doherty. They don't seem to realize that the Americans had fresh men for the doubles and that sometimes in America it is hot. If H. L. Doherty had played on the Wednesday and Thursday in the singles, and the weather had not been, as it was, propitious, he might have been a rag on the Friday. Apart from that, the Doctor was playing extremely well in practice against the Dohertys and we saw no reason *before the match* that he would not show the Americans some of his old quality. He was never in better training in his life, I should say. I don't even think he was overtrained, although he had taken off more than two stone in six weeks."

I give this explanation in justice to Mr. Collins, who has proved himself an efficient and generally a far-sighted captain, but I am bound to add that the net result (America won three of the four singles) of the international matches at Bay Ridge makes it now clear that the British captain would have been better advised had he left the brunt of the attack entirely in the hands of the Dohertys, as he did in 1903. The chances, it seems to me, were two to one in favor of H. L. playing. There were four singles and only one double. Pim's responsibility was therefore just double as much as the younger Doherty's and his pre-eminent standard twice as important. Only a month previously H. L. had become champion of England, and he had won the championship of Ireland the same year. Pim had been champion eight years previously; for some years he had been out of the tournament arena. Even the American journals expressed surprise at his selection. A shrewd judge of the game wrote: "Had the challenging side eliminated Dr. Pim and played on the brothers Doherty, it is easily conceivable they might have won two of the four singles matches as well as the doubles. Certainly Dr. Pim must be omitted from any critical analysis. He was simply a first-class man badly out of practice."

The matches themselves created immense interest. Over 5,000 people watched the play on the first day, over 6,000 on the second. The doubles, when the Dohertys beat Ward and Davis, actually attracted a crowd of 10,000—the largest assembly that had ever watched a lawn tennis match. The conditions were perfect. R. F. Doherty was decidedly unlucky in having to finish his match with Larned, postponed overnight on account of rain, in the morning and then play Whitman the same afternoon. Though this arrangement was unanimously agreed upon, R. F. was perhaps justified in subsequently remarking to me, "Whitman was fresh and I was not. I beat him at Newport afterwards, in the final of the American championship. It is a fair assumption I should have beaten him at Bay Ridge if I had not had the morning's strain and excitement."

As for the tactics pursued in this match, we are told that R. F. continued to battle for the net in the American fashion, and, though beaten in three straight sets, made a much better stand than was at first anticipated. "It is certain that R. F. Doherty owed his success against Larned to his recognition of the futility of English tactics, and it is at least safe to say that he will be stronger in the singles game when he leaves this country." It was in the doubles that the brothers convincingly demonstrated their superlative skill. This was probably the most remarkable doubles contest ever seen. Davis and Ward, the most spectacular team in lawn tennis annals, after playing in invincible style for nearly two sets, were gradually worn down and beaten out by the most heartbreaking precision and certainty of return. (The crowds filed out from the beautiful grounds of the Crescent Athletic Club still under the spell of the great tennis they had witnessed, and tried simultaneously to climb on one lone car of the Fort Hamilton line which had been thoughtfully provided by the trolley authorities to carry 6,000 people back to town.)

Dwight Davis, the donor of the cup, appears to have been the pivot upon which the doubles match turned: he it was who nearly won victory and who finally earned defeat. A whirlwind at first, his terrific smashing and twist service almost demoralized the Englishmen. He held himself in check a good deal in handling deep lobs and did not sacrifice points in attempting to kill those balls which other men volley with less speed; but towards the finish he missed many sharp volleys and low shots—his "kills" missed fire. Ward was a marvel of steadiness, but he was evidently less feared on the other side of the net than his partner, for even when Davis was palpably tiring in the second set, the Dohertys lobbed more to Ward than to Davis. H. L. seems to have handled the Americans' screw service with less embarrassment than R. F., and during the rallies was the "wheelhorse doing the lion's share of the work." He was very certain in all his strokes, but his return of the service was his best point. R. F. made nearly all of the killing strokes and also more errors. There seems to be little doubt that in gaining this memorable victory the Dohertys used more of the American style of play than any foreign team that had previously crossed the Atlantic.

1914

BROOKES-McLOUGHLIN DAVIS CUP MATCH

by S. Wallis Merrihew

Australasia played the United States on August 13, 14 and 15, at the West Side Tennis Club, Forest Hills, just outside of New York. The grounds were new and this was the first big event staged there. Stands seating 11,130 people had been erected, and, with those in and around the clubhouse and the enclosure courts, the number of those who watched was slightly in excess of 12,000. No such gallery had ever witnessed a lawn tennis match. . . . The gallery had assembled from all parts of the world.

Anthony Wilding and Richard Norris Williams 2d came out for the first match. The American had been enjoined to go all out at the start, instead of beginning slowly and feeling out his opponent. Williams did this and produced play that fell little short of the miraculous. He went to 3–0 and 4–1, sending the ball over so fast that often Wilding failed to connect with it. Then the reaction came and Williams slumped momentarily; his impetus carried him to 5–3, however. Then he went all to pieces and Wilding, playing carefully and letting Williams beat himself, won four games and the set at 7–5. Wilding won the second set at 6–2 and the third at 6–3. He was content to let Williams make errors, himself keeping the ball in play meanwhile. Williams tried to regain his grip but he could never do it long enough to count. He did make a stand in the eighth game, but it was the last he won. The gallery sat, dazed, almost unbelieving.

It was nearly four o'clock when McLoughlin and Brookes came on the court for their long looked-for meeting. A titanic battle ensued, from which the Californian emerged victorious after one of the finest and closest matches in the entire history of the game. The first set will go thundering down the ages as the greatest exhibition ever seen. McLoughlin won it at 17–15, and with it went all hopes of Brookes' winning. Only the possession of superabundant vitality and pre-eminent skill enabled the Californian to nose out ahead. The set lasted for well over an hour, and as it progressed the immense gallery sat spellbound and amazed. It did not seem possible that two men could make such shots and deliver such services as they did for a term long enough for three ordinary sets; and the suspense as to which would crack first became so intense that many of the spectators were at the end like rags that had been wrung out and hung up to dry.

That first set, won by McLoughlin at 17–15, was unequaled in Davis Cup annals until 1923, when it was exactly duplicated in a doubles match. It still stands as the most memorable of all sets in the contests for the trophy. From the splendid gallery its fame spread over the world, and in the days and years to come it was to be referred to, discussed, commented on and admired without stint. It was played on the court next to the clubhouse, and the grimness of the struggle, due to concentration on each stroke by the two men, was its outstanding feature. It has often been said of it that it was all service and volley. This is only partly true. Each player strove to make his service deadly, and each had a preference for volleying; but each played other strokes well and varied his game materially.

To 9–all games went with the service. McLoughlin stood far back, Brookes took his place inside the baseline, trying to meet the ball with a quick twist of the wrist. Brookes excelled in placing, McLoughlin in anticipation. Brookes' ground strokes were better than McLoughlin's, and the latter's service and overhead were superior. The Australian had his chance in the eighteenth game, when he reached 40–0 on McLoughlin's service; and as Brookes was "serving irresistibly," the win of McLoughlin's delivery apparently would ensure the set. But five times McLoughlin served his fast ball, "sending it humming across the net like a thunderbolt, and not giving his opponent a chance to get his racket on the first three deliveries." Then he served a twister, came in behind it and aced Brookes' return "with a matchless chop volley." A "burning service ace, which the Australian stood and watched go by," ended the game.

The battle of services went on. There was nothing to choose between the players. When McLoughlin got in a hole he came across with an ace; when Brookes was in danger he outmaneuvered his opponent and finally passed him. The crisis came in the thirty-first game. Brookes, serving, reached 40–15, and then got to advantage after deuce had been called. At long last McLoughlin got to advantage and drove hard to Brookes' feet for the game. The next game was bitterly contested and reached deuce. Then McLoughlin served two aces, and the set was his at 17–15.

The set was a marvel of evenness, and to the end the gallery feared that the "mighty Brookes, saturnine and grim, with his crouching position, his well-directed twisting shots, his deadly service and interceptions at the net," would win. Not until almost the end of the set was there confidence that the "youthful red-headed Californian, with his winning personality, his dash and brilliance, his fearsome service and dazzling smashes—for many of which he would leap in the air and bring his racket down on the ball like the club of the primitive caveman"—was equal to the task. When he had won the set he was more than ever the popular hero.

All saw that the set practically ended the match. Brookes had put nearly his all into it, and while he fought on, it was only because he was a fighter and not because he had any expectation of winning. McLoughlin was on the top of the wave, fresh, confident, resolved to press home his advantage. He now varied his game more, employing the lob to advantage, bringing off drop shots; but always there was the ability to slog the ball. Brookes lost his service in the third game, and at 5–3 McLoughlin hit the ball with tremendous speed and won a love game. At 3–all in the third set McLoughlin made his last great effort and by sheer speed won the next three games, ending with a "vicious smash of a low lob." . . .

American Lawn Tennis records these facts regarding the match: Played August 13, 1914 from 3:36 to 5:36 P.M. Day perfect, no wind. Sun bright, at times obscured. Barometer 30.06, temperature 76, humidity 46.

McLoughlin served 17 aces, 12 in the first set, while Brookes' total was 7. But Brookes scored 15 aces off McLoughlin's service, to only 3 by McLoughlin.

BROOKES VERSUS McLOUGHLIN—DAVIS CUP

by Al Laney

In the fateful summer of 1914, a schoolboy on blessed, unexpected holiday, with what seemed incredible good fortune, came into the presence of probably the most glamorous and exciting figure in tennis history, Maurice McLoughlin, in his moment of glory—and at the moment when the game itself burst into bloom, so to speak, as a genuine spectator sport.

It seemed to me, musing on destiny's strange ways, that the fact that so much of my adult life has been devoted to watching and recording the playing of games, especially tennis, was directly traceable to that combination of circumstances which permitted me, a teen-age Florida schoolboy, to be present in New York that blistering August week when a famous Davis

Cup Challenge Round was played at the new tennis club in Forest Hills with the guns of World War I already firing in Europe.

There was played on this occasion one of the most celebrated contests of sports history, the match in which McLoughlin, American, defeated Norman Brookes, Australian. This match may be said to have been the first truly "big" tennis occasion in this country, the first tennis encounter that really caught the imagination of the whole nation, and it did for tennis something comparable to what the victory of Francis Ouimet over Harry Vardon and Ted Ray, the great British golfers, had done for golf exactly one year earlier at Brookline, Massachusetts. It put tennis on the front page, as we are fond of saying, and its effect on the destiny of a tennis reporter very likely was as decisive.

The dramatic figure of McLoughlin had come storming out of the West with dynamic service and overhead smashes to electrify the small enclosed tennis world of the Eastern Seaboard and to draw non-tennis crowds to a game theretofore largely ignored and faintly despised by the public. The whole circumstance of McLoughlin's unheralded arrival on the sports scene was immensely exciting, and he quickly became the chief hero to a group of boys who had dared to play tennis publicly when it still was considered by many people a sissy game. The California Comet, he was called, a name with a fine ring to it, suitable for a hero, and the pictures of him, though perhaps not good by later standards, were very satisfying to young hero worshipers. There was one splendid shot, in *Leslie's Weekly,* I think it was, that showed the Comet leaping from the ground to make a "kill," and the caption referred to him as "flame thatched." (This one adorned the walls of my room for years.) We knew McLoughlin's record at Wimbledon, Newport, and elsewhere, as we knew Ty Cobb's exact batting average and how many times the villainous Three-Finger Brown of the Cubs had beaten our Giants.

We dreamed of being McLoughlin and longed to see him play. And then suddenly came the unbelievable good luck of a chance to be in New York that August week when the incredible Braves of 1914 were to be at the Polo Grounds and McLoughlin was to play at Forest Hills. For a teen-ager, this was the stuff of dreams, and the fact that all during that wondrous week I favored tennis over baseball, even with Matty pitching, is most significant. . . .

Play began on Thursday with Tony Wilding, the New Zealander, who had been Wimbledon champion for four years, against R. Norris Williams, described as "a young college boy from Harvard." . . . The big match, McLoughlin versus Brookes, the current Wimbledon champion, would follow, and there would be doubles on Friday. The experts were unanimous in the opinion that McLoughlin would have to beat both Brookes and Wilding if the United States, holder of the trophy, was to have any chance of retaining it. . . .

The stands were packed and there did not seem to be vacant space anywhere. An odd impression of the crowd that remains is of a solid sea of straw hats of the kind we called the straw kady. Looking down from the rim you could see nothing but the tops of those hats. Many of the women in the crowd wore larger versions with pins sticking out. A great many things have passed from the memory, but that picture of this ocean of straw remains. Every head among fourteen thousand seemed to have one, except for the occasional soft Panama, and so, too, for that matter, did mine.

Two white-clad figures appeared at the top of the steps leading down from the terrace to the court. Williams and Wilding. Since these were two of the finest players of the game I was to write millions of words about, it would be nice if I could recall something about their match. But I can find little, certainly nothing of importance. Undoubtedly I grew excited, cheered along with the others, and must have followed the play closely, since this was really the first tennis match I had ever seen, but practically everything I recall today about it I learned later by looking it up and reading about it in books. I know that they came and played before my eyes and that Wilding won in straight sets, but I recall only that the defeat of Williams put a greater burden on my man. I was there to see McLoughlin, not really to see tennis, and, strictly speaking, I did not see tennis, because when McLoughlin came onto the stage the action, now magnified, became larger than life, so that no really reliable report of that match could be made by me.

Nevertheless, the drama of it, often agonizing, can still be lived through a little. In that thirty-two-game service-governed first set, I lived and died with McLoughlin, and I never in the years since have witnessed what seemed to me so grim a fight or an athletic contest of any kind the winning or losing of which meant so much to me. I can well remember how those two looked as they came down the steps and stood for their pictures to be taken. Brookes, long of face and solemn, wore long sleeves and had in his hand a cap which he would wear throughout the match. McLoughlin's shirt was open at the neck and the sleeves were cut off at the elbow. He really did have that mop of hair I had read about, and altogether he was a most satisfactory-looking hero.

I had complete confidence in him and I watched every movement during the preliminary hitting of balls back and forth. They were playing on the far court by the terrace, but we could still see from our seats that McLoughlin smiled a lot. Brookes seemed very dour. My confidence was shaken many times before that terribly long first set was over. Brookes gave the impression he would never yield no matter how many thunderbolts our man might hurl at him, blows one never could have imagined possible with a tennis racket.

About halfway through, and after what seemed an eternity, Brookes, who had served first and thus was forcing McLoughlin to battle for his life every time the American served, was love-40 against the service. You would have to be a teen-ager again, I suppose, to suffer as I suffered then. But at this crisis, McLoughlin served three balls that Brookes could not even touch with his queer-shaped racket.

Other crises came later, near the end we could not know was near. Brookes again was within a point of winning the set, and each time the answer was the same, an unreturnable service. Was ever a boyhood hero more worthy of worship? I have read and reread everything about this famous match that I could lay my hands on, and visual memory is all mixed up with other people's observations and opinions. Where the emotions are so terribly involved some details are blurred, others enlarged out of all proportion.

One picture, though, must be my very own. It is of McLoughlin, all fire and dash, leaping from the ground to smash a lob and, as the ball bit into the turf and bounded impossibly away, of Brookes dropping his racket, raising both hands above his head in despair and calling on high heaven to witness his misfortune. This happened several times near the end of that tense set, and whenever in the years that have run like sand in the glass I have thought of this first exciting encounter with tennis of the highest class, this one picture repeats itself as if it actually were being seen again.

With McLoughlin winning this match for the United States, 17–15, 6–3, 6–3, the series was tied now and would go, the experts said, the way they had predicted: victory for Australia by three matches to two. And so it did. I do not remember about the doubles, I remember only McLoughlin in that match and the fact that Tom Bundy, his partner, wore a handkerchief around his head as though he had a splitting headache but actually to keep the perspiration out of his eyes—a practice which I adopted myself a little later. Neither do I remember much of Brookes and Williams in the match that decided the issue, but of Wilding and McLoughlin there were things to note.

I was called upon to make a decision on a problem with the enormity of which no schoolboy should have to contend. I had to make up my mind whether I should go to Forest Hills on Saturday to see McLoughlin play again in the match the experts said would mean nothing after Brookes had beaten Williams, or go to the Polo Grounds to see the Giants play the Braves in the final game of their series. After wrestling with the problem overnight I returned to watch the tennis and so deprived myself of the right later to boast, and thereby acquire distinction in my set, that I had seen the fabulous Braves beat the immortal Matty.

McLoughlin versus Wilding, where I watched my hero rather than carefully observing the match at the time, acquired a certain pathos and significance in later years, and I went over it carefully in the papers I had saved. It was the last tennis match Wilding would play, and McLoughlin never won another important victory. Two weeks later McLoughlin was beaten by Williams in the final round of the National Championship at Newport, and before spring came round again Wilding was in a grave in Flanders Field, killed in action in the early months of the war.

Dame Mabel Brookes has written of the final meeting between Brookes and Wilding in her delightful book, *Crowded Galleries*. "They all left for England immediately after the Challenge Round, Wilding to join his regiment. They met for the last time in Boulogne, across the English Channel, in a small dockside hotel that had that smell of new bread, tobacco, and lavatories that impregnates a certain type of French hostelry.

"Tony came," Dame Mabel recalled, "from nearby Belgium, where he was operating a trailer gun in the Westminster outfit. He was fit and full of energy. He looked handsome in the fatigue cap and uniform that was something like an airman's. As usual, he was untidy, one button dangling by a thread. He was leaving at dawn, and after a while bade a speechless shoulder holding farewell to him [Norman], for they were very close."

The account continues: "It was barely light when I threw back the shutters and the air came in sharp with a hint of autumn. . . . Tony strode out on the cobbled road, kicked his starter into action, contained, remote and lonely. He waved and wheeled out over the pavé to the bridge and, as he crossed and turned into the distance, he waved again. The smell of burning charcoal came up, mixed with the reek of exhaust from his bike, and drifted, ephemeral as the passing moment, leaving only memory. We never saw him again."

1919

JOHNSTON DEFEATS TILDEN FOR UNITED STATES CHAMPIONSHIP

by Richard Larned

William Johnston of San Francisco, California, regained the highest honors of American tennis yesterday afternoon at the West Side Tennis Club, Forest Hills, by defeating William T. Tilden 2d of Philadelphia, 6–4, 6–4, 6–3, in the final round of the national championship.

The one-sided victory came as a shock to those who had come to think of the tall Philadelphian as the greatest tennis player of the age, if not of all time; and it is still true that, when going at top speed, yesterday's runner-up is more impressive from a purely spectacular standpoint than any other man on the courts. But his defeat at the hands of the steady and reliable Johnston proved again the old contention that championships are won not by brilliant and versatile play so much as by the ability to use a few strokes with absolute assurance and that complete confidence which ultimately will drive the best of the sensational school into errors. The 1915 champion, in other words, is able to call upon his most effective game whenever he needs it most, as he proved this season in winning the national clay court title, in defending the Longwood Cup successfully, and again yesterday in his wonderful display against Tilden. The latter, however, employs such a huge repertoire of strokes that he can never be absolutely sure that they will all be at his command, and when something goes wrong or he finds himself facing unexpected opposition, he has no simple and infallible formula ready to fall back upon.

The forehand drive of William Johnston is unquestionably the greatest single tennis shot in the world, bar none. He seems able to use it with every possible degree of speed, with an accuracy that baffles the fastest court covering, and with a steadiness which has discouraged every opponent he has ever faced. No stroke has ever been developed by any other player to equal its efficiency and general dependability. Although the Californian prefers a fast, dry court, with plenty of speed on the other side of the net, he proved yesterday that he could control his drive just as well on a soft, slow surface, with generally an undercut ball instead of a topped drive to hit against. The adaptability of the new champion to supposedly unfavorable conditions was perhaps the most surprising feature of his victory. The surface should certainly have suited Tilden's chopping game, yet he constantly mistimed the ball, his greatest sin being the habit of hitting into the net.

Johnston, on the other hand, seemed not to care how the ball bounded or how much its pace varied. He was always able to drive it hard and accurately, and since he stubbornly refused to make errors, his rival's doom was sealed almost from the outset. Yet Johnston's forehand drive alone would not have won for him yesterday against the type of tennis that Tilden, even somewhat below par, could flash at intervals. It was the remarkable aggressiveness of the winner's backhand and service that actually kept him out in front. Johnston has never been noted for the shots he makes on his left side. He does not turn the face of his racket as most orthodox backhanders do, and he slices the ball with far less speed than he gets from his free-swinging forehand. But yesterday he not only had complete command of his backhand as a defensive stroke, but could use it consistently as a weapon of attack.

This was one reason for the hesitation which Tilden showed throughout the match in coming to the net. He found that even when he hit the ball hard to the traditionally vulnerable spot on the other side, it came back just as fast and accurately, passing him cleanly down the sidelines as he tried to volley. Discouraged by his lack of success at the barrier, Tilden early resigned himself to a back-court game, and at this he was absolutely no match for the Westerner. Johnston chased his tall opponent from corner to corner in the first two sets, and had him so exhausted by these tactics that in the final session, when Tilden's strokes were working far better, he did not have the strength to pull out a victory.

The crucial game of the match was the last one in the opening set. Tilden, trailing from the start, had broken through his opponent's service and was in a position to tie up the games on his own delivery and come through with one of his famous uphill fights in the face of the greatest odds. But after twice being within a point of the game, with a service ace and a cleanly placed volley, he made two fatal errors in succession and lost the set when Johnston, in turn, volleyed successfully. This reverse seemed to shake

Tilden's confidence more than any of his earlier mistakes of execution. He has gone through streaks of bad hitting, mistiming and wildness before, and has generally been able to pull himself together in time to avert disaster. But yesterday, when his supreme effort had been successful and he had recovered the game lost through a bad start, he found that his rival still had something in reserve, and it was the loss of his own service for the second time that broke his heart.

After that shock of surprise, the Philadelphian played as one who could not quite understand what was going on about him. He had made his habitual recovery, but it had not been sufficient. Now, with one hard-fought set already scored against him, he tried all the dazzling tricks of his equipment in turn, but nothing seemed to work. On the other side of the net Johnston was still plugging away, returning everything and waiting patiently for the inevitable error, or going in at the first opportunity and closing the rallies with impressive finality as a real opening offered itself.

Tilden now realized the hopelessness of a situation in which no one of a great variety of shots could be depended upon for sure results. His greatest need was for a fast drive, but his drive, unfortunately, was by no means sure of finding the court, since the ball rarely came with just the right bound for his free swing. His chop was steady and accurate enough but it did not suffice to keep Johnston in deep court, since he could volley it easily by correctly anticipating its line of flight. Most disappointing of all, perhaps, were the lobs that Tilden sent up as a last desperate resort, the lobs that baffled the great Brookes and drove the brilliant Williams into errors. Yesterday few of the soaring tosses fell within the lines, and the majority of these were so short that they were easily killed by the alert champion.

In fact, if Tilden's game can be said to have disclosed a real weakness yesterday, it was in lobbing, the foundation of successful defensive play. Using the theory that the best defense is a strong attack, he had in the past been generally able to keep his rivals from becoming too aggressive by the constant strain under which his own shots kept them, and had perhaps never before been brought to a point where absolutely nothing but good lobbing could avail. Here, again, the condition of the surface may have added to the difficulties of the loser.

The repeated delays caused by the rain seemed to have taken the edge off Tilden's game, whereas Johnston was, if anything, benefited by the two days' rest and entered the match with a vigor and keenness which the loser never showed. Rain threatened up to the actual time of starting, and a few drops fell while the veterans were still engaged in their preliminary bout. With the sky still overcast and the turf obviously soggy, there was little of the atmosphere that makes for spirited, energetic tennis.

Yet Johnston was able to adapt himself to conditions and Tilden was not. In spite of every handicap, the winner yesterday played by far the best tennis of his career, a game which, on that particular occasion, no one else in the world could have equaled. Whether it deserves to be placed unconditionally at the top, on the strength of this one amazing exhibition, is another question, which no amount of argument will settle. Johnston and

Tilden have met four times this season, and each has won twice. Yet the fact remains that Johnston's two victories came when national titles were at stake, whereas Tilden won the minor honors of the East-West encounter and the Newport invitation tournament.

1 9 2 0

TILDEN CROWNED KING OF THE COURTS

by Richard Larned

William T. Tilden 2d of Philadelphia is the tennis champion of the United States and of the world in general. His victory over William Johnston, the former national title holder, at the West Side Club, Forest Hills, yesterday afternoon, stamps him as not only the greatest of all living tennis players but, perhaps, the greatest of all time. It was a victory, however, completed only after five of the most terrific sets ever staged on a turf court, scored at 6–1, 1–6, 7–5, 5–7, 6–3. To what was probably the most dramatic scene in the history of lawn tennis was added the excitement of an airplane tragedy in which Lieutenant J. M. Grier of the U.S. Navy and Sergeant Saxe of the Army lost their lives in full view of the spectators, narrowly escaping a far more disastrous fall into the crowded stands themselves. . . .

The Tilden-Johnston struggle will go down on the records as the most astounding exhibition of tennis, the most nerve-racking battle that the courts have ever seen. It is not often that such a climax of competition lives up to every preliminary expectation. Yesterday, however, the wildest expectations were actually surpassed. Up to this time, the famous final of 1916, in which Richard Norris Williams 2d defeated Johnston for the championship, had been considered the apex of tennis history. But that great match faded into comparative insignificance yesterday.

Williams and Johnston played five sets of mechanically perfect tennis. Tilden and Johnston played five sets of incredible melodrama, with a thrill in every scene, with horrible errors leading to glorious achievements, with skill and courage and good and evil fortune inextricably mingled, and with a constant stimulus to cheers, groans and actual hysteria, so far as the spectators were concerned.

Those who had sympathies one way or the other, and this meant practically every one of the 10,000 or more in the crowd, went through more varieties of emotional reaction than the supposedly dignified and gentle game of lawn tennis could ever have been blamed for in the past. At times the mob spirit threatened to become unmanageable, as personal opinions were voiced from the stands in no uncertain terms. But Umpire E. C. Conlin kept a firm control of the proceedings throughout, and certainly no one was ever before given so difficult an assignment in the chair of arbitration. Rain, the airplane accident, a misunderstanding as to an important ruling, vitally affecting the result of the fourth set, and unusual frequency of close decisions by the linesmen all added to the umpire's troubles, but Conlin was not dismayed and finished his job in the same heroic spirit as was shown by the two men on the court.

To describe that amazing final to the most significant of all American tennis tournaments, a tournament that unquestionably carried with it the world's championship, would require the superlative of all the adjectives that the journalism of the game has either used up or discarded in the past. It is enough to say that all future discussions of the Olympian heights of tennis will probably begin with the question "Were you there when—?" and the answer will be either "You bet I was," or "Curses, no." For the proud possessors of the affirmative, no amplification is necessary. For the sad negatives, nothing can be done, for it will never happen again, at least not just that way.

Praise for the two contenders for the American championship of 1920 may be equally divided. There is plenty for both. Tilden's victory was a triumph of super tennis, a vindication of the game which the best judges have for some time considered invincible. But, if Tilden is considered the greatest tennis player that ever lived, Johnston is the gamest man that ever trod a court.

Armed with his wonderful forehand drive, his aggressive volleys, and his stubborn determination never to say die, the former champion for five sets resisted a dazzling, versatile game that theoretically should be rated at least twenty-five per cent ahead of his own. The difference between the two men in the one detail of service is convincingly emphasized by the stroke analysis.

Johnston did not serve a single ace in the entire match, and contributed more than his share of double faults. Tilden, on the other hand, had twenty technical aces to his credit, an average of four to a set, exclusive of the numerous occasions when an overwhelming service was miraculously returned by the courageous defender, only to lead to a sure score off the ground or on the volley.

It is by his service that the Tilden of yesterday will chiefly be remembered, for time and again it came to his rescue when all else had failed. But he had also a marvel of a backhand drive, a newly developed asset to his game, an offensive, not a defensive stroke, and one which scored equally well across court or straight down the line. Johnston's backhand, except for its accuracy of placement, was largely a defensive weapon. But, if the Californian had the worst of this comparison, he fared quite differently in the matter of volleying. Here he was distinctly Tilden's superior. Not only was he able to volley balls that would have knocked down an ordinary player, and to reach low, well-placed passing shots that could scarcely be seen in their flight, but he turned a majority of these extraordinary gets into actual factors in his attack, either scoring outright or forcing a defensive position which ultimately brought him the point. Tilden's volleying was too soft to finish the rallies, and depended too much on placement and undercutting for its success, whereas Johnston always picked the ball out of the air in a crisp, confident style that practically guaranteed results.

Overhead also Johnston was the better man yesterday, and he commanded a lob which proved exceedingly valuable in the pinches. But Tilden added a cruel chop to his terrific drives, and with the ability to mix up his ground strokes thus he could afford to take fewer chances by the aerial route. Johnston nearly tripled the number of points earned by his opponent in volleying and smashing. On the other hand, Tilden almost doubled his rival's record of ground placements. In the percentage of errors and earned points in general they were practically even, the new champion finishing a far greater number of rallies one way or the other, and therefore deserving a vast amount of credit for his statistical showing.

In the last analysis, however, it was the edge on service that told the story, and it was this tremendous difference that made Johnston's fight such an astonishing one. He more than justified his reputation of being the world's greatest finalist, the greatest "money player" living, for the tennis he offered yesterday would have annihilated anyone but a Tilden, and a super-Tilden at that.

In the fourth set, with Tilden needing only two points for the match, Johnston returned a smash at his feet with such a ridiculously impossible shot that Tilden himself joined in the astonishment of the spectators, and threw away the point in his amazement. Later in the same game, only one point intervened between the fighting defender and defeat, but he staved off disaster, and eventually pulled out the set. In the final session he again saved match point by a marvelously accurate placement off his backhand, and ultimately succumbed by barely missing the line in a desperate attempt to score.

As for Tilden, he also faced innumerable situations that called for more than ordinary courage, even with the advantage of his superior stroke equipment. Twice in the rubber he lost his service and had to accomplish the difficult task of breaking through in turn to save the match. When victory had seemed in his grasp in that fatal tenth game of the fourth set, only to vanish suddenly, it was peculiarly trying that rain should begin to fall immediately, ironically reminding him of what might have been, while the court was still dry. Added to this came a misunderstanding as to the replay of a point which was given against him, followed by the interruption which made a new start necessary.

But if Tilden showed courage and a commendable control of his nerves in these situations, the tennis that he exhibited in the opening set was something that stood on a pinnacle of supremacy, overwhelming in its magnificence, a unique display of matchless strength and skill that permitted no resistance, and took thought of nothing but its own perfection. That any one could hit a tennis ball so hard and so accurately against a national champion seemed utterly impossible, and it was not humanly possible for more than one set.

Tilden suffered an obvious letdown after that titanic exhibition of hitting, and after losing his service twice deliberately threw away the second set, making no effort to return the last few shots. The third was the crucial test, and here Tilden came through triumphantly after having lost his service and retrieved the loss immediately, finishing with a decisive break in which he earned three of his four points. He had the fourth set and the match on his racket, as stated above, but was foiled by Johnston's incredible get, and he lost the game on errors.

During the first rally of the next game, it began to rain, and the crowd instantly became a kaleidoscope of motion. Tilden looked inquiringly at Umpire Conlin, and evidently assuming that a let had been called, stopped playing. When they resumed, Referee Adee awarded the point to Johnston, reversing Conlin's decision. They stopped at 30–all, and when they returned to the court, after the rain had ceased, Tilden served three double faults which directly lost him the set. Trailing at 40–0 on the final game, he brought off two forehand wallops off service that completely beat Johnston by sheer velocity, but netted in his attempt to deuce the score.

In the last set, Tilden had to break through Johnston's service three times to win. The match point finally came up on an error following a net-corder from a half-volley, but Johnston saved it by poking the ball backhanded through an opening a few inches wide. A bad bound gave Tilden a service ace, and this time Johnston failed to save the situation, driving out after a great rally, for the set and match, 6–3.

It would be impossible to review the most important points and games in their regular order. Spectators will remember in particular some wonderful returns made by Tilden on the full run from far outside the court, with a slicing swing of the racket, on one of which he fell flat, but won the point. They will remember how beautifully Johnston anticipated his opponent's movements from side to side as he volleyed close up, invariably picking the right spot for his finishing shot. Several lobs that landed right on the baseline will stand out for those who delight in finesse of placement, as will the remarkable accuracy of both men in the fifth set, when they were too weary to trust to speed alone, but persisted in aiming at the sidelines and generally succeeded in hitting them. But above all will remain in the memory that downward stab of Johnston's racket as he returned a point-blank smash at his feet, and that amazing succession of service aces delivered by Tilden when he needed all his speed to win. It was a glorious victory.

TILDEN DEFEATS PATTERSON IN WIMBLEDON FINAL

from the Associated Press

William T. Tilden, 2d of Philadelphia won the British lawn tennis championship in singles here today. Tilden defeated Gerald L. Patterson of Australia, the titleholder, in the challenge round, 2–6, 6–3, 6–2, 6–4.

The American's victory was conceded to have been well earned, his game being characterized by tennis experts as the soundest and brainiest tennis ever seen on English courts. The technique and cleverness he displayed, although probably beyond the comprehension of the average spectator in the finer points, were not lost upon seasoned tennis followers.

It was commented, along this line, that the American tennis experts seemed to have realized, when Patterson was in the United States last year, that he was decidedly vulnerable on the backhand, owing to his unorthodox method of twisting his arm so as to bring the forehand face of his racket in use for backhand play, thereby locking his shoulder joints. This method usually collapses against an opponent who is keen enough to take advantage of the opening, and it did today.

Tilden in the first set opened with experiments all around the court and then settled down mercilessly to feeding his opponent's backhand, and, as the game progressed, Patterson got worse and worse under this method of attack.

Tilden exploited his famous cut-stroke to his opponent's backhand again and again in the last three sets, and Patterson was unable to get the spinning ball back over the net. He frequently hit into the bottom of the net. Then, when Patterson came up to the net, Tilden played a slower fast-dropping shot to his opponent's left hand. Almost invariably the ball was netted on the return.

These tactics were relentlessly exploited by Tilden, who showed Patterson, so far as the centre court crowds were concerned, in an entirely new role. Thousands of persons had believed he was unbeatable, only a few knowing he had a vulnerable joint in his armor.

In the first set Patterson led, 4–0, then 4–1 and 5–1, Patterson making a number of fine drives and serving magnificently. In the second set Tilden served first, taking the score to 2–0 and then 4–1. Patterson made it 3–5, and there was a protracted struggle for the ninth game, which Tilden finally won.

The third set went to 2 all, and then Tilden ran it out in the finest fashion. In the fourth set, after each man had alternately won, until Patterson led at 4–3, Tilden annexed three games in succession and won the set and match. The winner received a notable ovation. . . .

Charles S. Garland of Pittsburgh and Richard Norris Williams 2d of

Boston won the final in the British doubles championship from A. R. F. Kingscote and J. C. Parke of the British Davis Cup team. The Americans took three of the four sets played. The scores were 4–6, 6–4, 7–5, 6–2.

It was a red-letter day for Williams. He was the directing brain and outstanding personality of the match. His opponents served upon his backhand until they found he always made brilliant returns down the center line. They then attacked his forehand, only to find that the pace of his return often put the ball away. Williams' play generally was brilliant. In fast volley exchanges at the net he smashed finely, and he frequently sent over winning services which the Englishmen could not touch.

Garland did not start so well, but in the fourth set he played brilliantly. The features of his game were general all-round steadiness, great forehand driving and extraordinary quickness at the net. Sometimes he returned balls which it appeared impossible to get and scored on them.

1921

LENGLEN DEFAULTS TO MALLORY AT FOREST HILLS

by Al Laney

In August of that year [1921], all the papers turned loose full blast on that remarkable affair of Suzanne Lenglen and Molla Mallory. . . . The women's championship, held as a separate event then, was brought to New York for the first time that year, and none before or since has attracted the attention this one got. . . .

This extravagant affair, which came soon after the dawn of the Era of Wonderful Nonsense, provided me with an excellent exercise in tennis reporting by comparing my own observations with what appeared in all the papers. I found considerable disagreement between my own view and that of my new colleagues. Memory is notoriously faulty, especially where the emotions may be involved or prejudice present, but I really think I am secure here.

What is difficult to recall about the affair is the furor and sensation of it. A whole nation, seemingly, became exercised over what really was a small thing, making of it an international incident. I was also puzzled that there was no agreement among reporters presumed to be first class as to what had occurred in the highly charged atmosphere of the meeting of these two girls. The match had suddenly become important to papers on which tennis had been more or less ignored, and some of the commentators who spoke with great authority had never covered a tennis tournament before.

Women's tennis was not at the time very exciting. Molla—first as Miss Bjurstedt, a Norwegian, and then as Mrs. Franklin Mallory, an American—had won four of the last five U.S. titles and seemed likely to go on winning. The girls' tournament needed something to give it interest, and when it was learned that the great Suzanne would come for it, the papers began to whoop it up. Suzanne, as we have seen, had become something of a celebrity in 1914, when, still a child, she had won at St. Cloud. Her name, if not her figure, had become known in all the tennis-playing countries before the war, and she was still under twenty when the tournaments were resumed in 1919. Her first visit to Wimbledon for this renewal of that most famous of all tennis meetings had been sensational, and Suzanne quickly became a world-famous personality.

During the next two years she probably did more for women's tennis than any girl who ever played it. She broke down barriers and created a vogue, reforming tennis dress, substituting acrobatics and something of the art of the ballet where decorum had been the rule. In England and on the Continent this slim, not very pretty but fascinating French maiden was the most popular performer in sport or out of it on the postwar scene. From Biarritz to Monte Carlo, from Deauville to St. Moritz and Baden, she became the rage, almost a cult. Businessmen canceled appointments, and internationally famous hostesses postponed parties that conflicted with Suzanne's appearances because they knew no one would attend. Even royalty gave her its favor and she partnered King Gustav of Sweden in the mixed doubles more than once.

She became almost an obsession, attracting adoring crowds wherever she went, for she was more than a tennis player. She was acrobat, dancer, a spectacular artiste, actress and compelling personality. Just to see her crush some unfortunate girl 6–0, 6–0 was an event. She created fashions in dress followed by thousands of girls who could not hit a ball over the net, and her famous bandeaux were worn all over the world by women who never saw her.

Wherever Suzanne played she took the attention away from the men, and men treated her as a queen. She made the game popular in quarters where it hardly had been noticed, and she was compared to Pavlova and Bernhardt. Newspapers and magazines everywhere were forever full of her pictures in beautiful action, for the photographers and picture editors could resist her no more than the public.

Very few performers in any field have enjoyed such adulation. Everything she did on the court and off it, what she ate and what she wore, was important news. And together with all this, she brought to the courts a technique that was near perfection and a style of play that was the most wonderfully exciting the world had seen.

It was out of this splendid background that Lenglen made her first unhappy visit to the United States. In June she had won Wimbledon for the third time. She had not lost a set or come close to losing one anywhere since the war, and in these last two years she had played and beaten every girl in the world of any class, including, of course, Molla Mallory.

Suzanne's visit was in a way as an official representative of her country. She was invited to come to the United States to play in the championship and then to play a series of exhibitions to help raise money for the relief of the regions in France devastated by the war. A fund was being raised and it was under the auspices of the committee headed by Miss Anne Morgan, together with the United States Lawn Tennis Association, that the tour had been arranged. For this reason also the event created much interest. . . .

Lenglen was also, in a sense, returning the visit of Tilden and Mrs. Mallory, the two United States champions, who had gone to Paris in the early summer before playing at Wimbledon. So the papers made a great deal of the coming event, and the approach of the Maid Marvel of France, as she was called, was heralded flamboyantly in keeping with the time. . . .

Unfortunately for the buildup, Suzanne did not arrive on schedule. The arranging of the trip had taken some doing, and Lenglen pere, a poor sailor, refused to board a ship after agreeing most reluctantly that Suzanne could go. Monsieur Lenglen warned that the trip without him was not for the best. Suzanne took a later ship than at first planned, and it was delayed a little by storms. She landed in New York only a few days before she was scheduled to play her first match in the tournament.

When the draw had been made, with the French girl still at sea, it was seen that the big match to which everyone looked forward, the one against Molla, would come in the second round. The idea of a seeded draw, with the leading players arbitrarily placed so as to prevent such a meeting before the later rounds, had not yet been introduced.

Suzanne had been drawn in the first round against Eleanor Goss, a quite good American player whom she would have to play without having an opportunity to accustom herself to the strange new conditions, a decided handicap for a girl just off a ship. Even Tilden had found it impossible to play his game immediately after his arrival in France that summer. Suzanne was thought to be so wonderful that she would adjust more quickly to the faster balls and unfamiliar turf. She would not need practice, it was felt, and the match with Miss Goss would be quite enough to put her in top form for Molla.

Then Miss Goss defaulted, and Suzanne was required to go into court for her big test on the second day without benefit of a preliminary match. A lot was made of this default. It was announced that Miss Goss had withdrawn because of illness, but in some papers it was described as a clever bit of strategy by the "defenders." It was said that Miss Goss had been persuaded to withdraw so that the "invader" would be forced to come into the arena thus further handicapped. I am ashamed to say that I took some stock in this proposition for just a little while.

I am afraid I still believed it premeditated when I arrived at Forest Hills, but before the extraordinary climax, I had begun to resent the implications of it. I now doubt that it had any truth in it at all, even though I subscribed briefly. I had gone out early on this day, and . . . I saw coming toward me the familiar figure of Sam Hardy. . . . Sam was in tennis clothes, with a couple of rackets under his arm, and he said he had been practicing back there with Lenglen and that she had not seemed very keen for the match. I am quite certain he said nothing about illness, even though I cannot remember what he actually did say. If he had mentioned illness I certainly would have remembered, in view of what was going to happen soon after. . . .

When I had got settled in my seat and looked around I saw Suzanne sitting quietly in a box, with her mother beside her, waiting her turn. In two years she had changed into a world celebrity and outwardly she had changed greatly too. Gone was the long linen dress for a short sleeveless pleated one, more like a ballet skirt, and the funny little soft hat had been replaced by the now famous bandeau of many colors, a different one for each appearance.

Suzanne and Molla were preceded in the enclosure by two girls whose names have long since escaped me. . . . They played an interminable match, three long sets . . . By the time they were off the court and the preliminaries completed, it was getting on late afternoon. All this time Lenglen had been sitting there watching the match while the rest of us watched her. This was surely not good preparation. Molla had been more sensible. She rested somewhere out of sight.

Finally Molla came out of the clubhouse and Suzanne rose to meet her at the top of the steps leading down to the court level, onto which they came together with all sorts of French and American officials in their wake and photographers walking backward in front of them. This was the moment for which we had all waited—about ten thousand were there, the papers said. There was a burst of applause and some cheers.

Lenglen was dressed in the costume with which we had all become so familiar through pictures in the rotogravure sections . . . I do not remember the color of the bandeau that enclosed the dark, shining hair, but I noted that the white stockings now were rolled just above the knees. Molla also wore a band around her hair, but what a difference! The defending champion wore a serious, even a severe expression, and her costume was, by comparison, plain. She had pulled on a long, thin, dark sweater, and the white of her dress shone through. The sweater was caught and held tight at the waist by a narrow leather belt, and it had a sort of skirt falling down over the dress, which was inches longer than Suzanne's. This also was her usual costume, long familiar, and there is no doubt that she looked a little drab in it beside her glittering, volatile companion. But she also looked very menacing with her dark, swarthy Indian-like features.

Memory says that Suzanne came in like a queen to her ordeal . . . Since she was to show in a very few minutes that she was not herself and to declare that she was in fact ill, there may have been unnoticed signs of it from the very first. But, try as I will, I cannot remember any such indication which preceded the play.

However, when the match began with Mrs. Mallory serving, Suzanne did little more than tap the ball back over the net gently. We thought that she would take a little time to get started, so we were not disturbed as they changed courts for the first time. But the second game, which Suzanne served, went the same way to Molla, who hit the ball with great determination to the corners of the court, drawing feeble replies as Lenglen ran from corner to corner.

This gave the crowd a vague feeling of uneasiness. It was Suzanne's opponents who were supposed to run from corner to corner. We had been looking forward to acrobatics and pirouettes. At 40–love to Molla in the third game, Suzanne began to show the first signs of distress. She began to cough. She seemed to get hold of herself quickly, though, and suddenly she began to hit out. With drives shrewdly directed she won five straight points. She had won Molla's service and the crisis seemed to have passed. The coughing stopped.

But when they had changed sides again, Molla attacked with real viciousness. The champion hit deep and hard. There was a relentless air about her, and Suzanne's efforts at defense were again weak. When Molla rushed ahead to 4–1 the coughing began again. Suzanne stopped under the umpire's chair at the changeover after the fifth game. She shrugged a little helplessly and had a more violent fit of coughing.

As she took her place, the coughing continued. There was a nervous quality about it, and now Suzanne looked appealingly toward her mother. We were all a little dazed and puzzled too. This dazzling girl might not be able to hold the American champion in check, but surely she was better than this.

Molla took the two games she needed quickly and the first set, 6–2. Her dour expression relaxed and she smiled. This was the first set she or anyone else had won from Lenglen on any court in two years and more. Suzanne, of course, was conscious of it too, and it could hardly have made her feel better. Sitting there all disappointed, I remember thinking that now anyhow the match would have to go to three sets. I still could not imagine that the great Lenglen would lose in two.

I was sure of it for half a moment at the start of the second when Suzanne began to hit in the way we had all expected her to play. Now she would play her game, it seemed. The very first point produced a long exchange during which there came a stream of fine shots from the French girl's racket. But Molla finally won the point and the game at love. And then came the disappointing end, suddenly.

Suzanne was serving the second game of the set and the score had gone to love–30 against her. Here she served a double fault, a thing she never did. Apparently it was a signal to her. She walked unsteadily to the umpire's chair, looked up, shook her head, and said something. Molla came up too, said something to Suzanne and then to the official. In the stands we could not hear, but we saw Suzanne shake her head again, and we guessed what was going on. Suzanne was saying that she was ill and could not continue.

We saw Molla put her face close to Suzanne, speak some words and then run across to the clubhouse and disappear. Then we knew. No announcement was necessary. There was a mild burst for the American victory, but it subsided quickly as Suzanne sat there in the netcord judge's chair, a forlorn figure as the photographers rushed up to snap her in her misery. She got up after a bit and, with officials and photographers swirling about her, walked across the court and also disappeared into the clubhouse.

A faint but distinct hissing sound came from the stands as she crossed the terrace and passed from sight. It was a polite sort of hissing, but she certainly could not have failed to hear it or know its meaning. The crowd was branding her with that horrid American word "quitter."

In America we cannot abide a quitter. Our code is the die-for-dear-old-Rutgers code. We did not know then that in Europe they adopt the more sensible attitude that it is foolhardy to continue when ill. To retire from any athletic contest because of indisposition was the accepted thing, taken for granted. On that occasion, though, quite sensible people said unkind and untrue things, and some of the papers were especially caustic. For a little while after that day "to cough and quit" was a phrase heard often.

I left Forest Hills with a strong feeling of having been cheated, of not having seen the show that was advertised, and my resentment was great. I suppose everyone felt that way. I thought of the French girl with disfavor, but I really do not think now that I ever did accept the ugly word. I think I accepted the fact that she was not completely well, but I felt she at least could have gone on and made a match of it.

But when I joined the crowds at the station, and in the train on the way back to town, I heard people saying the nastiest things. Soon I began to swing over to Suzanne's side and found myself trying to make excuses for her. Then when I read all the scornful things in the papers the following days, I came to the quite erroneous conclusion that she probably would have won the match anyhow if she had decided to stick with it for a while longer. I did feel that she had not been feigning illness, as was said, and my opinion of the whole affair was reinforced by what happened months afterward.

Although she was said to have recovered quickly, Suzanne did not go through with her schedule of charity appearances. She did play an exhibition mixed doubles at Forest Hills, and she was reported in the papers to have played with the old verve, but I did not see it. Her chances to restore the balance came the following June when Mrs. Mallory went to Wimbledon again and reached the final. Against Suzanne in that match one newspaper report said that Molla "played shrewdly, courageously and probably as well as she ever played." But Suzanne required a scant twenty-six minutes to win, 6–2, 6–0.

The result should always be placed alongside the one at Forest Hills, for it is a better gauge of the relative tennis merits of these two. Unfortunately, Lenglen is remembered in the United States far more for the former than for the latter. It was her destiny, it seemed, to be remembered more for the clouds under which she left the two great tennis grounds of the world, Forest Hills in 1921 and Wimbledon a few years later, than for the bright sunshine in which she basked most of her tennis life.

Suzanne was to return to America in 1926 to join Vincent Richards and

Mary Browne in the first of a long series of exhibition tours under the banner of the fabulous figure of the Lawless Decade, Cash and Carry Pyle, of Bunion Derby fame. She was not much happier in this financially profitable venture, and earlier in the same year she figured in two more highly dramatic incidents before her dazzling career was done. The first was a match that attracted even more attention, the famous meeting with Helen Wills at Cannes. The other was the last, sad incident of her amateur days at Wimbledon, when they said she insulted Queen Mary.

TILDEN-SHIMIZU DAVIS CUP MATCH

by Al Laney

The Davis Cup matches had been held (at the West Side Tennis Club) for three years after the return of the trophy, with the United States defeating Japan, Australia and Australia again with the loss of only two of fifteen matches. Only one of these matches remains especially vivid, the meeting of Tilden with Zenzo Shimizu of Japan in 1921, about which I am again in disagreement with most tennis authorities.

Tilden was by now acknowledged everywhere as the world's finest player. He had won at Wimbledon in 1920 and 1921, and in their second final in the American Nationals, Johnston had failed to solve the problem of Tilden's new backhand in five exciting sets. . . .

As the climax of the 1921 season approached, Tilden was unbeaten in any important match for two seasons, but he still was thought to be surpassed in individual strokes by other players. His forehand was thought to have neither the pace nor the accuracy of Johnston's, his slices no better than Wallace Johnson's, his volley inferior to Richards', his overhead less decisive than McLoughlin's, and the famous cannonball service not noticeably faster than Patterson's.

As an all-court tactician Tilden was not rated with Brookes. He had not the wonderful touch, rhythm, and economy of movement of Williams, it was said, and Shimizu made far fewer errors while being a much better retriever.

The Tilden-Shimizu meeting on the first day of the Challenge Round was a famous tennis match played only a few weeks after that other celebrated affair of 1921, the Lenglen-Mallory match, and on the same turf. Shimizu won the first two sets, 7–5, 6–4, and was within two points of beating Tilden in the third. But Tilden pulled out the third set at 7–5 and then, after the rest period, won the fourth and fifth sets, 6–2, 6–1.

There is something strange about the accounts of this match and of the memory of it when people talked about it and wrote about it in later years.

It has been made a memorable tennis occasion, but other people's memories of it do not coincide with mine.

It usually is depicted as an occasion when Tilden, deliberately placing himself in a position that appeared hopeless, letting himself go, in fact, to the brink of defeat so as to display his unsurpassed ability to pull out of it, almost got caught. And the accounts, more often than not, intimated that it would have served the silly fellow right if he had got caught.

Tilden did have this reputation, and when you consider the number of times he pulled out a match within a point or so of defeat, it is not surprising. He had done it only a few months earlier against Brian Norton, the South African challenger, at Wimbledon. . . .

Tilden scored more important victories after seeming to be beaten than any other champion. He won these matches with super tennis, but I do not think it compatible with Tilden's greatness to hold, as many did, that he deliberately toyed with an opponent for the pleasure of snatching victory from his grasp. Against outclassed opponents he did not always use the full force of his game, since there was no need to, but I decline to believe that he let up against first-class players to tantalize and finally crush them. The fact that this occurred so often probably was part of the peculiar genius of the man. It may have been part of his feelings for showmanship, his real desire to give the crowd a full value and put on a proper show.

There was, for instance, an occasion somewhat later when, with H. LeVan Richards, probably the best tennis umpire we have had, in the chair, Tilden was playing someone who was normally a pretty good player but was now hopelessly outclassed. Seeing how easily and quickly he was going to win, Tilden began to offer up shots his opponent could make best, so as to produce longer exchanges. Big Bill also began a show of petulance and temperament that soon put the crowd in a hostile uproar. Tilden glared at linesmen after decisions that everyone could see were correct, stormed about the court, and called on heaven to witness the injustice of it all. At one point he stopped in mid-court, placed hands on hips, and shouted at the chair for all to hear, "For heaven's sake, Lev! Are you blind?"

This brought boos from the stands, just as it was calculated to do, and there were shouts of "Play the game, Tilden" and "Play ball." But when the last point was played and Tilden had won as inevitably he must with the greatest ease, though he had made the other man look quite good, he went to the chair and, extending his hand, said to Richards, "I'm sorry, Lev. I apologize. But they really deserved a show, don't you think?"

So Tilden was capable of such antics, but in the case of Shimizu I am certain the popular view is wrong. Tilden would never have taken such a chance with a player of Shimizu's known class, and the evidence, in any event as I remember it, is conclusive.

Tilden had been quite ill during Wimbledon and had got out of bed to win the Challenge Round match from Norton, who had won what was then called the All Comers Tournament. Fortunately for Tilden, the champion was not required to play through but stood out until a "challenger" was found. This method was abandoned the following year.

Tilden began this match with Shimizu with a ripe carbuncle, or boil, on his right foot, at the instep, I think. He was in much pain all through the first three sets, especially when he attempted to come forward. That is why Big Bill appeared so unaggressive. During the intermission after the third set, he got relief when a doctor came to the locker room, lanced the boil, and removed the pus. Tilden came back to the court with the wound tightly bandaged.

I am indebted for these details to Vinnie Richards, who had just recently won the national doubles title for the second time as Tilden's partner. . . . He was present when the foot was lanced, and since Tilden himself confirmed it in later years I do not think there can be any doubt. . . . Tilden never spoke of the handicap under which he played and never wrote about it in any of his books. He said many years later, after he had become a professional, that he never spoke of it because it would have been unfair to Shimizu, who played magnificently.

Tilden was a generous man where his opponents were concerned. Too generous, I thought he always seemed to give them a little too much the best of it. He refers to this match in his book *My Story*, published in 1948, as a "freak" match. He says there that the situation might not have arisen "if I had fully recovered from the illness which almost cost me my Wimbledon title."

"I was far from well," he continued. "I knew how Shimizu should be played, but he met my attack with a lobbing defense that ran me miles. I had reached 5–3 in the first set when suddenly the heat got me."

I never saw Tilden after he wrote this book, and he had not, in fact, too long to live. I puzzled over why, so long after the event, he should omit all reference to the boil on the foot. Had he also forgotten? The book is full of errors of fact and examples of faulty memory. I wrote Tilden asking about this but never received a reply. Only a few days before Tilden was found dead in his furnished room in California, Richards, then vice president of Dunlop Tire and Rubber Company, showed me a letter he had received from Big Bill asking, "Vinnie, could you please send me a couple of dozen balls and a racket or two? If I had them I think I could get some lessons to give. I need the money badly."

But the greatest tennis player the world has seen was dead when the packet arrived. He had less than five dollars in his pocket, and there was no one to care.

TILDEN DEFEATS JOHNSTON AGAIN

by Richard Larned

William T. Tilden 2d of Philadelphia is still the lawn tennis monarch of the world. By defeating William Johnston of San Francisco at the Germantown Cricket Club, Manheim, this afternoon in a bitterly fought five-set match, he retained his title of American champion and, by virtue of having beaten Gerald L. Patterson of Australia, holder of the so-called world's championship, in the semi-finals, he can justly lay claim to the highest position the game affords. No loftier pinnacle could be scaled in all tennis than Tilden climbed today, when he downed his foremost rival by scores of 4–6, 3–6, 6–2, 6–3, 6–4.

This is the third successive year in which Tilden has won the American title, and his victory today gives him permanent possession of the championship bowl, which has been in competition since 1911. There are five names on the cup besides Tilden's. William A. Larned and Robert Lindley Murray each won it once; and Maurice E. McLoughlin, Richard Norris Williams 2d, and Johnston each had two legs on it.

The final of the Veterans' National singles was won by Dr. Philip B. Hawk. He defeated his fellow Philadelphian Charles N. Beard, 6–0, 6–0.

The men's championship final was witnessed by the biggest gallery ever assembled in Philadelphia for a tennis match. It numbered only 12,000, for the reason that no more than that number could crowd their way into the stands or find a lodging place elsewhere from which to watch the proceedings. Every seat was taken and the unreserved section was filled an hour before the time of starting. People were standing three and four deep in the rear of the unreserved stand and in the back rows of the reserved stands. Even the aisles had their quota, and the stand set apart for officials and press contained scores more of spectators than it ever was intended to hold. They even crowded the roof of it. Hundreds who came the last minute had to be turned away.

It was one of the best-behaved galleries of the year. Applause was bestowed discriminatingly and wholeheartedly. At some particularly brilliant rally, the gallery would fairly yell its appreciation. Possibly Johnston was the crowd's favorite, and when he walked off the court a beaten man, the ovation accorded him was tremendous in volume and intensely moving in its sincerity. But it was a notably fair attitude that the gallery expressed all the time, and Tilden also had his ovation. The champion was playing before a home crowd and he never for a moment lacked full appreciation of his brilliant play.

Tilden's victory was attributable to the fact that he had larger physical resources than Johnston to fall back upon when the crisis of the match came in the fourth set. The Philadelphian had laid down his plan of campaign with rare acumen. He knew and feared Johnston's skill as equal to his own, but he also knew that in a long, hard five-set match in which he was required to do a great deal of running, Johnston had not the physical strength to hold to his fastest pace. Accordingly, Tilden was entirely unworried when Johnston took the first two sets. He was playing a waiting game. He made sure of the third set and reserved his big effort for the fourth and fifth. He was gambling on Johnston's questionable stamina, and the event proved that he gambled wisely.

The break came in the fourth and fifth games of the fourth set. Up to that time Johnston had been playing the game of his life. He had won two of the first three sets by a clearcut demonstration of super tennis. His forehand drive was mightier than Tilden's in the first two sessions and his backhand was as good as his forehand. Overhead he was at his best. Thus it was when he was leading two sets to one and with the games three–love in his favor in the fourth set.

If Johnston's strength had held up only ten minutes longer he would have been the 1922 champion. All he had to do was to maintain the pace of the first three games of the set. But he could not. His physical powers were not equal to the emergency.

To Johnston's legion of supporters in the gallery the sudden collapse of his game was heartbreaking. The abruptness of the transition was astonishing. After the rest period of ten minutes Johnston started the fourth set as though he intended to make a runaway of it. He won the first game to Tilden's 15 and the second to 30. He was playing with dash and power and every ball that left his racket traveled like a shot to the place he intended it to. His speed forced Tilden into errors and he pummeled the champion's backhand unmercifully. He finished the second game with a beautiful volley placement to Tilden's backhand. Johnston was crowding the net and getting away with it masterfully.

Then, on his own service, the Californian had a tough time winning the third game. Tilden had his back to the wall and was fighting with everything he knew. He was making unbelievable recoveries of shots that would have aced any other player in the world. Three times Tilden was within a point of the game, but each time Johnston set grimly and doggedly to work and pulled himself out of the hole. His court covering was wonderful. Finally he won the game by forcing Tilden to drive twice in succession into the net.

This was where the turning point came. Johnston's frail body was beginning to rebel seriously at the heavy demands upon it. He resisted well in the fourth game, but Tilden won it after deuce had been called. Tilden was taking the net more and hitting more decisively as he saw Johnston weaken. He scored two brilliant passing shots in the fourth game, killed the ball after good position-play in another rally, and finished it by forcing a net off service.

The beginning of the end was plainly discernible in the fifth game. Johnston's backhand was going to pieces. His returns were feeble and easily demolished by the champion, who was apparently as fresh as when he started. All the zip and power departed from the Californian's overhead shots. Given a setup, he could not put the ball away fast enough to keep Tilden from recovering it. From the fifth game on through the remainder of the set, Johnston scored only six points. Tilden was quick to see the state his backhand was in, and he pounded it in every rally. Johnston responded with error after error.

It was little short of tragic to see the Californian so suddenly bereft of his strength when most he needed it. The championship had been only three games away. It was all but in his grasp when he had to watch it fade away through no faltering of will and spirit, but because the flesh was weak. Almost tottering from exhaustion, Johnston struggled through the fifth set, putting his heart into every rally and sticking to his task like the splendid fighter he is. The breaks were all against him, and two bad decisions by a linesman were especially discouraging. Tilden drove the ball out in the opening game, but the linesman did not call it, and a long and exhausting rally ensued before Johnston finally won the point on a net by Tilden. Tilden won the game after deuce had been reached three times. The game was an additional drain upon the Californian's strength, but he won his service in the second game. This was a love game, and so, too, was the third, which Tilden won.

The point that gave Tilden the fourth game on Johnston's service was a heartbreaker. Tilden drove the ball in the final rally at least a foot beyond the baseline, but the linesman was blind to the error and the ball continued in play until Tilden scored a placement. Thus Tilden had a lead of 3–1, where Johnston should have had a chance of making it 2–all. Tilden's out was so manifest that the stands broke into righteous and vehement protest. The decision was inexcusable and marred an otherwise wonderful afternoon's work by Umpire Clifford Black and his associate officials.

The next two games were divided, and Tilden was leading 4–2. Then Johnston broke through in a deuce game, only to lose his own service promptly thereafter. Making his last stand, Johnston again won Tilden's service in the ninth game, summoning the last vestiges of his energy to charge the net and volley through for the winning placements. He strove gamely in the tenth game as well, but Tilden's hard hitting sent the points to 15–40, with the match point up. Johnston maneuvered Tilden out of range in the next rally and killed the ball. The next point decided the championship. Tilden, on his second return, dynamited the ball straight down the sideline for a clean passing shot off his forehand, and the match was over.

No summary is complete without a tribute to Tilden's wonderful headwork in planning his part of the match as shrewdly as he did. He was clearly outplayed in the early stages, but was always biding his time, waiting for the right moment to strike, and when the time came he struck heavily. Tilden played magnificently in the fourth and fifth sets. Some of his gets, particularly backhand half-volleys, fairly made the spectators gasp their amazement. Once he took the reins in hand, Tilden was attacking with every shot he sent across the net. His backhand slice worried Johnston greatly. The Californian seemed to have more trouble with it than with the champion's prodigious wallops off the forehand. When Tilden took the net in the final stages he decisively outplayed Johnston, great volleyer though the latter is. All through the match, in fact, Tilden made it extremely uncomfortable for his opponent at the net.

1 9 2 5

TILDEN DEFEATS LACOSTE IN DAVIS CUP SWEEP

by Allison Danzig

Four times within a point of defeat in the third set, William Tilden, national tennis champion, made a dramatic comeback today and defeated René Lacoste of France in the first of the final two singles matches in the Davis Cup Challenge Round.

Apparently hopelessly beaten in the third set, which found him on the verge of collapsing with the score 4–0 in Lacoste's favor, the Philadelphian summoned the very last of his physical reserve to stave off defeat, and the young Frenchman, like Shimizu in 1921, Johnston in 1922 and like Borotra on Thursday, went through the bitter disillusionment of having victory slip from his grasp. The score was 3–6, 10–12, 8–6, 7–5, 6–2.

William Johnston overwhelmed Jean Borotra, 6–1, 6–4, 6–0, giving the United States a clean sweep over the challengers.

Ten thousand spectators, among whom was Dwight F. Davis, Acting Secretary of War, who donated the cup bearing his name in 1900, filled the stands at the Germantown Cricket Club to witness the magnificent attempt of the twenty-year-old Wimbledon champion to accomplish what no player has been able to do in the six years that Tilden has been on the American team. Bewildered, almost stunned, they saw the bronzed phlegmatic youth from France run the world's recognized master ragged with a flawless exhibition of crafty, incisive stroking, taking the first two sets, and fight his way to a commanding lead in the third set.

That Tilden could rise to the emergency in this case seemed almost impossible, even to those who saw him pull out of his desperate plight against Johnston in the final of the 1922 championship. Dripping wet with perspiration and ice water, which he doused over his head at short intervals; dog-tired and labored in his breathing, the champion looked to be as badly spent as Borotra was on Thursday.

Lacoste had chased him in the same merciless fashion that the Philadelphian had sapped the strength of the Basque, and it appeared almost inevitable that he was going to win in exactly the same way. That Tilden won the match under the conditions is one more testimonial to his true championship caliber, to his ability to rise to unassailable heights under stress and confound his opponent.

Playing in his stocking feet, calling upon every shot he commands, measuring his strokes carefully and mixing them with superb generalship, Tilden hung on grimly. Four times he saved himself by a single stroke as the gallery burst into cheers, and, finally, three hours after play had been called, walked off the court the winner. Two hours and forty minutes of actual play were required for a decision in this struggle between the champion of America and the titleholder of Wimbledon.

Hardly before the gallery had been able to regain its composure, Johnston went out on the courts to complete the sweep for the United States by defeating Borotra. Less than forty minutes were required for the Californian to bring the play to an end. Hitting with devastating power, Johnston smothered Borotra in the back court and battered down his every effort at the net. The Frenchman, except for a spell in the second set, when he led at 4–2, was reeling and diving to get at his opponent's blistering placements, and Johnston rushed through to his victory. Not in years has he burned up the court as he did today. Borotra's speed of stroke was what he thrived on, and with tigerish eagerness he met everything on the nose.

Although the United States has gained a sweeping victory in the challenge round, its defenders were as sorely put to it as when the cup was brought back from Australia in 1920. France, playing in the challenge round for the first time, has shown that the days of America's undisputed supremacy are over and that America will have to look seriously to the future. It is a testimonial to the strength of the invaders that 10,000 spectators should have been drawn today in spite of the fact that the cup already had been won with the doubles victory yesterday. American tennis fans sense now the struggles that confront our cup defenders in the international matches, and the possibility of Johnston or Tilden being defeated today lured thousands to Germantown who attached no interest to the concluding matches of the Davis Cup series.

Lacoste, looked upon as an overrated player after his disappointing performance against the Australians, fulfilled today the promise that has been held out for him by European critics, who see in him a future world champion. Cool and undisturbed under any situation, a master strategist, this mere youth not merely outstroked and outlasted Tilden but he showed a cunning and an ingeniousness for forcing his openings that outwitted the player whose knowledge of tactics is looked upon as unsurpassed in the history of the game.

Whatever tactics the champion resorted to, whatever deception, Lacoste always anticipated his move and responded with a better one. Whether he chopped, dropped the ball over the net in an effort to score on a trap shot, or drove with all of the power of his mighty forehand and backhand, the ball invariably came back and in the most unexpected places. Probably never since he won the American title in 1920 has Tilden been so severely punished as he was in this match. There was hardly a minute in the first three sets when he was not on a mad dash to the corners for fast drives or tearing to the net to get an unexpected trap shot. During the major part of these three sets the American was running in circles, and before the second one was over he looked more tired and closer to the point of exhaustion than anyone has seen him since he reached the top. It is pertinent to ask whether Tilden's superb physical condition, one of the prime assets of his game, is not weakening.

Lacoste, by comparison, was as fresh as the proverbial daisy at the end of the match. Only occasionally did he take a sip of water, and he did not seem to even perspire. He was as immaculate when he walked off the court as he was at the start of the match. That the young Frenchman was arm-weary, however, was evident in the final set, for his shots were not clearing the net and did not have the sting and depth that they did in the earlier stages.

Tilden did not give the impression at the outset of being seriously concerned over the outcome of the match. He was hitting out with good length and stroking cleanly, but there was not the concentration and deadliness of purpose that characterized his play later in the match. Lacoste, on the other hand, was going out after every point, covering court thoroughly and getting back everything that Tilden sent over. The ability of the Frenchman to handle the champion's severest drives and cannonball service must have been disturbing to Tilden, for regularly Lacoste returned shots that would have been placements against almost any other player. As a rule, the Philadelphian had to earn his points three or four times before he was able to put the ball out of reach of the other.

Lacoste started right after the champion in the opening game, when he broke through at 4–1, mainly on Tilden's errors. The second game went to deuce eight times, with both players putting up fast, smart tennis. Tilden's service accounted for the third game, and he broke through in the fourth at 6–4 to tie the score at 2–all in games. Driving low and deep, getting sharp angles on his strokes and putting up an almost impenetrable defense, Lacoste took the next two games, outsteadying Tilden in long rallies. A lapse in control cost the Frenchman the seventh game, and he brought the set to an end by taking the eighth and ninth.

Tilden's seeming indifference, or confidence as to his ability to win in the end, was indicated by his failure to question a service ace by Lacoste in the eighth game, although the linesman faintly called the ball out.

Lacoste gave a great exhibition of hitting power in the final game, scoring on a kill and two drives down the lines. He was even better in the second set. He did not seem to know how to make an error in the rallies that were marked by sharp-angle stroking and jockeying for position. Hitting with crisp, deep drives, handling Tilden's cannonball service in unflinching fashion and going to the net with perfectly timed advances, he continually harassed Tilden and kept him on the run. In less than five minutes he took the first three games, in which Tilden got only two points. The Frenchman's service was a big asset for him and, except in the final set, when Tilden scored eight service aces, his service did not suffer by comparison with the champion's.

Tilden mixed up his shots with all his skill and won the fourth game, and the next three games also went on service, with both players making the most of their delivery. The score now stood 5–2. At this point the champion appeared to realize the size of the task ahead of him and he fought with everything he had until the end. He won the eighth game on service and, after being within a point of losing the set in the ninth, he pulled up from 15–40 with four winning shots, passing Lacoste for the last one. Cheers greeted the champion as he changed courts, and then began a desperate struggle in the tenth. Again Lacoste was within a point of the set, but Tilden, covering a prodigious amount of territory and making one marvelous get after another, saved himself and tied the score at 5–all.

The champion called on all his cunning and physical resources in an endeavor to carry on his rally, but Lacoste swept through the next game at love with two service aces, and continued to hold his delivery clear until the nineteenth game. Here at last Tilden broke through with two passing shots, one made after an amazing recovery of Lacoste's smashing drive to the corner, and took the lead for the first time in the match. He needed only to win on his service to take the set, but, weakened from the strenuousness of his exertions in the game before, he made four errors and the score was tied at 10–all. Lacoste was irresistible in the next game. Hitting to the corner, shortening length and changing pace in baffling fashion, he ran Tilden unmercifully and won the game at 5–3. Tilden won the first point of the next game after a long rally, and Lacoste then broke through for the set.

Fifty-three minutes were required for this set. Entire matches have been played in less time than this. . . .

As serious as was the position Tilden now found himself in, standing two sets down, it shortly became precarious. Lacoste, never letting down for a minute, took four games in a row at the start of the third set. Tilden was breathing heavily and it looked as though his legs would give beneath him as he fought in desperation to hold off the relentless attack of his young opponent. Almost never did Lacoste err, and practically every point Tilden won he had to pay dearly for.

In the first game the champion saw a lead of 40–15 slip away as Lacoste nicked the lines with drives and a backhand volley. In the next the champion pulled up from 15–40 to deuce and then saw his efforts go for naught as Lacoste laced his court with placements. Tilden rushed around like a race horse to hold off the attack, but it was unavailing. . . . The champion was helpless as the other took the third game at love, and his control vanished in the fourth when he double-faulted and hit out of court twice.

This was the point where Tilden started his comeback, the point from which the gallery was held at a feverish pitch of excitement until almost the last point of the match. Hitting with abandon, like a giant striking out at his tormentors, the champion scored three placements in the fifth game to break through at 4–1. Two cannonball service aces that were wildly cheered gave him the sixth, and he broke through again in the seventh when Lacoste, disconcerted by the speed of the other's attack, fell into error-making. The applause that greeted the champion now was almost deafening.

Tilden's rally was checked at this point. Lacoste, cool and calculating, broke through in the eighth, making a backhand drive at the end of a bitterly fought rally and following with a backhand drop volley that caught Tilden at the baseline. With the score 5–3 against him and only a game standing between him and defeat, Tilden broke through in the ninth and then tied the score at 5–5 by winning the tenth, taking both games mainly on Lacoste's errors. The Frenchman became dangerous again in the eleventh and took the game at love, to lead at 6–5.

It was in the twelfth game that the climax of the match was reached. Tilden, pitifully tired, made three errors in succession and trailed 15–40 on his own service. Only a point stood between him and defeat now. The gallery held its breath as the champion served. Lacoste drove out off the backhand. The tension was unrelaxed, for still Lacoste was at match point. When Tilden fought his way to the net and neatly dropped the ball over with a backhand volley, a storm of cheers went up from the stands. The score was deuce. Tilden drove out of court and for the third time Lacoste was at match point.

In the next rally Lacoste drove deep to Tilden's baseline. It looked as though the champion met the ball just before it hit the ground and his return went outside. This would have given Lacoste the match, but the linesman belatedly called Lacoste's shot out and the score became deuce again. For the fourth time Lacoste gained match point when Tilden hit into the net, but René became overanxious and drove out of court. Tilden gained the advantage on a placement that caught Lacoste going the opposite way and took the game on the Frenchman's net.

Something near to pandemonium reigned in the stands. For a minute the champion was cheered to the echo, the greatest demonstration of the week. Inspired by the sympathy and applause of the admiring gallery, Tilden drove his way to victory in the thirteenth game and broke through, and he won the next with a service ace and a streaking placement down the line for the set.

Lacoste had missed his big chance and it was felt by those who had seen the champion pull out of similar holes that it was the Frenchman's last chance. However, he threatened again in the fourth set, in which he took the first three games in quick succession. Tilden, raking the opposite court with placements, of which he made five in the seventh game, pulled up to 4–all, and, after being within two points of defeat in the tenth game, broke through in the eleventh and took the twelfth for the set.

Lacoste was beginning to tire now. His control was falling off and there was not the sureness and crispness to his strokes that there had been. The Frenchman seemed to realize his hopes had gone aglimmering, and this proved to be the case. Tilden let loose in devastating fashion in the final set and, with his cannonball service scoring for him repeatedly, took the set at 6–2. Lacoste made a brave fight for the fourth game, carrying Tilden to 16 points after trailing 0–40, but after that Tilden won as he pleased, dropping only three points in the last four games.

1 9 2 6

FIRST DEFEAT OF TILDEN IN U.S. CHAMPIONSHIP IN SEVEN YEARS

by Allison Danzig

Tennisdom was shaken to its foundations yesterday. The six-year reign of William Tilden came to an end, William Johnston also went down, and France placed three men in the semi-finals of the national championship at the West Side Tennis Club, Forest Hills. Six years of American supremacy on the courts vanished in the French holocaust that engulfed three of America's Big Four, leaving Vincent Richards as the only hope of the United States to keep the title from going overseas.

Tilden the invincible, the player whose magic with a racket has confounded the greatest players of the world and made America the mecca of tennis, whose conquests in America, England and Australia had left him in the position of an Alexander sighing for new worlds to conquer, at last has relinquished his scepter.

The tall, gaunt figure who has stood as the Mt. Everest of tennis, challenging all comers to their destruction, at last has toppled after reigning so absolutely for six years that he had come to be regarded as the most powerful potentate in amateur sports, immune to defeat in national championship play and capable of rising superior to any crisis through the sheer wizardry of his strokes.

Even the injury to his knee that paved the way for his defeat by René Lacoste last Saturday, his first in Davis Cup singles, had been looked upon as a negligible consideration, so supreme was the confidence in Tilden's mastery. But it was that injury that undermined the champion's great playing strength and left him, like Hercules, shorn of some of his power and unequipped to bring the plenitude of his resources to bear as Henri Cochet of France fought his way to victory in five sets at 6–8, 6–1, 6–3, 1–6, 8–6.

If ever a champion went down with colors flying, William Tilden was that champion yesterday. Fighting from behind most of the way during the two hours that the match lasted, the Philadelphian won the hearts of the 9,000 spectators in the stadium as he had never won them in victory as he gave himself unsparingly and with reckless disregard for his underpinning in his vain effort to withstand the demoralizing steadiness and craftily placed shots of his opponent.

The climax of the match, the point at which the gallery broke into the wildest demonstrations, was during the final set when Tilden, trailing at 1–4, rallied to volley Cochet dizzy with one of the most sensational exhibitions he ever gave at the net and pull up to 4–all. Every winning shot of the American was greeted with roars of applause and, with each successive game in the series of three, hearts became lighter with hope for an American victory.

When Tilden won the eighth game there were few who believed that the catastrophe would occur. The champion, it was agreed, was still the old champion, capable of lifting his game in an emergency to unassailable heights. But after leading at 40–15 on Cochet's service in the ninth game, Tilden had reached the end of his rope. The player whose last-minute pull-ups had brought him out of the jaws of defeat so many times in the past finally met his master.

Cochet, playing with the coolness of a veteran of twice his years and absorbing the champion's cannonball service and lightning drives with machinelike steadiness, confounded the American's most desperate efforts and checkmated his every thrust with counter-strokes of craft. Tilden's service enabled him to go into the lead at 6–5, and then the debacle came as the invader crushed all opposition in the next three games, in which Tilden got only four points.

Let full justice be done Cochet, the player who achieved what had been looked upon as the impossible. Fairness to Tilden necessitated consideration of the bearing his physical condition had upon the match, but fairness to the young Frenchman also calls for due acknowledgment of the fact that Tilden, even with the fullest support of his legs, would have been extended to the limit to prevail over Cochet and might well have failed.

Those who last saw Cochet in this country in 1922 were unable to comprehend how he could have beaten Richards abroad twice this year, but satisfactory explanation was furnished yesterday. No French player that ever came to the United States has given a more masterly exhibition than did Cochet against the champion. There was a confidence about this young player that those who have watched him in action abroad looked upon as a foreboding sign. Cochet was at his best for the first time in this country and went about his task as though he never had any doubt about the outcome.

This 24-year-old youth was coolness personified. In the face of Tilden's most devastating swipes he maintained the even tenor of his way, assimilating speed as though he was brought up on it and eternally getting the ball back as steadily as the patter of rain. Lacoste had come to be regarded as the most mechanically perfect player in tennis, but Cochet could have given him spades and a couple of rackets yesterday. At the end of a rally in the seventh game of the third set, Major A. P. Simmonds, the umpire, called out, "Advantage Lacoste." Cochet stopped in the act of serving and looked quizzically at the official, who raised his hat amidst the laughter of the spectators, to apologize for his mistake. But the mistake was easy enough to understand. Major Simmonds, like many another person there, must have been under the delusion this machinelike youth *was* Lacoste.

But Cochet was more than a machine. There was a tennis brain directing this mechanically perfect player's shots that left Tilden at his wit's end in trying to fathom its workings. It was not Cochet's strokes that were so irresistible but the craftiness with which they were employed. Off the ground the Frenchman was outclassed in speed and depth, for, as regards pace, his strokes for the most part were hardly more than defensive returns, crossing the net at high altitude and bouncing high off the turf to afford Tilden the opportunity to get set for his pasting returns. Playing safe against Tilden's blistering shots, Cochet awaited his opportunities to let loose with a forcing stroke—opportunities which he made himself by the changing direction and varying length he employed. Once he had the champion wide of the court and on the run, then Cochet's shots sought a lower level and deeper territory, and usually in the American's backhand corner.

If his ground strokes were lacking in severity, Cochet's volleys were the last word in finality. Any time that the Frenchman came to the net, he was a dangerous figure, deadly overhead and sure on the straight volley. As a rule, Tilden can dislodge any opponent who entrenches himself at the net, but he was always worried yesterday when Cochet bearded his forcing shots. Because Cochet is so deft a volleyer and handles his racket like an artist at close quarters, the champion knew that he must put the ball out of his reach or directly at his feet to stump him, and he could not hit the bull's-eye. Lobbing was out of the question, for Cochet handled everything overhead with unfailing precision.

Against an opponent of this caliber, who was a stonewall in his backcourt and a catapult at close quarters, Tilden never had a moment's peace of mind, except in the fourth set, when he carried all before him by the sheer fury of his attack.

The champion appreciated from the very start the size of the task facing him, for Cochet against Hunter had given him an inkling of what to expect, and for the first time in the tournament the gallery saw an aroused Tilden in the very first game—a Tilden who hit out with bludgeon strokes off the ground, capitalized his cannonball service for its full worth, jockeyed with all his cunning for positional advantages, and exploited his volleying game as few have seen him exploit it in all the years that he has held the title.

It is doubtful whether many appreciated how magnificent a volleyer Tilden can be until this match, so seldom has he felt it necessary to seek close grips with his opponents. There was a reason for his change in tactics yesterday, a change which he adopted on Wednesday also. The strain of plugging up the gaps in his backcourts called for greater demands upon his knee than the work of holding his position at the net, and for that reason Tilden the driver and chopper became a volleyer.

And what a volleyer the champion was! Even Richards at his best could not have performed more sensationally than did Tilden as he twisted and stooped and went through every sort of convolution in bringing off low drop volleys off his feet and smashes in the air. There were times, particularly in the fourth set and during the champion's rally in the final chapter, when it seemed that human resistance to this sort of shot-making was futile, but Cochet was never worried, and in due time put in his oar to take the play away from the champion with shot-making at the net that evoked almost equally thunderous applause. Everything that Tilden did well Cochet did also, and he was able to do it over a longer period, rising to irresistible heights in the final stages when Tilden was making the last desperate stand of a champion who felt his crown slipping away from him.

So totally absorbed were the officials, as well as the spectators, in this match that all thought of the other contests was forgotten until the last point was played, and as a result the three other matches got away to a late start.

Two hours after Tilden walked off the court a beaten man, Johnston also passed out of the play in five sets, the victim of Jean Borotra. Borotra, who had never before taken even a set from the Californian and who was subdued in three sets in the Davis Cup challenge round last week, blasted the hopes of Johnston just when it seemed that, with Tilden out of the competition, he had a real chance to break through and regain the title he held in 1915 and 1919. The score was 3–6, 4–6, 6–3, 6–4, 6–4.

Long before the Basque had finished his rally, which carried him to victory from the almost hopeless position of 0–2 in sets, Lacoste had disposed of Dick Williams, captain of the Davis Cup team and No. 4 in the American ranking, at 6–0, 6–3, 8–6, and Richards had eliminated Jacques Brugnon at 6–2, 6–1, 6–2.

The triumph of Borotra over Johnston was as unexpected as was the defeat of Tilden, but the gallery, dazed by the downfall of the champion, failed to show any great reaction to the upset. Anything was possible after Cochet's victory. Johnston has lost many a heart-breaking match during the six years that he has tried to break up the monopoly Tilden has held on the title, but yesterday's was in a way the most distressing one of all.

Leading at 2–0 in sets, the Californian looked to be a certain winner, and at last, it appeared, he would have the opportunity to test his strength against Richards in championship play. As he has always beaten Richards in a three-out-of-five-set match, there was reason for him to look forward with confidence to a test with the New York youth, and then would come his big opportunity to regain the crown. But for the seventh successive year Johnston's dream went up in smoke—the smoke of Borotra's lightning drives and darting volleys, and America's second-ranking player passed out of the tournament along with the world's first.

It was Borotra's volleying that decided the match. The spectacular Basque, unable to collect his forces in the first two sets in the face of the Californian's destructive forehand drives, took to the air in the third set, and out of the air, as he leaped for his volleys and overhead kills, came the shots from his racket that put the quietus upon Johnston.

The pace set by the Basque in the last three sets at times carried Johnston off his feet. Never for a minute did Borotra cease going to the net and everything that came within his reach there was doomed to destruction. Johnston's control in the later stages of the match was not at its best, and his forehand drive found the net with irritating persistence.

In the final set the Californian made a tremendous fight for the third game, winning it at 8–6 with a marvelous exhibition of volleying, and when he continued his deadly work at close quarters in the fourth, to lead at 3–1, it seemed that Borotra's rally was to be in vain. But the Basque, never discouraged and smiling his appreciation of his opponent's shot-making, came back to take the play away from Johnston at the net and ran three games in a row. This brilliant display of pyrotechnics by the Basque stung Johnston into dynamic action in the eighth and he broke through on three placements to tie the score at 4–all. That was his last game, though he led at 30–0 in the ninth. Borotra pulled even on the Californian's errors, lashed out from the net to break through, and the play came to an end in the tenth as Johnston's control lapsed in the face of his opponent's ruthless volleying.

LENGLEN-WILLS MATCH AT CANNES

by James Thurber

A rush of people struggling around a livid woman in pink-colored silk, a sudden rioting of flowers from somewhere, a bright glittering of silver in the sun. The crowd that watched from the stands was a little stupefied. It had all been too swift and too dazzling.

And then a girl in white walked silently away from the colorful, frenzied throne they were building around the woman in pink silk. The crowd that watched from the stands could comprehend it now. The silent girl in white detaching herself from the mad maelstrom was a note of familiar sanity. Helen Wills had been defeated and was going home.

She went home quietly, directly, without looking around, as she always does when a match is ended. The only color that relieved the whiteness of her face and of her dress, a whiteness so pathetically odd against that silver and red and pink-colored scene, was a bright flush on her cheeks. No one knew what she thought exactly. She didn't say anything—even when she was spoken to. But it wasn't a flush that comes from being ashamed or being crushed. It might well have been a flush of pride. At any rate, to the crowd that watched from the stands it was a sort of red badge of courage with as much significance as the glory that broke about the victorious head of Suzanne Lenglen.

Helen Wills was defeated yesterday on the Carlton court in Cannes by Suzanne Lenglen, 6–3, 8–6. Those were the statistics. But it was a match that transcended statistics. . . . They had said Helen Wills might not get a game. They had bet she wouldn't get six. She got nine. But those again are merely figures.

The heart of the game was that "Little Poker Face" from California met for the first time in the singles the greatest woman tennis player in the world since the time when Helen was fondling dolls, fought her with everything she had, smashed with her, drove with her, volleyed with her, until she had the French champion so greatly on the run that at times it seemed like the baseline on Mlle. Lenglen's side of the court was the dropping off place.

That was the heart of the game. The body of it was made up of a variety of things, very complicated things. But a component part that can not be overlooked was the fact that Suzanne Lenglen won a hard and brilliantly fought match, proved herself every inch the queen of the courts. If she was on the run at times, she almost broke Helen Wills' heart in a certain part of that tremendous second set when she sent her speeding from one alley-line to the other in a magnificent series of those sharp, accurate, hard-shot placements in which, at her best, she is the best there is.

She had to be the best to win in two sets yesterday. She may perhaps have to be a little better than the best to do it again. Helen Wills met a baptism of fire which was strange and new to her: she encountered a variety and a brilliance of technique that she has never encountered before. And having come through it so superbly, the unfinished sentence on everybody's lips yesterday was: "The next time . . .?"

Helen Wills, with the eyes of Lenglen on her across a net, all alone, for the first time, as the game began, was nervous. She showed it in her first quick wide-of-the-baseline returns of Suzanne's service. The Frenchwoman took an easy love game quickly. The next game was a little different, but neither player was yet warmed up. Wills saw the game go to 15–40 against her. Then abruptly it was deuce, her advantage, her game. And almost before the stands knew it she took the next game, by the same route exactly, on her opponent's service. 2–1 Wills.

Lenglen made up for it rapidly and irresistibly. She took two love games in succession and fairly toyed with the American in the second one. Then she made it ten straight points by going to 30–love in the sixth game. Wills held, to 30–40; then Lenglen took her third straight game to make the score 4–2, her favor. The seventh game was Wills' best in this set. She took it to 40–love on Lenglen's service, lost a point, and then shot over a nice winning placement.

With the score thus 4–3 in her favor, Lenglen asserted herself and beat Wills' service in the eighth game, four points to one. She went into the last game of the set with a nice high lob to begin with, shot over a placement to make it 30–love, lost a point, and took the next two—game and set.

Neither player had yet attained the form she was to show in the second set. Wills' early nervousness resulted in several wide outs and even more netted shots. They had been fairly even at the net, to which, however, they were yet to commit themselves for a real test. In her two straight love games the Frenchwoman's easy placements, that left Helen's racket wide of the ball in several cases, were abetted by Miss Wills' failure to take advantage of her opportunities.

The second set got off in a blaze of Wills. She took her first and only love game against the total of four that Suzanne scored in the two sets. After outshooting the French star to reach 30–love, Wills was helped to 40 when her opponent outed widely, and the California girl broke into her top-form stride in the next exchange, winning her love game by a pretty placement.

They were both now at it in earnest, and from this point on the game took on a thrilling aspect that kept spectators on the edge of their chairs, made hearts beat thickly in throats, and brought out involuntary shouts from the watchers.

With Lenglen serving the second game, Helen stepped into her first serve and began one of the most beautifully played point-battles of the match. She outplayed her opponent at this point in every phase of play, and the variety was becoming fast and furious. Wills took the next point also, only to yield the next two; then she made it 40–30, whereupon Suzanne forged to the front, deuced the game, and despite some of the most splendid brilliance of the afternoon, gained the advantage and the game.

Helen Wills was now in the match hammer and tongs, with fire in her eye and every trace of the nervousness which had visibly restrained her early play entirely vanished. She was playing not the greatest woman tennis player in the world but just a woman who happened to be finalist in the same match. With this attitude showing in every stroke, she served to 40–15 in the third game and then won it, four points to two. Score: 2–1, Wills.

At this point Helen Wills had Suzanne Lenglen on the run. She outplayed her at every turn in the fourth game, smashing through the Frenchwoman's service with the loss of only one point. Score: 3–1, Wills. But Suzanne Lenglen was not swept aside, partly due to a little overanxiety on the part of the American girl. Suzanne broke through Wills' service in return by the identical point score of the preceding game. Score: 3–2, Wills.

The Frenchwoman tied the count in the next game, winning it four points to one. But that was just the beginning of the struggle. The seventh game was one of the most thrilling and terrifically fought of the afternoon, and the Berkeley youngster won it in the end after it had gone four times to deuce. Moreover, she won it in spite of the fact that Lenglen had it in her grasp, 15–40, before the American, making good her reputation for hard, cool playing in a crisis, carried it to deuce, her ad, deuce again, Suzanne's ad, deuce again, Wills' ad, deuce again, Wills' ad and game. Score: 4–3, Wills.

On her serve, Lenglen took the next game, four points to two. It was in this hot sector of the match that Wills suffered one of her worst blows, a blow bad enough to break stuff less stern than the heart of the American fighter. With the score at 30–all, Lenglen outed, but the line judge failed to see or to call it. It practically presented this crucial game to the Frenchwoman. The stands yelled "out" in a chorus, but the heartbreaking "boner" was a *fait accompli*. Score: 4–4. The other blow that hit the American girl in the middle of this set was not a bad break but Lenglen's terrifically swift battery of placements all around the edges of the court that left the American panting.

Wills took the ninth game, however, in one of the most splendidly fought encounters of the set, replete with hard playing on both sides of the net. She served to deuce, her advantage, and game. The tenth game became Lenglen's fourth love game. Score: 5 5.

Both players were fagged, but Wills seemed suddenly a little ill in the bargain, for at one point in this terrific dueling, with Lenglen in place ready to serve, the youngster bent over and leaned pathetically on her racket. With her racket in the air and ball in hand, Lenglen had to call to the girl to get her to look up and receive the serve.

Later, however, the American rallied, while Lenglen was visibly fatigued —a fatigue that showed in every line of her face. The light was a little drained from her eyes and the lines around her mouth showed sheer misery. It seemed that at several points she was on the verge of stampede, and she evidenced it in one notable case by failing to play a stroke near the baseline and looking rather abjectly at the line judge. It was good and Wills won the point. Wills won the applause of the crowd in the terrific eleventh game when, with the points at love–40 against her on her service, she moved to 30–40 before yielding. Score: 6–5, Lenglen.

The next game was sheer tribute to Wills' "stuff." And incidentally it will go down as one of the most grotesque and thrilling and momentous games on record. Lenglen needed the game to win the set and match and the virtual championship of the world. It was her serve. It seemed to her that she could rest soon. And she had to rest soon. So did Wills.

Lenglen won the first two points. Wills fought with everything she had and won the next point. Lenglen went to 40–15. And here came the incident that brought the stands to their feet, cheering Lenglen, the "winner" of the great confrontation. She shot the ball perilously near the line. The line judge was silent. Silence means the shot is good. Lenglen upped her racket and prepared to quit the court. Wills started for the net, her hand out to congratulate the winner. The stands rose. And suddenly there was a conference of officials, and a loud voice announced, "40–30." Wills had been saved. The game went on. Wills took it to deuce, her advantage, game. Score: 6–6.

The next game was almost as nerve-wracking and it was again a great tribute to the American girl's remarkable grit in the face of defeat. On Helen's service, Suzanne rushed to 0–40. Then Wills rallied and fought back to deuce, then to her advantage. Lenglen deuced it, went to ad, and then took the game.

The next and last game, similarly, went to deuce twice. After Lenglen had stood at 30–15, Wills climbed to 30–40, Lenglen brought it to deuce, then to her advantage. Here the French star faltered and double-faulted. Deuce. But she came back, won the advantage again, and then the game, set, and match. There was the meeting at the net, and the "battle of the century" was over.

Wills, tired, game, defeated, but carrying a radiance all her own, left the court of honor with its cups and its flowers and its "bravos" to Suzanne Lenglen. Suzanne Lenglen was tired. Tired, pale and drawn.

"She knew she was in a match," someone breathed, a little awestruck. It was like seeing a goddess in pain. Even in her moment of glory she was, first of all, tired and worn. The youngster from America had had her on the run.

Both stars revived remarkably after a few hours' rest and took to the courts in a women's doubles final that was, in its way, almost as thrilling as the great match itself. Mlle. Lenglen and Mlle. Vlasto won it, 6–4, 7–5, from Miss Wills and Mlle. Contostavlos. All four played splendidly. Miss Wills was the weakest of all, perhaps, in the first set, but she made up for every fault by taking, almost single-handedly, the fifth, sixth and seventh games of the second set, all at love, in the most remarkably sustained brilliance of the whole day of playing. She won just about every point, and there might as well have been no one on the other side of the net.

THE GREAT MATCH

by A. Wallis Myers

The great match is over, and Mlle. Lenglen has won it. She won it in two sets, with the score of 6–3, 8–6. But the resistance offered by Miss Helen Wills over sixty minutes of a thrilling and level encounter proved the prophets to have been absurdly premature in their forecast of a romp-away victory. It is true that Suzanne won the first set with a satisfying margin, but she had to fight every inch of the court and every moment in the second set—a set of palpitating fluctuations, with scenes near and at its finish unprecedented in the annals of the game.

Let me describe briefly the dramatic incident in the twelfth game of this set before reviewing the match as a whole. Suzanne, leading 6–5 and almost breathless with her exertions, was serving and had reached 40–15. She had thus two match balls to close the great ordeal. There was a long, nerve-racking rally. Miss Wills played a withering forehand drive which hit the line plumb in the middle. Lord Charles Hope, who was officiating on this line, said nothing, as was only right and proper. But Suzanne evidently thought the ball was out and the match over. She tripped towards the umpire's chair, and Miss Wills followed her, though somewhat ruefully. The spectators rose in their seats, and some of the crowd burst on the court. Quietly, without any commotion, Lord Charles Hope made a beeline for the umpire's chair and informed him of the facts. Commander Hillyard, keeping his sailor's head in the crisis, requested the players to resume the struggle.

It was a terrible moment for Suzanne. She was obviously tiring and overwrought; she had drunk freely of brandy administered by her mother, and her French temperament, ever up and down, was reacting under the strain. She might easily, on taking up the cudgels again, have found them blunted and her cause lost. For a phase it seemed that Helen, reprieved after apparent defeat, would pull the match round and win a great triumph. She did save the twelfth game, and came within a point of winning the next. Americans, their shattered hopes once more buoyant, shouted their delirious approval when Miss Wills led once more. It is a great tribute to Suzanne that she did not falter at this menace. Drawing on her deeper experience, teasing Miss Wills with a shorter length, draining her opponent's last remaining stamina, she went out with sound defensive strokes.

It had been arranged that Mrs. Wills or Mme. Lenglen should present the cup to the winner. But this pleasant little plan could not be carried out. Immediately the match was really over, the excited, hysterical crowd stormed the court and mobbed both players. Tears were streaming down Suzanne's face; this was the greatest reaction of all. In vain were huge bouquets pressed on her; for once she was oblivious to congratulations. I imagine she was contemplating, in retrospect, the incident I have described. A French officer in uniform tried to cheer her by declaring that she had won two victories instead of one. She pinned a flower in his coat by way of acknowledging the compliment, but her heart seemed sore, and though she was lustily cheered from the surrounding roofs as she corkscrewed her way through the gesticulating mob to the Carlton Hotel, it was a rather wan and exhausted champion who sought the privacy of her room. Meanwhile, Miss Wills had slipped quietly away. She was a force absolutely spent in the last two games, for she had been fighting against odds all the time, fighting with superb courage and with a skill lacking only more experience to bring it greater reward.

In the second set Miss Wills had led 3–1. Like many another great match, this was one of fluctuations—first one and then the other would seem to be winning. After Miss Wills, beginning diffidently, had gained a 2–1 lead, Suzanne's reply of ten successive points seemed to suggest a swift conclusion. But of the next nine points, Mlle. Lenglen only won one. Then as a counter-stroke Suzanne took eight points to Helen's one.

But Mlle. Lenglen had been required to run much more than she had probably anticipated. The effort of retrieving the deep-length corner shots of Miss Wills was obviously taxing her strength. In the second set, her play became less provocative. In vain did she wait for Miss Wills to make a mistake. Helen took the first game to love, the third game from 30, and the fourth game from 15. Had the American not reduced her speed at this stage, relying on patience rather than on power, it is probable she would have placed a commanding lien on the set. But she drew in her horns and Suzanne's perfectly timed defense, with its fade-away shot on backhand, squared the set at 3–all. Miss Wills only won one point in the fifth and the sixth games. There was a tremendous fight for the seventh game. Miss Wills won it in the end because she came to the net at the psychological moment and volleyed decisively.

In the eighth game, Mr. Cyril Tolley, who was taking the sideline, gave a doubtful decision in favor of Mlle. Lenglen. For a second Miss Wills faltered, losing her valuable lead as a result. But she came back to the attack gallantly in the ninth game, and with strokes of astonishing accuracy and strength went ahead at 5–4. Defiance at this stage had paid her, but she made a fatal mistake in the next game of modifying all her strokes, doubtless hoping that Suzanne would compromise herself by error. Relieved of immediate pressure, Suzanne maneuvered for position with sure control. She won the tenth game to love and the eleventh game from 30. Miss Wills was now on defense when attack was so essential. Then came the memorable twelfth game, already mentioned.

Regarding the contest as a whole, it may be said indisputably that Miss Wills played a finer game than even her best friends expected. She was a match for Suzanne; she was unlucky in not winning the second set. Her tactics rather than her strokes were to blame. She exhibited speed, resource, and wonderful endurance. The hand and heart were perfectly sound; the head alone made mistakes. For Suzanne it was a great ordeal as well as a great triumph. One felt instinctively all through that she had counted on an easier victory. That she did not allow her emotional surprise to impair her control at the vital moment is a tribute to her ripe experience. She might so easily have lost the second set and been waging the third set at a physical and mental disadvantage.

Considering the crowd and the excitement, the officials may congratulate themselves that no greater disturbance occurred. When sightseers have removed tiles from a roof in order that they may peer on a tennis court a hundred feet below, when photographers are charging down the sidelines while play is in progress, when too eager partisans are shouting decisions from the stands, the wonder is that the two girls, under great physical strain, should have comported themselves so well.

TWO QUEENS

by Ferdinand Tuohy

Some spectacles will remain forever, even in a newspaperman's mind. Such a one was that of Suzanne Lenglen, lying on a bed on the sixth floor of the Carlton Hotel here at noon today, directly after her grueling victory over Helen Wills, 6–3, 8–6, in a simple game of tennis, yet a game which made continents stand still and was the most important sporting event of modern times exclusively in the hands of the fair sex.

A few minutes before, I had left her enthroned in a flowery bower in the middle of the tennis court, like a Broadway favorite after a successful first night. From a balcony high above the Mediterranean, I next glimpsed her being swept along a side street by a frantically cheering mob. Then she lay before me in complete whiteness of coat and skirt, capped by her vivid crimson face.

Only Mme. Lenglen moved about the room, arranging gifts of dolls and flowers above the furor still arising from the street, as I asked Suzanne how she had won, and waited while she gasped back to breath and then broke into a torrent of French, openly, perhaps challengingly, as if to say, "Now, for God's sake, will you English and Americans leave me alone for a moment and accept my supremacy, however much it may be getting boresome!"

In fact, I believe she said something very like that, though her first frantic thoughts were for her stricken father at Nice, while I fought with time to capture every notion, opinion, thought and reaction from the victor of Europe. Nor was Suzanne silent. She rebelled against being forced to play; maintained the champion's right to do what she pleases; explained away her indifferent display by her private worry and the public din during the match; developed praise for her rival, though somewhat grudgingly; and concluded on the defiant note that she, Suzanne, intended to remain enthroned for many years more.

With difficulty I dragged from the prostrate girl such grim little verbal bouquets as "Helen showed more intelligence than I imagined. She has style and production of strokes. She will improve."

Yet none of this—not even Helen's splendid drives and placings—worried Suzanne, according to Suzanne. A little more magnanimity might have issued from that white couch and its palpitating burden, and with little damage to the truth of the day, as most of those present saw it.

"*Elle se defende, la petite,*" said a French spectator of our amazing court-side champion.

"What a game Helen is putting up," echoed the serried Anglo-Saxon brigade. "She'll have her yet."

Suzanne, too, played like a champion. For many games in the memorable second set she fell steadily behind, yet she overhauled the challenger, to win fresher than Helen, and this afternoon the French girl gave one of the pluckiest performances ever seen on a tennis court when she was carried, in a collapsing state, to victory with Didi Vlasto in the women's doubles over Miss Wills and Helene Contostavlos. She is absolutely all in and is canceling tonight's celebration held here in her honor.

Since eight in the morning the entire social register of the Riviera, flanked by a goodly slice of the Almanac de Gotha and Debrett, had been fighting their way to the Carlton courts in one long procession of automobiles stretching out along the Nice and Monte Carlo road. And for three hours we sat there in the bleachers, 4,000 strong, just as when we were waiting for Dempsey and Carpentier, laughing hysterically at each trivial incident—as when chic women trod the skyline transparently on the rooftops or when the gendarmes engaged in arboreal pursuits in trying to compel the young locals to descend from the branches of trees.

Then each celebrity would be hailed on his entry as at a first night, and perilous jokes would be cracked anent the building of stands, which went on beneath us until Suzanne sent her first service over. At that moment one surely never beheld such a vivid rainbow effect beneath a blazing sun as was afforded by hundreds of the smartest women of Europe all assembled in their Helen and Suzanne frocks especially ordered for the occasion.

Once the game began we ceased to behave. Within we applauded each stroke while the rally still proceeded, cheering frantically when Helen excelled, while without, a thousand-strong company of locals rooted through the uplifted draping of Suzanne and France. From hotel windows and roofs hundreds of yards away little figures signaled their participation in the contest by waving handkerchiefs and flags at each point.

Repeatedly, poor susceptible Suzanne implored for calm, only for the turmoil to break out anew, sending her almost down in defeat before the outwardly unperturbed but inwardly quivering little poker face.

Then when the battle was at the tensest moment came the errors of linesmen, giving three outs against Miss Wills, all of which were in, and ending in letting Suzanne think she had won the match before she actually had. As events turned out, Helen proceeded to win two more games before the end. Upon this, of course, the dukes and movie men invaded the court one and all, and the limp and gasping Suzanne was held up in the midst of masses of floral offerings.

MY MATCH AGAINST MLLE. LENGLEN

by Helen Wills

I was happy when I persuaded my father and mother to let me go to the South of France. Both had thought that there wasn't really any reason for traveling such a long distance for tennis, because I could play all that I wanted to at home in California. Finally, my mother consented to go with me. The United States Lawn Tennis Association advised me not to go there for the tournaments and said that I could not be considered as their representative. But it seemed to me, at twenty, that the Riviera tournaments were the most alluring things in all the world.

So we started out, leaving California sunshine and tennis, shortly after Christmas, to journey six thousand miles to the South of France, where there would be more sunshine and more tennis. I found, when we arrived, that the sunshine was not nearly so warm as that in California, but that the tennis was worth having made the trip for. All the best players were gathered there for the tournaments that year—Mlle. Lenglen, who lived in Nice; Eileen Bennett; Betty Nuthall; Didi Vlasto, the pretty Greek champion; Lili Alvarez, the colorful Spanish player; and Helene Contostavlos, another excellent Greek player, who is a cousin of Didi. . . .

I was so eager to begin playing at once that I entered a tournament in Cannes the next day after arriving. The pink clay courts felt very different under foot from the asphalt courts to which I had been accustomed in California. The balls bounced differently too. There had been rain and the clay was damp, so that the bound was low. It was several days before my drives reached their usual form. And I found it difficult to be steady and accurate. . . .

In the South of France Mlle. Lenglen was queen. The whole of the Riviera was Mlle. Lenglen's home town. She lived in Nice, in a villa opposite the Nice Tennis Club, but so closely situated were all the towns that from a tennis point of view they were one. The first time that I saw Mlle. Lenglen in Nice was from the terrace on the top of the Nice Tennis Club. She leaned out of an upper window of her villa and waved at us. She was wearing a white tennis dress and a yellow sweater. Soon she was over on the terrace with us, welcoming us pleasantly to her home club.

Mlle. Lenglen knew every inch of every court on the coast, and it was not surprising that she chose the very excellent courts of the Carlton Club at Cannes for the scene of her appearance in the singles. The courts were owned and run by her good friends, the Burkes, who are well-known professionals. There are several Burke brothers. One of them used to practice with Mlle. Lenglen continually.

In California I had vaguely thought that if I were fortunate enough to win my preliminary matches, I would have the opportunity of meeting Mlle. Lenglen in a number of tournaments, and thereby learn a great deal about tennis. I was disappointed when I realized that these imagined meetings were to be boiled down into one, and that my whole visit to the South of France would have in it just one match with Mlle. Lenglen. . . .

The buzzing which had surrounded the tournament became concentrated on the final bracket. It had seemed to me that the week preceding and the week of the tournament had been entirely too hectic. No tennis match deserved the attention which this one received. . . . Our match was pounced upon by the newspaper correspondents, who waited on the courts or else in the bar at the corner. I know that I, and probably Mlle. Lenglen, too, was inclined to think that the outcome of the match meant more than it really did. It is not always easy to maintain a sense of proportion at a time like this. . . .

The court was a marvel of smoothness. The roller had done double duty. The seating facilities were very cramped, as there were not enough places for people who wished to see the match. The tickets had got into the hands of speculators and were being sold for four and five times what they had originally cost. The gates were so narrow and the ticket takers so stubborn—as they always are abroad—that there was much congestion around the one entrance. It was with difficulty that my mother and I got into the court at all.

The linesmen had been carefully chosen—men who had played tennis themselves, who were supposed to have an eye for a moving tennis ball. Among the linesmen was a titled Englishman of distinguished mien. On one line was an English golfer who had been a champion.

The match started with the usual spin of racket, the choosing of side and the preliminary rally. From the first I knew that Mlle. Lenglen was determined to extract the most out of her own game. She intended to bring forth the concentrated knowledge that had accumulated with her years of tournament play. She meant, also, to make the most of her understanding of strategy. She always did do these two things, for, curiously enough, she was one of the most consistent of players in her matches, contrary to general belief. But on this occasion she seemed to fix her mind on these two ideas with more determination than ever—or so I thought, because it was myself who was experiencing the full power of her concentration.

I also felt that she was saving her strength as much as possible—making her mind do the running instead of her feet. Indeed, it was I who was the stronger player physically, and the one who had the greater powers of endurance. But she was the superior in experience and in the understanding of the tactics of the game, as, in fact, she should have been, because she was seven years my senior.

Her favorite bit of strategy in our match was to keep me running back and forth, and then, at an opportune moment, to angle a shorter ball, so that I would have to run the longest distance for it—that is, on the diagonal, instead of sideways. Unless I made a very satisfactory return from this short ball, then she would be able to send a passing shot down the line.

Now, there is nothing particularly new about tactics of this variety in tennis; they have been often used. But probably never with the accurate touch which Mlle. Lenglen gave to them. In other words, she accomplished and carried to their ideal completion strategic plans which other players try but cannot always consistently finish.

As I remember, I had no definite plan of strategy or attack, because it was so difficult to find any way of attacking Mlle. Lenglen's game. And my three years of big-tournament play were not sufficient to warrant my being called a general of strategy. I felt that I could run as far on the court and for as long a time as Mlle. Lenglen. This was a consoling thought. I felt that I could meet enough of her balls so that the rallies would be prolonged. But as to the actual placing of the balls, I could not figure out a way beforehand. However, I hoped that the match itself might indicate what my strategic moves should be. As it turned out, my idea had been right about actual physical strength. As the match wore on, Mlle. Lenglen showed signs of weariness, and it was because of this that the second set went to the score of eight games to six. But clearly, throughout the match, Mlle. Lenglen was my superior as regards tactics and placing, and it was this which enabled her to win; coupled, of course, with her usual steadiness.

A thing that surprised me was that I found her balls not unusually difficult to hit, nor did they carry as much speed as the balls of several other of the leading women players whom I had met in matches. But her balls kept coming back, coming back, and each time to a spot on the court which was a little more difficult to get to.

It may seem that I am overdoing my description of my experiences when playing against Mlle. Lenglen. A match seven years ago—why, that is older than old news! But the interesting thing about it—at least to me—is that I believe that that match, for me, will be the unique experience of all my tennis-playing days. The reason being that Mlle. Lenglen was a unique player. No woman player that I have met since at Wimbledon or Forest Hills can compare with her in playing ability. Since Mlle. Lenglen showed how tennis can be played, there has been a marked rise in the standard of women's tennis, but no one has yet equaled her mastery and skill.

Unconsciously, I compare other matches that I play with the Lenglen one, and use it as a yardstick of measurement. To me, of course, at the time, with my game at the point where it might improve or cease to improve, the lesson was a most opportune one, and I feel that I learned things in that one match, as I said before, which have stuck with me ever since.

The match—the actual playing part of it—may be called uneventful, with the exception of one incident—at least from the point of view of the onlooker. The reason being that the white ball went back and forth, back and forth. Neither player did anything out of the ordinary, such as scolding ball boys or arguing with the linesmen. The comedy of the match was supplied by a eucalyptus tree that grew at the end of the court just behind the backstop. It was partly trimmed off, so that its shadows would not fall on the court, but in the leaves that were left were hidden more small boys than you would have believed possible. At intervals they fell out, or were dragged down by red-faced gendarmes who disturbed the peace more than the boys.

Several roofs of surrounding houses might have given way because of the unaccustomed weight of people, but did not. Americans, who were present in large numbers, clapped for their player, and the French for theirs. Patriotism holds true to form at a tennis match. I do not know which player the English onlookers wanted to have win. Perhaps they clapped for the ball itself, in the interests of pure sport.

From the eucalyptus-tree end of the court there were distractions, but both players were equally handicapped—perhaps Mlle. Lenglen more than I, because of her highly strung nature. A crowd of people from the town, unwilling to buy tickets, pressed against the backstop at one time and threatened to knock it over. Mlle. Lenglen, who was nearest, with a few sharp words, stilled the commotion. There was only one unusual incident in the play itself. Toward the end of the second set, Mlle. Lenglen needed only one more point to win the match. I sent over a ball down the line on her backhand that she thought was outside. She moved forward to the net and held out her hand for the final handshake. I thought, seeing her do this, that the match was over, so I went forward to the net too. Linesmen rose from their chairs and moved over to the court. Suddenly the voice of the Englishman on the line—Lord Hope—was heard at the end of the court. He said, "The ball was good! I did not call 'out'!" Then a number of people became excited. Some thought that Mlle. Lenglen would become upset and play badly, after the surprise of finding that she had not yet won the match, after all. But Mlle. Lenglen remained calm. This incident, better than any, shows that she was a truly splendid match player.

After our second handshake—for she won the second set a few games after this unusual incident—Mlle. Lenglen was immediately surrounded, where she sat on a chair by the umpire's stand, with crowds of linesmen and officials. She was weeping, now that the match was over. Above the heads of the circle about her was passed a great bouquet of American beauty roses.

So interested was I in the hubbub and general mass of gesticulating people who surrounded Mlle. Lenglen that I did not become aware, until some moments later, that I was standing entirely alone on the court. Turning my thoughts upon myself, I found that I did not feel so sad as I really should have, but at the same time I began to feel rather overcome at being in the middle of the court by myself. Then suddenly a young man whom I had met a few days before vaulted over the balustrade from the grandstand at the side of the court and came over to me. He said, "You played awfully well." It was Mr. Moody.

SUZANNE AND HELEN

by Al Laney

The golden sun of the Era of Wonderful Nonsense was somewhat beyond the meridian at the beginning of 1926, but the art of ballyhoo was at the peak. In sports, as in other areas of life, sensational occurrences took place more or less year long, rising to a summit with the defeat of Jack Dempsey by Gene Tunney in another Battle of the Century in September. In tennis the year also was on the flamboyant side, beginning in February, when the Musketeers put the handwriting plainly on the wall (for all to ignore) by sweeping the U.S. National indoor championships at the Seventh Regiment Armory in New York. With Tilden and Richards in the field, Lacoste and Borotra reached the final, and Lacoste became champion of the United States.

I was not in New York for the indoor tournament but the tennis parade began for me even earlier, and for France, three thousand miles from the armory. This was the meeting of two girls, one French, the other American, in an otherwise unimportant tournament on the French Riviera. Only a girls' tennis match, but it was blown up into a titanic struggle such as the world had never seen before. This was to be the only meeting of these transatlantic rivals, Suzanne Lenglen and Helen Wills, and it came on February 16 in the final round of an ordinary resort tournament at the small Carlton Club in Cannes, of which I had such pleasant memories.

By the time it came off it was of worldwide interest, and never again in the history of sport was such an event allowed to go on under such ridiculous and fantastic conditions. It probably could have filled Yankee Stadium the way it was built up, but it was played at a not very attractive club of six or so courts, with almost no facilities for dressing and with stands still being hurriedly knocked together when the crowds stormed the place the day of the match. . . .

The revival of the Riviera as a playground, both actual and in the imagination, had been rapid after the war, and tennis generally experienced a remarkably swift growth in France following the Armistice. . . . In the early 1920s clubs were springing up in every sizable community, and soon the yellow-red courts stretched completely around the coast of France from Menton, on the Italian border, to Boulogne, the far Channel port. Every resort along the way, Le Touquet, Deauville, Biarritz, and the others, scheduled tournaments during their "season" and offered inducements to the international name players to come. . . .

There had been a great influx of wealthy North American, English, and South American visitors; and refugees from the Russian revolution who had come through that upheaval with quantities of gold were spending almost as liberally as the grand dukes of old. Every nationality and every type was present—crooks, pimps, great ladies, and prostitutes by the hundreds, famous persons from stage and Hollywood, titled gentlemen from every European country where titles remained intact.

In this world Suzanne Lenglen ruled as the champion of champions, the queen of queens. Never beaten in her own country, she was a truly national figure, and a visit to the Riviera without seeing Suzanne play was like a visit to Rome without seeing St. Peter's. Every club between Cannes and Monte Carlo competed for her favors, and every function felt it had scored a triumph if Suzanne appeared. Her mere presence made any affair a success. For six years she had reigned unchallenged anywhere, but especially along the Azure Coast from December to March. She played tennis where she pleased, bestowing her favors where she could be induced in one way or another to bestow them, and very often she danced away the night at some brilliant social gathering, where she outshone all the ladies present, of whatever rank or stature.

This short glittering coastline belonged to Suzanne in a certain sense, and the plan of the young girl from California to come and play the tournaments was looked upon as an "invasion" of Suzanne's territory. Mademoiselle Lenglen was reported to have said she thought it "cheeky," although I do not know what the French word for cheeky might be. . . .

And what a contrast they represented! . . . Lenglen, a Latin and an actress to her fingertips, was slender, almost thin, with nothing about her figure suggesting the athlete, but supple, marvelously graceful, and full of accompanying acrobatics calculated to bring cheers from the crowd. An artist with a true sense of the dramatic.

She was far from beautiful. In fact, her face was homely in repose, with a long crooked nose, irregular teeth, sallow complexion, and eyes that were so neutral that their color could hardly be determined. It was a face on which hardly anything was right. And yet, in a drawing room this homely girl could dominate everything, taking the attention away from dozens of women far prettier or even notorious for one reason or another. She could, in an extraordinary way, make quite fashionable women appear just a little dull, if not actually dowdy, beside her. For an ugly girl she had more charm and vivacity than a hundred pretty girls you might meet. And Suzanne had suitors. Plenty of them.

Miss Wills, on the other hand, presented a picture of a typical young American girl, sturdy, well built and healthy-looking, with a strong suggestion of girlish simplicity. The picture of her as some sort of avenger was wholly false. The affair with Molla at Forest Hills was dragged up, and it was said that Suzanne had "cheated" an American girl of a proper victory, forgetting that Molla really was a Norwegian girl.

Miss Wills had done nothing more than announce from her home in Berkeley that she would go to France, when immediately the nonsense began to appear in the papers . . . Such experts on tennis as Blasco-Ibáñez, the popular Spanish novelist, were hired to comment beforehand and to "cover" the matches, and it was reported that some of them were receiving "fabulous" compensation. . . .

It would have been hard to choose a more unlikely ground for an event of such worldwide interest. The six courts of the club were squeezed into a small plot on a narrow, dirty street behind the Carlton Hotel, a few hundred yards back from the Croisette, and a narrow alley ran down one side. Normally there was a "center" court with small wooden stands along one side with seats for perhaps a thousand or so. Behind this was a one-story building, a garage, I think. Outside the grounds on the other side was a small factory of some sort from which came the wasplike buzz of machinery. Beyond and to one side of this were two or three small villas with orange tiles for roofs and with eucalyptus trees in front. High above were the towers of the Carlton Hotel. . . .

The Burkes had plenty of warning but were astonished like all the rest of us when people began clamoring to force into their hands three hundred francs each for seats. This was an enormous price for a Frenchman, with the franc at about twenty-five to the dollar. The promoters, eager to reap all the gain that was possible, decided to enlarge the stands and add other seats, but they decided very late. The sound of carpenters' hammers could be heard almost up to the start of the famous match. . . .

The arrival of Suzanne at the clubhouse entrance in her chauffeur-driven car from Nice was hailed by an outburst of cheering outside and the calling of her name. This was followed by a great roar when, someone said, she blew them kisses. Helen had to come only from the nearby Carlton, whose tower windows also were full of people watching. Probably she had preceded Suzanne, who always made certain of her "entrance."

Meanwhile the part of the crowd to which I belonged had made note of the great number of celebrities, including royalty in the person of ex-King Manuel of Portugal, the Grand Duke Michael, Prince George, and a number of maharajas and titled persons whose names escape me.

The suspense had begun to mount sharply, even before the two girls entered together, making a nice picture for the battalion of photographers that immediately engulfed them. Suzanne came like a great actress making an entrance that stopped the show, with flashing smile, bowing, posing, blowing kisses, full of grace and ever gracious. Helen, walking beside the Queen and, as befits a lady in waiting, just a little to the rear, came in calm, impassive, and unruffled, looking nowhere but in front. She seemed sturdy and placidly unemotional, although she must surely have been nervous. I noted for the first time that Miss Wills had large capable-looking hands, and I wondered if she really was the talented painter of pictures she was supposed to be. I don't suppose she took either literature or art very seriously at the time.

Suzanne wore a pure white coat with white fur collar over a short white dress, and her famous bandeau was of salmon pink. Helen wore her usual tennis costume, middy blouse and pleated white skirt, and she had a dark coat over the arm not full of rackets. When the photographers were induced to retire, and the girls were about to take the court, Helen removed her sweater. Suzanne wore hers all through the match, although the sun now was hot. When the flashing entrance smile had been turned off, it was seen that Suzanne had a somewhat strained, pinched look. There were dark lines and the eyes seemed drawn. She did not look well.

The officials came out to their places while the balls were being hit back and forth in the preliminary warmup, and it was noted that nearly all were English, chosen no doubt for their neutrality. . . .

The match lasted exactly one hour. Lenglen opened with a love game on her service, but Helen then began to hit her own faster drives deep, and controlled the back court exchanges just well enough to win the next two games for a 2–1 lead. She had won the champion's service, and when that service game was lost to a scoring shot from Helen's backhand off a fine Lenglen shot, you could sense the realization coming to Suzanne that she was in for a fight. No other girl ever had scored off such a shot. It must have been an unpleasant awakening. She knew now what she was facing. None could know it better. Here was an opponent her equal in controlled driving, and definitely more forceful. Helen's game was based on speed of stroke perfectly controlled, with drives more forceful than any woman's and many men's. Helen was not, however, Suzanne's equal in resourcefulness.

Helen had hit every backhand shot in these early games across court to the backhand line, often right into the backhand corner. These were shots of high quality, immaculate in their purity of execution, but they were sent to Lenglen's backhand, one of the most accurate and precisely controlled strokes and altogether one of the finest shots ever seen in the game of tennis.

It might be noted here that Miss Wills throughout her brilliant career continued to prefer the backhand cross-court shot to the one down the opponent's forehand line. I saw the latter shot so seldom from her that I suspected more than once in later years that either she could not make this more difficult stroke well or had no real confidence in it . . . I believed that day in Cannes, and still believe, that it was this lack, this one chink in an otherwise complete armor, that removed the chance that Miss Wills might have had to defeat Lenglen in their only encounter. . . .

At any rate, Lenglen was quick to see the advantage it gave her. After losing the second and third games, she began with great confidence to take these booming backhand drives pitching close to her own backhand corner, certainly the hardest and deepest she ever had encountered from another girl. Initially they had surprised her, but she was now not hurried by them and it seemed she even invited them by playing her own shots to Miss Wills' left side. Suzanne took the ball cleanly in the exact center of her racket and, with her slightly undercut stroke, placed her return to the spot her eye had picked out, very short down each of Miss Wills' sidelines.

This often brought Helen forward, and each time she came she lost the point. These coups were much easier for Suzanne to bring off than would have been similar shots hit deep to her forehand corner, but Miss Wills never attacked the forehand. She seemed to think at this time that the Lenglen backhand was the wing to attack, and attack it she did with great strength.

In spite of it, though, Suzanne won ten straight points from 2–1 in Miss Wills' favor. She won them with unyielding defense against the hardest thrusts Helen could manage and from which she herself would counter-attack with perfectly timed shots. These, placing Miss Wills in a losing position, were designed to draw errors. This was the game of women's tennis such as we would expect these two to play. Miss Wills was playing very well indeed and she was losing, but it took nearly perfect stroking and a well-conceived plan to check her. We expected that Miss Wills, with her equipment, would find the way to alter the course of play, and she did.

Having lost her service twice and now behind 2–4, she came to the net to volley for the first time in the seventh game and won it with a not very neat but effective push out of reach. Suzanne seemed now to have decided upon her plan of action, however, and to have regained her confidence, which had been disturbed by the unexpectedly strong resistance of the American girl. Helen could win only two points in the next two games as Suzanne captured the first set 6–3 to a great burst of cheering.

This seemed a convincing enough margin, but the set had been played under considerable stress, nevertheless, and Suzanne went to the chair to sip brandy before taking her place for the start of the second. She seemed already tired and nervous. The disturbing noises from the crowd annoyed her much more than they bothered Helen, and several times Suzanne had looked with an appealing gesture toward the spot where a vehicle of some kind had been drawn up alongside the fence with a shouting group sitting on top of it. She had first ordered them to be silent and then, being ignored, had pleaded with them, with the same effect.

Helen began the second set as Suzanne had begun the first, by serving a love game. This was the first time the strong and well-placed American service itself had been a decisive factor, and its sudden increase in power seemed to surprise Lenglen. All Miss Wills' shots, in fact, now appeared to carry more pace, or what the English call "devil," and, choosing well the proper ball on which to hit out, she placed Suzanne altogether on the defensive for a time. The greater speed of stroke of the American girl now was quite noticeable.

Helen went to a lead of 3–1, and she was serving so well it seemed to us unlikely she would lose a service game at all. If she did not, she would win the second set by 6–3, even without breaking the French girl's service again. At one point in the fourth game she had passed Suzanne cleanly at the net with a sharply angled forehand across the body. Suzanne stopped at the chair again for another sip of brandy before returning to her position. This seemed an ominous sign, and we thought that Suzanne never would survive a third set. But it gave her time to consider her position, which was, as a matter of fact, critical. With Miss Wills serving with a 4–1 lead in sight, Suzanne knew well that the capture of the American's service was imperative at this point. She dare not fall behind 1–4.

And then I think Miss Wills made the tactical mistake that may well have cost her the victory, although it is difficult to be sure in the light of what came later. Anyhow, serving for this commanding lead, Miss Wills appeared deliberately to reduce the pace of the game. Instead of pressing her advantage, she began to exchange deep and well-placed but slower drives with Suzanne.

Now, Miss Wills was not equipped to play this kind of game so well as Suzanne. Indeed, no girl that ever lived could do this. No matter where the ball was hit Suzanne could reach it with her marvelously fluid footwork and, given time for the stroke, she was again in control of the play. In such exchanges hers would be the last shot of each rally if it didn't end with an opponent's error. The shots that Helen missed now were those for which she was made to run and strain. Suzanne, for the second time, had a run of two games in which she lost only two points, both well earned by Helen. The score was now 3–3 and now surely the crisis was passed for Suzanne.

How wrong we were!

Now came the longest game of the match. With Helen serving, Suzanne was within a stroke of winning the game at 15–40 for a 4–3 lead and her own service to follow. Ten more points were to be played, however, and then Miss Wills won the game to give her that lead. Helen had brought out her very best game at this crisis, and we saw then the wonderful driving that only she in all the world could command and sustain over the next ten years or so.

The effect on Suzanne of losing this game from a winning position, and against play that indicated she might have met her match at last, was profound and visible. She was clearly surprised at such very strong resistance. She took more brandy and before taking up the balls to serve the eighth game, she appealed again to part of the crowd, now in a highly excited state, please to keep quiet.

As the play continued she appeared to falter, although actually she made no mistake in stroking at all. It was the way she looked. She seemed much more nervous, but at 30–all she received a small break that appeared to restore her a little while it depressed her opponent. Suzanne drove to Miss Wills' forehand line a ball that could not have been returned but appeared to have pitched just outside. Cyril Tolley, who was judging the line, gave no sign and then, when Miss Wills looked in inquiry at him, indicated that the ball had been good. If he had given it the other way, as Miss Wills clearly thought he should, she would have been one point away from a 5–3 lead, and in Lenglen's present state that might have been decisive.

Miss Wills lost the next point weakly, perhaps while contemplating what might have been, but she then served very well to reach 5–4. And now for the second time at a critical moment Miss Wills became tentative. And once more Lenglen's great skill at maneuvering an opponent lacking in aggression came to the fore. Again she drew Helen to a forward position where the American girl, unable to find room for her full-blooded drives, hit out or into the net. Suzanne thus won at love a game whose loss would have carried with it the loss of the second set and, very likely, the third also. This was, if partly the result of Miss Wills' strange quietude, even more the true champion's response to danger. It was characteristic, and a few minutes later we were to see an even more impressive demonstration of it.

Having survived these several dangers brilliantly, Suzanne now appeared to be moving straight to victory. She won Miss Wills' service surely, if not easily, from 30–all in the eleventh game and then in the twelfth, serving perfectly to prevent a forcing reply, went straight to match point at 40–15. And then, one stroke away from a two-set victory for Lenglen, there was a long exchange of deep drives at the end of which Miss Wills, finding at last a ball she could flog, sent a screaming forehand toward Lenglen's forehand corner. It had the look of a winning stroke, but the call of "Out" was heard and both players thought the match over.

Suzanne threw into the air the ball she had held in her hand throughout the rally and ran to the net to receive the traditional winner's handshake across the barrier. Before she could reach Helen, the court was full of people, a regular mob scene. They came from all directions, carrying huge baskets of flowers, and the photographers swarmed everywhere.

Through the throng of people and flowers, Lord Charles Hope, the lineman, pushed his way to the umpire's chair. Commander Hillyard leaned down to hear what was said amid the bedlam. Sir Charles explained that the ball had been emphatically good, not out. It was not he who had called but some volunteer official, of whom there were hundreds in the stands. Hillyard immediately changed the decision, made the score 40–30, and began an effort that at first seemed futile to clear the court so the match could be resumed. In those pre-loudspeaker days it took some doing. Many minutes passed before the facts could be communicated to the crowd, all of whom were standing and most of whom were shouting. But justice must be done and it was finally accomplished.

Confusion still reigned for a while, but in time all got back to their places. I could not see Lenglen's face when she first realized the situation. It must have been a study in dejection, for she had a sorrowful cast of feature even when in repose, and this for her was a tragic development. The highly charged emotional atmosphere had taken its toll of her nervous strength, but she had overcome all, including the strongest game she had ever faced, and come through successfully, still queen and still champion, at what cost only she probably knew. And now, exhausted from physical effort and nervous strain, she must go back and do it again under even worse strain. All was still uncertain and had to be played for.

And now Mademoiselle Lenglen confirmed and underscored her position as Queen of the Courts and one of the great champions of sports history. She had shown many petty traits of annoyance over trivial things and had acted in a haughty and arrogant manner many times in her years of triumph. Now, in her hour of trial, as the saying goes, she showed herself to be a real champion. Without a word or any outward sign, she walked steadily back to her place, picked up the discarded balls and served. Her face was drawn, but even when Miss Wills won the next point, also a match point, and then eventually the game, to draw even again at 6–all, there still was no sign.

When Miss Wills stood within one point of winning the following game, the thirteenth, a point that would have given her the lead at 7–6, there was at last a nervous gesture from Suzanne which seemed to indicate she might now be near collapse. But she steadied herself, recovered her concentration and won the game against the American's service, which was at its biting best now.

And so, serving once more for the match a good quarter-hour after she had thought she had it won, Suzanne came at last to her third match point. It had not been easy to arrive there, for Miss Wills resisted beautifully and with calm judgment. Suzanne had played with nearly perfect strokes, which, under the circumstances, showed a hardihood we none of us suspected in so highly emotional a creature. Then, in sight of the end once more, she reacted. Suzanne served a double fault, so rare a thing with her as to make one wonder if she were not really at the end of her resources.

But once again the champion gathered her remaining strength. This remarkable woman now played with a certainty and restraint, with unshaken nerve and fortitude, that was difficult to believe in the supercharged atmosphere after all that had gone before. Having served the double fault at match point, she then needed two more points to get out from deuce. For the first she fenced with Miss Wills until she drew an error. For the last one of all, her fourth match point, she carefully drew a weak reply from Helen and then she won in the champion's way by hitting a winner. It was, in a word, magnificent.

This time Suzanne did not run to the net. She stood almost in a trance, it seemed, in mid-court, and was there engulfed again by the rush of partisans, photographers and the baskets of flowers which returned for a monster horticultural display. I doubted she ever would reach the net, where Miss Wills waited to do the honors for the second time, if the photographers had not insisted upon it so they could take a thousand pictures of the kind photographers the world over must have.

Suzanne received an ovation beyond anything even she had previously experienced. Finally they sat her down on a bench at the side of the court and surrounded her with a wall of flowers until only her turbaned head showed above. She was surrounded also by a wall of hundreds of people, including lords and ladies, all pushing forward to congratulate and be near her. And directly behind where Suzanne sat, Helen stood for a few minutes, unnoticed, forgotten and alone in the midst of the thing. I watched as Miss Wills, with hardly room to extend her arms, pulled on her sweater. Then, still alone, she turned and began quietly to push her way back through the indifferent crowd toward the gate. She disappeared among them and no one seemed to care that she was gone.

I watched the scene for a while and then went out and found a seat along the Croisette, where I could sit in the sun and think about the strange match. I have been thinking about it in sunshine and shadow ever since, and the conclusion I reached while sitting on the bench in sight of the Mediterranean remains the same today.

I was to see Miss Wills many times afterward winning all her eight Wimbledon titles, all those in Paris and many of those at Forest Hills, besides her yearly Wightman Cup encounters. Suzanne was seen afterward only through the French championships, which followed in Paris three months later in May, and at her last Wimbledon that June.

My feeling about the Cannes match was then, and is now, that if it had been played under normal conditions Lenglen would have won more easily and more decisively. I think also that if she and Miss Wills had met later that same year, which seemed likely then but turned out not to be, Lenglen also would have won but probably less easily. If they had continued both to play the tournaments through the next years, however, I am certain that Miss Wills would have overtaken Suzanne and passed her.

This does not mean that I place Miss Wills at her peak above Lenglen at hers, for I believe the opposite. But Helen showed at Cannes that she already was close and still improving; and Lenglen, never very robust, already probably was declining a little in a tennis sense. She had been queen of Wimbledon for six years in 1926. Miss Wills first became champion there in 1927, after Suzanne's departure. If we add seven years to that date, we will see Miss Wills in 1934 also seriously challenged by players of lesser talent than her own.

These two wonderful performers were really of different tennis generations, and had they met more they must inevitably have come level and one passed the other, the one going up, the other down. It is ever the fate of even the greatest of champions to be superseded and, since in this case one great one followed immediately after another, we probably were denied a series of superlative women's tennis matches by Lenglen's retirement from amateur tennis that same year. They might have been matches such as we enjoyed during that period of two or three years when the rising Musketeers were catching up to and passing Tilden. They were, in fact, the very same years, and the finest of them were just ahead.

MOLLA MALLORY WINS BACK TENNIS CROWN

by Allison Danzig

The scepter in American women's tennis returned to Mrs. Molla Mallory yesterday. Time turned back at Forest Hills as the New York woman, holder for six years of the title, fought her way to a stunning victory over Miss Elizabeth Ryan of California to regain the crown which she lost to Miss Helen Wills in 1923 and to tie the record for all time of the number of championships won by a single player, either man or woman.

In all the thirty-nine years of the women's national championship, there has probably never been a more sensational victory scored in a final round than Mrs. Mallory's yesterday.

Trailing at 0–4 in the final set, in which she was within a single stroke of defeat in the fourteenth game, the New York woman threw the 3,000 spectators in the stadium into a frenzy of delight as she fought her way through four games in a row with a savageness of stroking that crushed all opposition. Miss Ryan, clearly the favorite from the start up to this point, wilted before the devastating attack which completely broke up her volleying game. She fought desperately through seven more games to hold off Mrs. Mallory's penetrating forcing shots, and then, amid screams of joy from the whole gallery, Mrs. Mallory brought the play to a climax by breaking through service and winning her own game for the match. The score was 4–6, 6–4, 9–7.

It is not often that a tennis gathering runs the gamut of emotions that those 3,000 spectators experienced yesterday. There were moments when the suspense was so terrific that it set hearts to pounding wildly as the match hung in the balance on a single stroke. Because Mrs. Mallory's cause was almost unanimously regarded as hopeless, the onlookers broke into applause at her every winning shot, cheered her on excitedly as she fought her way to victory in the second set, and then the safety valve was blown off as she staged her rally in the final chapter. The stadium fairly rocked as Mrs. Mallory won the last point, and of all those 3,000 people none was so unrestrainedly exuberant as the champion.

Mrs. Mallory danced with joy, throwing her racket into the air, waving to the cheering stands and unreservedly giving vent to her glee. One would have thought, as she received the championship cup from Jones W. Mersereau, president of the United States Lawn Tennis Association, that Mrs. Mallory was experiencing a new thrill. Certainly she showed greater happiness than she did over any of her victories in the past. And well she might. Looked upon as having passed the prime of her career and given little consideration as a championship contender, the New York woman showed that the same courageous fighting spirit and iron will to win that kept her at the top for seven years and that enabled her to triumph over Mlle. Suzanne Lenglen at Forest Hills in 1921 are still as strong as ever within her.

What other woman player has ever come from so hopelessly behind to win a championship final? William Tilden, with all of his great fifth-set rallies, could have done no better.

By winning the championship yesterday for the seventh time Mrs. Mallory equaled the record of victories scored by Richard D. Sears and William A. Larned, both of whom captured the men's title the same number of years, and of Mrs. Lambert Chambers, champion at Wimbledon seven times. Mlle. Lenglen has won at Wimbledon six times, while Tilden has captured the American title six times. Mrs. Mallory's other victories were scored in 1915, 1916, 1918, 1920, 1921 and 1922. In addition, she also won the patriotic tournament of 1917 (held in place of the championship because of the war), so that she has held the honors eight years in all, one more than any other player has ever held either the American or English crown.

Frustrated in her effort for the singles crown, Miss Ryan came back on the courts later to win the doubles championship with Miss Eleanor Goss. In the final round they defeated Miss Mary K. Browne and Mrs. Charlotte Hosmer Chapin, 3–6, 6–4, 12–10. In an exhibition Miss Penelope Anderson and Henri Cochet of France divided two sets with Miss Martha Bayard and Jacques Brugnon of France.

The singles final was remarkable for the closeness of the play. In both the first and second sets neither player ever held a commanding lead, and only in the first four games of the final set was the play one-sided. The point score and stroke analysis show how closely the two women were matched. Miss Ryan won one more point than Mrs. Mallory, 112 to 111, while the champion gained two more games, 19 to 17. Mrs. Mallory made eight more errors and seven more earned points than Miss Ryan.

It was the magnificent sharpshooting of Mrs. Mallory that decided the issue. The champion needed only to fall behind to become rampant, and she was never so deadly in her stroking as she was in overcoming the 4–0 lead of Miss Ryan in the final set, a lead that had been gained in hardly more than six minutes on Mrs. Mallory's inexcusable errors. In the next four games Mrs. Mallory scored nine placements of her sixteen points and in this set she made seventeen placements to Miss Ryan's nine. This remarkable accuracy and keenness of Mrs. Mallory in penetrating the openings completely broke up Miss Ryan's net attack. During the last twelve games the Californian scored only one winning volley.

Not only did Miss Ryan's short-court game become a total loss, but her chop strokes to deep territory made no impression whatever upon Mrs. Mallory in the late stages, contrasting with their effect earlier in the match, when they induced error-making repeatedly. Mrs. Mallory did not seem to know how to make an error any longer. Everything that came over the net was sent back like a bolt to open territory, keeping Miss Ryan on the run until she was badly tired and fell off in control.

Mrs. Mallory, to add the last straw, completely smothered her opponent's drop shots. These crafty trap strokes, which Miss Ryan made with such delicate finesse to catch Mrs. Mallory flat-footed in her back court in the first two sets, were now retrieved by a fleet-footed, keenly alert opponent every time and returned with winning shots.

Mrs. Mallory had the advantage of what might be called the "breaks" in the concluding stages, winning a number of points when the ball hit the top of the net and rolled the right way for her. But, on the other hand, she was the victim of a number of what seemed doubtful decisions, one of which cost her a point in the twelfth game that put Miss Ryan within 2 points of the match. Mrs. Mallory showed her fine sportsmanship by refusing to question the decision and silenced the crowd, which objected to it, with a wave of her arm. In the fourteenth game Miss Ryan was at match point but her errors in returning service—a weakness she showed throughout the match—cost her her opportunity.

Mrs. Mallory pulled out the game, and then there began a desperate struggle in the fifteenth. Miss Ryan gained a 30–0 lead. Mrs. Mallory pulled up to 30–all and then scored on a fluke return of service, the ball just getting over the net. Miss Ryan brought the score to deuce. Fighting desperately to get to the net, she found her efforts wasted when Mrs. Mallory scored on a net-cord placement, and the deciding break was made.

In the final game Miss Ryan showed her championship fiber. Trailing at 0–40 and with defeat only a point away, she fought Mrs. Mallory through the next four rallies and gained advantage point. Here her control waned as Mrs. Mallory pounded her base corners, and the champion took the next two points on errors for the match.

1927

TILDEN'S MYSTERIOUS COLLAPSE VS. COCHET
AT WIMBLEDON

by Al Laney

While the leading tennis players of the world were occupied in mid-June of 1927 with preliminary grass court play in and around London leading to Wimbledon, I was making the first of many visits to St. Andrew's, in Scotland, the shrine of golf, to see Bobby Jones carried off the final green of the Old Course by enthusiastic Scots. Bob had just won his second straight British Open title with a record score of 285 and it was a real mob scene, by which I believe I was more overwhelmed than Jones, who had captivated the Scots by his play and his manner.

I brought back only emotional thoughts of this historic golf occasion, but the 1927 Wimbledon, to which I returned immediately, remains for me the most exciting and dramatic tennis tournament I have known, and the easiest to remember. I think all who were there would say the same. This was partly, no doubt, due to the fact that it had been building up in the minds of the public for weeks because of the return of Tilden and his effort to repeat at the new tennis grounds his victory of six years earlier at the old.

In spite of his defeats by the Frenchmen, Tilden was still regarded in England as the world's greatest player, and it was thought only fitting that his "comeback" should be achieved at the headquarters of the game with all the Frenchmen in the field against him. They were all there, and the seeding had been arranged with a Tilden-Cochet semi-final and a Tilden-Lacoste final in view. It didn't work out that way. Neither Tilden nor Lacoste reached the final, and it was Cochet who authored most of the excitement as he survived a week-long series of crises to become champion.

It is unlikely that the public interest in this tournament right from its start ever has been exceeded. . . . On opening day there were at least five thousand in line waiting for what we call the general admission sales windows to be opened. Of course all reserved places had been sold months before. . . . When the real excitement began with the second Monday, we passed long lines when we came out at the end of each day. They were prepared to camp out all night to be sure of getting tickets at noon next day that would permit them to stand all afternoon on the concrete terraces of the center court. . . .

By the second Monday the unseeded Frank Hunter had come through to the quarter-final against Cochet, and here began the astonishing series of matches that brought the little Frenchman through to the title. In each of his last three matches against Hunter, Tilden, and Borotra, Cochet lost the

568

first two sets, was each time in sight of defeat, and then won the next three. After his narrow escape against Hunter on Monday, he had to play Tilden on Wednesday, and Big Bill, who had beaten him in Paris only a few weeks earlier, had been playing the most magnificent tennis.

This meeting of Cochet and Tilden was, of course, one of the most famous tennis matches ever played. I can still speak of it in detail because I kept the point score and notes made that day, but I could not explain it then and I cannot now. Tilden, having noted what happened to Hunter, went all out from the start to win quickly. He unleashed a withering attack of unanswerable speed. Drives from both wings, either "flat" or carrying top spin, were hitting the lines, out of reach or too swift to return, and the service often brought no reply at all.

Here was Tilden in all his majesty, "blowing his opponent off the court" with irresistible gusto, and at the end of the first set, which he won 6–2, I made a note to the effect that probably all but a very few of those looking on must have been amazed at the quality of the tennis, since they never had seen anything like it. Cochet seemed overwhelmed. Tilden's great pace and accuracy of stroke from any part of the court gave the little Lyonese no chance to organize a defense and no time in which to bring his own best weapons into play.

The Frenchman became a little more venturesome as the second set began, and his confidence increased enough so that he could at least attempt a counter-attack. He tried a crisp forcing shot to Tilden's short forehand, inviting the return across the body that could be volleyed out of reach. This got Cochet four games, but Tilden still won all the critical points and games, and it was clear that if Big Bill did not begin to make errors, all would soon be over.

And then, with the beginning of the third set, Tilden launched his most devastating attack. Never on that side of the Atlantic had he struck with such real violence. Cochet searched in vain for an effective weapon to stem the tide as Tilden went steadily on, literally hitting through his man, dominant, domineering and arrogant. It was the Tilden of 1921–1925 back on top, piling up the games. He seemed in a big hurry to get it over with. After banging his way to 5–1 with a cannonball that Cochet could not reach, Bill threw the two balls remaining in his hand over the net behind the service and could hardly wait for Cochet to gather them in and serve what we all thought would be the last game. In the competitors' stand just below the press box I saw Hunter hurrying out to be there when his doubles partner should come victorious from the arena. But Frank had still another hour to wait and no congratulations to give at the end of it.

For now the incredible happened. I have to keep referring to that point score, which I know to be accurate, to reassure myself. From 15–all in the seventh game, Tilden, going all out for a quick finish, hit three of Cochet's serves with all his force, but all three sailed beyond the lines, out of court. What matter? Tilden's service was to come and Cochet had won only two points against it during the third set.

They changed ends and Tilden waited impatiently, three balls in his left hand, for Cochet to take his place. But Tilden's sudden overhitting in the other game had not been due to his haste to get it over. Something had gone wrong. The cannonball missed the mark also, missed it rather badly, and Tilden hit every other ball out or into the net. He could not win a point. He lost his service at love and then another love game as Cochet served. Tilden was still trying to hit winners, and doing it with all the old pace, but now every ball went wild. The earlier stream of winning points became a stream of errors. From 15–all in that seventh game Cochet actually won seventeen points in succession, going from 1–5 down to 5–all and 30–0 before Tilden won a point, and yielding only four points altogether before winning the third set 7–5. Three of these points were in the last game, which Tilden managed to force to deuce when control of his cannonball returned momentarily.

People could not understand what had happened any more than I could. Tilden had said before going into court that he was "not going to let that little fellow get me into a long match," emphasizing the pronoun. And now, after seeming to have timed it perfectly, this had happened.

There is no rest period at Wimbledon after the third set, as there is at Forest Hills, and they went directly into the fourth set with no more than a quick mopping of brows. The match was not over. Tilden got back some of his effectiveness. The sudden check in the numbing attack, however, had given Cochet's own assets, smothered under the avalanche of lethal blows, a chance to operate. With the pressure off, he could work out a plan of campaign. He offered easy, soft strokes, refusing to give Tilden the pace from which to generate counter-speed.

Tilden pressed more and more to recover his accuracy but the initiative passed to the Frenchman, never to return. There were some periods of fine play in the last two sets, but they came when Tilden made desperate rallies to recover lost ground and the physical strain on him was great. He recovered from 2–4 down in the fourth set to 4–all, but the reaction was immediate and Cochet won the set, 6–4. Tilden had played the set very well, but he had expended great energy, only to lose it, and the possibility that he might win a fifth set now, it seemed clear to all, had gone.

Cochet, still fresh, took the net more often now to bring off his volleying coups. Tilden's formerly incisive passing shots had lost pace and Cochet, increasing the speed of his own forcing shots, was calling the tune in almost every game. Tilden, with a great effort, rallied again to win the enemy service in the fifth game and led by 3–2, with his own service to come, but the effort cost him so much he could do no more. It was the last game he could win. He was done physically and his face showed it. Two double faults followed immediately, two more in the eighth game and three errors in the ninth.

Tennis writers have a way of speaking of results which they did not expect as "stunning surprises" and in this case at least the use of the words is justified. People certainly were surprised, and I was, if not stunned, completely bewildered. I have discussed this match many times with many persons, one of them being Tilden himself, and I never have arrived at a satisfactory explanation of what happened, of why the greatest player of all could not win just one more game after the most brilliant play of a long career had taken him to the verge, as we say, of overwhelming victory. He could not win even one single point until it was too late.

It had not been an exhausting match at all up to that third-set collapse. There had been rain earlier and the day was cool. At one moment Tilden, in full possession of his physical and mental powers, seemed to be crushing his opponent with a withering attack, and in the next he was done, all control had left him and he was in distress.

Tilden declared vehemently some time after the match that the whole explanation could be found in Cochet's rising brilliantly to great heights in the face of defeat. This, of course, was nonsense, as Tilden very well knew. Some said that Tilden, having demonstrated beyond doubt twice within a month that he could beat Cochet, wanted to make sure that the little wizard would be chosen to play Davis Cup singles. This was, likewise, moonshine.

Another popular theory was that, when leading 5–1 in that third set, Tilden had noticed that the King of Spain had just entered the Royal Box and he decided to prolong the match a little to give Alfonso, a great fan, some tennis. And then, having relaxed, he couldn't get it back. Tilden assured me later that he had never been conscious at all of the royal visitor's arrival, and I believed him. I had not been conscious of it myself.

I think now that the explanation might be found in a remark Tilden addressed to me immediately after the match, or as quickly as I could reach the dressing room. "Maybe you were right," he said, and he said it with what I thought was scorn, but in a voice that carried a certain hatred too. He was referring to the statement that he had now passed his best years and could no longer call on that matchless stamina. Still he defeated Cochet in four sets later that year and Lacoste in five sets more than a year after.

F. R. Burrow, after eighteen years as referee of the tournament, remarked that the fact that Cochet ever got to the final "was the most astonishing event that has happened in my time at Wimbledon." That Henri ever won that final is even more so. Borotra had beaten Lacoste in the other semi-final, in which the Basque had used the crowd and its emotions almost as a weapon of victory. Against Cochet in the final, Borotra had six match points, the third of which also is a part of Wimbledon history.

Leading 5–3 and 40–30 in the fifth set, Borotra served and dashed in. Cochet hit the return down the middle and also closed in. There followed a lightning-like exchange of volleys at close range. It ended when Cochet scored with a stroke which I thought he had "scooped" up with a double hit. Others thought so too. The players looked to the umpire's chair and we all expected the call to be "Not up. Game, set and match to Mr. Borotra." It never came. Instead, the umpire called, "Deuce." The stroke had been ruled legal. Borotra served again and had three more match balls, losing one on a heart-breaking net cord, while Cochet was climbing to 5–all. Cochet eventually won 7–5 and the third Musketeer had become Wimbledon champion.

That was the end of my most memorable Wimbledon, but before the climax there was a women's match I cannot ignore since it looms so large in memory and was, in some ways, the finest I have ever seen. Helen Wills, after an absence of two years, returned to win the first of eight Wimbledon titles. Her final round opponent was Lili de Alvarez, the Spanish girl who, though never a champion, was one of the most exciting and attractive players of her sex the game has known.

That the señorita, dark and handsome and with flashing smile, played tennis wholly for fun was as obvious to me as it had been that Dick Williams did. And since they both gloried in the half-volley, preferring it even when the extreme danger of using it was apparent, I am wondering if there may be some special joy to be had from employing this stroke. In a game where girls not excessively talented take themselves with such deadly seriousness and sometimes even burst into tears on the court, the lovely, carefree, exuberant Lili was a refreshing change. I greatly admired her way of playing, and watching her has given me as much real pleasure as the play of any other girl I can think of. With it all, she was a person of rare and charming femininity.

Lili was good enough to be Wimbledon finalist three times. This was a quick match of only eighteen games, which Miss Wills won, 6–2, 6–4, because both her strokes and her physique were the more sturdy. But I doubt if any match ever played by two women could equal it for sustained attack on both sides of the net and the quality of strokes employed over such a long period.

This relatively short encounter was attack from first stroke to last. Both girls could hit winners off shots that themselves appeared to be winners, and in the whole match astonishingly few defensive strokes were employed. Miss Wills won the first set in a session of glorious hitting. The señorita instinctively favored the half-volley, and she could bring off this time-saving and exciting shot from anywhere in the court equally as well at her level of play as Cochet and Williams could at their higher level.

At the beginning of the second set Lili brought out a maneuver that I never was to see any other girl, with the one exception of Lenglen, attempt against Miss Wills. This was to exchange full-length drives from deep court and then to draw Miss Wills forward with a short, almost insolent, flick to the forehand line. With this plan, the señorita went to 4–3 after a series of unforgettable exchanges. But she was at advantage three times before she got the game, and by the end of it Miss Wills, though she had yielded, had caught on.

Miss Wills now set out to defeat the plan by sheer speed of stroke, which made the final half-volleying coup impossible to bring off. This brought them to the crisis of the match, the eighth game. It was an extraordinary session of tremendous hitting, and the last point of it produced a rally the equal of which I have never seen again in women's tennis. Such sustained hitting and such gorgeous shots by two girls had never taken place on this court, or, I imagine, anywhere else. Twenty strokes by each girl were counted, each hit to score, speed countered by more speed, until finally the señorita, perhaps in desperation, attempted once more to trap the other girl with her favorite coup and failed. The backhand half-volley curled out of court and the score was 4–all.

Both girls placed racket heads on the court for support and leaned exhausted over them while deluges of applause enveloped them. It was the end. The señorita could not recover her breath. She could win only one more point and, half-volley she ever so well, she never could win a set from Miss Wills. But for speed of attack and counter-attack, for quality of stroke employed over a sustained period, I am wondering if women's tennis did not here reach its highest point during my time. I have since seen flashes of perhaps similar brilliance by individual girls, but never a succession of games in which two girls played with such virtuosity of stroke at the same time.

LACOSTE DEFEATS TILDEN IN U.S. FINAL

by Allison Danzig

For the first time in the forty-six years' history of the tournament, the national tennis championship was won by a foreign player a second time yesterday when Jean René Lacoste of France retained the title which he succeeded to last year after the six-year reign of William T. Tilden 2d of Philadelphia had been brought to an end by Henri Cochet, another Frenchman.

In one of the greatest struggles that ever brought the championship to a conclusion, the 23-year-old Parisian triumphed over Tilden in three sets, frustrating the hopes of the American of equaling the record of seven victories established by Richard D. Sears and marking the first time that Tilden has failed to win a set from Lacoste in their many meetings on turf courts. The score was 11–9, 6–3, 11–9.

Close to two hours, an hour and fifty-three minutes to be exact, was required for a decision in this titanic struggle between the player who formerly stood as the invincible monarch of the courts and the youth who had succeeded to his position. Many a five-set match has been finished in far less time than that, but no five-set struggle that Tilden has lost or saved with one of his dramatic climbs to unassailable heights under stress has surpassed yesterday's harrowing battle between age and youth in the desperateness of the conflict and its appeal to the emotions, or in the magnificent quality of the play.

A gallery of 14,000 spectators, a gallery that packed the Forest Hills stadium to the last seat and that stood at the top of the last tier and in every other available space, looked down upon this terrific struggle, and at the end it knew that it had been privileged to see one of the most ennobling fights a former champion ever made to regain his crown.

Tilden, in the years of his most ruthless sway, was never a more majestic figure, never played more upon the heart-strings of a gallery than he did yesterday as he gave the last ounce of his superb physique to break through a defense that was as enduring as rock, and failed; failed in spite of the fact that he was three times at set point in the first chapter, in spite of the fact that he led at 3–1 in the second set, and once again in spite of the fact that he held the commanding lead of 5–2 in the third set and was twice within a stroke of taking this chapter.

He failed because youth stood in the balance against him—youth in the person of an untiring sphinx that was as deadly as fate in the uncanny perfection of his control, who assimilated the giant Tilden's most murderous swipes and cannonball serves as though they were mere pat balls and who made such incredible saves as to have broken the spirit of nine men out of ten.

But the spirit of Tilden was one thing that never broke. Long before the end of the match, yes, by the end of that agonizing first set which had the gallery cheering Tilden madly and beseeching him to put over the one vital stroke that was lacking, those marvelous legs of the Philadelphian were slowing up.

By the second set the fires of his wrathful forehanders were slumbering, and the third set found him a drooping figure, his head slunk forward, so utterly exhausted that not even the pitchers of ice water that he doused over himself could stimulate his frayed nerves, which must have ached painfully.

It was a spectacle to have won the heart of the most partisan French protagonist, the sight of this giant of the courts, once the mightiest of the mighty, flogging on his tired body in the unequal battle between youth and age. If there were any French partisans present, they did not make themselves known. One and all those 14,000 spectators were heart and soul for Tilden as he made his heroic fight to prevent the last of the world's biggest tennis crowns go the way of all crowns.

If they cheered him in the first set, if they raised the roof when he gained his lead of 3–1 in the second chapter and again when he slashed his way ahead at 5–2 in the third, the din was nothing compared to the ovation Tilden received when, later on in the final chapter, the Philadelphian came back like a man from the grave to save himself from defeat twice by a single point in the fourteenth game. That game was one of the most agonizing a tennis gallery ever sat through as a shell of a man staved off the inevitable by a classic exhibition of fighting entirely on nerve.

The gallery, hopelessly in the despond as the machine-like Lacoste pulled up from 2–5 to 5–all and then to 7–6, took one despairing look at the drooping figure of Tilden as Lacoste began to serve, and resigned itself to seeing the end. In spite of the fact that the American steeled himself and sent the ball back like rifle fire, he could make no impression against a youth who dug his chops out of the ground and made the most heart-breaking gets of his cannonball drives.

So Lacoste reached 40–30, one point away from victory. The suspense was terrific as the next rally began, and when Tilden pulled up to deuce on Lacoste's out, a sigh of relief went up. But the next moment Lacoste was again at match point as Tilden failed to return safely.

Again the French youth netted at the crucial point and the game went on and on until finally, after deuce had been called the fifth time, Lacoste drove out and Tilden whipped home a lightning drive down the line for the game.

How they cheered Tilden! And when he went on to win the fifteenth game at 4–1, with his cannonball service, to lead at 8–7, the crowd was fairly wild with delight. Visions arose again of victory for him, at least in this set, but they speedily vanished when Lacoste won the next two games, breaking through in the seventeenth as Tilden lost all control.

Once more the American aroused the gallery to a wild pitch when he broke through for a love game with two placements, but that was the end. Dead on his feet, Tilden fought Lacoste tooth and nail in the nineteenth, which finally went to the younger player at 8–6, as he scored on three placements in a row, and then, utterly at the end of his rope, he yielded quickly in the twentieth through his errors, to bring the match to an end.

It was a match, the like of which will not be seen again soon. As an exposition of the utmost daring and brilliancy of shot-making and equally of the perfect stage to which the defense can be developed, it has had few equals in the history of tennis.

On the one side of the net stood the perfect tactician and most ruthless attacker the game probably has ever seen, master of every shot and skilled in the necromancy of spin. On the other side was the player who has reduced the defense to a mathematical science; who has done more than that, who has developed his defense to the state when it becomes an offense, subconscious in its working but none the less effective in the pressure it brings to bear as the ball is sent back deeper and deeper and into more and more remote territory.

Both exponents of the attack and the defense were at their best yesterday, and the reaction of the gallery at the end was that it had seen the best that tennis can offer. As one of the spectators remarked, everything else will seem stale after this match. He had seen the zenith.

The defensive player won, but in no small measure it was because youth was on his side. As perfect as was Lacoste's defense, Tilden still might well have prevailed through the sheer magnificence of his stroking had not fatigue set in and robbed him of the strength to control his shots.

In the first set, when Tilden led at 7–6 and 40–love on his own service, it was his errors that robbed him of his big chance. His cannonball service failed him at this critical point, though it was only by a hair that he failed to put over an ace for the set, and when Tilden cannot put over an ace in a pinch he is usually tired.

Had the American put over that one point for which the gallery begged there is no telling who would have won the match. With the first set in the bag he could have loafed through the second and saved himself entirely for the third. Instead he had to keep going in the second, and while he switched from a driving to a chopping game that did not take so much out of him, still the strain was too much for him.

The day has passed when Tilden can maintain a burning pace for two full sets. He knows that as well as the next man, and so he plans his campaign to go "all out" in the first, coast in the second and come back strong in the third, relying upon the rest period to regenerate the dynamo for the fourth.

Had he won the first and relaxed in the second, it is hardly conceivable that he could have failed to make good his 5–2 lead in the third, which would have given him a 2–1 lead to work on after the intermission, with the psychological advantage on his side.

However, even had Tilden won the first set, it may be presuming too much to concede that he would have gone on to victory in the third. After all, this 23-year-old Lacoste is a wonder, a miracle-worker, and he might have stopped even a rampant Tilden at 5–2.

There are moments when Lacoste has had bad spells, when he is human, if to err is human, but those moments are rarer than an American victory over France. When he is in the hole and sets himself to the task, such moments are practically non-existent. You can drive away at him all the day long, mix chops, slices, drives and volleys in a mad melange, run him to the corners until he is dizzy, and always you get nothing for your pains but the chance to hit the ball again. It always comes back like no champion ever does.

The gallery, as partisan as it was, as whole-heartedly as it favored Tilden, could not help but be carried away by the incredible feats of Lacoste. Unmindful of the cheers for his opponent, playing a lone hand, the youthful invader concentrated upon his work and kept the ball in play—kept it in play when Tilden was sending his terrific service straight at him, kept it in play when he had to scramble to the far corners of the court for a blistering drive to his back-hand, and kept it in play when the American was loading his shots with such heavy spin that a spoon would have been needed by any other player to dig it out of the turf.

A defense so impregnable as that, a defense which confounded all of Tilden's ingenuity as he brought all of his artifices to bear, along with his devastating speed and power, should have undermined the morale of any opponent. That Tilden stuck to his guns and fought on as he has seldom fought before, in spite of the fact that he was on his last legs, while his adversary was flitting nimbly about the court on his toes, is to the American's glory.

In victory Tilden was never more magnificent a figure than he was yesterday in defeat, and Lacoste, in his years of triumph, was never greater than he was in the victory at Forest Hills.

Jean Borotra, Lacoste's teammate, who seldom before has been heard to extol the merits of his compatriots, could only shake his head at the end. "If René keeps on playing tennis like that," he said, "how is any one ever going to beat him?"

With the French and American championships both in his possession and victories to his credit over both Tilden and Johnston in the Davis Cup challenge round, the 23-year-old Parisian stands as the unchallenged monarch of the courts, the pride of France and her hope for a continuation of her sweeping success in the future.

All the honors belong to her. She has the Davis Cup, Cochet has the Wimbledon championship and Lacoste has the French and the American indoor and outdoor championships. What else is there to say, except that the season is over, and the French will all be back in the United States again after the Davis Cup challenge round matches in Paris in July?

LOTT CONQUERS LACOSTE AT SOUTHAMPTON

by Allison Danzig

A twenty-year-old youth from Chicago, with the courage of a lion, the trenchant racket of a Tilden and the generalship and self-command of the most seasoned internationalist, fought his way to a magnificently earned victory over the first ranking player of the tennis world today in one of the most stunning reversals in recent years.

René Lacoste of France, holder of the American and French championships, leading ace of the French Davis Cup team and conqueror of William Tilden in the challenge round last September and at St. Cloud in June, suffered the most crushing defeat he has met in almost four years when George M. Lott Jr. of Chicago, ninth in the American ranking, defeated him at 6–4, 6–3, 6–1 in the semi-final round of the annual Southampton invitation tournament.

A gallery of 1,500 spectators, one of the largest that has thronged the clubhouse porch and stands at the Meadow Club in the forty-four years' history of the event, looked on in bewilderment as the ruggedly built Chicagoan, with his "ventilated" blue beret, hammered the French invader into submission with a tigerish attack that put Lacoste on the defensive from the very start and kept him there without a moment's surcease to the end.

Lacoste never had a look-in. The player who had snatched victory from Tilden by a single point in the French championship, whose machine-like steadiness had prevailed over the volatile volleying of Borotra, the artistry of Cochet, the magnificence of Tilden, the daring of Dick Williams and the net play of Vincent Richards in 1926 to place him at the top of the tennis world, met his master in the twenty-year-old youth, and at the end could only say, "He was too good for me."

He might have said that he had been off the boat from France less than two weeks and that he had not had time to bring his game along to its peak. Tilden, who was a spectator at the match, said it for him, when he stated at the conclusion "That shows how far Lacoste has to go yet."

But making allowance for the fact that Lacoste was not at his best today, that he was glaringly poor in control and that he was never able to straighten out his backhand line drive, the fact remains that as Lott played today Lacoste at his best would have been extended to the limit to prevail over him and still might have failed.

It was the son of Thor that went out on the court today against the French ace, with a hammer in his hand that met the ball solidly on the nose and a rapier in reserve to administer the finishing thrust with drop shots of delicate finesse when brute force was not sufficient to prevail against the Frenchman's baseline defense.

This twenty-year-old youth had everything; he had a backhand that came out of the corners like a bolt from the blue to leave Lacoste standing in his tracks with a quizzical look upon his face like a man who had run into a stiff jolt. He had a forehand that ripped open wide gaps in the opposing court when it did not make the chalk fly in the corners for clean placements, and he had the killer's instinct in him to go forward behind these approaching shots and ram home his volleys before the harassed Lacoste could regain position.

He had a twisting service that further paved the way for his advances and that elicited a continual stream of errors from the other's racket, and he had a subtle touch and mental alertness that were too much for even so keen an anticipator and thorough a student of the game as Lacoste, as the American trapped him with drop shots and then lobbed over his head to send him scurrying from base line to net and back again.

It was a perfectly played game that Lott put up. Always he did the right thing and his touch was perfect, whether he was changing pace or spin to throw Lacoste off his stroke, switching from a driving to a chopping game or making his deft trap shots and marvelously gauged lobs.

Against an attack of such bewildering variety and terrific punch as this Lacoste was never able to assume command. It was always a defensive fight that he was making, and while his game is naturally a defensive one, his returns were not the penetrating shots that the tennis world is accustomed to.

With the ball coming back at him either like a bullet to his shoe tops or into remote territory up front or on the other side of the court, he was too cramped and too hurried in his stroking to maintain control or put the ball where he wanted it to go, which is usually as close to the lines as it can be put without going out.

The victory of Lott, so startlingly unexpected as it was, left the tennis colony here in a state that might be described by the legal fraternity as non compos mentis. For a whole week every one here had looked forward to a meeting between Lacoste and Tilden, and the one subject of conversation had been whether or not one of them would default, to prevent a meeting between them before the Davis Cup challenge round.

When Tilden went out on the courts this morning and annihilated Brugnon in the other semi-final in thirty-two minutes at 6–2, 6–1, 6–0, it seemed that the match was definitely on, for Lacoste had stated that he would not default, and with Tilden in the final round he was committed to play also.

The former champion had asked that the same ball boys who had worked in his match with Brugnon be used in the final, and had every expectation of meeting Lacoste.

Then along came George Lott to do what not one person in ten had conceded him more than an outside chance of doing, and the tennis world will now have to wait until the challenge round before the two Davis Cup aces will meet.

It might be suspected by some that Lacoste was not as keen to win today as he might have been under other circumstances, but any imputation that he sought, in defeat, a way out of a meeting with Tilden would be a slander upon his sportsmanship and an injustice to Lott.

If any one thought that the French invader welcomed defeat, his actions certainly spoke louder than suspicions. There was no mistaking his concern with the way the play was going against him, and at times such was his disgust over his errors that he slammed a ball into the net after the end of the rally.

No, Lacoste did not play his best tennis today, but it was not of his own choosing.

FRANCE'S FIRST DAVIS CUP CHALLENGE ROUND VICTORY

by Allison Danzig

The course of tennis umpire takes its way Eastward across the Atlantic. The longest reign in the history of the Davis Cup came to an end today and a new cycle began as France's invaders won the two final matches in the challenge round to capture the series with the United States at three matches to two at the Germantown Cricket Club and won the cup for the first time in the twenty-two times that the historic trophy has been competed for since 1900.

Thus ends the dominion of the English-speaking world in these international classics, which heretofore had been won only by the United States, Great Britain and Australia. Seven of America's ten victories have been gained since 1920, when the cup was brought back from the Antipodes. Australia has won it six times and Great Britain five.

France, to celebrate its first triumph, which marks the culmination of three successive years of effort in the challenge round and which was witnessed by the French Ambassador, Paul Claudel, will place the massive silver bowl and tray in the Louvre for keeping until it shall have been yielded to another nation.

The same two players who went to Australia to lift the cup in 1920 and who have been the mainstay of its defense ever since were the same two players who fought so gallantly but in vain today to extend America's tenure to another year, but the ravages of time had taken their toll, and youth, in the person of René Lacoste and Henri Cochet, carried the day.

To Cochet, the player who ended William Tilden's six-year reign as national champion last September and who triumphed over the Philadelphian again in the final at Wimbledon last July, fell the honor of winning the match that clinched the victory for France when he defeated William Johnston in four sets at 6–4, 4–6, 6–2, 6–4.

However, it is René Lacoste, the phlegmatic, sad-visaged young Parisian, on whom France should bestow the double palm, the Croix de Guerre and the Red Badge of the Legion of Honor, for it was his victory over Tilden in the first of the two singles matches today that really decided the series.

With the United States leading at two matches to one and Tilden playing in apparently invincible form, all signs pointed toward another American victory when the Philadelphian and his 23-year-old opponent went on the court. But the same machine-like defense, maintained inexorably against the most terrific pressure, which proved the undoing of Tilden in the challenge round last year, and again at St. Cloud in June, once more stood adamant against the 34-year-old veteran's shafts of lightning until the American had shot his bolt and his physical powers disintegrated.

By the middle of the third set Tilden's racket, the racket that had once been the symbol of the most autocratic power that ever held sway on the courts, had become a harmless bit of wood and string in the hands of a physically exhausted giant, and Lacoste relentlessly went onward to victory at 6–3, 4–6, 6–3, 6–2.

Nothing that the stage has to offer can equal in drama the scene that was enacted on the hallowed Germantown turf.

A crowd of 15,000 tennis fans stormed the gates, hundreds of whom were turned back. Also, so great was the throng that got inside that the two sections of the grandstand, the bleachers and the extra stands all proved inadequate to hold them. Hundreds sat in the aisles, stood on chairs and sat on the ground, and when Johnston and Cochet went on the court there was a mad rush for seats on the adjoining court that swept a score of police guards aside.

It was a thoroughly partisan gallery that looked down upon the play, a gallery that came scenting an American victory and which, when Tilden had been defeated and all hope had been abandoned, was so carried away by Johnston's great bid for victory over Cochet that it broke all bounds of tennis etiquette and cheered madly both the American's winning shots and Cochet's mistakes.

In the fourth set of the match, when Johnston, hitting into a streak of magnificent tennis that had Cochet reeling before his attack, pulled up from 2–5 to 4–5 and 30–0 on the French youth's service, the stands were in continuous uproar. In vain Umpire Paul Gibbons pleaded with them to remain quiet while the ball was in play. He might as well have tried to turn back the tide. Cheers, shrieks and storms of applause went up to the skies as they begged Little Bill to come on.

And who could blame them? Wasn't Johnston making one of the gamest fights to save the cup that had been seen in the long history of the matches? Johnston, the "has been" and the "hollow shell," as they called him after his crushing defeat by Lacoste on Thursday, was playing like one possessed, ripping the turf apart with his murderous forehand, volleying as no one had seen him volley in years, and battering the harried Cochet from pillar to post.

It would have been a strange gallery that could have controlled its mad excitement under the circumstances, and so the place became a seething furnace of human exhortations as the little Californian fought his way to within two points of tying the score at 5–all in the fourth set.

But at this critical point, with Cochet erring miserably and looking toward Captain Pierre Gillou in bewilderment, plainly at a loss how to regain command, Johnston faltered. Overanxiousness or perhaps nervousness that was partly the result of the uproar, interrupted the fluency of his stroking, the magic punch went out of his racket, and after he had been passed at the net he drove his backhand over the line, missed the line by an inch on a high volley, and, after a long rally, his forehand found the net.

The match was over, the cup had been won for France, and Cochet, in an ecstasy of happiness, threw his racket thirty feet high into the air as he ran forward to throw his arms around his adversary. At the same moment Captain Gillou and Lacoste, their faces beaming with delight, walked out on the court to shower Cochet with congratulations, and the genial Jean Borotra joined in the celebration.

For the next half hour the court swarmed with players, officials, spectators and photographers, who insisted on taking pictures of all the members of the two teams, the officials and everyone else who had any pretensions to being a tennis celebrity. The massive cup and tray were brought out. Ambassador Claudel entered into the ceremonies and President Jones W. Mersereau of the United States Lawn Tennis Association made the presentation speech as the prize was turned over to Captain Gillou.

Mme. Cochet, the wife of the 26-year-old youth from Lyons who had brought such glory to the valor of French tennis, was so overcome with happiness that she burst into tears and was still weeping a half hour after the play was over. It was an occasion that will remain forever in the memory of those who saw it, this first victory of France in the play for the cup that Secretary of War Dwight F. Davis offered in competition in 1900.

That it will be only the first of more victories to come for France is the lesson that is to be gained from the results of today's play. Tilden and Johnston have apparently seen their best days. Both are capable of playing as good tennis as ever they did in their lives, and this they both did today, but only for a certain number of sets. No longer is it possible for them to maintain the pace through a five-set match. While their physical powers endure they are as formidable as ever, but, unhappily for America's lost supremacy, the years have taken their toll of them and they must make way for the younger blood of France's masters of the court.

Tilden, victor over Cochet on Thursday and in the doubles with Frank Hunter over Borotra and Jacques Brugnon, undertook more than was within his physical capacity when he sought to bring victory practically single-handed to America today. It would have been the greatest triumph of the Philadelphian's long and glorious career on the courts had he been able to crown the three days of play with a victory that would have retained the cup for the United States. But almost from the outset the gallery had a premonition of what was to come.

Lacoste, driving with uncanny steadiness that characterizes his game at its best, was a stone wall against which the American wasted his strength in one long rally after another. Instinctively one felt that Tilden could not last against such pitiless efficiency, and it became apparent that he was going to have to pay dearly for every point he won. His only hope was to take every chance, hit for the lines with the smallest possible margin of safety and go to the net.

Tilden came to that understanding immediately himself, for he hit out for the baseline almost from the start. His range was badly off in the first set, his drives overreaching the chalk stripe by feet, and in spite of the fact that he was serving magnificently and volleying well his errors were far too numerous for him to make any headway against the flawless strokes of Lacoste. Tilden was taking all the chances, hitting the harder and lower over the net, but always the ball kept coming back, and at good length, and the points were to Lacoste. Lacoste did not make a single earned point in the opening set, Tilden contributing all 28 of his opponent's points on errors. Four of them came in the fourth game, when the only breakthrough service was made by Lacoste.

The second set found Tilden tightening in control, in spite of the fact that he was still taking chances with his length, and he now sought the net at every opportunity when he had the service. But the strain was telling on him, and, after he had broken through in the second game and won the third with three beautiful placements, one of them a kill, to lead at 3–0, he contented himself with holding his own service inviolate. Any shot that he had to scramble for he allowed to go unchallenged, particularly drop shots, and Lacoste won two service games at love, scoring 7 placements out of 8 points.

The crucial game of the set was the seventh. Lacoste gained a 40–0 lead on Tilden's service, and ordinarily the American would have made no effort to save the game, but he realized that if he lost his service it might mean the loss of the set, and he went to the net for two beautiful volleys that were cheered wildly. Lacoste's steadiness deserted him in this game and Tilden finally pulled it out at 7–5. The effort, however, told on him, and he lost the next two games, Lacoste pulling up from 15–40 to break through in the ninth after Tilden had twice been at set point. It looked serious indeed now for Tilden, for he was tiring badly and did not have the energy left to go to the net. The gallery was on tenterhooks when Lacoste began serving in the tenth. A placement off service and Lacoste's out gave Tilden a 30–0 lead and he carried it to 40–15 on a great kill from deep court. Lacoste pulled up to deuce on two errors, twice more saving the set by a point, but here he made one of his few unworthy errors in the match, flubbing a set-up shot near the net. That gave Tilden the advantage point and he took the set with a passing shot that was cheered to the echo.

With the sets one–all, there was more hope for Tilden, but one still had the feeling that the advantage lay with Lacoste as the fresher and more physically enduring of the two. Tilden had had no opportunity to spare himself as he did in the match with Cochet, when he coasted in the second set. He had to work just as hard in the second set against Lacoste as in the first, and that boded ill for him.

Both players relaxed at the start of the third chapter, and games went on service to 3–all. Tilden's aggressiveness asserted itself in the fifth when he scored on two blazing forehand drives across court and a gem of a volley. But this was the beginning of the end for him. His strength was exhausted and he had not enough left in reserve to control his shots. Lacoste took the next four games with the loss of only four points, and the gallery sat silent and depressed by the careless errors from Tilden's racket. The American was too weary and spent to do more than lift his racket.

The rest period did Tilden no good. Ten minutes of grace meant nothing to the veteran of 34 years. He had already given everything he had. He won only two points in the first two games of the fourth set, though he rallied to pull up from 0–40 and won the third game with two marvelous volleys. Tilden was too far gone to make good a lead of 30–0 in the fourth. Lacoste got eight points in a row on errors and one volley, and, after Tilden had made a last gallant effort in the sixth, to win it with two blasting drives, Lacoste won the seventh at love, and two beautiful crosscourt drives gave him the eighth for the set and match.

A perfect baseline defense that turned back everything with flawless precision had spiked the attack of the most spectacular player in the game. Tilden, for all his virtuosity and daring, had found that he did not have enough finishing shots to make any impression against a stone wall that catapulted back his most murderous smashes, and he realized the futility of opposition. Lacoste had robbed him of his confidence and will to win as well as his stamina.

The stroke analysis tells the story graphically. Tilden, while he scored 33 placements and 9 service aces to Lacoste's 21 and 1, made 100 errors to the other's 49. Lacoste was never more the machine.

After the defeat of Tilden the gallery resigned itself to the loss of the cup. Johnston, following his overwhelming defeat by Lacoste on Thursday, was looked upon as hardly more than a sacrifice offering for Cochet. It can be appreciated then what were the feelings of the thousands in the stands when the little Californian started out after Cochet with a savageness that took the

French youth by surprise. In the twinkling of an eye, Johnston had won the first game at 4–1 and rushed into a lead of 40–0 in the second, whipping his forehand through the court like a bullet.

The crowd was in a turmoil. Cheer after cheer went up and everyone asked his neighbor if this could be the same Johnston who couldn't get the ball over the net against Lacoste. At this point five errors in a row from Johnston's bat brought forth groans of disappointment, but they changed to cheers again when he won the third game at love and broke through at 5–3 to lead at 3–1. Cochet was slow to find himself against the hard hitting of Johnston, and his few excursions to the net resulted in errors. Beginning with the fourth game, however, the situation took on a different complexion. Cochet, as cool as ice and always master of himself, now steadied in control, added pressure to his strokes and began to make the ingenious shots that stamp him as the greatest artist of the courts. Johnston could not put the ball away. His errors began to mount, and Cochet took five of the six next games for the set.

Again the question presented itself as to how long Johnston could sustain his powerful driving. But to the surprise of everyone the little Californian came back stronger in the second set than he was in the first. Cochet was not as steady as he usually is at the start of this set and Johnston stayed on even terms to 3–all, both players losing their service games twice. In the seventh game the Californian electrified the gallery with four placements, two of them volleys, and two more blasting drives in the eighth carried him into a 5–3 lead. Johnston's volleying was now so perfect as he lifted the ball from his feet on the hardest shots, and he was forcing his openings so relentlessly with his cannonball forehand that Cochet, in spite of his miraculous recoveries, could not hold him off.

The stands were giving the Californian ovation after ovation, and hope sprang anew for an American victory. Johnston faltered for a brief period and lost the next game on errors, but the tenth found him sailing along again and Cochet, driven from corner to corner, finally yielded the set after a sensational duel at the net, where Johnston brought off three superb low volleys in succession. The pace was more than Johnston could stand, however, and he fell into a slump in the third set. His forehand found the net repeatedly. His backhand was vulnerable to Cochet's spinning drives to the corner. The French youth was stroking in his most inspired fashion, making the most impossible shots for placements. With the score 4–0 against him, Johnston aroused the gallery by taking the next two games with his aggressive driving and volleying, but his errors cost him the seventh, and Cochet broke through in the eighth after a long struggle in spite of Johnston's spectacular volleying and overhead smashing.

It was inconceivable now that Johnston could pull out the match against the more youthful and brilliant Frenchman. But again the California veteran surprised everyone by rallying with the score 2–0 against him and playing his best tennis of the match. From this point on the gallery was stirred to the depths, at one moment exulting as Johnston scored on a murderous forehand or biting volley, at the next moment despairing as he made a costly error. Both players were giving everything they had in the most bitterly fought rallies, and there were any number of close decisions on the lines that brought cries of protest from the stands when they went against Johnston.

Three times Johnston was at game point and he could not put over the necessary winning shot. As a consequence, he was always behind, though he had the chance to tie the score at 2–all and 3–all. When Cochet, after winning the second deuce game in succession, broke through at 8–6 in the seventh, in which Johnston led at 40–30, all hope was given up. Johnston was behind, 2–5, and Cochet had run him ragged in the seventh, passing him five times as Johnston sought to get to the net.

But at this point came the American's rally that set the gallery wild. Four smoking drives enabled him to break through in the eighth at 10–8 after Cochet had twice been at match point. The loss of that game had a disturbing effect upon the French youth, while Johnston, spurred on by his escape from defeat, as well as by the frenzied cheers of the spectators, pressed the attack in the ninth, pasting every ball on the nose, crowding the net to volley in sensational fashion and giving Cochet no rest. When he won the game at love the crowd cheered wildly. Cochet was a badly worried youth. His control was gone, as well as his confidence, and he was like a rudderless ship before the storm.

The suspense was terrific in the tenth game. Cochet, overanxious, whipped the ball into the net. Again he netted the ball in the next rally and the stands were in bedlam, cheering his errors. But, with the score 30–0 against him, the young invader took a grip on himself and passed Johnston as he closed in. Johnston's backhand drive overhit the line by an inch, making the score 30–all, and when the Californian put a high volley out of court by a hair a roar went up from the crowd, which protested that the volley hit the line. Cochet was now at match point again. He served. Johnston returned the ball safely. It crossed and recrossed the net as the gallery hung breathlessly on every stroke, and then Johnston's drive landed in the net and the match was over. Cochet had won the Davis Cup for France.

1929

TILDEN WINS SEVENTH U.S. TITLE

by Allison Danzig

The dominion of William Tilden over American tennis was re-established by title as well as in fact yesterday. Three years after his reign was brought to an end by an interlude of French triumphs, the 36-year-old Philadelphian captured the national championship for the seventh time, thereby equaling the record held jointly by Richard D. Sears and William A. Larned, and assuring himself of being ranked first in American tennis for the tenth consecutive time.

A gallery of 9,000 in the stadium of the West Side Tennis Club at Forest Hills witnessed the restoration of the crown as Tilden defeated Francis T. Hunter of New Rochelle in the final round of the forty-eighth annual tournament.

The match went to five sets, with Tilden trailing 2 to 1, but there never was any question as to the ultimate reckoning, and the final two chapters found the once invincible monarch of the courts electrifying the gallery as of yore with a withering onslaught of drives and service aces that brooked no opposition. The score was 3–6, 6–3, 4–6, 6–2, 6–4.

It was a happy Tilden who ran forward to the net to greet his beaten doubles partner while the cheers of the thousands paid tribute to a champion who had come back. Hunter, downhearted for the moment over his failure for the second successive year in the final of the championship, found his smile again and threw his arm around Tilden's shoulder as they posed before a battery of cameras while President Samuel H. Collom of the United States Lawn Tennis Association presented the champion with the challenge trophy. On that trophy René Lacoste of France holds two legs, gained in 1926 and 1927, while Henri Cochet of France was the winner last year, when he beat Hunter in five sets.

In defeating Hunter in the fifth set twenty-four hours after he had been carried to the maximum number of sets by John Doeg in a struggle of two hours and a half, Tilden showed that, for all his years, his staying powers are still as great as those of the younger generation of players. In both matches the champion produced his greatest tennis in the last two sets, when nothing less than his best was called for. The ability to rise to unassailable heights under stress that confounded his opponents in the days of his world supremacy was again in evidence in both of these struggles.

In the last meeting between Tilden and Hunter, in the Eastern championships at Rye, Tilden was the winner in three sets against a passive Hunter. It was a different Hunter yesterday, a Hunter fired with ambition to climb the last rung up the tennis ladder. The opening set found the rugged New Rochelle internationalist laying down a barrage upon Tilden's back court that had the Philadelphian running to cover up. Tilden's control was none too good at this stage and it was largely his service that was keeping him on even terms until the ninth game, when Hunter, hitting powerfully to the corners, effected the lone break in the set. How erratic was the tennis Tilden was playing in this set is shown by the fact that he made 27 errors, to Hunter's 17.

The second set saw Tilden tighten in control and add pressure to his strokes while his footwork was speeded up until he was retrieving everything in sight. Hunter stood firm in the face of this assault, but gradually he was forced to give ground as Tilden broke through in a long deuce game to gain a 3–0 lead. Try as he would, Hunter could not regain that lost ground and he was soon shaking his head, realizing the magnitude of his task against an aroused Tilden who covered court unflaggingly and whose backhand half-volleys from the baseline were repeatedly converting apparent winners for Hunter into points for himself.

After winning this set to draw level, however, Tilden patently slackened pace in the third set and Hunter, hitting furiously, gained a 4–0 lead with the loss of only five points. It seemed that Tilden was going to concede the set, but instead he now braced and launched a rally that took him to 4–5. With his service to come, it looked as though he was going to square the score, but Hunter checked this rally with a bombardment that exacted four errors from Tilden's racket, and Tilden left the court trailing, 2 sets to 1.

The onslaught that was looked for from the champion when he returned from the showers was immediately forthcoming. Hunter took the opening game of the fourth set on service and then Tilden set sail. Five games in a row fell to him, only one of them going to deuce, and not until he had gained set point at 40–15 in the seventh was Hunter able to stem the tide. In this set Tilden scored 11 placements to Hunter's 2.

The final set saw Hunter in his most dangerous mood and both men playing their best tennis of the match. To 2–all games went on service and then Tilden, mixing up his length and pace craftily, broke through in the fifth, after which he won the sixth for a 4–2 lead. This was sufficient to settle any doubts as to the outcome of the match.

Hunter was playing like a man possessed in the seventh, and he had Tilden running as he won the ninth to make the score 5–4, but the champion, playing coolly and with every confidence, finished matters in the tenth. Hunter made two ruthless returns of service, but Tilden's great recoveries put them to nought, and, with the score at 30–0, the champion put over a service ace and followed with another service that Hunter drove out of court, bringing the match to an end.

1 9 3 0

WOOD SHOCKS VINES AT SEABRIGHT

by Allison Danzig

In as bewildering a match as probably has ever been witnessed in the thirty-seven years' history of the invitation tournament of the Seabright Lawn Tennis and Cricket Club, Ellsworth Vines of Pasadena, California, finally met his Waterloo today after two weeks of amazing success that lifted him from obscurity to a dominating position among the younger generation of American tennis players.

With a gallery of 2,000 spectators looking on, unable to believe their eyes, the 18-year-old youth, who came out of the West unheralded two weeks ago to defeat Frank Hunter and Frank Shields in the metropolitan champion-ship and to repeat his triumphs over the same players on the Seabright courts, went down in overwhelming defeat in the final round of the tournament by the crushing margin of 6–2, 6–2, 6–0.

The player who administered this stunning setback to the all-conquering march of the Californian was not Tilden nor Cochet nor any other giant of the court of established reputation, but an even younger player than Vines, and, like him, unranked and unseeded in the Seabright draw. Sidney B. Wood, Jr., of New York is his name, and it is not likely to be forgotten by those who were privileged to witness the masterful way in which he carried out his preconceived plan of undermining the game of his towering oppo-nent and reducing it to impotency.

Seldom has a tennis gallery sat through a final-round match in such ominous silence as marked the ending of Vines's winning streak. The sight of the young player who had captivated all by his magnificent tennis going down in such ignominious defeat, utterly baffled by the methods of his opponent and helpless to produce his real game, was not a happy one, and a pall seemed to hang over the stands throughout the match, which lasted forty-five minutes.

It was not speed or magnificent shot-making that beat Vines, but a soft ball that raised havoc with his timing, ruined his pace, unsteadied his hand and completely disrupted his whole scheme of attack, leaving him utterly at the mercy of his opponent. Wood had not watched Vines in action here without learning that speed was the last thing in the world to give him.

Hunter and Shields and Richard Norris Williams 2d, who also fell a victim to the Californian, all had as much speed off the ground as he could hope to muster, and each of them had found it unavailing against Vines, who utilized the pace on their strokes to add to the velocity of his own. On leaving the courts yesterday, after he and Shields had defeated Vines and Keith Gledhill in the doubles, the flaxen-haired New York youth confided to several friends that he had learned the way he must play the Californian when they met today, and his analysis proved to be perfect.

That way was to give Vines nothing but soft shots, never to give him a short, high-rising ball on his forehand, and to concentrate on keeping the ball going back rather than to try for winners unless the opening begged for a fast drive. After the match Wood said: "I didn't try to win by trying to play brilliant tennis. I tried to prevent Vines from playing his best."

This, in the last analysis, tells the story of the match to perfection. It was not a brilliant match by any stretch of the imagination, for the play was one-sided and so marred by Vines's errors that Wood had little occasion to show the caliber of his forcing strokes.

On the other hand, Wood followed out his plan of battle exactly to the letter and with such consummate cleverness as to call for the highest praise, even if in so doing he lowered the quality of his tennis. In addition, the New York youth gave an exhibition of control that has been unequaled here all week, hardly a single inexcusable error being charged to him in the first set, and on the few occasions when Vines blazed away in characteristic fashion Wood turned back his terrific swipes with such magnificent back-hand recoveries as to win over a gallery whose sympathies obviously were for his opponent.

At the outset Vines set out to play his typical game, hitting hard and with daring. But he could not find his control or best pace, and Wood's disturbing soft returns and changes of pace on his service had him worried and faltering.

When the New Yorker had taken five games in a row with these subtle tactics, Vines, despairing of gaining control of his forcing strokes, changed to his opponent's own style of game, and the gallery looked on at an exhibition that resembled pat ball, with both players tossing the ball high above the net through the center of the court.

Two love games in a row then fell to the Californian and in the eighth game he led at 40–15 on his service. It looked like the Hunter match all over again, for on the day before Vines lost the first five games and then found his true form to go straight forward to victory.

But at this point, when the Californian seemed to have safely adapted himself to circumstances, his control deserted him again in the soft exchanges and he dropped the eighth game and the set. There was still hope for him, it was believed, for he had beaten Hunter after losing the first two sets in Brooklyn and again on these courts after dropping the first one. But the rally that was expected of the Californian never was forthcoming.

Vines won the first two games of the second set and then complete disintegration set in. From 0–2 Wood took twelve games in a row. Several times during these last two sets Vines lashed out furiously on his service and his drives, but he could not penetrate his opponent's marvelous defense and his control was found wanting. It seemed impossible for him to hit more than two hard shots in a rally and keep the ball in the court and out of the net.

There were some who thought that Vines made a fatal mistake in not going to the net and capitalizing his exceptional ability as a volleyer. But on the few occasions that he did gain the barrier safely he met with little success, so penetrating were Wood's passing shots.

TILDEN BEATEN BY DOEG

by Allison Danzig

Eleven years after he lost to William Johnston in the final of the 1919 tournament, William Tilden, seven times winner of the crown since 1920 and with the greatest European season of his career immediately behind him, suffered his first defeat at the hands of an American in the national championship yesterday as 10,000 spectators looked on incredulously at the stadium of the West Side Tennis Club, Forest Hills.

John Doeg, 21-year-old blond California giant, the same youth who gave Tilden his stiffest fight in the championship last year, accomplished what no other player save Henri Cochet in 1926 and René Lacoste in 1927 had been able to do in this tournament since Tilden first came to the throne a decade ago, and thereby frustrated the hopes of the 37-year-old Philadelphia veteran of breaking a record that has stood since Richard D. Sears won the title for the seventh time in 1887. The score was 10–8, 6–3, 3–6, 12–10.

Not since Lacoste lowered the colors of Tilden in the 1927 final has there been witnessed so magnificent a struggle at Forest Hills as was this two-hour battle in which the aging master fought with reckless courage and employed all the stratagems of his infinitely resourceful attack in the vain effort to repel the challenge of youth.

Such shots as the Philadelphian has not made in years electrified the gallery as of yore when none could stand against him. Cannonball service aces, and almost phenomenal recoveries that made the welkin ring were brought into the breach by Tilden as he stood with his back to the wall in the fourth set, but nought that he could do availed.

In the invincible service of his opponent and its faultlessly functioning volley adjunct, the defender faced a combination of forces that rode out the storm of his furious onslaught and finally quelled it, as another storm of cheers rolled out over the stadium in acclaim of the Californian's great victory.

The defeat of Tilden, which came like a bolt out of a clear sky after his victory at Newport and his remarkable record this year in Europe, where he won the English, German, Austrian, Italian and Dutch championships, almost made the gallery forget about the outcome of the other semi-final in which Sidney B. Wood Jr. met his master in Frank Shields.

Capitalizing his battering service to tremendous advantage and playing almost flawless tennis all the way, the strapping young New Yorker reversed the result of his previous meeting with Wood at Southampton to win at 6–2, 6–3, 4–6, 6–3.

The final today thus will bring together two of the youngest players ever to meet for the title and will witness the elevation of a new native champion for the first time since 1920. Shields will be 20 years old in November, and Doeg will be 22 in December.

The victory of Doeg over the defending champion was the climactic reversal of a week that saw Jean Borotra of France go down before Berkeley Bell, George Lott lose to Dick Williams, and Wilmer Allison bow to Shields. As unexpected as were these last three results, they were merely in the nature of minor surprises as compared to the downfall of Tilden.

Nothing that Doeg had done all season prepared anyone for yesterday's startling denouement, even though he had given a splendid account of himself in the South and came close to defeating Allison at Wimbledon. The difficulty he had experienced in defeating Francis T. Hunter on Thursday and the inefficacy of his ground strokes and volleying and the slump in his service were all the more reason for looking for a Tilden victory.

But the Doeg who went on the court against Tilden was not to be recognized as the same player who trailed Hunter two sets to one, nor was his magnificent performance to be reconciled with anything else he has done on American courts.

The herculean Californian has long had the reputation of possessing one of the most dreaded services the game has known. That service yesterday was one of the most destructive weapons ever let loose upon a tennis court, and, backed up by a volleying attack that never faltered, even in the face of Tilden's most savage and ingeniously directed drives, it invited comparison with the thunderbolts of another Californian of the same school of offense, Maurice McLoughlin.

In the four sets Doeg made the remarkable total of twenty-eight service aces, twelve of them coming in the final chapter, when he needed them most, as Tilden rose to his greatest heights. No less than fourteen times that service accounted for a love game, and time and again it came to his aid when he needed a point vitally to stave off the loss of an important game.

Tilden was never able to break through it in the first set, which was a duel of services that ended when the champion dropped his own in the last game. Once in the second set and once in the third were the only times that the Philadelphian could break through it.

As irresistible as was Doeg's service and as marvelous was his volleying, hardly less impressive were his ground strokes. The forehand chop that was thought to be a hopeless obstacle in the way of his climb to the heights was as adamantine as the Rock of Gibraltar, and his backhand drive and slice stood up equally well.

As for the champion, he played and fought against defeat like one. He did not appear to become seriously concerned about the outcome of the match until the third chapter, but throughout the four sets he was performing in close to his best style, in spite of the fact that he suffered a fall in the fifth game of the second set and limped thereafter.

Indeed, his most spectacular exploits came after his injury, when he drove himself on with reckless disregard of his underpinning, and in the final chapter, which had the gallery cheering deliriously, he made two passing shots in headlong flight from far off the court that equaled anything seen at Forest Hills in years.

Such shots as these are the hallmark of Tilden at his best and that Doeg should have held his service inviolate against them until he finally effected the lone break of the set in the twenty-second game is testimonial enough of the magnificent quality of his tennis.

DOEG DEFEATS SHIELDS FOR U.S. CHAMPIONSHIP

by Allison Danzig

A new tennis champion, the youngest to capture the national title in fifteen years and the first American to succeed William Tilden as the holder, was crowned at Forest Hills yesterday before the biggest crowd that has gathered in the stadium of the West Side Tennis Club since 1927.

In the final round of the forty-ninth annual tournament, with 13,000 spectators cheering them on frenziedly, John Hope Doeg, 21-year-old California giant, defeated the equally stalwart Francis X. Shields of New York at 10–8, 1–6, 6–4, 16–14 to carry the title back to the Pacific Coast for the first time since William Johnston came through in 1919. Tilden won his first championship in 1920.

In reality, the title will remain in the East, for Doeg stated before going on the court that he will make his home in New York and henceforth will confine himself to one or two tournaments a year, giving up Davis Cup play for a business career.

It was a fitting climax to the herculean Californian's last year of extensive competition that he should have come to the championship. After his victory over Tilden in the semi-finals and Frank Hunter in the round before—the two men that met for the title last season—defeat yesterday would have been a cruel trick of fate.

The same magnificent tennis that Doeg put forth against Tilden was offered against Shields, though his service was not consistently as effective, and those who witnessed his elevation looked upon one of the finest exhibitions that ever carried a player to the greatest prize the game awards in this country. But if defeat would have been cruel for Doeg, it was no less heartbreaking for Shields. The 19-year-old New York schoolboy, who had put out Wilmer Allison, Gregory Mangin and Sidney B. Wood, Jr., in advancing to the final, made a fight for the honors that will not be forgotten for years by those in the stands.

For two and a half hours the battle waged between these two young giants, with the play so close and the outcome hanging on so slender a thread time and again that the gallery was almost as exhausted at the end from the strain and excitement as were the contestants themselves. The fourth set, the longest one on record in a final round of the championship, requiring thirty games and an hour and twenty-two minutes for a decision, had the multitudes cheering frantically and fairly delirious with suspense. Four times Shields was within a stroke of winning the set to square the match—once in the eighteenth game, twice in the twentieth and again in the twenty-eighth. Each time Doeg's infallible volleying behind his service saved the day, and the match finally ended after the Californian had effected the lone break in the set in the twenty-ninth game.

It was a match that will linger long in memory as a superb exhibition of both tennis and the acme of good sportsmanship. Here were two strapping youths who both carried dynamite in their services and volleys, who scorned to temporize, who asked no mercy and never gave any, but who could give away points, regardless of the juncture, to rectify a possible mistake in their favor and give them not as charity but in the spirit of noblesse oblige and without quibbling or fuss.

From start to finish it was a ruthless battle of hammer and tongs, filled with spectacular shot-making and hair-raising recoveries and circumventions, and at no time were the proceedings such magnificent entertainment as they were in the final game as Shields catapulted himself about the court to stave off the inevitable with one miraculous shot after another.

Leading at 40–15 on Doeg's service in this game, Shields was forced to yield the next two points to his opponent's reverberating overhead smashes. Defeat was only two points away and in a moment it was only one point removed. The shots that the New Yorker made from this juncture until Doeg finally put over two unreachable volleys to end the match compare in their theatrical character with anything seen at Forest Hills in years. Electrifying backhand line drives from far off the court and returns of service that creased the chalk mark kept the stands in a state bordering on pandemonium until this pulsating struggle finally reached its conclusion.

In making one of his amazing recoveries Shields fell flat on his stomach and the wind was knocked out of him. It was several minutes before he was able to resume play and when he started to get out of the chair that was placed under him, Doeg put his hand on his shoulder and shoved him down again with the order to stay there until he had fully recovered. This gesture of the Californian was characteristic of the spirit in which the match was played all the way, even when the terrific strain was telling on the nerves of Doeg, and when the battle was over, each of the players had a friendly arm to throw around the other's shoulder.

It was almost dark when the play ended, and most of the spectators had been in the stands for nearly six hours. Owing to the almost interminable duration of the veterans' championship, which preceded the men's final and lasted nearly three hours, Doeg and Shields did not appear on the court until an hour and three-quarters after they were scheduled. Doeg was slow to get started as the first set got under way, and not until he was behind at 1–3 did he begin to pursue the even tenor of his way. From that point on he was invincible when he held the service in this set, his volleys and overhead smashes smothering everything and his ground strokes skimming the net at sharp angles to find unreachable territory.

Shields was serving even better than Doeg and was nailing the ball beautifully with immaculate length both on the forehand and backhand. After Doeg had drawn level at 4–all, there was nothing to choose between them, and a duel of services developed that was marked by a remarkable number of placements on both sides until the Californian broke through in the eighteenth game with three dazzling passing shots. Doeg made 23 placements in the set to 17 for his opponent.

The second set witnessed a surprising slump in Doeg's play. For some unexplainable reason he lost his aggressiveness and control, allowed Shields to take command of the situation, and was never a contender as the New Yorker, playing like a streak and serving three aces in the fourth game, rushed into a 5–0 lead. But with the start of the third chapter Doeg came back to the wars again and for the rest of the day the two young Goliaths fought each other to a standstill. Doeg was serving better now and Shields did not need to, so omnipotent was his battering delivery. The set was marked by a single break, in the ninth game, as Shields' backhand, magnificent all afternoon, failed him for one of the few times in the match.

The fourth set was the best of the match. For twenty-eight games there was not a single break in service, though Shields and Doeg both had to overcome leads of 30–0 and 40–15 several times to prevent them. How magnificently the points were being earned can be appreciated from the fact that Doeg made 36 placements and Shields 39, while the service aces were 5 and 8 respectively.

Some of Doeg's volleys in this set were almost unbelievable, particularly one that he made in the sixth game when Shields slammed the ball at him like a shot out of a cannon and the Californian blocked it to drop the ball over the net for a placement. In the seventh game Shields made three service aces in a row and in the ninth all four of his points were earned on superb placements. So magnificently was the New York youth playing now that Doeg could not afford to let down for a minute. Shields was handling his rival's service better and better and his cleverly placed returns of service to Doeg's feet had the Californian repeatedly in holes from which he extricated himself only by virtue of his superlative volleying and overhead smashing.

Shields had repeated opportunities but it was impossible to capitalize them in the face of Doeg's stonewall defense at the net, and time and again the New Yorker's legion of friends groaned as these opportunities went glimmering in the wake of the Californian's crosscourt volleys. A crosscourt passing shot finally enabled Doeg to break through in the twenty-ninth game. Then came the harrowing, nerve-wracking thirtieth game, and the next moment the thousands were hailing the crowning of a new champion, the first left-handed player to win the title since R. Lindley Murray came through in 1918.

BETTY NUTHALL FIRST FOREIGNER TO WIN U.S. WOMEN'S TITLE

by Allison Danzig

The women's national tennis championship has left the United States for the first time in the forty-three years of the tournament's history.

Miss Betty Nuthall, 19-year-old English girl, now sits on the throne vacated by Mrs. Helen Wills Moody and heretofore occupied only by residents of the United States, though two former champions, Molla Bjurstedt and May Sutton, were not Americans by birth. Mrs. Moody decided not to defend her title this year because of her disinclination to make the trip east from California so soon after her return from Europe.

Four thousand spectators, braving threatening skies, looked on from the stadium of the West Side Tennis Club at Forest Hills yesterday as Miss Nuthall completed her march through the championship field by defeating Mrs. Lawrence A. Harper of Oakland, California, at 6–1, 6–4, in a match that lasted thirty-six minutes.

Half an hour after she had received the championship cup, filled with American Beauty roses, from the hands of Walter Merrill Hall and P. Schuyler Van Bloem, the young British player returned to the courts to gain a second title.

With rain coming down so hard as to drive many of the onlookers to cover repeatedly, Miss Nuthall and Miss Sarah Palfrey of Boston overcame a 3–0 deficit in the final set to defeat Mrs. Harper and Miss Edith Cross of San Francisco, 3–6, 6–3, 7–5, in the final of the doubles.

Not since Hugh L. Doherty of England came through in the singles and carried off the doubles with his brother Reginald in 1903, had any visiting player scored a double triumph similar to Miss Nuthall's in American championships. There is a possibility that she may take back a third title with her when she returns to England, for she is to play in the mixed doubles at Boston this week with George M. Lott of Chicago.

The final between Miss Nuthall and Mrs. Harper started as a procession for the former that was reminiscent of the parades Mrs. Moody has habitually staged through these tournaments. Not until the English girl had established a 4–0 lead did Mrs. Harper begin to make a match of it, but once the lefthanded player from the Coast got her forehand chop and her flat backhand functioning properly in the second set, those in the stands who desired to see an American victory had plenty of occasion to cheer.

Indeed, while Miss Nuthall won by a comfortable margin, there was a time when her adherents had serious misgivings and the ultimate outcome of the match looked anything but foregone. By the margin of a single stroke Mrs. Harper, in the second chapter, lost what in all probability would have been an almost insurmountable lead.

Leading at 4–2, the Californian stood within a point of breaking through again in the seventh game for a 5–2 advantage. Miss Nuthall at this time was playing none too reassuringly.

The paceful, skimming drives which had countenanced no return in the first set as they beat a tattoo in the corners now had lost their fluency and length as her racket lost its smooth contact with the ball. Her first service, a battering weapon, no longer was offering difficulties to her opponent, and the cut that Mrs. Harper was imparting to the ball was confusing her repeatedly, to ruin her timing and lead her shots astray.

Mrs. Harper, meanwhile, was playing almost perfect tennis, mixing her spin and length and changing direction to keep Miss Nuthall scrambling across her baseline. Getting full length on her backhand, which she poked into the corners with surprising pace, considering the abbreviation of the stroke, the Californian went to the net to dominate the situation with deliberate volleys and overhead shots and in every department of the game she was giving decidedly the superior performance.

After breaking through in the fifth game and winning the sixth at 15 on Miss Nuthall's ragged stroking, Mrs. Harper went into a lead of 40–30 in the seventh. Only one point was lacking to enable her to effect a second break through her opponent's service for a 5–2 lead.

It was a critical moment, perhaps the deciding point of the match, if the tenseness of Miss Nuthall and the tension in the gallery were any indication. With everyone in the stands in breathless suspense, Miss Nuthall served, went to the net and her resounding kill of Mrs. Harper's lob saved the day.

After that one rally the crisis was past for Miss Nuthall. She still had to attend strictly to her knitting to the end, but once Mrs. Harper had failed to capitalize this big opportunity, her faultless game began to disintegrate. Two weak errors cost her the next two points and the game, and from there on Miss Nuthall, finding her coordination and pace again, blazed her way through the next three games also for the match. . . .

The next moment the English girl was running to the net, her face wreathed in smiles, to greet her opponent, as the gallery acclaimed the crowning of a new champion. Not since Mrs. Molla Bjurstedt Mallory came back in the absence of Helen Wills to regain the title in 1926 has anyone else taken the crown which the Californian first won in 1923.

Her victory gives Miss Nuthall the first leg on the new challenge trophy, the old one having been retired last year when Mrs. Moody carried off her second one outright with her sixth triumph.

TILDEN TURNS PROFESSIONAL

by Allison Danzig

Another of the world's most celebrated sports figures has followed Bobby Jones out of amateur competition via the motion pictures.

William Tatem Tilden 2d of Philadelphia, the ranking tennis player of the United States since 1920, mainstay of its Davis Cup team during those years, seven times winner of the national championship and generally recognized as the outstanding player of the past decade, if not of all time, informed Holcombe Ward, chairman of the Amateur Rule Committee of the United States Lawn Tennis Association, by letter yesterday that he has signed a contract with the Metro-Goldwyn-Mayer Film Corporation and announced his retirement from amateur tennis.

His letter to Mr. Ward follows:

> Dear Mr Ward:
>
> I wish to inform you that I have signed a motion picture contract with the Metro-Goldwyn-Mayer Film Corporation, the terms of which will violate the amateur rule of the U.S.L.T.A. Therefore I am announcing my retirement from amateur tennis to take effect immediately.
>
> Wishing the game of amateur tennis and the United States Lawn Tennis Association all success in the future and thanking you for many courtesies to me,
>
> Sincerely,
> William T. Tilden 2d.

This brief communication, ringing down the curtain on the amateur career of the most dramatic figure the game has produced, a figure whose stature in tennis has been commensurate with that of Jones in golf and whose exploits on the court and multiple controversies with the solons of the national association have made his name a by-word wherever the game is played, was the sole information forthcoming from Tilden last night. The former champion left his quarters at the Hotel Algonquin early in the evening and all efforts to reach him were unavailing.

The financial terms of his contract, the exact nature of the films he is to take a role in, aside from the fact that they will have to do with tennis; the number of pictures the contract calls for and their release dates all remain to be disclosed. Howard Dietz, representing the Metro-Goldwyn-Mayer Corporation, stated last night that it was the wish of Tilden that the amount of his remuneration be withheld in the public announcement.

Asked whether the figures approximated those called for in the motion-picture contract of Bobby Jones, who, it has been estimated, will receive $250,000 for the twelve one-reel educational films he will make for Warner Brothers, Mr. Dietz intimated that they will fall considerably below that amount.

The number of films the former champion will make, their exact character and the time of their first release, said Mr. Dietz, have not yet been determined upon. Tilden, he stated, is expected to leave for the Pacific Coast shortly and the first of his pictures probably will not be released until the tennis season opens early in the summer or just prior to its opening.

The signing of the contract automatically makes Tilden a professional in the eyes of the United States Lawn Tennis Association, even though there was some question of whether the same held true in the case of Jones, in whose footsteps Tilden has followed in his procedure of calling his own disqualification.

Section 5 of Article III of the by-laws of the U.S.L.T.A. states that a player will be considered to have forfeited his amateur status by "permitting or sanctioning the taking of tennis action motion pictures of himself and receiving remuneration in connection therewith."

Section 2 of the same article defines a professional tennis player as one who "is paid directly, or indirectly, for playing, engaging in, or teaching the game of tennis."

Tilden has appeared on the screen before, as well as on the stage, for a "consideration," but none of his roles has had any relation to tennis. He also has taken part in the making of motion picture films on lawn tennis of an educational nature, but these were sponsored by the U.S.L.T.A. and the former champion and the other players who lent their services did so gratuitously.

While Tilden has definitely ended his vivid career as an amateur with the signing of this contract, it does not necessarily follow that his playing days as a tournament competitor are over. It is possible that he may enter the arena of professional tennis and join the issue again with Vincent Richards, Karel Kozeluh and other leading players in the professional ranks.

Louis B. Dailey, president of the United States Lawn Tennis Association, reached at his home in South Orange, New Jersey, last night, had not previously heard of Tilden's retirement from amateur tennis. But he was quick to say that he wished Tilden all the success in the world.

Mr. Ward, to whom Tilden's announcement of his retirement was made, said last night that he had not received the letter and did not wish to comment until he had received it.

Tilden will be 38 years old on February 10, and while he undoubtedly has passed his prime on the courts he still ranks among the world's greatest players, and in 1930 amazed the tennis world with his performances on European courts, winning the championship at Wimbledon after an interlude of nine years since his previous victory there and defeating Jean Borotra of France in the Davis Cup challenge round.

Although he was beaten by John Doeg in the national championship at Forest Hills last September, his first setback at the hands of an American in this tournament since he lost to William Johnston of California in the 1919 final, he is still regarded by many as the country's foremost player and the general expectations are that he will be ranked either second or first in the forthcoming ratings to be released at the jubilee meeting of the U.S.L.T.A. in this city in February.

An interesting question arises from Tilden's present status in connection with the rankings. It will be recalled that in the rankings given out in 1927 for the season of 1926 Richards was left out because of the fact that he turned professional at the end of the 1926 season. Richards had defeated Tilden on several occasions during the season, and many felt that he was entitled to first place in the rankings. Richards, however, was left out and Tilden was rated at the top.

Whether the action taken in the case of Richards will be used as a precedent in Tilden's case remains to be seen. The fact that he has not played professional tennis may serve as a cause for making a distinction, though the fact remains that he is no longer an amateur.

The retirement of Tilden from the amateur lists will be received with dismay by thousands of tennis followers the world over. He has been so much a part and parcel of tennis, his name has been so synonymous with the game for the past decade, he has furnished so much of the interest in it with his flamboyant personality and his gifted racket, that it is almost inconceivable to them that he has played his last Davis Cup match, made his final bid for the national crown that he won the record number of times, and waged his last controversy with the lawmakers over the amateur rule and international play policy.

From beginning to end, the tall Philadelphian's amateur career has been a continuous series of dramatic episodes that have kept him in the international limelight above every other player even when his powers began to wane and his irresistible sway had been successfully challenged by Henri Cochet and René Lacoste of France.

A strong and forceful personality, distinctly a thinker and with the courage to battle for his ideas no matter how strong the opposition, he has repeatedly stood before national meetings, executive sessions and amateur rule and international play committees to challenge their dicta and strategy.

On many of these occasions the controversy centered around the famous player-writer provision of the amateur rule and while Tilden generally came off second best there were times when the association compromised and either changed its rule, as in 1924, when a committee of seven redrafted the code, or waived provisions, as last summer, when Tilden was allowed to write advance articles on the Davis Cup challenge round while a member of the team.

Perhaps the most celebrated of these many episodes came in 1928 when Tilden was removed as captain and member of the Davis Cup team on the eve of the interzone final with Italy in Paris. The repercussion following this action, taken because of his news articles on the play at Wimbledon a few weeks before, was so great as almost to bring about an international stringency and led to the intervention of the late Ambassador Myron T. Herrick.

Through the offices of Ambassador Herrick, who importuned the

U.S.L.T.A. to restore Tilden to the team for the sake of international good feeling, the former champion was permitted to take up his racket again for the United States, though on his return home he was brought up on charges in August of that year and suspended from amateur competition until the following February for violation of the player-writer provision by his Wimbledon articles.

Although the climax of his career as a player was passed in 1926, when he suffered his first defeat since 1919 in the national championship, Tilden's most glorious year, in many respects, was his last one as an amateur. Invading the lair of his French nemeses, the 37-year-old veteran proceeded to reawaken memories of his halcyon days by staging a procession through the tournaments of the Riviera and the national championships of country after country.

After carrying off thirteen singles trophies, thirteen in doubles and nine mixed doubles trophies on the Riviera, he won the championships of Italy, Austria and Germany, was runner-up to Cochet in the French championship, and then proceeded to Wimbledon to repeat his triumphs there of 1920 and 1921, with Wilmer Allison of Austin, Texas, assisting him by removing Cochet from the scene.

Tilden was never a greater figure than he was on the day the thousands in the packed stands at classic Wimbledon paid tribute to the victory of this "aging, doddering veteran" who had come back almost a decade after his last triumph to reclaim the most treasured individual prize the game offers. Although he lost later to Cochet in the Davis Cup challenge round and to Doeg in the national championship, the record of his amazing performances for the year will long stand as one of the most notable comebacks that sport has recorded.

LIST OF THE TWENTY-NINE TITLES
WON BY TILDEN IN U.S. TOURNEYS

Twenty-nine United States national tennis championships, comprising singles, doubles and mixed doubles, were won by William T. Tilden 2d. The list follows:

SINGLES

Grass—1920, 1921, 1922, 1923, 1924, 1925, 1929.
Clay—1918, 1922, 1923, 1924, 1925, 1926, 1927.
Indoor—1920.

DOUBLES

Grass—1918, with Vincent Richards; 1921, with Richards; 1922, with Richards; 1923, with Brian I. C. Norton; 1927, with Francis T. Hunter.
Indoor—1919, with Richards; 1920, with Richards; 1926, with Fred C. Anderson; 1929, with Hunter.

Grass—1922, with Mrs. Franklin I. Mallory; 1923, with Mrs. Mallory.
Indoor—1921, with Mrs. Mallory; 1922, with Mrs. Mallory; 1924, with Mrs. George W. Wightman.

1931

TILDEN BEATS KOZELUH IN PRO DEBUT

by Allison Danzig

William Tilden, formerly the invincible monarch of amateur tennis, made his bow to New York in the role of a professional last night when he defeated Karel Kozeluh of Czechoslovakia at Madison Square Garden in the first of a series of matches for the world's professional indoor championship. The score was 6–4, 6–2, 6–4.

A crowd of 13,800 spectators who paid in an estimated total of $36,000 saw the ranking American player of the past decade assert his supremacy over the foremost European professional in the most convincing fashion.

From beginning to end there was never any question of Tilden's superiority. His cannonball service, which brought roars from the crowd continually, his drastic forehand drives and his far greater variety of attack put Kozeluh squarely on the defensive in the back court and kept him there all the way. The match was over in an hour and five minutes.

Kozeluh, while he played brilliantly in spurts and displayed a number of his characteristic sensational recoveries, did not come up to the form expected of him. The fact that he arrived from Europe only last Saturday and had had little time in which to rid himself of his sealegs undoubtedly was responsible in part for his failure to make a better showing. Certainly he did not reach the standard he has maintained in the past in his matches with Vincent Richards. The Czechoslovakian was lacking his customary vitality and seldom asserted himself. His control was badly off and he was not as quick in getting to the ball as he is ordinarily.

Tilden held the match in his control by a clear margin. For the most part, he played with restraint, relying upon his drive and his chop and going to the net only when he wanted a particular point. With his service at its best, he knew that he had nothing to fear, for he sensed Kozeluh's shortcomings and he pursued the even tenor of his way without any great expenditure of effort, save in the delivery of his service. If the first match between the two championship contenders is any indication, Tilden should be clearly established the favorite to win five out of the nine matches which are to be played to determine the world professional indoor king.

It was a highly enthusiastic crowd that turned out for the professional debut of the recognized greatest player of his time, whose drawing power was attested to by the size of the gathering. Marking the return of lawn tennis to the Garden for the first time since Mlle. Suzanne Lenglen and Vincent Richards played there in the fall of 1926, last night's venture, arranged under the management of Jack Curley, was a decided success. While the tennis was not quite up to the grade expected, the gallery saw much to applaud and at times was uproarious in its demonstrations.

The officiating was as competent as any seen at Forest Hills, with a corps of linesmen on hand from the professional tennis association. Ball boys, nattily attired in white flannels and green slipovers, performed their duties efficiently, and the canvas court, built especially for Tilden's tour, offered a splendid surface, its broad white lines upon a green background being visible from the remotest seat in the gallery.

The match between Tilden and Kozeluh brought together, after years of effort, the player whose game has represented the highest attainment in the perfection of an all-court attack of infinite variety and devices, and the iron man of the courts who has developed the defense to a greater stage of efficiency than probably any other player in the history of the game with the possible exception of René Lacoste of France.

Here was the perfect foil—the man of flamboyant attack against the man of the gibraltaresque defense, brilliance and daring of shot-making against machinelike faultlessness in the methodical returning of the ball. In other words, it was the speed, daring and artifice of one of the cleverest manipulators of the attack against the more prosaic virtues of Kozeluh's steady hand and granite legs. Kozeluh's hand, however, was not so steady last night, nor did his legs stand him in their usual good stead.

Thus Tilden, obviously prepared to bring all the power and finesse of his heavy artillery and his rapier thrusts to bear, gained a hollow victory that was as decisive as it was unexpected by the great majority of tennis followers. Kozeluh won the opening game of the first set and that was the only time in the match that he led.

Kozeluh played entirely in the neighborhood of the baseline, and his efforts to draw Tilden out of position by angling his shots to the corners played right into the American's hands, for there is nothing that Tilden likes better than an angle on his drive, as William Johnston learned years ago. Johnston, incidentally, was in the gallery and was introduced to the crowd by Tilden before he went on the court.

Finding himself at a disadvantage in a driving game, Kozeluh sought to pull Tilden up to the net and lob over his head, but this strategy was to no avail, for the American gave one of the best exhibitions of overhead smashes of his career. In his volleying, too, Tilden was both sure and decisive, and Kozeluh's efforts to pass him down the sideline came to naught.

ALLISON AND VAN RYN WIN U.S. DOUBLES

by Allison Danzig

The prize that remained beyond the grasp of Wilmer Allison and John Van Ryn in the years when they were collectively sweeping all before them at Wimbledon as the American Davis Cup team, passed into their keeping today when they defeated Berkeley Bell of Austin, Texas, and Gregory Mangin of Newark, New Jersey, in the final of the golden jubilee national doubles championship at the Longwood Cricket Club.

One hour and five minutes after the start of the match the English champions of 1929 and 1930 were receiving the huge challenge cups, filled with roses, from Referee Richard Bishop, who presented them also with jubilee medallions and small gold tennis balls. The score was 6–4, 8–6, 6–3.

The windup of the longest national doubles tournament in many years, which was held up for four days by bad weather, did not bring out the highest quality of tennis, nor was the match nearly as spectacular or exciting as the semi-final yesterday between Bell and Mangin and Frank Shields and Sidney Wood.

For this, Van Ryn and Allison were in no way responsible, for they were keenly on edge and in perfect coordination and were prepared to meet the challenge of any team in the world.

Nor could Bell and Mangin be held accountable for the comparatively slow time of the play. They were used up pretty badly in their exhausting two-hour struggle with Shields and Wood, and in addition Mangin was suffering with a stiff neck, the result of a heavy fall that he took yesterday in making an overhead smash.

The deleterious effects of this spill were manifest in the erratic play of the Newark youth, whose whole game was undermined and whose volleying mistakes were disastrous, not only in the points they cost but in their effect upon the morale of his partner. Bell, although filled with misgivings over the errors of his teammate, made a game fight to stem the tide of defeat and his whiplash service and rattling volleys were winning applause all through the match.

Van Ryn and Allison were more temperate in their hitting than their opponents, particularly Van Ryn, but once they had worked up their opening through their careful, cooperative efforts they struck with full force for the finishing shot.

Van Ryn was the more restrained and deliberate of the two until the final set, when he was hitting with blazing speed off the ground and killing his overhead shots, while Allison all through the match was volleying and hammering overhead with daring and finality and was the most brilliant player on the court.

The champions constantly rushed the net to prevent their opponents from gaining their favored position and they were not only steadier at close quarters than were Bell and Mangin, but they were also much more effective off the ground.

The return of service is one of the most important shots in doubles, if not the most important, and Van Ryn and Allison distinctly had the edge over their opponents in this department, though Bell's service gave them trouble all along. Bell and Mangin could do little with Van Ryn's or Allison's service and this fact cost them opportunities to break through in three games of the second set, the only ones to go to deuce in that chapter.

In the final set Van Ryn and Allison were returning service in sensational fashion to score down the alley again and again, and it was these placements that broke Bell's service in the third game and took the heart out of the losing team.

Another break was made through Mangin in the sixth on his three volley errors and it looked as though the set would end at 6–1, but Bell's fiery drives enabled him to break through Van Ryn in the seventh and the bristling little Texan scored three service aces in the eighth to bring the score to 3–5 before the end came.

The break through Van Ryn was the only service game the champions lost in the match, though Bell and Mangin had opportunities to effect others.

SEVENTH U.S. TITLE WON BY MRS. MOODY

by Allison Danzig

The tennis champion without a crown assumed the royal purple again yesterday to restore the women's national title to the United States and reestablish her invincibility after a year's absence from the championship.

In the final round of the forty-fourth annual tournament at the West Side Tennis Club, Forest Hills, before a gallery that was held down to 4,000 spectators by the unfavorable weather, Mrs. Helen Wills Moody of California, conclusively defeated Mrs. Eileen Bennett Whittingstall of England at 6–4, 6–1, to capture the championship for the seventh time and complete her fourth year of competition without the loss of a set in singles.

Miss Betty Nuthall of England, whom Mrs. Whittingstall eliminated in the semi-finals, was the 1930 winner.

Technically, with her triumph yesterday, which gave her her first leg on the new cup put up last year, Mrs. Moody equaled the record held by Mrs. Molla Mallory of New York for the number of American singles championship victories.

But Mrs. Mallory stands in the records as winning eight national tournaments, and although one of them, that of 1917, is listed as a patriotic tournament and not a championship, the field was of championship class and by general disposition Mrs. Moody must yet win the crown again to duplicate the achievement of Mrs. Mallory.

The championship final failed to bring out the pulsating struggle that had been anticipated and within thirty-five minutes after Rufus Davis had called "play" from the umpire's chair the match was over.

As a matter of fact, Mrs. Moody's work had been accomplished once she had fought off the stirring challenge of Mrs. Whittingstall in the first set, a challenge that saw the slender British girl, trailing at 0–3, play magnificent tennis to win the next three games with the loss of only two points and stir the gallery to almost a frenzy of enthusiasm.

During these three games, in the last two of which Mrs. Whittingstall won six successive points with five placements and a service ace, the gauntlet was thrown down to the invincible Californian in such masterful fashion that there appeared to be every prospect of a tremendous battle in which Mrs. Moody might have to yield the first set she has lost since Miss Gwendolin Sterry of England wrested the opening chapter from her at Wimbledon in 1927.

Mrs. Whittingstall, far from being the oppressed and quiescent victim of the Californian's dreadnaught forehanders, was whole-heartedly the aggressor, carrying the attack to her opponent with so much speed and weight behind her drives and getting such depth and angles on them that Mrs. Moody was put squarely on the defensive.

When Mrs. Whittingstall won her third game in a row to square the score at 3–all the crowd fairly roared its delight. There was no mistaking where its sympathy lay and the sight of anyone outplaying Mrs. Moody was so novel as to captivate any gathering.

But with that one great effort, an effort that probably would have put her in the lead at 4–2 had it not been for a questionable decision on the service line in the third game, Mrs. Whittingstall was finished. She managed to win her next service game in the eighth to make the score 4–all, but after that she had nothing left in reserve except her nerve.

Mrs. Whittingstall, without being unfair to Mrs. Moody or minimizing the splendid tennis and courage the champion showed, was beaten before she went on the court. Her conquests of Miss Nuthall and Miss Jacobs on successive days were Pyrrhic victories that left her in possession of the field, but with her physical forces decimated.

Two bitterly fought three-set matches on successive days were too much for her slight physique, and in the final set yesterday she had neither the strength nor the control to stand up against Mrs. Moody's withering service and flawless drives.

The English girl, as badly spent as she was, never gave up the fight and collected her waning forces repeatedly to seek her fortune at the net. But it was obvious soon after she had won her last game of the match, the second of the final set, that she understood the fate that awaited her at the hands of her unerring, resourceful opponent, whose stamina had hardly been tapped and whose game gathered momentum as Mrs. Whittingstall's lost acceleration.

Mrs. Moody showed in this match, as she did throughout the championship, that she still has all of her old speed, though she does not use it as consistently as formerly, and in addition a variety and resourcefulness that were lacking to her game heretofore.

Her passing shots were seldom better attuned to penetrate the narrowest opening than they were in this match and their effectiveness did much to undermine the confidence of her opponent.

1 9 3 2

BOROTRA-ALLISON DAVIS CUP MATCH IN PARIS

by Al Laney

Extraordinary things kept happening in this [Roland Garros] enclosure year after year. Two of our own greatest players, Ellsworth Vines and Alice Marble, collapsed during matches on this court and were carried out unconscious. Vines had it happen while playing Perry in the 1934 interzone final, which the United States lost to Great Britain, 4–1. Miss Marble fainted during a French-American team match and was ill for many months after.

There was the final day of the Challenge Round of 1932 when Jean Borotra, putting on one of the finest acts of his entire career, using the volatile crowd as an instrument on which to play and as a weapon against his opponent, was said to have "stolen the Cup" after serving what clearly appeared to be a double fault at match point to Wilmer Allison.

This incident has been made much of and a certain amount of distortion has come into it in the retelling. I am convinced myself that the ball Borotra served was well beyond the line and that Allison should have been declared the winner of this fifth set and the match. But I am not at all convinced that it would have meant the winning of the Davis Cup by the United States team.

This was the fourth match of five and France was leading by two matches to one. Borotra had beaten Vines, and Cochet had beaten Allison, each in four sets on the first day, and Allison and John Van Ryn had beaten Cochet and Jacques Brugnon in a brilliantly played five-set doubles match on the second day. So that the victory of Borotra over Allison, which gave France the series, would have left the score tied at two matches—all if the ball in question had been called out. Then the final match, in which Vines defeated Cochet in five sets after losing the first two, would not have been merely an exhibition. In that event I thought, watching the play, that Cochet, drawing inspiration from the crowd and the situation, would have played less carelessly and probably would have won one of the three sets he lost.

In the first match of the series Borotra really had played one of the finest matches I can remember from him in defeating Vines 6–4, 6–2, 3–6, 6–4. It was a glittering display that he gave, for he was thirty-five years old and this was to be his final Davis Cup appearance as a singles player. He played with great cleverness and great energy for a man of his age, and when he had uncovered a weakness in Vines' backhand corner, his road to victory had been mapped out. To this sector he played a low ball with spin, and my old notes say that Vines never once was able to hit it safely down the line in the whole match. He was forced to play it across court and directly at the finest shot Borotra owned, the volley pushed straight down the forehand line and far out of reach. Even so, Vines could not make this cross-court shot effectively very often, and the defect in his backhand corner was glaringly revealed.

Vines had come straight from Wimbledon after defeating Bunny Austin 6–2, 6–2, 6–0 in the final with a withering attack that had astonished British observers and caused them to rate Vines as probably the greatest player of all time. I had seen that performance and had been very impressed by it too. Since Cochet had been beaten by Allison at Wimbledon two years earlier and had not survived the second round there in either 1931 or 1932, beaten each time by second-rate players, we all crossed to Paris in the full expectation that the Davis Cup would be won back for the United States. The shock and disappointment of what then happened at Auteuil may have led some of us to judge these encounters incorrectly and to give credence to that "stolen Cup" theory.

The confidence with which an aging Borotra handled the Vines blasts, and gradually led his man into error and even to double faulting, was the first shock. Borotra's conduct during this match was above criticism, and there could be only praise for his dazzling display of virtuosity. He knew the task he faced and he never faltered in pursuing his plan. Since we had been so certain of winning this point, the disappointment was great, but we had to admit that Vines was not yet the complete player we had supposed. But Allison had beaten Cochet in straight sets on his way to the Wimbledon final of 1930 and would no doubt get his country back even by doing it again two years later.

The same tactics of consistent attack got him the first set at 6–3 after he had been 3–5 down, but he never won another, and Cochet, coming back to the form he had shown in earlier years, had Wilmer in control in a fourth set. And so, after the doubles had been won by Allison and Van Ryn, we came on a hot, sultry Sunday afternoon to the controversial match.

Allison now had played nine sets and a hundred and nineteen games in two days, and he had to beat Borotra before this extraordinary crowd and under the most trying conditions imaginable. Else the series would be lost. France needed only one more point to retain the Cup. And this surely was one of the most unusual and dramatic tennis matches ever played with so much hanging on the result of it.

First of all, the court had been watered down until it was almost muddy, and it still was slow and heavy when play started. This was no doubt done to take some of the sting from the lightning strokes of Vines and to aid Cochet, in case the whole thing should go down to the final match. But in hampering Vines and favoring Cochet, they apparently forgot about Borotra, for he was terribly hampered at the start. The Basque could not get to the net behind his service in time for his volleying coups, and the bite was taken from his shots off the ground, which had been so full of guile against Vines on Friday. Allison, hitting winners all about the court and forcing errors, ran away to a two-set-to-love lead, with Borotra winning only four games. Of course this did not fool anybody. Borotra was not beaten so easily as this and Allison was sure to react from his nearly flawless play if the thing could be prolonged. Moreover, the sun was very hot. It had been drying and baking the court, and at the end of his eleventh set Allison's stamina may have been drained a little. At 3–all in the third set Borotra won Allison's service for the first time and all of a sudden the old Bounding Basque was back in court, leaping about and throwing the crowd into ecstasies, and running out the set.

The rest interval restored Borotra, but Allison's game had dropped far below the level he had maintained during the first two sets. His length was poor, his speed reduced, and he could no longer pass the volleyer. Borotra not only won the fourth set 6–2 but began here to lay the foundation of his fifth-set performance with a mild histrionic show. The Basque had come into court wearing a pair of those rope-soled beach shoes called espadrilles. These articles are not meant for so strenuous a pursuit as tennis and Borotra had burst one pair midway through the set and changed to another. Toward the end his toes came out again and he made a great show this time of not changing. All this was done to great head wagging by Borotra and delighted shouts from the crowd. Borotra knew very well how to stir an audience to response. He pretended to be shocked at their display. He shook his finger at them and the more he pretended to quiet them the more they roared.

Allison was greatly depressed by all this, but he threw it off and the stand he made is beyond praise. Borotra, seemingly now in command of the situation on the court as much as he was of the crowd, had gone to 2–1 in the deciding set. With a great effort Allison brought back his best game. Once more he was cheating the great volleyer and coming forward to hit winners himself. He was steady and calculating, and he went straight to leads of 4–2 and 5–3. And now came the first of those crises that caused the match to be underscored in tennis annals.

At 5–3 Allison three times came within a point of victory. On the first match point Borotra, lunging at a ball that seemed to have him beaten, struck the net tape with it and watched it drop safely on the American side of the net for the luckiest sort of salvation. On the next two match balls, however, the Basque played characteristically and boldly. He forced the errors on Allison and, winning the game, had a chance to serve himself back even at 5–all.

The saving of these points had stimulated Borotra and, serving shrewdly, he went to 40–0 in the tenth game. And here Allison turned the thing right around by bringing off a series of shots that stopped Borotra. Then the American appeared on his way to victory as surely as could be when suddenly Borotra stopped play and called attention to another burst shoe with the toes sticking out.

The crowd set up a wild shout for him to change. Someone had brought a new pair to the court and was displaying them plainly before the people. Borotra's actions said just as plainly, "No, no, no, never would I do such a thing while play is in progress." But, with the score at deuce, he finally consented to yield to the overwhelming pressure of the crowd. Allison stood a little disconsolately at the back of the court while the change was being made, and I suspect he was beaten right there.

Just the same Allison worked back to match point again when Borotra returned to serve. At this fourth match point to the United States, Borotra's first ball went into the net. The second, from where I sat directly above the service court, appeared to have hit so far beyond the line that there could hardly be any question that it was a fault, and Allison had won. But the linesman said it was good and, since Allison had let it go by without even offering at it, the score was deuce. Soon it was 5–all in games and then 7–5 to France, and Le Basque Bondissant had pulled yet another lost cause out of the fire.

The performance probably was Borotra's finest moment before the adoring home crowd, for it certainly was he who kept the Cup in France for another year.

VINES ESCAPES DEFEAT AGAINST SUTTER

by Allison Danzig

At the end of one of the longest semi-final round sessions in the history of the championship, Ellsworth Vines of Pasadena, California, the defending titleholder, remained in the running for the men's national singles tennis crown by the grace of two points last night and the consummation of the tournament with a Vines-Henri Cochet final still hung in abeyance.

Those two points represented the margin by which the 20-year-old Californian escaped defeat of the most ignominious sort at the hands of Clifford S. Sutter of New Orleans.

Sutter decisively outplayed the champion to win the first two sets, establish a lead of 3–0 and 30–0 in the third and come within two strokes of victory three times in the twelfth game of the third and once more in the twelfth game of the fourth set.

With a gallery of 9,000 looking on in suspense as he labored to find his way out of the morass of errors that were blighting one of the most devastating attacks in modern tennis, Vines extricated himself from his perilous position. With the aid of his cannonball service, he found the high road to victory, as Sutter's beautifully correct game began to disintegrate, and emerged the winner after over two and a half hours of play at 4–6, 8–10, 12–10, 10–8, 6–1.

Seldom has a gallery been held on the ragged edge of suspense over so long a period as was the experience of yesterday's assemblage. Manifestly in sympathy with the cause of the champion, in spite of the superb performance and splendid sportsmanship of his rival, the gallery, in the late stages, when it was obvious that Sutter's great bid had fallen just short of success, paid its most wholehearted tribute to the 22-year-old New Orleans stylist.

The strain and tension of this match, relieved with the escape of the champion from a fate that seemed almost inevitably in store for him, gave way to an emotional outburst of the stormiest character in the match that followed immediately.

Not since the meeting between William Johnston of California and Cochet in the Davis Cup challenge round at Philadelphia in 1926 has an American tennis gathering been so carried away as it was yesterday as Wilmer Allison of Austin, Texas, brightened the enveloping darkness in the stadium of the West Side Tennis Club at Forest Hills with a blazing attack that threatened to sweep Cochet to defeat.

Completely at the mercy of the French champion's masterful position play in the early stages and apparently headed toward summary defeat, the dashing Texan, one set down and trailing at 0–2 and 15–40 in the second chapter, suddenly galvanized the gallery into a roaring mass as he launched an irresistible net attack that put all the finesse and rapier thrusts of the French strategist to naught.

Through four successive games Allison carried all before him with his electrifying shot making and startling interceptions all over the court as he attacked like an enraged lion. Turned back twice at set point in the ninth game and repulsing Cochet twice from winning the set by the same one-point margin in the fourteenth, the young American Davis Cup star went on to win the set 12–10 and the third also at 6–4, to leave the stadium for the rest period amid a tremendous outburst of cheers.

The sun had long since sunk behind the horizon and the light was so poor that there was some question of whether the match would continue. It was thought extremely unlikely that Cochet would care to go on in the semi-darkness, particularly since the French champion had appeared to be so upset by the stormy enthusiasm of the gallery, with which the umpire, Ben Dwight, pleaded repeatedly as Cochet showed his displeasure over the outbursts.

But play was resumed after the conventional ten-minute intermission and Cochet, bringing all his powers to bear to confound the Texan's volleying attack with a superlative exhibition, took the set at 6–3 to square the match.

Any further play was now out of the question, for it was hardly possible to see the ball, and the match was called at 2 sets–all. Cochet won the first at 6–1, Allison the second and third chapters at 12–10, 6–4, and Cochet the fourth set at 6 3.

Editor's note: Cochet won the fifth set the next day, and in the final round he was beaten by Vines, 6–4, 6–4, 6–4.

1 9 3 3

CRAWFORD'S CLASSIC DEFEAT OF VINES

by Al Laney

The Wimbledon final of 1933 between Ellsworth Vines and Jack Crawford, the beautiful Australian stroke maker, is recommended to those who would place tennis players in neat lists numbered from one to ten. I consider this match the best final I ever saw at Wimbledon, and one of the most interesting matches seen anywhere. Vines came to it hailed by the British press as the greatest player of all time. They were thinking of his crushing victory over England's best player, Bunny Austin, in the previous year's final, finishing off with a love set that took less than ten minutes to play. Such powerful and controlled hitting over the last two sets of this 6–4, 6–2, 6–0 victory had, I believe, never been seen on a tennis court. It was simply devastating, and probably no player of the past or present could have matched it or stood up to it.

This was the picture we all still had in mind when Vines, having beaten Cochet 6–2, 8–6, 3–6, 6–1, in the semi-final, came out as champion to defend his title against the challenge of Crawford, the classic model of a tennis player. Crawford's game had a stately-domed sort of grandeur. It seemed as British as a three-volume novel in the paneled library of a manor house, as pre-World War I as a hansom cab. Though a very large man, he was a graceful and seemingly effortless mover, a fluent, easy-footed driver, with a strong, impressive personality expressed through a rare and charming amiability.

The Australian was a master strategist and a deadly, aggressive attacker with a mild manner, but, with all his aggressiveness, so sure an artist and so stylish and so courteous. He had command of every essential stroke and, attacking from the baseline, could use the entire court as few have been able to do. But for the asthma with which he battled through his whole tennis life, he probably would have been rated among the great. I do not think any tennis player has given me more genuine pleasure than Jack Crawford.

In his long sleeves and immaculate flannels Crawford made an impressive picture, in strong contrast to Vines, who was tall, slim and athletic enough, but slightly gangling and shambling for all that.

Certainly we did not suppose on the day they met that Vines would deal with Crawford as he had dealt with Austin, for the Australian was of a higher class, but we doubted that the beautiful stylist would be able to survive such an attack all around the court as Vines could launch. Vines did launch such an attack. It was just as severe and at times just as controlled as it had been against Austin. But Vines was beaten in a fifth set 4–6, 11–9, 6–2, 2–6, 6–4, and I doubt that anyone who saw the match would argue that Vines was not at his best. Crawford found the way to circumvent and counter Vines' far more powerful hitting and bring his own somewhat less spectacular assets to bear.

This was really a tennis match about as near heart's desire as I can remember, a thoroughly enjoyable thing in which the emotions were not so involved as to forbid a sort of detached admiration of both players. I am sure it must rank with the very best matches because of the pure pleasure it gave. For superlative play on both sides of the net, the blending of stroke and strategy, the unrelenting speed of service and considered counter-stroke, I cannot remember another to place above it.

Conditions were perfect, a rare thing, when they entered the court and began at a rather leisurely pace what was to be a marathon of fifty-six games. Then suddenly Vines, having won his first service game with ease, almost casually, stepped up the pace. He hit the baseline and deep sideline with two forehand drives no player could have returned, captured Crawford's service, and led 2–1. Then came streams of service aces and more forehand drives that made the chalk fly. As the last ball flew untouched and untouchable past Crawford to give Vines the first set, Jack smiled and bowed toward his opponent in acknowledgment, and we all wondered how the Australian could possibly check this enormous fire power long enough to bring his own less explosive but still deadly weapons into play.

We did not really think it possible, and at this point I was sure Vines would win, probably in straight sets. The burst of hitting had been so impressive that I was certain of it even though I knew well Crawford's artistry and resourcefulness and had learned long ago not to judge the outcome of a tennis match by the way it began.

Crawford was one of the finest of servers, but he seldom tried for an outright ace unless the point was critical. And he could take a fast service too. Vines had led 5–2 in the first set, but in spite of the explosive delivery he could not serve himself out in the eighth game. Looking back to that game from the end, one could see that there the key to victory had first been revealed. At the time, under the impact of Vines' tremendous blasting, it was attributed to a slight carelessness, with the set already well in hand and a lot to spare. What had been noted but not properly understood was that

Crawford moved in to take the service, hit down on a rising ball, blocked it back with a little spin, and waited. He won Vines' service and his own before Vines got the set.

Now began that long set of twenty games so vital to Crawford, since if he lost it he would have to win three sets in a row against that withering fire. During its progress I once or twice thought back to that long set I had seen Brookes and McLoughlin play in 1914 when Brookes, that other great Australian, had attempted to deal with the cannonball serve in the same way as Crawford was now doing. I did not really remember this from observation but from reading, but I had seen Cochet and Lacoste stand in to Tilden's service the same way, and Dick Williams could hit anybody's service for a winner at times. People forget that the fine player can take many, though not all, express services, striking down on the rising ball and letting repercussion come to his aid.

Crawford was standing right up to the ball and using the force of the serve itself to send it back fast and deep so that the server could not always get in behind the ball, had to stay back and exchange drives. Only the finest of players, of course, have this ability. It was not at all easy against Vines. Crawford seemed afraid to go to the net, for that was dangerous ground. Even so, it was there that Jack finally won the two successive games necessary to win the long, service-governed second set. Each time he advanced he hit deep to Vines' backhand corner after fencing a while from back court and then brought off the volleying coup with certainty.

The Australian thus revealed the weak spot in the American armor, the vulnerable spot which Vines, for all his avalanche of aces, deadly, long forehand cannonading, and devastating overhead, could not in the end protect. By searching it out and exploiting it, by steering the ball to this sector in the crises that lay ahead, Crawford made his still arduous task a little easier.

Vines played some of his finest and most resolute tennis in this second set, for he knew its value to Crawford. But Jack had begun with the service and so was always a game ahead when he had won. He could lose his own service and all would not be lost, for he could still get back even by winning Vines' service game. Vines, always a game behind when Crawford won, had never the stimulation of a service game in hand. He served each time after 4–all to save the set, never to win it, and, with this hanging over him through a dozen games, he played wonderfully well.

Those who would change the scoring rules to eliminate the deuced set have splendid motives, and most of their arguments are sound. But they never seem aware that they would also eliminate the drama, the excitement of these service battles when two fine players probe long and earnestly, searching to find a way in which the big serve can be overcome. How many fewer great moments there would have been in tennis without this.

Crawford had been probing and waiting since the match began, and now in the twentieth game of the second set that for which he waited arrived. However well Crawford handled the service, he could not win it so long as Vines could serve aces when in trouble. Now the big one at last missed the mark. Not one first service came into court and Crawford knew how to deal with the second. Now he could strike those beautifully controlled balls, low and spinning to the backhand corner, and reach the net before they came back. His volleys were decisive and they brought him back even at one set apiece.

Vines seemed discouraged a little in the third set and played below his best for the only time during the match. Crawford's pace of service and drive increased and, significantly, he several times threw up lobs that Vines could not handle effectively. In the fourth set the play returned to a high plane, sometimes to outright brilliance, but was somewhat less interesting because Crawford, falling behind early, appeared willing to yield the set since he was leading two sets to one, rather than make a strong and perhaps tiring charge to make up lost ground. He seemed to be resting a little, one thought, not stirring himself beyond trying to make Vines work a little harder for his games, looking toward the crisis of a fifth set and saving his ammunition for that.

Vines was serving altogether too well at this stage to hope for a break before he should win the set after he had once got ahead. And that fearsome service would have to be won twice if Crawford was to win the match in that fourth set. And so, after two hours of play, they came to the fifth set, dead level, each having won twenty-three games.

The culminating set was remarkable both for the very high quality of the play and the attitude of the crowd that filled every center-court space. It was completely impartial and hardly ever disturbed the progress of the play with either applause or those explosive outbursts that usually accompany a tense match. The whole thing now turned on whether Crawford, confident that he could hold his own service for a little while longer, could get one service game from Vines before he should have to yield one himself, through fatigue and strain.

It certainly did not seem possible the first time Vines served, for he never in his life served better, putting over four balls that either flew past or could be struck only at an angle out of court. But Vines also hit Crawford's service out of court in the third game and we sat forward now, wondering if the strain were telling and seeking signs of it. Had the perfect timing at last gone off? No.

More aces came in the fourth game for 2–all, and then in the fifth Crawford stood within a single point of losing his own service. With Vines still serving aces, to be 2–3 down probably would have been fatal. And now, alive to the danger, Crawford, with that deceptively easy, almost flat-footed service swing of his, cut the ball wide with spin to Vines' forehand service line and followed it to the net for a winning volley. It was the first time since play began that Jack had gone to the net behind a service.

The game was saved and on they went, with both men playing tennis that, in view of the length and strain of the match, was surprisingly good, full of forceful play, each attacking and defending with fine shots. Once more Crawford was a game ahead with his service won, and he came to 5–4 with some beautiful strokes, pulled out on the move, that once again caused the Vines backhand to yield to pressure.

With the first point of the tenth game we all felt that the real crisis might have arrived. Vines sent a blasting service to the forehand corner of the service court. Crawford, stepping in, blocked it back across court with a stroke that began at the shoulder and stopped as it met the ball, the racket canted backward. The shot was not very deep or difficult to handle, and Vines crashed a blistering forehand that barely cleared the net down Crawford's backhand line. It seemed that Jack would not be able to reach it at all, but he had begun moving before it was struck, and quickly, without seeming to hurry, he was there as Vines dashed for the net to cut off a possible reply.

And now Crawford, as calmly as though it were only a pregame warmup, threw a lob from corner to corner, exactly calculated as to height so that Vines could not back up and put it away as he had done so often earlier. Seeing that he was trapped, Vines turned and tacked in his forward progress and scrambled back to get behind the ball as it fell no more than an inch inside the baseline. He struck at it as it rose from the court but was so off balance that the ball bounced before it reached the net.

It was felt now that Crawford had, with that perfectly controlled lob off one of Vines' hardest thrusts, struck the decisive blow. And so he had. A spinning ball to the backhand corner on the next point and Vines missed it badly, hitting right into the bottom of the net. A little desperate at being behind 0–30 and within two points of defeat, Elly came in behind a serve off which he had taken a little to be sure it would be good, and Crawford, with perfect touch after more than two hours of tension-filled play, brought off a beautiful backhand passing shot. Love–40 now against the biggest service known to man, three match points in a row. Only one was needed. Crawford placed the ball on Vines' backhand again to draw the final error from a stroke that had gradually broken down under persistent pressure.

Crawford was Wimbledon champion at last, and that delicately struck backhand passing shot, moving slowly across the body of the rushing volleyer and just out of reach, and the lob with which he began the final game still are remembered perfectly, almost visually, so long afterward.

This was an occasion on which Vines, though beaten, justified many of the fine things said and written about him. He did not always play this well and his record, especially the Davis Cup record, is quite spotty. And a player's failures as well as his triumphs must go into the record. In 1931 and 1932 Vines was the acknowledged world champion and even, as we have seen, had been hailed in some quarters as the all-time greatest player after his overwhelming defeat of Austin. But the United States did not win back the Davis Cup until four years after Vines had become a professional.

CRAWFORD DEFEATS VINES

by A. Wallis Myers

Jack Crawford has made history for Australia and Wimbledon, bringing glory to both; and Ellsworth Vines helped to provide an epic. The final in which Vines, the American holder, was beaten by the Australian champion after five sets yielded one of the finest matches in the fifty-three-year story of the championship. My own experience of Wimbledon finals only goes back thirty-four years. Mr. S. A. E. Hickson, who was an umpire at the first and who witnessed his fifty-third consecutive final today, declares that for sustained quality of play, mutual attack in the service, and the tense excitement of the last phase, the two-hour contest which Crawford and Vines waged was Wimbledon's greatest match.

The mind passes back in swift retrospect. Renshaw and Lawford had historic fights in the 'eighties—genius against virility and confidence. Pim and Baddeley had several finals in which the science of the game was worthily revealed. The Dohertys showed us elegance of stroke play, refined in every branch, but their finals in the main merely advertised their supremacy. A great Australian, Norman Brookes, who predicted that Crawford would one day come into his own, had his famous challenge round with "H. L." in 1905. I took a line; it was a match to remember, but it had no climax, and only went to three sets. Wilding and Roper Barrett had a match for speculation six years later; the latter retired in a heat wave at two sets all.

Wilding's defending match against McLoughlin, another California giant, in 1913 had a family resemblance to yesterday's contest; it did not go beyond three sets. Neither the Cochet-Tilden match of 1927 nor the Cochet-Borotra match of 1930, memorable for their fluctuations, were finals. Lacoste played several finals against his countrymen . . . Wimbledon in truth has rarely ended with a "five-setter." There had only been ten five-set finals in the history of the meeting. Today's, for superlative play, refined coordination of strokes and tactics, continuous speed in service, and the fighting vigor of both men at the finish, must rank first.

It was a perfect day for play. Breezes were stirring even under an almost cloudless sky, but the walls of the giant stadium destroyed their force, and only occasionally was the ball deflected by a current. I detected a few empty seats; they were those of the photographers who had gone out momentarily to reload. Everybody who could buy or cajole a seat was there, and every living champion of the past seemed to be in the members' stand. Australians were there in force. The most excited was Mrs. Crawford, mixed doubles champion of Australia with her husband. (Vines was one of their opponents in the final.) I am told that she nearly fainted after Jack had won his title. Mrs. Norman Bayles, a well-known Australian hostess, was by her side to restore her. Mrs. Crawford was able to congratulate Jack through the dressing-room window. She had told me in Paris, her love for Wimbledon being what it is, that she would sooner her husband won the singles championship than that Australia should win the Davis Cup. His play yesterday almost deserved the double triumph.

SARAH PALFREY WINS AS HELEN MOODY'S SUB

by Allison Danzig

In the absence of Mrs. Helen Wills Moody, who was forced to remain in her hotel because of a sprained back, a 20-year-old Boston girl understudy "stole the show" as the United States swept the three opening Wightman Cup matches yesterday.

Never before in the eleven-year history of these international engagements has there been a day of such dramatic transpirings as attended the inaugural session at the West Side Tennis Club, Forest Hills.

First came the unexpected and decisive 6–4, 6–2 victory of Miss Helen Jacobs of Berkeley, California, over Miss Dorothy Round. The latter was Great Britain's chief hope, and she is renowned the world over for her feat this year in exacting the first set that Mrs. Moody has yielded since 1927. Shortly on the heels of this unlooked-for American triumph, gained through the efficacy of Miss Jacobs' chop on the soft turf and the brilliance of her volleying, came the announcement to the crowd of Mrs. Moody's illness.

The world's premier woman tennis player, a mainstay of every Wightman Cup team save one since 1923, had been lost to the defending forces at the eleventh hour. . . . Mrs. Moody first experienced the trouble with her back prior to the Wimbledon tournament, but she played through that event with a brace.

With the ace of the United States team thus lost to the defense, at least for the day, the hopes for an American triumph, running so strongly after the victory of Miss Jacobs, became dimmed. At the same time word spread among the 3,000 in the Stadium that Miss Alice Marble of California, third singles player and Mrs. Moody's doubles partner, also might not appear today. She was in poor condition as a result of her taxing struggles at East Hampton. . . .

Thus was the stage set for the entrance of Miss Sarah Palfrey of Boston. It was an entrance calculated to have unsettled the nerves of a much older and more experienced player than the sunny-faced slip of a Boston girl, to step into the shoes of Mrs. Moody in an international team match against the holder of the French championship.

Miss Palfrey rose to the occasion magnificently. Playing her first Wightman Cup singles match, she defeated Miss Margaret (Peggy) Scriven by the convincing margin of 6–3, 6–1, and later she came back to the court with Miss Jacobs to vanquish Miss Round and Miss Mary Heeley in doubles, 6–4, 6–2.

The enthusiasm engendered by the stirring, martial style of play of the Boston girl has seldom been equaled at a women's tennis match in this country. Sitting alongside the net as acting captain of the American team in Mrs. Moody's absence was Mrs. George W. Wightman of Boston, donor of the cup and the mentor of Miss Palfrey from the start of her youthful career.

One had only to glance at Mrs. Wightman's beaming countenance to understand the pride she took in the play of her protégée. One of the shrewdest court generals the game has produced, Mrs. Wightman had a keen appreciation for the aplomb and astuteness with which Miss Palfrey put her strategic precepts into practice.

The fine points of Miss Palfrey's changes of spin and pace and of her cunning in working up her openings may have been lost upon some in the gallery. No one could fail to appreciate the worth of her drastic forehand and the finality of her volleying, which stood forth so vividly in the doubles. Nor were the self-possession and absolute confidence with which this young understudy carried the attack to her opponents to be overlooked. Never for a moment did she show the slightest questioning of her ability to encompass the downfall of the valiant, hard-hitting Miss Scriven. The gallery went over to her en masse as she hewed industriously to the lines with her racing forehand drive and let her subtle drop volleys fall into unprotected terrain.

One questioned whether Mrs. Moody could have turned in a more masterful performance. Certainly there can be no question that even had the celebrated Californian been in the line-up, the day's reckoning could not have been more discouraging to the visiting team. Not even the satisfaction of winning a set was allowed the British on as one-sided a day of competition as these matches have brought forth. Their outlook as they go into the final session of competition this afternoon is forlorn indeed.

MRS. MOODY LOSES FIRST SET IN U. S. IN 7 YEARS

by Allison Danzig

Mrs. Helen Wills Moody lost a set yesterday.

The thing that had not happened in America since 1926 came about before the eyes of 8,000 excited spectators at Forest Hills as Mrs. Moody stood off the challenge of Miss Betty Nuthall of England, 2–6, 6–3, 6–2.

Something else happened yesterday that is without parallel in half a century of championship tennis play in this country.

In the second set, Mrs. Moody served in two successive games. The thirteen officials in attendance were as oblivious to the mistake as were the players themselves.

Between the two circumstances—Mrs. Moody losing a set and the unprecedented alteration in the order of the service—the neighborhood within the vicinity of the West Side Tennis Club was completely shaken out of its Sabbatic calm. It would be difficult to say which occasioned more surprise.

Within the official marquee spectators were incredulous as Miss Nuthall, hitting with a ferocity that actually made her listless opponent's plight seem hopeless, rushed through the opening set in twelve minutes. The sight of Mrs. Moody being relegated to the role which she customarily visits upon her opponents left the onlookers in a daze.

But the response was something totally different a little later when it dawned upon the officials that the regulations of the tennis code were being broken before their eyes in a national championship.

Fred L. Pond, chairman of the West Side Tennis Club tournament committee, rushed over to the box of Dr. S. Ellsworth Davenport 2d, president of the club, and as the latter hastened out to the umpire's chair the marquee buzzed with excitement.

The fact that the same thing had happened on the center court at Wimbledon this year in the match between Bunny Austin and Jiro Satoh of Japan, when Satoh served in two successive games, was offered partly in extenuation of the mistake.

Long after the play had ended for the day the episode was more the topic of discussion than the match itself.

To add to the day's dramatic record, Miss Freda James of England was seized with a cramp in the leg that brought a doctor on the court in the final stages of the doubles match. In this match Miss James and Miss Nuthall defeated Miss Helen Jacobs and Miss Sarah Palfrey, the defending champions, 6–4, 4–6, 7–5.

The final stroke of the match had hardly been made when a woman in the marquee, overcome by the excitement, fainted. It was ten minutes later before she was revived.

The unfortunate change in the order of the service, as greatly as it was deplored on the American side, can fairly be conjectured to have had little bearing on the final reckoning.

Mrs. Moody's service had been a handicap rather than an asset and she had broken through Miss Nuthall twice in this set for a 3–1 lead.

Miss Nuthall sportingly waived aside the idea that she had been affected by the situation. Tim Horn, the manager of the British Wightman Cup team, with equally fine sportsmanship, stated after the match that it absolutely had no influence upon her defeat.

Neither Miss Nuthall nor Mrs. Moody was aware of the mistake until the attention of the umpire, Rufus Davis, had been called to it, and half an hour after the match Mrs. Moody still had to be convinced that she had served twice in succession.

"They had better have somebody watch me hereafter," said the champion smilingly.

As the players changed sides following the fifth game, which Mrs. Moody had lost on her service, the Californian toed the backline and served, and it was not until several points had been played that the officials in the marquee went into action.

The regulations specify that if a player serves out of turn the player who should have served shall serve as soon as the mistake is discovered and that all points before the discovery shall be reckoned. But if the game shall have been completed before such discovery the order of service remains as altered. The latter procedure was followed.

Before the match was three minutes under way Miss Nuthall had won the first three games with the loss of only three points, breaking through service twice. Mrs. Moody broke through in the fourth, but then dropped the next two games, yielding the sixth after leading at 40–0.

The score was 5 to 1 and it looked like a runaway for Miss Nuthall. The British girl then went on to take the set at 6–2.

Miss Nuthall broke through in the first game of the second set, but then came the turn.

Mrs. Moody rallied for a 3–1 lead and the terrific tension was eased for the first time. It increased again in the fifth, however, as Mrs. Moody was broken through, and then came the alteration in the order of the service and Miss Nuthall broke through again to square the score at 3–all.

Miss Nuthall was holding command again and it looked desperate for Mrs. Moody. Her defeat in successive sets would have surprised no one.

But at this critical stage came the unlooked-for reprieve. The almost flawless control that the English girl had maintained began to waver. Mrs. Moody put on more pressure and captured the set at 6–3.

The American, up on her toes for the first time and hitting with better length, had her opponent on the run in the third set. Miss Nuthall's confidence had deserted her now, along with her control, and the play turned into a procession.

While beaten, Miss Nuthall had the satisfaction of taking the first set that Mrs. Moody has yielded in tournament singles on American courts since she was beaten by Mrs. Molla Mallory in 1926.

From 1927 on she had not lost a set until Miss Dorothy Round of England took the second chapter from her in the recent Wimbledon championship.

It would be unfair to detract in any way from the credit owing Miss Nuthall for the magnificent tennis she played yesterday. But at the same time the fact cannot be overlooked that Mrs. Moody obviously was sparing herself.

It was reported that the physician who has been attending her for her back injury had advised her strongly against playing and that she stay off the courts for six months. Mrs. Moody said, after the match, that her back was slow to "warm up," owing to the tendons being stretched. But she was quick to pay tribute to Miss Nuthall for the brilliance of her attack.

Mrs. Moody took her place in the final and there she awaits the winner of today's semi-final between Miss Round and Miss Jacobs. The victory of Miss Nuthall and Miss James also put them in the final of the doubles.

Editor's note: Miss Jacobs defeated Miss Round in the other semi-final, and in the final Mrs. Moody, trailing at 0–3 in the third set, defaulted to Miss Jacobs, explaining that she was unable to continue, owing to the pain in her back.

MY MATCHES AGAINST HELEN WILLS MOODY

by Helen Jacobs

My first national championship singles encounter with Helen Wills occurred in the 1927 tournament at Forest Hills. I think it may be said that she had reached the top of her form in that year. Driving with the same fury that marked her game in the Wimbledon final in July, when she won her first world's championship from Lili d'Alvarez (without the loss of a set), she seemed content to remain in the backcourt, hammering the ball relentlessly to the corners, alternating line drives with fast-dropping crosscourt shots. Seldom did she go to the net, depending largely upon lobs to offset the advantage of the net player against her. Although a recapitulation of the match showed that I earned more points than she, her errors were negligible in comparison with mine as I overhit the lines in an effort to match her length.

I had watched Helen often in practice against men in Berkeley. Most of them were able to defeat her without much trouble when they took to the net against her, played the drop shot [and] drew her to the net, where she was not naturally agile, very imaginative, or subtle with the volley. That, I knew, was the only game that could win from her; all the women players with skillful volleys and overhead knew this to be true. The difficulty was in making the opening to get to the net, for, aware of her limitations in that position, Helen had perfected a defense against the volleyer that required on the part of her opponent a baseline game as sound as the net game.

To play Helen Wills was to play a machine. There was little if any conversation, no joviality, and to this the gallery obviously reacted, becoming almost grim in its partisanship. The press had long since confused incompatibility with the elements of a "feud" in our matches, which became less agreeable to both of us as they inevitably occurred. I remember no laughter from the crowded stands, though admiring applause was often thunderous. Thus, one had a feeling, would one watch the Derby at Churchill Downs, some hoping for the favorite to win, others hoping that the challenger would come through. Helen Wills fought on the court much as Gene Tunney fought in the ring—with implacable concentration and undeniable skill but without the color or imagination of a Dempsey or a Lenglen.

Matches against her were fun only in the sense of the satisfaction that one derives from pitting one's skill against the champion's. Most of Helen's opponents whom I knew well and played often had the same impression. Yet all had the greatest admiration for her game, and if the indomitable quality of her match play could only be sustained by concentration that must exclude every possibility of diversion, that was her business, for it is the undeniable purpose of champions to win.

Helen defeated me in my first American championship final, 6–2, 6–1, in 1928. My only consolation was that I won half as many points in the first set as she did and a little better than half as many in the second, and that I had been beaten by a player who had not lost a set in her triumphant march to the English and United States singles titles. To say that Helen Wills was pre-eminent, actually unchallenged, in the world of women's tennis would be redundant. She stood head and shoulders above the field. Though the challenger might fight to the last ditch, she was invariably exhausted by rallies that might be prolonged to prodigious lengths if necessary or, at the least evidence of her faltering, concluded in merciless style.

In the spring of 1929, the United States Lawn Tennis Association announced that a team would be sent to Europe for a series of international matches. The team was to consist of Helen Wills and a partner of her choosing. In this year I was ranked second in the American lists and fully expected to be invited to join the team for the tour that would have seasoned my game tremendously. Instead, however, Helen selected Edith Cross, thereby creating almost as much controversial discussion as that which was to follow our match in 1933. I could see no justification for the decision, nor could I understand the Tennis Association's acquiescence in it, considering the fact that it customarily chose its own teams.

Though I missed out on that trip, a group of San Francisco and East Bay tennis enthusiasts, who felt as I did on the subject, sent me to England for the Wimbledon championships, where Helen and I met in the final. Our match was a repetition of the final at Forest Hills in 1928. Everything written about one would apply to the other; the same can be said of my 1930 final against her in the French championships. I had not acquired the finesse to defeat Helen Wills at Wimbledon. Neither of us played in the American championships in 1930, and I did not have the chance to play her at Forest Hills in 1932, for she did not compete that year. . . .

The 1933 season saw Helen extended to defend her title successfully in the Wimbledon final against Dorothy Round. She was forced to three sets for the first time since her initial victory in 1927. I played her that year in the final of the American championship. No tennis match within memory except the Lenglen-Mallory second-round match at Forest Hills in 1921 had quite such unpleasant repercussions as this one; none, I am sure, was more trying to both contestants.

There had been some doubts as to the value of my winning my first national championship in 1932, when, as I have written, Helen did not defend her title though she had won Wimbledon for the fifth time in July. With the opening of the 1933 season, it was considered almost certain that my reign as singles champion of my country would be short-lived; this, of course, in view of Helen's almost certain entry in the championships. A final match between us at Forest Hills was anticipated with much speculation—our supporters aligned vehemently against each other. . . .

Helen was trying for her eighth championship, having, by this summer of 1933, held the title in 1923, 1924, 1925, 1927, 1928, 1929, and 1931. I was defending a title won only one year before, and perhaps the more precious for that reason.

The gallery was not a particularly large one the day we played—a mid-week match, and uncertain weather, in addition to my tournament record against Helen Wills, were undoubtedly responsible. The day brought perfect tennis weather—no wind, not too hot—a day for exploiting all the shots Suzanne Lenglen had advocated: shots requiring accurate touch and little deflection by wind. It was also the ideal day for the volleyer who disliked more than anything else the drive that cannot be truly gauged or the lob that is pulled down toward the player by a sudden gust of wind.

I had determined that in this match I would go to the net at every opportunity. There was little sense standing in the backcourt swapping drives with anyone as superlative as Helen in that department. Of course, a net game was not enough of itself, but I had more confidence in my forehand than I had felt in years and was certain that it would stand up against the pounding I could anticipate from her, and also help to make the desired openings that would pave the way to the net. My backhand drive had seldom let me down.

It appeared, from the opening of the first set, that Helen was going to play me as she had done in every one of our meetings—playing chiefly to my forehand and, at the first evidence of my being off balance, using the short crosscourt drive to the opposite side. It was, at its best, a devastating placement, which I was determined to prevent. To do this I put everything I could into the force and placement of my service with the intention of drawing Helen out of court for the drive to the opposite side, then going to the net.

The first three games went with service. In the fourth I broke Helen's service, for a 3–1 lead. This lead seemed to inspire her to a stonewall driving defense in which she employed her familiar accuracy of corner placements, coupled with speed and pace. Games went to 3–3 as she broke my service. Then again service held to 6–6. For a while, during this stage of the first set, Helen also was playing for the net position, and it became a question of who would get there first. My backhand drive, particularly down the line, and my volley and overhead were serving me well enough to come within one point of the set at 5–4, but the fine variety of Helen's shots and her punishing steadiness saved the game for her. She was forcing me to hit lobs of difficult depth. Anticipating them, I had practiced smashing on an outside court for some time before the match began, and the practice was certainly justified. Helen Wills' lob can be a formidable weapon.

Breaking her service at 7–6 by the use of sliced drives to the corners and the volley, I ran out the set, 8–6. I had created a record for myself, winning my first set against Helen. It startled the press into wild activity. Typewriters and telegraphic instruments clacked furiously from the marquee. The set encouraged me, proving the wisdom of the net attack, which was certainly my chief weapon, and increasing my confidence in my forehand drive and slice as either aggressive or defensive shots on this day.

But one set was not the match. I had no illusions about the roughness of the road ahead of me. Helen was a fighter; she was a master of the drive and the lob. Her service required constant alertness and careful timing for the return. If I was to win, I must maintain my game at the same level for two more sets, if necessary, and hope that fatigue would impair neither my coordination nor my timing. I did not agree with those who claimed that a woman player could not attack at the net for three sets. In fact, I found it less tiring to go to the net, volley and smash, than to remain in the backcourt covering twice the ground in pursuit of Helen's magnificent drives.

But I had to continue to go to the net, and as the second set opened, it was apparent how difficult the task might become. Winning my service in the opening game, Helen lashed out with blistering drives, varied by deftly placed soft shots that gave her a quick 3–0 lead. With desperate risk, I went to the net on anything close to her backline and was lucky to smash lobs for winners until I drew level at 3–3. Two obviously erroneous decisions against each of us in the next game caused an uproar from the gallery. Right or wrong, they were so patently miscalled at such an important stage in the match that neither of us could resist throwing a point in an attempt to even matters.

A series of drives overreaching the baseline, forced by Helen's deep and paceful drives and her sudden short crosscourt shots, gave her three games running and the set at 6–3.

I was glad of the respite that came at the end of the second set, as I am sure Helen must have been. But she remained on the court, sitting on a chair at the umpire's stand, while I went to the dressing room to refresh myself. When I returned to the court after the ten-minute intermission, Helen opened the third set with service, going to 30–15 in spite of a double fault before I won the game. On my service two unretrievable drives by Helen forced errors from me and she led 0–30. Then, in turn, she overdrove twice, evening the score. A winning volley took me to 40–30, and a netted drive by Helen brought me to 2–0. Helen won the first point of the third game on a forcing service, but forehand and backhand passing shots, successful for me, and a forehand drive beyond the line by Helen gave me the lead at 3–0.

I turned to the ball-boy for the balls, speaking to him once and then again, before I realized that his eyes were fixed on the opposite court. I repeated my request before I turned to see that Helen had walked to the umpire's stand and was reaching for her sweater. It was a confusing moment. I hurried to the stand as Ben Dwight, the venerable umpire, announced that I had won by default. As Helen put on her sweater I went to her.

"My leg is bothering me. I can't go on," she said.

"Would you like to rest for a while?" I asked.

"No, I can't go on," she answered.

Officials, press, photographers rushed onto the court. It seemed unnecessary to subject her to this post-match ordeal. "If you're in pain there's no sense in continuing," I told her. "Why don't you leave before the photographers descend on us," I suggested. Helen left then, escorted from the court by one of the tournament officials.

I went back to the dressing room, where Molla Mallory was waiting for me. A radio commentator had asked her immediately after the match to broadcast a statement on the default in view of her experience with Suzanne Lenglen. She did, in biting terms, and was still full of it when we met.

There is no doubt that Helen, for her own sake, would have been wiser if she had remained on the court for the twelve points necessary for me to end the match in the third set. But what one does under the stress of emotion and pain cannot be calculated in the cold-blooded terms of the spectator. Helen's temperament had always been her most valuable asset. On this day it was her greatest liability.

Before I had finished dressing, Elizabeth Ryan came into the locker room in a state of wild excitement. Helen, her partner in the ladies' doubles, had announced that she would play the doubles final. Knowing the probable reaction of the gallery if she did, Elizabeth was determined to default. Fortunately, one of the officials, who had long been a friend of Helen's, persuaded her that she simply couldn't return to the court after the default.

As far as I was concerned, Forest Hills was real bedlam that day. A stream of reporters was in and out of my apartment until late in the evening; the phone never seemed to stop ringing. "Would I make a statement?" was a question that fell on my ears like a phonograph record stuck in a groove. There was nothing I could say. Of course, I was disappointed that the match had ended as it did—who wouldn't have been? But that was water over the dam. I had retained my championship and was happy about that. But how could I, how could anyone for that matter, dispute with Helen her statement that she felt on the verge of fainting when she defaulted. The fact that she walked back to her apartment in the Forest Hills Inn and later wanted to play the doubles final did not make her lot any easier with the reporters who knew of it, but I still did not feel that anything except the winning of my match concerned me.

There were repercussions of the match for months to come. The story of its ending was greatly distorted by many reporters, in most instances by those who obviously had not seen it. What I said to Helen was garbled by journalists whose hearing couldn't have extended to the umpire's chair. Some had it that I begged her to go on, the last request it would have occurred to me to make. Some wrote that she refused to shake hands and others that we shook hands, were photographed, and that she was then helped from the court. The truth of the matter is that, although we did not shake hands, Helen did not refuse to do so, nor was she assisted from the court. She left it, as soon as she had donned her sweater, under her own power.

She appeared next in major championship tennis in 1935 at Wimbledon. Beaten by Kay Stammers at the Beckenham tournament while she was again getting her "tournament legs," Helen had, with one exception (a three-set match against Fräulein Cepkova in the fourth round), a fairly easy time to the final of the Wimbledon meeting.

We met again, this time on an intensely hot afternoon with a slight breeze blowing. Both of us were playing well, but Helen went to a 3–0 lead in the first set before I could make much of an impression on the match. I believe she has always liked the fast Center Court turf, and she was hitting with wonderful length and great speed. The next three games to me evened the score, then Helen took the set, 6–3. The second set began with a determined net attack by Helen, surprising to anyone who had played her so often. It was only the functioning of my passing shots that enabled me to win this set, 6–3.

Up to this stage the match had not been as scintillating as our Forest Hills final of 1933. To defeat Helen once was to draw forth from her a more wary game; and having defeated her was to emphasize to the opponent the importance of taking chances at every opportunity, of playing boldly from backcourt and net, and yet of maintaining a sound defense and steadiness to match hers—a considerable challenge.

I think there was, in the beginning of the third set (which started without the ten-minute intermission that is customary in this country), some restraint in our hitting. But with the advantage of service, I was able to go to 4–2 and then, as Helen missed an easy smash, to 5–2. Helen won my service for 5–3. It was in that game that I held match point. At 30–15 in my favor, on Helen's service, a questionable sideline decision caused some delay before we could resume play. I hit a drive along Helen's forehand sideline that appeared to be in. Evidently the umpire thought it was in, but the linesman called it out. The umpire questioned the linesman, who repeated his call, and the game went on. With the score at 30–30, I won the next point to move to within one point of the match. After one of the longest rallies I can remember ever having survived, Helen, out of court on her backhand side, put up a shallow lob. The lob appeared to be headed for mid-court. I moved in to hit it, but a gust of wind caught it, pulling it in toward the net. By the time I was able to judge where it could best be hit, it was a short lob, very close to the net. I was almost on my knees for the smash, the ball hit the edge of my racket frame and rolled along the net cord before it fell onto my court.

That was really the end of the match. Though we were at 30–30 and deuce in the eleventh and twelfth games, Helen won the set at 7–5. She had made a magnificent comeback to win her seventh Wimbledon championship.

Unfortunately, some widely read members of the press reported what had been an exciting sporting test in such a manner that the so-called feud between us was the highlight of the reports. I, the loser, was represented as accepting defeat with tears in my eyes; Helen was represented as a far more jubilant victor than good taste would have dictated. These reports were so contrary to the facts as to make one wonder if it is not better not to report at all than to report inaccurately. Far from having tears in my eyes after this match with Helen Moody, I had enjoyed the match, for it had been a real test of skill and staying power, of tactics and strategy and nerve. Naturally, one regrets losing any big championship final, but it seems to me an unfair commentary on the behavior of women in competitive sport that it should be necessary, in order to create reader interest, to report the loser in tears and the winner gloating.

It has been my experience during eighteen years of tournament tennis that women are no more given to tears in defeat than men, nor is their enthusiasm in victory more excessive. To claim, even facetiously, that it is, is to lessen public regard for the important place that women have achieved, against immeasurable disadvantages, in all the games that Americans, Europeans and Asiatics love to play.

MRS. MOODY DEFAULTS TO HELEN JACOBS

by Allison Danzig

Mrs. Helen Wills Moody no longer rules the courts.

The reign of the world's pre-eminent woman tennis player, the most absolute in the annals of the game, came to an end at Forest Hills yesterday under dramatic circumstances that have been paralleled only once in the forty-six-year history of the national championship.

With the score standing 3–0 against her in the third set of her punishing final-round match with Miss Helen Jacobs, the defending title holder, Mrs. Moody walked to the umpire's chair and informed the arbiter that she was unable to play any longer.

The crowd of 8,000 spectators, thrilled by the magnificent play of Miss Jacobs and tingling with the expectancy of seeing Mrs. Moody beaten for the first time on any court since 1926, had little inkling of the nature of Mrs. Moody's remarks. It was not until the celebrated Californian took up her blue sweater and Miss Jacobs rushed to her . . . that the gallery sensed the significance of her action.

Mrs. Moody defaulted under physical distress, just as Mlle. Suzanne Lenglen had defaulted to Mrs. Molla Mallory early in the second set of their second-round championship match at Forest Hills in 1921. Exhausted by the terrific struggle that had been waged in a 14-game first set and feeling that she was on the point of fainting from the pain in her injured back, Mrs. Moody retired from the court and Miss Jacobs, amid the wild acclaim of the spectators, was declared the winner by 8–6, 3–6, 3–0 and default.

After the match Mrs. Moody gave out the following statement:

"In the third set of my singles match I felt as if I were going to faint because of pain in my back and hip and a complete numbness of my right leg.

"The match was long and by defaulting I do not wish to detract from the excellence of Miss Jacobs' play.

"I feel that I have spoiled the finish of the national championship and wish that I had followed the advice of my doctor and returned to California. I still feel that I did right in withdrawing because I felt that I was on the verge of a collapse on the court."

Thus came to a conclusion the most exciting women's tournament in years, with Mrs. Moody beaten for the first time in the championship since 1922 and Miss Jacobs established as the title holder for the second successive year. It was not, however, the end of the day's dramatic developments.

After it had been announced that Mrs. Moody would be unable to appear with Miss Elizabeth Ryan for the final round of the doubles against Miss Betty Nuthall and Miss Freda James of England, who won the title by default, an exhibition match was put on. Miss Alice Marble of San Francisco substituted for Mrs. Moody as Miss Ryan's partner against the British team.

With the score standing at 4–all in the second set, after the American pair had won the first set at 6–4, Miss Nuthall hit an overhead smash. The ball, traveling too fast for Miss Marble to get out of the way or to guard herself, struck the California girl in the eye. Miss Marble fell to the ground and there was great concern in the stands as officials and players rushed to her aid. After a few minutes, Rufus Davis, the umpire, announced that Miss Marble had suffered a painful injury and that Miss Nuthall and Miss James again had won by default.

It was a day such as will not soon be forgotten by those who sat in the stadium of the West Side Tennis Club. When Mrs. Moody lost a set last Sunday to Miss Nuthall, the first she had yielded in this country since 1926, there was excitement enough. But it was nothing compared to the stir created yesterday by the defeat of the player who had stood invincible against the best in the world since 1927. It was likened to the sensation of William Tilden's defeat in the men's championship at Forest Hills by Henri Cochet of France in 1926.

In spite of the fact that it was known that Mrs. Moody was not in the condition to show the full strength of her hand, it was difficult to believe that the player who had held such absolute sway could have met her master. Miss Jacobs had never been able to make the slightest headway against her, and even the defending champion's victory over Miss Dorothy Round in the semi-finals on Friday failed to shake the faith in Mrs. Moody's capacity to come through to the title.

The stunning reversal is to be explained on two scores. First, it would be a misrepresentation to say that Mrs. Moody was at her best. It was obvious from the outset that she was not hitting with anything like her accustomed severity. The speed that had subdued her opponents and left them with a feeling of hopelessness simply was not at Mrs. Moody's command yesterday. There was plenty of length to her shots and for the first two sets she was giving herself unstintingly to the desperate work of plugging up the gaps in her court against Miss Jacobs' inexorable forcing shots. But so far as her offense was concerned, Mrs. Moody was not to be recognized as the player of former years. In the final set her defense, too, folded up as she came to the end of her physical resources.

Having made allowances for the shortcomings in Mrs. Moody's prepared-ness for so strenuous an ordeal, it is now to be set down that these short-comings were accentuated by the brilliance of Miss Jacobs' play. The Berkeley girl Mrs. Moody faced yesterday was a far more dangerous opponent than she had been in any of their previous encounters. Uncertain with her forehand, erratic at the net, and lacking in confidence all through the season, Miss Jacobs was almost ignored from the start of the championship. There was some question, too, of whether she had the stamina to undergo the rigors of championship match play, for at Seabright she had fainted at her hotel and had been on the verge of a collapse after being defeated by Miss Sarah Palfrey in the final.

But against Mrs. Moody, Miss Jacobs was a great player, fighting with the heart of a champion. If she was in distress from her exertions, she never showed it until the second set, when Mrs. Moody's use of the drop shot compelled her to do a tremendous amount of running. Against Miss Round, it was Miss Jacobs' forehand chop that carried the day. Yesterday that chop was again tremendously important, remarkable for its uniform length and its accuracy. The Berkeley girl had other telling weapons. Her service was a big help, pulling her out of the hole repeatedly in the bitterly fought first set, and her volleying and overhead smashing were the most vivid seen in the tournament.

At the very start of the match it was apparent that Mrs. Moody had a battle on her hands. Miss Jacobs was hardly missing a thing from the back of the court and she was playing the ball so deep and changing direction with such fine judgment that Mrs. Moody was seldom given the chance to get set for her stroke. Under pressure at her baseline and forced to scramble for almost every ball that came over, Mrs. Moody had no alternative but to throw herself into the struggle without regard for her weakened back. Almost every rally was prolonged and the fur fairly flew without a letup in that long opening set. Miss Jacobs was getting fully as good length on her chop and her backhand as was her opponent and she was hitting the more crisply of the two. The lack of her usual drastic pace was plainly noticeable in Mrs. Moody's drives. Not only was the defending champion holding her own from the back of the court but at the net she was seldom to be denied. Mrs. Moody's lobs were too short and Miss Jacobs hammered them down time and again.

Miss Jacobs went into a 3–1 lead and Mrs. Moody got even at 3–all. From that point on games followed service until Miss Jacobs again broke through in the fourteenth. In three games in this set Mrs. Moody had commanding leads, only to dissipate them. The regularity with which Miss Jacobs extricated herself from difficulties must have had a disturbing effect upon her opponent.

When the former champion finally weakened and yielded the last two games of the set on errors, it was thought she would be at the mercy of her opponent in the second set. But Mrs. Moody, far from being resigned to defeat, changed her tactics, and the tide turned. Instead of hitting for length as she had been doing in the first set, Mrs. Moody now resorted to drop shots, alternately playing the ball short and deep. Miss Jacobs was now put on the defensive and was kept on the run between her baseline and the net in pursuit of trap shots and lobs, and Mrs. Moody quickly went ahead at 3–0. The champion got her second wind and came back to tie the score at 3–all, but after drawing level Miss Jacobs, sorely fatigued, was able to offer little opposition. Mrs. Moody took the next three games and when the players left the court for a ten-minute intermission it appeared to be either's match.

But the first game of the final set was all that was needed to reveal that Mrs. Moody's chances of carrying the day were remote. Two double faults gave the gallery an inkling of her weakened condition, and when Miss Jacobs, hitting with confidence and great severity, took the second game from 0–30, the end was in sight. On the last point of this game Mrs. Moody had an easy shot on her forehand, and when she feebly put the ball into the bottom of the net, there was not the slightest doubt of her helplessness. In the third game she made two weak efforts to get to the net, but each time Miss Jacobs passed her magnificently. The last shot of the match was a forehand drive by Mrs. Moody that overreached the line.

Mrs. Moody trailing at 0–3 on two service breaks, her defeat was now seen to be a matter of only a few more minutes. It came sooner than anyone expected, as the former champion defaulted at this point. It was unfortunate that Miss Jacobs had to be denied the satisfaction of winning a match in the only manner that a player finds satisfactory, and there can be no question that she would have won it with her racket had the play gone on to its logical conclusion. There were some who thought that Mrs. Moody might have continued, if only to go through the motions of playing. On the other hand, the fact must be faced that Mrs. Moody was running the risk of injuring herself permanently by going on in her weakened condition and with her back injury. Perhaps it would have been for the best if she had followed her doctor's orders during the Wightman Cup matches and given up tennis for the year. At any rate, she had the courage to undertake to play through the tournament.

After rushing out through one of the rear underground portals of the stadium, Miss Jacobs came back on the court to receive the championship trophy. The tumultuous cheering testified to the gallery's appreciation of her superb performance. Miss Jacobs had received Mrs. Moody's decision with sympathy, and her fine sportsmanship and her manner of conducting herself added to the popularity of her victory.

Not since the first year in which she competed for the women's title had Mrs. Moody met defeat in the championship. That was in 1922, when she was runner-up to Mrs. Mallory. In 1923, Mrs. Moody—then Helen Wills— wrested the crown from Mrs. Mallory and retained it in 1924 and 1925. She allowed it to go undefended in 1926, after undergoing an operation for appendicitis in Europe, where she had lost to Mlle. Suzanne Lenglen at Cannes in February. In 1927, Mrs. Moody came back to regain the championship, and she had won it every year since with the exception of 1930 and 1932, when she did not participate in the title tournament. She did not lose a set here or abroad from 1927 until Miss Round took the second chapter from her at Wimbledon this year. She had not lost a set in our championship since the 1925 final, when she was carried to three sets by Miss Kathleen McKane, and the last time she had been defeated was at Rye in August 1926. Mrs. Mallory that year vanquished her in three sets in the semi-finals of the New York State championship at the Westchester-Biltmore Country Club a week after Miss Ryan had defeated her in the final at Seabright in two sets.

In all those six years of Mrs. Moody's invincibility from 1927 on, Miss Jacobs had never succeeded in taking a set from her. Their first big meeting came in 1927, when Miss Jacobs, competing in the championship for the first time, reached the semi-finals and there lost to Mrs. Moody at 6-0, 6-2. The following year they met in the final of our championship and again Mrs. Moody won by the decisive margin of 6-2, 6-1. In 1929, in the final at Wimbledon, the verdict was 6-1, 6-2. In 1931, Mrs. Moody scored her most crushing victory of all, defeating Miss Jacobs in love sets in the final at Seabright. Last year, Mrs. Moody won the Wimbledon championship by defeating her California rival in the concluding round, 6-3, 6-1.

1934

VINES IN PRO DEBUT LOSES TO TILDEN

by Allison Danzig

William Tilden extended the official hand of welcome to Ellsworth Vines of Pasadena at Madison Square Garden last night—a welcome to the same fate that the Philadelphia tennis marvel visited upon Henri Cochet on the occasion of the French Davis Cup ace's professional debut last Fall.

Before a record-breaking tennis crowd for America of 16,000 spectators, who paid in $29,760 at the gate, the 41-year-old master added his celebrated 22-year-old rival to his long string of world famous conquests going back to 1920.

Not even the satisfaction of winning a set was permitted to Vines, who was playing his first match as a professional. Though his form was far superior to his showing as an amateur in 1933, though his cannonball service was setting the crowd wild and his ground strokes stood up magnificently in stretches, the tall, slim Californian never seriously threatened and went down at 8–6, 6–3, 6–2.

Tilden, playing with a fire and impetuousness that swept away all before it, including the years that hang on his broad shoulders, was the master of the situation from beginning to end. Before the fury of his cannonball delivery, which was seldom more terrorizing; the heartbreaking length and angles of his marauding drives and the resourcefulness and fertility of his devices Vines was faced with more than he could cope with.

The gangling young amateur champion of 1931 and 1932, who was handicapped by his lack of experience on indoor surfaces, had the Garden roaring when he pulled up from 1–4 to 4–all in the first set. He stood steadfast to 2–all in both the second and third sets, to revive the fading hopes of his many adherents in the tremendous throng.

But for all the dynamite in his racket and his unfaltering courage and perseverance, there was no gainsaying the generalship and relentless pressure of one of the most amazing iron men in the history of sport.

One hour and five minutes after Levan Richards had called "play" from the umpire's chair the match, the first in a series billed for the world's professional championship, was over and the huge crowd was paying tribute to victor and vanquished.

It was the greatest crowd that has seen a tennis match in this country, amateur or professional. It exceeded the throng that saw Tilden lose to René Lacoste of France in the 1927 championship final at Forest Hills by almost 2,000 and surpassed the professional mark of 1931 for the Tilden-Karel Kozeluh match at the Garden by 3,000.

It was a crowd that gathered from every class of society, and it not only filled every seat in the Garden, but hundreds were standing in the aisles. Many others sought admission to the huge enclosure, but in vain, the doors being closed on them.

Included in the brilliant assemblage clad in evening clothes in the boxes were Mr. and Mrs. Thomas H. Hitchcock, Jr., Bernard Baruch, W. Goadby Loew, Mr. and Mrs. William K. Vanderbilt, Geraldine Farrar, Ethel Barrymore and many other notables from society and the stage.

With the seats scaled from $5 down, the great outpouring was a testimonial to the lure of tennis and particularly to the magnetism of the names of Tilden and Vines, both former amateur champions.

The Californian underwent a season of continual disaster as an amateur in 1933, but such is the glamour of his fame and the appeal of his long awaited meeting with the player to whose mantle he was regarded as the heir that there were not seats enough in the Garden to accommodate the demand.

A percentage of the proceeds will be turned over to the Free Milk Fund for Babies, of which Mrs. William Randolph Hearst is chairman.

In addition to the meeting between Vines and Tilden, two other contests were staged on the benefit program. In the opening event of the evening, Bruce Barnes, the brilliant young Texan who has improved so amazingly since his amateur days, played Vincent Richards, former Davis Cup star, to 11–all in the first set. Owing to the length of the set and the lateness of the hour, the match was stopped at this point.

In the windup Vines and Richards, teaming together magnificently, crushed Tilden and Francis T. Hunter of New Rochelle, 6–1, 6–0.

Both of these engagements were exciting and held the interest of the spectators, but it was the meeting between Tilden and Vines that they had paid to see. The lateness with which the crowd arrived bespoke wherein its interest was centered.

The match started with Vines knocking the cover off every ball he hit, to stir the crowd to a frenzy as he won the opening game. To the very end, the Californian was continuing to blaze away with his machine-gun strokes, though he interpolated an occasional drop shot, but after that initial game Tilden had an answer to his speed.

The Philadelphian was not hitting as consistently hard as his younger opponent, but he utilized the pace on Vines's strokes, his hand and eye were surer, his range was more certain and his generalship was irresistible.

Under the pressure of his relentless attack to the corners, Vines seldom had the opportunity to get set for his shots and this accounted in large part for his errors. There were far fewer inexcusable errors by the Californian than he made in his last year as an amateur.

Vines's service was a heavy scorer, but no heavier than was Tilden's. The Californian made the more double faults and they cost him dearly, though certainly not nearly enough to have decided the outcome of the match.

More than anything else, it was Tilden's ground strokes that did that. The match was essentially a duel of services and drives, with Tilden having the advantage on both counts.

Vines sought to capitalize his fine net attack, and some of his most vivid shots were made on the volley and overhead, where he was greatly improved. But it was no easy task to get inside of Tilden's blazing, carefully gauged forcing shots, some of which exploded on the Californian's racket and caromed out of the court.

From both the forehand and backhand Tilden was hitting with equal deadliness, and it was particularly on the backhand that he excelled his opponent. Vines's forehand functioned magnificently and, had it not been for the amazing agility of the veteran in covering court, more games would have fallen to the younger player.

Nothing was more amazing to the crowd than the way the Philadelphia veteran, who was winning championships when Vines was a schoolboy, streaked across the baseline and up and down the court on one of the most remarkable pairs of legs sport has known.

The further the match progressed the more abundant seemed Tilden's resources. It required a great expenditure of effort for him to carry off the first set, in which Vines stood on even terms from 4–all to 6–all.

But after standing up under the Californian's battering service and ferocious drives, Tilden came back with a stronger attack in the second set. In the final set Vines led 2–1 on service and then Tilden opened up in earnest, to take five games in a row.

It was Vines, the younger player, who wilted and whose control deserted him as the miracle man of tennis turned loose an attack that for sustained control, power and brilliance of shot-making equaled the greatest flights of his amateur days.

TILDEN VICTOR OVER COCHET

by Allison Danzig

William Tilden stood more than ever the wizard of tennis last night.

A few strokes past midnight, after two hours of battle in one of the most taxing struggles of his long career, the 41-year-old ironman of the courts emerged the victor over Henri Cochet of France, his nemesis of their amateur days.

A crowd of 13,000 rose in their seats at Madison Square Garden to acclaim the Philadelphia veteran for a triumph that deserves to rank among the most meritorious performances accredited to him. The official paid attendance was 12,663 and the gross receipts were $20,066.09.

Fighting from behind almost the entire distance and with his strength apparently ebbing at the end of the drawn-out first set, Tilden came back in the face of Cochet's masterful defensive play to win at 7–9, 6–1, 4–6, 6–3, 6–3.

It was a comeback in the face of prohibitive odds, for at the end of that inaugural set, which found his younger adversary working miracles of interceptions in the best form of his amateur days, scarcely anyone believed that Tilden had a chance.

What chance did a 41-year-old man have against an opponent almost ten years his junior, who had beaten him in every meeting from 1928 through 1930 and whose game still showed the same confounding contraventions that had been Tilden's undoing year after year?

That was the logical question, but the only one Tilden asked was why he couldn't beat Cochet again after doing it in 1933 on the occasion of the latter's professional debut in Paris.

His answer was a fusillade of cannonball serves, a new antidote of drop shots to throw his opponent into confusion in the second set, and a resurgence of his backhand in the final two sets that put Cochet's deadly net attack completely to rout.

Cochet was probably never passed so often before in his career as he was in those last two sets. Tilden's backhand, so feared in his halcyon days, was nothing less than terrorizing in its accuracy, speed and range, and it eclipsed every other shot in the match.

It stood forth at its best when Cochet's backhand was crumbling, and more than either player's brilliant volleying or Tilden's service, lobbing and trap shots, it was the stroke of the night.

This stroke in particular and the match in general eclipsed all else seen in the two evenings of play in the international professional team competition, which ended in a score of 5 to 0 in favor of the American team.

There was no particular interest in the outcome of the series, which had already been clinched on Monday night, and it was taken as a matter of fact when Ellsworth Vines defeated Martin Plaa in the opening engagement last night, 13–11, 6–3, 6–3, after a rather disappointing exhibition.

What everyone was interested in was the renewal of the rivalry between Tilden and Cochet in their first meeting in this country since 1927. It was a beautiful match, not the best they have played perhaps, but nevertheless a match filled with magnificent shot-making of subtle shading and ingenious conception.

One could appreciate the high quality of its finesse and craftsmanship all the more by comparison with the first of the evening, in which victory was achieved almost entirely by superior hitting power.

Tilden won after substituting finesse for speed and power in the second set, when he resorted to his drop shots and changes of pace, spin and length. In the end, however, it was speed under control that won the match, and the amazing thing was that so much speed could be generated by the veteran after he had been on the court for almost two hours.

All of the delicacy and guile of Cochet's stroke production and tactics were set at naught by the cannonading from Tilden's racket, and well before the end of the final set the French professional had resigned himself to defeat.

PERRY FIRST BRITON TO WIN WIMBLEDON IN 25 YEARS

by Ferdinand Kuhn, Jr.

Fred Perry today gave England its first men's singles championship at Wimbledon since 1909—the year that he was born.

He won the title by inflicting a crushing defeat upon Jack Crawford of Australia in straight sets, 6–3, 6–0, 7–5. It was one of the most decisive finals seen at Wimbledon in many years, being even swifter and surer than Bill Tilden's defeat of Wilmer Allison in the all-American final in 1930.

It ended, too, in a way no old-timer at Wimbledon could remember having seen before. Perry was leading at 6–5 and advantage in the third set, with Crawford serving. The great crowd of 15,000 buzzed with excitement, for this was a moment England's tennis players had been trying for twenty-five years to reach.

A hush fell on the crowded stands. Crawford threw the ball into the air and served what looked like a sizzling ace, so fast and so wide that Perry couldn't touch it. Suddenly a voice rang out in the stillness. "Foot-fault!"

The crowd gasped and Crawford walked back to the baseline with misery written on his face. Perhaps he had rushed forward too eagerly, but there were thousands in the crowd who wished the foot-fault judge had been looking the other way just at that moment. Crawford was so shaken by the decision that he sent a miserable second service into the net, and the match was over.

The dethroned champion turned on his heels and bowed stiffly to the official who had called the costliest foot-fault ever seen at Wimbledon. Then he turned again and ran to greet the new champion, who had bounded over the net while the crowd cheered in delight and the movie cameras whirred to record the spectacle.

So the championship came back to England for the first time since A. W. Gore won it when Perry was a baby a month old. All the long years of Australian, French and American conquests had ended and an English youth of 25 had brought his own country back to supremacy on its own courts.

Perry was always the complete master today. He didn't make a half dozen bad shots in the whole match. He was lithe as a panther, always holding his opponent in check and beating Crawford at his own cool, cautious game. Once he performed the amazing feat of capturing twelve games in a row from the reigning champion. He was always steady and for three sets he played tennis that only wizards can play—fast, deep, accurate and supremely confident.

In the first two sets Perry returned Crawford's finest drives so easily that he made the Australian look anything but a champion. They would bound in the far corners in Crawford's old familiar way, but Perry was so speedy that he not only returned them but made attacking strokes off them. All Crawford could do was lose points and then slap his forehead or lift his clenched fists high in the air in disgust at his own performance.

Only once, toward the end of the third set, was Crawford able to make a fight of it, and then he came within two points of capturing the set. If he had done that he might have shaken Perry as he shook Frank Shields in the third set the other day. The games had swung back and forth with service after long and tense rallies in which Perry's shots skimmed the net so fast and so close the crowd could hardly see them. Finally, in the eighth game, Crawford broke through after bombarding Perry with wonderful lobs. Perry double-faulted then and lost the game on an unlucky net-cord ball that bounded out of his reach.

But Perry had learned his lesson from having watched Shields in the same circumstances Wednesday. He held on, steady as a rock, and evened the score at 5–all. He never tried to force matters, but was content to fight on Crawford's terms in long baseline rallies. He won the next game and the match because his ground strokes were just a shade steadier and swifter than Crawford's, and when he volleyed it was usually with crushing effect.

Perry now holds the American, Australian and British championships at 25—an achievement especially great because he started his tennis career without any of the advantages of wealth or social position other British players had. His father was a former Labor Member of Parliament, and the future champion started his climb toward the heights without any help except his own tennis genius.

"If I live to be 100 I'll never play so well again," he said after his victory. But there may be many more victories ahead of him in the Davis Cup matches and in the American championships.

LOTT AND STOEFEN DEFEAT ALLISON AND VAN RYN IN U.S. DOUBLES

by Allison Danzig

In a magnificent exhibition between the recognized world's two foremost teams, George M. Lott Jr. of Chicago and Lester B. Stoefen of Los Angeles successfully defended their national tennis doubles championship today on the courts of the Germantown Cricket Club.

A gallery of 3,500 spectators that filled the stands almost to capacity in spite of the threat of rain looked on spellbound at the sheer brilliance of the shot-making as the defending champions reversed the result of their Newport meeting against Wilmer Allison of Austin, Texas, and John Van Ryn of this city.

With the giant Stoefen bringing his tremendous hitting power to bear in almost terrorizing fashion, Lott confounding the opposition with the guile of his teasingly baited soft shots on the short slants and his lobs and neither countenancing any return with their ruthless services, the titleholders took the first two sets, faltered in the third and came back to eke out the fourth for the match. The score was 6–4, 9–7, 3–6, 6–4.

Allison and Van Ryn, former national and Wimbledon champions, put forth a grade of doubles qualified to have beaten any other team in the world. In full command of their game, eclipsing their rivals in their marvelous overhead smashing and hitting to the hilt from start to finish, they were in the fight every minute of the way.

As superb as they were, however, as magnificent as were Allison's volleying coups in the third set and as truly inspired as was Van Ryn's flashing performance in the fourth, the former Davis Cup combination was up against more pressure than it could withstand.

The dreadnought services of the champions, more than anything else, were the rocks upon which the opposition foundered. In conjunction with Stoefen's killing overhead play and bizarrely angled volleys and Lott's ingeniousness in opening up the court with his ferreting stratagems, those irresistible deliveries were too much for a great team.

In the first two sets there was only one game in which Van Ryn and Allison were able to carry the score to deuce when their opponents were serving, and in the second chapter Lott and Stoefen each won two games at love, with the agile Stoefen springing in for the return of service at the net like a tiger after its prey when his partner was serving, and Lott seldom having the opportunity to get in a blow when the Californian was toeing the baseline.

The superiority of Lott and Stoefen, particularly the latter, in their return of service, and the efficacy of Lott's lobs and masterfully designed short-angle shots in paving the way for them to wrest away command of the net exacted a break through Van Ryn in the first set and through Allison in the fifteenth game of the second chapter, in which Van Ryn and Allison were carried to deuce on three other services.

By the end of the second chapter the prospect of the challengers taking a set was highly remote. They had been playing as good tennis as was within their capacity under such deadly pressure, and Lott and Stoefen gave not the slightest indication that they were feeling the strain.

One might have reckoned that Van Ryn and Allison would have lost all heart by this point, with nothing to show on the scoreboard for the brilliant efforts they had put forth. But the former Davis Cup players are made of too stern fiber to reconcile themselves to defeat in the face of the vicissitudes of fortune, and they almost completely won over the gallery by their blazing comeback in the third chapter.

Under the fury and deadly accuracy of their hitting, particularly in the forecourt, Lott wavered in the sixth game. He managed to pull it out on his service, but the champions had shown enough evidence that the breaking point was at hand to inspire their opponents, and Van Ryn and Allison collected their forces for their greatest offensive of the match.

Before the sheer brilliance of their volleying attack, in which Allison was the master shot-maker, Lott and Stoefen were almost blown off the court in the seventh game and Van Ryn and Allison went after them savagely in the eighth. Stoefen's feared service was rammed back at him, the challengers tore up the court to volley like men possessed, and then Stoefen double-faulted and the champions had been broken through for the first time in the match.

There was no stopping Allison and Van Ryn now, and Van Ryn, who gave one of the finest exhibitions of his career after the first set, served in a manner to make the welkin ring and win the ninth game for the set.

Following the rest period, there was a comparative lull in the play with the resumption of competition in the fourth set. When Lott and Stoefen took liberties with Van Ryn's service in the second game and broke through for a 2–0 lead, it seemed that the former titleholders had shot their bolt.

Instead, they came right back to break through Stoefen as the latter was found wanting on his volleys and overhead smash, and then won the fourth on Allison's service, to make the score 2–all. It looked serious for the champions again now and, with Van Ryn threatening to put them into eclipse with his dazzling, aggressive hitting, Lott and Stoefen realized that the match was far from won yet.

The crucial point in the set came in the seventh game, with Stoefen serving. The champions fell behind at 0–30, pulled ahead to advantage and then lost the advantage.

In the next rally, with only a point needed to give them a vital break, Allison and Van Ryn broke up the formation of their opponents and had the court open on the right side for the coup de grace. But Allison, running in on the ball, played it too daringly for the line down the alley and just overreached the mark.

Reprieved by an inch, the champions salvaged the game on Allison's errors. Lott and Stoefen yielded the eighth to the Texan's service and went ahead to 5–4 as the Chicagoan won his game at love with a succession of volleys.

The end came with almost startling suddenness. With Van Ryn serving in the tenth, the score went to 30–all. Then he missed his low backhand volley in taking Stoefen's return of service, and in the succeeding rally Van Ryn found the net from the backhand to bring the play to a close an hour and a half after it started.

The victory marked Lott's fifth triumph in the national doubles. First he won the title with John Hennessey, then twice more with John Doeg and now he holds two legs with Stoefen on the massive challenge trophies, which have been in competition since 1919.

1935

THE TWO HELENS

by Al Laney

Queen Helen of Wimbledon saw defeat before the center court gallery today, looked it squarely and calmly in the eye and then came back to her throne in the finest and most courageous victory she has ever achieved since that faraway day when she first came swinging out of the West, pigtails flying, to herald the approach of the greatest woman tennis player of her time.

Mrs. Moody defeated Miss Helen Jacobs, 6–3, 3–6, 7–5, and became the Wimbledon champion for the seventh time, surpassing the record of Mlle. Suzanne Lenglen and equaling that of Mrs. Dorothea Lambert Chambers, but before she had done it the other Helen had been within one point of writing a new name on the championship roll. And when at last Mrs. Moody herself came to match point, thirty games had been played, and the two girls had been on the court nearly two hours.

No women's match in the longest memory at Wimbledon ever has been fought with such grimness or presented so many tense situations. It is not likely that Miss Jacobs ever played so well before or that she will ever come so close again and fail. She staked all on her unyielding defense against Mrs. Moody's unremitting attack and, although she defended wonderfully well for an hour and a half—so well, in fact, that she saw her greatest ambition about to be realized—her defenses finally crumbled under pressure of an attack that never let up from the first game to last.

From the point of view of excitement and tenseness that held 16,000 onlookers gripped in its spell, it was Wimbledon's greatest contest, and it definitely answered the question as to whether or not Mrs. Moody is as good as ever, the question Wimbledon wanted to answer in the affirmative but was afraid to before the abdicated queen had been crowned again.

Now it may be said without hesitation that Mrs. Moody is not the player she was, but it must be added that Mrs. Moody may look Miss Wills in the eye and smile unashamed. For if Mrs. Moody is not the player the tennis world knew as Miss Wills she still is the best woman player in the game, and, with Wimbledon behind her, it is not likely that she will be defeated again this year.

The two Helens walked into the arena, where the atmosphere already was beginning to get tense, exactly at 2 o'clock. Mrs. Moody, taller than her opponent and heavier, wore the familiar eyeshade, a dress that came to her knees, and a red coatee. Miss Jacobs, bare of head, wore a dark blue sweater to match the stripe in her shorts.

One thought of the long rivalry between these two leading women tennis players of the world and of their last dramatic meeting at Forest Hills, when Mrs. Moody retired at 0–3 in the third set. It was their first meeting since then. Only Miss Jacobs stood between Mrs. Moody and her ambition to stage a comeback and resume her position as the queen of the courts. Only Mrs. Moody stood between Miss Jacobs and the realization of the greatest ambition of her life—to be crowned champion at Wimbledon, an honor for which she had already fought three times in finals, only to fail.

So grim and determined did these two American girls from the same town 6,000 miles away (Berkeley, California) seem to be during the limbering up on an alien court before an alien crowd, that one felt that other things than tennis skill might decide the issue so important to both of them. It didn't seem that they were loosening up for a mere tennis match, for no game could be as grim as this one promised to be.

Imponderable and portentous factors had entered what should have been just a game of tennis between two pleasant and attractive girls. But Mrs. Moody has invested all matches in which she has participated this year with an electric thrill and this was picked up and communicated throughout the vast stands. Mrs. Moody toed the service line and every person in the stands sat forward. For the next hour and fifty minutes they were to get no relaxation from the tenseness that had gripped both players and spectators.

Receiving the first service, Miss Jacobs brought into play the chop stroke she has made her own and Mrs. Moody swung into the ball and hit for the corner. There was the story of the match given in the very first exchange. For thirty games to follow Mrs. Moody attacked and Miss Jacobs defended and each played her part superlatively well. Miss Jacobs defended as she has never done before and Mrs. Moody attacked and attacked, not as well as she has in the other years but well enough so that the finest defense she has ever met wasn't good enough to hold her. After nine games had been played she had the first set in hand and seemed beyond menace.

But Miss Jacobs, although her role was to defend, had an attacking service and she could come forward to stow the ball away when opportunity beckoned. And so Mrs. Moody, ever attacking, began to lose ground. The ball kept coming back to her with monotonous regularity, she was tempted into overhitting and Miss Jacobs had the second set by the same score. The match was squared once more. Through the second set Mrs. Moody stood in the middle of the baseline and hit, Miss Jacobs ran from corner to corner, covering miles of territory, but always throwing the ball back over the net and occasionally inserting a flat backhand drive that scored for her outright.

Toward the end of the set she began to show signs of fatigue. Crossing over, she sat for a moment on a rung of the umpire's chair and one wondered if she could last.

But Mrs. Moody didn't improve in the third set and Miss Jacobs, although tiring rapidly, was as steady as ever. Miss Jacobs, returning the ball softly to midcourt, prepared for a long rally each time the ball was put in play, ready to retrieve anything and wait for an error. Slowly she forged ahead and suddenly one realized that Mrs. Moody was in grave danger. She was playing as well as at any time during the match, but Miss Jacobs, with insidious chops, a fine service and a defense that refused to crack, was slowly drawing away from her.

Soon Mrs. Moody faced a deficit of 5–2 and Miss Jacobs needed only one more game for the match. She was never to get it, but during the tense few minutes in which the next few games were played none in the crowd believed that Mrs. Moody had a chance any longer. But she crept up to 3–5 by careful rather than forceful play, and now Miss Jacobs came as close as she could possibly come and lose.

Mrs. Moody faced match point against Miss Jacobs, an experience she had never known in any of their previous meetings. She faced it calmly, like a champion, far more calmly than the thousands who were looking on, and when she got safely past the crisis she took command of the match and went straight out, having won five games in a row. Miss Jacobs never came to match point again, and finally Mrs. Moody needed only one point to go out.

And when Miss Jacobs had hit out for the last point Mrs. Moody permitted herself the very un-Moodylike gesture of throwing her racket into the air and dashing to put an arm around Miss Jacobs' shoulder. She too was tired and could not have gone on much longer.

And Wimbledon welcomed back its queen with a burst of cheering not often equaled on this court. They had been generous to Miss Jacobs, too, and felt sorry for her now, but they were glad that Queen Helen was queen again.

MRS. MOODY'S SEVENTH WIMBLEDON TRIUMPH

by A. Wallis Myers

Wimbledon is over and its last day will live in lawn tennis history—a day when three of its finalists in successive matches were divided from a championship by only one stroke. . . . England has won three titles—the men's singles, the women's doubles and the mixed. The Dominions, through Australia, have taken another, making four for the Empire in the Jubilee Year. The fifth has gone for the ninth time to California.

By winning the women's singles championship for the seventh time, Mrs. F. S. Moody has equaled the record of Mrs. Lambert Chambers. But the ex-champion, who has now removed the "ex," reigning again after a year's retirement, has, in reality, a record more glittering than that of Mrs. Chambers.

Since she first became champion in 1927, Mrs. Moody has never tasted defeat at Wimbledon. Mrs. Chambers, as champion, was beaten three times—twice by another Californian, Miss Sutton, and once in the historic challenge round of 1919 by Mlle. Lenglen. Mrs. Chambers, great player though she was, only "played through" the championship four times and won. Mrs. Moody, coming to Wimbledon after the challenge round had been abolished, "played through" and triumphed on every occasion except the first—seven times out of eight.

How she saved herself from defeat on the eighth occasion, after her match against Miss Helen Jacobs seemed to be irretrievably lost, was witnessed by 16,000 spectators, almost as worn out mentally by excitement as the players themselves. The Chambers-Lenglen match of 1919, when the King and Queen were present at the old Wimbledon, was like the Moody-Jacobs duel only in that the loser, as on Saturday, was within a stroke of victory.

Then there was the international flavor, contrasting personalities, maturing against ripening talent. Then France through its girl champion was laying siege to a British stronghold; on Saturday the competitors, leaving the same base, had traveled 12,000 miles to play on a neutral court. Then the percentage of stroke error by both players was almost negligible; the net was rarely shaken by a mistimed drive. Then, although the day was hot and the tempo always tense, both champion and challenger used the standard strokes; they were driving in rhythm one against the other.

In Saturday's match Mrs. Moody was the copybook player, Miss Jacobs the one who defied convention. It was the plain drive against the chop—almost, one might say, style against stab. In the end, despite a challenge so well sustained and so enduringly pursued as to bring Miss Jacobs within sight and hearing of the victor's haven, the orthodox game and the purer strokes were vindicated.

Courage, as Stevenson has said, respects courage, and both these girls, inspired by the intensity of the other's, revealed more of it on Saturday than I have ever seen on a lawn tennis court. Yet valor, like the other virtues, has its limitations; it was the technique of Mrs. Moody which finally triumphed.

In fluent footwork Miss Jacobs was the superior of Mrs. Moody; without this supreme asset she never could have made those wonderful redemptions in the corner that startled both the crowd and her opponent. But Miss Jacobs, with all her great agility and her unbreakable heart, had not the "happiness of style" that belonged to her adversary.

Mrs. Moody's racket was "swung through" the ball rather than "swung" at it. There was always the smooth, even movement of the shoulders, initiated by a turn of the hips; the forcing forward of the forearm and the racket to meet the ball. In the smash she had not the decision of her opponent; she did not run as fast; but in the standard strokes of the game she was the mistress.

Because of its neatness and fluency, its anatomical security, Mrs. Moody's game was less exhausting and its value vindicated in the supreme crisis. When Miss Jacobs, throwing into the battle her last reserves of stamina, came to 5–2 and then to match ball in the final set—seeming almost certain to collect the prize which her crusade deserved—it was the easier and sounder rhythm of Mrs. Moody's strokes that, with less reaction in their train, saved the situation and turned defeat into victory.

To appreciate the "needle" character of Saturday's match it is necessary to grasp the close rivalry that has attended the careers of the two finalists. Before their struggle Mrs. Moody and Miss Jacobs had met eight times in two hemispheres. Always—and this fact tended to stiffen competition—they had played on courts away from their mutual home at San Francisco. Seven times, twice at Wimbledon, Miss Helen Wills or Mrs. Moody (the same person with the same calm insistence) had defeated Miss Jacobs without forfeiting a set; her superiority was acknowledged. Then, when Mrs. Moody did not defend her title of American champion at Forest Hills in 1932, Miss Jacobs assumed her mantle. It was a vicarious triumph, but the following year Mrs. Moody, wearing the Wimbledon crown, re-entered the lists. Here, Miss Jacobs thought, was her chance at last.

But the New York match of 1933 was not rounded off as both would have desired. When 3–love down in the final set, Mrs. Moody retired through physical incapacity. Miss Jacobs remained champion of America; not until two years later, until Saturday, was the test of their relative merits and their mutual quest for titles resumed.

ALLISON'S STUNNING VICTORY OVER PERRY

by Allison Danzig

A great champion lost his purple cloak of invincibility yesterday in the most staggering reversal witnessed at Forest Hills since William Tilden was toppled from his throne by Henri Cochet in 1926, and another champion, Miss Helen Jacobs, set a new record in American women's tennis.

With a capacity stadium crowd of 13,500 roaring spectators scarcely able to credit their eyes, Frederick Perry of Great Britain, monarch of amateur tennis and an almost prohibitive favorite to carry off our national title for the third successive year, went down before the machine-gun attack of Wilmer L. Allison Jr. of Austin, Texas, in the semi-final round, after falling heavily and injuring his right kidney in the opening set.

Beaten by Perry in five sets in last year's final and again in four sets last July in the Davis Cup challenge round, the 30-year-old American veteran turned in the masterpiece of his career. He electrified the great crowd with an exhibition of sustained speed and brilliancy such as has seldom been equaled in the championship.

Against the stark rapacity of Allison's assault, in which his lethal service, volleys, smashes, lobs and magnificent ground strokes all combined to lay down a withering barrage, the faltering Perry was seldom able to put his best foot forward and was hammered into submission in straight order.

Not even the satisfaction of a set was permitted the Briton. An hour and four minutes after Louis Shaw had called play from the umpire's chair the match was over at 7–5, 6–3, 6–3, and Allison had achieved his greatest triumph since he defeated Cochet at Wimbledon five years ago.

It was a triumph that assured an all-American final in the tournament for the first time since Ellsworth Vines and George Lott met for the title in 1931. Today the Texan will endeavor to carry an objective that he has stormed in vain over a span of ten years when he meets Sidney B. Wood Jr. in the concluding round.

The flaxen-haired New Yorker, who was Allison's unsuccessful rival for a singles berth on the Davis Cup team this year, gained his place in the final by defeating Bryan M. Grant Jr. of Atlanta, conqueror of Donald Budge, at his own soft ball game, 6–2, 4–6, 12–10, 6–2. . . .

For the first set of this championship final there were many whose only thoughts were of the disaster that had befallen Perry. The clubhouse of the West Side Tennis Club was besieged by officials and spectators curious to know the extent of the injury suffered by the British champion when he crashed at full length to the ground in the seventh game of the first set against Allison.

The mishap occurred in the first rally of that game as Perry rushed across his baseline in pursuit of a lightning forehand drive by the Texan straight down the champion's backhand line. Perry fell flat on his face and Allison came up the court in concern, but the British ace picked himself up and smilingly reassured his opponent that he was all right.

However, it soon became apparent that Perry was not entirely himself, even though he continued to tear around the court without sparing himself. He was putting his hand to his right side constantly and in the tenth game of this set he beckoned to P. Schuyler Van Bloem, vice chairman of the tournament committee, who came out on the stadium turf. Shortly after, other officials gathered in the exits under the stadium and a doctor was summoned.

Play continued without interruption and it was not until the match was over that Perry underwent an examination. Dr. Edward Knapp, assisted by Dr. Horace Ayers, examined him in the clubhouse and Dr. Knapp stated that he found a decided swelling on the front and back of his right kidney, which he diagnosed as evidence that the kidney had been displaced.

Perry was advised that, while the injury was not serious, he should abstain from any further play for a month. . . . It was reported that the British ace will undergo an X-ray examination today.

Debates were started and carried on spiritedly around the clubhouse as to whether Perry would have lost the match had he not suffered his injury. Without being unfair to Allison, it may be said unqualifiedly that Perry certainly did not play like the world beater whose racket had humbled all opposition at Wimbledon for the past two years in both the British championship and the Davis Cup matches and who had carried off the American and Australian crowns.

Perry, in the clubhouse, made light of his injury. Although dejected over his defeat, he gave full credit to Allison. "You can't win all the time," he said, "and I had it coming to me for a long time. The only trouble is that it came two days too soon."

Certainly few, if any, in the huge crowd looked for it to come in this match against a player whom he had consistently beaten. But Allison yesterday was an inspired player. Even had the defending champion not taken his bad spill the ultimate verdict, in the opinion of many, would have been unchanged.

The fact that Perry was desperately pressed to stay on even terms with the Texan up to the time of his mishap caused many to discount the effect of his injury. Allison had won his two first service games with a rush, had carried the champion to 10–8 in his first game and had broken through his second service game with two magnificent backhand passing shots to lead at 3–1.

Perry pulled up to 3–all as he got his ground strokes under control and the stage appeared to be set for a blazing duel when the defender met with his accident. As has been said, Perry continued to throw himself into the fray without reservations and stayed on even terms until he was broken through in the twelfth game.

Seldom in the memory of this observer have Allison's ground strokes stood up so invincibly as they did in this match. He fairly ate up Perry's speed, both from his forehand and backhand, and his counter-attack had his opponent scrambling almost frantically to close up the gaps in his court and was responsible for his losing his footing in the seventh game.

There was nothing but attack to Allison's game. Never for a moment did he resort to defensive measures or play safe. In perfect touch and a king for the day whose strokes could do no wrong, he went after the champion with almost berserk fury and it was beyond Perry's capacity to hold him in check.

Even when forced into a defensive position Allison continued to attack. Two of his most magnificent winning shots of the match were scored with Perry commanding the court. Both of them were lobs, which trapped the champion cold as he swept in to the net, and both of them came at game point.

The first one enabled Allison to break through Perry's service in the second game of the second set and the second was the instrument by which he effected a second break in the fourth game for a 4–0 lead.

Allison continued on to a 5–0 lead as Perry found the Texan's service an enigma, as he had been finding it continually through the match. Even the champion's most ardent adherents practically abandoned hope for him. Perry was no match for the other from the back of the court and his efforts to break up the American's net excursions failed through the lack of length on his lobs and the faulty range of his passing shots.

But at this desperate stage Perry rallied and Allison relaxed just a bit.

Game by game, Perry picked up on his opponent as the Texan's control faltered under the pressure of the other's attack. Three games in a row went to Perry with the loss of only two points.

When the Texan fell behind at 15–30 in the ninth game it looked serious indeed, but Allison rose to the occasion now in a fashion to bring tumultuous cheers from the crowd. A deep forehand volley brought him to 30–all, and also brought a gesture of protest from Perry toward the linesman on the baseline, for the champion thought the ball was out, and then the American delivered two scorching serves on Perry's backhand to win the game and the set.

The squelching of the champion's rally by these two services marked the climax of the match. If any doubt lingered as to the outcome, it was dissipated in the opening game of the final set as Perry double-faulted twice after being trapped by another lob.

After that Allison had only to hold his service, which he did with an exhibition of deadly volleying and serving that confounded the champion's most conscientious efforts to get back on even terms.

The match came to an end as Perry drove out of court on an attempted passing shot.

1 9 3 6

ALICE MARBLE ENDS HELEN JACOBS' REIGN;
PERRY SETS RECORD

by Allison Danzig

The four-year reign of Miss Helen Jacobs as national tennis champion was brought to an end by Miss Alice Marble at Forest Hills yesterday, and Frederick Perry of Great Britain averted defeat by two points against Donald Budge to set an all-time record in winning his third American crown.

With a crowd of 13,000 spectators cheering her on from the stadium of the West Side Tennis Club, the blond, beautifully proportioned girl from San Francisco and Palm Springs capped her comeback campaign following a two years' absence by defeating Miss Jacobs after it had appeared that the titleholder was the master of the court.

The score was 4–6, 6–3, 6–2, and Miss Marble's performance in the final set was one of the finest exhibitions of virtuosity and politic generalship the tournament has seen in years.

The wild excitement occasioned by the downfall of the defending champion, which balked Miss Jacobs in her effort to establish a new record of five consecutive victories in the championship, was a mere murmur, however, compared with the Niagara of the roar that was heard later in the afternoon as Budge threatened to lower the colors of the world's champion.

Leading by 5–3 in the fifth set of an almost interminable match that had been interrupted twice by rain and which was played for the most part in poor light with a highly keyed-up, moving crowd as the disturbing background to the flight of the ball, Budge tightened up at the critical juncture and blew his chance against a rampant Perry.

Once in the tenth game and again in the sixteenth, the red-haired youth from Oakland was only two points away from the greatest victory of his career, but on both occasions he was found wanting.

Two hours and forty-five minutes after Benjamin H. Dwight had got the match under way, Perry left the court the winner at 2–6, 6–2, 8–6, 1–6, 10–8, acclaimed as the first player from overseas in history to carry off our title three times.

It was a particularly sweet victory for the British champion, though for the greater part of the fourth set he appeared to be indifferent to the outcome, for it re-established him on the pinnacle in America after his defeat by Wilmer Allison last year, when he suffered a bad fall in the opening set.

For Budge, it was a heartbreaking experience after he had come so close to victory, but though beaten, the stalwart Californian with the murderous backhand proved definitely that he belongs among the great players of the world in his third season of championship competition.

Considering the conditions under which the match was played, he kept his concentration beautifully, far better than did Perry, who appeared to be distracted and annoyed by the wild enthusiasm of the crowd's devotion to his opponent's cause and so completely lost his touch and aggressiveness after his masterful performance in the third set as to leave the gallery mystified.

It was regrettable that rain should have intervened for the first time in the ten days of the championship to mar the prize match of the men's tournament. But in spite of the interruptions from the intermittent showers, which never discouraged the intrepid, enthusiastic crowd, some of the finest tennis Forest Hills has witnessed in years was on display.

The third set was a magnificent battle in which the rare excellence of Perry's ground strokes stood forth radiantly, and the final set brought forth some of the greatest shot-making of the season as the game but wilting Budge gave his last ounce of energy in the vain effort to stay the firm, skilled hand and masterful divination of the British champion.

So worked up was the gallery over the men's final that it almost forgot about the triumph of Miss Marble until Walter Merrill Hall, president of the United States Lawn Tennis Association, presented the championship trophies. But during the course of her ascension to the throne, the California girl could hardly have been more royally acclaimed.

Whether or not it was because the crowd, psychologically, is against the champion in sport, there was no mistaking that the great majority of the 13,000 spectators' sympathies were with Miss Marble. Considering the fact that Miss Jacobs was wearing a bandage on her injured thumb, which she was quick to disclaim as contributing to her defeat, one might have expected it to be otherwise.

On the other hand, there was the consideration that the challenger was making her return to the championship after overcoming an illness that at one time threatened to end her career on the courts. Two years ago Miss Marble was looked upon as the player of destiny in American women's tennis, born to wear the purple through the finest endowment of strokes and physical attributes of any player in the game.

Then, in the spring of 1934, as the third ranking player of the country, Miss Marble went abroad as a member of the Wightman Cup squad and during a match in Roland Garros Stadium in Paris against Mrs. Sylvia Henrotin she was stricken ill and collapsed.

That was the last seen or heard of the San Francisco girl in tennis until last year, when she took up her racket again on the Pacific Coast.

Under the coaching of Miss Eleanor Tennant of Palm Springs, a former first-ten ranking player, Miss Marble launched her comeback and made a radical alteration in her forehand, changing to the Eastern grip. Convinced that she was ready to return to championship play in the East after she had beaten Miss Carolin Babcock and other ranking players of California, she re-appeared in the East this summer.

The same masculine elements that had marked her game in 1933 were in evidence again, particularly the strength of her service and her command at the net. She won the Longwood Bowl tournament and the Seabright Bowl and then was beaten by Mrs. Henrotin at Rye in the Eastern championships. After that she went to the final at Essex and was beaten by Miss Jacobs in three sets.

When the national championship got under way there was conflicting opinion as to Miss Marble's chances.

As masterful as had been her game for the most part, at times she had played a very inferior grade of tennis.

At her best, it was admitted that the Palm Springs girl was the equal if not the superior of any of her rivals, but it was a moot question as to whether she had consolidated her game sufficiently to stand up against an opponent of the strength of Miss Jacobs. Her play at Forest Hills up to the final was not particularly outstanding, and after Miss Jacobs's thoroughly convincing performance in defeating Miss Katherine Stammers it was doubted whether Miss Marble could reverse the result of their meeting at Essex.

But Miss Marble saved her best tennis for the supreme day and was so much better than she had been in any other match of the season as to confound critical opinion. Miss Jacobs was not the same player she was against Miss Stammers, particularly in the final set, when her whole game collapsed feebly.

But Miss Jacobs's collapse was brought on by the pressure of a jolting, shifting attack that ran her unmercifully and exposed the inadequacy of either her chop or her topped forehand to stand against the flat, beautifully fluent drive of Miss Marble. It was not until Miss Marble appeared to be on the road to defeat that she played her finest tennis, after she had slumped and lost command of the first set and fallen behind at 0–2 in the second. The superiority of the challenger's weapons was established at the outset when she went ahead at 3–1. Miss Marble was hitting so deeply and serving so strongly that Miss Jacobs was desperately pressed to keep the ball in play. Neither her forehand chop nor backhand drive could withstand the pressure as she was kept running into the corners.

The crowd was unable to contain its delight over Miss Marble's play and she was squarely in command of the situation when, suddenly, her control deserted her and Miss Jacobs, fighting courageously, found the tide turning in her favor. Beginning with the sixth game, Miss Marble broke badly and the champion, getting everything back and lobbing effectively, took the set and went ahead at 2–0 in the second.

Miss Marble's chances of winning at this stage seemed slim indeed. But starting with the third game, she concentrated on Miss Jacobs's backhand, began to interpolate drop shots and from there on to the end of the match had the champion hopelessly on the defensive.

Miss Jacobs found it impossible to maintain position against her opponent's changes of length and direction. The pressure on her backhand was too much for her and she could not get to the drop shots which Miss Marble was bringing off.

Miss Marble was the master both with her ground strokes and with her volleys and smashes, which were bringing roars from the crowd. The champion sought to meet the issue at the net, but her overhead hitting was weak. She never knew where to expect the attack, was caught on the wrong foot repeatedly and her whole game broke down.

After the rest period, the play became even more one-sided, with Miss Marble giving an exhibition of targetry from the forehand that had the crowd cheering.

Miss Jacobs's chop was utterly inadequate, and she lost the first four games, winning only four points. Then Miss Jacobs, fighting valiantly, rallied. She pulled out the fifth game after Miss Marble had been within a point of a 5–0 lead, and then won the sixth on her service as her opponent's control wavered.

The crowd was now cheering on the champion for her game stand, and one wondered whether Mrs. Molla Mallory's rally of 1926, when she was down 0–4 in the third set to Miss Elizabeth Ryan, was to be repeated. But Miss Marble now lifted her game, broke down Miss Jacobs's backhand defense to win the seventh game at love and then broke through at 15 in the eighth as Miss Jacobs's control failed under pressure.

The Budge-Perry match started with the American at the peak of his game and setting so furious a pace as to keep the British champion on the defensive all the way. Budge's service was scorching in its speed and from both the forehand and backhand he was nailing the ball into the corners.

The cheers for the American's play subsided in the second set as Perry launched a counter-attack and put on pressure that took some of the starch out of his opponent's strokes. The British ace was serving the better of the two now and returning Budge's service regularly.

Budge's control broke under the pace and depth of Perry's drives and after the score had reached 2–all he dropped the next four games. There was a half-hour suspension after the seventh game, owing to the rain.

The third set was the best in the match in the high quality of the tennis on both sides. Budge's backhand and serve were off at the start and he fell behind at 1–3, but then he rallied and a magnificent battle developed.

Budge's backhand was now lashing the ball into Perry's backhand corner and opening the court for his drop volleys and cross-court punching volleys. So much better was his service that he won two games in succession at love.

Perry was hard pressed to stay on even terms, falling behind at 0–30 in the ninth, but then the champion hit into his best streak of the match. He was so irresistible from the back of the court that Budge found his own baseline untenable and was forced into volley errors when he came in. Perry won the thirteenth game at love with two service aces and broke through in the fourteenth at fifteen.

The champion looked like a champion indeed at this stage and when the players left the court for the rest period it seemed the match would end in the fourth set. Perry came out strong for the first game of the fourth chapter, but after leading at 40–30 and losing the game with a double fault, he suddenly slowed down perceptibly and lost his dash and aggressiveness.

Rain came up again and also the wind and the British ace slumped badly. At times he seemed to be totally unconcerned about his mounting errors or the outcome of the match, playing carelessly and making no effort to get to the net.

Budge, attacking impetuously and letting nothing disturb his concentration, staged a procession as Perry double-faulted four times and hit ball after ball into the net, particularly from his backhand. Then came the final set, which saw the gallery stage its noisiest demonstrations of the day.

Perry continued to remain in his back court and could do no better than stay on even terms, with Budge hitting so fiercely from both the forehand and backhand and serving so well.

Then the American broke through in the sixth game with a deadly smash and a backhand passing shot, and the stadium was in an uproar.

The cheers changed to groans when Budge slumped and lost his service in the seventh and then back to cheers as he broke through again in the eighth on Perry's errors.

It looked like Budge's match as he set himself to serve, with the score 5–3 in his favor, but the Californian broke under the strain, played badly and lost the game with a double fault. In the next game he pulled up from 15–40 to deuce, two points removed from victory, but then he tightened and gave Perry a set-up at the net and then hit out of court.

The battle fluctuated from there on until Budge was two points away from winning again in the sixteenth. Then Perry, serving irresistibly and going to the net for a smash, pulled out of the hole, and that was the end of Budge's hopes.

Weary from his constant running to the net and into the corners for Perry's fastidiously correct drives, the game American was at Perry's mercy and the aroused British champion showed none. Four beautiful drives from Perry's racket, two of them passing shots, cost the groggy Budge his service game and the champion ended the match with a service ace in the eighteenth.

1 9 3 7

RECORD CROWD SEES PERRY DEFEAT VINES

by Allison Danzig

Before a crowd of 17,630, the largest ever to witness a tennis match anywhere, Fred Perry of Great Britain signalized his entry into the professional ranks with a stunning victory over Ellsworth Vines of Pasadena, California, the world's professional champion, last night at Madison Square Garden.

Scarcely given an outside chance of winning in the almost unanimous consensus, the stalwart black-haired ruler of the world's amateur ranks for the past three years confounded the experts by defeating the hardest hitter of the courts, 7–5, 3–6, 6–3, 6–4. Superior physical condition, which has been so important a factor in Perry's subjugation of his amateur rivals, weighed heavily in the Briton's favor, more than to offset Vines' theoretical advantage in his greater familiarity with the conditions of indoor play.

Vines, the secret victim of an attack of influenza which kept him confined to his room at the Hotel Madison on Tuesday with a temperature of 102 and a sore throat, was a drooping figure in the final set, and only sporadically was his racket the terrorizing implement that has enabled him to rule supreme among the professionals for three years. Such was his distress that he was unable to appear for the doubles later in the evening and it was learned in the dressing room that he was running a fever of 101½ when he went on the court.

This is said without any intent of minimizing the achievement of Perry, who was acclaimed tumultuously for a victory so few expected and who himself was below par physically. The British champion, too, was suffering from a sore throat and a mild attack of the flu and in the afternoon, preparatory to leaving the Madison for a practice session at the Garden, he and Vines were joshing each other on their illnesses.

Vines, apparently, was the more grievously stricken of the two. At any rate, he looked much the weaker on the court, though it may have been that he was feeling the effects of his long tour of the Orient, and Perry was once more reaping the reward of his magnificent physical condition the year round and more careful conservation of his energies.

The record tennis gathering of all time that witnessed the downfall of Vines paid the unprecedented total of $58,119.50 at the gate, eclipsing the mark for the Tilden-Vines match of 1934 by more than $27,000. Another record was set in this long-awaited match between world's champions in the top price of $9.90 asked for tickets. The figure exceeded the previous high by $2.20, and no fewer than 1,208 spectators paid that price. Not only was every seat filled in the Garden, but hundreds were standing, and outside the police were turning away all who approached without tickets.

It was an unusually brilliant gathering that welcomed the black-haired son of John Bull in his premiere as a professional. It was the sort of crowd that turns out for an opening night at the theater or the opera. Fashionable society was out in large numbers to fill the boxes, and Broadway and Hollywood were strongly represented. It was the kind of setting that Perry, the movie actor, reveled in, no less than did the greatest trouper of them all, William Tilden, who was to have been Vines' doubles partner against Perry and George M. Lott Jr. of Chicago and Boston. Bruce Barnes of Austin, Texas, substituted for Vines. . . .

Francis T. Hunter and S. Howard Voshell, the promoters, could hardly have hoped for so great a success in their initial undertaking as was their reward last night for the months of effort put in by them and Bill O'Brien. . . . It was to be regretted that the most talked-of match of recent years did not come up to the crowd and the setting. Vines, for reasons mentioned, could not have been expected to show at his best, though no one knew until yesterday of his affliction, and Perry, playing under strange conditions and in less than perfect health, was also hardly prepared to show in his true colors.

As it turned out, the British pride played like the champion and Vines had one of those bad days such as overtook him when an amateur. It was one of those times when Vines could not control his wrathful speed and was lost in an unescapable morass of errors. The stroke analysis tells the story. Vines made almost twice as many earned points as did Perry, but he more than offset this advantage of 17 points by his excess of 29 errors.

The Californian's mistakes were the result in large part of his physical condition, but it would be unfair to Perry not to recognize that they were induced by the intelligence and design of the Briton. Perry concentrated throughout on Vines' backhand and it was the vulnerability of the American there that hastened his downfall. Once the weakness was exposed, Perry attacked it incessantly, and in the fourth set Vines' backhand crumpled completely.

The victor played a beautiful match in which attack and defense were skillfully blended. He could stay back and trade drives with Vines in magnificent rallies, waiting for the error or the winning opening, or he could go to the net and put away his volley with all the dispatch of Vines.

Perry's handling of Vines' service, too, was a vital factor. There were times when no one in the world could have returned it, but for the most part Perry solved it splendidly. He not only got the ball in play but scored outright winners with deftly shaded passing shots straight down or across court from the backhand. These returns of service had Vines shaking his head in discouragement, and Perry's own service added to Vines' discomfiture. . . .

In the doubles that followed, Tilden received a tremendous ovation when he walked on the court and another when he and Barnes left with a 6–3, 6–2 victory over Perry and Lott.

BUDGE–VON CRAMM DAVIS CUP MATCH

by Al Laney

Baron Gottfried von Cramm never won a singles title at Wimbledon or Forest Hills. The only major title the German baron ever did win was the French. He was unfortunate that the best years of both Perry and Budge overlapped his own, else he might well have been world champion more than once. Almost certainly he would have been. This titled aristocrat with a most beautiful game could beat the young Budge while Perry was champion, but by the time Perry had joined the professionals, Budge had advanced just enough to have a very slim edge over Cramm, as witness their five-set final at Forest Hills in 1937 and their memorable Davis Cup meeting that same year.

The latter match has been called the greatest ever played. Walter Pate, the American team captain, has insisted upon it so often since that many people who did not see it have accepted his judgment, because he is a man loved for his person and respected for his tennis knowledge. I think I was, on the whole, a more objective observer than Walter, and while I can almost agree with him, I cannot quite. I do not deny that he could be right, and I too have love and respect for him and am forever grateful for his kindness and help during these weeks of 1937. But there have been so many "great" matches. I have not seen them all, nor has Walter, but I have seen so many fine ones it is no more possible for me to rate them than to rate players. . . .

The day before the inter-zone final matches between the United States and Germany were to start on the Wimbledon center court, Pate called a press conference and, to the surprise of all those gathered, announced that Bryan Grant, the Atlanta player known to all as Bitsy, had been chosen to play singles with Budge. I knew Walter's tennis judgment to be quite sound and I could not understand this choice. Besides Budge, the team members were Gene Mako, his doubles partner, Frank Parker, Wayne Sabin and Grant. Whereas Grant had done nothing spectacular at the Wimbledon just ended, Parker had beaten Henner Henkel, the German number-two player behind Cramm, and had lost a close semi-final to Budge himself.

I suspected that the choice was not Pate's, but had been dictated in higher U.S.L.T.A. circles in New York. The tennis fathers had been for some time under a good deal of pressure to play Grant, a very popular little man. Southerners, and especially Atlantans, had charged discrimination, pointing out that Grant had beaten nearly everybody ranked above him at one time or another. This was true enough, for Grant was a great little competitor who could always be counted on to beat any man who played badly, although his own game appeared innocuous enough to those who did not note the absolute soundness of his method. The trouble now, though, was that on these big occasions men playing for their country seldom play poorly. . . .

I did not think it the correct selection, but I do know that all who saw the series can be grateful for the error. Had Parker been chosen he might well have beaten Henkel and there would have been no critical Budge-Cramm match on the third day to be writing about and telling about down through the years. On the first day, a Saturday, Cramm beat Grant, 6–3, 6–4, 6–2, and Budge beat Henkel, 6–2, 6–1, 6–3. Then Budge and Mako repeated their Wimbledon victory over Cramm and Henkel in the doubles on Monday, 4–6, 7–5, 8–6, 6–4.

So everything was going according to play, but in the first singles match on Tuesday Grant never had a chance against Henkel. The German won, 7–5, 6–2, 3–6, 6–4, beating Grant in the way Grant could be beaten, by superior force continually applied from close quarters. Henkel was not a top-class player by any means, but he could hit hard and volley decisively. . . . With the score now tied at two matches each, I looked forward to the deciding match between Budge and Cramm with confidence of an American victory, which surely would mean capture of the cup in the challenge round a week later. Perry had become a professional, and it was felt that Great Britain could no longer successfully defend against either the United States or Germany without him.

I never was so mistaken about how a tennis match would go. There was a surprisingly large crowd in the center court stands, and the big-match atmosphere of expectancy was there. It was as if the public had sensed what was to come where the experts had missed it. Cramm, who had been a great favorite in England for years, now was carrying British hopes. British crowds are loyal to their champions even when, like Budge, they are foreigners, but they also reckoned that they would have a much better chance of retaining the cup another year if the Germans should be the challengers. Budge won this match, but before he got through he had lost the first two sets, stood 1–4 down in the fifth, and Cramm had saved three match points before yielding in the fourteenth game. The final scores were 6–8, 5–7, 6–4, 6–2, 8–6. . . .

I prepared some notes on the styles of the players. . . . I still have these notes: "Cramm has a game of clean, wide drives and an offensive service that is mechanically perfect. What he lacks is a certain subtlety, an ability to break up the other fellow's game. This is more than a matter of strokes. Though he strikes the ball very quickly Cramm must have his feet planted and must address the ball, whereas a player such as Budge or Perry can perform miracles on the run. Yet Cramm can hit fine winners against Budge, and few players ever had a stroke to compare with his 'flat' backhand, with which he occasionally blinds the gallery.

"Whereas Cramm is all elegance, Budge presents an angular figure. It is strange that so great a player with so fine a game is yet so little graceful compared with the other great ones. But then Budge too is an individual, as Tilden was. When in form Budge presents no weakness. His forehand, though not a pretty shot, does not falter; his backhand is the world's best, and only Borotra, with his powerful punch down on the ball, has matched that acute-angled backhand return in recent years."

I had written these notes while watching the end of the Henkel-Grant match from the press box . . . People were saying how nice it was that the final match had now become a real one and not a perfunctory affair. It deserved to have significance, for it was a match between the Wimbledon champion, now rated the world's number one, and the finest player of Europe, the handsome owner of the most elegant game of all, whose misfortune had been to be born about the same time as Fred Perry, even as Little Bill Johnston had been a contemporary of Tilden. Now they were meeting to decide which country should advance to the challenge round against Great Britain. Since either was likely to defeat Britain, this one match would probably decide the fate of the cup. A great occasion, and they both rose to it, producing a wonderful match for tennis history. The play was absorbing from the start. . . .

Budge lost the first set and they were well into the second. Both were playing tennis of such a high quality that we could hardly think it would continue. But it did, and that is the principal reason people call this match the "greatest"—that the two finest amateurs in the world should play so superlatively well at the same time, during the same exchanges, over so prolonged a period.

Toward the end of the second set the crowd passed from enthusiasm to something near hysteria. Women would shriek now and then, men would yell, cheer and groan. . . . Cramm won the set . . . and they took plenty of time toweling themselves at the umpire's chair. I could just see across the Royal Box to the contestants' stand, and there sat Henkel in the front row, his very wide mouth wide open in an admiring grin when he caught Cramm's eye as the Baron came toward his end just beneath to receive service.

For two sets now Budge's wonderful backhand had been matched by the German's, and Cramm's forehand had been better at nearly every crisis where it had been put to the test. With these weapons Cramm brought off some of the most daring coups I have ever seen on a tennis court, and when the third set began the Davis Cup campaign on which the little band of players had set out so hopefully early in the summer was in the gravest danger of failure one step before success. At every one of the recurring crises of the first two sets Cramm had been a little more incisive, a little steadier, and a little more certain in his choice of stroke to meet the particular situation. He had never, I think, played as well as this and probably never would again. The German seemed poised for an even greater effort in the third set, trying to avoid the longer journey, knowing his chances probably would decrease as the match advanced.

The capture of the third set was, of course, a must for Budge. Cramm could lose it and still win the match, and he played scarcely less well than he had in winning the first two. It was a very close thing. One service break decided it. Don did not dominate, and the way things went he might easily have lost it. But he served out in the tenth game and there was great relief when they left the court for the rest period, which is the custom in Davis Cup play but is never allowed in the Wimbledon championships. . . .

Budge won the fourth set with what I felt was deceptive ease. The German was reacting from the strenuous efforts earlier and, I thought, saving his strength for the vital fifth set, to which he appeared to be looking all through the fourth. Budge served well, hit deeply, and Cramm decided to let the set go after falling behind. This was the only period during the long match when the issue was not really joined and the play of either man dropped from the earlier standard.

The fifth set began quietly with both serving well enough to win without strain. When Budge began service in the fourth game, 2–all seemed altogether likely and one of those long service-governed sets seemed in prospect. There had been no indication of what was to follow. Budge lost the first point with a weak forehand that led to a missed volley and the second with an even weaker forehand that Cramm hit for a winner. Love–30! And then the break.

Cramm was ahead 3–1 with Cramm's service to come. A love game followed and now it was 4–1. Budge's forehand had unaccountably reverted to the old method, and it had let him down. Now he must win Cramm's service twice and never lose his own again, else all hope of winning the Davis Cup this year would be gone. The situation was desperate, almost hopeless. But man's spirit is a worker of miracles. We reserve our greatest admiration for the man who, pushed into a corner from which there seems no escape, escapes death and achieves glory. Never was a tennis player in a tighter corner on so important an occasion as Budge at this stage, for Cramm was again playing magnificently.

It was at this moment as they changed courts that Budge is supposed to have reassured his worried captain, sitting at courtside, with words that have become part of tennis legend. "Don't worry, Cap, I'll make it." That's what we were told afterwards he said to Pate, with a little pat on the shoulder. I suppose he did say it, or something like it. Both Pate and Budge were so honest I refrained asking if it really was this way or thought up afterward, for fear of destroying a good story, and if this be one of those legends that grow after the event, Budge surely did give it credence. Don played a champion's game now. At this critical moment, when even one mistake might bring defeat, his aim was sure, his nerve steady, and he was at his wonderful best.

The faulty forehand became a champion's shot again. Budge won his service at love for 2–4, and, attacking with the same sort of boldness that had won the first two sets for Cramm, he captured the German's service also without the loss of a point. Two love games, eight straight points, against an opponent who had been outplaying him and who was still playing wonderfully well with victory in sight. I think we must count this one of the finest moments the game has known and I have never seen a champion in any sport do a better thing at so critical a moment.

When Budge served himself back even at 4–all, we felt that the tide, running overwhelmingly against him, had turned his way almost at the last possible moment. Cramm had not given up his advantage easily at all. The battle for Budge's service, coming after the two games in which the German had not won a point, was fierce and prolonged. Cramm had twice been within a point of winning it to lead 5–3, so that he would need only to hold service once for victory. At the first of these points the German hit a ball that seemed sure to be decisive. It was hit to the deep forehand. But here Budge pulled out the first of a series of forehand shots that were to take him safely out a little later after a series of exciting adventures. He scored with a ball hit with great speed straight down the enemy's backhand line.

Now at 4–all began the real battle for the match and the cup. The battle had run for more than two hours, and I think they are correct who call it great during the final stages. I doubt that any two other players ever performed so brilliantly after being in court so long in such a tense and critical situation with so much at stake. Playing for one's country is not the same as playing for an individual title. It carries a much heavier burden of responsibility and we were not to know until afterward what this match really meant to Cramm, on whom the pressure to produce a Nazi triumph was enormous. We may imagine what it would have meant to the Third Reich at this moment of 1937, with its philosophy of the Master Race, to have the Davis Cup, the famous emblem of world superiority, on display in Berlin. We ought to keep this in mind when we remember this match and how Cramm played it.

There came now two long deuced games in which winners were hit off balls that themselves appeared to be certain winners. Almost nothing was given away on either side. Cramm served and led 5–4, the last point a service ace. Only one game to win and Germany would be in the challenge round. Budge pulled back to 5–all. Cramm, serving as magnificently as at any time in the match, went to 6–5 with another love game, and was again within one game of victory. Once more Budge faced the crisis calmly. Neither did he lose a point in coming back to 6–all.

Even more calmly Budge brought off winners when Cramm, forcing still to the formerly shaky forehand, came to the net after preparing the way with that long, hard spinning shot dead into the corner of the court. Budge hit again straight down the line a ball at which Cramm lunged futilely as it passed him. The man with the world's finest backhand was now winning with shots as fine from the weaker forehand under extreme pressure. Cramm forced again to this sector and again was beaten, and Budge, sensing the moment, hit everything with all the force he had left. The German was serving as well as ever, it seemed, but Budge now brought his own game to its highest peak and Cramm could win only one point in this thirteenth game. For the first time since play began hours earlier, Budge was ahead, 7–6 in the fifth set. Now the time had come. The occasion had arrived for Budge, his team, and his country.

But the great effort to take Cramm's service, and finally to take the lead, had cost Budge. Fatigue also had arrived, slipping in unnoticed as tension continued over so long a period. Both men moved quite slowly to their places for the fourteenth game after pausing overly long at the chair. Budge took up the balls to serve, seemed about to do so, and then relaxed before striking the first ball.

There were to be no service aces this time. Instead we had a long, anxious, and excruciatingly tense game of tennis. The score went six times to deuce, and three times Budge was within a single point of victory. Each time Cramm played perfectly. The German would not yield. It seemed Budge could not get that final point and twice Cramm himself was within a point of winning the game, one point away from 7–all and a chance to fight on. A little unlucky too, it seemed, not to win one of those points.

And then, finally, after the sixth deuced point Budge won the advantage and stood for the fourth time one point away from victory. Three times Cramm had saved match point and seemed certain to save a fourth when Budge served weakly this time, giving the German a chance to step in and pound the ball to the forehand corner once more. Since Don could not come across court off such a ball, Cramm dashed in and crowded the other side. And Budge hit now the finest shot of the match, a truly gorgeous forehand as straight as could be down the line, swift, low, and certain. I can see the picture yet. The bending of the knees for the crouch—with Budge it was an ungainly squat—the lifting of the low spinning ball, with all the weight going into the swing as the knees straightened and locked. Cramm lunged to his left, hiding the ball from me as it flew on its way to pitch just beyond the service court, where a little puff of white marked the spot as it fell. He rose quickly and, without looking back, came around the net to congratulate Budge. No need to look back. He knew and we all knew the moment the ball was struck that it was a winner, and the wonderful match was over.

It is difficult to say here which of these men played the better, for they were about as level as two players can be in the scoring and in resolution and fortitude. Cramm showed that great flat forehand down the line and across court at its best. It was superior to Budge's version both in pace and execution. The backhands were about equal, and both could attack from this wing as few have been able to do. On the volley there was little, nothing really, to choose, for they both brought off many difficult shots brilliantly under pressure. Budge had a slight edge in service, although he did not serve actually at his very best. We took Budge's victory to be expected beforehand, and we could have only admiration in addition to surprise at Cramm's resistance. When shall we see another such wonderful tennis fight? I think we have not seen one since. . . .

The challenge round of 1937, played a week after, was an anticlimax. Parker, replacing Grant, defeated Charles Hare, 6–2, 6–4, 6–2, but lost to Austin, 6–3, 6–2, 7–5. Budge beat both with the loss of one set and, with the victory of Budge and Mako in the doubles over C. R. D. Tuckey and Frank Wilde, 6–3, 7–5, 7–9, 12–10, the United States won the series, 4–1, and brought the cup back home ten years after the French had taken it across the ocean in 1927.

BUDGE BEATS VON CRAMM FOR U.S. CHAMPIONSHIP

by Allison Danzig

The greatest record of conquest compiled by an American tennis player since the heyday of William Tilden was consummated yesterday as Donald Budge defeated Baron Gottfried von Cramm of Germany to come into his rightful heritage of the national championship.

Before a capacity gathering of 14,000 spectators, filling the Forest Hills Stadium for the second successive day and thereby establishing a new mark, the giant red-headed Californian scored his third consecutive victory of the season over his renowned rival from overseas, 6–1, 7–9, 6–1, 3–6, 6–1.

As Budge's backhand volley brought the two-hour struggle to a close a thunderous cheer went up from the great throng in acclaim of the player who brought back the Davis Cup almost singlehanded, who won the Wimbledon singles, doubles and mixed doubles and who now has claimed the diadem which escaped him by two points in last year's final with Frederick Perry of Great Britain.

In majestic isolation, Budge stands alone and pre-eminent in world amateur tennis, a great champion who can look back upon a long and arduous campaign filled with cruel responsibility and unmarked by a single instance of defeat on turf. The ablest players of Japan, Australia, Germany, England, France and of his own country had all in turn gone up against the lightning of his unrivaled backhand and the thunder of his service and overhead smash, and none of them, not even so magnificently armed and physically equipped a challenger as von Cramm, could stay the hand of the new California comet out of Oakland.

The elevation of Budge followed the crowning of a new champion in the women's singles. Señorita Anita Lizana of Chile, a country previously unheard from in championship American tennis, performed a feat that no other foreign player has accomplished in twenty-two years when she carried off the title in her first quest for it, as Miss Molla Bjurstedt, now Mrs. Mallory, did in 1915. . . .

In the first all-foreign final on record, the graceful, nimble-footed little champion from South America fairly captivated the gallery with her combination of speed, power, artistry and rhythmic motion as she quelled the hard-hitting onslaught of Mlle. Jadwiga Jedrzejowska of Poland with her baffling drop shots and marvelous top-spin backhand to win at 6–4, 6–2.

Considering that this was Señorita Lizana's first singles tournament in this country and that she had only a few days of preparation in the doubles at Longwood, her triumph stands out all the more vividly. In the entire tournament she did not lose a set, nor was she so much as carried to a deuce set. . . .

So came to an end the biggest season of tennis known in this country since the Davis Cup was carried away by France in 1927. . . . Only twice before has the stadium of the West Side Tennis Club been filled to capacity —once in 1927 when Tilden played René Lacoste and again in 1932 when Ellsworth Vines met Henri Cochet. On two successive days of the 1937 championship the box offices had to be closed down, with every seat disposed of.

Yesterday not a window was so much as opened except for reservations already purchased and the sale of 2,200 general admission tickets. Undoubtedly from five to ten thousand more could have been sold had there been accommodations. . . . Scalpers were offering as high as $8 for a ticket marked at $2.75.

All of this prosperity and revival of interest in tennis goes back to one player—Budge. The presence of von Cramm was a great magnet, and the blond German sportsman held the center of the stage almost every day, but it was the feats of Budge, against von Cramm and others, and particularly his winning back the Davis Cup after an absence of ten years, that started the revival. Like Maurice McLoughlin, the original California Comet, and Tilden, the Oakland giant captured the imagination and fancy of the public with the blasting power of his racket, and the turnstiles clicked as they had not in a decade.

For ten days Budge had been in semi-eclipse in the championship. He was winning his matches by such one-sided scores in coming down to the final that the spotlight was diverted to von Cramm, who was in difficulties in every match after his opening engagement. Yesterday belonged to Budge, or at least to Budge and von Cramm. This was the day the American public had been awaiting ever since their thrilling and deciding meeting in the interzone round of the Davis Cup play. It was the tennis "natural" of the year—the first singles clash on American turf between the two foremost amateurs of the world.

In all probability, the match failed to come up to the expectations of those who had thrilled to the accounts and broadcast of the great battle at Wimbledon. Von Cramm has not been quite the same player in America who led Budge by 4–1 in the fifth set abroad. The difficulty he had experienced in subduing opponents who were scarcely calculated to rate in the same class with him was evidence of that. But the fact that he had been able to lift his game each successive day to meet the requirements of the challenge gave substance to the hope that he might rise to the occasion when he found himself confronted by his rival of rivals.

In overcoming Bryan Grant's lead of two sets to one in the quarter-finals the German had given the gallery an inkling of the true capacity of his powers, and particularly in the fifth set of his semi-final with Robert Riggs, who led him two sets to none, had he revealed the sustained continuity of his flashing attack that had been so lacking all week.

But once again in the final von Cramm found it impossible to keep his game at the top level. The rapacity of Budge's attack, of course, was responsible in part for his shortcomings, but it was not the Baron's mistakes under pressure that caused his admirers distress. It was his deplorable errors on so many strokes that presented no difficulties that gave them anguish. Nevertheless, in spite of the unevenness of the play, the Baron made a fight of it that kept the crowd in suspense almost to the end and that was marked by shot-making of a character seldom seen more than once during the course of a season. When both men were going at full speed, tennis of the sheerest brilliance was on view and the applause at times was almost deafening.

Von Cramm was never able to get his hand and eye in, in the opening set. His return of Budge's high-kicking service was faulty, his backhand volley was going astray and his running forehand refused to function. Budge, hitting the full length of the court and keeping his opponent on the run, was clearly in command. Von Cramm was starting no better than he had against Riggs.

But with the second set the match took on a different aspect after Budge had won the opening game at love. Von Cramm settled into his game and now it was Budge who was doing the running, with his backhand under such pressure that he could not get the ball up to the net. Attacking mercilessly from both sides, taking the net both on his service and return of service and killing the ball from any position in the court, von Cramm had the stands roaring in admiration of his flashing play as he went to 3–1 and 40–0. Budge was helpless to get off the defensive.

At this point von Cramm fell into one of his inexplicable slumps and lost the next five points on errors and then the next two games also, to make the score 4–3 against him. The gallery was visualizing a three-set match now, but the Baron braced, found his touch and timing again and proceeded to play like a master. Budge met the attack superbly and for the remainder of the set the two great rivals kept the stadium in an uproar with the fury and brilliance of their efforts.

Von Cramm pulled out the twelfth game from 0–30, in spite of Budge's beautiful lobs, and averted the loss of the set by a point in the fourteenth, in which he volleyed and smashed magnificently to earn all five of his points. The deciding break was effected in the next game after a net-cord shot on his return of service had enabled von Cramm to draw level at deuce, and the German ace, serving irresistibly and smashing for the sideline, won the set. An idea of the brilliance of von Cramm's attack can be gathered from the stroke analysis, which shows that he earned 23 points to Budge's 11.

Budge's admirers were beginning to feel worried now. If von Cramm could sustain this form and keep putting on the pressure with his running forehand to close in for his finishing volleys and smashes, it was hard to see how he could lose. But with the start of the third set the Baron faded out of the picture. Budge, aroused by the loss of the second set, let loose an attack that found every weapon functioning at its best. Von Cramm had little to offer in resistance, piling up errors while the Californian held his own to almost the irreducible minimum for the set.

When the players left the court for the intermission the question in everyone's mind was whether von Cramm would come back to lift his game to its greatest heights as he had done against Grant and Riggs. His answer to the question soon raised disturbing doubts as to whether Budge had enough left in reserve to win. After a rather quiet start, the fourth set developed into a roaring battle in which von Cramm's magnificent straight backhand passing shots did such heavy execution as to set the stands wild. Von Cramm had caught on fire again and the American was fighting with his back to the wall.

To 3–all Budge managed to stay on even terms and then there was no stopping von Cramm. Budge became shaky overhead, where he had been hitting murderously. His return of service, particularly in taking the Baron's kicking ball high on the backhand, weakened and when he found his back court untenable his dashes to the net came to grief time after time as von Cramm whipped home his backhand straight down the line.

Again a net-cord intervened to contribute to Budge's loss of his service on the final point of the eighth game, and as the final set came up it looked like either's match, with the burden of the proof on Budge. But, indomitable fighter that he is, as he showed in coming back from 1–4 in the fifth set of their previous meeting, Budge met the challenge by letting loose with the full force of his battering attack. Von Cramm threatened up until the third game, but after Budge had pulled that one out with one of the greatest volleys of the day, a smoking backhand shot almost from the baseline, the battle was over.

Von Cramm, fighting with unwavering courage, gave himself unsparingly in the effort to stem the onslaught, but his control broke badly and he was rushed off his feet to defeat. Budge took the last five games of the set with the loss of only seven points as his opponent piled up 19 errors to 5, and the match of the year in the United States was over.

Budge stood the champion of his country, after having established himself as the champion of the world, and two genuine sportsmen and friendly rivals paid their respects to each other at the net as Umpire Benjamin H. Dwight congratulated them on their stirring exhibition.

1938

BUDGE'S GRAND SLAM

by Allison Danzig

The book was closed yesterday on the greatest record of success ever compiled by a lawn tennis player in one season of national and international championship competition.

J. Donald Budge of Oakland, California, stood as the first player in history to win all four of the world's major tennis titles in the same year when he defeated Gene Mako of Los Angeles in the Forest Hills Stadium in the final round of the national championship. The score was 6–3, 6–8, 6–2, 6–1.

The triumph of the 23-year-old red-headed giant, which followed upon the overwhelming victory of Miss Alice Marble of Beverly Hills, California, over Miss Nancye Wynne of Australia at 6–0, 6–3, in the shortest women's final on record, completed a campaign of unparalleled achievement on three continents.

No one before him has held at one and the same time the American, British, French and Australian crowns, all of which have fallen in 1938 to the rapacity of Budge's fifteen-ounce racket for a grand slam that invites comparison with the accomplishment of Bobby Jones in golf.

In this respect, at least, Budge takes precedence over William Tilden, the Frenchmen, Henri Cochet and René Lacoste, Ellsworth Vines, Wilmer Allison, Fred Perry, the Briton, and all the other great modern champions. Jack Crawford of Australia came closest to winning four major crowns when, in 1933, he won three of the titles and led Perry, two sets to one, in the American final.

To complete Budge's record of conquest for the year: He led the United States to victory in the defense of the Davis Cup against Australia at Germantown. He won the British and American doubles and mixed doubles and gained permanent possession of the mammoth Newport Casino Challenge Cup.

He leaves Forest Hills behind him, possibly for the last time, and heads for the Pacific Southwest championships at Los Angeles with the satisfaction of having won every singles match of consequence in which he started and of establishing a mark that promises to stand for many years. Here, truly, is one of the great competitors of sport and one of the most genuine sportsmen to grace the game.

A gallery of 12,000 looked on under a stinging sun as Budge made history. That the stadium was not filled to capacity was probably attributable to the conviction that the outcome of his meeting with his doubles partner was foreordained. Despite the amazingly fine tennis Mako had produced to concoct the defeat of John Bromwich in the semi-finals, few, if any, conceded the stalwart blond Los Angeles youth the slightest chance of staying the all-conquering march of the Oakland terror.

But if any had the notion that this was to be a Damon and Pythias act, they were speedily disillusioned. True, the play was animated by friendly manifestations across the net whose contagion was communicated to the gallery, particularly in the third set, when the crowd was roaring with mirth as the doubles champions trapped each other repeatedly with drop shots.

But there was no holding back on either side and there was no trace of amiability in the scorching forehand drives with which Mako caught Budge in faulty position inside the baseline or the murderous backhand and volcanic service which Budge turned loose.

If Mako had the satisfaction of being the only player in the tournament to wrest a set from the champion, it was not because Budge willed it that way. The circumstances under which it was won might have given rise to skepticism as to the validity of the achievement, for it was salvaged from a 2–5 deficit after Mako had slumped badly in the face of Budge's pitilessly raking bombardment.

Possibly at this point Budge, in the security of his commanding lead, may have relented and elected to relax the pressure of his cannonading on his helpless opponent, but if he proposed to go further than yield a game or two, his subsequent distress as his strokes got out of hand was a first class bit of acting, and he never pretended to thespian honors.

It would be considerably less than justice not to accord Mako that full measure of praise he deserves for the brilliant tennis he put forth in winning six of the next seven games. His flat forehand was striking like lightning. His backhand slice stood up unwaveringly from any angle. He used the lob and drop shot with his usual aplomb and success and his control was so steadfast that Budge got precious little that he did not earn.

The champion, struggling to regain his concentration and accuracy after getting only 3 points in three games, found his touch had deserted him. Nothing would work right for him and his footwork became faulty as he was caught out of position, or hit from his heels, while his smash failed glaringly.

It was a worried-looking Budge who stared at Mako's beautiful backhand drive that went passing by him for the final point of the set as the gallery cheered tumultuously.

With the start of the third set, command of the match reverted to the champion, and he was never seriously challenged again. Possibly Mako was content with taking that set, but whether he was or not, there was not much he could have done to stay the fate that speedily engulfed him.

Budge turned loose a tornado of controlled speed such as had been visited upon no other opponent in the tournament, with his service making the chalk fly on the lines, and Mako found that neither his drop shots nor lobs, nor blistering forehand drives could avail against the sharpshooting that scored 30 earned points for the champion in the last two sets.

When the match ended, Mako received an ovation from the gallery for a performance which, in conjunction with his victories over Bromwich, Franjo Puncec of Yugoslavia and Frank Kovacs, should earn him a high place in the 1938 rankings and possibly serious consideration from the Davis Cup committee in 1939.

UNSEEDED GENE MAKO UPSETS BROMWICH

by Allison Danzig

For the first time on record, an unseeded player gained the final round of the men's national tennis championship yesterday.

That bit of history was written into the book at Forest Hills as Gene Mako of Los Angeles furnished a stunning surprise at the expense of John Bromwich of Australia, to stand as the last barrier in the path of his doubles partner's quest of the first grand slam of the world's four major tennis crowns.

A gallery of 13,000 spectators, filling the stadium of the West Side Tennis Club almost to capacity after an interlude of six days in the play, saw the big blond Californian break up the game of the ambidextrous Bromwich on the slow turf with a distracting mixture of drop shots, lobs and short-angled backhand slices to deny him even the satisfaction of a set. The score was 6–3, 7–5, 6–4.

The victory of Mako, who ranks eighth in the country for 1937 but whose record for the current season in singles had hardly warranted his being designated as one of the eight seeded Americans in the championship, followed upon the almost miraculous escape of Miss Alice Marble in her match with Mrs. Sarah Palfrey Fabyan and preceded the conclusive triumph of J. Donald Budge over Sidney B. Wood Jr. at 6–3, 6–3, 6–3.

In the most exciting match of the day, Miss Marble, trailing by the precarious margin of 2–5 and 15–40 in the second set after losing nine successive games from 5–1 in the first, twice saved herself from defeat by a single stroke, to overcome Mrs. Fabyan at 5–7, 7–5, 7–5 with a magnificent fusillade of attacking shots. The blond California girl, champion in 1936, thereby qualified to meet Miss Nancye Wynne of Australia for the title. . . .

The defeat of Bromwich, who has been visualized as a future world's champion since his fine showing in the Davis Cup challenge round at Germantown, may be attributed in part to the fact that a week had intervened since he last played in the championship. Possibly the same circumstance accounts for the failure of Wood to offer a real challenge to Budge, against whose rapacity of stroke the New Yorker never was able, after the first few games, to find the touch that made him the complete master over Bryan Grant.

But while recognizing that the hiatus had not done Bromwich any good, the fact remains that Mako was laboring under the same handicap, and if the condition of the court, heavy from the week's rains, served the American's purposes, he is to be commended for utilizing them shrewdly to the utmost advantage.

After all, Mako's victory does not call for the explanation of a miracle after the fine tennis he had been playing throughout the tournament, in which he defeated Frank Kovacs, Franjo Puncec of Yugoslavia and Gilbert Hunt, the conqueror of Robert L. Riggs, and his five-set match with H. W. Austin at Wimbledon.

The big Californian defeated Bromwich primarily because he refused to meet him at the type of game the latter would have preferred. Instead of hitting with the young Australian, Mako employed variations to unsettle his opponent's strokes and shake his concentration and ultimately his confidence. The American learned something from his crushing defeat by Bromwich in the Antipodes.

Keeping the ball low on the slow turf with his backhand slice, interpolating drop shots constantly, and making big capital of his beautifully concealed lob, Mako seldom allowed his opponent to settle into the security of his devastating two-handed drive. Bromwich was continually being pulled up to the net to be trapped by lobs and masterful lob volleys or drawn wide by short angle shots that paved the way for passing drives.

The efficacy of these tactics was demonstrated convincingly in the second set. Bromwich started as though he would make short shrift of the opposition, hitting with so much speed and depth as to provoke error after error from Mako's backhand and go ahead at 4–1. But here Mako dug in, reduced his errors to a minimum and extracted the sting from the other's attack as he brought his mélange of drops, slices and lobs into play.

Bromwich, instead of sustaining his hard hitting, began to play Mako's game and resort to repeated drop shots. The direction of the play was taken away from him and when the set escaped him as his two-handed drive went off, his concentration and plan of attack were gone. He openly showed his distaste for the disrupting tactics of Mako as he was trapped by a drop shot to start the final set, double-faulting right after. Mako, playing with mounting confidence and attacking now with stinging drives and volleys as well, drew rapidly away.

1 9 3 9

HISTORY REPEATS IN AUSTRALIAN CUP VICTORY

by Allison Danzig

The clock turned back to 1914 today as an Australian tennis team won the Davis Cup preparatory to heading home to join the colors.

In a rally without precedent in the long history of the challenge round, the players from Down Under completed their sweep of the last three matches in the series with the United States at the Merion Cricket Club to reclaim the Davis Cup for Australia for the first time since 1919.

With the United States leading by 2 matches to 1 by virtue of the victories in the opening singles, Adrian Quist overcame Robert Riggs in a beautifully fought endurance contest, 6–1, 6–4, 3–6, 3–6, 6–4 and John Bromwich summarily squelched America's fading hopes with a crushing victory over Frank Parker, 6–0, 6–3, 6–1.

These two triumphs, in conjunction with their victory in the doubles yesterday, gave the Australians the verdict by 3 matches to 2, marking the first time since the cup was put in competition in 1900 that a team had lost the first two matches in the challenge round and still managed to win.

While president Holcombe Ward of the United States Lawn Tennis Association was turning the Davis Cup over to the victors in the presentation ceremonies on the courts, a cablegram was placed in the hands of Sir Norman Brookes, instructing Captain Harry Hopman and his team to return home by the first available ship. Twenty-five years ago Sir Norman received similar instructions to depart for war duty after he and Anthony Wilding of New Zealand had won the cup for Australasia from the United States at Forest Hills.

At first it was reported that the team would leave tonight for Los Angeles to sail on the 13th for the Antipodes, but late this evening it developed that there is still a chance that Quist, Bromwich, Hopman and Jack Crawford may compete in our national championships, beginning at Forest Hills on Thursday.

It seems that Sir Norman, president of the Australian Association, has two reservations on the S.S. *Monterey* of the Matson Line, sailing from Los Angeles on the 13th, and that he wishes to turn them over to the team, deferring his departure until his two daughters arrive here from England to join him and Lady Brookes in sailing on the *Mariposa* on October 10.

Captain Hopman, however, is unwilling to split up the team, stating that it won the cup as a team and will return as a team. He plans to call the Australian Association tomorrow from New York and ask that the men be allowed to play at Forest Hills and sail on the *Mariposa*. Sir Norman is understood to be making efforts to obtain two additional reservations on the *Monterey* so that the four players can leave together next week.

At any rate, the Davis Cup will leave these shores in the near future on a 10,000-mile trip, and it may be years before it will be seen again here. There will be no further competition until the new world war is over (there was a four-year lapse after the 1914 matches) .

As the winning players gathered around the cup, which apparently everyone but themselves had thought was sure to remain here after the opening day's matches, they were as happy as a lot of schoolboys. The fact that all of them might be carrying guns within a few months did not enter into their thoughts for the moment. That scrap could wait for a little while. All that counted at this time was that they had redeemed themselves magnificently, coming from far behind to achieve the victory which they had been favored to gain originally by odds of 3 to 1.

The triumph was wholeheartedly acclaimed by a crowd of 7,500, despite its keen disappointment over America's loss of the cup. How much the spectators wanted the trophy to stay here was evidenced in the enthusiasm with which they cheered Riggs as he came back brilliantly after losing ten successive games in the first two sets. His defeat, after he appeared to have the tiring Quist at his mercy at the start of the fifth set, left them depressed and fearing the worst.

Their fears were quickly realized, for it was soon perceived that Parker, with his totally inadequate and incessantly attacked forehand, was no match for Bromwich, who took the first seven games, lost the next three and then won ten more in succession before yielding the only other one that Parker got.

In winning today, Quist and Bromwich, particularly the former, vindicated the judgment of those who had visualized them as such dangerous threats before the series started. They were so much better than they had been on the opening day that there was no comparison. The greater speed of the turf, dried out by two additional days of sun, probably had something to do with it, and Sir Norman had predicted that in the role of underdogs they would play better tennis than they did when they were the big favorites.

Quist expressed the belief after his match that he had played the best tennis he has ever produced in this country and vouchsafed that his lack of a stiff test in months preparatory to his meeting with Parker on Saturday had been responsible for his faulty play on that occasion. Today, the 26-year-old Australian had his ground strokes functioning beautifully, and it was the strength of his drives, especially his powerful flat forehand, that enabled him to turn the tables on Riggs, who defeated him in the opening match of last year's challenge round series.

The gallery could scarcely credit its eyes as Quist ran ten games in succession after losing the first one of the match on his service. Riggs had turned in such a masterful performance against Bromwich that the crowd had complete confidence in his ability to clinch the cup, but here he was being played to a standstill.

Against the Australian's fast, deep drives, the American was hitting raggedly from both sides. He could not generate any pace, he was short of length and he was not volleying well, chiefly for the reason that his approach shots were not giving him adequate protection against so sharp a hitter as Quist. Quist got better and better and his superiority stood out particularly in the return of service. He was keeping his service high on Riggs's backhand and the American did not like it, and Riggs was not putting Quist's backhand under the pressure that did Parker.

In the second set Riggs called on his drop shots in the effort to break up Quist's drives, but neither they nor his lobs availed. The Australian continued to pound the ball back deep and get to the net for winning volleys and smashes, and Riggs continued to volley badly or to find himself passed. The play was getting closer now, with long deuce games the rule, but Riggs could not break up Quist's procession until the score stood 4–0. In the next game Quist reached 40–15 on two passing shots and a double fault, and here the tide turned. The pace of the bitterly fought games finally began to tell on the Australian and his errors enabled the other to salvage the game.

Riggs now forged ahead, fighting might and main and getting more speed and length on his shots as the opposition weakened. The crowd cheered him on and it seemed that he might save the set as he went to 3–4. But Quist, conserving his energies for his service, saved the vitally important eighth game from 15–30 to stay ahead at 5–3. When Riggs won the ninth quickly with his service, the gallery was prepared to see him get on even terms, for Quist was plainly fading. But the Australian had saved himself in the ninth again for his service, and after Captain Hopman had administered to him, he went out and took the tenth game at love for the set, Riggs presenting him with the first two points on weak returns of service that brought groans from the worked-up gallery.

The match was decided here in this second set. Riggs came back to win the third after some of the most sensational play of the match. At first Quist appeared ready to concede it. Then, at 0–2, he changed his mind as he perceived that Riggs was tiring too and presenting him with point after point on bad mistakes, and shortly they were going at it hammer and tongs again until Quist finally broke from fatigue.

After the rest period Riggs played his finest tennis of the match to break down Quist's resistance. The American had all his confidence now. He was timing his shots perfectly, and his drop volleys were working like a charm as he carefully opened the court, while his marvelous backhand lobs were keeping the other back. Quist looked like a very tired man as he lost the last four games of the set, with Riggs going along like a whirlwind, and when the American took the first game of the last set from 0–30 with two volleys and a smash, the crowd was sure the cup was safe. But Quist had far more in reserve than anyone suspected. He now came back into the fight with the same kind of tennis he had shown at the start.

Riggs, taken aback by the strength of the resistance, was forced on the defensive. His volleying touch deserted him. His lobs lost the necessary length and Quist's deadly forehand, which Riggs insisted on attacking, passed him beautifully time and again. Quist took five games in a row. Here Riggs braced and staged a rally that had the crowd in an agony of suspense and excitement. Fighting magnificently, Riggs pulled up to 4–5, saving a match point in the bitterly contested ninth game of 16 points, but Quist put everything he had into the tenth, attacked irresistibly at the net and with his service, and the match ended as Riggs's return of service overreached the baseline.

The match between Parker and Bromwich was an anticlimax despite the fact that it was the deciding one. After his victory over Quist, Parker's performance today was a keen disappointment and his forehand never before has looked so utterly inadequate. Bromwich hit nine out of every ten balls to the forehand and it was by everlastingly adhering to this plan that he won by his crushing margin.

The tennis was totally uninteresting to watch. At first the gallery started chuckling as the two players stood at their baselines and exchanged 30, 40 or even 50 drives, with hardly a volley, the first game lasting six minutes. But after a set of that, it had had enough, and some of the crowd began to leave.

Parker caused a flurry as he took three games in a row from 0–1 in the second set to lead, 3–1, attacking brilliantly at the net and smashing more decisively. But from then on he was at Bromwich's mercy, whether he stayed back or went forward. He could not keep the ball away from the Australian's double-handed drive, and no matter to which side he played it or how high he sought to keep it, it always came back. Bromwich won the next ten games with the loss of eleven points, dropped the next one and then ended the hopelessly uneven match.

RIGGS AND MARBLE TAKE U.S. TITLES

by Allison Danzig

Robert L. Riggs, Jr., of Los Angeles and Chicago and Miss Alice Marble of Beverly Hills, California, are the tennis champions of the United States, as well as of Wimbledon, for 1939, winners of probably the last big national tournaments of international representation until the roar of cannon shall no longer drown out the ping of rackets in the Old World.

The 21-year-old Riggs succeeded yesterday to the mantle of J. Donald Budge with a convincing demonstration of his mastery over the youth envisioned as another Ellsworth Vines. The immaturity of the stalwart, 19-year-old Welby Van Horn stood revealed under the searching challenge of Riggs's clever provocations, and the crowd of 10,000 gathered in the Forest Hills Stadium of the West Side Tennis Club groaned almost in unison as the boyish conqueror of John Bromwich, Wayne Sabin and Elwood Cooke went down in the final, 6–4, 6–2, 6–4.

For Riggs, the victory marked his first winning of the championship of his country. In conjunction with his triumph at Wimbledon, it gives him as good a claim as can be established for the year to the mythical world amateur crown, even though he lost to Donald McNeill in the final of the French championship and to Adrian Quist of Australia in the Davis Cup challenge round.

Miss Marble, unchallenged in her world supremacy in women's tennis, completed a season of uninterrupted conquest and retired the challenge trophy with her third triumph in four years by defeating Miss Helen Jacobs of Berkeley, California, 6–0, 8–10, 6–4. It was not, however, until Miss Jacobs, trailing at 3–5 in the second set, had thrown the stadium into a bedlam by winning that set and going ahead at 3–1 in the third, that the blond champion collected her disintegrating forces to hammer her way to victory over as game an opponent as she has ever faced.

All the excitement and nervous tension that were anticipated in the men's final developed in this meeting between the champion of the women's ranks and the player who ruled the courts a few years back.

Here was one of the most dramatic battles that women's tennis has produced in years, fought out for an hour and a half in gusty cross-currents of wind that raised havoc with the strokes, while the gallery roared and screamed its encouragement to Miss Jacobs. The crescendo of the enthusiasm was reached in the final game, a furiously disputed 20-point session in which Miss Jacobs five times came within a stroke of 5–all and twice stood off match point, only to yield finally to the defending champion's more powerful attacking weapons.

At the end there could be no question that the player with the superior strokes had prevailed, but neither could there be any doubt that Miss Jacobs had given a classic demonstration of how much sheer match-play courage counts for on the tennis courts.

Players with considerably better stroke equipment than Miss Jacobs possesses have gone out against Miss Marble and been blown off the court, counting themselves beaten before the striking of the first ball. Miss Jacobs, winner of our title four years in a row and also a Wimbledon victor, is made of far sterner stuff.

The terrible playing conditions, with the wind blowing at gale velocity, should have been particularly discouraging for Miss Jacobs, since she lacks Miss Marble's power to hit through so much resistance, though, of course, Miss Marble, too, was at a big disadvantage with her timing and judgment of distance ruined.

But, despite the fact that she could do nothing right in the first set, when the champion was hammering her backhand pitilessly and extracting errors there prodigally, Miss Jacobs refused to give up the fight. Instead, after dropping six games in a row, she dug in all the more fiercely in the second set.

With the second set both players sought the net, and Miss Jacobs was to bring the lob into the picture with striking success. Miss Marble was serving so well that Miss Jacobs was under great pressure, but she drew up from 1–3 to 3–all. The champion's forehand slumped badly, but she now recovered and went ahead to 5–3. It seemed the end for Miss Jacobs. But grimly the former champion fought her way out of the hole as the gallery cheered tumultuously.

The third set saw Miss Marble break through service in the first game and then fall into a slump of bad hitting from her forehand. Her backhand failed her, too, and Miss Jacobs went to 3–1. But it was now Miss Marble's turn to show the fiber of which champions are made. Never letting up in her hitting and crowding on pressure, she regained her confidence overhead and went on to triumph.

After Van Horn's amazing record of success, climaxed by his stunning defeat of Bromwich, a great men's final was looked forward to, but the California stripling was unable to come even close to the expectations of his host of admirers. Undoubtedly the energy he had used up against Cooke, Sabin and Bromwich told part of the story of his collapse against one of the cleverest players on the courts, and the disturbing wind, too, had its effect.

At the outset, and indeed for a good part of the opening set, it seemed that Riggs might be handled as roughly as were the others by this newcomer from the Pacific Coast, the second unseeded player in history to reach the final. Van Horn opened the match with a blasting service ace that brought forth a roar, followed it with another and took the game amid frenzied cheers.

But Riggs immediately let it be known that he had a service that could be just as effective, even though it has not been strikingly in evidence during the season. He showed, too, that though he hasn't the stark speed off the forehand that has Van Horn, he can hit through for winners from both that side and the backhand when he has maneuvered for the finishing shot, and he disclosed also, and what was more telling, that Van Horn had weaknesses that could be exploited.

Serving a high twist ball to Van Horn's backhand, keeping the ball down the middle to his forehand, to increase the youngster's tendency to crowd his powerful drive, interpolating drop shots, throwing up lobs and constantly mixing his speed and length, Riggs won the match not so much on his ability to finish off the rallies as on his success in provoking Van Horn into mistakes.

1 9 4 0

RIGGS DETHRONED BY DON MCNEILL

by Allison Danzig

Robert Riggs's one-year reign as national amateur tennis champion came to an end at Forest Hills yesterday after he had appeared to be launched on as unstoppable a procession as Miss Alice Marble had staged earlier in the day in defeating Miss Helen Jacobs, 6–2, 6–3, to win the women's crown for the fourth time.

In a hair-rising finish that galvanized the gallery out of its inertia of the early stages, blond 22-year-old Donald McNeill of Oklahoma City fought his way up from a two-set deficit to eke out victory over the defending title-holder from Chicago, 4–6, 6–8, 6–3, 6–3, 7–5, in the concluding round of the fifty-ninth annual tournament.

The final set of this two-hour struggle compares with any of recent years in the intensity of the drama that unfolded before the eyes of the 7,500 spectators in the stadium of the West Side Tennis Club. It was also notable for the fine sportsmanship shown by both players in the heat of a battle that had them, no less than the gallery, worked up to a feverish pitch as they fought under cruel tension for the victory that was to be snatched by so thin a margin.

Riggs, striving desperately to save what he had seemed to have sewn up, first when he stopped the blazing rally that McNeill launched at 1–5 and 15–40 in the second set, and again when he broke through to lead at 4–3 in the fifth set, was to be commended for the spirit in which he accepted two damaging decisions near the end, as well as the graciousness with which he met defeat and congratulated his antagonist.

McNeill, by his demeanor throughout the match, even when his robust strokes were failing him grievously in the first two sets, and his "throwing" of a point to offset one of the decisions in the final game, was equally to be applauded.

The integrity of one of the decisions was not to be questioned, though the rarity of its occurrence made it doubly bitter to take. The other was highly questionable. In the eyes of two competent sportsmen who were squarely in a position to pass judgment, it was dead wrong.

With the score at 4–all and deuce in the final set, McNeill made a backhand volley across court to Riggs's forehand sideline. The linesman serving there instantly signaled the ball as out and then hastily gestured with his hands to indicate that the shot was fair. Riggs had turned his back to the advantage court and did not know of the change in the decision until Umpire Benjamin Dwight called "advantage, McNeill."

674

The defending champion, who rarely questions a decision, turned at the call and then walked back toward the linesman, asking him why he had changed his ruling. The official maintained that the ball was good and Riggs, without further quibbling, accepted the costly decision and lost the next point and the game as McNeill passed him at the net with a beautiful forehand drive.

In the opening rally of the final game Riggs went forward and had a short high ball to deal with. The ball just barely reached the net and the defender gingerly endeavored to keep from touching the tape as he made his volley.

But instantly the umpire announced that his foot had touched the net and he had lost the point. At that critical stage, it was a bitter pill to swallow but Riggs took it without arguing.

McNeill, however, apparently did not like to win the point that way, even though the ruling was correct, and when he knocked Riggs's next service far out of court the stadium rang with applause. Such was the spirit in which these two rivals, who have fought each other to exhaustion a half dozen times this year, went at each other.

This was far from a great match. The errors on both sides doubled the earned points.

In the early stages McNeill's game was hopelessly out of hand and for the most part Riggs lacked the severity and accuracy off the ground that mark him at his best against a pacemaker, while his volleying, too, was not up to his capacity. Possibly the Chicagoan was still feeling the effects of the cold that had kept him in bed with a slight temperature on Friday, though this is not offered to disparage the merit of McNeill's courageously earned victory.

But if the quality of the play was not all that it might have been, the match had elements of greatness in the spectacular heights to which both men rose under nerve-racking pressure. Also there was a nobility to the spirit with which the trim, persevering McNeill came on after he had suffered adversity that might have broken the morale of a less self-reliant player, and few matches have kept a gallery keyed up to a higher pitch down to the bitter end.

By all rights, the Oklahoman should have been crushed in spirit when his thrilling rally from 1–5 and 15–40 in the second set came to naught. It was the same kind of rally that Riggs had staged against him at Rye in winning the third set, except that in this case the pull-up was made by virtue of some of the most magnificent shot-making seen throughout the tournament.

Four times McNeill saved set-point, pulling out both the seventh and eighth games from 15–40, with his top-spin backhand, bringing thunderous cheers from the stands. When the Oklahoman, after going ahead to 6–5 with his swirling assault, lost the next three games to be two sets down his plight seemed hopeless.

But they come no gamer and his refusal to accept defeat, along with Riggs's failure to hold his game together and keep on pressure, turned the tide. McNeill showed in the final set how brilliant a player he could be when in full cry, and some of his interceptions and redemptions, after being run ragged by lobs, had the stadium in a frenzy of delight.

The spectators were wholeheartedly, almost rankly, partial to the Oklahoman, and they fairly tore the place apart as he fought his way out of the hole in the final set. The shot of all that brought the house down came after Riggs had been reprieved at the first match point against him in the final game.

The champion went to advantage point, and in the next rally he tore for the net behind a strong approach shot to McNeill's backhand. His sharp cross-court volley, cut down with spin, seemed a sure winner, but McNeill, rushing pell-mell, took the ball on his forehand and whipped it back across court for a passing shot that was as close to the impossible as anything in tennis.

That great stroke so unnerved Riggs that he failed on his lift volley behind his next service, and the match ended as McNeill drove a beautiful backhand return of service at Riggs's feet.

McNeill's ascendancy to the championship capped two seasons of marked success and definite progress. Last year he won the French championship and this summer he took the national clay court, intercollegiate, Newport, Southampton and Baltimore tournaments and was a finalist at Rye.

1941

RIGGS AND MRS. COOKE WIN U.S. TITLES

by Allison Danzig

Robert L. Riggs of Clinton, South Carolina, is back on the national tennis throne and for the first time since 1908—unbelievable as it may seem—a native of the East reigns as women's champion in the person of Mrs. Sarah Palfrey Cooke of New York.

Displaced by Donald McNeill of Oklahoma as the head man of the amateur realm in last year's five-set final, the 23-year-old Riggs regained the championship yesterday by thoroughly outplaying Frank Kovacs of Oakland, California, as 12,000 looked on from the stadium of the West Side Tennis Club, Forest Hills. The score was 5–7, 6–1, 6–3, 6–3.

For one set the tall, loose Kovacs, who had held McNeill at his mercy Saturday in the semi-finals, put on a show of rapacious hitting that was eminently to the gallery's liking and that seemed beyond the capacity of Riggs's resisting powers, but after he had finished off the set with three successive blistering service aces there was nothing cosmic any longer in the game that has invited comparison on occasion with William Tilden's.

The outcropping of errors that had marred Kovacs's play became epidemic as he lost three love games to start the second set. It was perceived that there was too little real substance behind the gingerbread and tinsel that pull in the customers, and that the calculating, concentrating young man on the other side of the net was too resourceful, too smart and too fundamentally sound in his equipment to be beaten by spasmodic eruptions of power in the raw.

Mrs. Cooke, who has been a contender for the championship since she was a girl of 14 and who was runner-up to Miss Helen Jacobs in 1934 and 1935, finally achieved the reward for her years of perseverance as she defeated Miss Pauline Betz of Los Angeles, 7–5, 6–2.

At the age of 28, a year older than was Tilden when he first won the men's crown, the former Boston protégé of Mrs. George W. Wightman finds herself on the throne occupied for the past three years by Miss Alice Marble, now in the professional ranks.

Mrs. Maud Barger-Wallach was the last previous native of the East to win the women's crown. Since her triumph in 1908, Californians have monopolized the honor, except in the years of the ascendancy of Miss Betty Nuthall of Great Britain, Señorita Anita Lizana of Chile and Mrs. Molla Bjurstedt Mallory, who came here from Norway to become an American citizen and win seven national titles and the patriotic tournament in 1917 during the war.

Mrs. Cooke, beaten by Miss Betz twice on clay and once on turf during the season, played up to her full capacity yesterday, despite the violence of the wind, and her superior stroke production gained her the title.

Riggs's victory over Kovacs was a repetition of his triumph in the final at Southampton, their only other meeting of the season on turf. On that occasion the verdict was achieved in three sets and Riggs was never more masterful, thwarting Kovacs's violent speed with his marvelous counterblows.

The quality of the play was not as good yesterday, but it was not a day for good tennis. A strong wind, of almost gale violence at times, whipped across the court during both the men's and women's finals and played tricks with the ball. Considering the difficulty he was laboring under with his softer shots, Riggs played exceptionally fine tennis. He made far less errors than did Kovacs while scoring the same number of earned points.

It was more than control, however, that won back the championship for Riggs. He won with his head as much as with his hand, breaking up his opponent's attack after the first set and thereafter showing the greater potency in service, volleying and passing shots.

1942

PAULINE BETZ BECOMES NATIONAL CHAMPION

by Allison Danzig

The player who had conquered every rival and won every major women's tennis tournament on grass this season met her Waterloo yesterday in the final of the national championship at Forest Hills.

Miss Pauline Betz of Los Angeles and Rollins College is the new champion.

A fighter who stands up to adversity as have few other women players, the blond Californian ended the long winning streak of Miss Louise Brough of Beverly Hills, California, in a beautifully fought match as 8,000 looked on in the stadium of the West Side Tennis Club. The score was 4–6, 6–1, 6–4.

A year ago Miss Betz lost the championship final to Mrs. Sarah Palfrey Cooke after defeating her in two previous meetings. Yesterday it was her good fortune to turn the tables on the 19-year-old Miss Brough, who had beaten her in the finals at Rye and Manchester.

Miss Brough did not play quite so well at Forest Hills as she had elsewhere. Miss Mary Arnold carried her to three sets and so did Miss Helen Bernhard, whom she had overwhelmed at East Hampton.

Against Miss Betz, Miss Brough played like Alice Marble for a good part of the first set and at times in the third, but she paid the penalty for her extreme youth and lack of experience in failing to assert her hand boldly against an opponent who attacked at every opportunity.

Miss Brough has the best service and one of the finest backhands and is the most accomplished net player in the women's ranks. She is fast around the court, too. But she hung back too much and allowed her hitting to become tentative.

Miss Betz played her best tennis of the year. She has an extremely strong backhand and seldom has it served her so well, across court or straight. Her forehand, the vulnerable point of her game, stood up remarkably well, excelling her backhand at times in its pace and length.

From both sides Miss Betz was whaling the ball. She was tearing around the court with her usual abandon and taking heavy falls. She was rushing into the volleying position at every chance and her lobs were a particularly strong factor.

Probably it was Miss Betz's lobs that discouraged her rival from going to the net. They were not always of good length, but Miss Brough became chary of them and was not nearly so effective overhead as she usually is, putting even the short ones into the net.

In the opening set Miss Betz led at 3–1 and then lost the next four games, three of them at 6–4. In the second set Miss Betz lost her opening service and then ran six games in a row. Miss Brough was letting her rival take over the attack almost entirely and her control crumpled against Miss Betz's sweeping drives.

The third set was a stirring battle. Miss Betz's ground strokes were at their best and she was doing most of the volleying. Failure to take advantage of openings cost her important points, but she kept attacking regardless, while Miss Brough alternately played aggressive and defensive tennis.

Miss Betz broke through for a 3–2 lead with her volleys, lost her service and then effected the deciding break in the seventh. The match ended with Miss Brough hitting into the alley.

Lieutenant Gardnar Mulloy of the Jacksonville Naval Air Station and William Talbert of Cincinnati were crowned the new men's doubles champions. In the final they defeated Ted Schroeder of Glendale, California, and Sidney B. Wood Jr. of New York, 9–7, 7–5, 6–1.

1943

HUNT HALTS KRAMER TO WIN U.S. TITLE

by Allison Danzig

Lieutenant (j.g.) Joseph R. Hunt of the United States Navy is the new national amateur tennis champion.

With an exhibition of volleying and serving worthy of the best California tradition, the blond, powerfully developed naval officer, awaiting ship assignment for a return to sea duty, defeated Seaman John A. Kramer of the United States Coast Guard Academy yesterday in the final of the sixty-second annual tournament before 9,000 spectators at Forest Hills.

The match ended in the fourth set at 6–3, 6–8, 10–8, 6–0, two hours and eleven minutes after Umpire Harold Leban had called "play." In reality, the verdict was sealed with Kramer's loss of the exhausting, superbly fought third set after he had led at 5–4, with service following.

Weak from two hours of bitter competition under a hot sun, and still feeling the effects of the attack of indigestion which had confined him to his bed Saturday, the rangy 22-year-old California conqueror of Ecuador's Francisco Segura had nothing left when he came out for the fourth set.

The interval of rest could not reinvigorate the hand that had threatened at times to blast Hunt off the court, and would have, had it not been for the stout courage of the naval officer and the fidelity of his ground strokes against lethal speed.

Utterly spent and hardly able to move his feet, Kramer offered only the feeblest opposition in the final set. In eleven minutes Hunt, in full vigor, ran out six games in a row with the loss of only four points as Kramer, drooping and wan, allowed ball after ball to go unchallenged.

Paradoxically, the match ended with the champion "on the floor." As Kramer knocked the last ball out of the court, Hunt, turning at the baseline to run to the net and greet his opponent, fell to the ground in pain, seized with a cramp in his left leg, which had been bothering him through the last set.

Kramer walked over to his fallen rival and, with Hunt holding on to his leg, they shook hands on the turf as cameramen rushed to snap the unusual scene.

It was an unhappy ending for Kramer, who had such high hopes of winning the championship and who was the general favorite, particularly after he had ended Segura's 1943 sweep of American tournaments. In justice, though, to the 24-year-old Hunt, every inch the commanding figure a navy officer should be, it was brilliant, resourceful and shrewdly plotted tennis that brought about the undoing of the young Coast Guardsman.

Kramer was in full vigor at the outset and well might have won had not Hunt undermined his strength by keeping on pressure for so long a period. There were times when it seemed that Kramer's violent strokes could not be resisted, but Hunt was dead game and refused to become discouraged either by adversity or the uproarious demonstrations for his rival by the big crowd in the West Side Stadium.

Hunt not only was a magnificent volleyer who riposted with deft touch and wrist of steel from any level and depth, but he smashed overhead beautifully, and he served far more effectively than did Kramer, who had scored seventeen aces against Segura. He had the ground strokes to match Kramer's with his overspin forehand and underhit backhand, and he played his hand with a care, discernment and discrimination that extracted many errors.

Had Kramer been able to control his mighty forehand and dangerous backhand, his superior hitting power should have won, but Hunt, mixing his spin and pace, hitting straight at his opponent and interpolating drop shots, threw Kramer off his stroke. Also, by maintaining uniformly good length, he kept Kramer away from the net for the most part and commanded the volleying position.

Hunt's victory kept the title in the Navy. Ensign Ted Schroeder was unable to defend.

1944

PARKER BEATS TALBERT FOR U.S. TENNIS CROWN

by Allison Danzig

Man and boy-wonder, Frankie Parker came East annually from Milwaukee and California for more than a dozen years in fruitless quest of the national tennis championship. Mercer Beasley, his coach, suffered in silence with him as he endured the slings and arrows of outraged form experts sitting in judgment on a forehand that was never the same from season to season.

Today Sergeant Frank A. Parker of the Army Air Forces, Muroc Field, California, is the champion of the United States at the age of 28, one year older than was William Tilden when he began his matchless reign of world supremacy in 1920. Tilden will rejoice with Beasley in his elevation, for the master of them all was among the first to herald his rising star almost fifteen years ago.

In the final round of the sixty-third annual tournament yesterday, before 10,500 spectators in the Forest Hills Stadium of the West Side Tennis Club, Parker defeated William Talbert of Indianapolis, 6–4, 3–6, 6–3, 6–3.

The player who had eliminated Francisco (Pancho) Segura of Ecuador, the No. 1 favorite, in the semi-finals with the finest tennis to come from his racket found his polished weapons inadequate against the machine-like efficiency of Parker, one of the most thoroughly fit athletes to step on a court.

The match started as a procession, with Parker winning the first four games, developed into a real shooting match as the full strength of Talbert's immaculate drives and high-powered service was brought to bear to open the court for his volley and smash, and then, midway in the third set, the tide turned irrevocably in favor of Parker.

An hour and a half after the umpire, Harold Lebair, had got the match under way, the wiry, tight-lipped Army sergeant was running forward to greet his beaten opponent, with a muffled cry of exultation barely breaking the bounds of his habitual restraint.

It was the thrill of a lifetime for Parker when he stepped forward to receive from Dr. S. Ellsworth Davenport 2d, the referee, the challenge trophy for which he had fought for so many years. It was no less a thrill for the man who had stood by him and backed him so unswervingly, even in the face of ridicule—Mercer Beasley.

With Parker's victory the Army took over where the Navy had left off. Last year the crown was won by Lieutenant Joe Hunt, USN, who was to have defended his title but missed out by a week owing to bad weather delaying the completion of his flight training at Pensacola. . . .

Parker's victory was achieved in spite of the fact that it was the only tournament of the year in which he competed. It was thought that his lack of match play would militate against his chances, but he was in his usual flawless condition and had his game functioning at nearly top efficiency.

There were times during the play when his control fell off badly, but his forehand, which was attacked persistently, held up even better than his fine backhand, where he made most of his errors.

Talbert has the forehand and backhand to put anyone's strokes to a searching test, and Parker's forehand stood up staunchly, keeping beautiful length and making it difficult for Talbert to gain the net.

It was a task for both to get to close quarters, with the depth so good, but both came in and both volleyed smartly. Talbert was not as decisive at the net as he was against Segura for the reason that he was under far more pressure.

It was not a brilliant match, although the play reached brilliant heights, but it was a worthy final for a wartime championship, in which half of the contenders were from the armed forces.

1945

SARAH COOKE ENDS MISS BETZ'S
3-YEAR REIGN

by Allison Danzig

The three-year reign of Miss Pauline Betz of Los Angeles as women's national tennis champion ended in the Forest Hills Stadium yesterday. Back on the throne again sits Mrs. Sarah Palfrey Cooke of Boston, titleholder in 1941 and the only player from the East to win the crown since Mrs. Mallory's seventh triumph in 1926.

In a beautifully fought final that had the 10,000 spectators in a state of almost breathless excitement, with the outcome in doubt to the last stroke, Mrs. Cooke rose to her most shining moments when her fortunes seemed to be ebbing fast, to snatch victory from a valiant rival through the sheer brilliance and enterprise of her attack. The score was 3–6, 8–6, 6–4.

William F. Talbert of Wilmington, Delaware, invincible all season, faltered under a savage opening onslaught from Francisco (Pancho) Segura in the semi-finals of the men's singles, but rallied from 1–4 to assert his supremacy once again over his rival from Ecuador, 7–5, 6–3, 6–4. Talbert will face Sergeant Frank Parker of the Army Air Forces for the championship today, as he did a year ago, when Parker won in four sets. . . . Talbert was on the court for nearly two hours in the final of the doubles. With

Lieutenant Gardnar Mulloy, USNR, his partner in winning the 1942 championship, he stood off the challenge of Air Cadet Robert Falkenburg and S1/C Jack Tuero without reaching a decision. The match was called because of darkness, with the score 10–all in the third set and each side having a set. . . .

Before Mrs. Cooke and Miss Betz went on the court there was a short ceremony in observance of V-J Day. After the playing of the National Anthem, P. Schuyler Van Bloem, president of the West Side Tennis Club, expressed the nation's gratitude for the successful conclusion of the war.

The women's singles final was the stirring fight that had been anticipated. Mrs. Cooke had beaten Miss Betz at Rye and in the national clay court championship, as well as in the 1941 final at Forest Hills, and figured to be the blond Californian's most dangerous rival, even though Mrs. Cooke has been out of competition almost entirely since her triumph of four years ago.

Mrs. Cooke won because she had the better game and because she played it up to the hilt when anything short of her best would have been inadequate in the final stages. Miss Betz has a fine backhand, a courage that never wavers and more speed around the court than any rival in the top flight. All of these assets, however, were not enough. Mrs. Cooke had the better forehand and was more effective in the forecourt, particularly overhead. There was purpose and calculation in her every stroke and she had the weapons to profit by the openings her strategy effected.

With all her attributes, Mrs. Cooke had to play the finest tennis she has shown in years to overcome Miss Betz's magnificent resistance when the latter led, 4–3, in the final set, with her service following. The new champion's performance was almost perfection in the last three games. Her ground strokes were infallible and she hit so deep and at such angles that she had her rival running frantically to keep on the ball.

The spectators obviously were for the little player from New England. They had looked on silently as she lost five games in a row after leading, 3–1, in the first set. They had cheered her on as she went ahead, 5–2, in the second and had exulted when she stopped Miss Betz's rally to square the match. In the fluctuating final set they almost gave up hope for Mrs. Cooke at 3–4 and then roared forth encouragement as she launched her unbeatable rally to run the defending champion ragged and keep her under merciless pressure from every quarter. At 15–40 in the final game, match point, a breathless silence fell upon the scene and then cheers split the air as Miss Betz's volley went out of court to mark the crowning of a new champion.

The stroke analysis reveals how extremely close was the play. Miss Cooke made 63 errors to her rival's 62 and 39 earned points to Miss Betz's 44. Miss Betz won 6 more points than did the winner.

1946

BROWN BEATS PARKER WITH SENSATIONAL SPEED

by Allison Danzig

Tom Brown broke loose again yesterday and the two-year reign of Frank Parker as national amateur tennis champion came to an end at dusk in the Forest Hills Stadium.

Not since Ellsworth Vines was demonstrating his lashing speed in 1932 and 1931 has a tennis gallery seen such electrifying maceration of a fuzz-covered ball as was wrought by the 23-year-old Californian from San Francisco in defeating Parker, 6–3, 6–4, 6–8, 3–6, 6–1.

This was the same Tom Brown who came out of the Army unheralded to win ovations at Wimbledon as he toppled Francisco Segura of Ecuador and Franjo Puncec of Yugoslavia and won the first two sets from Yvon Petra of France in the semi-finals. If the British gallery took him to its bosom, the crowd of 8,000 spectators at Forest Hills yesterday did everything but tear down the stadium in its uproarious enthusiasm over the scorching all-court attack that was almost beyond credibility in its deadly targetry for the first two sets.

The match required close to two hours and forty-five minutes for a decision and, with few exceptions, the gallery stayed to see the kill, forgetting about dinner and all other engagements. Here was one of the dramatic spine-tingling moments of sport, the passing of a champion as game as they come, and the ascendance into the spotlight of a new young challenger for the throne who, despite his exploits of Wimbledon, had received no more than negligible consideration as a contender for the title.

Beaten at Orange by Felicisimo Ampon of the Philippines and denied so much as a set by Gardnar Mulloy of Miami at Newport, following his return from Europe, Brown had become the forgotten man as the championship got under way. His meteoric streak across the tennis horizon apparently had fizzled out, and Parker, John Kramer, Mulloy, William Talbert, Petra, Donald McNeill and Robert Falkenburg were the accepted headliners to reckon with.

So it was pretty much a thunderstruck gallery that saw the Frisco Flailer pick up again where he had left off at Wimbledon and stop the national champion in his tracks with a torrent of blazing forehand and backhand drives that for sheer rapacity exceeded anything to come from the racket of Donald Budge when he was the king of the courts.

The backhand drives that Brown brought off in the first two sets and at intervals thereafter had the gallery rubbing its eyes. Straight down and across court he was whipping the ball for winners, oftentimes while on the run beyond the alleys. At the start it was his lashing forehand straight down the line that was beating Parker, but as the play went on his backhand stood forth as his most dangerous stroke, and from both sides he was hammering for the winner with every swing of his racket.

The Californian has not been regarded as a good volleyer, but his play in the forecourt left little ground for criticism other than that he was making some of his shots too far back. His execution on volleys below the level of the net was surprisingly good and on the high ones he was absolutely deadly.

Parker, one of the finest defensive players the game has known, had no answer for the searing drives that were making the chalk fly on the lines. Nor could he check Brown at the net. His passing shots failed all through the first two sets and his own sallies to the net usually came to grief as the Californian whipped the ball beyond the reach of his racket.

There is no one, however, who stands up to adversity better than Parker or whose tenacity is harder to break. The target of the most withering attack ever turned upon him, an attack that scored the remarkable total of 91 earned points to his own 32 in the five sets, he refused to be stampeded by either the scintillating shot-making of his opponent or the rabidly partisan cheers that greeted Brown's every winning stroke and oftentimes his own errors.

Fighting with his back to the wall, Frank waited for the break in the storm of Brown's attack and then came on with some of the finest tennis he has ever produced to take control of the play. The tide turned so definitely in his favor that at the end of the fourth set Brown looked to be a beaten youth.

But Parker could not keep on the pressure that broke his rival's control. It may have been that he was paying the price for the fact that he did not play in a single grass court tournament all season except the national doubles, or it may have been that his glasses failed him in the fading light, as he stated after the match. At any rate the starch went out of his game in the final set and Brown went on the rampage again, to win storms of cheers from the gallery, which had all but resigned itself to his defeat a short time before.

The Californian is every inch the fighter that is Parker, with a concentration that is unshakable and the resolution of a bulldog. He was behind at 0–4 and 0–30 in the third set, and that should have discouraged anyone, but Brown refused to concede it and drew even at 4–all with another sensational burst of hitting from the backhand. His control finally buckled under the depth and calculation of Parker's strokes, which were functioning almost errorlessly, and he yielded the set despite the fact that he scored 27 earned points to the champion's 10.

In the fourth set Brown started by hitting four beautiful winners in the opening game. Then errors cropped up more and more in his play as Parker kept him under relentless pressure and ran him all over the court. When the champion took three games from 3–all, it seemed that he had the situation in hand and that his experience, accuracy and court craft, along with his ability to handle Brown's fiery service, would carry him to victory.

But no one suspected how little resistance the champion had left to offer. Brown whipped across two forehands and a straight backhand to win the opening game of the final set. Parker took the second at love, then the dikes burst. With the crowd roaring its delight, the Californian burned up the turf with his stabbing drives and the match ended as he ran wide of the court and sent a magnificent backhand through, after Parker had reached wide to bring off a stunning volley.

Brown now finds himself in the semi-final round of the championship and this afternoon will go against Mulloy, after Kramer plays Falkenburg. Mulloy expressed the belief that he would be able to repeat his victory of Newport over Brown, despite the latter's amazing performance yesterday. He will need to play with more fire, however, than he did yesterday in defeating Segura, 4–6, 6–4, 12–10, 6–3.

KRAMER HALTS BROWN TO WIN U.S. CROWN

by Allison Danzig

John Kramer had his rendezvous with his manifest destiny yesterday.

The 25-year-old Californian at last sits on the national tennis throne which was ticketed for his future occupancy from the time he first came East as a junior.

The victim of successive vicissitudes that upset the timetable of his elevation, the tall, sandy-haired ex-lieutenant of the United States Coast Guard toppled the meteoric new pretender to the crown, Tom Brown of San Francisco, in a manner to establish him as one of the real masters of the all-court attack and win the championship, 9–7, 6–3, 6–0.

With 14,000 spectators looking down from the packed embankments of the Forest Hills Stadium, Kramer slugged it out with the bombarding Brown in one long, blazing set. When the decision finally went against the 23-year-old Army veteran, after he had saved four set points in a thrilling tenth game and broken through service for a 7–6 lead, the conqueror of Frank Parker and Gardnar Mulloy had shot his bolt of lightning.

From then on Kramer was indisputably the master of the court, so sound and faithful to the tenets of orthodoxy and keeping on such grinding pressure with his lethal service, return of service and volleys that the lacerating drives of Brown were reduced to impotency in the final set.

Rushing ahead at 3–0 in the second set, Kramer fought off Brown's last outburst of sensational hitting in the ninth game. Four times again the youth from San Francisco saved set point amid roaring cheers, and twice he held advantage, a stroke away from an equalizing break.

When he lost the game and the set, Brown must have known beyond

question that he had met his master. Any lingering doubts that he may have
had were speedily resolved as the cool, poised youth on the other side of the
net kept his backhand under implacable pressure with a withering onslaught of forcing shots that broke down resistance and opened wide the
court for flying cross-court volleys.

In sixteen minutes Kramer swept through the final set at love, with his
every high-voltage stroke functioning faultlessly in carrying out an attack as
impeccably correct in its conception as it was sound in execution.

An hour and eleven minutes after Umpire Harold Lebair had called
"play," including the time-out taken to quiet the boos and uproarious
protests on decisions in the explosive opening set, Brown had come to the
end of his meteoric winning streak and Kramer was seated on the throne of
the mighty.

MULLOY BEATS TALBERT WITH SUPER TENNIS

by Allison Danzig

One of the great matches of lawn tennis was played today on the Meadow
Club turf.

Two hours and forty minutes after it began, William Talbert of Wilmington, Delaware, dragged himself wearily to a chair, on the verge of
collapse, a beaten man who had given one of the gamest exhibitions within
memory on a tennis court and stopped a rout in the third set, only to
succumb to utter exhaustion and the unquenchable spirit of his rival after
standing within two strokes of victory.

Gardnar Mulloy of Miami, Florida, was the winner of the match, the final
round of the fifty-sixth annual Southampton invitation tournament.

For two sets and a part of the third, Mulloy belonged among the real
masters of the racket of this or any day as he took eleven games in succession
from one of the finest stylists on the courts, to win the first two sets and lead
2–0 in the next.

After that, the almost unbelievable perfection of his virtuosity in making
any and every shot in the book began to yield to the inroads of fatigue, but
he was as full of fight as his opponent. He came on from 3–5 in the fifth set,
when his plight seemed hopeless, to eke out victory in a thrilling finish
seldom equaled for its tension and drama in Meadow Club history. The
score was 8–6, 6–0, 3–6, 2–6, 10–8.

The largest crowd to turn out here in recent years looked on as Mulloy
confounded expectations in defeating the second-ranking player of the
country and thereby scored his first triumph on turf over Talbert since the
latter first gained prominence as a member of the first ten.

It has been a long time since a Southampton gallery has seen tennis the equal of the Miamian's performance in the first two sets, or a fight to the death to compare with today's in thrills without end and the dead gameness of both men in playing on their nerve as they slugged it out to the point of physical collapse.

No one would have given much for Malloy's chances when Talbert, after standing within two strokes of victory in the tenth game and then falling behind at 5–6, won the next two games at love. But Mulloy became a rampant foe again in the fourteenth, ran Talbert all over the court and finally had his opponent at his mercy.

Talbert, a diabetic, looked as though he was about to keel over after losing the seventeenth game at love. He played like a man in a daze in the eighteenth, the last, but played brilliantly, nevertheless, until the agony of his ordeal ended with Mulloy's cross-court forehand volley.

Talbert was laboring under somewhat of a handicap in the match. His bandaged left knee was not securely under him and at times he played badly, while his overhead smashing was clearly affected. But Mulloy deserves full credit for a victory gained with the most brilliant kind of tennis and with a courage to match his opponent's.

The tennis that the Miamian put forth today was by far the best this observer has ever seen come from his racket. For two sets it came close to being as good as anyone has played anywhere at any time. It was so nearly perfect as to leave the gallery marveling at the succession of winners that sped from his flailing racket and broke down Talbert's control.

There are few players who can stand up to Talbert in the back court. Mulloy hit so deep and with so much pace from both sides that the pressure was on his opponent. The pressure was chiefly on Talbert's marvelous backhand, which Mulloy hammered and crowded with forcing shots that pulled Talbert wide enough to take some of the threat out of his down-the-line shot.

Mulloy was equally good at the net, where he volleyed decisively. His service had far more sting than in any previous match of the week, and his return of service was strong and deep.

U. S. REGAINS DAVIS CUP FROM AUSTRALIA

by Ted Schroeder with Alan Trengove

Very soon after World War II a tennis revolution swept Australia, and I like to think that I helped engineer it.

I'm referring, of course, to the changes that came about following the 1946 Davis Cup Challenge Round at Melbourne.

At that time Australian tennis players, the press and the public—more isolated than ever by a long war—were living in the past.

Your game here was virtually not out of the romantic long-flannelled-trousers era. And your concept of a champion was a fine stroker of the ball, with immaculate control and flowing shots from the back of the court. He was pretty to watch. But he was an anachronism.

Unknown to the Australians, Jack Kramer had perfected the serve-volley game. He had thought about it right through the war and had worked out what came to be known as percentage tennis, the only scientific way to play the game, under the present rules.

It was like turning a man loose with a machine gun against a line of kids with catapults.

The American team that came to Australia that year consisted of Walter Pate (the manager), Kramer, Frank Parker, Gardnar Mulloy, Bill Talbert and myself. . . .

Our singles players were expected to be Kramer and Parker, but since Parker had lost to John Bromwich 6–0, 6–3, 6–1 in the deciding rubber of the 1939 Challenge Round I couldn't see how he could possibly be chosen.

Australia was a clear favorite to retain the Cup. Bromwich was an experienced Cup player, and he and Adrian Quist were an outstanding doubles pair. Dinny Pails, the other Aussie singles player, was an up-and-comer.

However, as I've stated, we felt we were playing a superior type of game to the Australians'. By the 1950s you people would learn your lesson too well for our comfort, but in 1946 you were blithely innocent of what was going to hit you.

I gave myself a good chance of playing the singles instead of Parker, though I'd never played Challenge Round tennis up to then.

As a matter of fact, I hadn't played much tennis at all for the past few years. At 25, I was working as a sales engineer in commercial refrigeration, having been discharged from the Navy in December, 1945. My only tennis outside Southern California in 1946 had been in the Newport Invitational and the U.S. championships.

But back in 1941 I'd played the best tennis of my life in losing 7–5 in the fifth set of a U.S. championship semi-final to Bobby Riggs, a vastly under-rated player.

I knew that if I could get anyone into a fifth set I'd probably beat him. In a way, it was my only hope.

You see, I was always in sound condition, I played tactically, and if I could hang on long enough till the other fellow got tired, my determination usually saw me through. (It was when I ran into someone like Frank Sedgman, who had just as much determination, plus ability, that we nearly killed each other.)

Let me explain how I categorize tennis players.

There are those who have great ability, but nothing in the head and nothing in the heart. They are very ordinary players. There are others of limited ability who can think and fight. They are better players. And lastly there are the few great champions who combine ability with intelligence and courage.

I place myself in the second category, Kramer in the third.

Technically mediocre, I tried to compensate by getting the best out of what I had.

I couldn't hit anything except in the air. So the more chewed up a grass-court got—say, in a five-setter—the more it suited me. Bad bounces would drive Bromwich and Parker crazy. But me? Well, even on cement, which gives you a perfect bounce, I could play more wood shots than Sammy Snead in a whole tournament season.

Kramer didn't play in the Victorian championships before the Challenge Round because he didn't have to. Parker didn't front either.

I played, and lost 6–3, 6–3, 6–4 to Bromwich in the final. By December 23 I was much fitter, physically and mentally. . . . Mr. Pate left the choice of his singles players to the team, and the vote went 5–1 to me. . . .

The Aussies were jubilant. I remember one newspaper headline which said: "Pate Gives Cup Away." And in *The Sun* R. E. Schlesinger declared bluntly that our team was weakened by my selection.

I drew Bromwich in the first match, and there must have been only a handful of people in Melbourne who gave me the remotest chance of winning. One of them was me.

I figured there was no way Bromwich could force me. When you played Jack Kramer you had to force him or he would take the match away from you. There was never this pressure from Bromwich.

Boxing Day that year was hot and calm—perfect conditions for a net-rushing Californian. I was as tight as a drum when I stepped on to the Kooyong center court in front of a then record crowd of 14,000. But after I'd banged the balls around and the sweat was on my brow I felt great.

Brom, his yellow hair flopping over his bronzed face, soon had his cagy touch game under way. There was not much in it for a while. Then he forced me into some errors by swinging his service wide to my forehand and driving wide to that wing. He gradually assumed control and took out the set, 6–3.

I wasn't unduly worried. If I could tighten my game, I thought I could win one or two sets. In percentage tennis you win on the other guy's errors, not your own winners. You apply the pressure and wait for his errors to come.

It's like playing a slot machine. The longer a guy plays, the more the percentages are against him—and he must lose.

In the second set I approached the net on shots down the middle of the court, reducing Brom's margin to play his deadly angled shots.

When he tried to stem the tide by putting up lobs I was able to smash them with confidence. More and more, he was having to attempt difficult shots. I took the set 6–1.

The Aussie crowd could now see it wasn't going to be as easy as they expected. They were in for a further shock, for after losing the first two games of the third set, I took the next six games in a row.

By now, I was serving and smashing as well as I could, and picking up a lot of Brom's attempted winners. His double-handed forehand, which was a great shot, was not consistently effective.

Here again, the percentages were against him. To make a double-handed shot you must take a half-step farther to the right, and this means you have to take a half-step back in the other direction to position yourself for the next shot. Over five sets those half-steps use up a lot of energy.

We took a 10-minute rest, and then Brom came out and couldn't do a thing wrong. I played the same attacking game, but for the whole set Brom's passing shots worked like a dream. I got behind two service breaks, and then let the set go, 6–0, making sure I started with my serve in the fifth.

Once more the match had see-sawed. The crowd was sure again that the experienced Aussie was so much on top that he could not be beaten. I knew he could. If I kept winning my service in the fifth, how could I lose?

As it turned out, I broke through his first service. I remember one shot in particular. Brom had lobbed over my head on a crucial point, and instead of playing a defensive shot, I hit the ball across court off my backhand for a winner.

That was not percentage tennis, but it was a darned good shot and decided a game. You may play umpteen good shots in a match, but if you can play three or four at the right time nobody can beat you. This was one of those times.

I went to a 5–3 lead and knew that I had the match in the bag. Brom was going for drop shots in desperation, but a lot of them I got to.

On match point I hit a sharply angled backhand across court. It gave the Aussie no chance, and I threw my racket up in the air in jubilation. America had drawn first blood—and the Cup was just about ours.

In the second singles Kramer beat Pails, 8–6, 6–2, 9–7, and the following day we sewed it up by outgunning Bromwich and Quist in the doubles, 6–2, 7–5, 6–4.

I remember the scene very clearly, and how emotional I felt. Joe Hunt, one of my buddies, had been killed on a naval training flight during the war. He had played Cup tennis in 1938–39, and we had often yarned on warships how we would win the Cup back together.

So I went to the microphone in that Kooyong stadium and the words spilled out.

"Joe, the Dog-Faced Boy," I said, "wherever you are, I wish you were here today. We owe a lot to you."

And look what that 1946 Challenge Round has led to for me personally! I am now on my 27th visit to this country, the last 18 months of my life being occupied managing General Dynamic's activities in Australia and New Zealand.

I have more friends here than in America. And I repeat: I think I played a part in modernizing the Australian game. God and the LTAA willing, I hope to come here many more times, and see how that game is progressing.

1 9 4 7

KRAMER REPELS PARKER TO RETAIN CROWN

by Allison Danzig

John A. Kramer stands as the undisputed king of the realm of amateur tennis, but the crown of this Alexander of the courts was shaky on his head as the climax came to his season of world conquest, undoubtedly his last as a simon pure.

For two sets yesterday in the final of the national championship, the 14,000 spectators who filled the Forest Hills Stadium to the rim saw a world champion in one of the worst slumps of his career. With roaring enthusiasm they cheered Frank Parker, the almost forgotten man of tennis, as he extracted the sting from the most potent weapons in the game and had Kramer at the mercy of his baffling tactical moves, like a Samson shorn of his strength.

Not since Sidney Wood tamed the lethal strokes of Ellsworth Vines at Seabright in 1930 with his soft-ball strategy and reduced the Californian to a state of helplessness, has so cleverly designed and executed a plan of battle been in evidence on American turf as Parker employed in this match.

In the end, the plan failed, as the challenger's strength ebbed and the champion, extricating himself from a morass of errors, loosened the full fury of his attack to win at 4–6, 2–6, 6–1, 6–0, 6–3. But the gallery will long remember the thrill and the chill of those first two sets and also the tense final chapter as the 31-year-old Parker gave his heavily favored and younger opponent the scare of his life.

When Lawrence A. Baker, during the presentation ceremony at the end of the match, mentioned the challenger's name, the 14,000 fans broke loose with such tumultuous applause and cheers that the vice president of the United States Lawn Tennis Association had to pause for a full minute before continuing his remarks.

In winning the championship in 1944 and 1945, Parker was not nearly the hero he was yesterday in defeat—a defeat that raised him to the stature of a leading contender for the Davis Cup berth that he sought in vain in 1946 and 1947. Kramer is not expected to be around to defend the cup in 1948, with a big pot of professional gold in the offing, and even at the age of 32 Parker, who was tough enough to play an exhausting three-hour semi-final match with John Bromwich and came back the next day to challenge Kramer dangerously through the fifth set, will be welcomed with open arms.

Kramer's victory, consummated with the same display of sand and character that stamped his performance in hammering Jaroslav Drobny into submission after the Czech had outplayed him in the first set and broken through for a 3–2 lead in the second, brought his greatest year of play on turf to a close. Not since Donald Budge made his grand slam in 1938 has any amateur so bestrode the courts like a colossus.

The tall blue-eyed Californian, who received the William Johnston Trophy for his sportsmanship, won the championship at Wimbledon before successfully defending his national singles crown and taking the doubles with Ted Schroeder.

He led the American team that brought back the cup from Australia last December and then defended it this year. He did not compete for the French or Australian crowns, but there is little doubt that he could have added them to his conquest had he chosen. Forest Hills, in all probability, will not see him again as an amateur and it will not soon look upon his like, as a player of the very first class with all the virtues that are esteemed in sporting competition.

Sharing the day's honors with Kramer and Parker as the sixty-sixth annual championships came to a close was Miss Louise Brough of Beverly Hills. Playing the best match she has ever had at Forest Hills, the blond Californian confounded expectations by defeating Miss Margaret Osborne of San Francisco, champion of Wimbledon, 8–6, 4–6, 6–1, to succeed Miss Pauline Betz of Los Angeles as titleholder. . . .

The final of the men's singles provided almost as many thrills for the gallery that packed the stadium for the second successive day as did the match between Parker and Bromwich on Saturday.

Kramer's frame of mind possibly had a bearing on his poor showing for the first two sets. With a fortune awaiting him if he accepts the professional offers that have been held out to him, there was a far greater reward then a silver cup at stake for him in the match, and it is understandable if he was under an unduly great mental strain. It is possible, too, that his lack of competition in singles all season, between Wimbledon and Forest Hills, told on him, as it did on Parker a year ago.

But, conceding that this was the case, it tells only a small part of the story of the champion's harrowing hour before he found the road to victory. The big factor was Parker's shrewdly planned method of resistance and his success in carrying it out with remarkable fidelity until fatigue set in and Kramer got his high-powered strokes under control.

Parker's plan was comparable to Wood's against Vines seventeen years ago. There was not as consistent use of the soft ball, but the idea was the same. He knew it would be suicidal to hit with Kramer and give him the pace he thrives on. Instead, he continually changed speed, threw in soft, high floaters, used short angle shots and interpolated drop shots, followed by lobs that were deadly traps.

Always Parker concentrated on Kramer's backhand. He kept his service there, with a twist kicking to the left, and he invariably directed his floaters to the backhand. Kramer's backhand sagged badly and his forehand broke, too, as his confidence dwindled. Indeed, his whole game was affected as he piled up errors and became more and more concerned.

Kramer started strongly, winning the first game with a kill and volley and leading at 30–0 on Parker's service. Then his troubles began. His control broke and he proceeded to pile up errors and lose that game, the third at love and the fourth at 15. He lost nine successive points on errors. The crowd did not know what to make of it. Parker did, and he kept up his plan of attack to win the set. Kramer led at 30–0 again in the eighth and at 40–0 in the tenth and each time his return of service ruined his chances.

The champion scored 13 earned points in the set and Parker only 1, but he piled up 31 errors to the challenger's 13. The crowd looked for Kramer to find himself in the second set and put Parker in his place, but it got worse.

Kramer fought with all his might. His service was much improved and at the net his volley and smash were unanswerable, but his ground strokes were still out of control and he could not return service. He did not score a winning shot with his drive from either side until the eighth game.

The turn in the play came finally. Kramer started the third set with two service aces and a drop shot, and he was on his way. That drop shot meant much. It was the first of a number. He was changing his ways and resorting to subtlety instead of relying solely on power. Parker won the second game, then the champion hit four crunching volleys to take the third at love.

There was a desperate fight in the fourth. Finding his return of service, Kramer kept going in, and his volley and kill brought him out on top. After that, Parker's resistance dwindled and he elected to conserve his strength for the fourth set.

The fourth was a repetition of the third. Kramer was in full cry and his forehand was so deep and scorching that Parker was under far more pressure than he could withstand. He soon decided to save himself for the fifth set, and Kramer swept through six games in a row in his characteristic manner.

Parker was on his toes and full of cunning and fight as the final set got under way, and when he won the first game the tension was on again. Kramer wasn't out of the woods. He had a clever foe to contend with, dead game and still amazingly fast around the court. The champion took the second game at love and broke through in the third.

The sixth game was a critical one. Kramer double-faulted twice and was down, 0–40. The pressure must have been fearful, but he rose to the occasion like a champion. His blasting service came to his rescue and he rushed for the volley and kill and won 5 points in a row.

Seeing Them in Action

THE LATER YEARS

The Australian Davis Cup team of 1939 came on to take the cup from the U.S., 3–2, after losing the first two matches. Adrian Quist, Jack Crawford, John Bromwich, Harry Hopman and Norman E. Brookes receive it from Holcombe Ward and Walter Pate   (PHOTOWORLD–FPG)

Bobby Riggs won both at
Wimbledon and at
Forest Hills in 1939
and repeated his U.S.
title victory in 1941.
(PHOTOWORLD–FPG)

1936 to 1940 was
Alice Marble's era.
She took the American
title four times and the
Wimbledon one as well
in 1939. If she had
played more, some feel
she could have been
the greatest woman player
of all time.   (USLTA)

Sarah Palfrey Cooke,
U.S. women's singles titlist
in 1941 and 1945
(USLTA)

Ted Schroeder (left) won the
Wimbledon crown in 1949, and
in that same year Pancho Gonzales took the American title for
the second year running. Here
they are together before the
finals at Forest Hills, where Gonzales eked out a dramatic five-set
victory.   (PHOTOWORLD–FPG)

Jack Kramer's big game swept
Forest Hills in 1946 and 1947,
and in the latter year he also
took the All-England crown
at Wimbledon. (USLTA)

The fabulous doubles combination of Louise Brough and Margaret Osborne (duPont), who
won the U.S. women's doubles
nine times running from 1942
through 1950 and then did it
again from 1955–1957 inclusive.
They also picked up the Wimbledon title five times. Each
was also an outstanding singles
player: Miss Brough won the
Wimbledon four times and
Forest Hills once; Mrs. duPont
won the U.S. title three times
and Wimbledon once.

Gardnar Mulloy and Billy
Talbert, both marvelous
doubles players with any partner throughout the 1940s, but
best with each other, are on
the left in this picture of the
1946 U.S. Davis Cup team. On
Captain Walter Pate's other
side are Frank Parker and
Jack Kramer.   (USLTA)

Budge Patty, Wimbledon
champion in 1950; although
an American, he spent most
of his playing career on European courts.   (USLTA)

Although she eventually lost in a
rain-interrupted match that had
to be resumed for the final three
games the next day, the 23-year-
old Althea Gibson created a sensation at Forest Hills in 1950
when she was barely outlasted by
Louise Brough in a 6–1, 3–6, 9–7
match.   (WIDE WORLD)

A few years later Miss Gibson was
clearly the world's best, winning
both at Wimbledon and at Forest
Hills in 1957 and again in 1958.
Here she is (foreground) de-
feating Darlene Hard in the
Wimbledon final of 1957.
(WIDE WORLD)

Dick Savitt, Wimbledon and
Australian champion in 1951.
Although in later years he was
little more than a weekend
player, he remained a fierce
contestant.   (USLTA)

Australia's Frank Sedgman
took the American title in
1951 and 1952, and added the
Wimbledon crown as well
in the latter year.
   (WILSON)

The lethal two-handed forehand of Pancho Segura, who turned professional before attaining his peak and reached his heights as a pro (USLTA)

Maureen Connolly, unbeatable in her prime, who before she was 20 years old won the U.S. championship and the Wimbledon title three years running: 1951–1953 for the former, 1952–1954 for the latter. Injury cut her career short in her prime. (PHOTOWORLD–FPG)

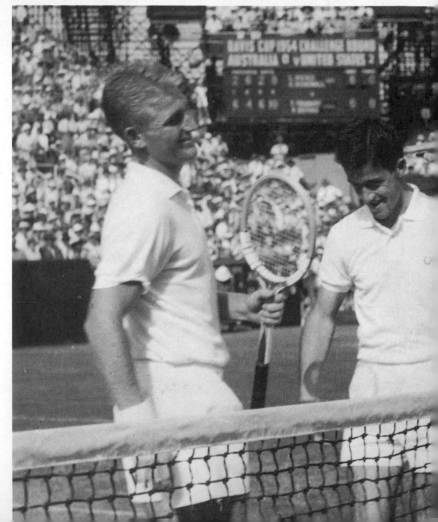

Here is Miss Connolly, at the age of 16, winning at Forest Hills against Shirley Fry.   (WIDE WORLD)

The most exciting Davis Cup win of modern times. After years of Australian domination, Vic Seixas and Tony Trabert take the third and deciding point by winning the doubles match over Lew Hoad and Ken Rosewall (on far side of net) in 1954.   (USLTA)

Jaroslav Drobny, the Czech, a long-time Wimbledon favorite of the crowd, finally captured the crown in 1954, defeating Rosewall.   (PHOTOWORLD–FPG)

Lew Hoad beat his fellow Australian, Ken Rosewall, in the finals of the 1956 Wimbledon tournament in four sets . . .   (WIDE WORLD)

. . . but two months later, at Forest Hills, Rosewall turned the tables on Hoad in the Forest Hills championship, also in four sets, to frustrate Hoad's last step toward sweeping a Grand Slam that year.　(WIDE WORLD)

In 1958 Alex Olmedo represented the U.S. in the Davis Cup and won it from Australia almost single-handed, taking both his singles matches and teaming with Hamilton Richardson to win the doubles. Here he gets a congratulatory embrace from Captain Perry T. Jones.　(PHOTOWORLD–FPG)

Maria Bueno of Brazil achieved the first of her many triumphs at Forest Hills and Wimbledon when she won the U.S. women's singles in 1959. The men's title was taken by Neale Fraser of Australia, who repeated in 1960 and won at Wimbledon as well. (USLTA)

Miss Bueno and Darlene Hard made a formidable doubles pair, teaming to win the U.S. title in 1960 and 1962, and the All England in 1960 and 1963. (USLTA)

Margaret Smith (later Margaret Court) won the first of her many national titles when she beat Darlene Hard in the finals at Forest Hills in 1962. She is in the far court here. The following year she broke through at Wimbledon for the first time. (WIDE WORLD)

The greatest of the Australian women players relaxes with her trophies after her Forest Hills triumph. (WIDE WORLD)

In that same year of 1962, the U.S. men's singles final was also contested by two Australians. Rod Laver (right) beat Roy Emerson in four sets and so completed a Grand Slam sweep of the Australian, French, British and American championships in one year, a feat accomplished only by Don Budge in 1938 prior to this time. (WIDE WORLD)

Manuel Santana, of Spain, who won both the U.S. and Wimbledon titles in the mid-1960s (USLTA)

Twenty years after his American championship victories in the late 1940s Pancho Gonzales beat Charles Pasarell of Puerto Rico on the Centre Court of Wimbledon in the longest match ever played in the All-England Championships: 22–24, 1–6, 16–14, 6–3, 11–9. The match took five hours and twelve minutes and, in addition to losing the first two sets, Gonzales had match-point against him on six occasions. The date: June 25, 1969 (WIDE WORLD)

A GALLERY OF
OTHER MODERN GREATS

Ann Haydon Jones
(USLTA)

Tony Roche
(USLTA)

Nancy Richey
(USLTA)

Arthur Ashe
(WIDE WORLD)

Billie Jean King
(USLTA)

John Newcombe
(USLTA)

Stan Smith
(USLTA)

Rod Laver
(USLTA)

**TWO NEW
ATTRACTIVE
CANDIDATES
FOR THE
GALLERY OF GREATS**

Chris Evert
(USLTA)

Evonne Goolagong
(USLTA)

KRAMER WINS WIMBLEDON

from the Associated Press

Jack Kramer of Los Angeles added the Wimbledon singles championship to his imposing list of tennis titles today by routing Tom Brown of San Francisco, 6–1, 6–3, 6–2, in one of the most one-sided finals ever played in the All-England tournament.

Kramer needed only 45 minutes to blow his fellow Californian off Wimbledon's famed center court as the Royal Family and 15,000 other spectators sat in virtual silence, completely awed by his mastery of the game.

The 25-year-old holder of both the outdoor and indoor titles in his own country drove Brown from the net with passing shots to the pocket, delivered a service that was unbreakable and never surrendered the offensive. In succeeding France's Yvon Petra and recapturing the trophy last brought to America by Bobby Riggs in 1939, Kramer demonstrated conclusively that he is the best amateur player in the world today. And he did it so mechanically that it looked simple and easy to the enthralled fans, many of whom stood in line all night for admittance to the big arena.

Kramer put Brown on the defensive when he broke his service in the third game of the first set with a battery of passing shots. From then on he was an unchallenged dictator. He forced with a service that was credited with only three clean aces but invited error by its speed. Whenever Brown failed to get length in his returns Kramer pounced to the net to kill mercilessly.

Brown, 24-year-old University of California law student, who finished his examinations just in time to get here for the tournament, had neither the power of stroke, variety of shot nor the speed to interrupt the favorite on his way to the title.

When King George, making his first Wimbledon visit since he played in the 1926 tournament, had taken his seat with Princess Elizabeth and Princess Margaret, Kramer and Brown ambled onto the worn lawn for their pay-off struggle. They faced the Royal box, dipped their heads and then turned to the match for which they had practiced together, eaten steaks at the same table and shared each other's nervousness in the locker room.

Their jitters told in the first two games, each winning his service on the other's errors. Then Kramer, first to shake off the tension, sprinted down the sideline to make a return that earned him a 2–1 lead. For that shot the spectators applauded. Then they relaxed in almost reverent respect for perfection as Kramer gobbled up the next four games, in which Brown got only three earned points.

By holding his first three services in the second set, Brown kept it level at 3–all. But Kramer broke up this tit-for-tat tussling by taking three games in a row. Any chance for the third-seeded Brown to rally faded when he dropped his service at love in the opening game of the third set. Like a man in a hurry, Kramer finished it off in the eighth game. As it was over, both players went to the Royal box, where the King presented the trophy to Kramer.

15,000 DEFY BLIZZARD FOR KRAMER'S PRO DEBUT

by John M. Ross

It was December 26th in New York City and it snowed. In fact, it snowed and it snowed and it snowed. And the old graybeards, who used to take immeasurable pride in retelling the story of the Great Blizzard of 1888, were silenced at last.

The storm of '88 lost its regal spot on the record books in mid-afternoon and it was still snowing. And Promoter Jack Harris, who was to introduce his so-called "tennis match of the decade" at Madison Square Garden that evening, peered gloomily out of his hotel window. "No one will go out to see a tennis match in this weather," he lamented.

His entourage echoed agreement.

They seemed so right. The great city already was paralyzed under a 20-inch blanket of white. Its vast transit system—buses, trolleys, elevated lines, railroads and even the subways—choked off. Stalled cars cluttered the streets and well-meaning snow plows were helpless. Thousands were stranded at their places of business at the end of the day. And, what's more, it was still snowing!

Yes, Harris and his extravaganza seemed doomed. He once thought the spacious Garden would bulge at the seams for this attraction. For, here he had the two finest tennis players in captivity—Big Jack Kramer, with the mightiest game in tennis, and pint-sized Bobby Riggs, unsurpassed as the game's defensive genius. The amateur king versus the pro champ! Fans had talked about this one for more than two years and had speculated on its outcome.

Now, it was apparent, they would settle the score in comparative privacy!

Several hours later, at 9:39 P.M. to be exact, with the snow now piled up at 25.8 inches, Jack Kramer took the court against Bobby Riggs while 15,114 people cheered. That's right, 15,114! . . .

How they got there, no one will ever know. And who knows how they got home, or when? But, there they were, 15,114 strong, in their heaviest winter armor—galoshes, boots, ski togs, earmuffs, etc.,—to see a tennis match on the worst winter's night in the history of New York. Some came on skis, others had to plow through snowdrifts four feet deep, making the journey from their homes on foot.

It was a testimonial to Riggs and Kramer and to tennis. But, it was a night that the performers had to take a back seat to the spectators. They really stole the show!

Before the main event was staged, Impresario Harris, beaming with joy, proudly announced that record-smashing gross gate of $55,730.50 had poured into his cash box and that the event was a sellout. Actually, 16,052 tickets were sold, and only 938 failed to conquer the blizzard. The startling "take" easily eclipsed the tennis box-office mark of $49,000, set by Ellsworth Vines and Fred Perry in their Garden match in 1937, and launched what should prove to be the most successful professional tour in the history of the game.

The New York press was so startled by the unbelievable turnout that it devoted columns of space to the story of the crowd alone. Perhaps Jimmy Powers, sports editor of the New York *Daily News,* sounded the keynote when he tabbed it "the greatest tribute to an indoor athletic event in the history of sport."

The brand of tennis played was not as glittering and some of the snowbirds had a right to be disappointed, particularly those in the Kramer camp.

Jake left his big game in the dressing room and came out with a severe case of what the theatrical people call "first night jitters." This is not meant to detract from Bobby Riggs's well-earned victory. Bobby, the greatest money player ever to wield a racket, won just as he predicted, in four sets, 6–2, 10–8, 4–6, 6–4. And he made the supposedly herculean task of trouncing the invincible boss of the amateurs look quite simple.

After appropriate introductions of the headliners by Alice Marble, the fans moved to the edges of their chairs to watch the "match of the decade." Kramer tightened up at the start and lost the first three games, Riggs breaking service on the second. His game lacked smoothness and he experienced considerable difficulty in keeping the ball in the court. At the end of 20 minutes, Bobby again broke Jack's big service in the eighth game after Kramer held the advantage, and took the opening set, 6–2.

The cool, methodical Riggs, who went into the match a 7–5 favorite, was outthinking the big Davis Cup hero at every turn. And outplaying him, too, at his own game. He discarded his defensive role and stormed the net time and again, and it seemed that each one of his strokes was a definite part of a well-organized plan.

The second set was the deciding factor of the match. Kramer seemed to settle down momentarily and moved to a 3–1 lead. After Riggs drew up to 3–2, Big Jake went off on a spree of eight errors and was down 3–4 as they went into the eighth game. Kramer steadied here to even the count, but he missed his big chance in the ninth game when Riggs was down 15–40 on his own serve. Bobby completely outwitted Jack here and saved the game.

That was the turning point, for Kramer came through with a love game on his own delivery to square it at 5–5. If he hadn't blown his big edge in the ninth he could have won the set. But Jack was finding out, like a good many of his predecessors have, that you can't give the cagy pro king the slightest opening.

Kramer fought hard to stay on even terms as the set wore on, turning back Riggs in the 12th game after the latter was at set point. But, after leveling off at 8–all, Jake lost the 17th game on his own errors and blew the next one on his own service as he slashed two successive volleys into the twine, giving Riggs the set, 10–8.

Bobby was playing Jack's backhand for all it was worth, hitting the ball so low that Kramer had to stoop to his shoetops for the pickup. As a result, Jack was unable to get his usual power behind these drives and Bobby had one less gun to worry about. The most amazing fact, however, was that Kramer's vaunted service, which was supposed to blast little Bobby off the court, was broken four times in the first two sets.

The third set conformed to the pre-match script, which Bobby had torn to bits in the first two stanzas. Big Jake hit hard and drove down the lines as the pro-Kramer gallery came to life. He kept Bobby on the baseline and the crowd envisioned a heroic Kramer rally such as the one he sported against Frankie Parker in the dramatic five-setter at the Nationals, last September.

Jack cracked through Riggs's delivery in the seventh game to take a 4–3 lead. He put the set away at 6–4, finishing up with two consecutive service aces.

The loss of the set didn't seem to disturb Bobby, who appeared to shift into low gear when Jack's game picked up. Leading two sets to one, Bobby knew he was in the driver's seat, and rather comfortable, at that.

When the big blond Californian jumped into a 2–love lead in the fourth set, Riggs appeared to be in hot water. But, like the seasoned campaigner that he is, Riggs coolly assembled his guns and went to work. He won the next three games with the loss of only three points. The count then went 4–all, with Riggs again holding the odd-game advantage on serve. Bobby stepped on the gas in the ninth game, winning it at love, and then smashed through Kramer's delivery in the tenth to win the set and match.

The match statistics clearly indicated a big edge for Riggs. There was a tremendous difference in the service department, where Kramer was supposed to rule supreme. Bobby out-aced Jack, 9–8, broke Kramer's service six times while losing his own only three times. Jack double-faulted a half dozen times, while Bobby was guilty of two.

Kramer led on placements, 55–22, but he netted the ball 46 times and drove out 69. Riggs was into the twine for 33 and too strong on 37 shots.

Editors' note: The 1937 Vines-Perry gate receipts were reported as $58,119.50.

PATTY-BROMWICH MATCH AT WIMBLEDON, 1947

by Gloria Butler

It is a matter of record that on Saturday, June 28th, 1947, the queues outside both entrances of Wimbledon were over a mile long.

For many weary years, the British people had been deprived of almost everything. As far as tennis was concerned, 1947 was the first post-war year in which most of the world's best players either returned to Wimbledon or appeared there for the first time; therefore the first Saturday—quarter-finals day—had a record-shattering crowd. People had started queueing up, complete with thermos flasks and rugs, at 5 P.M. on Friday in order to be first through the gates the following morning and first to have the doubtful privilege of standing like perspiring sardines to watch, among other matches, the battle between John Bromwich of Australia, the No. 2 seed, and Budge Patty, the relatively unknown young American.

John Bromwich was a two-handed wizard with endless stamina and unbelievable touch. He was not a hard hitter. His forte was disguise and a complete repertoire of strokes. He possessed a drop shot that looked like a forehand drive until the moment of impact, and among his great passing shots was the delicate lob that trapped the player leaning too close to the net. In this grass court championship he was considered by Kramer to be his greatest rival. His years of experience had deservedly earned for him the reputation of a formidable opponent.

Budge Patty had a far more limited amount of experience. He had yet to win honors in a major match on Wimbledon's famous Center Court. His game was as yet unsure from the baseline and he felt confident only at net. He had one additional disadvantage which would have been enough to keep most people out of tennis altogether. He suffered from extremely low blood pressure. He tired easily, and if the exhaustion was profound, he turned ashen with fatigue and had difficulty breathing.

Patty played the match according to a plan. He went all out for the first set, but, knowing that to stay on the baseline was dangerous against the steady, insidious shots of his opponent, he came to net repeatedly. Under this pressure, Bromwich gave momentarily and Patty took the first stanza, 6–4. In the second set, Bromwich came into his own, moving Patty about the court although the latter seemed careful not to try for the difficult shots. Bromwich took the set easily at 6–0, but it was won more from Patty's apparent disinterest than from the Australian's brilliant play. Many wondered why Patty did not make the effort to annex a lead of two sets to love. Wouldn't this have circumvented the match from going to a grueling five sets and save his much needed stamina? The truth of the matter was that Patty just did not have the strength to go into net for two successive sets and he knew it.

The third set was a repetition of the first: brilliant play by two great touch artists in a thrilling duel of thrust and parry. Patty edged past at 6–4 by again breaking Bromwich's serve. At the end of the set, Patty was at the end of his rope. As he started the fourth, few spectators would have given a plugged nickel for his chances. To the average onlooker, this stanza was a sad spectacle of a player too exhausted to attack or defend. A few even went out to tea convinced, after a look at the haggard youth walking apathetically from side to side of the court and making absolutely no effort to run for anything, that the sooner it was over, the better. They failed to realize they were witnessing a *chef d'oeuvre* in tactical maneuvering.

Patty's plan was to partition his strength, knowing that there is no rest period allowed at Wimbledon; players are not even permitted to sit down while toweling themselves off. By going all out for the first set, he could afford to take it easier in the second which, in turn, would give him enough energy for the third. Having won this set, he was genuinely exhausted, but his only hope for final victory lay in recuperating in the fourth set for the big effort in the fifth. There was nothing in his plan that called for Bromwich to recuperate too, so Patty did something that had never before been seen on the Center Court.

Every time Bromwich served, Patty parried with a delicate drop shot. When Bromwich returned it, Patty would watch the ball go by reflectively and walk over to receive the next service. On his own serve, he used the same tactics, dropping his return over the net and lobbing over Brom's head when the latter came in. Let Bromwich win the set while Patty rested!

At the end of the fourth set, won comfortably by Bromwich at 6–1, Patty had recuperated and, though still very fatigued, was less tired than he had been at the end of the third. Bromwich, an extremely astute player himself, realized the reason behind the seeming nonchalance of his opponent and knew that the fifth set was going to be a battle.

From the first point of the last stanza, Patty reverted to his net-rushing tactics of the first and third sets with a suddenness that startled many people long convinced of the outcome. But fatigue had enveloped him to such an extent that his reflexes were slower and Bromwich passed him time and time again. Yet he forced himself to come in, knowing it was his only chance. Patty's face was gray from fatigue, and one got the impression that he was lunging almost blindly as he tried to outguess Bromwich at the net. Sometimes he guessed right, sometimes not; then the painful walk to the baseline and the whole tottering business of getting into the net again. Across the barrier, an unhurried Bromwich alternated passing shots with judicious little lobs that just skimmed over the top of Patty's racket.

Then the Australian's serve was broken and Patty had the advantage. Literally reeling on his feet, Patty brought the score around to match point. The next point seemed interminable. Finally the Australian saw an opening down Patty's backhand alley and hit for it. Budge leaped to cut it off but was a fraction late. Suddenly, without any warning, his legs gave from under him and he fell flat on his face in the grass, his racket missing the ball by an inch. Despairingly, his glance followed its flight until it landed—six inches outside the baseline!

And so Patty, the young man with a plan and the genius of a Cochet, became the dark horse of Wimbledon 1947 and started on the road to tennis immortality.

GONZALES, RANK OUTSIDER, WINS U.S. TITLE

by Allison Danzig

The rankest outsider of modern times sits on the tennis throne today.

Unknown in the East until he made his first appearance on turf a year ago, Richard (Pancho) Gonzales, stalwart 20-year-old Californian from Los Angeles with the thundering service and the touch of a master in his volley, won the amateur championship of the United States yesterday in one of the most exciting finishes the tournament has known.

With darkness settling upon the stadium of the West Side Tennis Club in Forest Hills and the referee, Dr. S. Ellsworth Davenport 2d, prepared to call a postponement if a decision was not reached forthwith in the almost interminable third set, Gonzales leaped for the kill that had twice escaped him by a single stroke in his final-round match with Eric Sturgess of South Africa.

Amid the cheers of the 11,000 spectators who had taken successive drenchings during the long afternoon's showers, but stayed to the last in complete disregard of discomfort and the fading light, the strong young Californian steeled himself for the victory that must be now or possibly never, and gained it at the twelfth hour.

With the score 13–12 in Gonzales' favor in the third set, the Californian, who had been helpless to make any headway against Sturgess' service since he had twice stood at match point in the twelfth game, tore for the net, where he had given so dazzling a display all afternoon. Two unbeatable volleys, one a delicately turned drop shot, carried him to 40–15, once again a stroke removed from victory.

The gallery screamed from the excitement and tension, and then a big "shush" spread through the stands. In absolute silence Sturgess, a dead game antagonist who had grown stronger and stronger through this nerve-wracking last set, toed the line to serve. The ball came back; they were in a rally, with the crowd hanging on every stroke, and then came the shot that turned the place into a bedlam.

From his fine, if erratic, backhand, Gonzales whipped the ball like a bullet straight down. Sturgess, rushing in desperately, was caught a step short of position. His half-volley hardly got off the ground, to land in the net, and the seventeenth ranking player of the country and the last American seeded in the draw sat on the throne occupied by Jack Kramer for the past two years. The score of the match was 6–2, 6–3, 14–12.

The victory of the young Californian, whose record for the season had been lacking in any distinction except for a triumph over Gardnar Mulloy at Southampton and victories over Frank Parker and Jaroslav Drobny of Czechoslovakia in making his way to the final round of the championship, followed upon another exciting finish to the women's tournament.

In the longest final match on record since 1898 in the days when women played for the best of five sets, Mrs. William duPont of Wilmington, Delaware, the former Margaret Osborne, wrested the title from Miss Louise Brough of Beverly Hills, California, winner this year of the Wimbledon title. Escaping defeat by a stroke in the same twelfth game of the third set in which Sturgess had staved off disaster, Mrs. duPont finally crowned her years of effort by effecting the lone break in the record-breaking set to win the match at 4–6, 6–4, 15–13. . . .

Owing to the interruptions and the seemingly endless length of the third set of the women's final, during which the crowd showed its impatience to have the men's final get under way, the match between Gonzales and Sturgess had to be played in fading light and encircling gloom from the start and almost in darkness for the last fifteen minutes.

It was rather unfortunate for the fine sportsman from South Africa that he had to take the Californian's scorching service in such light, though he handled it very well when he had any chance at all, and Gonzales, whose court deportment is equally to be commended, commented upon this advantage in his remarks over the loudspeaker after President Lawrence Baker of the U.S. Lawn Tennis Association had presented the championship cup to him.

Gonzales, one of the youngest players to win the championship, established himself in the forefront of the candidates for the 1949 American Davis Cup team with his victory over Sturgess, if he had not done that in defeating Parker and Drobny.

His performance yesterday was not the equal of the tennis that has been played in the stadium by other champions, but it answered a number of questions in a manner much to his credit, and, considering his limited experience on grass and the fact that prior to 1947 he had been denied full opportunity of competing in California tournaments for a number of years, it is extraordinary that his game should have arrived at such maturity as he showed in the championship.

Against Drobny, the superbly built youth from Los Angeles had demonstrated one of the very strongest services in the game and his skill as a volleyer, as well as his ability to stay in a bitter fight and prevail in the face of discouraging vicissitudes.

Yesterday, against one of the real stylists of tennis, whose main strength is the classic game of developing an attack carefully prepared from the back of the court and carried forward with discretion and diplomacy, Gonzales showed that he has the ground strokes required of a player who aspires to reach the first class.

Ground strokes did not count for too much in the Drobny match except on the return of service. It was all service and volley, and the rallies were of short duration. Yesterday, there was a different kind of match.

It was a match fought chiefly from the back of the court. The volley was important and it was the stroke that won for Gonzales, but his service in the first two sets was not the battering assault weapon it had been against the player from Czechoslovakia, and he could not have got in so many winning shots from the net had his ground strokes not provided the proper approach to give him safe access.

It was thought that the Californian would have to serve at his best to win against so genuinely sound an opponent and so clever a strategist as Sturgess. After the effort he had expended with his delivery against Parker and Drobny there was some doubt as to whether it would be as formidable yesterday.

It turned out that his service was not that strong. Nevertheless Gonzales demonstrated his superiority in the first two sets and had the staying powers and the ability to lift his service in the third when Sturgess was playing his best tennis of the match and threatening more and more after escaping disaster in the twelfth game.

Sturgess did not quite come up to expectations yesterday until the late stages. Whether it was the poor light or the drabness of the weather, his ground strokes were not under the control he had shown all week and he was not as secure in his volleying. His backhand disappointed in particular and suffered by comparison with Gonzales's as the rivals concentrated in attacking the offside.

Three times Sturgess lost his service in the opening set while breaking through Gonzales' once. The seventh game proved the sterling worth of the American's backhand as he broke through for the third time, and he pulled out the eighth from 0–40 for the set.

The second set saw Gonzales still the master and making the fewer errors, although his service was still not functioning at its best. The poise and headiness of the youngster were shown as he broke through for the second time in the ninth game with the aid of a half-volley lob followed by a winning volley lob, and finally a beautifully turned drop shot that Sturgess saluted.

With the third set Gonzales began to explode service aces in his best fashion, and it was not entirely because of the poor light. It was well that he did, for Sturgess now began to play better and better. Gonzales went to 3–1 and 30–0, and his opponent drew even at 4–all. From then on it was a bitter fight and after Gonzales had passed up two match points in the twelfth game he was fighting to stay even.

Twice he had narrow escapes and, with Sturgess playing so brilliantly and holding his service so easily, it seemed that the match might well go to a fourth set on the morrow. Then the referee appeared upon the court and

Gonzales, realizing that the play might possibly take an altogether different turn if there was a postponement, immediately took his cue and lifted his game to win in a sensational finish.

1948

GONZALES AND SCHROEDER WIN THRILLING SEMI-FINALS

by Allison Danzig

The champion of the United States will play the monarch of Wimbledon in the tennis match of the year today and Forest Hills may see an outpouring of fans to put standing room in the Stadium at a premium.

In as exciting a pair of semi-finals as the national championship has provided in many seasons, Richard (Pancho) Gonzales of Los Angeles, the defending titleholder, and Frederick R. (Ted) Schroeder of La Crescenta, California, winner of the British crown, both were confronted with the specter of defeat yesterday and rose to the occasion like the fighting champions they are, to set up a tremendously appealing final.

Gonzales required only four sets to carry out his assignment, as compared with five for Schroeder, but the cool 21-year-old six-footer was subjected to as galling and humiliating a drubbing for the better part of an hour as any champion within memory has experienced before he was able to get his head above water and go on to victory over Frank Parker, 3–6, 9–7, 6–3, 6–2. Schroeder won from Bill Talbert, 2–6, 6–4, 4–6, 6–4, 6–4.

Forest Hills has heard a lot of cheering all through a week of exciting play, but the performance of Parker in winning the first set and harrying Gonzales unmercifully until the score stood 5–2 in the former's favor in the second chapter was nothing short of spellbinding upon the 13,000 who filled the stadium nearly to capacity.

Twice a winner of the crown and a wonderful competitor for more than fifteen years in the championship, the 33-year-old Parker surpassed anything he has ever shown before at Forest Hills with this almost unbelievably perfect exhibition of court craft and racket wizardry. Never before in the experience of this observer has anyone used the lob with such demoralizing precision, and not often has anyone combined such baffling, adamantine defensive genius with so much brilliance in attacking from every quarter.

Gonzales, twelve years Parker's junior, started out with the fight of a lion, seeking to let loose the full fury of his cannonball service and net attack upon the expressionless, trim figure across the net whom he had beaten in their three previous meetings. Plainly he was in the mood to make the kill with implacable dispatch, and that was what most everyone in the big gallery expected he would do.

In the very first game the crowd had a shock as Parker broke through from 0–30. It happened again in the third game, but the excitement had not really begun, for Gonzales retaliated each time, and when he won the fifth game on service to lead at 3–2 it seemed he was finally on his way.

Then came as shocking a half-hour of mortification as a defending champion has undergone at Forest Hills, and the crowd kept up a continuous roar as Parker ran his rival all over the court and made him look like a tyro. The regularity with which he threw lobs of perfect height and depth over Gonzales' head, to trap him as he came tearing in to the net and send him scurrying back frantically, reached the point where it was comical for the gallery, and shrieks of mirth rang out again and again.

There was nothing funny about it for Gonzales. He was fighting desperately, giving himself unsparingly in the effort to get to close grips with his opponent, and over and over he was running into a jolting counter-blow that left him confused and stricken, like a wounded king of the jungle. Like a king, he still kept attacking, and always the same thing happened.

Not only was Parker tossing lobs over his head. He was knocking back Gonzales' big service deep to the corner or short across court for winners or to extract the error, passing him at the net or forcing him into mistakes there and volleying himself like a master with crisp cross-court forehand winners or delicately turned drop volleys.

In three games Gonzales got just one point and then he lost the next one also, after leading at 40–15, as his first service refused to go in, and the set was gone.

It must have been a fearful jolt for the young champion to find himself so completely outclassed and outwitted. But his ordeal was to become more desperate as Parker went ahead to 5–2 in the second set. The pace slowed a bit, but the lob was still a deadly instrument in Parker's hand and Gonzales' first service refused to function.

The crisis came in the eighth game. Three times Parker stood within two points of gaining a lead of two sets to none, and had he succeeded there is no telling what might have happened. At this critical stage Gonzales' service finally came to his rescue. Five tremendous serves exploded from his racket in the game, three of them for outright aces, and Parker had missed his chance, as he missed it two years ago after giving Jack Kramer the scare of his life in the final.

The crowd gave Gonzales an earsplitting ovation as he took the game and there was no mistaking where its sympathy lay as he now took command, never to relinquish it except for a brief period of wavering that permitted Parker to save three set points in the twelfth game.

The young Californian deserved this tribute on a courage and resolution that refused to waver all the time he stood with his back to the wall, and for the rest of the set and in the next two the gallery saw him work the wrath of his terribly swift service and blazing volleys and overheads upon his weakening older opponent, who no longer could throw up those deadly lobs or take advantage of the openings he so skillfully worked up.

There were thrills and drama enough to satisfy any tennis gathering for an afternoon in this magnificently waged battle, but more were to come as Schroeder showed once again that he is a bulldog for fight in a 5-set match in overcoming the superb challenge of Talbert. . . .

Talbert, fourth ranking player of the country, who crushed Jaroslav Drobny in the quarter-finals and boasts two victories over Gonzales for the season, observed his thirty-first birthday yesterday and it seemed that he would really have occasion to celebrate royally, so dangerously did he challenge Schroeder.

No player in the amateur ranks has a sounder all-round game than the New York stylist, and the strength and fidelity of his ground strokes, as well as the excellence of his service and volleying, had the Wimbledon champion in trouble over and over. To come out on top against such sterling passing shots and returns of service, Schroeder had to prove that he belongs among the masters of the volley of his time, and his own ground strokes had to stand up to the searching test of the beautiful driving rallies with which the match was filled.

It was a strange match. In the first set Talbert led at 5–0, permitting his rival only six points to that stage. In the second set Schroeder went ahead by 5–1, and in the third Talbert again rushed to the front by 5–1. Each man in turn rose to brilliant heights to play his rival off his feet.

Schroeder played very badly at times, but he did so under the grinding pressure of Talbert's marvelous backhand and forehand, which returned service consistently low or deep to make the Californian's volley difficult. When he was in full cry, the dispatch of his volley and smash was too much for even as sharply armed an opponent as Talbert to resist, and in this match, as in the other, the younger man had the vitality and speed of foot to hammer out the victory against a tiring opponent who could not sustain his control.

In the second set Talbert rallied at 1–5 to come up to 4–5, and in the third it was Schroeder's turn to do the same thing. The Californian was attacking with such dazzling speed during his rally that it seemed there was no stopping him, particularly when he got to 40–15 in the tenth game on his service. But Talbert came through with three marvelous backhand returns of service, and a gasp went up from the crowd as Schroeder, on top of the net, failed on the easiest kind of an overhead smash, to lose the set.

There was real cause for concern on Schroeder's part as they left the court for the intermission, and when they returned the tension mounted as he lost his service in the fourth game after breaking through in the third. The Californian was fighting for his life now and, like Gonzales, he showed his mettle with the way he rose to the occasion, to force Talbert on the defensive with the speed and accuracy of his play.

In the final set, with Talbert definitely weakening, Schroeder went to 3–0 on two service breaks and his work seemed done. But once more Talbert challenged, to bring roars from the crowd as he broke back in the fourth from 0–30 and took the fifth at love. He made a fight for the sixth game and lost it and came back from 0–30 in the seventh, but it was evident now that Schroeder was too strong for him.

In the final game came some of the greatest excitement of the match. Schroeder, playing his volleys carefully, went to 40-0. Four times he stood at match point and each time he was denied, amid wild cheering. The fourth time his double-fault thwarted him, then he got the add again on a powerful service, and this time he finished matters as Talbert's backhand return of service found the net.

GONZALES AND DUPONT RETAIN CROWNS

by Allison Danzig

Richard (Pancho) Gonzales' reign as national amateur tennis champion was extended for a second year yesterday, and no holder of the crown has shown more perseverance in enduring and surmounting the barbs of adversity than did the 21-year-old six-footer from Los Angeles to defeat Frederick R. (Ted) Schroeder of La Crescenta, California, in the Forest Hills stadium yesterday.

Beaten in a record-breaking 34-game opening set—the longest ever played in a championship final—after five times requiring only a point to win it, and outplayed by a wide margin in the second as the inevitable reaction brought on the blight of apathy, Gonzales took the gallery of 13,000 and his tiring older opponent by storm as he came back to win at 16–18, 2–6, 6–1, 6–2, 6–4.

The women's title also was carried off for the second successive year by Mrs. William duPont, the former Margaret Osborne, of Wilmington, Delaware. In a one-sided final that contrasted with last year's epochal marathon, she defeated Miss Doris Hart of Jacksonville, Florida, 6–4, 6–1.

The veterans' championship was won for the sixth successive year by J. Gilbert Hall of New York. In the concluding round on the grandstand court he won from Wilmer Allison of Austin, Texas, former men's national titleholder, 6–3, 6–2, and maintained his record of never losing a set in all the years he has held the crown.

Gonzales, the victim of repeated setbacks during the year both at home and abroad, showed his characteristic genius for bringing his game to its peak in the big match that counts. He did that in the Davis Cup challenge round and he did it again in the championship.

One can hardly give the champion too much praise for his moral fiber. Almost invariably the loser of an opening set of anything like the length of yesterday's, which broke the 16–14 record set by John Doeg and Frank Shields in the 1930 final, loses heart as well and never is able to overcome the discouragement of the setback. So it seemed would be the case yesterday, as Gonzales slumped badly in the second set and appeared to be resigned to his fate.

For an hour and thirteen minutes through that thirty-four game opener the champion had fought his rival in a tremendous duel of service and volley. Seventeen times he had scored on unquestionable service aces, which must have set a record for one set, and he had matched Schroeder in winning one love game after another.

So devastating was Gonzales' service that never until the twenty-fifth game was Schroeder able to get to "deuce" against it. The only other time he got that far was the thirty-first game, until the lone break of the set was effected in the thirty-third.

In the thirtieth game came the most painful experience of all for the champion. Schroeder was behind at 0–40 as the champion threw two perfect lobs over his head, and the big crowd was ready to let loose with a thundering roar. Instead it cheered the Wimbledon titleholder for the great fight he made to pull out of that seemingly hopeless situation, twice as Gonzales' backhand failed on the return of service, as it did so often in the match, and the third time with one of Schroeder's overhead smashes.

Gonzales refused to become discouraged after missing that golden opportunity and won his next service. Then came the bitter blow. Behind at 0–40 in the thirty-third game, he emulated his rival in pulling up to deuce, to the thunderous applause of the crowd, and after Schroeder had gained advantage point on a net-cord shot, one of several by which he benefited, the champion brought the house down again with a searing service ace.

Then came a particularly bitter pill for the titleholder. In the next rally, an exciting exchange of lightning strokes, he executed one of his adroit drop volleys. The side linesman cried "out" and immediately an outburst of protests came from the stands.

Gonzales cried out too, then immediately accepted the decision with the fine sportsmanship Schroeder was to exhibit on the final point of the match and which both men showed throughout. In the next rally, the last of the set, the champion slipped as he made his volley and a gasp went up from the crowd as the ball fell into the net.

It seemed that the fates were against Gonzales. All the luck in the match had been with Schroeder, though it had not amounted to much, and that fact and the memory of the great opportunity he had missed at 40–0 were enough to have broken the spirit of most players after making so great a fight for seventy-three minutes—as long as many entire matches last.

To all appearances Gonzales was a beaten champion as the second set ended. But with the start of the third the big fellow lost no time in reassuring his admirers that he was in the fight again for all he was worth. It was the Gonzales of the first set with whom Schroeder had to reckon now, with his mighty service going full blast, his footwork speeded up and his volley doing deadly execution.

Four games in a row went to Gonzales without deuce being called once. Rifled service aces and blazing passing shots and volleys were speeding from his racket in a barrage of winning shots that had his rival helpless.

The ten-minute rest period did not serve to restore the vigor of Schroeder's game. He was offering more resistance, but his play lacked the vitality of his rival's. He could not return service nor was he attacking at the net as often or making the dazzling volleys for which he is feared.

With the final set, Schroeder dug in and made so strong a fight that the crowd was kept on tenterhooks almost to the very end. This was the famous fifth set, and no one had beaten him down the wire in four long matches at Wimbledon or in two in the championship against Frank Sedgman and Talbert.

Schroeder saved the first game from 0–30 and then had the crowd holding its breath as he got to 30–0 against Gonzales' service in the fourth. This was his chance, and, as it proved, his last one. His backhand failed him in trying to pass on an easy volley, and he never threatened to break through again. Nevertheless, he held his own service to 4–all even though Gonzales was both serving and returning service the better of the two.

As the play went on, the crowd could sense Schroeder's weakening in the opportunities he wasted with errors unworthy of him when he is fresh. Gonzales was missing chances, too, but not because of fatigue so much as from the nervous tension as he sighted victory.

Then came the break that decided the match. Against a clearly tiring Schroeder, Gonzales went on the attack. The return of service which had been so recalcitrant for most of the match now was functioning beautifully, to keep the ball at Schroeder's feet and extract the error or elicit a half-volley that enabled the champion to take the net position away from his opponent.

Every point in the final game brought cheers or groans, so worked up was the crowd. When Gonzales double-faulted to make the score 15–all, his first in three sets, they groaned. When he fell behind, 30–40, as he reached high up and hit a ball that was going out, they groaned again in extreme anguish.

A sigh of relief went through the crowd as the score reached deuce on Schroeder's backhand drive beyond the line. Then came a smash from Gonzales' racket that set the crowd wild with delight. Now came the final rally and Schroeder whipped a forehand down the line past Gonzales at the net. A gasp went up and then the place turned into bedlam as the linesman signaled it was out.

Schroeder, stunned by the call, cried out, and there were outcries from the stand. But the Wimbledon champion accepted the decision which meant failure to his great fight. Breaking into a grin, he pretended he was going to throw his racket at the official and then ran forward to offer his congratulations to the happy Gonzales as the crowd cheered.

1950

ALTHEA GIBSON LEADS LOUISE BROUGH

by Allison Danzig

Miss Althea Gibson of New York, the first Negro player to compete in the national championship of the United States Lawn Tennis Association, was leading Miss Louise Brough of Beverly Hills, California, Wimbledon title-holder, by 7–6 in the third and final set at Forest Hills yesterday when the match was interrupted by a cloudburst.

Close to 2,000 members of the gallery of 6,000—as many as could squeeze into the grandstand, find standing room or get a view from under the fence—saw Miss Gibson rally after playing badly in the opening set to produce such superior tennis with her powerful service and mannish net attack as to threaten the former national champion with defeat.

Outplayed from 3–all in the second set, in which her own game deteriorated badly, Miss Brough recovered after the rest period and broke through twice for a 3–0 lead in the third. She seemed to have the match under control, but here she wavered again and Miss Gibson, hitting beautiful winners from both forehand and backhand, using the lob cleverly and following service forward for crushing overhead smashes, came on in a fashion to bring cheers from the stands.

Breaking through service in the fourth, Miss Gibson lost her own again in the fifth and that looked to be the end of her hopes. But the New York girl hung on and Miss Brough, tiring from the running she had to do in the exciting rallies, particularly from going back for lobs, lost the next two games.

It was apparent now that anything could happen, so strongly was Miss Gibson playing and so unreliable was Miss Brough's service. The Wimbledon champion got to 5–3 and then it was that Miss Gibson stirred the gallery to its greatest excitement. Winning the ninth game, she went ahead to 40–0 in the tenth and the tension in the stands mounted.

Miss Brough pulled up to deuce with her volley and smash and was two points from victory. But Miss Gibson drove a hard forehand through in spectacular answer to a smash, for advantage point and a winning return of service gave her the game, for 5–all, as the gallery roared thunderously.

Continuing to play the same aggressive tennis and scoring brilliantly with service and two forehand volleys, Miss Gibson won the eleventh game, also, for 6–5. Miss Brough, behind for the first time in the match and in real peril, steeled herself in the twelfth and took it at love for 6–all.

The skies, which had been ominously dark for some time, grew blacker now and lightning flashed, while peals of thunder rolled over the scene. But hardly a person left the stands, so intense was the interest in the fight. Miss

Gibson then served and fell behind at 15–30 but got out of the hole with her service and forehand, to win the game and lead at 7–6.

A few drops of rain now fell and spectators started to leave. A request was made for them to stay in their seats, but hardly had the words been spoken when the deluge came. The crowd was trapped and most of the 2,000 were drenched before they could get out of the stands and run to get under the shelter of the stadium. One of the stone eagles at the top of the stadium was struck by a lightning bolt and toppled, but fortunately no one was injured as it plummeted to the ground.

That was the end of play for the day and the score stood at 1–6, 6–3, 7–6, in Miss Gibson's favor at the point of suspension. The match will be resumed at 12:45 today, with Miss Brough serving to start the fourteenth game of the final set and knowing that the loss of this game would cost her the match.

Editor's note: The next day Miss Brough won the third set, 9–7, for the match. She was beaten in the third round by Nancy Chaffee.

1951

SAVITT CRUSHES MCGREGOR IN WIMBLEDON FINAL

from the Associated Press

Dick Savitt of Orange, New Jersey, added the All-England lawn tennis championship to his Australian title today by crushing Ken McGregor of Australia, 6–4, 6–4, 6–4, in their final match before 15,000 on the center court.

A study in stroke perfection, the handsome 26-year-old Cornell graduate outclassed the Aussie Davis Cup star in every phase of the game. His superiority was so great most of the time that the tension which normally grips a Wimbledon final was almost totally missing.

Less than an hour elapsed from the time Savitt broke McGregor's service for a 3–2 lead in the opening set until he was accepting the big silver trophy from the Duchess of Kent, widow of the youngest son of the Late King George V, in the Royal box. He became the first player of any nation to win both the Wimbledon and Australian classics in the same year since Don Budge made his "grand slam" in 1938.

McGregor, who also was Savitt's victim in the Australian final last January at Sydney, had three chances to turn the tide under today's hot sun, but each time he failed as Dick lifted his own game to the heights. The first chance came with Savitt serving and leading at 5–4 in the opening set. McGregor forced the game to deuce and then to his advantage by charging the net for perfect stop volleys and cross-court smashes. Savitt pulled it back to deuce with a drop shot, took the advantage with a volley and then passed the onrushing McGregor for the decisive point.

The same situation arose in the second set. Again the tenth game went to deuce, with Savitt leading, 5–4, and twice McGregor needed only a single point to draw even. But Savitt beat him with a forehand cross-court pass and then the Australian lobbed out.

Savitt raced into a 5–1 lead in the third set before McGregor made a stand. The Aussie brought it up to 4–5, holding off two Savitt match points in the eighth game. He won the first point of the tenth game off Savitt's service, lost the next three on errors, and Savitt flashed a placement past McGregor's forehand for the victory. After exactly 61 minutes of play Savitt let out a shriek of joy that echoed through the crowded stands and flung his racket thirty feet in the air.

"It's wonderful," he declared with a broad grin as he walked up to receive the cup from the Duchess.

This was Savitt's first trip to Wimbledon, and his victory—the eighth by an American in the last nine championships here—was a personal triumph over temperament for the big, dark-haired New Jersey star. European experts who saw him lose in the French championships six weeks ago after holding a two-set lead over Drobny declared that Savitt had every stroke needed to win Wimbledon if he could only conquer his temper.

Two weeks ago he smashed his racket in a doubles match in the London championships after messing up a shot. But in this eleven-day grind his temper flared only once—in a third-round match against Kurt Nielsen of Denmark. He thought the linesmen were inaccurate and said so in a loud voice. At one point he stormed up to the umpire after a call went against him and he had to be ordered to resume play.

Today the big fellow was in almost flawless form. McGregor looked especially bad on return of service. Eleven times in the first set he got his racket on the ball but failed to get it back in play. Only twice in fifteen tries did the Aussie break Savitt's delivery. The first time was at the outset in the second set, when he jumped into a 3–0 lead and gave the fans visions of a stirring duel. Dick knocked that out of their heads in a hurry by hammering through six of the next seven games. Again, with Savitt leading 5–1 in the third set, McGregor pulled up to 3–5. Savitt lost the final point of the eighth on a double fault and the crowd applauded. It appeared to peeve Dick and he practically threw the next game away.

But that was all the fooling around Dick permitted himself. After McGregor had won the first point of the tenth game, Savitt poured his service across to take the next four points and the victory.

MAUREEN CONNOLLY WINS U.S. TITLE AT 16

by Allison Danzig

A 16-year-old California girl sits on the tennis throne, the youngest within memory to win the championship of the United States, at least since May Sutton was crowned in 1905.

Inevitably, Helen Wills Moody comes to mind with the elevation of Miss Maureen Connolly. The Berkeley belle of another generation was two months short of her eighteenth birthday when she won the title for the first time with her dreadnaught drives in 1923.

The golden-haired junior miss from San Diego will be 17 the seventeenth of this month. No player since Mrs. Moody has hit a ball of such velocity from both sides as Miss Connolly did yesterday at Forest Hills in defeating Miss Shirley Fry of Akron, Ohio, 6–3, 1–6, 6–4 in the final round of the championship.

No more than 2,500 people were in the stadium of the West Side Tennis Club to witness the elevation of a player who, if she can develop a strong service, may take her place on a pedestal with Mrs. Moody, seven times the winner of the championship. It was a slim gathering, compared to the galleries of 15,000 and 12,000 of the two previous days, and those who stayed away missed one of the tensest and most wearing fights of the entire tournament.

The final was so nerve-wracking in the concluding stages, with the outcome hanging in the balance to the last stroke, that Miss Eleanor Tennant, Miss Connolly's coach, was near collapse at the end. She had to be administered to in a box in the marquee as her pretty little protégée let out a scream of joy and ran forward to greet her beaten opponent.

Miss Fry, winner of the French championship, and the national and British doubles titles with Miss Doris Hart, was a wonderfully game antagonist who deserved a better fate for the adamant resistance she offered to the jolting drives that had exacted forthright capitulation from Miss Connolly's every other opponent in the tournament. Not even Miss Hart, champion of Wimbledon, had been able to wrest a set from the businesslike, remarkably poised youngster in the semi-finals, though she led at 4–0 in the first.

This was strictly a battle of attrition fought out almost entirely from long range. The pattern of the play was pretty much the same in game after game, rally after rally. Both girls might as well have left the volley at home, so little did it figure in the outcome.

Miss Connolly did not voluntarily seek the net until the last game of the second set and it was not until the sixth game of the final set that Miss Fry did so. Not a single passing shot was made until the very last game.

Perhaps had Miss Fry sought the net more often it might have been a different story, for she showed how good a volleyer she can be in the closing stages. But she was committed to a plan of battle that was predicated on defense rather than attack. She had seen Miss Hart's volleying ventures come to grief in the face of the lightning drives that streaked past her after gaining the 4–0 advantage, and the Ohio girl was resolved to fight it out on different lines.

It was a defense in depth that Miss Fry relied upon. Throughout the first set she made her stand well behind her baseline. There she took Miss Connolly's bombarding full-length drives at the top of the rise, after the full force of the blow had been spent in part.

With a tenacity that never wavered and a quickness around the court that permitted few balls to escape her racket, Miss Fry kept sending her opponent's lethal drives back. Her backhand bore the brunt of the defense, for it was to the backhand that both players were directing their shots.

As strong as was her resistance, Miss Fry in the opening set could not quite contain the barrage that was beating down in the vicinity of her baseline and making the chalk fly. But she made Miss Connolly pay dearly for almost every point she got in the expenditure of energy in long rallies.

Miss Fry led at 2–1 in the set on a break through service in the third game, but then her backhand had to yield to the constant hammering, and she lost the next four games and eventually the set. Miss Connolly did not find the net but once in the first four games and only three times in the set, despite the riskiness of her length and low trajectory, but she knocked many balls out of court in trying to break down her rival's resistance, and she also double-faulted three times.

When Miss Fry lost her service to start the second set it seemed that her tactics were a mistake and that she would be wise to bring the volley into play, as dangerous as it was to go forward against such length. Up to this time, she not only had not gone in but she also had hardly used a change of length.

Then came a turn in the play and Miss Fry's methods began to pay dividends, such big dividends as to throw fear into the gallery, which patently was devoted to the cause of her 16-year-old opponent though it was almost won over by the pluckiness of the Ohio girl.

Miss Connolly began to tire from the effort called for in sustaining her offensive barrage. She began to lose in length until Miss Fry was able to play inside of the baseline, and then Miss Connolly's control broke badly, on both the backhand and also the forehand, which was figuring more in the play now.

Miss Fry proceeded to take six games in a row, the last three of them going to deuce. Double faults contributed to Miss Connolly's loss of two of the six, but it was the Californian's fatigue that had brought about the turn in the tide.

Miss Fry was so steady, kept the ball so deep with her backhand and powerful forehand, and made her rival run so much that Miss Connolly broke under the strain. She became so discouraged, in fact, in trying to outhit Miss Fry that it was the champion who resorted to changes of length and the drop shot, which she did in the fifth game.

When Miss Connolly lost that game after leading at 40–15 it was evident that the match was to go to a third set. The second set ended with Miss Connolly seeking the net for the first time and bringing off a smash in the final game, only to lose it as she missed a volley.

The stroke analysis shows how the situation had changed. Miss Fry netted the ball only three times in the second set and made only eleven errors to Miss Connolly's thirty. The Californian scored seven placements to one for her rival, as she did in the opener, but her mistakes were beating her now.

The third set was an even fight every inch of the way in long, exhausting rallies. Miss Connolly broke through in the opening game and led at 40–15 in the second, only to yield it. From there on, service held until the final game in a fight that had the gallery on edge.

Both players in this set showed more variety in the way of changes of length, and the drop shot and lob were brought into play, as also were the volley and overhead. Miss Fry scored on her first volley of the match in the long sixth game.

Miss Connolly missed the chance to break through in that game but she passed up a bigger opportunity in the eighth, in which she led at 40–15 and then failed on four successive shots. It was almost too much for Miss Tennant. But, the little Californian eased the tension by taking the ninth quickly, with Miss Fry definitely showing her weariness, and then came the end.

Trailing at 15–40 as Miss Fry scored on a smash and the first winning passing shot of the day, Miss Connolly set the gallery wild as she won with an overhead, a drop shot and a magnificent backhand down the line that stopped the weary Miss Fry in her tracks. Two outs by Miss Fry followed, and it was all over.

SEDGMAN FIRST AUSTRALIAN TO WIN U.S. CROWN

by Allison Danzig

Frank Sedgman won the tennis championship of the United States yesterday, the only Australian to do so in the seventy years the tournament has been held and the first player from overseas to carry off the title since Fred Perry of Great Britain defeated Donald Budge in 1936.

In a repeat performance of his masterful display Monday against Arthur Larsen, the defending champion, the 23-year-old player from Down Under crushed Victor Seixas of Philadelphia in the final round, 6–4, 6–1, 6–1, as 12,000 looked on in the Forest Hills Stadium of the West Side Tennis Club.

Seixas, victor over the infection-hobbled Richard Savitt, champion of Wimbledon and Australia, was as helpless after the first set against the rare volleying skill and service of Sedgman as Larsen had been in the semi-finals. Seixas's defense collapsed and his attack never was sustained again after he had broken through service in the ninth game of the first set with a truly magnificent onslaught and then lost his own at love.

In forty-eight minutes, almost exactly the time required for him to dispatch Larsen, the blond, light-footed Australian had disposed of Seixas, allowing him only three more games than accrued to the defending champion. No one had beaten the Philadelphian this year with the exception of Sedgman, who won their meeting at Newport in three sets.

In winning his first national grass court singles title outside of his country, of which he was champion in 1950 and 1949, Sedgman yielded only two sets throughout the tournament—both to Tony Trabert of Cincinnati. He also carried off our national doubles crown, with Kenneth McGregor, and he stands more than ever as the backbone of Australia's forthcoming defense of the Davis Cup in the challenge round at Sydney in December.

Sedgman stands, too, as the fifth foreign player in history to win our singles title. Hugh Doherty of England was the first, in 1903; René Lacoste of France took it in 1926 and 1927; Henri Cochet of France in 1928; and Perry in 1933, 1934 and 1936. To complete an American sweep, Sedgman annexed the mixed doubles championship yesterday with Miss Doris Hart of Coral Gables, Florida.

Before the final of the men's singles and prior to the arrival of many in the gallery, a 16-year-old California girl achieved one of the season's most notable triumphs. With her amazing hitting power off the ground, Miss Maureen Connolly of San Diego defeated Miss Hart, the champion of Wimbledon and prime favorite in the tournament, 6–4, 6–4, to stand as the youngest player except May Sutton of California to reach the final round of the championship. . . .

The men's singles final had not been long under way before it became evident that the title was to go overseas. Sedgman was so sharp with his volleying, so destructive overhead and so strong with his service that Seixas's equipment was seen to be inadequate to check them. Along with his flashing finality of stroke, the Australian showed a quickness of foot and reaction and an ability to score in losing situations with breathtaking redemptions that were to all but take the heart out of his opponent.

Sedgman went ahead at 4–1, with Seixas's top-spin forehand failing him on the return of service and as a passing shot. Not until the ninth game did the American appear to have a real chance in the match. In that game Seixas reached sensational heights to set the gallery roaring. Twice he drove Sedgman away from the net and trapped him as he scored with three volleys and a straight forehand passing shot to break service. The Australian looked indeed to have met a foe worthy of his steel now. But in the next game

Seixas slumped, double-faulted, stared unbelievingly as Sedgman passed him with a slap at the ball as he ran like a deer beyond his alley, and lost his service at love.

After that it was no contest. Sedgman became a terror at the net in the second set with his facile volleys from any level or depth on both sides, and his destructive overheads. Seixas ceased to attack on his service, which lost some of its potency, fell off sharply in his control and was utterly unable to resist his rival's dazzling execution at close range. Eleven of the twelve placements Sedgman made in the set were volleys and smashes.

The final set saw Sedgman at the very crest of his attack. Seixas, after winning the first game and leading at 40–30 in the second, as he took to the net again, was helpless under the pitiless fire of the Australian's volleys and service. He got only six points in the last five games.

It was a bitter pill for the Philadelphian, who ranks eighth nationally and was seeded seventh in the tournament, to come to so crushing a defeat after eliminating McGregor of Australia, Herbert Flam, last year's finalist, and Savitt.

1952

CONNOLLY YOUNGEST WIMBLEDON CHAMPION SINCE 1905

by Allison Danzig

Hail to a new Queen of Wimbledon, the youngest American to be crowned All-England champion since May Sutton won in 1905.

On the famed center court, where Helen Wills scored eight triumphs, 17-year-old Maureen Connolly of San Diego, California, today won the prize of all lawn tennis prizes and did it on her first quest for the title. Not even the peerless Helen did that, her bid ending in defeat in the final of 1924, the year after she had won the first of her seven American championships at the age of 17.

With 17,000 persons filling the center court to the last bit of standing room on this warm day of brilliant sunshine, the blond little champion of the United States overcame the dangerous challenge of Louise Brough of Beverly Hills, California, in a punishing first set of superlative tennis, then won more comfortably in the second. The score was 7–5, 6–3.

Miss Brough, champion of Wimbledon in 1948–49–50, played as fine a quality of tennis in the opening set as has come from her racket in years. When her varied and powerful attack went for nought after she had broken through for a 5–4 lead, victory was beyond her ebbing strength against the quick, bustling youngster, who hammered away relentlessly with her jolting forehand and backhand, never lost her poise and concentration in any circumstance and was tireless in going up for drop shots and scurrying back for lobs.

Miss Brough led at 2–0 in the second set, lost a long third game and could do no more except for a final despairing stand. Miss Connolly pounded her out of the backcourt, whipped magnificent backhand passing shots and tossed perfect lobs beyond reach of her racket and went to 5–2.

In the next game, the petite San Diego dynamo they call "Little Mo" led by 40–0, match point. When the tall, blond Miss Brough, a big favorite with Wimbledon galleries, pulled out the game with her volleys, escaping disaster thrice by a stroke, the fans cheered her delightedly. In the ninth game she needed only a point to break through and she was playing more and more like the Louise Brough of the first set, attacking incessantly.

But Miss Connolly, sensing the danger of the situation if she should lose her service, set herself for the kill and stopped the threat on her fifth match point.

It was a joyously excited youngster who ran to the net to greet her opponent and doubles partner as Miss Brough, going forward to the last, knocked the ball into the net on her approach shot. There were tears of happiness in her eyes as the Duchess of Kent left the royal box to come on the court to present the championship gilt plate to Miss Connolly and congratulate both players on a match of stirring excitement.

Her Royal Highness then departed from the enclosure and left the new queen of Wimbledon to hold court while a score of cameramen swarmed feverishly around her. There wasn't a question in the mind of anyone present that the little 17-year-old girl was a queen of the courts every inch, worthy to wear the double crown of Wimbledon and Forest Hills and a vibrant personality who has invested women's tennis with more interest than it has attracted in years.

Miss Connolly cannot yet be said to be invincible. She does not yet command complete control of her wonderfully sound and fluent ground strokes. Her service and overhead are a bit shaky and, as much progress as she has made since last year with her net attack, the powerful passing shots of Miss Brough exposed a lack of strength on her volley that Miss Connolly will have to repair through hours of work on the practice court.

But recognizing these shortcomings, the San Diego youngster is still so good a tennis player and has so extraordinary a match temperament that none of her rivals can hope to beat her with anything less than an exceptional performance. No woman player since Helen Wills Roark has had such weight of stroke from both forehand and backhand as Miss Connolly. Few have matched her in quickness and celerity around the court and none within memory has excelled her in fortitude of spirit. She is so dead game, so unflinching in adversity and so clear-headed and poised when the going is rugged and discouraging, that one is almost tempted to predict it will be a rare occasion when she is beaten in championship play.

The confidence she gained from rising to the challenge of one trying test after another and winning at Wimbledon, where nervousness has afflicted more experienced players on the center court, in her first appearance here should make her all the more formidable an opponent henceforth.

This 17-year-old girl won over Wimbledon in spite of unfortunate publicity of which she was an innocent victim early in the tournament, and she came though to the championship where our ranking players in the men's tournament failed. . . .

The opening set of the women's singles was perhaps the finest of the tournament. Miss Brough, whose three-year reign as Wimbledon champion ended last year when she had an arm ailment, was at the peak of her game, with every stroke so obedient to her dictates that she seldom gave away anything.

Strong and deep off the ground and mixing her attack skillfully with changes of length and pace, she kept Miss Connolly under a pressure that never relaxed. Her service was much the stronger, though later it was to weaken and cost her rather dearly on double faults, and she hit with such power on her passing shots that Miss Connolly could not control her volleys.

Every game and almost every point was a fight. Miss Brough broke through in the fifth game with her passing shots. Then Miss Connolly, staying back, showed the beauty of her own passing shots and lobs to go ahead, 4–3. Miss Brough again gained the upper hand and broke through for a 5–4 lead. She was extracting errors with drop shots and attacking Miss Connolly's backhand successfully.

The tenth was the crucial game of the set and probably of the match. Miss Brough needed only to hold service to take the set and a terrific fight developed. Deuce was called repeatedly and three times Miss Brough was two points away from winning the set. Then Miss Connolly whipped through a terrific backhand passing shot and a strong cross-court forehand, each in answer to a volley, and took the game for 5–5.

Miss Brough had missed her chance and Miss Connolly took the next two games for the set.

In the second set Miss Brough started strong for a 2–0 lead and yielded the third game only after a wearing fight. The fourth game marked the beginning of the end for her. She double faulted twice, the second time on a footfault. The penalty seemed to unnerve her and she was tiring. Her errors mounted on her forehand as Miss Connolly hammered away and she began to chop and seek the net at every chance.

She could not stay in the backcourt and her volleying ventures were stopped dead by her opponent's passing shots.

Miss Connolly went to 5–2 and 40–0. Then Miss Brough made her game rally and saved four match points before the little Californian brought play to a close.

SEDGMAN DEFEATS DROBNY IN
WIMBLEDON FINAL

by Allison Danzig

Frank Sedgman won the All-England lawn tennis championship today, the first Australian to do so since 1933, and Maureen Connolly and Louise Brough will meet in an all-California women's final tomorrow.

The 24-year-old Sedgman, holder of the American title, lost the opening set to Jaroslav Drobny of Egypt and then went on to victory, reversing the result of their meeting in the final of the French championship.

The quality of the tennis was not particularly good and Drobny, discouraged by a gusty wind that made it risky to use his drop shot and lob, chief instruments of his victory in Paris, slumped badly in the middle of the third set and was helpless against the scintillating volley attack of the Australian. The score was 4–6, 6–2, 6–3, 6–2.

Sedgman succeeds Richard Savitt of Orange, New Jersey, who was ousted in the quarter-finals by Mervyn Rose of Australia, as champion. Jack Crawford was the last previous player from Down Under to win here. . . .

The wind boded no good for Drobny, with his delicately shaved strokes, and particularly with his lobs and drop shots, which stopped Sedgman on the wet, hard surface in Paris. Repeatedly the self-exiled Czech showed his discouragement over his inability to gauge the gusts as the ball went astray, and he used the drop shot very little, though this may have been in part because Sedgman was so quick in getting to it on the dry turf.

Sedgman did not play well in the first set except at the net. His ground strokes were erring constantly and his strategy in attacking Drobny's supposedly weak backhand did not pay dividends after the first few games. His service, too, was not functioning at its best. In the ninth game Drobny put three returns of service at Sedgman's feet and his errors on the volley and half-volley enabled the French champion to effect the lone break.

In the second set the Australian went on the attack in earnest, and Drobny was put on the defensive and kept there. Sedgman was going in on both his service, which was now sharper, and his return of service, and his passing shots discouraged his opponent from coming in. Drobny was clearly outplayed, with his backhand highly vulnerable.

The third set found both men playing rather badly and the first four games went against the server. Drobny's ripostes and drives down the line from the backhand were forcing Sedgman into backhand volley errors. To 3–all there was nothing to choose between them and then Drobny weakened and it was entirely Sedgman's match. The play turned into a stampede, with the Australian winning seven games in a row. A point from 0–5 in the fourth set, Drobny rallied and managed to win two games with his passing shots and volleys before yielding.

Sedgman, seeded first here three times in a row, finally achieved the last of the big turf court titles to elude him. He threw his racket joyfully to the side of the court and went forward to greet his beaten foe, who never has won one of the major grass court championships. The Duchess of Kent came down from the royal box to greet the players and present the cup to Sedgman.

DROBNY AND DORIS HART WIN FRENCH TITLES

by Allison Danzig

Jaroslav Drobny retained the French tennis championship today and Doris Hart of Miami, Florida, wrested the women's title from Shirley Fry of Akron, Ohio.

Before a gallery of 13,000 that filled Roland Garros Stadium to capacity, the left-handed Drobny, Czechoslovak exile now making his home in Egypt, defeated Frank Sedgman of Australia, 6–2, 6–0, 3–6, 6–4, on a soft court drenched by rain that began falling in the third game and held up play for half an hour.

At a disadvantage on the wet surface, Sedgman, champion of the United States and generally ranked as the foremost amateur in the world, was helpless against Drobny's clever lobs and passing shots. Sedgman's whole game disintegrated in the second set. The plight of the blond Australian was almost pitiful as he piled up errors under pressure of the new champion's masterful position play.

In the third set, Sedgman finally settled down after losing his service in the third game. He showed how magnificent a volleyer he is as he won five of the next six games. After the intermission, the Australian launched a blazing attack in the fourth set to lead, 40–15, then broke in control and lost four games in a row as the rain began to fall again.

Now came the most exciting part of the match as Sedgman rallied and attacked with dazzling backhand volleys and returns of service. Drobny, genuinely concerned, had game point for 5–love and game point for the sixth also, but he could not win either. He managed to win the seventh game for a 5–2 lead, but then came the most harrowing moments for him.

Sedgman won the eighth game and broke through in the ninth after a prolonged fight that found both men going to the net and bringing off beautiful winners. The gallery was on edge and every rally brought screams as the players fought with all their cunning and skill in the tenth game.

Sedgman led, 40–15, and it appeared serious for Drobny. The Australian was getting more dangerous by the minute and it seemed that he would have an even chance of winning if he could get to 5–all. The court was now drying out as the sun came out strong again and the Australian was covering ground rapidly to retrieve lobs and drop shots, and volleying with a security of footing that was impossible in the first two sets.

Realizing his danger if play went to a fifth set, Drobny came through in the emergency with three beautiful returns of Sedgman's service, which had not been functioning well for most of the match. After the score had gone to deuce twice, Sedgman volleyed out of the court and then failed on another backhand volley.

It was a jolting disappointment to Sedgman, who had not lost a set in the tournament, to fail again against Drobny as he had in the semi-finals last year.

At the same time, Drobny deserves the highest praise for his superb display under the conditions. His control was perfection for the first two sets and his court generalship was of the highest order.

Miss Hart defeated Miss Fry, 6–4, 6–4, and reversed the result of their meeting in the final here a year ago. It was the second French title for the Florida girl, who won here in 1950 and who is the present Wimbledon champion.

Miss Hart won the first five games. She had the better length and was the more effective at the net, Miss Fry failing on her volleys and also double-faulting.

Then the Ohio girl found her control and proceeded to outplay Miss Hart. She won four games in a row, saving a set point in the sixth and two more in the seventh.

In the tenth game, Miss Fry led, 40–15, on service and it seemed that she would even the match, but now she erred and Miss Hart pulled out of the hole and broke through for the set. As the second set got under way, Miss Hart weakened in control again and fell behind at 1–3. Then it was Miss Fry's turn to weaken and she lost the fifth game after being within a point of 4–1. She also lost the sixth game after lacking only a stroke to win it.

It was extremely hot during the women's match, and the heat seemed to affect Miss Fry. She had done a great deal of running, and her strength dwindled just when she seemed on the verge of squaring the match. Miss Hart won the seventh game also for 4–3. Miss Fry evened it at 4–all, and then Miss Hart ran the next two for the match.

1953

THE FRENCH CHAMPIONSHIPS

by Maurice Blein

Two 18-year-olds, Maureen Connolly and Ken Rosewall, won the laurels in the French lawn tennis championships at the Stade Roland Garros. A searching, tough championship went to youth. The slow brick-dust courts at Auteuil, Paris, give nothing. A rally that takes two shots to win on the lightning turf of Wimbledon needs four to get home here; a weakness of ground play never gets by. There was nothing lucky in the victories of these two prodigies. They were the best in the field.

Records were set up all around. No one so young as Miss Connolly has taken the French women's title before. This was the supreme test for San Diego's bustling youngster. Her skill on grass was undisputed, but could she make the grade on gruelling rubble?

Her answer was convincing. Her setback in Rome, when she lost the final of the Italian championship to Miss Doris Hart at her first singles attempt on hard courts, proved merely a dress rehearsal that had failed to go smoothly.

Wimbledon, Forest Hills, Australia and, now, France—Little Mo now holds them all, and all at the same time. No other woman has done so much; only one man did as much—Donald Budge.

Rosewall, also, is the youngest winner of the men's title and the first Australian victor in France since Jack Crawford in 1933. Like Miss Connolly, he won the Australian singles early in the year. What lies in store for this prodigiously solid youngster? He combines lightning reflexes—his speed on the ball is abnormal and comparable with that of Cochet—with a precision game. If his forehand at times looks uncertain, it is mainly because of the strength of the other wing. . . .

Rosewall can, without exaggeration, be hailed as a great champion, but it was not one of the greatest French championships. . . . Jaroslav Drobny, monarch of the hard courts, lost his throne. Enrique Morea, the big Argentinian, confirmed his increased lawn tennis stature. But perhaps the main issue in Paris this year was the familiar American-Australian rivalry. Vic Seixas, triumphant until his knockout in the last match, and Gardnar Mulloy led the American challenge. . . .

By the end of the third round both Seixas and Rosewall had made their mark as the outstanding men of the tournament. Both played with the air of potential champions, their games confident, immaculate and without weakness. Seixas and Rosewall, in fact, stole much of the thunder from Drobny, the holder, and Mulloy, the second seed. Morea eliminated Mulloy.

Before that, he brought the first seeding upset. He beat Mervyn Rose of Australia to reach the quarter-final. This was the most tremendous tussle of the middle of the tournament. . . .

The other seeding failure was Budge Patty, a man whom Paris claims almost as its own. It was an unlucky championship for Patty. As a touch player his game demands fitness and a keen eye more than normal. An attack of tonsilitis had robbed him of both. He reached the fourth round haltingly. There he met Felicisimo (Felix) Ampon, himself a touch player but normally lacking Patty's easy thrust and flair for the early ball. A jaded Patty never got into the match. He was slow, he fumbled. Ampon won in straight sets. It seemed long since that glorious year of Patty, 1950, when he had a series of heroic victories to win the French title and was equally impregnable at Wimbledon.

The Texan Bernard Bartzen had a good third-round win against the rising young Swede Stefan Stockenburg. Bartzen's next was Fausto Gardini. He forced Italy's gawky genius into a milling, exhausting fight in which endurance and mental strength counted more than strokes. Bartzen led two sets to one but could not make it. The exaggerated western-grip forehand of Gardini, his fantastic backhand, his pawky service—all these were plied with increasing effect under a burning sun, to counteract which Gardini often immersed his head in a bucket of water.

Lew Hoad had played so well in Rome that much was expected of him in Paris. He did not reach his promise. He invariably began well, faded, and then had to force himself to rediscover power of volley and service. Seixas was decisive and fluent against him in the quarter-finals and won in three sets. Drobny beat Gardini easily. Rosewall was even more impressive than Seixas in routing Ampon ruthlessly. Morea's win over Mulloy came after the American, with the coolness of a veteran court craftsman, had salvaged the first set from 2–5. Morea never lost heart and in the end he made Mulloy look a weary veteran.

In the semi-finals Rosewall beat Morea, and Seixas beat Drobny. Each was a splendid tussle rather than a great match. . . . In the final, as I saw it, Rosewall did everything to break Seixas's heart in the first game. With four shots, all made against the return of service, Rosewall won a love game and had the crowd on its feet. A sizzling forehand down the line, a snorting forehand across court, a perfect devilish drop and a backhand screamer— this was something like a start. The second game was cast in much the same mould. Seixas got just one point on his service. It was as if a boxer had landed two blows on the solar plexus in the first two seconds of a fight.

It was a copy book match by Rosewall. Seixas, by and large, played well, but he could not find a weakness anywhere. In the first set he pressed netward, but it was a disheartening effort, for Rosewall so often scampered across court to reach what seemed a winning volley to flash a dipping, screaming passing shot out of the blue. Later Seixas tried slowing the game up. This was productive of more Australian errors, but the little wizard never relinquished command. Seixas got the third set, but here one detected

Hopman's tactical advice, for there never was a doubt about Rosewall's win in the fourth set.

The women's singles was America's all through, quite apart from Little Mo. U.S. girls made up the last four—Miss Hart, Miss Shirley Fry, Mrs. Dorothy Head Knode and Miss Connolly—and there was never a doubt that they would. The semi-finals were straightforward. Miss Connolly swamped Mrs. Knode. Miss Hart asserted her superiority over Miss Fry, saving the first set from a 2–5 deficit.

The final was impressive mainly because lawn tennis history was being made. Miss Connolly was confident, masterful, utterly dominant. Her forehand was reputed uncertain. There was no trace of it. On the other hand Miss Hart, tremulous to begin and never at any time sure of herself, made it relatively easy for the great little player. Whatever plan of campaign she may have had was not effectively put into action. Miss Connolly triumphantly outpaced her and bustled and jerked between the games like a cheery sparrow. And well she might have done, because she was really good.

The doubles this year were relatively uneventful. Hoad and Rosewall ran through the men's like a comet. No weakness, no hesitation, no fumbling ever. There was no one to touch them. They did not lose a set. No pair forced a set to more than nine games. Miss Fry and Miss Hart won the women's doubles for the fourth year running. Miss Connolly and Miss Sampson, the other finalists, were outclassed.

DROBNY–PATTY MATCH: A WIMBLEDON RECORD

by Fred Tupper

Jaroslav Drobny defeated Budge Patty, 8 6, 16–18, 3–6, 8–6, 12–10, in a tennis match that lasted more than four hours and required ninety-three games, the longest singles contest in modern Wimbledon history. It was one of the finest matches seen here since the war.

As the clock struck nine amid sepulchral silence on the famed center court, Patty netted the last ball. The crowd rose to its feet cheering as one and the bravos rang for fully five minutes.

Here they were: Drobny, the imperturbable former Czech who tried for his first title here in 1938 and twice reached the finals, and Patty, the gay Adonis from Los Angeles and Paris who won it in 1950 and has just returned to form after three years of difficulty with his ankle. In tennis time, the sands are running out for both of them. Each was keyed for this effort.

Drobny possesses one of the big games still left in amateur tennis. His left-handed service has bite and heavy spin. His ground strokes are good and his overhead is dangerous. In contrast, Patty is a pure student of the game. To him the court is a geometric pattern and he the drawer of diagrams, exploiting every inch of space with his mastery of the volley.

And so, on the court they went in mid-afternoon, Drobny seeded fourth and the favorite; Patty holding two victories over him in three meetings here through the years. Drobny took the first set. Patty had three set points midway through the second and Drobny two much later. Two delicately angled volleys finally gave Budge the set.

Patty's keen flat serve was nicking the corners, and the follow volley as he came up behind it was punched into the holes he had planned. The third set was his and after two service breaks he was at 4–5 and 30–40, with Drobny serving. It was a match point and Patty gambled. He overdrove by half a foot. Twice again in the fourth set he had match point and twice Drobny served superbly to win it.

The former Czech was temporarily in command in the fifth and last set, going on to 4–2, but Patty broke through at love to knot it. Patty had three more match points in the twelfth game. But again a flat drive just missed and Drobny saved with overheads. At 10–all Referee John Legg was summoned to make a decision about continuing play in the fading light. He ruled they should go on.

With a last effort, Drobny took Patty's delivery, then held his own for the victory as the applause rang down.

"It's the first time I ever had a cramp," Drobny said.

"I thought I couldn't carry on," Patty declared later.

CONNOLLY'S GRAND SLAM; TRABERT CRUSHES SEIXAS

by Allison Danzig

An ex-sailor, less than three months out of the Navy, won the amateur tennis championship of the United States yesterday in as stunning a final-round reversal as Forest Hills has seen in many years.

With an onslaught of the leveling fire power of 16-inch rifles, Tony Trabert of Cincinnati silenced the guns of the favored champion of Wimbledon, Victor Seixas of Philadelphia, and in exactly one hour won the match, to the acclaim of 12,000 in the stadium of the West Side Tennis Club. The score was 6–3, 6–2, 6–3.

Preceding the triumph of the 23-year-old six-footer, one of the few to go through a championship without losing a set, Maureen Connolly of San Diego, California, carried off the women's crown for the third successive year.

In so doing she completed the first grand slam of the world's four major national championships. She had previously won the Wimbledon, Australian and French titles.

The little blond Californian, who will shortly attain the age of 19, repeated her victory of last year's final over Doris Hart of Coral Gables, Florida, whom she also defeated in a magnificent final at Wimbledon in July.

In forty-three minutes Miss Connolly, with her devastating speed and length off the ground and showing vast improvement since last year, took the match, 6–2, 6–4.

Miss Hart, a finalist five times and a strong hitter in her own right, resorted to every device, including changes of spin, length and pace, in an effort to slow down her opponent. But Miss Connolly went implacably on to victory in one of her finest performances. She was irresistible except for a momentary wavering when she stood within a stroke of ending matters at 6–2 in the final set and yielded two more games to Miss Hart.

The victory of Trabert over Seixas, the player with whom he is expected to shoulder the burden of America's challenge for the Davis Cup at Melbourne, Australia, in December, was achieved with the finest tennis to come from his racket this observer has seen.

It was disturbing enough for Australia that its two 18-year-old aces, Kenneth Rosewall and Lewis Hoad, failed to win a set in the semi-finals. The performance of Trabert in crushing the Wimbledon champion by almost as decisive a margin as did Sedgman in the 1951 final should be of even more concern Down Under.

On the best day Rosewall and Hoad ever had they could hardly have stood their ground against the all-court attack Trabert turned loose against Seixas.

Two years ago the rugged ex-sailor, who has the proportions of a football player, carried Sedgman to five sets in the championship. In 1952 he laid aside his rackets to serve in the Navy and was out of major competition except for the French championship while his aircraft carrier was in the Mediterranean Sea.

Since leaving the service in June, Trabert has been laboring hours daily in practice and physical conditioning work to bring his game back to where it was in 1951 and to get his weight down and regain his speed of foot.

At the Merion Cricket Club he met Seixas in the final and was crushed after a promising start. He won the Baltimore tournament, lost to Rosewall at South Orange and then met Seixas again at Newport.

The Philadelphian, with his speed and agility and his faultless volleying, won the first two sets, 7–5, 6–0, and then injured his knee early in the third set and lost the match. Trabert got little credit for the victory, under the circumstances.

Yesterday he went on the court again against Seixas. This time the

Wimbledon champion was thoroughly fit, with his knee completely healed, and primed with the confidence gained from his earlier victories over Hoad, Kurt Nielsen of Denmark and William Talbert of New York.

Seixas was favored in the final in spite of the excellence of Trabert's tennis against Rosewall. How was any one to suspect that Trabert would show the most punishing and solid ground strokes on display at Forest Hills in recent years or that they would wreak such havoc against an opponent who had made a shambles of the highly respected backcourt game of Talbert?

The explanation of the massacre that was perpetrated in the last two sets yesterday came down to the fact that Trabert on this day suddenly caught fire as he never had before and attained the mastery toward which he has strived over the years. On this day he measured up to a Donald Budge, a Jack Kramer in the fearful toll taken by his forehand and backhand, particularly the latter.

It is premature to rank him with those two former champions, but if he can sustain the form he showed against Seixas, the time may well come when Trabert will receive that recognition. At any rate, Australia has much to worry about as it prepares for the defense of the Davis Cup.

In his powerful serving and deadly play in the forecourt and in his speed in bringing off one amazing recovery after another for spectacular winners, Trabert was a foe for the best to reckon with. But his ground strokes were what broke Seixas' resistance and turned the match into something of a rout in the second set. The Wimbledon champion was harried at every turn, driven to the far corners and tied in knots as he tried to get his racket on the ball at the net.

In the final analysis, it was Trabert's top-spin backhand that made the match a nightmare for Seixas. The Philadelphian had beaten Hoad by putting his twist service high on the backhand preparatory to rushing in for the finishing volley. Such tactics also had worked successfully against other opponents. They did not succeed against Trabert.

In his overspin backhand Trabert had the antidote, and his return of service from the left side, falling low below the level of the tape and usually wide of Seixas' racket, wrecked the loser's net attack.

In game after game Seixas came rushing in, only to find himself passed or unable to take the ball at his feet with a regularity that finally left him at his wits' end, discouraged and baffled, though he kept going forward to the last.

The Wimbledon champion had little alternative. From the back of the court, with his looping forehand and undercut backhand, he was not sufficiently equipped to stand up to the long, heavy strokes that stemmed from Trabert's racket. He had to get in.

The inadequacy of his ground strokes was revealed in his inability to return Trabert's powerful service, which was usually directed to the backhand, or to make the passing shot on the run from the forehand as the Cincinnatian angled his following volley across the court. Trabert was using the tactics that his rival had employed so successfully against others.

The play turned into a rout for Seixas beginning with the fourth game of the second set, just before the players donned spikes, with a light rain falling.

In the opening set it had been an even fight until Seixas missed his chance to break through in the 18-point fifth game. Then he lost his service in the seventh as Trabert's returns forced him into volley errors. That was the margin of the difference between them in the set.

Up to this time there had been no inkling of the beating in store for Seixas. Indeed, few of his backers had lost faith in his capacity to win. When he took the opening game of the second set at love and won the third on the strength of his service, he seemed to be strongly in the running.

Then the storm broke and the spectators forgot about the sprinkle of rain as they looked on spellbound at the whirlwind that engulfed the clean-cut and wonderfully conditioned 30-year-old as Trabert swept through seven games in a row.

Trabert's service, with its length and varying speed and spin, extracted errors or scored outright in the fourth game. In the fifth his return of service had Seixas reeling and diving for the ball, to set up scorching passing shots and volleys. His service won at love in the sixth and Seixas had got just 2 points in the last three games.

Then came a magnificently fought seventh game, with Seixas battling might and main and scoring thrice at the net but yielding finally as Trabert scored six outright winners, four with his ground strokes. When Seixas lost the eighth game also, after leading by 40-0, it was seen to be all over.

Trabert continued his string of games to seven by breaking through at love in the first of the final set, making a sensational recovery of a cross-court volley, and taking the second game with a volley and two beautiful backhand drives. Seixas had a brief reprieve as his service picked up to win a love game in the third. Then he pulled out the fifth after being down 0-40.

When the Philadelphian broke through service for the first time in the match to draw even at 3–all, a spark of hope was revived. But Trabert came back like a tiger. The Cincinnati youth broke through in the seventh at love with another of his amazing recoveries and two passing shots down the line, won the eighth with two overhead smashes and then hit two hammering forehand returns of service that Seixas could not volley and finished matters with a tremendous backhand passing shot down the line.

With a cry of joy, Trabert tossed his racket into the air and then, after shaking hands with his opponent, turned and blew a kiss to his fiancée, Shauna Wood of Salt Lake City, Utah, who was seated in the marquee. Miss Wood, whom Trabert will marry in January, was called on the court to receive the winner's prize from Colonel James H. Bishop, president of the United States Lawn Tennis Association.

1 9 5 4

OLD DROB FINALLY WINS WIMBLEDON

by Fred Tupper

Jaroslav Drobny of Egypt defeated Ken Rosewall of Australia, 13–11, 4–6, 6–2, 9–7, today for the men's singles title in the All-England lawn tennis championships. And the thunderous applause that rang down the crowded center court at Wimbledon must have echoed wherever tennis is played.

For "Old Drob" had finally made it. He had been eleven times trying, first in 1938 as a 16-year-old ball boy from Prague. He had reached the semi-finals six times, the finals thrice, and at long last his dream had come true.

King Gustav of Sweden, Princess Margaret of Britain and the Duchess of Kent saw him achieve his goal.

"I was holding thumbs for you all the way," said the Duchess as she presented the huge silver loving cup to the left-handed Drobny. "The finest tennis I've ever seen," she added.

The finalists went on the court in the early afternoon. Drobny, 33 next month, faced Rosewall, 19—the aging tactician with the all-court game against the subtle young genius with the delicate lob and the best backhand in tennis.

Two rapier backhands knifed down the line meant the service break and a 2–0 lead for Rosewall as Drobny started shakily. But, cross-courting brilliantly off his own backhand, he was quickly even and then had four games running as Ken seemed tense and stiff under increasing pressure. Drobny was 5 to 4, with his own big serve to hold for the set.

But Rosewall came alive, as he was to do all afternoon in the crises. A gorgeous forehand passing shot down the line meant the game.

Drobny broke through again at 7–6; again Rosewall smashed him back, always forcing him on the backhand. Ken suddenly had a set point at 11–10, but Drobny just saved with a lunging smash return that clicked off the baseline.

Drobny was staying in the backcourt now, chopping deeply to either side, but concentrating chiefly on Ken's backhand in defiance of its reputation. His own strokes grew sharper and two forehands down the ribbon gave him the break and then the set at 13–11.

They were 4–3 in the second when Drobny lost his concentration briefly. A missed volley off his shoestrings and a flubbed drop shot had him in trouble. Then Ken whipped a flashing backhand across court to lead at 5–3. The pattern was becoming clearer.

It is axiomatic in big-time tennis that a server should follow his delivery to the net. But Rosewall's service has not the power of Drobny's and Ken went up only on service return.

Twice Drobny saved, once with an incredible return of a Rosewall smash, but the Australian made sure of his next volley and the set.

With the tide running against him, Drob abruptly shifted his whole game. He had been staying in backcourt; now he followed up his return of service.

Ken tried to pass him, but Jaroslav cut off his volleys dead to the corners. Then Rosewall pushed up a series of lobs but Drobny was simply lethal overhead. Quickly, the former Czech had the third set at 6–2.

This was beautiful tennis as each contrived for the narrow opening, the single shot that would pull the other off balance for the thrust and kill.

They were 3–all in the fourth set when a pair of searing forehands into the corner gave Drob the advantage. Three times he had it before Ken stumbled and his volley just drifted beyond the baseline.

At last Drobny was at 5–4 with his service, just where he wanted to be. There was hardly a sound in the huge crater as he toed the line.

He was 15–love. Then, as they had been all this long fortnight, the gods were with Rosewall. A backhand nipped the cord and popped in. Another backhand straight down the line and an overhead smash on the gallop broke Drobny's service. It was 5–5.

So near had Drobny come. He hadn't failed under the tremendous tension; he had been outgunned by a man who dared to fire all when he had to.

Still scrambling desperately, Drobny had an advantage in the fifteenth game, one more chance to break through. They traded drives and Drob hammered at the top of the net. The ball stuck there for a tantalizing split-second, then dropped over. Luck had evened up. Again he was ahead, again he had service to come.

Rosewall seemed exhausted now—a limp little figure bent almost double over the baseline as he waited for service. Once more Drobny was 15–love. Then Rosewall fired a backhand down the side and produced a roaring forehand across court, falling as he swung, to leave Drobny bewildered at the net.

Another point and it was 15–40. Drobny seemed about to fail again. Then it was level and a service ace that popped off the wood made it match point. Drobny smashed to the backhand. Ken netted.

For fully five minutes the 15,000 spectators cheered and waved. Some of them had queued all night to root for their favorite. Tickets sold as high as $30 apiece.

[A ticket speculator tried to sell Drobny a seat when the athlete showed up for the match, the United Press reported. "Sorry, I shall have to stand during the match," Drobny said.]

"That's it," said Drobny smiling, "and that's all. From here in, it will be fun."

MAUREEN CONNOLLY WINS THIRD WIMBLEDON TITLE

by Fred Tupper

Let it be placed on the record that Maureen Connolly of San Diego, California, won her third Wimbledon singles title today. In a swirling wind that raised eddies on the famous center court she defeated Louise Brough of Beverly Hills, California, 6–2, 7–5, and the manner in which she did it put her closer to her rightful niche among the tennis immortals.

Little Mo took the first set just as she had been expected to do, purposefully and ruthlessly, in 18 minutes. There was scarcely a chink in her armor.

She was firing her ground strokes for the corners, and as Louise raced from side to side retrieving, she would increase the pace and put the ball firmly away.

When the mood seized her, she would vary the tempo, and time and again, after a long baseline rally, out would come the most delicate of drop shots to spin just over the net and fade away.

All this was in the best Connolly tradition. Another chapter in the saga of invincibility that has carried her to triumph in every major tournament in which she has appeared the world over for the past three years.

But today she was meeting another champion in her own right, winner of Wimbledon three times herself in 1948, '49, '50 and now on the comeback trail after being sidelined with a "tennis elbow."

There is only one way left to play Miss Connolly. There is no use in slugging it out with her outright; it is foolhardy to force the net against the lightning of her passing shots. And so Louise attacked her down the middle of the court.

She fed her a diet of slow chops, high and deep, just inside the baseline. Maureen would take the cut-off with her drive, but Louise would slice it back interminably.

As Louise persisted, Maureen became impatient. Her fine edge was gone now and, disconcerted, she was having trouble with her service. Monotonously Louise kept pushing away, occasionally switching to her drive on the forehand, but always keeping the ball deep in play.

The points started to come now and then the games. She was 5–2 and the packed stadium, prepared by the press for a slaughter, was clapping Miss Brough's every winner.

Then came the deluge. Clenching her fists and muttering her own private words of encouragement, Maureen started to hit out. She produced the big shot on nearly every shot, the scorching backhand across court and the flat forehand down the line. Louise was back to the treadmill again, scampering all over the court in an increasingly hopeless attempt to retrieve.

Maureen was dead on target, each shot a bullseye. Against such cannonading, all resistance collapsed. Little Mo took five games running for the match.

SEIXAS AND DORIS HART U.S. CHAMPIONS

by Allison Danzig

Victor Seixas and Doris Hart were rewarded yesterday for their years of striving to gain the pinnacle of American tennis. They were crowned as the new champions of the United States in the Forest Hills Stadium.

The 31-year-old Seixas, competing in the tournament for the fourteenth time and in his third final, stopped the onrush of Rex Hartwig, conqueror of the defending champion, Tony Trabert, and Kenneth Rosewall.

With the crowd of 11,000 giving wholehearted support, the fast-moving, clean-cut Philadelphian rallied to win at 3–6, 6–2, 6–4, 6–4 as the favored 25-year-old Australian went into a decline after a brilliant opening assault.

Miss Hart, runner-up for the title five times without having won a set, stood on the precipice of a sixth failure before she achieved her first national singles title on grass. Three times only a point stood between her and defeat as she overcame Louise Brough of Beverly Hills, California, 6–8, 6–1, 8–6.

The victories of Miss Hart and Seixas both were much to the satisfaction of the gathering, after their years of effort in the championships. Each had won the British crown at Wimbledon and numerous other titles and international laurels, but their own championships meant far more to them.

The spectators sensed that this might be the last big opportunity for both, particularly for Miss Hart, with Maureen Connolly expected back in 1955. The little Californian was unable to defend the title she had won the past three years because of an injury she received while horseback riding.

Miss Hart's brother, Richard, sat in a box in the marquee to witness her long-awaited triumph. And there, too, Seixas's wife, father and mother watched.

The Australian Ambassador to the United States, Sir Percy Spender, witnessed the finals. He was called on by Colonel James H. Bishop, president of the United States Lawn Tennis Association, to address the crowd during the presentation of the men's cup. Sir Percy paid tribute to Seixas for his sportsmanship and the quality of his tennis and spoke of the high regard in which Vic is held in Australia.

Seixas's victory is a tribute to the Philadelphian's splendid match play qualities. He was not thought to have much chance of winning the tournament at the outset, when Trabert and Lewis Hoad were the prime favorites.

Seixas was indeed thought to be nearing the end of his years as a player of the top flight. His failure to win either of his matches in the Davis Cup challenge round last December was followed by defeats by Arthur Larsen in the French championship, by Budge Patty at Wimbledon, by Bernard Bartzen in the clay court championship and by Jack Frost at Newport.

Now, with his victories over Hartwig and Hamilton Richardson, who put out Hoad, Seixas is squarely in the Davis Cup singles picture again.

Seixas's form in the championship was his best all season. He was at the peak of his game both physically and in his stroke production, and he deserves the fullest credit for his victory, even though Hartwig did not play the tennis he had flashed against Trabert and Rosewall.

The Philadelphian made the most of his equipment and he never lagged in carrying the attack to his opponent. His speed and quickness, the effectiveness of his service, his strong return of service and his stanch volleying all contributed to the victory. Too, he found a vulnerable point in his opponent's game and exploited it by directing his twist service to Hartwig's backhand.

The Australian's inability to deal with Seixas's kicking service to his underhit backhand had much to do with the result. In the first set, though, he was so strong from every quarter that there did not seem much hope for an American victory.

Hartwig was serving like a streak and punching his volleys to the far corners. His ground strokes, particularly his backhand, were so good that Seixas was having trouble gaining the volleying position and was missing his volley and half volley. In the first set, Hartwig scored 14 earned points to 3 for Seixas.

Twice Hartwig broke through service in the first set, but in the second the wiry Australian suffered one of those lapses that had characterized his play in the past. His service suddenly cracked and two double-faults cost him the third game.

From that time, Hartwig was never the same player again except when he recovered to go from 0–2 to 4–2 in the fourth set. He had lost much of the sting of his strokes, particularly from the backhand, and his errors mounted.

Seixas maintained command in the third set, in which he won two love games on service, and broke through in the ninth as Hartwig's volleying slumped. In the final set Hartwig attacked and was stopped by looping passing shots to fall behind at 0–2. Then he rallied so brilliantly that it seemed a fifth set was in order as he won four games in succession.

At 2–4, Seixas's backhand came to his rescue while Hartwig's backhand buckled. Brilliant with the volley, Seixas had the ground strokes to stop the Australian at the net, and he ran out the next four games to win the match.

The women's final was not up to the best standard of either player. Miss Hart was a long time in finding herself. She did not hit with confidence nor her usual power off the ground in the first set, nor did she serve at her best. Her volleying was off most of all.

Miss Brough was not at her best either, missing particularly on her overhead, but by mixing her spin on her forehand and getting fine length on her backhand she provoked Miss Hart into errors or opened the way for the finishing volley. In the second set Miss Brough, finalist at Wimbledon this year, began to miss more and more and lost five games in a row.

The best tennis was played in the final set. Both were hitting more cleanly. Miss Hart was getting more pace and length off the ground and going to the net more. They fought on even terms to 4–all and then Miss Brough stood at match point in the tenth game.

The California girl hit the ball into the net then and Miss Hart was saved. Twice more in the twelfth game Miss Brough had match point, and each time her backhand return of service found the net. Thus saved three times, Miss Hart broke through in the thirteenth game as her opponent tired and failed on her backhand.

Miss Hart then served at her strongest in the fourteenth game and Miss Brough was helpless to return the ball safely.

RICHARDSON VICTOR OVER HOAD

by Allison Danzig

Hamilton Richardson gained the most significant victory of his tennis career yesterday with one of the memorable performances of the season.

In defeating Lewis Hoad of Australia in the quarter-final round of the national championship, the 21-year-old youth from Tulane University established himself in the first flight of the world's amateur players. At the same time, he projected himself prominently into the Davis Cup picture and lifted American hopes for the recapture of the world team championship trophy.

To the delight of a gallery of 8,000 in the Forest Hills Stadium of the West Side Tennis Club, Richardson defeated the 19-year-old player who led Australia's defense of the cup last December, 6–4, 7–5, 11–13, 4–6, 6–3.

The victory was all the more gratifying because it was gained after Richardson, a diabetic, had missed three match points in the third set and appeared to be fading in strength as he lost the fourth set.

The match was reminiscent of the final of the Newport tournament. There Richardson defeated Straight Clark in a four-hour endurance grind in which he stood at match point in the third set, and was five times within a stroke of defeat in the fifth set.

All season Richardson has been an improved player, after failing to make any marked progress during the last couple of years. The improvement has been made in the strengthening of his forehand and in his better understanding of the problem of living with diabetes.

Had he not found the solution to this problem he could not have lasted four hours at Newport nor overcome a player of Hoad's stature and more powerful weapons in two hours and forty minutes of exciting sport.

Never, within the memory of this observer, has Richardson shown so much solid all-round strength as he did yesterday. It is ground strokes that win most matches on turf, though the volley and the serve set up or account for many of the actual winning shots, and Richardson was so strong on both his backhand and forehand that Hoad's serve and powerful volley, along with a strong, fluent backhand, did not avail.

His backhand has been the Baton Rouge 6-footer's finest weapon right along. Yesterday, it was at its sharpest, knifing through on passing shots or knocking the ball back at Hoad's feet on the return of service. His service, while not the cannonball that is Hoad's, is fast enough in conjunction with the extremely good length he gets on it consistently.

Richardson maintained his game on a high level through the first three sets and, with Hoad in his best form of the week, the tennis was extremely good. A high percentage of the points was earned on merit rather than given on errors, and seldom was either man carried to deuce on his service.

One break through service decided each of the first two sets and both times Hoad lost at love. In the third, with Hoad leading at 5–3, Richardson got even and reached match point in the twelfth game and twice more in the twentieth. Hoad showed how magnificent a volleyer he can be in taking the ball low on his backhand to save two of these vital points.

When the Australian finally won the set, it was figured he would go on to take the match. So it seemed, all the more, when he won the fourth set, in which Richardson's serve weakened.

As they went into the final set Hoad was serving with great speed and apparently as fresh as ever, whereas Richardson's footwork was lagging and much of the sting was gone from his service. An Australian victory seemed very much in prospect, but suddenly the picture changed.

Possibly Richardson may have taken one of the quinine tablets he keeps with him. Whatever the reason, he hit a succession of stabbing winners to break Hoad's service in the sixth game, two from the forehand and the last a scintillating straight backhand passing shot.

The Australian, who had thought Richardson to be near the end of his rope, was completely taken aback by this outburst. He had fought with courage and concentration for nearly two and a half hours against an opponent who was much superior to the Richardson who beat Hoad at Newport in 1953, but this was too much.

His weapons failed him against such sharpshooting. As he greeted the Louisiana youth at the net, his manner and expression indicated that he recognized and paid his respects to Richardson's superiority, at least for this day.

The winner's mother, Mrs. Roger Richardson, was in tears in the marquee, so great was her happiness as she kissed her husband. "I was all prepared to smile in defeat," she said.

1955

TRABERT CRUSHES NIELSEN FOR WIMBLEDON TITLE

by Fred Tupper

Tony Trabert is the Wimbledon tennis champion. In a crushing display of power worthy of the best players of bygone eras, the American routed Kurt Nielsen of Denmark, 6–3, 7–5, 6–1, in the men's singles final of the all-England championships today.

It was Tony's thirteenth victory in his last fourteen tournaments. And it was the seventh triumph for the United States in the ten post-war championships here.

Not since Don Budge swept through in 1938 had any man so dominated Wimbledon. The Cincinnati siege gun with the wide grin and crew cut played twenty-one sets of singles during the fortnight and he won them all.

Even big Jack Kramer, considered the finest of the recent champions, dropped a set in taking the title in 1947.

"I've been dreaming of winning this one since I was in knee pants," said Trabert. "And I've been working on it for the past five years."

An overflow crowd of 18,000, including Princess Margaret, jammed every inch of this historic oval for the final. A thousand persons had queued all night.

Trabert was top-seeded and the favorite; the 24-year-old Dane, unseeded, was here because of his brilliant victory over Australia's Ken Rosewall in the semi-finals.

Trabert has the all-court game without a sign of a weakness. Nielsen has the big serve, the sharp volley and a suspected weakness on his ground strokes, particularly the forehand.

Kurt won the toss and the first game on service. Tony took his own and then went to work. A ripping backhand down the line, a passing shot, a double fault and then another backhand with a full swing and he was through to 3–1.

The pattern was already clear. Trabert was spinning his service to the Dane's forehand, pulling him out of court with the kick, and darting in to volleying position. Almost automatically he was slapping the return away.

The Dane's first serve is fast, but Tony was getting a good piece of the ball. He had two game points for another breakthrough at 4–2 but an ace pulled Kurt out of the hole.

It was 5–3 now, Kurt serving, and five times Tony had set point. Five times Kurt saved it, once magnificently with a backhand cross-court volley on the dead run. Tony finally tossed up a rolling lob that hit just inside the chalk and bounced away. It was his set, 6–3.

It now was 2–2 in the second set. Nielsen was much more accurate on return of service. His strokes were sharper and he was no longer blocking the ball but hitting for that thin bit of space open on either side as Tony charged the net.

Suddenly Kurt had game point, then another and finally slapped a cross-court volley off the damp grass to lead, 3–2. He held his service for 4–2 with an ace and the gallery, inevitably rooting for the underdog, was swaying with excitement.

Up to this point, Trabert had controlled his power. Now he opened up a notch. He had service for 4–3 and then he swung out with two full backhands, one across the court and the other savagely down the line. Kurt missed an overhead from mid-court and then, after a long exchange, Tony floated another spinning lob over his head for the break. It was 4–all, then 5–4 as Trabert hit his hardest serve of the day.

Quickly it was set point, but Kurt hammered an overhead down the ribbon and outgunned Tony from center with two perfectly punched volleys. The stay of execution was temporary.

Again Trabert had service easily and was at love–40 on two backhand passes and a swinging volley that nicked the line. He had three chances. He made it on the first, taking Kurt's service on the rise and backhanding it into the corner for set No. 2 by 7–5.

With his cramped forehand, Kurt couldn't break Tony's spinning deliveries and he was having increased trouble holding his own.

Utterly confident now, Tony was putting full weight into his volleys but still using his three-quarter serve. When Kurt did manage to get to the net, the American forced him back with a series of lobs, all delicate and all, almost monotonously, to the backhand corner.

With the score 1–all in the third set, Tony served and took the next game. Then the Dane double-faulted and that game was gone. Tony won again for 4–1 and it was Kurt's serve. Another double fault and Nielsen's spirit and control were gone, too. Tony slashed a backhand down the tape to break service.

Three serves, three dumped volleys and, finally, another lob that dropped tantalizingly into the corner slot. Trabert: 6–1.

The match was over. Tony flung his racket across court and bowed to the royal box.

The Duchess of Kent went to the court to award the large silver loving cup emblematic of the highest honor in amateur tennis.

For three years, Trabert has been considered the world's best. Today he proved it.

BROUGH DEFEATS FLEITZ FOR FOURTH
WIMBLEDON CROWN

by Fred Tupper

Louise Brough entered the hall of Wimbledon fame today. She drew on every shot in her memory book and improvised a few more on the spur of the moment to defeat Mrs. Beverly Baker Fleitz of Long Beach, California, 7–5, 8–6, for the All-England women's tennis championship.

The 31-year-old Beverly Hills, California, player won at Wimbledon three times running, 1948–50. Her fourth victory, a desperate struggle, placed her on a pedestal near Suzanne Lenglen and Mrs. Helen Wills Moody Roark. These two alone in modern times have won the title more often. Mlle. Lenglen won six times and Mrs. Roark eight times.

The match will live long in Wimbledon tradition. It rang on a high note from the first serve and enthralled a crowd of nearly 20,000. Mrs. Fleitz was the favorite. She had smothered Doris Hart in straight sets to reach the final and she had beaten Louise four times in a row around the world. She was rested and confident, faster afoot and infinitely better on ground strokes.

Louise played her the only way. She sliced one shot, drove another, always trying to break the lovely rhythm of Mrs. Fleitz's two-handed game. She lobbed and she drop-shotted. She even went to the net, but that proved damaging. Mrs. Fleitz passed her with consummate ease. Quickly in stride, Louise broke service and held hers. She was 3–1 when Mrs. Fleitz double-faulted twice and Louise dumped a teaser just over the barrier.

Then the little slugger found the range. She barreled the ball down one side, put away the return on the other. Her shots were faster and deeper, and all at once she led, 4–3, and again at 5–4 when Miss Brough unaccountably hit a short volley far over the baseline.

Louise took measures. She won her serve immaculately and then pulled the drop shot out of her repertoire. Mrs. Fleitz simply cannot handle the short ball and Broughie, biding her time, kept rallying from deep court and suddenly pushed in a couple of floaters for outright winners. She had broken service at love. In a tremendous rally Mrs. Fleitz fell down and then, unsettled, banged the next shot into the net. Louise had the set.

In the ascendancy now, Louise mixed every wile and stratagem she has picked up in the fifteen years since she was the American junior champion. A crisis came in the sixth game, Miss Brough serving. Five times Mrs. Fleitz had advantage, eight times in all the game went to deuce and finally Louise ripped a beautiful sliced backhand down the tape to lead 4–2.

Mrs. Fleitz merely hit the ball harder. No woman could stand against her pace now. She won ten points in a row on a brilliant barrage that left Louise shaking her head helplessly as the shots thundered by. The audience roared as Mrs. Fleitz reached 5–4. Louise took her serve, broke her rival's, and then the 25-year-old mother fired four rockets down the lines and it was 6–6 and anybody to win.

Louise was clearly tired now. She was resting between points and having difficulty throwing the ball into the air for service. Miss Brough finally struggled up to advantage on Mrs. Fleitz's service. Then came the shot of the match. A Fleitz drive down the left-hand side was weakly returned and Mrs. Fleitz hammered it down the other. Across court raced Louise. She lunged desperately and pulled off a gorgeous stop volley that just trickled over the net. It was, as she said later, "a determined bit of stretching." That shot did it. It was Louise to serve and 7–6. She was 40–15, faltered long enough to double-fault and then leaped in the air as Mrs. Fleitz weakly netted.

TRABERT BEATS ROSEWALL; REGAINS U.S. CROWN

by Allison Danzig

Tony Trabert regained the national championship yesterday and completed the finest record in amateur tennis since Donald Budge's grand slam of 1938 in the world's major tournaments.

Following Saturday's 6–4, 6–2, 6–1 victory over Lewis Hoad in the semifinals, the 25-year-old Trabert defeated Kenneth Rosewall, 9–7, 6–3, 6–3, in the final round before 9,000 in the Forest Hills Stadium of the West Side Tennis Club.

Thus, without yielding a set to them, the big fellow from Cincinnati disposed of the two 20-year-old Australians who had regained the Davis Cup from the United States in a 5–0 sweep.

It was Trabert's second United States championship. His first was gained in 1953.

Earlier in the day Doris Hart of Coral Gables, Florida, retained the women's title with a 6–4, 6–2 victory over Patricia Ward of England.

Trabert went through the entire tournament without the loss of a set. Rosewall, the champion of his country, was the only player to get more than four games from him in any one set.

Trabert won the Wimbledon championship, also without yielding a set. The French crown fell to him, too, together with our national indoor and clay court titles and numerous other prizes.

Lacking only the Australian crown among the world's four major championships, Trabert probably has a better claim to world pre-eminence than any other amateur, though Davis Cup success carries great prestige. In his position, he would be a big attraction for professional tennis. Jack Kramer, the promoter, is ready to sign him to a fat contract, if he says the word.

Trabert's clear-cut victories over Rosewall and Hoad brighten the United States' hopes of regaining the cup if he elects to remain an amateur.

Neither of the Australians was as keen or had as great an incentive in the championship as in the cup matches. Nevertheless, the improvement in Trabert's play was immensely heartening to American tennis officials. He was better prepared to show at his best than he had been in the challenge round following a four-week layoff.

Neither Trabert nor Rosewall came up to his form of the semi-finals, and the match did not quite measure up to expectations. The condition of the court, badly scarred and barren of grass in spots, was not conducive to the best grade of tennis. Nor was the cloudy, threatening weather, which kept many at home at their television sets.

Rosewall, possibly a bit more at a disadvantage than Trabert on the patchy turf because of his greater dependence upon his ground strokes, was shaky in his control at times. But he never gave up the fight. Unlike Hoad, who lost interest in his semi-final in the second set, the little Australian champion gave his best to the final point, though he seemed discouraged early in the final set.

In each of the three sets, Trabert was out in front and Rosewall rallied, only to falter each time against the American's stiffening opposition.

It appeared that Trabert was going to win almost as quickly as against Hoad when he broke service twice for a 4–1 lead in the opening set. Then Rosewall found his control with his lightning forehand and unsurpassed backhand, and Trabert broke badly in his volleying.

When Rosewall drew even at 5–all, breaking through in the sixth and tenth games on Trabert's errors at the net, there was concern for the Ohio star's prospects. It was believed that if he lost the set after dissipating his commanding lead, there would be no stopping Rosewall.

Trabert's service kept him in the running to 7–all and then Rosewall, who won four of his games in the set at love, weakened in his serving in the fifteenth game. He double-faulted, faltered in control, and Trabert sent a scorching cross-court forehand past him for the deciding break.

Once he had pulled out the set, Trabert was never headed. He went ahead again at 4–1 in the second set and once more in the third. His powerful serving, the depth and speed of his volley and his strong return of service kept him on top.

Rosewall's ground strokes, blazing sharp and bringing gasps from the gallery in the first set, failed to stand up under the constant pressure on the patchy turf. He made considerably more errors than is his wont, both from the back of the court and at the net.

In the second set Rosewall, at 1–4, broke Trabert at love, won the seventh game and had 40–15 in the eighth. There Trabert braced and his cannon-ball service, a clean drop shot made on the dead run, and a resounding overhead smash scored for him as he took the next eight points. The champion was too powerful, too alert and too good a shot-maker to be resisted.

When Trabert won the first three games of the third set, two of them at love, Rosewall seemed resigned to defeat. His superb backhand was failing him badly and he could not resist Trabert's volley, smash or his return of service. In every quarter Rosewall was being outplayed, and no one could have blamed him much if he had lost heart and submitted.

But, unlike some of his teammates, the little Australian fought to the bitter end. He broke service in the seventh with his lobs as Trabert's volley slumped again. And the gallery, though favoring Trabert, cheered Rosewall for his courage. But in the next game Rosewall's volley failed him three times, and Trabert sent a short cross-court forehand past him at the net to break through at love.

Trabert's powerful service, which scored ten aces in the match to Rosewall's one, brought the play to an end in the ninth.

1 9 5 6

HOAD DEFEATS ROSEWALL IN WIMBLEDON FINAL

by Fred Tupper

Lew Hoad advanced a step closer to tennis immortality today. As the crowd in the jammed stadium whistled in amazement he cut loose with a five-game burst of flawless hitting in the fourth set to defeat Ken Rosewall, 6–2, 4–6, 7–5, 6–4, for the men's singles title in the All-England lawn tennis championships.

It was a triumph of power over touch and it meant a third major crown on the world circuit so far this year for the 21-year-old Australian. Earlier Hoad won the Australian and French championships. He needs the American crown to reach the top pedestal of tennis. Only one man, Don Budge of the United States in 1938, has achieved a grand slam.

The stocky Hoad is a man of moods. When Lew is on his big game nobody in amateur tennis can stand against him.

At 2–all in the first set he struck his first streak. With three running forehands that shot into the corners he was through Rosewall for the first service break.

He held his own service and then broke through his fellow Australian again with a fantastic half-volley off a Rosewall smash and a forehand down the line. Serving well, he wrapped up the set.

Rosewall had yet to make his bid. He was slowly solving the secret of Hoad's service, a blur at times on the lightning-fast grass of the center court, and in the fourth game he hit two forehands on the rise that rocketed into the corners.

The exchanges were furious now and in one long rally Ken ran off the court, just got his racket on the ball and whipped it across to the far court as the crowd rose to its feet cheering. He riveted another forehand into the identical spot and the game was his. He led, 3–1.

Both were at the peak of their games now. Rosewall had the range of his ground strokes and Hoad, trying to break through the only way he knew how, went to the net on Rosewall's second serve in hope of controlling the volley.

Time and again Rosewall would push up lobs that fell inside the baseline or whip the ball through the tiny gaps at the net. Yet Hoad hung on.

Service seemed meaningless. They broke each other four times in a row and Ken finally took the set at 6–4.

At 1–all in the third, Rosewall double-faulted. Each point was so precious that every mistake was damaging. He made another, slipping on the grass while returning a volley. Hoad broke through his rival for a 3–1 lead. Yet minutes later, Rosewall somehow got the game back.

Stretching, Ken dumped a stop-volley over the net and then pulled out his fine forehand across court. On they went to 5–all. Again Ken fell, this time on a volley. Again he double-faulted. Hoad smashed down the line for the game and held his service at love for the set, 7–5.

With his back to the wall Rosewall made a final bid. A backhand volley into the open court broke Hoad's service in the second game. A backhand down the line followed by a stop-volley meant the fourth game. There he was at 4–1 in the fourth, still in the fight and a final set almost inevitable.

Then Hoad made his run. Three aces and it was 4–2. A drop-volley deftly sprinkled between two forehands and it was 4–3. Every shot clicked as he gambled for the corners.

He held service and Rosewall was helpless under the cannonading. Ken was forced into error after error. Two backhand volleys dropped sadly into the bottom of the net, two more were lofted over the back line. Hoad led, 5–4, and served beautifully to take the match.

Lew smiled now and waved his racket at his wife, who was in the stands. From the royal box came nods of recognition from Princess Margaret, Sir Anthony Eden, the Prime Minister of Britain, and Robert Gordon Menzies, Australia's Prime Minister.

ROSEWALL BEATS SAVITT IN U.S. CHAMPIONSHIP

by Allison Danzig

Victor Seixas stood as the lone American survivor with three Australians in the men's singles of the national tennis championships last night after the defeat of Richard Savitt in a display of racket virtuosity that approached the sublime.

The performance of little Kenneth Rosewall in defeating the rangy Savitt, 6–4, 7–5, 4–6, 8–10, 6–1, was as near to wizardry as anything this observer has seen on the courts in years. It left the 10,000 persons in the Forest Hills stadium stricken silent, with a sense of the futility of resistance.

With the score 3–4 and 0–40 against him on his service in the third set and the crowd heading for the exit, the hulking Cornellian from South Orange had galvanized the downcast gallery into a cheering, overjoyed throng.

With his mighty ground strokes, Savitt reached heights he never surpassed when he was the Wimbledon champion in 1951. Making a comeback after an absence of four years, he hammered his amazingly clever little opponent into submission in the third set and again in the fifty-minute fourth set.

The break-neck pace of the driving exchanges, the almost unbelievable control with which the two antagonists drilled the ball the full length of the court in utter abandon, was a sight for connoisseurs. Here was a player who had been in virtual retirement since 1952 taking on the second ranking amateur of the world and beating him at his own baseline game on one of the best days Rosewall ever had.

For two sets Rosewall had all but broken Savitt's spirit with his incredible control of the ball in returning service, in interpolating drop shots and throwing perfect lobs over the slow-footed American's head to confound and trap him. It didn't seem humanly possible that anyone could return a service as powerful as Savitt's with such hair-splitting accuracy, such exemplary length and such absolute regularity.

The American would put in his big serve and, instead of following for the volley, he would retreat behind his baseline to defend against the low-sinking drive that inevitably came back like a flash. Only with careful preparation in building up his approach shot would he seek the net.

And then would come a lob of perfect height and depth to send him scurrying back, after which he usually had to rush in again to retrieve a drop shot. Over and over Savitt appeared to have the winning position, only to be thwarted by the little Australian's amazing defensive coups.

Beaten in the first set after leading at 4–2 and again in the second after holding a 2–0 advantage, Savitt appeared to be outclassed. The sheer brilliance of Rosewall's tennis in rising to the challenge of those deficits convinced the onlookers that neither Savitt nor probably any other amateur in the world could beat him in his form of this particular day.

In no other match of the week had Rosewall approached such absolute mastery of his racket. The tennis that Savitt was playing probably would have beaten any other amateur with the exception of Lewis Hoad, even though he was getting his first service in play only occasionally. But it called for supertennis to stay the wizardry of Rosewall.

With the score 4–3 and 40–0 against him in the third set, Savitt seemed to be utterly beaten. And then three tremendous serves brought him to deuce. From then on the stadium was in an uproar.

Savitt pulled out the eighth game and took the next two for the set, attacking with a severity and accuracy that could not be resisted. Hopes sank again as he fell behind at 1–3 in the fourth set. He could not return service nor get his own first ball in play. And then came the most sensational games of the match.

Four successive games fell to the Cornellian as he hammered the ball to the far corners with his magnificent backhand and powerful forehand and followed them in for the finishing shot. Rosewall was now so hard pressed that he could not throw up perfect lobs or execute his drop shots successfully.

The effectiveness of Savitt's ground strokes was such that the little Australian found it expedient to go to the net despite his own superb backhand. On these occasions Savitt reached his greatest heights.

His passing shots, particularly from the backhand, had the crowd delirious with joy. It was no wonder that Rosewall's control, under the savage bombardment, broke down for the first time.

But once again Savitt let his lead slip away, as in the first and second sets, and hope faded as Rosewall pulled up to 5–all. Savitt missed another chance to break through in the thirteenth game. Then came the high spot of the afternoon.

Trailing at 0–30, he sent two smoking backhands past Rosewall at the net and broke through in the seventeenth game. Then, with the gallery in high excitement, he won the eighteenth on his third set point to even the match at two sets each.

It seemed either man's match now, but the gallery did not know that Savitt had spent his strength and had little left. His lack of competition, his lack of hard match-play week after week, season after season, had caught up with him. Five sets against an opponent of Rosewall's caliber and perfect fitness were too much for him.

After Rosewall had asked to be permitted to use spikes and the referee, Dan Johnson, had denied the request, the fifth set started. It was a procession. Savitt got only 1 point in the first three games and 3 in the first five. Fatigue marred his control and he piled up errors.

It was a disappointing finish to a match that for four sets had produced the greatest tennis of the tournament, if not of many tournaments. It was a real achievement for Savitt, after so long an absence, to have taken two sets from an opponent whose performance ranks with the greatest of Forest Hills.

ROSEWALL SPOILS HOAD'S GRAND SLAM

by Allison Danzig

Lewis Hoad's quest for the first grand slam in tennis since Don Budge's history-making success of 1938 fell short yesterday in the final of our Diamond Jubilee national championships.

Kenneth Rosewall, the little master of the racket who is Hoad's Davis Cup teammate and doubles partner, administered the jolting checkmate to the rugged blond youth who holds the championships of Wimbledon, France and his own Australia.

With a gallery of 12,000 looking on in the Forest Hills stadium and marveling at the breathtaking rapid-fire brilliance of the world's two ranking amateurs, the 21-year-old Rosewall defeated Hoad, 4–6, 6–2, 6–3, 6–3.

It was the first championship final between foreign players since 1933, and that year, too, another Australian, Jack Crawford, was thwarted in his bid for a grand slam by Fred Perry of Great Britain.

Shirley Fry of St. Petersburg, Florida, was crowned as the new women's champion. In a rather one-sided final she defeated Althea Gibson of New York, 6–3, 6–4.

Former Governor Thomas E. Dewey presented the Diamond Jubilee championship cup to Rosewall, the winner of our crown for the first time and the runner-up to Hoad in the Australian and British championships. Dewey hailed Rosewall as one of the greatest players he or anyone else ever had seen.

If there were any doubts about the little Australian measuring up to the caliber of a truly great player they were dispelled by his play in the championship. His performance in breaking down the powerful attack and then the will to win of the favored Hoad was even more convincing, considering the conditions, than his wizardry in his unforgettable quarter-final round match against Richard Savitt.

Against the powerful, rangy Savitt, Rosewall's ground strokes were the chief instruments of victory in a crescendo of lethal driving exchanges seldom equaled on the Forest Hills turf.

Yesterday's match between possibly the two most accomplished 21-year-old finalists in the tournament's history was a madcap, lightning-fast duel. The shots were taken out of the air with rapidity and radiance despite a strong wind that played tricks with the ball.

The breakneck pace of the rallies, the exploits of both men in scrambling over the turf to bring off electrifying winners, their almost unbelievable control when off balance and the repetition with which they made the chalk fly on the lines with their lobs, made for the most entertaining kind of tennis.

In time the gallery was so surfeited with brilliance that the extraordinary shot became commonplace, particularly by Rosewall.

The strain of the killing pace began to tell on Hoad, and when Rosewall got to his service in the second set and began to take the net away from him, Hoad's fortunes began to dwindle.

The blond Australian became shaky overhead and then his volleying went off, particularly on the backhand. It was fancied that his tremendous service and his powerful volley would be too much for his little opponent, but neither was up to its best standard, or at least it was made to seem so by the superlative quality of Rosewall's return of service and passing shots.

Rosewall's backhand has been rated the best in amateur tennis. It was terrorizing yesterday, so much so that Hoad's backhand, which had shown so much improvement this year, broke down.

It was not Rosewall's backhand alone but the accumulative pressure of his whole game that started Hoad on the road to defeat. The little fellow was a whirling streak on the court, on the ball like a hawk with unerring instinct and lightning reflex action, his racket flashing in perfect timing from the back of the court and in the furious give-and-take at the net.

How Rosewall managed to maintain such accuracy in the strong wind was a wonder to the thousands in the stands, and in time it was too much for Hoad and gave him a sense of his impending doom. He got off to a good start in the third set, leading at 2-0, but then Rosewall was on him with a fury that broke down his game. . . .

Ceremonies commemorating the Diamond Jubilee Anniversary of the United States Lawn Tennis Association were carried out on the stadium turf. Jean Borotra of France, Ted Avory and William Mellor of England, and Clifford Sproule of Australia were introduced by Renville H. McMann, the president of the U.S.L.T.A. Each delivered a short speech and presented gifts to the U.S.L.T.A. and its president. Borotra paired with Watson Washburn of New York in an exhibition against R. Norris Williams 2d of Philadelphia and Vincent Richards of New York, with Don Budge in the umpire's chair and William J. Clothier, national champion half a century ago, as the net umpire.

AUSTRALIA TURNS BACK U.S. DAVIS CUP CHALLENGE

by Allison Danzig

America's quest for the Davis Cup ended in failure today after Sam Giammalva, playing superbly in his first challenge round, and Victor Seixas had waged a stirring fight in the doubles match.

A crowd of 18,000 was absorbed by the tense fight throughout the four sets. The United States pair completely outplayed Lewis Hoad and Kenneth Rosewall of Australia in the opening set to win it by 6–1.

In the third and fourth sets the Americans stood within a stroke of 5–3 leads. But they missed those chances and luck was against them in the decisions on the line. Hoad and Rosewall went on to take the match, 1–6, 6–1, 7–5, 6–4.

With the victories they scored yesterday in singles over Herbert Flam and Seixas, the Australians had the three matches necessary to clinch the series and the cup will remain here for another year.

The doubles triumph was the tenth successive cup match Australia had won from the United States. It won the last two matches in 1954 when the Americans took the first three to reclaim the cup. Last year it scored a sweep of five matches.

Rosewall had a hand in five of those ten victories, winning four times in singles prior to today's doubles match. This undoubtedly is the last Davis Cup series in which Ken will play. He is expected to sign a professional contract with promoter Jack Kramer within forty-eight hours and to go on tour next month. . . .

There was one ray of hope for the immediate future of American tennis. That was the performance of Giammalva today and the experience he gained in challenge-round competition.

The 22-year-old Texan was chosen over Flam by Captain William Talbert to team with Seixas even though Sam plays the right court. This made Seixas, who is at his best on that side, take the backhand court. The choice was more than vindicated. Giammalva's play was praised by Talbert, Captain Harry Hopman of the Australian team and Kramer.

Giammalva made mistakes and his game can pick up in finesse. But the important thing was that he did not tighten up and lose his confidence in a big international test. He played his game for all it was worth and had the crowd with him a good part of the time. His overhead was the last word in finality, even though he missed at times. He stood up to Hoad in close-order volleying exchanges. He served blistering aces that won roars of approval.

The Australian players showed their mettle in rallying after their shaky start.

Rosewall was particularly at fault in the opening set. Neither his service nor his return of service was first class. He was missing his low volley in coming up behind his serve and he and Hoad were broken through. They won only the second game.

Rosewall was playing the forehand court despite the fact that his backhand is rated one of the great shots in tennis. He switched to forehand last year when he formed a partnership with Fraser after Hoad had been paired with Hartwig for the Davis Cup challenge round.

Hopman kept Ken in the right court when he and Hoad joined forces, in part to give him an opportunity to develop his forehand. Rosewall and Hoad won the Wimbledon, American and Australian doubles crowns this year.

When Rosewall lost his service to start the second set he and Hoad hardly looked like the world's best team. They were down 15–40 in the second game before they appeared to have a glimmer of hope.

A double fault by Giammalva started the turnabout. Then, with the help of one or two decisions on the line that the crowd seemed to question in a well-mannered fashion, the Australians won six games in a row for the set.

With the third set the United States was back in the fight. Rosewall was broken through in the fourth game after Giammalva had pulled out from 15–40 in the third in which he double-faulted twice. Leading by 3–1, the Americans yielded the fifth to volleys as the Australians set up winning shots with returns of Seixas' service. Then came the sixth game and a decision that hurt.

At 30–all Hoad served and Giammalva's return appeared to hit the sideline. The ball was called out and a stir went through the crowd. But the decision stood and Hoad won the next point with his volley for the game.

The crowd cheered Giammalva when he captured the seventh game at love. Then came the crucial eighth game. Rosewall was behind at 30–40 on service, a point removed from a 3–5 deficit.

In this emergency Hoad stepped in with a stabbing volley to reach the haven of deuce. The Australians went on to break through Giammalva for the set.

The final set following the rest period was a duplication of the third, except that Giammalva was outstanding even in defeat. The Texan blazed away with every weapon and Seixas, a wonderful fighter, could not keep his game on the same high level.

1957

ALTHEA GIBSON WINS WIMBLEDON

by Fred Tupper

Althea Gibson fulfilled her destiny at Wimbledon today and became the first member of her race to rule the world of tennis. Reaching a high note at the start, the New York Negro routed Darlene Hard, the Montebello, California, waitress, 6–3, 6–2, for the All-England crown.

Later Miss Gibson paired with Miss Hard to swamp Mary Hawton and Thelma Long of Australia, 6–2, 6–1, in the doubles for her second championship.

But the match of the day and the sensation of the year saw Gardnar Mulloy gain the honor of being the oldest man in Wimbledon history to win a title. The 42-year-old Denver executive teamed with 33-year-old Budge Patty, the Californian who lives in Paris, to upset the top-seeded

Neale Fraser and Lew Hoad, 8–10, 6–4, 6–4, 6–4, and break an Australian domination in the men's doubles that goes back seven years.

The shirt-sleeved crowd jammed in this ivy-covered inferno hailed Mulloy with a roaring ovation that must have echoed wherever he has played. The applause was deafening as Queen Elizabeth went down on the court to present a silver trophy to the American. . . .

The ladies took the stage amid a sea of waving programs as the temperature touched 96 in the shade. Miss Gibson was in rare form. She had beaten Darlene three times running in the past year and was off in high. Her big service was kicking to Miss Hard's backhand with such speed that Darlene could only lob it back. Behind her serves and her severe ground shots, Althea moved tigerishly to the net to cut away her volleys. Quickly she had four games running against one of the finest net players in the game. Darlene, white-faced in the heat, kept shaking her head at her failure to find an offensive shot. The set was gone in 25 minutes at 6–3.

Althea was unhurried. Her control was good and she calmly passed Miss Hard every time she tried to storm up to the barrier. The game grew faster as Miss Gibson's service jumped so alarmingly off the fast grass that Darlene nodded miserably as her errors mounted. It was all over in fifty minutes.

"At last! At last!" Althea said, grinning widely as the Queen congratulated her and presented the trophy. Althea flies home with her prize Monday evening.

It was Mulloy who was the master strategist in the staggering American victory over Fraser and Hoad. The artful ancient abandoned all pretext of playing the smash-grab Australian game. Cunningly he pitched the ball just over the net, mixing soft floaters with angled chip shots, and invariably he was the man who put the ball away at the end of the exchanges.

The games went with service in that long first set, but while the Australians were winning theirs easily, the Americans were struggling to hold. Mulloy saved a set point at 4–5 as he and Patty tangled rackets, but Budge was finally broken at love as he popped three volleys into the net. Then Mulloy took command. He hit four shots, all of them outright winners, to break Fraser in the first game of the second set. And then he had the crowd in stitches as he chased a Hoad overhead right into the stands and moved a spectator over so he could sit down. Returning on court, he won the point for the break through in the first game of the third set. The Americans took both sets at 6–4 as Patty backed Mulloy with his delicate volleying.

Hoad was making errors now, unable to dispatch the tantalizing soft stuff around his ankles. The Americans broke through him again to lead at 4–3 in the fourth. A Patty ace saved the next game and then Mulloy majestically served his game out at love for the match.

This was Gardnar's tenth appearance at Wimbledon. Patty has played here since the war. He won the singles in 1950. The delighted audience gave a concerted cheer, something reserved for old friends, at the Americans' victory. . . .

Queen Elizabeth's visit to Wimbledon today was her first since she became monarch. She wore a rose and white printed silk dress and straw hat. She entered the royal box just a few minutes before the Gibson-Hard match started.

ALTHEA GIBSON FIRST NEGRO TO WIN U.S. TITLE; ANDERSON ALSO CROWNED

by Allison Danzig

A lean, swift-moving athlete, striking rapier thrusts with his racket, yesterday became the first unseeded player within memory to win the national lawn tennis championship.

That was one of two counts on which history was made before 11,000 in the Forest Hills Stadium as unheralded Malcolm Anderson, from a cattle station in far-off Queensland, dispatched top-seeded Ashley Cooper in the second successive all-Australian final. The scores were 10–8, 7–5, 6–4.

Althea Gibson wrote the second red-letter entry for the archives. The first Negro player to win the crown of tennis crowns at Wimbledon, in July, and the first to represent the United States in the Wightman Cup matches, in August, she became the first also to carry off our national women's grass court title.

The girl who was playing paddle tennis on the streets of Harlem some fifteen years ago found herself, at the age of 30, at the pinnacle of tennisdom as she completed a year of almost uninterrupted conquest with a 6–3, 6–2 victory over Louise Brough.

It was against the same Louise Brough that Miss Gibson played the match that brought her into national prominence in 1950, when she came within inches of defeating the then Wimbledon champion. Althea had made history on that occasion, too, as the first player of her race to compete in the national championship.

The Vice President of the United States, Richard M. Nixon, introduced by President Renville H. McMann of the United States Lawn Tennis Association, presented the championship trophy, filled with white gladioli and red roses, to Miss Gibson. He made the presentations also to Anderson and to the runner-up in each event.

Miss Gibson, responding to the Vice President's congratulations, bespoke her gratefulness to every one in the stands and to all in tennis for the opportunity to play at Forest Hills. She offered thanks to God for her ability. She ended with an expression of hope that she might be able to wear her crown with dignity and humility.

Her remarks were followed by the longest demonstration of hand-clapping heard in the stadium in years.

Miss Gibson won the championship without the loss of a set. The most games any opponent was able to win from her in a set was four. Karol Fageros gave her her stoutest opposition in the opening round in a match that ended at 6–4, 6–4.

Sentimentally, the final day of the seventy-seventh annual tournament belonged to Miss Gibson. But no one fortunate enough to be in the stadium will soon forget the transcendent performance given by Anderson, a thin, dark-haired youth of 22 who was scarcely mentioned among the possible winners when the championships began.

Anderson's performance ranks with the finest displays of offensive tennis of recent years. His speed of stroke and foot, the inevitability of his volley, his hair-trigger reaction and facileness on the half-volley, the rapidity of his service and passing shots and the adroitness of his return of service, compelling Cooper to volley up, all bore the stamp of a master of the racket.

It was offensive tennis all the way, sustained without a letup. The margin of safety on most shots was almost nil. The most difficult shots were taken in stride with the acme of timing, going in or swiftly moving to the side.

Cooper, playing at his best, or the best he could under the strain of defending against so lethal and unrelenting an onslaught, shook his head over and over or stared at his opponent, unable to comprehend prodigies he was performing. Could this be, he seemed to be asking himself, the Anderson whom he had beaten in five of six previous meetings?

It was not the same Anderson, for those six meetings had been in Australia. The Anderson Cooper was facing now had "arrived" only in the past month.

Laid low by nervous exhaustion at home in February, stricken by heat prostration and also a broken toe at Wimbledon, and underweight and lacking in confidence in successive defeats in his early weeks in this country since then, Anderson did not find himself until he arrived at Newport. There he defeated Hamilton Richardson, our ranking player, breaking his serve at the start with four blistering returns of service that Richardson could scarcely touch.

Winning the Newport tournament gave Anderson the confidence he had been lacking. He came to Forest Hills primed for execution, and the fact that he was left out of the seeding of eight players, headed by Cooper, made him all the keener for victory.

Richard Savitt, who had beaten him at Orange and was thought to be our strongest hope, was crushed by Anderson, 6–4, 6–3, 6–1. That was a real shock, even though Savitt was ailing with a virus cold.

Next Anderson faced Luis Ayala, the fiery little Chilean who had beaten Richardson at Wimbledon and had come so close to defeating Savitt at Rye. The Australian youth knocked Ayala's searing service back so fast and whipped passing shots by him so regularly that Luis hardly knew what had hit him in a 6–1, 6–3, 6–1 rout.

Sven Davidson, the big, strong Swedish champion, holder of the French title and a winner from Victor Seixas at Wimbledon, was next in line. There were many who thought Davidson the most dangerous man in the field. They were almost right.

Davidson led Anderson by two sets to one before the latter won the match, one of the most magnificently fought of the tournament.

And then yesterday it was Cooper, rated at the age of 20 potentially the top amateur of the world. Victory in the final would establish Ashley definitely as the world's best, as holder of the American and Australian crowns and runner-up to Lewis Hoad at Wimbledon.

But it was Malcolm's match from the second game. He let loose with a blaze of savage hitting, projecting three whistling service aces. Then he shook Cooper's confidence with a half-volley, a backhand passing shot and a perfect lob to break service.

Cooper knew from this moment how accomplished and skilled a foe he had. There never was a moment when he was able to forget it.

Anderson wavered for one of the few times in the match in the eighth game when he double-faulted and failed three times with the volley. After that he hardly gave Cooper anything he did not earn, and only Ashley's strong service enabled him to prolong the match to the length he did.

The women's final was on the disappointing side in the quality of the tennis. Miss Brough, a former American and British champion, could not find her control. Miss Gibson, too, was erratic in the opening set. Both double-faulted, perhaps disturbed by numerous foot faults, and both erred off the ground and overhead.

They seemed tense and played cautiously. Both were tentative in their hitting. Miss Gibson let a lead of 30–0 escape her as she double-faulted twice in the second game. She led at 40–15 in the third and lost this game also. But after trailing at 2–3, Althea began to work into her stride and won the next four games.

In the second set Miss Gibson showed the tennis of which she is capable and her opponent, nervous and losing in confidence, continued to miss, particularly from her forehand. Miss Brough hit out boldly in the first game, to score twice on passing shots and break service. But her errors cost her the second game and from then on her hopes sank. The end came after she had saved two match points in the final game.

ROSEWALL SPOILS HOAD'S PRO DEBUT

by Allison Danzig

The little master of the racket who ruined Lewis Hoad's quest for a grand slam last year administered Hoad's first setback in singles as a professional yesterday.

With a control of the ball that was equal to any test of his virtuosity in shackling speed with marvelously wrought ripostes, Kenneth Rosewall thoroughly defeated his Australian Davis Cup teammate in the round-robin tennis tournament at Forest Hills. The scores were 6–3, 9–7, 4–6, 6–3.

The downfall of the blond champion of Wimbledon, playing in his first tournament as a professional under a record $125,000 contract, came as something of a shock, despite the fact that Rosewall had beaten him in our championship final last September and in their two other meetings since then in Australia.

Before the program ended in the early evening, the slim gallery of 2,500 was prepared for another shock. Pancho Gonzales of Los Angeles, the world champion, whose meeting with Hoad Sunday has been expected to draw a capacity crowd to the stadium, appeared to be headed for defeat, too. He trailed Frank Sedgman of Australia by two sets to one.

The 6-foot 3-inch champion looked to be in dire straits when he fell behind at 1–2 and 0–40 on his service in the fifth set.

The lithe, graceful Australian, operating with an ease and facility in the forecourt rarely seen, was so omnivorous in his volleying and so agile in his retrieving that Gonzales seemed to lack the guns to hold him off.

Pancho's big service, which was not at its best for the match because of a blister on his bandaged right index finger, came to his rescue at this critical moment.

Six times he denied Sedgman when he was within a point of breaking through in the fourth game, and he went on to win the two-and-a-half-hour match, 5–7, 7–5, 3–6, 6–3, 6–3.

The 30-year-old Australian, who has been out of competition since January and showed striking improvement over his form at the start of the tournament, came within a stroke of 4–all, after trailing at 2–4.

When he missed that last chance he knew he was a beaten man and Gonzales whipped the ball past him for four winners to break service at love in the final game.

Rosewall's return of service was so strong that it was almost enough in itself to have wiped out Hoad's theoretical superiority, since the Wimbledon champion's service is his most formidable weapon.

At the net the little fellow was almost unbelievably decisive from both sides and any level of the net or depth of the court. His overhead was the last word.

On top of this masterful stroke execution, Rosewall was a tactician of the first order, throwing up perfect lobs, always sensitive to the opening and confounding his opponent with a performance that approached perfection, except in service.

Hoad started alarmingly by double-faulting twice in succession, and it did not help his state of mind when a foot fault was called on him immediately.

His service failed him in his inability to get the first ball in play nearly often enough against an opponent so accurate and so decisive in his return of service, particularly from the backhand.

His volley found the net over and over in following his service in, and he was erratic both in returning service and with his attempted passing shots. Once a rally developed, Rosewall's ground strokes were usually the more reliable.

In the third set, Hoad hung on, hoping for a lull in Rosewall's attack. He stayed even, with his service improving, though in the eighth game he seemed near the end as he double-faulted to make the score deuce.

Then came a bit of encouragement. He broke through in the ninth as Rosewall double-faulted on the final point and he ended the set with a service ace in the tenth game.

When the players left the court for the intermission, it seemed that Hoad still had a fair chance of pulling out the victory. But any hopes his friends entertained for a strengthening of his game or for a letdown by Rosewall were quickly dispelled.

Rosewall took command from the opening game and his attack was so irresistible that it was quickly evident Hoad was doomed.

1958

BRITISH WIN WIGHTMAN CUP FIRST TIME IN 28 YEARS

by Peter Wilson

Great Britain's recovery of the Wightman Cup on the No. 1 Court at Wimbledon was the perfect sporting fairy story. It was in 1930 that Britain had last won—a year when none of the 1958 competitors on either side was taking any part in lawn tennis and when the majority of them were not taking any interest in anything as most of them were not born!

As a matter of interest, it is worthwhile recalling the two teams which clashed at Wimbledon 28 years earlier. The U.S.A. was represented by Mrs. Helen Wills Moody, Miss Helen Jacobs, Miss Sarah Palfrey and Miss Edith

Cross. The British players were Mrs. Holcroft Watson, Miss Joan Fry, Miss Phyllis Mudford, Mrs. L. A. Godfree and Miss Ermyntrude Harvey. Mrs. Moody won both her singles, of course, but Mrs. Watson beat Miss Jacobs, Miss Mudford beat Miss Palfrey and the British won both the doubles matches. Just to complete the picture, I am happy to record that I saw two of the British players, now long retired, fairly fizzing with excitement in the Members' Stand at Wimbledon.

Despite the long run of American successes, the overall home win did not come as a complete surprise. In my newspaper preview, I put the odds at 11 to 10 in favor of Britain, which was not too far out: the British girls won by 4 matches to 3, 9 sets to 8, and 81 games to 78. But what made the victory even more memorable than the length of time which it had taken to achieve it was the singles in which 17-year-old Christine Truman beat the reigning Wimbledon and U.S. champion, Althea Gibson. However, that did not come until the second day and it would be as well to take the matches in their chronological order.

On Friday, the first match was a clash between the leading players of the two nations, Althea Gibson and Shirley Bloomer. This was reckoned as one of the "certainties" for the United States—and so it turned out, with Miss Gibson winning 6–3, 6–4. Although, at times, Althea was as full of errors as a colander is full of holes, she had that extra yard of penetration with her ground strokes and her agility. The higher trajectory of Miss Bloomer's shots enabled the champion to advance to the net on poorish approach shots and, once there, make some acrobatic recoveries if she could not at once put the ball away.

As was only to be expected from one of the pluckiest girl fighters in the game, Shirley never threw in her racket and actually led 2–0 in the second set. However, there could only be one result. One player has much the harder service and can volley and smash, whereas the other makes tentative dabs like a nervous girl with a butterfly net. Althea, impassive as ever although clearly not satisfied with her performance, played just as well as she had to. . . .

Now a key match followed—Mrs. Dorothy Knode v. Christine Truman. If Britain were ultimately to triumph, they must win this match. In the stands, the thousands of schoolgirls who rimmed the court in their blazers and school uniforms like tiers of colored sugar on a cake "Oohed" and "Aahed" as their idol, who so recently had been one of them, warmed up. Mrs. Knode went into the lead, going to 3–1, with the English girl snatching at the ball when she came to the net. Gradually the 5'11" blonde started to get the rhythm behind her thumping forehands.

She levelled at 3–3, dropped behind again at 3–4 and then, with unexpected maturity, played a difficult baseline rally in which she was struggling to avoid being angled into the quicksands of the doubles court to break back for 4–4. In the next two games, the youngster was content to hang on and, with Dorothy fumbling too many volleys, the English girl took the first set at 6–4.

The second set was a very much more ticklish affair. Christine began a little too confidently. The drives which had been clipping the lines snapped back from the tape on the net. Volleys went gustily astray. An easy smash missed gave Dorothy a 3–0 lead. But again Christine rallied. Her fore-hand—*the* decisive shot in the match—clicked into its groove. Its momentum swung her up to the net, and once there she radiated confidence. Three-all was called. Miss Truman faltered from reaction, serving a double and volleying out.

Then Dorothy crumbled too. Two double faults and the netting of an easy forehand volley made it 4–4. At this stage the admittedly partisan observer felt, with Caliban: "Sometimes a thousand twangling instruments will hum about mine ears." The "twangling" was the noise of the players' nerves at snapping point. Christine shaped for a drop shot, changed her mind, went to drive and ended up by playing a half lob—into the doubles court! One of the worst and most astonishing strokes I have ever seen. Then she double-faulted. Thunder and lightning! Was she going to lose her grip on the match after all? But no. She produced a superb forehand line drive and Dorothy Knode's collapse was complete. She netted for Christine to go to 5–4, prodded a backhand out to give the English girl two match points in the next game and, after Christine had squandered one from the net, Dorothy surrendered rather tamely with a forehand error.

After a long interval, the two of them came back to contest the first doubles match, Christine in partnership with Shirley Bloomer and Dorothy combining with Karol Fageros. This was, in fact, the easiest victory of all the seven matches, the British taking just 40 minutes to win, 6–2, 6–3.

It started with an alarming misadventure for, with Shirley serving in the first game, doubt and despair chased themselves across her lively features and she had to dash to the umpire's chair while her light blue frilly hip-slip—I'm assured that's what it's called—slowly slid into a half-mast position. Fortunately this was only an embellishment to a more utilitarian and sturdy garment, but while Shirley, whose twenty-fourth birthday it was, was stepping out of it, I fancied I noticed a somewhat baffled look on the face of the beautiful Miss Fageros, who had been told a few weeks earlier that she must under no circumstances wear her gold lamé panties on the sacred lawns of Wimbledon under penalty of excommunication or some such dire fate. I guessed she might be thinking along these lines:

> Something frilly, something blue,
> Happy birthday, dear, to you.
> But if you can wear your slip so bold,
> Whatever's wrong with pants of gold?

So, at the start of the second day, Britain was leading by two matches to one and it was generally expected that the lead would be increased to 3–1 when Shirley Bloomer and Dorothy Knode went on to court. But this was the first of the upsets. . . .

It was a great comeback for Mrs. Knode—a very different player from the faltering and fumbling figure of the day before. She used oblique forehands to maneuver Shirley hopelessly out of position and then banged winners down the line. More important than these winners, however, was her tactical skill in using the slow, high-bouncing ball to break the rhythm of an opponent who, she knew, had no winning shots against any stroke which bounced shoulder high. In the end, Shirley was overdriving in a desperate attempt to hit outright winners. Her collapse was complete and rather pathetic, for she must have felt that it had cost her country the Cup.

Thus, when Christine Truman and Althea Gibson came on to court, the sides were level at 2 matches each. You could have got 5 to 1 against the English girl. Three times they had met in 1957—at Beckenham, Wimbledon and in the Wightman Cup played near Pittsburgh. Christine had never won a set and the last two scores against her had been 6–1, 6–1 and 6–4, 6–2. She started bravely enough, holding her service and capturing Althea's at love. She had two points for a 3–0 lead but lost the game with a double fault. Christine was still driving like an Indianapolis ace but she fluffed an easy volley to become 2–3 down. Then she missed a volley and another smash to lag further behind at 2–5. In the eighth game, Althea showed her mastery by making a winner from a kneeling position after having slipped. She served with all her old tigerish ferocity to win the sixth game in a row and the set at 6–2. It had lasted just over nineteen minutes.

Again Christine started well in the second set. She served, smashed and volleyed beautifully to win the first game. Althea made a lot of mistakes to lose the second. Christine hustled, hurried and harried her opponent from the net to go to 3–0. Althea served with the venom of a striking snake to make it 1–3. But now it was a real fight. Christine won the fifth game to love, playing like a veteran. . . .

Christine's superb dipping forehand returns of service caught the advancing champion in "mug's alley," halfway up and halfway back, with the ball at her feet. These forehands must have first suggested to the American that it was *possible*—although she must have thought it widely improbable—that she *could* be beaten. They also encouraged Christine to come up to the net herself.

Anyway, aided by an Althea double fault, Christine broke through again to lead 5–1, lost the next two games with the champion fairly hammering her backhand, and then leveled the match at 6–3 with a superb lob (Althea is as tall as Christine herself), a crosscourt forehand passing shot and an Althea drive which curved out.

At the start of the final set, you could still have got 2–1 against the teenager. Then she suddenly broke through for 3–2 with a truly memorable outright, winning forehand return off Althea's first service. The American immediately broke back, using more angle shots than a Continental film director. She served with masculine severity to regain the lead at 4–3. . . .

The snow maiden was disputing the net position with the sinuous, feline mistress of the volley. Sheer superior weight of shot on the forehand took Christine to 4–4, and two more of those tremendous "switchback" returns gave her the break at 5–4.

A frantically groped-for volley and she was 15–0 in the next game. Althea tucked a volley away for 15–all. A crosscourt backhand (how that wing had stood up under pressure!) made it 30–15. Vulcan couldn't have hammered a smash better than the one which took Christine to two match points. You suddenly realized that you'd forgotten to breathe for the last minute. Christine served—a fault and . . . another. Where are the stretcher bearers? Get me the oxygen. But this incredibly cool "cat" swung into action again as though she had as many match points as she needed. A brief rally, a backhand volley hooked out—AND CHRISTINE HAD WON! It was one of the most amazing women's victories I had witnessed in the 30 years I've been attending tennis matches. The whole affair had lasted 66 minutes. I felt 10 years older while it was going on and 5 years younger when it was over! Two things must be said. I have never seen a more sporting loser than Althea and, although she insisted that it was Christine's good play and not her own lack of form which had shaped the result, I must, in all fairness, record that she made many more mistakes than she does when she is at her best.

The rest was anticlimactic, even though the third singles match actually decided the destination of the Cup. In the clash between the two 19-year-olds—Ann Haydon and Mimi Arnold—the left-handed English girl was always slightly the more mobile, had the greater fluency at the net, and the swerve on her forehand always worried the stocky little Californian. . . . Undoubtedly, the most relieved person of all the thousands was Ann Shilcock who, with Pat Ward, had to play the final double against Althea Gibson and Janet Hopps—a match which would have been decisive had Ann Haydon not given Britain a 4–2 winning lead. . . . The American pair always looked the stronger and won fairly comfortably, 6–4, 3–6, 6–3.

Well—there it is. Let us hope it won't be another 28 years before Britain does it again. English girls have, in fact, won only once in the United States, and that was back in 1925. And, despite the fact that in Christine Truman and Ann Haydon the British have two better players than any Americans of the same age group, there might very well have been a different story had those two very popular players, Mrs. Beverly Fleitz and Miss Darlene Hard, been representing their country.

OLMEDO HELPS WIN DAVIS CUP FOR U. S.

by Jim Russell

Alejandro Olmedo looked down the court at world champion Ashley Cooper and prepared to serve. Umpire George Valentine called for quiet and repeated the score: "Forty–love."

There was a hush over the huge tennis stadium in Brisbane. A fast serve whipped down and Cooper, trying to return it, hit the ball high into the air. As it fell out of court, a side linesman called "out." The Peruvian sensation did a victory dance and yelled to Captain Perry Jones at the court-side, "We did it, Cap. We've won the cup!" And then, to the surprise of Olmedo, who, at one stage, thought the crowd was a little hard on him, 17,885 people rose in their seats and cheered for nearly five minutes.

Thus the United States of America regained the Davis Cup from Australia and broke what had become a dangerous stranglehold on its possession. Alex Olmedo, who had done no better than reach the quarter-finals of his two state championship tournaments since arriving in Australia, became the sensation of the country as he won both his singles and teamed with Hamilton Richardson to take the vital doubles.

This was one of the most amazing challenge rounds in postwar tennis history. It ranks with the 1951 tie in Sydney when Mervyn Rose could not get a point for Australia and Frank Sedgman won his three matches to give Australia a 3–2 win in the final match; and with the dramatic 1953 tie in Melbourne when Lew Hoad beat Tony Trabert to level the score at 2–all and gave Ken Rosewall a chance to rehabilitate himself in the last rubber against Vic Seixas, again winning the cup for Australia, 3–2. The final score here at Milton Courts was 3–2 for the United States. . . .

There were many side issues, but the real story behind the American win was better tennis when it was required. Ashley Cooper and Mal Anderson did not play as well as they can, not by a long shot. But on the other hand Alex Olmedo played above himself and, as the umpire said to the ballplayer, "If you don't believe you're out, read about it in tomorrow's paper." The only thing that counts is who plays the best when the chips are down, and this is what America's team did.

Fielding the Nos. 1, 2 and 3 amateur players in the world—Ashley Cooper, Mal Anderson and Neale Fraser—Australia had every reason to be confident of victory by at least 4–1 as the forty-seventh challenge round started. . . . The draw had been in favor of Australia, for Barry MacKay was the man local supporters feared might upset predictions. Olmedo, most people believed, would tighten up in a crisis as he had done on other occasions in his Australian season. And hadn't Anderson just beaten Cooper brilliantly in their last match at Kooyong two weeks earlier?

But we all reckoned without the strange complexity in Anderson's makeup that makes him so despondent at losing an opportunity, whether through his own poor play or his opponent's tenacity, that he presents himself as a sitting target for the next couple of games. In each of the three sets which he lost, Anderson held set points to break Olmedo's service and take the set. . . .

The court was heavy following a terrific storm the night before, and although the playing area was covered, dampness got through. Below the surface was a foot of water caused by seepage from surrounding high points. Anderson is always at his best on a fast, hard court, and he found the going too heavy for him. Perhaps there has never been a challenge round in history in which not one drop of rain has fallen during the playing of the tie, yet every player in the four singles and the doubles wore spikes at one stage or another during the match. Referee Cliff Sproule gave his reason for allowing this: "The match is between the teams. Whatever the captains agree upon within the rules of the game I will agree to." . . .

Australia's captain, Harry Hopman, said after Olmedo had won, 8–6, 2–6, 9–7, 8–6, "Alex was a shock. I didn't think he would play so well. It was a surprise to Mal, too, when Olmedo beat him. I was pleased enough with Mal's form." . . .

The Australian, Wimbledon and United States champion, Ashley Cooper, walked onto the court for his match with Barry MacKay with the appearance of a man of destiny. He must win this match to keep Australia with an even chance of victory, and the way he went about his opening serve convinced the great crowd he wasn't fooling. Three beautiful serves caught the big American flat-footed and gave him no chance as the score went to 40–0.

And then nervousness invaded Cooper just as it did in his final against Neale Fraser at Wimbledon in July when he held three match points which he muffed. MacKay won the five points needed to break service and followed with three more—eight in a row—to lead 40–0 and eventually take his own service to lead, 2–0. The Aussie did not recover in the set from this reverse and, with each winning his own service, Cooper was swept aside to lose the vital opening set, 4–6. But Ashley's greater experience stood by him and gradually he allowed the big American to pound his serves onto a flat, blocking racket, making him stretch to counter his own speed as the returns sped past him or dropped at his feet. The Australian won the second set, 6–3, the third, 6–2, and the fourth, 6–4. . . .

The standard of play in this rubber was not as high as in the opening singles nor was the tension so great. Nevertheless it was more gratifying to the appreciative crowd, who went home that evening fully sure that the cup would be retained by at least 3–2; even, the more confident predicted, 4–1. Among these was Harry Hopman, who felt that Cooper's service had not been as good as it might have, despite the fact that he served 21 aces in 19 games, to MacKay's 8. Cooper served six double faults to MacKay's eight and the match took one hour, 27 minutes, compared to the grueling two hours, 35 minutes of the first encounter.

Perry Jones said at this stage: "Barry is broken-hearted that he didn't beat Cooper. After all, it took the world champion to beat him. I thought we would be one–all today, but I hoped we would be two–nil. Now we can go on to win, 4–1. I have seen Alex play better. That boy's potential is terrific. He could be world champion in two years."

The sensational dropping from the American singles lineup of the No. 1 ranking American player, Ham Richardson, and the subsequent flare-up of emotions preceding the announcing of the teams, tended to cloud the issue of the possible result of the doubles. Now that we had seen Olmedo's fighting qualities and brilliant tennis ability, it was clear that he could beat Cooper on the final day if the Aussie's serve and general play did not lift a little higher. Anderson's dispirited display against Olmedo had left doubts in everyone's mind as to his ability to win against MacKay if the result went down to the last rubber. And, worse still, after his poor showing in critical stages of his match against Olmedo, would he be able to hold up his side of the court to allow Fraser, making his debut in challenge round tennis, to play his own brilliant doubles game without having to waste energy and concentration acting as court "mother"? On the other hand, would Richardson give of his best with the man at the courtside who, in his opinion, had treated him with such outrageous discourtesy, his captain, Perry Jones? Jones left no doubt as to the answer to this last one. "Ham knows he is not playing for me," he said. "He is playing for the honor of the United States. He is a fine boy, and when he walks on to that court he will play the game of his life."

To decide this vital rubber the players had to create a new record for the number of games played in a challenge round doubles. The previous record was 81 games; this one took 82 to decide. Olmedo and Richardson won, 10–12, 3–6, 16–14, 6–3, 7–5, from Fraser and Anderson.

For the first time since 1953, when Rosewall and Hoad were faced with the same task, Australia had to win the final two rubbers to save the cup. . . .

It was the afternoon of New Year's Eve. The opening rubber between Olmedo and Cooper packed more incidents into it than all the others combined. At one stage the referee, Cliff Sproule, and Olmedo had a gentle tug of war (one newsman reported it as a "wrestle") for possession of a towel. This was when, having fallen on the slippery court, Alex walked to the courtside and picked up a towel to wipe the mud off his hands and racket. Alex continued to towel himself as well, thus breaching the rules, a violation that Sproule tried to prevent the next time it happened. The result was a tugging match for the towel, with Olmedo winning. When he fell another time and lost his racket, Hopman rose from his chair and retrieved it for him. Olmedo took the racket from him but otherwise ignored Hopman as he continued to the stand and made with the towel again. . . .

Olmedo was brilliant with his catlike anticipation and powerful serving, backed up by splendid overhead and volley play. On this day he looked every bit the world champion, with Cooper an obvious 15-a-game inferior. Olmedo clinched the cup, winning his last game at love for the match, 6–3, 4–6, 6–4, 8–6.

Cooper's failure could be traced to two main factors. He served amazingly poorly, failing continually to get his first ball into play. Chalked up against him were eleven double faults to Olmedo's three. His second trouble was his inability to show complete concentration, a quality which marks him above other players with practically even equipment. Without wanting to make any excuses for him, I would hate to have been in his position, knowing that he had accepted a big professional offer, that he was playing his last amateur match, and that within two days he would be walking up the aisle to become a married man. One would need to be a superman to concentrate with all this and the fate of the Davis Cup depending on his match.

Bill Talbert wrote after the match: "Cooper was a very nervous performer. His service let him down badly and this affected the rest of his game." Hopman said: "Alex certainly played his best to beat our boys. Where he showed above them was his adaptability to all conditions. Coop was definitely not near his best. You can't compare his poor serving today with his first day's effort. The ebb point for Australia today was when Cooper's service started to falter." Mervyn Rose's opinion was: "Olmedo's skill in chipping back the service down the line and moving swiftly into the net was the match winner. Tactically I was disappointed with Hopman. Cooper did not vary his game and we didn't try very much new in the doubles. All the clever tactics seemed to come from the Americans. Olmedo deserves top marks. He used all the court wonderfully and moved as quickly as I have seen."

Although the fate of the Davis Cup had been decided, great interest still remained to see how Anderson would shape up against MacKay. . . . Anderson won in straight sets, 7–5, 13–11, 11–9.

After all official speeches had been made and everyone was leaving the court, the crowd set up a concerted chant, 18,000 voices calling out, "We want Alex!"

AUSTRALIAN FANS HAIL OLMEDO

by Will Grimsley

The Davis Cup, symbol of world tennis supremacy, is headed back to the United States today, thanks to the masterminding of a 70-year-old Californian and the playing of a young Peruvian.

It was Alejandro Olmedo who scored the points needed to crack Australia's monopoly, but it was Captain Perry Jones who organized and directed the successful campaign.

"It was a team job, the organized efforts of many," said Jones. He had fought to have Olmedo named to the squad over protests that a foreigner should not represent the United States. Then he recruited the best brains in the sport to help bring Olmedo and the United States to a 3–2 victory.

At the end all the knowledge and inspiration of the professional tennis promoter, Jack Kramer, and the professional champion, Pancho Gonzales, were thrown into the fight. Jones welcomed the help of the pros despite criticism.

Olmedo made himself the darling of Australia and the tennis hero of the world yesterday when he beat the world's recognized best amateur, Ashley Cooper, in the deciding match of the challenge round, 6–3, 4–6, 6–4, 8–6.

The 22-year-old son of a Peruvian court caretaker completely outclassed the holder of the Australian, United States and Wimbledon championships.

Afterward the crowd of 18,000 at Milton Courts interrupted the formal, stiff-backed cup presentation ceremony with cries of "We want Alex, speech Alex, give us Alex."

Olmedo went to the microphone. He thanked the people for their support and said: "I am happy for the United States and Peru that we were able to win."

Olmedo's stunning triumph over Cooper made a formality of the final match. In this one, Barry MacKay of Dayton, Ohio, lost to Mal Anderson, 7-5, 13-11, 11-9.

Olmedo won the opening singles from Anderson on Monday and teamed with Ham Richardson, America's No. 1 player, to win the doubles against Anderson and Neale Fraser Tuesday. MacKay lost the opening day's singles to Cooper.

Cooper made a fighting stand against Olmedo. Down 0-4 and 1-5 in the third set, he rallied and took three games in a row. In the fourth set Olmedo had a 4-3 lead and 40-love on his own service when Cooper, hitting all out, scrambled back to win the eighth game and knot the set.

But Olmedo roused himself for one final burst. He broke Cooper in the thirteenth game with a series of sharp service returns and won his own service at love, clinching the match.

He was in tears when he walked off the court as one of the most exciting Davis Cup figures of the generation.

Olmedo immediately dispelled rumors that he might turn pro. He wants to win the Wimbledon or United States championship before succumbing to Kramer's gold, and he wants to complete his studies at the University of Southern California.

Olmedo said that tactical tips from Kramer and Gonzales helped to bring him through.

"Gonzales told me Cooper couldn't move well and that I should keep him scurrying around the court," Alex said. "And Jack advised that when Cooper missed his first service I should start jumping around to worry him on his second."

Cooper, who ordinarily has one of the best services in the game, double-faulted eleven times. . . .

After receiving the cup from Sir William Slim, the Governor General of Australia, Jones placed it in Olmedo's hands.

Olmedo smiled broadly as the crowd laughed, then strode over and carefully placed the cup back on its stand.

Donald M. Ferguson, the president of the Lawn Tennis Association of Australia, said: "What a magnificent victory. On behalf of my association I congratulate Mr. Perry Jones and his wonderful team. They all played magnificently, but a special word of praise must go to the new star, Alex Olmedo."

PERU'S JUST WILD ABOUT OLMEDO

from the Australian Associated Press

Olmedo, Olmedo, Olmedo! All Peru's gone wild about him.

Thousands cheered in the streets today when news of the U.S. Davis Cup victory swept through Lima and his home town, Arequipa.

Alejandro Olmedo, the boy who rocketed to fame from nowhere—the boy who won't take out U.S. citizenship but is the hero of every American—is even more the hero of Peru.

President Manuel Prado cabled congratulations to Olmedo in Australia, where his singles victory over Ashley Cooper clinched the cup for the U. S.

The Chamber of Deputies gave a standing ovation when the news of his victory was received.

The Senate cabled congratulations and directed the Minister of Education to decorate him with the Order of Sports.

Among those glued to their radios were Olmedo's parents. His proud father, Salvador, wept when he first heard the news. Then he sent the following cable to his son: "We have cried at your victory, from happiness. You were always a good son and God is rewarding you. Keep it up, my son. All of Peru is watching you."

Mr. Olmedo told reporters: "My son, Alejandro, has given Peru its greatest glory in sports." His mother said she had made several visits to church, praying for her son's success. Alejandro's younger brother, Jaime, said in Lima, "I was sure he would win." Mr. Jorge Harten, president of the Peruvian Tennis Federation, who discovered Olmedo, said, "Without a doubt Olmedo is the No. 1 player of the world." He said he would try to bring Olmedo, Perry Jones, the U.S. Davis Cup captain, and other players to Peru.

1 9 5 9

OLMEDO DEFEATS SAVITT IN GREAT
INDOOR FINAL

by Allison Danzig

Alejandro Olmedo and Richard Savitt held a gallery of 3,500 enthralled at the Seventh Regiment Armory yesterday in one of the memorable tennis matches of all time.

For close to three hours the Peruvian youth who won the Davis Cup for the United States and the rangy defending champion waged battle with a continuous succession and profusion of master strokes as the big gathering looked on spellbound.

In the end, Olmedo was the winner, 7–9, 6–3, 6–4, 5–7, 12–10, and stood as the first player from South America to win the national indoor championship. But for the 32-year-old Savitt, no less than for the slight, wonderfully poised and game youth who stood up unflinchingly to the might of his cannonball service and sledgehammer drives, there was the satisfaction of sharing in a performance probably never surpassed in the 56-year history of the tournament.

Indoors or outdoors, it is not easy to recall when there has been such an exhibition of super shot-making, sustained to reach the crescendo of mad hitting and incredible volleying in the 22-game final set.

The powerfully built 6-foot-3-inch Savitt, winner of the Wimbledon and Australian championships in 1951, turned back the clock in this match with one of his shining performances. Against the inflexibly determined youth who had brought down Ashley Cooper and Malcolm Anderson in Australia with a hand of steely firmness and also of the most delicate touch, Savitt was every inch the player he was when he ranked with the world's best.

He was every inch the player in his projection of thunderbolts and he was also every inch the fighter. Seldom has he so won the hearts of a gallery as he did in this match with a spirit that held fast when all seemed lost. In the moments of greatest peril he fought back like a lion at bay and won one ovation after another from the enraptured onlookers.

Thus he fought when he trailed at 5–6 and 15–40 and saved two set points, going on to win the opening set. So he fought again when he fell behind at 4–5 in the fourth set and the end seemed at hand, with Olmedo serving. And in the thrilling final set, with the tension mounting in the service duel to the death, he hammered his dreadnought service and slugging drives and volleyed as seldom before to pull out of the hole over and over while Olmedo was winning his service without permitting him once to get to 40 until the very last game.

So tremendously convincing was the performance of Savitt, particularly in his staying powers through nearly three hours of punishing tennis, that it seems almost certain he will be under pressure to accept a place on the Davis Cup team. Year after year, since he went to Australia in 1952 as a member of the team, Savitt has declined a place on the team. He has demurred, with the explanation that he could not take the time from his oil business, and he has confined his tournament play to a few appearances yearly for the same reason. But now that the cup is finally back home and the challenge round will be held in this country, it may be that he will see it differently and help in its defense.

As for Olmedo, who came from the University of Southern California to compete for the indoor title for the first time, it is difficult to find superlatives to do justice to his play yesterday and all through the tournament. On a strange surface and in the unsatisfactory armory lighting, the Chief performed like the master craftsman he was in Australia, thrilling with the combination of his artistry on delicately wrought rejoinders and the lethal hitting power of his service and backhand, and his almost fantastic wrist action in volleying below the level of the net.

Not in recent years has a player come along who has so captivated tennis followers as has this modest, extremely likable youth whose good sportsmanship is one of his most winning qualities. The size of the crowds that turned out day after day at the armory is evidence enough of this. The fame he won with his victories in Australia, elevating him to the top place in the amateur ranks, was sufficient alone to account for the interest. But more than this, those who came to see were conquered by the skill of his accomplished hand in fashioning strokes of the most delicate subtlety and timing, as well as the more wrathful, and they came back again and again, as to a masterpiece in oil or tempera.

Olmedo plays with the soul of an artist. At the same time he fights with the courage of a gladiator. The combination was just an infinitesimal bit too much for Savitt.

Olmedo also won the doubles championship with Barry MacKay, whom he eliminated in the semi-finals of the singles. They defeated Gardnar Mulloy and Grant Golden in the final, 6–2, 6–4.

The stroke analysis shows that Olmedo scored 74 placements and 18 service aces, to Savitt's 68 placements and 28 aces.

MARIA BUENO WINS WIMBLEDON

by Fred Tupper

Gay, graceful Maria Esther Bueno of Brazil is the new queen at Wimbledon. The 19-year-old senhorita from Sao Paulo today realized all her enormous potential and defeated Darlene Hard of Montebello, California, 6–4, 6–3, on the center court oven. This snapped a string of American triumphs that dated back to 1938.

For Maria, the talent has been there a long time; the will to win grew this fortnight. Her fluent and almost flawless performance in 85-degree temperatures this afternoon was the second major triumph for South Americans in two days. Alex Olmedo of Peru, representing the United States, won the men's singles yesterday. . . .

Senhorita Bueno was born across the street from a tennis club and had a tiny racket in her hands at the age of 6. She burst like a comet into the bigtime a year ago and the wonder was simply when she would win her first crown. She took the Italian title then, but a combination of temperament and a strained shoulder cut her down for the rest of the season.

Her game is modeled on a man's. There are both the kicking and swinging serves, impeccable ground strokes and catlike coverage of court. She has everything except restraint, and that she had against Miss Hard today.

Darlene broke through service to win the first game, lost her own on two glorious passing shots that roared by her and then utterly failed to handle Maria's blazing service. She was cleanly aced by the Brazilian three times and barely got her racket on a dozen more serves.

The break that mattered occurred in the long tenth game. So uncertain was Darlene of her own service that she failed to follow it to net and a double fault gave Maria her first set point. Miss Hard saved it, but on the second she outrageously blooped a volley way behind the baseline.

At a game apiece in the second set, Darlene apparently pulled the same leg muscle that gave her trouble against Ann Haydon. She said later that it affected her game, but she was treated by a masseur before her doubles match.

Miss Hard was notoriously slower around the court and the senhorita, slashing her volleys away beautifully behind service, ran to 4–1. Darlene must dominate the net to win, but she was unable to force the pace against a girl who hits with more length and authority than any player since Maureen Connolly.

Senhorita Bueno had her own service to win and, as Darlene again volleyed long on match point, the Brazilian threw her racket high on court and burst into tears.

"I have never played better," she said in five languages to the journalists who clustered about her. "I am going back to Brazil and I am coming to Forest Hills."

"That service," said Miss Hard ruefully. "It's as good as Louise Brough's or Althea Gibson's." . . .

The American string in the ladies singles here goes back to the days of Helen Wills Moody. She won the title in 1938 for the last time. Helen Jacobs took it the next year and there have been thirteen consecutive American victories in the postwar period.

OLMEDO DEFEATS LAVER IN WIMBLEDON FINAL

by Fred Tupper

Alex (The Chief) Olmedo has won Wimbledon. The top-seeded Peruvian from Los Angeles enchanted a center-court crowd of 15,000, including Princess Margaret, with miracles of his own making in defeating unseeded Rod Laver of Australia today, 6–4, 6–3, 6–4.

His straight-set triumph was the climax of an amazing year for the 23-year-old University of Southern California senior. It established him as the best amateur tennis player in the world today.

Almost single-handedly, Olmedo brought the Davis Cup back to America from Australia last winter and later took the Australian and United States indoor titles.

Today he brought back the all-England lawn tennis championship, last won for America by freckle-faced Tony Trabert in 1955.

There's an extra dimension to Olmedo's game. He has the weapons essential for the modern game: the big serve, volley, and glorious freedom of swing on his ground strokes. But there's more. Today he confounded the red-headed Australian by deliberately using the lob to attack.

With his mind invariably on the move ahead, Alex shifted the 20-year-old redhead around the court like a chess piece. He was feinting for the coups to come.

Olmedo started fast against the left-handed Australian. He broke service in the first game, just as he had done against Ramanathan Krishnan, Luis Ayala, and Roy Emerson in the earlier rounds.

Olmedo was tuned up and Laver was not. The Australian has had a grueling fortnight. It took him nearly four hours to subdue Barry MacKay of Dayton, Ohio, in a furious five-setter Wednesday, and he has been further involved with doubles and mixed doubles. Laver was slow afoot and he was nervous.

Quickly, the Peruvian was 5–1, outpacing Laver on his ground shots and forcing him to err off the volley. There was a stunned silence in the packed stadium. It appeared to be a rout. Then the redhead switched his various services. He served flat on the left side down the middle and he swung it to the right side, always to the Olmedo backhand. He came alive with his heavily spun ground shots. Soon Laver was back in the match at 4–5. The Peruvian was unruffled. He held service for the set.

The battle was now joined in earnest. Rod was a step quicker getting up to the net and he led at 3–2 in the second set. It was the trap Olmedo had baited. He saved his service game and then came the lobs, high to the baseline and short to the sidelines. Backward pedaled Laver. Here came the drop shots, pulling the redhead in. Laver lunged up and netted. Olmedo had broken through at love.

It was deft, thinking tennis and it paid dividends. Off balance, Laver was confused and he was caught. Four games went to Olmedo in a row and the second set at 6–3 as he lobbed Laver off a volley with fingertip control.

Games went with service as Olmedo took a 5–4 lead in the third set. The panther had his man and it was time for the kill. He moved far inside the baseline to take service. A backhand passed Laver cleanly. A double fault gave Alex his second point. A flat forehand that hugged the sideline gave him match point.

Desperately, Laver saved with a volley. A backhand pass and a second match point for Olmedo. Laver saved it with a smash. Alex slashed another backhand into open court. A third match point. It came off. Laver, stumbling, volleyed into the net.

The Duchess of Kent went on the court to award Olmedo the challenge cup presented by the late King George V as the applause rang down from the terraces.

"I won't tell you my strategy," said Olmedo to the press. "It's a professional secret."

It was there for all to see.

FRASER AND MARIA BUENO WIN U.S. CROWNS

by Al Laney

Neale Fraser, a fine and attractive young man from Australia and a very good left-handed tennis player indeed, won the United States National title at Forest Hills yesterday by defeating Alex Olmedo, the Peruvian now domiciled in this country, in four sets in the final match of the 1959 championship.

Fraser won, 6–3, 5–7, 6–2, 6–4, thus repeating his victory over Olmedo in the recent Davis Cup challenge round. It was a better match than that one, much closer and more speculative, but Fraser now has definitely shown that he is superior to the man who returned the Davis Cup to the country of his adoption last December as Fraser himself now has returned it to Australia, along with our title. . . .

The women's title also went overseas, or perhaps it would be better to say over mountains since Maria Bueno, who added it to her Wimbledon title by defeating Christine Truman, the English girl, 6–1, 6–4, in the final, comes from Brazil. [For the first time, both the men's and women's championships have gone overseas in the same year.]

The finals were witnessed by a crowd of about 12,000 in the Stadium and this near capacity crowd very likely increased the total attending the championships of 1959 to a record number in the 79 times the tournament has been contested.

There was no doubt that this fine crowd wanted very much for Olmedo to win this match and be our champion as he is the reigning champion of Wimbledon and Australia. They showed it continuously but they really were not unfair about it even though at times they applauded Fraser's errors a bit too vociferously.

It was not a great final to rank with the best that have preceded it but it was a match full of quite good tennis and it was exciting enough to please the crowd from that point of view.

But first a word about Miss Bueno. When her game was at its best all during this tournament and especially in yesterday's final, she was the most exciting and the most rewarding player of the game we have had in her department of it since Alice Marble retired twenty years ago.

Not only is she the most graceful of players but she uses every shot known to the game and all of the court. So deft is she when riding along on the crest of her form that she makes one think instinctively of the incomparable Suzanne Lenglen herself.

No higher praise could be given any girl who plays this game and if Miss Bueno plays poorly at times we must remember that she is only 19 years old and ought to be even better and more rewarding to watch as the years pass.

As for the men's final, it should be pointed out first of all that Olmedo was not at his best, physically speaking, for the searching test to which Fraser was bound to expose him. This was evident very soon from the way the Peruvian served.

He served gently, making sure to get the ball in court. It was said that he had pulled a muscle in his right shoulder or strained one near the end of a mixed doubles match on Saturday in which, with Miss Bueno, he was playing Fraser and Margaret duPont, a match that was not completed.

Thus deprived of the full effect of one of his most potent weapons, Olmedo was badly handicapped. And he was further handicapped by his own persistence in trying to handle Fraser's now booming, now twisting delivery by standing inside the baseline.

In these two things, lack of an incisive service of his own and inability to take the other man's because of standing too close, we may find the reasons for Olmedo's defeat. Once an exchange was in progress he often played brilliantly, making repeatedly shots that probably no other amateur can match.

Fraser's second service he often attacked with great judgment, taking it on the rise and putting the big lefthanded Australian on the defensive quickly. And when straight, without spin, however hard, Olmedo was confident in these moments, and there were many of them. We saw some fine play, for Fraser retained always his almost incredible faculty for making an offensive shot, from a seemingly losing position.

Unfortunately, Fraser, although he was not serving quite so well as in the challenge round, did not miss often enough with the first ball nor take the cut off the second often enough. At the crises of the match—there was only one in the first set but any number thereafter—Fraser's service was both a game saver and a game winner.

The one break of service that Fraser got in the first set's sixth game made that one comparatively dull since he then bothered only to hold his own until the games ran out. The second seemed likely to go the same way when he took the Peruvian's service in the opening game.

But then in the tenth game, with a chance to win the set at 6–4 while serving, Fraser unaccountably grew unsteady and began to miss badly. The result was that he lost his game to love to square the set and lost it again two games later to square the match, hitting two easy smashes wildly out of court. But Olmedo had jumped to the attack in a wonderful way to force this turnabout.

At this time the crowd thought Olmedo, under the stimulation of such a recovery, might win, and there was actually some hope of it. But Fraser, too, saw the danger. He attacked the Olmedo service with a sort of viciousness in the third game and took it. That really was the end, although many more games were to be played.

Olmedo, gradually at first and then more rapidly, began to play less well. His wonderful volleying became less accurate. Fraser refused to make mistakes that counted heavily against him and went straight to his well-deserved victory.

1 9 6 0

ENGLAND WINS WIGHTMAN CUP

by Peter Wilson

For more than two decades the Wightman Cup, symbol of lawn tennis supremacy in the women's world, was, like the gold at Fort Knox, hidden away in the United States. For a couple of days each year it was produced, but this public view, I always felt, was just to prove to the British that it *did* exist and was, technically, "up for grabs" for either team. But it was more a technicality than a valid fact. Consider the post-war scores from 1946 to 1957 inclusive: 1946 and 1947 at Wimbledon and Forest Hills—a 7–0 "whitewash" to the U. S. A. 1948, Wimbledon, 6–1 for the U. S. 1949 and the Cup had started its peregrinations within the States, moving to Philadelphia, but the score had depressingly returned to 7–0—for the U. S., I hasten to add.

1950, still at Wimbledon and still 7–0. 1951—a new venue, Brookline, Massachusetts—and the tiniest improvement: back to 6–1. I was over for that match and I confess that I suggested it might be a good idea to suspend the competition for five years in order that a new generation of British players might arise who were not reared in the dismal tradition of defeat. But the slaughter went on. At Wimbledon, at Rye, New York, and at Wimbledon again, Britain failed to win a rubber. In 1955 at Rye we got one; at Wimbledon, in 1956, two—our best post-war performance!

Then, in 1957, the matches were played at a new American home, Sewickley, Pennsylvania—and as someone who has the happiest memories of the hospitality there, may I dare hope that this is a permanent future site? It was the U. S. 6 and Great Britain 1 again. A round dozen defeats and then Lewis Carroll had the line: "Calloo, callay, oh! frabjous day." Britain won

4–3 at Wimbledon—the first victory since 1930, with the score the narrowest possible, 4 to 3. True, last year we were beaten at Sewickley, but it was by the same "respectable" margin. Now Britain has won the Cup back again, once more by the odd match of the seven and, without exception, it was the most thrilling encounter I can remember in some 30 years of Cup going.

For the first time since 1936 the whole tie depended on the final match. On the first day Britain led 1–0, America leveled at 1–1 and drew ahead 2–1. On the Saturday it was even-steven at 2–2, the U. S. ahead 3–2, level again at 3–3 and a final 4–3 win for the home team. But apart from the prolongation of the thrills up to a 9–7 last set, the unpredictability of five of the seven matches made watching at times almost painful.

Let's take the contests chronologically. We had, of course, heard a lot of the potential of 17-year-old Karen Hantze, but it was still a mild surprise when she was chosen as one of the two top singles players. The whim of the draw decided that she should open against 21-year-old Ann Haydon, who had never lost a singles match in three previous Wightman Cup encounters. And what an opening Karen made. Trim, athletic, serious-looking but not overawed, she served with a crispness which took us back to the days of the young Alice Marble and she performed at the net as though she had built-in springs in her legs to race to a 4–0 lead. A couple of games to Ann and then the cute Karen took 8 points in a row and with them the first set.

Miss Haydon, a left-hander, prefers the crosscourt forehand drive, which, of course, goes to a right-hander's backhand, but it was clear that she would have to sacrifice her own favorite stroke in order to concentrate on Karen's more cramped forehand. After both girls had held their services to start the second set, there was a run of five against the deliveries. At 17 you can't serve as hard as Miss Hantze and not perpetrate some doubles, but in the eighth game this talented youngster whose personality illuminates the game had the temerity and the sense of tactics to vary her normal flat service with what I can only liken to a baseball pitcher's outside curve. She went to 5–3.

It was at this stage that someone irreverently suggested that Ann had got Hantze in her pants.

Haydon held her service, but, with the American girl leading by a set and 5–4, with her bombarding service to follow, it could have been all up for Ann. And then occurred one of those imponderable incidents which wreck prediction. Throughout the two days, Wimbledon's No. 1 court was to prove tricky and at times downright treacherous—the "shooter" being succeeded by the ball which "hung." But this was a new variant. At the Committee Box end the turf was cutting up in large lumps and these began to disturb young Karen's concentration. At one stage she actually asked the umpire whether she should replace one or get rid of it, and these horticultural cerebrations caused her to serve two double faults—six in five service games—and present Ann with the tenth game.

The young American led only once more in the match. That was at 9–8, but now confidence was flowing from Haydon's racket and, seeing is believing, Hantze was running around her forehand! Haydon leveled, held her own service, and then Karen presented her with two set points by serving her eighth and ninth doubles. The second one was enough.

And that, virtually, was the end of the match. At 17 you don't re-win games which you have had "in the bag." After the 10-minute interval the Birmingham (Warwickshire not Alabama) girl raced to 5–1. Her undercut backhand was forcing Hantze into forehand errors, her lobs were tantalizing instead of tame, she kept the pressure up, Miss Hantze's petals wilted and she was a sad lass at the end.

Then to the big guns. Darlene Hard and Christine Truman. These two were unofficially ranked third and second in the world last year, and on that basis I found their meeting unsatisfactory—more like a clash between two novice heavyweight boxers than the meeting of skilled practitioners. In forecast I had picked Darlene Hard, whom I saw win the French Championships, to beat Christine, but when the American began with three double faults in the first game I wondered if Truman's greatest asset was going to be Hard's nerves. Although she leveled briefly at 3–3, Darlene never really got on terms with herself or the wind, and an advancing Christine took the first set 6–4.

Just as America might well have won the first match, so Britain could easily have snaffled the second. A Darlene double and a backhand volley, which would have been apt only on the court of a lunatic asylum, gave Truman a breakthrough to lead 3–2. Then, in the nick of time, Darlene found her touch. Her passing shots seared over the net. Her volley had the irrevocable and irrecoverable effect of an auctioneer's hammer falling.

She made a run of 6 games which took her to a 2–0 lead in the third set. Truman still had the punch of her weightiest of all contemporary women's forehands, but against someone who rarely made the mistake of giving her two similar shots in succession she had neither the tactical nor the positional skill to bring her field gun to bear. Christine had one good game, the eighth, in which she drew up to 4–4, but the court's imperfections of bounce were bothering her more than Darlene, and in this final set the American girl never looked like anything but a winner.

Of the next match, the first of the doubles, the least said the better. The result was 6–0, 6–0 for the "H girls"—Hard and Hantze—gained at the expense of Ann Haydon and Angela Mortimer.

I never felt the result of the Christine Truman versus Karen Hantze match, which started the second day, was in any doubt. Against an opponent who set her no tactical problems and hit ball cleanly and flat, the big girl from Essex found her tiptop thumping power. Gradually the tremendous weight of her forehand knocked the heart and the stuffing out of Hantze, yet it was more like a man's match than a woman's for there were only two service breaks—both to Christine—the first in the twelfth game of the first set and the other in the fourth game of the second. With the possible exception of her Wightman Cup win against Althea Gibson two years ago, I don't remember seeing Christine play more satisfactorily.

The match in which Darlene Hard beat Ann Haydon was another in which the girl who first looked like winning ended up as the loser. Ann, fortified by four previous victories, displayed her particular brand of "stick-at-itness" and her backhand stood up well enough under a steady pounding. She took the first set and led 2–0 in the second. She then lost 10 games in a row, winning only 5 points in the last 6 of them! Of course Darlene, who this year has realized that it doesn't pay to persevere with a losing game, varied her play when she found herself trailing.

Ann had been scoring a lot of points with a forehand passing shot down the line. Darlene countered by staying back and scoring with crosscourt forehands, hooked at an unusual angle to the English girl's backhand. She also sliced and "faded" her backhand, getting some really remarkable angles on it as well as playing some tremendously confident touch stop-volleys. Ann won just 10 points in the final set and only one game of the last 13.

Now the pressure was on Angela Mortimer, veteran of the British team but this year demoted to third singles. She was meeting the American captain, Janet Hopps. Believe it or not (and if this were fiction I would have had to vary the plot) this was *another* match where, if you'd been betting, you'd have backed the wrong filly halfway through the second set.

Angela had her chance of winning the first. Although Janet was the more powerful, particularly when serving or volleying, the American girl was gripped by bouts of intermittent tension. One of these caused her to double-fault twice and then foot-fault. Angela, who had been trailing 2–4, leveled at 4–4 and then held her service. In the next game Janet was so strung up that she actually waited to receive service when she was 15–0 on her own service! The English girl had a set point in this game but her volleying, always rather reminiscent of a slightly frantic and pessimistic butterfly hunter with an inadequate net, let her down. She looked to be tiring as she lost the set at 6–8 after saving one set point with a volley which just about erased the maker's name from the racket.

Angela's backhand was a frail, floating, squeezed-up stroke and when, constantly misjudging the wind with her shots down the line, she trailed 2–4 in the second set, it looked as though our (Wightman) Cup of bitterness was to be filled. And then—collapse. Suddenly in the eighth game the robust-looking Miss Hopps was clutching her stomach. Miss Mortimer, who knows the fell clutch of physical handicap all too bitterly herself, ran her from side to side and broke through to lead 5–4.

When they changed ends, Darlene Hard ministered to Janet like a second reviving a boxer who has had a tough round. But it was no good. The jig was up and the American lost the next game at love. Nor was she ever in the fight in the third. Angela went to 5–0, having taken 9 games in a row. She dropped a love game, but then the final enemy of cramp knotted Miss Hopps' right leg and she played the last two points with tears streaming down her face.

Now with Janet having to partner Mrs. Dorothy Knode in the final doubles against Christine Truman and Mrs. Shirley Brasher, surely Britain's troubles were over—at least that's what we were telling ourselves in the half-hour interval. Not on your Nelly (which is English slang). Janet staged a most courageous recovery during the 30-minute break. She won her service in the opening game, Christine lost hers, Dorothy Knode won hers, Shirley lost hers—and presto! we were right in the consommé all over again.

I think Shirley will want to forget that set. The poor soul couldn't do a thing right. It was only a most astonishing leap volley from Christine, who was playing the heroine's part, which finally put us in front at 5–4. A smash from Hopps, dubiously given out, cost the U. S. the set.

Surely now we could relax. Some people may have been able to, but considering the scoreboard, which marked 3–0, 4–1 and 5–2 to the U. S., I wasn't one of them. At 5–4 Janet and Dorothy had a set point which Shirley, finally getting into the game, saved with a smash. At 6–5 Britain at last got to match point. It was now nearly 8 o'clock and play had started at 2:00.

We lost it! A volley hit Christine in the chest!

At 8–7, with Shirley serving, we had another match point. Shirley volleyed out. A third one and Shirley double-faulted. A fourth. Shirley volleyed out. Janet saved the fifth with a net-cord return of service. Shirley gave us a sixth with a volley down the doubles court, and at last Janet's forehand dropped out of court. Britain had won and the stock of Scotch, tranquilizers and fingernails was exhausted.

For the U. S. Darlene Hard, on the winning side in both her singles and one double, was outstanding. For Great Britain it was more of a team effort, with Christine Truman the most successful player. For the spectators it was murder!

MARIA BUENO WINS WIMBLEDON AGAIN; RALSTON AND OSUNA'S UNEXPECTED VICTORY

by Allison Danzig

Maria Bueno, the first player from South America to win the tennis championship at Wimbledon, extended her reign to a second year today.

Overcoming the strong resistance of Sandra Reynolds, the first representative of South Africa to reach the women's final, in the long opening set, the attractive 20-year-old Brazilian girl volleyed with rare skill in winning the second set at love for the match, 8–6, 6–0. An hour after the start of play, Senhorita Bueno was receiving the championship plate from the Duchess of Kent, to the applause of 15,000 filling every seat and every inch of standing room around the worn center court.

Far more exciting than the victory of the slender, graceful senhorita, which was accepted as foreordained, was the unprecedented triumph of a scratch combination playing for the first time in the men's doubles. After the galling ignominy of its failure to qualify a player for either the women's singles or the men's, won yesterday by Neale Fraser of Australia, the United States could take a sizable measure of satisfaction in the feat of Dennis Ralston of Bakersfield, California, in winning the doubles championship with Rafael Osuna of Mexico.

In the final round, the first to find two unseeded teams on the court since the adoption of the seeded draw in the 1920s, the tall, sandy-haired Ralston, who will not be 18 until July 27, and the 21-year-old Osuna defeated Michael Davies and Bobby Wilson of Britain, 7–5, 6–3, 10–8, saving two set points from 15–40 in the tenth game of the final set.

The exploits of Ralston and Osuna have caused something of a sensation. Not until the Beckenham tournament a few weeks ago had they ever paired together, and they had one other week of collective experience at Queen's Club. Neither had given any indication individually that they were in the class of the teams they defeated here, though Ralston is the junior champion of the United States. Osuna is a student at the University of Southern California.

The teams they conquered en route to the final included Rodney Laver and Robert Mark, Australian champions and rated as the world's best; Nicola Pietrangeli and Orlando Sirola, Italian Davis Cup pair; and Ulf Schmidt and Jan Lundquist, Swedish cup team. Davies and Wilson, who put out Fraser and Roy Emerson, defending champions, are Britain's cup tandem.

Osuna is an unbelievably fine doubles player, as quick as a jungle cat, just as rapacious in going for the kill with hair-trigger reflexes on the volley and in flattening the ball overhead. He has an innate sense of where to put the ball and a particularly good service. Ralston is surprisingly quick and easy of movement for his size and has an affinity for exploring open spaces. He volleys easily, with a sense of the vulnerable spot in the court, and is facile in the important half-volley. He is decisive overhead, and both his first and second service are placed beautifully and often go for aces.

Both youngsters have projected themselves squarely into the Davis Cup picture. Dave Freed, captain of the United States team, and James Dickey and Harold Lebair, vice president and treasurer, respectively, of the U.S. Lawn Tennis Association, congratulated Ralston and Osuna in the dressing room. Freed said that he is taking Ralston to Canada with the cup team and will try him out with various partners in search for a doubles team. Osuna, who failed to take part in the trials of the Mexican team, which is the United States' prospective opponent in the second round, said that he had received a cable today putting him on the Mexican cup squad. It is possible that he and Ralston may face each other in the cup matches.

Senhorita Bueno went into her match against Miss Reynolds with a healthy respect for her opponent. The slender girl from South Africa had beaten her a number of times on hard courts this year and her victories over Darlene Hard of Montebello, California, and Ann Haydon Jones of the British Wightman Cup team in the previous two rounds were indicative of how well she was playing on turf.

Miss Reynolds has one of the most feared forehands in women's tennis and she is a highly intelligent player in maneuvering and coming up with the right shot. In spite of the fact that her second service is weak and invites the receiver to come in on the return, Senhorita Bueno was chary about accepting the invitation. She became all the more chary when Miss Reynolds, after falling behind at 1–3, brought the lob and drop shot into play and pulled even. Soon the champion was lagging in following her own strong service to the net, in fear of the lob.

It was a tight fight all the way in the first set, with Senhorita Bueno hard pressed in driving exchanges. She was down at 0–30 in the eleventh game and it looked serious. But at this point the champion realized that she was not strong enough off the ground to overcome her opponent's powerful forehand and controlled backhand, and committed herself to getting to the net as early and often as possible. From then on it was her volleying and serving against the ground strokes of Miss Reynolds, who almost never went to the net.

After being in trouble again in the long thirteenth game and saving it with her volleys, the champion effected the deciding break in the fourteenth as she went in on her return of service. In the second set Miss Reynolds continued to offer strong resistance but Senhorita Bueno was performing like a master at the net. In the second game Miss Reynolds went ahead at 40–0 with stunning drives and the champion scored three times with drop shots in return of service and pulled it out.

That just about killed Miss Reynolds' last hope. She made a tremendous fight in the third, the longest, best-played and most exciting of the match, and when she lost it, after twenty points had been contested, she was near the end of her resources. Senhorita Bueno, going in on both her service and return of service, won the last three games with the loss of only three points.

The United States shared in the women's as well as the men's doubles championship. Miss Hard and Senhorita Bueno defeated Miss Reynolds and Renée Schuurman of South Africa in the final, 6–4, 6–0.

FRASER AND DARLENE HARD ARE U.S. CHAMPIONS

by Michael Strauss

Maria Esther Bueno, considered the queen of them all in women's tennis for these past two years, ran into an unexpected uprising in the national tennis championship final at Forest Hills yesterday.

The Brazilian senhorita, defending her crown, was beaten by Darlene

Hard, America's No. 2 player from Montebello, California, 6–3, 10–12, 6–4. As a result, the title won by Althea Gibson in 1957 and 1958, returned to the United States.

In the men's final, Neale Fraser, the sharpshooting stylist from Australia, conquered Rod Laver, his red-headed countryman, in a duel of southpaws, 6–4, 6–4, 10–8. Service breaks in the last game of each set enabled Fraser to win the championship for the second straight time.

Fraser has a service that he can make "kick" in either direction. It is his most feared weapon. Yesterday his tricky delivery was at its best. Laver was only able to pierce it once—in the third game of the second set.

The contest was a rubber match. Laver beat his Davis Cup teammate for the Australian crown early this year. In June, however, Fraser bounced back to conquer the red-headed bomber in four sets at Wimbledon. Yesterday Fraser was by far the more consistent performer.

There is little doubt that the developments in the women's encounter took the gallery of 7,000 by surprise. Senhorita Bueno has been winning the important matches with a sparkling, well-rounded repertoire of strokes. She was the big pre-match favorite. But Miss Hard was unimpressed. She sailed into the South American senhorita at the start with a confidence that gave her the role of aggressor. Her service was superb and her overhead deadly. After ten minutes, she boasted a 3–0 lead in games.

Senhorita Bueno, famed for her poise, power and poker face, never seemed able to gain full control of her game thereafter. She displayed moments of brilliance and long sieges of obstinacy. But after 1 hour and 45 minutes of play she succumbed.

For the American, the victory represented a dream come true. Five times before, she had failed in her quest of the national title. In 1958 she was beaten by Miss Gibson in the final. In 1959 she bowed to Senhorita Bueno in the semi-final, 6–2, 6–4.

"I never thought I'd do it," the Californian said after the match. "That girl never gives up. She hits winners when least expected. It's been a long time coming. It's great."

The gallery also thought it was "great." It rose and gave the American girl, a 24-year-old junior on leave of absence from Pomona (California) College, an ovation. She helped provide one of the most gripping women's matches seen in the big cement saucer in years.

Suspenseful moments were liberally sprinkled throughout the contest. The second set, by itself, had more thrills than often seen in a whole day's program on the field courts. The set was filled with drawn-out games. The ninth game, for example, was settled after 24 points. It was an old-fashioned neck-twister. With Miss Bueno on the service line and trailing 3–5, Miss Hard tried to end it then and there. The best she could do, however, was to gain one match point.

Senhorita Bueno finally broke Miss Hard in the twenty-second game after gaining a triple set point. The Californian held off the threat temporarily by acing her rival on the fourth point and volleying her out of position on the fifth. But Miss Hard then erred on a shot from the baseline.

The situation appeared far from bright for Miss Hard. She had missed numerous opportunities and seemed unable to provide the important shots when most needed. Miss Bueno, who had been having trouble with her short ground strokes, seemed to have finally found the touch. But when the girls returned for play in the third set, the Californian demonstrated that she was not ready to concede anything. She broke her opponent's service in the first game and took her own. Then the players exchanged breaks in the seventh and eighth games.

It seemed that Miss Hard's task might be made easier late in the ninth game when Senhorita Bueno went sprawling on the heavy turf after trying to return a drop shot. When the South American girl arose, she was shaking her right hand. Nevertheless, she was able to withstand her foe's charges during the game, which was the match's big breath-catcher. The South American took it on her service on the twenty-fourth point, a cross-court volley and a near service ace settling the issue. The long ninth game was a violation of the law of averages. Although it was teeming with sparkling shots by both players, Miss Hard gained only one match point, the seventh point of the game. After that the advantage points all went to the South American. But the Brazilian couldn't survive the second match point, in the next game. Miss Hard rushed into a 40–15 lead. Then she ended matters with a short forehand shot that caught her rival out of position.

For the 21-year-old Miss Bueno, the Wimbledon champion, the defeat marked the end of a reign that had made her the toast of courts around the world. In her younger days Miss Hard beat her frequently. Lately, however, the job had become difficult. In their get-together yesterday Miss Bueno seemed to adopt the strategy of watchful waiting. She was careful with her strokes at the start, always waiting for her opponent to make errors. Instead, the South American got into difficulties as Miss Hard clicked repeatedly, particularly with decisive cross-court volleys.

In the wake of Miss Hard's triumph, the developments in the men's engagement were only anticlimactic. Indeed, the match, pairing foreign players in a final for the fourth time in five years, seemed to be watched by the railbirds with only passing interest.

Fraser made his big move late in the first set. From 4–all he moved to a 2–0 lead in the second set. Laver retaliated with a service break in the third game, but he could not keep pace with his countryman. Neale broke him again in the tenth game to take the set.

Throughout the match, Laver's volley, his most potent weapon, missed connections repeatedly. Fraser, on the other hand, made fine use of his opportunities at the net and kept pecking away at his rival until able to get in his payoff shots. A big factor, too, was Neale's lobs. His lofting thrusts were flawless. But it was his service that made the big difference. Fraser works on the delivery line like a spitball pitcher in baseball. He masks his offerings. As a result, Laver never was sure what to expect.

1961

LAVER TROUNCES MCKINLEY AT WIMBLEDON

by Fred Tupper

Rod (The Rocket) Laver of Australia is the new champion at Wimbledon. And high time. The lithe, 22-year-old redhead, the runner-up the past two years, demolished Chuck McKinley of St. Louis, 6–3, 6–1, 6–4, on the center court in fifty-five minutes today.

It was the quickest men's tennis final here since Jack Kramer won from Tom Brown in forty-five minutes back in 1947.

And it confirmed what everybody from connoisseur to bookmaker knew: Laver is the best amateur in the world.

The Australian left-hander has been knocking at the door for some time. He was a finalist with Alex Olmedo here in 1959 and he lost to Neale Fraser of Australia in 1960. Over the past year, Laver has been the runner-up in the American, Australian and Italian championships.

Laver was tough and tournament-tested. McKinley was under suspension until May 1 for throwing a racket in Perth during the Davis Cup interzone final against Italy in Australia last winter. The stocky 20-year-old American has been studying at Trinity University in Texas. He played in his first tourney this year in Oklahoma late in May.

Since arriving in England, he won at Bristol, lost in the final of the London grass championship, and then acrobatically wove through the field into the Wimbledon final. Laver was seeded second here, McKinley eighth.

For a few minutes it was a fine match. McKinley started confidently, ripping his bullet service into the corners and sprinting up court behind it to volley. In the sixth game he had his one and only chance to break through.

Chuck was ahead 3–2 but down 40–0 on Laver's service. Two flat passing shots and a wide Laver volley got McKinley to deuce, and a cross-court volley to advantage. Sadly, he popped the service return low into the net.

Then Laver was away on a brilliant seven-game winning streak, continually forcing McKinley into errors. Chuck volleyed wide over the baseline, double-faulted on a netcord, volleyed into the net, and stared at a running Laver forehand that streaked by him.

Laver was serving continually to McKinley's backhand, alternately using his reverse-twist jumper or cutting the ball low to the right side. The Rocket took the eighth game at love and he had the next one and the first set on a backhand pass riveted to the sideline.

Nothing went right for McKinley. The little breaks never came. He couldn't handle Laver's service cleanly and he had no better luck with his own. The second set was soon gone. McKinley had won only 10 points in thirteen minutes.

Chuck thumped his racket on the burned grass and dug in. He was roaring around the court, chasing the redhead's looped ground strokes and the spinning lobs that arched over his head and disappeared.

Bravely McKinley held service to 4–all in the final set. Then came the holocaust. Laver braced himself for the breakthrough. He slapped a backhand down one line, banked a forehand down the other and then hammered a backhand squarely into the corner—three outright winners. McKinley hadn't touched one.

It was love–forty now. McKinley hurtled forward behind his service. Laver threaded his looped forehand through the hole for 5–4.

Quickly the redhead was at 40–15 and match point. Only then was there a flicker of nerves. He blooped a volley out and watched a flat backhand sail by him. He had match point again and bashed the ball in off the wood. That did it. Laver had won the all-England championship and Princess Marina, the Duchess of Kent, went to the court to praise him.

"I aimed every point for a winner," said the Australian. "Chuck was hanging around the edges and playing well."

"If I played well," said McKinley, "The Rocket played awful well."

ITALY DEFEATS U. S. IN DAVIS CUP

by William McHale

American tennis fans were understandably downcast a fortnight ago when they learned that for one reason or another none of their nation's top amateurs would be able to go to Italy to play for the Davis Cup. But Italy's tennis fans, oddly enough, were absolutely outraged. Still flushed from their victory over the best in the U. S. last year, the Italians were sure we had done it on purpose. "The United States has ridiculed the memory of Mr. Dwight Davis," snarled Italy's leading sports paper, *Corriere dello Sport,* as U.S. Cup Captain David Freed arrived in Rome with his crew of virtual unknowns—Jon Douglas, Don Dell, Marty Riessen and Whit Reed. "For years Italian tennis has waited for this moment—the Interzone Finals on the center court of Foro Italico—and now the U. S. tries to ruin the fiesta."

Corriere did not for one minute believe that America's top clay-court man, Tut Bartzen, had a sore wrist, that Chuck McKinley had to stay home in Texas or that Dennis Ralston was too naughty to play international tennis. "Knowing their inferiority on clay," said *Corriere* with a sneer, "the big guns of United States tennis have taken refuge in childish excuses. It's not very sporting."

As Captain Freed put his players to work practicing five hours a day on the mushy *en-tout-cas* courts of Mussolini's huge monument to sport, *Corriere* flatly predicted a feast for their own gladiators. "By the end of the first day's matches, we will be ahead two to nothing. By the following day we can pick up our airplane tickets for the trip to Australia," the paper declared. But, as it turned out, by the end of the first day's matches and to the ill-concealed fury of the Italian fans, the Italians themselves were behind one match and were well on their way to losing the second.

Roman tennis fans bear little resemblance to the well-behaved enthusiasts who politely applaud a good shot here and there at Wimbledon or Forest Hills. Following a tradition established in the days when Christians and lions were the main attractions on the local sports calendar, they scream their approval, roar their disapproval, and curse the umpire.

No athlete in all Italy is more responsive to this kind of rooting than Fausto Gardini, a knobby-kneed 31-year-old who was five times champion of Italy in the mid-'50s. Gardini quit the game six years ago to run the huge bakery business owned by his wife's father, but last summer he came back to tennis to win another national championship and help Italy beat the Swedes four to one in the European Zone finals. A stringy, expressive, cavorting clown, Gardini uses the crowd as his personal cheering section. During his matches last August the Swedes got so rattled by the booing and whistling Gardini claque that they huffily threatened to walk off.

Last Friday, as Gardini strutted onto the center court at the forum to meet America's brawny young Jon Douglas, he was greeted by a thunder of cheers from 6,000 patriotic throats. "Fausto, Fausto, Fausto," the fans chanted, waving the yellow paper hats they had bought to fend off the glaring October sun. To young Douglas, a short, husky onetime quarterback from Stanford University, it must have sounded like a Saturday afternoon at UCLA. Somewhat cowed by the demonstration, Douglas at first approached his opponent diffidently. A superb athlete but not a great tennis player, he seemed content to retrieve the Italian's shots without trying for any kills of his own. The first two sets were a series of long, dreamlike exchanges from backcourt to backcourt. Since Douglas missed more often than his opponent, he was soon trailing badly, and at each decisive point the Italian would throw back his head in a toothy grin and yell his triumph to the crowd, which would answer in a roar of Latin adulation.

Douglas was behind two sets to love and five games to two in the third set, and the crowd was hungry for the kill. *"Mazzalo, mazzalo"* (Slaughter the bum), shrieked the fans in ripe Roman fashion. But the young American suddenly dropped his waiting game and began rushing the net to slam into Gardini with all his muscular might. Taken by surprise, Fausto floundered, missed, dropped five straight games and lost the set to put the score at two to one his favor.

For nearly an hour after that the two men fought grimly, matching each other point for point, game for game. Then Douglas' young strength began to tell and the crowd's cheers grew anguished as its hero began to fade. "Fausto," they called, drawing out the final "ooo" in mournful tremolo like the end of an aria in *Rigoletto*.

When the American finally crashed through to win the set 10 to eight, Gardini collapsed like a pricked paper bag filled with hot air. He complained of cramps, staggered around the court pointing at his leg and grimacing the way Harpo used to after Chico slammed the piano cover on his fingers. In the final set the sulky Italian refused even to try. He served underhand like a Victorian maiden lady and waved his racket listlessly at the balls returning over the net. When Douglas took the set 6–0 and the match with it, the great Fausto slunk off to collapse in the arms of his team captain.

"Gardini," proclaimed the Italian papers soon after, "was beaten more by cramps than by the skill of his opponent."

It was well after 4 o'clock when unorthodox Whitney Reed took the center court in the second singles match against Nicola Pietrangeli, who is rated one of the best amateurs in Europe. Cheered by his teammate's victory and characteristically full of confidence, Reed refused to be intimidated. "I can take this guy," he told a friend, and then proceeded to do just that— almost. He chewed up the Italian's service and forced the normally impeccable Nicola into error after error on his own return. "Nicola, Nicola," moaned the disillusioned and unbelieving Italian fans in the lengthening shadows of darkness and defeat.

Indeed, if darkness had not overtaken Italy before the issue was forced, Reed might have gone right on to take the match and give the U. S. a commanding lead for the cup. As it was, however, the match was recessed with Reed leading two sets to love and Pietrangeli ahead four games to three in the third set. By next morning the Italian had regained his composure and was again at the top of his game. Reed seemed scarcely present as the Italian took the remaining games and sets almost effortlessly to win the match.

Sad to say, from then on the Americans never had a chance. On Sunday, Captain Freed chose Reed rather than Douglas, whose smashing play might have been more effective than Reed's delicate touch strokes on the soft surface, to team up with Donald Dell in the doubles. This untried combination was pitted against Orlando Sirola and Pietrangeli, a doubles team that had won 29 Davis Cup victories for Italy. The result was a U.S. defeat in four sets and the virtual end of American Davis Cup hopes for another year. Even the one set taken by Reed and Dell in the doubles was not so much won by the Americans as lost by their opponents during a spell when Sirola suddenly and unaccountably was unable to get the ball over the net. By the third set, however, the gigantic (6 feet 7 inches) carefree Italian player was back in form again, and from then on Italy's right to challenge Australia for the cup was never again in contention.

The doubles match which gave Italy its lead and the final singles matches which clinched the round went so predictably in Italy's favor that even the

Italian fans watched in relative quiet. During the first set of his decisive match against Pietrangeli—which was no match at all—young Douglas, only the sixth-ranked player in the U. S., fought tenaciously to hold his opponent to a 9–7 victory, but the effort took all he had. Pietrangeli won the next two sets easily, 6–3, 6–2, to capture the match and the round for Italy, leaving nothing in the way of glory for the agile—and miraculously recovered—Gardini but the formality of trouncing Reed in a five-set match that no longer mattered.

EMERSON AND MISS HARD U.S. CHAMPIONS

by Allison Danzig

Darlene Hard of Long Beach, California, extended her reign as women's national amateur tennis champion to a second year yesterday and Roy Emerson of Australia became the new men's titleholder.

It required only forty-seven minutes for Miss Hard to defeat Ann Haydon of Britain, 6–3, 6–4, in the final round of the tournament before 9,000 in the Forest Hills stadium.

The sturdy blond Californian, who had been out of competition for three months with hepatitis, carried the attack to her left-handed opponent with a vigor of volley and overhead that was overpowering.

Despite the strength of her ground strokes and her plucky tenaciousness, Miss Haydon, who holds the French championship and defeated the Wimbledon champion, Angela Mortimer of Britain, in the semi-finals here, was unable to resist the skill and éclat of her opponent in the forecourt.

And so Miss Hard, the only American to reach the quarter-finals of the championship, preserved one of the titles for the United States before the fifth all-Australian men's final since 1956 went on the court.

Emerson, the almost forgotten man of the tournament until his tremendously stirring five-set match with Rafael Osuna of Mexico in the semi-finals, gained probably the most significant victory of his career in defeating Rodney Laver, the Wimbledon titleholder, for the championship.

He had beaten Laver in the Australian championship in January in four sets but his performance yesterday was his crowning achievement.

In an hour and twenty-one minutes of blazing, almost electrifying tennis that had the gallery gasping at the fury of the hitting, the lean, dark-haired Emerson defeated the player looked upon as the world's best.

He did it without permitting Laver a set, and before the end, the quiet red-haired Wimbledon champion was all but crushed in spirit. The scores were 7–5, 6–3, 6–2.

In the first two sets against Osuna, Emerson's tennis was as good as had been seen at Forest Hills in years. He sustained an attack of crushing violence with hardly an unworthy error. His performance yesterday was of the same standard, though he had occasional lapses.

Australia need not fear if Neale Fraser, Wimbledon and American champion in 1960, is not sufficiently recovered from his recent knee operation to help in the defense of the Davis Cup. Emerson and Laver should handle the job quite adequately.

Laver did not play the match expected of him. He had not been performing up to his Wimbledon standard all week. Probably the fact that he had no real competition until he met Donald Dell in the quarter-finals had a deleterious effect on his game.

But though the slender, left-handed Australian youth made errors that were unworthy of him on his feared backhand and at the net, he played at times like a world champion.

He was nothing short of sensational in saving the first set by a stroke in the eighth game and again in the ninth. His ground strokes were lightning streaks and he volleyed like a fiend with the skill of a true master.

Unhappily for Laver, it was only by reaching such scintillating heights that he could hold Emerson in check, and it was beyond his capacity to maintain any consistency under the relentless pressure applied by his strong, wiry opponent.

Laver's spinning southpaw service is ordinarily one of the most troublesome in the game. But it had no terror for Emerson, with his great strength of return from both forehand and backhand. Only twice did the Wimbledon champion score an ace in the match.

Emerson's own service was exceedingly difficult to deal with, and behind it he volleyed as can few other players in the world, amateur or professional.

Overhead he was cataclysmic. He was tireless in keeping on the ball, and for the most part he had such wonderful control and so much comprehension in his resort to the lob and drop shot that Laver had to keep blazing away to earn a point.

Losing the opening set on a final double fault in the twelfth game, after Emerson had thrown a lob over his head and whipped through a return of service and a backhand passing shot to pull out from 0–30, Laver knew almost unbelievably cruel misfortune in the second set.

He lost the third game after leading at 40–0, the fourth from 30–0, the fifth from 30–0. He pulled even from 0–40 in the first and seventh games and lost them also.

It was enough to have broken the spirit of the most stout-hearted. It wasn't so much that Laver failed to take advantage of his opportunities. Emerson was a tiger for fight for every point in every situation, blazing away with his drives and volleying superbly.

Laver stayed in the fight with undiminished courage to 2–1 in the third set. Then his resistance and confidence were gone. Emerson was too strong, too accomplished from every quarter, and the Wimbledon champion lost heart and control.

Emerson won five games in succession with the loss of only five points, gaining three of them at love. He was still so strong at the end that he leaped high over the net as Laver's last backhand return of service went out of court.

Miss Hard swept ahead at 4–0 in the first set against Miss Haydon. The slender British girl had a big chance to break service in the opening game as she went ahead at 40–15 with two passing shots. Then Miss Haydon weakened and was able to offer little resistance. She rallied at 15–40 in the fifth game and won nine successive points as the Californian's control deserted her. But Miss Hard recovered, and her volleys and service exacted the set.

At the start of the second set Miss Haydon began to get more life into her game. She hit with greater pace and got more depth, went to the net more often and used the lob to repulse Miss Hard. It appeared she might make a match of it as she went ahead at 2–1.

Miss Hard's answer to the challenge was immediately forthcoming. Going in on her serve, her return of service and her splendid undercut backhand approach shot, she was irresistible with her volleys and won the next three games.

After Miss Haydon had taken the seventh, the Californian won the eighth at love and led at 40–0 in the ninth. Three times she was at match point, but her volleys went into the net under the pressure of Miss Haydon's passing shots and return of service, and the British girl was cheered as she pulled out the game.

Miss Haydon came within a stroke of leveling at 5–all before Miss Hard ended matters with a forehand cross-court passing shot.

1 9 6 2

WIMBLEDON TITLE TO KAREN SUSMAN

by Fred Tupper

It was Karen Hantze Susman day at Wimbledon today. The 19-year-old tennis star from Chula Vista, California, put a stop to an amazing string of upsets by Mme. V. Sukova of Czechoslovakia and brought the women's championship back to America for the first time since 1958.

Mrs. Susman, seeded eighth, won from Mme. Sukova, who was not seeded, 6–4, 6–4, as the Prague housewife pulled up crippled toward the end.

Then the lovely Californian with the classical style paired with Billie Jean Moffitt of Long Beach, California, and defeated Sandra Reynolds Price and Renée Schuurman of South Africa, 5–7, 6–3, 7–5, holding the doubles title they won here a year ago. It was a magnificent match that had the center court in turmoil. . . . The men's doubles championship went to Australia as Bob Hewitt and Fred Stolle defeated the unseeded Yugoslavs, Boro Jovanovic and Nicola Pilic, 6–2, 5–7, 6–2, 6–4.

Mrs. Susman raced through this Wimbledon without losing a set. Her rhythmic service and beautiful volleying are textbook material but she picked up match toughness as she went along. She won this afternoon under the greatest pressure, for Mme. Sukova is a grim, determined fighter of another school. She battles tenaciously for each point and she masks the direction of her ground game so astutely that Karen was caught off balance repeatedly in the early stages.

Mme. Sukova had knocked off the defending champion, Angela Mortimer, after trailing by a set and 1–3 in the second. She had beaten Darlene Hard, who was seeded second, and Maria Bueno, seeded third.

After dropping the first two games, Mme. Sukova broke through Karen's service, held her own at love and was just where she wanted to be at 3–2. The Californian pulled out the stops. She was curving her service away from the lunging Sukova forehand and rushing up to net to pound away the volley. She got that game back and she had the next with a brace of smashes to the far corners. Quickly she was at 5–3 and ahead 40–0 on the Czech's service. Three set points faded away as Mme. Sukova ran Karen around the court and plastered an overhead deep for the game. Karen had set point three times again in the next game. Mme. Sukova lobbed her, pushed a forehand down the line and then slashed a forehand across court. Karen got to that one on the dead run, volleyed it down the short side for the set at 6–4.

Mme. Sukova may appear ungainly, but she is efficient in the crises. With everything to go for, she hit a stream of winners over the whole court for a 3–0 lead in the second set. Karen wrenched her concentration back to the job. She broke back to 2–3 with her best game of the match—a backhand volley down one side, a forehand through the middle and then a lovely stop volley that fell dead on the scarred turf. It was glorious tennis and Mme. Sukova was on the run. Suddenly she pulled up, chasing a volley. Her right ankle, twisted the day before on the hotel stairs, was wrenched again.

Mrs. Susman never let up. She had five games running here from 0–3. Up loomed two match points. In a last effort, the Czech forced herself up court. She put away two smashes for 4–5. She staved off a match point in the tenth game with a forehand ripped down the chalk. Then she hit a high return. Karen measured it carefully and pounded it into the corner for the title.

Princess Marina came on court to hand Mrs. Susman the silver platter.

"She hides where she's hitting," said Karen later of her opponent. "For too long I didn't know where the ball was going."

Some 260,000 spectators crammed into the grounds during the championships, one of the largest attendances on record.

MEXICO DEFEATS U. S. IN DAVIS CUP FIRST TIME

by Allison Danzig

The United States was vanquished by Mexico in Davis Cup play today for the first time in fifteen meetings dating from 1928.

Beaten by Italy the last two years in the interzone final of the international tennis matches, the Americans now find themselves shut out of the final of their own zone. This had never happened before, though in 1936 they lost to Australia in the American Zone final at Philadelphia.

Rafael Osuna, a graceful, feathery-footed artist with a racket, scored the victory that made history at Chapultepec Sports Center. Apparently on the verge of exhaustion and taking recourse to oxygen to revitalize himself in the 7,800-foot altitude, he stemmed a rally that appeared to be carrying Jon Douglas of Santa Monica, California, to victory as the American won the third and fourth sets after losing the first two.

To the frenzied acclaim of the standing-room crowd of 3,200 that jumped to its feet almost every time he scored a winning shot or Douglas made a losing stroke, the 23-year-old Osuna swept through the final set with his finest tennis of the two-and-one-half-hour match. The racket that had lost its magic as his strength ebbed now became a flashing rapier. Douglas, who had looked like an almost certain winner after leading at 40–15 on his drooping opponent's service in the opening game of the fifth set, was overwhelmed.

With the excitement rising to the boiling point and his opponent finding it more and more difficult to maintain his admirable composure as the crowd cheered the American's errors, Osuna swept through five games. After losing the sixth, he ended the match in the seventh with his volleys. The scores were 9–7, 6–3, 6–8, 3–6, 6–1.

By winning the first of the last two singles matches Mexico increased its lead to 3–1 to seal the verdict. The Mexicans won the doubles yesterday after the opening two singles matches on Saturday had been divided. In the final match today Chuck McKinley of St. Ann, Missouri, defeated Mario Llamas, 2–6, 4–6, 7–5, 6–3, 6–3, after trailing at 4–5 on a service break in the third set. So Mexico won the series, 3–2. It will meet the winner of the match between heavily favored Yugoslavia and the British Caribbean team in the American Zone final here.

The anxiety of the gallery at 15–40 against Osuna in the first game of the final set with Douglas was demonstrated in the outbursts from the stands. Spectators were shouting encouragement to Osuna, urging him on. The umpire repeatedly had to request silence.

At this critical point, when Robert J. Kelleher, the United States captain, had every reason to be hopeful for an American victory, Douglas gave his exhausted opponent a reprieve. He missed four successive returns of service, three of them on the backhand, as he played for winners on the lines, and the game was lost to him.

It seemed that the thing for Douglas to have done was to keep the ball in play and prolong the rallies against an opponent who appeared ready to collapse from weariness and whose control was failing more and more.

Osuna gained a new lease on life as he pulled out the game. He then fell behind at 15–30 in the second game, but again he came on and broke service as Douglas failed twice on the backhand. The crowd was beside itself with joy as its hero went ahead at 3–0. Osuna, in turn, became more vital than he had been at any time previously in the match. It was as though he had drunk some magic potion. . . .

Osuna, leading at 5–0, yielded the sixth game at love to Douglas' four winning shots, saving himself for his service in the seventh. With the crowd cheering every shot, he went ahead at 40–15. Douglas saved two match points with stunning backhand passing shots. Then Osuna hit a volley for his third match point and play ended as Douglas hit out of court in answer to another volley.

Francisco (Pancho) Contreras, the Mexican captain, ran out and embraced Osuna. Fans rushed onto the court, and Osuna, an undergraduate at the University of Southern California in Los Angeles, was carried off in triumph.

The United States had missed a big chance to win the doubles match yesterday when it lost the opening set after leading at 6–5 and 40–15. Again today it appeared that Douglas had victory in his grasp against Osuna. When he went ahead at 40–15 to start the fifth set, the crowd was in the depths of despair. Osuna looked to be utterly spent and Douglas was punishing him severely with beautifully controlled lobs.

Osuna had been going to the net on his service and also on his return of service. Douglas had been playing a less strenuous backcourt game. The Mexican youth was undoubtedly feeling the effects of the wearing three-hour doubles match, and Douglas looked much the stronger physically. Even in the first set Osuna had been taking oxygen.

The 34-year-old Llamas was substituted for Antonio Palafox, who was troubled with a pulled stomach muscle. In Saturday's opening singles McKinley had beaten Osuna, 6–2, 7–5, 6–3, and Palafox defeated Douglas, 6–3, 6–1, 3–6, 7–5. Yesterday Osuna and Palafox won the doubles from McKinley and Dennis Ralston of Bakersfield, California, 8–6, 10–12, 3–6, 6–3, 6–2.

LAVER COMPLETES GRAND SLAM

by Allison Danzig

Rodney Laver of Australia achieved the first grand slam in men's tennis since 1938 when he won the national championship yesterday. For the first time, the women's title also went to an Australian player.

The holder of the Wimbledon, Australian and French championships, the red-haired, left-handed Laver completed his sweep of the world's four major titles by defeating his Davis Cup teammate, Roy Emerson, in the final round. The scores were 6–2, 6–4, 5–7, 6–4.

A year ago, Emerson had beaten Laver in the final here in three sets.

The gallery of 9,000 in the Forest Hills stadium of the West Side Tennis Club acclaimed the 24-year-old champion with a standing ovation as he walked off the court.

Waiting to congratulate him as he reached the marquee was Donald Budge, also a redhead, and the only other player to achieve the grand slam.

Laver was born the same year that Budge won four titles.

"I feel so happy, I don't know what to say," said Laver after the championship cup had been presented to him by James B. Dickey, the first vice president of the United States Lawn Tennis Association. "I only wish I may be able to come back next year and defend this cup."

Emerson, whom Laver had also defeated in the Australian, French and Italian championship finals, said: "I would like to congratulate Rod for his fantastic record in matching Don Budge in winning the four major championships."

"He has beaten some great players in the finals," he added, as the crowd roared in appreciation.

Budge, called to the microphone, said, "If anyone ever deserved winning the grand slam, Rod Laver certainly deserved to win it. I was lucky in not having to compete against such a player as Rod, and Roy's sportsmanship has been impeccable. A lot of our boys and players from other countries could learn something from them."

Margaret Smith is the Australian girl who made history in carrying off the women's crown. Like Laver, she too is red-haired.

The tall 20-year-old Miss Smith ended the two-year reign of Darlene Hard of Long Beach, California, defeating her, 9–7, 6–4, in the final after saving set point in the fourteenth game.

Only once before had an Australian reached the women's final. Nancye Wynne of Australia was the runner-up to Alice Marble in 1938.

Miss Hard, who practically ruined her chances of winning with sixteen double-faults, was so emotionally distraught that she gave way to tears after losing the sixth game of the second set.

Miss Hard had been aggravated by close calls on the lines against her, as well as by her lost opportunity in the first set and her five double-faults in the third game of the second set. She found it too much when another call went against her in the sixth game.

Fighting to break service and get back on even terms in the set, she had volleyed the ball deep at advantage point for Miss Smith in the game. Miss Hard was going back to receive service, thinking she had won the point, when the official on the baseline belatedly called the ball out.

Miss Hard stopped in her tracks as if stunned by the call, which gave the game to Miss Smith. She put her hand to her eyes and wept. Then she walked to the rear of the court and stood with her face to the canvas backstop, continuing to weep.

It was a trying ordeal for Miss Smith, and it became more difficult for her when the gallery roared its encouragement to Miss Hard as the American got back into the fight and won the seventh game with her skillfully turned volleys.

In the next game, the Australian girl broke badly. After Miss Hard had scored with a return of service, Miss Smith double-faulted and missed twice on her fine backhand, which had been so steadfast and had scored so often for her. She lost her service at love.

It seemed that the defending champion was strongly back in the running. Miss Smith, however, regaining her composure and returning service beautifully from both sides, broke through easily in the ninth game as the Californian double-faulted.

Miss Smith then ran out the last game at love with her powerful service, which had been so big a factor in her victory, along with her strong backhand volley. Miss Hard appeared to slam her last two returns of service carelessly out of court and into the net, as if in a hurry to have the match over with.

Laver, for the first two sets of the men's final, was almost as irresistible as he had been in overwhelming Rafael Osuna of Mexico in the semi-finals.

Emerson is one of the world's toughest competitors. He had led Laver, two sets to none, in the French final, and two sets to one in the Italian. He was not serving at his best, however, and he could not cope with Laver's rifle-fire return of service, failing on his lift volleys.

Laver, even though he was not getting his scorching first service in play as often as usual, was completely in command in the first two sets. He was both chipping and stroking his backhand return and hitting his forehand with topspin. At the net, he was ruthless with his volley and overhead.

In the very first game, Rocket Rod hit four of his fearful backhand returns of service and broke through. He broke service again in the eighth as Emerson double-faulted three times, and his emphatic volleys ended the set in the tenth.

Emerson's service improved in the second set and he showed what a masterly volleyer he is. He won his games decisively, but he had one letdown and yielded the long seventh game to Laver's cracking backhand returns of service.

Emerson had not once reached 40 on Laver's service, and it appeared he would never do so. Then Rod began to weaken in his serving and return of service. The gallery cheered Emerson on as he broke through for the first time in the eighth game of the third set. Two lucky net-cord shots helped.

Roy's two double-faults in the ninth enabled Laver to retaliate, and the latter saved three set points to even the score at 5–all. Then in the twelfth game, Emerson returned service from the backhand in the fashion of Laver, both chipping and stroking for winners, and he won the set. It was only the second set Laver had yielded in the entire tournament.

The crowd applauded Emerson enthusiastically as he left for the rest period, and it continued to cheer him as he broke Laver's service in the fourth game of the fourth set to get back on even terms after losing the first game.

Then came the break that sent Laver on his way to victory. Emerson faltered in his volleying, missing twice on high backhands as Laver tossed up lobs, and yielded the fifth game.

Emerson had one chance to save himself. He got to 40–30 in the last game, scoring with a marvelous cross-court forehand passing shot. Then Laver ran the next three points and it was over. He had his grand slam. . . .

So ended the most exciting and most international championships held in recent years. Thanks to Colonel Edward P. F. Eagan's People-to-People Sports Committee, which airlifted some seventy players from Europe in a chartered plane, thirty-five nations were represented in the tournament. The Soviet Union sent players here for the first time.

The attendance far exceeded last year's. Colonel Eagan presented a citation to Mrs. Gladys Heldman, the editor and publisher of *World Tennis,* who represented his committee in marshaling the players, raising the funds for their transportation and housing and dining them for two weeks.

J. Clarence Davies, the chairman of the U.S.L.T.A. championship committee, said that it was the most successful tournament in almost thirty years.

1 9 6 3

THE CHAMPIONSHIPS OF ITALY

by Gloria Butler

Rome 1963 . . . white marble statues and sunshine . . . players who entered but never appeared . . . chaos in the men's singles as unseeded Martin Mulligan won his first major title over fifth seeded Boro Jovanovic . . . order in the women's singles as seven of the eight seeds reached their expected brackets and favored Margaret Smith won her second Italian title over second-seeded Lesley Turner . . . confusion in the thinning ranks because the French Championships started before Rome finished and because player after player had to cancel reservations on planes, trains and in packed Paris hotels . . . and over it all, the vital, enthusiastic and madly partisan Italian crowds, cheering vociferously for native sons and shouting over the double-faults of foreigners.

The first event of moment was the non-appearance of Manuel Santana, the No. 2 seed. The Spaniards had only just shaved through the day before in the Davis Cup against Germany, and they were so exhausted emotionally (and perhaps also from the celebrations that undoubtedly followed) that they canceled their entries at the last minute. Since Ingo Buding, who had played on the German team in the same encounter, also did not show and since both he and Santana were in the top half of the draw (so were non-appearing Couder and Arilla), this left the way open for a few surprise results. One was the emergence of a nearly unknown young Italian, Giordano Majoli, who ranks No. 11 in his country. He reached the quarter-finals by means of a win over Bob Hewitt. Bob has always had problems with his temper, and his emotions were put through a real meat grinder in this match. He was faced not only with a slightly partisan umpire and linesmen but a 100% partisan Italian crowd—and is there any other country where a crowd is more partisan? Under this barrage, young Majoli, who is certainly not in the same class as Bob Hewitt, pulled off a big win, 0–6, 6–3, 7–5, 6–4.

Another fourth-round surprise was the elimination of Sweden's Jan Erik Lundquist, generally considered the best player in Europe, by Ronald Barnes of Brazil. The crowds were behind Barnes to a man, perhaps because they felt Latin nations should stick together. Lundquist's sweeping strokes and greater facility of style availed him little. Time after time the ball went sailing over the baseline by feet. One had the impression the court was just too small for him. Barnes is, of course, a very dangerous player, quick as a cat, and he finally won 6–3, 1–6, 8–6, 13–11. Nicki Pietrangeli, not seeded for the first time in years, played the entire tournament with a broken finger and still managed to get to the quarters, where he lost to eventual finalist Jovanovic, 6–4, 6–3, 6–4.

Poker-faced Mike Sangster played alternately brilliant and sloppy tennis to reach the quarter-finals, beating Fred Stolle in four sets and losing a very close match to Emerson. Mike appears to carry a big weight on his shoulders. There are times when he acts as though he hates the game and everything in it. He is an enigma to officials, press and players alike—perhaps even to himself—because his potential is so enormous. At any rate, he showed so much talent (as well as so much sloppiness) in his match with Roy that Emmo was lucky to win, although Roy specializes in being down two sets and still winning. In this one he had unbelievably bad patches. His length was appalling—either mid-court on his backhand or over the fence on his forehand—but he finally won, 4–6, 4–6, 6–4, 6–4, 6–0.

The stars of two of the most delightful matches of the tournament were two old-timers who showed everyone how the game should be played. Fausto Gardini, who looks even more long-legged and awkward than ever, gave eventual champion Mulligan a terrific run for his money. The emotional Fausto raised his arms upwards to the God of the Italians to request his blessings, shook his racket with vehemence to encourage himself, called upon the galleries for vocal encouragement, and yelled "dai dai" after pulling off shots that first-time visitors to Italy had never before seen. He raked the court with his spoonlike drives, keeping Mulligan on the run. Through all the dramatics the little Aussie managed to remain calm, even though the crowds to a man were pulling for Fausto. Marty went about his business with quiet dispatch, proving that it *is* possible to win a match in Italy against an Italian.

The other old-timer who caused old hearts to flutter was Jaroslav Drobny, who played amazing tennis to down Wimbledon semi-finalist John Fraser in four long sets, young Aussie hope Tony Roche in five sets, and Bill "The Crocodile" Alvarez, also in five sets. This last match was one of the most attractive of the tournament. Alvarez, the Colombian, is a fascinating player because he is one of the few men on the circuit with a real personality, although his opponents seldom appreciate it. And for good reason. In the first place, he happily runs for hours and gets everything back. In the second, he employs every trick in the game, legal or illegal. The objects of his attention are ballboys, linesmen, umpires and spectators. In addition, the grillwork around the court, the net posts, any convenient chair and, needless to say, the net and his poor overworked racket come in for their share of abuse. He is also a consummate staller, taking longer to towel off, longer to walk to his side of the court, and longer to sip some water than anyone else. Combined with the pantomime is a never-ending flow of imprecations in Spanish. If, by the end of Act II, any of his opponents can still play tennis, it is a miracle.

It was a hilarious match because all of Alvarez's antics affected Drobny not one whit. While the Colombian walked in circles at one end of the court or tossed his racket on the ground and stamped on it, Drob calmly stood in the receiving position, unperturbed by the dramatics. He drop-shotted Alvarez without mercy, and what touch Drob still has! The whole panoply of shots in the game came off his racket in glorious sequence, and he made the Crocodile look like a puppet at the end of a string. The gallery cheered for Drobny and booed Alvarez. Near the end of the match, Alvarez sat down hard and then had difficulty getting up because of cramps, but nobody believed him. Such is the price of over-showmanship. He certainly appeared to have cramps badly, but then he would run like a rabbit after the next shot. Drob ran out the match at 4–6, 2–6, 6–3, 6–3, 6–4. In the next round he played Jovanovic and quite obviously had nothing left. The score was 6–2, 6–1, 6–1.

Nicola Pilic of Yugoslavia had an easy draw to the semi-finals, for Santana had defaulted and Hewitt had been eliminated. He only had to beat little Majoli, and with his deep shots and greater strength of play he won by 6–4, 6–4, 6–3.

Boro Jovanovic, who came through to the semi-finals over Drobny and Pietrangeli, then trounced Roy Emerson, 6–4, 6–3, 6–4. Roy seemed slow and lethargic. The bullnecked Boro, who thrives on slow clay, hit beautiful passing shots whenever Roy ventured to net. The Aussie's game received a setback when he went home in mid-season to see his new son. He missed shots which normally he would make, although Boro played very well and at a fast pace. The other semi-final between Pilic and Mulligan was played on a rather heavy court, which took a bit of the bite off Nicki's shots. He missed more balls than the consistent Mulligan and finally went down in four sets, 1–6, 6–2, 6–2, 6–3.

The final between Jovanovic and Mulligan was played under very wet circumstances and on a heavy court. The sting of Boro's shots was offset by the court, and Mulligan, who can run anything down, kept the pressure on. He never gives anything away. To beat him, his opponent has to crush him, and there are not many of the present group who can do this consistently. He is, in fact, a much better player than many give him credit for. Although Boro led 4–1 in the fourth set, his concentration seemed to melt. Mulligan pulled out a rather uninteresting final, 6–2, 4–6, 6–3, 8–6.

The women's singles was dominated by the towering figure of Margaret Smith. Everyone was so sure she would win that it was only a matter of watching her take the opposition apart. Just as Margaret was a heavy favorite against the field, so was Lesley Turner heavily favored to reach the final. Jan Lehane and Ann Haydon Jones were expected to reach the semi-finals, which they did without problems. The only upset in the entire women's singles occurred in the first round when America's Judy Alvarez beat Renée Schuurman of South Africa.

ROSEWALL'S CLASSIC AGAINST LAVER

by Allison Danzig

Kenneth Rosewall won the professional lawn tennis championship of the United States yesterday with a performance that ranked as one of the classics of Forest Hills.

A master of the racket in the execution of every variety of stroke, the little black-haired Australian routed his fellow countryman, Rodney Laver, in the final round of the tournament, 6–4, 6–2, 6–2.

The crowd of 5,000 in the stadium in sultry, threatening weather witnessed an unforgettable exposition of the art, science and vigor of lawn tennis at its finest.

The match was no contest after the first set, with Laver's mighty strokes reduced to ruin as his confidence was destroyed and his touch fled. The authority and almost infallible precision with which the calculating Rosewall disarmed the youth who had completed his grand slam on the same turf as the world amateur champion last year exerted a fascinating spell, however.

In receiving the championship bowl from Senator Jacob Javits, Republican of New York, at the end of the 68 minutes of play, Rosewall said that he was fortunate that he caught Laver on one of Rodney's bad days. It was one of the most harrowing, unhappy days Laver has known. Rosewall kept him under merciless, continuing pressure that brought his game to the point of almost total collapse.

With his unsurpassed ground strokes, Rosewall returned Laver's wrathful, spinning service in a fashion to extract the volley error. Rosewall's passing shots were equally provocative. His lobs were a torment. Always, it seemed, he had his left-handed, red-haired opponent straining for the ball or scrambling back in pursuit. While his service was not nearly as violent or loaded with spin as Laver's, Rosewall maintained such good depth and used so many variations that Laver failed over and over on his return of service, particularly from the backhand. At the net, too, the champion was the superior. Laver is murderous in volleying above the level of the net, but Rosewall's mastery of the low volley was close to perfection, and from the backhand he was unbelievably secure. Above all else, it was the inflexible challenge of Rosewall's ground strokes—unstrained, purposeful and beautifully timed—that ruined the day for Laver.

Laver resisted unflinchingly in the first set and came within a stroke of a 4-2 lead, pulling out the third game from 0-40 and the fifth from 15-40. Once Rosewall's ground strokes rifled back his service regularly in the second set, however. Laver's whole game fell apart, no matter how courageously he resisted. . . .

The championship, the first professional tournament at Forest Hills since 1959, did not draw as well as had been hoped. This was attributable in part to the extreme heat of the first two days and the threatening weather on the last two days.

OSUNA AND MISS BUENO MAKE HISTORY

by Allison Danzig

Latin America had its day of greatest glory on the tennis courts yesterday as Australia was in eclipse, along with the United States.

For the first time, a player from Mexico carried off the United States amateur tennis championship as Rafael Osuna, with an almost unparalleled combination of tactical cleverness and craftsmanship of stroke, defeated Frank Froehling 3d of Coral Gables, Florida, 7–5, 6–4, 6–2.

The standing acclaim showered upon the lithe, lightning-quick youth from Mexico City by the 11,000 in the Forest Hills Stadium was mild compared to the ovation given to Maria Bueno of Brazil.

With one of the most electrifying bursts of super shot-making produced by a woman in the championship, the slender, graceful girl from Sao Paulo overwhelmed favored Margaret Smith of Australia after trailing at 0–3 and 0–40 in the second set of the final. Miss Bueno regained the title she won in 1959, 7–5, 6–4.

So Latin America stands triumphant in the field of 176 men and 96 women from 34 nations who entered the championships.

Australia, which had placed the finalists in the men's singles every year since 1956 except 1959, failed to qualify a representative for the quarter-finals. The defeat of Miss Smith, the Wimbledon and Australian champion and the winner at Forest Hills a year ago, added to the disappointment Down Under.

The United States, shut out of the women's semi-finals for the first time, at least had the satisfaction of placing a representative in the men's final for the first time since 1955.

Only once before had the men's and women's championships been carried off in the same year by foreign players. Neale Fraser of Australia won the men's title in 1959, sharing honors with Miss Bueno.

Brazil has been put on the tennis map as never before. In addition to the triumph yesterday of Miss Bueno over the player who was looked upon as almost invincible, Ronald Barnes of Brazil scored a stunning victory over Dennis Ralston, and Tomas Koch, Barnes's countryman, came within a stroke of defeating Chuck McKinley, the Wimbledon champion, who lost in the semi-finals to Osuna.

Secretary General U Thant of the United Nations presented the trophies to the winners and runners-up. He was assisted by J. Clarence Davies Jr. of New York, the chairman of the championship committee of the United States Lawn Tennis Association, and Edward Turville of St. Petersburg, Florida, the president of the U.S.L.T.A. . . .

The final of the men's singles was unusual for the tactical pattern followed by Osuna. His big problem was to solve the violent trip-hammer service of Froehling. The service had been a big factor in the tall Florida youth's amazing defeat of Roy Emerson of Australia, the player most favored to win the championship, as well as Bobby Wilson of Britain and Barnes.

In the first game Froehling, who was unseeded in the draw, let loose the full thunder of his service to win it at love. When Osuna, at 0–40, dropped 10 feet behind the baseline to receive the next service, the gallery roared with mirth.

But Osuna was not being funny. Throughout the match he was continually changing his position in taking the cannonball first service. At times he stood in close and met the ball on the rise, attempting to chip it low with his rapier backhand. But more and more he stayed far back, took the catapulting ball at the top of the bounce and lobbed it back.

The lob was Froehling's undoing more than anything else. Not only on the return of service but in the rallies too, Osuna threw up his parabolas with striking accuracy, even going all the way to the backstop at times to make them. Froehling's overhead, made with an unorthodox stroke, failed him as he was called on to bring down lob after lob.

It was particularly the lobbed return of service that undermined Froehling's game, ruining his timing and upsetting his procedure of going in for the volley. He turned the tables on Osuna on occasion by tapping his overhead for a drop volley, instead of smashing the ball. And he varied his first service, changing from the cannonball to a slower spin. But the lob was his nemesis, and more and more as the match progressed.

Osuna added to his opponent's difficulty by continually changing his position, suddenly falling back or rushing in, as Froehling was starting his service. Also, Osuna changed his tactics when he was serving.

For the most part, he followed his service in for his marvelously executed volleys, which came to his rescue over and over when Froehling's return of service or passing shot appeared to have him beaten. But at times Osuna remained in the back court, and his changing pattern posed a further problem for the Florida youth.

Despite Osuna's tactical cleverness in maneuvering and his great volleying skill and rapier thrusts from his chipped backhand, Froehling challenged him to the hilt for the first two sets.

Froehling volleyed with violent impact behind his service and he could hit stunning returns of service from both sides. His forehand was much the more reliable, and at times he ran around the ball to take it on his strong side. Some of his finest winners came from the backhand, but it was there that he made most of his errors.

Osuna had all he could do to stay even in the first set, and then came a decision that could have been upsetting for Froehling.

In the 10th game, with the score 15–30 against Osuna on his service, Froehling hit a blazing backhand return of service. The ball appeared to strike the baseline, making the chalk fly. When the linesman called it out, there was a strong outburst in protest from the gallery, including boos. But the decision stood, and instead of the score being 15–40, it was 30–all.

Froehling said after the match that one point did not make a match, even though he was upset by the decision. But his fortunes waned from that point on. Osuna pulled out the game and broke service in the 11th as Froehling failed on three overhead smashes and a volley. Osuna won the 12th with two volleys and a final service ace for the set.

When Froehling double-faulted twice starting the second set and lost his service, it seemed that the disputed point might have been his ruination. But he recovered and set the gallery to cheering as he broke service with his ground strokes in the second game and then sent through two blistering aces to win the third.

Osuna, winning his service at love in the fourth game, broke through in the fifth as Froehling faltered against the return of service. The Florida youth could not get back on even terms, but he fought so superbly in the long deuce games that Osuna was desperately pressed to hold him off.

Only Osuna's lobbed returns of service and his magnificent volleying enabled him to stay on top. There were five prolonged games in the set and he won four of them.

When Froehling finally yielded the set, after saving 5 set points, it was obvious that he was beaten. Lobs ruined him in the first game of the third set and his control worsened in the second. Then came his last stand as he pulled even at 2–all, hitting two marvelous backhands to break service in the fourth.

The fifth was a tremendous game, but although Froehling hit two powerful overheads and two volleys, he lost it. Osuna then ran out the next three games, and the match ended after Froehling had hit three stunning forehand returns of service to save match points.

Miss Bueno had given Miss Smith her greatest fight in the 1962 championship and yesterday the girl from Brazil, who was stricken with hepatitis in 1961, improved on her performance of a year ago.

Miss Bueno won the opening set on her stronger serving and return of service, as well as her sound volleying. Miss Smith's backhand failed her, particularly on the return of service, and her usually powerful service was not functioning. She double-faulted in losing the third game and, after retaliating in the 10th, she double-faulted twice in the 11th. That cost her the set.

With the start of the second set Miss Smith became a different player. She refused to make errors any longer and the strength of her service, volley and ground strokes overpowered Miss Bueno. Winning the first three games with the loss of only 2 points, the Australian girl went ahead at 40–0 in the fourth. Miss Bueno looked to be helpless and resigned to the loss of the set.

Then came five successive errors from Miss Smith, four on the return of service, and the whole picture changed. Miss Smith won the fifth game, and that was the last one she won.

With the score 1–4 and 0–30 against her, Miss Bueno set the gallery wild with the dazzling strokes that stemmed from her racket. Her service was never so strong. Her volleys and overhead smashes were the last word, and she hit blazing winners from the backhand and threw up lobs in an overwhelming assault.

From 30–0 in the fifth game Miss Bueno yielded only 5 points as she ran five games in a row, amid cries of "bravo." When she hit her final backhand volley for the match, Miss Bueno tossed her racket in the air and jumped with happiness.

CHUCK MCKINLEY IS WIMBLEDON CHAMPION

by Lance Tingay

Chuck McKinley, who gave the impression of being made of India rubber, became Wimbledon's men's singles champion right worthily. That can be gainsaid by no one and he became the third of a distinctive trio. Donald Budge won the title in 1938 without losing a set to anyone. Tony Trabert did so in 1955 and McKinley did just this in 1963. What with the drain to professionalism, the men's singles event at Wimbledon may not be quite what once it was, but to win the title in 21 straight sets is not a feat to be achieved by ordinary mortals.

At the same time it was a most curious win because McKinley pulled it off without ever having to meet another seeded player. That was hardly McKinley's fault, for he overwhelmed all that the luck of the draw and the seeding committee threw against him. McKinley himself was the fourth seed, and his status as such and that of Roy Emerson at No. 1 and Manuel Santana at No. 2 were about the only decisions by Wimbledon's seeding committee with which anyone was in agreement.

During the course of the eight days over which the men's singles was played there was the extraordinary happening, or, rather, lack of happening, that no seeded man ever clashed with another. It made for lively interest as the event progressed, but it was hardly indicative of good seeding.

McKinley bounced, darted and jabbed his way through the field. The opening set of 16 games in the final against the unseeded Fred Stolle was the longest he had to play through, in actual number of games conceded as a whole; his second round against another Australian, Alan Lane, was the hardest he had to endure. He never looked like not winning in any set he played, though I do not think it was until he beat Wilson in the quarter-final that he began generally to be looked upon as the likely champion.

The controversial seeding list was (1) Emerson, (2) Santana, (3) Fletcher, (4) McKinley, (5) Mulligan, (6) Darmon, (7) Lundquist, and (8) Sangster. This year the allocation of the seeds in the draw followed a different system. Formerly the situation of Nos. 1 and 2 used to be decided by lot, as were those of Nos. 3 and 4 and then Nos. 5 to 8. Under the new rules the draw order was automatically in the run of 1, 8, 4, 5, 6, 3, 7, 2. Which is the fairer method? So when the seeding was published before the start of the meeting, it was possible to indicate the quarter-final matches. None of them came about. Sangster departed in the first round, Fletcher and Darmon in the second, Mulligan and Lundquist in the fourth. A different seeding committee would not have omitted Dennis Ralston, Rafael Osuna or Ramanathan Krishnan. Possibly the omission of Osuna was a blessing in disguise, for he met Santana in the third round and that match, a magnificent one, provided the masterpiece of the meeting. Bungert's quarter-final against Emerson was the other great match of Wimbledon. . . .

From time to time lawn tennis has sublime moments. When Wimbledon reduced to the last 16 it supplied such a magic spell as Santana memorably beat Osuna, 2–6, 0–6, 6–1, 6–3, 6–4. A more beautiful, entrancing match I have not seen for years and when at the end of nearly 100 enchanting minutes the thousands of spectators stood up and cheered and cheered, there were not a few who did so with tears in their eyes. If the finger of fate were to point to me and I were to hear the words "See one more match and then come away," this would be such a contest I would wish to watch. A magnificent symphony, with not a discord in it, was played out on the center court and it should have been the final. Santana won after losing the first two sets. He and Osuna won the same number of games. More than that, he and Osuna won the same number of points—132 to 132—but all that was merely incidental to what made it transcend the majority of lawn tennis matches. . . .

From first to last it was a contest where brilliance on the one side served merely to provoke greater virtuosity on the other. From time to time there were human failings, even double-faults, but never, I think, did either player project a mundane shot. The proportion of first services that were good was enormous and so, too, was the quality of service return. If a lob were hoisted, it raised the chalk on the baseline nine times out of ten. If a passing shot was projected, it rarely failed to be within an inch of the line. Everything flowed, and to frame the grandeur was the generous sportsmanship of both men. They played with a smile and they acknowledged each other's genius. Nor did they delay the conflict by pausing between the games.

On the mere record of the score—and in few matches can it have mattered less to the spectators, for, indeed, one was so captivated with the sublimity of the exchanges that one required a conscious effort of will from time to time to note which player was which—Osuna won the first two sets easily. He lost only two games out of the first fourteen. Santana took 16 out of the next 21 games to be 4–1 up in the fifth set. Yet none of this was one-sided. Every rally had uncertain issue and every great stroke was liable to provoke a greater. It is easy to see in retrospect that Osuna drained too deeply of his virtuosity in the first two sets. Santana was not, as he rarely is at the start of a match, at his best. But all the margins between these artists were minute.

Had it been anyone but Santana, one would have assumed the Spaniard to be a beaten man after the first two sets. The second set was curious in that of its sixteen minutes eight were occupied by the opening game. Santana had eight chances to win it but he was denied them all, and Osuna took it after deuce was called on nine occasions. Osuna then gained the set for the loss of only four further points, with his opponent wearing an air of resignation.

Two sets in arrears, Santana then found his most moving harmonies. There was a sharpening to his service sufficient to avert the winners Osuna had been making from it earlier. His forehand began to create those deadly winners that only he can project with consistent surety. The balance had shifted, not by much, but nevertheless inexorably. With Santana 4–1 in the fifth set, the symphony was augmented by a crescendo of tension as Osuna started to clear the deficit against him. The Spaniard maintained the advantage that had been created by a service break in the second game to be 5–3, but when he served in the next game a loud chord signaled Osuna's insistent effort of revival. Osuna broke Santana's service and the last shot was a superb stop volley, so shrewdly and unexpectedly deployed that Santana, wrong-footed by its boldness and delicacy, slipped flat on his face on the baseline.

As Osuna served to make it 5 games–all, Santana himself dipped into another reserve of genius. Osuna found himself 30–40 and sent down a telling serve. The backhand passing shot across the court that it provoked would have beaten any player in the world at any time. The artists had nothing left then but to be silent as they fell in each other's arms in mutual congratulation. It was left to the crowd to provide the last resounding chords of this majestic symphony. The rapturous applause went on and on, and so great an acclaim had not been heard at Wimbledon since Patty and Drobny ended their historic battle on the same court ten years before. . . .

Quarter-finals. Three victories more mundane than otherwise and a major sensation marked the translation of eight survivors to four. Wimbledon came to its singles semi-final without its top seed, Emerson. The man who beat him was the unseeded Bungert. . . . Erect as a ramrod, stiff as a poker but fluent none the less, Bungert led all the way against Emerson but kept slipping back. Emerson was behind all the way and kept climbing back. How the Australian fought to keep in the championship and what heartbreaks German supporters must have had! Bungert is not notably a quick finisher and before now he has lost matches he was on the brink of winning. When at last he won his seventh match point against Emerson, Germans at least must have been thankful.

The basic secret of Bungert's win was his readiness to harry Emerson at all times. To this end he stood close in to take all the Australian's serves. It was attack and punch, and punch and attack all the way. But Emerson eluded and slipped and ducked, and it seemed right to the end he might avoid the knockout blow. Thus it was that Bungert first poised himself for the opening set with his service to come at 5–4. It eluded him and he did not get the set until 8–6. Then, Emerson was back on level terms, taking the second set, 6–3. Up came the German once more, 6–3. Then Emerson again, for despite Bungert being 2–0, 40–15, the Australian was home at 6–4 to make it two sets–all.

There were two service breaks early in the fifth set and they were both had by Bungert. He got to 5–2 with his service to follow, and an exultant audience—the German, being the underdog, was the favored man by a Wimbledon crowd, who always puts its loyalties thus—clung to every move. At 40–30 he served for the match, but the backhand volley that followed his delivery pitched over the sideline. He reached his second match point and here he was presented with a smash which, without being dead easy, was certainly far from hard. Bungert placed it somewhere in the tramlines. A third match point came his way and here Emerson saved it well with a forehand pass that was unanswerable.

Bungert was shaken by all this and double-faulted. Another backhand pass gave Emerson the game and renewed life. Germans were in despair, for they remembered not so long before when in the Davis Cup tie between Germany and Spain Bungert led 5–2 in the fourth set of the fifth rubber against Couder and had five match points and lost not only that match but the tie.

Emerson was not free from tension either. He served and became 15–40. A dashing, courageous volley forced a German error and that was match point four turned away. He followed it with another winning volley from the backhand and that was match point five that had come and gone. With a forehand, Bungert made a winning return of service to get to match point for the sixth time. There was a hectic rally then and a scrambled defensive lob from the German fell almost on the line, bouncing high. Emerson played it as an overhead and projected a winner plumb on the same line on the other side. It looked a line ball to me but both Bungert and, seemingly, the umpire thought it was out. Bungert dropped his racket in frustration and looked as if he would weep. But one point later he reached match point for the seventh time and on this occasion there was no disputing the merits of his forehand pass. The top seed was out. In all, Emerson saved 25 game points during this match. But he could not save the last point of all.

The outcome of the semi-finals left the hardy denizens of the press box at Wimbledon quite bewildered. There were those who had confidently predicted a German-Spanish final and the end of Australian and American domination of the men's game, and they had more explaining to do than most. The hardy core of lawn tennis writers had not gone as far as that, and McKinley's bouncing, confident win over Bungert was not unexpected. Stolle's sharp victory over Santana was like a slap in the face, and not only to the writers either. The Spaniard was a well-loved player at Wimbledon on both the score of personality and for his artistic game. It was almost a mute crowd that watched Stolle beat him, not because anyone disliked Stolle in the least—who could?—but because it was incredible that Santana could fall so short of what was expected. A McKinley-Santana final was what was wanted and, to use a schoolboy's term, it seemed a "dirty swindle" that it had not come about.

If Stolle was not a popular winner on the court, he afterwards held the greatest press conference ever. "Where's that guy Lance Tingay," he declaimed, "who said Santana had the best forehand in the world? . . . Do I love playing lawn tennis? Of course not, I'm an amateur." I must hand it to Stolle; he handled his affairs like a veteran.

And he handled Santana, too, with a competence few thought he had. First and foremost, it was his tremendous return of service that gained him his win. It really was superb and mostly directed from the backhand, for it was to that side that Santana directed most of his deliveries. One wondered why, until there occurred the odd occasion the Spaniard switched to the other wing. His forehand return was even better, and I hardly think there was one rally when Santana, coming in on his service, had any choice but to volley upwards from his feet. Only one thing marred Stolle's flat, sharp, immaculate play. He double-faulted twelve times, though never on any vital point.

Yet, give Stolle all the credit in the world, no one can deny that Santana was but a shadowy representation of his better self. In that he was terribly disappointing. Somewhere he had about him a casket of rare lawn tennis jewels. As he dipped into it on the center court on that Wednesday afternoon, he pulled out about two rich specimens and the rest were bad imitations.

At no time did the match follow a Santana pattern. For one thing, he gained an early ascendancy and that is far from typical. Santana rarely leaps ahead. Rather he comes from behind. He broke Stolle's service at love in the third game of the match and led 5–3. At 5–4 he served for the set and after being love–40 got to set point. I suppose it was the most vital point of the match. Both men moved in to the net and Santana, with a forehand error, was worsted in the volleying exchange. He lost the next point also, then double-faulted to make it 5 games–all. Santana held serve to be 6–5 but he was never in front again. Stolle became inexorably firm, pacemaking without error. Santana's defenses were overwhelmed.

In the third set Santana partially checked Australian domination. He captured Stolle's service at love in the sixth game and built a 5–2 lead. There was, though, no genius to implement the advantage. Stolle yielded only eight points in taking the next five games. The Australian bludgeon was irresistible. The sword of the Spanish conquistador was blunt. Accordingly the unseeded Stolle was in the final.

Nor was the dignified Bungert true to his own best self. He missed the easy shots as well as the difficult ones. McKinley never was more dynamic and, apparently with springs in his heels, he darted and jabbed in a sizzling fury of never-ceasing aggression, banging home sharp volleys as if he were swatting flies and conveying the impression he had the ability to be everywhere on the court at the same time. Bungert's effort to hustle McKinley, as he had hustled Emerson, by taking his service return early, met with no success. How to hustle a man who is himself the supreme hustler on the court? Bungert's backhand met the major share of McKinley's pressure, and it broke down against it.

Basically the match was one-sided and McKinley had only one check. In the third set he failed to hold his service at 5–4. Bungert fought his way back into the match, reached 6–5, and, on McKinley's service, was three times within a point of the set. On all occasions McKinley forced a German error, squared at 6–all after a game of four deuces, and then accelerated out to victory.

So there was the final, the fourth-seeded McKinley against the unseeded Stolle. Whatever way it fell it was bound to be a final unique to Wimbledon. If Stolle won, it would be the first unseeded victory since seeding began in 1927; and if McKinley, the first champion to come through without having met a seeded player.

McKinley's translation of himself into the status of Wimbledon singles champion came after 79 minutes of lawn tennis against Stolle that were good—better, in fact, than some recent finals—without being great. The potent factor of his win was his baffling variety of service. With fast ones, spinning ones, directed this side and that, with never the same ball twice, he baffled a less flexible Stolle into submission. This was despite the fact that throughout the final the quality of service return was good.

For the first fourteen games, until seven—all in the first set, two strong players stood toe to toe without any sign of yielding either way. The bold and excellent quality of service return did nothing to prevent service domination. Each was expert enough to make, from the forehand wing, shots that tested the full ability of the volleyer as the serve was followed netwards. In this McKinley's incredible speed of foot stood him in wonderful stead, for he was quick thinking and nimble enough to position himself for a full-blooded stroking return, even when Stolle served his fastest.

The watershed of the conflict was clear. Having shared both games and points equally, Stolle led 40–15 in the 15th game. An agile and teasing lob beat him utterly and, having been frustrated thus delicately, he was never quite the same again. He double-faulted to be brought to deuce and he afterwards double-faulted to lose his service. McKinley's winning impetus was, temporarily at any rate, irresistible. He plied four service winners one after another to clinch the set at 9–7 and Stolle, still shaken, opened the second set with another double-fault.

McKinley bounced his able and agile way through that second set in only 15 minutes. There was Australian bankruptcy then while American business boomed. The fight, as a fight, was not then entirely over but there was not a lot of significance left. In the third set McKinley, who never lost a service game at all, had two games when he came within a point of doing so and these, coming when he had two sets behind him anyway, hardly constituted a major crisis. Finally McKinley broke Stolle's service in the tenth game to win the set and championship.

MARGARET SMITH FIRST AUSTRALIAN TO WIN WOMEN'S WIMBLEDON CROWN

by Fred Tupper

Margaret Smith has won Wimbledon. The 20-year-old Australian triumphed over nerves and a last-ditch surge by Billie Jean Moffitt of Long Beach, California, and took the one crown that had eluded her. The scores were 6–3, 6–4.

She confirmed what everyone had known all along—that she's the best woman tennis player in the world. . . .

The finish of the women's doubles had a center court crowd of 17,000 squirming in its seats. Miss Hard and Maria Bueno of Brazil led 5–2 and 40–0 in the second set. They then dropped 5 match points before they downed Miss Smith and Robyn Ebbern of Australia, 8–6, 9–7.

In the men's doubles, Rafael Osuna and Antonio Palafox, the Davis Cup combination from Mexico, defeated Pierre Darmon and Jean Claude Barclay of France, 4–6, 6–2, 6–2, 6–2.

Miss Smith was top-seeded at Wimbledon in 1961 but lost to Christine Truman. She was top-seeded again in 1962 only to be rudely dispatched by Miss Moffitt after she led in the third set by 5–2.

Under enormous pressure today Big Margaret, as Miss Smith is called, stood firm in the clutch and became the first Australian to win the All-England women's championship. Bruising the ball with the speed of her ground strokes, she broke through the 19-year-old Billie Jean at love to lead 3–2 in the first set and then hit two devastating forehands to reach deuce at 5–3.

Miss Moffitt swung a first service wide that creased the line as Miss Smith hit it into the net. It was called out. The umpire reversed the call. Margaret slashed a forehand across court, then banged a backhand down the line. She had the set at 6–3.

The Australian was keyed for the kill and her service bit into the corners. She roared up to the net to punch away the volleys and she ate up Miss Moffitt's weak second serve.

Suddenly Miss Smith was at 4–0, and it seemed over. In a final desperate stand, Miss Moffitt shook off the malaise that had hobbled her serve and had taken the sting from her volley.

The American had been in serious straits before in this tournament and had survived. She had rallied to beat Lea Pericoli of Italy in three sets, and had upset Lesley Turner of Australia in three more.

There still was time. Billie Jean banged a backhand through the hole. Miss Smith foot-faulted and then double-faulted. Miss Moffitt tossed up a lob and cut off the volley. She rapped another drive and broke through at love.

Serving, she dumped a half-volley off her shoetops across court, hit a volley away and then caught Margaret off-balance. Seven points in a row and it was 2–4. Miss Smith held her service and slashed a forehand across court for match point.

Billie Jean smashed it. She volleyed into one corner and then the other. It was 3–5, Miss Smith to serve. Miss Moffitt was hitting the ball with all she had. She had broken through to 4–5, with her own serve due.

This was the test for the Australian. She had cracked before in the crises because of nerves. She had temporized when she should have hit out. Now she went for the big shot. A forehand ripped down the line, another forehand hit the tape and a third disappeared out of reach into the far corner.

Two more match points to come. Billie saved the first and then volleyed across court.

Margaret moved in on the dead run and lashed the ball to the line. She had won.

1964

EMERSON AND BUENO CHAMPIONS OF WIMBLEDON

by Lance Tingay

Just about 260,000 enthusiasts watched a good Wimbledon this year, 12,000 more than the year before. We had a political Wimbledon for the first time, with players from the Iron Curtain countries scratching rather than play South Africans; we had a lineswoman sound asleep, we had a tremendous women's singles final, with the Brazilian Maria Bueno coming back in her full majestic glory to take the crown from Margaret Smith. We had the Australian Roy Emerson winning the men's singles all through. In retrospect it was easy to see how he never looked like not taking the honor.

We had some sublime failures. The redoubtable Miss Smith, for instance, looked like a certainty to take the women's singles right through until the last match. Chuck McKinley yielded his crown because he never quite got going. Dennis Ralston hardly started. Rafael Osuna did not, I think, do his talents justice. Manuel Santana lost mobility when he hurt his ankle.

Even an all-Australian men's singles final at Wimbledon did not deter crowds from queueing overnight to have a look at it. Wimbledon was, in fact, very much its charming self, the crowds inspired by the players, the players in turn inspired by the crowds.

The men's singles seeding list was universally held to be a good one. Such criticism that could be made of the order— (1) Emerson, (2) McKinley, (3) Santana, (4) Osuna, (5) Ralston, (6) Stolle, (7) Pietrangeli and (8) Mulligan—was minor and technical, reflecting shades of opinion this way and that. Certainly no one disputed Ralston's position at fifth. He flew into London over the weekend, had a brief practice at the International Club's garden party at Hurlingham on the Sunday prior to the start of the meeting, went on the court at two o'clock on the first Monday and by four forty-five made himself eligible for the consolation plate.

The demands of the intercollegiate championships and the demands of Wimbledon were in conflict. Wimbledon will not be taken lightly. Its pristine turf is good but demanding. Some of its players are, naturally, better than others but all are of one mind. No player is going to beat them until they have expended the last ounce of effort. England's Tony Pickard was in such a frame of mind. Ralston was perhaps unlucky to meet Pickard on a day when the latter's near-genius, rather than his essentially erratic nature, was uppermost. Pickard, No. 8 in the British ranking list, gained the finest win he ever had in all his career (after Ralston won the first two sets and led 3–1 in the third) .

That was Wimbledon's opening sensation. It was not a good day for the United States. Frank Froehling acquired plate status as well. The man who beat him was Greece's young Nicolas Kalogeropoulos, who, having nosed out in an opening set of 22 games, nosed out in a fifth set of ten. Most enthusiasts were expecting a prestige win such as this from the Greek sooner or later. Ralston out, Froehling out—all this made good company for Britain's Bobby Wilson, who went out also. . . .

It was still a good seeding list, but Nos. 7 and 8 withered early. Marty Mulligan proved sterile and so did Nicola Pietrangeli. His fellow Australian, Bob Hewitt, was much too good for Mulligan. France's Pierre Barthes beat Pietrangeli. . . . There was also a near sensation that would have been tremendous had it come off. Once in watching lawn tennis over many years I have seen a player (or rather, in my case, players, for it was doubles) get to match point and then have to forfeit because of injury. Manuel Santana nearly did just that. On the center court he mastered Russia's Tomas Lejus with the efficiency one expected. A victory course followed easily and the score piled up to 6–4, 6–2, 5–2, 40–30 in favor of Santana. At that stage Lejus projected a short ball just over the net. In chasing forward, Santana fell and twisted his ankle, straining his Achilles tendon. With some difficulty he managed to stand up after an interval. He had enough, but only just enough, mobility in reserve to play four more points. It sufficed to give him victory after Lejus had had, and missed, a point for the game. It was lucky for Santana that he was serving.

McKinley took something of a mauling in this round. The 19-year-old Brazilian, Tomas Koch, did not quite get as far as he did last year at Forest Hills against him when he held match point, but he did take a narrow issue to the fifth set. . . . Emerson took rather a mauling also. Nikki Pilic, the Yugoslav left-hander, detained him on the center court for a long time, despite the fact that the match was delayed while Pilic had medical treatment. Not only had he got a boil on his neck but there was a torn muscle as well.

Heroics were undertaken by the German, Wilhelm Bungert, semi-finalist in 1963. How close can one get to a match without winning? South Africa's Keith Diepraam, a nice, neat player, though hardly of the majestic fluency which Bungert can pull off, had two sets to one and led 5–1 in the fourth. At 5–4, he had four match points and Bungert saved the lot. The German victory was had comparatively easily in the fifth set after all that.

Two Danes made up the company of the last 32. What was remarkable about this was that they were brothers, Torben and Jorgen Ulrich. The bearded Torben gave up the game because of his health some time ago and his comeback was pretty effective. His victim at Wimbledon at this stage was the young Australian Davis Cup man, Tony Roche, a fine scalp for a player perhaps ten years or so past his peak. Arthur Ashe put out Cliff Richey. This was a hard five-setter, Ashe coming back after Richey had taken the first two sets. . . . Ron Holmberg and Marty Riessen had their contest called at 12–all in the first set because of failing light. They resumed the next day. Holmberg was the victor and I record the score here and now. It was 14–16, 11–13, 6–4, 6–2, 10–8. That is 90 games. The longest at Wimbledon is the 93-game affair played between Jaroslav Drobny and Budge Patty in 1953.

Third round. First the politics, intruding into the dignity of Wimbledon for the first time. The score sheets read A. Segal (South Africa), walkover. A. Metreveli (U.S.S.R.), retired. This is exactly what took place. Soon afterwards young Metreveli was shaking Segal by the hand, saying, "Of course there is nothing personal in this." Of course there was not. But the edict had gone forth, doubtless from some quarter of the Kremlin, that Russians and South Africans were not to meet. . . . Later in the day Hungary's Istvan Gulyas, who had been delighted to find a partner in Segal for the men's doubles, withdrew also from that event. Instructions had gone forth. All of which was a pity. I never yet met a lawn tennis player who concerned himself with politics and, as far as I can see, the main objection one player might have towards another is the quality of his service, certainly not the activities of his government. So Segal had a free ride into the last 16. . . .

Santana survived this round with the help of pain-killing injections in his ankle which enabled him to run, though scarcely with full mobility. There were Spanish heroics here, for he beat Gene Scott despite (1) being behind one set to two and (2) trailing 2–5 in the fifth set. A great-hearted player, Santana, and he came through because even with diminished powers he could, when pressed, wield those snaky passes and deft, unexpected thrusts that so bedevil all opposition. McKinley had another rough passage. The bearded Dane, Torben Ulrich, 35 years old, yielded one set to three but had points to win two of the sets he lost. . . . The sixth seed, Fred Stolle, had a close call also and that after roaring through the opening set against Antonio Palafox by 6–0. He had two sets to love. For all that he came within a point of trailing 3–5 in the fifth set, where he finally hauled out 11–9. The suave German, Wilhelm Bungert, met Britain's Mike Sangster and won in four sets. Ashe continued nicely in this round. Bill Bond could not get a set from him. Mike Belkin, parading at Wimbledon with the benefit of nomination by Canada despite his American ranking, did not take happily to the center court and Bob Hewitt mastered him readily. . . .

Fourth round. Emerson, Hewitt, McKinley and Abe Segal were the first to break the barrier into the last eight. Those who were looking for the potential champion at this time picked on Emerson. I was rather surprised that Ashe did not do better against him and had the impression that he was rather below his best on Wimbledon's second showplace, court number one. Ashe managed to build a 4–1 lead in the second set, but could not implement the advantage. Emerson was streamlined, fast and efficient. He looked as forthright as a No. 1 seed should. Whether McKinley looked like a defending champion as he beat Britain's Billy Knight, the last home survivor in the event, is another question. There were a lot of rough edges to Mc-

Kinley, especially on the backhand wing. But for his speed of foot and his forehand power he might have got into much trouble. . . .

A day later Osuna, Bungert, Stolle and Christian Kuhnke followed into the quarter-final brackets. Kuhnke beat Santana, and it was a nostalgic moment to see so good a man brought down, for one could not help but think that had it not been for his ankle injury it would probably not have taken place. The year before, in the quarter-final stage, Santana beat Kuhnke pretty easily. The consolation was that Santana lost to a good man. Santana was always behind. He salvaged the third set after dropping his serve in the opening game but when in the fourth he fell behind 1–4, the leeway became too great for him to make up. From start to finish it was a match packed with fine touch strokes, gems of delicacy illustrating lawn tennis as an art rather than crude athleticism.

Another connoisseur's match in this round was Osuna's victory over the lesser Spaniard, Jose Arilla. Here again strokes learned in the demanding control school of hard courts were wedded well to the faster demands of turf. Bungert conquered Jorgen Ulrich after dropping the opening set, Stolle beat the young Greek Nicolas Kalogeropoulos far more easily than anyone expected. So that was the last eight into line. Four of the seeds had survived. Only Abe Segal of South Africa was in the quarter-finals for the first time.

Quarter-finals. McKinley, the second seed; Stolle, the sixth; Emerson, the first; and Bungert, not seeded at all, won the quarter-finals. Three of the matches no one will particularly remember. That in which Bungert put out Rafael Osuna was memorable. Just one year before, on the same day and on the same court, court one, and in the same round, Bungert played an electric match and beat Emerson. Osuna is a great volleyer and perhaps the fastest man in the world on court. He is, moreover, champion of the United States. Bungert made him look second rate. He plucked him from the tournament, as if he were a player of no account. It took genius to reduce Osuna like that. And what a genius Bungert was! In seventy-one minutes he played as he rarely can have played before, not so much hitting the ball as meeting it with a sharp caress that still held control seconds afterwards.

Bungert is slender, tall and unbending, as dignified as a Prussian guardsman. His footwork tends to break every rule in the book. His wrist is astonishing. Only he, in my experience, can, from the wrong foot anyway, take a ball on the half-volley on the forehand side and project it over the net with top spin as surely as if he had the ball on the end of a piece of string. He played an immaculate game with such sharp and dominating ground strokes that it was small wonder that Osuna was turned into a dejected loser. The Mexican's sting was extracted from the start. Bungert treated his service with contempt and by the end of the first set Osuna ceased on his second delivery trying to get to the net at all. It was virtual suicide if he did.

Bungert's most telling returns of service were from his backhand, and from the left-hand corner he positively flayed the ball to the corner. The wonder was that Osuna persisted from this court in serving to that wing, since such a course was to invite rather more than an even chance of destruction. Then there were deft lobs and teasing angles to frustrate Osuna when he was in the forecourt. All round and in every way Bungert was the puppet master, with Osuna as a doll dancing to his bidding. The Mexican was never in the match. . . . Naturally all German supporters were delighted. They were less delighted by Kuhnke, whom Stolle eliminated with a forthright readiness not expected at this stage of the meeting. Stolle was precise and sure. There was never a doubt about the outcome. Nor was there between Emerson and Bob Hewitt. The latter's easy course came to an abrupt end. Emerson never wavered. If there were any signs that Emerson was keying up his strength it was on his service. He served with real dash. Hewitt never got to grips with it. McKinley lost the third set to Segal, and I must hand it to this genial 33-year-old that he should bring out so much to force the defending champion thus far. Even so, McKinley still looked more of a rugged than a polished player.

It was on the second Monday, the day of the men's quarter-finals, that the august management committee delivered their rebuke to the Russians. Sergei Likhachev and Anna Dmitrieva scratched to South Africa's Terry Ryan and to Rhodesia's Pat Walkden. On Saturday, an official communiqué pointed out, the manager and trainer of the Russians were told that in the event of their winning they would be required to play against a South African and, that being so and their wishing not to play, it would be courteous to retire at match point so as to let their opponents go through. Such, indeed, is the custom everywhere.

"It is regretted," stated the Wimbledon management committee with dignity and bite, "that this advice was not accepted." This was tantamount in lesser circles to a kick in the jaw.

Afterward the point was put to the Russians, "Ah, yes," it was said, "we did not quite understand the advice but even if we had we would not have followed it. You see, we have come here to play lawn tennis, not to indulge in politics." If I had logic like that I could prove I was the finest lawn tennis player in the world.

Semi-finals. There have been better matches than those which took Emerson and Stolle to the sixth all-Australian final in nine years, and there have also been many worse. Stolle avenged his final defeat of the year before by beating Chuck McKinley, 4–6, 10–8, 9–7, 6–4, and had its quality been maintained at the level of the first set and for the first part of the second, it would have rated a memorable contest. Stolle maintained his standard better and in the end beat a ragged champion. It was a day of Australian revenge all round, for Emerson reversed the outcome of 1963 by beating Bungert, 6–3, 15–13, 6–0. . . . Bungert, a genius against Osuna, was much less so against Emerson. The Australian was all efficiency, workmanlike to his fingertips. . . .

The final. Emerson beat Stolle, 6–4, 12–10, 4–6, 6–3, to become the champion at his ninth attempt. They were on court two hours and 41 minutes, but 34 minutes of this were taken up by three interruptions for rain during the second set. It was not the greatest of contests. There have, though, been many worse finals, and the most remarkable aspect of it was that each man played to the best of his capacity. Nerves have often ruined the last match.

Two factors contributed most to Emerson's victory. The first was his electric speed of foot. The second was his ability to return service adequately. Stolle lost his service five times, Emerson twice. This followed the pattern of the statistics related to the number of times service was returned into court. Overall Stolle got back the service only 67 times in 127 chances. Emerson got it back 108 times out of 157. Stolle's deficiencies in this matter were most marked in the first and fourth sets. . . . Yet I would assess Stolle's service to be faster than Emerson's. Stolle, though, double-faulted eleven times, to but thrice for Emerson.

Emerson had a minor crisis in the second game of the match when he was within a point of yielding his opening serve. A service winner averted this threat and when, seven games later, the roles were reversed, Emerson jumped on the chance at once. With a lightning backhand volley he took Stolle's service to lead 5-4 and served out the next game with confidence to clinch the set. More errors were unforced than otherwise. There was staccato speed and ruthlessness on the part of both men. This was not a final in which shaky nerves played any part.

In the second set Stolle began to handle Emerson's serve incomparably better. Even so when the next service break occurred it was he who suffered it. The seventh game was a wavering one of four deuces and in the end Emerson had broken through to lead 4-3. Then came his first service loss and 4-all. With this recovery Stolle indicated that the match was not beyond his winning. When Stolle was 5-4 came a real crisis for Emerson. He fell to 30-40 on service, set point for Stolle. His answer was a fast delivery down the middle which Stolle could not get back, and with a backhand volley and another service winner he saved the game.

At six games-all, 30-all, with Stolle serving, a drizzle interrupted play for ten minutes. Thirteen minutes later, with the score 9 games-all, there was another interruption, for nine minutes. It was becoming a menace. Seven minutes of play brought the score to 10-all, 15-all, Stolle serving, when a heavy downpour brought a 15-minute cessation. On return this time the court was pretty slippery, a factor more vital to the more rigid Stolle than the swifter moving Emerson. On taking up his service game Stolle got only one more point before Emerson had broken through. Emerson dashingly served the next game out to love to secure the set at 12-10 and lead two sets to love.

When in the opening game of the third set Stolle fell to love-40, it looked all over. Emerson would have broken through then had he not, on his third game point, missed an easy forehand shot into an open court. Stolle kept himself alive after all. More than that, Stolle pulled out some superb returns in the tenth game to capture Emerson's service to love. That was the set, 6-4 to Stolle, a fine comeback effort. The discomfiture of Emerson, however, was purely temporary. Stolle delivered two double-faults, his eighth and ninth in the match, in the first game of the fourth set. Emerson, aided by these gifts, broke through, and from that stage on his victory course was a formal exercise. Stolle ceased to be at all effective against his service and Emerson again broke through in the ninth game to win the set 6–3 and so, with mercurial dash, assume the glories of a Wimbledon singles championship. . . .

Women's semi-finals. Margaret Smith, who was great, and Maria Bueno, who was great, uncertain, maddening, inconsistent and a superb fighter, came through the semis. Smith beat Billie Jean Moffitt, 6–3, 6–4, after being 1–4 in the second set. Bueno beat Lesley Turner, 3–6, 6–4, 6–4, after being 2–4 in the third set. There was nearly a Smith-Turner final, an all-Australian affair to match the men. With all respect to Lesley, who is now such a fine player, Wimbledon crowds did not want that. They were delighted when Bueno won. Margaret was devastating against Billie Jean. In the first set her expertise in every department of the game was unanswerable. She made just three errors and I am not at all sure those were really of the unforced variety. Whoever had won between Bueno and Turner would have been applauded for a fighting victory. It was not great lawn tennis but it was a great fight. Great shots there were a-plenty, but errors also, especially on the part of a sometimes majestic, sometimes delinquent Maria. The broad issue was between Lesley's strength off the ground and Maria's net play. . . .

Final round. Maria Bueno regained the crown she had won in 1959 and 1960 when she beat Margaret Smith, 6–4, 7–9, 6–3, after one hour, 28 minutes. When it ended, the crowd, a little short of 15,000, did not know whom to applaud the more. They cheered Bueno in victory and they cheered Smith in consolation. Above all, they cheered one of the best women's singles finals played at Wimbledon, certainly the best in the last decade. In simple terms, the artist beat the athlete. But the artistry and the athleticism displayed were tremendous and not until the last minute of the match was it clear as to who was to be the victor. If occasionally both players fell short of their own talents, these periods merely served to illustrate that they were, after all, humans and not machines.

Knowing how disloyal Miss Bueno can sometimes be to her own genius, there were many who feared that Smith might take the last match at a canter. Her earlier progress had been impeccable. That this was not to be was signaled early in the match when Maria built a lead of 3–1. Three games later, though, the Australian was 4–3 after Bueno had been 40–15 and advantage point for a 4–2 lead. What was vital in this set was the ninth game. Here Margaret yielded her service to 15, giving the last point on a double-fault which appeared to indicate the Brazilian resistance had shaken her. Bueno, despite love–30, held her serve in the next game to take the set, 6–4. At no time in this set or in either of the next two was there a stroke played that was not positive. Mistakes there certainly were but never lack of resolution. The net was the objective of both. I do not think Bueno missed a smash at any time.

The second set lasted 47 minutes and it was one of rich qualities. If Smith had again signaled her tension by double-faulting on the opening point, she soon put this phase behind her. Her aggression flowed with athletic skill and she pounded, pounded, pounded, always moving forward. Soon she was 4–love and 40–15. It was at this point her service power diminished and her forehand lost its zip. Bueno climbed back to 4–all. The next game, with Smith serving, was a contest in itself. Margaret was 40–15. Maria came five times within a point of taking the game. Smith, despite two doubles, at last got it on her fifth chance. Bueno double-faulted twice in the tenth game but won it. Then Smith saved herself from 15–40 to lead, 6–5. Bueno leveled again. In the 13th Smith refound confidence in her forehand and won it and the 15th both at love for 8–7. The Brazilian yielded her service to 30 and that was set to Smith and one set–all.

Bueno had imperious power but, compared with Smith's trained muscles, it had the more fragile look. The Australian served first and won to 15. Bueno responded, to love. Then Smith to 15 again. A minor crisis followed, Bueno being 30–40 before she squared the issue. A love game to Miss Smith was the last the Australian had. At that stage, 3–2 to her in the final set, she had taken eleven more points than her opponent. In the last stages this deficit was wiped away and passed. Bueno held her own service to love for 3–all. Her batteries seemed recharged. Smith lost some strength of arm and when she yielded her service to 15 she had, in fact, lost the match. Bueno made it 5–3, winning service to 15. In the ninth a now-tired Miss Smith double-faulted to be love–30. Her last winning shot was a fine forehand that forced a Brazilian volley error—15–30. Then 15–40 when Smith, made to stretch wide for a forehand volley, found the net. The Australian smashed to save match point but it was not angled wide enough. Bueno just reached the ball and luckily projected a perfect half-volley return.

If Smith had served a little better, perhaps she would have had the title instead. It was a close-run thing and was surpassed in quality only by the Little Mo versus Doris Hart final of eleven years before.

AUSTRALIA REGAINS DAVIS CUP FROM U. S.

by Al Laney

The Davis Cup, emblem of world supremacy of tennis, was handed into the keep of the Australian team once more yesterday after Roy Emerson, rated now even more than ever the world's leading amateur player, defeated Chuck McKinley, the No. 1 player of the defending team, in the fifth and deciding match of the 1964 Challenge Round.

In a single's match postponed from Sunday after Fred Stolle had evened the count by defeating Dennis Ralston in a long five-setter with too little of the day remaining, Emerson beat our man in four sets, 3–6, 6–2, 6–4, 6–4, to give Australia the victory by three matches to two.

The teams had split the opening singles matches on Friday when McKinley defeated Stolle, and Emerson beat Ralston, and the United States had taken a 2–1 lead on Saturday when McKinley and Ralston defeated Emerson and Stolle in the one doubles match.

The deciding match, which never had a chance of being played as scheduled on Sunday because of morning-long rain that prevented the start of play until well past mid-afternoon, was one of the most interesting of the five. It was never speculative for long, however, after McKinley, playing very well, certainly as well as he had played in defeating Stolle, had surprisingly won Emerson's big service twice on his way to capturing the first set.

In each of the following three sets Emerson won McKinley's service in the first game and encountered little serious difficulty in holding his own. In the second he won the American's service twice, and one felt he might have repeated in the others also if it had been necessary to victory.

The match was interesting because the tactics employed by Emerson at the start, having proved ineffective, were changed over quickly and played in the only way in which McKinley can be beaten. Even when he had changed and really got control of the play, he was in danger each time he became just a little careless. For McKinley, a tough little competitor, brought roars from the crowd every time he was given a chance.

In the first Chuck brought more than roars. He brought yells and shrieks and hand-clapping between points. For this was the most pleasant surprise of the tournament. Emerson was playing him from the back of the court and McKinley was superior in this maneuver, fencing until he could find a ball to bang, and then hitting out for the forcing shot that would let him into forecourt for a volley or else an outright score.

This was very good tennis all around, for Emerson was not missing much, but McKinley was definitely on top and went out with a flourish in the ninth game. At this moment hope was high, for our man had clearly outplayed the best.

Alas, it never burned so brightly again. Emerson calmly and almost quietly, it seemed, turned the thing right around. From the opening game of the second set to the last one of the fourth it was at all times a question of which man could get to the net. Emerson seemed able to do so now whenever he made the effort. McKinley almost never could, either behind his own service or against Emerson's much harder and deeper one.

Chuck stuck to his guns with much determination. Every opportunity he was given he took. But although he could put Emerson in trouble now and then he never could carry the thing through to a successful conclusion, which would have been the capture of the Australian's service to get back even and go on from there.

Emerson played wonderfully well through the second and third sets after he had got the break he needed. Now and then he had to put on extra effort because of dropping behind while serving, but he always seemed to have the right shot close at hand.

McKinley never ceased trying to get to close quarters but hardly ever could do it against Emerson's incisive delivery and only rarely when he himself was serving. He fought a good fight in defense of the Cup but it was clearly a losing one all through the closing sets, and now the United States will have to go to Australia next year in an effort to bring it home again as McKinley and Ralston did last December.

1 9 6 5

SANTANA AND MISS SMITH WIN U.S. TITLES

by Allison Danzig

Manuel Santana yesterday became the first player from Spain ever to win the tennis championship of the United States, and Margaret Smith of Australia established beyond question that she is the premier woman player of the world in adding the American title to the Wimbledon crown she holds.

In the final round of the 50th anniversary tournament to be held at the West Side Tennis Club in Forest Hills, Queens, the 27-year-old Santana, the architect of Spain's first Davis Cup victory over the United States, defeated Cliff Drysdale of South Africa, 6–2, 7–9, 7–5, 6–1.

The match was interrupted by rain for 40 minutes after Drysdale had pulled up from 1–5 to 5–all in the third set, and many of the gallery of 11,000 that turned out in the stadium despite the threatening weather had departed before Santana staged a stampede following the resumption of play.

Miss Smith, who had lost only nine games in five matches in advancing to the final round, overcame the exceedingly strong challenge of Billie Jean Moffitt of Long Beach, California, to win, 7–5, 8–6, after trailing at 3–5 in both sets and twice standing within a stroke of losing the second in the tenth game.

Senator Robert F. Kennedy presented the trophies to the winners and runners-up in both events and congratulated them on the excellence of their performances. Assisting him were J. Donald McNamara, president of the club, and Martin Tressel of Pittsburgh, president of the United States Lawn Tennis Association.

Cries of "bravo" greeted Santana as he walked off the court in victory, and he was serenaded by Spanish singers in the marquee and feted later at the clubhouse by a Spanish band.

He had achieved what no other player of his country—neither Manuel Alonso or Andres Gimeno—ever accomplished in winning one of the world's major grass-court titles. In 1961 he stood as the first Spaniard to win the French title, on a slow clay-type court, on which he has commonly been supposed to be far more effective than on turf.

This notion was all but dispelled by Santana's performances at Forest Hills, where he also defeated Arthur Ashe, the conqueror of Roy Emerson of Australia, the defending titleholder, to qualify for the final.

Drysdale, the first player from South Africa to reach our final since 1948, had beaten Dennis Ralston, the ranking player of the country, and Rafael Osuna of Mexico, the 1963 champion, en route to the final. Also he was a semi-finalist at Wimbledon.

With his dangerous two-handed backhand, his strong service, his amazing recovery ability, his command of the lob and his skill as a volleyer, as well as his fine court temperament and fighting qualities, the tall South African youth offered the rugged opposition to bring out the best in Santana's game.

The best was not always forthcoming, and there was a definite lag in Santana's play in the third set, after he had stood at set point three times in the 12th game of the hour-long second set and let it get away from him.

But when he applied himself to his task and brought all his craftsmanship and court craft to bear, he stood revealed as one of the soundest, most versatile and accomplished stroke manufacturers and cleverest tacticians in the game.

Santana has at his command every variety of stroke and spin. His looping forehand and lob, his overspin backhand, so confounding to the volleyer; his chipped forehand and his artfulness around the net all combine to qualify him to meet any challenge. Also, he moves easily and he is able to maintain position with seemingly little effort for the reason that he is so sure in his anticipation.

His service is not as spectacular as some, but he can make the chalk fly when pushed, just as he can nail his forehand. He is the complete tennis player, of which there are few, and his triumph at Forest Hills should win him the world-wide recognition that has been accorded him only in Europe, where he is looked upon as unbeatable on clay.

The women's final provided highly exciting tennis, with both girls hitting powerfully from the back of the court and volleying with an authority and a frequency not often seen in women's play.

Miss Moffitt, who defeated Miss Smith at Wimbledon in 1962 and lost to her in the final there in 1963, rushed the net behind almost every service and volleyed and hammered overhead in a fashion to bring roars from the gallery. From both the forehand and backhand she drove with burning pace and fine length and she flew around the court in a maximum expenditure of energy that was worthy of a better fate.

In both sets she broke service in the opening game with her chipped returns and her skillful use of the lob and drop shot. Concentrating on Miss Smith's backhand, she maintained her lead to 5–3 each time, only to be thwarted by the strong play of her opponent in the emergency.

Miss Smith was not as consistent as she was in defeating Nancy Richey in the semi-finals. Her control was not so good, she did not serve so well nor volley so decisively. But when she found herself in danger she rose to unassailable heights and brought off the big shot so regularly that Miss Moffitt's beautiful all-round performance went for nought. . . .

It was announced that the championships set records with gross receipts of approximately $300,000 and a total attendance of more than 90,000. The gate receipts came to $215,000.

1966

KING AND SANTANA
QUEEN AND KING OF WIMBLEDON

by Maureen Connolly Brinker

A King became the international queen of tennis as America's Billie Jean (Moffitt) King, in one of the most exciting world championships of the past few decades, upset three-times world champion Maria Bueno, 6–3, 3–6, 6–1, in a tense, hard-fought battle on Wimbledon's center court before 17,000 spectators. Sharing the honors of tennis royalty was Spain's popular Manuel Santana, who gained his crown at the expense of America's Dennis Ralston in an excellent three-set final, 6–4, 11–9, 6–4.

It was a very popular victory for both champions. For Billie Jean in particular the win ended a long uphill battle to snare the number one position in ladies' tennis. Twice before the bouncy Californian came mighty close to the coveted crown—once in 1963 when she lost in the final to Australia's Margaret Smith, 6–3, 6–4, and last year when Maria Bueno defeated her in the semis by the very close scores of 6–4, 5–7, 6–3.

This year, however, Billie Jean was not to be denied. She faced a most difficult draw and, at times, found herself in serious trouble. In her quarter-final encounter with South Africa's Annette Van Zyl, for example, Billie Jean was down 0–3 in the third set. In earlier rounds she often was down, struggling to control her big game. But as the tournament progressed, Billie Jean progressed. By the time she entered her semi-final encounter against defending champion Margaret Smith, Mrs. King was on top of her game and certainly playing well above her opponents.

Santana also had a difficult struggle to find championship form, but with each succeeding round his touch game and strong serve gained in sharpness and precision. It is a testimonial to this fine versatile player that he could develop an attacking game the equal of any player—with perhaps the exception of Roy Emerson—yet maintain his excellent defensive pattern necessary in acquiring frequent service breaks. It was this very versatility that formed the pattern of his game against more powerful opponents and allowed him to extricate himself from many dangerous positions.

Manuel's road to the pinnacle was made easier, of course, by Emerson's unfortunate injury in the quarter-final round. Playing against the vastly improved Owen Davidson of Australia, Emerson ran into the umpire's chair while chasing an elusive drop shot and dislocated his shoulder in the third game of their second set. Although he remained on court, Emerson was unable to approach his normal caliber of play and quickly succumbed to his powerful left-handed opponent. With Emerson's exit, all eyes turned on Davidson. He had distinguished himself in earlier rounds by defeating several fine players and, in his semi-final encounter with Santana, carried the Spaniard to five long sets, only to lose 5–7 in the fifth. Although Santana was eventually to win the title, Davidson clearly was "the man of the hour." . . .

The earlier rounds were marked with a few stunning upsets. Most notable was that of Bob Hewitt over Fred Stolle, the No. 3 seed, in four sets, 6–2, 6–3, 4–6, 6–2. Because Stolle's game is built around a powerful delivery, it is essential that this facet of his play be working consistently. Such was not the case. Stolle double-faulted heavily on adverse game points, handing service breaks to Hewitt on a silver platter. Hewitt, on the other hand, was consistent with his well-placed serves, catching a rather heavy-footed Stolle in compromising positions. Fred was tired and discouraged, battling the hungry and enthusiastic Hewitt, who sensed victory after the first set.

The earlier rounds produced some sad moments for several of America's key players. Clark Graebner met the inspired Davidson and lost, 6–3, 3–6, 8–6, 6–1. It would be difficult to find error in Clark's play other than that his first service was not working with its usual force, allowing Davidson to attack off Graebner's second delivery. But Davidson really played superb tennis against the Yugoslav Pilic in the first round, Graebner in the second, and the very tough Tom Okker of the Netherlands in the third before meeting and beating the injured Emerson in the quarters.

Marty Riessen tried a tactical change in an attempt to subdue the fourth-seeded Santana but the switch came too late. Knowing that Manuel had been bothered by a shoulder injury while playing the Brazilian Davis Cup tie, Riessen abandoned the serve-for-serve, volley-for-volley style of play of the first set and a half and began hitting high lobs off of every conceivable ball, even service returns. The idea was to break up the well-established rhythm of the Spaniard and to test the overhead ability and physical soundness of the questionable limb. Although Santana continued strong throughout the second set, the high balls definitely bothered him in the third—more mentally than physically. He objected to this style of play and even served a few underhanded balls in response to this tennis tactic. But all is fair when one is playing to win, and the contest in the third set makes one wonder what might have happened had Riessen attempted the lob game from the first point of the match. As it was, the score ended 6–3, 6–2, 10–8.

Another early match in the men's division that caused a ripple of surprise was the loss by fifth-seeded John Newcombe of Australia to his former compatriot, Ken Fletcher, who now lives in Hong Kong. Fletcher was strong off the ground, particularly on the forehand, and able to pass Newcombe at net when John was slow in approaching behind chip shots. In the fourth round, America's Cliff Richey pressed second-seeded Tony Roche before losing, 4–6, 4–6, 4–6. It was apparent that the Texan still has much room for improvement. The most notable differences between Roche and Richey were in their second serves and returns of serve. Richey's second delivery needs more length because, at present, it rarely holds an opponent back. Roche, on the other hand, has a tremendous "kicker" that falls close to the line and rarely allows an opponent an offensive shot. Richey also seems to be in need of a chip return of service that falls at the feet of the oncoming net-rusher. Cliff now tries to hit every shot hard and flat, with the result that his serve returns carry much too high over the net and never vary in pace. Roche quickly grooved his volleys to the pace.

The two minor upsets in the quarter-finals were Davidson's win over top seed and defending champion Roy Emerson (seeking his third Wimbledon singles title), 1–6, 6–3, 6–4, 6–4, and seventh seed Cliff Drysdale's surprise of second-seeded Roche, 9–7, 6–2, 6–2. Emerson began the match against Davidson in routine fashion, taking the first set, 6–1. Roy was beginning to hit top form following a month of heavy training prior to this championship when the unfortunate accident took place. With Davidson serving at one–all and 15–30 in the second set, Davidson interrupted a long rally with an excellent drop shot. Emerson chased the ball down but slipped on the wet turf and slid into the umpire's stand. His left shoulder crashed into the stand and was dislocated. From that point on Emerson merely went through the motions.

Drysdale's match against Roche featured a closely contested first set in which the Australian had six set points. But South Africa's Drysdale, putting up a tremendous fight, passed Roche with his two-handed backhand and, in so doing, seemed to break Roche's spirit. At any rate, Tony never got back into the match following Drysdale's recovery and seemed at times to be barely trying for wide balls. Following his save of the six set points (three at 4–5, two at 5–6 and one at 6–7), Drysdale won 13 of the next 16 games. In defense of Roche, one could point to the ankle injury that had reoccurred at the Queen's tournament the week preceding Wimbledon. Tony had to default there.

Ralston met Hewitt (the upset winner over Stolle) and won, 7–5, 6–2, 11–9. Ralston was bothered by his old nemesis, double faults, and was averaging one per game in both the first and third sets. Hewitt started rather fast in the match, taking a 3–0 lead. But in the fourth game Ralston reached his stride, stopped making careless volley errors . . . and, despite a hard struggle in the third set, looked the winner all the way.

On center court Santana was battling a difficult circular wind and an inspired Ken Fletcher. Calling upon his ground-stroking resources, Santana just defeated the quick Aussie by a narrow margin, 6–2, 3–6, 8–6, 4–6, 7–5.

Fletcher had more than his share of chances. He continually broke the Spaniard's serve, only to double-fault in his own service games. Fletcher had a real chance to take the match when he led, 5–4, in the fifth set but he missed some crucial forehand passes and made two very careless forehand volleys to drop his serve at love. From 5–5 Manuel got down to business, placed his first serve in and volleyed deeply. Receiving in the final game, Santana fully applied himself, took the offensive and successfully ended the match.

The two men's semi-finals surely set endurance records. The Santana-Davidson encounter ended in a 6–2, 4–6, 9–7, 3–6, 7–5 victory for Manuel while Ralston barely edged out Drysdale, 6–8, 8–6, 3–6, 7–5, 6–3. It required six hours and 20 minutes to determine the two men's finalists and it was an exhausted center court audience that then turned its attention to doubles play. As in the Santana-Fletcher encounter, the Davidson-Santana match featured numerous service breaks. Service standard was high but quality of service return was even better. Davidson often took the lead only to find Santana retaliating with loop returns that slid by the net-rushing Australian. It was Santana's defense rather than offense that saved the day for him. . . .

Fantastic is the word for the fifth set, which must rank as one of the greatest comebacks in tennis history. Down 5–1 in the set, Davidson staged a tremendous rally to pull up to 5–5. But this great effort took its toll of the Australian's strength, and Santana, aided by some magnificent top-spin passing shots off both wings, took hold of himself to win the next two games and match.

Ralston was a bit fortunate in his match against Drysdale. The South African had played two five-set matches in as many days (one singles, one doubles) and simply gave out midway through the fourth set. Up to this point Drysdale was gaining the upper hand. He was helped by Ralston's self-criticism and consequent poor play. When Ralston hits one of those self-deprecating moods, his opponents just have to be patient and the games will come. Drysdale served well in this encounter with few double faults. His first delivery had great power and he was using a bit more spin on his second service as a safety measure. Ralston knew that Drysdale had been through a run of difficult matches and therefore employed many lobs in an effort to tire him. This tactic worked out well in the fourth set as the South African began stretching for overheads and failed to put them away. . . .
In the fifth set Ralston made the necessary breakthrough in the third game, and went to 4–1 with another break. Drysdale immediately retaliated with a break of his own but simply could not keep up the pace. Games followed service for the set, 6–3, and match.

The final between Santana and Ralston produced some glorious tennis. Making fewer errors, Santana clinched the championship, 6–4, 11–9, 6–4.

Dennis used a wide slice serve to Manuel's forehand in an attempt to open the court for the volley. But Santana did not seem bothered by the wide balls and returned an amazing percentage for outright winners. Santana employed much of the same tactics he had against Davidson—

approaching high down the middle for time to gain the net and to cut down his opponent's passing angle. Santana also served extremely well and extricated himself from several awkward positions with outright aces throughout the match. Games followed service until the ninth, first set, when Ralston hit short approaches which allowed Manuel the use of his top-spin drives. With a 5–4 break, Santana took his service with the loss of only one point.

Ralston took a 4–1 lead in the second set, aided by a net-cord shot that won the fourth game. But Dennis couldn't hold the lead as his first service failed him in the seventh game. Santana took advantage of the serving lapse to move in on Ralston's second delivery and dump returns at the American's feet. Games followed evenly to 9–all, when Santana again broke Dennis with some effective forehand drives and then served out the set.

There was only one service break in the third set and that came in the third game when Santana made some truly fantastic returns off Ralston's hardest serves. After this break, Santana kept the pressure on with excellent serving. Ralston tried to break up Manuel's game with lobs, but Santana's overhead was working beautifully and he discouraged this tactic with fine overhead winners. At 5–4 Manuel employed Ralston's tactic of slicing wide to the forehand and quickly ran out the match, 6–4.

On the distaff side, the early rounds also produced some exciting tennis although few minor upsets. The only seed to bow out was Norma Baylon of Argentina, No. 8, who bowed to the left-handed Dutch girl, Trudi Groenman, 4–6, 6–4, 6–4. Some of the seeded American girls, however, had a difficult time reaching the quarter-finals. Billie Jean King had a tough opener against British Wightman Cupper, 19-year-old Winnie Shaw, and had to rely on her big volley and Shaw's inexperience to pull out, 6–2, 8–6. But the bouncy Californian's closest game occurred against the tall Australian girl, Karen Krantzcke, who was playing in her first Wimbledon. Billie Jean found herself down, 2–5, set point in the first set by virtue of Karen's booming serve and exceptionally good forehand. Billie seemed to ignore the Aussie's weak backhand until the set was almost lost. When she reversed tactics and began serving and attacking this side, the tide of battle quickly changed and the American went to 6–5. The score leveled at 6–6 and, following a rain break, Mrs. King came back strong to win, 9–7, 6–2.

While Billie Jean was having trouble, her partner in the No. 1 U.S. ranking, Nancy Richey, barely squeaked through a three-set win over Britisher Rita Bentley, 3–6, 6–4, 6–2. Nancy was down one set and 0–4 before she settled down to business by steadying her strokes and eliminating short-court errors. Most lady competitors realize that Nancy cannot be matched stroke-for-stroke from the backcourt and they concentrate, instead, on feeding her "nothing" balls down the middle or in chipping short to draw her in to the net. This lack of pace often results in an upset of Nancy's tempo.

The two outstanding matches in the fourth round saw 17-year-old Rosemary Casals of California challenge third-ranked Ann Jones on center court before bowing, 6–2, 6–3 while second-seeded Maria Bueno dropped a set to the much improved Australian, Judy Tegart, 6–3, 4–6, 6–2. The young

Casals made a most impressive mark in her first Wimbledon visit. She played most aggressively—hitting for outright winners on 80 per cent of the shots—and certainly gave promise of great potential a few years hence. It was this very aggressiveness, however, that proved a drawback in this match. Rosemary tried to make brilliant shots off practically every ball, when an early placement to open court would have served her purpose. This undoubtedly is due to lack of experience; time teaches patience and the value of an errorless game. The only disturbing factor in Rosemary's game is a questionable forehand. She has a rather "roundhouse" backswing that causes her to hit with excessive top spin. She meets the ball late on grass and, as a consequence, errs often. A shorter backswing and secure chip shot would be preferable. . . .

At the opposite end of the draw, Bueno carried too much volleying power for the unorthodox stroking of France's Françoise Durr, winning 6–4, 6–3. The other two matches, however, were closely contested as Billie Jean King outlasted South Africa's Annette Van Zyl, 1–6, 6–2, 6–4, while Ann Jones beat Nancy Richey, 4–6, 6–1, 6–1. . . . The Richey-Jones battle saw the American girl break the first cardinal rule in tennis: Never change a winning game. Finding great success with the drop shot-lob combination, Nancy used it relentlessly in the first set and wisely altered her length and pace. This tactic deprived the English girl of the pace which she needs for her tough, angled game. There were five service breaks in the first set, with the key ones going to Nancy in the fifth and seventh games. Ann fought off three set points in the ninth game to pull up to 4–5 but Nancy won the next game and set.

In the second set Nancy reverted to her usual hard-hitting game and dropped five games in a row. Nancy managed to hold one service game but that was all. At the start of the final set it became evident that Nancy was having difficulty bending and moving. She didn't chase short balls and was quite slow in pushing off. She was down again 5–0 before breaking Jones, but the match was virtually over as Ann was too grooved in her angles and loop forehands to lose control. I could not help but wonder if Nancy were bothered by her old knee injury as her motions varied greatly from the start of the match.

The two semi-final matches produced some of the most exciting tennis of the tournament. One provided a major upset when Billie Jean King knocked out reigning champion Margaret Smith in straight sets, 6–3, 6–3, and the other—the Jones-Bueno encounter—offered the sheer drama that only a world championship brings. In the King-Smith match Billie Jean's use of the lob was the telling factor. From the very start, the American never allowed Smith to crowd the net for the volley. Realizing that Margaret approaches the forecourt at rapid speed, King intermixed chop returns with these lobs to keep the Aussie off balance. Smith helped the dynamic American get away to a quick 3–0 lead by serving two double faults in the second game. It was obvious that Smith was uneasy over the match as she had difficulty in moving—barring injury, a sure sign of tension. King, on the other hand, played faultless and absolutely brilliant tennis. Unlike her earlier rounds, there were no careless volleys or loose ground strokes. Instead, Billie Jean's racket whipped out winners, and the set was quickly run out at 6–3.

Smith, however, started the second set most positively, winning her service at love. King suffered a slight letdown, dropped her delivery and was behind 0–3. But in the fifth game Billie Jean delivered a series of splendid backhand returns that put her back into the match. King again broke Smith's serve to lead 4–3. In the eighth game Smith held game point and a chance to rebreak King and even the match. Billie Jean hit a ball that was carrying deep into court. Margaret thought it was out but the linesman called it good, and from this point on the Australian lost her impetus. She became upset while Billie Jean maintained her concentration and strong play to win that important game. With a 5–3 lead, King produced some magnificent volleys to take the match and to stage one of the finest victories of her career.

But for drama and emotional exhaustion, the Jones-Bueno duel must be recognized as one of the finest in Wimbledon history. Both girls displayed the best in offensive and defensive play, the best in fighting spirit, and the best example of two unique styles locked in a desperate battle. In the end, it was Bueno's great ingenuity and incredible flair that earned the victory.

As was anticipated, Bueno carried the attack to Jones. Maria opened the match by breaking Ann at love. The English girl was not getting good depth on her drives, allowing Bueno to take the ball early on the rise (her favorite position) and to force the play. Ann managed to win the Brazilian's delivery in the fourth game by virtue of some fine forehand passing shots, only to see her own service fade before the wilting drives of her opponent. Jones was not serving particularly well and this gave Maria the vital openings. Ann also was a bit sticky moving after the return of serve, which placed her in a late position for her second shot. The end result of this slowness of foot was that Ann's shots were rising to the volleyer instead of dipping low. At 5–3 Maria broke Ann at 30–40 for the set.

Bueno again attacked in the second set. Serving badly, Jones dropped her delivery in the fourth game but immediately applied pressure for a re-break. Each girl dropped another service and soon the score was 4–all. They battled back and forth, with the Brazilian trying quickly for net position and Jones doing her best to hold Maria back. With a 9–8 lead, Bueno held two match points, only to be denied this early victory by the battling Britisher. Evening the score at 9–all, Ann again broke Maria for the vital one-game lead and finished off the set at 11–9 with a high backhand volley placement.

Then Jones incredibly lost touch completely. Almost before spectators realized what was happening, Ann was down 0–5, apparently suffering a complete letdown from the second set. Then Bueno began to play cautiously and Jones, having little to lose, grew rather bold and mounted a net attack. From 1–5 down, Jones broke Bueno and held delivery. But, sensing danger, Bueno put out a surge of power and, with great serving, reached 40–0, match point. Bueno was denied again as Jones hit outright winners from good services to save the game and pull up to 4–5, with her own service to follow. Having saved five match points already, Jones tempted fate again by hitting loose ground strokes and falling behind 0–40. But Ann did the impossible! Coming to net behind hard, flat serves, she punched away ball after ball and, gaining momentum, tied the match 5–5.

Bueno was stunned. Eight match points gone! The Brazilian reacted as might be expected—with hesitant play. But down 0–30, Maria produced some brilliant half-volleys to level and then win the game. With the ninth match point against her at 30–40, Ann Jones netted a forehand drive to finally bow out 7–5. This match was dramatic testimony to the fighting qualities of both girls.

As so often happens in the world championship, the final match was a bit disappointing. Although Billie Jean achieved the finest win of her career in topping Maria Bueno, 6–3, 3–6, 6–1, her victory was due more to the nervous, inhibited play of the Brazilian than to anything else. This is not to say that Billie Jean played any less than an excellent game of tennis. She was patient in positioning herself, secure in her service return, and very forceful with her own delivery. The great disappointment was in Bueno's inability to pass through the nervous state and into the realm of exciting tennis. She remained taut throughout the match and rarely produced the caliber of tennis of which she is capable.

Billie Jean again employed a predetermined tactic, as she had against Smith. When serving, the American kept the ball breaking wide to Maria's forehand, which opened up the backhand court for her first volley. When receiving, Billie Jean was careful to keep the first ball deep, attacking behind her drives at every possible opportunity. When Bueno did come into net, Billie Jean used the same effective lob as against Smith, keeping Maria constantly off balance. King knew that if Maria grooved her strokes, it would be difficult to break up her rhythm. She also knew that Maria is not moving as rapidly as in the past and so she sacrificed some speed for accurate placements.

The match started with King serving, and the vital, and only, service break in the set came in the fourth game. Both girls served a fair share of double faults (8 for King) but Billie also put in a fair share of forceful first serves. Maria, on the other hand, was catching the tape with her hesitant first delivery and serving quite short on the second one. Although she opened the 5–3 game with a double fault, Billie Jean quickly controlled her errors and ended the first set with a lovely display of volleying.

In the second set Bueno got off to a fast start as King suffered a slight letdown and began using the lob too much. Bueno hit some lovely overhead winners and took advantage of King's short volleys. The second game was the only service break of the set. Billie Jean had one serving lapse in the match—in the eighth game—when she served three consecutive double faults in the backhand court. But Maria could not take advantage of these errors to break service and wound up the set on her own delivery at 6–3.

In the final set the first few games were extremely tense. Both girls played safe balls until the court opened up. Billie Jean was much quicker in grasping control of play and broke Maria in the fourth game to take a 3–1 lead. From that point on, there was no looking back for the American. She played safe volleys and relied on her opponent for the error. From a commanding 5–1 position, Billie Jean served out the set with a love game.

STOLLE, UNSEEDED, WINS U.S. CHAMPIONSHIP

by Richard Evans

The boomerang came back. Having been chucked into the outback of Forest Hills and Wimbledon during the previous twelve months, when not one of their number could win a place in either of the world's two leading grass court finals, the Australians came back—and in such profusion that the United States singles championships of 1966, men's division, should be spoken of hereafter with an Aussie twang. They not only provided the winner, Fred Stolle; the runner-up, John Newcombe; one other semi-finalist, Roy Emerson; and two other quarter-finalists, Owen Davidson and Bill Bowrey; but six of the seven seeds that were beaten in straight sets—an incredible fact in itself—were beaten by Australians.

(The seeds in order were Manuel Santana, Emerson, Dennis Ralston, Tony Roche, Arthur Ashe, Cliff Drysdale, Clark Graebner, and Cliff Richey. Stolle defeated Emerson, Ralston and Graebner; Newcombe beat Santana and Ashe; Mark Cox put out Roche; Bowrey beat Drysdale; and Davidson put out Richey. Santana was the only one to win a set in defeat, in the semi-finals. In the other semi-final Stolle butchered Emerson by the incredible score of 6–4, 6–1, 6–1, with an astonishingly fine display of serving and returning service.) . . .

And so it was Stolle and Newcombe to offer the final installment in the form-shattering saga of Forest Hills 1966. That these two should have emerged from the pack of hungry Australians that had been running amok in the draw was hardly surprising in retrospect, for they had produced, round by round, the most ruthlessly efficient tennis of the tournament. Yet anybody who had been bold enough to back them at the start would have deserved to be a rich man. Never in the history of Forest Hills had two unseeded players reached the final, and not since Mal Anderson—another Australian, of course—achieved the feat in 1957 had an unseeded player won the title. It had been an extraordinary week, but, short of some terrible accident or incredible recovery from the brink of defeat, there could be no more surprises now. Both players—27-year-old Stolle, the veteran finalist, and 22-year-old Newcombe, the teenage prodigy who was at last coming good—had an equal chance of victory, and the most the near-capacity crowd could hope for was an entertaining match of high quality tennis. They got it.

There was not much evidence of quality or equality, however, in the opening game as Stolle, having elected to serve, immediately wished he hadn't: he served two double faults to lose the game. That was just the gift Newcombe was looking for, and he roared away to a terrific start, serving like a bomb and volleying with tremendous confidence. Few players look quite so thoroughly aggressive and out-for-the-kill on court as Newcombe. With his huge springy stride, square shoulders and handsome features that contort and grimace with every mighty effort he makes, he seems to be hell-bent on landing the knockout punch before the referee stops the fight. At this stage, and for most of the match, his greatest punch was his service, which he hit with frightening power on the first delivery and unusual force on the second. Considering how much he chanced with that aggressive second serve, it was tribute to his accuracy that he produced no more than five double faults, three of those coming in the last three games of the fourth set.

The initial break was sufficient to bring Newcombe the first set, 6–4, despite the rise in Stolle's own game. Service, however, was the dominant factor, and 21 games passed in the second set with only two hints of a breakthrough. Stolle threatened first. At 5–4, he reached 40–30 on Newcombe's service with a belligerent forehand passer off a short smash. But Newcombe produced a service special on set point. Next it was Newcombe's turn to force the issue as he played a beautiful point at 9–all, retrieving a smash, pushing Stolle back onto the baseline with a great lob and following up with a drop volley that Fred could only glare at. Stolle double-faulted after that, and a fine service return down the line put him within a point of losing the game. But he survived as he received the blessings of the gods when Newcombe fell trying to reach a drop shot on the first point of the 22nd game and hurt his ankle. It was not serious but it took the edge off his speed and restricted his mobility when trying to move to the right. Perhaps if anyone had to have some luck in this match it was right that it should be Fred, for he has been on the wrong end of a final often enough in the past. Yet it was a cruel stroke for "Newk," who had been playing superbly up to this point. When a smash went out of court to put him 0–40 down, recovery was beyond him, and Stolle took the set, 12–10.

Having finally got a hand on the control throttle, Stolle never let go. His return of service improved, almost reaching the pitch of perfection it had achieved against Emerson, and his own service began to wear away at Newcombe's energy. A break for 5–3 gave him the third set, and, agreeing to forgo the ten-minute break because Newcombe was afraid his ankle would swell up, he struck again against service in the opening game of the fourth. But Newcombe immediately leveled at one–all. It was, nonetheless, his last gesture, for his service began to crack towards the end of the set and a double fault lost him the ninth game at love. Stolle reached 30–0 in the next game, turned from mid-court to walk back to the baseline and took three very long, very deep breaths. With his first major grass court title just two points away, he was suddenly feeling the tension. But he had watched Emmo from the wrong side of the net often enough at Wimbledon and elsewhere to know what to do, and he kept cool enough to make those two points his own. At last, Fred Stolle was the champ, the No. 1, and none deserved it better. But although a loser this time, it seemed that John Newcombe had arrived in a big way, for he had never played this well away from home. Ah, well, just another Aussie champion, biding his time.

MARIA BUENO IS WOMEN'S CHAMPION AGAIN

by Mary Hardwick

The great Maria Bueno, whose poise, artistry and exquisite touch are a joy to behold, and the tremendously talented Rosie Casals, the most exciting personality to rise from the ranks of the juniors since Little Mo Connolly burst upon the Forest Hills stage in 1951, gave the championships their finest hour with the epic semi-final battle which opened in the brilliant sunshine on the final weekend.

Both girls played some of the best tennis seen in the stadium for over a decade. Bueno eventually won in a match that had the packed stadium cheering repeatedly. Maria won the toss and chose to receive. She broke Rosie's service immediately and the set was soon hers at 6–2. Rosie was playing well: she seldom made a loose shot, scrambled for every ball, served furiously and continued to attack. Maria relaxed momentarily and a few errors crept into her game. The tiny Californian took command and reached 5–2 in the second set.

Maria, playing with the coolness of a great champion, fought back to 5–all, only to be thwarted by the gallant and crowd-pleasing challenger. Rosie held serve to lead 6–5. She was hitting magnificent top-spin forehands and scintillating winners from every part of the court. In the next game she had three set points. Maria saved them with beautiful serving and a magnificent smash. When Rosie lost her serve for 6–7, the match seemed over. But here Maria showed the strain and dropped her own service for 7–all. The little challenger from Golden Gate Park twisted and turned with acrobatic abandon, volleyed off her toes and passed Maria frequently. Rosie had her fourth set point at 8–7, but again Maria's coolness in the face of the unlimited energy of her uninhibited opponent helped her to level. At 9–all Maria had two points for the game but Rosie saved them with a lucky mis-hit off her racket handle and a "never say die" spirit. At 10–all the Brazilian faltered for the first time. There were some loose shots and an unwillingness to chase Rosie's lobs. Rosie closed it out on her fifth set point, 12–10.

After the rest period the great battle continued. The champion soon got a service break. Maria was somewhat weary of limb but her elegance was still unruffled. She closed out the match, 6–2, 10–12, 6–3, as the fans thundered their appreciation of the thrilling play.

The other semi-final was in great contrast to the epic on the stadium court. Nancy Richey was a strong and worthy winner over 19-year-old Kerry Melville of Australia (who had put out Billie Jean King). The match was played in the grandstand enclosure under the early evening shadows. The crowd flocked in and the seats were full, a tribute to Nancy's quiet personality and the attractive game of the charming Australian.

Nancy began strongly, hitting deep to the corners, and was soon 3–1. Kerry used her powerful forehand to level at 3–all. She was making the U.S. No. 1 work for every point, but the greater consistency of the Texan controlled most of the rallies. Nancy took the set at 6–3. Both girls have almost identical games—flowing deep drives off both wings, followed by a net attack only after a drive has opened up the court. Nancy, much more mature, was always the better of the two in winning the vital points and she ran out the second set 6–2.

The final. Maria Bueno won her fourth championship by crushing Nancy Richey, 6–3, 6–1. The first six games were evenly fought and both girls had uncertain moments. But at 3–all Maria found her range. She smashed with confidence and generated great pace off the ground to break into the lead at 4–3. From that moment on she played with the authority born of the knowledge of her own greatness. She is perhaps not quite as mobile as of old, but there are still brilliant shots in her repertoire, and the natural instinct of when to use them has never deserted her.

Nancy never stopped fighting, but her limitations of service power and her inability to vary her attack must always be exposed against a player of such skill as Bueno. After Maria won the first set, 6–3, she dominated the stage. There were moments when she showed disdainful contempt for her own errors—the frailty of a mistimed volley—but she was the complete artist as she swept onward to victory, 6–3, 6–1. Nancy had done as well as she could. Naturally she was bitterly disappointed at the outcome, but at least she knows that Maria at Forest Hills was a very different player than she had been at Wimbledon.

FOX'S AMAZING SWEEP IN LOS ANGELES TOURNAMENT

by Jeff Prugh

When the curtain ascended, the cast of characters read like a Cecil B. DeMille production: Roy Emerson, Fred Stolle, John Newcombe, and Tony Roche from Australia; Manuel Santana from Spain; Dennis Ralston and Arthur Ashe from the U. S. But the ending was strictly out of Alfred Hitchcock.

Who should happen to come along and emerge the hero? Why, none other than Allen Fox, of course. Allen Fox? That's right—Allen Fox, a guy who rides a motorcycle out of economic necessity, who studies post-graduate psychology out of vocational necessity, and who plays a defensive, patty-cake game of tennis out of physical necessity.

Physically, Fox seems miscast on a tennis court. He has thickly-muscled arms and legs that look as if they were borrowed from a weightlifter, and his sawed-off stature—all 5 feet, 7 inches of it—is about as awe-inspiring as that of an exercise boy at Hialeah. Mechanically, Fox is not a picture-book tennis player, either. We give you, for example, Exhibit A—the service. The hips swivel as if he were doing calisthenics; the arm coils in an unorthodox windmill-like fashion; and the delivery, for all its excess motion, is anything but overpowering.

Needless to say, the foregoing would scarcely qualify anybody to play the title role September 15–25 in Los Angeles' most glittering tennis extravaganza—the 40th annual Pacific Southwest Championships. Naturally, the person whom everybody had in mind for the male lead was, instead, an Emerson, a Stolle, a Santana, or perhaps, for the second year in a row, a Ralston. After all, each had been battle-tested from a summer of strenuous campaigning at Wimbledon, Forest Hills, and the Eastern circuit, while Fox was in a UCLA research lab, of all places, observing nervous systems of rabbits.

Moreover, Fox had just been in Philadelphia, attending his brother's wedding, and only decided to enter the tournament at the last minute. Nobody paid his entry fee for him, either, except Allen Fox. "Why, this title," he said laughingly, "cost me a whole nine bucks."

And when the seeding committee rated him No. 7 among domestic players and put him in a bracket that was loaded with perhaps the mightiest guns of any tournament this year, it clearly was open season on Fox. The world's foremost three players (Emerson, Santana, and Stolle) each took shots at him. And so did the world's No. 7 player (Roche). But the little Ph.D.-to-be scrambled spectacularly around the Los Angeles Tennis Club's center court and emerged without a scratch, not losing a set to any of them.

Not only did he knock off—in order—Santana, the king of Wimbledon; Roche, the French and Italian champion; Stolle, the U.S. titlist; and Emerson, the Australian champ (prompting Fox to remark, "That means I win the 'Grand Slam' "), but he won an audition for the U.S. Davis Cup team, which plays the Brazilian squad November 5, 6, 7 at Porto Alegre, Brazil.

"You bet he'll get a tryout," said the team captain, George MacCall, after Fox won the Pacific Southwest title for the first time by turning back Emmo in a surprisingly easy 6–3, 6–3 finale. "Any guy who can knock off these four guys on successive days certainly deserves every opportunity."

At 27, Fox would be the elder statesman—by three years—of the U.S. squad, yet would have but a modicum of Davis Cup experience, having won a single match against Iran in 1963 and having been a non-playing member in 1961.

Before Fox could cool off from his furious finish in the Pacific Southwest, MacCall hastily entered him in the Pacific Coast Championships the following week at Berkeley as the first step toward making the six-man entourage that would go to the South American championships in Buenos Aires before proceeding to the Interzone confrontation with Brazil on clay.

While clay is not Fox's surface, he says he likes it just the same. "I played on it for a year in Europe," he said, "and I play a control game, anyway, so that shouldn't matter too much." Tactically, Fox's control game was not hampered on cement, either, much to the red-faced chagrin of his victims and to the delight of a transistor radio-equipped gallery which found somebody else to cheer about besides the Dodgers.

If anyone's style was cramped on cement, it was that of Santana, who was making his first Pacific Southwest appearance in seven years and whose right ankle was not quite up to par after he had reinjured it at Forest Hills. "Those drop shots of his," said Fox, who wore down Manolo, 10–8, 6–2, on a searing 90-degree afternoon, "are not nearly so effective on this surface. They bounce too high. The footing is better than on grass, too, so I was able to cut off his passing shots."

Next came the quarterfinals and Roche, who fell so swiftly, 6–4, 6–1, that Fox had enough stamina left to go practice for a half-hour afterward with Cliff Richey (whose sore arm and thumb kept him out of competition).

Then came Stolle, who had been playing every bit as well as he did at Forest Hills and who had just demolished Rafael Osuna in 48 minutes, 6–3, 6–2. Miraculously, Fox broke Stolle's bullet service three times after trailing, 5–3, in the first set and broke early in the second to go ahead, 2–1, on the strength of two backhand passing shots in a row. From there, Fox never looked back in an 8–6, 6–4 semifinal victory that was more convincing than the scores indicated.

In the showdown for the title, Emerson was not quite the same methodically skillful player who had outlasted Ralston the previous day, 6–1, 7–9, 8–6, in a battle of smashes and lobs. But it was Fox's unerring backhand returns that cut off the power in Emmo's service and reduced his effectiveness. What's more, Fox scored most of his key break points on artistic, pinpoint lobs that seemingly hypnotized Emmo into submission in a match that took just 47 minutes. "It seemed like two hours," said Fox.

For the most part, Fox employed the same strategy against Emerson as he did Stolle. "Emmo is more mobile, though," said Fox. "He gets into the net a lot faster than Fred. Yesterday I was hitting them at Fred's feet. Today, I had to lob Emmo, and it worked."

Said Emerson afterward: "Everything I hit, he hit right back to me."

It was a fitting climax, indeed, to a tournament that had enjoyed its finest box-office success in years (all box seats had been sold out by opening day). A homegrown boy, Allen Fox, had made good. He was the darling of a highly partisan crowd, and he won the admiration of his victims, too.

As Cliff Sproule, manager of the Australian team, was saying when it was all over, "I think we'll stop raising kangaroos back home. Maybe we ought to raise some foxes, instead."

1967

THE AUSTRALIAN NATIONALS

by Adrian Quist

The War Memorial Drive tennis courts at Adelaide in South Australia are situated a few minutes away from the heart of the city, an ideal location for a sports arena. The courts are surrounded by trees and are only a stone's throw from the river on one side and from the world-famous Adelaide Cricket Oval on the other. The atmosphere is peaceful and gracious. In the background one sees the spires of St. Peter's Cathedral, and as spectators stroll past the gates of the cricket grounds to the courts, they pass a statue of a world-famous aviator who was born in South Australia and died in England. It is a memorial to Sir Ross Smith, erected by the people of South Australia, to commemorate the first successful flight by airplane from England to Australia, November 12–December 10, 1919.

The beautiful green grass courts at Adelaide are fast and true and they are the equal of Wimbledon. Therefore it was a fair test of skill on turf for the players, and the Championship was a great personal triumph for Roy Emerson. At the age of 30 he was thought to be past his peak, but he proved himself once again the best amateur in the world. His victim in the final was Arthur Ashe, whose languid, easy-going court manner has built up for him a reputation in Australia as a casual customer who works hard when the occasion demands. Last year Arthur captured the imagination of sportswriters and public by trimming both Emerson and Stolle in his first Australian tournament. When he left the country, he had impressed us as a gifted player with easy and natural movements, a great first service (the foundation of his game) and an attractive manner. However, his tennis seemed to lack that basic solidity necessary to reach championship heights, and although players agreed he was good on grass because he gained maximum value from his service, he was unpredictable and this lack of steadiness which is associated with "the unpredictable" gave him no chance of beating the best six or seven players on clay. . . .

The two main overseas contenders for the Australian title were Ashe and Cliff Richey. It is interesting to watch young Richey in action. At the moment he is a very good player who is desperately striving to become a great one. He played a fine match to beat left-handed Ray Ruffels in five sets in the last 16, and his quarter-final match with the greatly improved Tony Roche was very close. Roche won in five sets, but at two sets–all it was anyone's game. In the beginning of the match, when Roche snatched an early lead, the young American fought so hard to recover lost ground that the shots he missed were the result of highly accelerated emotion. Cliff has already made great strides by learning to control his temper, and he wants so hard to become a great player that one senses this in every movement he makes. A great deal will depend upon the next twelve months, and at the moment John Newcombe and Tony Roche both have an edge on him. The Australians relax when they are away from the game, whereas Cliff plays tennis mentally 24 hours a day. Perhaps if he could ease this inner tension, it would help him when he actually faces an opponent. I suggest my old friend, Don Budge, might teach him to throw the ball higher when he serves. His delivery is causing him to double-fault and he throws the ball too low in his efforts to reach the net.

Returning to Ashe, the American had no real opposition until he clashed with Owen Davidson in the quarter-finals. . . . Ashe won with fantastic ease, and his attitude toward the match was good. While Arthur was concentrating on every shot, Owen's attitude was much more casual. . . .

Now that Fred Stolle has turned professional, Australia is pinning its hopes on Newcombe and Roche to fill the singles berth on the 1967 Davis Cup team. Therefore it was important from the local viewpoint that Newcombe should beat Ashe. The two men took the court after the tremendous Emerson-Roche marathon in the late afternoon of January 28. Play was postponed because of darkness, with Arthur leading 12–10, 9–all. Spectators were admitted free on the next day (Sunday) and they came by the thousands, filling every seat in the stands. Even the sea gulls showed up, flying overhead at regular intervals. Perhaps it was the beautiful birds who inspired Ashe to greater heights, for he served a total of 37 aces. Newcombe, who had led at 5–2 in the second, only won it at 22–20, and the shot he made to break Ashe's serve for a 21–20 lead was purely a reflex motion. At 30–40 Ashe unleashed a bullet. John made a last second thrust with his racket and a crosscourt backhand flew past Arthur for a winner. Newcombe's face registered shocked surprise while Arthur's shoulders twitched up and down in disbelief. It was a marathon contest of 81 games in which service dominated. Ashe had served 37 aces, but Newcombe was not far behind with 26. Although the match lacked the all-around quality of the Emerson-Roche contest, it was a hard, bitter struggle with neither player giving an inch. I can never recall Ashe concentrating so hard, and when he lost the marathon second set he never flickered an eyelid. He won the third and fourth sets, 6–3, 6–2, but had he lost interest for even one game, I do not believe he could have won. Newcombe was waiting for some sign from Arthur which might indicate that concentration was slackening, but nothing happened except the flashing of rackets lashing out at forehands and backhands which, on many occasions, swept past the incoming Newcombe for outright winners. Arthur is still loose with many volleys and is not certain overhead, but when his first serve is functioning he is a very formidable grass court player. He finished off the match with two untouchable aces.

Emerson's path to the final was a much more dangerous one. He ran into trouble against young Bill Bowrey, winning out at 4–6, 6–4, 11–9, 16–14. Emmo had to fight to hold almost every service game, and the hot conditions and the consistency of Bowrey's passing shots would have broken the heart of a lesser player. But Emmo, his dark, saturnine face set in grim lines and his white floppy hat pulled down to ward off the hot sun, finally ran Bowrey right into the ground. . . .

The following day Emerson returned to the fray to face the greatly improved Tony Roche. Once again Emerson battled his way through 83 games in the hot sun—and it was the younger man who wilted. Emmo won the third set, 15–13, and Roche took the fourth, 15–13. But Roy knew before the match started that he would have to stay with every shot, that Roche had improved his first service and that his backhand was also better. Roy remained calm whereas Roche, who had matched Emerson shot for shot, began to show signs of strain in the fifth. Time and again Tony had been catching Emerson flat-footed with his backhand, but in the end it was Roy's persistence that finally caused Roche to falter. Emmo raced across court to save a few impossible shots—just enough to upset Roche, as one could see by looking at his face. He stared in amazement as Roy raced around in the heat. It was one of the finest tennis matches seen in Australia in the last ten years, and to outlast his young rival Emerson played as well as he has ever played in his career.

Thirty minutes after the women's singles match was over, Roy Emerson and Arthur Ashe strolled quietly through the crowd and onto the beautiful green Center Court. It was very hot and the spectators were sitting quietly and expectantly. They looked at Ashe as they would at any celebrity. They had read about his tremendous serving against Newcombe, and running through their minds was the thought that the unpredictable American might beat out the four-time Australian Champ. After all, Emmo was 30 and he should have been feeling tired after his close match against Roche. But no one is in better condition than Roy.

The first eight games were even, with both players clinging desperately to service. Suddenly a light southeasterly breeze sprang up and blew across the court. It was 4–all, with Ashe serving. The American double-faulted three times in the breeze and the score was love–40 for Emerson. Ashe served two thunderbolts to climb back to 30–40, pounded another big one in but Roy fumbled it back into play and Arthur missed a sitter. This was the service break and, as it turned out, the end of the match. Try as he did, Arthur could never get back into the play. Emerson raced through the second set, 6–1, and had gained enough confidence to guess fairly accurately the direction of Arthur's first service. I believe this was the reason for his success since it was noticeable that Ashe tried to increase the speed of his serve beyond his capacity. Consequently he overhit or found the net. Arthur made a determined bid for the third set when two great backhand passing shots broke through Emerson's opening service. Ashe led 2–love but failed to hold the advantage because he missed too many first volleys. Emerson achieved consistency on Ashe's first serve by pushing the ball into play. I am quite satisfied that Arthur is capable of missing the easiest shots imaginable, just as he is capable of playing the greatest ones. The court manners of both players were impeccable, and not for one second did Ashe stop fighting. He has beaten Emerson on previous occasions and he sensed right through the contest that he could win, even after trailing two sets to love. . . .

The ladies' singles missed the dominating personality of the seven-time champion, Margaret Smith. In Australia she was practically unbeatable and as yet there is no young player capable of stepping into her shoes.

Among the most impressive of the visitors was Rosemary Casals. She made something happen during every match and she reminded me of an India rubber ball—never still, bounding around the court, making many great shots and some very bad ones. At the moment Rosemary is too erratic, but when she learns to control her game this young American could become a very great player. Lesley Turner beat her in a close three set semi-final. . . .

The final between Nancy Richey and Turner was played in bright sunshine before a capacity crowd. Nancy was dressed in shorts and shirt with a short-sleeved sweater plus eyeshade and elastic bandage over her left knee. This was quite a contrast to the short mini tennis dress worn by Lesley. The American girl tackled this match just as an Australian wood-cutter would compete for the world's championships. Slowly and deliberately she pounded her drives, first to one corner, then to the other, just as the axeman chops his way through the logs. Lesley ran from side to side. The second set was close but, slowly, the precision shot-making of Richey broke up the Australian girl's game. The only emotion displayed by either player was the quaint skip of joy Nancy gave when she threw her racket in the air as the last shot flew over the baseline. Shirley Fry was the last foreigner to win the Nationals crown (ten years ago in 1957), and therefore the little skip of pleasure was understandable.

Nancy is not yet a great player. She is studied and methodical, something like a wound-up clock. Her grand strokes are solid and she eliminates errors but she does not have fast reflexes or lightning racket work. On the credit side, Nancy never quits and it takes a mighty good shot and a lot of bustling to throw her out of gear. Margaret Smith could do it, but Margaret is not around now and so Nancy's precision shot-making could win a few more big titles this year.

GONZALES' CHALLENGE TO LAVER

by Allison Danzig

In the autumn of his career, 39-year-old Richard (Pancho) Gonzales gave one of his most impressive performances yesterday in standing off the world champion, Rodney Laver of Australia, for 2 hours 55 minutes before accepting defeat in the final of the $15,000 professional indoor tennis tournament at the 71st Regiment Armory. The scores were 7–5, 14–16, 7–5, 6–2.

A slim rainy-day gathering of hardly more than 1,500, including Mayor

Lindsay and his family, cheered its encouragement for Gonzales as he won the 85-minute second set and challenged his youthful opponent with undiminishing vigor to 5–all in the third.

Up to this point, the big black-haired Californian, formerly the king of the courts, had lost his service just once in almost 2½ hours of play on the fast rubber court. It was truly an astonishing achievement against an opponent more than 10 years his junior, to whom Gonzales's craftily chipped and flicked returns of service were continuing anathema.

And then, in an instant, Gonzales, in one of his most heroic hours, lost the favor of the crowd, or most of it, and the magnificent tactical and physical effort he had made went down the drain, along with the resplendent image he had created. As Laver finished the 10th game with a service ace, Gonzales walked forward to the net and spoke severely to him, requesting that he take more time on his service. A linesman revealed after the match that Gonzales had made a passing remark during the play about Laver's "quick-serving him."

If such was the case, it was not apparent to this observer, though the rather slow-moving former champion might require more time to settle himself for the service than is normally needed. Never, so far as known, has Laver, a quiet, unassertive player, been faulted for his sportsmanship.

Gonzales's remark, audible in the stands, brought an outburst of boos. As play was resumed and Laver hit a blazing backhand return of service for a winner to start the 11th game, the most explosive cheer of the day went up. When Gonzales won the next point with a cannonball service ace, there was a responding roar, evidence that the Californian had not lost all his friends.

But from then on, Gonzales was never in the match again. Missing two volleys as he went in behind his service, which had scored the more aces in the match, he lost the game with a final double-fault, and Laver pulled out the 12th from 0–30 with two passing shots and an overhead for the set.

Following the intermission, Gonzales won the opening game of the fourth set after it had gone to deuce, and then Laver overwhelmed him. Hitting his ground strokes with a fury and control that had been lacking up to this time, and getting his wickedly spinning first service in play with a regularity heretofore lacking, the red-haired southpaw from Down Under raced through five games with the loss of only 7 points.

Gonzales stemmed the onslaught momentarily to win the seventh game, and then Laver finished the match in the eighth.

Gonzales took his defeat with good sportsmanship. He extended a friendly hand to his opponent, gathered his rackets and walked off amid a warm demonstration from the stands. Laver's salute from the crowd was every bit as warm as he left.

BILLIE JEAN KING SWEEPS WIMBLEDON

by Fred Tupper

Mrs. Billie Jean King has done it again. The bouncing, bespectacled 23-year-old from Long Beach, California, defeated an old rival, Mrs. Ann Jones of Britain, in precisely one hour today to take the coveted Wimbledon tennis crown for the second year in a row.

Before an enormous center court crowd—some of whom had queued all night—the top-seeded Mrs. King won, 6–3, 6–4, in a fascinating, fluctuating battle of styles amid gusts of wind that whipped the canopies over the Royal Box, kicked up puffs of dust on this sacred patch of turfdom and made playing conditions far from easy.

Today was Billie Jean's finest four hours. She came off court shortly after 7 P.M. wearily grinning in delight with all three women's titles—singles, doubles and mixed doubles—for the first triple sweep since Doris Hart pulled it off in 1951.

Yesterday, John Newcombe of Australia beat Wilhelm Bungert to take the men's singles.

In this topsy-turvy Wimbledon, where six of the eight male seeded players were gone by quarter-final time and the reigning champion, Manuel Santana, was upset by Charles Pasarell of the United States on opening day, Billie Jean was the only player in the field to justify her singles seeding.

The emergence of Roger Taylor of Britain into the semi-finals and of third-seeded Mrs. Jones into the finals, after six years reaching the semi-finals, brought vast crowds through the gates. The final attendance figures of more than 300,000 were the largest in the 81-year history of the All-England lawn tennis championships.

By her singles victory this afternoon Billie Jean became the first woman to win the title twice since Maria Bueno of Brazil did it in 1959 and 1960.

Mrs. King was the favorite because over the years, around the world, she had won 10 of her 13 matches against Mrs. Jones on the big occasions. Billie Jean was favored, too, because this was where she first made her reputation at the age of 18 by knocking out the great Australian, Margaret Smith, and where she blasted Miss Bueno to reach her first final at 19.

The Californian's big serve and volley game thrives on the fast grass of center court, and she was off to a splendid start. She held her first service, with three advantage points against her, but then she dived pell-mell into the attack.

Mrs. Jones had a plan today. She had survived an early onslaught by Rosemary Casals in the semi-finals by discarding her stonewall base-court game and taking command of the net. So on her opening service Ann bustled netward and Billie Jean fired her rockets.

A backhand ripped down the line, another shot across court, a lob pulled

Mrs. Jones back so that Billie Jean could volley a winner, and then another backhand streaked down the tape for the breakthrough.

Billie Jean just held her service to 3–love and suddenly was at 4–1 with a point for another break. It was beginning to look like a rout. The partisan crowd clapped perfunctorily as Mrs. King had the first set at 6–3.

Billie Jean quickly broke service again with two breathtaking ground shots through the holes. So there she was at 2–1 in the second set, riding high, with her booming service to come.

But Ann is not that easy to beat. Patiently she was slowing down Billie Jean, giving her a mixture of spin chops and lobs. Six times in that vital fourth game, the Briton had points to win it.

As the wind swirled around the court, Mrs. King began to miss the low volley. "I can't do it," she cried in distraction, but she held service to 3–1.

Mrs. King lost her next service, though, as Mrs. Jones increased the pressure, slapping a backhand shot down the line as the stadium exploded. They were at 3–all now, with Mrs. Jones toeing the service line.

With a magnificent volley, Billie Jean was at deuce and had the game as she wrong-footed the Briton again with a backhand down the line. It was more than the crowd could bear.

Billie Jean was serving for the match and, in a dying surge, Mrs. Jones was at advantage. Four times this afternoon she had been poised for a breakthrough. Once she had made it.

With the scent of victory near, the American fired her cannonballs into the corners. A last looping Jones drive slipped over the baseline, and Mrs. King again had her Wimbledon.

"It was my service that did it," she said. "And I wanted to win this one for my coach." Her coach, Frank Brennan of Upper Saddle River, New Jersey, suffered a heart attack here yesterday and was said to be resting comfortably in a hospital.

Editor's note: In the women's doubles final, Mrs. King and Rosemary Casals dethroned Maria Bueno and Nancy Richey, 9–11, 6–4, 6–2. Mrs. King and Owen Davidson of Australia defeated Miss Bueno and Ken Fletcher of Australia in the mixed doubles final, 7–5, 6–2.

NEWCOMBE WINS WIMBLEDON CROWN

by Fred Tupper

John Newcombe has won Wimbledon. The 23-year-old Australian demolished Wilhelm Bungert of Germany, 6–3, 6–1, 6–1, over 70 minutes today in an anticlimax to this wonderful fortnight, where reputations were shattered, upsets were routine and a new tennis generation made its breakthrough.

There have been other disappointing finals since the war. Jack Kramer allowed Tom Brown six games in 1947 in just 42 minutes, the fastest final ever; Lew Hoad lost five to Ashley Cooper in 1957; and Rod Laver five to Martin Mulligan in 1962.

Newcombe's shattering victory was the eighth for an Australian in the last 11 years, and the big burly man from Sydney, seeded third, was one of only two seeded players to reach the quarter-finals.

"I've wanted to win Wimbledon since I was ten," said Newcombe. "I thought I could win it when I got the service break I lost back in the first set."

Newcombe had a relative picnic all the way through. He dropped two sets in all, one to Stan Smith, the American No. 11, and the other to Nikki Pilic of Yugoslavia, the only player to extend him. The Australian has learned his trade well. He started playing tennis at 6, was coached weekends until he was 10, played his first Wimbledon at 18, and at 19 was the youngest Australian ever to play in a Davis Cup challenge round, with the United States the opponent.

Newcombe's shots are out of the textbook, hit with tremendous power. He is a net rusher and crowds it, probably too closely, but he is fit and fast enough to retreat for the smash or lob. His most effective weapon is that huge service, which he banged in game after game with brutal consistency this afternoon. It was like a hammerlock on Bungert. He broke it in the third game, but never after that.

Bungert is one of the last true amateurs, a shy, humorous man who enjoys his tennis and plays about six weeks a year, mostly for the fun of it. Yet the rigid stance, the jerky movement, the stoical mien all portray the Prussian image. He hit some ground shots standing at attention.

Wilhelm had a miraculous Wimbledon until this afternoon. The 28-year-old Düsseldorf sports dealer is a touch player and somehow always found it in the crisis. He takes the ball quickly on the rise, hits it suddenly at awkward angles for winners and is an effective volleyer. He played four 5-set matches, dropped nine sets on his way to the final and, he said later, "packed my bags four times during the fortnight."

In the early minutes today the German looked dangerous. At one-game-all, he struck like lightning. A forced error, a forehand rifled across court, a backhand down the line and another forced error gave him the game at love. He led, 2–1, with his service to come, and promptly made a botch of it. Three times he double-faulted in that long game, missed an easy smash and flubbed two volleys. Newcombe smiled with relief when he won it.

They were at 3–4 on service, Bungert leading 40–15, when the vital break came. Wilhelm just missed with a couple of volleys, and at add-out Newcombe crashed a forehand across court into the clear to lead, 5–3. He had the set in 25 minutes. From then on it was just a formality. Newcombe hurtled his service thunderbolts, Bungert became impatient and hurried his shots. Big John won his last service at love, and beamed as Princess Marina came on the court and handed over the silver cup. "Champagne tonight," he said.

WIMBLEDON'S FIRST PRO TOURNAMENT

by David Gray

"The amateurs have the best tournaments and we have the best players. It's a pity we can't get together," said Jack Kramer some time ago, stating the Great Dilemma for the 552nd time. It is good to report that over that quaint feast which the British call August Bank Holiday, the All-England Club took a large step in the direction of bridging the gap. Helped by BBC, who wanted a major attraction for color television, they held a professional tournament on the holy turf of the Center Court, until then wholly reserved for amateur feet.

The prize to the winner was $8400 out of a total purse of $35,000. It was the highest in the game's history and after a slow start (next time someone ought to do some serious work on publicity for All-England and the Pros), the experiment was an exciting success. Only half of the 9,500 seats were taken on the first day but there was "Standing Room Only" for the semi-finals and the finals. The grand climax was a singles battle in which Rod Laver defeated Ken Rosewall, 6–2, 6–2, 12–10.

Places in the tournament were gained by good performances in recent match play, with two notable exceptions. Pancho Gonzales, whose only summer outing had been at Fort Worth, and Lew Hoad, a reluctant competitor nowadays, were invited because it was agreed they would pull in the crowds. Gonzales and Hoad repaid the compliment by entertaining the crowd from teatime to dusk with a match which Hoad won by 3–6, 11–9, 8–6 and which more or less saved the first day.

They had to follow three slightly disappointing matches. First, Stolle had the unenviable task of facing Laver. From the start Rod looked as though he were going to win the tournament. Stolle, long-legged and sad-eyed, gazed at Laver reproachfully across the net. It didn't seem fair for anyone to be so good. Dennis Ralston fared even worse. He couldn't control his service—7 double-faults made it just like old times—and he couldn't find a foothold. One hadn't seen anyone fall so often on the famous turf since the days when Karen Susman used to play there. Gimeno, amiable and elegant, beat him 6–1, 6–2. Butch Buchholz did better, but all his confidence and certainty seemed to disappear at the moment when a rather discomposed Rosewall was struggling. Buchholz, beaten 5–7, 6–2, 6–3 in the end, won the first set and at 3–3 in the third looked more enterprising than the Australian, but two crops of double double-faults in successive games spoilt his chance.

Up to then the applause had been polite, respectful but a little cold. Then Hoad and Gonzales provided the real stuff. Pancho, at 39, looked sharp and fit, and he quickly took the initiative. Hoad, seven years younger, was suffering from a shortage of match play and the passing of time. At first he did not move at much more than a jog-trot: waning autumn was the mood of his first set. Some lovely shots were full of the old majesty, but they made his decline all the more melancholy. Gonzales, the old black panther, teasing him and wounding him, took the first set easily, but suddenly the old magic began to flow back into Hoad's shots. His daring and authority returned. Gonzales was tired and found it difficult to maintain the pressure. When Hoad captured the second set, Wimbledon became alive. You stopped thinking how good Lew had once been and started to applaud the brilliant and bold strokes he still could make. The match no longer had merely an antiquarian interest but a dynamic existence of its own. In the third set Hoad twice had to win his own service from 0–40 and both times he frustrated the older player. When Hoad finally won with a forced lob which eluded Gonzales and dropped on the middle of the baseline, Pancho hit a ball so hard and so high out of court that it landed somewhere in Bristol. Furiously he threw down his racket before congratulating Hoad. Did I hear someone say that enthusiasm and the desire to win diminish with the years?

Hoad could not repeat the trick of recapturing the past in the semi-finals. Rosewall beat him 6–2, 6–2, winning seven successive games from 2–2 in the first set. As with every Hoad-Rosewall match, there was a fascinating contrast in style and character. Rosewall was wonderfully economical, his length immaculate, his lobbing was the perfect means of turning defense into attack, and his concentration and discipline were astonishing. He aimed at perfection. Hoad was splendidly imperfect. He must have been tired after his long battle on the previous evening, but he was still in the mood to play well. Everything he did was extravagant—he hit powerful and spectacular winners and, enjoying living dangerously and dying well, he made mistakes on an equally large scale. Rosewall punished him remorselessly for every untidy stroke.

Ken must have found this exercise in the art of restraining a powerful hitter good practice for dealing with Laver but, if anything, Gimeno came closer to puzzling the top professional in their semi-final, which Laver won 6–3, 6–4, than Rosewall did in the final. Gimeno rallied beautifully and there were two games in which he might well have captured Laver's service, but the Australian knew where to serve when in danger. Gimeno was vulnerable to the low ball on the backhand. On three crucial occasions the return was a grope rather than a shot.

The final was an important contest for the pros. The Center Court at Wimbledon is the biggest shop-window in the game. Success meant continuation of the event. Success is judged by the gate and the quality of the play, both of which were outstanding. And yet Laver and Rosewall cannot have felt the same burden of tension that Newcombe and Bungert labored under when they played the amateur final two months before. At the amateur Wimbledon the drums of history, publicity and national pride never stopped beating. Most of the world takes an interest in the outcome. People care less if Laver beats Rosewall or vice-versa. It isn't a national tragedy if one man gets £3000 and the other only £2000.

The pros begin with a background of confident achievement and the fact that they play each other so often and know each other's strengths and weaknesses so well takes some of the strain from even their biggest occasions. The prize at Wimbledon may have been the highest ever, but the contenders had been rivals week in and week out for five years. It was no wonder that, compared with the amateurs, their approach to this match seemed unemotional, almost clinical. There were even times when that elusive thing called "heart" seemed to be missing—but the compensation was that it was possible to watch the two greatest masters of the game attacking each other with businesslike determination and taking risks which their talent made it possible for them to calculate to the last degree of audacity. What they did was to show how good first-class lawn tennis on grass can be. Either Rosewall or the occasion brought the best out of Laver. The quality of the returns of service, Rod's fierce backhands, Rosewall's elegant passing shots and Laver's serving in the first two sets were superb. Having grown used to margarine, it was good to be reminded of the taste of butter.

In the first set Rod was 0–40 down on service at 2–1, pulled it out to be 3–1 and then took seven more games in a row. There was never much doubt that Laver would win, but he could not maintain the breathtaking pace of his first two sets and as soon as the pressure slackened Rosewall made his challenge. Ken led 5–2 in the third and Laver had to save three set points before he regained the ascendancy and pocketed the major share of the cash. Afterwards Gonzales and Gimeno won the doubles with great gusto, and Gimeno beat Hoad 6–3, 6–3 in the playoff for third place. . . .

It is a pity that no one thought of staging this event five years ago. The pros then would have looked even more impressive than today.

GRAEBNER'S MIRACLE AGAINST LESCHLY

by Allison Danzig

Clark Graebner worked a miracle yesterday and stands as the first United States player to reach the final round of the national men's grass court tennis championship since 1963.

To the tumultuous cheers of 13,000 in the Forest Hills Stadium in Queens, the ruggedly built youth from Beachwood, Ohio, the conqueror of Roy Emerson in the quarter-finals, defeated Jan Leschly after being all but demoralized in the first two sets by the incredibly fine tennis of the talented, fast-moving Dane.

Helpless to win more than a single point on Leschly's left-handed service in any game until the seventh of the third set, unable to get his powerful service to function in anything like the fashion it did against Emerson, and staggered by the regularity with which Leschly knocked back his service and threaded the narrowest opening with his passing shot, Graebner looked to be a hopelessly beaten and dispirited young man at the end of the second set. And then, to the astonishment and joy of the big gallery, which had resigned itself to his defeat, Graebner picked up in strength and confidence as Leschly let up just a bit in his attack and began to make errors for the first time. They cheered him hopefully as he broke service for the first time in the eleventh game and won the third set, exulted as he did it again in the fourth set and roared their solid encouragement as he went on to victory in the fifth, with his service sending the ball catapulting for aces.

As the umpire called the score, 3–6, 3–6, 7–5, 6–4, 7–5, Graebner, tossing his steel racket in the air, went sailing across the net. At the same time the good-natured Leschly went flying across from his side, too, and then, with the crowd shrieking with mirth, jumped back across, and the two players fell into each other's arms.

It was an appropriate finale to a match in which Graebner had called a point against himself as the ball from Leschly's racket, unknown to anyone else, ticked his own on the way to overreaching the baseline. Graebner thereby lost his service as he appeared on the verge of ending the match in the tenth game of the final set. Leschly took repeated close calls against him on the lines and foot-faults with good sportsmanship.

Today Graebner, who has confounded all expectations after a season barren of particular distinction, will play John Newcombe of Australia, the champion of Wimbledon and runner-up to Fred Stolle of Australia in the final here a year ago. Newcombe defeated Gene Scott of New York, the victor over Owen Davidson Friday, in the other semi-final, 6–4, 6–3, 6–4.

Scott, who also had surpassed expectations in getting so far in the tournament, offered a strong challenge for the first two sets with his clever backhand returns of service, his solid serving and his tactical soundness. In both sets, after having lost his service, he had big chances to get back on even terms. It was not until the third set that Newcombe showed the full strength of his game. His first service began to go in and he hit his backhand with his accustomed eclat, and Scott was helpless to hold him in check.

Mrs. Billie Jean King of Berkeley, California, the Wimbledon champion, and Mrs. Ann Haydon Jones of Britain, the Wimbledon runner-up, will meet for the women's crown. Mrs. King defeated Françoise Durr, the champion of France, 6–2, 6–4, and Mrs. Jones won by the same score from Lesley Turner of Australia.

Jaroslav Drobny of Britain, who won the men's championship at Wimbledon in 1954, retained his national senior title. He defeated Gardnar Mulloy of Miami in the final, 6–8, 6–3, 6–1.

It is not often that anyone plays the magnificent tennis that Leschly did for two sets yesterday and comes off the court the loser. His mastery of the racket was little short of wizardry, so consistently did he do the seemingly impossible. His spinning service was so fast and unreachable that Graebner could only make futile stabs at it. More remarkable was the fidelity of his backhand in knocking back the American's service for winners, or putting him under fearful strain in making his volley, and in knifing through slits for passing shots.

His volleying had the touch of a Cochet in its nonchalant ease. Overhead he was cataclysmic. And most confounding of all, such was his speed and balance that he could dash far beyond the sideline for a volley that looked to be beyond redemption and hit a stunning winner past the dazed and unbelieving Ohioan.

No one could have faulted Graebner if he had thrown in the sponge against such super tennis as this, particularly since his service was so recalcitrant and he could not summon any touch, either at the net or in his ground strokes. That Graebner did not abandon the fight and went on to victory is a testimonial to his great fortitude. For a few minutes near the end it appeared that he might let the match get away from him after he had put on a stampede that carried him through three love games in a row and 14 successive points early in the final set.

Losing the fifth game and the opportunity virtually to seal matters after leading at 40–15 on Leschly's service, he nevertheless went to 5–3. The Dane won the ninth game at love and the gallery was prepared to see Graebner serve out the match in the tenth. Instead, he lost his service after having voluntarily given up the point that would have made the score 30–15 in his favor, and Leschly was back in the running at 5–all. But in the eleventh game Graebner tossed up three lobs and Leschly, who had hardly missed one for the first three sets, put all of them in the net or out of court and lost his service. In the next game he went from 0–30 to 40–30, a stroke from 6–all, but Graebner's service thwarted him, and the match of 2 hours, 37 minutes came to an end.

NEWCOMBE AND MRS. KING WIN U.S. TITLES

by Allison Danzig

John Newcombe of Australia and Mrs. Billie Jean King of Berkeley, California, added the United States championship to their Wimbledon titles yesterday and stand indisputably as the monarchs of amateur tennis the world over.

The 23-year-old Mrs. King became the first player of this country since 1961 to win the women's title when she repeated her victory in the Wimbledon final over Mrs. Ann Haydon Jones of Britain, 11–9, 6–4, as 10,000 looked on in the stadium of the West Side Tennis Club at Forest Hills, Queens.

Mrs. King stands also as the first woman player to win the triple crown of singles, doubles and mixed doubles in both the British and American championships since Alice Marble garnered them in 1939. Rosemary Casals of San Francisco and Owen Davidson of Australia were her doubles partners.

Newcombe, also 23, who was runner-up a year ago to Fred Stolle of Australia, ended the striking progress of Clark Graebner of Beachwood, Ohio, through the tournament by winning the final, 6–4, 6–4, 8–6. They had met also at Wimbledon, where Newcombe was the winner, 17–15, 6–3, 6–4.

So the title went to a player other than a representative of the United States for the 12th successive time since 1955, when Tony Trabert was the winner.

Harold Brown, the Secretary of the Air Force, presented the trophies to the champions and runners-up. He was assisted by Robert J. Kelleher, the president of the United States Lawn Tennis Association, and Henry Benisch, the president of the West Side Tennis Club.

The presence of a home player in the final of the men's championship for the first time since 1963 probably accounted for the crowd of 10,000 that turned out despite threatening weather following a morning rain.

Graebner's unexpected success in having defeated Roy Emerson in a match lasting almost three hours and his sensational comeback victory over Jan Leschly of Denmark, after he had lost the first two sets, in another marathon of 2 hours 37 minutes had nurtured hopes that at long last a player of this country would win the championship.

These hopes were dispelled before the match was 10 minutes under way. Newcombe had not been playing too impressively in the tournament, but now he demonstrated immediately that he was razor sharp and in the mood for swift execution.

Fast on his feet, merciless in fighting with all his fury for every point and intimidating with his service and backhand return of service, he got on top at once. After Graebner had won the opening game on service, the big Australian took the next five games, and the glum gallery had a sense of Graebner's impending doom.

Graebner's service was not functioning. He was double-faulting and failing to get the first ball in play, and Newcombe was knocking back the second serve for winners or to provoke the volleying error or to set up the winning shot for him.

When Newcombe broke service at love to start the second set as Graebner double-faulted on the final point, the futility of the American's cause was apparent. Graebner made a brave fight in the long second game, only to be thwarted by two successive aces, and Newcombe won his next three service games at love.

Then came a turn, and hopes began to revive. Newcombe lost some of his fire in the third set and Graebner's service began to hit for aces, while his backhand was suddenly performing like his opponent's. He was passing Newcombe and forcing him into repeated volleying errors.

Could Graebner be on the way to repeating his rally against Leschly? It seemed he could as he went ahead at 5–2, breaking service with four beautiful backhand returns and serving aces galore in game after game to the cheers of the gallery.

But Newcombe, regaining his control, came back on the attack with power and accuracy and a deadliness at the net that put him again in command. He ran through three games with the loss of only 3 points.

Graebner caused a final stir as he hit three successive aces to win the 11th game, but after that he could win only 3 more points.

Mrs. Jones gave Mrs. King her stiffest fight of the tournament, in which the champion did not lose a set. The performance of the left-handed British player was all the more commendable because she was handicapped by the recurrence of a pulled hamstring muscle that had her hobbling at times in the first set and caused her to fall in pain in the fourth game of the second set.

Mrs. King ran to her opponent's assistance, as did the referee, Dan Johnson, and linesmen. Mrs. Jones resumed play shortly to a burst of applause.

Mrs. King won largely on her speed and volleying ability. But she was challenged severely throughout. The games were unusually prolonged and the two sets required an hour 37 minutes.

1968

RICHEY WINS U.S. INDOOR CHAMPIONSHIP

by Allison Danzig

Cliff Richey attained another peak in his tennis career today.

The 21-year-old Texan, winner of the national clay-court title in 1966 (as was his sister Nancy in the first sister-brother crowning) and victor in both of his singles matches in the 1967 Davis Cup fiasco against Ecuador, succeeded Charles Pasarell of Puerto Rico as the United States indoor champion.

Before a capacity crowd of 4,000 at the Civic Center [Salisbury, Maryland], Richey defeated Clark Graebner of Beachwood, Ohio, and received one of the most prolonged demonstrations of his career. Graebner, who follows the Texan in the ranking at No. 4 and who was runner-up for the national grass-court championship at Forest Hills last year, had eliminated Pasarell in the semi-finals here, but was unable to win a set today.

Troubled by the raw blisters in the palm of his right hand and perhaps feeling the effects of his 3 hours 12 minutes of play against Pasarell yesterday, Graebner was unable to bring the full might of his service to bear, perceptibly softened his whole game in the second set and was beaten, 6–4, 6–4, 6–4.

Richey's progress to the final round was marked by victories over Stanley Smith of Pasadena, California, who had eliminated Arthur Ashe, and Jan Leschly of Denmark, a semi-finalist at Forest Hills. He did not consistently play the quality of tennis he did in those two triumphs, but he is an extraordinarily determined competitor of unsurpassed desire and intensity of purpose, and his skill at the volley and overhead, his quickness of movement, his fine backhand and his service enabled him to hold command of the court.

Graebner, who was first troubled with blisters during his match with Pasarell, has a casual manner and a rather languid way of moving that can be deceptive. Today they typified his lack of confidence, owing to the condition of his hand, and he seldom played with any fire or brought to bear the full power of service and stroke that he commands. His forehand return of service was unreliable and too often he failed on vital shots when there was little provocation and the opening was presented.

Richey won the opening set on a break in the seventh game when he hit one of his many fine straight backhand passing shots and threw up a lob and Graebner double-faulted.

In the second set, which found Graebner letting up on his service and stroking the ball softly on his passing shots, the Texan hit three passing shots, two from the backhand, to break through in the fifth game.

Graebner retaliated in the sixth, the only time he broke service, with two clever returns of service for winners and two others that extracted the volley error. But the Ohioan's control weakened badly in the seventh and he found the net five times to lose the game and ultimately the set.

The outcome of the match was now seen to be fairly inevitable. Graebner obviously did not have the vitality or the security of stroke to rise to the challenge of a two-set deficit.

The gallery was sympathetic and gave him its full-hearted encouragement, and it seemed he might get back into the fight as he won his first two service games decisively. But after losing the fourth game despite his four beautiful winning strokes, he yielded his service in the equally long fifth to Richey's four blazing backhand passing shots, three in succession down the line.

Graebner was unable to get back on level terms as Richey's service scored heavily, and shortly the Texan was tossing his racket into the air in jubilation and leaping across the net to greet his beaten foe.

The doubles championship was won by Tomas Koch of Brazil and Tom Okker of the Netherlands. In the final round they defeated Smith and Robert Lutz of Los Angeles, 6–3, 10–12, 8–6.

Late last night Smith and Lutz won, 13–11, 4–6, 6–3, from Bobby Wilson and Mark Cox of Britain, who had beaten Pasarell and Ronald Holmberg in the quarter-finals, 26–24, 17–19, 30–28, in 6 hours 20 minutes.

Pasarell received an award for his outstanding sportsmanship.

BOURNEMOUTH: THE WORLD'S FIRST OPEN

by Linda Timms

It was a long, hard winter. But finally, on April 22nd, when the politics had to stop, Open tennis came to life. The first Open tournament in the world, the 1968 Hard Court Championships of Great Britain, took place at the West Hants Club, Bournemouth, and from the moment the first touring professional stepped on the center court it all went like something which was meant to succeed. The ILTF talked Britain out of flinging Pandora's Box wide open; they may or may not be glad to know that, when the corner of the lid was lifted, no hideous troubles jumped out, only an abundance of excitement and promise.

In a way it was an odd tournament. The distant prospect was magnificent, but when the draw appeared it looked so disappointing that one could almost envisage a flop. It turned out to be one of the most thrilling weeks anyone could remember. The professional entry consisted of George Mac-Call's team (Rod Laver, Ken Rosewall, Andres Gimeno, Pancho Gonzales, Roy Emerson and Fred Stolle) plus the British official coach, Owen Davidson, and a figure from the past, Luis Ayala, now coaching in Puerto Rico, who paid his own fare in order to compete. But where the world's leading "amateurs" should have come, there was just a big gap; no top class foreign player competed. It is not clear why: perhaps they were afraid of contaminating themselves in this most confused of seasons, but the fact is that when it came time to be counted, not one of the world's or even of Europe's top ten turned up.

The remaining entry—all the British players (except Mike Sangster) and a sprinkling of lesser Australians—looked a couple of classes below the pros. And, indeed, the most consistent money-winner of them all, Ken Rosewall, took the cup and the first prize of £1000. But it was Mark Cox, the British No. 3, who for a mere £50 expenses and £4 semi-finalists' prize, showed them all the way home. To the immense delight of all concerned for the Open game (except perhaps Gonzales and Emerson) he demonstrated that it doesn't necessarily take a Santana or a Pietrangeli to beat a professional and set a tournament alight.

The only respect in which the amateurs showed caution, in fact, was over the expenses-prize money option. Almost all of them went cannily for the flat rate of £50 for the week plus the old amateur prizes. Most of them, of course, made a slight profit this way in the face of such opposition. But Mark Cox would have won a £250 prize he could never have dreamed of, and Virginia Wade, who retained her title, eschewed the £300 which the British women regarded as such an inadequate first prize compared with the men's rewards.

On court, by contrast, the amateurs were all robust aggression and optimism. They realized that it was not they but the professionals who were being thrown to the lions; that they had nothing to lose and history to make, while the pros were defending their august position for the first time in the rough-and-tumble of free competition. The pressure was heavily on the professionals: for once, who stole their purse stole trash; it was reputation that at all costs they must not lose. They may have taken a harsher battering than they anticipated, but when the tension subsided, it was clear that they were not diminished so much as everyone else was exhilarated. The word started to get around: they are human, they have nerves, they can make mistakes, they can be upset by an inspired opponent just like any mere Wimbledon champion. Realization of such evident truths can do nothing but whet the appetites of both players and spectators for more of the same. Paradoxically, the pros gained more from the startling results at Bournemouth than if they had swept the board.

It really was Mark Cox's week. He beat Pancho Gonzales, 0–6, 6–2, 4–6, 6–3, 6–3, and Roy Emerson, 6–0, 6–1, 7–5, before losing 6–4, 6–1, 6–0, to Rod Laver at his totally uncompromising best. At this time, Cox had never even played a Davis Cup singles. After spending three years at Cambridge University with only limited time for tennis, he gave himself two years to make it as a tennis player, and only began to show real improvement on the Caribbean circuit this spring. When he met Gonzales, who had just majestically annihilated Clay Iles from the baseline, Cox was strong, fit, fast and in form. Gonzales, on the other hand, at nearly 40, had not played a five-set match for five years. Cox, after a first set which made him wonder if he would get a game in the match, prodded the old man-eater with more and more daring. Gonzales prowled, snarling and wounded, but could not make the kill, and Cox's fierce forehand and young legs put Gonzales out of the first Open tournament.

Gonzales, we said, is an old man now, unaccustomed to unfamiliar opposition. It will be different when Cox plays Roy Emerson, the fittest of the fit and the newest recruit. All very logical, but neither Cox nor Emerson nor anyone else had any use for logic when Cox won twelve of the first thirteen games. It still makes one look twice when one sees the score sheet, but the simple answer is that Cox was as strong and confident as before, showing no signs of reaction from the previous day. Emerson played terribly badly. His forehand had been unreliable in his first round match when it did not matter, and in this match he never controlled it at all until the third set when, with all the fighting spirit that won him two Wimbledon titles, he led 4–1 and reached set point at 5–4. But when he missed, his resistance collapsed. Cox broke him to love, winning 11 points in a row, and on the first match point Emerson put a forehand appropriately into the net. No one begrudged Cox such a superb victory and no one now could possibly breathe the word "fluke"—two in two days must mean something. But it was sad for Emerson, the last player on whom anyone would wish such a humiliating defeat.

All parties are over sometimes, and Cox's time to call it a day came in the semi-final. His score against Laver was inglorious but his performance was not. Laver, who had the advantage now of knowing what he was up against, paid him the compliment of pulling out all stops. He turned on that combination of brilliance and total accuracy which at its highest is almost unplayable. Cox lived with it only briefly, but the length and quality of the rallies said much for him, even if he did not win many. He lost in three quick sets.

In contrast the other half was quiet and orderly. Rosewall allowed no hindrance in coming through to the final, not even from Gimeno who had been looking in splendid form.

The final itself was in many ways a disappointment. First, after a week of Wimbledon weather, it rained, just to remind us that we were still at good old Bournemouth. The first part of the match was played in bitter cold and steadily mounting drizzle. It was abandoned with Rosewall leading 3–0 in the third set, and when it was resumed at the ungodly hour, for the pros, of 10 A.M. the next day, he won quickly 3–6, 6–2, 6–0, 6–3. The standard of play in the match was lower than one had hoped, mainly because Laver utterly failed to reproduce his semi-final form. He seemed out of sorts with the conditions, himself, and in particular his backhand. Now and again he roused himself to win a breathtaking rally, but most of the time Rosewall, hitting cleanly and economically, dictated matters from the baseline. Still, one can hardly complain; finals often fail to live up to the earlier rounds, and this tournament was too good to be marred even by a final infinitely worse than this one.

For years, the women's event predominated at Bournemouth; this time, it was definitely a side issue. No professional took part, and as a result Virginia Wade, the holder, was top seed. Her chances were greatly improved by the much regretted last-minute withdrawal of an ailing Julie Heldman, who should have met her in what could have been a fascinating final. As it turned out, the runner-up was Winnie Shaw who . . . attacked bravely but lost her accuracy when forced to play at Virginia's pace. The score was 6–4, 6–1.

When it first became clear some months ago that Bournemouth would stage the world's first Open, it seemed faintly ironical. One had been carping for years about the wretched weather, the lack of first class players and the general need for the LTA to *do* something. They certainly did something; they dropped into the lap of the Hard Court Championships committee the fattest and juiciest plum of them all. It is satisfying to be able to conclude that Bournemouth, 1968, was equal to all its opportunities. . . . Six times as many tickets as usual were sold in advance, the center court seats were packed solid for most of the week, and the total gate receipts were just over £12,000. If anyone doubted that Open tennis would galvanize public interest overnight, here was their answer.

It was a little surprising that overseas countries, both for and against the Open game, did not send observers to see the unimaginable phenomenon actually take shape. If they had come, they would have seen, as we did, that there is nothing bizarre or monstrous or shocking about amateurs playing professionals. On the contrary, it seemed natural, straightforward and obvious, and one could only wonder why it had never happened before. And that is the best argument of all for Open tennis.

FEDERATION VOTES FOR OPEN TOURNAMENTS

by Fred Tupper

In a historic decision, the International Lawn Tennis Federation voted unanimously today for open tennis. That means that professionals will be allowed to compete against amateurs in a limited number of tournaments. Not one dissenting voice was heard as the entire agenda was approved with resounding applause at this extraordinary general meeting, fittingly enough held in the Place de la Concorde.

"It was an incredible result achieved here," said Bob Kelleher, president of the United States Lawn Tennis Association, "in a spirit of highest cooperation and friendliness."

Until today, the federation had adamantly voted down over the years all attempts to introduce open tennis. In 1967 at Luxembourg, the open proposal was defeated, 139 votes to 83. The British had made approval possible. In an unparalleled decision, they announced last October they would make the 1968 Wimbledon tournament an open. They said that in the future all players in Britain would be simply "players," not amateurs or professionals. And the British said they were ready to risk expulsion from the federation to make open tennis possible. Country after country fell into line, and today the world agreed.

Specifically, the federation approved these things:

"Retention of the notion of amateurism in the rules of the I.L.T.F., as its removal would indisputably weaken the ideal which the I.L.T.F. has the duty to protect and develop." Creation of officially recognized amateur championships; for example, championships of Europe, etc.

"Rights of national associations to self-determination regarding the status of their players, except where relations with professionals are concerned. On this point, in view of international complications, a common international policy must be established by the federation. Professionals may play against other players only in events organized by a national association or an affiliated body if that event has been declared open to all by the federation.

"Creation of a strictly limited number of open tournaments under the authority of the federation, each one sanctioned by the federation."

The words need translation. What the federation is prepared to recognize is the following categories of tennis players: the "amateur" who is not paid, the "registered" player, who can profit from the game while not making tennis his profession, and the "professional," who makes his money from teaching or playing in events not organized by the national associations.

Everybody seemed happy.

"It's a wonderful thing," said 70-year-old Jean Borotra, who had won Wimbledon as long ago as 1924. "Amateurism is preserved. I've been repaid for the six months it took out of my life to make this possible." The British were pleased. They continue their own interpretation of "players" as just that, neither amateurs nor pros, but they recognize the rights of other nations to call them what they want.

The United States voted for open tennis at Coronado, California, in February and had worked here solidly behind the scenes all week for its success. Kelleher will now reconvene the adjourned Coronado meeting next Saturday at Dallas to decide where and if the U.S.L.T.A. will stage an open tournament this year.

Under the new conditions the open tourney would logically be held in Forest Hills, Queens, the site of the national amateur championships, in early September.

"I don't know whether Forest Hills wants an open," said Kelleher. "We'll know at Dallas." Another site, he intimated, might be Cleveland, where Davis Cup and Wightman Cup matches have been successfully held.

There is bound to be bickering in a Committee of Management meeting tomorrow, when it must be agreed how many open tournaments will be apportioned to each country this year. The British, for example, have asked for nine. The number will undoubtedly be reduced under protest. The Australians are reported to want opens for their various states, possibly as many as six. The French will probably have one to replace their national championships at Roland Garros Stadium in Paris in May.

Further difficulties are foreseen in the administration of when and where some categories of players can play others. But in the flush of victory today, these matters seem irrelevant.

"You have to creep before you can crawl," Kelleher said, "and the evolutionary process will take time."

The federation has 65 member nations. The meeting was attended by 86 representatives from 47 nations.

PARIS BLUES

by Linda Timms

Traditionally, Paris in the spring stands for youth, hope and romantic idealism; in lawn tennis terms it now means disillusion and disingenuousness. From October 5th, 1967, to March 30, 1968, the British Lawn Tennis Association had conducted a campaign for honest open tennis which was impressively brave, uncompromising, outspoken and unflinching in the face of opposition. The annual general meeting of the L.T.A. had voted overwhelmingly on December 14th in favor of their council's resolution "that all reference to amateurs and professionals be deleted from the rules." We were, it seemed, committed irrevocably, beyond possibility of conciliatory maneuver, and the International Lawn Tennis Federation would have to make up its own mind what to do about us.

Can it really be true that, after all the sound and fury, we shall have just four open tournaments in Britain in 1968, and that the Federation now recognizes not one category of players, not two as previously, but four? Yet such was the outcome of the extraordinary general meeting of the I.L.T.F. in Paris on March 30th. There are so many ways of regarding the Federation's decisions—after all, chaos must have a kaleidoscope of facets—that it is best to start with such hard or semi-final facts as did emerge.

First, the Swedish resolution in support of Britain, which was the original reason for the convening of the meeting, was withdrawn. This was the result of urgent preliminary lobbying in which it became clear that when it came to the crunch, neither Australia nor the United States was prepared to stand by Britain in defying the rest of the Federation. Instead, therefore, the meeting simply considered "The Report of the Committee of Management on the Subject of Amateurism," which was essentially based on those findings of the subcommittee on amateurism which the L.T.A. had so scornfully dismissed in February.

On the Saturday morning, basking in the kind of unseasonal sunshine that made one feel it must be time to be on the way to the Stade Roland Garros, we were stopped in our tracks by this document, which, though one tried not to credit it, was indeed the writing on the wall. The committee of management unanimously—that is, with the support of its British member, Mr. Eaton Griffith, included—adopted the following recommendations:

(1) The retention of the notion of amateurism in the rules of the I.L.T.F., and the creation of restricted amateur championships.

(2) The right of national associations to self-determination regarding the status of players *except where relations with professionals are concerned* (my italics).

(3) The creation of a strictly limited number of open tournaments, each one sanctioned by the I.L.T.F.

It emerged later that the four categories of players to be recognized by the Federation are as follows: amateurs, registered players, players (any form of combination of the preceding two) and professionals. The professional is defined as one "who gains pecuniary advantages either from the teaching of the game . . . or from taking part in events which are not organized by the national association of the country where they are held (a touring professional)." The registered player, on the other hand, is "authorized to derive material profit from the game whilst not making lawn tennis his profession." This profit-making amateur (haven't we met him somewhere before?) may play practically anywhere, while the touring pro has been pushed even more firmly outside the official fold, if that is possible; in this so-called new age of liberalism, he may not play in "any event organized by a national association . . . which has not been declared open by the I.L.T.F."

Amid a plethora of doubts, complications, refinements and perplexing discussion points, a few things were immediately clear. First, Britain has, on the surface at least, embraced the very principles which she contemptuously rejected in February. Existing gulfs have been widened, an enormous group of top-class players lost to the majority of tournaments, and chaos is come again. On the credit side, we have, at least, some open tournaments; and as little as eight months ago the Federation had rejected these events as an experiment. . . .

At the press conference at the end of the March 30th meeting, the management committee of the Federation appeared together: John Eaton Griffith, Jean Borotra, Giorgio de Stefani, Basil Reay and Pierre Geeland, sitting in a row. Signior de Stefani looked gloomy and Mr. Eaton Griffith distinctly uncomfortable, both understandably so. M. Borotra, smiling and gracious as ever, did most of the talking. It was not, of course, surprising that he should be delighted; the registered, or authorized, player was his brainchild as long as eight years ago, and at last it has come to life—if an idea so sterile can be said to have any life. M. Borotra said this was "a historic day," memorable for an "honorable compromise . . . a spirit of tolerance and liberalism." The I.L.T.F. had, he claimed, gone 90 per cent of the way to meet British requirements.

Throughout these proceedings one sat first bewildered, then sardonic (at times some members of the British press were practically guffawing in disbelief) and finally disgusted by the confusion and palpable falseness of the whole business. Mr. Eaton Griffith steadfastly refused to acknowledge that there was any clash between the British rules, which omit all references to amateurs and professionals, and the new Federation rules, which hold the touring pros at a distasteful arm's length. Questioned later, other British representatives stuck to their blandly optimistic view of the situation: Herman David said, "We have got very nearly all we wanted; I am sure that before very long the rest will come." And the L.T.A. chairman, Derek Hardwick, agreed: "We have got 99.9 per cent of what we want."

Both, indeed, declared themselves well satisfied with what had happened, but when the hard details came out the next day it was hard to see why they should be. Surely whatever one's hopes for the future, it is to say the least somewhat unsatisfactory when a country which regards all players as equal can have only four open tournaments: Wimbledon, Queen's, Bournemouth and Beckenham. Not even these are well chosen: Queen's, as everyone knows, is not really a tournament at all, and we have been warned that we are only being allowed this "generous" quota because of the special commitments we have already taken on this year. "Never again" was the threat.

In commenting on this whole weekend's work, it is essential to declare one's partisan British interest, to acknowledge the special difficulties of other countries, but at the same time to make clear that one's biased position is not really a nationalistic one but a radical one. It was Britain who chose to lead the campaign for all those who want to abolish false distinctions in the game; she has accepted plenty of praise so far and it is on her that any disappointment now must inevitably focus.

The bitterest critics used the words "sell-out" and "carve-up"; the staunchest establishment defenders maintained that the concessions were only minor. The whole occasion generated a lot of feeling, but sincerely held principles should involve emotion and there was here a major clash of priorities. By refusing to be rigidly defiant, the British delegation chose to prevent the break-up of the Federation and preserve a superficial smiling unity, even though they did not carry out the mandate of their own AGM. Just how cynically they have done all this remains to be seen in the next few months. Taking the sanguine view, the whole British strategy seems based on the conviction that the Federation's ideas are so unworkable anyway that the system is bound to collapse. In this belief they have been willing to play along for the moment to avoid a row. After all, Wimbledon will be open in any case.

It is on this very point that one feels disillusioned and deflated. The L.T.A. have always maintained that they did not just want an open Wimbledon; they wanted to abolish the "living lie" of amateur tennis— Herman David's words. It was on principle that the L.T.A. council recommended the deletion of the words amateur and professional, and on principle that the AGM endorsed it. Now the I.L.T.F. have, with Britain's vote in support, legalized old shamateurism writ large in the form of the registered player—a move which Derek Hardwick, consciously echoing the L.T.A.'s phrase of February, still called "the quintessence of hypocrisy."

The British may win the war in the end this way—they seem confident that they will—but in adopting such a strategy they have tarnished their shining armor and sacrificed their previously unassailable moral leadership. Playing politics, winning devious diplomatic victories in shades of gray, may be all right in one way; but when your very purpose is to root out cynical expediency, it is supping with the devil. We must just hope that the British spoon is long enough.

THE PEACEFUL REVOLUTION

by Lance Tingay

On the 30th June, 1789, in the tennis court in the Place de la Concorde, Paris, the First Republic of France came into being. That was one revolution that changed the face of the world. On the 30th March, 1968, in the Automobile Club in the Place de la Concorde, Paris, just a few yards away across one corner of that great concourse, lawn tennis had its own revolution. And without bloodshed. Even without hard words. Without even one dissenting vote.

It was unbelievable. Last December Great Britain raised the revolution. Last March that revolution was accepted as a fact. Britain yielded some ground and accepted the fact that instead of all her tournaments being Open, only four would be. But sham amateurism was abolished from the face of lawn tennis.

There is now no need for the lawn tennis enthusiast to gaze bleakly at his friends, to shift uneasily from one foot to another and try to explain that the word "amateur" is a technical definition that has nothing to do with not making money from the game. He can tell his friends, in fact, that the amateur and professional distinction is really dead. There are those players who accept the discipline of the amateur associations. There are those who do not. Those who do not may play against those who do at Open tournaments, and control of the game is firmly in the hands of those who have always administered it.

For that, in effect, was the outcome of the emergency session of the ILTF in Paris. I think all delegates must have gone home reasonably happy.

The delegates from Eastern Europe were happy because in the new definitions was the word "amateur" in as big letters as they care to print it. Their leading players were still beautifully amateur. All the clerks in the Ministries of Sport, the majors in the Army, the technical assistants at sports stadia—all, thanks to pure socialism, able to pursue the practice of lawn tennis with unswerving zeal—were still free to play the game purely for the love of it.

The same delegates were happy because in due recognition of not voting "no" they were granted the solace of being promised specifically amateur championships, particularly one for Europe. (Incidentally, when a wire service report reached the Tass Agency in Moscow that the Paris vote had been unanimous, it was at once queried and its accuracy disputed on the grounds that the Russian delegate could not possibly have said "yes.")

The delegate from Australia was happy because for the first time in years his nation was not assailed as a hide-bound reactionary to all reform in the game.

The delegates from France were happy because at last their brain child,

857

the "registered player"—that is, the shamateur made legal—was now a possibility. But they were realistic, too. They stressed that they did not regard him as an amateur.

The delegates from Great Britain were happy because they had got away with an outrageous rebellion, because they had shocked the lawn tennis world into at last doing something about the absurd state of the game, because they had not been expelled from the international scene and because on reflection the concessions they had made would give them greater control of the game in Britain than they might otherwise have had.

The Irish delegate was happy because he had been instructed to vote on whichever side seemed to be winning the battle and he was able to do just that.

The Swedish delegates were happy because by their initiative in calling the meeting they had averted chaos in the game. I hope they were happy too because someone thanked them for their action. I do not know if anyone did.

Some delegates were happy because, though they could not care less about the outcome one way or the other, they were in Paris for the first time. One talks of a permissive society. There are spots in Paris where it is more permissive than most. The only time some delegates were unhappy was when they came to settle their bills. Even four-minute milers have ceased to try and keep up with the cost of living in Paris.

There are no doubt many loose ends to be tidied up. It will be some time before it is quite clear as to who can play in which sort of tournament. The International Federation has laid down various categories of players but the only one that matters is that which gives nations the right of self-determination to make their own definitions.

In effect, there are now just two categories—those who accept the disciplinary control of their national association and those who do not. If one nation cares to state that only redheads can take money for playing, that is all right with the Federation. If another cares to insist that no player can accept a lift in a car without penalty, that is all right too.

There were no delegates representing the top professionals of the world. Had there been, they might not have been among the happy ones. Britain would have given them everything. The Federation insisted on rationing their corn.

It is not, though, a bad ration. No one knows yet how many Open tournaments the world will end up having. But it will be a pretty fair number and the kudos of the great titles will be able to be gained.

A lot of people in the revolution of 1789 lost their heads under the guillotine. Were there casualties in 1968? Some British tournaments must have felt they were. Three of the four British tournaments granted permission to be Open—Wimbledon, the Hard Court Championships at Bournemouth and the London Championships at Queen's Club—are LTA events. The only independent British tournament to be Open is the Kent meeting at Beckenham. The organizers of the West of England Championships at Bristol the same week reckoned on being Open and will not be. I doubt if

they will take the rebuff without making their views heard. And British
tournaments like those at Newport and Hoylake and so on, which were also
planning on Open lines, have reason to be aggrieved. They will claim that
their supporting votes last December were gained by false representations.

But I suppose there will not be actual bloodshed.

FIRST FRENCH OPEN CHAMPIONSHIPS

by Rex Bellamy

The center court of the Stade Roland Garros has glittered with enchantment this past two days. The vast amphitheater has smoldered with heat. Its
steep banks, tightly packed with spectators in summer colors, have been a
dazzling sight. The players must have felt like ants, trapped at the foot of a
giant rockery in full bloom.

With its blend of sharpness and subtlety the tennis matched the setting in
both character and quality. The professionals, used to playing indoors,
looked at the brightness and beauty around them and felt, perhaps, that
such gloriously "open" tennis as this was made for the gods.

Appropriately, the professionals kept their dignity, though some were
challenged by players who, for part of a match, were able to lift their games
to the same level. This was true yesterday of Herb FitzGibbon, an American,
who played so well that he had Ken Rosewall in a corner at one set all and
5–1 in the third. Rosewall played wonderful tennis then, saving three set
points, and almost stopping the heart with the lashing facility of his ground
strokes. There were puffs of dust as the ball bit into the court like a bullet.
The mighty crowd made thunderous noises—and then fell back into the
intimidating silences peculiar to vast assemblies.

Today it was the turn of another American, Cliff Richey. At one set-all,
he took Roy Emerson (the reigning champion) to 14 games in the third set
and then 20 in the fourth—for which Richey had a set point. Yet the hard
opposition of FitzGibbon and Richey became but shadows in the memory as
Ricardo Gonzales today exposed the richest texture of his game in beating
Istvan Gulyas by 6–4, 6–2, 6–2.

This was an extraordinary result because the little Hungarian, runner-up
here two years ago, was expected to tax Gonzales to the full and possibly
beat him. But Gulyas, a modest man, did not fancy his chances against a net-
rushing professional. Perhaps, in a sense, this was a clash between a big man
and a small man.

In any case, Gonzales today made tennis look the loveliest of games. He
was efficient, but he was romantic. His serving and smashing were explosive.

His ground strokes, stop volleys and drop shots had the delicacy of feathers blown by a gentle breeze. At times he seemed to have too much respect for the ball to hit it hard. Instead, he whispered to it, like a fond parent lulling a child to sleep. To watch Gonzales was to think in terms of poetry and music. He did not play the game. He composed it.

Perhaps, because of the professionals, perhaps because of the strikes, perhaps because of the glorious weather, perhaps because of all three, the receipts here are more than 10 times as high as last year's figures. But income does not yet equal expenditure. Open tournaments are expensive promotions.

LAVER WINS FIRST WIMBLEDON OPEN

by Lance Tingay

When Rod Laver, now undisputed world lawn tennis champion, enters the Wimbledon championships next year, it might be as well if he were given the prize money and asked if he minded stepping down. The tournament might then become more exciting. If Laver continues to play as he did in the final today, there will be no contest worth the description.

Laver beat Tony Roche, 6–3, 6–4, 6–2, in an hour. If not the briefest of Wimbledon finals, it was among the most shattering. That this remarkable left-hander would dominate the first open Wimbledon was expected. There have been favorites in the past who have gone through the meeting as a whole more one-sidedly, notably Jack Kramer in 1947. Laver, though, has achieved lawn tennis immortality, not by being the champion of the first open Wimbledon, but by climaxing the achievement with a display of such immaculate mastery that, given a repetition, no other man in the world could hope to hold him in check.

One knew Laver to be a maestro. He was when he was an amateur, as witness his unique performance in taking the six big championships—those of Australia, Italy, France, Wimbledon, Germany and the United States—in 1962. After that he dominated the more confined world of professionalism. It could not be more fitting that so splendid a performer should win the premier open championship.

He paced himself well during the course of the fortnight. He paced himself perfectly in the final. Poor Tony Roche! He is a good player and he played quite well this afternoon. Yet all he could do, all he was allowed to do, was to be a foil to his opponent's high skill. How galling it must have been for him to play his heart out, to reach standards of stroking that were first class, only to be permitted merely an ignominious hour on the court.

The highest tribute I can pay Roche is that he did well enough to make Laver bring out his finest game. The more searching his shots, the more Laver raised his own standard. I suppose the most striking aspect of Laver's high quality is his ability to make a shot virtuosity when under pressure. It was heartbreaking for Roche to project what would normally have been a sure winner, merely to provoke the unplayable.

Two efforts at searing passing shots by Roche were instances in the second set. Most players would hardly have seen the ball, so fast did Roche project it. Laver answered with a stop volley that died as soon as it passed over the net. Afterwards he admitted there was luck about it, but then he is the sort of man who creates such luck. A rally or two later a similar deadly ball was projected by Roche. This time, Laver made the same response with unerring touch, and with intention in every split second of his quick reaction.

The match was never exciting because the outcome was so inevitable. I suppose there was tension in the opening stages, for it happened that Roche held all his first three service games to love. . . .

Laver was not without some failings. His own first service he got into court less often than he might, though so deep and swinging was his second ball that it hardly mattered. Then there were his double-faults, five in all before the match was over. Failings? No one can be perfect all the time. . . . At no time did Roche ever break through Laver's service. In all, there were three games and five rallies when he was within two points of doing so, but always Laver surely took back the chance.

Roche may console himself that this was Laver's third Wimbledon title—and his hardest yet. In 1961 Laver beat Chuck McKinley for the loss of only eight games, and in 1962 he brought down Martin Mulligan for the loss of only five. Roche managed nine games, with Laver's standard of performance at its highest level. I doubt if there are many players in the world who could have done so well.

BILLIE JEAN KING AGAIN WIMBLEDON QUEEN

by Fred Tupper

Mrs. Billie Jean Moffitt King is still queen of Wimbledon.

The bespectacled Californian, wan and listless most of the way, won her third title in a row on raw courage and some knifing volleys in beating seventh-seeded Judy Tegart of Australia, 9–7, 7–5, over 70 minutes on the center court today.

Mrs. King seemed a pale carbon of the exuberant extrovert who set tennis aflame here a few years back. Wide of grin and brash of manner, she made history in 1962 by bouncing out the favorite, Margaret Smith (now Mrs. Court), in the first round. The public loved it. The "Moffitt Mob" would hem in the sidecourts to hear as much as watch her.

"Throw in your nickels and dimes," she would say. "This is the worst show on earth."

It was far from that today, but it was not vintage King. She was subdued. She moved slowly around the court, and it was not until early in the second set that a flicker of a smile glinted across her face.

On the other side was Miss Tegart, a big broth of a girl who, at 30, had blossomed late. She had been trying for seven years and the pieces suddenly had fallen into place.

She had beaten second-seeded Mrs. Court over three sets and demolished third-seeded Nancy Richey of the United States, 6–3, 6–1, with the finest tennis of this tournament. A laugh on her lips, ponytail askew, she had overnight become the darling of Wimbledon.

Mrs. King was lucky to be on the court at all. In the semi-final, Mrs. Ann Jones of Britain had led her by a set and 5–4 with her service to come. She had Mrs. King on the hook and couldn't reel her in. Great match player that she is, Mrs. King had the resolution and somehow found the shots to win.

Today Miss Tegart was uncertain. Her devil-may-care attitude vanished, carried away by center-court jitters.

The American had the first service game and the service break, too, in a long, vital game. She was at advantage point four times as Miss Tegart volleyed into the net, missed a forehand down the middle, foot-faulted and then stared at a cross-court forehand that fled by her. In an exchange around the net, Mrs. King whipped a topspin forehand short to the sideline to lead, 2–0, and then 4–1.

But there was trouble ahead. Mrs. King was not getting her first service in, and her second was short without much pace.

Miss Tegart began to bang the ball. In the seventh game she slashed a backhand pass down the line, hit a forehand that Mrs. King muffed and then pasted another backhand to the line for the break to 3–4.

The American was shaking her head. She seemed unable to move. Bravely she held her service, because she could still get up to the net in time to scythe away those lovely backhand volleys.

Miss Tegart was scampering around the court, but double-faults were haunting her, and she blew the 16th game with her sixth double-fault and three flubbed volleys as the crowd groaned with her.

With that hurdle cleared, Mrs. King was happier. A wild yell at an error was a familiar sign. She served her first ace in the third game, hammered a couple more in the fifth and smiled at her parents in the players' stand.

Miss Tegart was determined to make a fight. She had length and spin on her service and was booming up for the volley. With the crowd's cheers to nourish her, she hit three splendid shots, one after the other, in the ninth game with the score at 4–all.

In some frantic infighting at the barrier, the Australian slapped a volley through a hole, scored with a forehand on the run and then slammed a backhand to Mrs. King's shoelaces for vantage point.

This was the test. Mrs. King met it with courage, volleying away the dangers to hold service.

Five–6 now, the Australian serving. Shrewdly Mrs. King changed tactics. She dinked a return just over the net, placed a forehand to the wide side and chipped another return short as Miss Tegart underhit. Love–40, three match points to come.

A delicate lob drifting on the breeze left Miss Tegart wrong-footed. She blooped it out. Mrs. King threw her racket aloft and hurtled up to the handshake. The wide grin was back. She had become the first woman to win here three times since Maureen Connolly swept the titles in 1952: 53–54.

"There was nothing wrong with me," Mrs. King said later. "Judy goes fast, and I went slow. I've had to learn to go slow to concentrate."

She thought about it, then said: "I guess I won this Wimbledon on sheer fight. I wasn't prepared either mentally or physically. But I'll be back one more time."

For her victory in this first Wimbledon open, Mrs. King earned $1,800, but she said it would go toward her $10,000 a year guarantee as a pro.

In the almost inevitable five-set match that is played when Australians meet in the doubles final, John Newcombe and Tony Roche defeated Ken Rosewall and Fred Stolle, 6–3, 6–8, 5–7, 14–12, 6–3, in an all-pro slugfest that ebbed and flowed nearly three hours. . . .

Mrs. King did it again later. She paired with Rosie Casals to win from Françoise Durr and Mrs. Jones in a thrill-stabbed doubles final, 3–6, 6–4, 7–5.

ASHE FIRST NEGRO TO WIN MEN'S U.S. TITLE

by Neil Amdur

Arthur Ashe achieved another milestone in his marvelous tennis career today when he won his first United States amateur singles title in five tension-filled sets.

In a 2-hour-45-minute final that delighted a capacity crowd of 4,200 at the Longwood Cricket Club, the 25-year-old Army lieutenant served 20 aces as he beat Bob Lutz of Los Angeles, 4–6, 6–3, 8–10, 6–0, 6–4.

It was Ashe's ninth attempt at the grass-court crown and his most significant singles achievement since emerging from Richmond as the country's first prominent Negro male player.

The exciting match was in doubt all the way. In the final game of the fifth set Lutz, the unseeded darling of the tournament, gained a 40–15 lead on Ashe's serve in an effort to break back. But Ashe subdued his 20-year-old rival on the fifth match point when Lutz netted two service returns at deuce.

The triumph assured Ashe No. 1 amateur singles ranking in the United States. He had been No. 2 three consecutive years.

Mentally tired from the pressure of Davis Cup play and catch-up matches early in the tournament, Ashe said he would take three days off and fish and hunt before practicing for the first United States open at Forest Hills, Queens, beginning Thursday.

Lutz also was tired and tense from his consecutive singles upsets over Cliff Richey, Bob Hewitt and Clark Graebner, and his emotion-packed doubles title victory yesterday with Stan Smith.

"I seemed to lose my rhythm and timing in the fourth set," said the handsome Californian, who served 19 double-faults and lost eight straight games after intermission. "I'm not ashamed of losing to the No. 1 player, though. I've had a great week."

Ashe's victory, the first for an American since Tony Trabert triumphed in 1955, completed the most hectic 10 days in tournament history. Other finals won today by Mrs. Margaret Smith Court and Maria Bueno in the women's doubles and by Mary Ann Eisel and Peter Curtis in the mixed doubles, coupled with the Smith-Lutz triumph and that of Mrs. Court in women's singles, provided a sweep of the five titles by top-seeded entries.

Until Ashe took control in the fourth set with a service break in the first game, a break that Lutz later said was "a key game," the Californian seemed on the verge of joining Fred Stolle and Mal Anderson, who had won the championship without being seeded.

Lutz won a 63-minute third set and a 2–1 lead in sets when Ashe netted an easy touch volley and double-faulted on the seventh set point. It was one of his few double-faults in the match.

The 90-degree weather and occasional wind gusts seemed to take some of the sting from Ashe's normally decisive serves and volleys as he struggled through seven deuce games in the set. Then, in a most unusual bit of strategy, Ashe stayed at courtside and changed shirts during the 10-minute intermission while Lutz retreated to the locker room.

When Lutz returned to the court, he was not the same player. His first serve, which had been 62 per cent effective in the first three sets, was only 47 per cent effective in the last two.

Lutz also changed aluminum rackets several times, and the different tension strung into each racket seemed to affect his serving touch. Ashe, meanwhile, had no trouble holding serve and finished with 20 aces.

Ashe served well when he had to, though, especially in the last game. He always brings in the big one when he has to.

FIRST U.S. OPEN CHAMPIONSHIPS

by Herbert Warren Wind

About midway between the first open Wimbledon, which ended shortly after the Fourth of July, and the first United States Open Tennis Championships, which began shortly before Labor Day, it became clear to me, as I thought ahead to our championships, that my major concern was whether Ken Rosewall and Richard (Pancho) Gonzales would come through with good, solid performances at Forest Hills. I expected neither of them to win. For Gonzales, that was simply out of the question. He is forty years old—an age when an extraordinary athlete can flout the laws of nature on isolated afternoons now and then but certainly not throughout a seven-round championship in which a contestant must play a series of matches with, at most, a day between them to recuperate in. Rosewall's case is somewhat similar yet somewhat different. At thirty-three he is physically capable of standing up to the rigors of a protracted championship, but the hard fact of the matter is that the years have also begun to catch up with this brilliant Australian and he is now a discernible shade past his tennis peak. While he can still hold his own against anyone on a slow surface, he is a lot more beatable on a fast surface, like grass, than he was two or three years ago. At Wimbledon, for example, where he was seeded second, he was defeated by Tony Roche in straight sets in the fourth round—the round after Gonzales was eliminated by Alex Metreveli, a young Russian.

As I say, I didn't expect Rosewall to go all the way at Forest Hills—like almost everyone, I thought that Rod Laver would repeat his Wimbledon triumph without much trouble—but I wanted both him and Gonzales to be in much better form than they had exhibited in England, so that, however long they lasted, they would leave an imprint on our first Open befitting two exceptional champions, each of whom had reigned for years as the best player in the world (Gonzales, roughly from 1954 to 1960, and Rosewall from 1960 to 1965) but had had the misfortune to be past his prime when open tennis finally arrived. . . .

No one who ever saw Gonzales in his heyday was likely to forget it. It was not only that he combined power and touch and tennis sense as few players before him had done but that he projected one of the strongest personalities in all of sport. Saturnine and disputatious, an unrepentant loner, this tall, graceful man who moved like a panther seemed forever to have a chip on his shoulder. When the galleries rooted for his opponent (galleries invariably attach themselves to the underdog), Gonzales seemed almost to welcome it, as if to say, "Who needs you?" During his reign, he didn't change an iota.

Rosewall is quite a different person. . . . Shortly after the 1956 Davis Cup Challenge Round, Rosewall turned professional. For a twenty-two-year-old, he had compiled an astonishing record: he had never won at Wimbledon (though he had reached the final twice), but he captured the three other major titles—the French in 1953, the Australian in 1953 and 1955, and the American in 1956, when he defeated Hoad in the final. (Hoad, incidentally, did not turn pro until July of 1957.)

Rosewall had accomplished much, but how he had accomplished it was at least as important. In a period in which just about every other player of world class was an exponent of the so-called big game—the big serve followed by the volley or smash—Rosewall was that comforting anachronism, the baseliner with superb ground strokes who won points by outmaneuvering his opponent. A cool, neat, economical workman with an extremely pleasant court personality, he prepared his points carefully. When the structure of a rally suggested it, he did not hesitate to move up to the net—he was a very deft volleyer—but he concentrated on the forecourt only in those rare matches in which he was making no headway against a determined opponent and felt he had to change his pattern of play. (He did this in winning a marvelous five-set match with Dick Savitt at Forest Hills in 1956, for example.) For all his ability, however, there was some doubt whether he would enjoy equal success as a pro, because most of the time he would be facing Gonzales and the other serve-and-volley virtuosos on fast indoor courts that favored their style of play.

There was increased doubt, and not a little sadness, when Rosewall himself, as soon as he turned pro, went over to the serve-and-volley game. With the least powerful serve of any of the great players since René Lacoste, he seemed ill-equipped for this, and few people were surprised that Gonzales had little difficulty with him on their coast-to-coast tour in 1957, winning fifty of their seventy-six matches. Then Rosewall amazed everybody all over again. Gradually he became adept at the big game. ("I felt I had to try to play that way, because, under the conditions, it was the easiest way and the most certain way to victory," he told me recently. "Indoors, the percentages for making good passing shots are very low.") He improved his forehand, which had a tendency to be loose, by cutting down the length of his backswing. This put his return of service in a class by itself. He beefed up his own serve a bit, but what really made it click was his incredible quickness in getting to the return and dispatching an aggressive volley. Before too long, he was beating Gonzales as often as not, and after Gonzales went into semi-retirement Rosewall succeeded him as the world professional champion. . . . He held the championship until 1965, when Laver took over. . . .

In the spring of 1963, the pros assembled at Forest Hills for one of their infrequent tournaments on grass, and this enabled me to catch Rosewall when he was just about at his zenith. He was so far superior to all his opponents, Laver included, that none of his matches was even remotely close. That week, by a happy chance, I discovered the secret of one aspect of Rosewall's skill that had always fascinated, and mystified, me: How come he was always perfectly positioned for each shot when men of comparable agility weren't? During the final, when Rosewall was on the far side of the court, I had the inspiration of holding up my hand in such a way that it blocked off the near side and I could focus wholly on how Rosewall moved to the ball from shot to shot. My guess was that I would find that he took quite a few more steps than the average player—maybe fifteen on some shots. What I found was that he often took as many as thirty. The instant after he had executed his stroke, he began repositioning himself, with a series of quarter and half steps, and all the while that he was studying the stroke his opponent seemed to be planning, he continued to shift his position, with a dozen or so noodling little steps; then, when the return was on its way—and he was already darn close to where it was coming—he went on adjusting, with a succession of tiny sidesteps. No wonder the ball arrived so regularly in his "strike zone." And since he was always on balance, no wonder he had such exquisite timing that the ball exploded off the face of the racket.

In sum, Rosewall, thanks to his inherent artistry, made even the serve-and-volley game a delight. How Rosewall at his peak would have fared against Kramer, Gonzales and Laver at *their* peaks, I cannot say, but I do know that for me, as for many others, Rosewall stands as the most attractive player of the postwar era. Certainly no other player has given me nearly as much pleasure. For these reasons, and for the additional one that he is now starting down the far side of the slope, I wanted him to have a very good Forest Hills.

Although Forest Hills can't compare with Wimbledon as a spectacle, as an occasion, or as an institution, there was little to choose between the two history-making Opens in terms of straight tennis. The only player of renown who appeared at Wimbledon and not here was Manuel Santana. If Wimbledon gained a special evocative aura from the high number of former champions who returned, either to play in peripheral events or simply to be on hand, this was equally true of Forest Hills. In the senior men's doubles, for instance, nostalgia flowed like wine when Bobby Riggs and Pancho Segura confronted Don Budge and Frankie Parker in the quarter-final round. . . .

The first open Forest Hills also resembled the first open Wimbledon in its unpredictability. From the moment, early in the tournament, when Fred Stolle fell before young Peter Curtis of England, the seeded players were treated roughly. To say the same thing in a slightly different way, no fewer than thirteen professionals were ousted by amateurs, and even if this statistic is qualified by the observation that two-thirds of the players who have turned pro in recent years had not been colossi in their amateur days, it does indicate the prevalence of the unanticipated. Whatever the reasons, tennis, long the most form-abiding of sports, isn't that way at the moment. The most startling upset took place in the fourth round when Laver, the heavy favorite to win the championship, was put out by Cliff Drysdale of South Africa, 4–6, 6–4, 3–6, 6–1, 6–1. (Note the decisiveness of the scores of the last two sets.) In the second round, Laver had barely avoided elimination at the hands of Tomas Koch of Brazil. . . .

Gonzales, after a bye and an easy second-round match, came up against

Mal Anderson, who, at thirty-three, is still a redoubtable player. The Gonzales we saw against Anderson was an entirely different Gonzales from the tired old man of Wimbledon. His pride had obviously been wounded by his performance there, and he meant to do something about it. Having got his weight down to a hundred and seventy-five pounds, he looked years younger and he moved years younger. Against Anderson, he played an almost perfect match, expending his limited reserves of energy at just the right moments. In each set, when he had his chance for the pivotal service break he seized it, and he wrapped up the match quickly, 6–4, 6–4, 6–4. . . .

In the next round, when Gonzales met Roche, the young Australian who was a finalist at Wimbledon and was seeded second at Forest Hills, the stands were so passionately pro-Gonzales that on several occasions they went too far, even applauding Roche's double-faults. In truth, though, Gonzales did play a rousing match. In winning the first set, 8–6, he fought off four set points in the tenth game, broke through Roche in the thirteenth with two bravura forehands, and then held his service at love. In the second set when Roche, leading 4–1 in games and 40–15 on his service, became a little careless, Gonzales pounced on his errors like a cat on a mouse, and before you knew it he had broken Roche's service twice. That was it, really: Gonzales, 8–6, 6–4, 6–2. There are a lot of men who can hit a tennis ball with authority but very few who are gifted match players, like Gonzales. What it requires, at bottom, is true resolution and infinite care. . . . Only a man who wants terribly to win can work so hard and steadily at the task of winning.

Gonzales's victory over Roche took him to the quarter-finals, where he opposed Tom Okker, a twenty-four-year-old Dutchman, who is currently the fastest man in tennis. Again, Gonzales gave it everything, but this time it wasn't enough, and he went down, 14–16, 6–3, 10–8, 6–3. . . . In the semi-finals Okker met Rosewall in the lower half of the draw; and in the upper half Arthur Ashe, Jr., who had eliminated Roy Emerson and Drysdale, met his fellow-American amateur and Davis Cup teammate, Clark Graebner. . . . Rosewall's opponent in the quarters was Dennis Ralston, but what would ordinarily have been a very good match turned out to be no match at all. Handicapped by a torn stomach muscle, Ralston could serve only at half speed and, in general, offer little more than token resistance. . . .

Until this year, Okker was just a respectable internationalist. Then he suddenly blossomed. He won the South African and Italian championships, and in the Queen's Club tournament, prior to Wimbledon, he knocked off three professionals, Laver among them. A slim (five-ten, one-forty) young man with a handsome Ivy League face, Okker is what is currently called in this year of change a "registered player.". . .

Rosewall vs. Okker proved to be the finest match of the championship—crisp and entertaining tennis, filled with dramatic exchanges. In the first set . . . the trim little Australian was keeping the ball away from Okker's dangerous top-spin forehand, he was making Okker do a lot of running, and he was moving very well himself. However, in the tenth game, when Rosewall was serving for the set, we had the first adumbration of the course the match was to take. Down 30–0, Okker fought his way to deuce with two placements—hit while he was running at full tilt—and a forehand drive that Rosewall volleyed into the net. He went to ad on another volley error by Rosewall, and took the game by whipping a forehand down the line off Rosewall's first service. Four games later, he broke through Rosewall's service again, to win the set, 8–6.

The rest of the way, except for a shaky passage in the third set, Okker was just a little too much for Rosewall to handle. His speed afoot was something to behold. In addition, Okker possesses terrific reflexive speed in handling a racket, and I think that what may, more than anything else, have convinced Rosewall of the impossibility of his task was finding that in those rat-tat-tat volley exchanges at close quarters the shot that should have won for him kept coming back. Okker in four sets: 8–6, 6–4, 6–8, 6–1. In all this there was, of course, a lavish splash of irony. Rosewall had played very well—well enough to have won most matches—but he was up against the one type of opponent he could not contain: a young Rosewall.

Finally, the finals. I have devoted so much attention to the heartening adventures of the old boys that, I fear, I will be discussing the new young champions all too briefly. However, Arthur Ashe and Virginia Wade should be strutting their stuff for many years to come, so there should be ample opportunity to make amends.

The ladies first. In Miss Wade, the first British girl to carry the day at Forest Hills since Betty Nuthall did it in 1930, we have a new and refreshing tennis personality. . . . She made her way past four strong opponents— Stephanie DeFina, Rosie Casals, Judy Tegart and Ann Jones—to reach the final. There she outclassed Billie Jean King, the defending champion, 6–4, 6–2, hitting out all the way and never losing her nerve or her purpose. . . .

As finals go—they are generally anticlimactic—the men's final between Ashe and Okker was a superior one. Ashe won it in five sets, 14–12, 5–7, 6–3, 3–6, 6–3, and, as the scores indicate, it was closely fought all the way. However, it was a decidedly less interesting match than the Okker-Rosewall duel. It produced a paucity of rallies, for one thing, and, for another, Okker did not play as brilliantly. Both of these phenomena—an absence of rallies and a less than glittering performance by his opponent—occur in just about every match that Ashe plays. They are curious affairs, Ashe's matches, often boring and exciting at the same time. Ashe, you see, hits a tennis ball harder and faster than anyone else has for years. He simply blows it past his opponents. On a good day it goes in a lot, and on a bad day it goes out a lot. As a result you can have long successions of points that are over almost before they have begun. That is what makes for the boredom. What makes for the excitement, of course, is the sheer velocity of Ashe's strokes. The odd thing is that he has a rather wispy build for a power hitter: he is six feet, one inch tall but weighs only a hundred and fifty-five. The secret of his power is fantastic coordination. For example, on his cross-court backhand— his best stroke, apart from his serve—he doesn't appear to swing especially hard at the ball, but it travels like a shot. His method of serving is simplicity itself. He bounces the ball twice, tosses it about a yard above his head, leans forward, and cracks it. It goes like a blur. In the first set alone against Okker, he scored fifteen aces—not that that is anything unusual for Ashe. Moreover, he possesses endless energy and can keep the cannonading up for hours.

Ashe's admirers have long speculated about the heights he might reach if he modified his all-attack style by adding to his repertoire some more restrained strokes on which he could rely during those afternoons when his control is off—and on which he could call during his good afternoons, too, in those tactical situations that require a whisper rather than a thunderclap. Ashe is only twenty-five, and in time he may develop a more complete tennis vocabulary and move closer to Tilden and Vines. However, the game he now plays is the game he has always played, from the time he emerged as a sensational talent when he was just a boy in Richmond, Virginia. Since he was barred from playing in that city's tournaments because he was a Negro, he transferred to an integrated high school in St. Louis, and during his years there he won the United States interscholastic championship and the United States junior indoor championship. He went on to the University of California at Los Angeles on a tennis scholarship. His first considerable victory came at Forest Hills in 1965, when, in the quarter-final round, he met Emerson, then the No. 1 amateur, and blasted him off the court. After that, everyone expected the world of Ashe. This put a tremendous burden on him, which became still heavier in the next two years, when, serving in the Army, at West Point, and consequently under-tennised, he had disappointing tournament seasons. This year, although he is still in the Army, he has finally come on to fulfill his vast promise. He won the Madison Square Garden Challenge Trophy by defeating Emerson. At Wimbledon it took Laver to stop him, in the semi-finals. The week before the Open he won the United States amateur championship, at Longwood. Then, at Forest Hills, he topped it all off.

I cannot conceive of a more popular victory. Ashe is not only a very fine young man but a very rare young man. Intelligent, calm, honest and natural, he is the antithesis of the spoiled American tennis hero. In the midst of all the usual pressures and, in his case, some added ones, he has had the strength of character to go his own way—to enjoy his tennis and his friends as much as possible, and avoid the folly of trying to be all things to all men and all media. There couldn't have been a better winner of our historic first Open.

To end on a light note: money. As an amateur Ashe received only expenses—twenty dollars a day. Gonzales took home $4,250 and Rosewall $9,000. The registered players made the largest hauls. Okker won $14,000 and Miss Wade $6,000.

1 9 6 9

THE FRENCH CHAMPIONSHIPS

by Rex Bellamy

The French championships are the game's finest advertisement. The surface, clay, is grueling to play on, yet provides the most exacting test of ability and the most satisfying spectacle. The entry is the best outside Wimbledon.

All is grandeur and pathos. The grandeur is public—the protracted, absorbing exercise in tactics, technique and physical and mental stamina. The pathos is private—the drained, exhausted bodies crumpled on the masseur's table or the dressing-room benches.

These are great but cruel championships. Nowhere else is the aesthetic potential of the game so fully explored, or the physical cost of it so sadly apparent.

The round of 16 in the men's singles summed it all up. We saw some superb tennis that day. But, at the end of it, the human wreckage of the men's dressing room was a pitiful sight. Manuel Santana, his head in his hands, was heaped on a bench. He was a broken man. John Newcombe, a superman at his physical peak, fell back onto the massage table like a crumbling pack of cards. . . .

This year the championships were better and tougher than ever. On the first page of the program there were a lot of new names under the heading "comité du tournoi." A new regime had taken over French tennis. Their organization—not least their thoughtfulness about the small things—was admirable. . . .

There were plenty of tough matches before Rod Laver and Margaret Court completed the second legs of their "grand slam" attempts. The crowds were gratifying and gratified. The fun soon started. Billie Jean King, who has yet to win "big" on a slow court, was taken to a 7–5 third set by Vlasta Vopickova. . . . Ilie Nastase, that gay Rumanian, an expert on clay, was suffering from an abscess on a tooth, and was beaten by Stanley Matthews, ranked only tenth in Britain. Dennis Ralston was taken to five sets by Patrick Proisy, ranked only twelfth in France.

Day Two: and the most attractive match in the men's first round, Santana vs. Cliff Drysdale, was played under floodlights. Santana came from behind to win easily in a heavy shower, with Drysdale handicapped by a pulled muscle. . . . Stan Smith came back from two sets and 1–4 down to beat Boro Jovanovic, a specialist on these courts. . . . Roger Taylor had to scratch because he could not grip a racket: his hand was still bruised and swollen after its impact with the perimeter of Bob Hewitt's left eye in a Berlin dressing room.

Kristy Pigeon worked hard and well in an unfamiliar slow-court role but was thoroughly beaten by Ann Jones. "It was like playing a backboard," said Miss Pigeon. . . .

On Day Three, Allan Stone (Australia) beat Nikki Pilic; Wieslaw Gasiorek (Poland) beat Butch Buchholz; and Rosemary Casals and Françoise Durr narrowly edged their way through nervous marathons with Virginia Wade and Helen Gourlay. . . . Miss Casals took 125 minutes to beat Miss Wade, who served for the match three times and had two match points (she put a smash and a backhand into the net). Miss Casals had the greater flair and, on the big points, the firmer nerves. She finally won two love games for the match. . . .

Roy Emerson and Fred Stolle, both former champions, beat fellow professionals Ray Moore and Marty Riessen. Ken Rosewall played some lovely tennis to whip Milan Holocek (Czechoslovakia).

Day Four—and Peaches Bartkowicz could not cover the court fast enough to check the fast-flowing tide of Kerry Melville's forehands. Santana beat the huge, intimidating Rumanian, Ion Tiriac, in a delightful match on the new "show" court. At the end of the day, the 6 foot 4½ inch Dick Crealy, ranked third in Australia, led Laver, 6–3, 9–7, 2–6. One of the most effervescent and engaging characters in the game, Crealy played well and led on merit. . . . But at the end of the day Crealy was lunging in vain as Laver's winners blazed down the lines. It was like trying to pluck bullets out of the air. Rain reprieved him.

On Day Five, Laver won. But neither he nor Crealy regained his best form of the previous day. Crealy led, 4–3, in the fifth but did not get another game. . . . Arthur Ashe, still learning about clay, played well to crush Barry Phillips-Moore, an Australian slow-court expert. Ralston was humiliated by the rising young Yugoslav, Zeljko Franulovic, who lost only three games. "I played nine sets yesterday, and I was tired," said Ralston. Cliff Richey and Stan Smith, "the Leaning Tower of Pasadena," joined Ashe in the last 16, though Smith was taken to five sets by Premjit Lall (India).

This took us to Days Six and Seven, the first weekend. These were days of enchantment, as both singles were cut to the last eight. Here was a sunny microcosm of life as a whole—its loveliness, its drama, its pathos. That new "show" court staged a superb match rising to a genuinely great finish. John Newcombe beat Jan Kodes, 6–1, 6–4, 0–6, 8–10, 11–9. In the fourth set Newcombe served for the match at 7–6. In the fifth, Kodes led, 4–1, had two points for 5–2 and, later, was twice within two points of winning. Newcombe finished him with two pulverizing aces from 10–9 and 30–15.

Santana played his compatriot, Andres Gimeno, for the first time in nine years. For two sets Gimeno was outclassed. Santana's game was all caressing brushwork and delicate artistry. But, at the crux of the third set, Santana pulled a muscle and at 0–1 in the fifth retired. How cruel tennis can be! Tom Okker's willowy brilliance frustrated the brave little Richey. Emerson (who looked as if he had had too much clay) and Ashe (who looked as if he had not had enough) lost to Franulovic and Stolle, respectively. Laver and Rosewall played like masters. In the women's event, Mrs. Jones, short of match play, was 0–4 down before taking 12 straight games for the match against Tiiu Kivi (Russia). Lesley Bowrey had her revenge for the 1967 final, in which she was beaten by Miss Durr.

Day Eight—Tony Roche took two hours and six minutes to beat Franulovic in five sets. Rosewall took 26 minutes longer to beat Stolle in four. . . . Franulovic justified his new reputation. Again his mature temperament and his instinctive flair for the game were apparent. He asked Roche a lot of awkward questions. But his second service and his forehand volley were suspect. Roche had an advantage in pace, punch and experience. He came from behind to win all the first four games of the fifth set, though Franulovic had five game points on the way. That string of deuce games showed us who was the better man on the big points. Roche finished the match with a love game—two service winners and two aces. The Rosewall-Stolle match inevitably lacked the excitement of new discoveries. Each knows the other's game well. Rosewall failed to recapture his 1968 form, but Stolle played remarkably well. Both looked weary by the time Rosewall, from a defensive position, hit a scorching backhand down the line for the match.

On Day Nine, Okker beat Newcombe (as he did in the Monaco final) in five sets and Laver beat Gimeno in four. The Okker-Newcombe match lasted for two hours and eight minutes. It was a glorious and often great spectacle. Kodes had already drained Newcombe's mental stamina. More important was the double fault that cost Newcombe his service at 1–all in the fifth set. Most important of all was Okker, who played wonderfully exciting tennis in a match dominated by earned points. But Newcombe hit the shot of the match—a ferocious smash-cum-passing shot from seven yards behind the baseline. Once Laver had settled down to work, there was no doubt about the outcome—even Gimeno knew that. Laver always had the greater capacity for taking profitable initiatives.

Margaret Court and Nancy Richey—both 26, both former champions, both at the top of their domestic rankings—beat their closest domestic rivals. Mrs. Court had a fine match with Miss Melville, who served for the first set twice. . . . Mrs. Court was enviably sound and resourceful, especially in the forecourt. Miss Melville gambled too heavily on the drop shot. In a predictably less spectacular match, Miss Richey demonstrated that she had all Julie Heldman's virtues and, thanks to her experience, slightly more variety. Miss Heldman made most of the errors. But from a set and 2–4 down, she doggedly pushed the second set to 9–7. Miss Richey's was a precarious win.

Day 10 was bleak and breezy, when Mrs. Jones conceded all of two games to Miss Casals. Mrs. Bowrey conceded only six to Mrs. King. In both cases the clay-court inexperience of the losers was apparent. This led us to Day 11–and the men's semi-finals, in which the "old" pros of the National Tennis League beat the rising stars of World Championship Tennis.

Rosewall beat Roche in straight sets. Laver beat Okker in four. As matches, both were disappointing. It was another gray day—overcast now by a shadow from distant Mexico, where Rafael Osuna had been killed in an air crash. The flags were at half-mast. The crowd stood for a minute's silence. Beside the net, holding an empty racket cover, was Osuna's last opponent, Bill Bowrey.

Rosewall and Roche measured each other carefully for a spell. There was a mutual respect between them. But Roche broke to 4–2 and then reached 40–love on his own service. At this stage the match was bursting with promise—but it was never fulfilled. Rosewall's confidence increased, Roche's decreased. Rosewall's superiority on the big points became ever more evident. Finally he was hitting to a superb length and hustling the erratic Roche all over the place. The second match had a similar pattern: a close first set, with youth to the fore, followed by a steady decline, as Laver's authority expanded. There was some gorgeous tennis in the first set, in which the players married speed to subtlety. Once they flirted dangerously with the laws of ballistics with a thunderous exchange of top-spin drives. But the bubble of expectation was burst by a second set in which Laver was so "hot" that he raced to 6–0 in 14 minutes at the cost of only eight points. This was great tennis. Laver came down from the clouds eventually, but he was still too good for Okker. You could say that Roche and Okker were both consumed by the flames their early form ignited.

On Day 12, Mrs. Court and Mrs. Jones (who each had won the title twice before) again qualified for the women's final. Mrs. Court beat Miss Richey, 6–3, 4–6, 7–5, in 97 minutes. The Australian recovered from 2–5 down in the third set and was twice within two points of defeat. This was a perfect example of the way she can raise her game in adversity. It was an absorbing match in which both players used every inch of the court. Mrs. Court asked her sharpest questions from the forecourt, Miss Richey from the baseline. At the crux of the match, Miss Richey became tense and Mrs. Court became bold. At 1–4 down in the third set, Mrs. Court felt twinges of cramp and, in desperation, decided to "go in." She lost only one more game, and had a point for that. After leading 5–2 Miss Richey did not get past 30 again. Mrs. Jones lost only three games to Mrs. Bowrey. She was always the sounder and, thanks to her drop shots and her forecourt game, the more versatile. . . .

So to Days 13 and 14, the last weekend. The championships ended in dazzling sunshine, with the center court so crowded and colorful that it seemed hemmed in by vast banks of flowers. Laver beat Rosewall in straight sets in 93 minutes. Mrs. Court beat Mrs. Jones, 6–1, 4–6, 6–3, in 78 minutes, after Mrs. Jones had pumped new life into a dying match by winning six successive games from 1–4 down in the second set. This was Mrs. Court's 22nd major singles title—eight Australian, one South African, three Italian, three French, two Wimbledon, three German and two American. We shall be lucky if we see again such a superb combination of tennis player and athlete. Her one flaw, as a competitor, is that she remains a country girl at heart—sometimes overawed by the biggest of occasions. But for that, her peerless record would be even better. Now her severity of volley, smash and service was matched by good ground strokes, especially on the backhand. Mrs. Jones drew on every ounce of her skill, sense and courage. Like the fine professional she is, she pounced on her one chance to get into the match. . . .

[In the men's final] the sunny occasion had the flavor of an exhibition by two masters of the game. But in competitive terms it was commonplace. Laver's length was better. It enabled him to keep Rosewall under the sort of pressure that enforces errors. Rosewall's length was just wayward enough to give Laver chances to attack. Laver was also as quick as a cat, so that Rosewall usually had difficulty putting the ball away.

"I was lucky," said Laver, "in that my form stayed all the way through."

Rosewall, of course, was French champion as far back as 1953. Someone asked him if he was still the same weight. (He looks it.) "I'm a bit heavier in the pocket," he said with a straight face.

These were memorable championships, unusually well organized. The song makes a fuss about "April in Paris." But May and June will do for me!

RECORD WIMBLEDON MATCH WON BY PANCHO GONZALES

by Fred Tupper

Let it go down in the record books that Richard (Pancho) Gonzales has won from Charles Pasarell, 22–24, 1–6, 16–14, 6–3, 11–9.

It was the longest match in Wimbledon tennis history, 5 hours 12 minutes, and had the most games, 112. It was played over two days, first in darkness, then in sunshine. It pitted the greatest player of his time against a man who for three years running in the early stages has set Wimbledon's center court afire.

Everything else at the $80,000 open tournament today paled into insignificance: Rod Laver was two sets down before he beat Premjit Lall of India, and Arthur Ashe was two sets down before he defeated Terry Ryan of South Africa.

Gonzales is a tennis legend. It was 21 years ago that he won his first national championship at Forest Hills at the age of 20. He won again in 1949, then turned professional. Through the 1950s he was almost unbeatable, the top man in the game.

Pasarell is 25 years old. He, too, has been the American No. 1. In 1967 here he defeated the defending champion, Manuel Santana, in the first round; last year he took Ken Rosewall to five sets in the second round, both Wimbledon classics.

They first went on court yesterday evening a few minutes before 6 o'clock, the old lion and the tough, rangily built Puerto Rican. That story has been written: how Pasarell held 11 set points before he won the 46-game first set, which equaled the record for the longest set here; and how he took the second set at 6–1 after Gonzales had raged in protest at playing in the darkness, unable to see the ball properly. The match was called then, 2 hours 20 minutes after it had started.

The sun came out as they went on the center court this afternoon. It warmed the back of the old lion. Now he could see.

The third set was supposed to be a formality. How could a man of 41 spring back after that grueling ordeal?

The 15,000 fans who saw it could tell you. Some of the sting has gone from Pancho's blazing serve; it was not notable. He cannot cover court as fast as in his heyday, but he gets to where he's going. Perhaps he cannot hit the ball so hard any more, but he can put it where he wants to.

Pasarell serves harder, runs faster, cracks the cover off the ball.

That third set went 30 games. It took an hour and a half. Seven times Pancho had set point before he won it as Charlito sprayed a backhand over the sideline.

Gonzales took the fourth set at 6–3 as Pasarell double-faulted on set point.

The strain was telling on Gonzales. He wasted no motion. He went for the balls he could hit; he let others go by. His aim was to hold service, to throw every ounce of strength into keeping the ball hard and deep. But he was fading.

At 4–5 he was at love–40, three match points against him. He won them all. At 5–6 he was love–40 again, three more match points to stave off. A smash in deep court, a drop volley, a thunderbolt serve, and he had done it, ending the game with the wristiest of stop volleys that slid over the net.

There were shouts of "bravo! bravo!" and prolonged applause when the men changed sides. At 7–8, there was the seventh match point, but Pasarell lobbed over the line.

It was a question of raw courage now. How long could Pancho go on? He was leaning on his racket between exchanges, flicking globules of sweat off his brow.

At 9–9 Pasarell played a bad game. He double-faulted, hit a volley wide, a lob over the baseline and another volley just out. Gonzales served for the match. A serve, a smash to deep court and a backhand volley that creased the sideline put him at match point. In sepulchral silence Gonzales toed the tape to serve. Then Pasarell lobbed out. Gonzales had taken 11 points in a row. He had clawed his way back and won.

He shuffled off to the dressing room, head up. The cheers reverberated around the court and followed him in. If he never comes back again, that will be a fitting epitaph.

"I'm a little tired," he said.

There was a vast crowd around the No. 4 enclosure where Laver, his whole game out of gear, was two sets down to Lall. At 3–4 in the third set, Lall pulled up, rubbing his leg and apparently hobbled by cramp. He missed two smashes and lost that game. He didn't win another one. Match to Laver, 3–6, 4–6, 6–3, 6–0, 6–0.

Ashe takes longer and longer to get started. Against Terry Ryan, a 26-year-old South African, he served badly, failed to find his rhythm and trailed, 3–6, 4–6.

The American No. 1 took the next three sets, serving very well.

"I like to win the last point," he said. He won it with an ace.

The previous longest match was in 1953 between Jaroslav Drobny and Budge Patty. It went 93 games and lasted 4¼ hours without an interruption. Drobny won.

ANN JONES ENDS MRS. KING'S WIMBLEDON REIGN

by Fred Tupper

Mrs. Ann Jones ended today the three-year reign of Mrs. Billie Jean King as Wimbledon women's tennis champion. The 30-year-old British left-hander, a dogged competitor, won by 3–6, 6–3, 6–2 in 70 minutes before 15,000 excited fans jammed around center court.

Some of the fans had yelled "Out! Out!" at close line calls and at one point the yelling prompted Mrs. King to curtsy to the crowd.

"The crowd was making the calls before the balls hit," Mrs. King said after the match. "The curtsy was a nice way of saying be quiet."

An official request for quiet came from the umpire, Laurie McCallum.

"I wanted to win fair and square," Mrs. Jones said. "I did not want the crowd to put Billie Jean off. I felt slightly embarrassed about being in England. I wanted to win, but I wanted to win fair and square."

Mrs. Jones was the better player and she became the first British woman to win since Angela Mortimer defeated Christine Truman in 1961. Mrs. Jones had been in the semi-finals eight times in the last 11 years and lost to Mrs. King in the final two years.

Her inspiration came from her tremendous victory over the world's No. 1, Mrs. Margaret Court of Australia, in the Wednesday semi finals. Given little chance then, she blew an early lead and lost the first set, but stuck to her guns and triumphed on persistence.

Early in the match, Mrs. King dominated the court, serving well, volleying beautifully and finding wide openings for her backhand. At a game apiece, she was dead on target. She slapped a backhand down the tape, a backhand into the clear across court and another backhand through a hole for a service break.

Soon she was at 5–3, with Ann serving. That backhand thumped into the corner to put her at set point and in some infighting around the net, Mrs. King volleyed into open space for 6–3.

Mrs. Jones had been having trouble reaching the low bouncers and was not swinging true on the shot. Mrs. King had the first game of the set at love and was at game point on Ann's serve with a lob to the baseline and a wristy shot that slid over the net and dropped dead. But that game eluded her.

Three times she hoisted windblown lobs to deep court as Ann smashed back, curving one to the corner for deuce and starting a blazing run that gave her game after game. Mrs. Jones was transformed now, coming in on everything and jerking Mrs. King around court with low, spinning volleys.

Billie Jean was at 2–1 with three points for the break and missed them all. She was down 1–4, and then pulled herself together. Sharp volleys and a forehand into the corner brought her to 2–4, deep serving to 3–4.

She was love–30, Ann serving, with 10 points in a row. It looked like a new game. But Ann rushed to advantage and a swinging southpaw serve pulled Mrs. King far out of court and into error.

A forehand from the baseline was so accurate that Billie Jean could get only the wood on it as it thundered by. Set to Mrs. Jones at 6–3.

Mrs. King was at 15–40, Ann's service, in the first game of the decider on a backhand across court that nicked the line. The crowd didn't like it. A group in the open stand behind Mrs. King shouted "Out! Out!" The umpire called for silence.

Billie Jean lost that game, then won the next, but she was demoralized. She couldn't get her first service in. She lost her touch on the volley. Those spinners were fluttering around her shoetops as she became enmeshed in a defensive web. She tried to blast her way out, but Mrs. Jones was in control, with cheers driving her on. At 1–4, Mrs. King flubbed some volleys and double-faulted on game point.

The match was there for the taking and so were the butterflies for Ann.

"I kept thinking of Nancy Richey," she said, alluding to the quarter-final match in which she had led, 5–1, and was pulled back to 5–all.

Ann served a wild game and lost it. She was soon at 15–40 with two match points. Mrs. King saved them both with volleys and wristed a dropshot over for ad-in. The postponement was futile. At the third match point she double-faulted again. There was bedlam.

Princess Anne came on court to present the huge silver platter. Mrs. Jones takes $3,600 for winning (Mrs. King won $1,800). She receives honors as a member of the British Empire next Tuesday. Her cup is full after 13 years of trying.

The Australians, John Newcombe and Tony Roche, retained their doubles title by defeating Tom Okker of the Netherlands and Marty Riessen of Evanston, Illinois, 7–5, 11–9, 6–3.

LAVER DEFEATS NEWCOMBE FOR FOURTH WIMBLEDON TITLE

by Fred Tupper

Rod Laver has won the Wimbledon championship for the fourth time.

The Australian carrot-top fought back with an irresistible seven-game surge today to defeat John Newcombe, 6–4, 5–7, 6–4, 6–4, in one of the best finals in Wimbledon history.

And so the wiry left-hander enters the halls of tennis immortals. He is the first man to take the title four times since the challenge round was abolished in 1922 and the first man to take it four times in as many attempts. He won it in 1961 and 1962 as an amateur, turned professional in 1963 and then won the first open last year.

Laver has also taken the Australian and French crowns this year and needs the United States title at Forest Hills next month for the grand slam. The last man to make it was Laver in 1962, and then the pros were not competing. The only other man to do it was Don Budge in 1938.

Laver was top-seeded and a 5-to-4 betting favorite when this wonderful Wimbledon began. But he never had a tougher match over his years here than against Newcombe this afternoon.

Big John burst into the limelight this spring. He won the Italian and British hard-court titles and made a mockery of his sixth-seeded position here by demolishing the second favorite, Tony Roche.

This final was supposed to be a contrast in styles, the blazing ground strokes and imaginative improvisations of the 30-year-old redhead against the big service and inflexible tactics of the 25-year-old Newcombe.

It didn't work out that way. Rod served beautifully and Newcombe dinked and lobbed and hit soft shots with such consummate cunning that at one stage it seemed probable that he would win.

It was a slugfest at the start, tennis as good as you could see, with the ball moving as fast as the eye could follow. In a marvelous point, with the players scrambling all over the court, Laver shot out of nowhere to slash a volley down the line and then break Newcombe's service for 2–1.

The redhead went to 4–3 and was serving when John tried another ploy. He teased Laver with a running lob, hoisted another high and deep that was smashed out and then dropped a dink over the net that pulled Laver up, whereupon John pitched a topspin lob over his head for the break-back. He was in the set at 4–all.

For a moment there Laver had looked mortal. Not so. Taking dead aim he whipped a backhand across court and fired another one down the tape for the next game and took the set with an ace.

Newcombe persevered. In the eighth game of the second set he floated a chip to the sideline, threaded a backhand through a needle and then

879

chipped to Laver's feet to lead, 5–3. But the big Australian double-faulted to start the next game and double-faulted to end it.

Twice he had broken Laver, twice he had been broken back immediately. Then he made it. He hammered a forehand down the middle and Laver was long on the return. He stretched him with a cross-court backhand, which Laver netted. Second set to Newcombe as the crowd roared approval.

Laver was losing his touch. At 1–2 in the third set he messed up a low volley, sprayed a shot too far, hit a half-volley over the line and double-faulted.

Newcombe held his serve to 4–1 and there were mutterings in the stands. He seemed clearly on top. Was the unthinkable to happen? The great Margaret Smith Court was a certainty to win the women's title and she had fallen. And a crisis was staring Laver in the face.

He hit a couple of lobs to take the first point in the seventh game and then he struck a wonder shot. With a snap of his wrist he hit a backhand spinner at such an inconceivable angle that it cleared the net by inch fractions. Then he backhanded a shot through the middle and was at 3–4.

It was savage, searing stuff and turned the whole match in a twinkling. The winners streamed off Laver's racket, hit to impossible places.

In the seven-game streak he had the third set and was 2–love in the fourth. Then it was a question of holding service. As he toed the line at 5–3, one match point escaped, but he buried a high lob diagonally across court for the set and match. . . .

"It was my toughest match here ever," Laver said. The victory was worth $7,200. . . .

After a rainy first day, perfect weather helped bring the total attendance to 300,000. This Wimbledon was to be remembered for Pancho Gonzales's record 5-hour-12 minute, 112-game victory over Charles Pasarell, the fantastic first-set performance of Arthur Ashe against Laver and the victories of Mrs. Jones over Mrs. Court and then Mrs. King.

STAN SMITH WINS NATIONAL GRASS TITLE

by Neil Amdur

Stan Smith, the tallest player in American tennis, closed in on a coveted Davis Cup singles assignment and No. 1 national ranking today with a 9–7, 6–3, 6–1 victory over Bob Lutz for the national grass-court championship.

In beating his doubles partner, college teammate and close friend for the eighth time in nine meetings, the 22-year-old Smith took another significant step in his bid for the prestigious top spot. He previously won the national indoor and Eastern championships this year.

The 6 foot 4 inch Californian currently is No. 3 behind Arthur Ashe and Clark Graebner. But he has 2–0 won-lost records against each this year, is 2–0 against Lutz and has won three of five singles matches with Charles Pasarell, another member of the well-balanced American Davis Cup team. . . .

Smith, from Pasadena, has played Davis Cup doubles and won the crucial doubles point with Lutz in last year's 4–1 challenge round triumph over Australia. But he has never played singles and would have to replace either Ashe or Graebner, last year's successful regulars.

Smith, an independent professional, played confidently against Lutz in collecting the $4,000 first prize. . . . He is a soft-spoken giant, whose sportsmanship and sincerity have made him one of the most popular players. On the court he is almost impossible to lob over, has improved his agility, developed delicate touch at the net and has such an unusually long reach that passing him either down the line or cross-court requires superb threading. If there has been a weakness in his game, it has been a tendency to underestimate his innate talent and physical attributes. Recent victories have induced a breakthrough toward greater confidence.

Today's match, played in 94-degree weather before a crowd of 4,000, lasted 97 minutes. Smith lost only 14 points on service. . . . The crucial game came with Lutz serving at 7–all. At 15–30 Lutz popped a string on his aluminum racket while slapping a backhand wide. He changed rackets, and the difference in touch and tightness was evident when he netted a forehand approach volley on the next point and lost the game by driving another low volley past the baseline.

The Australian team of Dick Crealy and Allan Stone won the $1,000 men's doubles title by beating Bill Bowrey of Australia and Pasarell, 9–11, 6–3, 7–5. The women's doubles final went to Mrs. Margaret Smith Court of Australia and Virginia Wade of Britain, 6–1, 6–3, over the American duo of Mrs. Mary Ann Eisel Curtis and Valerie Ziegenfuss.

U. S. WINS BACK WIGHTMAN CUP

by Neil Amdur

The Wightman Cup returned to the United States today when Julie Heldman won her second singles match of the series, 6–3, 6–4, from Winnie Shaw of Britain.

In posting the winning fourth point in the seven-point competition, the 23-year-old New Yorker offset Virginia Wade's formidable 6–3, 2–6, 6–4 conquest of Nancy Richey in today's opening match.

It was Miss Wade's most impressive single performance since she beat Mrs. Billie Jean King for the United States open title last year. It came against America's top-ranking player, on unfamiliar asphalt courts, with light balls, and with Britain's back to the baseline.

Miss Heldman, the American No. 2, was the heroine of this 41st annual series, which the United States won for the 34th time, including its 18th consecutive triumph in this country.

Miss Heldman defeated Miss Wade, 3–6, 6–1, 8–6, in the pressure-packed first match, last Saturday. Before she walked on court against Miss Wade, Julie was named a substitute in doubles when Miss Richey developed arm trouble.

Fortunately, the match had no effect on the outcome, but Miss Heldman, voted the outstanding performer in the series, and Jane (Peaches) Bartkowicz of Hamtramck, Michigan, beat Miss Wade and Miss Shaw 6–4, 6–2, for a final 5–2 American triumph. The crowd of 4,827 at Harold T. Clark Stadium [in Cleveland] brought the three-day attendance total to 15,025.

Today's two singles matches were studies in contrast, with Miss Wade and her opponent lashing at each other while Misses Heldman and Shaw softballed strategically from the baseline.

Service meant little in the Heldman-Shaw duel as they freely traded 12 breaks during the 60 minutes. Neither could hold serve until the sixth game of the first set when Julie finally carried at love, helped by a forehand placement and three errors by Miss Shaw. She broke again for the set in the 10th game as Winnie banged two volleys into the net and slapped errantly at an overhead.

Miss Wade and Miss Richey exchanged the first two sets. One service break, in the seventh game at 15, decided the final set after Nancy had gallantly held in a fifth game that played to deuce eight times, twice to Miss Wade's advantage. . . .

Miss Richey was not without opportunity in the last set. She had two break points in the second game and led, 30–love, in the sixth game. But Virginia, a miss of many moods, had her tenacious face on today, perhaps eager to vindicate her erratic play for most of this year and to reverse a disputed three-set loss to Miss Richey during the South African championships. . . .

In regaining the sterling silver cup, the United States finds itself in possession of the three symbols of international tennis supremacy, the Davis Cup, Wightman Cup, and Federation Cup for the first time since 1963. Miss Heldman, a newcomer to Wightman Cup competition, also played on the victorious Federation Cup team.

LAVER DEFEATS ROCHE FOR GRAND SLAM

by Neil Amdur

Rod Laver achieved the second grand slam of his tennis career yesterday.

With all the competitive trademarks of the true champion, the 31-year-old king of the court overcame Tony Roche, his 24-year-old Australian countryman, 7–9, 6–1, 6–2, 6–2, in the final of the United States Open championship at the West Side Tennis Club in Forest Hills, Queens.

With the $16,000 first prize, the richest singles payoff in the sport, Laver lifted his professional earnings this year to a record $106,000. He also entered the record books as the only player to have achieved two sweeps of the Australian, French, British and American championships, the international events that make up the grand slam.

Don Budge registered the first slam in 1938. Laver completed his initial sweep in 1962, but as an amateur and with such established pros as Richard (Pancho) Gonzales, Ken Rosewall, Lew Hoad and Tony Trabert ineligible for the competition. The situation has been changed with the approval of open tournaments. . . .

Laver and Roche had to wait 1 hour 35 minutes until a rented helicopter could dry the center court, which had been dampened by the morning rain.

"The playing conditions made it very difficult," Laver said. "The ground was very soft, the speeds of the bounce made it tough to return, and you were sliding all over."

The fine line that separates Laver from Roche, Arthur Ashe, Roy Emerson and others is his ability to concentrate on the big serve or decisive volley at 15–30 or 30–40. . . .

Roche, who collected $8,000 as runner-up, could have felt the physical strain of his three-hour semi-final with John Newcombe on Sunday. . . . But when the big money goes on the line, the winning strokes are Laver's. Except for last year's first open here, when he lost to Cliff Drysdale in the quarter-finals, Laver has won every major tennis money event in the world. . . . Comparing Laver with the stars of other eras—Gonzales, Jack Kramer, Budge and Tilden—might be treasonous in tennis' sacrosanct society, but the Rocket has met every challenge with the discipline and dedication worthy of a place in the hall of heroes. . . .

In winning here at Forest Hills, the richest tournament in the world with its $137,000 purse, Laver overcame psychological hazards, as well as such quality pros as Dennis Ralston, Emerson, Ashe and Roche, his chief tormentor this year. Rain had washed out two complete sessions and delayed the final one day. His tense semi-final match with Ashe had been halted by darkness in the third set and finished the following day.

Meanwhile in Newport Beach, California, Laver's wife, Mary, had also been experiencing delays. The couple's first child was three days overdue and Laver had been calling every morning to make sure everything was all right. Mrs. Laver reported yesterday by phone before her husband walked onto the stadium court for the final, "I've been telling him everything's fine and to concentrate on his tennis," she said.

If there was a touch of nostalgia to this tournament it came in the women's doubles final yesterday, in which Françoise Durr and 33-year-old Darlene Hard upset the top-seeded team of Mrs. Margaret Court and Virginia Wade, 0–6, 6–4, 6–4.

The crowd of 3,708 (6,200 tickets had been sold) cheered lustily, particularly for Miss Hard, a former national champion, who had replaced Miss Durr's regular partner, Mrs. Ann Haydon Jones.

LAVER COMPLETES HIS SECOND GRAND SLAM

by Roy Blount, Jr.

One thing worked out neatly at the U.S. Open at Forest Hills last week: the best player in the world won. By defeating a fellow Australian, Tony Roche, 7–9, 6–1, 6–2, 6–2, top-seeded Rod Laver added the U.S. Open title to the Australian, British and French ones and completed the Grandest Slam, or at least the first Grandest Slam, or at least the first Grand Open Slam in tennis history. Laver has now won five of the seven big-four tournaments held since the creation of open tennis, and it looks as though the sport will have to be opened considerably wider, to include angels, highly trained kangaroos or something as yet unenvisaged, before anyone else will be in Laver's league.

As a factor at Forest Hills, though, the hard-nosed Aussie lefthander would have to take second place to the weather, which let everyone down. "I live in a near-tropical country, where we have monsoon rains, and I have never seen 5½ inches of rain in 24 hours before," groused Owen Williams, the South African tournament director who was brought in to transform the U.S. Open but was hard pressed to do more for it than the rain did to it. The 13-day tournament grossed nearly twice as much—$500,000 would be a good guess—as last year, but Williams estimated that the rain—which canceled play on two days, interrupted it on three other days—cost the enterprise some $100,000. . . .

On Saturday, when showers of considerable force first delayed play and then interrupted the taut semi-final match between Laver and Arthur Ashe, some 11,000 sodden fans huddled together under the stands. . . . A tarpaulin cover and the use of hovering helicopters as improvised drying-off devices failed to keep the courts truly playable. They gave rise to bad bounces ("You get to know the patches after a while," noted semi-finalist John Newcombe), they got so chewed up around the baselines that, when a player bounced a ball preparatory to service, it frequently got away from him and on Saturday, at least, they sounded downright squishy from the stands. . . .

The grass wasn't the only thing that failed to hold up. The U.S. Davis Cup team was also washed away. Bob Lutz lost to Tony Roche in the first round—no disgrace—but on one horrible afternoon Clark Graebner, Stan Smith and Charlie Pasarell all disappeared. Graebner had to default with a twisted ankle, Pasarell lost to a lesser Australian, Terry Addison, and most stunningly, Smith got beaten by Ilie Nastase, one of two Rumanians who will challenge for the Davis Cup later this month. Most disappointing of all, the No. 1 U.S. doubles team of Smith and Lutz lost in the third round, in straight sets, to Earl Buchholz and Ray Moore, virtually a pickup team. . . . The U. S. should still be comfortably favored over Rumania in the Davis Cup, but the open was still a blow to U.S. court prestige.

It was something of a leap forward for capitalism, however—to a good many fans' irritation. It may be inconsistent to applaud the elimination of hypocritical amateurism and then complain about having COME TO MARLBORO COUNTRY emblazoned on the new $167,000 Forest Hills scoreboard, but then there was also "Spalding" on the front and back of the ballboys' shirts and "Pepsi" on the drink cooler behind the umpire's stand and the new IBM board proclaiming ponderous and not always comprehensible statistics. . . .

There were other rough spots in the proceedings. Leaflets were handed out in protest of Williams' back-home implication in apartheid, and Ashe announced that he had had to talk an unnamed group of protesters out of an attempt to disrupt the tournament. The world's and history's only prominent black male player said he told the dissidents to give him time to get himself admitted to the South African meet in March—a project to which Williams is lending his support. Finally, Vice President Spiro Agnew, in presenting women's singles champion Margaret Smith Court her trophy and check, stimulated a good deal of heavy murmuring in the stands by announcing that runner-up Nancy Richey . . . would surely "continue to improve."

And yet, despite the unfriendly elements and possible grounds for complaint, there were many times during the tournament when the tennis and a beer were worth all they cost and more. The still-arresting Pancho Gonzales . . . won a picturesque five-set match from long-haired Dane Torben Ulrich before bowing out to Roche in the fourth round. . . . Roche and Newcombe fought magnificently through five semi-final sets before Roche finally won, 3–6, 6–4, 4–6, 6–3, 8–6. And Laver—hitting winners off Ashe's big serve, clipping the corners with looping top-spin ground shots and contriving by acrobatics or foresight to be in the right place again and again—earned every one of the 16,000 dollars he won in the richest tennis tournament ever. The U.S. Open was on uncertain footing in more ways than one, but it imported a lot of class.

U. S. DEFEATS RUMANIA TO RETAIN DAVIS CUP

by Frank DeFord

The SDS called it "a ruling class festival," but the sad truth is that if this is the best that the capitalistic pigs—and the Commie red rats, too, for that matter—can manage to amuse themselves with, then the Establishment is certainly on shaky ground. The real tennis ruling class was a hemisphere away last week, at home in Australia, as the U. S. whipped Rumania 3–0 (5–0 if you collect Green Stamps) in the Davis Cup Challenge Round in Cleveland.

Routs in the Challenge Round are not to be sneezed at and, Lord knows, we get them regularly enough, since the archaic rules permit the defending nation to sit on the sidelines all year and expend energy only in doctoring up the home courts. By the time the challengers arrive, weary and spent after a year of tussling with opponents scattered all over the good green earth, what little chance the challengers might have had is pretty well dissipated. By itself, this situation almost managed to destroy all tennis interest in Australia, where a succession of Indias and Mexicos showed up for euthanasia exercises every Christmas.

While it is still boring, discriminatory new rules have succeeded cleverly in making the Challenge Round rather senseless, too. With only petty jealousy—and the traditional death wish—as motivation, international amateur mastodons (from the smaller countries, mostly) have opened the Davis Cup up to pros. That is, certain pros. Selected pros, those whom the national organizations can control. Which is to say, as one high amateur official does: "Look, there's no mumbo jumbo to it. We're keeping the contract pros out. Anybody else can play. It's that simple." The result is that the best team in the world—the Australians: Laver, Newcombe, Roche, Rosewall, Emerson, Stolle—is included out, since it is all under contract for good American dollars. The U.S. team could beat Rumania before breakfast every day playing on Jell-O and not turn a head. Only tennis could take its premier event, the Challenge Round, and transform it into the Runner-up Bowl.

So it is hardly surprising that there was no television of the Cleveland event and previous little other press coverage. True, Clevelanders, who, unlike their brethren in Sydney and Melbourne, are not experienced in these massacres, hardly left a seat empty in the Harold T. Clark Stadium, but then the fantastically diligent Cleveland tennis organization pulled in 15,000 paying customers for the girls' Wightman Cup a few weeks ago, and P. T. Barnum lunged from his grave with admiration at that news. At last Saturday's deciding doubles match, however, even some of the most patriotic Buckeyes had begun to cheer for the Rumanians, chauvinism taking a back seat to the hope of getting one's money's worth.

It was a forlorn hope, though, even on the challengers' side of the net. Ilie Nastase, the attractive young Rumanian, was candid enough to say afterward that he and his teammates had never really figured on more than two points—beating Stan Smith twice in the singles. Nastase and his partner, Ion Tiriac, had been a good enough team to get to the finals of the French championships and had been undefeated in their first six Davis Cup matches this year, but Nastase just wrinkled his nose at the suggestion that he and Tiriac thought they had a chance against Smith and Bob Lutz in the doubles. "We had only 10 days to practice on this court," he said. "Sure, we beat the British at Wimbledon on the grass, but it takes too long to learn how to run on this kind of court."

The Clark court had been slow for the Wightman Cup, making for long, exciting rallies, but by the Challenge Round the cement surface had been painted lengthwise and buffed for speed so that in the opening match Arthur Ashe beat Nastase 6–2, 15–13, 7–5—48 games in which there were only four points during which the ball went over the net five times. It was dull; Ashe won more with cold efficiency than with his usual élan. Nastase kept playing it safe, hitting cross-court, as if he were still home on surfaces that some top international players consider the slowest in the world. "The clay instincts are completely different," Ashe said afterward, with some sympathy—and bitter memories too, perhaps since so many fast American games came a cropper on slow courts in recent years.

Australia was not altogether absent in Cleveland. Denied permission to employ Laver and his cohorts this year, the Aussies, fielding two koala bears and a wallaby, were eliminated from the cup months ago. Somewhere along the line after this, however, Harry Hopman, the irascible, perennial Australian captain, surfaced as coach of the Rumanians. For Hopman, a master technician and strategist, it was the ultimate chance at playing Pygmalion with a team that, before this year, had won a grand total of eight Davis Cup matches in 25 years. He took charge. While Captain Gheorghe Cozbuc sat by the court, smiling graciously and providing his players with water, Hopman scribbled notes furiously in the stands. Earlier—although he is 62—he had hit vigorously with his charges in practice and ushered them about paternally, instructing them, as he always did his Aussies, in the evils of a free press.

The old master did not have enough to work with, though, and, especially after Nastase beat Smith at Forest Hills, there was no chance that the Americans would take their challengers lightly. Under Captain Donald Dell and Coach Dennis Ralston (ineligible to play as a contract pro) the U.S. team was well briefed, in good shape and a happy ship, rocked only slightly when Dell had to decide who should play the second singles with Ashe. Off his play this year and his potential—and despite the loss to Nastase—Smith was expected to be the choice. Cliff Richey, however, beat Smith in practice, and Dell had shown a disposition in the past to go with a hot player. But he called the team together Wednesday and said Smith was it. "If I don't go with the big serve on this surface," he explained, "we're giving up a natural advantage."

Smith, then, felt perhaps as guilty as dismayed when he came into the locker room down 2–1 in sets to Tiriac in the second of the opening day's matches. What drama could be distilled from the proceedings was here, for if Tiriac won and showed Smith vulnerable the Rumanians still had two more shots at him and a chance for the upset. "I'm letting all you guys down," Smith said, shaking his head.

"No, Stan," Dell replied, "if you lose you're not letting anyone down but yourself." There was no false banter; Dell only emphasized that Smith should concentrate more on getting his big first serve in.

On the other side of Roxboro Junior High, in the Rumanian locker room, Tiriac was fuming. An utterly charming man away from the court, he is singularly perverse on it, complaining, glowering, stalking and weaving like a bull at bay.

Now he was unhappy because he could not get any hot water for a shower. Ashe, better versed in the intricacies of American plumbing, had found an obscure valve so that he and his teammates had plenty of water. Tiriac had to go back out cold on a raw, windy day, and he promptly lost serve at 15 in the first game. Warmed up, neither he nor Smith could break the other thereafter, and the set went to the American 6–4 to tie the match at two sets apiece.

Despite their good size, both Tiriac and Nastase have more guile than power. Indeed, their simple inability to put away easy volleys was a significant element in their defeat. But they were tireless dandies, and Tiriac had gone ahead of Smith with a series of beautiful flip-wrist backhands down the line.

Now, as the last set proceeded with close games, Smith began to pass Tiriac with his own (but harder) backhands down the line. At 4–4, with Tiriac serving under a threatening dusk, Smith's backhands got him to love–40. Tiriac came back with four straight points, and he would have held serve with the next point, but he hit a typically soft smash, Smith was able to retrieve it and passed him with another backhand in the next exchange. At last, after four deuces, Smith broke serve with his fifth winning backhand of the key game of the whole match. He held serve at love to put the U. S. up 2–0 and effectively conclude matters.

Smith and Lutz ended things for real the next day 8–6, 6–1, 11–9. That they played well together again and, more important, that Smith showed he could come from behind against a wise and trying opponent under pressure, establishes the Americans as more formidable than ever. It is especially unfortunate, then, that all that can be said with assurance is that they are champions of the Davis Cup and the second-best national tennis team in the world.

1970

THE FRENCH CHAMPIONSHIPS

by Rex Bellamy

The French championships may have been the most significant in the early history of open tennis. The 1968 edition was the first major open tournament. The 1970 edition was the first major open tournament to be boycotted by the contract professionals—or, more accurately, by the men who control them. Why the boycott, and what effect did it have?

The split occurred partly because of bad relations between the French and the pro groups (politicians are more reluctant than players when it comes to forgiving and forgetting), and partly because the French would pay only what the players earned on court. The pro groups insisted on a corporate fee before playing. Both sides were adamant.

The firmness of the French—in accepting the boycott, and keeping the prize money at its record high level—was widely admired and brought them a pat on the back from the players. Arthur Ashe, Zeljko Franulovic, Lew Hoad, and Ilie Nastase, representing the independent professionals, publicly congratulated the French on setting "a major precedent" and "adhering to the principle of fair play."

The absence of the 24 contract professionals had no effect on the championships except that, during the second week, the quality of the men's singles was slightly lower than usual. Crowds and receipts alike were almost identical with the 1969 figures. This was a sharp blow to the prestige of the contract professionals. In addition, they did their reputations no good by "ducking" the toughest championships in the game.

The difficulties of the pro groups, in meeting management costs and players' guarantees, are widely appreciated. But they are swimming against the tide of opinion in demanding from open tournaments any money except what they earn on court. They overrate their market value. Their ultimate bargaining weapon (that no major championships can succeed without them) has been shattered. They have been reminded of the old Irish saying that the only thing worse than being indispensable is being dispensable.

The prize money in Paris was the same as Wimbledon's (give or take a few dollars according to the rate of exchange). But since the players were taxed 20 per cent, many earned less than they would have done under the old expenses system.

The organization of the championships fell down only in the manning of lines and scoreboards (on some of the outside courts, there were no scoreboards to man). But in every other respect these were gloriously successful championships. Huge crowds swarmed into Roland Garros day after day, so that the center court often looked like a giant rockery in full bloom. The weather was so consistently hot that it was a test of endurance merely watching tennis, never mind playing it. Towards the end, gusty breezes swirled clouds of dust across the courts. Inevitably, the championships were more grueling than ever.

Mrs. Court won her 26th major singles title (nine Australian, two South African, three Italian, four French, two Wimbledon, three German, and three United States). She became the first woman since Helen Wills to win the French title four times. Her prize was 17,800 francs, less tax. Miss Niessen, eight months older and 2 in. taller, became the first German since the war to reach the women's singles finals of any of the "Big Four" championships. She has played the best tennis of her career since she switched to metal rackets last November.

Jan Kodes, runner-up for the Italian championship two months earlier, won his first major title and became the first Czechoslovak champion since Jaroslav Drobny in 1952 (this year, Drobny won the veterans' event). The French championship, like the Italian, had its first East European men's final.

Kodes, a tight-lipped little introvert who moves fast and hits screaming passing shots down both lines, bounced through in straight sets until he came up against Ion Tiriac in the round of 16. Tiriac led by two sets to one in a tempestuous and disputatious match. Overall, Kodes looked the sharper operator in more than one sense. The Czechoslovak then whipped Martin Mulligan in straight sets. We put a stop watch on this, just for fun, and discovered that although the match lasted 88 minutes, the ball was in play for only 28 minutes 20.9 seconds.

Against Goven, Kodes was again two sets to one down (and Goven was serving for a 3–0 lead in the fourth). This was something else. Can you imagine a young Frenchman playing a semi-final on the center court at Roland Garros? Kodes had 11,001 opponents—Goven and the crowd, who made an explosive din whenever their man won a point. At times Kodes had a glassy-eyed look of utter bewilderment. He must have felt like an early Christian thrown to the lions. But although the inspired Goven played some aggressive, quick-footed tennis, Kodes was the better man and eventually proved it.

That crisis over, Kodes played one of the finest matches of his life to crush Franulovic, 6–2, 6–4, 6–0, in an astonishing 66-minute final. "He played so well that I was under pressure all the time," said Franulovic, whose nonchalant flair had endeared him to the Parisian public. He had his chance. The crux of the match came in the 10th game of the second set. With all in the balance, and Kodes apparently going off the boil after a lusty start, Franulovic served two double-faults in an abominably loose game. That put him two sets down. After that, Kodes was too far in front to be inhibited and Franulovic was too far behind to be anything else. The Yugoslav scored only 10 points in the third set.

Franulovic's luck had run out. He had been taken to five sets by Wieslaw

Gasiorek, Ashe, and Richey. The Ashe match was a beauty, and ended with high drama and a baying crowd. In the fifth set, Franulovic achieved a lucky break to 5–3. His racket flew from his hand, over the sidelines, as he hit a winning stop volley. A chancy backhand fell slap on the line. A net cord by Ashe gave Franulovic the opening that clinched the break. The match was like that, its shifting patterns dictated by fractions of an inch. Serving for the match, Franulovic disputed a call as he went love–30 down.

The crowd yelled. Both men recovered from the unsettling dispute to play some hot points before Franulovic won on his third match point. Casually but swiftly, he took a loose ball from his pocket and tossed it after his winning stop volley: it seemed that he legally "lost" the point that won him the match.

If this was close for Franulovic, it was nothing to his semi-final with Richey. This throbbing drama, disputed before an enthralled crowd, lasted more than three hours and contained one of the most extraordinary twists in the history of the championships. From a set and 1–2 down, Richey won 16 games out of 20 to lead by two sets to one and 5–1.

The pale-eyed Texan was all bouncing, surging authority, hitting some glorious passing shots, pressing forward all the time, and hardly missing a shot. The seeds of his eventual frustration were probably sown in the fifth game of the fourth set, when Franulovic hit a forehand that landed on or close to the baseline. Richey grabbed the ball before the linesman called, and then vehemently argued the point with linesman and umpire in turn. The crowd swung behind Franulovic.

Richey nevertheless reached 5–1, two breaks up. Twice he served for the match. The first time he lost the game to 30, serving two double-faults. The second time, at 5–3, he reached 40–15, two match points. But he volleyed into the net and then double-faulted again. His service had lost its rhythm and the match was swinging away from him. He conceded six successive games and the set with them. Franulovic calmly accepted his reprieve and regained his touch.

In the fifth set Richey had break points for 4–2 and 5–3. Then Franulovic had a chance and seized it. He had plucked success from the jaws of defeat. But there was never a hope that he would do the same against Kodes.

Kodes collected 56,000 francs, the biggest first prize outside Forest Hills. But it went to his country, not himself. The leading Czechoslovaks have contracts to the effect that their earnings from the Italian, French, and German championships go back into the development of their national game. As a youngster, Kodes himself used to benefit from this scheme. Renata Tomanova, runner-up for the girls' championship in Paris, is among the present-day beneficiaries.

Let us take a cursory look at the rest of the championships. For a time they were dominated in many ways by the iron men of east Europe, players with faraway faces and strange-sounding names. Among these was the new Hungarian champion, Szabolcs Baranyi, whose backhands down the line tamed "The Bear," Barry MacKay, and stretched Manuel Santana. Later the Spaniard was beaten by Goven in a nerve-twanging, crowd-imposed drama on the center court, where nine years earlier Santana had become the first Spaniard to win a major title.

Another old favorite, Hoad, reached the last 16, delighting the customers by marrying power with delicacy, by ruthlessly attacking anything short— and merely by being Hoad. At the other end of the age scale was 19-year-old Adriano Panatta of Rome, who also reached the last 16. We noted the exceptional youth of the last four men—Kodes 24, Goven 22, Franulovic 22, and Richey 23. It was Richey who disposed of the top seed, Nastase—a superb athlete and resourceful stroke player, lank hair flopping as he pranced about the court with his slightly pigeon-toed gait. But Nastase seemed jaded. His length was poor and he could not hit as hard as he needed to.

In the women's event, Karen Krantzcke, her confidence boosted by the role she played in Australia's Federation Cup success, beat Judy Dalton (her teammate a week earlier), Françoise Durr, and Virginia Wade and then led Miss Niessen 3–1. Miss Krantzcke was to win only 17 more points.

"The strain of concentrating so hard for so long hit me like a bomb at 3–1," she said.

Esme Emanuel, who has been studying at San Francisco State College for the past three years, played almost flawless clay-court tennis to lead Julie Heldman 6–3 and 4–1. Miss Heldman, no longer quite the player she was last year, could make nothing of Mrs. Court, who by this time (the semifinals) was playing devastating tennis. Meantime, Miss Niessen had disposed of Billie Jean King for the third time in four matches this year. It took her 93 minutes and it was a lot like that Richey-Franulovic match. Agile, flexible, and hitting harder, Mrs. King outclassed the leggy German in a 6–2 first set and had 16 break points (yes, 16) in the second.

Three times Miss Niessen held her service from love–40 down. Logically, she was done for. But somehow she held on and at 7–6 her enviably good backhand earned her a break for the set. The rest was anticlimax. Mrs. King had a break point for 2–1 in the third set but was promptly afflicted by cramp and scored only four more points. She hobbled through the rest of the match merely as a formality, hitting the ball only when it came her way.

The women's final was a far tougher match than Mrs. Court's 6–2, 6–4 win may suggest. The heat was fierce. Both players poured with perspiration under their sun hats. They worked each other cruelly hard. In gaining a 6–3, 3–0 lead (she had a point for 4–0), Mrs. Court played some of the most athletic, resourceful, and accomplished clay court tennis of her career. But Miss Niessen's length, drop shots, and cool tennis brain enabled her to draw level at 4–all. A sudden rash of errors in the ninth game snapped the German's tenuous thread of authority. Overall, she was outclassed. But she had contributed admirably to an exhausting match that contained some gorgeous tennis.

When Miss Durr shared the women's doubles title for the fourth successive year, it gave an appropriately Gallic touch to a championship in which, merely by sitting or standing in the sun, we had learned exactly what happens to a steak under the grill.

IT ALMOST CAME UP ROSES FOR ROSEWALL AT WIMBLEDON

by Walter Bingham

Pity Ken Rosewall. Sixteen years ago he stood on Wimbledon's center court in the finals against Jaroslav Drobny, a 19-year-old boy against a Wimbledon favorite. Drobny won, a popular decision, and little sympathy was wasted on Rosewall. Surely he would have other opportunities. Two years later Rosewall reached the finals again and this time he lost to his doubles partner, Lew Hoad. When Rosewall turned pro, he became ineligible for Wimbledon and by the time open tennis arrived, Rod Laver had supplanted him as the best player in the world.

And yet last week, on a damp, humid afternoon, there was Ken Rosewall, now 35, back on center court and in the finals, back for perhaps his last try at the one major title he had never won. Across the net was John Newcombe, another Australian—this was the 10th All-Australian final in the last 15 years—a big, strong, good-looking 26-year-old with a crashing serve and volley and the stamina to run all day. It would be pleasant to report that little Ken, with his lightning backhand and delicate touch, cut the bigger man down, as almost everyone in London wanted him to do. In truth Newcombe won and it was not really close, that is if you can call a five-set match not close.

Rosewall won the first set by breaking Newcombe's big serve in the 11th game and then holding his own.

But for the next hour it was all Newcombe. Whenever Rosewall missed with his first serve, Newcombe would take the weak second one on his forehand, perhaps the strongest in tennis, and pin Rosewall back on his heels. Newcombe won the second and third sets 6–3, 6–2 and when he immediately broke Rosewall to start the fourth set, the rout appeared to be on. Rosewall looked exhausted, and he would seize the brief rest periods to sit at the base of the umpire chair, waiting until Newcombe took his position on the court before rising.

Losing 1–3, Rosewall fell behind love–30 on his serve and it seemed certain that Newcombe was about to apply the crusher. There then occurred one of the most remarkable reversals in Wimbledon history. Rosewall won four straight points to make it 2–3. He won four more on Newcombe's serve to even the set. Four more made it 12 straight points and 4–3 Rosewall. Again Rosewall broke Newcombe, held his own serve and won the set 6–3. From that black moment in the fifth game he had won 20 out of 23 points.

The applause around the stadium was, by Wimbledon's standards, enormous—but it was applause for a dying man. Newcombe may be young, but he does not shake up easily. Leading 2–1 in the fifth set, he broke Rosewall's serve and rattled off four more games in a row for the match. For Newcombe it was his second Wimbledon title—he won in 1967—while Rosewall had only the sad distinction of the most years between losses in the finals.

In women's singles, the title went to another Australian, Margaret Court, who survived a strained left ankle and a marathon final match with the only woman in the world fit to rally with her, Billie Jean King. The girls are old rivals. In 1962 they met in the first round—it was Miss Smith and Miss Moffitt then—and Billie Jean, an unknown, startled everyone by upsetting Margaret, who was seeded No. 1. In the years since then, Billie Jean had won three Wimbledon titles, Margaret two. This year Margaret had already won the Australian and French championships, so at Wimbledon she was seeking the third leg of the grand slam.

Wimbledon treasures its great matches and this year's Court-King battle has already been stashed away as a classic. To recount all the peaks and valleys is impossible, but it should be remembered that the girls were on center court for 2½ hours in a 14–12, 11–9 match that set all sorts of endurance records.

For most of the first week of Wimbledon it was a quiet tournament, with plenty of time for ice lollies in the tea garden. The crowds were enormous, lured by the sunny weather, and at the top of the day, which at Wimbledon is about 6 P.M., it was impossible to move along the pathways between the outside courts.

For the players the early days were much like a class reunion, for it is only at major championships such as Wimbledon and Forest Hills that all of them get together. Laver confided that this was the first time he had ever come to Wimbledon feeling on top of his game—a staggering thought— then went out and crushed young Butch Seewagen to open the tournament. Newcombe admitted his back was better than last year, when he had been forced to sleep on the floor of his London hotel room. "Bit embarrassing, you know," he said, "looking up to the wife to say goodnight."

It was on Saturday of the first week—middle Saturday, the British call it—that the tournament suddenly came alive. Laver, winner of four Wimbledon titles and 31 consecutive matches, took center court for his fourth-round test against Roger Taylor, a rugged lefthander from Yorkshire. Almost from the start it was clear that Laver was dramatically off form. In the first set Taylor was no better and he gave it away to the champion 6–4. But as Taylor watched Laver's first serve miss repeatedly and saw him hit shots low into the net or far wide of the lines, he realized he could win and his game improved. Nothing Laver did was right—a truly remarkable negative performance—and he dropped the next three sets, winning only seven games. At match point, with the capacity crowd hardly believing it and with thousands of people outside the stadium watching the electric scoreboard, Laver double-faulted away his title.

Less than an hour after Laver's defeat, America's third-seeded Arthur Ashe was on center court, his chances of winning the title now greatly increased. Against him was Andres Gimeno, a seasoned and underrated Spaniard, but not in Ashe's class on grass. When Ashe had heard about Laver, he had said to himself: "Just give me four more good matches." As it turned out, he didn't get even one. Playing with supreme casualness, which is his style, he went down without a gurgle in three straight sets.

Ashe's defeat capped a disastrous fourth round for U.S. players. Six of them had been among the last 16 in the tournament. After the round, only Clark Graebner remained. Ashe, Dennis Ralston, Stan Smith, Marty Riessen and young Tom Gorman, who had upset Cliff Drysdale to reach the fourth round, all lost, winning only three sets among them.

The second week of the tournament the weather changed, turning gray and cold. The London newspapers had a field day with Taylor, just as they had in 1967 when he had reached the semifinals. TAYLOR THE FANTASTIC was one headline. He was "the Sheffield steelworker's son" and "full of true Yorkshire grit." His left arm was "a shining scimitar." Taylor made the semis again by rolling over Graebner, but Rosewall, who had reached the round by upsetting Tony Roche in one of the really good matches, beat him in four sets to "shatter the golden dream," as the papers screamed the next day.

Gimeno also reached the semifinals, beating unseeded Bob Carmichael, while Newcombe defeated Roy Emerson in five bitterly fought sets—another good match. Against Newcombe, Gimeno was tense and uncomfortable and he was never in contention.

So it was Rosewall against Newcombe and if sentiment counted it would have been Rosewall in straight sets. The BBC put Drobny and Hoad on television and both picked their former Wimbledon opponent to finally win one. So did Jack Kramer, who was acting as the BBC color man. When Rosewall rallied to win the fourth set, older newsmen in the press section, those who have seen every Wimbledon since Borotra and Lacoste were having at it, began warming to one of the epic stories. But John Newcombe wouldn't allow it. "It's not that I was unsympathetic," he said later. "But let's face it, I wanted to win, too." Then he turned to Rosewall, who was sitting beside him. "You're going to Bristol next week, aren't you? Good. You can win that."

SUDDEN DEATH AT FOREST HILLS

by Walter Bingham

The climax of a major tennis championship often arrives well before the finals, and if it were legal, all play should be suspended at that point. Cut and print, everybody go to lunch. That's certainly the way it was at Forest Hills last week, at least from a U.S. standpoint. Again it was an all-Australian men's finals, just like the ones your grandfather told you about, the same kind that have been going on forever. This year it was Ken Rosewall beating Tony Roche, while in the ladies' division Margaret Court was completing her grand slam by beating Rosemary Casals. Another chorus of *Waltzing Matilda,* please.

The tournament should have ended Thursday morning shortly before the start of the men's quarter-finals. There had already been enough memorable matches to savor during the long winter, and, of the eight remaining players, four were Americans. Yes, four. That hasn't happened much lately.

The prospects for the day were delicious. Dennis Ralston against Cliff Richey, for instance, two guys you won't find at the same dinner table by choice—and in this case the U. S. couldn't lose. Ralston was the hero of the hour, having knocked out top-seeded Rod Laver in five exciting sets, by far the biggest win in a checkered career. Richey, too, had beaten a former champion, Manuel Santana, the deft but aging Spaniard. It promised to be an intriguing match, temper vs. temper.

The winner would meet Roche, the only one of the leading Australians without a Wimbledon or Forest Hills title thus far, or an unknown, Brian Fairlie of New Zealand, who had slipped through a weakness in the draw to reach this round. Perhaps he could slip past Roche, too.

Stan Smith had made it to the quarter-finals by beating Roy Emerson, the first time in his life he had ever done so. Now he was to face another Australian legend, Rosewall, who at 35 had looked as brilliant as he did when he won at Forest Hills in 1956.

Finally, there was the feature attraction, Arthur Ashe, the 1968 winner, against John Newcombe, the current Wimbledon champion. A battle of serves, bomber against bomber, two classy heavyweights. Ashe had not looked much like a champion since he beat Tom Okker in the finals two years ago, but in his fourth-round match, again against Okker, his skill suddenly had revived, the explosive serve, the lightning returns.

So that was what was on tap for the day, Thursday, September 10, those four matches plus an assortment of other goodies—women's singles and all kinds of doubles. With some luck, the U. S. could place three players in the semis. Maybe even the New Zealander could win. No Aussies at all. Imagine!

Which is why the tournament should have ended right there. Rosewall and Smith were the first to take center court, and they weren't out there long. Smith is normally a strong server, but against Rosewall, one of the best returners in the game, he seemed to be pressing. He double faulted nine times, and in three sets he won only six games. Throughout the brief encounter he looked like a dinosaur trying to stalk a mongoose. So long, Stan.

Next came Richey and Ralston. (Meanwhile, on an outside court, Fairlie was definitely not slipping by Roche, losing in three straight sets.) As Ralston was to say later, he felt dead from the start, an emotional letdown following his victory over Laver. Richey won in three sets.

Late in the afternoon, with the light beginning to fade, Ashe and Newcombe took the court in what many people regarded as a sort of finals in the quarter-finals, for surely either man was as good or better than anyone else playing that day. Ashe lost the first set 6–1, looking remarkably like the Arthur Ashe who lost so easily to Andres Gimeno at Wimbledon in late June. But in the second set his tremendous serve began to rip past Newcombe and the two players reached 6–6, which at Forest Hills this year meant sudden death, a nine-point tie breaker, first player to win five points wins the set.

Newcombe reached a commanding position at 3–3 with three serves coming up, but Arthur hit the first of them for a winner and was at set point. Then Ashe did what he does all too often, the thing that prevents him from being the best player in the world. Newcombe served, and Ashe hit the ball in the net. Newcombe served again, and again Ashe hit the ball into the net. Simple. Newcombe never had to hit a volley with match point against him, for Ashe never put the ball into play. Ashe hits as many great shots as anyone in the world, but he doesn't hit enough good ones. He won the third set, but Newcombe won another tie breaker in the fourth to close out the match.

So there it was. Three Aussies in the quarter-finals, three in the semis. Four Americans in the quarter-finals, one in the semis.

The destruction of the U.S. forces was completed two days later in the semifinals when Roche humiliated Richey in three sets, the last one 6–1. The other match was a gem, Rosewall gaining revenge for his loss in the Wimbledon final by giving Newcombe a lesson in the return of serve, as well as assorted other strokes.

In the finals Rosewall completed a remarkable tournament by beating Roche in four sets, again showing a younger, harder-hitting countryman that tennis can be an art and that sheer power can be stopped by a delicate touch. Rosewall had one desperate moment. At one set apiece he served at 5–6 in the third and three times allowed Roche to reach set point. Each time he saved himself. Winning the game to make it 6–6, he then crushed Roche in sudden death. Essentially, that was it. Rosewall broke Roche's first serve in the fourth set and quickly won 6–3. In seven matches he lost only two sets. When he won 14 years ago he lost four, which obviously proves he is twice as good as he was then.

Long after it is forgotten exactly which Australian did win at Forest Hills in 1970, it will be remembered that this was the first year of sudden death and sets with odd-looking scores of 7–6. What a success it turned out to be! As Ashe said following his second tie breaker with Newcombe: "When I went to serve at 2–4, you could have heard a pin drop. The silence was spooky."

What the nine-point tie break was designed to do was put an abrupt end to a set that might have continued—who knows how long? A score of 16–14 may look exciting in agate type, but any two clods with big serves and no strokes can produce a set like that. Sudden death cleared them off the court. Better yet, it provided the most exciting moments of the tournament. On center court, whenever a set reached 6–6, a large red flag was unfurled inside the stadium signaling a tie break was about to begin. Smaller red flags were used on the outside courts, so that wandering fans could hustle along the pathways to watch the crucial points.

The format was simple: Ashe, say, would serve two points, then Newcombe two. The players would change sides, Ashe would serve twice more, and finally Newcombe three. Ah, you might argue, an advantage for Newcombe, serving five times, but in practice the sudden-death sets seemed to split about even between those who served first and those who received. In one memorable example, when Nikki Pilic beat Pancho Gonzales, Pilic won two serves, Gonzales two, Pilic two more. Now Pancho had his three serves coming up, which looks good on paper, but on the court it was 2–4, triple set point against him. Under that pressure, Gonzales dumped his first volley in the net for the set, whereupon he hit the ball he would have used for his second serve out of the stadium.

There were other exciting sudden deaths. In an early ladies' match, Virginia Wade and Sharon Walsh, a promising California teen-ager, reached four points apiece. Since Miss Walsh had lost the first set, it was match point against her, set point against Miss Wade. A nervous rally developed, both girls afraid to go for a winner. Finally Miss Wade took the net, forcing Miss Walsh to try a passing shot. The result was a long, loopy shot which Miss Wade confidently let go, only to watch it fall like a dying duck on the baseline. Set to Miss Walsh.

The players, as a group, were leery of the new rule. Gonzales, an old dog, found it difficult to learn the new trick. "I use up more energy in a tie break than I do in a whole set," he said. "I may have a heart attack out there." Laver said he would prefer to play the 12-point sudden death in which a player must win by two points, reasoning that under the current system you can win every point you serve in an entire set and still lose.

In one form or another, sudden death is almost certain to be a part of tournament tennis from now on. It should be pointed out right here that the tie break is the creation of James Van Alen, the 68-year-old Newport millionaire, who for 12 years has been urging—no, badgering—tennis to modernize its scoring system. Surely you have heard of VASSS, the Van Alen Simplified Scoring System—one, two, three, as in table tennis. It is true that Jimmy can come on awfully strong when he starts in on the subject of updating the tennis scoring system to accommodate such things as television, but tennis needs to be hit over the head with a sledgehammer before it will change anything. Last year Van Alen finally got the USLTA to incorporate sudden death into its official rules, and this year, with the help of Bill Talbert, the tournament director, he convinced the USLTA to try sudden death at Forest Hills. As it became an instant success, there were signs last week that the USLTA would have you believe it thought up the system. For the record, it did not. Old Jimmy Van Alen did. Now if he's any good at all, he'll figure out a way for U.S. tennis players to beat the Aussies.

THE TENNIS REVOLUTION UNABATED IN 1970

by Allison Danzig

The revolution in tennis that began in 1968 with the sanctioning of open tournaments, permitting amateurs to compete with professionals, continued through 1970 with mounting repercussions, dissension and one history-making innovation—the first major change in scoring since the original badminton or table tennis method of playing for 21 points gave way, in 1877, to the 15–30–40, deuce-advantage games, and sets won on six games.

The solution of the problem of ending the dishonesty and "shamateurism" of secret payments to amateurs, the principal motive of the British in forcing through the acceptance, at long last, of open competition by the International Lawn Tennis Federation in 1968, led to the creation of one bête noir after another and greater acrimony than ever.

For three years now, tennis has been in a constant state of flux, undergoing changes unimaginable to graybeards of the establishment that was unchallenged in its authority for some four-score and ten years. New categories of players were created, and England erased the demarcation between amateur and pro, calling everyone simply a "player." Tennis joined the affluent society as money poured in from increasing attendance, television and commercial sponsors. More and more promoters got into the act to share the new wealth. The earnings—in prize money and from fringe benefits—of the leading pros, who had been outside the pale and whose tournaments were looked upon as hardly more than exhibitions until they were welcomed back to Wimbledon, Forest Hills and Roland Garros (France) in the national open championships, soared until they are making as much as many of the top golfers. Rod Laver earned $201,453 in prize money in 1970. Ken Rosewall, the sensation of the year in winning the U.S. Open and finishing as runner-up to John Newcombe at Wimbledon at the age of 35, and displacing Laver (the autocratic monarch of tennis for five years and artisan of a second grand slam in 1969) as the winner of the Martini & Rossi Player-of-the-Year Award, amassed $140,455.

Amateur regulations were emasculated to the point that virtually every player of reputation was competing for prize money as a "contract" pro or "independent" pro, and amateur fixtures of long standing had to put up $10,000 to $25,000, and more, or stage a talentless show, or give up. Such was the exodus of players into the ranks of the contract pros during these three years that Australia, winner of the Davis Cup fifteen times in eighteen challenge rounds between 1950 and 1967, lost the trophy to the United States' "independent" pros in 1968 and was ignominiously ousted by Mexico in an early round in 1969 and by India in 1970. In both of those years the United States scored 5–0 sweeps, over Rumania in 1969 and over West Germany in 1970.

The regained supremacy of the United States may possibly end in 1971 for the same reason that Australia plummeted. Two of the mainstays of the American team, Arthur Ashe and Bob Lutz, changed from "independent" pros, who operate in the fold of the U.S.L.T.A. and are thus privileged to play in the Davis Cup matches, to "contract" pros, whose allegiance is to promoters and are ineligible for the matches.

Ashe and Lutz signed with World Championship Tennis, Inc., backed by Texas multimillionaire Lamar Hunt, as contract pros after the Davis Cup matches. During the United States Open Championship Mr. Hunt, after merging his group of eighteen players with six of the rival National Tennis League and Tennis Champions, Inc., including Laver, Rosewall and Pancho Gonzales, announced that W.C.T. was putting on a "world championship" tour of 20 tournaments for a million dollars in prize money, open to the 32 "ranking" players. He then proceeded to sign up nine more players, including Ashe and Lutz.

The contract pros operate outside the jurisdiction of the International Lawn Tennis Federation, and in setting up this tour Hunt's group came into conflict with the I.L.T.F.'s Grand Prix circuit of some 20 tournaments, for which $1,500,000 will be at stake in 1971. Hunt holds virtually all the aces, with Laver, Rosewall, Newcombe, Tony Roche, Ashe, Gonzales, et al.

The U.S.L.T.A. threatened to bar all contract pros from its prize-money tournaments but deferred action. Following an emergency meeting of an I.L.T.F. committee in London in November, a summit conference in Dallas reached a settlement that seemed to assure that the contract pros will compete in the United States, Wimbledon and French Open Championships.

On top of this, women players staged a revolt against the U.S.L.T.A. late in 1970. Dissatisfied with the prize money offered them in the Pacific Southwest Championships, they took part, instead, in a commercially sponsored "Virginia Slims" tournament in Houston. When the U.S.L.T.A. refused to sanction this event if they were paid $5,000 in prize money, eleven players, led by Mrs. Billie Jean King, former Wimbledon and U.S. champion, signed professional contracts at one dollar each with *World Tennis* magazine and its publisher, Mrs. Gladys M. Heldman. A women's curcuit of "Virginia Slims" tournaments was set up.

Thereupon, the players, most of them ranked in the world's first ten, were notified that they were ineligible to compete in the U.S.L.T.A. sponsored tournaments. Mrs. King and Nancy Richey (now Mrs. Kenneth Gunter) and Julie Heldman, the first and second ranking players in the 1969 U.S.L.T.A. list, were thus lost to the Wightman Cup and Federation Cup teams for 1971, along with Rosemary Casals, Mrs. Mary Ann Curtis and Peaches Bartkowicz. Mrs. King, ineligible for the teams (along with Miss Casals) in 1968 and 1969 as a contract pro, regained her eligibility in 1970 when she did not renew her contract and played the stellar role in the victory of the U. S. over the British in the Wightman Cup matches, defeating Mrs. Ann Jones, who had ended her reign as Wimbledon queen in the 1969 final, and then pairing with Miss Bartkowicz to win the deciding doubles match. The Federation Cup was won by Australia, which beat West Germany in the final after the latter had eliminated the U. S. in the semifinals.

The premier woman player of the world, Mrs. Margaret Smith Court of Australia, did not join the rebellion. Mrs. Court became the first player of her sex to achieve a grand slam since Mrs. Maureen Connolly Brinker won the Wimbledon, American, French and Australian crowns in 1953.

Standing out above all else in a year of turmoil, innovations and record-breaking prize money and attendance was the change in the scoring method. Since, in 1884, the height of the net at the posts was lowered to 3 feet, 6 inches and, in 1887, sets in the championship were changed to three out of five for all rounds and 'vantage sets were ordered subsequently for all rounds, the fundamentals of tennis remained unchanged for roughly eighty years, except for variations in the foot-fault rule, until the "sudden death" tie-break was used in 1970.

With the permission of the I.L.T.F. to experiment with it, the U.S.L.T.A. used the tie-break in its Open Championship at Forest Hills, New York. When the game score reached 6–all in the set, the decision was reached forthwith in a contest for the best five of nine points. The player (A) whose turn it was to serve next at 6–all served two points. His opponent (B) served the next two, after which they changed sides. A then served two more and B served the final three points (if necessary). Most of the top pros favored a 12-point playoff, rather than the 9, for a 2-point, rather than a 1-point, winning margin and equalizing the number of times each served. In the 9-point playoff the player who served last would start service in the next set.

The tie-break was used also in the U.S. Professional Championship, the Marlboro Open (formerly Eastern Grass), the Pacific Southwest, the Pacific Coast and Phoenix Thunderbird tournaments. Wimbledon is reported to be preparing to use the tie-break in 1971.

James H. Van Alen of Newport was the originator of the 9-point tie-break. He introduced VASSS (Van Alen Simplified Scoring System) some ten years before, playing sets of 31 points—a reversion to lawn tennis' original scoring method. His purpose was to control the length of matches. The U.S.L.T.A. would not accept his system, since it has to conform to

I.L.T.F. regulations, but it did put VASSS in its year book for those who wished to use it in club, handicap and other minor tournaments. It finally adopted the tie-break to put an end to sets of marathon length and thus make tennis feasible for television—a highly important consideration.

Polls taken at Forest Hills showed that spectators and officials were heavily in favor of the tie-break and that the players were less enthusiastic about it. Most of them preferred the 12-point rather than 9-point play-off.

In the U.S. Open final, Rosewall defeated Roche, 2–6, 6–4, 7–6, 6–3, and received $20,000 first prize. (The winner of the tie-break after 6–all wins the set by the score of 7–6.) In the semi-finals Rosewall beat Newcombe, 6–3, 6–4, 6–3. Newcombe defeated Ashe in the quarter-finals, 6–1, 7–6, 5–7, 7–6, after Ashe eliminated Tom Okker of the Netherlands, whom he had beaten in the 1968 final. The shock of the tournament came in the defeat of Laver in the fourth round by Dennis Ralston, 7–6, 7–5, 5–7, 4–6, 6–3. Ralston then lost, 7–6, 6–3, 6–4, to Cliff Richey, who in turn was beaten by Roche, 6–2, 7–6, 6–1. Richey finished on top with the most points and $25,000 in the Grand Prix circuit of tournaments. Ashe was runner-up with $17,500.

In the women's final Mrs. Court defeated Miss Casals, 6–2, 2–6, 6–1, after beating Miss Richey in the semi-finals. Miss Casals had eliminated Virginia Wade of England, 1968 champion, in the semi-finals. Mrs. King did not enter as she had undergone a knee operation. Eighth-seeded Pierre Barthes of France and Nikki Pilic of Yugoslavia won the men's doubles. Newcombe and Roche, No. 1-seeded team, lost to Charles Pasarell and Erik Van Dillon in their first match. Mrs. Court and Judy Tegart Dalton won the women's doubles.

Under the management of tournament chairman Joseph F. Cullman 3d and tournament director William Talbert, who succeeded Owen Williams of South Africa, the U.S. Open drew a paid attendance of 122,996, it was announced—21,000 over the 1969 figures. The prize money amounted to $169,000.

At Wimbledon, Newcombe was the winner over Rosewall by 5–7, 6–3, 6–2, 3–6, 6–1. Laver fell before Roger Taylor of England in a stunning reversal. Mrs. Court beat Mrs. Billie Jean King, 14–12, 11–9, in the women's final, the longest at Wimbledon since Louise Brough defeated Mrs. Margaret Osborne duPont, 10–8, 1–6, 10–8, in 1949. Mrs. Ann Haydon Jones, 1969 champion, did not defend her title. Newcombe and Roche won the men's doubles and Mrs. King and Miss Casals the women's.

None of the contract professionals competed in the French Open, as their demands for "appearance" money were rejected. Nevertheless, the tournament attendance was reported to have exceeded the 1969 figures. In the first all-Eastern European final the championship has known, Jan Kodes of Czechoslovakia defeated Zeljko Franulovic of Yugoslavia, 6–2, 6–4, 6–0. Kodes received $10,000 in prize money and, it was reported, turned it over to the Czech government and tennis federation. Mrs. Court beat Helga Niessen of West Germany in the women's final, 6–2, 6–4. Miss Niessen eliminated Mrs. King in the quarter-finals, the American suffering leg cramps. Ion Tiriac and Ilie Nastase of Rumania defeated Ashe and Pasarell in the men's doubles final and Françoise Durr and Mrs. Gail Chanfreau of France beat Mrs. King and Miss Casals for the women's title.

Ashe was the winner of the Australian Open, defeating Richard Crealy in the final, 6–4, 9–7, 6–2, after winning from Ralston in the semi-finals, 6–3, 8–10, 6–3, 2–1, and default, Ralston retiring with a back injury. Ralston had beaten Newcombe in the quarter-finals, 19–17, 20–18, 4–6, 6–3, in 4 hours and 43 minutes of play. The 93 games set a record for the tournament (Laver and Roche played 90 games in the 1969 final). Crealy put out Roger Taylor, Okker and Stan Smith, and Taylor eliminated the No. 1-seeded player, Roche. Smith and Bob Lutz won the doubles title. In the women's final Mrs. Court beat Kerry Melville of Australia. In the Italian championship Nastase was the winner over Kodes, and Mrs. King defeated Julie Heldman, 1969 champion, after which they paired to win the women's doubles.

In the Davis Cup matches Germany reached the challenge round for the first time when it defeated Spain, 4–1, in the interzone final, after eliminating India, the Soviet Union, Belgium, Egypt and Denmark. The Germans offered feeble opposition to the U. S. until Christian Kuhnke carried Ashe to 6–8, 10–12, 9–7, 13–11, 6–4 on the final day. This was the longest Davis Cup match ever played. Richey was chosen over Stan Smith as the U. S.'s other singles player by Edward Turville of St. Petersburg, Florida, the new captain of the team, and the Texan played notably well. Not since 1949 had the United States won the cup more than two years in succession. Spain beat Brazil, Yugoslavia, France, Belgium and Sweden en route to the interzone final. India beat Australia for the first time. Yugoslavia put out Rumania, 1969 challenger, and England, European Zone finalist in 1969, lost to Sweden in the first round. South Africa was banned from the cup matches because of its apartheid policy, and Rhodesia withdrew after Czechoslovakia refused to play its team. In Federation Cup matches Israel, Hungary and Poland withdrew in protest against South Africa's entry.

Tony Trabert and Mrs. Shirley Fry Irvin, former Wimbledon and United States champions, were elected to the National Lawn Tennis Hall of Fame. Enshrined with them in ceremonies in the Forest Hills Stadium were Clarence J. (Peck) Griffin, national doubles champion with the late William Johnston, and Perry T. Jones, Davis Cup captain in 1958 and 1959 and director of the Pacific Southwest championships for many years.

Mr. Jones, trailblazer in junior tennis development in Southern California, was unable to attend the ceremonies, owing to illness. He died later in the year. Mrs. Jean Hoxie, famous for her coaching school at Hamtramck, Michigan, where she helped countless young players, and Lester Stoefen, winner of the national doubles championship twice with George Lott and member of the Davis Cup team, also died in 1970.

1971

ROD LAVER'S INCREDIBLE STREAK AND $160,000

by Fred J. Podesta

A selected field of the greatest players in the world. The biggest prize money in tennis. Head-on competition with the winner taking all the money. A direct challenge in each match for superiority. These were some of the elements that guaranteed unusual happenings in the 1971 Tennis Champions Classic, the richest of all tennis events, and what happened was not only unusual, it was one of the greatest of all performances in any sport—and assuredly the greatest ever in the sport of tennis.

Rodney G. Laver, the red-haired 32-year-old Australian, accomplished what was regarded by everyone connected with the game—by players, fans, the press—as totally impossible. He ran through 13 consecutive matches against the finest players in the world and emerged unbeaten and richer by $160,000.

"On one of his very best days, Bill Tilden might have had a chance against Laver." The speaker was a man associated with tennis for decades, a man who has seen them all—from Bill Tilden through Don Budge, Jack Kramer, Pancho Gonzales, Lew Hoad—and now he had just seen the incredible skill of Rod Laver as he sent a match point whistling to the deepest corner of the court in a Classic victory.

There were those who challenged Laver's dominance. In 1962, he had become only the second man in history to achieve the Grand Slam of Australia, France, Wimbledon and Forest Hills. But the Big Four were amateur events then, and the best players were professional. In three of the four final matches, Laver defeated the same opponent.

In 1969, Laver again swept the four titles, and this time the tournaments were open to all players—and he defeated a different opponent in each final, establishing himself beyond doubt as the finest player in the game. Many said that this marked his peak and that he would never again approach the mastery he displayed that year.

In 1970 he won $57,500 in the first Tennis Champions Classic and shattered all money-won totals, but failed in three Grand Slam tournaments that he entered.

And then the 1971 Classic began. Who could win thirteen matches in succession against Ken Rosewall, John Newcombe, Tony Roche, Roy Emerson, Arthur Ashe, Tom Okker, Roger Taylor and Dennis Ralston? The obvious answer was no one. Laver looked over the field and said with assurance that there was no way possible for one man to run that gauntlet. That's what he said . . . but he also saw that here was an opportunity to establish his mastery over each player and win the greatest amount of money ever, and all in a period of two and one half months.

"I was nervous when Kenny and I began," Laver said. Rosewall scored a break and took a 3–1 lead in the opening set.

Nervous he was, but not that nervous. Rosewall, the Forest Hills champion, went down 6–3, 6–2, 7–5, with match point a blazing service ace. Ken murmured, after his strongest challenge had been blunted in the third set, "It's just that whatever I hit, Rod hit better."

Someone asked Rod if he thought he could keep going, and he smiled and said: "I doubt it. The competition is just too keen, and it's difficult to keep your game on top."

The date was January 2 in Madison Square Garden, and Laver had earned his first $10,000.

"I knew this match with Rod was coming, and that is what I have been preparing for. He's been the only player on my mind," said Wimbledon champion John Newcombe on the eve of his Classic confrontation with Laver.

"I was tired. I'd be a fool to say otherwise. Three hours is a long time," said Laver in the locker room after winning a bitter, exhausting, five-set war from Newcombe.

"He never ceases to amaze me," said Newcombe, who had come back from a two-set deficit to square the match by taking the fourth-set tie break, seven points to five. It was obvious that Laver was in deep trouble, but in deepest trouble his greatest play emerges, and with tactics and shots described by the press as "fantastic," Laver fought off Newcombe in the final set.

Of his rival's astonishing play in that fifth set, Newcombe could say: "When I make a truly great shot, I look up and thank God. Rod takes his for granted."

The score was 6–4, 6–2, 4–6, 5–7, 6–4. The date was January 9 in the Rochester War Memorial Auditorium, and Laver's earnings reached $20,000.

"Everybody's out to knock my head off, you know," said Rod Laver as he prepared to meet the challenge of Tony Roche.

"I don't know how I could have lost that one," grumbled a disconsolate Tony Roche in the dressing room after an astonishing five-setter in which Roche, who had taken Laver's U.S. Pro championship in 1970, had Laver at match point in the fourth set. Trailing 4–5 and serving, Laver netted a volley at deuce and Roche needed one point for victory. But Tony netted a forehand drive for deuce again and Rod, given a life, grabbed the game with two backhand cross-court volleys, then raced through the tie break to capture the set. The fifth set of the two-and-one-half-hour match was easy for Laver, leaving Roche to shake his head in disbelief and disgust that he had failed.

"I thought I had absolutely no chance," smiled Laver in looking back at the drama of match point. "No chance whatsoever," he repeated.

The date was January 13 in the Boston Garden. The score was 7–5, 4–6, 3–6, 7–5, 6–1. Laver's earnings reached $30,000.

"I don't understand how Rod can win all that money," said Roy Emerson. The personable Australian veteran, winner of more amateur titles than Laver, and who came into the professional world at a comparatively late age, was waiting for his Classic shot at Laver. Emerson knows how to beat Rod, and he coaches and explains how one can cope with his long-time friend and foe. But when Roy goes onto the court, it is as if he never saw the man before, and he quickly became Rod's fourth victim. It took Emerson two sets to find a chink in Laver's armament, and he pushed it as far as he could, carrying the third set to tie break—but to no avail.

Mary Laver smiled at courtside. Staying with Rod all the way through the Classic, and spending her spare time shopping.

Her husband had defeated Emerson, 6–2, 6–3, 7–5. Laver's earnings were now $40,000—and the date was January 16 in the Philadelphia Spectrum.

"I wish I had been in the Classic a year ago," said Arthur Ashe as he made ready to launch his career as a contract professional. Ashe, winner of the first U.S. Open in 1968, was next in line for Laver. In 1970 Arthur had read of men fighting for $10,000 in a single match—and wished he could be part of that kind of competition. Now he was, and all he had to do was defeat Rod Laver.

"He takes advantage of everything," Ashe was saying in the dressing room. Arthur had given everything he had, and the crowd had been with him, and he had forced two sets into sudden death—but there was no denying Laver.

"I'm very unhappy with my first service," said Laver. But his second wasn't all that bad, as Ashe ruefully admitted. The two tie break sets went to Laver. "I just can't seem to take those tie breaks," Ashe sighed.

The date was January 21 in Madison Square Garden. The score was 7–5, 6–4, 7–5 and Laver's earnings reached $50,000.

"You can't afford to dream," said Laver as he approached the sixth match. His opponent would be Tom Okker, the Flying Dutchman, regarded by experts as a man who has all the strokes, all the skills, and once he puts them all together . . .

And Okker put them all together—almost. After the first two sets, Tom had Rod on the ropes. Okker won both sets in breath-taking tie breaks. But the game is stamina too, and in the face of Laver's ferocious counterattack Okker's strength waned, Laver's waxed.

The date was January 23 in the Detroit Olympia. The score was 5–7, 5–7, 6–2, 6–2, 6–2. Laver's earnings reached $60,000.

"It's getting easier as I go along," Laver said. "I don't mean it the way it sounds," he added hastily. "It's just that—well . . ."

Laver was getting ready to take on Ashe making his second bid. And while the first match had been fiery and furious over three sets, Rod was being nothing more than himself when he said it seemed to be getting "easier." With six straight victories, tie break tensions, the shock of being down match point to Roche behind him, Laver was beginning to think, beginning to believe that he could do the impossible—go all the way.

The crowd again was very much pro-Ashe, and when Arthur took the first set the cry went up that now, at last, someone would halt Laver. But the cheers strangled in the throat as Laver, gearing his play a notch higher, fought back and grappled the momentum away from Ashe.

"I made too many errors at the wrong time," a despondent Ashe muttered. Five double faults contributed to Ashe's defeat, one which Laver categorized as "a poor match on my part. I was much too relaxed in the beginning."

The date was January 28 in Madison Square Garden. The score was 3–6, 6–3, 6–3, 6–4. Laver's earnings were now $70,000.

"He's No. 1 in my book," said Roger Taylor, "but I'd be lying if I said I thought I'd lose." It was now Taylor's turn, the very same Taylor who had turned the biggest upset of the 1970 season when he brought Laver down in the fourth round at Wimbledon. Could he possibly check Laver again?

"I almost think it's a dream," said Laver in awe. He had taken brisk and deadly revenge on Taylor, although the Britisher had gone down with all guns blazing.

"I made the mistakes in the second set," Taylor said glumly. He had led 5–2, but then Laver was all over the court and the match went out the window for Taylor. "I missed two smashes and an easy lob," Roger recalled. You do not make mistakes like that against Laver.

The date was February 3 in the Los Angeles Forum. The score was 6–3, 7–5, 6–2. Laver's earnings were now $80,000.

"I feel I'm better prepared for this match than I was for our first," said Tom Okker as he went out on the court to challenge Laver once again.

And Okker was right. The young Dutchman played perhaps the finest tennis of his life. He had every shot, every move—but Laver had the answer to every shot, every move. It was, to that date, the greatest tennis Laver had played, and it was after this match that the grizzled veteran observer had said that maybe, just maybe, Tilden might have had a chance.

At one point, Okker caught Rod flat-footed in the forecourt but Laver, in desperation, raced backward, caught up with the ball, ran around it and put it away. Okker dropped his racket in astonishment and the spectators, even the umpire in the chair, howled in disbelief and admiration.

In the locker room, Okker declared flatly that he had played as well as he had ever played, perhaps better than he had ever played, "but I was never even in the match. I couldn't believe some of those shots. He couldn't believe them himself," Okker moaned.

The date was February 6 in Madison Square Garden. The score was 6–1, 6–4, 6–3. Laver's earnings were now $90,000.

"I'm not afraid of him." Dennis Ralston was speaking, and he meant it. A veteran to all pressures, Ralston is one of the few men never dominated by Rod Laver, and in 1970 had sent Laver out of the Forest Hills event. But Dennis still has the temper that made him famous. . . .

"Here we go again," Ralston moaned to himself at the start of the second set. The call had been dubious at best, and in exasperation Ralston flung a ball toward the lineman—"not at him," Ralston insisted. But the hostility of the fans, the tenseness of the situation, with him leading Laver, cracked Ralston's concentration—and against Laver that is always fatal.

The date was February 17 in Madison Square Garden. The score was 3–6, 6–1, 6–4, 6–3, and Laver's earnings were now $100,000.

"The other fellows are pushing the panic button," said Laver. "They're trying too hard."

"Anything can happen, can't it?" asked Roy Emerson as he strode onto the court for his last shot at Rod.

Anything can happen, and anything almost did too, but Laver was not going to be denied, now that he had come this far. The match was long and skilled, as the old rivals who knew each other's style, even thoughts, waged war for five sets—with Laver winning.

"I don't know how he does it," sighed Emerson after it was over. "How can he get up for so many big matches?"

The date was February 19 in the New Haven Arena. The score was 6–3, 5–7, 6–3, 3–6, 6–3. The Laver earnings were now $110,000 in just seven weeks.

Laver had swept all of the $10,000 winner-take-all regular season events, and now moved into the last two tests, where the money was even greater.

"I'm determined to keep my cool, no matter what happens," said Rod as he prepared to face Ralston in the semifinal.

"We all know he can be beaten," Ralston insisted. "I just go out there with the idea of winning, and determined not to let anything break my concentration this time." Dennis didn't lose his concentration, yet could do nothing against the juggernaut Laver had become. "I was struggling to get pace on my first serve," explained Ralston. "Dennis has played better," said Laver.

Laver had now won 12 in a row and observed, "I don't feel unbeatable, but if my opponents feel I am—well, that's terrific."

The date was March 18 in Madison Square Garden. The score was 6–3, 6–4, 7–5—and Laver's earnings stood at $125,000.

And so came #13 for Rod. The final match to complete the impossible and it was Okker, who had led him two sets to love the first time, Okker the victim of some of the greatest tennis Laver ever displayed in their second test, Okker who would make this last desperate stand.

"I do not like to lose," Laver said. "I can't understand anyone who is a good loser. If you go into a match with the idea that if you lose, you will be a 'good loser,' you are going to be a loser."

Okker walked onto the court, and like Don Quixote tilted his lance and charged. The first set was a bristling one, with the young Dutchman standing up to serves, the lobs, the drops, the dinks, the impossible retrieves—and losing the set in sudden death. And then the tide was inexorable. For Laver, the golden dream was about to become a reality, and he was not to be denied that reality.

The applause began to grow at the end of the second set. Applause in a special way—applause as a salute to what the fans saw happening as game after game dropped into Laver's column, bringing him to the ultimate victory. When it was over, applause and awe surrounded Laver as he accepted the final check.

The date was March 19 in Madison Square Garden, and the score was 7–5, 6–2, 6–1. Laver's earnings stood at $160,000.

"At the very outset," Laver said, "I totally agreed with everyone that it was virtually impossible for any one player to go through this Classic undefeated. I have done just that—and I do not believe it either."

EVONNE GOOLAGONG'S WIMBLEDON

by Walter Bingham

When she came out from under the green enclosure beneath the royal box and strolled onto center court, she appeared to be smiling. *Smiling.* Now you just don't do that at Wimbledon, especially for the finals. When you play a match on that hallowed lawn the knees should turn to jelly and the elbow to stone; you are supposed to look humble and reverent and, above all, scared stiff. Margaret Court knows how to do it properly. She has won the championship three times but there she stands, looking scared stiff. So where does this 19-year-old kid, this Evonne Goolagong, get off waltzing out there as if she were about to play a practice match?

What she did to Mrs. Court when play began just isn't done either. This is the sort of thing that happened: Evonne would hit a short second serve— one of the few weaknesses in her game—and Margaret would move in, crack a deep return and continue confidently to the net, a winning position. But then Evonne would rifle a cross-court backhand, or forehand, an inch over the net and maybe an inch inside the line. Over and over again. She gave a vivid demonstration of how wide and how long a tennis court can be, and in the process she destroyed the defending champion 6–4, 6–1. On previous days she had beaten Nancy Richey Gunter 6–3, 6–2 and Billie Jean King 6–4, 6–4. Six straight sets from the reigning queens. So goodby, Nancy, goodby, Billie Jean, goodby, Margaret. And hello, Evonne.

Evonne Goolagong was hardly unknown before the tournament began. In fact she was seeded third, thanks to her spectacular improvement since last year's Wimbledon, where she was beaten in the second round. Early this year she barely lost to Mrs. Court in the finals of the Australian championship, beat her in the Tasmanian championships, and last month beat her on clay in Paris to win the French championship. The world had learned that she was from the Australian Outback town of Barellan in New South Wales, that she was part aborigine, that she was one of eight children of a sheep shearer. When she was 10 she was spotted by Vic Edwards, a leading Australian tennis coach, who liked her movement on court. When she was 14 he made arrangements with her parents for Evonne to move in with him and his wife so that he could coach her daily.

Edwards had publicly predicted that Evonne would win at Wimbledon in 1974, but last month on a hunch he phoned his wife from Paris and told her to join him and Evonne in London. The family—for that is how they feel about one another—stayed in a flat, eating in, with Mrs. Edwards washing the dishes and Evonne drying. Before matches Edwards would watch Evonne warm up with Kim Warwick, a young Aussie, correct minor flaws and caution her about playing a "walkabout," his term for falling asleep on the court—a failing she has displayed in the past. Only once did Evonne do that at Wimbledon, losing a set—the only set she lost—to Lesley Hunt 1–6 before beating her 6–2, 6–1.

A moment after Evonne, the champion, had shaken hands with Margaret Court, she looked up to where the Edwardses were sitting, crinkled her nose and waved to them. Later she announced she would celebrate by "going to a disco." And what would the stern Vic Edwards say about that? "Tonight I have the right of way," Evonne answered. At 19, she may have the right of way in women's tennis for years.

CHRIS EVERT AT FOREST HILLS

by Roy Blount

In the end, Chris Evert fell somewhat short of becoming the new Evonne Goolagong at Forest Hills last week. But the poker-faced 16-year-old Florida ingenue with a two-fisted backhand and nothing to lose did provide the flash of life that the 1971 U.S. Open so desperately needed. Like many a New York production, the show was saved by a skirt.

The championships, threatened by tedium, bogged down by controversy and eventually awash in rain, will be remembered as the one spurned by the big names and brought to life by a little girl. As one European newsman put it snidely, "Shirley Temple is alive and well and living in Forest Hills." To most of the audience, however, she was a savior, more Joan of Arc than Shirley Temple. Many of the world's top contract professionals, including anticipated favorite Rod Laver, 1970 champion Ken Rosewall, Cliff Drysdale and Fred Stolle, had declined to take part in the $160,000 Open, citing fatigue. By being tired Rosewall became the first Forest Hills champ not to defend his title in nearly 30 years—excluding those who rendered themselves ineligible by turning pro in the days when the tournament was an amateur affair. Aussie John Newcombe did show up to lend his mustache and dashing ways to the competition for $15,000 first-place money, and he was seeded first. He was also first to go, knocked out in his opening match by unseeded Czech Jan Kodes, who took the occasion to describe grass-court tennis as "a joke."

There was also a shortage of big-name women. Defending champion Margaret Court was pregnant, the 20-year-old Miss Goolagong was back home in Australia savoring her Wimbledon victory and Virginia Wade was injured.

Then along came slim, blonde, sloe-eyed Chris, hotly pursued by more TV camera crews and adjective dispensers than had ever been seen at Forest Hills, or perhaps in the whole borough of Queens. Miss Evert, who took two weeks off from Fort Lauderdale's St. Thomas Aquinas High School to be on hand, was riding a string of 44 straight winning matches, dating back to February. However, only one of those wins—a 6–1, 6–1 trimming of Miss Wade Aug. 23 in the match that gave the U.S. the Wightman Cup over England—made her look like a real threat to the top-seeded Billie Jean King at Forest Hills.

That besting of Miss Wade was significant because it was on grass. The other stirring upsets Chris had pulled off since last September over such distinguished elders as Mrs. King, Mrs. Court and Françoise Durr had been on clay—a soft, uniform surface. Few observers expected Chris's defensive, counterpunching tactics and classic looping ground strokes from the backcourt to be formidable on quick, tricky grass, which favors the aggressive player who hits hard, moves to the net and gets plenty of spin on the ball.

And yet on the patchy swards of Forest Hills Miss Evert *was* formidable. Tournament Director Billy Talbert recognized a hot property and moved her directly into the stadium court for her first match. After beating Edda Buding easily, Chris faced Mary Ann Eisel Curtis, one of the best American grass players. "I was petrified," Chris said of her center-court experience. But she looked amply loose beating Mrs. Curtis 4–6, 7–6, 6–1, coolly staving off six match points in the second set with long forehands and backhands that just landed in. Then she came from behind twice more to defeat Miss Durr (2–6, 6–2, 6–3) and Australia's Lesley Hunt (4–6, 6–2, 6–3). In each case she stayed at the baseline and kept hitting two-handed backhands and fluid forehands that ran her opponents from side to side until they wilted and lost their poise. When they came in, she hit past them. When they stayed back, she stranded them with nifty drop shots. Her unimposing serves sufficed. She seldom showed emotion, and she looked so young. The crowd went wild.

Tennis fans are not supposed to go wild. But these did not just clap politely for Chris, they yelled and whooped and grew so partisan as to cheer her opponents' errors. One misguided enthusiast even yelled "Out!" and caused Chris to let up on a ball that was in. Except in that one instance, the fans helped make Chris a testing opponent.

They also helped make her unpopular among the other women players, despite a general agreement that she was, well, a nice kid personally. It was said that Chrissiemania was turning the stadium atmosphere into that of "a baseball game"; that Chrissie herself hit "garbage" strokes; that she had "a kid's concentration," because she had nothing else on her mind; that she was so locked into her own rhythm and careful steady breathing that sometimes she served before her opponent was quite ready.

One woman player who spoke out against all this grumbling was Billie Jean King, the unquestioned master of the lady pros who had already won $60,000 this year. "Chris has really helped women's tennis," she said. "What it needs is more personalities. If any of the other girls feel jealous about the attention she's received, they should stop and think beyond their own little worlds." Billie Jean also declined to shudder at the notion of a tennis crowd's sounding like a baseball crowd. "I like demonstrative crowds," she said. "People who pay their hard-earned money for a ticket ought to be able to make noise. Maybe the girls could wear earmuffs."

Billie Jean did observe that Chris had the advantage enjoyed by a baseball rookie just up from the minors whose weaknesses the pitchers had not found yet. And the 27-year-old veteran pointed out that Chris "is on the crest of a wave. I hope she enjoys it now, while she can."

This was said a couple of days before Mrs. King set up the beachhead upon which Miss Evert's wave broke at last. Their face-off came in a stimulating semifinal match on Friday before an overflow of press and TV representatives and a crowd of 13,000 that included Spiro Agnew and Senator James Buckley.

Neither Chris nor Billie Jean was intimidated by the crowd, which displayed great enthusiasm for them both. Nor was Chris intimidated by Billie Jean, but the 27-year-old pro quickly confirmed Miss Evert's own suspicions that her game was not forceful enough to stop a first-rate player on grass.

Each held service until Billie Jean, trailing 2–3 in the first set, broke through and won seven straight games. Billie Jean stayed back for a while, refusing to give Chris a good passing-shot target. But she kept Chris's rhythm disrupted with a strong serve, with diversely spinning groundstrokes and with drop shots. And an occasional lob exposed Chris's lame overhead. Gradually Billie Jean worked her way to the net, where she was able to score with smashes much more consistently than Chris was able to pass her. There were many fine rallies that left the crowd with no cause to regret the Evert boom that had brought so many of them there, but the final score was 6–3,

6–2 King. Thus Mrs. King's status as top American woman remains secure, as does Miss Goolagong's as the tennis world's flashiest young meteor maid. Evonne hits with more zing and has fewer gaps in her game than Chris.

But Chris, four years younger than Evonne, is already an established drawing card, and her life—along with her "kid's concentration"—stands to become more complicated. ("Your mind is always being interrupted," Billie Jean warned her during the full-scale joint press conference following their match. "Your life is not your own except for the few hours you spend asleep at night.") For instance, the King-Evert match had its overtones of tennis politics. Though no one on either side would admit it publicly, the World Championship Tennis people were rooting for King, since the furor over Evert tended to take attention away from the absence of Laver, Rosewall and the other WCT pros. Of the missing pros only Laver admitted that the International Lawn Tennis Federation's decision to ban WCT players from open tournaments beginning next year influenced his decision not to show up at Forest Hills, but in effect if not intent there was a partial boycott of the tournament by WCT. On the other hand, ILTF and USLTA people were clearly delighted to see such a boycott upstaged by a slip of a girl.

Chris had no comment on all that. She was headed back to St. Thomas Aquinas High—and the rains came to Forest Hills.

STAN SMITH BEATS KODES FOR U.S. OPEN TITLE

by Neil Amdur

Stan Smith, a rejected ballboy, won the United States Open tennis championship yesterday.

The second-seeded Californian, currently serving a two-year tour of duty in the Army, put down the grass-court heroics of Jan Kodes, the unseeded, 25-year-old Czech, 3–6, 6–3, 6–2, 7–6, before a crowd of 12,879 at the West Side Tennis Club in Forest Hills, Queens.

The women's singles final, also delayed three days by rain, went to top-seeded Mrs. Billie Jean King, who beat second-seeded Rosemary Casals, her keenest rival on the tour, 6–4, 7–6, for the ninth time in 10 meetings this year.

It was the first time in 16 years that Americans had swept the singles titles.

Smith's victory was the finest achievement in a career that has brought continued artistic improvement. With this title and as runner-up to John Newcombe at Wimbledon earlier the angular, 6-foot-4-inch blond must be considered among the top three or four players in the world, perhaps behind Newcombe, Rod Laver and Ken Rosewall.

Such status is a far cry from that gloomy day a decade ago when Smith, an ambitious junior, offered his services as a ballboy for a Davis Cup match, but was turned down because officials thought he was too clumsy to run across the court and pick up balls.

Yesterday he moved on the lawn in the stadium with the controlled grace of an athlete who had spent long, perhaps frustrating hours jumping rope and exercising to improve his balance, coordination and timing.

He leaned into returns of serves with adroit skill, was impeccable on the difficult half-volley and managed 68 percent of his first serves (66 of 97), with enough diversity to thwart his rival's potent passing game.

"I changed strategy after the first set," the mustachioed victor said, sipping champagne sent by his racquet manufacturer. "I was serving hard in the first set, and he was hitting everything back. So I slowed it down and tried to hop the ball on the grass."

The contrast of Smith's range and power with Kodes's tenacious talents off the ground made for an exciting, well-played match despite four service breaks in the fourth set.

Early in the second set, the players hit five successive winners on returns of serves, volleys, and shots from difficult angels. Smith broke Kodes for 2–1 in the third set off a short second serve, which he ran around to take on his forehand and hammer cross-court for a winner.

"I was feeling very tired," said Kodes, who needed five sets to beat Ashe in the semifinals on Tuesday and perhaps felt the effects of a hot, mid-afternoon sun. "My serve was very weak."

Kodes converted 62 per cent of his first serves. But Smith demonstrated in the 12th game of the fourth set, and again in the tiebreaker for the match, that his serve had precision and power.

Serving at 5–6 in a tense stadium, Smith carried the game at love without hitting a volley. The last three points were an unreturnable flat serve deep to Kodes's forehand and two aces, the second of which took a bad bounce, bolstering the Czech's contention that grass courts might not be the joke he thought they were, but that "grass is grass, you know."

Smith and Kodes had won four tiebreaker sets apiece during the tournament.

"The tiebreaker really demands a different technique," said Smith, whose concentration on the court is another outstanding trademark. "You have to change your thinking."

Kodes won the first two points of the tiebreaker on serve. Smith put in a spin-serve ace for 1–2, but the trim, inspired Czech slapped a forehand cross-court winner.

Leading by 3–1 and with an opportunity to win the 5-of-9 point playoff and the set on service, Kodes lost the next two points. More specifically, Smith won them.

The Californian again ran around his backhand on Kodes's second serve and slapped a forehand winner cross-court. Then he answered the Czech's best flat first serve with another cross-court return for a winner, this time off the backhand.

THE LAST DAVIS CUP CHALLENGE ROUND

by Neil Amdur

The Davis Cup challenge round ended today the way it began 71 years ago, with a United States victory.

Stan Smith, a 24-year-old Californian on loan from the United States Army, produced the decisive third point in the five-match series against Rumania with an 8–6, 6–3, 6–0 rout of Ion Tiriac.

Smith's 1-hour-35-minute triumph before an enthusiastic crowd of 5,500 at Julian J. Clark Stadium gave the United States a 3–1 lead and reduced the fifth match in the competition, between Frank Froehling and Ilie Nastase, to formality.

Nastase led, 6–3, 2–0, when late afternoon rain suspended play in their match. Harry Hopman, the referee, said the match would be completed tomorrow.

The challenge round began in 1900 between players from the United States and Britain, but will be discontinued next year by a vote of the Davis Cup nations. The change will force the United States, as defending champion, to play through the long elimination series to the final round along with other countries, instead of meeting the survivor of the interzone matches under the challenge format that became the symbol of the competition.

Rumania's hopes of becoming the fifth nation to hold the cup seemed doomed from the time that the 82d Airborne Army Band played the wrong Rumanian national anthem, a pre-revolutionary tune on opening day and Smith beat Nastase with surprising ease.

Even heavy rains last night and early this morning failed to slow or soften the clay court in the stadium, factors that would have aided Tiriac and Nastase. In fact, after a rented helicopter was called in and gasoline was ignited to help dry the playing surface, the court played more like slow asphalt than fast clay.

Smith, who learned the game on fast California cement, slipped and landed hard on his right wrist in a prematch practice and said he moved and played "tentative" in the first set.

When the 32-year-old Tiriac gamely played off a set point in the 10th game and broke back for 5-all, Smith admitted, "I thought I might be in for a long day."

However, Tiriac's experience (52 cup singles matches to Smith's four) could not counter the American's effective flat first serve, deep approach shots and decisive overheads and volleys.

Smith broke serve in the 13th game by attacking the Rumanian's short second serve, driving deep to the backhand and answering Tiriac's shallow lob with a winning overhead.

Tiriac's last stand was at break point on Smith's serve in the second game of the second set. Playing the point beautifully, the bushy-haired, mustachioed Rumanian moved Smith out of position at the base line, rushed the net and had an open court for an easy overhead. But he overhit Smith's short lob past the base line; Smith held serve, and promptly broke Tiriac at 15, helped by two double faults.

It was a satisfying victory for Smith, as well as for Edward A. Turville, the United States captain, and American tennis, in general.

It was only eight years ago that the 6-foot-4-inch Smith applied to the Los Angeles Tennis Club for a job as a ball boy at another Davis Cup match between the United States and Mexico. He was turned down at the time because officials thought he was too clumsy and gawky to run across the court.

PART III
Technique

THE SPIN OF THE BALL

by William T. Tilden 2d

Most tennis players look upon the ball that is used as merely something to hit. It is not an individual, separate factor in their play, like their opponent. They use it as a means to an end. Let me suggest the ball for a moment as an individual. It is a third party in the match. Will this third party be on your side or against you? It is up to you.

The ball will do as it is told. Suggest (with your racket, not your tongue) that the ball curve this way or that and it obeys. It is the power of your suggestion that determines how well your wishes are carried out.

Every ball has an outside and inside edge every time it comes to you. I admit it is round, yet to the player the side nearest you is its inside edge and that away from you its outside edge; and the edge you hit determines the curve and spin of the ball on your return. Why should we curve or spin the ball?

1. We do it to gain control of our shot.
2. We do it to fool our opponent.
3. We do it by accident.

Let me recommend that you confine your activities to the first two of these, for the third will happen anyway.

Curve and bound will be affected not only intentionally by your shot but quite unintentionally by wind, air friction and poor court surface. Tennis matches are often won by conditions, and the man who is sufficiently master of his game to turn conditions to his account is the one who will usually win. The factor in the game most affected by external conditions of wind, heat and playing surface is the ball. Its weight, bounce, flight, and even size, vary with varying conditions. It is for this reason that the mastery and complete knowledge of spin and curve of the ball is of paramount importance to a tennis player. I prefer to make the ball follow my suggestions, rather than chase it around at those of my opponent.

Let me open this discussion by a sound tennis maxim:

"Never give your opponent a chance to make a shot he likes."

The whole object of putting twist, spin, cut, curve (or whatever term you prefer to describe your control of your stroke) on the ball is to force your opponent into error.

I may sound unsporting when I claim that the primary object of tennis is to break up your opponent's game, but it is my honest belief that no man is defeated until his game is crushed, or at least weakened. Nothing so upsets a man's mental and physical poise as to be continually led into error. I have often seen players collapse in a match after they have netted or driven out a crucial point which they should have won. It is with a view not only to your own stroke but to the effect on your opponent that leads me to say, "Never make any stroke without imparting a conscious, deliberate, and intentional spin to the ball."

There are two fundamental facts as to spin:

1. *The more spin the less pace, and vice versa.*
2. *Top spin tends to drop; slice or cut spin tends to rise.*

Spin may be imparted either by a long follow-through, which, in my opinion, is the soundest method for all ground strokes, drives or slices; and by a wrist movement, which is preferable in volleying. This latter is essentially a slice or undercut spin.

Remember that where a shot is designed to defend, the spin should tend to bring the ball toward the center of the court; when a shot is used for attack, the spin can be used to curve the ball either way, according to the direction of your passing shot.

Slice shots tend to curve toward the sideline closest to the point from which the stroke is made, and are thus apt to go out over the side. Top spin tends to curve the ball toward the center of the court.

The slice is a right-hand pitcher's "in-curve," while the top spin is analogous to the "out-drop." In hitting a slice or under-cut shot the racket passes under the ball and inside (closer to the body). The top-spin shot is hit with the racket head outside the ball and passing up and slightly over it.

Every player who desires to attain championship heights must understand the value of spin on the ball. Spin means control. Knowledge of how to use it assures a player of a versatile defense and attack.

The most useful, and, in the main, the most used service carries slice spin. The rotation of the ball causes it to curve and bounce from the server's right to his left, or, in other words, towards his opponent's forehand. The object of this service is to force your opponent to reach for his return, causing his shot to either slide off his racket or to pop weakly in the air. The spin will tend to make his shot travel down the backhand sideline of the server's court unless he acutely pulls his stroke across court, a difficult and dangerous shot. To offset the natural trend out of the return of this slice service I advocate meeting the service with a flat racket and imparting top spin by a long follow-through, thus neutralizing the twist of the serve.

The reverse twist, so popular among beginners, as something unique in their experience, is not a sound service.

This reverse twist is imparted by hitting the ball from *below* and behind and carrying the racket up sharply from right to left, with a sharp lifting motion. The ball travels in a high, looping parabola, with a fast shooting drop, which, on hitting the ground, hops to the forehand of the receiver.

The first few meetings with this freakish delivery are apt to be disastrous until the receiver recognizes the hop and the excessive twist away from the curve of the ball—the reason for its name, reverse twist. Once that is gauged, all one needs to do to handle the service is to advance on the ball, meet it at the top of the bound with a firm, fast stroke and a flat racket face. The twist, still on the ball as it leaves the ground, again reverses and, acting as top spin, holds the receiver's drive in court. I know of no service so ideal to drive hard as the reverse twist.

The American twist, also a reverse as to curve and bound, but far more effective and useful, is one of the greatest assets to a player. It is the service which made Maurice E. McLoughlin famous. It is used by R. N. Williams, Watson Washburn and myself as the foundation of our delivery, although we all mix it up with the slice.

The ball is struck behind the head with the racket traveling from left to right and up over the ball, imparting a distinct "outdrop" top spin. The ball curves from the server's right to left and bounces from his left to right and high or, in other words, to your opponent's backhand, generally his weakest point. The great twist with which it hops from the ground tends to pull his stroke out over the sideline. For this reason the receiver should always strive to pull an American twist service into court and allow a large margin of safety at the sideline.

I am discussing twists in service in detail because, in service, twist rather than speed is the essential point. It is by twist and placement, rather than by speed, that you can force your opponent on the defensive at the opening of the point. Speed alone is easy to handle. It must beat the other man clean or his return will force *you* on the defensive by your own speed turned back on you. The cannonball service, a delivery of which I am supposed to be a leading exponent, is almost without twist, hit with a flat racket face and quite incapable of control or placement except by accident. Richards, Johnston and Williams, if they can put their racket on the ball at all, and they usually can, all handle my cannonball flat service more easily than either of my spin deliveries. So I strongly urge, from personal experience, base your service on a twist of some sort.

Let me turn to the use of spin in actual play, once the service has been delivered. Remember that, as a general rule, top spin or a flat twistless shot is offensive, the basis for attack; while a slice, or under-cut, back-spin shot is defensive. Top spin carries control, speed and pace. Under cut carries control and direction but no speed.

Against the net man, who is storming the barrier, all passing shots should be hit with top spin. In the first place, top spin will drop more quickly and force him to volley up from below the top of the net. Secondly, the shot carries more speed and as much control as slice. The reverse of the spin of a top shot when it is volleyed tends to cause it to rise up in the air unless the volley is perfectly hit, while a slice, when volleyed, pulls down off the racket, often for a kill. There can be no two views about the advantage of top spin over chop or slice against a net attack when striving for a passing shot.

Let us consider the defensive lob for a moment—the attempt to gain time when you are forced off your feet by your opponent's attack. Here the under-cut lob is the better choice. The under cut tends to hold the ball longer in the air, as the friction of its spin reacts. Also, when struck, it comes down rapidly, often forcing the net man to hit into the net. The slight gain in time itself may give you time to recover your position, even if your opponent makes his kill. Top-spin lobs, or the so-called "loop drive," are useful only as a surprise, never as a sound defense.

Admitting the foregoing, the question arises as to spin from the baseline when both players remain in the backcourt. Here is where the under-cut shot, with its tantalizing hesitation of bound, advances to almost equal footing with the top spin. The top spin will win outright more often than the under cut, owing to its greater speed and severity, but I am of the opinion that the under-cut shot is more apt to force your opponent into error. There is less labor involved in making the slice shot, while its irregularity of twist is greater than that of the top-spin shot, and therefore harder to judge accurately.

The ideal combination is a mixture of the two. Personally, I study my man and lay my attack accordingly. I form the basis of my game on a top-spin drive, using the slice shot to mix pace, speed and depth.

Certain players are peculiarly susceptible to error from certain twists. A sliding chop to the forehand of Johnston or Williams is fairly effective, while against Wallace Johnson or Vincent Richards it is a waste of time; yet this shot will almost alone defeat Shimizu or Kumagae.

If I were to lay down a general principle to follow, I would advise slicing to a player who prefers a high bounding ball to drive, and top-spin driving to the man who likes to slice or chop his return. It is quite a difficult feat to chop a chop, yet it can be done successfully at times, as Robert Kinsey proved in his crushing defeat of Wallace Johnson in the 1923 championship.

A VIEWPOINT OF THE GAME

by William T. Tilden 2d

It was just half a century ago that I lifted a tennis racket for the first time and, with dire results, hit my first tennis ball. There was something about the delightful sound of ball on gut, even if slightly marred by the jingle of glass from the broken window, that entered my soul with a never-to-be-forgotten thrill. It was a new emotion to my six years, but one that now, at fifty-six, still carries the thrill—even if not the broken glass. I can, at least, hit the ball in the court most of the time.

I urge you—play tennis! Tennis is the most valuable sport that any individual can learn, even more so than golf. It is the most universally played of all athletics, and its rules are the same the world over. A good game of tennis is the open-sesame on every continent and in almost every nation. Language is no barrier to tennis players, since whether a ball is out or in can be seen and understood without spoken words. Individual sport is always more valuable than team sport in adult life, since team sport requires too much effort to organize in the press of the business world. Tennis, by its small requirements of time and playing space, and its comparatively inexpensive equipment, lies within the reach of practically everyone. The tremendous increase in public courts in almost all cities has taken the game away from the classes and put it in the hands of the masses, which is a healthy and splendid thing in every way. Even our schools and colleges, steeped in the English tradition of team sport rather than individual sport, are gradually yielding to pressure and giving more and more importance to tennis. The steady growth of tennis courts at schools and colleges, together with the increase in the number that provide professional coaching for their students, shows that at last the importance of the individual sport for the adult life of the citizens of the future has been recognized by our educators.

Certainly the greatest benefit that tennis gives its followers is the means to keep physically fit. It is a game that can be played practically from the cradle to the grave—and it is apt to aid in postponing the latter many years. I started to play tennis at the age of six—and I was not unique in that. King Gustav of Sweden was still playing in his late eighties. . . . It is a game that can be carried on along with practically any form of human endeavor. The businessman, doctor, lawyer, actor, singer, writer, etc., are all able to find enough leisure time to play and, by so doing, increase their productivity by better physical condition.

The better one plays tennis, the greater its rewards, materially, spiritually, and psychologically. The champion, whether he is the champion of the world or just champion of the particular city block where he lives, is a big man in his own world and carries added weight socially and in every other way. The great players who attain international fame gain rewards in travel and the chance to meet peoples of other lands that no amount of money could buy. . . .

Therefore, I urge all who can to play tennis, and if you do play it, play it to the very best of your ability and opportunity. Enjoy it as a game, keep it a sport. If you become great in it, the material rewards will come to you without your playing it with that in mind. . . .

Most people who take up tennis seem to feel that it isn't worth the effort unless they can master the game in a short time. I can only say that I have never discovered any short cut to learning tennis. I feel that the player who is willing to learn slowly and soundly from the basic foundation of the game will benefit in the end. He will go ahead far faster than one who superficially picks up a flashy but unsound style in a short time, and then stops working. Weeks spent in laying a sound groundwork of correct strokes at the start will save years in the end.

There is nothing mysterious about tennis. It is a game of sound scientific principles that anyone with an average mind and body can learn to play well if he will take the trouble to work at it. The great champions are not born but are made by their own—and at times their coaches'—efforts. In the years I have played tennis, I have looked for a born tennis player, but I have yet to find one. The best I have been able to do is to find a gifted athlete, but only long, hard work made the player. The two greatest naturals in tennis I ever saw were Vincent Richards and Frank Kovacs, but yet neither had quite the willingness to do the long serious practice work that produces a champion of champions and an all-time great.

I believe that one can learn to play tennis in a year or less—but it takes five years to make a Tennis Player and ten years to make a Champion. Much that is the trouble with tennis today is due to the unwillingness of promising youngsters to go through the proper preparations in laying a sound scientific foundation. The result is that once the first flush of youth and athletic prowess starts to fade, the modern game disintegrates because it has no solid and intelligent foundation on which to depend. Speed and power are essential in the equipment of every great player, but they alone cannot suffice. Attack alone or defense alone is not enough; a combination of the two, with the knowledge of how to employ them, is what makes your F. J. Perry, Ellsworth Vines Jr., Donald Budge, or Bobby Riggs. It was not until Jack Kramer added defense to his attack in his professional tour with Riggs that he established himself as the outstanding player of the world.

The success of the California game of hard hitting as exemplified by Vines, Budge, and Kramer might have done serious damage to the total picture of tennis if it had not been offset by the equal success of the subtleties and intellectual defense of Perry and Riggs. But all these great stars produced their outstanding performances only after learning the incontrovertible lesson that the combination of attack and defense, in proper blend, is the maximum tennis skill. The reader may feel that this explanation should come as a summing up, but to me, if the proper picture is drawn at the beginning, then all that follows takes its place in logical order within the frame. The player who really desires to go high must have an ethical and technical background that will explain the game of today. The champion of today owes his game to the champions of yesterday, just as he will add his bit to the champion of tomorrow. The wise student should learn all he can about the styles and methods of the great players of the past, every bit as much as he does of the players of the present.

It is the fashion of the moment to view with patronizing contempt, as slightly obsolete, the game of any player who has been in the tennis world for a decade. As for anything older than that, the modern youngster either knows nothing or considers it a dead issue. Where would our culture, education, and art be if this became the fashion in these worlds? Why, then, should we ignore our valued heritage in athletics? School and college coaches should hold regular classes in their sports that would provide accurate knowledge on the changing methods of their games, and of the great stars of the past. . . .

There is nothing that Jack Kramer does today that players of the past have not done equally well. There are some very valuable things of the past that have been lost in the wild scramble for speed and power. These should be recovered and brought back into the repertoire of the modern player.

Much of the present-day type of tennis is due to the effect of the official propaganda of the United States Lawn Tennis Association on young players.

During the past two decades the U.S.L.T.A. has built up the finest and best-organized junior development system of any nation in the world. Much of our international success has been due to this, since we have encouraged and increased competition among our boys and girls from their earliest teens. By so doing, we have ingrained the spirit of competition, developed the will to win, and given the opportunity for champions to mature. Naturally, along with all its virtues, such a large organizational plan would also develop its attendant weaknesses, chief of which is the armchair theorist who crept into power and established himself as a coach or tennis expert. Often he is merely an interested, well-meaning crackpot who knows little or nothing about the actual development of the tennis game from either its technical or its tactical side. These earnest but incompetent people take immediate result rather than sound development as their criterion of correct method, often without ability to see below the surface to the foundation. The success of such hard hitters as Vines, Budge, and Kramer so impressed these armchair coaches that they induced the U.S.L.T.A. to start a steady stream of propaganda to its juniors that, summed up in a few words, amounts to "Hit like hell and run to the net."

The result of this method, used almost exclusively by these inexperienced and unwise coaches, is that from 1940 to 1950 junior tennis has steadily declined in class in the United States, although more of it is played than ever before. . . .

How can real tennis players develop under that sort of advice? The immediate result, which anyone who knows anything about tennis technique can see at first glance, is the deterioration of all ground strokes among the youngsters of today. This is particularly true of that basic shot and most important stroke in tennis, the forehand drive. There are many well-produced backhands, but even these are inclined to be unsound and too aggressive. The defensive chop and the medium pace and slow drive have practically disappeared from the game, and all one sees is a bunch of kids trying to reach the net behind shots that are pitifully uncertain. If almost all these kids were not amazing volleyers and servers, they would have no chance at all, and, in fact, they have none now when they meet a really first-class ground-stroke player, like Perry or Riggs, who can also volley when needed.

The official attitude of the U.S.L.T.A. should be overhauled and modified. The need of attack should definitely be stressed to all young players, but not overstressed as it is today. If the line of learning, and the method of teaching it, could be set by a group of such great stars as Eleanor Tennant, Vincent Richards, Fred Perry, Alice Marble, Donald Budge, and Bobby Riggs, rather than by such unpractical theorists as do it today, the standard of junior tennis would start an immediate rise and in a comparatively short time reach a new peak. . . .

Something drastic is needed to bring back a balanced and intelligent method to American tennis, and to take full advantage of the wealth of superlative material that is today only realizing a small fraction of its true worth. I see boys and girls with wonderful natural ability held back and practically condemned to mediocrity because they are almost forced along a path that can only develop a portion of their abilities. It is a crying pity that this is so, when it could be avoided by a wise advisory board.

The predominance of the California group, where tennis is played on concrete courts, is partially responsible for the overstress on attack. On concrete, cement, and asphalt, power pays off while defense and finesse are almost useless. Yet less than 5 per cent of all world tennis is played on such hard courts. Over 85 per cent is played on some form of clay or dirt court, while grass, with its 10 per cent, is still the most important surface, since the United States, English, and Australian championships are all played on it. On grass, and even more definitely on clay courts, defense and finesse, variation of spin, speed, pace, and depth, have equal importance with sheer power. All of those players whose goal is international competition should recognize that they must not allow themselves to be held within the limitation of the game as played generally in their home locale. Just as California and the Pacific Coast overstress attack, so do the East, South, and Middle West place too much reliance on defense. The wise player attempts to learn both styles, since in major competition only a blend of both can carry a man to the very top.

It is a pity that so far nothing has really been done to standardize court surfaces. The greatest single step forward that tennis could take would be for the International Lawn Tennis Federation to adopt one standard surface as the only one on which recognized tournaments could be held. It will never be. England, Australia, and, to a lesser degree, the United States would fight to hold grass as the standard, yet grass is impossible to grow in many countries where tennis is very popular. Some form of clay (like En-Tout-Cas) or dirt is a possibility and even practical almost all over the world, but the tendency of this surface to slow up the game—overstress defense and underplay attack—makes it far from universally popular. Even within a great country like the United States, various sections have such definite prejudices that they would battle to protect their own favorite type of court. I am positive it would take more than a major earthquake ever to wean California away from the hard court. It is sincerely believed—and possibly correctly, though I doubt it—that much of that state's success is due to the hard court. Personally, I think it is the fact that the climate allows all-year play, coupled with the splendid organization of tennis, that keeps California at the top in this country. After all, Oregon and Washington have the hard courts, as do Arizona and New Mexico, but they haven't the other two factors.

Therefore, just as long as a tennis player will be called on to play on varied court surfaces, just so long must he strive to have a real all-court game capable of meeting all conditions with the best possible style of play.

Everything today points to one thing. Too much emphasis is laid on physical effort, quick result, and snap judgment. In the increased rush of modern living, the need for thoughtful, careful planning and preparation has been overlooked and sacrificed. Too great publicity on victory, and not enough appreciation for the sound, complete artist, has built up a fear of immediate defeat in many of our young players. So they are not willing to work slowly toward a real goal. Everything I write here about tennis today is written in the hope that the youngsters who read it will gain the knowledge that there is no need for all the rush toward immediate success.

Tennis should always be played with the head consciously directing the racket. Every shot should be played with a definite intention behind it, one that will make it of value to the player who hits it.

The viewpoint on tennis that stamps a tennis player is that the game is a science and an art. It can reach its highest expression only if a player is willing to study and practice in an attempt to master the game in all its varied facets. . . . What I have learned I owe to those who preceded me, my own contemporaries, and those who have followed me. Do not scorn to learn from those you can beat. There is much to be learned from them. Remember always that even more can be learned in defeat than in victory, if you suffered that defeat when you gave your best. And keep in mind that, no matter how great you are, there is always the possibility of someone greater.

THE GENERAL TECHNIQUE OF ALL STROKES

by William T. Tilden 2d

Strokes are the weapons with which you fight your tennis battles. The better the weapons, the greater the chance of victory. Still, you must always remember that weapons alone never won a war. It is the way in which they are used that determines their usefulness. It is extremely important, almost necessary, to have good strokes, but strokes are not the end—only the means to the end. Therefore, do all in your power to learn good strokes, but never be satisfied to be just a shot maker. Shots alone never won a tennis match or crowned a champion. Above all, never allow yourself to become too stroke-conscious. Correct form is beautiful and a fine thing to attain, but in every important match there is some crucial period when form must go by the board and the result—getting the ball back any way, with two hands and the wood of the racket if necessary—becomes the deciding factor. So once more I say work for good strokes in all departments, but always regard them as merely your means to put the ball into the right place at the right time. A badly produced shot to the right place is always better than the most beautiful shot in the world to the wrong place. The first wins, the second loses, so keep your perspective on what strokes mean in tennis.

There are several generalities about strokes that carry through the entire list and should always be borne in mind:

1. For the same effort—the less spin, the more speed, and conversely, the

more spin, the less speed. From this it can be seen that the flat shot is almost always the attacking shot, while the spin is more often defensive.

2. On all drives the racket head in its backswing should be dropped below the line of the stroke and the ball is struck on the lower outside surface, with the racket head hitting up on the ball, which gives a tendency toward top spin.

3. On all chops, slices, and volleys, the racket head should be above the line of the shot in its backswing and hit down slightly on the ball, which gives a tendency toward back spin.

4. On all shots—drives, chops, slices, volleys, smashes, services—the racket head should hit directly through the ball and at the place in your opponent's court where you wish to place the ball. The secret lies in that geometric axiom "A straight line is the shortest distance between two points."

Under no circumstances use flourishes or exaggerated movements in stroke production. The essence of good form is absence of "form." Watching all the great stars, you are seldom conscious of what they do before they hit the ball. It is the actual hitting of the ball itself that is important, and that is what sticks in your mind with these players. Everything they do is so simple and natural that it is unobstrusive. Once more you find an example of the simplicity of true greatness. In every form of human endeavor the real masters of the job make whatever they do look so easy. They have eliminated all the waste motion and useless effort, and all that remains is the sheer necessity of their art. That is what really good form does in tennis. Strive to make all your strokes sound, sane, solid, and simply produced. Freak shots, even such remarkable strokes as Pancho Segura's two-handed forehand, or the remarkable two-handed shots of John Bromwich, or the ambidextrous cleverness of Beverly Baker, are never as sound as the orthodox style and will ultimately break up under enough pressure. Stay away from tricks and freak strokes. They won't pay dividends.

In learning strokes the order of work is clear-cut and definite:

1. Learn the correct racket grips.
2. Learn the correct footwork and body position.
3. Learn to hit the ball.
4. Learn to hit the ball correctly.
5. Learn to hit the ball correctly to a certain place.
6. Learn to hit the ball correctly to a certain place hard, or slow, or at even pace.

THE GRIPS

The first step in acquiring good strokes is to learn the correct grips. (Notice I said grips, not grip, for no one grip will do for all strokes.) You will hear much talk about the three schools of gripping the racket:

The Eastern grips, which are correct; the Continental grip, which is included in the Eastern style for certain strokes; the Western grip, which is obsolete and discarded today by experts.

Since I am convinced that the Eastern grips are best, I will discuss them only, for in doing so I bring in the Continental, or Universal, grip where it belongs.

The Eastern Grips. There are three distinct grips within the Eastern school:

1. The forehand drive grip—the key grip from which you learn the others.

2. The backhand drive grip.

3. The Continental grip, or Eastern service, which is used for all strokes *except the drive.*

1. The Forehand Drive Grip. Hold the racket in the left hand so the short strings are perpendicular to the ground, with the handle pointing at you. Then (assuming you are right-handed) place the palm of the right hand flat against the flat side of the handle at the back (or right-hand side), away from the direction you would hit the ball (to the left), so that the handle and your arm make a straight line. Close the fingers firmly around the handle with the fingers spread comfortably. Notice that now the face of your racket and palm of your hand are in the same hitting plane and that there is practically no broken line at the wrist. This is the key grip of the Eastern school and is the one that should always be learned first.

2. The Backhand Drive Grip. Still holding the racket as described above, learn the move to the second grip, the background grip. Move the hand backward (or counter-clockwise) a quarter circle turn until the palm of the hand is *on top* of the handle, with the flat side of the top resting in it and the arm still making nearly a straight line with the handle. Close the fingers firmly around the handle, with the thumb *diagonally across* the handle, *not straight up the back.* In hitting the ball, you use the opposite face of the strings from the forehand. These two grips, as described, are used to hit all flat and top-spin drives, forehand and backhand. They are not used for any strokes except drives.

3. The Continental Grip. This grip, which is also known as the Eastern service grip or the Universal grip, is used for the chop and slice stroke, the volley, the smash, the lob, and the drop shot, as well as for the slice, twist, and cannonball service. It should never be used to drive, particularly off the forehand, where it lacks power. Halfway between the handle positions of the forehand and backhand grips is a slanting surface of the handle. Starting from the original forehand key position, move the hand an eighth circle turn backward or counter-clockwise (which is half of the way to the backhand grip), until the palm of the hand lies on this slanting surface of the handle. Then close the fingers firmly around the handle, let the thumb take a natural diagonal position across the handle, and depress the wrist, making an angle with the handle of the racket that will bring the head of the racket above the wrist. The hand in position is not materially changed, only eased between forehand and backhand.

Do not grip the racket so tightly that it will cramp the arm muscles, but do not go too far the other way by holding the racket so loosely that it will turn easily in the hand. The time to hold the racket firmly is at the moment of impact with the ball. Many players feel that they haven't time to change the position of the hand on the racket handle. Actually, they have more than enough provided they know how to do it. Do not attempt to turn the racket in the hand but move the hand on the handle, keeping the racket still. Do this by steadying the racket in your left hand and moving the right hand into the correct position by sliding it around the handle. Remember that correct grips are a vital part of a sound shot. Even if at first these grips seem slightly unnatural, stay with them until they are mastered. Many players have great difficulty in learning to serve with this grip, because it does not feel natural to them, but let me strongly urge you to stay with it until you have it, since time has proved it is by far the best service grip.

THE DRIVE

by William T. Tilden 2d

We will now take up the key stroke of tennis, on which all sound tennis games are, or should be, built.

The drive, on both wings, is the most important single stroke in tennis. It is played probably twice as often as all the other strokes combined. It is the key to all back-court games, and since a player must make at least one ground stroke before he can volley (when he is not the server) you can see that ground strokes will always be more important than the net game. The drive is the only shot in tennis which is equally important in attack and defense. It can be used to win points outright by blasting speed or subtle placement and it can also be used to keep the ball going back when you are being attacked by your opponent. It is capable of wider range of speed and angle than any other shot. Therefore, the wise student will learn to hit a drive first of all shots, and will strive to make it as sound and solid as practice will produce. A great many players will work hours to learn a backhand drive under able coaching but will be satisfied with almost any sort of natural poke on the forehand. There are few good forehands in tennis today. Actually, the forehand is more important than the backhand because it is, or should be, used more often.

The basic method of hitting either drive is the same in attack and defense. It is only in the power of the swing of the racket head and the direction of the stroke that the difference is to be found. Do not try to develop one type of drive in defense and another in attack—one way to hit cross-court and another to hit straight—because by so doing you will fail to have the ability to go from one to the other with no indication of what you intend to play.

The secret of a sound drive lies in the early preparation of the shot and the placing of the feet in correct position to keep your body sideways to the net, your rear end out of the way of the ball, and the weight moving forward with the stroke.

On all drives, no matter how high or low the point of contact with the ball may be, the head of the racket must be dropped below the line of your shot. At the moment of hitting the ball, the racket face should meet the lower outside surface of the ball with a slightly upward and definitely forward motion, and continue to the very end of the full arm swing.

Do not turn the racket face over the ball with your wrist, or "lift up" across the ball, to impart top spin. The fact that you have hit slightly up on the ball with the flat racket face, and followed through, will give you all the tendency to top spin that you need. Do not attempt to gain direction by "hooking" or twisting your drive. Let the flat face of your racket go directly at the place you want the ball to go.

To drive cross-court from your right to left, lean a shade forward, letting the weight definitely go out on the left foot before the ball is struck, and meet the ball on a line with the left hip, or, in terms of time, hit it early.

To hit straight, or even from your number 2 court off to your right, keep your weight evenly divided between your feet and let the ball come back to a line with your belt buckle before you meet it, or, in terms of time, hit it late.

All drives should be hit waist-high! If the bound of the ball is too high to take it waist-high where you are standing, pick up your carcass and get in position where you can. Either move in and meet it waist-high as it comes up, which is dangerous even for experts and is used only in attack by them, or take the better and safer course and move back, letting the ball cross the top of the bound, and, as it falls to the waist, hit it. Should the bound of the ball be so low that it never rises to your waist, then you must bend your knees and take your waist down to the ball, but still hit it waist high. Do not stand up like a cigar store Indian to these low shots and then use the shovel shot. It is no good.

The Mechanics of the Forehand Drive: 1. As the ball approaches, drop the racket head down and back, behind the body. 2. Step across directly toward the right sideline with the left foot so your rear end is turned away from the ball. 3. Allow the weight to go forward toward the left foot, passing on to it just before or just as you hit the ball. 4. With the eye never leaving the ball until you actually hit it, swing the racket head around the body so the flat face of the racket, with the short strings up and down, meets the ball on the lower right rear surface (away from you) and, with a *stiff wrist and firm grip* on the racket, swing directly through, continuing the swing until the racket head has traveled around your body and ends on your left with its opposite face turned to your opponent's court.

Few players realize that the follow-through is the thing that controls the drive. The reason so many players balloon shots into the backstop is that they swing into the ball, and as soon as they hit it they stop the racket. The ball, with no spin to take hold of it, goes "poof" into the air. Timidity, fear

of error, often stops a player from finishing his follow-through and results in
the very thing he fears, whereas if he had had the courage to hit the ball
and follow through, he would have made his shot. Never hit a drive without
completing the arc of your swing, and that is just as true of the slowest,
easiest shot as it is of the hardest. Indecision will ruin any shot. Make up
your mind, and then play the ball with definiteness and decision to the very
end of your swing.

The Backhand Drive. Everything I pointed out in the *Mechanics of the
Forehand Drive* is equally correct for the backhand if you substitute right
for left and vice versa. You step over with the right foot directly toward the
left sideline, let the weight pass on to the right foot, and meet the ball on its
lower left surface. The one great difference in the backhand lies in the point
where the racket face contacts the ball. All forehands are hit directly in
front of the body in a space between the lines of the front (or left) hip and
the back (or right) hip. . . . (Remember that the player is standing sideways.) On the backhand, the ball should be met sooner, that is, nearer the
net. The latest point to hit a backhand drive is the line of the front (or
right) hip, and from there to a point about two feet forward of the hip will
produce the best results. The earlier you meet the ball the sharper cross-
court will your shot go. The reason for swinging soon is easily seen, since if
you allow the ball to get on a line with the body, the arm must swing back
against the body, and at the moment of hitting it is still cramped in its
swing. The secret of a good backhand lies in the freedom of the swing and
the long follow-through. Most players have a tendency to poke at a backhand, so there is little control or power to the shot.

The main uses of the drive are 1. To return service (both attack and
defense). 2. To make passing shots against the net player (attack). 3. To
advance to the net behind a forcing shot (attack). 4. To hit clean winners
(attack). 5. To open your opponent's court and maneuver him out of
position (subtle attack). 6. To get yourself out of trouble when you are
forced into bad position (defense).

From these six uses you can see that the drive is primarily an attacking
shot but not necessarily so and, if used as an attack, is very often not an
outright winner but is used to build up the point for a winner—often from
the net. Therefore, it should carry a fairly high average pace but only at
times should it be slugged with full power. Too many modern players have
only one drive, and that is at the top of their power. The sound average-
pace drive, and the slow drive, with its insidious weapon of variation, are the
greatest losses of tennis today, and they must be regained.

MATCH PLAY TACTICS AND TENNIS PSYCHOLOGY

by William T. Tilden 2d

Over the entrance to the great center court at Wimbledon, England, and also over the marquee steps to the stadium of the West Side Tennis Club, Long Island, are identical signs. They carry two lines from Rudyard Kipling's "If": "If you can meet with Triumph and Disaster, And treat those two impostors just the same . . ."

In those two lines Kipling gave the perfect picture of what a great tennis player must have, and both tennis associations, British and American, recognized it. It is a long but effective way to saying one word—Courage! When I use the term "courage" here I do not merely mean that wonderful quality that is part of courage, known colloquially as "guts." Certainly that quality is also needed by a champion, but it is momentary, perhaps fleeting, and but an infinitesimal part of the entire picture of courage.

Courage embodies patience, philosophy, and the vision to lift your eyes to the goal far ahead. It is the ability, in spite of discouragement, disheartening disappointments, even apparent failure, never to lose sight of that goal, or belief in yourself and your ultimate victory.

It takes five years to make a Tennis Player and ten years to make a Champion. If you set out to be champion, you must have the courage to look ten years ahead, and never waver or hesitate, even during those awful periods of growing pains when your game seems to be getting nowhere. You will lose to players you know you should beat, and all your best friends either look the other way when you play or tell you bluntly that you are just a dub and always will be. Every great player goes through such periods. I know I did. I wish I had a dollar for every time I definitely made up my mind at night that I'd give up the game forever. Many were the evenings when I burned my rackets in imagination, only to be out on the court the next day, just as full of enthusiasm, confidence, and love of the game as ever. Perhaps that quality isn't courage, only pigheadedness, but whatever it is, a person must have it, if he is ever going to become a real tennis player.

Progress in tennis is usually very slow and not very easy to see. There are long periods in the development of every first-class player when he feels he is standing still. Do not look for improvement on a day-to-day or week-to-week basis. If you're lucky and going up fast, the quickest visible improvement is month by month, but it is more likely to be a seasonal one. It takes patience and philosophy to get you over this hump. The sounder and more carefully you lay your foundation, the better grounded in technique your strokes during your early years, the slower may be the progress. You may get some terrible lickings from flashy naturals who have played only half as long as you have, and whose strokes look like windmills. You may find yourself wondering why you waste all this time on correct form when, in a short time, some dub with no idea of what he's doing can beat you. "Perhaps," you tell yourself, "I'm crazy and I'd better give it all up." That is the time your courage must come to your aid and to keep your eyes on that distant goal of perfection. It can keep you plugging, and if it does, about a year later, you run into the same dub and you make a remarkable discovery—now he's a pushover. You beat him so easily, you wonder how you could ever have lost to him. Actually, during that year, all you did was to gain a mastery of what you had, but had not been able to control, a year before.

Every stroke that you gain control of, so that it is really dependable, takes at least six months of hard, intensive work in actual match play. If you make the mistake of attempting to work on too many shots at a time, you will gain control of none. The service and ground strokes can be learned and worked on together, but for your first year you should not attempt anything about the net game beyond learning the mere mechanics. The next year you can afford to start going in a great deal. In fact, turn for a while from a baseliner to a net player, and then gradually blend the two styles. The third year you can start to mix in the backspin shots, and soft volley. The fourth, you should take to work on variation of strokes and variety of spin, speed and pace. Finally, you add the half-volley and drop shot, and if you have reasonable control of all these, you have become a tennis player, instead of just someone who plays tennis. You see that determination, patience and vision of the ultimate goal are required to carry you along this sort of road. An added difficulty is the fact that each new shot you start to learn upsets to some extent the ones you have already mastered, with the result that each year you will suffer some unexpected and discouraging defeats.

Once the technical mastery of all these shots is yours, then experimentation in match play is needed to show when and where each will serve you best. It will take you several years to gain the knowledge that you will need to meet all players and all situations. During that time you will lose matches to players you know you should beat, but you will have the inspiration of a few upset victories over stars who are as surprised as you are at the result. Those victories are merely the signposts of your regular game of the future, and you should treasure them to boost your courage for the long road to tennis heights. Do not make the mistake of considering that one or two good wins means your job is done. They are merely indications of what is to come in the next few years.

Many young players get delusions of grandeur after their first few big victories. They suddenly realize that they are God's gift to tennis, that they know all there is to know about the game, and right there they start down the path to tennis oblivion. Confidence and belief in one's self are almost essential to success, but conceit is the one certain poison to kill all chance of it. Take your victories and defeats in stride, and keep your feet on the ground and your head a trifle smaller than your hat. Success is a dangerous wine, particularly to the young. It can make you as drunk with your own importance as any liquor. It is during the time of your first success that the philosophical quality of your courage must come to your aid. All those good old bromides like "The bigger they come, the harder they fall" carry real truth. Take your game seriously and regard it with respect. Play it always to the best of your ability, but for heaven's sake don't believe your publicity and start taking yourself too seriously. Conceit and fatheadedness can ruin your physical condition, your match temperament, and your future in an incredibly short time.

One of the early symptoms of conceit is an attitude of disparagement toward one's opponent and his game. This is a growing attitude today among the juniors, and a most distressing one. I have watched so many kids recently who seemed to take a good shot by their opponent as a personal insult instead of giving it the admiration that was its due. Instead of saying, "Good shot!" sincerely, as a true sportsman would, they say, "Good God!" . . . These offenders hate to admit any other person's equality, let alone superiority. . . . Behind much of conceit is fear, rooted in an inferiority complex and camouflaged by the swagger and the boast. There are many dangerous, regrettable examples of such conceit in the tennis world. One finds the player who, having won a good match, avoids his defeated opponent thereafter whenever possible, afraid to give him another chance, but he always lets the world know he won the last time they met. There is the reverse situation where the player, once beaten, tries to stay away from any event where he might meet his conqueror again, afraid of another licking. There is the great practice player, the man who hits like a demon when he is playing for fun, but who, when the chips are down in a match, ladles everything and loses ignominiously. Yet he always tells of his great victories in practice, and invariably forgets his tournament record. All these players are on the wrong foot. They are afraid! Play tennis without fear of defeat and because it's fun and you enjoy it, or don't play at all. There is no disgrace in defeat. . . . Explanations and alibis take your mind off the really important thing, which is, or should be, your match. If done to excess this sort of thing will destroy your concentration and bring about the very thing you fear, defeat.

There is no time in any hard-fought tennis match for your mind to wander if you want to win. Conceit makes you too self-conscious and is apt to set your mind thinking about how you look, or what the gallery is saying about you, when it should be centered on your tactics and your opponent. There is a great difference between confidence and conceit, but many players never find out what it is. The knowledge of what you have in your own game, the sincere belief that it will win, *provided* it is played to the best of your ability and the limit of your physical resources if necessary— that is confidence and it will carry you far. The attitude that you are so good you need not try, that you are so great that your opponent must fear you, and that you are past the point where you can learn anything more is conceit. That will beat you consistently and if it becomes a habit will completely ruin your game. The dividing line is very thin, and extremely easy to cross. You should be on your guard at all times against the insidious inroads of your ego. . . .

Before you can really "dish it out" in tennis, you have to learn to "take it." Only by going through the mill of many defeats can a player gain the experience needed to show him what shot to play, and when and where to play it. Champions are born in the labor of defeat. It takes all phases of courage to go through the years when defeat is your portion a large part of the time, and realize, amid all your discouragement, that you are steadily forging ahead toward your goal. If you learn something of tactics or the psychology of match play in a losing match, as you should if you analyze it afterward, you have taken another step toward the complete mastery of your game.

EXPLOITING YOUR OPPONENT'S WEAKNESSES

Tennis matches are won by the man who hits the ball to the right place at the right time most often. That right place may be determined by the possibility of making a clean winner, but more often it's a place from which an opponent will make an error on his return shot. Nothing is so disconcerting or upsetting to a player as to miss. A magnificent shot, which beats him completely, doesn't cause him much mental anguish because, if he's a sportsman, he will admire it and then not worry about it any more. On the other hand, each time he sees an important shot of his own sail out of court or into the net, a player becomes more nervous and less likely to win a match. The more errors he makes, the less likely are his chances of pulling his game together on subsequent points. Remember that in first-class tournament tennis, 70 per cent of all points end in error, a net or an out, and only 30 per cent end in winning placements or service aces. (Of course, the percentage of points ending in an error is even higher in poorer caliber tennis.)

This fact gives birth to the first great rule in general tactics: *Keep the ball in play and give your opponent another shot at it, rather than risk an error by taking an unnecessary chance.*

Notice the word "unnecessary" in that rule. Naturally, if you are presented with a weak shot, be ready to take advantage of it. But the keynote of good tactics is to be content to keep the ball going and move your opponent around his court unless:

1. You see the big opening and decide to hit out for a winner, or

2. You are forced into an almost hopeless position, with little chance to extricate yourself, and you decide that the gamble carries practically no extra risk, and may conceivably turn the tables in your favor.

Let your opponent be the one to take the *unnecessary* chances, and the one who will pile up the majority of those 70 per cent errors. You are playing the percentage if you do so, and you'll beat your opponent if you are otherwise evenly matched. However, always be ready for the opening to win outright, while you are keeping the ball going. You are "playing your hooked fish"—getting ready to land him. The best tennis tacticians play *a defensive game with an offensive mental attitude.*

The first thought that you should have, when you step onto a court for a match, is "What are my opponent's weaknesses? Where will he miss most?"

You should start at once, even during the warm-up, to watch for the signs that point to weaknesses.

The beginning of any tennis match has somewhat the same quality as that shown by two boxers feeling each other out before risking their respective attacks. Much of that exploration can be achieved during the warm-up period if you are clever about it, and the chances are that your opponent will be quite unaware of the fact that you are doing anything except warming up. The way to do it is to vary your first shots to him: a drive, a chop—a fast shot, then a slow one. Stick in a mid-court shot and watch what he does with it. Does he walk in and hit it hard, and then come in to volley, or does he just hit it back, and then retire to the baseline again? Did he show any sign of hesitancy in hitting your backspin slice? Did he attempt to meet speed with speed, or did he show timidity in returning your fast drives? What was the form of your ground strokes?

You should be able to get some leading hints about two aspects of your opponent's tennis game by the end of the warm-up period. They are:

1. The type of game he will probably elect to play against you, which, unless he knows something about you, is undoubtedly his most natural and strongest game.

2. Any weaknesses in stroke production he may have, which are likely to be obvious if the form of his ground strokes is faulty in certain respects.

Let's take up these two aspects in detail, and see what indications your opponent may give you that will help you determine how to plan your own offense.

The Type of Game Your Opponent Will Probably Play. If, at the end of the warm-up, you are of the opinion that he is going to defend from the baseline and doesn't like speed, you should attack in the first game, going to the net behind fast drives. If, on the other hand, you think he will turn out to be a slugger (a much more likely thing these days), start your match in a slow, soft tempo, using distinct variation of spin and depth. By so doing you are attempting to upset the hitter at the very outset, by forcing errors from him. In any case, start all matches with a slow enough tempo and pace so that your own energies will be able to build in power and pressure, no matter how long the match continues. The modern "neck or nothing" type of game usually goes off like an explosion, but if the original impetus fails to carry to victory, there is no reserve left for a rally. You should space every match so that you still have a final physical and mental reserve to call upon, a little unexpended energy to bring up for victory in a final set. Too many players waste valuable energy in rushing a match unnecessarily. The wise player learns to relax *physically* between points, games, and sets, even though he never can relax *mentally* until the match is over.

Walk, don't run, into position. Don't stall deliberately, but you are entitled to a reasonable time in which to get ready, so take it, even if your opponent is stewing and fidgeting to get started on a point. Play your own game, not his. If you are playing a rusher, slow up the tempo. If you are up against a staller, keep him moving a shade faster than he likes. There is nothing unsporting about this—you are simply taking your rights under the rules. The proper tempo of a match for you is the one you like, and you should make every effort to set it. When two players start a match, it is always a battle to see who will dominate the match, and who will be pushed around. One player or the other will ultimately impress his tennis personality on the other. The one who does will win, because by so doing he forces the recognition of impending defeat upon his opponent. One of the surest ways to achieve this state of affairs is to set your own tempo and hold it. Do it courteously, with all due regard for your opponent's rights, but do it. An attitude of calm confidence goes a long way toward maintaining a mental edge. The more you can make your opponent feel that you expect to win, intend to win, and there's nothing he can do to shake your confidence and determination, the harder it is for him to hold his own concentration. That old school bromide "A man who won't be beat can't be beat" may be ripe corn, but there's a lot of truth in it.

Weaknesses in Stroke Production Your Opponent May Display by the Form of His Ground Strokes. During the warm-up period there are several indications of this sort which you can use later to your advantage.

a. The form of the shot, particularly with respect to the backswing and feet. If you meet a player with a roundhouse backswing, starting high, or a man who faces the net while making a stroke, you will know at once that he is vulnerable to a low backspin shot into the deep corners. He is also an easy mark for a speedy shot aimed directly at him, since he will be caught with his racket too high and forced to crowd his return. Any player who faces the net when he hits his shots can't get down to the ball and still keep his body out of the way of his swing, on low, short shots. He will also have trouble on shots that keep going away from him and make him reach, since he cannot throw his weight out on a balancing foot, as he could if he stroked from the sideways position. Therefore, the sharply angled cross-court shot will tie this man into knots.

b. A definite tendency to run around a ball that should be played on the backhand, and to take it on the forehand. The fact that your opponent is so eager to stay away from playing a shot off his backhand means that he is weak off that side, but watch out in trying to exploit that weakness. He has probably built up his greatest strength, his forehand drive made from the backhand court, to cover it. . . . The way to play this obvious weakness is to hit once to the side or corner of the forehand court, in order to open up the backhand court, and then attack the latter. Against a man with a backhand weakness, it is also good to go to the net once you have placed the ball solidly on that side, for the return is likely to be a weak one.

c. A tendency to hang back on the baseline when it is logical to come to the net. This probably means your opponent possesses an uncertain volley or overhead. Try him out early in the match by using short shots, and even a drop shot or two. Then, if he stays in at the net, as he almost must do, hit directly at him once with great speed, try one soft, angled passing shot, and toss up a lob. His method of playing these shots will confirm your suspicions if he is poor at certain aspects of net play. If he is, draw him in whenever possible, and then give him every chance to make errors by playing to his weakness.

d. A continuous net attack. This is likely to mean uncertain ground strokes. You should use every method, including lobbing, to force your opponent away from the net during the early games. If unsuccessful in doing so, go in a good deal on your own service, so that at least he is forced to play every second game from the back court. That will offer enough of a chance for his weakness to show up, if he has it.

All of the above can be summed up in another important tactical rule: *Never give your opponent a shot he likes to play if you can avoid it.* (There is an exception to this rule, which will be discussed a little later on, but the rule is an excellent one under most circumstances.)

No one, not even the greatest tactician in the world, can lay down specific rules of tactics for any given point, or series of points, and have them work out every time. You may start a point with a definite idea of just how you will play it to win, have things seeming to go well, and then any one of several occurrences may take place and force you to change your plans. You may play a weaker or shorter shot than you intended, and your opponent will take the attack away from you. Or you may start out to exploit your opponent's weakness only to have him make a lucky shot off it, or even an unexpectedly good shot, which leaves him in a favorable position if you continue the attack you planned. Or you may have guessed wrong on what your opponent himself planned to do. He may come in when you thought he was going to stay back, with the result that carrying through your original plan would now be fatal. In all of these circumstances, and others like them, you must discard your original ideas and bring up fresh ones to meet the new situation.

Do not be mechanical or pigheaded about your tactics. Always keep an open mind, aware of the whole picture and ready to change plans at any time if it seems wise. Far too many players make up their minds to play a certain point, game, set or even match in one way, and stick to it even when it's obvious that they're getting nowhere with it. That is neither courage nor determination—it is stupidity. There are two generalities of tactics which should be borne in mind in this connection:

Never change a winning game.

Always change a losing game.

The first seems obvious. You would think that anyone would know enough to follow that rule, but for some perverse reason it seems to work the other way with some players. A man will build up a winning lead by staying back and pounding his opponent's backhand. Then, suddenly, for no understandable reason except perhaps a desire to finish in a blaze of glory, he begins to rush the net, starts losing points, and ends by being defeated. Perhaps the reverse takes place. He builds up his lead by going to the net constantly but, just as he should be finishing his man off, suddenly retires to the baseline and eventually loses. Perhaps he gains his lead by slow finesse and changes to speed for no reason, or vice versa. In each case he changes a winning game before he has won, and by doing so he gets just what he deserves—a licking.

Conversely, it is equally stupid to insist upon playing to the end a type of game that is losing badly. If you do, you are certain to lose. You may lose anyway, but you might better try to win with something else. If you can't win from the baseline, go to the net. If you have been going in, and it hasn't been working, stay back and see if you can outsteady your opponent. Try out something new, if what you have previously been trying has failed.

There is another approach to this tactical problem, which is that your opponent is never completely beaten until you have broken his morale, and made him conscious of his impending defeat. Pounding a weakness is one way to do it. It is the longest, often the surest, and certainly the most universally used method. A method I frequently prefer is quicker, more exciting, and perhaps more dangerous, but if it's successful it inflicts the most lasting of all defeats. It is to *play your opponent's strength until you break it*. (This, of course, is the exception to the tactical rule of not giving your opponent a shot he likes to play.) Believe me, once a player finds his favorite shot won't win for him, his whole game collapses. If he can't win with his strength, he can't win at all. Once a player admits defeat to himself, he is through, even though he plays on gamely and tries to hide it. Certainly, the very fact that you attack his strong point with assurance and confidence will shake him, if you get away with it a few times. It makes him aware of your strength of purpose and will to win, and keeps tremendous mental pressure on him that is worth much to you in a long match. It takes courage and determination on your part to attack his strength, but if you do it of your own volition you are prepared for his reply, and you can tune your own game accordingly.

Finally, in sizing up your opponent, be prepared for the deliberate "goat-getter," the man who sets out consciously to irritate you and destroy your concentration. If you are prepared for him you have the battle half won before it starts. The goat-getter is usually a fresh gent who starts out by telling you, or hinting to you on the way to the court, how easily he will win. He is then apt to stall around and generally foul up the court so that it's almost impossible to set a tempo to the match and hold it. He isn't really trying to set a tempo to the pace of the play, which is what I have advised you to do; he is merely attempting to upset you by his disregard of ordinary tennis court manners. The greatest weapon against the goat-getter is to ignore his verbal or physical "needling" completely. Go your own way, pay no attention to his remarks, play if anything a shade more slowly than he does, and give no show of irritation even if you are burning up inside.

But do not go out onto the court looking for trouble. Most players are good sportsmen, and their occasional lapses from courtesy are due to thoughtlessness or carelessness, and are not intentional. You can always delude yourself into believing you are being cheated or needled, if you start looking for trouble. If you do, you can completely destroy your own concentration, even though the fancied offense that bothered may not really have been present at all. Close calls can always give rise to differences of opinion, but just call them as you see them, without prejudice or favor. Call them as impersonally in your own match as you would if you were a linesman in a match between strangers. Only on the shot on which you are really uncertain should you give the benefit of the doubt to your opponent. If you are fair and impartial yourself and believe your opponent to be the same, you are playing the game. You may both make mistakes at times, but they will be honest mistakes and they should be forgotten, with no hard feelings, by the next point. Thinking about past points you have lost, whether because of bad decisions or unlucky breaks, only costs you present points as well, because your mind is not on your job.

GENERAL TACTICS AND STRATEGY

The first-class court general and tactician is the man who not only knows all the technical answers but is also trying to exploit the psychological element to the detriment of his opponent. Such a man is always consciously aware of the logical reply to the shot his opponent plays, and also which sequence of shots of his own will pay off most frequently. He knows that he must wait out all spin shots until they have crossed the top of the bound. A slice or chop (or even, to a lesser degree, a heavily topped drive) carries all the "devil" with which it has been hit through the air, right on through its bounce to the top of the bound. Until that point, it is almost certain to twist off the racket face and slide away as an error unless your return stroke is perfectly timed. However, at the top of the bound the spin dies, and as the ball falls it can be hit as easily and surely as if it were the bounce off a flat shot. If you do try to take a spin shot before it reaches the top of the bound, hit it flat and firmly to kill the effect of the spin. Do not chop a chop.

Here are some axioms on the best ways of handling your returns of various strokes:

1. The answer to a chop is a drive.
2. The answer to a drive may be either a drive or chop—a drive for attack, and a chop for defense.
3. The answer to a smash is usually a lob, occasionally a drive or a chop.
4. The answer to a volley is usually a drive, occasionally a lob.
5. The answer to speed is backspin.
6. The answer to backspin is the flat drive.

There are certain mechanical combinations of shots that are sound tactically, provided you do not become so wedded to them that you play them stubbornly every time, with no variations:

1. Three drives in a row to the same corner, and then a sharp, slow cross-court to the other side.
2. Four drives from alternate corner to corner, and then the cross-court drop shot.
3. Alternate corner to corner until you decide your opponent is set in the rhythm, and then the slow, straight short shot back to the same side of court as your last shot.

4. First a drop shot, then a lob deep to the opposite side of the court.

5. First a drive, then a chop, then a drive, then a chop, and so forth, with continually varying depth until an error is forced.

These are only a few samples of the sorts of patterns an acute court strategist knows; he's always ready to try out new and unexpected things also. He watches his opponent make his shot, so he can be prepared to handle whatever spin may be hit at him. Watching where an opponent's racket head meets the ball will always give you the tip-off on the direction in which the ball will bounce. If the ball is hit *above the waist,* it will bounce in the same direction as the racket head was traveling when it hit and followed through on the ball. On the other hand, if an opponent hits the ball *below the waist,* the ball will bounce in the *opposite* direction from that in which the racket head travels on the follow-through.

You should never hit any shot in match play without a definite intention behind it. If you drive, think of driving and of no other type of stroke. Even more important, on that shot think with decision where you will hit the ball, and why. Every shot should be hit to a definite place, in a definite way, for a definite purpose, and not just hit back over the net for no particular reason except to get it into your opponent's court. Make up your mind before you hit the ball that you are going to do one of three things:

1. Attack with this stroke, going out for an aggressive shot, or

2. Maneuver your opponent and open his court by playing a medium-pace shot, with a safe margin of error, to the widest reach away from his position, or

3. Defend with this stroke, if you sense you are in difficulty, by playing a slow, floating drive or a well-spun slice, to change the tempo and give you time to recover.

Obviously, there are shots other than the ones cited above that you will sometimes use in these situations, but the point is that you must recognize that you are either going to attack, maneuver, or defend and play your shot accordingly without vacillating.

Whichever of these three choices you decide upon, keep in mind the follow-up shot you will use if your opponent returns the ball. Are you going in to the net to win, or will you stay back and work on your opponent's position further before hitting out for the point? Where will his logical return come, and to what position should you move to be ready to meet it? And when it does come, what type of shot will your next one be?

Unless he is trying for an outright winner, a good player always hits his shot with his next shot in mind, and a really fine court general is usually planning two strokes in advance of the one he is then hitting. . . . There are several types of baseline rallies that, unless deliberately broken up by one player or the other, will follow an almost invariable pattern. The most general type is the cross-court exchange to deep court. The one seen most often is the backhand-to-backhand variety. The forehand-to-forehand variety seldom continues for more than three exchanges. To break up either type of cross-court exchange, there are two excellent shots. One is the faster straight shot, paralleling the sideline, into the deep corner. The other is a slow and very sharply angled cross-court shot, which is still in pattern with the exchange, but has very different depth and pace, and possibly has different spin as well.

Another rhythmic pattern you often see is one player hitting cross-court every time, and the other hitting straight returns. This makes both men run back and forth across the back court almost equal distances. To break this up, the man who has been hitting cross-court can insert a slow, high slice down the center, or straight. The man who has been hitting straight can break up the pattern by hitting a slow, sharply angled drive cross-court. Either of these methods changes the rhythms of the point and is very likely to force an error from the other man. Obviously, one way to break up any back-court exchange is for either player suddenly to go in to net. However, if the baseline exchanges are carrying good depth, it is a dangerous experiment and usually results in the advancing player being passed, or forced into error, while trying to get up far enough to reach a volley position. It is better to break up the rhythm of these back-court rallies by a change of pace, spin, depth, and direction from the baseline, than it is to risk an ill-considered and improperly prepared advance to the net.

One certain tactical stratagem is to decide what feature of your opponent's game you will attempt to exploit, and then hop on it at the beginning and never leave it until you are convinced it will not break. It may be his weakness or his strength, but whichever you elect, stay with it until you can see how the picture is working out. If you're winning with it, keep going the same way as long as the general tide of play is going in your favor. Only when you're convinced that the method you have selected isn't going to win for you should you change to something else, but be sure to do so then. Otherwise, stay with your plan of campaign the whole way. On individual points you often will be forced to change plans, and you must always use enough variety to keep your opponent guessing, but maintain one definite point upon which to center the pressure you are trying to apply, and do not wander from it. I often see players who seem just to be hitting a tennis ball with no very definite plan behind their play. For a while they hit to their opponent's forehand and then, for no reason, shift to his backhand. Or they stroll in toward net when they've made no proper preparation for an advance. If, behind these changes in play, there were real thought and reason for the shift, I would agree completely with the strategy, but when it's done without purpose it's sheer whim, and not strategy. It's valueless in that case. Consistent pressure centered on one point, disguised by enough variation to keep your purpose hidden, will produce the best results.

The margin of difference between a champion and a good tournament player is very small. Many times there is no difference in stroke equipment. I know many players with the finest technical games who have never made much of a mark in the tennis world. What is the dividing line between the champion and the merely good player? It lies in that intangible quality which makes the champion produce his best under pressure, and the other man his worst. I believe that the champion will miss just about as many shots as the second-class man, but he will miss them at different times. The champion seldom misses a shot he should make at a critical moment. His serve never fails under pressure, whereas the second-class player, good as he is, misses in the pinch when playing the champion, and that's when it counts the most. It takes years of match play to school a player to make, and not err, when the match hangs on the result of a shot. He must be so completely master of himself and his game that he remains calm and confident, no matter how crucial the situation. I have always felt that Rudyard Kipling summed up the qualities of the champion as well as it can be done, in his lines from "If":

> If you can force your heart and nerve and sinew
> To serve your turn long after they are gone,
> And so hold on when there is nothing in you
> Except the will which says to them, "Hold on" . . .

Oh, yes! Those lines indeed describe a champion!

FOOTWORK AND THE PRESERVATION OF RHYTHM AND BALANCE

by Suzanne Lenglen

By footwork I do not mean just running about, but the use of the feet.

Your feet are the pivot from which the work is done. You must be easy upon them. Do not allow them to hold the ground flatly, for then movement in any direction will not be instant, and a fraction of time will be lost which cannot be made up.

It starts from the beginning, which is the receipt of service. Be upon your toes, ready to take off in response to the message from your brain.

Not a bad plan in order that this may become natural, and not be forced, is to walk about on your toes when you are dressing in the morning and to go up and down stairs on your toes. Even those who are, by ill luck, flat-footed can in this manner strengthen the arch of the instep.

If you do not start the rally on your toes, you will be apt to be digging your heels into the ground when you run. This jars and throws you out of your stride.

Note carefully whether you are able to move with more ease one way or the other. If that is found to be the case, take every chance of thrusting to the slower side, never dodge it.

Practice moving backward with your face to the net, keeping the weight of the body forward.

When you move sideways remember that it is done by a push or fling of the leg on the side to which you are going, but that the impulse is taken from the foot on the other side.

Never run too fast. Run with short steps or sort of jumps. I cannot emphasize enough the fact that the singles court is not so big as it appears. From the center to the sides it is but 13½ feet, not quite two and a half times your height, between three and four strides. To the net from the baseline it is 39 feet, about ten strides. And so on; you can work out every distance.

Over-running is a thing to which you must pay great heed. Nothing is more calculated to throw you out of your balance and to disturb the preservation of your rhythm.

The secret of rhythm is the joint working of the eye, the brain, and the body, and this is contained in self-control.

Do not permit yourself to be flustered or to become acutely conscious of your stroke production, or to be dreadfully aware of your racket.

Lawn tennis players are constantly catching things like crabs because they allow one portion of their stroke production to get through to their minds above the rest. It immediately exceeds, and balance is gone.

Beware lest the exercise you are giving your right arm should lend it greater weight than the left.

Go through at home, with the racket in the left hand, the movements which you do with the right. At first you will be awkward, but in a very short time you will be able to carry them out. The evening-up of both sides of the body will improve your balance. People are not by nature right-handed or left-handed only. Children are rather prone, I believe, to use the left hand before they are taught that they must use the right.

Correct the tendency you will have to begin all your forward movements by a pressure of your stronger leg. Discover as soon as you can which is the weaker and strengthen it by use.

The arm which does not hold the racket does not for that reason wave idly like a tassel, nor hang rigid like a rod. It has a compensating influence, keeping the racket arm by counter-balance from overdoing the job. It is nearly always held up, across, or at angles to the body, with the elbow bent. If it is not, there is something wrong with your rhythm. It is one-sided. It is ragged. To the spectator you have an awkward appearance. To yourself you have a sense of half-measures.

Never allow any stroke to have a jerk in it. Whenever there is a jerk, there is a jolt to some nerves, as, in another way, when you run or after a jump land on your heels instead of on your toes. A series of such jerks and jolts will tell upon you in a long match and you will tire before you should.

Be careful that the body leans forward, riding upon the hips but deriving its impulse from the feet, upon which you should be able to sway, as from a root or socket.

Practice that sway so that you may be able to throw your whole weight into the blow you give the ball. That blow starts, as I have said, and cannot say too often, through the feet to the center of the racket, which is equivalent to the palm of the hand. In the true understanding of this principle is the foundation of footwork, balance, and rhythm—and good lawn tennis.

THE WOMAN'S GAME

by Molla Bjurstedt Mallory

"Take the net as soon as you can—and don't let her pass you." I heard this instruction given to a young girl by a man ranking in the first ten. The girl took the advice eagerly—as though it were new and unusual. A few weeks later I saw her playing; she was faithfully following the principle in so far as reaching the net was concerned but she was being passed at will. Her opponent, who had not nearly as much tennis ability, was winning rather easily.

The admonition to play the volley game is perfectly sound; the style is most effective—if you can play it.

I have never known a girl or a woman who could play a net game in singles through three hard sets—who could reach the net, volley consistently, and keep the pace. And yet I do not know how many thousands are trying to progress in this style of game under the impression that first-class tennis is not to be achieved without imitating Mr. Maurice McLoughlin. Mr. McLoughlin, at his best, is a marvelous player; he can do things which an ordinary human is foolish to attempt. And he must be in the most splendid physical and mental condition to play his own peculiar game. No other man has ever yet been able to put over a railroad serve, follow up to the net, and play the ball almost continuously in the air; it demands more energy and endurance than even the trained man possesses. Mr. Johnston, the present champion, and Mr. Williams, the 1914 champion, have flashes of the McLoughlin game, but they find hard driving more economical of effort and just as effective in point getting.

If the men in the first flight cannot play the hard serving, smashing game, how foolish it is for the average girl to experiment with it!

No woman has the strength, the reach, or the quickness of the skillful tennis man, and to play consistently at the net requires the ultimate in strength, reach, and quickness. It is silly to take the net and be passed by the first return, but only extraordinary speed and reach will avoid being passed, while just as uncommon spryness is needed to go back to the baseline for the lobs. I have never had much difficulty in passing an inveterate volleyer or in forcing her back by hard drives, and while she is exhausting herself, I am consuming comparatively little energy.

The best volleyer that I have ever seen among women is Mrs. George W. Wightman (Miss Hazel Hotchkiss). She is deadly at the net; she is the best partner to be found among all the women for mixed doubles because there she can show her volley skill; but she cannot often keep up the pace of her game through three sets of singles. I have played against her many times and she always leads me until the effort of her game begins to wear her down. I am considerably stronger than most women but I could not play the man's game.

I think it best for a woman to realize that she is a woman and to adopt a style of tennis play which will call for all the generalship and strength which she can claim—but not for more.

Any girl will find her best tennis by concentrating on the drives rather than on the service, and by making use of the volley only when circumstances promise an ace.

Accuracy and speed from the baseline make up the game of tennis for women. It is not a spectacular style, but it wins. I do not for a moment advocate pat ball and I do not consider it enough merely to make a return. I have nothing of gentleness in my own game, but I do not attempt the impossible—and I hold the net game for women approaches the impossible.

The baseline game is almost universal abroad, although English women volley much more than is generally supposed. The average of play abroad, taking the whole tournament season, is somewhat higher than in the United States. I think this is because the women in England, Germany, and France give vastly more attention to their form in driving. American women waste so much time in a vain attempt to learn to volley that they neglect the foundation of their game.

I have yet to know a first-class volleyer among women who has consistently won from a hard-hitting baseline player. Mrs. Bundy (Miss May Sutton) is a hard and accurate driver; it was her driving that brought her the English championship, although she plays extremely well overhead when such play is needed. She drove so well that some of the English women thought they could break up her game if only they could dislodge her from the command of the drive. In the championship singles of 1905 Mrs. Larcombe (then Miss E. W. Thomson) planned to win from Miss Sutton with a volley game. She lured Miss Sutton to the net by a short drop drive and then lobbed the return high to the baseline; this gave her the chance to reach the net, where she caught Miss Sutton's return of the lob with a sharp cross-court volley for the ace. Miss Thomson won five out of the first seven games by these tactics, but she ran herself off her feet in the winning; she became feebler and feebler, while Miss Sutton was as fresh and strong as at the beginning. Having worn herself out, Miss Thomson lost all control and Miss Sutton ran out that set and then took the second set and the match without the least trouble. Possibly Miss Thomson might have won had she been able to keep up her starting pace—but she went the way of all women volleyers. I am fairly certain that, someday, a girl will burst out with the ability to play the fast game through the course of two tournament sets; that girl will be, beyond question, a champion. But there is no sight of her as yet. Closely pressing the desire to play the net game is the yearning after a service which will always score aces.

Many girls have the notion that tennis is a one-stroke game. They act as though the game started and stopped with the delivery of a non-returnable service ball. Of course a non-returnable service would be a distinctly worthwhile acquisition for any player, man or woman; the super-girl of whom I have just spoken might attain such a service and score aces as she pleased, but I have yet to meet the unreturnable service.

The service is merely the stroke which puts the ball into play; it may be made with more speed and precision than the subsequent strokes of the game, because it is executed at leisure, but it is not the game itself, and undue attention to the service will not only exhaust a player but it is also apt to result in a slacking of the play after service.

Rather than work for a non-returnable service, one had better cultivate an accurate service of fair speed that does not require too much strength. Save your strength for the drives, because no matter how hard you may serve, a first-class player will nearly always find a way to return; the service aces are not numerous enough to warrant the effort in trying for them, while the attempt to score on the service may easily gain as many double faults as aces.

The ranking women players are not the players with the swiftest services. I have never been able to develop more than fair speed and accuracy on the service; Mrs. Bundy has almost as bad a service as I have; Mrs. Wightman has little speed but excellent placement.

A few girls try to learn the fast twisting services which some male players use—the reverse twist for instance—but when they do develop that service, they seldom have another stroke at command, and they will beat themselves if you give them half a chance; if they serve a very fast first ball, they will either have a slow and easily killed second ball or they will put over the second ball at the pace of the first and therefore make frequent double faults. Bothering with the complex services is not worthwhile; the effort of the delivery is too exhausting.

The point which I wish to make is this: a woman has physical limitations—she is not so strong or so enduring as a man and she must acknowledge these limitations when playing tennis. She can play a certain sort of game very well indeed while another sort of game is quite beyond her. By mixing the two extremes she will have a game which is neither one thing nor the other, but by developing along the right lines she will attain a technique that makes for good tennis. The woman's game emphasizes hard drives and accuracy and minimizes the plays, such as the volley and the twisting services, which make huge drafts on energy.

I believe in accuracy and speed. Both are the results of style. Therefore a player needs style. Style represents that method of executing a stroke which has been found to produce results with the least possible exertion. With proper form the hard drive does not represent mere brute strength but perfect timing and the concentration of the weight of the body on the ball. Without this coordination one may hit at the ball very hard indeed without making a really fast drive. Every person will not find the same style comfortable, but it is very rare that a grotesque style gives results. Some players win in spite of their style, but it will usually be found that these players have picked up faults in the beginning which they have not been able to overcome and therefore their ultimate playing style is only the result of a bad start.

When you have gross faults of style it is well to try out thoroughly with a good professional or a skilled player. If, after exhaustive experiment, you find that better style does not improve your game, then you may let well enough alone. But only one player in every thousand will do well to stay with a fundamentally bad style. It is far better to begin tennis all over again and spend two or three years in thoroughly reforming your bad habits.

Some few elements must be common to every style which is worthy of the name; without these elements the style is so bad that persistency is foolish. Among these elements are the (1) foot work and its close associate (2) body momentum and (3) the swing and the follow through. Unless the feet are well managed, a player will not reach the ball in proper position for the stroke, and, if she is not in proper position, she will not add weight to the swing of the racket; even the strongest arm will not put the pace on a ball that is given, almost without effort, by a slight concentration of the force of the body at exactly the right moment. I am not enough of a scientist to know why following through helps speed and control so much—because it starts after the ball has left the racket. I am told that the follow-through is valuable because it forces one to start the stroke well before the impact with the ball and thus insures a firm, even, forceful swing. Certainly speed and control are not possible without taking the stroke through at least half a circle. Everyone knows how a golf ball pops off from a shakily swung club; a tennis ball acts in precisely the same way if the racket be rudely poked at it. The full, true stroke is essential.

Although it may not be given to everyone to play first-class tennis and many will not have ambitions in that direction, yet more fun is to be had from the game by playing well rather than poorly. And any girl, without a serious physical defect, may learn to play a passable game of tennis.

Tennis seldom comes naturally; one may have the strength, the speed, and the eye by nature, but form is a question of hard, painstaking work. The best players practice tirelessly—they are playing every day through the open season and often play indoors a good part of the winter. They do not expect to play half a dozen times a year and also play well. I take a professional every little while to help me out on some part of the game where I feel especially weak.

I know splendid players who apparently have not a single natural aptitude toward the game, but by intelligent practice they have learned the game best suited to them—and they play it. Mrs. Barger-Wallach is not strong, but she has acquired a tennis game far above average. Mr. Johnston is very slightly built.

Tennis does not need brute strength as much as coordination. Coordination is a matter of training; tennis resolves itself into form and training. If one has strength and speed in addition to form and coordination, so much the better for the eventual game, but it is a mistake to imagine that only the natural athlete can profitably take up tennis.

There is no tennis age; the limit is mental. I have partnered with the Crown Prince of Sweden against the King and my sister. Of the two men the King is the better player. In Germany the Countess of Schulenberg enters the tournaments at scratch; her daughter, in the twenties, has a handicap. I know a dozen women over fifty who will give anyone a stiff game; and I also know girls of fifteen and sixteen who are masters of every stroke. I should hardly advise the very young girls or the women past fifty to enter the first-class tournaments, because the nervous strain of playing through is considerable; but tournament play engages only a small number of players and is not to be considered the end of tennis. The real object of tennis—the object of any sport—is to gain health and have a good time.

I think any girl or woman will be helped by playing tennis.

Strength, quickness, grace, agility, and general good health are the rewards.

It is a mistake to imagine that a woman should have only gentle, lazy exercise. A normal woman needs an outdoor sport which will stir her blood and her brain.

Droning through a set of motions is a mere waste of time.

Tennis has every element of the perfect exercise for women. There is no bodily contact and hence no danger of injury, but there is the strongest kind of competition. The fighting spirit is developed, and I think a girl ought to have as much pluck and fighting spirit as a man. It helps in everything to be able to clench the teeth and say, "I'm going to win."

And then tennis keeps the player in the open air amid the most healthful surroundings; you have to move quickly, your hand and your foot must obey your mind and you are forced to forget poses and all that unnatural sort of thing. A girl is the better for knowing she is alive.

Tennis is not too violent. A weak woman may adapt her game to the limits of her physique; she will play a gentle game until more strength permits her to play harder and faster. I have played twelve hard sets in a single afternoon and then danced all the evening without finding myself harmed. Of course this would be too much for an unseasoned player—but then an unseasoned player could not keep on her feet so long.

Tennis is not for the girl who wants a milk-white face covered with paint and powder; if that is the ideal of feminine beauty, tennis and every other outdoor game must be avoided. But I think a coat of tan and a freckle or two are normal. I have no patience with the languishing made-up beauty; she is not much more human than a dressmaker's dummy.

Play tennis if you wish a lithe, slim figure, a clear, healthy complexion, and a coordinated body and brain.

The points in the woman's game are

1. Accuracy in placement.

2. The development of the driving baseline game as opposed to the net game.

3. The accuracy and not the speed of the service.

4. The conservation of energy.

5. The grounding of the knowledge that a stroke is not well played unless the ball goes to the intended spot.

6. As much speed as is consistent with accuracy.

WINNING DOUBLES

by George Lott

Willie Keeler, one of baseball's immortals, was once asked the secret of his fabulous hitting. Shifting a large cud of tobacco from right to left, little Willie maintained: "I hit 'em where they ain't." His grammar may have left something to be desired but his theory was perfect. It applies not only to baseball but to tennis. Almost every move, stroke, and thought should stem from Willie's thesis. There are other similarities between baseball and tennis—the throw in baseball, which is similar to the serve, and the team-work in baseball, which must be also carried on by a successful doubles team. Individual skills must be blended. Just as the shortstop and second baseman coordinate on the double play, so must the doubles team work together.

When I was active in the game, one of the questions I was asked most often was how I won so many doubles titles. My standard reply was that I had good partners. In those days I was trying to appear modest, but now that I have had plenty of time to reflect, I am certain that truer words never were spoken. A doubles team is as good as its weakest link. When selecting a partner, assuming that you pick one of equal ability, choose one with whom you get along well and whom you like personally. I always felt that one of the main reasons that the team of Allison and Van Ryn was so great was their deep personal friendship.

If you are a student of human nature, you can be helpful to your partner's morale by applying your knowledge. Some players should be kidded, other need a pat on the back, and still others need to be prodded. There are some whom you know are trying their best, and to them you offer nothing but encouragement. I used to kid John Hennessey occasionally by telling him, after he blew a point, that for an Irishman he wasn't so hot. This usually brought forth an immediate winner, along with a look that needed no words. When Johnny Doeg and I were in a tough match, I usually mentioned somewhere along the line that I would like to see a display of the "famous Doeg heart." More than likely a few service aces would follow. If Les Stoefen was in a wild streak, I would casually mention that a couple of good-looking girls in the third row were giving us the eye. This would bring him to strict attention to the matter at hand, and before I knew it we had won the match and were sitting in the third row, investigating the situation. Van Ryn needed to be patted on the back, which was easy since he always played well.

If there is something you can say to help your partner, say it. Never argue with him; don't even have a heated discussion. If things are not going well, make suggestions but don't put them in the form of an order. Complete harmony is essential.

The serving team always has the advantage, and it does not require a mathematical genius to figure out that if your side always wins service, the worst you can do is end up in a dead-heat. And so it behooves us to find ways and means of not only holding this advantage but of increasing it: there is nothing more disconcerting to a doubles team than to lose their opponents' serves easily, then struggle hard to hold their own.

I will assume that we all know the necessity for putting the first ball into play and will proceed from there. The opponents' weaknesses and strengths should be studied. This information should be utilized to full advantage. A case in point is the series of close matches Doeg and I had with Bill Tilden and Frank Hunter; one of the decisive factors was whether or not I could hold my serve. Winning Doeg's delivery was fairly easy because he could do it on power alone. My serve depended more on placement, with a modicum but not an overwhelming amount of power.

The Tilden and Hunter returns of serve presented several problems. Hunter possessed one of the best forehands in the world and he crowded the service court so much that it was difficult to expose his fairly weak backhand. At first I attempted to serve from the normal position with an American twist to his backhand down the center service line (Hunter played the right court). This was not successful because Frank was a genius at running around this type of delivery, and his low, dipping forehand was extremely difficult to handle. Next I tried serving from a wider position to get a wide slice to his forehand, but this forced Doeg to cover the down-the-line possibility and left me to cover the center as well as the right alley. I would find myself looking up at Tilden on my volleys, and this was not only unsightly but unprofitable.

Finally I found by trial and error that the most advantageous position to serve to Hunter was from as close to the center service line as I could possibly get. From this position I alternated a fast slice to his forehand sideline with a semi-fast flat serve straight down the center. If he crowded the center, up came the slice; if he gave ground toward his forehand, down the center went the ball to his backhand. This semi-fast flat serve reached his point of contact a fraction of a second sooner than a high kicking twist, and so it prevented him from running around the ball to get his murderous forehand drive on it. The solution we found did not always work, but it was more successful than anything else we had attempted. With a receiver of this type, it is absolutely necessary to get the first ball in.

Serving to Tilden was not exactly child's play either. If we served to his backhand, it was usually Katy-bar-the-door, so accurate with it was he. Our solution was to serve the first ball to his forehand, hoping to volley the return deep to his backhand corner, thus opening up the court, making his return a difficult one, or anticipating a lob by pretending to close in at net.

These sorts of tactics must be varied to be effective. At certain scores, such as 30–0, 40–0 or 40–15, another approach should be used. The pace or the theme must be varied. Occasionally the server may even stay back just for the surprise, although I must admit that a wide-awake team would eat up this sort of move. Sometimes the server can try hitting to the opponent's strength, for even the strong and alert are caught napping at times. These ventures provide change of pace and tempo, and they prevent the opponents from getting into a groove.

Return of Service. Here is where the battle rages. There are few players who have been able to win points from the receiving end on power alone. In the main, it is thrust and parry, with the object being to create an opening for the kill. Therefore one tries to make the server hit up on the return, drive the opponents away from the net, or force an error. Since the server has the advantage of putting the ball in play, the forcing of an error is the most difficult as it must depend upon power or a very deep lob.

One year at the National Doubles, I saw the use of the lob on return of serve break up two of the best overheads in the world at that time. The Kinsey brothers, Howard and Bob, left Gerald Patterson and Pat O'Hara-Wood of Australia with a pair of very stiff necks at the conclusion. But the Californians were magnificent lobbers, sending the ball always to within a foot or two of the baseline, retrieving the smashes and lobbing again with perfect depth. Before the match, the consensus was that the lobbing Kinseys would be murdered. 'Tweren't so. If any player actually does lob within a foot of the baseline on service return, he will win a lot of doubles matches if he has the rest of the game to go with it. Not all of us are given that knack; neither do most of us have the ability to knock the cover off the ball on the return. The first was an attribute of the Kinseys and the second a talent of Bill Johnston, Vines and Budge.

My preference on return of serve was for variety—bullets, lobs, change of pace and deception. I believe *power* should be tempered to fit one's control, the *lob* should be used for surprise, and the *soft shot* or dink should be deceptively mixed in; this combination offers the receiving team the best chance of winning service breaks. The vast majority of doubles matches are won from the net, and this assortment of shots is best utilized to obtain the doubles position for the kill. A fine doubles player will produce these three strokes with the same motion, just as a baseball pitcher throws a fast ball, curve, or change of pace with the same action. If he telegraphs the pitch, he gets an early chance at the showers. So will the tennis player if he Western Unions his returns. If the receiver lacks deception, his partner, who is standing at net in a poaching position, is apt to be turned down for life insurance—if he lives long enough to apply for it.

Teamwork comes with experience and with a knowledge of each other's movements and reactions. The most notable examples of what almost seemed like intuition were from Allison–Van Ryn and, in later years, Mulloy-Talbert. Signals were used when an attempted poach was about to be tried. I believe that hand signals are risky, although they do work. I preferred to tell my partner what I was going to do, and we had an agreement as to what we should do if we were overheard. Sometimes it is possible to speak softly but with clarity in the hopes that one will be overheard. The two teams mentioned above were so familiar with each other's reactions that they knew instantaneously what their partner would be doing. New teams should have long talks together and should go over every situation that might possibly arise.

There is an old and untrue adage that partners should play parallel to each other. The sooner this is forgotten, the better. The proper court position is the one that will enable you and your partner to hit down on the ball or which will force your opponents to hit up. There are many times, of course, particularly when your team is receiving, when you will be in trouble because of position. The best parry is to return the ball softly to the opponents' feet in order to get back into even balance. The lob-volley can also be evoked under these circumstances. If you find yourself in an utterly hopeless position, the best thing to do is to run toward the ball to cut down the angle—unless you are nervous about getting hit. It is surprising how often you can rescue a point with these tactics.

SUMMARY

1. Hold service
2. Use the best available means to get to net
3. Force your opponents to hit up
4. Do not become stereotyped
5. Encourage your partner
6. Make all the easy shots; the difficult ones will take care of themselves
7. Your plan should be to force errors or to "hit 'em where they ain't."

THE CONTINENTAL GRIP

by Fred Perry

Throughout my long tennis career I traveled around the world five times and played successfully in many countries. From time to time, my game was described as unconventional, unorthodox and one scribe even likened it to ping-pong. Perhaps this was because I once held the world's championship in that particular sport. At any rate, it is true that some of the shots I used were similar to my table tennis strokes.

It was said that no other tennis player could make the same kind of forehand; that if my wrist were not as strong as the proverbial ox, I could never have produced the shot at all. I do not see how this statement can be entirely correct when many of the players in Europe—the Continent in particular—use the same grip. You have only to go to the European capitals to see this for yourself. It is a fact that the grip I used, the Continental grip, is the best for low-bounding balls and anyone who has played on the slow rubble courts of the Continent knows the ball does not bounce very high.

With this grip, the racket is held the same as an ax, that is with the "V" formed between the thumb and first finger which rests along the first bevel of the handle when the racket is at right angles to the floor. By holding the racket in this manner, the wrist is in front of the racket which aids in making a powerful return on wide balls. If the Eastern grip is used, the wrist is behind the racket so that the power imparted to the ball is a pushing rather than a pulling force. If this were the best way to achieve power, surely locomotive engines would be placed behind the coaches.

When playing on Continental courts, I found it much easier to hit a ball hard from a low bounce and still keep it in the court by employing the Continental grip. The Eastern grip is much better for a high-bounding ball. However, with the present trend toward fewer grass courts it would seem that the Continental grip is more useful. I always played with one grip and I didn't have to change the position of my hand or finger to make any kind of shot. With the Continental grip, I saved time, increased accuracy and could make "snap" shots in close volleys at the net more easily.

From the day I started playing, I based all my strokes on the forehand drive. It was the one shot I knew how to make and the only one on which I could rely in difficulties. If I got in trouble, I just prayed that my opponent would hit the ball to my forehand and come to the net. In that case, at least, I had a fifty-fifty chance of winning the point. Then came the task of modeling the rest of my game around this particular shot and that was no easy matter. My forehand became better and better, mainly because I used it at every available opportunity, so that the rest of my shots looked mediocre by comparison. However, I worked hard to cut down the errors in order to make the rest of my game as safe as possible, planning to leave the "fireworks" to my forehand.

In order to gain speed, I was advised to play the ball early, which means hitting it before it reaches the top of its bounce. Dick Williams was one of the first to employ the "early-ball game" and Henri Cochet, the great French star, continued that style. Cochet was one of the first to win matches by flustering his opponents and causing them to make their shots quickly. By hitting the ball on the rise as he did, he was able to make it in stride and work his way to the net without losing time in getting his feet properly positioned.

I studied his game for a long time and discovered that he made the shot with the wrist alone. The whole weight of his body moved through the ball as he hit. The momentum of his stride carried him at least two paces nearer the net in the same movement so that he was in a volleying position before his opponent realized it. In this manner, he was able to combine three movements in one. The speed of his run, together with the added momentum of his body movement, imparted a lot of pace to the ball without apparent effort. The quickness with which he flicked the ball off the court helped him considerably in disguising the direction of his shot.

In adopting this shot, I found my table tennis experience aided me and I was able to disguise the direction of my shots not only from half-court, but from the base-line as well.

Close study of my forehand drive revealed that the whole weight of my body was put into practically every shot and that I pivoted from the hips with each stroke. It was from this pivot that the pace was obtained and the wrist governed only the direction. By opening the wrist—that is, by keeping the wrist in front of the hand—the ball was directed down the backhand line; and by closing the wrist—by bringing the hand in front of it—the ball traveled to the opponent's right-hand court.

I would advise any would-be-adopters of this style to be extremely careful when they start out. It is a great strain on the wrist and time must be spent in strengthening the muscles for this purpose and naturally the only way to build up any muscle is to use it continuously. I do not see any reason why your wrist should not develop sufficiently for you to adopt the so-called Continental forehand. It will not take you any longer to learn this particular style than any other and I think it will pay in the long run.

So much then for the early-ball forehand drive. As for the running forehand used by Cochet, the ball must be taken well away from the body and it is not necessary to hit hard. Gauge your run so that you can hit the ball immediately after it has bounced, practically on the half-volley. It is necessary to start the shot before the ball bounces so that your timing will be correct. As you hit it, and it is only necessary to stroke it moderately or you are liable to lose your balance, allow your weight to go through the ball. The momentum of your run, which should be made with long strides, gives the ball a lot of speed and at the same time you are already on your way to the net.

The shot is dangerous because the margin of error is small. The least deviation in the bounce of the ball and you are sunk. You may be lucky and get it into play but the pace is gone. If you want to make this shot with any degree of accuracy, you must not be discouraged by a few errors. You must have confidence in it and make it without any thought of the consequences if you miss.

I found this shot to be the most useful in my repertoire, as it can be used to turn defense into attack at any moment. You must remember, however, that once you start out on one of these running forehands you have to go through with it, as the actual making of the shot and the gaining of the volleying position tie-in together. I found that by running close to the ground, and by that I mean running with my body bent in readiness for the stroke, I was much more sure of bringing it off without error. In this way, many movements are combined. The run is made close to the ground so that you do not have to bend down to hit the ball, and in addition, you are already on your way to the net, all in one movement.

In my travels, I was often asked what grip I thought was most useful and naturally I expressed favor for the Continental grip. I grant you that it is perhaps not the best for every shot, but I do think for volleys, backhands and forehands it is advantageous. The Eastern grip is perhaps better for service and overhead. In all my years of active tennis I never found a player whose service could equal those of the Americans. I don't know if any of the European players can learn the cannonball serve with conditions such as they are in Europe. For instance, they use a slower ball and the surface of the court further retards the ball when it bounces.

I believe that if I had adopted the Eastern grip for service I could have gained a lot of pace, but I feel sure that the adoption of such a grip would have hindered the rest of my game as I would have been afraid that I was using the new grip at the wrong time. To anyone wishing to play the game seriously, my advice would be to learn one grip, the one which comes most naturally, and stick to it no matter what anyone tells you. All the various grips and styles of making shots have their various advantages, but unless you feel comfortable and confident in the way you hold the racket, you will never reap the full reward of your efforts.

HOW IT FEELS TO BE A BEGINNER

by Sarah Palfrey

It's a rather strange yet exhilarating sensation to find yourself on a tennis court for the first time with a racket in your hand, seeing all that space around you and white lines going in different directions. For this very reason it is a good idea to begin tennis at an early age if possible. The younger you are, the less awkward you'll feel and the more you will laugh at yourself when you fall flat on your derrière while chasing a backhand or lob.

At what age should one start? Actually there can be no accurate answer to this, because so much depends on the individual. The more natural ability and enthusiasm you have, the better. Height makes a difference, too—it helps if you're not too short. Many youngsters can start comfortably at eight or nine (my brother was enjoying it at five), while others have to wait a few more years. My son Jerry, at twelve, was just beginning to get fun out of the game. He had, however, played ping-pong and other ball games before, which helped train his eye.

Equipment. The first thing you'll need to begin playing is a tennis racket.

It should be the best you can afford, and in order not to spend your money foolishly you should take along a "knowing" adult when you go shopping, or else get the advice of a good club pro. It's important to get the proper weight, balance, and handle for your age and size. All the well-known sporting goods concerns carry good frames. Some are sturdier than others and will last longer; some are whippier or livelier than others but will warp sooner. Don't forget, in choosing your racket, that you must allow ¾ of an ounce for the gut. So if you buy a racket that weighs 12½ ounces unstrung, it will be 13¼ ounces strung. The average weight racket for a girl is from 13 to 13½ ounces strung; for a boy, from 13½ to 14 ounces strung. Girls usually prefer lighter rackets with smaller handles. The main thing, however, is to select one that suits *you;* it must have a good "feel" as you swing it.

The gut in the racket, by the way, is just as important as the frame. I've seen so many beginners flourishing expensive rackets (that they have picked up at sales) strung with soft, mushy gut. No one can do justice to his game with a badly strung racket. The gut will do lots of the work for you, if you'll give it a chance. Another decision for you to make now concerning the stringing is whether to choose nylon or real gut (which is quite a bit more expensive, doesn't last as long, and frays in wet weather). Obviously if you're a beginner unless you're a millionaire, you won't think twice about choosing the nylon. But get a good grade of nylon and have it strung by a man who knows his business. If you can afford two rackets and are a good player, then you may splurge and get one of each: use the one with nylon for practice and in damp weather, and save your good one for matches and important occasions.

Keep your racket (or rackets) in a rubberized canvas case and a press whenever it's not in use, and it will give you many seasons of happy tennising. Naturally, if you outgrow your racket, you'll have to buy another, but you can always pass down your first one to a younger friend or member of the family. You may even make a trade.

Prices for rackets run anywhere from ten to thirty dollars apiece. So you see there's a wide range to choose from. A good re-stringing job costs from five to nine dollars for nylon, depending on the quality of the nylon, and may go as high as eleven dollars for high-grade or tournament gut.

Besides a racket, the other big expense is a supply of balls. Buy (or share) a can of balls as often as you can, because it's hard to control the balls when they become light and the fuzz wears off. The cost for a can of three varies from $1.80 to $2.75. Keep an eye out for store sales and remember you can buy good used balls at sanctioned tournaments.

Now you've got a racket and balls. All you need is wearing apparel, which should be comfortable and white (white is traditional and, believe it or not, will make you *feel* like a tennis player), and a good pair of flat rubber-soled sneakers.

The most important matter when you start actually playing, whether you're ten or twenty, is to find someone to show you how to hold the racket correctly. This helps you to avoid all sorts of bad habits, which are so hard to undo later.

Watch . . . and Practice. Another fine idea for a beginner is to watch the good players whenever possible, either in tournaments or practice. It's amazing how much you can learn by watching. The trick here is *not* to watch the ball after it has been hit, but to keep your eye on the player himself, watching his strokes, movements, footwork, and court positions. Notice how the good player will start moving for the next shot the second the ball leaves his racket, while the poorer player will pause a bit to see where his own shot is going, thus wasting precious "getting-back-into-position" seconds.

At the Longwood Cricket Club, our home club in Chestnut Hill, Massachusetts, my four sisters (Polly, Lee, Mianne, and Joanna), our brother John and I used to attend all the big tournaments held at the club. And they were important tournaments: the National Doubles, the Long-wood Bowl, and the Massachusetts State. There we followed our favorite heroes from court to court in awe—players like Bill Tilden, Billy Johnston, Helen Wills, Molla Mallory, and the great players who came from overseas to play in the National Doubles. From these champions we learned a tremendous amount. After watching them all afternoon, we'd rush home to the court on our farm in the country and play until darkness, trying to imitate them as best we could.

We realized how lucky we were to have a court of our own to play on from spring to fall. It was a clay court, and we had to take care of it by ourselves, doing all the watering, rolling and laying-down of the tapes. We also had the advantage of ready-made, eager opponents day in and day out, each trying to beat the other. To prove what a great boon this was, all five of us sisters had won National Junior titles by the time we were eighteen.

Polly, the oldest (who now has a daughter of her own), won the National Junior Girls' Doubles with Fanny Curtis; Lee, the second oldest (now the mother of two daughters), won the National Junior Indoor Doubles with Marjorie Morrill; Mianne, the third sister (now the mother of five), won the National Junior Doubles and the National Junior Indoor Doubles three times each with her next younger sister (me), as well as the National Women's Indoor Singles once; and the fifth sister, Joanna (she now has four children), won the National Junior Indoor Doubles with me. Our only brother, John, the youngest member of the family, won a couple of Massachusetts State Junior Doubles titles, but he was too busy with more important pursuits to give tennis his full attention. We all agree that he could have won a national title if he had seriously tried.

Most beginners aren't so fortunate and have to scurry around to find their opponents and courts. It's not terrifically difficult, but it does take time. If possible, find an opponent who is better than you, even if you have to give him or her frequent home-cooked meals or tickets to the movies. Use your ingenuity; it will be worth it. If you play against someone as bad as you are in the beginning, neither one of you will improve much, because the ball will seldom be returned.

The best method to start, if you are really a beginner, is to cajole a parent, relative, or close friend to toss the balls to you underhand. He, or she, will stand near the net on the same side as you (who will be in the middle of the court on the baseline) and throw you a few easy forehands, which you won't be made to reach for at first; then a few easy backhands, also within easy reach; then alternate shots, first forehand, next backhand, then forehand again. In this way you will get loads of shots to hit and will soon acquire a sense of timing and a feel for the ball, without worrying about footwork—yet.

Do be nice to your helper afterwards, because it's pretty boring work. If you can afford a professional, so much the better. He *has* to help you; he's being paid for it. And his help will pay off for you. . . .

Another suggestion for you right now is to do just what you're doing: read a book. This gives you time to think things over at your leisure without being rushed and confused. I shall never forget my older sister Lee's experience with Bill Tilden's book. At the age of twelve, she had borrowed it from a friend, and her nose was buried in it for days. It meant everything to her, not only for what it said, but because it had been written by Tilden, her idol. Dreading the day when she would have to return it, she began to copy it all out in longhand, painfully, slowly, word for word. Our mother and father were so amused when they discovered what was going on behind the closed bedroom door that they mentioned the story to some friends at a dinner party (Lee by this time was about a third of the way through). The friends happened to know a friend of Tilden's, and so, we later discovered, it all got back to Tilden himself. A week later, with no warning, a package arrived by mail for Lee. It was an autographed copy of The Book! It said, "To Lee Palfrey, who was kind enough to care to copy my book. Bill Tilden." Lee, of course, walked on air—and the rest of us were touched with reflected glory.

As a sequel to this story, in four years, when I was twelve, I helped Bill Tilden lose the semi-final round of the mixed doubles in a senior grass-court tournament at the Agawam Hunt Club in Rhode Island. However, we became firm friends thereafter, and he helped me with my game many times in the years that followed.

Reading in itself doesn't do much good, though, if you don't practice what you're reading about. A good idea at this stage is to find a practice wall or backboard against which you can practice hitting balls to yourself. Many clubs have these. (They should, even if they don't.) If you don't belong to a club, there are other substitutes: a handball court in the park; the wall of a school gym when not in use; even a garage door. All that is needed are a flat surface and a backstop. . . .

Althea Gibson started her brilliant tennis career by playing paddle tennis on a Police Athletic League play street in Harlem. She was the champion of the block. This led to learning regular tennis on a handball court with two second-hand rackets given to her by a friend, bandleader Buddy Walker, who thought she showed unusual ability. This, in turn, led to her playing on a real court.

I used to practice against a twelve-foot space of brick wall in back of our house in Brookline. The ground was too uneven for the ball to bounce, so I had to hit all shots on the fly. This must have helped me to become a good volleyer and doubles player, since volleying became the best part of my game. After paying for too many broken windows, my parents decided it would be less expensive to have a wooden wall nailed to the inside of the far end of our garage. My sisters and I painted a white line the height of a tennis net and practiced happily, even in wintertime. Why our neighbors didn't complain about the noise I'll never understand.

One advantage in practicing by yourself is that you escape the embarrassment of looking foolish in front of others when you try frantically to make contact with the ball. For some of you, though, who may have slow reflexes, a practice board is too fast and is definitely not for you. The ball comes off the wall much too quickly and won't give you enough time to get set. You can graduate to it later on. . . .

Types of Courts. As you probably know, there are different types of courts throughout the country. In the East one is apt to find grass, clay, composition, and wood courts (in indoor armories). Grass courts favor the aggressive player, because the ball bounces fast and low, making it easy for a good server and volleyer to put the shot away. Clay courts on the other hand favor the speedy retriever, because the ball bounces slower and higher, giving him more time to get to the ball. The slower the clay court, the more difficult it is to put a volley away.

Composition courts are somewhere in between grass and clay: the ball bounces higher than on grass and faster than on clay. It's a very good surface that is growing in popularity and requires little upkeep. Wood courts, more than any other surface, really favor the "big" serve and volley. The ball shoots and skids by so fast that a player needs very quick reflexes, hardly any backswing and 20–20 vision.

In the Far West you find hardly any courts that are not cement or asphalt (like Grasstex). These courts favor the aggressive player, since the ball bounces fast and high. (You'd better get a good pair of tennis shoes: these courts can be rough on the feet.) . . .

No matter how you start, the main thing is not to get discouraged when you don't improve as fast as you think you should or when you fan ten shots in a row. You will find that the few good shots you make as time goes on will more than compensate for the many bad ones. The only times you should feel discouraged are when you give up too easily or when you're too lazy to try. If this happens, you should sit down and have a fight-talk with yourself—not about tennis but about *you.*

THE VOLLEY

by Sarah Palfrey

Volleying, to me, is really the most exciting part of tennis. When you try it, you'll see why. Besides the fun of the shot itself, sudden and dramatic, the whole situation is exhilarating: you are at the net; you've made a forcing shot, your opponent is on the run—and you are ready for the kill! I don't believe you'll ever get over feeling proud of yourself when you finish off a point this way.

Of course, things don't always work out right. You may run into trouble; perhaps your forcing shot turns out to be "not forcing" and the tables are turned. Suddenly you are the one on the run and the best you can manage is a desperation return. But it's easy to forget the failures, the times you've been passed. For a good volleyer there's always another chance, another point that needs to be ended with finality. For the volley is the finishing shot par excellence, whether it turns out to be an immediate winner or so devastating to your opponent that the winner inevitably follows on the next shot. The second alternative is more usual—and you will be wise to settle for it.

Today the volley is an essential part of your tennis equipment—if you want to win. Rallies, in the best men's matches, nearly always end at the net; and this is happening more and more often in women's matches too. Volleying is now incorporated into the tempo of modern tennis. It would be hard to find a good player today who has the patience or sees any reason for the long, monotonous backcourt rallies which used to be so common.

Think of the famous match which took place years ago on the Riviera between Mrs. Satterthwaite and Lucy Valerio. They made tennis history, but it certainly seems like ancient history today. I can hardly believe that it ever really happened. The story goes that these two women had a rally which lasted so long that the ball went back and forth over the net well over two hundred times. Some spectators grew bored, went off to have tea, came back—and found that the same point was in progress. Two men playing a match on the next court finished their whole first set. No one knows the exact number of balls hit because no one started to count until the rally had begun to look spectacular, but unquestionably they set a world's record for the number of balls hit in one point of tournament play. How could they bear to do it?

The answer of course is that neither of them knew how to volley. Today the situation would be impossible. Any modern player would certainly take advantage, sooner or later, of a short or weak return and force matters by running in to the net.

It was Mrs. Wightman who, as Hazel Hotchkiss, in 1909 first introduced the volley into women's tennis in this country and showed what a woman could do at the net. And she has never stopped showing us. Thanks to her amazing anticipation, quick reflexes and clever placing of the balls, she was and is able to volley back the hardest balls in the most uncanny way. It was she who taught me to love volleying; I couldn't help, from the beginning, absorbing her enthusiasm, imitating her style, and trying to learn some of her tricks. We often used to volley to each other at close quarters.

If you didn't know before, you must have gathered by now that a volley is hitting a ball in the air before it bounces. The hitter is usually up at the net—that is, between the net and the service line. This is the conventional volleying position. But when I am asked where you ought to stand for volleying, my answer is that it all depends on the individual's height and reach. The nearer you are to the net the easier it is for you to hit down on the ball with severity. At the same time, however, you must be able to cover all possible lobs. So unless you are very tall and have a long reach, or happen to be playing doubles with an obliging partner who will chase your lobs for you, it's dangerous to stand too close to the net. Only trial and error will determine your own best position.

The volley is not a full stroke; it's more of a punch. For the forehand volley you can use either the service grip or the forehand grip. I use the service grip because it involves less changing for the backhand when you haven't much time. It's possible, if you get caught, to hit a backhand volley with the service grip. But you'd really be stuck if you had to hit a backhand volley with a regular forehand grip. The best backhand grip is like the drive, with the thumb up the handle: this adds power and punch to your shot. For either volley, holding the racket an inch or so farther up the shaft than usual will give you extra control.

You will find that by resting your racket in your left hand at all times between shots, and by using the fingers of your left hand to help you shift grips, you will soon be able to make the changes rapidly.

In hitting a volley, keep the racket head *above* your wrist and hit down, across and under the ball, as you do for the cut or chop. This is easy when the ball is high or medium high. But when the ball is low the shot is more difficult: you must bend your knees way down in a crouching position, so that when you hit the ball the racket head will still be above the wrist. In this way you can still cut the low balls and lift them just over the net.

You never need much backswing for a volley, and the faster the ball comes to you the less backswing and follow through are necessary. For a very fast ball, hold your wrist firm to withstand the shock of impact and almost block the ball, using your opponent's speed. For a slower ball you need more backswing because you must use your own power and give the ball a real punch.

It often happens that you haven't time to get your feet around sideways to the net. Try, in spite of your feet, to get your shoulders turned around.

One of the most important rules of volleying is to keep your eyes and feet on the alert all the time. Then you will be able to get ready in time to hit the ball in front of your body and your reflexes will automatically speed up. When people are surprised or caught napping they are rushed and become flustered.

When and how is the volley most effectively used? As you will soon find out, there is a right time and a wrong time to run in to the net, and there is a good way and a bad way to do it. This is especially true in singles, where you have no partner to share the court with you.

The best time to run in is always immediately after a forcing shot, either a ground stroke or a serve. Very few people have good serves to follow them in consistently in singles. Furthermore, it's tiring to do so. If you find that you can, more power to you! Otherwise, follow your serve in occasionally, as a surprise. The better your opponent, the better your forcing shot must be. It's a mental hazard to some people just to see an opponent running in to the net. Against such people, of course, your forcing shot doesn't have to be very good: you can bother them by running in on practically anything. Against players who have an outstanding weakness, either on the backhand or forehand side, your forcing shot needn't be remarkable, if properly directed to the weakness. But when you are up against a good player who has no outstanding weaknesses you must be wary and bide your time. Wait for the right opportunity, when your opponent is out of position or has sent you a weak or short return, to make a *good* forcing shot and follow it in. To be really good, this forcing shot needn't be hit hard, but it must be *deep* and *well placed*. If you hit it too hard, as a matter of fact, you may not give yourself time to get far enough in to the net.

The better your forcing shot is, the less difficult your volley will have to be. Don Budge's forcing shots, for instance, are so good that when he gets to the net he almost always has an easy put-away volley to make. On the other hand, players like Jean Borotra and Wilmer Allison, who used to run in on practically anything, including a prayer, had to call on all their brilliance to make phenomenal volleys, which they were fortunately able to do.

Some players prefer to use a chop as a forcing shot, because it bounces low and gives them time to get to the net. Mrs. Wightman and Bunny Ryan have used the chop very successfully, as have Johnny Doeg and Berkeley Bell. The trouble with using a chop regularly, as I have said before, is that its slow flight gives your opponent a little extra time to get set—and to pass you. Unless your chop is an awfully good one or your opponent particularly minds chops, you're wise to depend on your drive and use your chop for variety.

In doubles, when you have a partner to help you, the volley is always effective and the sooner you can get up to the net the better. Try, if possible, to follow your serve in to the net. You will discover that a not-too-hard, deep serve gives you more time to get to the net than a fast one which is not well placed. If you are receiving, try to run in behind the return of service. The more successful your return (the lower the better) the easier your next volley will be.

In doubles, try above all things to keep your volleys as low as possible, without hitting the net, so that your opponent must hit *up* to you and you can hit *down* to him. The closer to the net you are, therefore, the easier it will be for you to volley down. But watch out for the lobs!

When you get caught, as you may often be, on your way to the net, you will be forced to make a very difficult shot, the low defensive volley. Your best bet is to bend your knees, cut the ball, not too hard, and aim low to the top of the net. You will thus put your opponent in a difficult situation. . . .

Vinnie Richards and George Lott are two of the greatest volleyers I have ever seen. Vinnie can hit a volley from any height in any direction, with extraordinary consistency and pace. George relies a little more on touch and finesse; he often interrupts a fast exchange with a subtle lob-volley. He too is amazingly accurate. And both can handle any speed.

Alice Marble volleys remarkably like a boy; she is both quick and powerful. She uses considerable wrist motion and is, for this reason, more brilliant on some days than others. (A shot made with a flexible wrist calls for pretty fine timing; it's hard to be consistently accurate.) At its best, Alice's touch is wonderful.

To be a good volleyer you need an aggressive spirit and must actually love being up at the net. This spirit is present in some people and not in others. But it can be developed to a surprising degree as you gain confidence in your volleying stroke itself and as, through practice, you learn to feel comfortable at the net. Standing up there at close range understandably frightens many people at first, especially women who are playing doubles against men. Remember that it's fatal to cringe back, hoping that the ball won't come your way. Try instead to think and actually to feel, "I hope I can get a crack at this one!" Only work and more work will help to develop this attitude for you. Once you begin to learn how to volley in practice, you will stop being fearful in a match.

You will also discover that the stroke isn't half as much of a stroke as you had thought and that you have more time for everything than you had expected. Learn above all to raise your racket quickly and to meet the ball squarely in the shortest possible space of time with the least possible fuss and windup. Try to follow my instructions on all the preliminaries. *Expect every ball to come to you*—and you will learn to love volleying.

If you intend to play serious tennis you will have to volley—whether you love to or not. If, on the other hand, your ambition goes no further than to play sociable tennis, friendly doubles matches, you will still find that the fun of volleying is always worth the effort. You needn't be an expert to try, nor particularly young. King Gustav of Sweden, who is over eighty and still plays tennis, loves to volley. Naturally, he doesn't run in to the net. (Running in is the most strenuous part of volleying; once you are in, it takes less exertion to hit a volley than a ground stroke.) But he stands at the net whenever he can. Since he is very tall, he can afford to stand in close, and he puts away all sorts of shots within reach.

If you are getting on in years, or for any reason lack the physical equipment for volleying, of course play a backcourt game and enjoy as many years of tennis as possible. (I suspect that Mrs. Wightman, however, will be volleying at ninety.) But if you are young and active, I doubt you'll be able to resist the quick give-and-take of volleying in a doubles match.

THE VOLLEY

by William Talbert

Why are so many good baseliners such poor volleyers?

Lack of practice, particularly on clay courts. They get passed so often when they come to net that they stay back where they know at least they can keep the ball in play. A good player must hit 50,000 to 100,000 groundstrokes a year but only 5000 to 10,000 volleys at most. Unless he makes a conscious effort to practice his volley, it is obviously going to be weaker than his groundstrokes.

The reason it is so hard to practice volleys is that it requires another player to hit them to you at net. Most players prefer to play. The way to practice volleys, of course, is to get some player to feed 50 or 100 balls slightly away from you. This makes you alert and willing to move, while at the same time giving you the necessary practice on the stroke. While your opponent is feeding you volleys, you can give him practice, for example, on forehands down the line. Two players can help each other out this way.

What is the correct grip for the volley?

The Continental or service grip because it requires no switch of grips during a fast exchange at net. Many players use the Continental grip on low volleys or when hurried, but switch to the Eastern grip when they have time. In a fast exchange it is virtually impossible to switch grips and every good player is therefore able to hit volleys with the same grip off either side merely by using the opposite face of the racket.

Continental grip users on the volley: Larsen, Rosewall, Hopman, Gonzales, Riggs, Patty (the biggest Continental of them all and the most feared forehand volley in the game today), the youngsters Holmberg and MacKay, Gene Mako (The Cat), Frank Shields (a Western forehand and a Continental volley!), Doris Hart (whose strokes were Continental anyway), Margaret duPont and a host of others. The big Eastern style volleyers are: Budge, Schroeder, Kramer and Wilmer Allison, all of whom excelled at net play. Sammy Giammalva is one of the outstanding youngsters who will be a hard-hitting Eastern-style volleyer in the style of the above.

Where should a player stand to practice his volley?

Don't stand on top of the net! You will never learn proper volleys and, moreover, if you intend to play this way, you will be lobbed over repeatedly. In good tennis, a player is helpless in this position, the only exception being when a player anticipates where he thinks the ball will be and moves in for the kill. This happens more often in doubles than in singles because the partner can protect on the lob. On the other end of the spectrum, the poor volleyer stands a chance of getting hit or not being ready since those extra few feet are vital in allowing time to get ready.

The proper place to stand is roughly halfway between the net and the service line, although individual preference will vary within a few feet either way. Mostly, however, bigger players will prefer to stand a bit forward. If you choose to stand behind the halfway line, you must excel in the half-volley since this is the beginning of the "trap area." The basic principle is to stand as close as you can and still be able to cover your own lobs; then, if the ball comes slow or high, you can move forward for the kill.

Should you come in toward the center in singles play?

The only people (and these are very rare) who come in down the center in singles play are those who practice "Center Theory"—i.e., they hit their approach shots directly down the middle in order to give their opponents the least angle for the passing shots. The most famous exponent of this theory was the great Wilmer Allison. This was a controversial theory in the middle thirties, and the opposite point of view has prevailed in all other good players. It is definitely harder to pass the volleyer when he hits straight down the center on his approach, but his first volley must be a winner or else he is in trouble. Very few are gifted enough volleyers to utilize this technique effectively.

Today's volleyer hits for a corner on his approach shot and comes in roughly halfway between that alley line and the center. Consideration of the geometry of the court will tell you why. The opponent must either aim down the line or hit a very sharp short crosscourt, which is very difficult.

Don't ever come in on a short, sharp crosscourt, for you give your opponent a tremendous opening on the down-the-line shot. If you do get a short ball to move in behind, always hit down the line without regard to where your opponent is unless you have an obvious winner and will end the point on the one shot. The good players learn their backhand or forehand chips down the line, not to play to an opponent's weakness, but as the proper position play on all short balls. This holds true in both doubles and singles, for if the opponent reaches them, he is in command. . . .

How should the racket be held while waiting for the volley?

The racket is held in front of you, slightly to the left, and the head is pointed slightly upwards at approximately a 30° angle. The poor player should emphasize this precision in waiting for two reasons: It helps to keep him alert and it is the easiest position from which to move to either side. It also prevents him from holding his racket awkwardly, which is a detriment to the beginning of every stroke. The elbows should be in close to the body, for hard volleys are hit with that forward punch like a boxer.

Should the knees be bent?

Yes, slightly. No athlete can start well from a straight-kneed position. If the beginner is on his toes with knees slightly bent and left foot slightly forward, he will be ready to move in any direction while maintaining good balance. This advice is given to prevent the beginner from remaining flat-footed. The perpetual motion of bouncing on the toes (feet never leave the ground) makes you alert to the ball.

How big is the backswing?

The smaller the better, and always with a bent elbow. This makes for a contained volley along the lines of a boxer's punch. Schroeder was the greatest advocate of this principle, for his backswing started a foot in front of him and he could actually see the ball through the racket face. Volleys are hit in front of you or very slightly to the side. The Eastern backswing begins *in front of* the body. The Continental backswing starts in front of but to the side of the body. Naturally, this can't be true if you are reaching wide, but the principle still stands that you hit the ball as far in front of you as you can. The total volley swing need not be more than six inches or a foot. The follow-through is also very short, for you punch, then get ready for the next volley. If you take a long follow-through, you can actually be hit in close net play!

The one exception to the short backswing and follow-through is in the drive volley. This is not a basic stroke and is not recommended until you have mastered the punch volley. Don Budge and Lew Hoad are masters of this stroke, for it is a stroke. There is a backswing and a follow-through and the ball is hit flat or with a slight amount of overspin as in the drive. It is hit best on balls of shoulder height. Unfinished players should never attempt this stroke until they have mastered the shoulder-high volley. My reasoning is that every bit of volleying practice they get is necessary, and it grooves the player into punching all balls at net. You are not yet Budge or Hoad; when your volley is more than adequate, then you can experiment with drive volleys.

Should you slice volleys?

There is underspin on all volleys unless they are high kills similar to overheads, or are drive volleys. You have to have underspin to control the ball, and the underspin should be more pronounced on balls under net height. For underspin, the racket face is tilted slightly upwards and the travel of the racket head is slightly downward. Hold your racket on the forehand side with bent elbow so that arm and racket are directly in front of you for Eastern or slightly to the side for Continental. Then, with racket face turned slightly upward, move in with the body and push forward approximately one foot with the forearm. The elbow bend at the beginning is about 90°, and there is still a faint elbow bend at the finish. This is the whole volley! It is a one-foot motion of the forearm and a forward movement of the body. The backhand volley is hit with exactly the same motion—a one-foot block or punch.

Should there be any wrist movement or wrist break?

In the forehand Eastern volley, there is a definite wrist break at the start. The wrist is laid back, but is then kept firm throughout the one-foot punch with occasional variations for direction. If you want to hit crosscourt, the wrist does move forward slightly. However, avoid slapping the ball with the wrist and never allow the wrist to straighten out completely. A straight wrist on an Eastern forehand volley is an impossibility—you have no strength in your wrist at the 180° angle and no way of controlling the ball.

The Continental forehand volley emphasizes the cocked wrist rather than the laid back wrist. In other words, the racket points upward. This means that the Continental volleyer hits more to the side since the position of the wrist would be extremely awkward on all but very high volleys.

The backhand volley grip, which is the same for Continental and Eastern, has a slightly cocked wrist. Again you cannot hit it with a straight wrist since you lose all control and power.

What happens when you have to stretch wide for a volley?

The elbow has to straighten out, for you have to use your maximum reach. Otherwise the principles remain the same: the less swing, the better; the shortest block possible. The stretch volleys make pretty pictures, but you are in more control of the stroke if you are contained and hit it close in.

Where should you stand in doubles play at the net position?

The net man, whose partner is serving, should stand as far to the center as he can while still protecting his alley. He is there for a purpose, namely, to cut off as many returns of serve as possible. If he stands toward the alley, he does no one any good and he forces the server to cover more ground coming in. If the net man does not get any balls hit toward his alley during the course of a set, he is protecting it too much and he is not putting any pressure on the receiver.

The server should, if at all possible, get at least two feet inside the service line for his first volley. The good net rusher who is serving can get in as far as he wants unless the return of serve is drilled at him. Doubles is a game of chance and offense, and the receiver may sometimes take a chance on a big shot. The server must run in with his racket available for quick movement. His aim should be to hit the ball in front of him, straight down the middle if the receiver's partner is not there to cut it off.

Server and partner each take up their position in the center of their section of the court. If the ball is hit to the left alley in the opponents' territory, *both* players shift toward the left, for the extremely sharp crosscourt passing shot is a difficult and rarely tried stroke. The middle has to be covered, and this is covered by the man farthest from the alley.

If a lob is hit over one player's head and his partner elects to take the ball, this player must immediately and swiftly move to the other side of the court and then get down low enough so that his partner is free to hit the overhead wherever he chooses.

Should the receiver's partner stand up at net?

The answer has to be yes in all good doubles since the net position is the dominating one. It is difficult to break serve, and although you will get balls hit past you at net, you stand your best chance to break serve if you are there to cut off volleying mistakes by your opponents. It is not uncommon for all four players to be at net in good doubles, for the receiver will also try to come in behind his serve. In the great Davis Cup doubles match played against Australia at Forest Hills last year, the receiver's partner was always at net. One of the very few doubles matches on record in which the receiver's partner did not stand in was Schroeder-Mulloy versus Bromwich-Sedgman in the 1950 Challenge Round. Ted elected to stay back when Gardnar received.

How should the young player practice his volleys?

As said above, he should spend a number of hours each week practicing with a willing friend who will, after all, get something out of it as well. In singles practice, he should follow up every short ball even though he does not yet feel at home at the barrier. This will strengthen the depth of his approach shots and will give him the feel of the attacking game. I would also suggest that occasionally he follow his serve into net as a change of pace, and as he progresses farther in tennis, he can make more and more incursions to the barrier.

In doubles, he *must* take the net position at all times. There is no point in getting on the court with three other players if you are going to try to play singles on the doubles court. It is even more ridiculous in practice to stay back. The only exception is a 10- or 11-year old who, if not yet capable of volleying, should stay off the doubles court completely. The reason the Australian players are so good so young is because they are at home at net and start learning the volley along with their groundstrokes.

DROP SHOTS AND DROP VOLLEYS

by William Talbert

The drop shot and the drop volley are the whipped cream of a player's game. They are not basic strokes in the sense that a player cannot win without them, yet there has never been a champion who has not used them on occasion and with discretion. A few champs have developed their drop shot technique to the point where it is a major weapon in their attack, but such players are certainly the exception. Among the most accomplished in this art are Doris Hart, Ken Rosewall, John Bromwich, Bobby Riggs, Art Larsen and Jaroslav Drobny.

The drop shot is a complement to the forcing game. Hard hitters, whether they possess touch or not, develop drop shots and drop volleys to take advantage of the tremendous openings in the short court. Best examples are in the women's field where hitters such as Maureen Connolly, Beverly Baker Fleitz and Dottie Knode, masters of speed rather than spin, acquired the knack of dumping the ball just over the net for winners. Don Budge is the prime exponent of this technique in men's tennis. He has designated it "the dump shot," for he actually uses little spin and depends on softness and gravity rather than backspin to control his length.

I mentioned before that the drop shot should be used with discretion. This cannot be emphasized too much, for improper use will make it a point loser. Only a few great drop shot artists are able to use it effectively from the baseline. The shot is far more effective and less likely to boomerang when the deliverer is standing close to the net: the drop shot from the baseline hangs in the air for a long time, giving one's opponent a chance to run for it, while the drop shot hit from the net area is likely to be an outright winner.

There are certain players against whom the drop shot should be used quite a bit. These are those who tire in a long match, those who are slow of foot and those who cannot hit short, low balls well. In each case excessive use should be avoided for it will change a winning strategy into a losing one. A few years ago Ham Richardson was a good example of the first category; both Rosewall and Drobny have exploited Dick Savitt's slowness of foot; and players such as Darlene Hard and Beverly Fleitz have low, short weaknesses on the right and left side respectively. The Savitt example is a rather unusual one. As the match progresses, Dick gets faster and faster, making the drop shot less and less effective. This only goes to prove the Don Budge adage that the drop shot should be used less often in the later stages of a match.

Drop shotters often lose matches by refusing to temper their strategy. There is no more helpless feeling than to see your opponent bear in on your drop shot before it has even bounced. If this happens with any frequency, the stroke should be abandoned immediately. Players such as Rosewall, Hoad and Connolly are so light on their feet and anticipate so well that the drop shot is effective against them only when they are well out of court, and then any kind of dump shot is effective. Gonzales and Sedgman are also in this category, the latter being so quick that he can return seemingly perfect stops. Little Mo always had the edge over Doris Hart since she nullified the latter's superb execution of the drop shot by her trigger-quick anticipation. Against these players the drop shot should be used extremely sparingly and primarily to keep them from establishing a rhythm. As little as two or three drop shots in a match is sufficient for this purpose.

The great drop shotters have both disguise and spin. The beginning of their stroke is identical with their normal ground stroke action. As impact is approached, the motion is slowed up and the racket face is turned under to impart backspin. One cannot hit a drop shot with a fast motion since that would be a chop and would impart forward motion to the ball. It requires practice to achieve a balance of spin and trajectory.

The more backspin you use, the harder you can hit the ball but the less control you have. Backspin makes the ball spin in backward circles as it moves forward; this motion creates a drag on the ball which slows its forward movement. However, the extreme open face of the racket allows little margin for error since the slightest mistiming leads to hitting the ball on the wood. A large dose of backspin will cause the ball to bounce backwards over the net. Everyone has seen and laughed at this on occasion, but the percentage on such a shot is ridiculously small. It is a trick shot used for amusement purposes only, not for serious tennis.

Controlled backspin is the key to the successful drop shot. On a waist-high ball, the stroke is hit at about 30° off the vertical—i.e., the racket face is open by that amount. The follow-through after the hit is in a downward direction and can be as short as a foot. The stroke is hit to the side and in front of the body as in regular ground strokes. From the standpoint of accuracy and control, drop shots could be hit exactly as volleys; however, this would be a signal to your opponent that you were going to drop shot, and all the advantage of disguise would be lost. If the player keeps in mind that the hit of the drop shot is like the hit of the volley and if he adds to it his regular ground stroke wind-up, he will find himself aided in learning its execution.

Since the drop shot is an underspin shot, players with slice backhands find it very easy to acquire on the left side. It is more difficult to learn on the forehand side since so few players undercut their forehands. Once again, if they think in terms of forehand volleys, they will get a better conception of the technique.

The easiest balls off which to hit drop shots are soft ones when one has time to get set. The artists of the game—Rosewall, Drobny, Bromwich, Larsen, Hart and Riggs—can make drop shots off speed since they never seem to be off balance. The average tournament player can neither neutralize speed nor be sufficiently set to accomplish a satisfactory drop shot off speed. This is the great fallacy of the statement so frequently made by male players in regard to women's tennis: "All you have to do to beat so-and-so is drop shot her." It is far easier said than done if so-and-so is hitting deep drives with pace to the corners.

Drop shots can best be learned against players inferior to you. The fact that you are superior means that you are reaching the majority of their balls and are therefore set. Don't try to learn your drop shot against a better player or in a tournament!

Drop volleys are used more often than drop shots since the position at the net means that more points will be won if the ball barely drops over. On the other hand, drop volleys are more dangerous to the executor than drop shots since the point is immediately lost if your opponent can reach the ball.

Consequently a good rule would be not to use the drop volley if there is a good alternative chance for a winner on a deep volley.

Drop volleys should never just be dumped over the net. There should always be sharp angle to one side or the other. In singles play, drop volleys are made against hard passing shots, which means more touch is required than in the drop shot. Players like Welby Van Horn, Pancho Gonzales and Althea Gibson execute the drop volley to perfection by simply turning their racket under at the moment of impact. The player who is learning the drop volley will find that the execution is easier in doubles where the pace can be softer under certain circumstances. Surprisingly enough, the drop volley finds a place when all four players are at net, provided enough angle and spin are used to work one's opponent and keep the ball low. Here the shot might more properly be called a dink.

The method of execution depends upon a slight amount of wrist at the moment of impact. The racket face is slightly open for the volley. At the hit, the wrist turns so that the racket face sweeps under the ball. The racket face is almost completely open at the finish of the stroke as compared with the only slightly open face on the regular volley. The reason for the difference is that with the volley, you use the speed of the oncoming ball as part of the returning speed; with the drop volley, you are trying to neutralize that energy. The only way to dissipate this speed is with spin. Pancho Gonzales is actually able to counteract this speed in the only other way permitted by the laws of physics: he moves his racket slightly backwards in a tiny little motion. However, *you* are urged to try backspin. The Gonzales backwards motion can be executed only by a handful of racket artists.

In conclusion, the drop shot and the drop volley are special strokes limited to special occasions. They should be part of the repertoire of every player, but they should be used with the greatest possible discretion.

THE BACKHAND

by William Talbert

What is the correct backhand grip?

The soft part of the palm is placed on top of the racket handle with the fingers spread naturally. The space between the forefinger and middle finger can be a half inch or even more, and the thumb comes diagonally around the handle. I am stressing the position of the fingers in order to avoid the hazards of the "hammer grip." This latter style, in which the fingers are bunched together, puts the hand in an unnatural position; it lessens the area of contact between the hand and the racket and thereby lessens the control of the hand over the racket. It also cramps the muscles of the hand and wrist and thereby allows less flexibility of movement. In the last ten years, only two or three great players out of 50—Pancho Gonzales, Tom Brown and Art Larsen—have been able to use this grip successfully, even though it is prevalent among the majority of club or public park players. Fortunately, it is the easiest defect in a player's stroke equipment to change and it can be literally altered overnight.

A good many players, particularly in past years, have placed the thumb up the back of the handle. This gives a feeling of security to a beginner whose grip is still uncertain, for the racket cannot weave in his hand as he hits the ball. However, there are two major objections to this stiff thumb method. First, the position of the thumb tends to pull the whole grip around so that the palm is behind the racket handle rather than on top of it. This grip creates a tendency to lead with the elbow, the consequences of which will be described later. Secondly, the thumb position tends to set the wrist so that it cannot be moved as fluently for control and disguise of the stroke by spin. The player has traded stability for fluency. Among the great players who have used the thumb up the handle are Helen Wills Moody, as well as many of her contemporaries, but lately only Tony Trabert remains as a prime exponent of this almost-vanishing technique.

The grip we are advocating is known correctly as the Eastern backhand or the Continental backhand, both of which are identical. It is practically the same as the service grip or the Continental forehand. The Western backhand, now practically extinct, pulls the palm almost under the racket handle, thus forcing the player to hit the ball with his elbow pointed high in the air. It is awkward, unnatural and completely ineffective against low shots.

Can you use the "open stance" in hitting a backhand?

It is used only under two circumstances, the sideways stance being the only proper method in normal baseline play. The open stance is almost a necessity against a powerful first service when there is no time to swing the body around and the delivery must be blocked. It can also be used on certain approach chip shots when the player literally runs into the ball, but it is made at the sacrifice of pace in order to reach the net position safely and quickly. The player should always choose the sideways stance whenever circumstances permit, which is most of the time. He can then combine accuracy with power in a natural stroke.

The backhand is hit from the shoulder, but if you face the net you can hit only with the arm. Using the shoulder action brings power without effort since the entire body weight backs up the stroke; using the arm alone cannot possibly bring pace without a jerky motion. The only hazard in the sideways stance is the possibility of blocking yourself from forward motion by allowing the right foot to step across the body rather than toward the net. No power can be achieved when the body is moving sideways; a real effort should be made to step toward the net with the right foot.

What is the correct waiting position?

The waiting position is identical for both forehand and backhand. The player is crouched like a boxer, alert on the balls of his feet and with a low center of gravity. The bend should be from the knees rather than from the waist: leaning over from the waist makes you top heavy while you can achieve stability of balance by bending from the knees. The perfect ready position enables the player to move instantaneously in either direction, and when you are up against a strong player, every fraction of a second counts. Attention to the ready position is a primary aid to good concentration, and the player who never lets his weight sink to his heels is far more likely to make a good return than a lazy opponent.

The arms are held naturally in front of the body, with the elbows bent at the side or slightly in front of the body. The fingers of the left hand gently cradle the throat of the racket and will actually not leave the racket until the backswing is completed. The legs are comfortably separated, perhaps a foot and a half apart. Since the emphasis is on the natural, the racket head should point some 30° left of center so that the right wrist is completely relaxed. Don't try to point the racket straight in front of you since you will have to bend your right wrist awkwardly and straighten your left arm in order to do so. The right hand can be either in the forehand or backhand position, depending upon personal preference. Whichever waiting grip you favor you must use every time since the basis of all good tennis is to have automatic and grooved responses. The waiting position should be so ingrained that it never varies from one season to the next. It must become a reflex action that instinctively alerts muscles and body.

Do you favor a high backswing on the backhand?

A high backswing is certainly permissible and it is part of the semi-circular wind-up typical of every player in tennis today. It is not a necessity, but the semi-circular swing that starts high and ends low gives a natural rhythm to the stroke. It is feasible to take the racket straight back at waist level, yet there is not a top player in the game today who does not use some sort of a modified Figure 8 wind-up. The roundhouse backswing is a handicap on any fast surface, so one should attempt to keep the backswing as neat and small as possible. Even so, some natural players have used large flourishes, Pat Todd being a prime example, and their backhand has still been a forceful, attacking weapon. But it was really in spite of the flourish, not because of it, for no extra power can be gained by wielding the racket high above the head.

As the racket reaches its zenith on the backswing, it is above shoulder height and the face is frequently open. As the backswing is completed, the racket comes down to waist level and the face is perpendicular to the ground. Then the racket comes upward again on the follow-through to complete the Figure 8 motion. It is important to remember that the racket *must come down to waist level before the hit* and the racket face cannot be open at this point unless one wishes to slice. Players who slice exclusively and have never learned to drive use the same wind-up but, on reaching the zenith, come diagonally down to the ball with the face still open instead of bringing the racket down to waist level and then coming up and over the ball.

There are two ways of taking the racket back, either of which is satisfactory. In both cases the left hand remains on the racket until the wind-up is completed. In the one instance, the left hand remains at the throat as the racket is drawn back. The length of this backswing is limited by the trajectory of the left arm and it is therefore highly recommended for those with too flossy an action. In the other instance, the fingers of the left hand slide down to the handle and help carry the racket back in what appears to be a two-handed grip. This also cuts down on the enormous circular wind-up.

What makes some backhands look so awkward?

In most cases it is because the elbow is leading the arm. Sometimes the problem begins in the backswing, for instead of taking the arm straight back with elbow close in to the body and at wrist level, the player allows the elbow to protrude. It loses all contact with the body and is at a much higher level than the wrist. When the backswing is completed and the drive begins, once again the elbow leads, while the wrist and racket trail until the elbow is snapped forward suddenly. The player is using only his forearm instead of his shoulder and body. It is ungainly, to say the least, and there is nothing to say in its favor. This problem is always associated with the Western backhand but is also in frequent evidence amongst players with solid Eastern grips but very little training. The solution is to keep the elbow locked against the body in the backswing and to hit temporarily with a straight arm until the old behavior pattern is forgotten. Eventually the elbow may be allowed to bend slightly, although the utmost precaution should be taken to see that it never leads the wrist.

Should the body bend during the hit?

The emphasis should be on the knee bend, although there is a slight body curve typical of the natural athlete. Never reach for a ball by bending from the waist as this is accompanied by a backward pull of the hips. The correct method of getting down to the ball is to allow the knees to flex with the legs well separated. Surprising as it may seem, the player who best gets down to low balls is Lew Hoad, who never bends from the waist at all. Sven Davidson is also a master of the supple legs and erect torso.

How is the backhand drive executed?

The short Figure 8 backswing has already been recommended. The player is now in the following position: his body is sideways to the net, his right shoulder is pointing to the ball and, assuming the ball is going to bounce at waist height, the arm and racket head are at or slightly below waist level and are parallel to the ground. The elbow is bent at approximately a 45° angle and is held reasonably close to the body. The legs are bent and well separated, and the right foot will step toward the net as the ball is hit.

Contact with the ball is made slightly in front of rather than to the side of the body, and the arm is almost straight at the moment of impact. The arm moves as a whole from the shoulder; *there is no separate forearm motion.* The action is from the shoulder, not from the elbow or the wrist. It is as though the entire arm were being thrown from its position at below waist level to the top of the fence behind the opponent's baseline.

Should wrist be used in the backhand?

The amount of wrist that is used is dependent upon the individual player. There have been great backhands with almost no wrist action, whatsoever, and there have been equally great backhands in which the wrist movement was the prominent feature. A player with a great deal of natural talent can get away with more wrist flick than a player who depends mainly upon consistency. Use of the wrist is always a dangerous feature since the snap action requires split-second timing. In its favor are added power and last-minute change of direction, and yet a solid backhand can be taught which will have both pace and disguise but a minimum of wrist. It is absolutely impossible to hit with a completely locked wrist, Tony Vincent notwithstanding, but the solid backhand involves a wrist motion of only 15°, as compared with the 130° movement of a wrist snap.

When the wrist is completely locked, there can be no control of direction by means of minor adjustments of the wrist. A very slight amount of wrist movement gives fluency to the stroke, yet this motion is so small that the ball can be met slightly behind or ahead of the anticipated spot, for there is more than a foot of leeway. A very wristy shot requires the most exact timing, for there is no leeway whatsoever since the wrist action is occurring at such a violent rate. Therefore limit your wrist movements to what you can do with safety; add your wrist action later if you so desire, but use a minimum of wrist to begin with so that steadiness and control are not sacrificed for an occasional flashy shot.

Where should the follow-through end?

There is a certain amount of leeway permissible. The racket head travels up and normally ends at about shoulder height pointing toward the net or slightly past it. The stroke can be finished slightly before this level is reached, particularly on the down-the-line shot. It is not wise to carry the follow-through around the body since it forces the hips and shoulders to pivot around and therefore prevents you from getting ready quickly for the next shot. Don't cut the follow-through too short for by doing so you are fighting the momentum of the racket as it goes through the ball and will therefore lose power or will end up with a jerky shot.

Should the racket head ever drop?

No. The head should never be below the extension of the arm. Get down to the ball instead and keep the same angle of the wrist in relation to the arm for all your backhands.

How do you get power on a high backhand?

There is no problem whatsoever if you come through the ball and follow through at a slightly higher level. The common error is to pull away from the ball by leaning on the rear foot. Treat the high backhand just as you would a backhand at any other height, moving into it as you hit.

What is a slice backhand and is it recommended?

The racket face is open during the hit and the follow-through is slightly below the ball height rather than up toward shoulder level. The result is underspin (the ball spins round and round in the air, the top of the ball constantly moving backwards, away from the direction of the hit). This underspin slows down the flight of the ball and is an extremely useful weapon where speed and a low dipping trajectory are not desired. It is an important part of a player's repertoire *after* the backhand drive has been fully conquered. It cannot take the place of the drive as a forcing shot, but it has a good many uses when properly employed. Most of the leading players have a slice in addition to their topspin drive; only a few slice exclusively.

A slice can be used to dig up a low ball when coming to net. With the same slice action, one can also execute the drop shot. Sharp crosscourt angle shots, in which touch rather than power is required, become rather easy with this motion. Slice may also be used to retrieve a ball, for it hangs in the air while the player gets back into position. It is highly useful, therefore, in the defensive lob. It should never be used as a passing shot since the slower pace allows the net man more time to reach the ball and since the ball tends to travel upward as it crosses the net. A slice is most effective on wet grass where it hardly comes off the ground and least effective on high-bouncing cement.

Pancho Gonzales is a good example of a player with both a fine drive and a good slice. Bobby Riggs used the slice for control and the drive for power and could do both beautifully. Doris Hart also mastered both shots and could produce either at will. Ken Rosewall and Art Larsen are also in this category. The players who did have backhand weaknesses were those who favored the slice over the drive, and in this grouping I place Vic Seixas, Neale Fraser, Jaroslav Drobny and even Jack Kramer. The players who use the drive almost exclusively are Don Budge, Dick Savitt and Tony Trabert, all of whom have made the backhand a fearsome weapon. The conclusion must therefore be that a strong backhand drive is a basic necessity, whereas the slice alone will not suffice.

Is a flat backhand desirable?

The absolutely flat backhand is a rarity and is only used in special instances. Topspin or underspin in small amounts is generally used for control, although a completely flat backhand can be hit with safety on a high, short ball where the racket trajectory is down. A flat shot neither dips nor rises, and only gravity pulls it down; slight spin, either top or slice, will make the ball dip or rise at the player's will. What is known as a flat backhand is therefore a *relatively flat* backhand, where the amount of spin used is minimized. Don Budge, who has the best backhand the game has ever known, and Ken Rosewall, possessor of one of the finest backhands in the game today, both hit relatively flat backhands with great frequency. Don's having a little topspin and Ken's a little underspin. Doris Hart and Maureen Connolly both hit with a minimum of spin from the left side. Even though these four great players chose to hit with very little spin, many outstanding backhands have been characterized by quite a good deal of topspin. Among the great topspin artists are Tony Trabert, Lew Hoad, Pat Todd and Pauline Betz. Dick Savitt is somewhere in between these two categories while Frank Sedgman leans toward the flat stroke.

What is topspin?

Topspin is imparted by drawing the racket face over the ball in such a manner that the ball spins round and round in the direction of the net, the top of the ball constantly moving forward. Technically, air pressures are created by this spin which literally tend to shove the ball down. Thus a topspin ball may be hit in a relatively high trajectory so as to gain high net clearance, and yet it will still drop within the boundaries of the court. If a flat ball were so hit with the same speed, it would sail far out; if a slice ball were similarly hit, it would sail even farther out because air pressures would be created by the backspin which tend to lift the ball up. This is the same principle which makes an airplane fly and is one facet of the Bernoulli Theorem.

On the backhand stroke, a small amount of topspin is naturally produced by the rising forward swing at the end of the Figure 8 movement *if* the racket face is held perpendicular to the ground. If the face is open, backspin or slice is produced. Another way to produce topspin is by a wrist roll when the ball is hit, Lew Hoad being the prime exponent of this method. His is more like a table tennis shot and is dependent upon a powerful wrist under complete control. Other players rarely use such heavy wrist movements to gain topspin, the preferred method being to start the forward motion with the racket low and to end high.

The topspin or roll drive has everything in its favor. It has speed, control and safety. The amount of topspin used varies with the individual, but seldom does one see a player with excessive amounts since it is so hard on the wrist and arm to produce in large quantities.

What is a backhand chop?

The chop is simply an abbreviated slice. The backswing is smaller and the follow-through is short. If you like, it is a volley hit after the ball has bounced. In recent years, players have tended to use the term "chip" instead of "chop." It has a slightly different connotation since it primarily refers to a coming-in shot. It is not as ineffective as the old "chop" since momentum is given to the chip by running into the ball.

The chip has become one of the commonest shots in the game today. Many young players have not even bothered to learn the drive but instead use this weak chip shot to seek the net position as fast as possible. It does get them into the barrier where they put the pressure on their opponent, but it is never as forceful as the drive and it is utterly useless in a baseline rally or as a passing shot. The only time the chip should be used in my opinion is to dig up a low, short ball when approaching the net.

When should sidespin be used?

Sidespin can be used effectively on a down-the-line shot. Since it is achieved by pulling the racket face across the ball during the forward hit, the ball naturally tends to go to your opponent's forehand. It can be hit equally well by players with topspin or underspin. It is so difficult to use on the crosscourt that it has become almost exclusively a down-the-line weapon. It is a recommended shot because it is easy to produce, it can be hit with comparative safety, it carries a spin that is heavy on the opponent's racket and the direction of the shot is not signalled to the opponent in the windup.

The windup is exactly the same as on the drive. The underspin player will hit the ball with the racket face slightly open and the topspin player will hit the ball by lifting up with his racket. As ball and racket meet, the arm pulls across the body, thus making the ball spin sideways as it travels forward.

Should the return of serve be blocked?

It is always preferable to drive the ball when there is sufficient time. It is a rare player whose second serve is so strong that the return cannot be driven, but many players have a first delivery that carries so much speed that it becomes almost mandatory to block the ball. In this category are the first services of Pancho Gonzales, Lew Hoad, Dick Savitt, Neale Fraser, Ham Richardson and a good many others. These serves come with such lightning speed that it is hard to get one's racket on them, much less drive them. It takes a Don Budge or a Dick Savitt to drive such a ball, the majority of us being content to block the ball back. Lew Hoad and Pancho Gonzales frequently block heavy services, and they have learned to use this return with a considerable amount of skill and placement.

The block is not a stroke at all. The racket is merely held in place, and the speed of the other man's ball rebounds from your racket. If any forward motion is added, the block emerges into the chip, which is the shortest stroke in the game. The block should not be used against any but the most forceful serves since against weak serves the rebound action will not be sufficient to return the ball over the net.

When you are pulled wide, should you try merely to return the ball or should you seek to hit a winner?

It depends upon the position of your opponent. If he is in the backcourt, the best thing you can do is to roll the ball safe and deep toward the center of your opponent's baseline. This gives you a chance to get back into position. If you try the long crosscourt, you leave yourself vulnerable since your opponent can reply down the line to your unguarded forehand side;

similarly, if you try to hit down the line, your opponent can hit a sharp forehand crosscourt to this unprotected territory.

If your opponent is at net, you have your choice of the three passing shots—down the line, crosscourt or lob. The down-the-line or crosscourt shots must be hit low and hard, whereas the lob can be either an aggressive or defensive one. The important thing to remember is not to hit only down the line or only crosscourt when you are caught wide. Vary your shots so that your opponent cannot anticipate your move.

DON'T CHANGE YOUR GRIP

by Edward Moylan

No greater injustice can be done to a young player than to force him to change a natural grip into a less natural but more orthodox one. There are a number of players with Western or Continental grips who are being urged by other players who should know better to shift to the more recognized Eastern grip. If a grip is natural to the player, there is no reason on earth why he should spend three or four years re-adjusting it. I have never known a top player who changed his grip and thereby developed a great shot. . . .

The world is full of great players with unorthodox grips. Pancho Segura has a highly unusual but excellent two-handed forehand; Doris Hart uses the Continental, as did Fred Perry; Pancho Gonzales's grip is an Eastern with Continental tendencies; Frank Shields has a big Western forehand; Gar Mulloy verges slightly toward the Western; Ted Schroeder hits his overheads with a forehand grip. Many of the great players seem to have grips that are peculiar to themselves although they are frequently just variations of the Eastern.

I started out with a Continental grip, which was the natural one for me. Bill Tilden advised me to change to an Eastern solely because he hit the ball that way. It took me two years to learn it, yet I would never urge such a change for anyone else. There is no need to alter the natural to conform with a pattern.

The most famous grip changer of all time was Sidney Wood. He had a classical Continental forehand which he hit well, but he was talked into changing to the more respectable Eastern by well-meaning friends. His forehand was never the same again. As a matter of fact, it was never the same two years in a row; he appeared every spring with a new variation on the Eastern.

Don Budge is the best example of a player who made the shift from a natural grip to a more artificial one with extreme success. His original

Western forehand was sound and solid, but he changed to the Eastern in order to be able to handle low balls on a grass surface. The old forehand was excellent, but the new one was probably even better. But I believe that Don was one of the few players who accomplished the change with more on the plus side of the ledger than on the minus.

Every professional has probably at some time been approached by an anxious mother who urged him to change her child's grip because somebody told her that her son "would never be any good unless he did change." The good teacher will not automatically alter a grip because it is the recommended one; he will first consider the individual and then determine what is best for his pupil.

In group instruction, I think we would all favor the standard Eastern grips being shown to the beginner. As the player develops, he will find his own distinctive style—perhaps a slight shifting of the fingers to the Continental or the Western. The wise teacher will hesitate before teaching a shift back toward the standard Eastern.

One postscript: I am speaking of *grips,* not of strokes. Stroke defects in wind-up, hit and follow-through should be corrected but grips, in the main, should be left untouched.

BATTING THE BALL

by Jack Kramer

There are a number of players who look good and don't win, probably because they have their choice of shots and stop to think. There is not time to think on a tennis court: the less you think, the better off you are. That is why it is better to have one good shot and use it repeatedly than to have two or three. As an example, when I hit an approach shot, I pick my spot and hit it even though I know my opponent will be there. *I always hit every short forehand down the line* unless, of course, I have an easy high ball that I can put away crosscourt with no chance of error. Then, when I come in, my opponent will either hit the backhand down the line where I am waiting or he will try one of the most difficult shots in the game, the short backhand crosscourt, which only Don Budge and Frank Kovacs could ever hit consistently. Most opponents will flail at the ball, making 20% placements to 80% errors, so that the percentage is with me.

When I first played Frank Sedgman on the tour, he would hit most of his forehand approach shots down the line, but every so often he would try a crosscourt ace, which is the hardest shot in the game. All he had to do was hit one wrong forehand at game point and he'd be out of the set. Why was the forehand crosscourt wrong to try? He'd make a few placements, but too often he'd hit the tape or the return would not be strong enough. In the latter case, he left a wide-open court and lost the point. On our tour, he probably gave me ten service breaks by attempting the forehand crosscourt approach shot! Now Frank has developed a nice slice down the line; he takes his short balls and lazes them within a few feet of the spot he has picked.

Some players never seem to learn. They have all the shots but they think on the court instead of playing the ball as they are supposed to. I know one circuit player who hits the ball as well as anyone, but he doesn't win. He will try a shot and it will miss by a few inches, and a few minutes later he'll try the same shot. To play a winning game, you cannot make errors. Make your opponent make the errors. *The difference between a great player and a good one is that the great player misses fewer easy shots.* Matches are won on errors, not on placements, and one learns to play winning tennis when one forces one's opponent into errors.

One thing I have noticed about many of the top-flight players is that they cannot spring back as well after hitting a forehand as they can from a backhand. Dick Savitt, for example, is weak on the wide forehand, as am I, because of that inability to get back into position. Only Fred Perry could get himself back into court, perhaps because of his open stance. Pancho Segura also had the knack of seldom hitting a ball from which he could not get back into position.

The greatest weakness of good players comes in overplaying the ball, i.e., hitting it harder than they should or, in general, simply trying too tough a shot. *Only Bobby Riggs never overplayed his shots.* Occasionally I have seen Pancho Segura, when losing to Gonzales, get desperate and press. Then he would try too tough a volley or too good an approach shot instead of being content to throw the ball back. I remember watching Sedgman and Gonzales play their opening pro match in Los Angeles. As early as 2–all in the first set, with ad for Pancho, Sedgman tried a second serve ace. As soon as we saw that, we knew he was out of the match.

Don Budge is now hitting the ball better than he ever did, yet in a good match he'll try too tough a shot, whereas before he would have played the ball more safely. However, Don has a reason for pressing: he feels he cannot get back into court and, knowing that he is out of condition, he tries the more difficult shot. The same thing happened on my tour with Bobby Riggs. We played evenly for the first two dozen matches, but when I started to go out ahead, he began to hit his passing shots into the alley because he was trying for the "great" shot. . . . Budge improved me because I could not serve and come in against him and he forced me to learn to play him from the baseline.

Professional tennis today is a serve and volley game. If you don't come in on your second serve, your opponent will come in and will force *you* into the errors. That's why Segura, who never volleyed as an amateur, is a great volleyer now. That was Riggs's defense against my game—take the net away from me and force me to play a game I didn't know—the defensive game.

He made me learn the lob and he, in turn, learned to play his best as a server and volleyer. When Riggs was at his peak, no one could outserve Bobby; he got as many errors and weak returns off his serve as his opponent—partially, I must admit, because of his great return of service. This was due to the fact that Bobby had the greatest anticipation in history, particularly on return of serve.

By the time Budge had finished playing on the last tour, he was serving and coming into the net both to keep his opponent back and because it was less exhausting than staying back. As he came in, he forced his opponent to attempt to pass him and thereby he forced the errors; when staying back, he tried for the placements while his opponent forced Don's errors.

Just as Don had to change his game, so would the other great stars of the past were they playing today. Gottfried von Cramm, the great ground stroke artist, would be a net rusher like the rest of us since that is the only defense against an attacking game. It is too tough to cope with an attacking game by staying in the back court. Picture Ken Rosewall against Sedgman or Segura! That's why I am convinced that von Cramm would play as do Gonzales or Sedgman were he in competition in these days. He would have no more rallies from the baseline—he would simply serve and come in. I also think Budge, if he were starting today, would serve and come in rather than stay back and trade ground strokes. The game has changed! *Tennis is serve and volley, with a good passing shot required when you have the ad point.*

There are only three players against whom you could not serve and come in—Budge, Kovacs and Bromwich. Brom came over the ball and made you half-volley, while Budge and Kovacs drove the ball too well to allow the percentages to be in your favor. I have been in the game 20 years, yet only these three were capable of keeping me back. Dick Savitt had the weakness of being a little slow of foot in the forehand court, while Trabert appears tough, but not as tough as the Budge-Kovacs-Bromwich trio. Against these latter, one jockeyed around to see who could get into the net first. Even during Don's last tour, the players discovered they could not serve and come in against him. Incidentally, I have found that Gonzales, Schroeder and Sedgman were never difficult to come in against, mainly because they all used an undersliced backhand return of serve.

Some players have the winning system of serve and volley but lack the ground strokes to back them up. No one can win a match these days without a good return of serve and a good passing shot. Eddie Moylan has one of the best ground games in tennis today, but why hit a great shot if you don't come in behind it? If you come in on a fine forehand down the line, how many players can really make consistent fine passing shots to keep you in hot water?

When Bill Tilden was in his prime, no one could touch him—until the Frenchmen came along. They finally got the idea that it was far less foolish to come into net and force Tilden into the errors than to stay back and allow the master to jerk them around the court.

There is only one problem. The public does not yet understand the serve-and-volley game. It's boring. Someone serves, comes into net, and either makes a good volley or forces an error. Occasionally, a perfect passing shot is made. There are no back-court maneuvers; the ground stroke artists don't win. What to do? There are only two choices: change the game or interest the public in volleying tennis. . . .

Segura and I had a discussion about the value of the serve-and-volley game. I claimed I could beat him from the back court. We played three matches—three great matches—under our own rules, which were: the server could not volley the first return and the receiver must also wait one stroke before coming in.

There are other ways of changing tennis to make it a better spectator sport. One could make the server stand two feet behind the baseline, one could shorten the service court, or one could soften the balls. I sincerely believe something should be done as the game is becoming less and less attractive to the spectators.

FIVE POINTS FOR BEGINNERS

by Richard (Pancho) Gonzales

1. Always keep your eyes on the ball.
2. Bend your knees in making your stroke on the forehand and backhand.
3. Get down to the ball for the volley.
4. On the service, guard against foot-faults. They can become a habit if not corrected early.
5. In serving strike the ball at the top of the toss.

THE SERVE AND HOW TO VARY IT

by Richard (Pancho) Gonzales

Picture in your mind a chain reaction in which the body moves in to the ball, the shoulder moves in to the ball, the elbow extends and the wrist snaps through the ball. There, simplified, you have the service action. The power comes from the coordinated speed of the action.

In modern lawn tennis the emphasis has shifted increasingly on to big serving, and it is not easy to recall a champion in recent years who got by without a powerful service weapon. The advantage of having a big service is in the pressure it puts on one's opponent. As the match progresses he begins to fear that if he loses his own service it will cost him the set. The strong server may also be able to conserve more energy than his opponent by winning his service games more easily. He should be more confident of his condition lasting in a long set or a long match.

I concede that the possession of a big service alone isn't enough to become a champion. A player needs other strokes as well. But a player with an outstanding service and fair ground strokes has the foundation for a successful career.

Early in my own career I relied a lot on my service, my ground strokes being only moderate. In the final of the United States singles championship at Forest Hills in 1949 it was my service that saved me and enabled me to beat Ted Schroeder. Not for another two or three years, until I played many matches on clay courts, did the rest of my game improve. To survive on clay courts you just have to have sound ground strokes.

In my time I have played against many players with great serves. Probably the greatest was Jack Kramer, who hit the ball very hard (his service was timed at 110 m.p.h.) and was extremely accurate and deceptive. Frank Sedgman is another good server, with a consistently hard first service which he follows with tremendous speed in to the net to volley away winners. Lew Hoad has a hard and deceptive service that has always presented me with difficulty. Barry MacKay, because of his height, can send down balls at terrific angles and has great power. However, he usually directs his service to the backhand, and though it travels at high speed, it is not as difficult to handle as the more deceptive services of Kramer and Hoad. Bobby Riggs was a small player, but he accurately served to the corners, pulling his man out of court. Another hard and baffling server was the Czechoslovakian-born left-hander, Jaroslav Drobny, now a naturalized Briton.

In the average match, 50 per cent of points are won by serves, the rest by volleys and ground strokes. There admittedly are traps in making such generalizations. A person like Kenneth Rosewall might win only one point a game on his serve, and the rest by volleys and ground strokes. On the other hand, I might win three points a game with my serve and only one with volley and ground strokes. It all depends on the strength of the player's service. But obviously if it's possible to win 50 per cent of points by service the stroke deserves at least 50 per cent of your effort to perfect it.

My serve was natural from the very beginning. I had one coach, a high school coach by the name of Spears, who told me that if I threw the ball up a little higher and a little farther behind my head I would get more spin on the ball. Following his advice, my serving improved almost overnight.

At home there is a guy named Charles Pate, three years older than me, who has done more to remind me of my faults than any other player I have ever known. If I am serving badly he invariably can put his finger on the fault. He will come over and tell me what I am doing wrong; usually I'm not throwing the ball enough and not reaching for it.

In all these years of lawn tennis, years in which I have managed to beat off many players' challenges, I have never become overconfident with my service. I have practiced my serve just as much as, if not more than, any of my other strokes. Sure, you have to practice on your weaknesses. But you mustn't overlook practicing your strength. Your game will always be built around your strength.

Let me tell you how I serve. My grip, which is orthodox, is very important. It's almost the backhand grip, but perhaps not quite all the way.

In singles I stand about six inches from the center line when serving into the deuce court, and about two feet away from the center line when serving into the advantage court.

The stance for each service is exactly the same, thus increasing the deception. One of the big secrets in serving is in disguising the delivery in order to keep the opponent off balance.

The flat serve is hit by snapping the wrist and opening the face of the racket just as the ball is hit. I aim the flat serve primarily to the backhand corner, and, being right-handed, I follow through on my left side.

For the slice serve I swing the racket away from my body, hitting around the ball and again following through on my left side. The ball is thrown up about nine inches in front of my forehead (though higher, of course) and into the court, so that I have room to hit around it. The slice is used for drawing the opponent out of court, especially if he has a weak forehand, and it is effective on grass, on which the ball stays rather low. It is an offensive shot, used in the top company almost as much as the flat serve.

The twist serve is hit by dropping the head of the racket behind the back, then swinging up and over the ball. For this serve the ball must be thrown behind the head, and the follow-through of the racket is high and to the right of the player's body. The twist, or American twist, as it is often called, is mostly a consistent serve used as a second serve, because it clears the net comfortably and cuts back into the court with a greater margin of safety.

Incorrect tossing up of the ball in serving causes as many errors as any other one factor. You must practice and practice and then practice still more to synchronize the toss of the ball and the swing of the racket.

The position of the ball in the air varies by two, three or maybe four inches between the first serve and the second serve. You throw it to a height about an inch or two beyond the point you can reach with your racket. At the ball's zenith you go up on the toes of your left foot, stretching as far as you can in striking it.

On the first serve you should hit the ball just at the moment it starts to fall. On the second serve the ball can be allowed to drop two or three inches before you go up to meet it. From this position you will be able to impart the spin which will bring the ball into the court. Because the back has to be arched in order to get spin on the ball, the twist serve is the most tiring of all. Otherwise, I have found that big serving doesn't necessarily use up undue energy.

Whether a player should go flat out for a cannonball on his first serve depends largely on the quality of his opponent. A flat serve bothers some players more than the spin serve. You must react very much like a baseball pitcher, varying your serves to keep the other guy off guard and off balance, but serving mostly to his weakness, whether it be the forehand or the backhand. Sometimes the court surfaces are inferior and it may pay, therefore, to make sure your first ball goes into play by sending over your second spin serve first. Then you can hurry in and command the net position.

While the second serve cannot be quite as severe a weapon as the first serve, it can be more aggressive than most players make it. Practice the second serve by hitting it deep and to the corners. This will give you confidence. Your first serve will be as good as your second serve allows it to be. If you are sure that you can hit a second serve without double-faulting, you will get more of your first serves into play. But the knowledge that your second serve is poor will make you miss more first serves through fear of double-faulting. You have to work on that second serve to make it as consistent as it possibly can be.

Before serving, you should stand relaxed behind the baseline, bouncing the ball once prior to beginning your windup. The left foot ought to be planted firmly by the baseline, two or three inches behind it, with the left shoulder pointing toward the net.

Your body must move freely as you transfer the weight from the ball of the left foot onto all of the toes, which bear most of the strain as you reach up for the ball.

Do not hesitate on your forward motion. The tendency to fall into the court is perfectly natural and is part of a good service. As you fall forward you regain balance and are ready to move off in any direction for the return. Normally, in regaining balance you take one step into the court, occasionally two, and these steps ought to be made quickly to prevent being caught in the middle of the court on a deep shot.

Rhythm comes with practice. The service is a continuous motion from start to finish, and if you relax and swing freely you ultimately will fall into a rhythm.

I like to see players taking their time with their service, analyzing their action and trying to do something extra with the ball. Outwardly, they should go through some ritual of approaching the baseline and bouncing the ball in the same way each time. That will help them to get into a groove. But while they go through this drill they must be thinking. They must put thought into their second serve, using their first serve as a guide. If the first ball was too long, the racket must be brought into the ball sooner to pull the second serve down. And if the first serve finished in the net, the racket has to be swung farther out to carry the second ball deeper.

Most of the time when I am serving I try to penetrate my opponent's weakness. Normally, the more his weakness is attacked the more errors he will make. Once in a while, however, I will serve to his strength in an attempt to stop him from getting set for one particular shot. I do this especially on my second serve.

People can remember that over the years Pancho Segura was devastating with his forehand, and yet, throughout my career, I felt I won many points serving to his forehand, simply because he crowded his backhand, opening up the whole of his forehand court. It was a calculated risk which a lot of players wouldn't have taken. It is very dangerous playing in to as great a shot as Segura's forehand.

Too many players follow their serves in to the net irrespective of some factors that should discourage them. You must assess your serve and your opponent's ground strokes before gambling everything on a rush to the net. If your serves are falling short it is suicidal to follow them in. You must wait for the ball on which you can be more offensive.

The other guy's return of service may be extremely accurate. In that case you'll have to wait longer and try to maneuver yourself into a more aggressive position. Of course, you may have no ground strokes at all. Then you haven't much choice; you are safest at the net.

Wind and sun can pose problems for players of all standards. I wish I knew the answers. The only attitude to take on a windy day is to concentrate harder and make allowance for the strength of the wind. In serving into the wind, naturally you have to hit harder to get the ball deeper. Hitting with the wind, you ease up on your shot, allowing the wind to carry the ball to a good depth. It's not a bad idea to shorten the service action. There will be less risk then of mistiming.

As for finding yourself looking directly into the sun when serving, all I can suggest is that you adjust your stance to the right or the left. The fact is that the wind and the sun, and all other weather conditions, affect both players. Accept this from the start. Try to use the conditions to the best of your ability, and don't allow them to upset you. What it really comes down to is strength of character.

Some players feel that confidence in the whole of their game mainly hinges on their serving. I don't know why this should necessarily be so, unless all they have is a big service. Confidence, to my mind, comes from hitting the ball in the middle of the racket and executing winning shots.

But I agree that a bad spell of serving in the middle of a match can break a player's morale. If he can't get his first serve into play he becomes that much more apprehensive. What ought he to do? Well, he must concentrate more and look more intensely at the ball. Sometimes a player will take his eyes off the ball before it is struck; this is the cause of numerous faults. He must stretch up for the ball at its highest point as he swings. And, if necessary, he must ease up on the power. It sounds obvious, but many players don't seem to realize that you must get the serve in to have a chance. A slower serve is better than a cannonball that never goes in.

Be careful of foot-faults, which occur more frequently in club tennis than is generally realized. The most common foot-faults are usually caused by lack of concentration—perhaps by a player unthinkingly walking up and stepping on the line as he serves. If you form a habit of deliberately placing your left foot two or three inches behind the baseline you will avoid this.

Other foot-faults are caused by the left big toe, as it bears the weight, turning onto the line; by the left foot creeping onto the line; and by taking a small steadying step onto the line. These faults can be eliminated if you back as much as four to six inches behind the baseline before serving.

I doubt whether I have been foot-faulted more than a dozen times during my career. My left foot is very firm. I know that I can place it within half an inch of the line without risking a foot-fault.

When I started playing the game the rules forbade the back foot from crossing the line before impact, and I must have been foot-faulted about a half dozen times on this clause. I solved the problem by stepping back six inches. Now, of course, the rule doesn't operate.

Height is a great advantage in serving, for it allows a player to hit the ball with greater angle. A tall man has this extra angle and he can hit the ball harder with a greater margin of safety. The smaller man has to put spin on the ball to get it to hook into the court. He thereby loses power. Two small men who've developed great serves are Rod Laver and a player of the past, Bobby Riggs. Jaroslav Drobny, whom I've already mentioned, wasn't too tall, either. Lew Hoad, who has a fine serve, is five feet, eleven inches, but most of the best servers are at least six feet. I stand a little over six feet, three inches, and Barry MacKay is about six feet, four inches.

Change of pace in serving is often worth a few points. The receiver may be standing a foot or two behind the baseline waiting for the fast first serve. A slower, spinning ball may catch him by surprise and give you a little more time to close in on the net. If, however, he has quick reflexes and a strong return of service you are taking a risk. He will be away ahead of the ball, unworried by the change of pace.

One of the curious aspects in many long sets between two good servers is that finally, when there's a break, the other player breaks back immediately. Although it causes excitement in the gallery, it shouldn't really happen. The player who has the set in his grip by breaking through first either relaxes from overconfidence or suffers a mild letdown. The pressure has built up while the games were going with service and when, after sustained effort, he takes his opponent's service, he has a nervous reaction, missing volleys that up till then he'd been putting away. The answer is to concentrate harder, move in more quickly to a volley and watch the ball like a hawk.

When you get into the position of having victory within your grasp you must call on all your "killer" instinct and try to close out the match without the loss of a point. Don't relax on the first point when you are serving at 5–4, 9–8, or whatever the score is. Move in immediately and close out the set as quickly as you can. Then concentrate even harder in the second set, because overconfidence and lack of concentration will automatically become a hazard, causing you to drop service early in the set.

So often your strategy in serving must be governed by the state of the game and the ability of your opponent. At 5–4, for instance, you might feel that it's important to get to the net more quickly, so you serve a little more slowly, providing yourself with more time in which to go forward and make a sound volley.

It pays always to be offensive with the first service, because an attacking delivery gives you two chances of winning the point. But in a tough match, when I see my opponent is tired, I may try to conserve my energy by discarding my cannonball and making sure my first serve goes in. The fact that he is weary means that my opponent will have just as much trouble returning a consistent first service—even though it lacks my full power.

A number of present-day players have developed the habit of holding only one ball when they serve. I cannot see any merit in it. Most players can hold two balls in one hand quite comfortably, and, with practice, it becomes easy to retain one ball while throwing the other into the air. Those who keep one ball in the pocket of their shorts may be creating a pressure on a leg muscle, causing them to get cramps or tire that particular muscle much faster than muscles in other parts of the body.

As for throwing one ball aside when the first ball is good, I don't know that it is fair to the opponent. Some umpires rightly have ruled interference when this has been done.

New balls in a match, or balls that become wet and heavy, demand added concentration. It is an advantage to have new balls to serve, because they travel about one tenth faster. A wet, heavier ball will drop as much as five or six feet shorter than a dry ball. One has to concentrate on hitting through it with the center of the racket in order to get it deeper.

It shouldn't be beyond anyone to develop a strong service as long as he sets out observing the right principles. Women have more difficulty because they are not as strong physically. A little girl is more content playing with dolls and dresses and helping round the house than in building up her muscles. Boys meanwhile play sports such as baseball, basketball and, in Britain, cricket, in which they use a motion that can be incorporated later into a tennis service. Consequently, when they start playing tennis, boys find it more natural to serve than girls. And, of course, they have stronger forearms anyway. Wrist action, as I have said, is important in generating service power.

All of us in trying to improve our service will occasionally serve double-faults. They needn't be discouraging. I have served many in my time, not because of a fault in my swing or any nervousness, but through aiming for the lines and the corners. I have great confidence in my service and I figure that going for the lines pays off. Don't, therefore, be distracted by double-faults, if you are trying to play boldly.

Finally, never serve in a lazy manner when practicing. Serving hard over the years will develop those muscles that are used in serving. Practice as often as you can, hitting your serves to the corners and lines, and slicing the ball off short to the forehand. Have confidence in this and every other serve so that in a match you know exactly what you can do with each ball. Your game will grow accordingly.

THE SERVICE

by Frank Sedgman

In top flight tennis, there are no poor services. I can think of a few players of international fame who have never been able to hit a hard, flat ball, but they made up for their lack of pace by utilizing disguise, depth and place-ment. However, the big, flat service gives the player a tremendous edge over his opponent, and if the delivery is strong enough, he can win matches simply by cudgeling the ball with all his might. There have been two notable cases in history where a major title was taken by a serve alone— John Doeg won the U.S. Singles in 1930 and Bob Falkenburg won Wimble-don in 1948.

Most of the leading professionals in Jack Kramer's troupe have powerful deliveries, Pancho Gonzales's being the most noteworthy. In no part of the serve is he ever at fault. His body swings into the service just at the moment of impact, and he has great flexibility of arm in delivering a flat or twist service. His is the toughest delivery among the current pros. Only Lew Hoad excels Pancho in a serve wide to the forehand. Pancho Segura's is the easiest service to take, and then comes Ken Rosewall. Tony Trabert's first service is very powerful, but he utilizes excessive spin for his second serve. Rex Hartwig also relies more on spin than speed, and I think his delivery would be far more effective if he flattened it. Kramer's service is still very good. From the same toss, he can either slice wide or hit down the middle.

I have several defects in my own service, one being that my hips are too far forward before I hit the ball. I know I also have a pause in the action. This used to bother me until I watched Cary Middlecoff drive a golf ball. He has a distinct pause of almost a second at the top of his swing. However, all the best serves in championship tennis such as those of Gonzales, Hoad and Kramer have a smooth, continuous action. A young player should never deliberately cultivate a hitch, and that is what a pause in the action is.

Harry Hopman got me to start a rocking motion in the service. I would bend forward on the front foot, then rock back and go into the swing, which was good for rhythm. I decided this was wasted motion and I later dispensed with it. Hopman also taught Rosewall this same rock, which is very appar-ent on his delivery. Gonzales and Hoad, however, start on the back foot and have no swaying motion.

Many of the Aussies seem to have acquired a peculiarity native to our country. Rex Hartwig, Ken Rosewall and Lew Hoad keep their elbow close into their side just before the hit. Lew has a good serve and an excellent action despite this, but I feel Ken and Rex could improve their delivery by raising that elbow above the right shoulder as do Gonzales and Trabert.

Gonzales and Hoad have perfect weight distribution at the hit. As I said before, my hips are already into the court before impact. Tony Trabert also starts leaning in quickly. Trabert has another peculiarity of twisting his body too far around from the court.

If I had to choose the best serve I ever encountered, it would be a toss-up between Gonzales's and Kramer's. I never saw Ellsworth Vines, but I believe his delivery was on the same high level. My third choice is left-handed Jaroslav Drobny. His serve was a classic. He could bamboozle you with it more than any other player. He could use a kick, slice or flat serve all in the same game, and they would all get results—i.e., they would force an error. The fourth best service belonged to Bob Falkenburg, who had a nice rhythmical action and who could hit unbelievable serving streaks. During this period, his first serve was as good as Pancho's. Lew Hoad is my choice for No. 5, followed by Geoff Brown at No. 6. Geoff had a fantastic service for a man of his relatively short height. However, he used a lot of unnecessary energy on the wind-up. As a result, he would start off like a whirlwind, but at the end of the fifth set he would be thoroughly exhausted.

There are others with good deliveries. Barry MacKay has a fine action and he uses his height well. He goes for aces on the second service all the time, and this may or may not pay off; when he is serving well he wins, but otherwise double-faults can cost him the match. Billy Talbert has a fine delivery. He can disguise direction with that short swing. Dick Savitt's heavy serve is hit extremely well. He found the short swing the most effective, and he eliminated all preliminary wind-ups. Budge Patty's serve is similar to Talbert's. It is harder to handle than most because it bounces low and has a lot of sidespin. The action is not as smooth as Bill's but it is just as effective.

There are two serves that have not looked impressive to the spectator but which were reasonably good when all factors were considered. Pancho Segura is a little fellow who gets the most out of his height. He holds the racket at the very end, with the butt hitting the middle of his palm. Jack Bromwich never had an offensive delivery, but he kept the ball low, he always got his first serve into play and it was always well directed. Neither Pancho nor Jack ever hit a loose serve.

The average player should remember the examples of Bromwich and Segura when tempted to go for a big first serve. Most club players will attempt a tremendous first delivery, but if it never looks like getting in, it is a waste. A player should hit the serve as hard as he can while still being able to maintain control.

I believe the twist service to be a dangerous one. It can go short and get the server in trouble, particularly against an opponent who is good off the ground. Only Drobny, Gonzales and Hoad could combine speed and placement with the twist for effective use. The slice is an easy one to learn and it can be hit with good pace. The ball stays low and moves off the court rather than directly to the opponent.

There are several factors common to the serves of Kramer, Gonzales and Hoad. There have been relatively good serves where all these factors were not included, but I would consider them reasonably essential for a big delivery. First, the weight starts on the back foot and does not transfer forward until the moment of the hit. Secondly, the body should be sideways to the net. Third, the tip of the butt end of the racket is held inside the palm so that no edge is projecting. Fourth, the elbow points upward at the end of the backswing. There have been good servers such as Vic Seixas who choked the racket, faced the net and leaned forward before delivery. You may be able to get away with an idiosyncrasy, but you'll need the talent of a Seixas to pull it off successfully.

QUALITIES THAT MAKE A WINNING PLAYER

by Doris Hart

Much has been written on the basic fundamentals for the beginning tennis player. I, too, could write reams on how to hit a forehand or backhand, or how to serve, but I don't intend to do so here. Certainly, I accept the fact that one must learn the proper strokes to become a good player. But what about those who have mastered the strokes but lack or know little about the qualities that make up a winning player? I believe that too much emphasis has been placed upon the beginner and not enough on the more advanced player in the texts and articles and advice treatises. Therefore, I would like to share with the more advanced players some of the things I have learned in my years of playing tennis. . . .

Learning to play a really outstanding game of tennis is like learning any other art or skill. You may have instruction for an hour every day, but then you spend at least three hours practicing. To develop all the shots in tennis you must also have expert instruction and then practice, practice, and practice. You may be one of those fortunates blessed with natural aptitude for the sport. You find that it is not too difficult to make certain strokes, and your progress is more rapid then that of the average beginner. But that is no reason to grow lax and consider practice periods a waste of time. Maureen Connolly, a great champion at twenty, practiced five hours a day. Surely if a champion believes in constant practice, that must be an indication of how important it is.

As in any career, many sacrifices are required to get ahead in tennis, but they are well worth making, believe me. If you learn this at an early age, your rewards will be great. But there are many who work diligently and yet never quite make the grade. Even though you may never reach championship heights you will still get many advantages from your prowess in tennis. No other amateur sport affords the same opportunities for travel and for meeting interesting people all over the world. Tennis is a form of education in itself.

Now that I have made it clear how I feel about tennis, let us move ahead.

Let us say that you are progressing and decide that you are ready for tournament competition. This is the best way to put into practice all that you know about the game, and learn more about tennis. Tournament play produces many important factors for winning tennis. The main ones are tactics, concentration, and experience.

I am assuming that you are past the beginner stage and on the way to becoming a good player. You are playing tournaments now but for some reason you are not getting positive results. Physically you outshine your opponents, mentally you are considered above average, you practice hard and spend many hours on the court. Yet there is something lacking. What is it? I honestly believe that almost every player has experienced this situation.

The day usually comes (unfortunately not for everyone) when you seem to find the key to your problems. Actually, it is a combination of certain qualities that you have developed through competition. Use of tactics is one. Tactics play an important role in tennis. Without tactics, how can you win? There are a few instances when sheer physical force may win a match. For example, playing against a rabbit (tennis slang for a bad player) you can win just by hitting the ball with great speed even though you make numerous errors. The outcome is usually certain against such an inferior player.

But if you play that same type of game against a player of your own caliber, what then? You would certainly have to change the slam-bang routine and begin to use tactics, or all would be lost. Haven't you often seen a player hit the ball with beautiful flowing strokes, executing every shot in the book, and yet lose to a hacker (slang for an unorthodox player) who hits the ball entirely wrong and against all forms of stroke production ever taught? The player who possesses both correct stroke production and tactics has an excellent opportunity to succeed.

Tactics are simply a form of planning. If your opponent has an outstanding weakness, then by using tactics you play that weakness. You try to analyze your opponent's game in order to detect any flaws in his mode of play. Most players prefer to play an offensive type of game, but you must be able to resort to defensive tactics when the situation requires. I always found that the best way to discover any weakness against a new opponent is to make him hit every shot during the five-minute warm-up before the match. Naturally, if you have played your opponent before, then you should have a good idea as to how you will play him.

As the game progresses you may have to alter your tactics. Perhaps you found a slight weakness in the forehand and suddenly that shot became stronger. Do you continue to play the forehand? If you do, you may find yourself on the losing end of the match. But do remember one very important point: *Never change a winning game.*

I myself have been a victim of this costly mistake. Having a secure lead I have at times decided to try out that new drop shot or that down-the-line forehand I had been practicing. Before I knew it, I had lost control of the match and allowed my opponent to raise his game and go on to victory.

This is a common fault and only through constant competition can it be overcome. But it cannot be accomplished without thinking, and thinking involves *concentration*. Unless your thoughts are entirely concerned with the strokes and other factors of the game, you cannot produce top form. Yet it is almost impossible to teach a player to think. It is entirely the individual's problem, but you can encourage and suggest concentration. When you become a good player, thinking and instinct go hand in hand. Everything comes to you automatically.

Mercer Beasley, a great coach who did much for my tennis, once told me, "Doris, if you had only started thinking years ago, the game would have been much easier for you." How true! Again I quote "Beas": "Why make things hard when there is an easy way?" A good player can make an inferior player move about the court as if he were dangling on a string, and this mainly because the top player not only controls all the shots but thinks out a system for putting his opponent out of position in order to reduce the running on his own part. I am sure that you have witnessed this scene many times. It is a tragi-comic situation.

Frank Parker, a great champion, was noted for his powers of concentration. It was said that you could almost see him thinking out loud, so intense was his concentration. Maureen Connolly had the greatest concentration of any woman player in the world. Also, she never considered a match won or lost until the last point had been played. Shirley Fry is another exponent of this very important and necessary quality.

For years I suffered from a lack of concentration. I tried hard to overcome this fault, but for some reason my thoughts would wander and this had a definite effect on my game. In between points I would find myself watching the match on the court next to mine or gazing off into the stands to see if I recognized anyone! Things like this tend to break up any concentration that you may have, and at that time I had very little. Fortunately I overcame this failing, but it took years.

I was often accused of letting up in a match and not going all out to defeat my opponent. I soon learned that the will to win was important, and the so-called killer instinct had to be developed. You may classify this as a form of temperament. And temperament certainly enters into the make-up of sportsmanship. . . .

Now we come to the fighter in tennis competition. . . . By fighting I mean a form of determination to win no matter how black the outlook. It is no disgrace to lose if you have given your best effort and fought to the end. However, to lose a match without trying and to give in because your chances of victory are slim develop a reputation for poor sportsmanship for the offending player. This kind of player always has a million excuses to explain his losses and lacks the guts to go down to defeat fighting. A fighting spirit is essential, and if you are incapable of acquiring this valuable asset, then your hopes of ever becoming a great champion are indeed limited.

The old adage of learning from one's mistakes applies to tennis, too. After winning or losing a match you must analyze your game and figure out the shots that you scored with the most, or how your opponent was able to defeat you. This method will help you overcome any weakness that may stand in your path to success. One thing of which you can be certain is that your opponent will not divulge the secret of how he defeated you! That is a problem for you alone to solve. This can be called experience.

They say in all walks of life that experience is the best teacher. Have you ever seen a junior player winning or extending a champion in a tournament match? If so, you probably said to yourself, "He can't possibly win. He will tighten up and lose because he is playing the champion." From my own experience when a junior, I know that this is a most natural reaction when competing against a top-flight player. The reason for the champion's winning is *experience*. He is able to make the right shot at the right time. He never hurries or forces himself into errors. He feels confident, while the junior keeps thinking to himself that he cannot possibly continue playing such good tennis. Actually, as far as being able to hit all the shots, he could do so, but being able to produce the winning shots is difficult for the junior. Some people assume that the junior is suffering from a bad case of nerves, or to use the tennis slang, the lock, steel elbow, choke—or, as the Australians put it, the waving waddies! Actually it is none of these. The novice is not capable of defeating a first-class player, and the paralyzing thought creeps into his mind and affects his game at the critical moments.

But there are cases of steel elbow and the like in tennis matches. I've experienced a slight tightening of the arm a few times myself. On such occasions you find it difficult to stroke the ball properly. Some players find it impossible to play championship tennis. In championship play you must have complete control over your nerves at all times, no matter how tremendous the strain involved.

Under pressure everyone reacts differently, but one can usually distinguish a champion by his coolness and control under trying conditions. Every player, from the champion to the rabbit, experiences nerves before an important match in some form or another. Sometimes the attack may come even during the match. Anyone who denies this is not being quite honest. The nerves symptoms show in a variety of ways. One person may have trouble eating—it's just impossible to swallow. Pauline Betz would often lose her lunch before a match and could never control her jitters until the match began. Sometimes a player will be found laughing or talking too much, or his hand will be shaking so badly you wonder how he will be able to hold on to his racket. These are telltale symptoms of nerves, plain to any other player who has probably experienced them in his own time.

However, once the match begins, most players usually lose their nervousness. They start concentrating on the game and soon forget about everything but the immediate problem of hitting the ball over the net and placing it where their opponent isn't.

These are but a few of the many problems you will encounter in the game of tennis. But, if you have the ability to devise tactics, master the power of single-minded concentration on the game in progress, gain all the experience you possibly can, and never cease to strive to improve the quality of your game, then, I believe, you are on the road to success. Even to championship! And I wish you luck. Sincerely.

A NEW VIEW OF GRIPS

by Tony Trabert

Sometimes a top player will tell you that he has just changed his forehand grip. His statement is accurate but subject to explanation; he has not made an absolute switch, viz., from Eastern to Continental, and the change is not as prominent to the outsider as it is to the player. He has *modified* his grip, but the change to him is violent since it gives him an extraordinary new "feel." Sometimes all he has done is to spread his fingers more and switch an eighth of a turn, but to him the change appears radical.

These modified alterations in grips can be of great help to a player who has been having a problem with a stroke. The first premise to accept in making such changes is that there is no such thing as a perfect grip suitable to every player. For several decades American coaches have overemphasized the importance of the Eastern forehand. They ignore the most prominent fact in post-war tennis, which is that almost every great Australian player has had a semi-Continental forehand. My own theory is never to change a natural grip unless the player is having problems with it, e.g., he has been having long spells of "no feel" or it wilts under pressure.

Here is an example of what can be done to help a player with a forehand problem. In this particular case, the player has an Eastern grip but for the last two years he has had less and less success with the stroke. Sometimes he plays the ball too close to the body, sometimes his wrist is wobbly and sometimes his preparation is late. This last factor is not indigenous to the Eastern but, strangely enough, his lack of confidence on the stroke may cause late preparation. The player is asked to experiment with a slight variation in grip; even if he decides to stick with the old, he will at least get the feel of a new type of approach. In other words, he does not have to commit himself to a permanent change unless the experiment proves something to him.

The change offered to this player is relatively minor: he moves the "V" between thumb and forefinger leftwards so it is almost on top of the racket and at the same time he spreads his fingers more (the forefinger, from being wrapped around the racket, now points toward the racket head). He still will have to "switch," i.e., move his hand more to the left, when he hits a backhand, but his forehand is now "approaching" the Continental.

Within 15 or 20 minutes the player will know whether he likes the new grip. He may find it gives him more power, that it enables him to hit down-the-line with greater ease, that he is no longer taking the ball too close to his body. More important still, that wrist wobble which was so evident in his extreme Eastern may now work to his advantage in the semi-Continental; he has acquired a *controlled wrist action*.

It is up to the player, not to the teacher or coach, to decide after a fair experiment if he wants to return to the old grip or accept the new. The suggestion of switching the grip should never be made to *any* player with a confident stroke, no matter how unorthodox or extreme the old grip appears to be. It is only when a stroke has repeatedly failed the player for a long period of time that the thought of switching grips should enter the picture. Leave the solid, big Western or the firm Eastern or the confident Continental alone. Experiments in changes are for the unsolid, wobbly, hesitant stroker only.

THE LOB: HOW TO AND WHEN

by Chuck McKinley

Young players underrate the importance of the lob. They do not recognize its uses nor the effects it can have on the outcome of a match. When I was a junior and I watched such pros as Gonzales and Segura, I noticed only the big serve, the big volleys and the hard-hit balls; I was unaware of the effectiveness of the lob as used by them, since my mind was oriented only to power play. I did not realize the value of the shot: the player with a great lob will *pass* the net man more often because the latter is worried about the threat of a ball going over his head. . . .

Manuel Santana, the 1966 Wimbledon Champion, is one of the best lobbers in the game. So is Roy Emerson, the No. 1 Australian. He is especially effective off the backhand because he passes so well and his opponent can never judge when he will be lobbing. Rafael Osuna also lobs to good advantage, but with him it is more a matter of necessity since he does not have the great ground strokes of a Santana. Dennis Ralston has a fine lob although he does not use it as often as he should. One of the greatest players of all time, Maureen Connolly, had a magnificent lob. Through the use of the lob her ground strokes became even bigger. She was murderous off forehand and backhand, but she could loft a ball over her opponent's head as well. If I know my opponent will never lob, I will get so close to net that I can cut off almost every passing shot. If I, who am a small player, can do this, think what Pancho Gonzales can do against an opponent who never lobs!

Among the pros, Pancho Segura is probably the best lobber. He holds his forehand until the last minute, then hangs a lob over his opponent's head. This is the reason that Gonzales calls the Segura forehand one of the best shots in the game. Segoo can dump it at your feet, belt one by you or loft it over your head with the same motion. It is a most deceptive shot, which is the criterion of a good offensive lob. Both Rod Laver and Ken Rosewall make tremendous use of the lob. Gonzales also lobs well but it is often an unnoticed part of his game. . . . Laver, Rosewall and Gonzales can do something else besides hitting hard.

There are four occasions when you must lob. First, lob when you are in deep trouble to stay in the point. Second, lob when a player gets too close to net (even if you hit the shot badly) to make him stay back. If you don't have a knack for the lob, you still must use it. Third, lob to change the pace of the match. Fourth, lob for tactical reasons. If your opponent has a bad overhead, lob him. Not every player, even in the top echelon, has a good overhead. . . . Even if the opponent has an excellent overhead, one must lob to keep him honest. . . . Great lobbers of the past include Bobby Riggs and Bitsy Grant. . . .

When Butch Buchholz and I were young players, we met Ramanathan Krishnan and Naresh Kumar in the first round of the Wimbledon Doubles. The Indians found they could not volley with us and so they began to lob on almost every point. Butch and I had good overheads but, as the match progressed, it became exceedingly difficult to hit them. It was one of the toughest matches I have ever played and we only won in five long sets. . . .

The man who can couple lobbing ability with good passing shots and sound ground strokes has a tremendous advantage. The ability to lob alone will not win for you. No one shot can win a match.

There are two kinds of lobs, the offensive and the defensive, and there are three ways to hit them—with overspin, underspin or no spin. Santana, Laver and I use overspin effectively as an offensive shot. An overspin lob is usually an outright winner if the player does not touch it since it is almost impossible to chase the ball down once it has gone over your head. The actual stroke production of the overspin lob begins just as a regular ground stroke; it looks like an overspin forehand or backhand and only the follow-through is different. Therefore it catches the opponent by surprise. I felt that my use of the overspin lob was the turning point in my final against Fred Stolle at Wimbledon. . . .

Once the overspin lob bounces, it jumps away from the court. If you let it bounce, you are in bad trouble. You have to decide whether to hit it on the fly, and the indecision as to what to do can cause you to make an error.

The underspin lobs tends to bounce straight up. However, it can still be an offensive shot. It can be hit lower, with just enough height to get it over the opponent's head. A player with an underspin backhand should use an underspin lob because it will be more deceptive. Gonzales therefore uses underspin on his backhand lob. Santana is one of the very few players who can topspin a backhand lob. The topspin lob accelerates when it bounces, whereas the underspin lob slows up.

The offensive lob is used to win a point and therefore it has to be deceptive. The stroke production must be similar to the passing shot of the player; otherwise it will not fool anyone. Emerson comes closest to hitting a "no spin" offensive lob on his backhand. He simply lofts the ball over his opponent's head. I do not recommend this shot because it requires a great deal of feel; most players need spin control for the lob. . . .

I developed an offensive lob by watching Santana and Laver. One day, when I was practicing with Dennis Ralston, I said jokingly: "Let me show you my Santana and Laver lob." I tried it and, to my surprise, it worked. It became one of the most effective shots in my game.

A vital factor in lobbing is preparation, regardless of what kind of lob you hit. Almost every great lobber has the ability to get the racket back quickly, thus disguising the shot. The lob need not always be disguised. For example, there are times when you must hit a straight defensive lob; it is evident that this is going to be your tactic since you can barely get to the ball. When you do have the time, the quicker you can prepare, the more apt your opponent will be to look for a passing shot. The element of surprise is just as important as depth in a lob. . . . Preparation means not only getting the racket back quickly but getting the feet in position as though for a passing shot. This preparation is important not only for good execution of the lob but for all shots.

Although all tactical statements have their exceptions, I would say that, as a rule, you should not lob when you are standing well inside the baseline and the shot coming to you is not pressing. The court is shorter and the passing shot here will be more effective.

Everyone tries for depth on the lob. The nearer the ball lands toward the baseline, the better the shot is. However, there are varieties of height on the lob. It depends upon the situation and the type of lob.

Most players train themselves to lob over the backhand. However, a player limits himself if he only practices lobs to the backhand side which, theoretically, is the most difficult lob to return since the opponent has to go to the backhand corner. One must be able to lob over the forehand of the opponent as well since this becomes important in doubles or when one faces a lefty in singles.

After you have lobbed, you must decide how far behind the baseline you will stand to retrieve the ball. It depends, of course, on the type of overhead your opponent hits. He may angle, he may hit deep or he may aim for one side of the court only. His overhead may be very powerful or not so strong but well placed. All of these factors have a bearing on your position. For example, you would not stand in the same place to return an Osuna overhead as you would to return an Emerson overhead. Osuna angles rather than overpowers, whereas Emerson normally hits very hard and deep. Additionally, you must keep in mind the type of court you are playing on. On clay you have more time because the ball comes off the court more slowly. Cement, grass and wood are much faster.

If you have lobbed over your opponent's head successfully, my suggestion is that you move to net to try to cut off the return. All you need is an adequate volley. Your opponent is moving away from the court, perhaps with his back to you. In such a situation it does not take much of a volley to end the point. Keep in mind that not too many players, once the ball has gone over their heads, will try a passing shot. The normal return will be a lob.

The lob is a full stroke. One of the common faults in lobbing is the lack of follow-through. Every great player who hits a bad lob will question himself as to whether or not he has failed to follow through. The lob is not a short, quick stroke; it requires a long finish. The control comes in this follow-through. The backswing is the same as the backswing of your ground stroke. . . . The follow-through of the lob is slightly more elevated than that of a passing shot. You end higher but you do not hit the ball straight up in the air. Don't think about hitting the ball upwards but rather think "forward and upwards." The lob that goes straight up and ends short is a loser.

The lob is not used often enough in doubles today, and this is most unfortunate. Great teams in the past such as Mulloy and Talbert, Kramer and Schroeder or George Lott and any of his various partners, used the lob to great effect. Normally in doubles it is a defense-oriented shot because there is so much volleying in tandem play. But a lob off return of serve is very effective. One should also lob when in trouble because it is difficult for the opponents to hit an overhead by or between two players who have only half the court to cover. The Australians have always been great lobbers in doubles. John Bromwich had a particularly well-disguised doubles lob. Neale Fraser was an excellent lobber and his partner, Roy Emerson, would do the rest by standing on top of the net and picking off the balls.

The lob can be overdone. If the opponent knows that there is no threat of anything but the lob, he will be ready and patient enough to win every point. But our young players are not guilty of overlobbing; they do not lob enough. It is the least used stroke in their repertoire. When I learned to lob, I felt for the first time I could develop into a complete player. Without a lob a player can conceivably play a great match, but why do it the hard way?

THE OVERHEAD

by Chuck McKinley

In an earlier article I discussed the importance of the lob as a primary tactic. The riposte of the lob is the overhead, and the reply to a man who lobs very well is to hit an overhead that is a winner.

Every net-rusher must have a good overhead, but even the non-volleyers have to acquire a smash adequate enough to end the point. The function of the overhead is to end the point, not necessarily by smashing hard but by depth or angle. If you are unable to put away your overhead, anyone with tennis intelligence will lob high and, hopefully, with depth; if you simply put the ball back in play, you are starting the point all over again and have lost the advantage of the attack.

There have been only a handful of players among the many in top-flight competition who did not have good overheads. . . .

I would never have been able to go to net because of my size (5'8") if I had not been able to hit a good overhead. It was strong enough to keep a lot of players from lobbing me and I was therefore able to get much closer to net and to be more effective when volleying. Pancho Gonzales has one of the great overheads of all time. He goes back very quickly, which is one of the main factors in hitting an overhead well (to get into position as quickly as possible). Gonzales both hits the ball hard and places it well. Ken Rosewall has a good overhead but uses a different style. He does not powder the ball but places it so well that even if you get to it you are in an uncomfortable position and have to hit another defensive lob instead of a passing shot. One doesn't necessarily have to be a net-rusher in order to hit a good overhead. Dick Savitt, the Wimbledon Champion in 1951, had a great overhead although he was not a serve-and-volley player. He ended the point when he hit the smash. Even baseline players must work on the overhead since there are so many times when they must go to net.

The smash is not as important in the women's game. . . . Normally women do not attack as much as the men, although the best of today's players—Billie Jean King, Maria Bueno and Margaret Smith—attack constantly and have excellent overheads which they hit with pace and accuracy. The majority of women play back, coming in only on the short ball, and therefore the need for a good overhead is not as great. Nancy Richey and Lesley Turner are not particularly strong overhead because their ventures to net are infrequent. . . .

In the execution of the overhead, the most important factor is to get into position as quickly as possible. This is true of all strokes but particularly so on the overhead since it is vital to get back from the net quickly; otherwise the lob will go over your head and you will lose the dominating position of the net. Once you are in the proper position, you can hit the ball with authority and control.

The grip for the overhead should be the one that is most natural for you. I believe this is true for all strokes. The comfortable grip for you will probably be somewhere between your backhand and forehand grip, leaning a bit toward the backhand. In other words, it approximates a Continental, although any grip is satisfactory as long as you hit the overhead well.

Footwork is vitally important in preparation. Your weight should be on the balls of your feet. Many times you are going to have to jump for the overhead. This requires precise timing and therefore a great deal of practice. It isn't easy to hit a jump overhead. Ideally, you don't want to jump if you don't have to and yet it is extremely important to go *up* for the ball. Never wait for the lob to come down since the ball may come close to your body and force you to hit in cramped fashion. Your arm is bent rather than straight when the ball gets too close, and your body is hunched instead of stretching so that it is difficult to hit through the ball.

The backswing on the overhead is shorter than on the serve, although there is the same full follow-through. The reason for the short wind-up is that the lob is coming down from a great height and this requires precise timing. The bigger the preparatory swing, the less precision. Instead of taking the racket back with a circular motion, lift it quickly, and let it drop behind your shoulder in the "back-scratching" position. This abbreviated preparation allows you to hit the ball with less worry about the timing.

The follow-through is very much the same as on the serve. The ball is hit approximately in the same position that you would hit the serve although at times, due to the effectiveness of the lob, you cannot hit it exactly where you would choose. Ideally speaking, you would like to hit it slightly to your right and a little in front of you if you are a right-hander. Go up after it and make contact before it cramps you to the point where you cannot extend your arm fully on the hit. If, when the ball is coming down, you did not swing but let it drop, it should hit you on the top of your head or on your right shoulder.

One of the most difficult balls to hit is a very high lob which arches deep into the court. First, you have to back up quickly and, second, you have to hit a ball that is coming straight down, which is never easy. Most lobs are not that tough. When the very high lob would land inside the service line, I would let the ball bounce rather than try to hit it on the fly, which is difficult from the viewpoint of timing. If the ball is going very deep, generally you should not let it bounce. However, on a windy day when the ball is blowing all over the place, you might want to let the ball bounce to decrease the possibility of error. I often let the ball bounce because I knew I could hit a bouncing overhead from practically any spot in the court. Some players do not like to let the ball bounce, and yet a bouncing overhead can sometimes be easier to hit than one where the ball is falling rapidly. Some players feel that you should never let the overhead bounce because you then relinquish your position at net. This theory has a great deal of validity except for the player who can hit the bouncing overhead very well or when the conditions warrant letting the ball bounce. The procedure for hitting the ball after it bounces is exactly the same as for the overhead taken in the air, except that you can take a little larger backswing. Still, the simpler the backswing, the better.

All overheads should be hit flat or with very little spin. If you are going to put any spin on the ball, use slice. If you do slice, the ball will still carry after it bounces instead of slowing up as it would if you tried to put twist on it.

The most important factor in an overhead is consistency. It will help you to win many matches because, even if you cannot knock the ball out of play, you have not made an error and thereby lost the point. You can build a big overhead by starting from consistency. Gradually you learn to hit the ball harder, deeper and in the correct spot. Of these four attributes of the good overhead—consistency, depth, placement and pace—the most important is consistency. Next comes placement. If your opponent is on one side of the court and he has lobbed, the other side of the court is wide open. You must know how to hit to either side. At times an angle overhead or a straight-down-the-middle or a straight-down-the-sideline is the correct shot, depending upon where your opponent is and how far back in the court you are standing. If you are back near the baseline, it is going to be very difficult to angle the ball and you would be better off hitting your overhead either straight down the middle of the court or straight down one of the sidelines. If you try to hit a sharp angle, you will have trouble clearing the net.

You should hit the overhead just at that pace where you can still control it. The emphasis is on the control. Sometimes you will aim for depth but there are situations when you will want to hit the ball and angle it off. Generally, if you are going to angle to try to knock the overhead by your opponent, go for depth. When you get a short overhead which would bounce inside the service line, you must decide whether you are going to hit it in the air or let it bounce. The one overhead your opponent can never return is one that you bounce over the fence. In practice you may not want to bounce the ball out of the court boundaries and thereby lose the ball, but in a tournament you don't care. You simply want to win the point.

Among players who primarily use placement and depth is Rafe Osuna, who specializes in angling off overheads rather than hitting them hard. Players who depend primarily on speed in hitting the overhead are Roy Emerson and myself. I hit the overhead quite well and hard, but Roy has a little bit of difficulty with the high lob. This is because of his long wind-up, which puts him in trouble when the ball is coming straight down. Whenever you run into a player with a big wind-up on the overhead, I would advise you to lob very high.

There are times when you should not hit an overhead. If a lob has caught you by surprise, it is difficult to struggle back and risk the chance of an error in trying to hit an overhead. Let the ball bounce, go back and play a defensive shot, probably a lob because your opponent has undoubtedly closed in at net; if you try a passing shot, the chances for error are too great. If it is a windy day, let more overheads bounce. If you have a tremendous wind behind you and the lob is not too high, the wind will hold the ball up sufficiently so that you can run back, play a groundstroke and come right back into net.

Every young player should practice both lobs and overheads. The success or downfall of many of our players in top-flight competition depends upon their mastery of these two shots. If you want to practice your overhead, find someone who wants to practice his lob. . . . This practice is essential to the development of a good overhead. One must give it a great deal of time and patience because there are so many factors involved in developing a smash. There is not only stroke production and timing but also the difficulty of returning a high, deep lob and a bounce overhead under windy conditions. It requires practice and more practice.

In a long five-set tennis match you will have to hit many overheads. You will be in good condition if you have regularly practiced the overhead. . . .

Frequently you will run up against someone who has a great overhead. Then you must make your lobs a little better. But the lob is only effective if you are hitting good passing shots. When I play against someone who has a good overhead, I do not necessarily lob him. Instead I try to lob just when he is expecting me to hit a passing shot. This is not as easy as it sounds, but if you do not lob him, he will close in to the net and you will have much more difficulty in passing him, even though he may not be a good volleyer.

After you have lobbed, what do you do? If you have hit a deep lob, do not retreat in the court, because it is very difficult for a player to knock away an overhead from a position near the baseline. If he hits the overhead from deep in the court, you may catch him trying to get back to net with a ball at his feet, which is always a tough shot. . . . It is difficult to outguess a player when he is hitting an overhead because, after all, he knows where he is hitting it and you do not. I always tried to learn where my opponent liked to hit his overhead and as I watched him play other matches I would mentally make a note of any tendency to hit crosscourt, to the backhand, down-the-line or wherever, depending upon his position and the kind of lob he was given. If he does have a pattern, one can spot it by careful observation.

The overhead is one of the most important shots in the game of doubles. When I played with Dennis Ralston I never had to worry whether he would miss when he went back to smash, and I would close in and try to pick off the weak return or the lob that would follow. But if you have no confidence in your partner or if he does not have a good overhead, you would be a little leery of playing in on the next shot since your partner might not hit the overhead hard enough to elicit a weak return. Hit the overhead to the spot where it is easiest to win the point. This is a matter of judgment, which is true of all tennis shots. But there will be certain times when your opponents leave the middle open. If they have covered the middle, then you can angle off the overhead. The difficulty of the lob will be your criterion as to where you should hit the ball.

In doubles you rarely hit an overhead softly. You might be afraid to hit one of the opponents, but you must hit the ball hard enough even though one of the opponents is standing or might be moving to the point where you are aiming. Big-time doubles is an aggressive game. You never deliberately aim at an opponent but if you ease up for fear of hitting him, he will run in front of your overheads and knock them off. I emphasize again that I am not advocating hitting the overhead at an opponent. I never did that in my entire playing career. But you must hit the overhead with authority and you cannot worry about an opponent if he happens to run in the direction where you are hitting. A baseball pitcher will occasionally throw a ball inside, not because he is trying to knock the batter down but to let him know that he is not always going to have it his way.

Sometimes in doubles it is hard to decide whether you or your partner should take the overhead. As a general rule, the player in the left court (the man playing the backhand side) has a better view of a ball that is coming down the middle of the court and of what the opponents are doing. He is not backing away or moving to his left; he is going to his right to hit the ball. It would be the reverse for left-handers. In doubles competition with my partner, Dennis Ralston, we always let the other know who was going to hit the ball. If Dennis said "Mine" I would let him hit it. If I said "Mine," even though I might have to go a little farther, Dennis knew from experience that in my judgment I would hit the ball and win the point. If one player has a better overhead than the other, he should hit the majority of overheads provided it is convenient and the ball is in the right spot. . . .

Regardless of your stature in tennis or the maturity of your game, the overhead is vital. A player without an overhead, just like a player without a lob, is missing something basic in his overall game structure. I was very fortunate in that my tennis coach, Bill Price of St. Louis, got me started at a very young age in learning the overhead. He told me: "You are not as tall as the others and therefore you have to hit an overhead better than anyone else." I learned through hard work and good teaching. These are the two factors that will determine how far you go in acquiring any stroke.

Among the important points to remember are position, grip, the ability to get under the ball, when to let it bounce, when not to let it bounce, how to hit an overhead in doubles, how to hit an overhead in singles, when not to hit an overhead and *the importance of consistency*. When I was playing tournament tennis, I never thought of consistency; I only thought of ending the point. But keep in mind that I had worked hundreds of hours hitting overheads to the point where I never had to be afraid that a player would lob when I came to net. Because my opponents had respect for my overhead I was able to volley that much better although I did not have the reach of other players nor the height on hitting overheads. Never let a coach tell you that you are too short to develop a net game. You are never too short if you can hit an overhead, and this you can learn through hard work. You can compensate for any deficiency, whether it be physical or lack of soundness of the stroke, through hard work. Hard work and desire will go a long way in developing a good overhead—or any other stroke.

THE RETURN OF SERVE

by Dennis Ralston

The return of serve is the second most important stroke in tennis; only the serve takes priority. Basically it must have consistency since you are bound to lose every game in which you receive if 50% of your returns are errors. The great players are not only consistent but they either have penetration on the return or superb accuracy or enough touch to put the server in difficulty. But first and foremost, the return of serve goes in.

There is no one way to return serve. It depends upon the kind of player you are and whether or not you are weak or strong in one department. For example, most players do not have the groundstroke equipment or the timing to return serve consistently by pounding drives off big deliveries

(Don Budge and Dick Savitt were exceptions). Some drive off one side and chip off another, some lob, some underspin and some topspin. One player with a truly fine return of serve did nothing but chip or hack, but he was athletic and a great competitor with a feel for where the ball should go. This was Vic Seixas, winner of Forest Hills and Wimbledon. Most players would not deliberately imitate Vic and could not possibly copy Don Budge. However, there are a few elements common to both players which can be an asset to anyone.

When you return serve, your thoughts should be only on watching the ball coming off your opponent's racket. Your eyes and mind are keyed to the ball, not to what you will say if you win the match or what the score will be if you win that point. If the serve is a big one, you do not have time to think about what you will do with the ball; your movement has to be "instinctive." This comes only from hitting thousands and thousands of returns of serve on both fast surfaces and slow ones. A third element common to all good returns of serve is the posture: feet are spread 12" to 18", knees are flexed (slightly or to a great extent), the racket points more or less in the direction of the net and the racket head is up rather than down. Now that I have stated the three factors which I believe to be basic to a good return of serve—concentration, instinctive hitting and a good ready position—I would like to mention the variations that are frequently seen.

When returning serve in the forehand court, I generally stand a foot or more from the forehand alley line; when returning in the backhand court, my position is right by the alley line to tempt the server to hit wide to my forehand. Most players with good backhand returns of serve will place themselves as I do, but those who have mighty forehands and relatively weak backhands will leave even more of a forehand opening on either side. Before Frank Froehling developed a good backhand, he would stand inside the alley when receiving serve in the backhand court and he waited with a forehand grip. It was as though he were saying: "Okay, guys, serve to my forehand." He opened up his forehand side because he would have done anything to keep from hitting a backhand. Pancho Segura has one of the best forehands in the game and he still runs around as many backhand returns of serve as possible to clobber a two-handed forehand. I offer the server a little room to entice him to hit to my forehand and I run around backhand returns of serve more than most of the players (Froehling and Segura excepted). But the average top player has a better backhand return of serve than a forehand. It is not that the latter is bad; it is often more forceful but, conversely, it is less consistent.

The spot where you stand—inside the baseline or behind it—on return of serve depends upon a) the server, b) the surface and c) your own ability to take the ball on the rise. Rafe Osuna was quick enough (and brave enough) to stand way in, even on grass against a big serve. But in his famous match against Froehling in the finals of Forest Hills he often took up his position 15 feet behind the baseline since Frank could only hit the serve hard and deep and could neither angle nor dink it. I have heard that Herb Flam played 10 feet back on return of serve against Dick Savitt on grass. I do not know of any other players, other than Osuna and Flam, who elected to play this far back. Osuna played far in frequently because he felt his eye was quick enough to take the net off his own return. Alex Olmedo is the only current pro who returns serve from well inside the baseline. Most of the other touring pros stand neither well in nor way back; they move in on second serve and they stand back against a big server. I sometimes stand a little farther back than most, especially if my opponent is serving well or if I am having trouble seeing the ball because it is growing dark or the lights are bad.

When I was a young boy, I learned to play on cement and one of my frequent opponents was my dad. He had a big topspin serve and I could not handle it until I stepped in and took it on the rise. I could now get it before it spun away, and the taking of the serve on the rise was invaluable to me when playing on grass.

The knees are never stiff when you are waiting for the service. Still, one hears stories of the great Art Larsen who stood for delivery with the casual air of a man waiting for a bus. His feet were together, he stood straight and his racket dangled by his side with the head pointing to the ground. Of course it is possible to turn sideways or hold your racket over your shoulder like a sergeant on parade, but why make it more difficult? If the idea is to give yourself a handicap, you might try closing your eyes and not opening them until the serve has been hit.

Most players will bend their knees more on grass, where the bounce is low, than on clay or cement. I crouch on grass, but my knees are only slightly flexed on other surfaces. Again, if I am receiving a big serve, I stand two feet behind the baseline and the knees and back are only slightly bent. Although I am not aware of it, I have been told that I start in a crouched or semi-crouched position and then I straighten up as the serve is hit. . . . I never move after taking my position unless I plan to run around the backhand and take the serve on the forehand.

Most players with good returns of serve keep both feet on the ground as they receive. Ken Rosewall has an excellent return of serve (as I write this article, he has not missed a backhand return of serve in two weeks) and he never takes his feet off the ground. However, pictures of Don Budge show him returning serve off the backhand with both feet in the air. If you have a backhand return of serve like Don's you can dance a *pas de deux* and still hit a winner.

The racket head should be pointed upward and toward the net. If it points toward your backhand alley, you are going to be slow in getting the racket back for a forehand return. If the racket head points down, you have an extra motion of raising it after the serve has been hit. The serve will often come so fast that you will be late.

Players with an Eastern forehand usually wait with a forehand grip. I have a Continental and so my backhand and forehand grips are the same. Occasionally on clay I hit with a slight Eastern to get more topspin. Then, believe it or not, sometimes I will wait with a forehand grip—and sometimes with a backhand. But don't do as I do; do as I say.

The Hit. The wrist should always be firm, as it must be on all strokes. The receiver can either hit with a locked wrist or whip the ball with his wrist if he is as strong as Hoad or Laver; he can never hit it with a floppy wrist.

Most good returns of serve are hit with a short stroke. You have to see the ball awfully well to take a big drive against a cannonball. Rosewall, with one of the best returns in the business, holds his racket head high and brings his racket back only a little behind his shoulder; he does not attempt the big sweeping drives that he uses in groundstrokes. The return of a big service is like a short punch drive and the follow-through is also curtailed in order to be ready after the server has hit his first volley. If you take a long, lovely follow-through, by the time you get back to the ready position you are just in time to applaud the winner volley your opponent made.

The long return of service is possible only on a clay surface where the opponent is staying back. Here you can use that long, flowing stroke and elegant follow-through.

Strangely, the forehand return of serve action is slightly longer than the backhand. I don't take any backswing at all on the backhand but I do take a *soupçon* of one on the forehand. . . .

The best forehand returns of serve in the pro game belong to Rod Laver, Pancho Segura, Butch Buchholz and Andres Gimeno. Butch and Andres are actually pretty good off both sides. Laver either rolls or chips his forehand return. He has a good backhand return of serve also, but he is more dangerous on the forehand. Segura, of course, has accuracy and angle on his great two-handed shot. Rosewall's forehand return of serve has often been called his weakest shot, but I know a lot of players who would like to have it. It is actually not a weak shot at all; it is excellent. It only suffers when compared to his backhand return.

Most of the leading players have a better backhand return of serve than a forehand. Roy Emerson is excellent on the backhand side, but his forehand return is not consistent. He can knock a few by you on the forehand but he hurts you more on the backhand. Arthur Ashe has a better backhand than forehand return. Ditto for the girls—Billie Jean King, Margaret Smith and Maria Bueno. They can all knock off forehand winners but the shot is slightly suspect since an occasional forehand will carom off the fence. In no case do any of these players have a bad forehand return; it is simply that they miss less on the backhand. Among other amateurs with fine service returns are Manolo Santana (consistent off both sides) and Charlito Pasarell (an excellent forehand). It should be added that the returns of Ashe and Pasarell are not as consistent as those of Emerson and Santana. . . .

One of the best returns in the game belongs to Pancho Gonzales. He does not knock the ball through you, but he dips, angles, dinks, always gets the ball back and forces his opponent to do something. He knows what he is trying to do, which is the asset that unsteady amateurs lack. When Fred Stolle first played Gonzales he found himself against an opponent who never gave him two similar returns. First Fred would be stretching wide and low on the forehand volley, and next he would be crouching to pick up a backhand volley from his shoelaces. He never found Gonzales returning wildly into the net or the fence. It is much easier to play against an erratic cannonball return than against the wiles of the tricky, heady Pancho.

Other players with good returns of serve are Clark Graebner (a good forehand and a backhand that he chips well) and Marty Riessen (he is consistent and, although he does not hurt you, he makes you volley up). There are not many great players in the game like Mike Sangster who completely lack consistency on return of serve. Most of the big boys are consistent, even if they have to shovel the ball back.

The direction of the return of serve depends upon the service and the server. As I said earlier, there is no time to think when returning a big serve on a fast court. Reactions must be automatic. If the big serve goes to your forehand in the right court, you will hit it more often down the line because to hit it crosscourt you have to be early. Against this type of serve, I am more concerned with getting the ball in play than anything else.

Here are some alternatives on the riposte to a serve to the forehand in the right court: 1) against a big serve on a slow court, I try to hit deep and down the line so as not to open up the court too much (a deep crosscourt return would allow the opponent to hit deep to my backhand, thus forcing me to run the entire width of the court) ; 2) if the opponent is coming in behind serve and I am running around my backhand, I may go for the crosscourt; 3) if the surface is slow, I hit for depth, and if it is fast I try to keep my return short and low; 4) on a fast surface against a big serve I have no plan unless, without even consciously knowing it, I spot an opening in the hundredth of a second that I am allowed for "thinking."

These returns are the kind that are proper for me. Rod Laver, with his big topspin forehand, often goes for the crosscourt. Alex Olmedo, who chips off return and moves in, is aiming to take the net away from the server. But it takes an Olmedo to meet the ball on the rise, move in like greased lightning and leap the width of the court for the volley.

On a forehand return of serve in the ad court, I mostly go for the down-the-line (to the server's forehand) since one of the most difficult shots in the game is to return "reverse crosscourt." When playing the ad court, a serve to the forehand is either a "bad" serve or a slice to pull you wide. When you are pulled wide, the safest shot is down-the-line. I like to have someone serve wide to my forehand in the backhand court or wide to my backhand in the forehand court since I like to reach and I end up after my return in the center of the court. You can see how a wide serve to the forehand in the forehand court or a wide serve to the backhand in the backhand court, particularly one that breaks wide, leaves the receiver out of position and past the alley. If the receiver then returns crosscourt, he has left one side of his court completely open.

A dink return is a defensive play; the ball is usually angled and hit without real pace to force the incoming server to volley up. The chip is a more aggressive shot. It can be used offensively as a wedge to take net behind return of serve. Gonzales can both dink and chip: he dinked against

Stolle when returning first serve but he chipped and moved in against Fred's second delivery. The chip is a short volley motion hit with no back-swing; the dink is a soft drive with good direction (if it is to be effective). The drive return of serve is the clean ball, the dink is the confuser and the chip is the weapon of the net-rusher.

Both Rafe Osuna and Tony Roche chip the backhand (Rosewall drives it with underspin). The chip has less speed than the drive, and the Osuna or Roche chip ball simply floats in. I use the chip against a second serve with topspin, especially on clay, since it gives me a chance to move in; I drive when my opponent hits a flat serve. Chuck McKinley was very effective with the topspin drive, but he could also chip when he wanted. Seixas, of course, was the top chipper in the game. Rod Laver drives and occasionally chips, but his drives are more effective.

The return of serve is not a fixed shot. There are certain basics in hitting a good return, but the variations of good returns are enormous and they change depending upon the server, the surface and the capabilities of the receiver. Lea Pericoli lobs every return and wins many matches by doing so; Don Budge drove every ball and won the Big Four; Osuna chips, Laver topspins, Rosewall undercuts and Gonzales plays tricky dinks. Lea would be no good if she drove nor would Budge have been the World Champion if he had dinked. Osuna is better off attacking behind a chip and you, too, will be getting the most out of your game if you utilize what you can do best. BUT do not leave your whole court open by returning crosscourt when you are pulled wide. Most important of all, kick back the return if you have to, but be sure to get that return in the court.

THE FOREHAND

by Rod Laver

"I'll tell you about a bloke called Bromwich," said Charlie Hollis.

"I've seen him hit twenty-five good shots to win a point. Not once did his concentration waver. He planned where he would put every shot well in advance of its execution. The length of his ground shots was so good not one of the twenty-five was more than two or three feet from the baseline. He'd put four in a row on a spot the size of a handkerchief."

We were going through the technique of playing the forehand drive, which Charlie considered the most difficult in tennis, and he was driving home to us the value of driving to a consistent length.

I seldom hit the forehand flat because I am a little fellow and I can't get right over the ball the way big men like Jack Kramer, Jack Crawford, Lew

Hoad and the other great forehand players have done. Charlie summed it up when he said, "Short blokes can't hit flat balls. Big men don't need spin but the little runts like you do." You can get good length with the topspin I use, if not the pinpoint accuracy of Bromwich.

We would lay tins on the court just in from the baseline and I'd try to hit them with forehand drives. I got so I could do it fairly often if I used topspin, which made the ball dip down when it looked likely to go out over the baseline. If I tried to do the same with flat forehands the ball would invariably be too long.

A newcomer to tennis once watched the famous Gerald Patterson spray forehands time after time yards over the baseline. "He hits the ball well but he seems to be accustomed to playing on a larger court," said the newcomer. You'd know what he meant if you saw me trying to hit nothing but flat drives.

Many things can go wrong with your forehand, but most of them concern the backswing. It's amazing how you can suddenly develop a looping backswing after months of taking the racket head back in the right groove. The fundamental slogan in producing a strong, fluid forehand from any position in the back of the court is: low ball, low backswing; high ball, high backswing.

The backhand frequently is the first stroke people play in tennis, but for years whenever people played Ken Rosewall they always attacked on his forehand side. Under pressure in the pro ranks Rosewall improved his forehand tremendously, but I'd still rather go to the net on a ball hit to his forehand than on one aimed at that devastating backhand of his. I've heard it argued that one reason Rosewall had the early trouble with his forehand was that he was a natural left-hander, but how this reconciles with his great backhand I wouldn't know.

I was too young to see them, but wherever I have talked with people about tennis, it seems to be conceded that the greatest forehands belonged to Fred Perry and Bill Tilden. Tilden, it is said, got tremendous power into his forehands, Perry, uncanny accuracy. The forehand drive was their main weapon in winning world championships. Jack Crawford always rates Perry's forehand the greatest the game has known, so it must have really been a fantastic shot. Jack himself had a terrific forehand. I have heard good judges say they saw Harry Hopman running the wrong way again and again in matches against Crawford because he could not pick up which way Crawford was going to hit it.

Novices often make the mistake of playing the forehand facing the net. Instead, the shot should be hit with the body side-on to the net. You set up the shot by taking that step forward and across the body with the leg farthest from your racket arm. Now take your racket back with the forearm parallel to the ground as the weight swings on to that front foot. Move into the shot by thrusting your body forward, with the wrist relaxed until the moment of impact. Keep the racket head going as you strike the ball, taking it across the body in the follow-through. The worst mistakes you can make are to back-pedal as you make the stroke or to take your eye off the ball.

Stay in control, never indulge in unrestrained slogging. Rhythm, smoothness and timing produce far more power than bashing.

The grip for the forehand is the basic Eastern wherever the shot is played from. The time to hit it is as soon as possible after it bounces without converting it into a half-volley. The place is on the forehand side of the body—never try to run around a backhand so you can take it on the forehand side.

Never hit a forehand off the back foot—always when you are moving into the ball. By hitting it while the ball is still on the rise after bouncing you gain a yard or so on the man at the other end of the court. You might get more forehands back if you stay back and hit them as the ball drops, but you will never be a champion unless you can hit them on the rise.

The forehand is the tennis shot most frequently used to set up winners, the shot on which most players go to the net. "A brilliant attacking forehand can be wasted if the player making it did not move into position at the net to take advantage of the weak reply or defensive lob," Harry Hopman wrote in the newspaper during that coaching course.

We had gone home to Rockhampton after the course ended with mixed reactions. Hopman has confirmed Charlie's view that lack of the "killer" instinct was the flaw in my make-up. "He's too little," Hop had said. "He can't breathe with a sunken chest like that." This meant if I really wanted to progress I would have to go into the gymnasium to try to cure or strengthen these physical shortcomings. Hop has always been a great believer in strong breathing as a cure for nervousness on the court and even as a protection against cramps.

"Laver is a left-hander who is one of the best prospects for Davis Cup we have in Australia," wrote Hopman in one of his coaching course reports. "I would not be surprised if he developed into the best player Queensland has produced. Of course, he is some years and a tremendous amount of work on his game and experience away from that goal—but, fortunately, he knows it."

I was fifteen, about to sit for school examinations, when I got yellow jaundice. I had to be isolated on a remote property run by a cousin. When I got well I didn't feel like repeating the year to pass exams I'd missed. Reg Clemens, Queensland manager for Dunlop Sports Company, came to town and offered me a job in Brisbane working with another promising tennis youngster, Frank Gorman, where I could get regular practice against a better caliber player than was available at home. Dunlop's hired me as a messenger boy at 4 pounds, 17 shillings, 6 pence a week, and off I went to the South, happy to know that I was pursuing the only kind of life I cared about.

THE TOPSPIN FOREHAND

by Rod Laver

My forehand is not the conventional shot. I hit it with quite a lot of wrist and, frequently, with a great deal of topspin. It was not a taught shot; it gradually grew from an Eastern forehand into a Continental wrist flick. It can hardly be called a safe shot since I sometimes close the hitting surface of the racket just as I make contact with the ball. Therefore if my timing isn't exactly right, I don't have good control. With the Eastern grip you can get a much flatter hitting surface and, consequently, a safer stroke.

Mal Anderson is one of the few Australians with an Eastern forehand. He and I were taught by the same coach, Charles Hollis. I had an Eastern grip, too, but I found the Continental a more comfortable one. My racket handle was tapered toward the end and I held it with the butt at the end of my palm. Both of these factors may have made it easier for me to switch to the Continental. Hollis did not try to stop the change. He never told me: "You won't go anywhere with that shot." He felt he shouldn't stop me from doing what was natural for me and what I wanted to do.

In the beginning with my Continental I could not control the ball well because my wrist was not strong enough. The stroke improved on my second trip overseas. We practiced all day long and my arm would be tired at nighttime, but I felt I had more control because my wrist had become stronger.

I have always felt that it was important to experiment with spins. At one point in my youth, I would hit a forehand with so much topspin (on the lob) that my follow-through ended over my left shoulder. But I made too many errors on this shot (win one, lose three) and so I discarded it. The heavy topspin shot, hit with a wrist snap, was a very effective one for me when I was confident: I could make better shots from bad positions. But when the confidence was lost, there was not much margin.

The topspin Continental stroke is based on timing and rhythm. My wrist is ahead of the racket until just before the hit when the racket is whipped at the ball. I like the topspin for a number of reasons: I can hit the ball very hard and still keep it in play, the ball doesn't sail over the baseline, and if it falls short it dips and is tough to volley.

I never hit the same shot twice. On my regular forehand from the baseline in a groundstroke exchange, I try to flatten my shot, hit through the ball and keep my follow-through lower to avoid excessive topspin and to get better length. On approach forehands, I sometimes try a little slice (it is too long a stroke to be called a chip). However, if the ball is slow and sits up, I will topspin the return. Usually this will end the point one way or the other, except occasionally on slow clay. The ideal approach shot to my mind is either a very slight topspin or slice for depth, particularly on low balls.

It was very easy for me to obtain spin. It was my natural game. Lefties as a rule seem to take better to spin, and had I been a right-hander I might have had an Eastern forehand. The only way I could never hit the ball was to take the racket straight back, wait and hit. My forehand always had to be in motion and the circular backswing seemed very natural. Of course on a fast surface I shorten the backswing into a more compact stroke or a semi-block, but on clay I have time for a big, full swing at the ball.

The point of contact on a Continental wrist stroke is by the side, although I often hit the ball in front of me on return of serve.

My preference in teaching is the Eastern grip with side to net. Those who advocate teaching an open stance to beginners are starting with the complicated shots instead of the basic ones. A good player has to stretch on a wide forehand, which he hits with an open stance, but you don't teach the game that way. If a youngster who is taught an Eastern grip with side to net gradually develops a Continental style, nothing should be done to stop him. After he is taught the fundamentals, he will get his own hitting ideas.

When I stretch on a wide forehand, I am more at ease than when returning a ball that comes down the center. It is easier for me to hit when I move toward the ball. I have hit so many balls that when I get there, my feet are in the right position.

My backhand is a more accurate shot than my forehand, but none of the pros serve to my forehand regularly. Because of the topspin, the ball is returned to their feet, making it difficult for them to half-volley or volley. Occasionally the pros will come in on my forehand. On a deep ball I usually go crosscourt but if it is short I will hit down the line because of the spin I have on the ball. You can pass the net man quicker down the line.

In baseline rallies normally I will hit crosscourts. When I approach net I go down the line quite often. I play the point to make my opponent hit to my backhand volley: I try to close up half the court and the opponent's opening is the crosscourt. Of course this attack depends on how good the opponent's forehand is. On passing shots I generally hit down the line or lob with a lot of topspin (especially in doubles where I play the left court).

There are many great players whom I have not seen, such as Jack Kramer, but among the champions I have played, I would pick Pancho Segura's forehand as the best. Another tough forehand is Lew Hoad's. He hits the same kind of heavy topspin that I do and moves in on the ball. Jaroslav Drobny also had a fine spin forehand which won him a lot of matches. Butch Buchholz has the best forehand among the current pros and Manuel Santana among the amateurs.

With my forehand stroke as it is, I rarely drop shot and then only on clay. I will drop volley on the forehand, but when I drop shot it is just a dump when the opponent is out of court. It is not an effective shot for me because I can't disguise it with my big backswing.

Despite the fact that the Eastern stroke is basically safer than the Continental, a natural player should never be forced to hit an Eastern if his bent is toward the Continental. I encourage individualism. The fellow with the free swing and the wrist action should not be stifled, particularly if he has the timing. However, excessive wrist can be ironed out a little, and perhaps if I had been Billy Knight's coach I would have discouraged his excessive topspin because it lacked the speed to get by the net man. However, it is always sad to see a natural hitter forced into a pattern that is not his own and robbed of his court personality by an unimaginative coach.

TAKING THE BALL IN FRONT

by Andres Gimeno

The champion is distinguished from the good player by one characteristic. It is *not* the grip: Laver, Santana, Rosewall, Emerson, Gonzales and Hoad all have slightly different methods of holding the forehand. It is *not* the bending of the knees. It is *not* the open or the closed stance on the forehand. It is *not* the length of the wind-up or the follow-through. It is *how far the player hits the ball in front of him*.

The top twenty players in the world, professional and amateur, hit the ball several inches farther in front of them than the 80 players who are just behind them. These 80, in turn, hit the ball several inches farther in front of them than do the next two hundred players. The mediocre or bad player hits the ball by his side. The bad player lets the ball drop and then hits it by his side.

It is not enough just to hit the ball well in front of you. It must be done with a *firm wrist*. The player with the wishy-washy or sagging wrist is letting the ball control his racket instead of controlling it with his own firmness.

The good player lets the ball come to him; the great player goes to the ball. Don Budge with a different grip would still have been a great player. Don Budge hitting the ball by his side would never have reached tennis immortality. Pancho Segura, a little champion with a great forehand, would finish his wind-up and start moving forward when the ball was still a good ten feet in front of him. Roy Emerson has a weakness on the forehand simply because he takes it six inches later than would Segura. Ken Rosewall's backhand is infinitely better than his forehand: the backhand is hit more in front of him.

If the player hits the ball in front of him with a firm wrist, the follow-through takes care of itself. One cannot stop short because the whole weight is moving forward. My definition of a "choke" forehand is a ball that is hit late (by the player's side). In this case, there may not be a follow-through. I would describe this forehand as a push, not as a drive.

The key to championship tennis is hitting the ball well in front of you with a firm wrist.

A ROAD TO IMPROVEMENT

by Tony Roche

When Tony Roche was 16 years old, he came to the U. S. for the first time to play in the Orange Bowl. He was seeded second, lost in straight sets to Mike Belkin in the Juniors and was then beaten in the Sunshine Cup by Charlie Pasarell, also in straight sets. The next year he defeated Mike Belkin easily to become the Orange Bowl Champion.

Later that day, when I asked Tony what his goals were in tennis, he replied in that confident Tarcutta brogue: "To become the No. 1 player in the world. What else?" It was an answer one expects to hear from a young champion. But after I watched Roche in the latter stages of last year and early this season, it was evident to me—and everyone else—that, at the age of 24, he was closing in on the coveted No. 1 spot in tennis.

Where did it all begin and how has it progressed? Tony himself tells us how.

It is considered unusual for an Australian to be a good clay court player. Most of the promising Aussies learn to play in Sydney or the other big cities where the courts are grass. I learned on two clay courts in Tarcutta and so my groundstrokes were always more suited to clay.

I change my game and even my grips when I go from clay to grass. I feel I have more time on clay to make the shot and so I use much more topspin. On grass, I move my grip around on the forehand, using a Continental, which means the knuckle of my forefinger is nearly on top of the racket. On clay I grip the racket like I would a frying pan. The Continental grip is good for grass because you don't have time to make the shot. I also take a bigger backswing when I play on clay.

I always had a heavy topspin forehand. In my younger days, my backhand was a heavy slice. Now I try to come over the backhand more (hit it with topspin). When you play against men who move fast, underspin is not a good shot—unless you hit it well—because it does not have enough speed. You can get the speed and depth if you come over the ball, and so the most aggressive backhands are hit with topspin.

The best way to learn is to learn by yourself. You, and only you, will know your own capabilities. If Harry Hopman or Donald Dell or someone else you respect makes a suggestion, you may know in your own mind that you will not feel comfortable doing it. In tennis you must be an individual. You must develop your own style or technique by your own creativity.

The champion cannot be a sloppy player. When I was young I thought I had a fair amount of ability, but I could never string two matches together. I would play a good match one day, then do terribly the next. Now that each match I play is for money, I am forced to concentrate harder. As amateurs, we played small tournaments where it did not mean that much to lose. Nobody likes to lose, even if it is a small tournament, but you tend to get sloppy playing against fellows whom you know you are going to beat. You can only improve by playing against better men.

My improvement since turning professional has shown up most in my second serve. It used to be short; now it has good depth. Additionally, I can keep the ball in play a lot longer. This seems to be true of most of the amateurs who turned touring pro: second serves and steadiness both took an upward jump.

The backhand volley is probably my best stroke. I get down to the ball and seem to generate more pace off the ground when it hits than I do with the forehand volley. However, I wouldn't mind swiping some of the other strokes of my fellow professionals. First I would steal the Gonzales serve. He has an easy motion which doesn't take anything out of him and he disguises it very well. It is deep and heavy and he can serve slice, flat or with topspin. I have a heavy serve; it has spin but it is by no means fast. Perhaps I would borrow the left-handed serve of Neale Fraser (in exchange, I would let him keep his backhand). Neale had a wonderful motion, and he could hit slice, flat or kick.

Next I would take Ken Fletcher's forehand and Rod Laver's backhand. I would appreciate Ken Rosewall's return of serve, which is the most consistent in the game as well as the most varied. Although I have never seen Lew Hoad at his best, I have heard enough about him from the other players. I would be willing to take his overhead and volley, which were practically perfect.

But it is not enough to have all the equipment. Fletcher has the best forehand in the game but he does not work hard enough. Even with good equipment, you must learn to play against a variety of games. When I turned pro, I wasn't sure how I would do against the established professionals. I knew I could hold my own fairly well in our group because five of our original eight players were amateurs together. I knew how these fellows played and I knew their games, but I wasn't sure how long it would take to beat the great pros like Laver and Rosewall. I was happy and surprised when I beat them much earlier than I expected.

My first big win was over Rosewall at Longwood last year in the quarter-final round of the U.S. Pro Championships. It was the first time I had ever played one of the older pros. The victory gave me confidence against him when we met the next month at Wimbledon. If I hadn't played him before, I would have been much more nervous.

Rod Laver crushed me at Wimbledon but I did much better in our next meetings. We both play the same type of game—topspin forehand and undersliced backhand. At Wimbledon he played too well. But at Madison Square Garden in November I found out a little more about how to play him. Fortunately our group has two other left-handers, Roger Taylor and Nikki Pilic, while Laver doesn't have any other lefties in his group to prepare him for a match against me.

Rod likes to move to the ball. He plays well when he is running wide. If you serve wide, he likes to take a fling at it. The same is true of his volleys. He likes to dive for them. He plays these shots well, but if you hit into his body he has a bit more trouble. This is the type of analysis you can make only after playing against a particular man, although you can spot quite a lot from watching. During the match I am always conscious of what I must do, although it doesn't always work. Before I serve, I concentrate on what serve I am going to hit. Everybody goes through some sort of ritual. I look at my feet and make a few moves with my left arm before I unwind. When I play Rod, I try to serve into his body. You can't do this every time because the opponent will get grooved. You must mix up your serves.

Never in the history of the game has the outlook been so good for a top professional star. This can provide the motivation for a good player to get better and it can attract more athletes into tennis. . . . And it is here, in the U. S., that the greatest interest in tennis will show.

THE SECRET OF BALL CONTROL

by Bob Harman

There's at least one in every tennis club: the slam-bang neck-or-nothing player who hits every ball as if he wants to batter it to smithereens. He never can understand why he has so much difficulty persuading anybody, of high or low estate on the tennis ladder, to step onto a court with him. Even the club's topflight players make excuses when he suggests a game.

It can't be the way he plays tennis, he says to himself. Isn't his game as spectacular as anyone's? Doesn't he hit drives that are veritable bullets? There must be something else wrong. He wonders if he has galloping halitosis, or if club members think he beats his wife.

What he may never know—unless he reads this book—is that people dislike playing with him for the simple reason that he hits the ball too hard.

Does that make tennis players sound like sissies? It shouldn't. What a tennis player wants is a duel of drive and counterdrive—a chance to hit some balls and keep on hitting them—some running and some maneuvering. What he gets against a slugger is a lot of work picking up balls.

Sluggers are the pariahs of the tennis courts because they hit virtually nothing except aces and errors. Mostly errors. There are no rallies. You hit one ball to a slugger, and then you walk into position to start the next point, because he's either socked it into the net or backstop, or else he's murdered it with an untouchable placement. His placements, when he makes them, look impressive, but actually they're sheer luck. He never knows where the ball is going. He habitually sacrifices control for speed—and nobody enjoys playing with a man who lacks control.

Such a speed demon is not a good player. He hits harder than the really good players do. Even the great international stars don't try to pulverize the ball, except on service and an occasional overhead smash. Oh, their drives are faster than a club player's but not as much faster as you might think. The acoustics of a tennis stadium make each impact of racket against ball sound like a gunshot, and spectators at the big tournaments assume that the drives must therefore be red hot—but if you were playing against a tournament star you'd be surprised to find that his drives don't travel as fast as those of your club pest.

Tournament players know that it is useless to wallop a drive with their full strength because they can't control its flight if they do. About the only great champion who persistently tore the cover off the ball was Ellsworth Vines. His drives flickered across the court like summer lightning, clearing the net by perhaps half an inch and hitting no more than six inches inside the baseline. Vines is the only man in the modern history of the game who could murder the ball and still put it where he wanted it. When he was right, he could have crucified most of the legendary champions of other years. But he had to practice relentlessly to keep himself at the very peak of his game because his strokes gave him such a tiny margin for error that he could be beaten badly if his form got even a trifle ragged. In one big match he went down something like 6–0, 6–1, 6–1 against Bitsy Grant, the dinker par excellence whose greatest assets were steadiness and the ability to keep getting the ball back. Just like the slugger in your own club, Vines was either very good or very bad, the main difference being that Vines was usually the former and your acquaintance is usually the latter.

Although the man who murders every ball is an annoyance or a joke to other players around the club, he differs only in degree from most of his clubmates. They don't realize it, but nearly all of them make the same mistake he does, to a less glaring degree. They hit too hard.

Ask any club pro, or any school coach, and he'll tell you the same thing: the besetting fault of the average player is hitting too hard. Nearly all once-a-week tennis enthusiasts try to use a racket as a battering ram instead of a precision instrument.

How about you?

Haven't you found that you frequently beat yourself through failure to control the course of your shots? Are you driving ball after ball a foot or two into foul territory? Are you smacking one into the back fence, or the next court, or the bottom of the net every now and then? If so, the reason is almost certainly that you're hitting too violently to be accurate. You sometimes take such a ferocious whack that you hurry your swing, jerk at the ball, ruin your follow-through, and make a wild shot that depends entirely on blind luck to put it inside or out.

To cure all this, the prescription is simple:

Relax. Take it easy. Forget about trying to hit aces.

The way to beat your friends—and the way to enjoy tennis—is to hit a medium-paced ball, with control. If you'll slow down your drive a bit, take a full backswing, and a full follow-through, you'll find yourself placing the ball where you want it.

You'll also find yourself having more fun. The boys who go into tantrums and apoplexy on a tennis court, who throw rackets over the fence, who spend half their time hating the game and their partners and themselves are the boys who murder the ball and therefore fail to control it. How much happier they'd be if only they would settle for a smooth, graceful, accurate drive with moderate power! Then they would know where the ball was going when they hit it; they wouldn't be cursing and praying as they watched its flight. They could relax and think ahead to the next move by the opposition. They'd make far fewer errors and therefore wouldn't lose their temper. The whole atmosphere on the court would change, and every-one would enjoy the game more.

In all sports, easy does it. The boxer who takes a terrific roundhouse swing, and grunts with the effort of his punch, isn't the one who knocks out opponents. He can't aim his blows, and when they do land he hasn't got his weight behind them. A straight puncher like Joe Louis who looks smooth and graceful even when he's knocking a man silly, is ten times as deadly as a wild, berserk swinger. Jack Dempsey could put a fighter to sleep with a hook that traveled no more than six inches.

Louis and Dempsey and all the other killers of the ring put their legs, hips, and shoulders into their punches, not just their arms. The big-league baseball pitchers throw with their whole body. The home-run hitters use an easy, flowing swing that produces power, not by the speed with which they move the bat, nor by great effort of their arm muscles, but by the weight of their body behind the bat. Golfers who drive a ball a mile never hurry their swing. Whether it's a soccer ball, a hockey puck, a discus, or a tennis ball that you're propelling, the secret of power lies in a fluid, graceful, not-too-fast motion that gets your weight into it.

Just remember that fundamental principle, and you'll probably hit the tennis ball much better. If you've been playing tennis for ten years or more, you're not likely to make many revolutionary changes in your stroke technique. . . . Right now you should begin sharpening your game by making one simple resolution: resolve to slow down your shots and not to try to murder any more drives.

The Sin of Wrist-Flicking. When you try to murder a drive, you probably draw the racket around behind your shoulder, flick it across your body in a sort of roundhouse hook with a vicious twist of your wrist, and end the swing with the racket coming to rest somewhere behind your left armpit. It's a stroke that is seen on tennis courts every day. That wrist-flicking drive looks spectacular because it really makes a ball smoke. Even if the shot lands far outside, as it usually does, the spectators' eyes pop—and maybe the opponent's eyes pop too—because the shot obviously took physical strength, and obviously traveled with murderous speed.

Yet it's a bad shot. You practically never see it in big-time tennis. It demands too much effort of the wrist and forearm, and more important, it's a jerking, flicking shot which can't be controlled. You can't aim anything when you flick it. The only way to aim anything, when you're throwing or hitting it, is to move your hand in the same straight line that you want the object to follow.

So you'd better forget about that spectacular wrist-flicking drive. Forget about hitting with a roundhouse swing, and think about driving with a smooth, straight motion in which your racket follows through along the same line that you intend the ball to go. Surprisingly, the average wrist-flicker doesn't need to make any drastic change in his stroking technique in order to get rid of his fault. He needs to keep only two thoughts in his mind:

1. Before hitting the ball, remember to hit it more slowly than usual.

2. During and after the hit, remember to follow through. Follow-through is vital. And don't forget that it must be a follow-through in the direction of the ball's flight, not a follow-through toward the sideline.

Try it. You'll be amazed to find that you've stopped flicking your wrist, stopped jerking, stopped hooking. Just by stroking slowly and following through you'll straighten out your swing and control the placement of your shots. Your shots won't travel as fast as they did when you flicked your wrist, but they'll travel fast enough, and they'll land inside the court instead of outside.

Your greatest temptation to use this wrist-flicking shot will come when you're at the net and your opponent sends across a floater. The ball looks as big and soft as a balloon and you mentally smack your lips as you prepare to plaster it. So you flick your wrist and hit with all your might, and what happens? You belt it into the top of the net, or barely outside the line.

Club players miss these easy kills again and again. They hurry the shot, try to hit it too hard, and feel like biting a piece out of someone's leg when they miss. Even the professionals succumb to temptation on these easy kills sometimes. . . . We all have to keep a tight grip on our rash impulses when we get a chance for a kill at the net. We have to keep reminding ourselves, whenever such a shot comes up, to take our time, aim the shot, and slow down enough to make it good. Steel yourself to do this, and you'll spend much less time in that special little hell occupied by tennis players when they miss easy shots.

"Feel" the ball. Maybe you're not sure, when you hit your drives, whether you're stroking well. You can't see yourself, and perhaps there's no expert on hand to watch your form and criticize it. So, even though you're struggling to get rid of that wrist-flicking style of stroke, you're not sure whether you have succeeded.

There's one easy way to check up on yourself. You can tell whether your stroke is good or bad just by the feel of the ball against your racket—and therein lies the big secret of stroking smoothly and controlling your shots. Feel the ball!

When you follow through properly, with your racket moving in the same direction as the ball, the ball will naturally be flattened out against your racket for an instant longer than it would be otherwise. Therefore you'll feel a heavy, solid, soul-satisfying thwack of the ball against gut while you're hitting it.

It's that longer contact between ball and racket that gives accuracy. Conversely, it's the instantaneous glancing contact of racket moving in a different line from ball that sends the ball flying off at unpredictable tangents whenever you hit it with that murderous flick of your wrist.

In every good stroke—whether it's a drive, a volley, a lob, or a smash—the racket must meet the ball squarely and solidly. Whenever it does, you'll get an unmistakable feel of solidity against the racket, of gut and ball in contact during an appreciable interval of space and time. You'll feel that good substantial thump all the way through your racket and up your arm.

Always stroke *through* the ball, and it will feel good against your racket. Furthermore, it will go where you want it. Just make your whole arm motion, from start to finish of the swing, follow the line you want the ball to travel. That's all you have to do. If your racket moves along that line, the ball will too, and you'll find yourself controlling your shots.

Constant attention to the feel of the ball, as your racket strikes it on every shot, will give you instant warning if your shots are getting sloppy. Among tournament players you'll often hear remarks like "I lost my feel." What they mean is that they lost their follow-through, thereby losing the solid feel which they'd learned to expect in hitting the ball.

This feel is almost as important in volleying as it is in driving. A good volley should feel solid to you. If it doesn't, you're hurrying, jerking, and hitting the ball a glancing blow—most common fault of club players at the net—and, while it may travel with the speed of sound, its destination is unpredictable. Don't stroke a volley, just get your racket squarely into the path of the ball; then block it back, or "punch" it back if you want more speed. Get your shoulder and body into the hit, which will give you controlled power, and you'll feel that rich smack when you hit.

Some topflight players are said by their opponents to hit a very "heavy" ball. Maybe you've heard the expression. Don't let it confuse you. What it means is a ball that comes at you with more speed than you expect. Don Budge always hit an extremely "heavy" backhand. When you played to his backhand, you'd see him take an apparently easy swing, and you'd think his drive would be a soft one. But as it crossed the net you'd realize it was faster than you thought. By this time you'd started your swing, and therefore Budge's ball nearly knocked your racket out of your hand when you hit it.

The reason a Budge backhand felt heavy was that opponents misjudged the speed with which the ball would travel. Don had a way of gliding forward and stepping into the ball which increased the speed of impact, even though his racket hardly seemed to swing at all. Similarly, Pancho Segura's two-handed stroke produced more power than it appeared to, and was forever surprising players by the speed at which it ricocheted off the ground. Consequently he had a reputation for hitting heavy balls. Kramer's forehand is a heavy one too because he's loose as ashes when he hits it, and his racket doesn't look as if it's moving quickly. His long arm gives him more leverage than you realize, and he pours the rest of his weight into the stroke with such superb smoothness that you think his effortless-looking drive will produce an average-speed ball.

There are players who bang the ball hard yet aren't afraid to hit a heavy ball simply because they move with such obvious speed and violence that opponents realize the ball will come fast. Such players generally burn themselves out quickly—and seldom stay near the top for very long. Tom Brown is a perfect example. He hits his drives with terrific force. His racket fairly flashes as he whips it through a stroke; there's nothing effortless about his attack on a ball. Brown went up like a skyrocket in international competition, and went down just as fast. He got to the finals at both Forest Hills and Wimbledon one year, with his blazing speed under perfect control, but his control slipped a little in the finals and he was beaten rather badly. Since then a lot of obscure players have been walking all over him. He still hits the ball just as murderously but he's lost the razor-edge of his accuracy, and he seems to have used up some of his strength. . . .

You may never get good enough to acquire a reputation for hitting heavy balls. Such deceptive smoothness usually takes years of daily polishing. But if you'll forget about bashing the stuffing out of a ball and work for easier strokes with the smooth follow-through that gives you a solid feel against your racket, then you'll be able to enjoy tennis for the rest of your life. You'll control your shots, you'll be relaxed and happy while you're playing, and you'll be a popular opponent in any tennis gang you join.

INDEX

*Italic page numbers indicate an article by,
rather than about, the person under consideration.*